WANT TO

- MAKE A
- DETERMINE TIMES FOR ROASTING, BROILING, OR PANFRYING MEATS ?
- REDUCE SODIUM IN YOUR DIET?
- CARVE A ROASTED BIRD?
- MAKE A SENSATIONAL TIRAMISU?
- TAKE THE GUESSWORK OUT OF GRILLING?
- SHOP FOR FISH?

A wealth of new information and terrific new recipes make this great American classic even better

Better Homes and Gardens®
NEW COOK BOOK

BETTER HOMES AND GARDENS®

NEW COOK BOOK

BANTAM BOOKS

NEW YORK   TORONTO   LONDON   SYDNEY   AUCKLAND

BETTER HOMES AND GARDENS® NEW COOK BOOK
A Bantam Book / published by arrangement with Meredith Corporation

PUBLISHING HISTORY
Meredith edition originally published November 1930
Better Homes and Gardens® Family Book Service
edition / October 1963
Latest Meredith edition / August 1989
Bantam edition / October 1979
Bantam revised edition / October 1982
Bantam 10th revised edition / May 1993
Bantam 11th revised edition / December 1997

The red plaid cover design is Registered in
U.S. Patent and Trademark Office.

ISBN 0-553-57795-6

Published simultaneously in the United States and Canada

Bantam Books are published by Bantam Books, a division of Bantam
Doubleday Dell Publishing Group, Inc. Its trademark, consisting of the
words "Bantam Books" and the portrayal of a rooster, is Registered in U.S.
Patent and Trademark Office and in other countries. Marca Registrada.
Bantam Books, 1540 Broadway, New York, New York 10036.

PRINTED IN THE UNITED STATES OF AMERICA

OPM   11   10   9   8   7

CONTENTS

INTRODUCTION

For generations, novice and experienced cooks alike have relied on the *Better Homes and Gardens® New Cook Book* for recipes that combine excellent flavor, ease of preparation, and balanced nutrition—everything you and your family need. Now completely updated and improved, America's best-selling cookbook promises to continue that tradition.

INSIDE THIS EDITION

As we prepared this new edition, we talked to people just like you to find out what you want and need in your favorite cookbook. Not surprisingly, time, convenience, and health were priorities for many of you. We also examined the vast array of new products on the market, and we took a fresh look at the most recent dietary guidelines. As a result of all our research, this edition reflects the preferences of today's cooks. You'll still find many of the classic recipes you've always loved, but you'll find so much more. For example:

■ We've reorganized the Special Helps section from earlier editions into Cooking Basics and made it the first chapter so you have an overview of essential information. We updated this comprehensive reference to include identification of many newly available fruits and vegetables (see page 22). We also give new information on the use of basic ingredients such as butter versus margarine (see page 4) and describe ingredients for ethnic cooking (see page 23).

■ We've brought back menu-planning information, including shopping and timesaving strategies, to help you speed preparation of everyday and special-occasion meals. For a wide range of sample menus, see page 41.

■ We've flagged recipes that are low in fat and quick to fix. For extra time savings, we've included at-a-glance reference information on preparation and cooking times, plus suggestions for make-ahead cooking and storage.

■ To help you prepare balanced, nutritious meals, we've included hundreds of low-fat and no-fat recipes, plus a nutrition analysis with every recipe. (For an explanation of the nutrition analysis, see page 36.)

■ Most important, and as always, every one of the more than 1,200

recipes in this edition was developed and tested for outstanding flavor, consistency, and nutritional value in the Better Homes and Gardens® Test Kitchen.

We hope that, like past generations, you will enjoy this cookbook for years to come. If you have any questions or comments, we would enjoy hearing from you. Please contact us at this address:

Better Homes and Gardens® New Cook Book
Meredith Corporation
1716 Locust Street, RW-240
Des Moines, IA 50309–3023

AN AMERICAN STAPLE

The *Better Homes and Gardens® New Cook Book* has held a treasured spot in America's kitchens since 1930 when the book was introduced. In that first edition, released during the Great Depression, readers could find dozens of recipes for preparing wild game and homemade mayonnaise, icebox cookies that were true to their name, and numerous dishes made with fresh produce—though there wasn't a tossed salad in the entire volume.

Since that time, each edition of the *New Cook Book* has reflected changes in America's tastes, cooking techniques, and lifestyles. During World War II, the book included details for canning and preserving crops from the Victory gardens grown by patriotic Americans. In the 1960s, recipes reflected a growing interest in ethnic foods, such as Chinese and Italian cooking. In the 1970s, brand-new recipes capitalized on the timesaving features of crockery cookers and microwave ovens.

To date, more than 30 million copies of the *New Cook Book* have been sold. It has become as much a staple in American kitchens as a sack of flour or a dozen eggs, with every dog-eared and food-stained page confirming its role in the family.

READING OUR RECIPES

The recipes throughout this book are simple to read and follow, thanks to these standard features:

Each recipe begins with at-a-glance times for preparation and cooking, plus the oven temperature, as needed.

These flags designate recipes that are quick to prepare and low-fat (or no-fat), helping you choose dishes that fit your time constraints and dietary needs.

Preparation steps are numbered for easy reference.

Each and every recipe includes a nutrition analysis.

SHRIMP IN GARLIC BUTTER

START TO FINISH: 20 MINUTES

`Fast`   `Low-Fat`

- 1 **pound fresh or frozen medium shrimp in shells**
- 2 **tablespoons butter or margarine**
- 3 **cloves garlic, minced**
- 2 **tablespoons snipped fresh parsley**
- 1 **tablespoon dry sherry**

1. Thaw shrimp, if frozen. Peel and devein shrimp (see photos 1 and 2, below). Rinse shrimp; pat dry with paper towels.
2. In a large skillet, heat butter or margarine over medium-high heat. Add shrimp and garlic. Cook, stirring frequently, for 1 to 3 minutes or till shrimp turn pink. Stir in parsley and sherry. Serves 4.

Nutrition Facts per serving: 126 cal., 6 g total fat (4 g sat. fat), 146 mg chol., 218 mg sodium, 1 g carbo., 0 g fiber, 14 g pro. **Daily Values:** 13% vit. A, 8% vit. C, 2% calcium, 14% iron

Many recipes include suggestions for easy variations, storage methods, and make-ahead directions.

■ **Scallops in Garlic Butter:** Prepare as above, except substitute 12 ounces fresh or frozen *scallops* for the shrimp. Thaw scallops, if frozen. Rinse scallops; pat dry with paper towels. Cut any large scallops in half. Cook and stir the scallops and garlic in butter or margarine for 3 to 5 minutes or till scallops turn opaque.

Nutrition Facts per serving: 114 cal., 6 g total fat (4 g sat. fat)

1. To peel a shrimp, open the shell lengthwise down the body. Start at the head end and peel back the shell. Gently pull on the tail to remove it.

Photographs and captions that clearly show techniques and methods guide you step by step toward making a successful dish.

2. To devein a shrimp, use a sharp knife to make a shallow slit along the back from the head to the tail end. Locate the black vein and remove it.

TESTING RECIPES FOR PERFECT RESULTS

In the Better Homes and Gardens® Test Kitchen, we're serious about great taste and proper nutrition—so much so, in fact, that we test and retest every single recipe until we're sure it will turn out perfectly every time.

Since 1928, the Test Kitchen has painstakingly tested each recipe published in the many Better Homes and Gardens publications, ensuring that it meets high-quality standards. Our home economists work in kitchens equipped with the same appliances you have at home, perfecting recipes so you don't have to.

After our home economists prepare each recipe, they present the dish to a panel of peers and food editors, who judge the recipe according to strict criteria. You can cook with assurance knowing that we're looking for perfect taste, texture, and appearance. To ensure it will work well for you, we also evaluate each recipe to make sure it meets the following guidelines.

■ Instructions are clear, using standard, easy-to-follow cooking methods and terms.

■ Cooking times, preparation instructions, and serving sizes are realistic.

■ The recipe is made from ingredients that are readily available across the country and includes suggestions for substituting one ingredient for another.

■ If applicable, the recipe includes timesaving methods, such as

the use of prepackaged or convenience ingredients.
■ When possible, the recipe calls for an entire can or package of an ingredient to avoid waste.

Thanks to our Test Kitchen, you can trust all the foods in this cookbook to meet your high standards for excellent flavor, ease of preparation, and balanced nutrition.

COOKING
<u>BASICS</u>

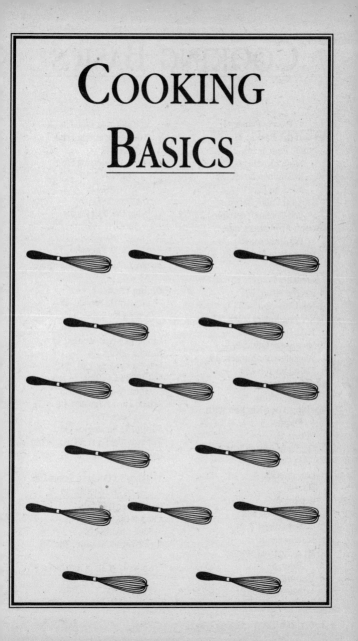

COOKING BASICS

PANTRY PRIMER

STOCKING YOUR KITCHEN WITH STAPLES

A well-stocked kitchen helps you cook faster and more efficiently. The following are foods no kitchen should be without.

CHEESE

The texture and flavor of cheese are determined by the kind of milk used. Most cheeses are made from cow's milk, but some types are made from the milk of goats, sheep, and other animals. They also may be classified as natural or process.

■ Natural cheese is made directly from milk curd and ranges from fresh, soft, and mild to aged, firm, and robust. Natural cheese is neither reprocessed nor blended. Popular natural cheeses include blue, Brie, cheddar, feta, Parmesan, and Swiss.

■ Fresh cheese is natural cheese made directly from milk curd and is not aged (ripened). Some of the most popular fresh cheeses include cottage cheese, cream cheese, and ricotta.

■ Process cheese is made from natural cheese that has undergone additional steps, such as pasteurization, or has been enhanced with ingredients for flavoring, a softer texture, or extended shelf life. Process cheeses include American cheese and cheese spreads.

When buying cheese, avoid wet or sticky packages or a cheese that has a shrunken rind, cracked edges, or uneven texture. For storage information, see page 489.

EGGS

Like any perishable food, eggs need special handling. Purchase clean, fresh eggs from refrigerated display cases. At home, refrigerate them promptly in their original carton. Do not wash eggs before storing or using them, and discard eggs with cracked shells. For the best quality, raw eggs should be used within one week, though they can be refrigerated safely for as long as five weeks. If you set out eggs before cooking, be sure to use them within two hours. For additional information on safe handling, see page 462.

■ **Egg size.** The recipes in this book were developed and tested using large eggs. If you purchase eggs in other sizes, adjust the number you use to ensure success when preparing our cakes, soufflés, egg-thickened sauces, or recipes such as meat loaf, in which egg binds the ingredients together (see chart, below). For most other recipes, the egg size isn't critical.

■ **Beating eggs** (see tip on page 47).

■ **Separating eggs.** To separate a yolk from the white, use an egg separator. Separating the egg yolk from the egg white by passing the yolk from shell to shell is not considered safe.

■ **Using raw eggs.** Using uncooked or slightly cooked eggs in such recipes as mayonnaise, meringue pies, or Caesar salad can be hazardous, especially to people vulnerable to salmonella such as the elderly, infants, children, pregnant women, and the seriously ill. Commercial forms of egg products are safe because they are pasteurized, which destroys salmonella bacteria (see tip, page 473).

EGG EQUIVALENCE CHART

If you use an egg size other than large, you may need to increase or decrease the number of eggs you use in our recipes (see Egg Size, below). Use these suggested alternatives:

1 large egg = 1 jumbo, extra-large, medium, or small egg

2 large eggs = 2 jumbo, 2 extra-large, 2 medium, or 3 small eggs

3 large eggs = 2 jumbo, 3 extra-large, 3 medium, or 4 small eggs

4 large eggs = 3 jumbo, 4 extra-large, 5 medium, or 5 small eggs

5 large eggs = 4 jumbo, 4 extra-large, 6 medium, or 7 small eggs

---

FATS AND OILS

■ **Butter.** For rich flavor, butter is usually the fat of choice. Salted and unsalted butter can be used interchangeably. However, if you use unsalted butter, you'll need to increase the amount of salt in the recipe. You can store butter in the refrigerator for up to a month or in the freezer for 6 to 9 months.

Some recipes in this book list butter before margarine. Our Test Kitchen made this distinction for certain recipes when the type of fat used is especially critical to the outcome of the recipe. For more information, see Margarine, below, and the tip boxes on pages 302 and 395.

■ **Margarine.** Made from vegetable oil, true margarine is 80 percent fat. In most recipes, it can be used as a substitute for butter. Margarine look-alikes, called spreads, contain less fat and more water; this can affect the texture and quality of baked goods or crunchy coatings. If you use a spread, it should contain no less than 60 percent vegetable oil (read the product label for this information). Like butter, margarine and spreads can be stored in the refrigerator for up to a month or in the freezer for 6 to 9 months.

MEASURING BUTTER AND MARGARINE

To measure sticks of butter or margarine, follow the markings on the wrapper. For unwrapped butter or margarine, soften it, then measure as for shortening.

■ **Shortening.** A vegetable oil that has been processed into solid form, shortening commonly is used for baking or frying. Plain and butter-flavored types can be used interchangeably. Store shortening in a cool, dry place, discarding it if it has an odor or appears discolored. To measure shortening, use a rubber spatula to firmly press it into a dry measuring cup, removing as many air bubbles as possible. Level it off with the straight edge of a spatula. Shortening also is available in sticks; measure it like butter or margarine (see tip, above).

■ **Lard.** Made from pork fat, lard is sometimes used for baking. It's especially noted for producing light, flaky piecrusts.

■ **Cooking oils.** Liquid at room temperature, cooking oils are made from vegetables, nuts, or seeds. Common types include corn, soybean, canola, sunflower, safflower, peanut, and olive. Some are available seasoned with herbs and spices. Other oils with a mild flavor include avocado, walnut, sesame, hazelnut, and almond. You can store most oils on your shelf for up to a year. Nut-based oils, though, may turn rancid over time; store them in tightly capped containers in a cool, dark place for up to 3 months, or refrigerate them for up to 4 months.

■ **Nonstick cooking spray.** This spray is used to bypass the mess of greasing pans; a 1¼-second spray replaces a tablespoon of butter, margarine, shortening, or cooking oil. Use the spray only on cold baking pans or skillets, as it can burn or smoke if sprayed onto a hot surface. For safety, hold pans over your sink or garbage can when spraying to avoid making your floor or counter slippery. In cooking, you can substitute cooking spray for oil when stir-frying, but use it only over medium heat.

FLOUR

■ **All-purpose flour** is true to its name, as it can be used for baking, thickening, and coating. Milled from a combination of soft and hard wheats minus the bran and germ, all-purpose flour comes enriched (with vitamins and minerals) and may be bleached or unbleached. To substitute all-purpose flour for cake flour, use 2 tablespoons less all-purpose flour for each cup of cake flour in your recipe.

■ **Flours for specific uses.** Many flours milled from either soft or hard wheat are available for specific uses. These include bread flour (for yeast breads), pasta flour (or semolina flour), and pastry flour. Cake flour, milled from soft wheat, is perfect for fine and feathery cakes, but it's too delicate for general baking. Self-rising flour is an all-purpose flour with added salt and a leavening, such as baking powder. It is used for nonyeast products and may be substituted for all-purpose flour in quick breads by omitting the salt, baking powder, and baking soda called for in the recipe. Instant-type flour has a granular texture and blends easily into hot or cold liquids without lumping.

■ **Whole wheat flour.** Also called graham flour, whole wheat flour is coarse, since it is made by grinding the entire wheat kernel. It is used in breads and some cookies, but generally is not recommended when a delicate product is desired. It may be substituted for up to half of the all-purpose flour called for in most recipes; the end product is likely to have a coarser texture and may have less volume.

GELATIN

This dry ingredient is available in unflavored and flavored forms. When using gelatin, make sure it is completely dissolved. To dissolve one envelope of unflavored gelatin, place it in a small saucepan and stir in at least $1/4$ cup of water, broth, or fruit juice. Let it stand 5 minutes to soften, then stir it over low heat until the gelatin is dissolved. To prevent problems with gelatin setting up, do not mix it with: figs, fresh pineapple (canned pineapple is not a problem), gingerroot, guava, kiwifruit, and papaya.

Some recipes call for gelatin at a certain stage of gelling. "Partially set" means the mixture looks like unbeaten egg whites; at this point, solid ingredients may be added. "Almost firm" describes gelatin that is sticky to the touch; it can be layered at this stage. "Firm" gelatin holds a cut edge and is ready to be served.

HERBS, SPICES, AND SEASONINGS

Dried herbs and spices will keep for months when they're tightly covered and stored in a cool, dry place. Look for the freshness date on the container and replace them past this date or when their color or aroma seems weak. Whole spices stay fresher longer (up to 2 years) than ground spices (about 6 months). Refrigerate red spices, such as paprika, to preserve their flavor and color.

Fresh snipped herbs add flavor that can't be matched by dried. If you don't have an herb garden within reach, buy fresh herbs at a farmer's market or grocery store. Store fresh herbs in the refrigerator with their stems plunged in water and plastic over the leaves; use them until they start to wilt—usually about a week. Because fresh herbs generally are less intense than dried, you can experiment with them, varying the amount in recipes as desired.

SEASONING BLENDS

For quick seasoning, these popular blends can't be beat.

■ **Barbecue seasoning.** This zesty combination includes salt, sugar, garlic, hot red pepper, hickory smoke flavor, onion, and other spices. Sprinkle it onto meats before grilling, roasting, or broiling.

■ **Cajun seasoning.** This seasoning is a fiery blend of white, black, and red pepper; garlic; salt; and onion. If you like your foods spicy, sprinkle this seasoning into crumb coatings or directly onto fish, poultry, or meat before cooking.

■ **Fines herbes** *(feenz-ERB).* This French phrase describes a mix that usually contains chervil, parsley, chives, and tarragon. Use it in place of herbs in gravies, sauces, creamy soups, and poultry stuffings.

■ **Herbes de Provence.** Thyme, marjoram, rosemary, basil, fennel, sage, and lavender are blended together in this French classic from the Provence region. Add it to poultry stuffings, creamy pasta dishes, soups, and salad dressings.

■ **Jamaican jerk seasoning.** A favorite in the Caribbean, jerk seasoning contains salt, sugar, allspice, thyme, cinnamon, onion, and red pepper. It adds tropical taste to fish, meat marinades, and salad dressings.

■ **Lemon-pepper seasoning.** A mixture of mainly salt with black pepper and grated lemon peel. It adds a delicate lemon flavor to poultry and vegetables.

■ **Mexican seasoning.** This peppy mixture includes cumin, chili peppers, salt, onion, sweet peppers, garlic, oregano, and hot red pepper. Use it to perk up ground meat for meat loaf, burgers, and meatballs. Or add it to tacos, fajitas, enchiladas, and other Mexican dishes.

■ **Old Bay seasoning.** Old Bay is a blend of celery salt, mustard, pepper, bay leaves, cloves, pimiento, ginger, mace, cardamom, and cassia. Use it in coatings for fish or chicken, or in crab cakes and other seafood dishes.

■ **Pizza seasoning.** This favorite mix of flavors includes oregano, basil, fennel, garlic, onion, and other Italian herbs. Besides spicing up pizza, it's an excellent addition to burgers, salad dressings, chicken, popcorn, buttered French bread, and pasta dishes.

FRESH HERBS

Check our list of the most popular culinary herbs and their uses to help you select herbs.

■ **Basil.** With a minty, clovelike aroma, basil perks up spaghetti sauce, sandwiches, vinegars, sauces, fish, and poultry. Cinnamon, lemon, and anise basils have a basic basil flavor, plus the taste for which they're named.

■ **Chervil.** Fresh chervil may be hard to find, but its distinctive anise-tarragon flavor is worth the search. Use it to season soups, vegetables, and salads, bearing in mind that the dried form loses some of its intensity. Crush dried chervil after measuring to release more of the flavor.

■ **Chives.** Snip the mild onion-flavored leaves as you need them; just like grass, they grow back after cutting.

■ **Cilantro.** Also known as fresh coriander or Chinese parsley, cilantro adds an aromatic flavor to salsas and sauces. Season to taste; a little goes a long way.

■ **Dill.** A familiar herb for peas, its delicate taste also is excellent with fish and seafood and vegetables.

■ **Mint.** Peppermint has a sharp, pungent flavor; spearmint is more delicate. Both have a sweet, refreshing flavor and cool aftertaste. They are usually used in desserts, but try small amounts of them in salads, marinades, and vegetable dishes.

USING DRIED HERBS FOR FRESH

To use dried herbs, crush them after measuring to release their flavor. Because dried herbs have more intense flavor than fresh, you can make the following substitutions.
■ For strong-flavored herbs such as dillweed, marjoram, rosemary, sage, tarragon, and thyme, substitute $1/2$ teaspoon dried herb for each tablespoon of fresh herb.
■ For mild-flavored herbs such as basil, mint, oregano, and savory, use about 1 teaspoon dried herb for each tablespoon of fresh herb.

■ **Oregano.** Popular as a pizza spice, oregano offers a robust, pungent flavor. Use it in bean soups, sauces, and pasta salads.

■ **Parsley.** Often reserved as a garnish, the snipped leaves provide a mild, fresh taste to almost any dish. Use parsley in moderation; too much can make a dish taste "grassy." There are two main types, curly-leaf and Italian.

■ **Rosemary.** Often paired with lamb, this aromatic herb has a bold flavor described as piney and perfumy. It's delicious sprinkled over any roasted meat and in tomato-based dishes (try it in place of or in addition to basil).

■ **Sage.** Slightly bitter, with a musty mint taste, sage is the primary herb in poultry seasoning. Often used to flavor stuffings and sausages, it also complements most vegetables.

■ **Sweet marjoram.** With its delicate, mild flavor, sweet marjoram can be used to season almost any meat and vegetable dish. This variety is less pungent than wild or pot marjoram.

■ **Tarragon.** Essential to French cuisine, tarragon has a spicy, sharp flavor with licorice-like overtones. It is excellent with poultry and in marinades for grilled meats.

■ **Thyme.** Possessing a minty, yet lemony aroma, thyme seasons chicken, vegetables, and Creole dishes. You may want to follow one cook's adage: "When in doubt, use thyme."

LEAVENINGS

Leavening ingredients are essential in helping batter and dough expand or rise during baking. If omitted, the baked products will be heavy and tough. There are two types of leavenings: natural and chemical. Natural leavenings include yeast (as in bread), hot air (as in angel food cake and soufflés), and steam (as in popovers and cream puffs). Chemical leavening agents include baking soda and baking powder. For best results, store yeast, baking soda, and baking powder in a cool, dry place and use them before the expiration date on the package.

MILK AND MILK PRODUCTS

■ **Whole, low-fat, and skim milk.** These differ only in the amount of fat they contain and in the richness of flavor they lend to foods. As a result, they can be used interchangeably in cooking. All our recipes calling for milk were tested using 2-percent milk (meaning it contains 2 percent fat).

■ **Nonfat dry milk powder.** When reconstituted, this milk product can be used in cooking.

■ **Evaporated milk.** Made from either whole milk or low-fat milk, canned evaporated milk has had 60 percent of the water removed. It is not interchangeable with sweetened condensed milk.

■ **Sweetened condensed milk.** This product is made from whole or low-fat milk that has had water removed and sugar added. It is not interchangeable with evaporated milk.

■ **Cream.** Light cream and half-and-half contain more fat than milk, but not enough fat to be whipped. In contrast, whipping cream or heavy cream contains up to 36 percent milk fat. To beat whipping cream, chill a deep bowl and the beaters of an electric mixer in the freezer. (Cream whips better if it is very cold.) Beat the cream on medium speed until soft peaks form. One cup cream yields 2 cups whipped. Use whipped cream immediately or chill it for no more than 1 hour (see tip, page 456).

■ **Cultured dairy products.** These include buttermilk, yogurt, and sour cream. Buttermilk is skim or low-fat milk to which special bacteria have been added to make it thick and tangy. In recipes, you can use sour milk in place of buttermilk (see tip, page 261). Sour cream traditionally is made from light cream and has a sweet taste; low-fat and no-fat versions are also available. Yogurt, made from whole, low-fat, or skim milk, is thick and creamy with a tangy flavor. Fruit and sweeteners often are added.

PRODUCE

Fruits and vegetables offer a world of fresh flavors and juicy possibilities. In many recipes, fresh produce is interchangeable. Sampling a wide variety of fruits and vegetables will help you learn which items may be substituted successfully.

SWEETENERS

If stored in an airtight container in a cool, dry place, all sweeteners will keep indefinitely. Transfer sugars that come in boxes (especially brown sugar) to sealed plastic bags or airtight containers to avoid lumping.

■ **Sugar.** When a recipe doesn't specify type but calls for sugar, use the white granulated kind. Measure it by spooning it into a cup and leveling it off. Recipes calling for powdered sugar (or confectioner's sugar) refer to granulated sugar that has been pulverized; cornstarch often is added to prevent it from caking. Powdered sugar usually requires sifting before measuring. Brown sugar, another popular ingredient, is a mix of granulated sugar and molasses; the amount of molasses determines whether the sugar is light or dark. To measure brown sugar, spoon it into a measuring cup, packing it down with your hand or the back of the spoon as you add more; level off the top. When the measuring cup is turned over to remove the sugar, the packed brown sugar should hold its shape.

■ **Corn syrup.** A nearly flavorless sweetener, it usually is used in frostings, candies, and glazes, and cannot be substituted for other sweeteners.

■ **Honey.** The flavor of honey depends on the flowers from which the nectar came, but most honey is made from clover. Honey and maple syrup sometimes can be substituted for sugar in recipes—es-

SELECTING FRESH FRUITS

When picking fruits, look for plumpness, tenderness, and bright color. Fruits should be heavy for their size and free from mold, mildew, bruises, cuts, or other blemishes. Some fruits—apricots, avocados, bananas, kiwifruit, nectarines, peaches, pears, and plums—are picked and shipped while still firm, so they may need additional ripening. **To ripen,** place them in a small, clean paper bag. (A plastic bag is not recommended because it doesn't allow fruit to breathe and can produce mold on the fruit from moisture trapped in the bag.) Loosely close the bag and store it at room temperature. Feel free to mix varieties of fruit in the same bag. To speed up the ripening process, place a ripe apple or ripe banana in the bag with the underripe fruit. Check fruit daily and remove any that yields to gentle pressure. Enjoy ripe fruit immediately or remove fruit from the bag and transfer it to the refrigerator for a few days to retard further ripening.

Fruit	How to Choose	How to Store
Apples	Fruit is sold ready for eating. Select the variety for intended use.	Store apples purchased in a plastic bag in refrigerator; store bulk apples in cool, moist place.
Apricots	Look for plump, fairly firm fruit with deep yellow or yellowish orange skin.	Ripen firm fruit as directed above* until it yields to gentle pressure and is golden in color. Refrigerate ripe fruit for up to 2 days.
Avocados	Soft fruit can be used immediately (especially good for guacamole). Avoid bruised fruit with gouges or broken skin.	Ripen firm fruit as directed above* until it yields to gentle pressure; refrigerate.

Bananas	Choose bananas at any stage of ripeness, from green to yellow.	Ripen at room temperature until they have a healthy yellow color. Very ripe bananas are brown.
Berries	If picking your own, select berries that separate easily from their stems.	Refrigerate berries in a single layer, loosely covered, for up to 2 days. Rinse just before using.
Cherries	Select firm, brightly colored fruit.	Refrigerate in a covered container for up to 4 days.
Citrus	Size, shape, and color differ with each variety. All fruit is ripe when sold. On oranges, a greenish tinge on skin doesn't affect quality.	Keep 2 to 3 weeks in the crisper drawer of refrigerator.
Cranberries	Fruit is ripe when sold. Avoid soft or bruised fruit.	Refrigerate for up to 4 weeks or freeze for up to 9 months.
Grapes	Look for plump grapes without bruises, soft spots, or mold. Bloom (a frosty white cast) is typical and doesn't affect quality.	Refrigerate in a covered container for up to 1 week.
Kiwifruit	Choose fruit that is free of bruises and soft spots.	Ripen firm fruit as directed above* until skin yields to gentle pressure; refrigerate up to 1 week.
Mangos	Look for fully colored fruit that smells fruity and feels fairly firm when pressed.	Ripen firm fruit as directed above* and refrigerate for up to 5 days.

Selecting Fresh Fruits (continued)

Fruit	How to Choose	How to Store
Melons	Pick fruit with a sweet aromatic scent, not a strong smell that could indicate overripeness. Melons should feel heavy for their size and should be well shaped. Avoid wet, dented, bruised, or cracked fruit.	Ripen as directed on page 12* and refrigerate for up to 4 days.
Nectarines and Peaches	Look for fruit with a healthy golden yellow skin without tinges of green. Ripe fruit should yield slightly to gentle pressure.	Ripen as directed on page 12* and refrigerate for up to 5 days.
Papaya	Choose fruit that is at least half yellow and feels somewhat soft when pressed. The skin should be smooth.	Ripen as directed on page 12* until yellow and refrigerate in a covered container up to 1 week.
Pears	Skin color is not an indicator of ripeness because skin color of some varieties does not change much as the pears ripen. Look for pears without bruises or cuts. Choose a variety for intended use.	Ripen as directed on page 12* until pear yields to gentle pressure at the stem end. Store ripened fruit in the refrigerator for several days.

Pineapple	Look for a plump pineapple with a sweet, aromatic smell at the stem end. It should be slightly soft to the touch, heavy for its size, and have deep green leaves.	Refrigerate for up to 2 days. Cut pineapple lasts a few more days if placed in a tightly covered container and chilled.
Plums	Find firm, plump, well-shaped fresh plums. Each should give slightly when gently pressed. The bloom (light gray cast) on the skin is natural and doesn't affect quality.	Ripen as directed on page 12* and refrigerate for up to 5 days.
Rhubarb	Look for crisp stalks that are firm and tender. Avoid rhubarb that is wilted looking or with extra-thick stalks.	Wrap stalks tightly with plastic wrap and refrigerate for up to 1 week.

Selecting Fresh Vegetables

Take a few minutes in the produce section and inspect each vegetable before you buy. Look for plump, crisp, bright-colored vegetables that are heavy for their size (this indicates moistness). Avoid vegetables that are bruised, shriveled, moldy, or blemished. Follow these guidelines for selecting and storing fresh vegetables. In most cases, rinse vegetables just before using. For preparation and cooking information, see pages 1082 through 1096.

Vegetable	How to Choose	How to Store
Asparagus	Choose firm, straight stalks with compact, closed tips. Avoid stalks that are either very thin (less than 1/8 inch) or very thick (more than 1/2 inch), because they may be stringy.	Wrap the bases of fresh asparagus spears in wet paper towels and keep tightly sealed in a storage container in the refrigerator for up to 4 days.
Beans	Select fresh beans that are bright-colored and crisp. Avoid bruised or scarred beans or ones that are rusty with brown spots or streaks. Bulging, leathering beans are old.	Rinse fresh beans and refrigerate in a storage container.
Beets	Select small or medium beets; large beets tend to be pithy, tough, and less sweet.	Trim the beet greens, leaving an inch or two of stem. Do not cut the long root. Store unrinsed beets in an open container in the refrigerator for up to 1 week.

Broccoli	Look for firm stalks with deep green or purplish green heads that are tightly packed. Avoid heads that are light green or yellowing.	Keep broccoli in a covered container in the refrigerator for up to 4 days.
Brussels Sprouts	Pick out the smaller sprouts that are vivid green; they will taste the sweetest. Large ones may be bitter.	Refrigerate in a covered container for up to 2 days.
Cabbage	No matter what the variety (red, green, Savoy, Napa), the head should feel heavy for its size. Cabbage should have bright leaves, free of withered or brown spots.	Refrigerate in a covered container for up to 1 week.
Carrots	Check a bag for straight, rigid, and bright orange carrots.	Refrigerate the carrots in plastic bags for up to 2 weeks.
Cauliflower	Look for solid heavy heads with bright green leaves. Avoid those with brown bruises or yellowed leaves.	Refrigerate in a covered container for up to 4 days.
Celery	Look for crisp ribs that are firm, unwilted, and unblemished.	Refrigerate, tightly wrapped, for up to 2 weeks.
Cucumbers	Select firm cucumbers without shriveled or soft spots.	Keep salad cucumbers in your refrigerator for up to 2 weeks. Pickling cucumbers should be picked and used the same day.

Selecting Fresh Vegetables *(continued)*

Vegetable	How to Choose	How to Store
Eggplant	Look for plump, glossy, heavy eggplants. Skip any that are scarred or bruised. The cap should be fresh-looking and free of mold.	Refrigerate whole eggplants for up to 2 days.
Mushrooms	Fresh mushrooms should be firm, fresh, and plump and have no bruises. Size is a matter of preference. Avoid spotted or slimy mushrooms.	Store fresh mushrooms, unwashed, in the refrigerator for up to 2 days. A paper bag or damp cloth bag lets them breathe so they stay firmer longer.
Okra	Look for small, crisp, bright-colored pods without brown spots or blemishes. Avoid shriveled pods.	Store okra, tightly wrapped, in the refrigerator for up to 3 days.
Onions, Leeks, and Shallots	Select dry bulb onions and shallots that are firm, free of blemishes, and not sprouting. Leeks and green onions (scallions) should have fresh-looking tops and clean white ends.	Keep dry onions in a cool, dry, well-ventilated place for up to several months (shallots for up to 1 month). Fresh green onions and leeks should be tightly wrapped and refrigerated for up to 5 days.
Peas and Pea Pods	Select fresh peas, snow peas, or sugar snap peas that are crisp and bright-colored. Avoid shriveled pods or those with brown spots.	Store, tightly wrapped, in the refrigerator for 2 to 3 days.

Peppers	Fresh peppers, whether sweet or hot, should have bright color and good shape for the variety. Avoid shriveled, bruised, or broken peppers.	Refrigerate in a covered container for up to 5 days.
Potatoes	Look for clean potatoes that have smooth, unblemished skins. They should be firm and have a shape that is typical for their variety. Avoid those that have green spots or are soft, moldy, or shriveled.	Store potatoes in a well-ventilated, dark place that is cool and slightly humid, but not wet. Bright lights cause them to develop green patches that will have a bitter flavor. Avoid refrigerating potatoes; cold temperatures cause potatoes to turn overly sweet and to darken when cooked.
Root Vegetables (Parsnips, Rutabagas, Turnips)	Choose vegetables that are smooth-skinned and heavy for their size. Sometimes parsnips, rutabagas, and turnips are covered with a wax coating to extend storage; cut off this coating before cooking.	Refrigerate for a week or more.
Spinach	Leaves should be crisp and free of moisture. Avoid spinach with broken or bruised leaves.	Rinse leaves in cold water and thoroughly dry. Place the leaves in a storage container with a paper towel and refrigerate for up to 3 days.
Sweet Potatoes and Yams	Choose small to medium, smooth-skinned potatoes that are firm and free of soft spots.	Store in a cool, dry, dark place for up to 1 week.

SELECTING FRESH VEGETABLES (continued)

Vegetable	How to Choose	How to Store
Tomatoes	Pick well-shaped, plump, fairly firm tomatoes.	Let ripen in a brown paper bag (see page 12*), then use within 3 days. Store only ripe tomatoes in the refrigerator.
Winter Squash	Avoid cracked or bruised squash.	Store the whole squash in a cool, dry place for up to 2 months. Store cut squash, wrapped in plastic, for up to 4 days in the refrigerator.
Zucchini and Summer Squash	Because of its tender skin, it is almost impossible for a zucchini to be blemish-free, but look for small ones that are firm and free of cuts and soft spots.	Refrigerate dry squash, tightly wrapped, for up to 5 days; fresh-from-the-garden squash may be stored for up to 2 weeks.

pecially in baked goods—but you may have to adjust the liquid and the leavening.

■ **Maple syrup.** This syrup is made from maple sap that is boiled down until it thickens. Maple-flavored syrup is a blend of pure maple syrup and corn syrup and usually can be used in place of the real thing.

■ **Molasses.** This sweetener is made by reducing and blending sugarcane juices into a syrup. For a more robust flavor, use dark molasses instead of light. Blackstrap molasses isn't considered a sweetener because most of the sugar has been removed. It has a pungent, intense flavor.

■ **Artificial sweeteners.** Because these have unique attributes, they should not be used unless a recipe calls for them specifically.

THICKENERS

■ **Flour and cornstarch.** All-purpose flour often is used to thicken saucy mixtures. Cornstarch produces a more translucent mixture than flour and has twice the thickening power. Before adding either of them to a hot mixture, stir cold water into a small amount of one of them or combine with cold water in a screw-top jar and shake until thoroughly blended. It is very important that the starch-water mixture be free of lumps to prevent lumps in your sauce or gravy.

■ **Quick-cooking tapioca.** This is a good choice for foods that are going to be frozen. Unlike flour- and cornstarch-thickened mixtures, tapioca mixtures retain their thickness when reheated.

BEYOND THE BASICS

TROPICAL FRUITS

Supermarkets across the country now carry an expanded array of refreshing, flavorful fruits from tropical climates. Many of them are sold unripened; to ripen them, store the fruit at room temperature for a few days until it yields to gentle pressure. For best results, handle ripe fruits gently and refrigerate them until you're ready to use them.

■ **Cactus pear or prickly pear.** This oval fruit tastes like watermelon but with a slight peach-pear flavor. The fruit may be spooned and eaten straight from the shell or peeled and cut up. The seeds are edible, too.

■ **Carambola.** Also called a starfruit, this tastes like a combination of lemon, pineapple, and apple. It is sweet and bright yellow when ripe; unripe fruit is greenish and tart.

■ **Cherimoya.** Also called custard apple, this heart-shaped fruit has a creamy white interior with large black seeds. The ripe fruit has a custardlike texture with a hint of banana flavor. Cherimoya turns a dull brownish green when ripe.

■ **Feijoa.** This egg-shaped fruit has pale yellow to green flesh with a pear-like texture. The tiny seeds are edible, but discard the bitter skin.

■ **Guava.** This juicy fruit tastes like lime, kiwifruit, banana, and berries all rolled into one. Though the seeds are edible, they're usually discarded.

■ **Kiwifruit.** With a flavor reminiscent of strawberry, melon, and peaches, this fuzzy, brown-skinned fruit is entirely edible—skin, seeds, and all.

■ **Mango.** In the middle of this fruit's golden flesh is a large seed that clings to the meat. Cut away as much of the fruit as you can with a sharp knife and enjoy the spicy peach flavor and perfumelike fragrance.

■ **Passion fruit.** On the outside, this ripe fruit looks shriveled and dented. Inside, the juice and edible seeds are lush and tangy. Use a spoon to eat the meat straight from the shell.

UP-AND-COMING VEGETABLES

An ever-growing variety of fresh vegetables are now available, providing an excellent opportunity to add new flavors and textures to your meals. The following descriptions will help you make new selections with confidence.

■ **Bok choy.** This variety of Chinese cabbage has long, white, celerylike stalks and large, dark green leaves. Its texture is crisp like celery, and its flavor is much like mild cabbage. To use bok choy in cooking, slice the stalks and shred the leaves.

■ **Broccoli raab.** Also called rapini, this vegetable looks like a stalk of broccoli with sprouting spinach leaves. Both the stems and leaves have a somewhat sharp and bitter flavor. Broccoli raab must be kept well-chilled because it deteriorates quickly under warm conditions. To use it in recipes, tear it into bite-size pieces, discarding any wilted portions.

■ **Cactus leaves.** Plucked from the prickly pear cactus, these leaves are similar to green beans, with an avocadolike aftertaste. When cooked, they are soft and crunchy, with the slipperiness of okra.

Chayote. This pear-shaped squash also is called mirliton, the preferred name in Cajun and Southern cuisines. It has delicate green- or white-ridged edible skin, and the moist flesh tastes like a cross between an apple and a cucumber. Use chayote in cooking as you would zucchini or other summer squash.

Fennel. A bulbous vegetable, fennel has celerylike stalks and feathery, bright green leaves. Its light licorice flavor mellows upon cooking. Discard the tough upper stalks and save the leaves for a delicate garnish.

Jerusalem artichoke. Also called a sunchoke, the Jerusalem artichoke can be eaten raw or cooked. Though it has a crisp texture, its flavor is reminiscent of a sweet potato.

Kohlrabi. This vegetable has a sweet, mild, turniplike flavor, and the leaves taste like spinach. Peel it before cooking or eating raw.

Mesclun. This is actually a mixture of piquant, delicate, young salad greens. The mix varies, but it is always a combination of flavors, textures, and colors.

Plantain. When cooked, a ripe plantain tastes similar to a banana; pick a black plantain for the ripest, fullest flavor. Ripen green or yellow plantains at room temperature.

ETHNIC INGREDIENTS

The authentic flavors of Mexican, Italian, and Asian cooking have migrated to America's home kitchens. The following lists include the ingredients characteristic of these cuisines.

MEXICAN INGREDIENTS

Beans Also known as frijoles (free-HO-lays), beans are used to flavor soups, sauces, and salads, and to complement or replace meat in dishes served with tortillas. The most common variety is the pinto bean, which is used to make refried beans. Other types include garbanzo, black, and fava beans.

Blue corn When choosing chips, tortillas, or even cornmeal, check out the versions made from blue corn. While it tastes the same as other cornmeals, the blue color adds interest to food presentation.

Chili peppers Available fresh and pickled, these peppers come in many sizes, colors, and degrees of hotness. The best known are serrano and jalapeño, both of which are fiery hot; poblano and anaheim peppers are much milder.

Chipotle (chi-POHT-lay) **pepper** The chipotle is a jalapeño pepper that has been dried and smoked.

■ **Chorizo** *(chuh-REE-zo)* This spicy Mexican pork sausage is available in bulk or link. It's delicious in fillings for tortilla-based dishes.

■ **Cumin** *(CUH-min)* Often found in chili powder, this nutty, slightly bitter, ground spice or seed peps up chili, beef, fish, and soups.

■ **Jicama** *(HEE-kah-mah)* Jicama is a potatolike tuber with a mild, slightly sweet flavor. It has a crunchy texture either raw or cooked.

■ **Masa Harina** *(MAH-sah ah-REE-nah)* A special mix you can purchase for making tortilla dough. Masa *(MAH-sah)* is a dried corn dough used as the base for corn tortillas and tamales. Generally it is not available ready-made.

■ **Papaya** This pear-shaped fruit is known for its mellow, buttery taste. Remove the black seeds before eating.

■ **Salsa** The catsup of Southwestern cuisine, salsa is a sauce usually made from finely chopped tomatoes, onions, chilies, and cilantro.

■ **Tomatillo** *(toe-mah-TEE-yo)* This green, tomatolike vegetable comes wrapped in a husk. With a tart, lemony flavor, it is usually cooked and used in sauces and salsas.

■ **Tortilla** This small, thin, flat bread is made from corn or wheat flour and usually is wrapped around a filling.

ITALIAN INGREDIENTS

■ **Artichoke** This firm-leafed globe vegetable usually is steamed and served with a dipping sauce. To eat one, see the note on page 1028.

■ **Balsamic vinegar** (see page 952).

■ **Caper** This flower bud of the caper bush has a pungent, slightly bitter flavor. Capers are usually pickled.

■ **Mushrooms** Porcini, or cèpes, the most prized fresh wild mushroom in Italy, is known for its large, meaty, slightly rounded cap. The crimini mushroom is shaped like a button mushroom but is light tan to dark brown in color.

■ **Olives** The color of Italian ripe olives can vary from purplish red and brown to jet black. They are packed in oil or brine, which may be flavored with herbs or citrus peel.

■ **Olive oil** (see page 951).

■ **Pancetta** *(pan-CHEH-tuh)* The Italian version of bacon, it is seasoned with pepper and other spices, then salt-cured.

■ **Parmesan cheese** Parmigiano-Reggiano cheese is an aged hard cheese made from cow's milk. In the United States, Parmesan often is imitated. The results are different from the cheese made in Italy, where quality is strictly regulated.

■ **Prosciutto** *(proh-SHOO-toh)* Sweetly spiced, this ham is salt-cured to eliminate moisture then air-dried. The resulting rose-colored meat has a slight sheen.

■ **Tomatoes** For cooking, plum and Roma tomatoes are preferred, as they have fewer seeds, firmer flesh, and less juice. Recipes often call for dried tomatoes, which have an intense, sweet flavor and a chewy texture. They may be packed in olive oil.

ASIAN INGREDIENTS

■ **Bean sauce and paste** Both products are made from fermented soybeans and have a salty bean flavor. They can be used inter-changeably.

■ **Bean threads** These thin, almost transparent noodles are made from mung bean flour. They also are called bean noodles or cello-phane noodles.

■ **Chili oil** This fiery oil, flavored with chili peppers, is used as a seasoning.

■ **Chili paste** Made from chili peppers, vinegar, and seasonings, this condiment is very hot; use it sparingly.

■ **Dried mushrooms** Despite their shriveled appearance, dried mushrooms swell into tender, flavorful morsels. Simply soak them in warm water, rinse them and squeeze out the moisture, then cook them in recipes as you would fresh mushrooms. Popular choices include oyster, wood ear, and shiitake mushrooms.

■ **Fish sauce** This thin, salty condiment is made from fermented fish. Use it sparingly to season foods during cooking and at the table.

■ **Gingerroot** This brown-skinned, knobby root has a fibrous flesh that adds spicy-sweet flavor to stir-fries. Slice or grate it (peeling isn't necessary), discarding the fibers. Wrap whole gingerroot in paper towels and store for up to a month in the refrigerator. Or, place cut-up ginger in a small jar. Fill jar with dry sherry or wine and refrigerate it, covered, for up to 3 months.

■ **Lemongrass** Loved for its delicate, lemonlike flavor, lemongrass is available in fresh, dried, or powdered forms. Remove tough outer portion of the stalk and slice tender inner part before adding it to dishes. You may substitute ¹/₂ teaspoon finely shredded lemon peel for 1 tablespoon lemongrass.

■ **Rice sticks and rice papers** Ultrathin rice sticks puff up and get crisp when fried. Use round, flat rice papers as wrappers for spring rolls.

■ **Rice vinegar** This slightly sweet vinegar with a subtle tang is made from rice. If you don't have any on hand, substitute white or white wine vinegar.

■ **Shrimp paste** This paste is a strong-flavored, thick mixture of fermented shrimp, chili peppers, and curry. Dilute it with water and use it sparingly.

■ **Soba noodles** These thin dried noodles are made from buckwheat flour.

■ **Tamari** A dark, thin sauce, tamari is made from soybeans. For a substitute, use soy sauce.

■ **Tamarind paste** The tart taste of this thick, brown paste comes from the fruit of the tamarind tree.

■ **Toasted sesame oil** This aromatic reddish brown oil is made from toasted sesame seed. A little oil goes a long way.

■ **Tofu** Also called bean curd, tofu is made by curding soybean milk. It has little flavor of its own but easily absorbs flavors of other foods. Soft tofu works best for whipping, blending, and crumbling. Use the firm type for slicing and cubing. Submerge tofu in water in an airtight container, and it will keep for up to 1 week in the refrigerator. Change water daily to keep it fresh and moist.

KITCHEN APPLIANCES AND EQUIPMENT

For greatest convenience and versatility in preparing family meals, equip your kitchen with the following basics.

BLENDER

This kitchen helper trims preparation time by instantly blending, chopping, and pureeing foods. For best results, follow these guidelines:

■ Cut fresh fruits and vegetables, cooked meats, fish, and seafood into $1/2$- to 1-inch pieces before adding them to the blender.

■ Stop your blender often and check the size of the food pieces. Blenders work quickly and easily can overblend or overchop food.

■ Cube soft cheese before blending it with liquid ingredients.

■ When blending thick mixtures, stop the blender often and use a rubber spatula to scrape sides of the container.

■ For better control, blend large quantities of foods in several small batches.

■ For slushy drinks, add ice cubes, one at a time, through the opening in the lid as the blender is running.

■ If you're preparing creamy salad dressings, add the oil through the opening in the lid as the blender is running.

CROCKERY COOKER

A hardworking kitchen helper, this basic appliance cooks meals while you're away, and it keeps party dips and sauces warm all evening. The long, slow cooking process produces tender meats and full-flavored stews. Remember that a crockery cooker differs from a slow cooker (see tip, page 985).

ELECTRIC MIXER

While you can choose from a wide array of mixers—with and without attachments—there are basically two kinds on the market. The handheld portable mixer will do well for most recipes. But if you do a lot of cooking, you may want to invest in a heavy-duty stand mixer, which will free you up while it's operating. Many of the stand mixers can knead bread dough and handle large amounts of thick batter.

FOOD PROCESSOR

A food processor does many of the same jobs as a blender and electric mixer, and it slices and shreds as well. Unlike an electric mixer,

KEEPING KNIVES SHARP

A sharp knife is essential. Keep your knives in prime condition by sharpening them before each use with a handheld sharpening steel or stone. With the steel or stone in one hand, hold the knife in your other hand at a 20-degree angle to the sharpener. Draw the blade edge over the sharpener, using a motion that goes across and down at the same time. Turn the blade over, reverse directions, and sharpen the other side an equal number of times.

STOCKING YOUR KITCHEN

The equipment needed to prepare food can be broken down into three groups: preparation and cooking gadgets, range-top cookware, and bakeware. Outfit your kitchen with this basic equipment and you'll be able to make almost any recipe in this book.

Preparation and Cooking Gadgets

Bottle opener
Can opener
Chef's knife
Clear glass liquid measuring cup
Colanders
Corkscrew
Flexible metal spatulas
Grater and/or shredder
Kitchen scissors
Kitchen timer
Ladle
Long-handled fork
Long-handled spoon
Meat mallet
Meat thermometer
Oven thermometer
Pancake turner
Paring knife
Pasta server
Plastic cutting board
Rolling pin
Rotary beater
Rubber spatulas
Serrated knife
Set of dry measuring cups
Set of measuring spoons
Set of mixing bowls
Sharpening steel
Slotted spoon
Small and large strainers
Tongs
Utility knife
Vegetable peeler
Wire cooling rack
Wood cutting board
Wooden spoons

Range-Top Cookware

4- or 6-quart covered pot or kettle
1-quart covered saucepan
2-quart covered saucepan
3-quart covered saucepan
6- or 8-inch skillet
10-inch ovenproof skillet with cover
12-inch skillet
Nonstick skillet

Bakeware

2-quart rectangular baking dish (12×7$\frac{1}{2}$×2-inch)
3-quart rectangular baking dish (13×9×2-inch)
2-quart square baking dish

(8×8×2-inch)
9×9×2-inch baking pan
15×10×1-inch baking (jelly roll) pan
8×1½-inch round baking pans
9×1½-inch round baking pans
Baking sheet
Various sizes of round, deep casserole dishes

6-ounce custard cups
8×4×2-inch loaf pan or dish
9×5×3-inch loaf pan or dish
Muffin pan
9-inch pie plate
Pizza pan
Roasting pan with rack
10-inch tube pan

though, a food processor can't whip foods such as potatoes or cream.

Microwave Oven

Microwave ovens vary in wattage according to the manufacturer and model. All recipes in this book were tested in ovens that provide 600 to 700 watts of cooking power. If you own a 1,000-watt oven, your food will cook faster than our recipe times suggest. If you own a low-wattage oven (less than 600 watts), your recipe may need additional time.

Thermometers

■ **Candy/deep-frying thermometer.** The calibrations on this instrument are higher than a meat thermometer to accommodate the temperatures required for candy and deep-fat frying. It is equipped with a handy clip for attaching to the side of the pan. For more information, see page 297.

■ **Instant-read thermometer.** This handy gadget can be plunged into any food to give you an internal reading in seconds. Use it for verifying the temperature of dense casseroles or thin cuts of meat and fish. Do not leave it in a hot oven.

■ **Meat thermometer** (see tip, page 620).

■ **Refrigerator/freezer thermometer.** This verifies whether the appliance is chilling correctly. For food safety, refrigerators should be set as cold as possible without freezing milk or lettuce—generally about 40°. Freezers should be set at 0° or lower.

BAKING PANS AND DISHES

For the recipes in this book, a baking pan refers to a metal pan, and a baking dish refers to an oven-safe glass container. (When using glass or ceramic cookware in the oven, reduce the baking temperature by about 25°.)

Use baking pans:
■ For a golden, crisp crust when baking cookies, breads, or cakes.
■ For all broiling, since glass dishes cannot withstand the high temperatures.

Use baking dishes:
■ For dishes with acidic ingredients, which can cause metal to react and discolor food.
■ For moist casseroles—especially those made with eggs, because metal can discolor them.
■ For a more attractive presentation of the food.

MAKE-DO COOKWARE

When you don't have the exact utensil called for in a recipe, try one of these substitutions:
■ **Covered casserole:** Cover a baking dish with foil.
■ **Double boiler:** Place a metal or heat-resistant glass bowl in a saucepan. The bowl should be wide enough so its bottom doesn't touch the bottom of the pan.
■ **Food mill:** Force food through a strainer set over a bowl or pan.
■ **Pastry bag:** Snip the corner from a heavy plastic bag.
■ **Pizza pan:** Use a baking sheet, building up the pizza crust edges to hold toppings.
■ **Sifter:** Pour flour or powdered sugar into a sieve set over a bowl, then stir it with a spoon to force the grains through the holes.
■ **Soufflé dish:** Substitute a straight-sided casserole with the same volume.

KITCHEN SAFETY

Keeping food safe to eat involves four simple rules.
■ **Use clean hands, clean food, clean utensils, and clean surfaces.**
Bacteria live everywhere; always wash and dry your hands with clean cloths before handling food. Wash kitchen towels, cloths, and sponges often. Rinse fresh fruits and vegetables with water before eating or preparing them. Rinse poultry before cooking. Wash plastic

cutting boards, knives, and other utensils with hot sudsy water after every use and before using with another type of food. This is especially necessary after handling raw meat and poultry. Never put cooked meat or poultry on the same plate or in the same container that held the raw meat, unless it has been thoroughly washed first.

■ Keep hot foods hot.

Thorough cooking is needed to kill harmful bacteria that may be present in raw eggs, fish, poultry, and meat. From a safety standpoint, hamburger that is red in the middle, steak and roast beef that are rare or medium-rare, and eggs that are runny are undercooked. Cook red meat to 160° and poultry to 180°; use a meat thermometer to check temperature. For a visual check for proper doneness, follow these tips: Red meat is brown or gray inside; poultry and pork juices should run clear; fish flakes easily with a fork; and egg yolks and whites are firm and set.

If you use a microwave oven for thawing, complete the cooking as soon as the food is thawed. Do not partially cook foods, stop, then finish cooking later; bacteria may grow before the second cooking time. When cooking in a microwave oven, stir the food or rotate the dish to help prevent hot and cold spots. Observe the standing time suggested in recipes or on package directions to allow the food to finish cooking. Use a meat thermometer to check for doneness.

If you have leftovers, refrigerate or freeze them in covered containers as soon as possible. Divide large amounts into small, shallow containers for more rapid cooling. Remove poultry stuffing and store in a separate container. Reheat leftovers in a covered container to retain moisture. Bring sauces, soups, and gravy to a full boil, stirring during cooking. Heat other leftovers to 165°, stirring occasionally.

■ Keep cold foods cold.

Check packages before purchasing; refrigerated food should be cold to the touch, frozen food should be rock solid. Take purchased groceries straight home to the refrigerator or freezer. Check appliance temperatures periodically (refrigerator should be 40°, freezer 0° or lower). Put packages of fresh meat, poultry, and fish on a plate in the refrigerator if you plan to cook them within a few days, otherwise place them immediately in the freezer. Thaw and marinate foods in the refrigerator, not on the kitchen counter. Keep eggs in the covered egg carton in the refrigerator. Store cheese, cream, milk, sour cream, yogurt, margarine, and butter in the refrigerator, tightly covered.

■ If in doubt, throw it out.

Contaminated food can smell, look, and taste perfectly normal, so never taste a food you suspect is contaminated. Even one bite could make you ill. This is especially true for pregnant women, infants, the elderly, and individuals with weakened immune systems.

For more on food safety, see pages 462 (eggs), 652 (meats), and 819 (poultry).

SAFE PICNICKING

Keep cold foods in an insulated cooler that has been cleaned and cooled before packing. Chill the cooler by filling it with ice for at least 30 minutes before packing it with food. Refrigerate foods before putting them in the cooler. Wait until just before leaving home to pack your cooler. In addition to ice or ice packs, pack frozen foods, such as cans of juice, to thaw along the way and help keep other foods cold. On the drive to a summer outing, don't put the cooler in the car trunk. Once at the picnic site, set the tightly closed cooler in a shady area and add ice often.

Handle hot dishes wisely, too. Just before you leave home, take hot foods from the oven. If desired, transfer hot food (such as baked beans, soups, and casseroles) to an electric slow crockery cooker for extra insulation. Wrap the covered dish, container, or crockery cooker in heavy foil, several layers of newspaper, or a heavy towel. Then place in an insulated container to tote. The food should stay hot for up to 2 hours. If there is electricity at your picnic spot and you have a crockery cooker, your food will stay warm for hours on the low-heat setting (add additional liquid as needed).

MEAL PLANNING

"What are we having to eat?" is a daily question. The following information can help you plan delicious, healthful meals that fit your schedule.

HEALTHY ADVICE

Increasing evidence supports the notion that what we eat affects how we feel and even whether we'll live a long, healthy life. More often debated are the roles played by specific foods. Instead of trying to keep track of all the claims and counterclaims, remember two words: variety and moderation. Eating a variety of foods and choosing specific foods in moderate amounts are daily goals no matter what your age.

DIETARY GUIDELINES

The 1995 recommendations from the United States Department of Agriculture (USDA) are based on medical and scientific research, and include the following.

1. Eat a variety of foods.
2. Balance the food you eat with physical activity; maintain or improve your weight.
3. Choose a diet with plenty of grain products, vegetables, and fruits.
4. Choose a diet low in fat, saturated fat, and cholesterol.
5. Choose a diet that's moderate in sugars.
6. Choose a diet that's moderate in salt and sodium.
7. If you drink alcoholic beverages, do so in moderation.

THE FOOD GUIDE PYRAMID

The Food Guide Pyramid (see next page) can help you eat to meet the dietary guidelines (see above). The Pyramid retains the four-food-group concept, but also shows you how to apportion your family's choices among the various food groups. As you can see by its broad base, the Pyramid emphasizes eating lots of fruits, vegetables, grains, pasta, and breads. These foods supply important nutrients that contribute to overall good health and may help prevent certain diseases, such as heart disease and cancer. The small triangle at the top of the Pyramid shows that fats, oils, and sweets should play a limited role in your daily diet. Foods high in fat are strongly linked to obesity and an increased risk for heart disease and some forms of cancer.

The Pyramid also tells how many servings in the major groups you should strive to eat every day. You need the most servings (6 to 11) from the bread, cereal, rice, and pasta group. No number of servings is recommended for the group at the top of the Pyramid (fats, oils, and sweets) because you should eat these foods sparingly. Throughout the Pyramid, tiny circles (which symbolize fat) and tiny triangles (which symbolize sugar) show that foods in these groups might contain fat and added sugar, too.

Refer to the list on page 35 to determine serving sizes for many common foods. Keep in mind these caveats:

Food Guide Pyramid
A Guide to Daily Food Choices

KEY
● Fat (naturally occurring ▼ Sugars
and added) = (added)

These symbols show fats, oils, and added sugars in foods.

Fats, Oils, & Sweets
USE SPARINGLY

Milk, Yogurt,
& Cheese
Group
2-3 SERVINGS

Meat, Poultry, Fish,
Dry Beans, Eggs,
& Nuts Group
2-3 SERVINGS

Vegetable
Group
3-5 SERVINGS

Fruit
Group
2-4 SERVINGS

Bread, Cereal,
Rice, & Pasta
Group
6-11
SERVINGS

Source: U.S. Department of Agriculture/U.S. Department of Health and Human Services

■ The total number of servings you need from each group will depend on your age, gender, size, and activity level. Aim for the minimum number of servings.
■ If you eat a significantly larger portion than the suggested serving size, count it as more than 1 serving.
■ For children ages 6 or older, use the same serving size as you would for an adult.
■ For children ages 2 to 5, count two-thirds of the adult size as one serving, except for dairy foods (for which the serving sizes are the same).
■ Consult your doctor for advice on feeding children younger than age 2.

▓ Bread, cereal, rice, pasta

1 slice bread or 1 dinner roll
1 ounce ready-to-eat cereal
$^1/_2$ cup cooked rice, cereal, or pasta
$^1/_2$ of a hamburger or hot dog bun

▓ Vegetables

1 cup mixed green salad
$^1/_2$ cup cooked or raw chopped vegetables
$^3/_4$ cup vegetable juice
$^1/_2$ cup tomato or spaghetti sauce
$^1/_2$ cup cooked dry beans (if not counted as a meat alternate)

▓ Fruits

1 medium apple, banana, orange, pear, or peach
$^1/_2$ cup cooked, canned, or frozen fruit
$^1/_4$ cup dried fruit
$^3/_4$ cup fruit juice (100% juice)

▓ Milk, yogurt, cheese

1 cup milk or yogurt
$1^1/_2$ ounces natural cheese
2 ounces process cheese

▓ Meat, poultry, fish, dry beans, eggs, nuts

2 to 3 ounces cooked lean boneless meat, poultry, or fish
$^1/_2$ cup cooked dry beans (if not counted as a vegetable)
2 to 3 equivalents of 1 ounce of meat (2 tablespoons peanut butter or 1 egg
   is equivalent to 1 ounce of meat)
$^1/_3$ cup nuts (walnuts, pecans, or peanuts)

USING FOOD LABELS

Today's nutrition labels, which appear on most food cans, packages, and boxes, make choosing healthful foods for your family easier than ever. The wisest, quickest way to benefit from food labels is to pay close attention to the daily values.

To have a balanced diet, you need a certain amount of specific nutrients every day. The daily values (expressed in percentages) tell how much of the recommended amount of a nutrient is in a serving of that food. You can use these daily values to figure out how a food fits into your total diet.

Thinking in terms of points will help you use the daily values. You start every day with 100 percentage points for each of the nutrients listed on the food label. For example, you're allotted 100 points for saturated fat, 100 points for cholesterol, 100 points for dietary fiber, and so on. Each time you eat a serving of food, you subtract the specific number of percentage points for each nutrient contained in that serving from 100. (Remember, the "points" are listed under the % Daily Value on each food label.)

For example, the label at right shows that an 8-ounce serving contains a 4 percent daily value for fat. Once you subtract that from your 100-percent allotment, you're left with 96 points of fat for the rest of the day. At first glance, it may seem as though the goal is to hit that target number of 100 percent for each nutrient. But that isn't always the case. It's good to fall below the 100 level for fat, sodium, and cholesterol. On the other hand, overshooting the 100 mark for essential vitamins and minerals isn't a problem. In fact, if you consistently come in low with essential nutrients, you should eat more foods that are high in those nutrients.

The daily value percentage for each nutrient is based on a specific serving size. To tell how each food fits into your total diet, as well as to judge whether yours is a balanced diet, follow the serving sizes listed on the label. (The Food and Drug Administration requires that similar foods be consistent in their serving amounts.)

The daily values are based on a 2,000-calories-a-day diet. That number is an average intake of calories for all Americans. Depending upon your age, gender, weight, and activity level, you may require more or fewer calories per day.

With all the concern about fat in our diets, more and more low-fat food products are available. Before buying low-fat and no-fat

Nutrition Facts
Low-Fat Milk

Serving Size: 8 fl oz. (240 ml)

Amount Per Serving

Calories 100	Calories From Fat 20

	% Daily Value*
Total Fat 2.5 g	4%
Saturated Fat 1.5 g	8%
Cholesterol 10 mg	3%
Sodium 130 mg	5%
Total Carbohydrate 12 g	4%
Dietary Fiber 0 g	0%
Sugars 11 g	
Protein 8 g	

Vitamin A	10%	•	Vitamin C	4%
Calcium	30%	•	Iron	0%

*Percent Daily Values are based on a 2,000 calorie diet. Your daily values may be higher or lower depending on your calorie needs:

		Calories	2,000	2,500
Total Fat	Less than		65 g	80 g
Sat Fat	Less than		20 g	25 g
Cholesterol	Less than		300 mg	300 mg
Sodium	Less than		2,400 mg	2,400 mg
Total Carbohydrate			300 g	375 g
Fiber			25 g	30 g

Calories per gram:
Fat 9 • Carbohydrates 4 • Protein 4

products, give the labels a careful reading. These alternative products still have calories, and they can still add fat to your diet.

NUTRITION FACTS: HOW TO MAKE THEM WORK FOR YOU

With each recipe, we give you useful nutrition information you easily can apply to your own needs. First, see "What You Need" (below) to determine your dietary requirements. Then, refer to the Nutrition Facts listed with each recipe. Here, you'll find the calorie count and the amount of fat, saturated fat, cholesterol, sodium, carbohydrate, fiber, and protein for each serving. Along with the Nutrition Facts per serving, you'll find the amount of vitamin A, vitamin C, calcium, and iron noted as a percentage of the Daily Values (see "Using Food Labels," page 35). To be more accurate, follow the suggested number of servings.

HOW WE ANALYZE

Our Test Kitchen uses a computer analysis of each recipe to determine the nutritional value of a single serving. Here's how:

■ The analysis does not include optional ingredients.

■ We use the first serving size listed when a range is given. For example: Makes 4 to 6 servings.

■ When ingredient choices appear in a recipe (such as margarine or butter), we use the first one mentioned for analysis. The ingredient order does not mean we prefer one ingredient over another.

■ When milk is an ingredient in a recipe, the analysis is calculated using 2-percent milk.

■ When Nutrition Facts are not given for a variation, it means the values are similar to those listed for the main recipe.

WHAT YOU NEED

The guidelines below suggest nutrient levels that moderately active adults should strive to eat each day. As your calorie levels change, adjust your fat intake, too. Try to keep the percentage of calories from fat to no more than 30 percent. There's no harm in occasionally going over or under these guidelines, but the key to good health is maintaining a balanced diet most of the time.

■ **Calories:** About 2,000

■ **Total fat:** Less than 65 grams

■ **Saturated fat:** Less than 20 grams

■ **Cholesterol:** Less than 300 milligrams

■ **Carbohydrates:** About 300 grams

- **Sodium:** Less than 2,400 milligrams
- **Dietary fiber:** 20 to 30 grams

LOW-FAT RECIPE FLAGS

Recipes that meet our low-fat criteria are flagged with this symbol:

Low-Fat

To meet this designation, a main-dish serving must contain 12 or fewer grams of fat. For side-dishes or desserts, the serving must contain 5 or fewer grams of fat with these exceptions:
- 3 or fewer grams of fat for bread and vegetable side dishes
- 2 grams or fewer per appetizer
- 2 grams or fewer per cookie

SHOPPING STRATEGIES

Grocery shopping can become a more efficient process with the following methods for saving time and money.
- Start by getting organized before you head to the store. Whenever possible, plan a week or two of menus. Review the Food Guide Pyramid recommendations as you plan meals. Also look at your local newspaper ads to take advantage of weekly specials.
- Shop during down times when the market isn't crowded. That way you can take your time to discover new foods, and it gives you a chance to read the nutrition facts on labels.
- Shopping with a list is the best way to keep impromptu purchases to a minimum. Keep an ongoing list in your kitchen to jot down foods as you think of them.
- Gather coupons you plan to use and mark those items on the list. At the store, compare brands and prices to find the best buys.
- Know the difference between impulse buying and bargain hunting. Unadvertised specials for items you routinely use can mean savings even if the item isn't on your list.
- Avoid grocery shopping when you're hungry—you're more likely to buy extra items on impulse.

TIMESAVING TIPS

Even busy people can cook from scratch by planning their kitchen time wisely and relying on today's convenience products. Here are

LOW-FAT COOKING TIPS

Many of the recipes in this book can be prepared using lower-fat ingredients or cooking techniques. Consider some of these slimming tricks each time you fix a recipe:

■ Use low-fat or no-fat dairy products. Lower-fat sour cream, yogurt, and cheese can be substituted in recipes at a substantial fat and calorie savings. Reduced-fat or fat-free cream cheese can be used as a substitute in any recipe (cheesecakes, dips, sauces), but you may notice a difference in flavor or texture.

■ Use small amounts of strong-flavored cheese rather than a lot of mild cheese.

■ To mimic the flavor and creaminess of sour cream, use buttermilk instead. It's as low in calories and fat as 1-percent milk.

■ Use evaporated skim milk in place of light or heavy cream in soups and sauces.

■ Remove the skin from poultry. (You can do so after cooking since the meat doesn't absorb much of the fat.)

■ For the leanest option when preparing ground meat recipes, ask your butcher to grind skinned, boneless turkey or chicken breast.

■ Use Canadian-style bacon. Ounce for ounce, it has 116 fewer calories than regular bacon.

■ Use nuts sparingly; toast them to enhance their flavor.

■ Use very little fat in cooking. Instead, use nonstick pans, spray coating, or a small amount of broth or water to sauté or "fry" vegetables or meat.

some of our favorite ways to make home cooking quicker and easier than ever.

■ Before starting any meal preparation, read all recipes thoroughly. You'll also save time by assembling ingredients and utensils before you begin.

■ Make preheating your oven the first step with any baked or broiled recipe so the oven is ready when you are.

■ Overlap cooking steps. While you're waiting for one part of the recipe to heat or cook, cut or mix the other ingredients.

■ Rely on boneless, thin cuts of meat and poultry that cook quickly—usually in less than 20 minutes.

■ Convenience products give you a jump on cooking by doing some of the work for you. Items such as shredded cheese, minced fresh garlic, frozen chopped onions, precut vegetables, refrigerated doughs, and cubed meat for stir-fries or stews often cost more, but the time saved may be worth the extra cost to you.

■ Chill ingredients ahead. If your refrigerator space or your time is limited, chill canned fruits, vegetables, or meats in your freezer for 30 minutes before using. (Remove the food from the cans before freezing and place in a container. In case you don't use them, you don't want a can to burst in your freezer.)

■ Concentrate on a main recipe. Start with one recipe for the entrée, then round out your meal with quick-to-fix or already prepared foods such as steamed vegetables, a frozen side dish, fresh fruit, or a bakery dessert.

■ Add favorite ingredients to quick-fix products. For instance, spread purchased cheesecake with seedless raspberry preserves and decorate with fresh fruit. Or, make a simple main dish by stir-frying strips of pork or beef, then adding a package of frozen Oriental vegetables and serving over rice.

RECIPE TIME ESTIMATES

The timings listed with each recipe should be used as general guidelines. Consider the following points as well.

■ Preparation (Prep) times with recipes have been rounded to the nearest 5-minute increments.

■ Listings include the time to chop, slice, or otherwise prepare ingredients, such as cooking rice when a recipe calls for cooked rice.

■ When a recipe gives an ingredient substitution, the calculations are made using the first ingredient.

■ When a recipe gives an alternate cooking method, such as stovetop or oven directions, timings refer to the first method.

■ Timings assume some steps can be performed simultaneously.

■ The preparation of optional ingredients is not included.

■ Recipes that are designated as Fast can be prepared and served in 30 minutes or less.

■ Make a mix unique with a few tasty additions. Top brownie mix batter with almond brickle pieces and chocolate pieces before baking. Add orange or lemon peel or nuts to sweet muffins. Add chili peppers and shredded cheese to corn muffins.

■ Stock your pantry with items that can be turned into a quick meal. Family favorites include biscuit mix, canned soups, quick-cooking rice mixes, pastas and pasta sauces, cheese, and eggs.

GUIDE TO GREAT MENUS

You're in for rave reviews when you serve a meal that's nutritious, attractive, and delicious. But it does take a bit of organizing to harmonize all the parts of the meal.

First think about the flavor of your main course. Usually one highly seasoned food at lunch or dinner is enough. For example, alongside hot and spicy chili offer mild accompaniments such as corn bread. If you're serving a delicate fish, be sure the other dishes don't overpower it. With most dinners, one starchy dish (potatoes, rice, pasta, beans, or corn) is plenty. Bread can be served anytime.

Next consider the texture and temperature of the foods. It's best to serve some hot foods and some cold foods as well as soft and crisp foods.

Think visually, too. How will the foods look together on the plate? This includes color and shapes of ingredients. An all-white meal of poached fish, mashed potatoes, and bread pales next to poached fish with steamed green beans and rye rolls. Also, a meal with all the same shapes is less interesting than one with varying shapes.

Even when two recipes aren't served at the same time, consider how each dish adds character to the meal. Plan a dessert that rounds out dinner—a light sweet following a hearty meal or a rich dessert with a light entrée.

SAMPLE MENUS

You can try the following variety of menus. The page number is listed for recipes in this book. Other items are generic.

EASY DINNER FOR 4

Pork Tenderloin Sandwiches, 650
Orzo Pilaf, 771
Creamy Coleslaw, 920 (or purchased)

CASUAL DINNER FOR 4

Stuffed Mushrooms, 65
Turkey-and-Broccoli-Filled Lasagna Rolls, 751
Spinach Toss, 915
Crisp breadsticks
Double Chocolate Chunk Biscotti, 405

SUNDAY DINNER

Swiss Steak, 629
Biscuits Supreme, 239
Fried Green Tomatoes, 1070 (or sliced fresh tomatoes)
German Chocolate Cake, 261

COOKOUT FOR 4

Grilled Fish Sandwiches, 579
Grilled vegetables, 597
Cold rice or pasta salad (purchased or homemade)
Low-Fat Cheesecake, 430

VEGETARIAN MEAL FOR 4

Guacamole and Tortilla Crisps, 69, 68
Spicy Black Beans and Rice, 107
Assorted fruits, such as melon wedges and grapes

LOW-FAT DINNER FOR 6

Oven-Fried Chicken, 823
Mixed Grain Casserole, 128
Steamed carrots with lemon
Brown-and-serve rolls
Individual Meringue Shells, 426 (with fresh fruit)

FIX-AND-FORGET SUPPER

Old-Fashioned Beef Stew, 981
Dill Batter Bread, 203
Chocolaty Velvet Ice Cream, 450

WEEKEND BRUNCH FOR 6 TO 8

Dijon Chicken Strata, 488
Orange Bowknots, 210
Mixed fresh fruit
Iced Coffee, 144

SPECIAL-OCCASION DINNER

Marinated Prime Rib, 621
Horseradish Sauce, 965
Steamed asparagus
Hot cooked orzo, 774
Dinner Rolls, 194
Truffle Cake, 432

OPEN HOUSE BUFFET FOR 20

Spicy Party Cheesecake, 93
Easy Chicken Pâté, 75
Polynesian Meatballs, 90
Sour Cream Fruit Dip, 66
Orange-Rosemary Pound Cake, 286
Raspberry Truffle Brownies, 377
Spiced Fruit Punch, 150

THANKSGIVING

Hot Spiced Cider, 149
Roast Turkey with Old-Fashioned Bread Stuffing, 865
Candied Sweet Potatoes, 1066
Steamed Brussels sprouts or broccoli
Whole Wheat Potato Rolls, 198
Cranberry Relish, 973
Mince-Apple Pie, 780

MEXICAN FIESTA

Toasted Chili Nuts, 62
Chili Rellenos Casserole, 486
Spanish Rice, 100
Assorted fresh fruits
Orange Sherbet, 449

ITALIAN FLAIR

Crostini with Dried Tomato-Feta Spread, 82
Chicken Marsala, 828
Easy Risotto, 106
Sesame Asparagus, 1031
Tiramisu, 431

Rumaki, 94
Eggrolls, 94
Cashew Pork and Pea Pods, 662
Hot cooked rice, 139
Sorbet with fortune cookies

DINING ETIQUETTE

Just as important as the food you create for dining is the mood. Whether setting the table with fine china and silver or casual dinnerware and tumblers, you can enhance the experience by setting the table right. Don't forget—a minute spent lighting a candle or putting a favorite memento in the center of the table can make family or guests feel welcome and nourished by more than just the food.

SETTING THE TABLE

Over the years customs have evolved to define where plates, glasses, and flatware should be placed on the table. Even at a casual meal people expect to find pieces in a certain spot.

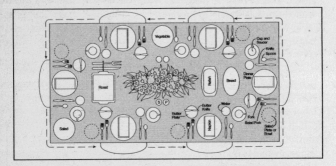

For a family meal (see above), arrange the plate in the center of each place setting. Add the forks, knives, and spoons around the plate, with the first items to be used set on the outside. Forks are placed to the left of the plate. The spoon and knife (blade side turned in) go on the right of the plate. Dessert spoons and forks and coffee spoons may be placed horizontally at the top of the dinner plate or brought to the table at serving time. Bread-and-butter plates (if needed) go to the left of the dinner plates above the forks (unless salad is served, then the salad plate is placed to the left of the forks).

Glasses are placed above the knife to the right of the plate. If more than one beverage is served, start at the outside edge of the place setting and arrange glasses in the order in which they will be filled. Water goes closest to the plate and can be poured before guests are seated. Cups and saucers can be placed to the right behind any glasses.

Tablecloths, table runners, or place mats at the table are optional—napkins aren't. Generally, dinner napkins are larger, up to 24 inches square; luncheon and breakfast napkins are a few inches smaller; cocktail napkins are either 4 by 6 inches or 6 by 8 inches. Paper napkins are fine for casual meals. For barbecues and other messy meals, consider using dish towels or bandannas. Fold the napkin in any attractive shape and place it on the plate to the left of the forks or above the dinner plate (parallel to the edge of the table).

BUFFET-STYLE SERVICE

Serving food buffet-style is the easiest way to serve groups of eight or more people. Arrange the table in a logical serving sequence with plates first followed by the main dish, vegetables, salad, and bread (see below). Place napkins and flatware at the end of the line or at tables where guests will eat. Glassware, beverages, desserts, and plates can be included on the serving table if space allows or on separate tables.

A two-line buffet will allow a large number of guests to be served quickly. For a smaller group, or if your space is limited, use a similar arrangement on a counter or on a table placed against the wall.

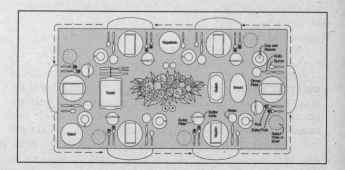

GUIDE TO COOKING TERMS AND TECHNIQUES

Success in the kitchen starts with an understanding of cooking vocabulary. Knowing the difference between terms such as fold and beat leads you to consistently delicious results. This glossary defines the most often used terms and techniques that appear in everyday recipes.

■ **Al dente** (see tip, page 729).

■ **Bake.** To cook food, covered or uncovered, using the indirect, dry heat of an oven. Usually used to describe the cooking of cakes, other desserts, casseroles, and breads (see Roast).

■ **Baste.** To moisten foods during cooking with pan drippings or a sauce in order to add flavor and prevent drying.

■ **Beat.** To make a mixture smooth by briskly whipping or stirring it with a spoon, fork, wire whisk, rotary beater, or electric mixer (see tip, right).

■ **Bias-slice.** To slice a food—often a vegetable or a partially frozen piece of meat—crosswise at a 45-degree angle. This technique often is used for ingredients in Oriental dishes.

■ **Blackened.** A popular Cajun cooking method in which seasoned fish or other foods are cooked over high heat in a super-heated heavy skillet until charred. At home, this is best done outdoors because of the large amount of smoke that is produced.

■ **Blanch.** To partially cook fruits, vegetables, or nuts in boiling water or steam; also used to loosen skins from tomatoes, peaches, and almonds. This is an important step in preparing fruits and vegetables for freezing.

■ **Blend.** To combine two or more ingredients until smooth and uniform in texture, flavor, and color; may be done by hand or with an electric blender or mixer.

■ **Boil.** To cook food in liquid at a temperature that causes bubbles to form in the liquid and rise in a steady pattern, breaking on the surface. A rolling boil occurs when liquid is boiling so vigorously that the bubbles can't be stirred down. To parboil is to boil a food until it is partially cooked; vegetables can be parboiled before stir-frying.

■ **Bouquet garni.** A bundle of herbs, often tied in a cheesecloth bag, used to flavor soups, stews, stocks, and poaching liquids. In traditional French cooking, the herbs used are thyme, parsley, and bay leaf.

■ **Braise.** To cook food slowly in a small amount of liquid in a tightly covered pan on the range top or in the oven. Recommended for less-tender cuts of meat.

■ **Breading.** A coating of crumbs, sometimes seasoned, used on meat, fish, poultry, and vegetables. Often made with soft or dry bread crumbs (see Crumb).

■ **Brine.** Heavily salted water used to pickle or cure vegetables, meats, fish, and seafood.

■ **Broil.** To cook food a measured distance below direct, dry heat (see also Panbroil).

■ **Brown.** To cook food in a skillet, broiler, or oven in order to develop a rich, desirable color on the outside, add flavor and aroma, and help seal in natural juices.

■ **Butterfly.** To split foods such as shrimp or steak through the middle without completely separating the halves, then spreading the halves to resemble a butter-

BEATING EGGS

Beating whole eggs, egg whites, or egg yolks to the just-right stage is critical for many recipes.

■ **Slightly beaten eggs.** Use a fork to beat the whole egg until the yolk and white are combined and no streaks remain.

■ **Beating egg whites until soft peaks form.** Place the egg whites in a clean glass or metal bowl (do not use plastic). Beat the whites with an electric mixer on medium speed or with a rotary beater until they form peaks with tips that curl over when the beaters are lifted. Any speck of fat, oil, or yolk in the bowl will prevent the whites from whipping.

■ **Beating egg whites until stiff peaks form.** Continue beating egg whites on high speed until they form peaks with tips that stand straight when the beaters are lifted.

■ **Beating egg yolks.** Beat the egg yolks with an electric mixer on high speed for about 5 minutes or until thick and lemon-colored.

fly. The food cooks more quickly because twice as much surface area is exposed to heat.

■ **Candied.** A food—usually a fruit, nut, or citrus peel—that is cooked in a sugar syrup.

■ **Carve.** To cut or slice cooked meat, poultry, fish, or game into serving-size pieces.

■ **Chill.** To cool a food to below room temperature in the refrigerator or freezer, or over ice.

■ **Chop.** To cut foods with a knife, cleaver, or food processor into smaller pieces (see tip, page 49).

■ **Coat.** To evenly cover food with crumbs, flour, or a batter. Often done to meat, fish, and poultry before cooking.

■ **Cream.** To beat a fat, such as margarine, butter, or shortening, either alone or with sugar to a light, fluffy consistency. May be done by hand with a wooden spoon or with an electric mixer. This process incorporates air into the fat so baked products have a lighter texture and better volume.

■ **Crimp.** To pinch or press pastry or dough together using your fingers, a fork, or another utensil. Usually done for a piecrust edge (see Flute).

■ **Crisp-tender.** A term that describes vegetables that are cooked until just tender but still somewhat crunchy (a fork can be inserted with just a little pressure).

■ **Crumb.** A fine particle of food that has been broken off a larger piece. Dry bread, cookie, and cracker crumbs can be made in a blender or food processor, or by putting the large pieces into a heavy plastic bag and pressing with a rolling pin.

■ **Crush.** To smash a food such as seasonings in your hand or with a mortar and pestle to release flavor and aroma.

MAKING CRUMBS

Crumbs often are used as a coating, thickener, or binder. Bread crumbs can be either soft or fine and dry, and usually are not interchangeable in recipes.

■ For 1 cup of cracker crumbs, you'll need 28 saltine crackers, 14 graham crackers, or 24 rich, round crackers.

■ To make soft bread crumbs, use a blender or food processor to break fresh bread cubes into fluffy crumbs.

■ To make fine dry bread crumbs, place very dry bread in a plastic bag and finely crush it with a rolling pin (see Crumb). You also can buy fine dry bread crumbs; store the opened canister in the refrigerator indefinitely.

■ **Cube** (see tip, at right).

■ **Curdle.** To cause semisolid pieces of coagulated protein to develop in a dairy product. Can occur when foods such as milk or sour cream are heated to too high a temperature or are combined with an acid food such as lemon juice or tomatoes.

■ **Cut in.** To work a solid fat, such as shortening, margarine, or butter, into dry ingredients, usually with a pastry blender.

■ **Dash.** A measure equal to $1/16$ teaspoon. Can be measured by filling a $1/4$-teaspoon measure one-fourth full.

■ **Deep-fat fry** (see Fry).

■ **Deglaze.** Adding a liquid such as water, wine, or broth to a skillet that has been used to cook meat. The liquid is poured into the pan after the meat is removed and is used to help loosen the browned bits in the pan to make a flavorful sauce.

■ **Dice** (see tip, above right).

■ **Dip.** To immerse food for a short time in a liquid or dry mixture in order to coat, cool, or moisten it.

■ **Dissolve.** To stir a solid food and a liquid food together to form a mixture in which none of the solid remains. Heat may be needed (see Gelatin, page 7).

■ **Drawn.** A term referring to a whole fish, with or without scales, that has had its internal organs removed. Also can refer to melted butter.

■ **Dredge.** To coat a food, either before or after cooking, with a dry ingredient, such as flour, cornmeal, or sugar.

■ **Dress.** To remove the internal organs and heads from fish, poultry, and game. Or to toss salad ingredients with salad dressing.

■ **Dust.** To lightly coat or sprinkle a food with a dry ingredient, such as flour or powdered sugar, either before or after cooking.

■ **Emulsion.** A suspension of two liquid or semiliquid ingredients, such as oil and vinegar, that don't naturally dissolve into each other.

■ **Entrée** *(ON tray).* A French term that originally referred to the first course of a meal or to food served between the soup and meat courses. In the United States, entrée refers to the main dish of a meal.

CHOP IT UP

■ **Cube** means to cut into uniform pieces, usually $1/2$ inch on all sides.

■ **Dice** means to cut into uniform pieces, usually $1/8$ to $1/4$ inch on all sides.

■ **Mince** refers to chopping a food into tiny irregular pieces.

THE RIGHT WAY TO MEASURE

Using the correct measuring utensil for ingredients is another secret to success. Don't interchange liquid measuring cups for dry ones. Liquid measuring cups hold up to 1, 2, or 4 cups liquid and have the incremental markings printed on the outsides of the cups. Dry measuring cups are stackable and come in increments of ¼, ⅓, ½, ⅔, ¾, and 1 cup. Measuring spoons can be used for dry and liquid ingredients.

■ **For liquid ingredients,** use a glass or clear plastic liquid measuring cup placed on a level surface. Bend down so your eye is level with the marking on the cup. For small amounts of liquid (1 tablespoon or less), fill the appropriate measuring spoon to the top without letting it spill over.

■ **For dry ingredients,** spoon the ingredient into the appropriate dry measuring cup or measuring spoon, and level off the excess with the flat side of a knife or spatula.

■ **Filet** *(fi LAY)*. Usually refers to a small, boneless piece of meat. Also refers to the process of cutting lean poultry or fish into boneless pieces. Filet mignon *(fi LAY mean YOHN)* is a slice of beef tenderloin.

■ **Fillet** *(FILL uht)*. A boneless piece of fish cut lengthwise from the side of the fish. Or a boneless piece of poultry breast.

■ **Flake.** To gently break a food into small, flat pieces.

■ **Flute.** To make a decorative pattern or impression in food, usually a piecrust.

■ **Fold.** A method of gently mixing ingredients—usually delicate or whipped ingredients that cannot withstand stirring or beating. To fold, use a rubber spatula to cut down through the mixture, move across the bottom of the bowl, and come back up, folding some of the mixture from the bottom over close to the surface.

■ **Fry.** To cook food in hot cooking oil or fat, usually until a crisp brown crust forms. To panfry is to cook food (may have a very light breading or coating) in a skillet in a small amount of hot fat or oil. To deep-fat fry (or French fry) is to cook a food in enough hot fat or oil to cover the food until it is crisp. To shallow-fry is to cook a food, usually breaded or coated with batter, in about an inch of hot fat or oil. To oven-fry is to cook a food in a hot oven, using a small amount of fat, so that it has the flavor and appearance of a fried food.

■ **Garnish.** To add visual appeal to a finished dish.

■ **Giblets.** The edible internal organs of poultry, such as the liver, heart, and gizzard; also may include the neck and wing tips.

■ **Glacé** *(gla SAY)*. A term used to describe a food that has a glossy coating.

■ **Glaze.** A thin glossy coating on a food.

■ **Gluten.** An elastic protein present in flour, especially wheat flour, that provides most of the structure of baked products (see Knead).

■ **Grate.** To rub food—especially hard cheeses, vegetables, or whole nutmeg or ginger—across a grating surface to make very fine pieces. A food processor also may be used (see Shred).

■ **Grease.** To coat a utensil, such as a baking pan or skillet, with a thin layer of fat or oil. Also refers to fat released from meat and poultry during cooking.

■ **Grind.** To mechanically cut a food into small pieces, usually with a food grinder or a food processor.

■ **Hors d'oeuvre** *(or DERV)*. A French term for small, hot or cold portions of savory food served as an appetizer. Often eaten as finger food or served with toothpicks or wooden skewers.

■ **Jelly roll.** Dessert made by spreading a filling—usually jelly, pudding, ice cream, or flavored whipped cream—on a sponge cake and rolling it up into a log shape (see recipe, page 279). When other foods are shaped "jelly-roll style," this refers to the log shape with a filling inside.

■ **Juice.** The natural liquid extracted from fruits, vegetables, meats, and poultry.

■ **Julienne.** To cut food into thin matchlike sticks about 2 inches long. For easier cutting, first cut food into slices about 2 inches long and $1/4$ inch thick; stack the slices and cut them lengthwise into strips $1/8$ to $1/4$ inch wide.

■ **Knead.** To work dough with the heels of your hands in a pressing and folding motion until it becomes smooth and elastic; an essential step in developing the gluten in many yeast breads (see tip, page 171).

■ **Marble.** To gently swirl one food into another; usually done with light and dark batters for cakes or cookies (see Marble Cake recipe, page 264).

■ **Marinade.** A liquid in which food is allowed to stand in order to flavor or tenderize it. Marinate refers to the process. Do not use a metal container. Do not marinate meats, poultry, or fish at room temperature more than 30 minutes.

■ **Mash.** To press or beat a food to remove lumps and make a smooth mixture. This can be done with a fork, potato masher, food mill, food ricer, or electric mixer.

■ **Measure.** To determine the quantity or size of a food or utensil (see tip, page 50).

■ **Melt.** To heat a solid food such as chocolate, margarine, or butter over very low heat until it becomes liquid or semiliquid.

■ **Mince** (see tip, page 49).

■ **Mix.** To stir or beat two or more foods together until they are thoroughly combined. May be done by hand with a wooden spoon, a rotary beater, or an electric mixer.

■ **Moisten.** To add enough liquid to a dry ingredient or mixture to make it damp but not runny.

■ **Mull.** To slowly heat a beverage, such as red wine or cider, with spices and sugar.

■ **Oven-fry** (see Fry).

■ **Panbroil.** To cook a food, especially a meat, in a skillet without added fat, removing any fat as it accumulates.

■ **Pare.** To cut off the skin or outer covering of a fruit or vegetable, using a small knife or a vegetable peeler.

■ **Partially set.** A phrase that describes a gelatin mixture that is chilled until it is the consistency of unbeaten egg whites; fruits, vegetables, or nuts are added at this stage so they will stay evenly distributed and not sink to the bottom or float to the top (see Gelatin, page 7).

■ **Pectin.** A natural substance found in some fruits that makes fruit-and-sugar mixtures used in jelly- or jam-making set up. Commercial pectin also is available.

■ **Peel.** The skin or outer covering of a vegetable or fruit; also may be called the rind. Also refers to removing the covering.

■ **Pipe.** To force a semisoft food, such as whipped cream, frosting, or mashed potatoes, through a bag to decorate a food.

■ **Pit.** To remove the seed from a piece of fruit.

■ **Plump.** To allow a food, such as raisins, to soak in a liquid.

■ **Poach.** To cook a food by partially or completely submerging it in a simmering liquid.

■ **Pound.** To strike a food with a heavy utensil to crush it. Or, in the case of meat or poultry, to break up connective tissue in order to tenderize or flatten it.

■ **Precook.** To partially or completely cook a food before using it in a recipe.

■ **Preheat.** To heat an oven or utensil to a specific temperature before using it.

■ **Process.** To preserve food at home by canning. Or to prepare food in a food processor.

■ **Proof.** To allow a yeast dough to rise before baking. Also a term that indicates the amount of alcohol in a distilled liquor.

■ **Puree.** To change a solid food into a liquid or heavy paste, usually by using a blender, food processor, or food mill; also refers to the resulting mixture.

■ **Reconstitute.** To bring a concentrated or condensed food, such as frozen fruit juice, to its original strength by adding water.

■ **Reduce.** To rapidly boil liquids, such as pan juices or sauces, so that some of the liquid evaporates, thickening the sauce or concentrating its flavor.

■ **Rind.** The skin or outer coating, usually rather thick, of watermelon, bacon, cheese, and citrus fruits.

■ **Roast.** A large piece of meat or poultry. Also a dry-heat cooking method used for meats, poultry, and vegetables in which the food is cooked, uncovered, in an oven or over a fire (see Bake).

■ **Roux** *(ROO)*. A French term that refers to a mixture of flour and a fat cooked to a golden or rich brown color and used for thickening in sauces, soups, and gumbos.

■ **Sauté** *(saw TAY)*. To cook or brown a food in a small amount of hot fat.

■ **Scald.** To heat a liquid, often milk, to a temperature just below the boiling point, when tiny bubbles just begin to appear around the edge of the liquid.

■ **Score.** To cut narrow grooves or slits partway through the outer surface of a food to tenderize it or to form a decorative pattern.

■ **Scrape.** To use a sharp or blunt instrument to rub the outer coating from a food such as carrots.

■ **Sear.** To brown a food, usually meat, quickly on all sides using high heat to seal in the juices. May be done in the oven or on top of the range.

■ **Section.** A pulpy segment of citrus fruit that has had the membrane removed; also the process of removing the segments. Use a sharp paring knife to remove the peel and white rind (see Peel). Working over a bowl to catch the juice, cut into the center of the fruit between a section and the membrane. Turn the knife and slide it along the other side of the section, next to the membrane, cutting outward.

■ **Shred.** To push food across a shredding surface to make long, narrow strips or very thin strips (finely shred). A food processor also may be used. Lettuce and cabbage may be shredded by thinly slicing them (see Grate).

■ **Shuck.** To remove the shells from seafood, such as oysters and clams, or the husks from corn.

■ **Sieve.** A circular utensil with wire mesh or tiny holes through which food is passed. Foods are put through a sieve to separate small particles (such as removing seeds from pureed berries), to separate liquids from solids, and to puree a food. Also refers to the process of passing a food through the utensil.

■ **Sift.** To put one or more dry ingredients, especially flour or powdered sugar, through a sifter or sieve to remove lumps and incorporate air.

■ **Simmer.** To cook a food in liquid that is kept just below the boiling point; a few bubbles will form slowly and burst just before they reach the surface.

■ **Skim.** To remove a substance, such as fat or foam, from the surface of a liquid.

■ **Slice.** A flat, usually thin, piece of food cut from a larger piece. Also the process of cutting flat, thin pieces (see Bias-slice).

■ **Snip.** To cut food, often fresh herbs or dried fruit, with kitchen shears or scissors into very small, uniform pieces using short, quick strokes.

■ **Steam.** To cook a food in the vapor given off by boiling water.

■ **Steep.** To allow a food, such as tea, to stand in water that is just below the boiling point in order to extract flavor or color.

■ **Stew.** To cook food in liquid for a long time until tender, usually in a covered pot; also the mixture prepared this way.

■ **Stir.** To mix ingredients with a spoon or other utensil to combine them, to prevent them from sticking during cooking, or to cool them after cooking.

■ **Stir-fry.** An Oriental method of quickly cooking small pieces of food in a little hot oil in a wok over high heat while stirring constantly.

■ **Stock.** The thin, clear liquid in which the bones of meat, poultry, or fish are simmered with vegetables and herbs; usually richer and more concentrated than broth; gels when cooled.

■ **Toast.** A slice of dried bread. Also the process of heating nuts, seeds, or coconut in the oven or on the range top until they are slightly browned to enhance their flavor (see tip, page 234).

■ **Toss.** To mix ingredients lightly by lifting and dropping them using two utensils.

■ **Weeping.** A condition in which liquid separates out of a solid food, such as jellies, custards, and meringues.

■ **Whip.** To beat a food lightly and rapidly using a wire whisk, rotary beater, or electric mixer to incorporate air into the mixture and increase its volume.

■ **Zest.** The colored outer portion of citrus fruit peel. It is rich in fruit oils and often used as a seasoning. To remove, use a grater, fruit zester, or vegetable peeler; avoid the bitter white membrane beneath the peel.

COOKING AT HIGH ALTITUDES

When you cook high in the sky, recipe adjustments need to be made because of lower atmospheric pressure. (If you are unsure about the altitude of your area, contact your county extension office.) For example, water boils at a lower temperature, so foods cooked in water will take longer to cook. When water boils at lower temperatures, moisture evaporates more quickly, causing foods to dry out more quickly during cooking or baking. Unfortunately, since ingredients and proportions vary by recipe, no simple formula exists. If you live more than 1,000 feet above sea level, your best bet is to become familiar with how altitude affects food, then experiment with recipe ingredients and amounts to find the balance suitable for your location. Measure amounts carefully and keep a record of the amounts you use and the results you achieve each time you cook. The following high-altitude tips will help you get started.

BAKING

For cakes leavened by air, such as angel food cakes, beat the egg whites only to soft peaks. Otherwise, your cakes may expand too much. When making a cake that contains 1 cup or more of fat, you may need to reduce the shortening by 1 to 2 tablespoons and add an egg to prevent the cake from falling. The leavening, sugar, and liquid in cakes leavened with baking powder or baking soda may need adjustment, too.

Cookies, biscuits, and muffins, on the other hand, are more stable than cakes and need little adjustment. If necessary, experiment by slightly reducing the sugar and baking powder, and increasing the liquid.

For cakes and cookies, increase the oven temperature about 20 degrees and slightly decrease the baking time. These steps will keep cakes from expanding too much and cookies from drying out.

For yeast doughs, allow the unshaped dough to rise only until doubled in size, then punch the dough down. Repeat this rising step once more before shaping the dough. Also, if your yeast dough seems dry, add more liquid and reduce the amount of flour the next time you make the recipe. Flours tend to be drier at high altitudes and sometimes absorb more liquid.

RANGE-TOP COOKING

When boiling foods at high altitudes, increase the cooking time. This is necessary because liquids boil at lower temperatures at high altitudes. Also increase the amount of liquid, as it will evaporate more quickly. Do not increase the heat because your food might scorch.

For deep-fat frying, fry foods at a lower temperature for a longer time. Since the moisture in the food has a lower boiling point, food fried at the recommended sea-level temperature will be crusty but underdone. Lower the temperature of the fat 3 degrees for each 2,000 feet you live above sea level.

For candies, decrease the end-point temperature given in the recipe by 2 degrees for each 1,000 feet of elevation. This step is necessary at high altitudes because rapid evaporation causes candies to cook down more quickly.

When canning foods at high altitudes, adjust the processing time or pressure to guard against food contamination. If you plan to use the boiling-water method of canning, contact your county extension office for detailed instructions. For information on pressure canning at high altitudes, see page 345.

To blanch vegetables for freezing, heat 1 minute longer than the sea-level directions if you live more than 5,000 feet above sea level.

MICROWAVE COOKING

Because the air is thinner at high altitudes, foods that puff, rise, or foam during microwave cooking often expand more. That means you'll need slightly larger containers to prepare beverages, sauces, soups, cereals, candies, cakes, and breads. Since water boils at a lower temperature at high altitudes, you may need to increase the cooking time for foods cooked in liquid, such as vegetables, rice, and stews.

COOKING ABOVE 7,500 FEET

For altitudes above 7,500 feet, baking time may actually be less. At such high elevations, the dry air may influence cooking times more than the low boiling point. Dry air means faster evaporation, more drying, and, in many cases, faster cooking. Carefully watch food during baking and check recipes for doneness before the suggested minimum timings.

FURTHER INFORMATION

For more information on cooking at high altitudes, contact your county extension office or write: Colorado State University Food Science Extension Office Fort Collins, CO 80523-1571.

APPETIZERS
& SNACKS

APPETIZERS & SNACKS

CRUNCHY PARTY MIX

PREP: 15 MINUTES   BAKE: 45 MINUTES

Oven 300°

Keep some of this crispy snack mix on hand—freeze some of it for up to 4 months.

    1 cup margarine or butter
    3 tablespoons
        Worcestershire sauce
  1/2 teaspoon garlic powder
        Several drops bottled hot
        pepper sauce
    5 cups tiny pretzels or
        pretzel sticks
    4 cups round toasted oat
        cereal
    4 cups bite-size wheat or
        bran square cereal
    4 cups bite-size rice or corn
        square cereal or bite-
        size shredded wheat
        biscuits
    3 cups mixed nuts

1. Heat and stir margarine or butter, Worcestershire sauce, garlic powder, and hot pepper sauce till margarine melts. In a large roasting pan combine pretzels, cereals, and nuts. Drizzle margarine mixture over cereal mixture; toss to coat.

2. Bake in a 300° oven 45 minutes, stirring every 15 minutes. Spread on foil; cool. Store in an airtight container. Makes 20 cups.

Nutrition Facts per 1/2 cup: 165 cal., 11 g total fat (2 g sat. fat), 0 mg chol., 237 mg sodium, 14 g carbo., 2 g fiber, 3 g pro.
Daily Values: 8% vit. A, 11% vit. C, 1% calcium, 11% iron

PLANNING A PARTY MENU

Plan a party menu you can prepare easily and serve with confidence. Select favorite recipes you are comfortable with, and try out new dishes before serving them at the party.

■ Imagine how foods will look and taste together. Balance rich, highly flavored foods with simple, fresh items. Don't forget practical matters such as how much refrigerator space is available and how many appetizers you can keep warm at the same time. Plan one or two hot appetizers that can be made ahead and heated just before serving. Also choose appetizers you can prepare early and serve without last-minute attention.

■ When you serve appetizers buffet style, choose foods that guests can pick up easily. Too many choices that must be spooned out, sliced, or spread can cause people to bunch up around the buffet table.

■ **Cajun-Style Party Mix:** Prepare Crunchy Party Mix as above, except increase bottled hot pepper sauce to 1 tablespoon and substitute 3 cups *pecan halves* for mixed nuts.

Nutrition Facts per ¹/₂ cup: 153 cal., 11 g total fat (1 g sat. fat)

SWEET SPICED WALNUTS

PREP: 10 MINUTES   BAKE: 20 MINUTES   OVEN 325°

Fast

    1 egg white
    5 cups walnut halves or pieces
    1 cup sugar
    1 teaspoon ground cinnamon
 ¹/₄ teaspoon ground nutmeg
 ¹/₄ teaspoon ground allspice

1. Grease a 15×10×1-inch baking pan; set aside. In a large bowl beat together egg white and 1 teaspoon *water* with a fork. Add nuts; toss to coat. In a small mixing bowl combine sugar, cinnamon, nutmeg, allspice, and ¹/₂ teaspoon *salt*. Sprinkle sugar mixture over walnuts; toss to coat.
2. Spread nuts in prepared baking pan. Bake in a 325° oven 20 minutes. Spread on waxed paper; cool. Break into pieces. Store in an airtight container. Makes 7 cups nuts.

Nutrition Facts per 2 tablespoons: 83 cal., 7 g total fat (1 g sat. fat), 0 mg chol., 21 mg sodium, 6 g carbo., 0 g fiber, 2 g pro. **Daily Values:** 0% vit. A, 1% vit. C, 0% calcium, 1% iron

---

TOASTED CHILI NUTS

PREP: 5 MINUTES   BAKE: 12 MINUTES   Oven 350°

Fast

    2 tablespoons margarine or butter
    2 tablespoons Worcestershire sauce
    1 teaspoon chili powder
 ¹/₄ teaspoon onion salt
 ¹/₄ teaspoon ground red pepper
    2 cups walnut or pecan halves or pieces

1. Combine margarine, Worcestershire sauce, chili powder, onion salt, and red pepper. Cook and stir till margarine melts. Spread nuts in 9×9×2-inch baking pan. Drizzle with margarine mixture; toss.
2. Bake in a 350° oven for 12 to 15 minutes or till toasted, stirring occasionally. Spread on foil; cool. Store in an airtight container. Makes 2 cups nuts.

Nutrition Facts per 2 tablespoons: 111 cal., 11 g total fat (1 g sat. fat), 0 mg chol., 63 mg sodium, 3 g carbo., 1 g fiber, 2 g pro. **Daily Values:** 2% vit. A, 6% vit. C, 1% calcium, 3% iron

TRAIL MIX

START TO FINISH: 5 MINUTES

Fast

> 4 cups granola
> 1 6-ounce package mixed dried fruit bits or 1¹/₃ cups raisins
> 1 cup peanuts or broken walnuts or pecans
> 1¹/₂ cups mixture of any of the following: shelled sunflower seeds, coconut, candy-coated milk chocolate pieces, candy-coated peanut butter-flavored pieces, candy-coated fruit-flavored pieces, or candy corn

1. In a large bowl combine all ingredients; toss to mix. Store in an airtight container in a cool, dry place. Makes 8 cups mix.

Nutrition Facts per ¹/₂ cup: 271 cal., 12 g total fat (5 g sat. fat), 0 mg chol., 93 mg sodium, 38 g carbo., 2 g fiber, 7 g pro. **Daily Values:** 2% vit. A, 0% vit C, 2% calcium, 9% iron

FLAVORED POPCORN

START TO FINISH: 10 MINUTES

Fast

Flavor your popcorn with one of three zesty seasonings.

> 6 cups warm popped popcorn (about ¹/₄ cup unpopped)
> 2 tablespoons butter or margarine
> 2 tablespoons Parmesan cheese, 1 tablespoon American cheese food, or 1 teaspoon taco seasoning mix
> 1 tablespoon finely snipped parsley (optional)

1. In a large mixing bowl toss together the warm popped popcorn and the butter or margarine. Immediately sprinkle with the Parmesan cheese, American cheese food, or taco seasoning, and, if desired, the parsley. Toss to coat. Makes 6 appetizer servings.

Nutrition Facts per serving: 83 cal., 5 g total fat (3 g sat. fat), 12 mg chol., 78 mg sodium, 8 g carbo., 1 g fiber, 2 g pro. **Daily Values:** 4% vit. A, 1% vit. C, 2% calcium, 2% iron

POTATO SKINS

PREP: 20 MINUTES   BAKE: 50 MINUTES   Oven 425°

Save baking time by cooking the potatoes in the microwave on 100% power (high) for 15 to 20 minutes, rearranging them once.

> 6 large baking potatoes, such as russet or long white
> 2 teaspoons cooking oil
> 1 to 1½ teaspoons chili powder
>   Several drops bottled hot pepper sauce
> ⅔ cup chopped Canadian-style bacon or 8 slices crisp-cooked, crumbled bacon or turkey bacon
> ⅔ cup finely chopped tomato (1 medium)
> 2 tablespoons finely chopped green onion (1)
> 1 cup shredded cheddar cheese (4 ounces)
> ½ cup dairy sour cream (optional)

1. Scrub potatoes and prick with a fork. Bake in a 425° oven for 40 to 45 minutes or till tender; cool.

2. Cut each potato lengthwise into 4 wedges. Scoop out the inside of each potato wedge, leaving a shell about ¼ inch thick. Cover and chill the leftover fluffy white part of potatoes for another use.

3. In a small bowl combine the oil, chili powder, and hot pepper sauce. Using a pastry brush, brush the insides of the potato wedges with the oil mixture. Place the potato wedges in a single layer on a large baking sheet. Sprinkle wedges with bacon, tomato, and green onion; top with cheese.

4. Bake about 10 minutes more or till cheese melts and potatoes are heated through. If desired, serve with sour cream. Makes 24 wedges.

■ **Make-ahead directions:** Prepare as above, except cover and chill assembled potato wedges for up to 24 hours before baking.

Nutrition Facts per wedge: 64 cal., 2 g total fat (1 g sat. fat), 7 mg chol., 97 mg sodium, 8 g carbo., 1 g fiber, 3 g pro. **Daily Values:** 2% vit. A, 8% vit C, 3% calcium, 1% iron

STUFFED MUSHROOMS

PREP: 25 MINUTES   BAKE: 8 MINUTES   Oven 425°

> 24 large fresh mushrooms, 1¹/₂ to 2 inches in diameter
> ¹/₄ cup sliced green onions (2)
> 1 clove garlic, minced
> ¹/₄ cup margarine or butter
> ²/₃ cup fine dry bread crumbs
> ¹/₂ cup shredded cheddar or crumbled blue cheese (2 ounces)

1. Rinse and drain mushrooms. Remove stems; reserve caps. Chop enough stems to make 1 cup.

2. In a medium saucepan cook the chopped stems, green onions, and garlic in margarine or butter till tender. Stir in bread crumbs and cheese. Spoon crumb mixture into mushroom caps. Arrange mushrooms in a 15×10×1-inch baking pan. Bake in a 425° oven for 8 to 10 minutes or till heated through. Makes 24 mushrooms.

Nutrition Facts per mushroom: 41 cal., 3 g total fat (1 g sat. fat), 2 mg chol., 58 mg sodium, 3 g carbo., 0 g fiber, 1 g pro. **Daily Values:** 3% vit. A, 1% vit. C, 1% calcium, 2% iron

■ **Sausage-Stuffed Mushrooms:** Prepare as above, except omit margarine or butter and cheese. Reduce bread crumbs to 2 tablespoons. Cook ¹/₂ pound bulk *Italian sausage* with stem mixture till sausage is no longer pink. Drain fat well. Stir 2 tablespoons grated *Parmesan cheese* and the bread crumbs into sausage mixture.

Nutrition Facts per mushroom: 38 cal., 3 g total fat (1 g sat. fat)

■ **Pepperoni-Stuffed Mushrooms:** Prepare as above, except omit cheese. Stir ¹/₄ cup chopped *pepperoni* and ¹/₂ teaspoon *dried Italian seasoning,* crushed, into the crumb mixture.

Nutrition Facts per mushroom: 39 cal., 3 g total fat (1 g sat. fat)

SOUR CREAM FRUIT DIP

PREP: 10 MINUTES   CHILL: 1 TO 24 HOURS

If you're counting calories, try the Yogurt Fruit Dip (see below).
You'll cut the calories nearly in half and eliminate all the fat.

 1/4 cup apricot or peach preserves
   1 8-ounce carton dairy sour cream
 1/8 teaspoon ground cinnamon
     Apple, pear, or peach slices

1. Cut up any large pieces of fruit in the preserves. In a small mixing bowl stir together the apricot or peach preserves, sour cream, and cinnamon. Cover and chill for 1 to 24 hours. Serve with fruit slices. Makes 1 cup dip.

Nutrition Facts per tablespoon dip: 44 cal., 3 g total fat (2 g sat. fat), 6 mg chol., 8 mg sodium, 4 g carbo., 0 g fiber, 0 g pro. **Daily Values:** 3% vit. A, 0% vit. C, 1% calcium, 0% iron

■ **Yogurt Fruit Dip:** Prepare as above, except substitute one 8-ounce carton plain *yogurt* for the sour cream.

Nutrition Facts per tablespoon dip: 23 cal., 0 g total fat

DILL DIP

PREP: 10 MINUTES   CHILL: 1 TO 24 HOURS

For colorful dippers, serve carrot or zucchini sticks, broccoli or
cauliflower flowerets, radishes, and mushrooms.

   1 8-ounce package cream cheese, softened
   1 8-ounce carton dairy sour cream
   2 tablespoons finely chopped green onion (1)
   2 tablespoons snipped fresh dill or 2 teaspoons dried dillweed
 1/2 teaspoon seasoned salt or salt
     Milk (optional)
     Assorted vegetable dippers, crackers, or chips

1. In a medium mixing bowl beat cream cheese, sour cream, green onion, dill, and seasoned salt or salt with an electric mixer on low speed till fluffy. Cover and chill 1 to 24 hours. If dip thickens after chilling, stir in 1 or 2 tablespoons milk. Serve with vegetable dippers, crackers, or chips. Makes about 2 cups dip.

Nutrition Facts per tablespoon dip: 40 cal., 4 g total fat (2 g sat. fat), 11 mg chol., 45 mg sodium, 1 g carbo., 0 g fiber, 1 g pro. **Daily Values:** 4% vit. A, 0% vit..C, 1% calcium, 0% iron

■ **Creamy Blue Cheese Dip:** Prepare as above, except omit dill and seasoned salt or salt. Stir $^1/_2$ cup crumbled *blue cheese* (2 ounces) and $^1/_3$ cup finely chopped *walnuts* into the beaten cream cheese mixture.

Nutrition Facts per tablespoon dip: 56 cal., 5 g total fat (3 g sat. fat)

SALSA

PREP: 15 MINUTES   CHILL: 4 HOURS

Low-Fat

Adjust the hotness of this no-cook salsa to your liking by adding some jalapeño peppers or bottled hot pepper sauce.

  2 14$^1/_2$-ounce cans chunky pasta-style tomatoes
  1 4-ounce can diced green chili peppers
  $^1/_4$ cup thinly sliced green onions (2)
  $^1/_4$ cup snipped cilantro or parsley
  2 tablespoons lemon juice
  $^1/_8$ teaspoon pepper
  1 clove garlic, minced
  1 recipe Tortilla Crisps (see next page)

1. Drain tomatoes, reserving $^1/_3$ cup juice; discard remaining juice. Combine tomatoes and reserved juice, chili peppers, green onions, cilantro or parsley, lemon juice, pepper, garlic, and $^1/_4$ teaspoon *salt*. Cover and chill at least 4 hours before serving. Serve with Tortilla Crisps. Cover and chill leftovers up to 2 weeks. Makes about 2$^3/_4$ cups salsa.

Nutrition Facts per tablespoon salsa: 1 cal., 0 g total fat, 0 mg chol., 218 mg sodium, 2 g carbo., 0 g fiber, 0 g pro. **Daily Values:** 5% vit. A, 9% vit. C, 1% calcium, 1% iron

TORTILLA CRISPS

Fast	Low-Fat

*Choose plain or Cinnamon Tortilla Crisps to serve with salsa
or other dips or spreads.*

12 7- or 8-inch flour tortillas

1. Cut each tortilla into 8 wedges. Spread one-third of the wedges in
a 15×10×1-inch baking pan. Bake in a 350° oven 5 to 10 minutes or
till dry and crisp. Repeat with remaining wedges; cool. Store in an
airtight container at room temperature up to 4 days or in the freezer
up to 3 weeks. Makes 96 crisps (24 appetizer servings).

Nutrition Facts per serving: 57 cal., 1 g total fat (0 g sat. fat), 0 mg chol., 84 mg sodium,
10 g carbo., 0 g fiber, 2 g pro. **Daily Values:** 0% vit. A, 0% vit. C, 1% calcium, 3% iron

■ **Cinnamon Tortilla Crisps:** Prepare as above, except combine ¹/₂
cup *sugar* and 1 teaspoon *ground cinnamon*. Brush ¹/₄ cup melted
margarine or butter over tortillas; sprinkle with cinnamon-sugar mixture. Cut each tortilla into 8 wedges.

Nutrition Facts per serving: 90 cal., 3 g total fat (1 g sat. fat)

CHILI CON QUESO

Fast

  ¹/₂ **cup finely chopped onion (1 medium)**
   1 **tablespoon margarine or butter**
1¹/₃ **cups chopped, seeded tomatoes (2 medium)**
   1 **4-ounce can diced green chili peppers, drained**
   1 **cup shredded American cheese (4 ounces)**
   1 **cup shredded Monterey Jack cheese (4 ounces)**
   1 **teaspoon cornstarch**
   1 **teaspoon bottled hot pepper sauce**
    Tortilla or corn chips

1. In a saucepan cook onion in margarine or butter till tender. Stir in
tomatoes and chili peppers. Simmer, uncovered, for 10 minutes.

2. Toss cheeses with cornstarch. Gradually add cheese mixture to saucepan, stirring till melted. Stir in hot pepper sauce; heat through. Serve with chips. Makes 1³/₄ cups dip.

Nutrition Facts per tablespoon dip: 35 cal., 3 g total fat (1 g sat. fat), 6 mg chol., 94 mg sodium, 1 g carbo., 0 g fiber, 2 g pro. **Daily Values:** 3% vit. A, 5% vit. C, 4% calcium, 0% iron

---

GUACAMOLE

PREP: 15 MINUTES   CHILL: UP TO 24 HOURS

  2 **medium very ripe avocados, halved, seeded, peeled, and cut up**
¹/₂ **of a small onion, cut up**
¹/₂ **of a 4-ounce can (¹/₄ cup) diced green chili peppers, drained,**
    or several drops bottled hot pepper sauce
  1 **tablespoon snipped cilantro or parsley**
  1 **tablespoon lemon or lime juice**
  1 **clove garlic, minced**
¹/₄ **teaspoon salt**
²/₃ **cup finely chopped, peeled, seeded tomato (1 medium)**
    (optional)
    Tortilla chips

1. In a food processor bowl or blender container combine avocados, onion, chili peppers or hot pepper sauce, cilantro or parsley, lemon or lime juice, garlic, and salt. Cover and process or blend till mixture is smooth, scraping sides as necessary. If desired, stir in tomato. Transfer to a serving bowl. Serve immediately or cover and chill up to 24 hours. Serve with chips. Makes 2 cups dip.

Nutrition Facts per tablespoon dip: 22 cal., 2 g total fat (0 g sat. fat), 0 mg chol., 23 mg sodium, 2 g carbo., 1 g fiber, 0 g pro. **Daily Values:** 1% vit. A, 3% vit. C, 0% calcium, 0% iron

SALMON AND PESTO SPREAD

PREP: 30 MINUTES   CHILL: 6 HOURS

For a different shape, put this layered spread in a 3-cup mold. Don't forget to line the mold with plastic wrap.

- 1 7¹/₂-ounce can red salmon, drained, flaked, and skin and bones removed
- ¹/₂ of an 8-ounce package cream cheese, softened
- 2 teaspoons snipped fresh dill or ¹/₂ teaspoon dried dillweed
- ¹/₄ cup refrigerated purchased pesto
- 1 8-ounce package cream cheese, softened
- ¹/₄ cup margarine or butter, softened
- 2 tablespoons snipped chives
- ¹/₄ teaspoon coarse ground pepper
  Fresh dill or chives (optional)
  Assorted crackers or bread

1. Line the bottom and sides of a 7¹/₂×3¹/₂×2-inch loaf pan with plastic wrap; set aside.

2. In a medium mixing bowl stir together salmon, the 4 ounces cream cheese, and the 2 teaspoons dill. Spread evenly in the bottom of the prepared pan. Chill 10 minutes; spread pesto over salmon mixture. In the same mixing bowl stir together the 8 ounces cream cheese, margarine, the 2 tablespoons chives, and pepper. Drop by spoonfuls over pesto; spread over pesto. Cover and chill at least 6 hours.

3. To serve, invert pan onto a serving platter; remove plastic wrap. Let stand at room temperature for 15 minutes. If desired, garnish with additional fresh dill or chives. Serve with assorted crackers or bread. Makes 2 cups spread.

Nutrition Facts per tablespoon spread: 73 cal., 7 g total fat (3 g sat. fat), 16 mg chol., 100 mg sodium, 1 g carbo., 0 g fiber, 2 g pro. **Daily Values:** 6% vit. A, 0% vit. C, 1% calcium, 1% iron

FRUIT SALSA

PREP: 30 MINUTES   CHILL: 6 TO 24 HOURS

Low-Fat

If you plan to chill this salsa more than 6 hours, stir in the strawberries just before serving.

1 cup finely chopped strawberries
1 medium orange, peeled and finely chopped ($^1/_3$ cup)
2 large or 3 small kiwifruit, peeled and finely chopped ($^2/_3$ cup)
$^1/_2$ cup finely chopped fresh pineapple or one 8-ounce can crushed pineapple (juice pack), drained
$^1/_4$ cup thinly sliced green onions (2)
$^1/_4$ cup finely chopped yellow or green sweet pepper
1 tablespoon lime or lemon juice
1 fresh jalapeño pepper, seeded and chopped (optional) (see tip, page 111)
1 recipe Cinnamon Tortilla Crisps (see page 68)

1. In a mixing bowl stir together the strawberries, orange, kiwifruit, pineapple, green onions, sweet pepper, lime or lemon juice, and, if desired, jalapeño pepper. Cover and chill for 6 to 24 hours. Serve with Cinnamon Tortilla Crisps. Makes about 3 cups salsa.

Nutrition Facts per tablespoon salsa: 6 cal., 0 g total fat, 0 mg chol., 0 mg sodium, 0 g carbo., 0 g fiber, 0 g pro. **Daily Values:** 0% vit. A, 13% vit. C, 0% calcium, 0% iron

---

CHEDDAR CHEESE BALL

PREP: 45 MINUTES   CHILL: 4 TO 24 HOURS

1 cup finely shredded cheddar cheese
1 3-ounce package cream cheese
2 tablespoons margarine or butter
1 tablespoon milk or dry white wine
1 tablespoon finely chopped green onion
1 tablespoon diced pimiento
1 teaspoon Worcestershire sauce
Dash bottled hot pepper sauce
$^1/_3$ to $^1/_2$ cup snipped parsley or finely chopped walnuts or pecans
Assorted crackers

1. Bring the cheeses and margarine to room temperature. Add milk, green onion, pimiento, Worcestershire sauce, and hot pepper sauce; beat till combined. Cover and chill 4 to 24 hours.

2. Shape mixture into a ball; roll in parsley or nuts. Let stand 15 minutes. Serve with crackers. Makes 1½ cups spread.

Nutrition Facts per tablespoon spread: 41 cal., 4 g total fat (2 g sat. fat), 9 mg chol., 54 mg sodium, 0 g carbo., 0 g fiber, 2 g pro. **Daily Values:** 4% vit. A, 3% vit. C, 3% calcium, 0% iron

■ **Blue Cheese Ball:** Prepare as above, except omit pimiento, add ¼ cup crumbled *blue cheese* (1 ounce) to cheese mixture, and substitute chopped *almonds*, toasted (see tip, page 234), for parsley or nuts.

Nutrition Facts per tablespoon spread: 54 cal., 5 g total fat (2 g sat. fat)

SMOKY CHEESE BALL

PREP: 35 MINUTES   CHILL: 4 TO 24 HOURS

  2 8-ounce packages cream cheese
  2 cups shredded smoked cheddar, Swiss, or Gouda cheese
½ cup margarine or butter, softened
  2 tablespoons milk
  2 teaspoons steak sauce
  1 cup finely chopped nuts, toasted (see tip, page 234)

1. Bring cheeses and margarine to room temperature. Add milk and steak sauce; beat till fluffy. Cover; chill for 4 to 24 hours. Shape mixture into a ball. Roll in nuts. Let stand for 15 minutes. Serve with *assorted crackers*. Makes 3½ cups spread.

Nutrition Facts per tablespoon spread: 74 cal., 7 g total fat (3 g sat. fat), 13 mg chol., 72 mg sodium, 1 g carbo., 0 g fiber, 2 g pro. **Daily Values:** 6% vit. A, 0% vit. C, 3% calcium, 1% iron

---

MEXICAN EIGHT-LAYER DIP

PREP: 15 MINUTES   CHILL: 4 TO 24 HOURS

  2 to 3 cups shredded lettuce
  1 9-ounce can bean dip
¼ cup picante or taco sauce
  1 8-ounce carton dairy sour cream

1 6-ounce container frozen avocado dip, thawed
1 cup shredded cheddar or Monterey Jack cheese (4 ounces)
$^{1}/_{4}$ cup sliced green onions (2)
2 tablespoons sliced or chopped pitted ripe olives
$^{2}/_{3}$ cup chopped, seeded tomato (1 medium)
Tortilla chips or crackers

1. On a platter arrange lettuce, leaving a 2-inch open rim at edge of platter. Combine bean dip and picante sauce. Spread bean mixture over lettuce, making a layer $^{1}/_{4}$ inch thick. Next layer sour cream and avocado dip. Top with cheese, onions, and olives. Cover and chill 4 to 24 hours.

2. Before serving, sprinkle with chopped tomato. Arrange the chips or crackers on the platter around spread. Makes 16 appetizer servings.

Nutrition Facts per serving dip: 102 cal., 8 g total fat (3 g sat. fat), 14 mg chol., 186 mg sodium, 5 g carbo., 1 g fiber, 4 g pro. **Daily Values:** 8% vit. A, 6% vit. C, 6% calcium, 3% iron

---

NACHOS

START TO FINISH: 20 MINUTES   Oven 350°

Fast

*You can zap this Tex-Mex appetizer in your microwave, too.
Microwave on 100% power (high) for 2 to 3 minutes
or till the cheese melts.*

6 cups tortilla chips
1 15-ounce can black beans or pinto beans, rinsed and drained
$^{1}/_{4}$ cup thick and chunky salsa
$1^{1}/_{2}$ cups shredded cheddar or colby-and-Monterey-Jack cheese (6 ounces)
1 recipe Cilantro Cream (see page 74) (optional)
Thick and chunky salsa (optional)

1. Spread tortilla chips on an 11- or 12-inch ovenproof platter or on a baking sheet; set aside.

2. Combine beans and the $^{1}/_{4}$ cup salsa; spoon over chips. Sprinkle with cheese. Bake in a 350° oven for 5 to 7 minutes or till cheese melts.

3. To serve, if desired, spoon Cilantro Cream atop nachos and pass additional salsa with nachos. Makes 8 servings.

■ **Cilantro Cream:** In a small bowl stir together ¹/₂ cup *dairy sour cream* and 2 tablespoons snipped *cilantro or parsley*.

Nutrition Facts per serving: 226 cal., 12 g total fat (6 g sat. fat), 22 mg chol., 426 mg sodium, 22 g carbo., 4 g fiber, 10 g pro. **Daily Values:** 8% vit. A, 3% vit. C, 16% calcium, 7% iron

---

SALMON AND DILL CANAPÉS

PREP: 15 MINUTES   CHILL: UP TO 24 HOURS

You also can spread or pipe the salmon mixture on ¹/₄-inch-thick slices of cucumber.

  1 4-ounce piece smoked salmon, flaked, with skin and bones removed
¹/₂ of an 8-ounce tub cream cheese
  2 tablespoons sliced green onion (1)
  1 tablespoon snipped fresh dill or 1 teaspoon dried dillweed
  1 tablespoon lemon juice
    Dash pepper
24 slices party rye bread
    Fresh dill (optional)

1. In a small mixing bowl combine salmon, cream cheese, green onion, the 1 tablespoon dill, lemon juice, and pepper. Cover; chill up to 24 hours.
2. To assemble canapés, spread 1 to 2 teaspoons of the salmon spread on top of each bread slice. If desired, garnish with additional fresh dill. Makes 24 canapés.

Nutrition Facts per canapé: 34 cal., 2 g total fat (1 g sat. fat), 6 mg chol., 83 mg sodium, 2 g carbo., 0 g fiber, 2 g pro. **Daily Values:** 1% vit. A, 0% vit. C, 0% calcium, 1% iron

---

CAJUN TUNA SPREAD

PREP: 15 MINUTES   CHILL: 3 TO 24 HOURS

If you like things peppery hot, the combination of tuna and a blend of Cajun flavors is sure to tempt your taste buds.

1   3-ounce package cream cheese, softened
3   tablespoons mayonnaise or salad dressing
1   teaspoon paprika
$^1/_4$ teaspoon ground black pepper
$^1/_8$ teaspoon garlic powder or 1 clove garlic, minced
$^1/_8$ teaspoon ground red pepper
1   $6^1/_2$-ounce can tuna, drained and broken into chunks
$^1/_4$ cup finely chopped red or green sweet pepper
2   tablespoons thinly sliced green onion (1)
    Assorted crackers

1. In a small mixing bowl beat cream cheese, mayonnaise or salad dressing, paprika, black pepper, garlic powder or garlic, and ground red pepper with an electric mixer on medium speed till well combined. Stir in the tuna, sweet pepper, and green onion. Cover; chill for 3 to 24 hours. Serve with crackers. Makes $1^1/_2$ cups spread.

Nutrition Facts per tablespoon spread: 35 cal., 3 g total fat (1 g sat. fat), 7 mg chol., 46 mg sodium, 0 g carbo., 0 g fiber, 2 g pro. **Daily Values:** 2% vit. A, 3% vit. C, 0% calcium, 1% iron

---

EASY CHICKEN PÂTÉ

PREP: 20 MINUTES   CHILL: 6 TO 24 HOURS

*Purchase a 2- to 2$^1/_2$- pound deli-roasted chicken to use for the
cooked chicken. Remove and discard the skin
and bones before chopping.*

3   cups chopped, cooked chicken
$^1/_2$ cup dairy sour cream
$^1/_4$ cup snipped parsley
3   tablespoons chopped green onions (2)
3   tablespoons dry sherry or dry white wine
1   clove garlic, minced
$^1/_4$ teaspoon lemon-pepper seasoning
$^1/_4$ teaspoon salt
1   tablespoon snipped parsley or chopped walnuts, toasted (see
      tip, page 234)
    Assorted crackers

1. In a food processor bowl combine chicken, sour cream, the $^1/_4$ cup parsley, green onions, sherry, garlic, lemon-pepper, and salt. Cover and process till mixture is smooth.

2. Line a 3-cup bowl or mold with plastic wrap; spoon in chicken mixture. Cover and chill for 6 to 24 hours. To serve, invert the bowl onto a platter; remove wrap. Sprinkle with the 1 tablespoon parsley or walnuts. Serve with crackers. Makes about 2¹/₂ cups pâté.

Nutrition Facts per tablespoon pâté: 30 cal., 1 g total fat (1 g sat. fat), 11 mg chol., 18 mg sodium, 0 g carbo., 0 g fiber, 3 g pro. **Daily Values:** 1% vit. A, 1% vit. C, 0% calcium, 1% iron

---

CHICKEN LIVER PÂTÉ

PREP: 10 MINUTES   COOK: 10 MINUTES   CHILL: 3 TO 24 HOURS

  2 slices bacon
¹/₂ pound chicken livers
¹/₂ cup chopped onion (1 medium)
  1 clove garlic, minced
  2 to 3 tablespoons milk
¹/₄ teaspoon ground nutmeg or ¹/₈ teaspoon ground allspice
    Assorted crackers

1. In a large skillet cook bacon till crisp. Remove bacon from skillet, reserving 2 tablespoons drippings. Drain and crumble bacon; set aside.
2. Add livers, onion, and garlic to reserved drippings. Cook and stir over medium heat 5 minutes or till livers are no longer pink; cool slightly.
3. In a food processor bowl or blender container combine bacon, chicken liver mixture, the 2 tablespoons milk, nutmeg, ¹/₄ teaspoon *salt*, and ¹/₈ teaspoon *pepper*. Cover; process till well combined. (Add 1 tablespoon milk if mixture appears stiff.)
4. Line a 1¹/₂-cup mold or bowl with plastic wrap; spoon in mixture. Cover; chill for 3 to 24 hours. To serve, invert mold onto a platter; remove wrap. Serve with crackers. Makes 1 cup pâté.

Nutrition Facts per tablespoon pâté: 22 cal., 1 g total fat (0 g sat. fat), 56 mg chol., 18 mg sodium, 1 g carbo., 0 g fiber, 3 g pro. **Daily Values:** 43% vit. A, 3% vit. C, 0% calcium, 5% iron

SWISS FONDUE

Classic nutty-sweet Emmentaler and smooth-melting Gruyère
combine with cherry-flavored kirsch in this
traditional cheese fondue.

    3 cups shredded Gruyère or Swiss cheese (12 ounces)
    2 cups shredded Emmentaler, Gruyère, or Swiss cheese (8
       ounces)
    3 tablespoons all-purpose flour
   12 1-inch-thick slices herb bread or French bread, cut into 1-inch
       cubes, and/or precooked broccoli or cauliflower flowerets
 1½ cups dry white wine
   ¼ cup milk
    2 tablespoons kirsch or dry sherry
   ⅛ teaspoon ground nutmeg
   ⅛ teaspoon white pepper
       Paprika (optional)

1. Bring shredded cheeses to room temperature; toss with flour and
set aside.
2. To toast the bread cubes, place on a baking sheet and bake in a
350° oven 5 to 7 minutes or till crisp and toasted; set aside. To precook broccoli or cauliflower, in a saucepan bring a small amount of
water to boiling. Add flowerets; simmer, covered, 3 minutes or till
crisp-tender. Drain and rinse with cold water; set aside.
3. In a large saucepan heat wine over medium heat till small bubbles rise to surface. Just before wine boils, reduce heat to low and
stir in the cheese mixture, a little at a time, stirring constantly and
making sure cheese is melted before adding more. Stir till the mixture bubbles gently.
4. Stir in milk, kirsch, nutmeg, and white pepper. Transfer mixture
to a fondue pot. Keep mixture bubbling gently over a fondue
burner. (If mixture becomes too thick, stir in a little more milk.) If
desired, sprinkle with paprika. Serve with toasted bread cubes and/
or broccoli or cauliflower flowerets. Makes 3 cups fondue (12 appetizer servings).

Nutrition Facts per serving: 294 cal., 15 g total fat (9 g sat. fat), 49 mg chol., 300 mg
sodium, 16 g carbo., 0 g fiber, 16 g pro. **Daily Values:** 15% vit. A, 0% vit. C, 41% calcium,
5% iron

SPINACH DIP

Fast

  1 tablespoon margarine or butter
$^1/_4$ cup finely chopped onion
  1 clove garlic, minced
  1 8-ounce package cream cheese or fat-free cream cheese, cut up
$^1/_4$ cup milk
  1 10-ounce package frozen chopped spinach, thawed and well
    drained
$^1/_4$ teaspoon finely shredded lemon peel
  1 tablespoon lemon juice
  2 teaspoons Worcestershire sauce
    Several drops bottled hot pepper sauce (optional)
  4 slices bacon, crisp-cooked, drained, and crumbled, or $^1/_4$ cup
    finely chopped red sweet pepper
  1 to 2 tablespoons milk
    Assorted vegetable dippers

1. In a medium saucepan melt margarine over medium heat. Add onion and garlic; cook till onion is tender, stirring occasionally. Add cream cheese and the $^1/_4$ cup milk; cook and stir till smooth.
2. Stir in the spinach, lemon peel, lemon juice, Worcestershire sauce, and, if desired, hot pepper sauce; heat through. Stir in *half* the bacon or red sweet pepper and the 1 to 2 tablespoons milk to reach desired dipping consistency. To serve, transfer to a serving bowl. Sprinkle with remaining bacon or sweet pepper. Serve warm with assorted vegetable dippers. Makes $1^1/_2$ cups dip.

Nutrition Facts per tablespoon dip: 49 cal., 4 g total fat (2 g sat. fat), 12 mg chol., 63 mg sodium, 1 g carbo., 0 g fiber, 1 g pro. **Daily Values:** 11% vit. A, 4% vit. C, 2% calcium, 1% iron

WHITE BEAN DIP

PREP: 20 MINUTES   CHILL: 4 TO 24 HOURS

Low-Fat

*For striking presentation of this tangy, Greek-style dip, line the
serving bowl with purple kale leaves or a variety lettuce such as red-
tipped leaf lettuce.*

  $^1/_4$ cup soft bread crumbs
  2   tablespoons dry white wine or water
  1   15- to 19-ounce can cannellini beans or great Northern beans,
        drained and rinsed
  $^1/_4$ cup slivered almonds, toasted (see tip, page 234)
  3   cloves garlic, minced
  2   tablespoons lemon juice
  2   tablespoons olive oil
  $^1/_4$ teaspoon salt
  $^1/_8$ teaspoon ground red pepper
  2   teaspoons snipped fresh oregano or basil or $^1/_2$ teaspoon dried
        oregano or basil, crushed
      Fresh basil or oregano leaves (optional)
  1   recipe Tortilla Crisps (see page 68) and/or assorted vegetable
        dippers

1. Combine bread crumbs and wine or water; set aside to soak for
10 minutes.
2. In a food processor bowl or blender container combine beans, almonds, garlic, lemon juice, olive oil, salt, and red pepper. Cover and
process or blend till almost smooth. Add bread crumb mixture; blend
till smooth. Stir in 2 teaspoons oregano or basil. Cover; chill 4 to 24
hours to blend flavors.
3. To serve, transfer to a serving bowl. If desired, garnish with fresh
basil or oregano leaves. Serve with Tortilla Crisps and/or vegetable
dippers. Makes about 2 cups dip.

Nutrition Facts per tablespoon dip: 22 cal., 1 g total fat (0 g sat. fat), 0 mg chol., 23 mg
sodium, 2 g carbo., 1 g fiber, 1 g pro. **Daily Values:** 0% vit. A, 1% vit. C, 0% calcium, 1%
iron

HOW MUCH AND HOW MANY?

How many appetizers do you need per person for a party? Consider the kinds of appetizers served—if they are hearty or light—and whether or not a meal is soon to follow.

If a meal will be served shortly after the appetizers, allow four or five per guest. If a late meal is planned, figure six or seven per guest. When appetizers are the meal, plan eight or nine per guest.

MINI PEPPERONI CALZONES

PREP: 30 MINUTES   BAKE: 10 MINUTES   Oven 425°

Start with refrigerated pizza dough for great pizza taste in minutes.

1 10-ounce package refrigerated pizza dough
1 recipe Pepperoni Pizza Filling (see below)
1 beaten egg
2 to 3 tablespoons shredded Parmesan cheese (optional)

1. Unroll pizza dough. On a lightly floured surface roll dough into a 15-inch square. Cut into twenty-five 3-inch squares. Spoon a slightly rounded teaspoon of Pepperoni Pizza Filling atop each dough square. Use 2 teaspoons *water* to brush edges of each dough square. Lift a corner of each square and stretch dough over the filling to the opposite corner, making a triangle. Press edges together and seal well with fingers or a fork.
2. Arrange calzones on a greased baking sheet. Prick tops with a fork. Mix egg and 2 teaspoons *water*, brush over calzones. Bake in a 425° oven for 10 to 12 minutes or till golden. During the last 3 minutes of baking time, if desired, sprinkle with Parmesan cheese. Let stand for 5 minutes before serving. Makes 25 calzones.

■ **Pepperoni Pizza Filling:** In a small bowl stir together ¹/₃ cup finely chopped *pepperoni*, ¹/₄ cup finely chopped *green sweet pepper*, ¹/₄ cup *pizza sauce*, 2 tablespoons finely chopped *onion*, and ¹/₂ teaspoon *dried Italian seasoning*, crushed. Use immediately or cover and chill for up to 24 hours.

Nutrition Facts per calzone: 43 cal., 2 g total fat (1 g sat. fat), 10 mg chol., 99 mg sodium, 5 g carbo., 0 g fiber, 2 g pro. **Daily Values:** 1% vit. A, 3% vit. C, 1% calcium, 6% iron

---

QUESADILLAS

PREP: 10 MINUTES   COOK: 2 MINUTES PER BATCH   Oven 300°

Fast

In place of the bacon or sausage, add some chopped cooked chicken or vegetables.

>   2 **cups shredded colby-and-Monterey-Jack cheese (8 ounces)**
>   6 **7- or 8-inch flour tortillas**
>   3 **tablespoons canned diced green chili peppers, drained**
>   3 **tablespoons chopped green onions (2)**
>   3 **slices bacon, crisp-cooked, drained, and crumbled, or ¼ pound bulk Italian sausage, cooked and drained**
>   **Salsa (optional)**

1. Sprinkle ⅓ cup cheese over half of each tortilla. Top with chili peppers, green onions, and bacon or sausage. Fold tortillas in half, pressing gently.
2. In a 10-inch skillet cook quesadillas, 2 at a time, over medium heat for 2 to 3 minutes or till lightly browned, turning once. Remove quesadillas from skillet; place on a baking sheet. Keep warm in a 300° oven. Repeat with remaining quesadillas. To serve, cut quesadillas into wedges. If desired, serve with salsa. Makes 6 appetizer servings.

Nutrition Facts per serving: 280 cal., 16 g total fat (1 g sat. fat), 39 mg chol., 459 mg sodium, 20 g carbo., 0 g fiber, 13 g pro. **Daily Values:** 8% vit. A, 7% vit. C, 27% calcium, 10% iron

CROSTINI WITH DRIED TOMATO-FETA SPREAD

Fast

To make it easier to slice, partially freeze the French bread loaf first.

- $1/2$ of a 7-ounce jar oil-packed dried tomatoes
- 1 8-ounce loaf French bread (baguette)
- $1/4$ cup finely chopped onion
- 1 teaspoon capers, drained, or 1 tablespoon chopped pitted ripe olives
- 1 clove garlic, minced
- 1 3-ounce package cream cheese, softened
- 2 tablespoons milk
- 1 cup feta or soft goat cheese (chèvre), crumbled (4 ounces)

1. Drain the tomatoes, reserving oil; set aside. Bias-slice the bread into forty $1/4$-inch-thick slices. Arrange bread on baking sheets. Lightly brush 1 side of each slice with some of the reserved oil. Bake in a 400° oven 4 minutes. Turn slices over and bake 4 minutes more or till light brown.

2. Meanwhile, finely chop the tomatoes. In a small bowl stir together the tomatoes, onion, capers or olives, and garlic; set aside. In a small mixing bowl beat the cream cheese and milk with an electric mixer on medium speed till smooth. Stir in the feta or goat cheese till nearly smooth.

3. To serve, spread cheese mixture on the oiled side of toasts. Top with a small amount of tomato mixture. Serve immediately. Makes 40 crostini.

Nutrition Facts per crostini: 37 cal., 2 g total fat (1 g sat. fat), 5 mg chol., 81 mg sodium, 4 g carbo., 0 g fiber, 1 g pro. **Daily Values:** 1% vit. A, 4% vit. C, 1% calcium, 1% iron

QUICK PIZZA BREADSTICKS

Fast

*These cheesy herb breadsticks also go great with
a bowl of tomato soup.*

1 10-ounce package refrigerated pizza dough
2 tablespoons margarine or butter, melted
$1/2$ cup grated Parmesan or Romano cheese
2 teaspoons dried Italian seasoning, crushed
$1/4$ teaspoon garlic powder
$1/8$ teaspoon ground red pepper
1 8-ounce can pizza sauce, warmed

1. Lightly grease a large baking sheet. Unroll pizza dough and transfer to the prepared baking sheet. Using your hands, press the dough into a 12×9-inch rectangle. Brush the dough with the margarine or butter.
2. In a small bowl stir together the Parmesan or Romano cheese, Italian seasoning, garlic powder, and red pepper. Sprinkle mixture over dough. Using a sharp knife, cut dough crosswise into twelve 1-inch strips. Cut dough in half lengthwise to make 24 strips.
3. Bake in a 425° oven for 10 to 13 minutes or till golden brown. Serve with warm pizza sauce. Makes 24 breadsticks.

Nutrition Facts per breadstick: 48 cal., 2 g total fat (1 g sat. fat), 2 mg chol., 143 mg sodium, 5 g carbo., 0 g fiber, 2 g pro. **Daily Values:** 3% vit. A, 3% vit. C, 2% calcium, 2% iron

BRUSCHETTA

*These toasted and tomato-relish-topped Italian appetizers were
created to use up day-old bread.*

    1 cup pitted ripe olives
    2 cloves garlic, minced
    2 teaspoons balsamic vinegar or red wine vinegar
    1 teaspoon capers, drained
    1 teaspoon olive oil
1¹/₃ cups chopped red and/or yellow tomato (2 medium)
  ¹/₃ cup thinly sliced green onions (3)
    1 tablespoon snipped fresh basil or oregano or 1 teaspoon dried
        basil or oregano, crushed
    1 tablespoon olive oil
  ¹/₈ teaspoon pepper
    1 8-ounce loaf French bread (baguette)
    2 tablespoons olive oil
  ¹/₂ cup grated or shredded Parmesan cheese

1. For olive paste, in a food processor bowl or blender container
combine olives, garlic, vinegar, capers, and the 1 teaspoon olive oil.
Cover and process or blend till a nearly smooth paste forms, stopping and scraping the sides as necessary.

2. For the tomato topping, in a small bowl stir together chopped
tomatoes, green onions, basil or oregano, the 1 tablespoon olive oil,
and pepper.

3. For the toast, cut bread into ¹/₂-inch-thick slices. Use the 2 tablespoons olive oil to lightly brush both sides of each slice. Place on an
ungreased baking sheet. Bake in a 425° oven about 5 minutes or till
crisp and light brown, turning once.

4. To assemble, spread each piece of toast with a thin layer of olive
paste. Top each with about 2 tablespoons of the tomato topping and
sprinkle with Parmesan cheese. Return slices to the ungreased baking sheet. Bake in a 425° oven for 2 to 3 minutes or till cheese starts
to melt and toppings are heated through. Serve warm. Makes 24 appetizers.

■ **Make-ahead directions:** Prepare as above, except cover and chill
the olive paste and tomato topping for up to 2 days. Place the

cooled toast in an airtight container and store at room temperature for up to 24 hours. Assemble and bake as directed.

Nutrition Facts per appetizer: 62 cal., 4 g total fat (1 g sat. fat), 2 mg chol., 125 mg sodium, 6 g carbo., 0 g fiber, 2 g pro. **Daily Values:** 1% vit. A, 3% vit. C, 3% calcium, 2% iron

COWBOY CAVIAR

PREP: 15 MINUTES   CHILL: 12 HOURS

Low-Fat

Scoop up some of this salsalike appetizer with a cracker or tortilla chip.

    1 15-ounce can black-eyed peas, rinsed and drained
 $^1/_4$ cup thinly sliced green onions (2)
 $^1/_4$ cup finely chopped red sweet pepper
    2 cloves garlic, minced
    2 tablespoons cooking oil
    2 tablespoons cider vinegar
    1 to 2 fresh jalapeño peppers, seeded and chopped (see tip, page 111)
 $^1/_4$ teaspoon cracked black pepper
       Dash salt
       Assorted crackers or tortilla chips

1. In a bowl combine black-eyed peas, green onions, sweet pepper, garlic, oil, vinegar, jalapeño pepper, black pepper, and salt. Cover and chill overnight.
2. To serve, transfer to a serving dish. Serve with crackers or tortilla chips. Cover any leftovers; chill for up to 4 days. Makes 2 cups dip.

Nutrition Facts per tablespoon dip: 18 cal., 1 g total fat (0 g sat. fat), 0 mg chol., 21 mg sodium, 2 g carbo., 1 g fiber, 1 g pro. **Daily Values:** 1% vit. A, 4% vit. C, 0% calcium, 1% iron

Buffalo Chicken Wings

Prep: 15 minutes   Bake: 35 minutes   Oven 375°

You'll need the creamy blue cheese dressing to cool down the heat from these wings doused with hot sauce.

12 chicken wings (about 2½ pounds)
2 tablespoons margarine or butter
½ to one 2-ounce bottle hot pepper sauce (2 tablespoons to ¼ cup)
   Bottled blue cheese salad dressing
   Celery sticks

1. Cut off and discard wing tips (see photo 1, below). Cut each wing into 2 sections (see photo 2, at right). Rinse and pat dry.
2. In a foil-lined 15×10×1-inch baking pan arrange wing pieces in a single layer. Bake in a 375° oven for 20 minutes.
3. Meanwhile, in a small saucepan melt the margarine or butter. Stir in hot pepper sauce. Drain off fat from wings. Brush wings with margarine-pepper sauce mixture. Bake 10 minutes more. Turn wings over and brush with mixture again. Bake 5 to 10 minutes more or till tender and no longer pink. Serve wings with blue cheese dressing and celery sticks. Makes 24 pieces.

Nutrition Facts per piece: 30 cal., 2 g total fat (0 g sat. fat), 9 mg chol., 26 mg sodium, 0 g carbo., 0 g fiber, 3 g pro. **Daily Values:** 1% vit. A, 1% vit. C, 0% calcium, 0% iron

1. Use a sharp knife to carefully cut off the tips of the wings. Discard the wing tips.

2. Spread the remaining wing portions open. With a sharp knife, carefully cut each wing at its joint into two sections.

SAUSAGE BITES

START TO FINISH: 30 MINUTES

Fast

1$^1/_2$ cups bottled barbecue sauce
$^2/_3$ cup orange marmalade
$^1/_2$ teaspoon dry mustard
$^1/_8$ teaspoon ground allspice
$^3/_4$ pound fully cooked bratwurst, cut into $^1/_2$-inch-thick slices
$^3/_4$ pound fully cooked kielbasa, cut diagonally into $^1/_2$-inch-thick slices
$^1/_2$ pound small fully cooked smoked sausage links
1 8-ounce can pineapple chunks, drained

1. In a large saucepan combine barbecue sauce, orange marmalade, dry mustard, and allspice. Cook and stir till bubbly. Stir in bratwurst, kielbasa, smoked sausage links, and pineapple chunks. Cover and cook over medium-low heat about 20 minutes more or till heated through, stirring occasionally. Makes 20 appetizer servings.

■ **Crockery-cooker directions:** Combine barbecue sauce, orange marmalade, dry mustard, and allspice in a 3$^1/_2$- or 4-quart crockery cooker. Stir in bratwurst, kielbasa, and smoked sausage links. Cover and cook on the high-heat setting for 2$^1/_2$ to 3 hours. Stir in pineapple chunks. Serve immediately or keep warm on the low-heat setting for up to 2 hours.

Nutrition Facts per serving: 198 cal., 13 g total fat (5 g sat. fat), 32 mg chol., 578 mg sodium, 12 g carbo., 1 g fiber, 7 g pro. **Daily Values:** 1% vit. A, 5% vit. C, 2% calcium, 5% iron

ONION RINGS

PREP: 15 MINUTES   COOK: 2 MINUTES PER BATCH

Keep the fried rings warm in a 300° oven while you're cooking the remaining batches.

$^3/_4$ **cup all-purpose flour**
$^2/_3$ **cup milk**
 1 **egg**
 1 **tablespoon cooking oil**
$^1/_4$ **teaspoon salt**
   Cooking oil or shortening for deep-fat frying
 4 **medium mild yellow or white onions, sliced** $^1/_4$ **inch thick and separated into rings**

1. For batter, in a medium mixing bowl combine flour, milk, egg, the 1 tablespoon oil, and salt. Using a rotary beater, beat just till smooth.

2. In a large skillet heat 1 inch oil or shortening to 365°. Using a fork, dip onion rings into batter; drain off excess batter. Fry onion rings, a few at a time, in a single layer in hot oil for 2 to 3 minutes or till golden, stirring once or twice with a fork to separate rings. Remove rings from oil; drain on paper towels. Makes 6 appetizer servings.

Nutrition Facts per serving: 216 cal., 13 g total fat (2 g sat. fat), 38 mg chol., 116 mg sodium, 21 g carbo., 2 g fiber, 5 g pro. **Daily Values:** 3% vit. A, 7% vit. C, 4% calcium, 6% iron

OYSTERS ROCKEFELLER

PREP: 40 MINUTES   BAKE: 10 MINUTES   Oven 425°

*Traditionally, these oysters are placed on a bed of rock salt in a
shallow pan to balance them and keep them from spilling as they
bake. If you don't have rock salt, simply crumple a large piece of foil
to help them balance.*

    2 cups torn fresh spinach
  1/4 cup finely chopped onion
   24 oysters in shells
    3 tablespoons margarine or butter, melted
    2 tablespoons snipped parsley
    1 clove garlic, minced
      Several drops bottled hot pepper sauce
      Dash pepper
  1/4 cup fine dry seasoned bread crumbs
      Rock salt

1. In a saucepan cook spinach and onion in a small amount of boiling water for 2 to 3 minutes or till tender. Drain; press out excess
moisture.

2. Thoroughly wash oysters. Using an oyster knife or other blunt-
tipped knife, open shells. Remove oysters and dry. Discard flat top
shells; wash deep bottom shells. Place each oyster in a shell.

3. Combine spinach mixture, *2 tablespoons* of the margarine or butter, the parsley, garlic, hot pepper sauce, and pepper. Spoon 1 teaspoon spinach mixture atop each oyster. Toss together the bread
crumbs and the remaining margarine or butter. Sprinkle over
spinach-topped oysters.

4. Line a shallow baking pan with rock salt about 1/2 inch deep.
Arrange the oysters atop. Bake in a 425° oven 10 to 12 minutes or till
the edges of oysters begin to curl. Makes 24 (8 appetizer servings).

Nutrition Facts per serving: 85 cal., 5 g total fat (1 g sat. fat), 23 mg chol., 196 mg
sodium, 5 g carbo., 0 g fiber, 4 g pro. **Daily Values:** 16% vit. A, 7% vit. C, 3% calcium,
21% iron

POLYNESIAN MEATBALLS

PREP: 45 MINUTES BAKE: 25 MINUTES   Oven 350°

Get a taste of the tropics with these cilantro- and peanut-studded meatballs that are skewered with pineapple and brushed with sweet-and-sour sauce.

  1 **beaten egg**
$^{1}/_{4}$ **cup fine dry bread crumbs**
  2 **tablespoons snipped fresh cilantro or parsley**
  2 **cloves garlic, minced**
$^{1}/_{4}$ **teaspoon salt**
$^{1}/_{8}$ **teaspoon ground red pepper**
  1 **pound lean ground beef**
$^{1}/_{4}$ **cup finely chopped peanuts**
  1 **fresh pineapple, peeled and cut into bite-size chunks or one 20-ounce can pineapple chunks (juice pack), drained**
  1 **recipe Sweet-and-Sour Sauce (see page 964) or $1^{1}/_{4}$ cups bottled sweet-and-sour sauce**

1. In a mixing bowl combine egg, bread crumbs, cilantro or parsley, garlic, salt, and red pepper. Add the beef and peanuts; mix well. Shape into 36 meatballs. Place in a 15×10×1-inch shallow baking pan. Bake in a 350° oven for 20 minutes or till no longer pink. Remove from oven; drain.

2. Thread a pineapple chunk and a meatball on a wooden toothpick. Return to the shallow baking pan. Repeat with remaining fruit and meatballs. Brush with some of the Sweet-and-Sour Sauce. Bake 5 to 8 minutes more or till heated through.

3. In a saucepan heat remaining sauce till bubbly. Brush meatballs and fruit with additional sauce before serving. Serve remaining sauce in a bowl alongside meatballs. Makes 36 appetizer skewers.

TO PREPARE PINEAPPLE

To clean fresh pineapple, remove crown, and cut off top and base. Cut off wide strips of peel. Remove eyes from pineapple by cutting narrow wedge-shaped grooves diagonally around fruit, following pattern of eyes.

■ **Make-ahead directions:** Cool cooked meatballs. Cover and chill for up to 2 days. Assemble skewers as directed; bake for 10 minutes or till hot.

Nutrition Facts per skewer: 59 cal., 2 g total fat (1 g sat. fat), 14 mg chol., 102 mg sodium, 7 g carbo., 0 g fiber, 3 g pro. **Daily Values:** 0% vit. A, 3% vit. C, 0% calcium, 3% iron

---

BRIE EN CROÛTE

PREP: 30 MINUTES   BAKE: 20 MINUTES   Oven 400°

Jalapeño pepper jelly adds zing to this rich, buttery appetizer.

    $1/2$ of a $17^1/4$-ounce package frozen puff pastry, thawed (1 sheet)
    2 tablespoons jalapeño pepper jelly
    2 $4^1/2$-ounce rounds Brie or Camembert cheese
    2 tablespoons chopped nuts, toasted (see tip, page 234)
    1 slightly beaten egg
      Apple and/or pear slices

1. Grease a baking sheet; set aside. Unfold pastry on a lightly floured surface; roll into a 16×10-inch rectangle. Cut into two 8-inch circles; reserve trimmings.

2. Spread jelly over top of each cheese round; sprinkle with nuts. Lightly press nuts into jelly. Combine egg and 1 tablespoon *water;* set aside.

3. Place pastry circles over cheese rounds. Invert cheese and pastry. Brush edges of circles with egg mixture; pleat and pinch edges to cover and seal. Trim excess pastry. Place rounds, smooth sides up, on prepared baking sheet. Brush egg mixture over tops and sides. Cut small slits for steam to escape. Using hors d'oeuvre cutters, cut shapes from reserved pastry. Brush shapes with egg mixture; place atop rounds.

4. Bake in a 400° oven 20 to 25 minutes or till pastry is deep golden brown. Let stand 10 to 20 minutes before serving. Serve with apple and/or pear slices. Makes 2 rounds (12 appetizer servings).

Nutrition Facts per serving: 193 cal., 14 g total fat (4 g sat. fat), 38 mg chol., 216 mg sodium, 13 g carbo., 0 g fiber, 6 g pro. **Daily Values:** 5% vit. A, 2% vit. C, 3% calcium, 1% iron

PHYLLO TRIANGLES

PREP: 30 MINUTES   BAKE: 15 MINUTES   Oven 375°

$^{1}/_{2}$ **pound bulk hot Italian sausage or pork sausage**
$^{1}/_{4}$ **cup finely chopped onion**
$^{1}/_{2}$ **cup ricotta cheese**
$^{1}/_{2}$ **cup shredded mozzarella cheese (2 ounces)**
$^{1}/_{2}$ **teaspoon dried oregano, crushed**
12 **sheets (18×14 inches) frozen phyllo dough, thawed**
$^{1}/_{2}$ **cup margarine or butter, melted**
 1 **cup meatless spaghetti sauce (optional)**

1. For filling, in a skillet cook sausage and onion till sausage is no longer pink. Drain fat; pat dry with paper towels. Combine sausage-onion mixture, cheeses, and oregano; set aside.

2. Lightly brush a sheet of phyllo with some of the melted margarine. Place another sheet of phyllo on top; brush to edges with margarine. Keep remaining phyllo covered with plastic wrap to prevent it from becoming dry and brittle.

3. Cut the 2 layered sheets crosswise into 6 equal strips, each 14 inches long and 3 inches wide. Spoon 1 well-rounded teaspoon of filling about 1 inch from an end of each dough strip. To fold into a triangle, bring a corner over filling so it lines up with the other side of the strip. Continue folding strip in a triangular shape. Repeat with remaining sheets of phyllo, margarine, and filling.

4. Place triangles on a baking sheet; brush with margarine. Bake in a 375° oven about 15 minutes or till golden. If desired, serve with spaghetti sauce. Makes 36 triangles.

Nutrition Facts per triangle: 67 cal., 5 g total fat (1 g sat. fat), 6 mg chol., 115 mg sodium, 4 g carbo., 0 g fiber, 2 g pro. **Daily Values:** 3% vit. A, 0% vit. C, 1% calcium, 2% iron

■ **Spinach Phyllo Triangles:** Prepare Phyllo Triangles as above, except omit sausage filling and spaghetti sauce. For filling, cook one 10-ounce package *frozen chopped spinach,* $^{1}/_{2}$ cup chopped *onion* (1 medium), and 1 clove *garlic,* minced, according to spinach package directions. Drain well in a colander. Press back of spoon against mixture to force out excess moisture. Combine spinach mixture with $1^{1}/_{2}$ cups finely crumbled *feta cheese* (6 ounces) and $^{1}/_{2}$ teaspoon dried *oregano,* crushed. Continue as directed.

Nutrition Facts per triangle: 72 cal., 5 g total fat (2 g sat. fat)

■ **Make-ahead directions:** Prepare Phyllo Triangles as above except place the unbaked triangles in a covered freezer container; freeze up to 2 months. Bake as directed. Do not thaw the triangles before baking.

SPICY PARTY CHEESECAKE

PREP: 20 MINUTES   BAKE: 40 MINUTES   CHILL: 3 TO 24 HOURS   Oven 350°

  2 8-ounce packages cream cheese, softened
  2 cups shredded Monterey Jack cheese (8 ounces)
  1 8-ounce carton dairy sour cream
  3 eggs
  1 cup salsa
  1 4-ounce can diced green chili peppers, drained
  1 8-ounce carton dairy sour cream
  1 6-ounce container frozen avocado dip, thawed
$^2/_3$ cup chopped, seeded tomato (1 medium)
  1 recipe Tortilla Crisps (see page 68), or purchased tortilla chips
     or large corn chips
    Fresh cilantro or parsley sprigs (optional)

1. Beat cheeses with an electric mixer till light and fluffy. Beat in 1 carton sour cream. Add eggs all at once; beat on low speed just till combined. Stir in salsa and chili peppers.

2. Pour into a 9-inch springform pan. Place on a baking sheet. Bake in a 350° oven 40 to 45 minutes or till center is almost set. Immediately spread remaining carton sour cream over top of cheesecake. Cool on a rack. Cover; chill 3 to 24 hours.

3. To serve, remove sides of pan. Spoon avocado dip around edge of cheesecake and sprinkle with tomato. Cut into wedges and serve with Tortilla Crisps. If desired, garnish with cilantro. Makes 20 appetizer servings.

Nutrition Facts per serving cheesecake: 205 cal., 19 g total fat (10 g sat. fat), 77 mg chol., 242 mg sodium, 3 g carbo., 0 g fiber, 7 g pro. **Daily Values:** 22% vit. A, 9% vit. C, 11% calcium, 4% iron

■ **Lower-Fat Party Cheesecake:** Prepare as above except substitute *reduced-fat cream cheese, reduced-fat Monterey Jack cheese, and light dairy sour cream* for the regular products. Substitute $^3/_4$ cup *refrigerated or frozen egg product* (thawed) for the eggs. Omit the avocado dip.

Nutrition Facts per serving cheesecake: 167 cal., 11 g total fat (7 g sat. fat), 37 mg chol.

Rumaki

PREP: 15 MINUTES   MARINATE: 4 TO 24 HOURS   BROIL: 8 MINUTES

$^3/_4$ **pound chicken livers (about 12 livers)**
$^1/_4$ **cup dry sherry**
$^1/_4$ **cup soy sauce**
 2 **tablespoons brown sugar**
 2 **tablespoons cooking oil**
$^1/_4$ **teaspoon garlic powder**
$^1/_8$ **teaspoon ground ginger**
$^1/_4$ **cup water**
 1 **8-ounce can sliced water chestnuts, drained**
12 **to 14 slices bacon, cut in half crosswise**

1. Cut livers in half; quarter any extra-large livers. Place livers in a plastic bag set inside a deep bowl. Combine sherry, soy sauce, brown sugar, oil, garlic powder, ginger, and water; pour over livers. Marinate in the refrigerator for 4 to 24 hours, turning bag occasionally.

2. Drain livers. Wrap a bacon piece around a liver piece and water chestnut slice. Secure with a wooden toothpick. Place on a lightly greased broiler pan. Broil 4 inches from heat 8 to 10 minutes or till livers are no longer pink, turning once. Serve warm. Makes 24 to 28 appetizers.

Nutrition Facts per appetizer: 53 cal., 3 g total fat (1 g sat. fat), 58 mg chol., 227 mg sodium, 2 g carbo., 0 g fiber, 3 g pro. **Daily Values:** 43% vit. A, 4% vit. C, 0% calcium, 6% iron

Egg Rolls

PREP: 25 MINUTES   COOK: 15 MINUTES   Oven 300°

 8 **egg roll skins**
 1 **recipe Pork Filling (see below)**
    Shortening or cooking oil for deep-fat frying
 1 **recipe Sweet-and-Sour Sauce (see page 964), bottled sweet-and-sour sauce, or prepared Chinese-style hot mustard**

1. For each egg roll, place an egg roll skin on a flat surface with a corner pointing toward you. Spoon about $^1/_4$ cup Pork Filling across and just below center of egg roll skin. Fold bottom corner over filling, tucking it under on the other side. Fold side corners over filling, forming an envelope shape. Roll egg roll toward remaining corner. Moisten top corner with water; press firmly to seal.

2. In a heavy saucepan or deep-fat fryer heat 2 inches melted shortening to 365°. Fry egg rolls, a few at a time, 2 to 3 minutes or till golden brown. Drain on paper towels. Keep warm in a 300° oven while frying remainder. Serve warm egg rolls with Sweet-and-Sour Sauce. Makes 8 egg rolls.

■ **Pork Filling:** Cook ½ pound *ground pork*, 1 teaspoon grated *gingerroot*, and 1 clove *garlic*, minced, for 2 to 3 minutes or till meat is no longer pink; drain fat. Add ½ cup finely chopped *bok choy or cabbage*, ½ cup chopped *water chestnuts*, ½ cup shredded *carrot*, and ¼ cup finely chopped *onion*. Stir-fry 2 minutes more. Combine 2 tablespoons *soy sauce*, 2 teaspoons *cornstarch*, ½ teaspoon *sugar*, and ¼ teaspoon *salt*; add to skillet. Cook and stir for 1 minute; cool slightly.

Nutrition Facts per egg roll: 317 cal., 22 g total fat (4 g sat. fat), 23 mg chol., 527 mg sodium, 22 g carbo., 0 g fiber, 9 g pro. **Daily Values:** 19% vit. A, 4% vit. C, 2% calcium, 10% iron

---

MELON AND PROSCIUTTO

START TO FINISH: 20 MINUTES

Fast   **Low-Fat**

You also can wrap prosciutto around pear wedges. First brush the cut edges of the pears with a little lime or lemon juice.

   1 **large cantaloupe or honeydew melon or half of each melon**
   3 **ounces very thinly sliced prosciutto or fully cooked ham**

1. Cut cantaloupe or honeydew melon in half and remove seeds. Using a melon baller, scoop out pulp, or cut pulp into bite-size cubes.

2. Cut prosciutto or ham into 1-inch-wide strips. Wrap a strip of prosciutto around each melon ball. Fasten prosciutto with a toothpick. Makes about 36 appetizer servings.

Nutrition Facts per serving: 17 cal., 1 g total fat (0 g sat. fat), 0 mg chol., 44 mg sodium, 2 g carbo., 0 g fiber, 1 g pro. **Daily Values:** 8% vit. A, 18% vit. C, 0% calcium, 0% iron

CRAB AND CITRUS COCKTAIL

START TO FINISH: 15 MINUTES

Fast **Low-Fat**

- $^3/_4$ **pound cooked lump crabmeat**
- 1 **orange, peeled and sectioned**
- 1 **grapefruit, peeled and sectioned**
  Lettuce leaves
- 1 **recipe Cocktail Sauce (see page 965)**

1. Combine crabmeat and fruit sections. Divide mixture among 6 lettuce-lined cocktail cups or glasses. Spoon 1 tablespoon of the Cocktail Sauce over each. Makes 6 appetizer servings.

Nutrition Facts per serving: 90 cal., 1 g total fat (0 g sat. fat), 57 mg chol., 326 mg sodium, 8 g carbo., 1 g fiber, 12 g pro. **Daily Values:** 3% vit. A, 44% vit. C, 6% calcium, 4% iron

---

SHRIMP COCKTAIL

PREP: 1 HOUR   CHILL: 4 TO 24 HOURS

Low-Fat

- $1^1/_4$ **pounds fresh or frozen shrimp in shells**
  Lettuce leaves
- 1 **recipe Cocktail Sauce (see page 965)**
  Lemon wedges

1. Thaw shrimp, if frozen. Peel and devein shrimp (see photos, page 528).

2. In a large saucepan bring 3 cups *water* and, if desired, 1 teaspoon *salt* to boiling. Add shrimp. Simmer, uncovered, for 1 to 3 minutes or till shrimp turn pink, stirring occasionally. Drain shrimp; rinse under cold water. Chill 4 to 24 hours.

3. To serve, prepare Cocktail Sauce. Arrange the chilled shrimp in 6 lettuce-lined cocktail cups or glasses. Spoon 1 tablespoon of the sauce over each serving. Serve with lemon wedges. Makes 6 appetizer servings.

Nutrition Facts per serving: 78 cal., 1 g total fat (0 g sat. fat), 116 mg chol., 357 mg sodium, 4 g carbo., 0 g fiber, 13 g pro. **Daily Values:** 7% vit. A, 11% vit. C, 2% calcium, 13% iron

Beans, Rice, & Grains

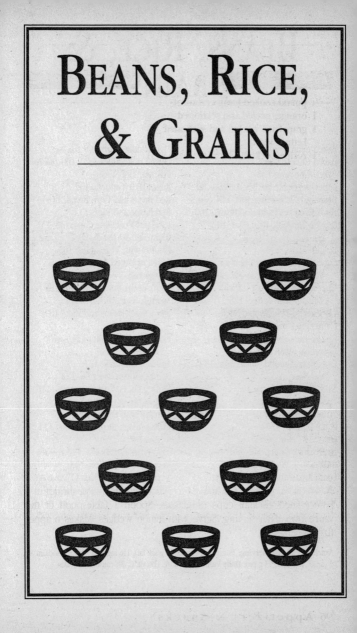

BEANS, RICE, & GRAINS

RICE PILAF

PREP: 10 MINUTES   COOK: 25 MINUTES

Low-Fat

*For ease of preparation, stir in purchased cooked bacon pieces
instead of cooking and crumbling bacon strips.*

  1/2 cup chopped onion (1 medium)
  1/2 cup sliced fresh mushrooms
  1/4 cup chopped celery or green sweet pepper
    1 clove garlic, minced
    1 tablespoon margarine or butter
 1 1/2 cups water
  3/4 cup long grain rice
 1 1/2 teaspoons instant chicken or beef bouillon granules
  1/8 teaspoon pepper
    2 slices bacon, crisp-cooked, drained, and crumbled

1. In a saucepan cook onion, mushrooms, celery or sweet pepper,
and garlic in hot margarine or butter till tender but not brown. Carefully stir in water, uncooked rice, bouillon granules, and pepper.
Bring to boiling; reduce heat. Cover and simmer about 15 minutes or
till the rice is tender and liquid is absorbed. Stir in crumbled bacon.
Makes about 3 cups (4 side-dish servings).

Nutrition Facts per serving: 188 cal., 5 g total fat (1 g sat. fat), 3 mg chol., 424 mg
sodium, 32 g carbo., 1 g fiber, 4 g pro. **Daily Values:** 3% vit. A, 6% vit. C, 2% calcium,
12% iron

OVEN-COOKED RICE

PREP: 10 MINUTES   BAKE: 35 MINUTES   Oven 350°

Low-Fat

*Vary this side dish by substituting 3/4 cup quick-cooking
barley for the rice.*

 1 1/2 cups boiling water
    1 tablespoon margarine or butter
  3/4 cup long grain rice

1. In a 1-quart casserole combine boiling water and margarine or butter; stir till melted. Stir in uncooked rice and ½ teaspoon *salt*. Cover and bake in a 350° oven about 35 minutes or till rice is tender and liquid is absorbed. Fluff with a fork. Makes about 2¼ cups (4 side-dish servings).

Nutrition Facts per serving: 152 cal., 3 g total fat (1 g sat. fat), 0 mg chol., 304 mg sodium, 28 g carbo., 0 g fiber, 3 g pro. **Daily Values:** 3% vit. A, 0% vit. C, 1% calcium, 9% iron

■ **Oven-Cooked Rice Pilaf:** Prepare as above except substitute boiling *chicken broth* for the water. Omit salt and stir in ¼ cup sliced *green onion,* ¼ cup chopped *celery,* and ¼ cup chopped *carrot* with the uncooked rice.

Nutrition Facts per serving: 175 cal., 4 g total fat (1 g sat. fat)

SPANISH RICE

PREP: 10 MINUTES   COOK: 25 MINUTES

Low-Fat

    ½ cup chopped onion (1 medium)
    ½ cup chopped green sweet pepper
    1 clove garlic, minced
    1 tablespoon cooking oil
    1 28-ounce can tomatoes, cut up
    ¾ cup long grain rice
    1 teaspoon sugar
    1 teaspoon chili powder
      Several dashes bottled hot pepper sauce
    ½ cup shredded cheddar cheese (optional)

1. In a large skillet cook onion, sweet pepper, and garlic in hot oil till tender. Stir in undrained tomatoes, uncooked rice, sugar, chili powder, hot pepper sauce, ⅛ teaspoon *pepper,* and 1 cup *water.* Bring to boiling; reduce heat. Cover; simmer for 20 to 25 minutes or till rice is tender and most of liquid is absorbed. If desired, sprinkle with cheese. Makes about 5 cups (6 to 8 side-dish servings).

Nutrition Facts per serving: 145 cal., 3 g total fat (0 g sat. fat), 0 mg chol., 223 mg sodium, 27 g carbo., 2 g fiber, 3 g pro. **Daily Values:** 9% vit. A, 45% vit. C, 3% calcium, 13% iron

SHOPPER'S GUIDE TO RICE

Rice, often called "the world's leading bread," has many uses. You can serve it in casseroles, soups, salads, and even desserts. The various types and processing methods increase the grain's versatility. Here's a sampling of what's available.

■ **White rice:** Long, medium, and short grain are the three types. The shorter the grain, the more starch it contains. It is the starch that causes rice to stick together when cooked. Long grain rice cooks up light and fluffy.

■ **Arborio rice:** A short grain, white rice. It is preferred in risotto as it contributes to the traditional creaminess of the dish. Look for Arborio rice in larger supermarkets and specialty food shops.

■ **Instant and quick-cooking rice:** Popular because of their short cooking times, instant and quick-cooking rice are partially or fully cooked before they're packaged.

■ **Brown rice:** An unpolished rice grain, it has the bran layer intact. Pleasantly chewy and nutty in flavor, brown rice requires a longer cooking time.

■ **Converted rice:** Also called parboiled rice, this white rice is steamed and pressure-cooked before it's packaged. This process helps to retain nutrients and keep the grains from sticking together when cooked.

■ **Aromatic rices:** The aroma of basmati, Texmati, wild pecan, or jasmine rice is irresistible. They taste like toasted nuts or popped corn. Look for them in food markets featuring Indian or Middle Eastern foods or in some larger supermarkets.

■ **Wild rice:** Not a grain at all, wild rice is a marsh grass. It takes three times as long to cook as white rice, but the nutlike flavor and chewy texture are worth the wait. Wash wild rice thoroughly before cooking.

INDIAN-STYLE PILAF

PREP: 5 MINUTES   COOK: 25 MINUTES

Fast

- ¹/₂ cup chopped onion (1 medium)
- ¹/₄ cup sliced celery
- 1 tablespoon margarine or butter
- ²/₃ cup long grain rice
- 2 tablespoons snipped fresh parsley
- 1¹/₂ teaspoons instant chicken bouillon granules
- ¹/₂ teaspoon curry powder
- ¹/₈ teaspoon ground allspice
- ¹/₂ cup raisins
- ¹/₄ cup chopped peanuts

1. Cook onion and celery in hot margarine till tender. Stir in uncooked rice, parsley, bouillon, curry powder, allspice, ¹/₄ teaspoon *salt*, ¹/₈ teaspoon *pepper*, and 1¹/₂ cups *water*. Bring to boiling; reduce heat. Cover; simmer 15 minutes or till rice is tender and liquid is absorbed. Add raisins and peanuts. Makes about 2 cups (4 side-dish servings).

Nutrition Facts per serving: 261 cal., 8 g total fat (1 g sat. fat), 0 mg chol., 510 mg sodium, 44 g carbo., 2 g fiber, 6 g pro. **Daily Values:** 4% vit. A, 8% vit. C, 3% calcium, 14% iron

---

BROWN- AND WILD-RICE PILAF

PREP: 15 MINUTES   COOK: 45 MINUTES

Low-Fat

1. In a medium saucepan cook 1 cup sliced fresh *mushrooms* and ¹/₄ cup sliced *green onion* in 1 tablespoon hot *margarine or butter* till tender. Carefully add one 14¹/₂-ounce can *chicken broth;* bring to boiling. Stir in ¹/₂ cup uncooked *brown rice;* ¹/₃ cup uncooked, rinsed and drained *wild rice;* ¹/₄ cup shredded *carrot;* ¹/₂ teaspoon *dried basil*, crushed; and ¹/₈ teaspoon *pepper*. Return to boiling; reduce heat. Simmer, covered, about 40 minutes or till the rices are tender and most of the broth is absorbed. Stir in ¹/₂ cup frozen *peas*. Simmer for 3 to 5 minutes more or till heated through, stirring occasionally. Makes about 3¹/₂ cups (4 side-dish servings).

WILD RICE WITH WALNUTS AND DATES

PREP: 15 MINUTES   COOK: 1¼ HOURS

Serve this pilaf-style side dish alongside broiled chicken or fish.

   2 cups chopped celery (4 stalks)
 ¼ cup chopped onion
   1 tablespoon margarine or butter
   1 cup wild rice, rinsed and drained
   1 14½-ounce can chicken or beef broth
   1 cup water
 ⅓ cup pitted whole dates, snipped
 ¼ cup chopped walnuts, toasted (see tip, page 234)

1. In a large skillet cook the celery and onion in hot margarine or butter about 10 minutes or till tender but not brown. Add the uncooked wild rice. Cook and stir for 3 minutes more. Carefully add chicken or beef broth and water. Bring to boiling; reduce heat. Cover and simmer for 50 to 60 minutes or till rice is tender and most of the liquid is absorbed. Stir in snipped dates and walnuts. Cook, uncovered, for 3 to 4 minutes more or till heated through and remaining liquid is absorbed. Makes about 5 cups (6 to 8 side-dish servings).

VEGETABLE FRIED RICE

PREP: 35 MINUTES   COOK: 20 MINUTES

Be sure the cooked rice is thoroughly chilled before you start so the rice grains won't stick together during stir-frying.

   8 dried mushrooms
   1 beaten egg
   3 tablespoons soy sauce
   3 tablespoons dry white wine or water
   1 tablespoon cooking oil
   1 cup loose-pack frozen green beans, thawed and well-drained
   1/2 cup bias-sliced celery (1 stalk)
   1 small onion, halved and sliced (1/3 cup)
   1/2 of an 8-ounce can bamboo shoots, drained
   2 cups chilled cooked rice (see page 139)
   1/4 cup unsalted peanuts

1. Soak mushrooms for 30 minutes in enough warm water to cover. Rinse well; squeeze to drain thoroughly. Chop mushrooms, discarding stems. Combine egg, soy sauce, wine or water, and 1/8 teaspoon *pepper*. Set aside.

2. Pour cooking oil into a wok or large skillet. (Add more oil as necessary during cooking.) Preheat over medium-high heat. Add thawed green beans, celery, and onion; stir-fry for 3 to 4 minutes or till crisp-tender. Remove vegetables from the wok. Add the mushrooms and bamboo shoots; stir-fry for 1 minute. Return all vegetables to the wok. Add cooked rice. Drizzle egg mixture over rice, stirring constantly. Cook and stir for 6 to 8 minutes or till mixture is heated through. Sprinkle with peanuts. Serve immediately. Makes about 4 cups (4 side-dish servings).

Nutrition Facts per serving: 264 cal., 10 g total fat (2 g sat. fat), 53 mg chol., 808 mg sodium, 36 g carbo., 2 g fiber, 8 g pro. **Daily Values:** 4% vit. A, 8% vit. C, 4% calcium, 14% iron

RISOTTO WITH VEGETABLES

PREP: 15 MINUTES   COOK: 30 MINUTES

Risotto (rih ZOT oh) is a classic Italian dish in which Arborio rice is first browned, then simmered in broth and constantly stirred so it absorbs the liquid. The finished product has a creamy consistency and a tender, but slightly firm, texture.

    2 cups sliced fresh mushrooms
  1/2 cup chopped onion (1 medium)
    2 cloves garlic, minced
    2 tablespoons olive oil or cooking oil
    1 cup Arborio rice
    3 cups vegetable or chicken broth
  3/4 cup bite-size asparagus or broccoli pieces
  3/4 cup seeded and diced tomato
  1/4 cup shredded carrot (1 small)
    1 cup shredded fontina or Muenster cheese (4 ounces)
  1/4 cup grated Parmesan cheese
    3 tablespoons snipped fresh basil or parsley
      Tomato slices (optional)

1. In a large saucepan cook mushrooms, onion, and garlic in hot oil till onion is tender. Add uncooked rice. Cook and stir over medium heat about 5 minutes more or till rice is golden.

2. Meanwhile, in another saucepan bring broth to boiling; reduce heat and simmer. Slowly add *1 cup* of the broth to the rice mixture, stirring constantly. Continue to cook and stir over medium heat till liquid is absorbed. Add another *1/2 cup* of the broth and the asparagus or broccoli to the rice mixture, stirring constantly. Continue to cook and stir till liquid is absorbed. Add another *1 cup* broth, *1/2 cup* at a time, stirring constantly till the broth has been absorbed. (This should take about 15 minutes.)

3. Stir in the remaining *1/2 cup* broth, the tomato, and carrot. Cook and stir till rice is slightly creamy and just tender. Stir in fontina or Muenster cheese, Parmesan cheese, and basil or parsley. If desired, garnish with tomato slices. Serve immediately. Makes about 4 cups (4 main-dish or 6 to 8 side-dish servings).

Nutrition Facts per main-dish serving: 406 cal., 19 g total fat (8 g sat. fat), 38 mg chol., 1,050 mg sodium, 48 g carbo., 2 g fiber, 16 g pro. **Daily Values:** 35% vit. A, 21% vit. C, 23% calcium, 23% iron

EASY RISOTTO

PREP: 5 MINUTES COOK: 30 MINUTES

Low-Fat

In this simplified version, the constant stirring required by the classic recipe is eliminated.

- 1/3 cup thinly sliced green onion (3)
- 1 tablespoon margarine or butter
- 2/3 cup Arborio or long grain rice
- 2 cups water
- 1/2 teaspoon instant chicken bouillon granules
- 1/4 cup grated Parmesan or Romano cheese

1. In a medium saucepan cook green onion in hot margarine or butter till tender but not brown. Add uncooked rice. Cook and stir for 2 minutes more. Carefully stir in water, bouillon granules, and dash *pepper*. Bring to boiling; reduce heat. Cover and simmer for 20 minutes (do not lift cover).

2. Remove from heat. Let stand, covered, 5 minutes. Rice should be tender but slightly firm, and the mixture should be creamy. (If necessary, stir in a little water to reach desired consistency.) Stir in cheese. Makes about 2 cups (4 side-dish servings).

Nutrition Facts per serving: 168 cal., 5 g total fat (2 g sat. fat), 5 mg chol., 263 mg sodium, 25 g carbo., 0 g fiber, 5 g pro. **Daily Values:** 6% vit. A, 2% vit. C, 8% calcium, 9% iron

---

HEARTY RICE SKILLET

PREP: 5 MINUTES COOK: 20 MINUTES

Fast   **Low-Fat**

- 1 15-ounce can black, garbanzo, or kidney beans, rinsed and drained
- 2 cups loose-pack frozen mixed vegetables
- 1 14 1/2-ounce can stewed tomatoes, cut up
- 1 cup water
- 3/4 cup quick-cooking brown rice
- 1/2 teaspoon dried thyme, crushed, or dried dillweed
  Several dashes bottled hot pepper sauce (optional)

1　10³/₄-ounce can condensed tomato soup
¹/₃　cup slivered almonds, toasted (see tip, page 234)
¹/₂　cup shredded mozzarella or cheddar cheese (2 ounces)

1. In a large skillet stir together beans, vegetables, undrained tomatoes, water, uncooked rice, thyme or dillweed, and, if desired, hot pepper sauce. Bring to boiling; reduce heat. Cover and simmer 12 to 14 minutes or till rice is tender. Stir in soup; heat through. Before serving, stir in almonds and sprinkle with cheese. Makes 4 main-dish servings.

Nutrition Facts per serving: 329 cal., 9 g total fat (2 g sat. fat), 8 mg chol., 1,206 mg sodium, 53 g carbo., 7 g fiber, 18 g pro. **Daily Values:** 39% vit. A, 81% vit. C, 16% calcium, 24% iron

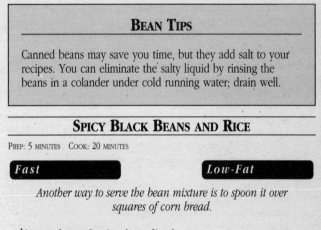

BEAN TIPS

Canned beans may save you time, but they add salt to your recipes. You can eliminate the salty liquid by rinsing the beans in a colander under cold running water; drain well.

SPICY BLACK BEANS AND RICE

PREP: 5 MINUTES　COOK: 20 MINUTES

Fast　　　　　　　　　**Low-Fat**

Another way to serve the bean mixture is to spoon it over squares of corn bread.

¹/₂　cup chopped onion (1 medium)
4　cloves garlic, minced
2　tablespoons olive oil or cooking oil
1　15-ounce can black beans, rinsed and drained
1　14¹/₂-ounce can Mexican-style stewed tomatoes
¹/₈　to ¹/₄ teaspoon ground red pepper
2　cups hot cooked brown or long grain rice (see page 139)
¹/₄　cup chopped onion (optional)

1. In a medium saucepan cook the ¹/₂ cup onion and garlic in hot oil till tender but not brown. Carefully stir in beans, undrained tomatoes, and ground red pepper. Bring to boiling; reduce heat. Simmer, uncovered, for 15 minutes.

2. To serve, mound rice on serving plates; make a well in each mound. Spoon the black bean mixture into wells. If desired, sprinkle with the ¹/₄ cup chopped onion. Makes 4 main-dish servings.

Nutrition Facts per serving: 280 cal., 8 g total fat (1 g sat. fat), 0 mg chol., 620 mg sodium, 47 g carbo., 7 g fiber, 11 g pro. **Daily Values:** 7% vit. A, 29% vit. C, 5% calcium, 12% iron

---

SOUTH-OF-THE-BORDER PIE

PREP: 20 MINUTES   BAKE: 25 MINUTES   Oven 350°

Low-Fat

Cumin and chili powder give this main-dish pie its south-of-the-border flavor.

- ¹/₂ cup chopped onion (1 medium)
- 2 cloves garlic, minced
- 1 tablespoon olive oil or cooking oil
- 1 to 2 teaspoons chili powder
- 1 teaspoon ground cumin
- ¹/₄ teaspoon salt
- 1 15-ounce can red kidney beans, rinsed and drained
- 1¹/₂ cups cooked brown rice (page 139)
- 1 cup shredded cheddar cheese (4 ounces)
- ³/₄ cup milk
- 2 beaten eggs
  Nonstick spray coating
  Chopped green sweet pepper (optional)
  Salsa (optional)

1. In a saucepan cook onion and garlic in hot oil till tender but not brown. Stir in chili powder, cumin, and salt. Cook 1 minute more; cool. Stir in beans, cooked rice, cheese, milk, and eggs.

2. Spray a 10-inch pie plate or quiche dish with nonstick coating. Spoon mixture into pie plate. Bake, uncovered, in a 350° oven about 25 minutes or till the center is set. Let stand 10 minutes. If desired, sprinkle with sweet pepper and serve with salsa. Makes 6 main-dish servings.

Nutrition Facts per serving: 258 cal., 12 g total fat (5 g sat. fat), 93 mg chol., 367 mg sodium, 27 g carbo., 5 g fiber, 14 g pro. **Daily Values:** 12% vit. A, 2% vit. C, 18% calcium, 13% iron

---

BLACK-EYED PEAS AND RED BEANS

PREP: 1¼ HOURS   COOK: 1 HOUR

If you like, omit the dry red beans and use 1 cup total of dry black-eyed peas.

- ½ **cup dry red beans**
- ½ **cup dry black-eyed peas**
- 1 **bay leaf**
- ½ **teaspoon salt**
- 3 **slices bacon**
- 1 **cup chopped red, yellow, and/or green sweet pepper**
- 1 **cup chopped onion (1 large)**
- 3 **cloves garlic, minced**
- 1 **teaspoon dried thyme, crushed**
- ⅛ **teaspoon ground red pepper**
  Dash ground black pepper

1. Rinse red beans. In a large saucepan combine red beans and 3 cups *water*. Bring to boiling; reduce heat. Simmer for 2 minutes. Remove from heat. Cover and let stand for 1 hour. (Or, place beans in water in a large saucepan. Cover and let soak in a cool place for 6 to 8 hours or overnight.)

2. Drain and rinse red beans. Return beans to pan. Add black-eyed peas, bay leaf, salt, and 3 cups fresh *water*. Bring to boiling; reduce heat. Cover and simmer for 45 to 60 minutes or till beans and peas are tender. Drain; discard bay leaf.

3. Meanwhile, in a large skillet

FOR BEAN COUNTERS ONLY

How many beans do you need to buy when a recipe calls for a cup measure? Here's a guide to follow. One pound of dry beans equals 2¼ to 2½ cups uncooked beans or 6 to 7 cups cooked beans, depending on the variety. A 15-ounce can of beans contains about 1¾ cups drained beans.

cook bacon till crisp. Drain on paper towels, reserving 1 tablespoon drippings in skillet. Crumble cooked bacon; set aside.

4. Add sweet pepper, onion, garlic, thyme, red pepper, and black pepper to skillet. Cook and stir till vegetables are tender. Stir in red beans, black-eyed peas, and bacon; heat through. Makes about 4 cups (3 main-dish or 6 side-dish servings).

Nutrition facts per main-dish serving: 315 cal., 8 g total fat (3 g sat. fat), 9 mg chol., 472 mg sodium, 45 g carbo., 8 g fiber, 17 g pro. **Daily Values:** 19% vit. A, 82% vit. C, 6% calcium, 35% iron

---

STUFFED GREEN SWEET PEPPERS

PREP: 45 MINUTES   BAKE: 15 MINUTES   Oven 400°

Low-Fat

    4 large green sweet peppers
    1 15-ounce can black beans, rinsed and drained
    1 8³/₄-ounce can whole kernel corn, drained
    ¹/₂ cup chopped onion (1 medium)
    ¹/₃ cup long grain rice
    1 to 2 jalapeño peppers, chopped (see tip, page 111)
    ¹/₈ teaspoon salt
    2 tablespoons snipped fresh cilantro or ¹/₂ teaspoon dried
        cilantro
   ³/₄ cup shredded reduced-fat Monterey Jack cheese (3 ounces)

1. Fill a large pot half full of water; bring to boiling. Meanwhile, cut tops from sweet peppers; remove seeds. Chop sweet pepper tops; set aside. Add whole sweet peppers to boiling water; return to boiling. Reduce heat and cook, covered, for 4 to 5 minutes or till just tender.

2. Meanwhile, in a medium saucepan combine the chopped sweet pepper tops, black beans, corn, onion, uncooked rice, jalapeño peppers, salt, and 1 cup *water*. Bring to boiling; reduce heat. Cover and simmer about 15 minutes or till rice is tender. Stir in cilantro and *half* of the cheese; toss to mix. If necessary, let rice mixture stand, covered, about 5 minutes or till water is absorbed.

3. Fill sweet peppers with rice mixture. Place in a 2-quart square baking dish; sprinkle with remaining cheese. Bake, uncovered, in a 400° oven about 15 minutes or till cheese melts. Makes 4 main-dish servings.

Nutrition Facts per serving: 248 cal., 5 g total fat (2 g sat. fat), 15 mg chol., 602 mg sodium, 42 g carbo., 7 g fiber, 16 g pro. **Daily Values:** 8% vit. A, 107% vit. C, 17% calcium, 17% iron

---

HANDLING CHILI PEPPERS

Because chili peppers, such as jalapeños, contain volatile oils that can burn your skin and eyes, avoid direct contact with them as much as possible. When working with chili peppers, wear plastic or rubber gloves. If your bare hands do touch the chili peppers, wash your hands well with soap and water.

TORTILLA-BLACK BEAN CASSEROLE

PREP: 25 MINUTES   BAKE: 30 MINUTES   Oven 350°

Low-Fat

This Tex-Mex favorite also can be served as a side dish for 10 to 12 people.

   2 cups chopped onion (2 large)
1 1/2 cups chopped green sweet pepper (2 medium)
   1 14 1/2-ounce can tomatoes, cut up
 3/4 cup picante sauce
   2 teaspoons ground cumin
   2 cloves garlic, minced
   2 15-ounce cans black beans or red kidney beans, rinsed and
     drained
  12 6-inch corn tortillas
   2 cups shredded reduced-fat Monterey Jack cheese (8 ounces)
   2 medium tomatoes, sliced (optional)
   2 cups shredded lettuce (optional)
     Sliced green onion (optional)
     Sliced pitted ripe olives (optional)
 1/2 cup light dairy sour cream or plain yogurt (optional)

1. In a large skillet combine onion, sweet pepper, undrained tomatoes, picante sauce, cumin, and garlic. Bring to boiling; reduce heat. Simmer, uncovered, for 10 minutes. Stir in beans.
2. Spread one-third of the bean mixture over the bottom of a 3-quart

rectangular baking dish. Top with *six* of the tortillas, overlapping as necessary, and *1 cup* of the cheese. Add another one-third of the bean mixture; top with remaining tortillas and remaining bean mixture.

3. Bake, covered, in a 350° oven for 30 to 35 minutes or till heated through. Sprinkle with remaining cheese. Let stand 10 minutes.

4. If desired, top with tomato slices, shredded lettuce, green onion, and olives. If desired, serve with sour cream or yogurt. Makes 6 to 8 main-dish servings.

Nutrition Facts per serving: 379 cal., 11 g total fat (4 g sat. fat), 27 mg chol., 889 mg sodium, 57 g carbo., 10 g fiber, 25 g pro. **Daily Values:** 10% vit. A, 121% vit. C, 16% calcium, 26% iron

---

RED BEANS AND RICE

PREP: 1¼ HOURS   COOK: 3 HOURS

Cover and refrigerate any leftovers for up to 3 days or freeze up to 3 months.

   1 **pound dry red beans or dry red kidney beans**
   1 **1-pound meaty ham bone or 1 pound meaty smoked pork hocks**
   1 **large onion, chopped (1 cup)**
   3 **cloves garlic, minced**
   2 **bay leaves**
   ½ **to ¾ teaspoon ground red pepper**
  12 **ounces smoked sausage, chopped (2¼ cups)**
   4 **cups hot cooked rice (see page 139)**
     Sliced green onions (optional)

1. Rinse red beans or red kidney beans. In a large pot combine beans and 6 cups *water*. Bring to boiling; reduce heat. Simmer for 2 minutes. Remove from heat. Cover and let stand for 1 hour. (Or, place beans in water in pot. Cover and let soak in a cool place for 6 to 8 hours or overnight.) Drain and rinse beans.

2. Return beans to pot. Add ham bone or pork hocks, onion, garlic, bay leaves, red pepper, and 6 cups fresh *water*. Bring to boiling; reduce heat. Cover and simmer about 2½ hours or till beans are tender, stirring occasionally. (Add additional water during cooking, if necessary.)

3. Remove meat. When cool enough to handle, cut meat off bones;

coarsely chop meat. Discard bone. Return chopped meat to pot; stir in sausage. Return to boiling; reduce heat. Simmer, uncovered, for 20 to 30 minutes more or till a thick gravy forms, stirring occasionally.

4. Remove bay leaves. Serve the bean mixture over rice. Season to taste with salt and pepper. If desired, sprinkle with green onions. Serves 8.

Nutrition Facts per serving: 447 cal., 15 g total fat (5 g sat. fat), 36 mg chol., 551 mg sodium, 57 g carbo., 3 g fiber, 23 g pro. **Daily Values:** 0% vit. A, 11% vit. C, 5% calcium, 38% iron

■ **Red Beans and Corn Bread:** Prepare as above, except serve bean mixture over squares of Corn Bread (see recipe, page 226).

Nutrition Facts per serving: 561 cal., 24 g total fat (7 g sat. fat)

TWO-BEAN TAMALE PIE

PREP: 25 MINUTES   BAKE: 20 MINUTES   Oven 400°

> **Low-Fat**

Top this main-dish casserole with salsa and a spoonful of sour cream.

   $^3/_4$ cup chopped green sweet pepper (1 medium)
   $^1/_3$ cup chopped onion (1 small)
    2 cloves garlic, minced
    1 tablespoon cooking oil
    1 15-ounce can kidney beans, rinsed, drained, and slightly mashed
    1 15-ounce can pinto beans, rinsed, drained, and slightly mashed
    1 6-ounce can vegetable juice cocktail ($^2/_3$ cup)
   $^1/_4$ cup snipped fresh cilantro or parsley
    1 teaspoon chili powder
    1 teaspoon ground cumin
   $^1/_2$ cup yellow cornmeal
   $^1/_2$ cup whole wheat flour
    1 teaspoon baking soda
   $^1/_4$ teaspoon salt
    1 egg
   $^1/_2$ cup buttermilk or sour milk (see tip, page 261)
    1 4-ounce can diced green chili peppers
    2 tablespoons cooking oil
   $^1/_2$ cup shredded cheddar cheese (2 ounces)

1. Grease a 10-inch quiche dish or a 2-quart square baking dish; set aside.

2. In a medium skillet cook sweet pepper, onion, and garlic in the 1 tablespoon hot oil till tender but not brown. Stir in kidney beans, pinto beans, vegetable juice cocktail, cilantro or parsley, chili powder, and cumin. Heat through. Spoon bean mixture into the prepared dish.

3. In a medium mixing bowl stir together the cornmeal, flour, baking soda, and salt. In another bowl combine egg, buttermilk, chili peppers, and the 2 tablespoons oil. Add to cornmeal mixture, stirring just till combined. Fold in cheese. Spread cornmeal mixture evenly over top of bean mixture. Bake, uncovered, in a 400° oven about 20 minutes or till golden. Makes 6 main-dish servings.

Nutrition Facts per serving: 328 cal., 12 g total fat (3 g. sat. fat), 46 mg chol., 960 mg sodium, 44 g carbo., 6 g fiber, 16 g pro. **Daily Values:** 11% vit. A, 41% vit. C, 15% calcium, 25% iron

---

BEAN AND CHEESE BURRITOS

PREP: 15 MINUTES   BAKE: 10 MINUTES   Oven 350°

Fast

Save some fat and calories by using fat-free refried beans and reduced-fat cheese.

   6 7- or 8-inch flour tortillas
   1 cup chopped onion (1 large)
   1 tablespoon cooking oil
   1 16-ounce can refried beans
   1 cup shredded cheddar cheese (4 ounces)
      Shredded lettuce
      Salsa

1. Stack tortillas and wrap tightly in foil. Heat in a 350° oven for 10 minutes to soften.

2. In a skillet cook onion in hot oil till tender. Add beans. Cook and stir till heated through. Spoon about ¼ cup of bean mixture onto each tortilla just below center. Divide cheese among tortillas. Fold over edge nearest filling just till filling is covered. Fold in sides till they meet; roll up. Place on a baking sheet. Bake in a 350° oven about 10 minutes or till heated through. Serve with lettuce and salsa. Makes 3 main-dish servings.

Nutrition Facts per serving: 622 cal., 25 g total fat (10 g sat. fat), 40 mg chol, 1,324 mg sodium, 76 g carbo., 8 g fiber, 26 g pro. **Daily Values:** 16% vit. A, 37% vit. C, 37% calcium, 38% iron

---

BAKED BEAN QUINTET

PREP: 10 MINUTES   BAKE: 1 HOUR   Oven 375°

Low-Fat

> 1 cup chopped onion (1 large)
> 6 slices bacon, cut up
> 1 clove garlic, minced
> 1 16-ounce can lima beans, drained
> 1 16-ounce can pork and beans in tomato sauce
> 1 15¹/₂-ounce can red kidney beans, drained
> 1 15-ounce can butter beans, drained
> 1 15-ounce can garbanzo beans, drained
> ³/₄ cup catsup
> ¹/₂ cup molasses
> ¹/₄ cup packed brown sugar
> 1 tablespoon prepared mustard
> 1 tablespoon Worcestershire sauce

1. In a skillet cook onion, bacon, and garlic till bacon is done and onion is tender but not brown; drain. In a mixing bowl combine onion mixture, all beans, catsup, molasses, brown sugar, mustard, and Worcestershire sauce. Transfer mixture to a 3-quart casserole. Bake, covered, in a 375° oven for 1 hour. Makes 12 to 16 side-dish servings.

■ **Crockery-cooker directions:** Prepare bean mixture as above. Transfer to a 3¹/₂- or 4-quart electric crockery cooker. Cover and cook on low-heat setting for 10 to 12 hours or on high-heat setting for 4 to 5 hours.

Nutrition Facts per serving: 236 cal., 3 g total fat (1 g sat. fat), 5 mg chol., 768 mg sodium, 46 g carbo., 8 g fiber, 11 g pro. **Daily Values:** 2% vit. A, 15% vit. C, 7% calcium, 29% iron

OLD-FASHIONED BAKED BEANS

PREP: 1 HOUR   COOK/BAKE: 3¾ HOURS   Oven 300°

Low-Fat

  1 pound dry navy beans or dry great Northern beans (about 2⅓
      cups)
¼ pound bacon or salt pork, cut up
  1 cup chopped onion (1 large)
½ cup molasses or maple syrup
¼ cup packed brown sugar
  1 teaspoon dry mustard
½ teaspoon salt
¼ teaspoon pepper

1. Rinse beans. In a large pot combine beans and 8 cups *water*.
Bring to boiling; reduce heat. Simmer for 2 minutes. Remove from
heat. Cover and let stand for 1 hour. (Or, place beans in water in
pot. Cover and let soak in a cool place overnight.)

2. Drain and rinse beans. Return beans to pot. Stir in 8 cups fresh
water. Bring to boiling; reduce heat. Cover and simmer for 1 to 1½
hours or till tender, stirring occasionally. Drain beans, reserving liquid.

3. In a 2½-quart casserole combine the beans, bacon or salt pork,
and onion. Stir in *1 cup* of the reserved bean liquid, the molasses or
maple syrup, brown sugar, dry mustard, salt, and pepper.

4. Bake, covered, in a 300° oven about 2½ hours or to desired consistency, stirring occasionally. If necessary, add additional reserved
bean liquid. Makes 10 to 12 side-dish servings.

Nutrition Facts per serving: 231 cal., 2 g total fat (1 g sat. fat), 3 mg chol., 168 mg
sodium, 44 g carbo., 0 g fiber, 10 g pro. **Daily Values:** 0% vit. A, 5% vit. C, 9% calcium,
23% iron

SHORTCUT BAKED BEANS

PREP: 10 MINUTES   COOK: 15 MINUTES

Fast   **Low-Fat**

  1 16-ounce can pork and beans with tomato sauce
  1 15-ounce can red kidney beans, drained
¼ cup catsup

2 tablespoons brown sugar
1 tablespoon cooked bacon pieces
2 teaspoons dried minced onion
2 teaspoons prepared mustard

1. In a medium saucepan combine pork and beans, kidney beans, catsup, brown sugar, bacon pieces, minced onion, and mustard. Cook over low heat about 15 minutes or to desired consistency, stirring often. Makes 4 or 5 side-dish servings.

■ **Oven directions:** Combine all ingredients in a 1½-quart casserole. Bake, uncovered, in a 350° oven about 45 minutes or to desired consistency.

■ **Crockery-cooker directions:** Double all ingredients and combine in a 3½- or 4-quart electric crockery cooker. Cover and cook on low-heat setting for 5 to 6 hours or on high-heat setting for 2½ to 3 hours. Makes 8 to 10 side-dish servings.

Nutrition Facts per serving: 243 cal., 2 g total fat (0 g sat. fat), 9 mg chol., 955 mg sodium, 50 g carbo., 12 g fiber, 14 g pro. **Daily Values:** 4% vit. A, 11% vit. C, 8% calcium, 35% iron

---

VEGETARIAN LENTIL PILAF

PREP: 15 MINUTES   COOK: 30 MINUTES

Low-Fat

1 cup chopped green sweet pepper
1 cup chopped yellow sweet pepper
1 cup sliced celery
1 cup chopped onion and/or red onion
4 cloves garlic, minced
2 tablespoons olive oil or cooking oil
1 cup lentils, rinsed and drained
1 14½-ounce can (1¾ cups) vegetable or chicken broth
⅛ teaspoon powdered saffron or ½ teaspoon ground turmeric
2 medium tomatoes, seeded and chopped
1 cup frozen peas, thawed
¼ cup snipped fresh cilantro or parsley

1. In a large pot cook the sweet peppers, celery, onion, and garlic in hot oil till onion is tender but not brown. Add lentils, vegetable or chicken broth, and saffron or turmeric to the vegetable mixture.

Bring to boiling; reduce heat. Cover and simmer about 30 minutes or till lentils are tender and liquid is absorbed. Stir in tomatoes, peas, and cilantro or parsley. Heat through. Season to taste before serving. Makes 4 main-dish servings.

Nutrition Facts per serving: 309 cal., 8 g total fat (1 g sat. fat), 0 mg chol, 501 mg sodium, 48 g carbo., 5 g fiber, 17 g pro. **Daily Values:** 10% vit. A, 98% vit. C, 6% calcium, 42% iron

---

LENTIL-RICE PATTIES

PREP: 25 MINUTES   COOK: 55 MINUTES

> ### Low-Fat

$2^3/_4$ cups water
$^1/_2$ cup chopped onion
$^1/_3$ cup brown rice
  2 cloves garlic, minced
$^3/_4$ cup lentils, rinsed and drained
  1 15-ounce can garbanzo beans, rinsed and drained
$^3/_4$ cup regular rolled oats
  2 slightly beaten egg whites
$^1/_4$ cup snipped fresh basil or $1^1/_2$ teaspoon dried basil, crushed
  1 tablespoon Worcestershire sauce
  2 dashes bottled hot pepper sauce
$^1/_2$ cup chopped walnuts or almonds, toasted (see tip, page 234)
    Nonstick spray coating
  8 whole wheat hamburger buns, split and toasted

1. In a medium saucepan combine water, onion, uncooked brown rice, and garlic. Bring to boiling; reduce heat. Simmer, covered, for 20 minutes. Add lentils. Cover and simmer 25 minutes more or till rice and lentils are tender. Remove from heat.

2. Add garbanzo beans to saucepan; mash the mixture. Stir in oats. Let stand 5 minutes.

3. Combine the egg whites, basil, Worcestershire sauce, hot pepper sauce, and $^1/_2$ teaspoon *salt;* add to mixture in pan, stirring to combine. Stir in nuts.

4. Using about $^1/_2$ cup mixture for each, shape into eight $^1/_2$-inch-thick patties. Spray a 12-inch skillet with nonstick spray coating. Cook the patties over medium heat for 7 to 10 minutes or till light brown, turning once. Serve the patties on buns. If desired, top with *lettuce, onion,* and plain nonfat *yogurt.* Makes 8 main-dish servings.

Nutrition Facts per serving: 350 cal., 8 g total fat (1 g sat. fat), 0 mg chol., 570 mg sodium, 57 g carbo., 8 g fiber, 15 g pro. **Daily Values:** 1% vit. A, 13% vit. C, 9% calcium, 33% iron

---

MEATLESS TACOS

PREP: 5 MINUTES   COOK: 35 MINUTES

If you like lots of taco flavor, look for the taco-seasoned shredded cheese at your supermarket.

  $^1/_2$ **cup water**
  $^1/_4$ **cup lentils, rinsed and drained**
  $^1/_4$ **cup chopped onion**
   1 **8-ounce can tomato sauce**
  $^1/_2$ **of a 1$^1/_8$- or 1$^1/_4$-ounce envelope (5 teaspoons) taco seasoning mix**
   8 **ounces firm or extra-firm tofu, drained and finely chopped**
   8 **taco shells, warmed**
 1$^1/_2$ **cups shredded lettuce**
   1 **medium tomato, chopped**
  $^1/_2$ **cup shredded cheddar cheese**
  $^1/_2$ **cup salsa**

1. In a medium saucepan combine water, lentils, and onion. Bring to boiling; reduce heat. Cover and simmer about 30 minutes or till lentils are tender and liquid is absorbed.
2. Stir tomato sauce and taco seasoning mix into lentils. Simmer, uncovered, for 5 minutes. Stir in tofu; heat through. Spoon into taco shells. Top with lettuce, tomato, cheese, and salsa. Makes 4 main-dish servings.

Nutrition Facts per serving: 385 cal., 18 g total fat (5 g sat. fat), 15 mg chol, 1,100 mg sodium, 42 g carbo., 3 g fiber, 23 g pro. **Daily Values:** 17% vit. A, 34% vit. C, 24% calcium, 64% iron

■ **Bulgur Tacos:** Prepare as above, except increase water to $^3/_4$ cup and substitute *bulgur* for lentils. Cover and simmer water, bulgur, and onion for 12 to 15 minutes or till bulgur is tender and liquid is absorbed.

Nutrition Facts per serving: 344 cal., 18 g total fat (5 g sat. fat)

CHEESE-AND-TOFU-STUFFED SHELLS

PREP: 45 MINUTES   BAKE: 25 MINUTES   Oven 350°

Tofu is a high-protein soy product that absorbs the flavors of the ingredients it's cooked with.

12 jumbo pasta shells
$^1/_4$ cup shredded carrot (1 small)
 2 tablespoons sliced green onion (1)
 8 ounces tofu, drained
$^1/_2$ cup low-fat ricotta cheese
$^1/_2$ cup shredded cheddar cheese (2 ounces)
$^1/_2$ cup shredded mozzarella cheese (2 ounces)
 1 beaten egg white
$^1/_4$ teaspoon salt
$^1/_4$ teaspoon pepper
 1 14$^1/_2$-ounce can tomatoes, cut up
$^1/_2$ of a 6-ounce can ($^1/_3$ cup) tomato paste
 1 teaspoon dried basil, crushed
 1 teaspoon dried oregano, crushed
$^1/_2$ teaspoon sugar
$^1/_4$ teaspoon garlic powder
$^1/_4$ teaspoon fennel seed, crushed (optional)
   Grated Parmesan cheese (optional)

1. Cook pasta according to package directions; drain. Rinse with cold water. Drain and set aside. Meanwhile, in a saucepan cook carrot and green onion in a small amount of water till tender; drain.
2. For filling, in a medium mixing bowl mash tofu with a fork. Stir in the carrot-onion mixture, ricotta cheese, cheddar cheese, $^1/_4$ cup of the mozzarella cheese, the egg white, salt, and pepper. Set aside.
3. For sauce, in a saucepan combine undrained tomatoes, tomato paste, basil, oregano, sugar, garlic powder, and, if desired, fennel seed. Bring to boiling; reduce heat. Simmer, uncovered, for 10 minutes.
4. Stuff each cooked shell with about 1 rounded tablespoon of the filling. Place shells in an ungreased 2-quart square baking dish. Pour sauce over shells. Bake, covered, in a 350° oven about 25 minutes or till heated through. Sprinkle with remaining mozzarella cheese. If desired, serve with Parmesan cheese. Makes 4 main-dish servings.

Nutrition Facts per serving: 349 cal., 15 g total fat (7 g sat. fat), 32 mg chol., 532 mg sodium, 31 g carbo., 3 g fiber, 25 g pro. **Daily Values:** 43% vit. A, 43% vit. C, 36% calcium, 56% iron

---

SPICY STIR-FRIED TOFU

PREP: 20 MINUTES   COOK: 5 MINUTES

Fast   **Low-Fat**

Look for tofu in the store's refrigerated section. Select the firm variety for this recipe as it keeps its shape better for the pita filling.

- 1 10¹/₂-ounce package firm or extra-firm tofu, drained and chopped
- 1 cup green sweet pepper strips (1 medium)
- 1 small red onion, cut into strips
- 2 tablespoons snipped fresh cilantro
- 2 teaspoons chili powder
- ³/₄ teaspoon salt
- ¹/₂ teaspoon ground cumin
- ¹/₄ teaspoon garlic powder
- ¹/₄ teaspoon pepper
- 1 tablespoon olive oil or cooking oil
- 1 tablespoon lime juice
- 5 large whole wheat pita bread rounds or 8-inch whole wheat tortillas
- ³/₄ cup alfalfa sprouts
- 1 tomato, seeded and chopped
-    Salsa (optional)

1. For filling, in a medium mixing bowl combine tofu, sweet pepper, onion, cilantro, chili powder, salt, cumin, garlic powder, and pepper. In a large skillet cook filling, uncovered, in hot oil about 4 minutes or till vegetables are crisp-tender. Stir in lime juice.

2. Spoon filling onto one side of each pita round or tortilla. Top with alfalfa sprouts and tomato. Fold opposite sides of pita round or tortilla over filling; skewer closed with toothpicks. If desired, serve with salsa. Makes 5 main-dish servings.

Nutrition Facts per serving: 303 cal., 10 g total fat (1 g sat. fat), 0 mg chol., 683 mg sodium, 43 g carbo., 2 g fiber, 17 g pro. **Daily Values:** 7% vit. A, 30% vit. C, 12% calcium, 46% iron

SPINACH-RICE CASSEROLE

Start preparations by thawing the spinach so that it will be ready to stir into the mixture.

$^1/_3$ cup chopped onion (1 small)
1 clove garlic, minced
1 tablespoon cooking oil
1 14$^1/_2$-ounce can whole Italian-style tomatoes, cut up
1 teaspoon dried oregano or basil, crushed
8 ounces tofu (fresh bean curd), drained
2 cups cooked brown rice (see page 139)
1 10-ounce package frozen chopped spinach, thawed and well drained
$^1/_2$ cup shredded Swiss cheese (2 ounces)
$^1/_2$ teaspoon salt
$^1/_4$ teaspoon pepper
1 teaspoon sesame seed, toasted (see tip, page 234)

1. In a large saucepan cook the onion and garlic in hot oil till onion is tender but not brown. Add undrained tomatoes and oregano. Bring to boiling; reduce heat. Simmer, uncovered, about 3 minutes.
2. Place tofu in a food processor bowl or blender container. Cover; process or blend till smooth; add to tomato mixture. Stir in cooked rice, spinach, *¼ cup* of the Swiss cheese, salt, and pepper.
3. Grease 4 individual 16-ounce casseroles or one 2-quart rectangular baking dish. Spoon mixture into casseroles or baking dish. Bake, uncovered, in a 350° oven for 30 to 40 minutes or till heated through. Sprinkle with remaining Swiss cheese and sesame seed. Makes 4 main-dish servings.

Nutrition Facts per serving: 321 cal., 14 g total fat (4 g sat. fat), 13 mg chol., 525 mg sodium, 34 g carbo., 3 g fiber, 18 g pro. **Daily Values:** 47% vit. A, 37% vit. C, 30% calcium, 52% iron

MEATLESS SKILLET LASAGNA

PREP: 15 MINUTES   COOK: 15 MINUTES

Fast

The cheeses and spaghetti sauce are the ingredients in this main dish that will remind you of lasagna. Tofu replaces the lasagna noodles.

- 1 15¹/₂-ounce jar (1¹/₂ cups) meatless spaghetti sauce with mushrooms
- 1 8- or 10¹/₂-ounce package firm or extra-firm tofu, drained
- 3 cups loose-pack frozen broccoli, French-style green beans, onions, and red peppers
- 1 cup ricotta cheese
- ¹/₄ cup grated Parmesan cheese
- ¹/₂ teaspoon dried oregano, crushed
- ¹/₄ teaspoon pepper
- ¹/₂ cup shredded cheddar or mozzarella cheese (2 ounces)

1. In a large skillet heat *1¹/₄ cups* of the spaghetti sauce over low heat. Thinly slice the tofu and arrange half of the slices in the skillet with the sauce. Run cool water over the vegetables in a colander to thaw. Press with hands to remove excess liquid. Sprinkle vegetables into skillet.

2. Stir together the ricotta cheese, Parmesan cheese, oregano, and

EATING MEATLESS

Pasta, dairy products, eggs, dry beans, lentils, tofu, rice, and other vegetables and grains are important ingredients that go into meatless main dishes.

■ If your meatless recipes include dairy products, watch out for fat and calories. Some of the healthier dairy choices include skim milk, fat-free and low-fat yogurt, fat-free and light sour cream, reduced-fat cheeses, and low-fat cottage cheese.

■ If you are eliminating all animal products from your diet, it's critical that the foods you eat are nutritionally balanced so that you get the protein, vitamins, and minerals your body needs. Strict vegetarians should be aware that their intake of certain nutrients, such as iron, calcium, zinc, vitamin B_{12}, and vitamin D, may end up being lower than recommended.

pepper. Drop by spoonfuls over vegetables in skillet. Top with remaining tofu slices and spaghetti sauce. Cover and cook over low heat for 10 to 15 minutes or till mixture is heated through. Sprinkle with cheddar or mozzarella cheese before serving. Makes 4 main-dish servings.

Nutrition Facts per serving: 375 cal., 22 g total fat (9 g sat. fat), 39 mg chol., 906 mg sodium, 21 g carbo., 5 g fiber, 26 g pro. **Daily Values:** 52% vit. A, 112% vit. C, 44% calcium, 51% iron

POLENTA

PREP: 30 MINUTES   CHILL: 30 MINUTES   BAKE: 20 MINUTES   Oven 350°

No-Fat

This is a three-way recipe: Bake, cut into wedges, and top with sauce for polenta; serve it as a cereal with milk; or slice, fry, and serve it with margarine and syrup.

  1 **cup cornmeal**
  1 **cup cold water**

1. In a saucepan bring $2^{3}/_{4}$ cups *water* to boiling. Meanwhile, in a mixing bowl combine cornmeal, the 1 cup cold water, and $^{1}/_{2}$ teaspoon *salt*.
2. Slowly add cornmeal mixture to boiling water, stirring constantly. Cook and stir till mixture returns to boiling. Reduce heat to low. Cook for 10 to 15 minutes or till mixture is very thick, stirring occasionally.
3. Pour hot mixture into a 9-inch pie plate. Cool; cover and chill about 30 minutes or till firm. Bake in a 350° oven about 20 minutes or till hot. Cut into wedges. If desired, serve with *spaghetti sauce, pizza sauce, or taco sauce,* and sprinkle with grated *Parmesan cheese*. Makes 6 side-dish servings.

Nutrition Facts per serving: 84 cal., 0 g total fat, 0 mg chol., 183 mg sodium, 18 g carbo., 1 g fiber, 2 g pro. **Daily Values:** 0% vit. A, 0% vit. C, 0% calcium, 6% iron

■ **Cornmeal Mush:** Prepare as above, except do not transfer cooked mixture to pie plate. If desired, serve hot with *milk, margarine, butter, honey, or sugar*. Makes 4 side-dish servings.

Nutrition Facts per serving: 126 cal., 1 g total fat (0 g sat. fat)

■ **Fried Cornmeal Mush:** Prepare as above, except pour hot mixture into a 7¹/₂x3¹/₂x2-inch loaf pan. Cool; cover and chill for several hours or overnight. Turn out of the pan and cut mush into ¹/₂-inch-thick slices. In a large skillet heat 3 tablespoons *cooking oil, margarine, or butter* over medium heat. Add 5 slices of mush and fry for 10 to 12 minutes on each side or till brown and crisp. Repeat with remaining slices. If desired, serve with *margarine or butter* and *honey or maple-flavored syrup*. Makes 7 side-dish servings.

Nutrition Facts per serving: 116 cal., 5 g total fat (1 g sat. fat)

CHEESE AND BASIL POLENTA WITH TOMATO-BASIL SAUCE

PREP: 1¹/₂ HOURS   CHILL: 2 TO 24 HOURS   BAKE: 40 MINUTES   Oven 350°

    1¹/₂ cups shredded fontina or mozzarella cheese (6 ounces)
    ¹/₃ cup grated Parmesan or Romano cheese
      2 tablespoons snipped fresh basil or 2 teaspoons dried basil,
          crushed
      1 cup yellow cornmeal
    ¹/₂ teaspoon salt
      1 recipe Tomato-Basil Sauce (see below)
          Fresh basil (optional)
          Grated Parmesan or Romano cheese (optional)

1. In a medium mixing bowl stir together fontina or mozzarella cheese, the ¹/₃ cup Parmesan or Romano cheese, and basil. Set aside.
2. For polenta, in a medium saucepan bring 3 cups *water* to boiling. Meanwhile, in a mixing bowl stir together cornmeal, salt, and 1 cup *cold water*. Slowly add cornmeal mixture to boiling water, stirring constantly. Cook and stir till mixture returns to boiling. Reduce heat to very low. Cover and simmer for 15 minutes, stirring occasionally.
3. Immediately transfer one-third of the hot mixture to a greased 2-quart square baking dish. Sprinkle with half of the cheese mixture. Repeat layers, ending with the hot mixture. Cool for 1 hour. Cover with foil and chill several hours or overnight till firm.
4. Bake polenta, uncovered, in a 350° oven about 40 minutes or till lightly browned and heated through. Let stand 10 minutes. Serve with Tomato-Basil Sauce. If desired, garnish with additional basil and sprinkle with Parmesan or Romano cheese. Makes 6 main-dish servings.

■ **Tomato-Basil Sauce:** In a medium saucepan cook ³/₄ cup chopped *onion* and 2 cloves *garlic,* minced, in 2 tablespoons hot *margarine or butter* till onion is tender. Carefully stir in two 14¹/₂-ounce cans whole *Italian-style tomatoes,* undrained and cut up; half of a 6-ounce can (¹/₃ cup) *tomato paste;* ¹/₂ teaspoon *sugar;* ¹/₄ teaspoon *salt;* and ¹/₈ teaspoon *pepper.* Bring to boiling; reduce heat. Simmer, uncovered, about 20 minutes or to desired consistency. Stir in ¹/₄ cup snipped *fresh basil* or 1 tablespoon *dried basil,* crushed. Cook 5 minutes more. Makes about 3¹/₃ cups sauce.

Nutrition Facts per serving: 292 cal., 15 g total fat (7 g sat. fat), 37 mg chol., 769 mg sodium, 27 g carbo., 3 g fiber, 13 g pro. **Daily Values:** 24% vit. A, 30% vit. C, 22% calcium, 13% iron

---

BAKED GNOCCHI

PREP: 25 MINUTES   CHILL: 1 HOUR   BAKE: 25 MINUTES   Oven 425°

Italian for dumpling, gnocchi (NO-key) goes well with meat or poultry.

1¹/₂ **cups milk**
   2 **tablespoons margarine or butter**
³/₄ **cup milk**
¹/₂ **cup quick-cooking farina**
   1 **beaten egg**
¹/₃ **cup grated Parmesan cheese**
¹/₄ **cup grated Parmesan cheese**

1. Bring the 1¹/₂ cups milk and margarine to boiling. Mix the ³/₄ cup milk, farina, and ¹/₄ teaspoon *salt;* slowly add to boiling milk, stirring constantly. Cook and stir 3 to 4 minutes or till thick. Remove from heat; gradually stir hot mixture into egg. Stir in the ¹/₃ cup Parmesan cheese. Pour into a greased 2-quart square baking dish. Chill 1 hour or till firm.
2. Turn out of baking dish. Cut into 4×1-inch rectangles. Sprinkle tops with the ¹/₄ cup Parmesan cheese. Place on a well-greased baking sheet. Bake in a 425° oven about 25 minutes or till golden. Serve warm. Makes 5 side-dish servings.

Nutrition Facts per serving: 227 cal., 11 g total fat (5 g sat. fat), 60 mg chol., 445 mg sodium, 19 g carbo., 0 g fiber, 12 g pro. **Daily Values:** 16% vit. A, 1% vit. C, 25% calcium, 6% iron

■ **Spinach Gnocchi:** Prepare as above, except reduce milk to 1¼ cups. Cook one 10-ounce package *frozen chopped spinach* according to package directions. Drain in a colander, pressing out as much liquid as possible. Stir spinach into hot farina mixture with the ⅓ cup Parmesan cheese.

Nutrition Facts per serving: 232 cal., 11 g total fat (5 g sat. fat)

GRITS

START TO FINISH: 15 MINUTES

Fast   **No-Fat**

1. Bring 2 cups *water or chicken broth* and ¼ teaspoon *salt* to boiling. Slowly add ½ cup *quick-cooking grits,* stirring constantly. Cook and stir till boiling. Reduce heat; cook and stir for 5 to 6 minutes more or till water is absorbed and mixture is thick. If desired, serve with *margarine, butter, or milk.* Makes 2 side-dish servings.

Nutrition Facts per serving: 144 cal., 0 g total fat, 0 mg chol., 274 mg sodium, 31 g carbo., 0 g fiber, 4 g pro. **Daily Values:** 5% vit. A, 0% vit. C, 0% calcium, 10% iron

---

BAKED CHEESE GRITS

PREP: 10 MINUTES   BAKE: 25 MINUTES   Oven 325°

   2 cups water or chicken broth
  ½ cup quick-cooking grits
   1 beaten egg
   1 cup shredded American or cheddar cheese (4 ounces)
   1 tablespoon margarine or butter

1. In a saucepan bring water or chicken broth to boiling. Slowly add grits, stirring constantly. Gradually stir about ½ cup of the hot mixture into the egg. Return egg mixture to saucepan and stir to combine. Remove from heat. Stir cheese and margarine or butter into grits till melted.
2. Spoon grits into a 1-quart casserole. Bake in a 325° oven for 25 to 30 minutes or till a knife inserted near the center comes out clean. Let stand 5 minutes. Makes 4 or 5 side-dish servings.

Nutrition Facts per serving: 222 cal., 13 g total fat (7 g sat. fat), 80 mg chol., 458 mg sodium, 16 g carbo., 0 g fiber, 10 g pro. **Daily Values:** 18% vit. A, 0% vit. C, 15% calcium, 7% iron

BARLEY-VEGETABLE MEDLEY

START TO FINISH: 35 MINUTES

Low-Fat

  1 cup fresh or frozen whole kernel corn
 1/2 cup quick-cooking barley
 1/2 cup chopped onion (1 medium)
 1/2 cup chopped green sweet pepper
 1/2 cup coarsely shredded carrot
  2 teaspoons instant beef bouillon granules
 1/2 teaspoon dried basil, crushed
 1/4 teaspoon dried thyme, crushed
 1/4 teaspoon dried oregano, crushed
 1/8 teaspoon pepper
  1 large tomato, chopped

1. Bring 1 1/2 cups *water* to boiling. Stir in corn, barley, onion, sweet pepper, carrot, bouillon granules, basil, thyme, oregano, and pepper. Return to boiling; reduce heat. Cover and simmer about 10 minutes or till barley is tender, stirring occasionally. Drain barley mixture. Stir in tomato. Cook and stir about 1 minute more or till heated through. Makes 6 side-dish servings.

Nutrition Facts per serving: 100 cal., 1 g total fat (0 g sat. fat), 0 mg chol., 306 mg sodium, 22 g carbo., 3 g fiber, 4 g pro. **Daily Values:** 42% vit. A, 22% vit. C, 1% calcium, 7% iron

---

MIXED GRAIN CASSEROLE

PREP: 10 MINUTES BAKE: 1 HOUR   Oven 350°

Low-Fat

Looking for a meatless main dish? Make four larger servings out of this side-dish casserole.

  2 medium carrots, halved lengthwise and thinly sliced (1 cup)
  1 cup fresh small mushrooms, quartered
  1 cup canned black beans, rinsed and drained
  1 8 3/4-ounce can whole kernel corn, drained, or 1 cup frozen
     whole kernel corn
  1 cup vegetable broth
 1/2 cup pearl barley

$^{1}/_{3}$ **cup snipped parsley**
$^{1}/_{4}$ **cup bulgur**
$^{1}/_{4}$ **cup chopped onion**
$^{1}/_{4}$ **teaspoon garlic salt**
$^{1}/_{2}$ **cup shredded cheddar cheese (2 ounces)**

1. In a $1^{1}/_{2}$-quart casserole combine carrots, mushrooms, beans, corn, broth, barley, parsley, bulgur, onion, and garlic salt. Bake, covered, in a 350° oven about 1 hour or till barley and bulgur are tender, stirring once halfway through baking time.

2. Sprinkle with cheese. Cover; let stand 5 minutes or till cheese melts. Makes 6 side-dish servings.

Nutrition Facts per serving: 187 cal., 4 g total fat (2 g sat. fat), 10 mg chol., 530 mg sodium, 33 g carbo., 7 g fiber, 10 g pro. **Daily Values:** 83% vit. A, 13% vit. C, 9% calcium, 14% iron

---

CABBAGE ROLLS WITH BULGUR AND VEGETABLES

PREP: 45 MINUTES   BAKE: 15 MINUTES   Oven 400°

Low-Fat

Keep sodium in check by using reduced-sodium chicken broth and low-sodium tomato sauce.

$1^{1}/_{2}$ **cups chopped fresh mushrooms**
  1 **small zucchini, quartered lengthwise and sliced (1 cup)**
$^{3}/_{4}$ **cup reduced-sodium chicken broth or beef broth**
$^{1}/_{2}$ **cup chopped green sweet pepper (1 small)**
$^{1}/_{2}$ **cup chopped red sweet pepper (1 small)**
$^{1}/_{2}$ **cup bulgur**
  1 **teaspoon dried basil, crushed**
$^{1}/_{2}$ **teaspoon dried marjoram, crushed**
$^{1}/_{2}$ **teaspoon dried thyme, crushed**
$^{1}/_{4}$ **teaspoon pepper**
  8 **medium cabbage leaves**
$^{1}/_{4}$ **cup finely shredded or grated Parmesan cheese**
  2 **teaspoons lemon or lime juice**
$^{1}/_{8}$ **to** $^{1}/_{4}$ **teaspoon bottled hot pepper sauce**
  1 **8-ounce can low-sodium tomato sauce**
  2 **tablespoons finely shredded or grated Parmesan cheese**

1. In a large saucepan combine mushrooms, zucchini, broth, sweet peppers, bulgur, basil, marjoram, thyme, and pepper. Bring to boiling; reduce heat. Cover and simmer for 5 minutes. Remove from heat; let stand, covered, for 5 minutes.

2. Meanwhile, fill a Dutch oven with water; bring to boiling. Cut out center vein from cabbage leaves, keeping each leaf in one piece. Immerse leaves, 4 at a time, into the boiling water for 2 to 3 minutes or till leaves are limp. Drain well.

3. Stir the $1/4$ cup Parmesan cheese and lemon or lime juice into bulgur mixture. Place about $1/4$ cup of the bulgur mixture on each cabbage leaf; fold in sides. Starting at an unfolded edge, carefully roll up each leaf, making sure folded sides are caught in the roll. Stir hot pepper sauce into tomato sauce. Spoon about $1/3$ cup of the tomato sauce into a 2-quart square baking dish. Place cabbage rolls in dish. Spoon remaining sauce over cabbage rolls. Bake, covered, in a 400° oven about 15 minutes or till heated through. Sprinkle with the 2 tablespoons Parmesan cheese. Makes 4 main-dish servings.

Nutrition Facts per serving: 173 cal., 3 g total fat (0 g sat. fat), 7 mg chol., 280 mg sodium, 28 g carbo., 8 g fiber, 10 g pro. **Daily Values:** 18% vit. A, 151% vit. C, 13% calcium, 16% iron

WHEAT BERRY AND PASTA PILAF

START TO FINISH: $1^{1}/_{2}$ HOURS

Low-Fat

Wheat berries are the whole wheat kernel with just the hull removed.

   5 **cups water**
$1^{1}/_{4}$ **cups wheat berries**
  $^{3}/_{4}$ **cup orzo (rosamarina)**
   2 **cups sliced fresh shiitake or button mushrooms**
   1 **cup thinly sliced carrots (2 medium)**
   1 **$14^{1}/_{2}$-ounce can chunky pasta-style tomatoes**
   1 **8-ounce can low-sodium tomato sauce**
  $^{1}/_{2}$ **cup dry white wine**
  $^{1}/_{2}$ **teaspoon instant beef or chicken bouillon granules**
  $^{1}/_{2}$ **teaspoon fennel seed, crushed**
     Dash ground red pepper

1. For pilaf, in a large saucepan bring the water to boiling. Add wheat berries. Reduce heat. Cover and simmer for 1 hour. Add orzo. Cook, uncovered, about 10 minutes more or till wheat berries and orzo are tender. Drain off any excess liquid. Cover to keep warm. Set aside.

2. Meanwhile, for sauce, in a medium saucepan cook mushrooms and carrots, covered, in a small amount of boiling water about 4 minutes or till carrots are crisp-tender; drain. Stir undrained tomatoes, tomato sauce, wine, bouillon granules, fennel seed, and red pepper into the mushroom mixture. Bring to boiling; reduce heat. Simmer, uncovered, about 25 minutes or to desired consistency, stirring occasionally.

3. To serve, spoon pilaf onto dinner plates. Top with sauce. Makes 4 main-dish servings.

Nutrition Facts per serving: 366 cal., 1 g total fat (0 g sat. fat), 0 mg chol., 622 mg sodium, 87 g carbo., 6 g fiber, 14 g pro. **Daily Values:** 155% vit. A, 56% vit. C, 10% calcium, 39% iron

---

RICE AND VEGETABLE CASSEROLE

PREP: 20 MINUTES   BAKE: 30 MINUTES   Oven 375°

$^1/_2$ cup chopped green or red sweet pepper
$^1/_2$ cup chopped onion (1 medium)
$^1/_2$ cup chopped celery or one 4-ounce can diced green chili
    peppers, drained
1 clove garlic, minced
1 tablespoon margarine or butter
$1^1/_2$ cups cooked rice, bulgur, wheat berries, or barley (see pages
    138–140)
$^1/_2$ of an 8-ounce tub ($^1/_2$ cup) cream cheese
$^1/_4$ teaspoon ground cumin, ground coriander, or dried basil,
    crushed
    Milk
$^1/_2$ cup shredded cheddar cheese

1. Cook sweet pepper, onion, celery (if using), and garlic in margarine till vegetables are tender.

2. Meanwhile, in a bowl combine cooked rice, cream cheese, chili peppers (if using), cumin, $^1/_4$ teaspoon *salt,* and $^1/_4$ teaspoon *pepper.* Stir in vegetable mixture. Transfer to a 1-quart casserole. Bake, covered, in a 375° oven about 25 minutes or till heated through. If mixture seems stiff, stir in milk, a tablespoon at a time, to moisten.

Sprinkle with cheese. Bake 2 to 3 minutes more or till cheese melts.
Makes 5 or 6 side-dish servings.

Nutrition Facts per serving: 226 cal., 14 g total fat (7 g sat. fat), 37 mg chol., 305 mg
sodium, 18 g carbo., 1 g fiber, 6 g pro. **Daily Values:** 11% vit. A, 16% vit. C, 10% calcium,
6% iron

GRANOLA

PREP: 10 MINUTES   BAKE: 30 MINUTES   Oven 300°

  2 cups regular rolled oats
  $^1/_2$ cup flaked coconut
  $^1/_2$ cup coarsely chopped slivered or sliced almonds, or chopped
      peanuts
  $^1/_2$ cup shelled sunflower seeds
  $^1/_4$ cup sesame seed
  $^1/_2$ cup honey or maple-flavored syrup
  $^1/_3$ cup cooking oil

1. Combine the oats, coconut, almonds or peanuts, sunflower seeds,
and sesame seed. Combine honey or syrup and oil; stir into oat mixture. Spread evenly in a greased 15×10×1-inch baking pan. Bake in a
300° oven for 30 to 35 minutes or till lightly browned, stirring after
20 minutes.
2. Remove from oven; immediately turn out onto large piece of foil.
Cool; break into clumps. Cover tightly and store at room temperature
for up to 2 weeks. For longer storage, seal in freezer bags and
freeze. Makes 6 cups (twelve ½-cup servings).

Nutrition Facts per serving: 238 cal., 15 g total fat (3 g sat. fat), 0 mg chol., 45 mg
sodium, 24 g carbo., 1 g fiber, 5 g pro. **Daily Values:** 0% vit. A, 0% vit. C, 2% calcium, 8%
iron

■ **Raisin-Date Granola:** Prepare as above, except after removing
granola from the oven, stir in ½ cup *raisins* and ½ cup snipped *pitted dates*. Makes 8 cups (sixteen ½-cup servings).

Nutrition Facts per serving: 208 cal., 11 g total fat (2 g sat. fat)

STORING BEANS AND GRAINS

Dry beans are easy to keep and can be stored at room temperature up to 1 year or even longer in the freezer. Cooked dry beans (see chart, pages 136–137) can be refrigerated for up to 3 days or frozen for up to 3 months.

Whole grains have a shorter storage life because they contain an oil-rich germ that can become rancid. Therefore, purchase whole grains in smaller quantities. Keep all grains in tightly covered containers. For specific grains, follow these storage guidelines:

■ **Pearl and Scotch barley:** up to 1 year in a cool, dry place. (Other forms of barley: up to 9 months in a cool, dry place.)

■ **Buckwheat:** up to 3 months in a cool, dry place, up to 6 months in the refrigerator, or up to 1 year in the freezer.

■ **Bulgur:** up to 6 months in a cool, dry place or indefinitely in the freezer.

■ **Cornmeal:** up to 6 months in a cool, dry place or up to 1 year in the refrigerator or freezer.

■ **Oats:** up to 6 months in a cool, dry place or up to 1 year in the freezer.

■ **Rye berries:** up to 5 months in the refrigerator or freezer.

■ **White and wild rice:** indefinitely in a cool, dry place.

■ **Brown rice:** up to 6 months in a cool, dry place.

■ **Whole or cracked wheat:** up to 6 months in a cool, dry place or up to 1 year in the freezer.

■ **Wheat bran:** up to 1 month in a cool, dry place, up to 3 months in the refrigerator, or up to 1 year in the freezer.

■ **Wheat germ:** up to 3 months in the refrigerator.

CINNAMON-RAISIN OATMEAL

PREP: 10 MINUTES   COOK: 10 MINUTES

Fast   Low-Fat

To cook one serving at a time, use ³/₄ cup water and ²/₃ cup oat mixture.

1½ cups quick-cooking rolled oats
1 cup raisins or mixed dried fruit bits
¼ cup chopped nuts (optional)
¼ cup packed brown sugar
½ teaspoon ground cinnamon
¼ teaspoon salt
¼ teaspoon ground nutmeg
Milk (optional)

1. Stir together oats, raisins or dried fruit bits, nuts (if desired), brown sugar, cinnamon, salt, and nutmeg. Cover tightly and store at room temperature. Makes about 2⅔ cups mix (four ⅔-cup servings).
2. For 4 breakfast servings, in a medium saucepan bring 3 cups *water* to boiling. Slowly add oat mix to boiling water, stirring constantly. Cook for 1 minute, stirring constantly. Cover; remove from heat. Let stand 1 to 3 minutes or till desired consistency is reached. If desired, serve with milk.

Nutrition Facts per serving: 277 cal., 2 g total fat (0 g sat. fat), 0 mg chol., 144 mg sodium, 63 g carbo., 3 g fiber, 6 g pro. **Daily Values:** 0% vit. A, 2% vit. C, 4% calcium, 16% iron

---

CRANBERRY-ALMOND CEREAL MIX

PREP: 20 MINUTES   COOK: 20 MINUTES

Low-Fat

Keep this cereal mixture on hand and cook one or two servings at a time.

1 cup regular rolled oats
1 cup quick-cooking barley
1 cup bulgur or cracked wheat
1 cup dried cranberries, snipped dried apricots, or raisins
½ cup sliced almonds, toasted (see tip, page 234)
⅓ cup sugar
1 tablespoon ground cinnamon
¼ teaspoon salt
Milk (optional)

1. Stir together oats, barley, bulgur or cracked wheat, cranberries, almonds, sugar, cinnamon, and salt. Cover tightly and store at room temperature for up to 6 months. Makes about 4²/₃ cups mix (seven ²/₃-cup servings).

2. For 2 breakfast servings, in a small saucepan bring 1¹/₃ cups *water* to boiling. Add ²/₃ cup of the cereal mix to boiling water. Reduce heat. Cover and simmer 12 to 15 minutes or till cereal reaches desired consistency. If desired, serve with milk.

■ **Microwave directions:** For 1 breakfast serving, in a large microwave-safe cereal bowl, combine ³/₄ cup *water* and ¹/₃ cup *cereal mix.* Microwave, uncovered, for 9 to 11 minutes on 50% power (medium) or till cereal reaches desired consistency, stirring once during cooking. Stir before serving. If desired, serve with milk.

Nutrition Facts per serving: 340 cal., 5 g total fat (1 g sat. fat), 0 mg chol., 91 mg sodium, 68 g carbo., 10 g fiber, 10 g pro. **Daily Values:** 0% vit. A, 0% vit. C, 5% calcium, 19% iron

---

FRUIT MUESLI

START TO FINISH: 10 MINUTES

Fast

The German word muesli (MEWS-lee) means mixture. This version of the breakfast cereal contains cereal, nuts, and dried fruits.

  4 **cups multigrain cereal with rolled rye, oats, barley, and wheat**
  1 **cup regular rolled oats**
³/₄ **cup coarsely chopped almonds or pecans, toasted (see tip, page 234)**
  1 **cup toasted wheat germ**
  1 **6-ounce package mixed dried fruit bits**
¹/₂ **cup unsalted shelled sunflower seeds or Grape Nuts cereal**
¹/₂ **cup dried banana chips, coarsely crushed**
     Milk or nonfat plain yogurt (optional)

1. In a bowl stir together multigrain cereal, rolled oats, almonds or pecans, wheat germ, dried fruit bits, sunflower seeds or cereal, and banana chips. Cover tightly and refrigerate for up to 4 weeks. If desired, serve with milk or yogurt. Makes 8 cups mix (twelve ²/₃-cup servings).

Nutrition Facts per serving: 284 cal., 11 g total fat (3 g sat. fat), 0 mg chol., 12 mg sodium, 40 g carbo., 2 g fiber, 9 g pro. **Daily Values:** 3% vit. A, 1% vit. C, 3% calcium, 14% iron

COOKING DRY BEANS, LENTILS, AND SPLIT PEAS

Rinse beans, lentils, or split peas. (See special cooking instructions below for black-eyed peas, fava beans, lentils, and split peas.) In a large pot combine 1 pound beans and 8 cups cold water. Bring to boiling; reduce heat. Simmer for 2 minutes. Remove from heat. Cover and let stand for 1 hour. (Or, omit simmering; soak beans in cold water overnight in a covered pot.) Drain and rinse. In the same pot combine beans and 8 cups fresh water. Bring to boiling; reduce heat. Simmer, covered, for time listed below or till beans are tender, stirring occasionally.

Variety	Appearance	Cooking Time	Yield
Black beans	Small, black, oval	1 to 1½ hours	6 cups
Black-eyed peas	Small, cream-colored, oval (one side has a black oval with a cream-colored dot in the center)	Do not presoak. Simmer, covered, for 45 minutes to 1 hour.	7 cups
Cranberry beans	Small, tan-colored with specks and streaks of burgundy, oval	1¼ to 1¾ hours	7 cups
Fava or broad beans	Large, brown, flat, oval	Follow these soaking directions instead of those above: Bring beans to boiling; simmer 15 to 30 minutes to soften skins. Let stand 1 hour. Drain and peel. To cook, simmer 45 to 50 minutes or till tender.	7 cups

Bean	Description	Cooking Time	Yield
Garbanzo beans or chickpeas	Medium, yellow or golden, round and irregular	1½ to 2 hours	6¼ cups
Great Northern beans	Small to medium, white, kidney-shaped	1 to 1½ hours	7 cups
Lentils	Tiny, brownish green, disk-shaped	Do not presoak. Use 5 cups water. Simmer, covered, about 30 minutes.	6 cups
Lima beans, baby	Small, off-white, wide, oval	45 minutes to 1 hour	6½ cups
Lima beans, large (butter beans)	Medium, off-white, wide, oval	1 to 1¼ hours	6 cups
Navy or pea beans	Small, off-white, oval	1 to 1½ hours	7 cups
Pinto beans	Small, tan-colored with brown specks, oval	1¼ to 1¾ hours	6½ cups
Red beans	Small, dark red, oval	1½ hours	6½ cups
Red kidney beans	Medium to large, brownish red	1 to 1½ hours kidney-shaped	6⅔ cups
Soybeans	Small, cream-colored, oval	2 to 2½ hours	7 cups
Split peas	Tiny, green or yellow, disk-shaped	Do not presoak. Use 5 cups water. Simmer, covered, about 45 minutes.	5½ cups

COOKING GRAINS

Use this chart as a guide when cooking grains. Measure the amount of water into a medium saucepan and bring to a full boil unless the chart indicates otherwise. If desired, add ¼ teaspoon salt to the water. Slowly add the grain and return to boiling. Simmer, covered, for the time specified or till most of the water is absorbed and grain is tender.

Grain and Amount	Amount of Water	Cooking Directions	Yield (four 1/2- to 3/4-cup servings)
Barley, quick-cooking pearl, 1¼ cups	2 cups	Simmer, covered, for 10 to 12 minutes.	3 cups
Barley, regular pearl ¾ cup	3 cups	Simmer, covered, about 45 minutes. Drain, if necessary.	3 cups
Buckwheat groats or kasha, ⅔ cup	1½ cups	Add to cold water. Bring to boiling. Simmer, covered, for 10 to 12 minutes.	2 cups
Bulgur 1 cup	2 cups	Add to cold water. Bring to boiling. Simmer, covered, for 12 to 15 minutes.	3 cups
Cornmeal 1 cup	2¾ cups	Combine cornmeal and 1 cup cold water. Add to the 2¾ cups boiling water. Simmer, covered, about 10 minutes.	3½ cups

Grain	Water	Directions	Yield
Farina, quick-cooking, ¾ cup	3½ cups	Simmer, covered, for 2 to 3 minutes, stirring constantly.	3 cups
Hominy grits, quick-cooking, ¾ cup	3 cups	Simmer, covered, about 5 minutes.	3 cups
Millet, ¾ cup	2 cups	Simmer, covered, for 15 to 20 minutes. Let stand, covered, for 5 minutes.	3 cups
Oats, rolled, quick-cooking, 1½ cups	3 cups	Simmer, covered, for 1 minute. Let stand, covered, for 3 minutes.	3 cups
Oats, rolled, regular 1⅔ cups	3 cups	Simmer, covered, for 5 to 7 minutes. Let stand, covered, for 3 minutes.	3 cups
Quinoa, ¾ cup	1½ cups	Rinse well. Simmer, covered, about 15 minutes.	2¾ cups
Rice, long grain white 1 cup	2 cups	Simmer, covered, about 15 minutes. Let stand, covered, for 5 minutes.	3 cups
Rice, regular brown 1 cup	2 cups	Simmer, covered, about 45 minutes. Let stand, covered, for 5 minutes.	3 cups
Rice, wild 1 cup	2 cups	Rinse well. Simmer, covered, about 40 minutes or till most of the water is absorbed. Drain, if necessary.	2⅔ cups
Rye berries ¾ cup	2½ cups	Simmer, covered, about 1 hour. Drain.	2 cups

Cooking Grains (continued)

Grain and Amount	Amount of Water	Cooking Directions	Yield (four 1/2- to 3/4-cup servings)
		(Or, soak berries in 2½ cups water in the refrigerator for 6 to 24 hours. Do not drain. Bring to boiling; reduce heat. Simmer, covered, for 30 minutes.)	
Wheat berries ¾ cup	2½ cups	Simmer, covered, for 45 to 60 minutes. Drain. (Or, soak and cook as for rye berries.)	2 cups
Wheat, cracked ⅔ cup	1½ cups	Add to cold water. Bring to boiling. Simmer, covered, for 12 to 15 minutes. Let stand, covered, for 5 minutes.	2 cups

BEVERAGES

BEVERAGES

Amaretto Dessert Coffee, 144 *Fast No-Fat*
Café Latte, 145 *Fast Low-Fat*
Candy Milk Shakes, 156 *Fast*
Cappuccino, 145 *Fast Low-Fat*
Chocolate Eggnog, 154
Chocolate-Mint Dessert Coffee, 143 *Fast No-Fat*
Chocolate-Orange Dessert Coffee, 143 *Fast No-Fat*
Coffee, 143 *Fast No-Fat*
Cookie Milk Shakes, 156 *Fast*
Daiquiri Punch, 160 *Fast No-Fat*
Dessert Coffee, 143 *Fast No-Fat*
Eggnog, 154
Espresso, 144 *Fast Low-Fat*
Fresh Lemonade Base, 156 *No-Fat*
Frozen Margaritas, 161 *Fast No-Fat*
Fruity Yogurt Sipper, 158 *Fast Low-Fat*
Glogg, 152 *Low-Fat*
Hot Buttered Cider Sipper, 150 *Fast Low-Fat*
Hot Chocolate, 147 *Fast*
Hot Cocoa Mix, 148 *Fast Low-Fat*
Hot Mocha, 147 *Fast*
Hot Spiced Cider, 149 *Fast No-Fat*
Ice-Cream Punch, 152 *Fast Low-Fat*
Iced Coffee, 144 *Fast No-Fat*
Iced Tea, 146 *Fast Low-Fat*
Irish Dessert Coffee, 144 *Fast No-Fat*

Kiwi-Limeade Slush, 157 *No-Fat*
Lemon Sherbet Float, 157 *Low-Fat*
Lime Daiquiris, 159 *Fast No-Fat*
Lime Sherbet Float, 157 *Low-Fat*
Low-Fat Eggnog, 155 *Low-Fat*
Low-Fat Hot Cocoa, 147 *Fast Low-Fat*
Malts, 156 *Fast*
Milk Shakes, 155 *Fast*
Mocha Dessert Coffee, 143 *Fast*
Mocha Milk Shakes, 156 *Fast*
Mocha Mix, 148 *Fast Low-Fat*
Nonalcoholic Eggnog, 154
Orange Breakfast Nog, 158 *Fast Low-Fat*
Peach Daiquiris, 160 *Fast No-Fat*
Raspberry Daiquiris, 159 *Fast No-Fat*
Raspberry Tea, 146 *No-Fat*
Sangria, 153 *No-Fat*
Slushy Punch, 151 *No-Fat*
Spiced Fruit Punch, 150 *No-Fat*
Spiced Hot Chocolate, 147 *Fast*
Spiked Slushy Punch, 151 *No-Fat*
Strawberry Daiquiris, 159 *Fast No-Fat*
Strawberry-Lemonade Slush, 157 *No-Fat*
Sun Tea, 146 *Fast No-Fat*
Tea, 146 *Fast No-Fat*
White Hot Chocolate, 148 *Fast*
Wine Spritzer, 159 *Fast No-Fat*

COFFEE

START TO FINISH: 10 TO 15 MINUTES

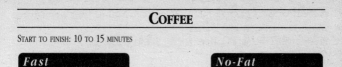

Fast   **No-Fat**

    1 to 2 tablespoons ground coffee (for each 6-ounce cup)
    ³/₄ cup cold water (for each 6-ounce cup)

■ **Drip Coffee:** Measure coffee into filter-lined coffeemaker basket. For electric drip coffeemakers, pour cold water into water compartment. Place pot on heating element; let water drip through basket. For nonelectric drip coffeemakers, pour boiling water over coffee in basket. Let water drip into pot. When coffee is finished dripping, remove basket; discard grounds. Keep coffee warm over low heat.

■ **Percolator Coffee:** Pour water into a percolator. Stand stem and basket firmly in pot. Measure coffee into basket. Replace basket lid and cover the pot. Bring the water to boiling. Perk gently for 5 to 8 minutes. Let coffee stand for 1 to 2 minutes. Remove basket from pot. Keep coffee warm.

Nutrition Facts per serving: 4 cal., 0 g total fat, 0 mg chol., 4 mg sodium, 1 g carbo., 0 g fiber, 0 g pro.

DESSERT COFFEE

START TO FINISH: 10 TO 15 MINUTES

Fast   **No-Fat**

    ²/₃ cup hot strong coffee
        Desired coffee flavoring (see choices below)
        Whipped cream (optional)
        Ground cinnamon or nutmeg (optional)

1. Stir together hot coffee and desired flavoring. If desired, top with whipped cream and sprinkle with cinnamon. Makes 1 (about 6-ounce) serving.

■ **Chocolate-Orange Dessert Coffee:** Stir 1 tablespoon *chocolate-flavored syrup* and 1 tablespoon *orange liqueur* into hot coffee.

■ **Chocolate-Mint Dessert Coffee:** Stir 1 tablespoon *chocolate-mint liqueur* into hot coffee.

■ **Mocha Dessert Coffee:** Stir 1 tablespoon *chocolate-flavored syrup* and 1 tablespoon *coffee liqueur* into hot coffee.

■ **Irish Dessert Coffee:** Stir 1 tablespoon *Irish whiskey* and 1 teaspoon *brown sugar* into coffee.

■ **Amaretto Dessert Coffee:** Stir 1 tablespoon *amaretto or hazelnut liqueur* into hot coffee.

Nutrition Facts per serving: 83 cal., 0 g total fat, 0 mg chol., 14 mg sodium, 16 g carbo., 0 g fiber, 1 g pro. **Daily Values:** 0% vit A, 0% vit C, 0% calcium, 2% iron

---

ICED COFFEE

START TO FINISH: 10 TO 15 MINUTES

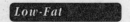

Fast   **No-Fat**

To make coffee cubes, freeze regular-strength coffee in ice-cube trays.

    ¹/₄ to ¹/₃ cup ground coffee
    1 teaspoon ground cinnamon (optional)
    Ice cubes or coffee cubes

1. Measure coffee and, if desired, cinnamon into filter-lined coffeemaker basket. Pour 3 cups *cold water* into water compartment. Prepare according to manufacturer's directions. Serve over ice cubes or coffee cubes. Makes 4 (6-ounce) servings.

Nutrition Facts per serving: 11 cal., 0 g total fat, 0 mg chol., 11 mg sodium, 2 g carbo., 0 g fiber, 1 g pro. **Daily Values:** 0% vit A, 0% vit C, 1% calcium, 3% iron

---

ESPRESSO

START TO FINISH: 10 TO 15 MINUTES

Fast   **Low-Fat**

1. Using a drip coffeemaker, add 1 cup *cold water* and ¹/₃ cup *French roast or espresso roast coffee,* ground as directed for your coffeemaker. Brew according to manufacturer's directions. (If using an espresso machine, use manufacturer's suggested amounts of ground coffee and water.) Pour into 4 demitasse cups or small cups. Serve with *sugar cubes or coarse sugar.* Makes 4 (2-ounce) servings.

Nutrition Facts per serving: 2 cal., 0 g total fat, 0 mg chol., 2 mg sodium, 0 g carbo., 0 g fiber, 0 g pro.

■ **Cappuccino:** Brew 1 recipe Espresso (see recipe, above). In a small pan warm 1 cup *low-fat milk* over medium heat till hot, but not boiling. Transfer milk to a food processor bowl or blender container. Process or blend till milk is frothy. (If using an espresso machine with a steaming nozzle, heat and froth milk according to manufacturer's directions.) Divide espresso among four 5- to 8-ounce cups. Top with frothy milk. Sprinkle with *ground cinnamon or grated chocolate*. If desired, serve with *sugar*. Makes 4 (4-ounce) servings.

Nutrition Facts per serving: 32 cal., 1 g total fat (0 g sat. fat)

■ **Café Latte:** Prepare 1 recipe Cappuccino (see recipe, above), except increase the low-fat milk to 2 cups. If desired, serve with *sugar*. Makes 4 (6-ounce) servings.

Nutrition Facts per serving: 63 cal., 2 g total fat (1 g sat. fat)

STORING COFFEE AND TEA

Unopened packages of vacuum-packed roasted coffee and jars of instant and freeze-dried coffee can be kept at room temperature at least a year. Opened packages should be stored in containers that are airtight and moisture-proof. Instant and freeze-dried coffee can be stored at room temperature. Whole beans and fresh ground coffee will keep in the refrigerator for 2 to 3 weeks or in the freezer for 2 months (freezing is not recommended for dark-roasted espresso blends). If you buy coffee beans, grind only as much as you need; if beans are frozen, thaw amount needed before grinding.

To preserve the flavor of tea, store it in airtight containers, keeping different types separate to maintain their distinct flavors. If properly sealed against air, tea can be kept at room temperature up to 2 years.

TEA

START TO FINISH: 15 MINUTES

Fast　　　　　　　　　　　**No-Fat**

   3 to 6 teaspoons loose tea or 3 to 6 tea bags
   4 cups boiling water

1. Warm a teapot by filling it with boiling water. If using loose tea, measure tea into a tea ball. Empty teapot; add tea ball or tea bags to pot. Immediately add the 4 cups boiling water to teapot. Cover; let steep 3 to 5 minutes. Remove tea ball or tea bags; serve at once. Makes 5 (about 6-ounce) servings.

■ **Iced Tea:** Prepare as above, except use 4 to 8 teaspoons loose tea or 4 to 8 tea bags. Steep; cool at room temperature 2 hours. Serve over *ice cubes.* Store in refrigerator. Makes 5 servings.

■ **Sun Tea:** Place 6 to 8 tea bags in a 2-quart clear glass container. Add 1$\frac{1}{2}$ quarts *cold water;* cover. Let stand in full sun or at room temperature 2 to 3 hours or till desired strength. Keep the container away from combustible material. (Sunlight coming through glass and liquid can concentrate a beam of light that may start a fire.) Remove tea bags. Serve over *ice cubes.* Store in refrigerator. Serves 8.

Nutrition Facts per serving: 2 cal., 0 g total fat, 0 mg chol., 7 mg sodium, 1 g carbo., 0 g fiber, 0 g pro.

RASPBERRY TEA

PREP: 10 MINUTES   CHILL: SEVERAL HOURS

No-Fat

Float fresh raspberries on top of this iced tea for a summer refresher.

   2 cups fresh or frozen red raspberries
   4 or 5 tea bags
   5 cups boiling water
   Ice cubes

1. Place raspberries and tea bags in a glass bowl. Pour boiling water over raspberries and tea bags. Cover; let stand 5 minutes. Remove bags. Strain berries from mixture; discard berries. Cool several hours.

If desired, chill. Serve over ice cubes. Makes 6 (about 6-ounce) servings.

Nutrition Facts per serving: 12 cal., 0 g total fat, 0 mg chol., 6 mg sodium, 3 g carbo., 1 g fiber, 0 g pro. **Daily Values:** 0% vit. A, 8% vit. C, 0% calcium, 1% iron

---

HOT CHOCOLATE

START TO FINISH: 15 MINUTES

Fast

   2 ounces unsweetened or semisweet chocolate, coarsely chopped, or $^1/_3$ cup semisweet chocolate pieces
$^1/_3$ cup sugar
   4 cups milk
    Whipped cream or tiny marshmallows (optional)

1. In a medium saucepan combine unsweetened or semisweet chocolate, sugar, and $^1/_2$ *cup* of the milk. Cook and stir over medium heat till mixture just comes to boiling. Stir in remaining milk; heat through. Do not boil.

2. Remove from heat. If desired, beat milk mixture with a rotary beater till frothy. If desired, top each serving with whipped cream or marshmallows. Makes 6 (about 6-ounce) servings.

Nutrition Facts per serving: 171 cal., 8 g total fat (4 g sat. fat), 12 mg chol., 82 mg sodium, 22 g carbo., 1 g fiber, 6 g pro. **Daily Values:** 10% vit. A, 2% vit. C, 17% calcium, 5% iron

■ **Hot Mocha:** Prepare as above except stir 1 tablespoon *instant coffee crystals* into chocolate mixture with remaining milk.

Nutrition Facts per serving: 173 cal., 8 g total fat (4 g sat. fat)

■ **Spiced Hot Chocolate:** Prepare as above except stir $^1/_2$ teaspoon *ground cinnamon* and $^1/_4$ teaspoon *ground nutmeg* into chocolate mixture with remaining milk.

Nutrition Facts per serving: 172 cal., 8 g total fat (4 g sat. fat)

■ **Low-Fat Hot Cocoa:** Prepare as above except substitute $^1/_4$ cup *unsweetened cocoa powder* for the chocolate and use *skim milk*.

Nutrition Facts per serving: 115 cal., 1 g total fat (0 g sat. fat)

HOT COCOA MIX

START TO FINISH: 15 MINUTES

Fast   **Low-Fat**

For a no-fat version of this wintertime favorite, omit the powdered nondairy creamer.

> 3¹/₂ cups nonfat dry milk powder
> 2 cups sifted powdered sugar
> 1 cup powdered nondairy creamer
> ¹/₂ cup sifted unsweetened cocoa powder

1. In a mixing bowl combine dry milk powder, powdered sugar, nondairy creamer, and cocoa powder. Store in an airtight container.
2. For each serving, place ¹/₃ cup of the mix in a mug and add ³/₄ cup *boiling water*. Makes about 5¹/₂ cups mix (16 servings).
■ **Mocha Mix:** Prepare as above, except stir ¹/₂ cup *instant coffee crystals* into mix. Makes about 6 cups mix (18 servings).

Nutrition Facts per serving: 143 cal., 3 g total fat (0 g sat. fat), 6 mg chol., 87 mg sodium, 21 g carbo., 0 g fiber, 9 g pro. **Daily Values:** 10% vit. A, 1% vit. C, 18% calcium, 2% iron

WHITE HOT CHOCOLATE

START TO FINISH: ABOUT 15 MINUTES

Fast

To cut fat, substitute low-fat milk or evaporated skim milk for half-and-half.

> 3 cups half-and-half or light cream
> ²/₃ cup white baking pieces or chopped white chocolate baking
>   squares
> 3 inches stick cinnamon
> ¹/₈ teaspoon ground nutmeg
> 1 teaspoon vanilla
> ¹/₄ teaspoon almond extract
>   Ground cinnamon (optional)

1. In a saucepan combine ¼ *cup* of the half-and-half, baking pieces, stick cinnamon, and nutmeg. Stir over low heat till baking pieces are melted.

2. Add remaining half-and-half. Cook and stir till heated through. Remove from heat. Remove stick cinnamon. Stir in vanilla and almond extract. If desired, sprinkle each serving with ground cinnamon. Makes 5 (6-ounce) servings.

Nutrition Facts per serving: 224 cal., 17 g total fat (10 g sat. fat), 39 mg chol., 56 mg sodium, 15 g carbo., 0 g fiber, 4 g pro. **Daily Values:** 13% vit. A, 1% vit. C, 11% calcium, 0% iron

---

HOT SPICED CIDER

PREP: 10 MINUTES   COOK: 15 MINUTES

Fast   **No-Fat**

    8 cups apple cider or apple juice
¼ to ½ cup packed brown sugar
    6 inches stick cinnamon
    1 teaspoon whole allspice
    1 teaspoon whole cloves
    8 thin orange wedges (optional)
    8 whole cloves (optional)

1. In a saucepan combine cider and brown sugar. For spice bag, place cinnamon, allspice, and the 1 teaspoon whole cloves on a double-thick, 6-inch-square piece of 100% cotton cheesecloth. Bring corners together and tie with a clean string. Add bag to cider mixture.

2. Bring to boiling; reduce heat. Cover and simmer 10 minutes. Meanwhile, if desired, stud orange wedges with cloves. Remove spice bag; discard. Serve cider in mugs with studded orange wedges, if desired. Makes 8 (about 8-ounce) servings.

Nutrition Facts per serving: 145 cal., 0 g total fat, 0 mg chol., 9 mg sodium, 40 g carbo., 0 g fiber, 0 g pro. **Daily Values:** 0% vit. A, 4% vit. C, 1% calcium, 9% iron

HOT BUTTERED CIDER SIPPER

PREP: 10 MINUTES   COOK: 10 MINUTES

Fast   **Low-Fat**

    4 cups apple cider or apple juice
    3 tablespoons honey
    2 tablespoons lemon juice
    1 teaspoon whole cloves
    1 teaspoon whole allspice
    4 inches stick cinnamon, broken
  1/4 to 1/3 cup brandy
    3 teaspoons butter or margarine
      Stick cinnamon (optional)

1. In a saucepan combine apple cider, honey, and lemon juice. For spice bag, place cloves, allspice, and broken stick cinnamon on a double-thick, 6-inch-square piece of 100% cotton cheesecloth. Bring corners together and tie with a clean string. Add bag to cider mixture.

2. Cover and heat cider; do not boil. Discard bag; stir in brandy. Ladle mixture into mugs; top each serving with 1/2 *teaspoon* butter. If desired, use stick cinnamon as stirrers. Makes 6 (6-ounce) servings.

Nutrition Facts per serving: 156 cal., 2 g total fat (1 g sat. fat), 5 mg chol., 25 mg sodium, 32 g carbo., 0 g fiber, 0 g pro. **Daily Values:** 1% vit. A, 6% vit. C, 0% calcium, 5% iron

SPICED FRUIT PUNCH

PREP: 25 MINUTES   COOK: 15 MINUTES   CHILL: 2 TO 24 HOURS

No-Fat

To serve this punch without alcohol, substitute two 1-liter bottles of chilled club soda or carbonated water for the wine.

  1/3 cup sugar
   12 inches stick cinnamon, broken
  1/2 teaspoon whole cloves
    4 cups apple juice, chilled
    1 12-ounce can apricot nectar, chilled
  1/4 cup lemon juice
    2 750-milliliter bottles dry white wine, chilled

1. In a saucepan combine $^1/_2$ cup *water*, sugar, and spices. Bring to boiling; reduce heat. Cover and simmer 10 minutes. Chill, covered, 2 to 24 hours.

2. Strain spices from sugar water and discard. Combine with fruit juices. Pour into punch bowl; add wine. Makes 24 (about 4-ounce) servings.

Nutrition Facts per serving: 81 cal., 0 g total fat, 0 mg chol., 5 mg sodium, 10 g carbo., 0 g fiber, 0 g pro. **Daily Values:** 1% vit. A, 10% vit. C, 0% calcium, 2% iron

SLUSHY PUNCH

PREP: 15 MINUTES   FREEZE: 4 TO 24 HOURS

No-Fat

    1 cup sugar
    2 ripe medium bananas, cut up
    3 cups unsweetened pineapple juice
    1 6-ounce can frozen orange juice concentrate
    2 tablespoons lemon juice
    1 1-liter bottle carbonated water or lemon-lime carbonated
       beverage, chilled

1. Combine $2^3/_4$ cups *water* and the sugar till sugar dissolves. In a blender container combine bananas, *half* of the pineapple juice, and the orange juice concentrate. Cover; blend till smooth. Add to sugar mixture. Stir in remaining juices. Transfer to a 13×9×2-inch baking pan. Freeze for 4 to 24 hours.

2. To serve, let mixture stand at room temperature 20 to 30 minutes. To form slush, scrape a large spoon across frozen mixture; spoon into punch bowl. Slowly pour carbonated water down side of bowl; stir. Makes 23 (about 4-ounce) servings.

Nutrition Facts per serving: 73 cal., 0 g total fat, 0 mg chol., 10 mg sodium, 18 g carbo., 0 g fiber, 0 g pro. **Daily Values:** 0% vit. A, 27% vit. C, 0% calcium, 1% iron

■ **Spiked Slushy Punch:** Prepare as above, except add $1^1/_2$ cups *rum or vodka* with juices. Let the frozen mixture stand for 5 to 10 minutes before scraping. Makes 26 (about 4-ounce) servings.

Nutrition Facts per serving: 94 cal., 0 g total fat

ICE-CREAM PUNCH

Fast **Low-Fat**

> 2 quarts vanilla ice cream or lime, orange, lemon, or raspberry
>   sherbet
> 1 12-ounce can frozen lemonade concentrate, thawed
> 2 1-liter bottles lemon-lime carbonated beverage, chilled

1. Spoon ice cream by tablespoonfuls into a punch bowl. Add 1½ cups *cold water* and the lemonade concentrate; stir just till combined. Slowly pour carbonated beverage down side of the bowl; stir gently to mix. Makes 32 (about 4-ounce) servings.

Nutrition Facts per serving: 113 cal., 4 g total fat (2 g sat. fat), 15 mg chol., 34 mg sodium, 20 g carbo., 0 g fiber, 1 g pro. **Daily Values:** 3% vit. A, 5% vit. C, 3% calcium, 0% iron

GLOGG

Low-Fat

Use a vegetable peeler to peel the orange, making sure to get only the outer orange part and as little as possible of the bitter white layer.

> 1 750-milliliter bottle dry red wine
> ½ cup raisins
> ½ cup gin, vodka, or aquavit
> ⅓ cup sugar
>   Peel from 1 orange
> 8 inches stick cinnamon, broken
> 6 whole cloves
> 2 cardamom pods, opened
> ¼ cup blanched whole almonds

1. In a large saucepan stir together the wine; raisins; gin, vodka, or aquavit; and sugar. For the spice bag, place orange peel, cinnamon, cloves, and cardamom in the center of a double-thick, 6-inch-square piece of 100% cotton cheesecloth. Bring the corners of the cheesecloth together and tie with a clean string. Add the spice bag to the saucepan with the wine mixture.

2. Heat mixture to simmering. Simmer, uncovered, for 10 minutes. Do not boil. Remove the spice bag and discard. Just before serving, stir in almonds. Makes 8 (about 4-ounce) servings.

■ **Crockery-cooker directions:** In a 3½- or 4-quart electric crockery cooker combine ingredients as above. Cover and cook on low-heat setting for 3 hours. Remove the spice bag and discard. Just before serving, stir in the almonds.

Nutrition Facts per serving: 177 cal., 2 g total fat (0 g sat. fat), 0 mg chol., 61 mg sodium, 18 g carbo., 1 g fiber, 1 g pro. **Daily Values:** 0% vit. A, 2% vit. C, 1% calcium, 5% iron

SANGRIA

PREP: 20 MINUTES   COOL: 30 MINUTES

No-Fat

1 lemon
1 orange
½ cup sugar
½ cup water
1 750-milliliter bottle dry red or white wine, chilled
1 to 2 cups carbonated water, chilled
2 tablespoons brandy
Ice cubes

1. Cut lemon and orange into ¼-inch-thick slices. Place the 4 end slices from the lemon and orange in a saucepan; set aside remaining slices. For syrup, add the sugar and the ½ cup water to the saucepan. Bring to boiling, stirring till sugar dissolves. Remove from heat; cool for 30 minutes. Squeeze juice from cooked fruit into the syrup. Discard cooked fruit.

2. In a pitcher combine remaining fruit slices, syrup, wine, carbonated water, and brandy. Serve over ice. Makes 10 (about 4-ounce) servings.

Nutrition Facts per serving: 100 cal., 0 g total fat, 0 mg chol., 54 mg sodium, 12 g carbo., 0 g fiber, 0 g pro. **Daily Values:** 0% vit. A, 2% vit. C, 0% calcium, 2% iron

EGGNOG

PREP: 15 MINUTES   COOK: 10 MINUTES   CHILL: 4 TO 24 HOURS

  6 beaten egg yolks
  2 cups milk
  1/3 cup sugar
  1 to 3 tablespoons light rum
  1 to 3 tablespoons bourbon
  1 teaspoon vanilla
  1 cup whipping cream
  2 tablespoons sugar
    Ground nutmeg

1. In a large heavy saucepan mix the egg yolks, milk, and the 1/3 cup sugar. Cook and stir over medium heat till mixture just coats a metal spoon. Remove from heat. Place the pan in a sink or bowl of ice water and stir for 2 minutes. Stir in rum, bourbon, and vanilla. Cover and chill for 4 to 24 hours.

2. Just before serving, in a mixing bowl beat the cream and the 2 tablespoons sugar till soft peaks form. Transfer chilled egg mixture to a punch bowl. Fold in the whipped cream mixture. Serve at once. Sprinkle each serving with nutmeg. Makes about 10 (4-ounce) servings.

Nutrition Facts per serving: 201 cal., 13 g total fat (7 g sat. fat), 164 mg chol., 71 mg sodium, 13 g carbo., 0 g fiber, 6 g pro. **Daily Values:** 19% vit. A, 1% vit. C, 7% calcium, 3% iron

■ **Chocolate Eggnog:** Prepare as above, except stir 1/4 to 1/3 cup *chocolate-flavored syrup* into egg mixture before chilling.

Nutrition Facts per serving: 211 cal., 13 g total fat (7 g sat. fat)

■ **Nonalcoholic Eggnog:** Prepare as above, except omit the rum and bourbon. Increase the milk to 2 1/4 to 2 1/2 cups.

Nutrition Facts per serving: 191 cal., 13 g total fat (7 g sat. fat)

LOW-FAT EGGNOG

PREP: 10 MINUTES   COOK: 10 MINUTES   CHILL: 4 TO 24 HOURS

Low-Fat

   4 cups skim milk
   1 12-ounce can evaporated skim milk
   1 8-ounce carton frozen egg product, thawed
   $^1/_2$ cup sugar
   $^1/_3$ cup light rum
   1 teaspoon vanilla
     Skim milk
     Ground nutmeg
     Stick cinnamon

1. In a large saucepan, cook and stir the 4 cups skim milk, evaporated skim milk, egg product, and sugar over medium heat about 10 minutes or till slightly thickened. Do not boil. Place the pan in a sink or bowl of ice water and stir for 2 minutes. Cover and chill for 4 to 24 hours.

2. Stir in rum and vanilla. Stir in additional skim milk till desired consistency is reached. Sprinkle each serving with ground nutmeg. Serve with stick cinnamon as stirrers. Makes 12 (4-ounce) servings.

Nutrition Facts per serving: 129 cal., 2 g total fat (0 g sat. fat), 3 mg chol., 113 mg sodium, 16 g carbo., 0 g fiber, 7 g pro. **Daily Values:** 10% vit. A, 2% vit. C, 16% calcium, 3% iron

MILK SHAKES

START TO FINISH: 5 MINUTES

Fast

   1 pint vanilla, chocolate, strawberry, butter brickle, cinnamon,
     or coffee ice cream
   $^1/_2$ to $^3/_4$ cup milk

1. Place the ice cream and milk in a blender container. Cover and blend till smooth. Serve immediately. Makes 2 (about 8-ounce) servings.

Nutrition Facts per serving: 294 cal., 16 g total fat (10 g sat. fat), 63 mg chol., 137 mg sodium, 34 g carbo., 0 g fiber, 7 g pro. **Daily Values:** 19% vit. A, 2% vit. C, 20% calcium, 1% iron

■ **Malts:** Prepare as above, except add 2 tablespoons *instant malted milk powder* with the milk.

Nutrition Facts per serving: 360 cal., 17 g total fat (10 g sat. fat)

■ **Mocha Milk Shakes:** Prepare as above, except use chocolate ice cream. Add 2 teaspoons *instant coffee crystals* with the milk.

Nutrition Facts per serving: 298 cal., 16 g total fat (10 g sat. fat)

■ **Candy Milk Shakes:** Prepare as above except use only vanilla or chocolate ice cream. Add 6 *bite-size chocolate-covered peanut butter cups or* one 1¹/₈-ounce bar *chocolate-covered English toffee*, broken up, to blended mixture. Cover; blend just till candy is coarsely chopped.

Nutrition Facts per serving: 432 cal., 24 g total fat (14 g sat. fat)

■ **Cookie Milk Shakes:** Prepare as above except use only vanilla or chocolate ice cream. Add 4 *chocolate sandwich cookies or* 4 *chocolate-covered graham crackers* to blended mixture. Cover; blend just till cookies are coarsely chopped.

Nutrition Facts per serving: 394 cal., 20 g total fat (11 g sat. fat)

FRESH LEMONADE BASE

PREP: 20 MINUTES   COOK: 15 MINUTES   CHILL: UP TO 3 DAYS

No-Fat

    2¹/₂ cups water
    1¹/₄ cups sugar
     ¹/₂ teaspoon finely shredded lemon or lime peel
    1¹/₄ cups lemon or lime juice

1. For a lemonade or limeade base, in a saucepan heat and stir water and sugar over medium heat till sugar is dissolved. Remove from heat; cool 20 minutes. Add peel and juice to sugar mixture. Pour into a jar, cover, and refrigerate for up to 3 days.
2. For each glass of lemonade or limeade, combine equal parts base and water in ice-filled glasses; stir. Makes 8 (about 8-ounce) servings lemonade or limeade or about 4 cups of the base.

Nutrition Facts per serving: 104 cal., 0 g total fat, 0 mg chol., 2 mg sodium, 28 g carbo., 0 g fiber, 0 g pro. Daily Values: 0% vit. A, 23% vit. C, 0% calcium, 0% iron

FRESH SQUEEZED JUICE

When you need fresh squeezed citrus juice to use in a recipe or just want it to drink, try these helpful juicing tips.

■ Choose fruits that are heavy for their size; they'll contain more juice.

■ Before squeezing fruit, leave it out at room temperature for 30 minutes. Roll each piece of fruit on the counter under the palm of your hand a few times.

■ Or, save time by using the microwave oven to warm a lemon, lime, or small orange before juicing it. Halve the fruit and heat it on 100% power (high) for 20 to 45 seconds.

■ **Lemon or Lime Sherbet Float:** For each serving, place 1 or 2 small scoops *lemon or lime sherbet* in a tall glass. Pour ¹/₂ cup *lemonade or limeade base* and ¹/₂ cup *carbonated water* over the sherbet. Serve immediately.

Nutrition Facts per serving: 256 cal., 2 g total fat (1 g sat. fat)

■ **Strawberry-Lemonade Slush:** For each serving, in a blender container combine ¹/₂ cup *fresh or frozen unsweetened strawberries,* ¹/₃ cup *lemonade base,* and 1 tablespoon *sugar.* Blend till smooth. With blender running, add ¹/₂ cup *ice cubes,* 1 at a time, through opening in lid till mixture becomes slushy. Pour into a tall glass; serve immediately.

Nutrition Facts per serving: 158 cal., 0 g total fat

■ **Kiwi-Limeade Slush:** For each serving, in a blender container combine 1 peeled and sliced ripe *kiwifruit,* ¹/₃ cup *limeade base,* 1 tablespoon *sugar,* and several drops *green food coloring.* Cover; blend till smooth. With blender running, add ¹/₂ cup *ice cubes,* 1 at a time, through opening in lid till mixture becomes slushy. Pour into a tall glass and serve immediately.

Nutrition Facts per serving: 182 cal., 0 g total fat

ORANGE BREAKFAST NOG

START TO FINISH: 5 MINUTES

Fast **Low-Fat**

1¹/₂ cups buttermilk
¹/₂ of a 6-ounce can (¹/₃ cup) frozen orange juice concentrate
2 tablespoons brown sugar
1 teaspoon vanilla
2 or 3 large ice cubes

1. In a blender container combine buttermilk, orange juice concentrate, brown sugar, and vanilla. Cover and blend till smooth. With blender running, add ice cubes, 1 at a time, through opening in lid. Blend till smooth and frothy. Makes 2 (about 10-ounce) servings.

Nutrition Facts per serving: 198 cal., 2 g total fat (1 g sat. fat), 7 mg chol., 198 mg sodium, 38 g carbo., 0 g fiber, 7 g pro. **Daily Values:** 3% vit. A, 123% vit. C, 19% calcium, 3% iron

FRUITY YOGURT SIPPER

START TO FINISH: 5 MINUTES

Fast **Low-Fat**

Make this icy drink fruitier by substituting fruit-flavored yogurt instead of vanilla.

1 ripe large banana or 2 medium peaches, peeled and pitted
1¹/₂ cups milk
1 8-ounce carton vanilla yogurt
1 to 2 tablespoons powdered sugar
¹/₂ cup ice cubes

1. Cut fruit into chunks. In a blender container combine the fruit, milk, yogurt, and powdered sugar. Cover; blend till smooth. With blender running, add ice cubes, 1 at a time, through lid opening. Blend till smooth. Makes 4 (8-ounce) servings.

Nutrition Facts per serving: 139 cal., 3 g total fat (2 g sat. fat), 10 mg chol., 79 mg sodium, 24 g carbo., 1 g fiber, 6 g pro. **Daily Values:** 7% vit. A, 7% vit. C, 15% calcium, 1% iron

WINE SPRITZER

START TO FINISH: 5 MINUTES

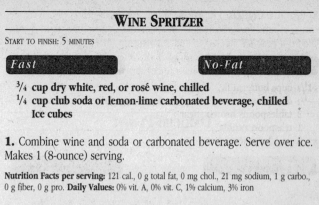

Fast   **No-Fat**

$^3/_4$ cup dry white, red, or rosé wine, chilled
$^1/_4$ cup club soda or lemon-lime carbonated beverage, chilled
Ice cubes

1. Combine wine and soda or carbonated beverage. Serve over ice. Makes 1 (8-ounce) serving.

Nutrition Facts per serving: 121 cal., 0 g total fat, 0 mg chol., 21 mg sodium, 1 g carbo., 0 g fiber, 0 g pro. **Daily Values:** 0% vit. A, 0% vit. C, 1% calcium, 3% iron

---

LIME DAIQUIRIS

START TO FINISH: 10 MINUTES

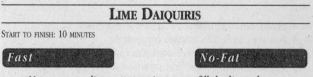

Fast   **No-Fat**

*No reason to dirty a measuring cup—fill the limeade can
to measure $^2/_3$ cup rum.*

1 6-ounce can frozen limeade or lemonade concentrate
$^2/_3$ cup rum
$2^1/_2$ to 3 cups ice cubes

1. In a blender container combine limeade or lemonade concentrate and rum. Cover and blend till smooth. With blender running, add ice cubes, 1 at a time, through opening in lid. Blend till slushy. Makes 6 (about 4-ounce) servings.

Nutrition Facts per serving: 110 cal., 0 g total fat, 0 mg chol., 1 mg sodium, 14 g carbo., 0 g fiber, 0 g pro. **Daily Values:** 0% vit. A, 5% vit. C, 0% calcium, 0% iron

■ **Raspberry or Strawberry Daiquiris:** Prepare as above, except use *half* of a 6-ounce can ($^1/_3$ cup) frozen limeade or lemonade concentrate. Add one 10-ounce package *frozen red raspberries or sliced strawberries* and, if desired, $^1/_3$ cup *sifted powdered sugar*. Makes 7 (4-ounce) servings.

Nutrition Facts per serving: 113 cal., 0 g total fat

■ **Peach Daiquiris:** Prepare as above, except use *half* of a 6-ounce can ($^1/_3$ cup) frozen limeade or lemonade concentrate. Add 3 *ripe medium peaches,* peeled, pitted, and cut up ($1^1/_2$ cups), or $1^1/_2$ cups *frozen unsweetened peach slices.* If desired, add $^1/_2$ cup *sifted powdered sugar.* Makes 8 (about 4-ounce) servings.

Nutrition Facts per serving: 77 cal., 0 g total fat

DAIQUIRI PUNCH

START TO FINISH: 10 MINUTES

Fast   *No-Fat*

If using fresh strawberries, remove stems and caps. For frozen strawberries, thaw the berries after measuring; do not drain.

  6 cups fresh or frozen unsweetened strawberries
  1 6-ounce can frozen limeade concentrate
$^3/_4$ cup light rum or unsweetened pineapple juice
  1 16-ounce bottle lemon-lime carbonated beverage, chilled
  2 cups ice cubes or crushed ice
    Fresh strawberries (optional)

1. In a blender container or food processor bowl, place *half* the strawberries at a time. Cover; blend or process till smooth. Transfer blended berries to a large pitcher. Stir in limeade concentrate and rum. If desired, cover and chill for up to 24 hours.
2. Just before serving, stir in carbonated beverage and ice. If desired, garnish with whole berries. Makes 8 (7-ounce) servings.

Nutrition Facts per serving: 146 cal., 0 g total fat, 0 mg chol., 9 mg sodium, 25 g carbo., 2 g fiber, 1 g pro. **Daily Values:** 0% vit. A, 109% vit. C, 1% calcium, 3% iron

FROZEN MARGARITAS

START TO FINISH: 10 MINUTES

Fast   **No-Fat**

     1 6-ounce can frozen limeade concentrate
   ²/₃ cup tequila
   ¹/₂ cup orange liqueur
     4 cups ice cubes
     1 or 2 limes
       Coarse salt

1. In a blender container combine limeade concentrate, tequila, and orange liqueur. Cover; blend till smooth. With blender running, add ice cubes, 1 at a time, through hole in lid, blending till slushy.

2. Cut a thick lime slice; cut slice in half. Rub slices around rims of 8 glasses. Invert glasses into a dish of coarse salt. Pour mixture into prepared glasses. Slice remaining lime into 8 thin slices. Garnish glasses with slices. Makes 8 (4-ounce) servings.

Nutrition Facts per serving: 121 cal., 0 g total fat, 0 mg chol., 1 mg sodium, 15 g carbo., 0 g fiber, 0 g pro. **Daily Values:** 0% vit. A, 4% vit. C, 0% calcium, 0% iron

COMMON TYPES OF WINE

Type	Flavor	How to Serve
APERITIF WINES **Dry Sherry, Dubonnet, Lillet, Madeira, Vermouth, White Port**	Very dry to fruity with a bitter finish.	Chilled before a meal to stimulate appetite.
DESSERT WINES **Late-harvest wines, Marsala, Muscat, Sauternes, Sherry, Sweet Port, Tokay**	Sweet and full-bodied.	Chilled or at room temperature with dessert or after a meal.
WHITE TABLE WINES **Chablis,* Chardonnay, Riesling, Sauvignon Blanc**	Dry to medium sweet.	Chilled, but not ice cold, with food or as a cocktail.
BLUSH OR ROSÉ WINES **Grenache Rosé, White Zinfandel, Tavel**	Medium sweet to dry. Always fruity.	Well chilled as a cocktail or with foods.

RED TABLE WINES		
Bordeaux, Burgundy,* Cabernet Sauvignon, Merlot, Pinot Noir	Medium dry to dry. Rich flavors with firm acidity.	At cool room temperature with rich and flavorful foods.
SPARKLING WINES		
Blanc de Blancs, Blanc de Noirs, Champagne,* Spumante	Very dry to sweet, fruity (Spumante) to tart and crisp (Champagne).	Well chilled as a cocktail. Also suited for lighter foods and celebrations.

*French wines labeled Burgundy, Chablis, or Champagne are produced according to specific guidelines. In the United States, however, the same names are used generically (see Wine Glossary, pages 164–166).

WINE GLOSSARY

■ **Beaujolais:** *(Bo-zho-LAY)* From an area south of Burgundy, France, known for producing a pleasantly fruity, light-bodied red wine from Gamay grapes that is best consumed young.

■ **Bordeaux:** *(Bore-DOE)* From a wine-producing area in western France. Both white and red versions are made with flavors ranging from light and fruit-fresh to strong and hard-edged.

■ **Burgundy:** From a wine-growing district in east central France that produces both reds and whites. The name often is given to bulk generic blended red wines produced in the United States.

■ **Cabernet Sauvignon:** *(Ka-ber-NAY so-vee-NYAWN)* Best-known red wine grape and can be used alone and in a variety of blends. Grown in many countries; each locale produces a slightly different flavor reflecting its growing conditions. Usually high in tannin; improves with storage.

■ **Chablis:** *(Shah-BLEE)* A true French Chablis—dry, fresh, and fruity—is a white Burgundy made from Chardonnay grapes. In the United States, Chablis is used as a generic term for all bulk blended white wines.

■ **Champagne:** *(Sham-PAIN)* French Champagne is a specific wine made by a process known as *méthode champenoise*. Any sparkling wine that is produced in the United States may be labeled Champagne if it is bottled using this method.

■ **Chardonnay:** *(Shar-don-AY)* A versatile grape grown worldwide and used in many varietal and blended white wines and Champagnes. Flavor is fresh and fruity with subtle differences determined by the growing conditions and country.

■ **Chenin Blanc:** *(SHE-nin BLAWnk)* A versatile white-wine grape most often used in dry wines. Fresh, fruity flavor is more acidic than generic blended white wines.

■ **Chianti:** *(Key-AN-tee)* The red table wine of Italy that is produced in Tuscany. Italian wines that meet certain standards of high quality are labeled *denominazione di origine controllata* (D.O.C.) or *denominazione di origine controllata e garantita* (D.O.C.G.).

■ **Gewürztraminer:** *(Geh-VERT-stra-me-ner)* A tough-skinned pinkish blue grape usually from Alsace, France, but also grown elsewhere. The resulting white wine has a spicy accent and may be dry to semisweet.

■ **Merlot:** *(Mare-LOW)* A red grape that may be blended with Cabernet Sauvignon and Cabernet Franc to make traditional French red Bordeaux wines. It also is becoming popular as a varietal that is smoother than Cabernet Sauvignon.

■ **Muscat:** *(MUS-kaht)* A grape used in Italy to make light, bubbly wine (Asti Spumante) and in other countries to make a sweet dessert wine.

■ **Pinot Blanc:** *(PEA-no BLAWnk)* A dry white wine with a fruit finish from Alsace, France, and other regions.

■ **Pinot Noir:** *(PEA-no NWAR)* A versatile grape used for fresh, light red wine or richer, smooth, plum-flavored red wine. It also is used for Champagne.

■ **Port:** Traditionally made in Portugal where it is aged at least three years, it may be aged for more than 40 years. Similar-style fortified wines produced elsewhere must state the country of origin. It can be white or amber but is most often ruby red and sweet.

■ **Riesling:** *(REEZ-ling)* A grape often ranked with Chardonnay as the most popular for white wines. Often called Johannisberg or White Riesling when grown in the United States. Usually thought of as being from the German Rhine and Mosel districts and having a floral aroma and fairly sweet, fruity taste. With aging, it develops richness and body as well as a honeylike aroma.

■ **Sauternes:** *(So-TERN)* From the area of Bordeaux, France, known for excellent sweet white wines. The Sémillon grapes develop "noble rot" in which a beneficial mold, *botrytis cinerea,* causes the grapes to shrivel, thus concentrating their juices and resulting in a richer wine flavor.

■ **Sauvignon Blanc:** *(So-vee-NYAWN BLAWnk)* A grape originally made famous in Loire, France, for wines such as Pouilly-Fumé that have the scent of newly mown grass and a refreshing, clean taste. California wineries can label it Fumé Blanc.

■ **Sherry:** A fortified wine that may be dry (served cold as an appetizer) or sweet (served at room temperature after meals). It has a nutty flavor from its long aging period in wooden casks before bottling.

■ **Zinfandel:** *(ZIN-fan-del)* A versatile grape used by California wineries to make a fruity red wine as well as a rosé labeled "White Zinfandel."

BREADS

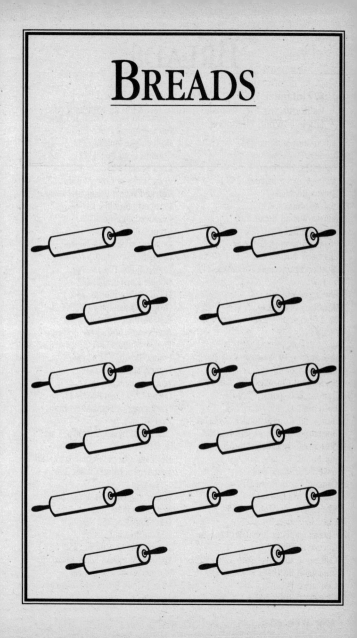

BREADS

WHITE BREAD

Low-Fat

5³/₄ to 6¹/₄ cups all-purpose flour
   1 package active dry yeast
2¹/₄ cups milk or buttermilk
   2 tablespoons sugar
   1 tablespoon butter, margarine, or shortening
1¹/₂ teaspoons salt

1. In a large mixing bowl combine *2¹/₂ cups* of the flour and yeast; set aside. In a medium saucepan heat and stir milk, sugar, butter, and salt just till warm (120° to 130°) and butter almost melts. Add milk mixture to dry mixture. Beat with an electric mixer on low to medium speed for 30 seconds, scraping the sides of the bowl constantly. Beat on high speed for 3 minutes. Using a wooden spoon, stir in as much of the remaining flour as you can.

2. Turn the dough out onto a lightly floured surface. Knead in enough of the remaining flour to make a moderately stiff dough that is smooth and elastic (6 to 8 minutes total) (see tip 1, right). Shape dough into a ball. Place in a lightly greased bowl, turning once to grease surface of the dough. Cover; let rise in a warm place till double in size (for 45 to 60 minutes) (see tips 2 and 3, right).

3. Punch dough down (see tip 4, right). Turn dough out onto a lightly floured surface. Divide dough in half. Cover; let rest 10 minutes. Mean-while, lightly grease two 8×4×2-inch loaf pans.

4. Shape each portion of dough into a loaf by patting or rolling. To shape dough by patting, gently pat and pinch each portion into a loaf shape, tucking edges beneath (see tip 5, right). To shape dough by rolling, on a lightly floured surface, roll each portion into a 12×8-inch rectangle. Roll dough up, jelly-roll style, starting from a short side (see tip 6, right). Seal with fingertips as you roll.

5. Place the shaped dough in the prepared loaf pans. Cover and let rise in a warm place till nearly double in size (for 30 to 40 minutes).

6. Bake in a 375° oven about 40 minutes or till bread sounds hollow when you tap the top with your fingers (if necessary, cover loosely with foil the last 10 minutes of baking to prevent overbrowning). Immediately remove bread from pans. Cool on wire racks. Makes 2 loaves (32 servings).

Nutrition Facts per serving: 91 cal., 1 g total fat (0 g sat. fat), 2 mg chol., 112 mg sodium, 17 g carbo., 1 g fiber, 3 g pro. **Daily Values:** 1% vit. A, 0% vit. C, 2% calcium, 6% iron

TO PREPARE DOUGH

1. To knead, fold dough over and push down with the heel of your hand. Turn, fold, and push down again. Repeat process until smooth and elastic (see tip, page 178).

2. Cover the dough with a clean towel. Let it rise in a draft-free place, such as the upper rack of a cool oven with a bowl of warm water placed below it on the lower rack.

3. You can tell if dough has doubled and is ready to shape by pressing two fingers $1/2$ inch into the dough. Remove fingers; if indentations remain, it is ready to punch down.

4. Punch down the dough by pushing your fist into its center. Next, use your fingers to pull edges of the dough to the center.

5. To shape dough, gently pat each half into a loaf, pinching and tucking the edges beneath the loaf. Place each shaped loaf seam side down in a prepared pan.

6. Or, roll each half of dough into a 12×8-inch rectangle. Tightly roll up, jelly-roll style, starting from a short side. Pinch seam to seal. Place seam side down in pan.

WHOLE WHEAT BREAD

PREP: 30 MINUTES   RISE: 1¾ HOURS   BAKE: 40 MINUTES   Oven 375°

Low-Fat

     3 to 3½ cups all-purpose flour
     1 package active dry yeast
   1¾ cups water
    ⅓ cup packed brown sugar
     3 tablespoons butter, margarine, or shortening
   1¼ teaspoons salt
     2 cups whole wheat flour

1. In a large mixing bowl stir together *2 cups* of the all-purpose flour and the yeast; set aside. In a medium saucepan heat and stir water; brown sugar; butter, margarine, or shortening; and salt just till warm (120° to 130°) and butter almost melts. Add water mixture to dry mixture. Beat with an electric mixer on low to medium speed for 30 seconds, scraping the sides of the bowl constantly. Beat on high speed for 3 minutes. Using a wooden spoon, stir in whole wheat flour and as much remaining all-purpose flour as you can.

2. Turn dough out onto a lightly floured surface. Knead in enough of the remaining all-purpose flour to make a moderately stiff dough that is smooth and elastic (6 to 8 minutes total) (see tip 1, page 171). Shape the dough into a ball. Place dough in a lightly greased bowl, turning once to grease surface of the dough. Cover and let rise in a warm place till double in size (for 1 to 1½ hours) (see tips 2 and 3, page 171).

3. Punch dough down (see tip 4, page 171). Turn dough out onto a lightly floured surface; divide in half. Cover; let rest 10 minutes. Mean-while, lightly grease two 8×4×2-inch loaf pans.

4. Shape each portion of dough into a loaf by patting or rolling (see tips 5 and 6, page 171). To shape dough by patting, gently pat and pinch each half into a loaf shape, tucking edges beneath. To shape dough by rolling, on a lightly floured surface, roll each half into a 12×8-inch rectangle. Roll up, jelly-roll style, starting from a short side. Seal seams with fingertips as you roll.

5. Place the shaped dough in the prepared pans. Cover and let rise in a warm place till nearly double in size (for 45 to 60 minutes).

6. Bake in a 375° oven for 40 to 45 minutes or till bread sounds hollow when you tap the top with your fingers (if necessary, cover loosely with foil the last 10 minutes of baking to prevent overbrowning). Immediately remove bread from pans. Cool on wire racks. Makes 2 loaves (32 servings).

Nutrition Facts per serving: 83 cal., 2 g total fat (1 g sat. fat), 0 mg chol., 84 mg sodium, 16 g carbo., 1 g fiber, 2 g pro. **Daily Values:** 0% vit. A, 0% vit. C, 0% calcium, 5% iron

■ **Wheat Germ Bread:** Prepare as at left, except reduce whole wheat flour to 1½ cups and add ½ cup *toasted wheat germ*.

Nutrition Facts per serving: 83 cal., 2 g total fat (1 g sat. fat)

■ **Oatmeal Bread:** Prepare as at left, except substitute *quick-cooking or regular rolled oats* for the whole wheat flour. Increase the all-purpose flour to 4¼ to 4¾ cups total.

Nutrition Facts per serving: 92 cal., 2 g total fat (1 g sat. fat)

HOW TO MAKE BREAD WITHOUT A MIXER

All of our yeast breads are made using an electric mixer. However, if you don't have an electric mixer, you can beat the dough by hand. Here's how:

Prepare the dough as directed, except when the recipe says to beat the mixture using an electric mixer, use a wooden spoon to beat the dough by hand instead. When mixing by hand, be sure to beat the mixture until it is smooth (it may take longer than the 3 minutes given in most recipes). Also note that with hand-mixed dough, you most likely will need to use the maximum amount of flour to knead into the dough.

FRENCH BREAD

PREP: 40 MINUTES   RISE: 1¹/₂ HOURS   BAKE: 35 MINUTES   Oven 375°

No-Fat

Baguettes are a long, thin version of French bread, providing more crunchy crust per bite.

5¹/₂ to 6 cups all-purpose flour
  2 packages active dry yeast
1¹/₂ teaspoons salt
  2 cups warm water (120° to 130°)
    Cornmeal
  1 slightly beaten egg white
  1 tablespoon water

1. In a large mixing bowl stir together *2 cups* of the flour, the yeast, and salt. Add the warm water to the dry mixture. Beat with an electric mixer on low to medium speed for 30 seconds, scraping the sides of the bowl constantly. Beat on high speed for 3 minutes. Using a wooden spoon, stir in as much of the remaining flour as you can.

2. Turn the dough out onto a lightly floured surface. Knead in enough remaining flour to make a stiff dough that is smooth and elastic (8 to 10 minutes total) (see tip 1, page 171). Shape the dough into a ball. Place dough in a lightly greased bowl, turning once to grease surface of the dough. Cover and let rise in a warm place till double in size (about 1 hour) (see tips 2 and 3, page 171).

3. Punch dough down (see tip 4, page 171). Turn dough out onto a lightly floured surface. Divide dough in half. Cover and let rest for 10 minutes. Meanwhile, lightly grease a baking sheet. Sprinkle with cornmeal.

4. Roll each portion of the dough into a 15x10-inch rectangle. Roll up, jelly-roll style, starting from a long side; seal well. Pinch ends and pull slightly to taper. Place seam side down on prepared baking sheet. In a small mixing bowl stir together egg white and water. Brush some of the egg white mixture over loaves. Cover and let rise till nearly double in size (for 35 to 45 minutes). Using a sharp knife, make 3 or 4 diagonal cuts about ¹/₄ inch deep across the top of each loaf.

5. Bake in a 375° oven for 20 minutes. Brush again with some of the egg white mixture. Continue baking for 15 to 20 minutes more or till bread sounds hollow when you tap the top with your fingers. Immediately remove bread from baking sheet. Cool on wire racks. Makes 2 loaves (30 servings).

Nutrition Facts per serving: 80 cal., 0 g total fat, 0 mg chol., 109 mg sodium, 17 g carbo., 1 g fiber, 3 g pro. **Daily Values:** 0% vit. A, 0% vit. C, 0% calcium, 7% iron

■ **Baguettes:** Prepare as above, except divide dough into 4 portions. Shape into balls. Cover; let rest 10 minutes. Meanwhile, lightly grease 2 baking sheets or 4 baguette pans; sprinkle with cornmeal. Roll each portion of the dough into a 14×5-inch to 16×5-inch rectangle. Roll up, jelly-roll style, starting from a long side; seal well. Pinch ends and pull slightly to taper. Place seam side down on prepared baking sheets or baguette pans. Continue as directed, except reduce the second baking time to 10 to 15 minutes. Makes 4 baguettes (28 servings).

Nutrition Facts per serving: 85 cal., 0 g total fat

RYE BREAD

PREP: 40 MINUTES   RISE: 1½ HOURS   BAKE: 35 MINUTES   Oven 375°

Low-Fat

3½ to 4 cups all-purpose flour
  2 packages active dry yeast
  2 cups warm water (120° to 130°)
  ¼ cup packed brown sugar
  2 tablespoons cooking oil
  2 cups rye flour
  1 tablespoon caraway seed
  · Cornmeal

1. In a large mixing bowl stir together *2¾ cups* of the all-purpose flour and yeast. Add warm water, brown sugar, oil, and 1 teaspoon *salt.* Beat with an electric mixer on low to medium speed 30 seconds, scraping sides of bowl. Beat on high speed 3 minutes. Stir in rye flour, caraway seed, and as much remaining all-purpose flour as you can.
2. Turn dough onto a floured surface. Knead in enough remaining all-purpose flour to make a moderately stiff dough that is smooth

and elastic (6 to 8 minutes total) (see tip 1, page 171). Shape into a ball. Place in a greased bowl; turn dough once. Cover; let rise in a warm place till double (about 1 hour) (see tips 2 and 3, page 171).

3. Punch dough down (see tip 4, page 171); turn onto a floured surface. Divide dough in half. Cover and let rest 10 minutes. Meanwhile, lightly grease a baking sheet; sprinkle with cornmeal.

4. Shape by gently pulling each portion into a ball, tucking edges beneath. Place on prepared baking sheet. Flatten each dough round slightly to 6 inches in diameter. Or, shape each half into a loaf by patting or rolling (see tips 5 and 6, page 171). Place in two greased 8×4×2-inch loaf pans. Cover and let rise in a warm place till nearly double in size (for 30 to 45 minutes).

5. Bake in a 375° oven 35 to 40 minutes or till done (if necessary, cover loosely with foil the last 10 minutes of baking to prevent overbrowning). Immediately remove from baking sheet or pans. Cool on wire racks. Makes 2 loaves (24 servings).

Nutrition Facts per serving: 112 cal., 1 g total fat (0 g sat. fat), 0 mg chol., 91 mg sodium, 22 g carbo., 2 g fiber, 3 g pro. **Daily Values:** 0% vit. A, 0% vit. C, 0% calcium, 7% iron

■ **Peasant Rye Bread:** Prepare as above, except reduce rye flour to 1 cup. Stir in ¹⁄₂ cup *whole bran cereal* and ¹⁄₂ cup *yellow cornmeal* with rye flour.

Nutrition Facts per serving: 109 cal., 2 g total fat (0 g sat. fat)

MARBLED LOAF

PREP: 50 MINUTES   RISE: 1¹⁄₂ HOURS   BAKE: 30 MINUTES   Oven 375°

Low-Fat

    3 to 3¹⁄₂ cups all-purpose flour
    1 package active dry yeast
1¹⁄₂ cups milk
    2 tablespoons sugar
    2 tablespoons cooking oil
    2 tablespoons dark molasses
1¹⁄₄ cups rye or whole wheat flour

1. In a large mixing bowl combine *2 cups* of the all-purpose flour and yeast. In a saucepan heat milk, sugar, oil, and 1¹⁄₂ teaspoons *salt* just till warm (120° to 130°). Add to dry mixture. Beat with an electric mixer on low to medium speed 30 seconds, scraping bowl. Beat on high speed 3 minutes. Divide batter in half. To 1 portion of batter, stir in as much remaining all-purpose flour as you can. Turn onto a floured surface. Knead in enough remaining all-purpose flour to make a moderately stiff dough that is smooth and elastic (6 to 8 minutes total) (see tip 1, page 171). Shape into a ball. Place dough in a greased bowl; turn once.

2. To remaining batter stir in molasses, rye flour, and as much of the remaining all-purpose flour as you can. Turn onto a floured surface. Knead in enough remaining all-purpose flour to make a moderately stiff dough that is smooth and elastic (6 to 8 minutes total) (see tip 1, page 171). Shape into a ball. Place in a greased bowl; turn once. Cover and let both dough portions rise in warm place till double (1 to 1¼ hours) (see tips 2 and 3, page 171). Punch both portions down (see tip 4, page 171); cover and let rest 10 minutes. Lightly grease an 8×4×2-inch loaf pan; set aside.

3. On lightly floured surface roll each portion into a 12×8-inch rectangle. Place dark dough atop light; roll up, beginning at a short side. Place seam side down in prepared pan. Cover; let rise till nearly double (30 to 45 minutes). Bake in a 375° oven 30 to 35 minutes (if necessary, cover loosely with foil the last 10 minutes of baking to prevent overbrowning). Remove from pan; cool on a wire rack. Makes 1 loaf (16 servings).

Nutrition Facts per serving: 148 cal., 2 g total fat (1 g sat. fat), 2 mg chol., 212 mg sodium, 27 g carbo., 2 g fiber, 4 g pro. **Daily Values:** 1% vit. A, 0% vit. C, 3% calcium, 9% iron

---

SAVING TIME WITH QUICK-RISING YEAST

The bread recipes in this chapter were tested with active dry yeast. You can, however, prepare these recipes (except Sourdough Starter) using quick-rising active dry yeast. Just follow the same directions, keeping in mind that the dough should rise in about one-third less time, especially during the second rising step.

KNEADING YEAST BREAD

Kneading is an important part of making yeast breads. It causes a protein structure called gluten, which gives body to the final product, to develop. To knead, fold the dough over and push down on it with the heels of your hands, curving your fingers over the dough. Give the dough a quarter turn and repeat the process of folding and pushing down (see tip 1, page 171).

Continue kneading until you obtain an elastic dough and stiffness specified in recipe. The best guide for reaching proper stiffness is to follow the timings given in the recipe. To double-check, here's a description of each of the stiffness terms used in these recipes.

■ Soft dough is very sticky and used for breads that don't need kneading, such as the Citrus-Nutmeg Puffs on page 211.

■ Moderately soft dough is slightly sticky and is used for rich, sweet breads. This dough is turned out onto a floured surface and kneaded for 3 to 5 minutes.

■ Moderately stiff dough is not sticky and is slightly firm to the touch. It usually requires 6 to 8 minutes of kneading on a lightly floured surface and is used for nonsweet breads.

■ Stiff dough is firm to the touch and will hold its shape after about 8 to 10 minutes of kneading. It's used for breads with a chewy texture, such as French Bread on page 174.

SOURDOUGH STARTER

PREP: 10 MINUTES   STAND: 5 TO 10 DAYS

    1 package active dry yeast
2½ cups warm water (105° to 115°)
    2 cups all-purpose flour
    1 tablespoon sugar or honey

1. Dissolve yeast in ½ *cup* of the warm water. Stir in the remaining warm water, flour, and sugar or honey. Beat till smooth. Cover with 100% cotton cheesecloth. Let stand at room temperature (75° to 85°) for 5 to 10 days or till mixture has a fermented aroma and vigorous bubbling stops, stirring 2 or 3 times a day. (Fermentation time depends on room temperature; a warmer room will hasten the fermentation process.)

2. To store, transfer Sourdough Starter to a 1-quart covered plastic container and refrigerate.

3. To use, stir starter. Measure desired amount of cold starter. Bring to room temperature. Replenish starter after each use by stirring ³/₄ cup *all-purpose flour,* ³/₄ cup *water,* and 1 teaspoon *sugar or honey* into remaining starter. Cover with cheesecloth; let stand at room temperature 1 day or till bubbly. Cover with lid; chill for later use. If starter isn't used within 10 days, stir in 1 teaspoon *sugar or honey.* Continue to add an additional 1 teaspoon *sugar or honey* every 10 days unless the starter is replenished.

SOURDOUGH BREAD

PREP: 1 HOUR   RISE: 1¼ HOURS   BAKE: 30 MINUTES   Oven 375°

Low-Fat

   1 cup Sourdough Starter (see page 178)
5¹/₂ to 6 cups all-purpose flour
   1 package active dry yeast
   3 tablespoons sugar
   3 tablespoons butter or margarine
 ¹/₂ teaspoon baking soda

1. Measure Sourdough Starter; let stand at room temperature 30 minutes. Combine 2¹/₂ *cups* of the flour and the yeast; set aside. Heat and stir 1¹/₂ cups *water,* sugar, butter, and 1 teaspoon *salt* just till warm (120° to 130°) and butter almost melts. Add water mixture to dry mixture. Add Sourdough Starter. Beat with an electric mixer on low to medium speed for 30 seconds, scraping bowl. Beat on high speed for 3 minutes.

2. Combine 2¹/₂ *cups* of the remaining flour and the baking soda. Add to yeast mixture. Stir till combined. Stir in as much remaining flour as you can.

3. Turn dough onto a lightly floured surface. Knead in enough remaining flour to make a moderately stiff dough (6 to 8 minutes total) (see tip 1, page 171). Shape dough into a ball. Place dough in a greased bowl; turn once. Cover and let rise in warm place till double in size (for 45 to 60 minutes) (see tips 2 and 3, page 171).

4. Punch dough down (see tip 4, page 171). Turn onto a floured surface. Divide in half. Cover; let rest 10 minutes. Lightly grease a baking sheet.

5. Shape by gently pulling each portion into a ball, tucking edges beneath. Place on prepared baking sheet. Flatten each slightly to 6 inches in diameter. Using a sharp knife, make crisscross slashes across tops of loaves. Cover and let rise in a warm place till nearly double in size (about 30 minutes).

6. Bake in a 375° oven 30 to 35 minutes or till bread sounds hollow when you tap the top (if necessary, cover loosely with foil the last 10 minutes of baking to prevent overbrowning). Immediately remove bread from baking sheet. Cool on wire racks. Makes 2 loaves (24 to 36 servings).

Nutrition Facts per serving: 131 cal., 2 g total fat (1 g sat. fat), 4 mg chol., 133 mg sodium, 25 g carbo., 1 g fiber, 3 g pro. **Daily Values:** 1% vit. A, 0% vit. C, 0% calcium, 9% iron

---

SOURDOUGH CORNMEAL LOAVES

PREP: 50 MINUTES   RISE: 80 MINUTES   BAKE: 35 MINUTES   Oven 375°

Low-Fat

      1 cup Sourdough Starter (see page 178)
4¹/₂ to 5 cups all-purpose flour
      1 package active dry yeast
      2 tablespoons honey
      2 tablespoons butter or margarine
   ¹/₂ cup cornmeal
      Cornmeal (optional)

1. Measure Sourdough Starter; let stand at room temperature 30 minutes. Combine *2 cups* of the flour and yeast; set aside. Heat and stir honey, butter, 1¹/₂ cups *water*, and 1 teaspoon *salt* just till warm (120° to 130°) and butter almost melts. Add starter and water mixture to dry mixture. Beat with an electric mixer on low to medium speed for 30 seconds, scraping bowl. Beat on high speed 3 minutes. Stir in ¹/₂ cup cornmeal and as much remaining flour as you can.

2. Turn dough onto a floured surface. Knead in enough remaining flour to make a moderately stiff dough that is smooth and elastic (6 to 8 minutes total) (see tip 1, page 171). Shape into a ball. Place in a greased bowl; turn once. Cover and let rise in a warm place till double in size (about 50 minutes) (see tips 2 and 3, page 171).

3. Punch dough down (see tip 4, page 171). Turn dough out onto a floured surface; divide in half. Cover and let rest for 10 minutes. Lightly grease two 8×4×2-inch loaf pans. If desired, sprinkle pans with the additional cornmeal.

4. Shape each portion of dough into a loaf by patting or rolling (see tips 5 and 6, page 171). Place in prepared pans. Cover; let rise in a warm place till nearly double in size (for 30 to 40 minutes).

5. Bake in a 375° oven for 35 to 40 minutes or till bread sounds hollow when tapped (if necessary, cover loosely with foil the last 10 minutes of baking to prevent overbrowning). Remove from pans; cool on wire racks. Makes 2 loaves (32 servings).

Nutrition Facts per serving: 89 cal., 1 g total fat (0 g sat. fat), 2 mg chol., 75 mg sodium, 18 g carbo., 1 g fiber, 2 g pro. **Daily Values:** 0% vit. A, 0% vit. C, 0% calcium, 6% iron

---

ONION AND OLIVE FOCACCIA

PREP: 30 MINUTES   RISE:1¹/₃ HOURS   BAKE: 25 MINUTES   Oven 375°

Low-Fat

Using bread flour rather than all-purpose flour results in a chewier bread. Either way, it's hearty.

   3¹/₄ to 3³/₄ cups bread flour or all-purpose flour
   1 package active dry yeast
1¹/₄ cups warm water (120° to 130°)
   1 tablespoon olive oil or cooking oil
1¹/₂ cups chopped onion (3 medium)
   2 cloves garlic, minced
   2 tablespoons olive oil or cooking oil
   1 cup sliced pitted ripe olives and/or snipped oil-packed dried
       tomatoes, drained
   2 tablespoons snipped fresh rosemary or 2 teaspoons dried
       rosemary, crushed

1. In a large mixing bowl combine *1¹/₄ cups* of the flour and the yeast. Add the warm water, the 1 tablespoon oil, and 1 teaspoon *salt* to the dry mixture. Beat with an electric mixer on low to medium speed for 30 seconds, scraping sides of bowl constantly. Beat on high speed for 3 minutes. Stir in as much of the remaining flour as you can.

2. Turn dough onto a lightly floured surface. Knead in enough remaining flour to make a stiff dough that is smooth and elastic (8 to 10 minutes total) (see tip 1, page 171). Shape dough into a ball. Place in a lightly greased bowl; turn once. Cover and let rise in a warm place till double in size (about 1 hour) (see tips 2 and 3, page 171).

3. Punch dough down (see tip 4, page 171). Turn onto a floured surface. Divide in half. Shape each portion into a ball. Place on 2 lightly greased baking sheets. Cover; let rest 10 minutes.

4. For topping, in a medium skillet cook onion and garlic in the 2 tablespoons oil, covered, over low heat 3 to 5 minutes or till onion is translucent, stirring occasionally. Uncover; cook and stir just till onion begins to brown. Remove from heat. If using olives, stir into onion mixture; set aside.

5. Using your hands, flatten each ball to about 12 inches in diameter. Make ¹/₂-inch-deep indentations every 2 inches. Spoon onion mixture atop dough. Sprinkle with rosemary. Cover and let rise in a warm place till nearly double in size (about 20 minutes).

6. Bake in a 375° oven 25 minutes or till golden. If using dried tomatoes, sprinkle atop bread during last 5 minutes of baking. Remove from sheet; cool on wire racks. Makes 2 rounds (24 servings).

Nutrition Facts per serving: 95 cal., 3 g total fat (0 g sat. fat), 0 mg chol., 71 mg sodium, 15 g carbo., 1 g fiber, 3 g pro. **Daily Values:** 0% vit. A, 0% vit. C, 0% calcium, 5% iron

■ **Blue Cheese and Walnut Focaccia:** Prepare as above except omit the onion, garlic, olives and/or tomatoes, and rosemary. Brush the shaped dough with the 2 tablespoons olive oil or cooking oil. Sprinkle with 1¹/₂ cups chopped *walnuts* and 1 cup *crumbled blue cheese or shredded Swiss cheese*. Continue as directed.

Nutrition Facts per serving: 136 cal., 8 g total fat (2 g sat .fat)

CRACKED WHEAT BREAD

PREP: 40 MINUTES   RISE: 1³/₄ HOURS   BAKE: 35 MINUTES   Oven 375°

Low-Fat

Cracked wheat is whole wheat kernels broken into fragments. If you can't find it in your grocery store, check local health-food stores.

   2 **cups boiling water**
   1 **cup cracked wheat**

3¾ to 4¼ cups all-purpose flour
  1 package active dry yeast
  ¼ cup sugar
  1 tablespoon butter, margarine, or shortening
1¼ cups whole wheat flour
  ¼ cup unprocessed wheat bran

1. In a medium saucepan, combine the boiling water and cracked wheat. Let stand, covered, for 5 minutes. Drain well, discarding liquid. Set cracked wheat aside.

2. In a large mixing bowl stir together *1½ cups* of the all-purpose flour and the yeast; set aside. In a medium saucepan heat and stir 1¾ cups *water,* sugar, butter, and 1 teaspoon *salt* just till warm (120° to 130°) and butter almost melts. Add water mixture to dry mixture. Beat with an electric mixer on low to medium speed for 30 seconds, scraping the sides of the bowl constantly. Beat on high speed for 3 minutes. Using a wooden spoon, stir in the drained cracked wheat, the whole wheat flour, and wheat bran. Stir in as much of the remaining all-purpose flour as you can.

3. Turn the dough out onto a lightly floured surface. Knead in enough of the remaining all- purpose flour to make a moderately stiff dough that is smooth and elastic (6 to 8 minutes total) (see tip 1, page 171). Shape the dough into a ball. Place dough in a lightly greased bowl, turning once to grease surface of the dough. Cover and let rise in a warm place till double in size (about 1¼ hours) (see tips 2 and 3, page 171).

4. Punch dough down (see tip 4, page 171). Turn dough out onto a lightly floured surface. Divide dough in half. Cover and let rest 10 minutes. Lightly grease two 8×4×2-inch loaf pans.

5. Shape each portion of dough into a loaf by patting or rolling (see tips 5 and 6, page 171). Place in prepared loaf pans. Cover; let rise in a warm place till nearly double in size (30 to 40 minutes).

6. Bake in a 375° oven for 35 to 40 minutes or till bread sounds hollow when you tap the top with your fingers (if necessary, cover loosely with foil the last 10 minutes of baking to prevent overbrowning). Immediately remove bread from pans. Cool on wire racks. Makes 2 loaves (32 servings).

Nutrition Facts per serving: 80 cal., 1 g total fat (0 g sat. fat), 0 mg chol., 71 mg sodium, 16 g carbo., 1 g fiber, 2 g pro. **Daily Values:** 0% vit. A, 0% vit. C, 0% calcium, 6% iron

HONEY AND GRANOLA BREAD

PREP: 30 MINUTES   RISE: 1¹/₄ HOURS   BAKE: 35 MINUTES   Oven 375°

*Store whole wheat and rye flours in the freezer—they will
stay fresher longer.*

   3 to 3¹/₂ cups all-purpose flour
   2 packages active dry yeast
1³/₄ cups milk
  ¹/₂ cup honey
  ¹/₃ cup butter, margarine, or shortening
   1 teaspoon salt
   2 eggs
   2 cups whole wheat flour
   1 cup granola
   1 cup rye flour
  ¹/₂ cup cornmeal
  ¹/₂ cup quick-cooking rolled oats
  ¹/₄ cup slivered almonds, toasted and chopped (see tip, page 234)

1. In a large mixing bowl stir together *2 cups* of the all-purpose flour
and the yeast; set aside. In a medium saucepan heat and stir milk;
honey; butter, margarine, or shortening; and salt just till warm (120°
to 130°) and butter almost melts. Add milk mixture to dry mixture
along with the eggs. Beat with an electric mixer on low to medium
speed for 30 seconds, scraping the sides of the bowl constantly. Beat
on high speed for 3 minutes. Using a wooden spoon, stir in the
whole wheat flour, granola, rye flour, cornmeal, rolled oats, almonds, and as much of the all-purpose flour as you can.
2. Turn dough out onto a lightly floured surface. Knead in enough
of the remaining all-purpose flour to make a moderately stiff dough
that is smooth and elastic (6 to 8 minutes total) (see tip 1, page 171).
Shape the dough into a ball. Place dough in a lightly greased bowl,
turning once to grease surface of the dough. Cover and let rise in a
warm place till double in size (for 45 minutes to 1¹/₄ hours) (see tips
2 and 3, page 171).
3. Punch dough down (see tip 4, page 171). Turn dough out onto a
lightly floured surface. Divide dough in half. Cover; let rest 10 minutes. Meanwhile, lightly grease a large baking sheet.
4. Shape by gently pulling each portion of dough into a ball, tucking
edges beneath. Place each dough round on the prepared baking

sheet. Flatten each ball slightly to 5 inches in diameter. Cover and let rise in a warm place till nearly double in size (for 30 to 40 minutes).

5. Bake in a 375° oven about 35 minutes or till bread sounds hollow when you tap the top with your fingers (if necessary, cover loosely with foil the last 10 minutes of baking to prevent overbrowning). Immediately remove bread from baking sheet. Cool on wire racks. Makes 2 loaves (24 servings).

Nutrition Facts per serving: 209 cal., 6 g total fat (2 g sat. fat), 22 mg chol., 137 mg sodium, 35 g carbo., 3 g fiber, 6 g pro. **Daily Values:** 4% vit. A, 0% vit. C, 3% calcium, 11% iron

---

MIXED GRAIN BREAD

PREP: 30 MINUTES   RISE: 1½ HOURS   BAKE: 30 MINUTES   Oven 375°

Low-Fat

3½ to 4 cups all-purpose flour
2 packages active dry yeast
1½ cups milk
¾ cup water
½ cup cracked wheat
¼ cup cornmeal
¼ cup packed brown sugar
3 tablespoons cooking oil
1½ teaspoons salt
1½ cups whole wheat flour
½ cup rolled oats
Rolled oats

1. In a large mixing bowl combine *2 cups* of the all-purpose flour and the yeast; set aside. In a medium saucepan combine milk, water, cracked wheat, cornmeal, brown sugar, oil, and salt. Heat and stir over medium-low heat just till warm (120° to 130°). Add to dry mixture. Beat with an electric mixer on low to medium speed 30 seconds, scraping sides of bowl often. Beat on high 3 minutes. Using a wooden spoon, stir in whole wheat flour, the ½ cup rolled oats, and as much of the remaining all-purpose flour as you can.

2. Turn dough out onto a lightly floured surface. Knead in enough of the remaining all-purpose flour to make a moderately stiff dough that is smooth and elastic (6 to 8 minutes total) (see tip 1, page 171). Shape into a ball. Place in a lightly greased bowl, turning once to grease the surface of the dough. Cover and let rise in a warm place till nearly double in size (about 1 hour) (see tips 2 and 3, page 171).

3. Punch dough down (see tip 4, page 171). Turn dough out onto a lightly floured surface. Divide in half. Cover and let rest for 10 minutes. Lightly grease two 8×4×2-inch loaf pans.

4. Shape each portion into a loaf by patting or rolling (see tips 5 and 6, page 171). Place in prepared pans. Cover; let rise in a warm place till double in size (about 30 minutes). Brush tops of loaves with water; sprinkle with additional rolled oats.

5. Bake in a 375° oven for 30 to 35 minutes or till bread sounds hollow when you tap the top with your fingers (if necessary, cover loosely with foil the last 10 minutes of baking to prevent overbrowning). Immediately remove bread from pans. Cool on wire racks. Makes 2 loaves (32 servings).

Nutrition Facts per serving: 102 cal., 2 g total fat (0 g sat. fat), 1 mg chol., 107 mg sodium, 19 g carbo., 1 g fiber, 3 g pro. **Daily Values:** 0% vit. A, 0% vit. C, 1% calcium, 7% iron

---

EGG BREAD

PREP: 30 MINUTES   RISE: 1½ HOURS   BAKE: 25 MINUTES   Oven 375°

Low-Fat

4³/₄ to 5¹/₄ cups all-purpose flour
  1 package active dry yeast
1¹/₃ cups milk
  3 tablespoons sugar
  3 tablespoons butter or margarine
¹/₂ teaspoon salt
  2 eggs

1. In a large mixing bowl stir together *2 cups* of the flour and the yeast; set aside. In a medium saucepan heat and stir milk, sugar, butter or margarine, and salt just till warm (120° to 130°) and butter almost melts. Add milk mixture to dry mixture along with the eggs. Beat with an electric mixer on low to medium speed for 30 seconds, scraping the sides of the bowl constantly. Beat on high speed for 3 minutes. Using a wooden spoon, stir in as much of the remaining flour as you can.

2. Turn dough out onto a lightly floured surface. Knead in enough of the remaining flour to make a moderately stiff dough that is smooth and elastic (6 to 8 minutes total) (see tip 1, page 171). Shape the dough into a ball. Place in a lightly greased bowl, turning once to grease surface of the dough. Cover and let rise in a warm place till double in size (about 1 hour) (see tips 2 and 3, page 171).

3. Punch dough down (see tip 4, page 171). Turn dough onto a lightly floured surface. Divide dough in half. Cover and let rest for 10 minutes. Lightly grease two 8×4×2-inch loaf pans.

4. Shape each portion of dough into a loaf by patting or rolling (see tips 5 and 6, page 171). Place dough in prepared pans. Cover and let rise in a warm place till nearly double (about 30 minutes).

5. Bake in a 375° oven for 25 to 30 minutes or till bread sounds hollow when you tap the top (if necessary, cover loosely with foil the last 10 minutes of baking). Remove bread from pans. Cool on wire racks. Makes 2 loaves (32 servings).

Nutrition Facts per serving: 87 cal., 2 g total fat (1 g sat. fat), 19 mg chol., 72 mg sodium, 15 g carbo., 1 g fiber, 3 g pro. **Daily Values:** 2% vit. A, 0% vit. C, 1% calcium, 5% iron

---

■ Cinnamon Swirl Bread: Prepare Egg Bread as on page 186, except instead of shaping into loaves, on a floured surface roll each portion of dough into a 12×7-inch rectangle. Brush lightly with water. Combine ½ cup *sugar* and 2 teaspoons *ground cinnamon*. Sprinkle half of the sugar- cinnamon mixture over each rectangle. Roll up, jelly-roll style, starting from a short side. Pinch seam and ends to seal. Place seam side down in prepared loaf pans. Rise and bake as directed. If desired, drizzle warm loaves with 1 recipe *Powdered Sugar Icing* (see page 291).

Nutrition Facts per serving: 99 cal., 2 g total fat (1 g sat. fat)

■ Challah: Prepare Egg Bread as on page 98, except substitute 1¼ cups *water* for the milk and *pareve margarine* for butter. Prepare as directed through step 2. Punch dough down; divide in thirds. Cover; let rest 10 minutes. Roll each third into an 18-inch rope. Place ropes on a large baking sheet 1 inch apart and braid (see tip 3, page 190). Cover; let rise 30 minutes or till nearly double. Brush braid with 1 beaten *egg yolk* and sprinkle with 2 teaspoons *poppy seed*. Bake as directed. Makes 1 braid (32 servings).

Nutrition Facts per serving: 83 cal., 2 g total fat (0 g sat. fat)

HERB AND CHEESE BUBBLE LOAF

PREP: 40 MINUTES RISE: 1½ HOURS BAKE: 35 MINUTES   Oven 375°

2½ to 3 cups all-purpose flour
1 package active dry yeast
1 cup milk
1 tablespoon butter or margarine
1 cup shredded cheddar cheese or Swiss cheese (4 ounces)
¼ cup butter or margarine, melted
2 tablespoons snipped parsley
½ teaspoon dried oregano, crushed
½ teaspoon dried marjoram, crushed

1. In a large mixing bowl combine *1 cup* of the flour and the yeast; set aside. In a small saucepan heat and stir milk, the 1 tablespoon butter, and ½ teaspoon *salt* just till warm (120° to 130°) and butter almost melts. Add milk mixture to dry mixture. Beat with an electric mixer on low to medium speed for 30 seconds, scraping sides of bowl often. Beat on high speed 3 minutes. Stir in cheese and as much of the remaining flour as you can.

2. Turn dough onto a floured surface. Knead in enough remaining flour to make a moderately stiff dough that is smooth and elastic (6 to 8 minutes total) (see tip 1, page 171). Shape dough into a ball. Place in a lightly greased bowl; turn once. Cover; let rise in a warm place till nearly double in size (about 1 hour) (see tips 2 and 3, page 171).

3. Punch dough down (see tip 4, page 171). Turn dough out onto a lightly floured surface. Cover and let rest for 10 minutes. Meanwhile, lightly grease a 1½-quart casserole or a 9x5x3-inch loaf pan. Stir together the ¼ cup melted butter, parsley, oregano, and marjoram. Set aside.

4. To shape, on a floured surface roll out dough from center to edges, forming an 8x6-inch rectangle; cut into 48 pieces. Gently pull each portion of dough into a ball, tucking edges beneath. Roll each ball in butter mixture. Arrange balls, smooth sides up, in prepared casserole or pan. Cover; let rise in a warm place till nearly double (30 to 40 minutes).

5. Bake in a 375° oven 35 to 40 minutes or till bread sounds hollow when tapped (cover loosely with foil the last 10 to 15 minutes of baking to prevent overbrowning). Remove bread from casserole or pan. Serve warm. Makes 1 loaf (16 servings).

Nutrition Facts per serving: 135 cal., 6 g total fat (4 g sat. fat), 17 mg chol., 155 mg sodium, 15 g carbo., 1 g fiber, 4 g pro. **Daily Values:** 7% vit. A, 2% vit. C, 6% calcium, 7% iron

WALNUT-FILLED BRAID

PREP: 40 MINUTES   RISE: 1½ HOURS   BAKE: 30 MINUTES   Oven 350°

You can use a food processor or blender to grind the nuts, but be careful not to grind them too long. Process or blend until the nuts are fine, but stop before they become a paste.

3¼ to 3¾ cups all-purpose flour
  1 package active dry yeast
¾ cup milk
¼ cup sugar
¼ cup butter or margarine
½ teaspoon salt
  2 eggs
  1 egg yolk
⅓ cup apple, currant, or mixed fruit jelly
1½ cups ground walnuts
  1 egg white
  1 tablespoon water

1. In a large mixing bowl stir together *1¾ cups* of the flour and the yeast. In a medium saucepan heat and stir milk, sugar, butter, and salt just till warm (120° to 130°) and butter almost melts. Add milk mixture to dry mixture along with the whole eggs and egg yolk. Beat with an electric mixer on low to medium speed for 30 seconds, scraping the sides of the bowl constantly. Beat on high speed for 3 minutes. Using a wooden spoon, stir in as much of the remaining flour as you can.

2. Turn the dough out onto a lightly floured surface. Knead in enough of the remaining flour to make a moderately soft dough that is smooth and elastic (3 to 5 minutes total) (see tip 1, page 171). Shape dough into a ball. Place dough in a lightly greased bowl, turning once to grease surface. Cover; let rise in a warm place till double in size (for 1 to 1¼ hours) (see tips 2 and 3, page 171).

3. Meanwhile, for filling, in a small saucepan heat and stir the jelly over low heat just till melted. Stir in walnuts; set aside. In a small mixing bowl beat together egg white and water; set aside.

4. Punch dough down (see tip 4, page 171). Turn dough out onto a lightly floured surface. Divide dough in half. Cover and let rest for 10 minutes. Meanwhile, lightly grease a baking sheet.

5. Roll each portion of the dough into a 12×10-inch rectangle. Cut each rectangle into three 10x4-inch strips. Spread a scant 3 tablespoons of the filling down the center of each strip (see tip 1, right). Brush egg white mixture on edges. Fold long sides of dough over filling; seal (see tip 2, right).

6. To shape, place the 3 filled ropes, seam sides down, 1 inch apart on half of the prepared baking sheet. Loosely braid the ropes of dough, working from the center to each end (see tip 3, right). Press the ends together to seal and tuck them under the loaf. Braid the remaining 3

TO PREPARE BRAID

1. Using the back of a spoon, spread filling down center of each strip and to within $1/4$ to $1/2$ inch of all 4 edges.

2. Carefully fold the long sides of the dough over the filling. Using your fingers, pinch the dough to seal.

3. Starting in the middle, loosely braid by bringing the left rope over the center rope. Next bring right rope over new center rope. Repeat to end. On the other end, braid by bringing alternate ropes over center rope to center. Press ends together to seal; tuck under.

ropes. Brush loaves with some of the egg white mixture. Cover and let rise in a warm place till nearly double (about 30 minutes). Brush loaves again with egg white mixture.

7. Bake in a 350° oven about 30 minutes or till bread sounds hollow when you tap the top with your fingers (if necessary, cover loosely with foil the last 10 minutes of baking to prevent overbrowning). Immediately remove bread from baking sheet. Cool on wire racks. Makes 2 loaves (32 servings).

Nutrition Facts per serving: 116 cal., 6 g total fat (1 g sat. fat), 24 mg chol., 58 mg sodium, 14 g carbo., 1 g fiber, 3 g pro. **Daily Values:** 3% vit. A, 0% vit. C, 1% calcium, 5% iron

■ **Almond-Filled Braid:** Prepare Walnut-Filled Bread as above except substitute *apricot or peach preserves* for the jelly and ground *almonds* for the ground walnuts.

Nutrition Facts per serving: 117 cal., 5 g total fat (1 g sat. fat)

PEPPER-CHEESE BREAD

PREP: 40 MINUTES   RISE: 1¾ HOURS   BAKE: 35 MINUTES   Oven 375°

*For a more robust flavor, freshly grate the Parmesan
or Romano cheese.*

  2¾ to 3¼ cups all-purpose flour
  1 package active dry yeast
  1½ to 2 teaspoons cracked black pepper
  ½ teaspoon salt
  1 cup warm water (120° to 130°)
  2 tablespoons olive oil or cooking oil
  1 cup shredded provolone or mozzarella cheese (4 ounces)
  ½ cup grated Parmesan cheese or Romano cheese
  1 slightly beaten egg white
  1 tablespoon water

1. In a large mixing bowl stir together *1 cup* of the flour, the yeast, pepper, and salt. Add warm water and olive oil. Beat with an electric mixer on low to medium speed for 30 seconds, scraping the sides of the bowl constantly. Beat on high speed for 3 minutes. Using a wooden spoon, stir in as much of the remaining flour as you can.

2. Turn the dough out onto a lightly floured surface. Knead in enough of the remaining flour to make a stiff dough that is smooth and elastic (8 to 10 minutes total) (see tip 1, page 171). Shape the dough into a ball. Place dough in a lightly greased bowl, turning once to grease surface of the dough. Cover; let rise in a warm place till nearly double in size (1 to 1¼ hours) (see tips 2 and 3, page 171).

3. Punch dough down (see tip 4, page 171). Turn dough out onto a lightly floured surface. Cover and let rest 10 minutes. Meanwhile, lightly grease a large baking sheet.

4. Roll the dough into a 12×10-inch rectangle. Sprinkle provolone or mozzarella and Parmesan or Romano cheeses on top of the dough. Roll up, jelly-roll style, starting from a long side. Moisten edge with water and seal. Pinch ends and pull slightly to taper. Place seam side down on prepared baking sheet. In a small mixing bowl combine egg white and water. Brush some of the egg white mixture over the top of the loaf. Cover loaf and let rise in a warm place till nearly double in size (about 45 minutes).

5. Using a very sharp knife, make 3 or 4 diagonal cuts about ¼ inch deep across the top of the loaf. Bake in a 375° oven for 15 minutes.

Brush again with some of the egg white mixture. Bake for 20 to 25 minutes more or till bread sounds hollow when you tap the top with your fingers. Immediately remove bread from baking sheet. Cool on a wire rack. Makes 1 loaf (16 servings).

Nutrition Facts per serving: 129 cal., 5 g total fat (2 g sat. fat), 7 mg chol., 191 mg sodium, 16 g carbo., 1 g fiber, 6 g pro. **Daily Values:** 2% vit. A, 0% vit. C, 8% calcium, 7% iron

TIPS FOR SUCCESSFUL YEAST BREADS

■ Recipes usually give a range on the amount of flour. Start with the minimum amount and knead in as much of the remaining flour as you can.

■ Yeast is a living organism that's killed by high temperatures; its respiration is slowed by cold temperatures. Use a thermometer to make sure you heat the liquid mixture to just the right temperature.

■ Proof (raise) yeast breads in a draft-free location between 80° and 85°. To use your oven for proofing, place a bowl of dough in an unheated oven with a large bowl of hot water set on the oven's lower rack.

■ Check the dough to see if it has risen enough by pressing two of your fingers 1/2 inch into the center. Remove your fingers. If the indentations remain, the dough has doubled in size and is ready for the next step.

■ For the second rise, don't let the dough rise above the top of the pan because the dough needs room to rise more as it bakes.

■ You can check the doneness of a yeast bread by tapping the top of the loaf with your fingers. If it sounds hollow, the bread is done. (Check rolls and coffee cakes for golden brown tops.) If the sides of the loaf are pale when you remove it from the pan, put it back in the pan and bake longer. Cover top of the loaf with foil if it is getting too brown.

■ If you live at a high altitude, expect yeast dough to rise faster than at sea level. The higher the altitude, the faster dough rises (see page 55 for additional information on high-altitude baking).

■ Store yeast breads at room temperature; they become stale quicker when chilled.

OATMEAL-MOLASSES ROLLS

PREP: 40 MINUTES   RISE: 1½ HOURS   BAKE: 12 MINUTES   Oven 375°

Low-Fat

2¾ to 3¼ cups all-purpose flour
1 package active dry yeast
1 cup milk
⅓ cup molasses
¼ cup butter, margarine, or shortening
½ teaspoon salt
2 eggs
¾ cup whole wheat flour
¾ cup quick-cooking rolled oats

1. In a large mixing bowl stir together *2 cups* of the all-purpose flour and yeast. In a medium saucepan heat and stir the milk; molasses; butter, margarine, or shortening; and salt just till warm (120° to 130°) and butter almost melts. Add milk mixture to dry mixture along with the eggs. Beat with an electric mixer on low to medium speed for 30 seconds, scraping the sides of the bowl constantly. Beat on high speed for 3 minutes. Using a wooden spoon, stir in whole wheat flour, rolled oats, and as much of the remaining all-purpose flour as you can.

2. Turn dough out onto a lightly floured surface. Knead in enough of the remaining all-purpose flour to make a moderately stiff dough that is smooth and elastic (6 to 8 minutes total) (see tip 1, page 171). Shape the dough into a ball. Place dough in a lightly greased bowl, turning once to grease surface of the dough. Cover and let rise in a warm place till double in size (about 1 hour) (see tips 2 and 3, page 171).

3. Punch dough down (see tip 4, page 171). Turn out onto a lightly floured surface. Divide dough in half. Cover and let rest for 10 minutes. Meanwhile, lightly grease two 8×8×2-inch or 9×9×2-inch baking pans.

4. Divide each portion of the dough into 16 pieces. To shape, gently pull each dough piece into a ball, tucking edges beneath.

5. Place the shaped rolls in the prepared pans. Cover and let rise in a warm place till nearly double in size (for 30 to 40 minutes).

6. Bake in a 375° oven 12 to 15 minutes or till golden brown. Remove rolls from pans. Cool on wire racks. Makes 32 rolls.

Nutrition Facts per roll: 83 cal., 2 g total fat (1 g sat. fat), 16 mg chol., 55 mg sodium, 13 g carbo., 1 g fiber, 2 g pro. **Daily Values:** 2% vit. A, 0% vit. C, 1% calcium, 5% iron

DINNER ROLLS

PREP: 45 MINUTES   RISE: 1¹/₂ HOURS   BAKE: 12 MINUTES   Oven 375°

Low-Fat

Make this dough into butterhorns, rosettes, Parker House rolls, or cloverleaf rolls following the shaping directions on page at right. You can freeze the baked rolls for up to 3 months.

4¹/₄ to 4³/₄ cups all-purpose flour
  1 package active dry yeast
  1 cup milk
¹/₃ cup sugar
¹/₃ cup butter, margarine, or shortening
³/₄ teaspoon salt
  2 beaten eggs

1. In a large mixing bowl stir together *2 cups* of the flour and the yeast. In a medium saucepan heat and stir milk, sugar, butter, and salt just till warm (120° to 130°) and butter almost melts. Add milk mixture to dry mixture along with eggs. Beat with an electric mixer on low to medium speed for 30 seconds, scraping sides of bowl constantly. Beat on high speed 3 minutes. Using a wooden spoon, stir in as much of the remaining flour as you can.

2. Turn dough out onto a lightly floured surface. Knead in enough remaining flour to make a moderately stiff dough that is smooth and elastic (6 to 8 minutes total) (see tip 1, page 171). Shape the dough into a ball. Place in a lightly greased bowl; turn once. Cover; let rise in a warm place till double (about 1 hour) (see tips 2 and 3, page 171).

3. Punch dough down (see tip 4, page 171). Turn dough out onto a lightly floured surface. Divide dough in half. Cover; let rest for 10 minutes. Meanwhile, depending on what shape of roll you wish to make (see photos, at right), lightly grease baking sheets or muffin cups.

4. Shape the dough into desired rolls and place on prepared baking sheets or in muffin cups.* Cover and let rise in a warm place till nearly double in size (about 30 minutes).

5. Bake in a 375° oven for 12 to 15 minutes or till golden. Immediately remove rolls from pans. Cool on wire racks. Makes 24 to 32 rolls.

Nutrition Facts per roll: 114 cal., 3 g total fat (2 g sat. fat), 25 mg chol., 103 mg sodium, 18 g carbo., 1 g fiber, 3 g pro. **Daily Values:** 3% vit. A, 0% vit. C, 1% calcium, 7% iron

Butterhorns: On a lightly floured surface, roll each portion of the dough into a 12-inch circle. Brush with melted butter or margarine. Cut each circle into 12 wedges. To shape, begin at the wide end of a wedge and loosely roll toward the point. Place point side down, 2 to 3 inches apart, on prepared baking sheets.

Rosettes: Divide each dough portion into 16 pieces. On a lightly floured surface, roll each piece into a 12-inch-long rope. Tie in a loose knot, leaving 2 long ends. Tuck top end under roll. Bring bottom end up and tuck into center of roll. Place 2 to 3 inches apart on prepared baking sheets.

Parker House Rolls: On a lightly floured surface, roll each portion of dough to ¼-inch thickness. Cut dough with a floured 2½-inch-round cutter. Brush with melted butter or margarine. Using the dull edge of a table knife, make an off-center crease in each round. Fold each round along crease with larger half on top. Press folded edge firmly. Place rolls 2 to 3 inches apart on prepared baking sheets.

Cloverleaf Rolls: Divide each portion of dough into 36 pieces. Shape each piece into a ball, pulling edges under to make a smooth top. Place 3 balls in each muffin cup, smooth sides up.

■ **Whole Wheat Dinner Rolls:** Prepare as above, except substitute 1¼ cups *whole wheat flour* for 1¼ cups of the all-purpose flour that is stirred in at the end of step 1.

Nutrition Facts per roll: 113 cal., 3 g total fat (2 g sat. fat).

■ **Herb-Onion Dinner Rolls:** Prepare as above, except add 1 tablespoon *dried minced onion* and ½ teaspoon *dried basil, oregano, or Italian seasoning,* crushed, to milk mixture.

Nutrition Facts per roll: 115 cal., 3 g total fat (2 g sat. fat)

■ **Rye-Caraway Dinner Rolls:** Prepare as above, except add 2 teaspoons *caraway seed* to milk mixture and substitute 1¼ cups *rye flour* for 1¼ cups of the all-purpose flour that is stirred in at the end of step 1.

Nutrition Facts per roll: 111 cal., 3 g total fat (2 g sat. fat)

■ **Batter Dinner Rolls:** Prepare as above, except reduce the all-purpose flour that is stirred in at the end of step 1 to 1¼ cups. (Use a total of 3¼ cups all-purpose flour.) Spoon batter into greased muffin cups, filling half full. Cover and let rise in a warm place till nearly double (about 45 minutes). Brush roll tops with milk, and, if desired, sprinkle with *poppy seed or sesame seed.* Bake in a 375° oven for 15 minutes or till golden brown. Makes 18 rolls.

Nutrition Facts per roll: 129 cal., 4 g total fat (2 g sat. fat)

■ **Hamburger or Frankfurter Buns:** Prepare Dinner Rolls as above, except divide dough into 12 pieces. Cover and let rest for 10 minutes. For hamburger buns, shape each portion into a circle, tucking edges under. Place on a greased baking sheet. Using your fingers, slightly flatten circles to 4 inches in diameter. For frankfurter buns, shape each portion into a roll about 5½ inches long, tapering ends. Place on a greased baking sheet. Continue as directed. Makes 12 buns.

Nutrition Facts per bun: 228 cal., 7 g total fat (4 g sat. fat)

■ ***Make-ahead directions:** Cover shaped rolls loosely with plastic wrap, leaving room for rolls to rise. Chill 2 to 24 hours. Uncover; let stand at room temperature 30 minutes. Bake as on page 194.

BREADSTICKS

PREP: 40 MINUTES RISE: 1³/₄ HOURS BAKE 10 MINUTES Oven 425°

Low-Fat

You can make these breadsticks either way you like them—thin and crispy or thick and chewy.

2¹/₄ to 2³/₄ cups all-purpose flour
1 package active dry yeast
³/₄ teaspoon salt
³/₄ cup warm water (120° to 130°)
2 tablespoons olive oil or cooking oil
1 tablespoon sugar or honey
1 egg yolk
1 egg white
    Sesame seed, poppy seed, or grated Parmesan cheese
    (optional)

1. In a large mixing bowl stir together *1 cup* of the flour, the yeast, and salt. In another bowl combine warm water, oil, sugar, and egg yolk. Add water mixture to dry mixture. Beat with an electric mixer on low to medium speed for 30 seconds, scraping the sides of the bowl constantly. Beat on high speed for 3 minutes. Using a wooden spoon, stir in as much remaining flour as you can.

2. Turn the dough onto a lightly floured surface. Knead in enough remaining flour to make a moderately stiff dough that is smooth and elastic (6 to 8 minutes total) (see tip 1, page 171). Cover and let dough rise till nearly double in size (about 1 hour) (see tips 2 and 3, page 171).

3. Punch dough down (see tip 4, page 171). Cover; let rest 10 minutes. Grease a baking sheet.

4. Divide dough in half. Divide

TO SIFT OR NOT TO SIFT

You usually can skip the sifting of all-purpose flour because most of it is presifted. However, flour does settle during shipping, so it's a good idea to stir through the bag or canister just before measuring to make the flour lighter. Then gently spoon it into a dry measuring cup and level it off with a spatula.

each portion into 8 pieces. On a floured surface, roll each piece into a 12-inch-long rope for thin, crispy sticks or into a 6- to 8-inch-long rope for thick, chewy sticks. Place 2 inches apart on prepared baking sheet. Cover; let rise till nearly double (about 45 minutes).

5. Beat together egg white and 1 tablespoon *water* till frothy. Brush over breadsticks. If desired, sprinkle with seed or cheese. Bake in a 425° oven about 10 minutes or till golden. Remove from baking sheet. Cool on a wire rack. Makes 16 breadsticks.

Nutrition Facts per breadstick: 83 cal., 2 g total fat (0 g sat. fat), 13 mg chol., 105 mg sodium, 13 g carbo., 1 g fiber, 2 g pro. **Daily Values:** 2% vit. A, 0% vit. C, 0% calcium, 5% iron

■ **Whole Wheat Breadsticks:** Prepare as above, except substitute 3/4 cup *whole wheat flour* for 3/4 cup of the all-purpose flour that is stirred in at the end of step 1.

Nutrition Facts per breadstick: 82 cal., 2 g total fat (0 g sat. fat)

WHOLE WHEAT POTATO ROLLS

PREP: 40 MINUTES   RISE: 1 1/2 HOURS   BAKE: 15 MINUTES   Oven 375°

Low-Fat

There's no need to wait for leftover mashed potatoes to make soft potato rolls. With this recipe, you can make them anytime you want.

   2 1/4 cups to 2 3/4 cups all-purpose flour
   1 package active dry yeast
   1 cup milk
   1/4 cup butter or margarine
   1 tablespoon sugar
   1/2 teaspoon salt
   1/4 cup instant mashed potato flakes
   1 egg
   1 cup whole wheat flour

1. In a large mixing bowl combine *1 cup* of the all-purpose flour and the yeast. In a medium saucepan heat and stir the milk, butter, sugar, and salt just till warm (120° to 130°) and butter almost melts. Stir in the potato flakes. Let stand for 1 minute. Add milk mixture to dry mixture along with the egg. Beat with an electric mixer on low to medium speed 30 seconds, scraping sides of bowl. Beat on high speed 3 minutes. Using a wooden spoon, stir in the whole wheat flour and as much of the remaining all-purpose flour as you can.

2. Turn dough out onto a lightly floured surface. Knead in enough of the remaining all-purpose flour to make a moderately stiff dough that is smooth and elastic (6 to 8 minutes total) (see tip 1, page 171). Shape the dough into a ball. Place dough in a lightly greased bowl, turning once to grease the surface of the dough. Cover and let rise in a warm place till double in size (about 1 hour) (see tips 2 and 3, page 171).

3. Punch dough down (see tip 4, page 171). Turn dough onto a lightly floured surface. Divide in half. Cover and let rest for 10 minutes. Lightly grease two 8-inch round baking pans.

4. Divide each portion of the dough into 12 pieces. To shape, gently pull each dough piece into a ball, tucking edges beneath. Place shaped rolls in prepared pans. Cover and let rise in a warm place till nearly double in size (for 30 to 40 minutes).

5. Bake in a 375° oven for 15 to 20 minutes or till golden. Immediately remove rolls from pans. Cool on wire racks. Makes 24 rolls.

Nutrition Facts per roll: 86 cal., 3 g total fat (1 g sat. fat), 15 mg chol., 73 mg sodium, 14 g carbo., 1 g fiber, 3 g pro. **Daily Values:** 2% vit. A, 0% vit. C, 1% calcium, and 5% iron

---

BRIOCHE

PREP: 1 HOUR   RISE: 8¾ HOURS   BAKE: 15 MINUTES   Oven 375°

   1 **package active dry yeast**
 ¼ **cup warm water (105° to 115°)**
 ½ **cup butter or margarine**
 ⅓ **cup sugar**
   4 **cups all-purpose flour**
 ½ **cup milk**
   4 **eggs**

1. Stir yeast into warm water to soften. In a mixing bowl beat butter, sugar, and ¾ teaspoon *salt* till fluffy. Add *1 cup* of the flour and milk. Separate 1 egg. Add the yolk and remaining 3 whole eggs to beaten mixture (refrigerate egg white to use later). Add softened yeast; beat well. Stir in remaining flour till smooth. Place in a greased bowl. Cover; let rise in a warm place till double (about 2 hours). Refrigerate dough 6 hours. (Or, omit 2-hour rising time and refrigerate dough up to 24 hours.)

2. Grease twenty-four 2½-inch muffin cups; set aside. Stir dough down. Turn dough out onto a floured surface. Divide dough into 4 portions; set 1 portion aside. Divide each of the remaining 3 portions into 8 pieces for a total of 24.

3. To shape, pull each piece into a ball, tucking edges beneath. Place in prepared muffin cups. Divide the reserved dough portion into 24 pieces. Shape into balls. Using a floured finger, make an indentation in each large ball. Press a small ball into each indentation. Combine reserved egg white and 1 tablespoon *water*. Brush over rolls. Cover; let rise in a warm place till double (45 to 55 minutes).

4. Bake in a 375° oven 15 minutes or till golden, brushing again with egg white mixture after 7 minutes. Remove from pans; cool on racks. Makes 24.

Nutrition Facts per roll: 130 cal., 5 g total fat (3 g sat. fat), 46 mg chol., 125 mg sodium, 18 g carbo., 1 g fiber, 3 g pro. **Daily Values:** 6% vit. A, 0% vit. C, 1% calcium, and 7% iron

---

BAGELS

<small>PREP: 1½ HOURS   RISE: 20 MINUTES   BAKE: 25 MINUTES</small>   Oven 375°

No-Fat

> 4¼ to 4¾ cups all-purpose flour
> 1 package active dry yeast
> 1½ cups warm water (120° to 130°)
> ¼ cup sugar

1. In a large mixing bowl combine *2 cups* of the flour and the yeast. Add the warm water, *3 tablespoons* of the sugar, and 1 teaspoon *salt* to the dry mixture. Beat with an electric mixer on low to medium speed 30 seconds, scraping bowl. Beat on high speed for 3 minutes. Using a wooden spoon, stir in as much of the remaining flour as you can.

2. Turn dough out onto a floured surface. Knead in enough remaining flour to make a moderately stiff dough that is smooth and elastic (6 to 8 minutes) (see tip 1, page 171). Cover and let rest 10 minutes. Grease a baking sheet.

3. Working quickly, divide dough into 12 portions; shape into smooth balls. Punch a hole in center of each; pull gently to make a 2-inch hole. Place on prepared sheet. Cover; let rise 20 minutes. (Start timing after first bagel is shaped.)

4. Broil bagels 5 inches from heat 3 to 4 minutes, turning once (tops should not brown). Meanwhile, in a deep 12-inch skillet or large pot bring 6 cups *water* and the remaining 1 tablespoon sugar to boiling. Reduce heat. Simmer bagels, uncovered, 4 or 5 at a time, for 7 minutes, turning once. Drain on paper towels. Place drained bagels on a well-greased baking sheet. Bake in a 375° oven 25 to 30 minutes or till tops are golden. Makes 12.

Nutrition Facts per bagel: 166 cal., 0 g total fat, 0 mg chol., 179 mg sodium, 35 g carbo., 1 g fiber, 4 g pro. **Daily Values:** 0% vit. A, 0% vit. C, 0% calcium, 13% iron

■ **Onion Bagels:** Prepare as above, except stir 2 tablespoons *dried minced onion* into the flour with the yeast.

Nutrition Facts per bagel: 169 cal., 0 g total fat

■ **Raisin Bagels:** Prepare as above, except stir in ³/₄ cup *raisins* with the all-purpose flour that is stirred in at the end of step 1.

Nutrition Facts per bagel: 193 cal., 0 g total fat

■ **Whole Wheat Bagels:** Prepare as above, except substitute 1¹/₂ cups *whole wheat flour* for 1¹/₂ cups of the all-purpose flour that is stirred in at the end of step 1.

Nutrition Facts per bagel: 165 cal., 1 g total fat (0 g sat. fat)

ENGLISH MUFFINS

PREP: 45 MINUTES   RISE: 1¹/₂ HOURS   COOK: 25 MINUTES

Use a fork, not a knife, to split the muffins before toasting. It creates a surface that has plenty of peaks and craters to hold butter and jam.

5¹/₄ to 5³/₄ cups all-purpose flour
  2 packages active dry yeast
  2 cups milk
¹/₄ cup butter, margarine, or shortening
  2 tablespoons sugar
  1 teaspoon salt
    Cornmeal

1. In a large mixing bowl stir together *2 cups* of the flour and the yeast; set aside. In a medium saucepan heat and stir milk; butter, margarine, or shortening; sugar; and salt just till warm (120° to 130°) and butter almost melts. Add milk mixture to dry mixture. Beat with an electric mixer on low to medium speed for 30 seconds, scraping the sides of the bowl constantly. Beat on high speed for 3 minutes. Using a wooden spoon, stir in as much of the remaining flour as you can.

2. Turn the dough out onto a lightly floured surface. Knead in enough remaining flour to make a moderately stiff dough that is smooth and elastic (6 to 8 minutes total) (see tip 1, page 171). Shape the dough into a ball. Place dough in a lightly greased bowl, turning once to grease surface. Cover and let rise in a warm place till double in size (about 1 hour) (see tips 2 and 3, page 171).

3. Punch dough down (see tip 4, page 171). Turn dough out onto a lightly floured surface. Cover and let rest for 10 minutes. Roll dough to slightly less than $1/2$-inch thickness. Using a floured 4-inch biscuit cutter, cut dough into rounds, dipping cutter into flour between cuts. Reroll as necessary. Dip both sides of each muffin into cornmeal. (If necessary, to make cornmeal adhere, lightly brush muffins with water.) Cover and let rise in a warm place till very light (about 30 minutes).

4. Cook muffins, four at a time, in an ungreased electric skillet at 325° for 25 to 30 minutes or till golden, turning every 5 minutes. (Keep any remaining muffins in the refrigerator for up to 8 hours.) Or, cook over low heat on an ungreased large griddle or in several skillets for 25 to 30 minutes or till golden, turning frequently. Cool on wire racks. Split muffins horizontally. To serve, toast or broil muffin halves. Makes 12 muffins.

Nutrition Facts per muffin: 253 cal., 6 g total fat (2 g sat. fat), 8 mg chol., 234 mg sodium, 43 g carbo., 2 g fiber, 7 g pro. **Daily Values:** 6% vit. A, 0% vit. C, 4% calcium, 17% iron

■ **Whole Wheat English Muffins:** Prepare as above, except substitute $1^1/2$ cups *whole wheat flour* and $1/2$ cup *cracked wheat* for 2 cups of the all-purpose flour that is stirred in at the end of step 1.

Nutrition Facts per muffin: 247 cal., 6 g total fat (2 g sat. fat)

DILL BATTER BREAD

Low-Fat

This speedy yeast bread rises just once and requires no kneading.

    2 cups all-purpose flour
    1 package active dry yeast
  1/2 cup water
  1/2 cup cream-style cottage cheese
    1 tablespoon sugar
    1 tablespoon dillseed or caraway seed
    1 tablespoon butter or margarine
    1 teaspoon dried minced onion
  1/2 teaspoon salt
    1 beaten egg
  1/2 cup toasted wheat germ

1. Grease a 9x1½-inch round baking pan or a 1-quart casserole; set aside.

2. In a large mixing bowl stir together *1 cup* of the flour and the yeast; set aside.

3. In a medium saucepan heat and stir water, cottage cheese, sugar, dillseed or caraway seed, butter or margarine, dried onion, and salt just till warm (120° to 130°) and butter almost melts.

4. Add cottage cheese mixture to dry mixture along with the egg. Beat with an electric mixer on low to medium speed for 30 seconds, scraping the sides of the bowl constantly. Beat on high speed for 3 minutes. Using a wooden spoon, stir in the wheat germ and the remaining flour (batter will be stiff).

5. Spoon batter into the prepared pan or casserole. Cover and let rise in a warm place till double in size (for 50 to 60 minutes).

6. Bake in a 375° oven for 25 to 30 minutes or till golden. Immediately remove bread from pan or casserole. Serve warm, or cool the loaf on a wire rack. Makes 1 loaf (8 servings).

Nutrition Facts per serving: 179 cal., 4 g total fat (2 g sat. fat), 32 mg chol., 213 mg sodium, 28 g carbo., 1 g fiber, 8 g pro. **Daily Values:** 3% vit. A, 0% vit. C, 2% calcium, 15% iron

SOFT PRETZELS

PREP: 1½ HOURS   RISE: 1¼ HOURS   BAKE: 24 MINUTES   Oven 475°

Low-Fat

    4 to 4½ cups all-purpose flour
    1 package active dry yeast
 1½ cups milk
 ¼ cup sugar
    2 tablespoons cooking oil
    1 teaspoon salt
    2 tablespoons salt
    3 quarts boiling water
    1 slightly beaten egg white
    1 tablespoon water
       Sesame seed, poppy seed, or coarse salt

1. In a large mixing bowl stir together *1½ cups* of the flour and the yeast; set aside. In a medium saucepan heat and stir milk, sugar, oil, and the 1 teaspoon salt till warm (120° to 130°). Add milk mixture to dry mixture. Beat with an electric mixer on low to medium speed for 30 seconds, scraping the sides of the bowl constantly. Beat on high speed for 3 minutes. Using a wooden spoon, stir in as much of the remaining flour as you can.

2. Turn the dough out onto a lightly floured surface. Knead in enough of the remaining flour to make a moderately stiff dough that is smooth and elastic (6 to 8 minutes total) (see tip 1, page 171). Shape the dough into a ball. Place dough in a lightly greased bowl, turning once to grease surface of the dough.

DON'T CROWD THE OVEN

When baking several long, individual, or round loaves of bread at the same time, you'll need an extra-large (17×14-inch) baking sheet. If you don't have a baking sheet this size, go ahead and shape the loaves on two smaller baking sheets and let them rise as directed. However, bake only one at a time, placing the second baking sheet in the refrigerator. Don't bake the two smaller sheets at the same time because not enough air will circulate in the oven.

Cover and let rise in a warm place till double in size (about 1¼ hours) (see tips 2 and 3, page 171).

3. Punch dough down (see tip 4, page 171). Turn dough out onto a lightly floured surface. Cover and let rest for 10 minutes. Meanwhile, lightly grease 2 baking sheets.

4. Roll dough into a 12×10-inch rectangle. Cut into twenty 12×½-inch strips. Gently pull each strip into a rope about 16 inches long. Shape into pretzels (see photo, below).

5. Carefully place pretzels on prepared baking sheets. Bake in a 475° oven for 4 minutes. Remove from oven. Lower oven temperature to 350°.

6. Dissolve the 2 tablespoons salt in the boiling water. Lower pretzels, 3 or 4 at a time, into boiling water. Boil for 2 minutes, turning once. Using a slotted spoon, remove from water; drain on paper towels. Let stand a few seconds. Place about ½ inch apart on well-greased baking sheets.

7. In a small mixing bowl stir together egg white and the 1 tablespoon water. Brush pretzels with some of the egg white mixture. Sprinkle pretzels lightly with sesame seed, poppy seed, or coarse salt. Bake in a 350° oven for 20 to 25 minutes or till golden brown. Immediately remove from baking sheets. Cool on wire racks. Makes 20.

Nutrition Facts per pretzel: 119 cal., 2 g total fat (0 g sat. fat), 1 mg chol., 226 mg sodium, 21 g carbo., 1 g fiber, 3 g pro. **Daily Values:** 1% vit. A, 0% vit. C, 2% calcium, 7% iron

■ **Whole Wheat Soft Pretzels:** Prepare as above, except substitute 1½ cups *whole wheat flour* for 1½ cups of the all-purpose flour that is stirred in at the end of step 1. Continue as directed.

Nutrition Facts per pretzel: 121 cal., 2 g total fat (1 g sat. fat)

Shape each pretzel by crossing one rope over the other about 4 inches from each end, forming a circle. Holding an end of the rope in each hand, twist once at the crossover point. Fold pretzel in middle and lay the ends over the bottom edge of the circle. Moisten the ends, tuck them under the circle, and press to seal.

CINNAMON ROLLS

4 to 4⅓ cups all-purpose flour
1 package active dry yeast
1 cup milk
⅓ cup sugar
⅓ cup butter or margarine
½ teaspoon salt
2 eggs
3 tablespoons butter or margarine, melted
½ cup sugar
2 teaspoons ground cinnamon
1 recipe Powdered Sugar Icing (see page 291)

1. In a large mixing bowl combine *2 cups* of the flour and yeast; set aside. In a medium saucepan heat and stir milk, the ⅓ cup sugar, the ⅓ cup butter, and salt just till warm (120° to 130°) and butter almost melts. Add milk mixture to dry mixture along with eggs. Beat with an electric mixer on low to medium speed 30 seconds, scraping bowl. Beat on high speed 3 minutes. Using a wooden spoon, stir in as much of the remaining flour as you can.

2. Turn dough onto a floured surface. Knead in enough remaining flour to make a moderately soft dough that is smooth and elastic (3 to 5 minutes total) (see tip 1, page 171). Shape dough into a ball. Place dough in a lightly greased bowl; turn once to grease dough. Cover and let rise in a warm place till double in size (about 1 hour) (see tips 2 and 3, page 171).

TO PREPARE ROLL

1. Brush each dough rectangle with butter and sprinkle with the sugar-cinnamon mixture. Starting from a long side, carefully roll up dough.

2. Seal the seam by pinching the dough with your fingers, beginning at one end and working toward the other.

3. To easily cut rolled dough, place a piece of heavy-duty thread under it. Bring the thread around the sides and cross it at the top; pull in opposite directions quickly.

3. Punch dough down (see tip 4, page 171). Turn onto a lightly floured surface. Divide in half. Cover and let rest 10 minutes. Lightly grease two 9×1¹/₂-inch round baking pans.

4. Roll each portion of the dough into a 12×8-inch rectangle. Brush the melted 3 tablespoons butter over dough. Combine the ¹/₂ cup sugar and cinnamon; sprinkle over dough. Roll up, jelly-roll style, starting from a long side (see step 1, below left). Seal seam (see step 2, below left). Slice each roll into 12 equal pieces (see step 3, below left). Place in prepared pans.* Cover and let rise in a warm place till nearly double (about 30 minutes).

5. Bake in a 375° oven for 20 to 25 minutes or till golden. Cool slightly; remove from pans. Drizzle with Powdered Sugar Icing. If desired, serve warm. Makes 24 rolls.

Nutrition Facts per roll: 161 cal., 5 g total fat (1 g sat. fat), 19 mg chol., 102 mg sodium, 27 g carbo., 1 g fiber, 3 g pro. **Daily Values:** 6% vit. A, 0% vit. C, 1% calcium, 7% iron

■ **Cinnamon and Chocolate Rolls:** Prepare as above, except add ³/₄ cup *miniature semisweet chocolate pieces*. Sprinkle them over the dough on top of the sugar-cinnamon mixture.

Nutrition Facts per roll: 185 cal., 6 g total fat (3 g sat. fat)

■ **Caramel-Pecan Rolls:** Prepare dough through step 3 as at left, except do not grease pans. After dough has been punched down and while it is resting for 10 minutes, in a small saucepan combine ²/₃ cup packed *brown sugar*, ¹/₄ cup *butter or margarine*, and 2 tablespoons *light corn syrup*. Heat and stir over medium heat till combined. Divide between two 9×1¹/₂-inch round baking pans. Sprinkle ¹/₃ cup *chopped pecans* in each pan; set aside. Continue to shape and bake rolls as directed, except reduce cinnamon to 1 teaspoon, immediately invert baked rolls from pan, and do not drizzle with icing.

Nutrition Facts per roll: 205 cal., 9 g total fat (2 g sat. fat)

■ ***Make-ahead directions:** Cover shaped rolls loosely with plastic wrap, leaving room for rolls to rise. Refrigerate for 2 to 24 hours. Uncover and let stand at room temperature for 30 minutes. Bake as directed above.

LEMONY MORAVIAN SUGAR BREAD

PREP: 1 HOUR   RISE: 1 HOUR   BAKE: 20 MINUTES   Oven 375°

    1 cup Sourdough Starter (see page 178)
3¹/₂ cups all-purpose flour
    1 package active dry yeast
  ¹/₂ cup granulated sugar
  ¹/₂ cup milk
  ¹/₄ cup butter or margarine
    2 lightly beaten eggs
    2 teaspoons finely shredded lemon peel (set aside)
    2 tablespoons lemon juice
  ³/₄ cup packed brown sugar
  ¹/₃ cup butter or margarine
    1 teaspoon ground cinnamon

1. Let 1 cup Sourdough Starter stand at room temperature 30 minutes. Lightly grease a 13×9×2-inch baking pan or 3-quart baking dish. Set aside.
2. In a large mixing bowl combine *1¹/₂ cups* flour and yeast. In a saucepan heat and stir granulated sugar, milk, ¹/₄ cup butter, and ¹/₂ teaspoon *salt* just till warm (120° to 130°) and butter almost melts. Add milk mixture to dry mixture. Add starter, eggs, and lemon juice. Beat with electric mixer on low to medium speed 30 seconds, scraping bowl. Beat on high 3 minutes. Stir in peel and remaining flour.
3. Transfer dough to prepared pan. Using floured hands, pat dough evenly into pan. Cover; let rise in a warm place till nearly double (about 1 hour).
4. In a saucepan combine brown sugar, ¹/₃ cup butter, and cinnamon. Heat and stir till melted and smooth. Using a wooden spoon handle, poke holes in dough. Pour brown sugar mixture over dough. Bake in a 375° oven 20 to 25 minutes or till golden. Serve warm. Makes 12 servings.

Nutrition Facts per serving: 326 cal., 10 g total fat (6 g sat. fat), 60 mg chol., 213 mg sodium, 52 g carbo., 1 g fiber, 6 g pro. **Daily Values:** 13% vit. A, 2% vit. C, 3% calcium, 16% iron

HOT CROSS BUNS

PREP: 35 MINUTES RISE: 2¼ HOURS BAKE: 12 MINUTES   Oven 375°

    4 to 4½ cups all-purpose flour
    1 package active dry yeast
    ¾ teaspoon ground cinnamon
    ¼ teaspoon ground nutmeg
      Dash ground cloves
    ¾ cup milk
    ½ cup butter or margarine
    ⅓ cup sugar
    3 eggs
    ⅔ cup currants or raisins
    ¼ cup diced candied orange peel (optional)
    1 beaten egg white
    1 recipe Powdered Sugar Icing (see page 291)

1. In a large mixing bowl combine *2 cups* flour, yeast, cinnamon, nutmeg, and cloves. In a pan heat and stir milk, butter or margarine, sugar, and ½ teaspoon *salt* till warm (120° to 130°) and butter almost melts. Add milk mixture to dry mixture. Add eggs. Beat with an electric mixer on low to medium speed 30 seconds, scraping bowl. Beat on high 3 minutes. Stir in currants and orange peel (if desired), and as much remaining flour as you can.

2. Turn out onto a lightly floured surface. Knead in enough remaining flour to make a moderately soft dough (3 to 5 minutes total). Shape into a ball. Place in a greased bowl, turning once. Cover; let rise in a warm place till double (about 1½ hours).

3. Punch dough down. Turn onto floured surface. Cover; let rest 10 minutes. Divide dough into 20 portions. Shape portions into smooth balls. Place balls 1½ inches apart on greased baking sheet. Cover; let rise till nearly double (45 to 60 minutes).

4. Using a sharp knife, make a crisscross slash across top of each bun. In small bowl combine beaten egg white and 1 tablespoon *water*. Brush mixture of egg white and water over rolls. Bake in a 375° oven 12 to 15 minutes or till golden brown. Cool slightly. Drizzle Powdered Sugar Icing into slashes atop each bun. Serve warm. Makes 20.

Nutrition Facts per bun: 188 cal., 6 g total fat (3 g sat. fat), 45 mg chol., 118 mg sodium, 30 g carbo., 1 g fiber, 4 g pro. **Daily Values:** 6% vit. A, 0% vit. C, 2% calcium, 9% iron

ORANGE BOWKNOTS

5¼ to 5¾ cups all-purpose flour
1 package active dry yeast
1¼ cups milk
½ cup butter, margarine, or shortening
⅓ cup sugar
½ teaspoon salt
2 eggs
2 tablespoons finely shredded orange peel
¼ cup orange juice
1 recipe Orange Icing (see top of next page)

1. In a large mixing bowl combine *2 cups* of the flour and yeast; set aside. In a medium saucepan heat and stir the milk, butter, sugar, and salt just till warm (120° to 130°) and butter almost melts. Add milk mixture to dry mixture along with eggs. Beat with an electric mixer on low to medium speed 30 seconds, scraping bowl. Beat on high speed 3 minutes. Using a wooden spoon, stir in the orange peel, orange juice, and as much of the remaining flour as you can.
2. Turn dough onto a floured surface. Knead in enough remaining flour to make a moderately soft dough that is smooth and elastic (3 to 5 minutes total) (see tip 1, page 171). Shape dough into a ball. Place dough in a lightly greased bowl; turn once. Cover; let rise in a warm place till double in size (about 1 hour) (see tips 2 and 3, page 171).
3. Punch dough down (see tip 4, page 171). Turn onto a lightly floured surface. Divide in half. Cover and let rest 10 minutes. Meanwhile, lightly grease 2 baking sheets; set aside.
4. Roll each portion of the dough into a 12x7-inch rectangle. Cut each rectangle into twelve 7-inch-long strips. Tie each strip loosely in a knot. Arrange knots 2 inches apart on prepared baking sheets. Cover and let rise in a warm place till nearly double in size (about 30 minutes).
5. Bake in a 400° oven about 12 minutes or till golden. Immediately remove rolls from baking sheets. Cool on wire racks. Drizzle with Orange Icing. Makes 24 rolls.

■ **Orange Icing:** In a small mixing bowl combine 1 cup *sifted powdered sugar* and 1 teaspoon finely shredded *orange peel*. Stir in enough *orange juice* (1 to 2 tablespoons) to make icing easy to drizzle.

Nutrition Facts per roll: 167 cal., 5 g total fat (3 g sat. fat), 29 mg chol., 95 mg sodium, 27 g carbo., 1 g fiber, 4 g pro. **Daily Values:** 5% vit. A, 4% vit. C, 2% calcium, 8% iron

CITRUS-NUTMEG PUFFS

PREP: 25 MINUTES   RISE: 1½ HOURS   BAKE: 20 MINUTES   Oven 375°

Want hot rolls for breakfast? Make this batter the night before and refrigerate the covered rolls overnight instead of letting them rise the second time. The next morning, let them stand at room temperature for 10 minutes while your oven preheats.

    2 cups all-purpose flour
    1 package active dry yeast
  ²/₃ cup milk
  ¹/₄ cup sugar
    3 tablespoons butter or margarine
    1 tablespoon finely shredded orange peel
  ¹/₂ teaspoon salt
    1 egg
    2 tablespoons sugar
  ¹/₄ teaspoon ground nutmeg

1. In a large mixing bowl stir together *1 cup* of the flour and the yeast; set aside. In a small saucepan heat and stir milk, the ¹/₄ cup sugar, butter or margarine, orange peel, and salt just till warm (120° to 130°) and butter almost melts. Add milk mixture to dry mixture along with the egg. Beat with an electric mixer on low to medium speed for 30 seconds, scraping the sides of the bowl constantly. Beat on high speed for 3 minutes. Using a wooden spoon, stir in the remaining flour.

2. Cover; let rise in a warm place till double in size (about 1 hour) (see tips 2 and 3, page 171). Lightly grease twelve 2¹/₂-inch muffin cups; set aside.

3. Stir batter down. Spoon batter into prepared muffin cups, filling each half full. In a small mixing bowl combine the 2 tablespoons sugar and nutmeg. Sprinkle about ¹/₂ teaspoon sugar-nutmeg mixture atop batter in each muffin cup. Cover and let rise in a warm place till nearly double in size (for 30 to 40 minutes) or refrigerate overnight.

4. Bake in a 375° oven 20 minutes or till golden brown. Immediately remove from cups. Cool slightly on wire rack. Serve warm. Makes 12 puffs.

Nutrition Facts per puff: 134 cal., 4 g total fat (2 g sat. fat), 26 mg chol., 130 mg sodium, 22 g carbo., 1 g fiber, 3 g pro. **Daily Values:** 4% vit. A, 1% vit. C, 2% calcium, 7% iron

---

STOLLEN

PREP: 25 MINUTES RISE: 2¾ HOURS BAKE: 18 MINUTES   Oven 375°

     4 to 4¹/₂ cups all-purpose flour
     1 package active dry yeast
   ¹/₄ teaspoon ground cardamom
  1¹/₄ cups milk
   ¹/₂ cup butter or margarine
   ¹/₄ cup sugar
     1 egg
     1 cup raisins or currants
   ¹/₄ cup diced mixed candied fruits and peels
   ¹/₄ cup blanched almonds
     1 tablespoon finely shredded orange peel
     1 tablespoon finely shredded lemon peel
     1 cup sifted powdered sugar
     2 tablespoons hot water
   ¹/₂ teaspoon butter or margarine

1. Combine *2 cups* of the flour, yeast, and cardamom. In a saucepan heat and stir milk, ¹/₂ cup butter, granulated sugar, and ¹/₂ teaspoon *salt* till warm (120° to 130°) and butter almost melts. Add to flour mixture along with egg. Beat with an electric mixer on low speed 30 seconds, scraping bowl. Beat on high speed 3 minutes. Stir in as much remaining flour as you can. Stir in raisins, candied fruits and peels, almonds, and peels.

2. Turn dough onto a floured surface. Knead in enough remaining flour to make a moderately soft dough (3 to 5 minutes total) (see tip 1, page 171). Shape into a ball. Place in a greased bowl; turn once. Cover; let rise in a warm place till double (about 1³/₄ hours) (see tips 2 and 3, page 171).

3. Grease baking sheets; set aside. Punch dough down (see tip 4, page 171). Turn onto a floured surface. Divide into thirds. Cover; let rest 10 minutes. Roll one portion into a 10×6-inch oval. Without stretching, fold a long side over to within 1 inch of opposite side; press edges to lightly seal. Place on prepared baking sheet; repeat with remaining dough. Cover; let rise till nearly double (about 1 hour). Bake in a 375° oven 18 to 20 minutes or till golden. Remove from baking sheets; cool 30 minutes on a rack. Combine powdered sugar, hot water, and $^1/_2$ teaspoon butter; brush over warm bread. Makes 3 loaves (48 servings).

Nutrition Facts per serving: 83 cal., 3 g total fat (1 g sat. fat), 10 mg chol., 47 mg sodium, 14 g carbo., 0 g fiber, 2 g pro. **Daily Values:** 2% vit. A, 0% vit. C, 1% calcium, 3% iron

---

BOSTON BROWN BREAD

PREP: 15 MINUTES   COOK: 2 HOURS

$^1/_2$ **cup cornmeal**
$^1/_2$ **cup whole wheat flour**
$^1/_2$ **cup rye flour**
$^1/_2$ **teaspoon baking powder**
$^1/_4$ **teaspoon baking soda**
 1 **cup buttermilk or sour milk (see tip, page 261)**
$^1/_3$ **cup light molasses**
 2 **tablespoons brown sugar**
 1 **tablespoon cooking oil**
$^1/_4$ **cup raisins or chopped walnuts**
    Cream cheese, softened (optional)

1. Well grease a $7^1/_2$×$3^1/_2$×2-inch loaf pan; set aside. In a large mixing bowl combine cornmeal, flours, baking powder, baking soda, and $^1/_4$ teaspoon *salt*.

2. In a mixing bowl combine buttermilk, molasses, brown sugar, and oil. Gradually add milk mixture to flour mixture, stirring just till combined. Stir in raisins. Pour into prepared loaf pan. Grease a piece of foil. Place the foil, greased side down, over the loaf pan. Press foil around edges to seal.

3. Place loaf pan on a rack in a pot. Pour hot water into pot around loaf pan till water covers 1 inch of loaf pan. Bring water to boiling; reduce heat. Cover; simmer 2 to $2^1/_2$ hours or till a wooden toothpick inserted near center comes out clean. Add additional boiling water to the pot as needed.

4. Remove loaf pan from pot; let stand 10 minutes. Remove bread

from pan. If desired, serve warm with cream cheese. Makes 1 loaf
(14 servings).

Nutrition Facts per serving: 94 cal., 1 g total fat (0 g sat. fat), 1 mg chol., 94 mg sodium,
19 g carbo., 1 g fiber, 2 g pro. **Daily Values:** 0% vit. A, 0% vit. C, 4% calcium, 6% iron

---

BUTTERMILK-OAT BREAD

PREP: 25 MINUTES   BAKE: PER BREAD MACHINE DIRECTIONS

Low-Fat

1-POUND LOAF

   $^3/_4$ **cup buttermilk**
   1 **tablespoon honey**
$1^1/_2$ **teaspoons butter or margarine**
$1^3/_4$ **cups bread flour**
   $^1/_3$ **cup rolled oats, toasted***
   $^1/_2$ **teaspoon salt**
   1 **teaspoon active dry yeast or bread machine yeast**

$1^1/_2$-POUND LOAF

$1^1/_4$ **cups buttermilk**
   2 **tablespoons honey**
   1 **tablespoon butter or margarine**
$2^3/_4$ **cups bread flour**
   1 **cup rolled oats, toasted***
   $^3/_4$ **teaspoon salt**
   1 **teaspoon active dry yeast or bread machine yeast**

1. Add all of the ingredients to a bread machine according to manufacturer's directions. Bake the bread using the regular or white setting. Makes 1 loaf (16 to 24 servings).
***Note:** For toasted rolled oats, place oats in a shallow baking pan.
Bake in a 350° oven for 15 to 20 minutes or till oats are lightly
browned, stirring occasionally; cool.

Nutrition Facts per serving: 73 cal., 1 g total fat (0 g sat. fat), 2 mg chol., 83 mg sodium,
14 g carbo., 1 g fiber, 3 g pro. **Daily Values:** 0% vit. A, 0% vit. C, 1% calcium, 4% iron

SAGE-WHEAT BREAD

PREP: 10 MINUTES BAKE: PER BREAD MACHINE DIRECTIONS

Low-Fat

Our Test Kitchen recommends using 1 teaspoon of yeast for either size of loaf.

1-POUND LOAF

1 cup milk
1½ teaspoons shortening
1⅓ cups whole wheat flour
⅔ cup bread flour
¼ cup cornmeal
2 teaspoons brown sugar
1½ teaspoons snipped fresh sage or ¼ teaspoon dried sage, crushed
½ teaspoon salt
1 teaspoon active dry yeast or bread machine yeast

1½-POUND LOAF

1⅓ cups milk
1 tablespoon shortening
2 cups whole wheat flour
1 cup bread flour
⅓ cup cornmeal
1 tablespoon brown sugar
2 teaspoons snipped fresh sage or ¼ teaspoon dried sage, crushed
¾ teaspoon salt
1 teaspoon active dry yeast or bread machine yeast

1. Add all of the ingredients to a bread machine according to the manufacturer's directions. Bake the bread using the wheat, regular, or white setting. Makes 1 loaf (16 to 24 servings).

Nutrition Facts per serving: 76 cal., 1 g total fat (0 g sat. fat), 1 mg chol., 75 mg sodium, 14 g carbo., 2 g fiber, 3 g pro. **Daily Values:** 1% vit. A, 0% vit. C, 1% calcium, 5% iron

BANANA-WALNUT BREAD

PREP: 10 MINUTES   BAKE: PER BREAD MACHINE DIRECTIONS

*Whether your bread machine makes 1- or 1¹/₂-pound loaves, we have
the instructions here. Just follow the ingredient list
for the appropriate size.*

1-POUND LOAF

¹/₂ cup milk
¹/₃ cup mashed ripe banana
1 egg
1 tablespoon butter or margarine
2 cups bread flour
2 tablespoons sugar
¹/₂ teaspoon salt
¹/₈ teaspoon ground cinnamon (optional)
1 teaspoon active dry yeast or bread machine yeast
¹/₂ cup chopped walnuts or pecans, toasted (see tip, page 234)
1 recipe Powdered Sugar Icing (see page 291)

1¹/₂-POUND LOAF

²/₃ cup milk
¹/₂ cup mashed ripe banana
1 egg
2 tablespoons butter or margarine
3 cups bread flour
3 tablespoons sugar
³/₄ teaspoon salt
¹/₄ teaspoon ground cinnamon (optional)
1 teaspoon dry yeast or bread machine yeast
³/₄ cup chopped walnuts or pecans, toasted (see tip, page 234)
1 recipe Powdered Sugar Icing (see page 291)

1. Add ingredients to a bread machine according to manufacturer's
directions, adding the banana with the milk. Bake the bread using
regular or white setting (use the light color setting, if available). Drizzle cooled loaf with Powdered Sugar Icing. Makes 1 loaf (16 to 24
servings).

Nutrition Facts per serving: 114 cal., 4 g total fat (1 g sat. fat), 17 mg chol., 84 mg
sodium, 17 g carbo., 1 g fiber, 3 g pro. **Daily Values:** 2% vit. A, 1% vit. C, 1% calcium, 5%
iron

BANANA BREAD

PREP: 15 MINUTES   BAKE: 50 MINUTES   Oven 350°

For the fullest banana flavor, select bananas that are beginning to turn dark.

1½ **cups all-purpose flour**
1½ **teaspoons baking powder**
¼ **teaspoon baking soda**
¼ **teaspoon ground cinnamon**
1 **egg**
1 **cup mashed bananas (3 medium)**
¾ **cup sugar**
¼ **cup cooking oil**
1 **teaspoon finely shredded lemon peel (optional)**
½ **cup chopped walnuts or pecans**

1. Grease the bottom and ½ inch up the sides of an 8×4×2-inch loaf pan; set aside. In a medium mixing bowl combine the flour, baking powder, baking soda, cinnamon, and ⅛ teaspoon *salt*. Make a well in the center of dry mixture; set aside.
2. In another bowl combine the egg, bananas, sugar, cooking oil, and, if desired, lemon peel. Add egg mixture all at once to dry mixture. Stir just till moistened (batter should be lumpy). Fold in nuts.
3. Spoon batter into the prepared pan. Bake in a 350° oven 50 to 55 minutes or till a wooden toothpick inserted near center comes out clean. Cool in pan on a wire rack for 10 minutes. Remove loaf from pan; cool on rack. Wrap and store overnight before slicing. Makes 1 loaf (16 servings).

Nutrition Facts per serving: 154 cal., 6 g total fat (1 g sat. fat), 13 mg chol., 75 mg sodium, 23 g carbo., 1 g fiber, 2 g pro. **Daily Values:** 0% vit. A, 3% vit. C, 3% calcium, 5% iron

ADJUSTING CONVENTIONAL RECIPES FOR BAKING IN BREAD MACHINES

There's no great secret to converting conventional yeast bread recipes for use in your bread machine. Just follow these tips.

■ Using the minimum amount of flour in the recipe (where a range is given), reduce the amount of flour to only 2 cups (for a 1-pound-loaf machine) or 3 cups (for a 1½-pound-loaf machine). Reduce all ingredients—including the yeast (one package equals about 2¼ teaspoons)—by the same proportion. For example, for a 1½-pound-loaf bread machine, a recipe using 4½ cups flour and 1 package yeast would be decreased by one-third to 3 cups flour and 1½ teaspoons yeast.

■ If the bread uses two or more types of flour, add the flour amounts together and use that as the basis for reducing the recipe. The total flour used should be only 2 or 3 cups, depending on the size of your machine.

■ Use bread flour instead of all-purpose flour, or add 1 to 2 tablespoons gluten flour (available at health-food stores) to the all-purpose flour. Rye breads usually need 1 tablespoon of gluten flour even when bread flour is used.

■ Make sure the liquid ingredients are at room temperature before starting.

■ Measure the ingredients as you would for any other recipe. Add them in the order specified by the bread machine manufacturer.

■ Add desired dried fruits or nuts at raisin bread cycle, if your machine has one. If it doesn't, add them according to the manufacturer's directions.

■ Do not use light-colored dried fruits, such as apricots and light raisins, because the preservatives added to them can inhibit yeast performance. Choose another fruit, or use the dough cycle and lightly knead in the fruit by hand before shaping the loaves. (**Note:** When making the dough only, after removing the dough from the bread machine, it may be necessary to knead in a little more flour before shaping it. Knead in just enough additional flour to make dough easy to handle. If necessary, let dough rest 5 minutes before shaping. The dough will be very elastic and letting it rest makes it easier to shape.)

■ For breads containing whole wheat or rye flour, use the whole wheat cycle, if available.

■ For sweet or rich breads, use the light color setting or sweet bread cycle, if your machine has one. Monitor the bread carefully because with some machines, using the sweet bread cycle can result in breads that are slightly underdone or gummy in the center.

■ The first time you try a new bread in your machine, watch and listen carefully. Check the dough after the first 3 to 5 minutes of kneading. If your machine works excessively hard during the mixing cycle, if the dough looks dry and crumbly, or if two or more balls of dough form, add 1 to 2 tablespoons of extra liquid. If dough looks very soft and is unable to form a ball, add more flour, 1 tablespoon at a time, until a ball does form. Record how much additional liquid or flour you add so you can adjust your future recipes accordingly.

MAKING BETTER QUICK BREADS

These simple suggestions will help ensure your bread-baking success.

■ Check the bread 10 to 15 minutes before the minimum baking time is reached. Cover it with foil if it's browning too fast.

■ After baking, let the loaves cool completely on a wire rack, then wrap them in foil or plastic wrap and store at room temperature. Store the bread overnight before slicing and eating. This allows the flavors to mellow and makes the loaves easier to cut.

■ Don't be concerned about a crack down the top of the loaf. It is typical of quick bread.

ZUCCHINI BREAD

*When the markets are brimming with zucchini, look for the small
ones—they're young and their skins are more tender.*

1 1/2 cups all-purpose flour
  1 teaspoon ground cinnamon
  1/2 teaspoon baking soda
  1/4 teaspoon baking powder
  1/4 teaspoon salt
  1/4 teaspoon ground nutmeg
  1 cup sugar
  1 cup finely shredded, unpeeled zucchini
  1/4 cup cooking oil
  1 egg
  1/4 teaspoon finely shredded lemon peel
  1/2 cup chopped walnuts or pecans

1. Grease bottom and 1/2 inch up sides of an 8×4×2-inch loaf pan;
set aside. In a medium mixing bowl combine the flour, cinnamon,
baking soda, baking powder, salt, and nutmeg; set aside.

2. In another medium mixing bowl combine sugar, shredded zucchini, cooking oil, egg, and lemon peel; mix well. Add dry mixture
to zucchini mixture. Stir just till moistened (batter should be lumpy).
Fold in walnuts or pecans.

3. Spoon batter into the prepared pan. Bake in a 350° oven 55 to 60
minutes or till a wooden toothpick inserted near center comes out
clean. Cool in the pan on a wire rack for 10 minutes. Remove loaf
from pan. Cool completely on the wire rack. Wrap and store
overnight. Makes 1 loaf (16 servings).

Nutrition Facts per serving: 148 cal., 6 g total fat (1 g sat. fat), 13 mg chol., 83 mg
sodium, 22 g carbo., 1 g fiber, 2 g pro. **Daily Values:** 0% vit. A, 1% vit. C, 1% calcium, 4%
iron

■ **Apple Bread:** Prepare as above, except substitute 1 cup finely
shredded, peeled *apple* for the shredded zucchini. Continue as directed.

Nutrition Facts per serving: 151 cal., 6 g total fat (1 g sat. fat)

BREAD SPREADS

Add a tasty zip to your breads by serving them with one of these yummy spreads. You can stir a spread together in about 5 minutes, but let it chill at least 1 hour before serving to allow its flavors to blend.

NUT BUTTER

Stir together ¹/₂ cup finely chopped *almonds or walnuts;* ¹/₄ cup *butter or margarine,* softened; and ¹/₄ cup *apricot or peach preserves.* Makes 1 cup.

CITRUS BUTTER

Stir together ¹/₂ cup *butter or margarine,* softened; 1 tablespoon *powdered sugar;* and 1 teaspoon finely shredded *orange or lemon peel.* Makes ¹/₂ cup.

BREAKFAST BUTTER

Stir together ¹/₂ cup *butter or margarine,* softened, and 2 tablespoons *honey or maple- flavored syrup.* Makes ¹/₂ cup.

ONION-PARMESAN BUTTER

Stir together ¹/₂ cup *butter or margarine,* softened; 2 tablespoons grated *Parmesan cheese;* and 2 teaspoons sliced *green onion.* Makes ¹/₂ cup.

HERB BUTTER

Stir together ¹/₂ cup *butter or margarine,* softened; and ¹/₂ teaspoon each *dried thyme and marjoram,* crushed, or 1 teaspoon *dried basil,* crushed. Makes ¹/₂ cup.

PIMIENTO BUTTER

In a blender container or food processor bowl, combine one 4 ounce jar *sliced pimientos,* drained; 1 tablespoon *anchovy paste;* and 1 clove *garlic,* minced. Cover and blend or process till pimientos are pureed and mixture is smooth. Stir pimiento mixture into ¹/₂ cup *butter or margarine,* softened. Makes about 1 cup.

NUT BREAD

   3 cups all-purpose flour
   1 cup sugar
   1 tablespoon baking powder
   $^1/_2$ teaspoon salt
   $^1/_4$ teaspoon baking soda
   1 beaten egg
   1$^2/_3$ cups milk
   $^1/_4$ cup cooking oil
   $^3/_4$ cup chopped almonds, pecans, or walnuts

1. Grease the bottom and $^1/_2$ inch up the sides of a 9×5×3-inch loaf pan; set aside. In a large mixing bowl stir together flour, sugar, baking powder, salt, and baking soda. Make a well in center; set aside.
2. In a medium mixing bowl combine the egg, milk, and cooking

---

PICK A PAN FOR QUICK BREADS

Sometimes a single large loaf of quick bread is just what you need. Other times, you may want several small loaves to give as gifts or to sell at bazaars. If the pan size given in our recipe doesn't fit your needs, use this chart to convert the recipe to the size desired. Fill your pans about two-thirds full. If you have batter remaining, use it to make muffins. Remember, the baking times in this chart are approximate and may vary with the recipe.

Pan Size	Baking Time
One 9×5×3-inch loaf pan	1 to 1$^1/_4$ hours
One 8×4×2-inch loaf pan	50 to 60 minutes
Two 7$^1/_2$×3$^1/_2$×2-inch loaf pans	40 to 45 minutes
Six 4$^1/_2$×2$^1/_2$×1$^1/_2$-inch loaf pans	30 to 35 minutes
Twelve 2$^1/_2$-inch muffin cups	15 to 20 minutes

oil. Add egg mixture all at once to dry mixture. Stir just till moistened (batter should be lumpy). Fold in nuts.

3. Spoon batter into the prepared pan. Bake in a 350° oven for 1 to 1¼ hours or till a wooden toothpick inserted near center comes out clean. Cool in pan on a wire rack for 10 minutes. Remove loaf from pan. Cool completely on the wire rack. Wrap and store overnight before slicing. Makes 1 loaf (18 servings).

Nutrition Facts per serving: 187 cal., 7 g total fat (1 g sat. fat), 14 mg chol., 153 mg sodium, 28 g carbo., 1 g fiber, 4 g pro. **Daily Values:** 1% vit. A, 0% vit. C, 7% calcium, 7% iron

■ **Cranberry Nut Bread:** Prepare as above, except add 2 teaspoons finely shredded *orange peel* to the dry mixture. Fold 1 cup coarsely chopped *cranberries* into batter along with nuts.

Nutrition Facts per serving: 191 cal., 7 g total fat (1 g sat. fat)

■ **Blueberry Nut Bread:** Prepare as above, except add 1 teaspoon finely shredded *lemon peel* to dry mixture. Fold 1 cup fresh or frozen *blueberries* into batter along with the nuts.

Nutrition Facts per serving: 192 cal., 7 g total fat (1 g sat. fat)

PUMPKIN BREAD

PREP: 15 MINUTES   BAKE: 1 HOUR   Oven 350°

    1 cup all-purpose flour
    1 cup packed brown sugar
    1 tablespoon baking powder
    1 teaspoon ground cinnamon
 ¼ teaspoon salt
 ¼ teaspoon baking soda
 ¼ teaspoon ground nutmeg
 ⅛ teaspoon ground ginger or ground cloves
    1 cup canned pumpkin
 ½ cup milk
    2 eggs
 ⅓ cup shortening
    1 cup all-purpose flour
 ½ cup chopped walnuts
 ½ cup raisins

1. Grease the bottom and $^1/_2$ inch up the sides of a 9×5×3-inch loaf pan; set aside.

2. In a large mixing bowl combine 1 cup flour, the brown sugar, baking powder, cinnamon, salt, baking soda, nutmeg, and ginger or cloves. Add pumpkin, milk, eggs, and shortening. Beat with an electric mixer on low speed till blended. Beat on medium to high speed for 2 minutes. Add the 1 cup flour; beat till blended. Fold in the walnuts and raisins.

3. Spoon batter into prepared pan. Bake in a 350° oven 60 to 65 minutes or till a wooden toothpick inserted near the center comes out clean. Cool in pan on a wire rack for 10 minutes. Remove loaf from pan. Cool completely on a wire rack. Wrap and store overnight. Makes 1 loaf (18 servings).

Nutrition Facts per serving: 189 cal., 8 g total fat (2 g sat. fat), 27 mg chol., 138 mg sodium, 28 g carbo., 1 g fiber, 3 g pro. **Daily Values:** 35% vit. A, 1% vit. C, 8% calcium, 10% iron

---

LEMON BREAD

PREP: 15 MINUTES   BAKE: 50 MINUTES   Oven 350°

If you're squeezing a fresh lemon for juice, remember to shred the lemon peel first.

$1^3/_4$ cups all-purpose flour
$^3/_4$ cup sugar
2 teaspoons baking powder
$^1/_4$ teaspoon salt
1 beaten egg
1 cup milk
$^1/_4$ cup cooking oil
2 teaspoons finely shredded lemon peel (set aside)
1 tablespoon lemon juice
$^1/_2$ cup chopped almonds or walnuts
2 tablespoons lemon juice
1 tablespoon sugar

1. Grease the bottom and $^1/_2$ inch up the sides of an 8×4×2-inch loaf pan; set aside.

2. In a medium mixing bowl stir together the flour, the $^3/_4$ cup sugar, baking powder, and salt. Make a well in the center of the dry mixture; set aside.

3. In another medium mixing bowl combine the egg, milk, cooking oil, and the 1 tablespoon lemon juice. Add egg mixture all at once to the dry mixture. Stir just till moistened (batter should be lumpy). Fold in the almonds or walnuts and lemon peel.

4. Spoon batter into the prepared pan. Bake in a 350° oven for 50 to 55 minutes or till a wooden toothpick inserted near center comes out clean. Meanwhile, stir together the 2 tablespoons lemon juice and the 1 tablespoon sugar. While bread is still in the pan, brush lemon-sugar mixture over the top of the loaf. Cool in pan on a wire rack for 10 minutes. Remove loaf from pan; cool on the wire rack. Wrap and store overnight before serving. Makes 1 loaf (16 servings).

Nutrition Facts per serving: 153 cal., 6 g total fat (1 g sat. fat), 14 mg chol., 91 mg sodium, 22 g carbo., 0 g fiber, 3 g pro. **Daily Values:** 1% vit. A, 3% vit. C, 5% calcium, 5% iron

---

RAISIN-CARROT BREAD

PREP: 20 MINUTES   BAKE: 55 MINUTES   Oven 350°

$^3/_4$ **cup raisins**
$^1/_4$ **cup rum or orange juice**
1$^1/_2$ **cups all-purpose flour**
$^3/_4$ **cup sugar**
  2 **teaspoons baking powder**
  1 **teaspoon ground cinnamon**
$^1/_2$ **teaspoon salt**
$^1/_4$ **teaspoon ground allspice**
  1 **beaten egg**
  1 **cup finely shredded carrots (about 3 large)**
$^1/_4$ **cup cooking oil**
$^3/_4$ **cup chopped walnuts**

1. Grease the bottom and $^1/_2$ inch up the sides of an 8×4×2-inch loaf pan; set aside. In a small mixing bowl stir together the raisins and rum or orange juice; set aside.

2. In a medium mixing bowl stir together flour, sugar, baking powder, cinnamon, salt, and allspice. Make a well in center of dry mixture; set aside.

3. In another medium mixing bowl combine egg, carrots, and cooking oil. Stir in raisin mixture. Add egg mixture all at once to the dry mixture. Stir just till moistened (batter should be lumpy). Fold in the walnuts.

4. Spoon the batter into the prepared pan. Bake in a 350° oven for 55 to 60 minutes or till a wooden toothpick inserted near center comes out clean. Cool on a wire rack 10 minutes. Remove from pan. Cool completely on the rack. Wrap; store overnight before serving. Makes 1 loaf (16 servings).

Nutrition Facts per serving: 179 cal., 7 g total fat (1 g sat. fat), 13 mg chol., 120 mg sodium, 25 g carbo., 1 g fiber, 3 g pro. **Daily Values:** 20% vit. A, 1% vit. C, 4% calcium, 6% iron

---

CORN BREAD

PREP: 15 MINUTES   BAKE: 20 MINUTES   Oven 425°

Decide how much sugar to use according to how sweet you like your corn bread.

  1 **cup all-purpose flour**
  1 **cup cornmeal**
  2 **to 4 tablespoons sugar**
  1 **tablespoon baking powder**
$^1/_2$ **teaspoon salt**
  2 **beaten eggs**
  1 **cup milk**
$^1/_4$ **cup cooking oil or shortening, melted**

1. Grease the bottom and $^1/_2$ inch up the sides of a 9×9×2-inch baking pan; set aside.
2. In a medium mixing bowl stir together the flour, cornmeal, sugar, baking powder, and salt. Make a well in the center of the dry mixture; set aside.
3. In another bowl combine the eggs, milk, and cooking oil or melted shortening. Add egg mixture all at once to dry mixture. Stir just till moistened.
4. Spoon batter into the prepared pan. Bake in a 425° oven for 20 to 25 minutes or till a wooden toothpick inserted near the center comes out clean. Cool on a wire rack. Makes 8 or 9 servings.

Nutrition Facts per serving: 222 cal., 9 g total fat (2 g sat. fat), 56 mg chol., 301 mg sodium, 29 g carbo., 1 g fiber, 6 g pro. **Daily Values:** 4% vit. A, 0% vit. C, 14% calcium, 11% iron

■ **Double Corn Bread:** Prepare as at left, except stir one 12-ounce can *whole kernel corn with sweet peppers,* drained, into the batter.

Nutrition Facts per serving: 254 cal., 9 g total fat (2 g sat. fat)

■ **Green Chili Corn Bread:** Prepare as at left, except fold 1 cup shredded *cheddar or Monterey Jack cheese* and one 4-ounce can *diced green chili peppers,* drained, into the batter.

Nutrition Facts per serving: 283 cal., 14 g total fat (5 g sat. fat)

■ **Confetti Corn Bread:** Prepare as at left, except stir ¹/₂ cup shredded *cheddar cheese,* ¹/₄ cup finely shredded *carrot,* and ¹/₄ cup finely shredded *zucchini* into the batter.

Nutrition Facts per serving: 282 cal., 14 g total fat (5 g sat. fat)

■ **Corn Sticks or Corn Muffins:** Prepare as at left, except spoon batter into greased corn stick pans or muffin pans, filling pans ²/₃ full. Bake in a 425° oven for 12 to 15 minutes or till brown. Makes 24 to 26 sticks or 12 muffins.

Nutrition Facts per corn stick: 74 cal., 3 g total fat (1 g sat. fat)

No Ledges on the Edges

Are there rims around the edges of your nut breads and muffins instead of more evenly rounded tops? There's a simple remedy to this problem: Grease the baking pans or muffin cups on the bottom and only ¹/₂ inch up the sides. This will let the batter cling to the sides of the pan or muffin cup instead of sliding down during baking.

CHEESE AND BEER BREAD

PREP: 15 MINUTES   BAKE: 35 MINUTES   Oven 375°

Low-Fat

A blend of savory flavors makes this a perfect bread to serve with a bowl of soup or a salad.

2¹/₂ cups all-purpose flour
  2 tablespoons sugar
2¹/₂ teaspoons baking powder
  1 teaspoon dried oregano, crushed
¹/₂ teaspoon baking soda
¹/₂ teaspoon salt
¹/₂ teaspoon dried basil or marjoram, crushed
  1 12-ounce can (1¹/₂ cups) beer
  1 cup shredded cheddar cheese (4 ounces)
  1 tablespoon chopped, seeded fresh jalapeño pepper (optional)
    (see tip, page 111)

1. Grease the bottom and ¹/₂ inch up the sides of an 8×4×2-inch or a 9×5×3-inch loaf pan; set aside.
2. In a large mixing bowl stir together the flour, sugar, baking powder, oregano, baking soda, salt, and basil or marjoram. Add the beer, cheddar cheese, and, if desired, jalapeño pepper. Stir just till combined (batter should be lumpy).
3. Spoon batter into the prepared pan. Bake in a 375° oven for 35 to 40 minutes or till golden. Cool in pan on a wire rack for 10 minutes. Remove from pan. Serve warm, or cool completely on rack. Makes 1 loaf (16 to 18 servings).

Nutrition Facts per serving: 109 cal., 3 g total fat (2 g sat. fat), 7 mg chol., 208 mg sodium, 16 g carbo., 1 g fiber, 4 g pro. **Daily Values:** 2% vit. A, 0% vit. C, 9% calcium, 6% iron

CHEDDAR SPOON BREAD

PREP: 25 MINUTES   BAKE: 45 MINUTES   Oven 325°

For a punch of pepper, use Monterey Jack cheese with jalapeño peppers.

  1¹/₂ **cups milk**
    ¹/₂ **cup cornmeal**
      2 **cups shredded cheddar cheese or Monterey Jack cheese (8 ounces)**
      1 **tablespoon butter or margarine**
  1¹/₂ **teaspoons baking powder**
      1 **teaspoon sugar**
      4 **eggs**

1. In a large saucepan stir together the milk and cornmeal. Cook, stirring constantly, over medium-high heat till mixture is thickened and bubbly; remove from heat. Add cheese, butter or margarine, baking powder, sugar, and ¹/₄ teaspoon *salt*. Stir till cheese melts.
2. Separate eggs. Add yolks, one at a time, to cornmeal mixture, stirring after each addition just till combined (mixture will be thick).
3. In a large mixing bowl beat egg whites with an electric mixer on high speed till stiff peaks form (tips stand straight). Stir about one-third of the beaten egg whites into the cornmeal mixture. Gently fold remaining beaten egg whites into cornmeal mixture till combined. Spoon mixture into an ungreased 2-quart casserole or soufflé dish.
4. Bake in a 325° oven for 45 to 50 minutes or till a knife inserted near the center comes out clean. Serve immediately. Makes 8 servings.

Nutrition Facts per serving: 235 cal., 16 g total fat (9 g sat. fat), 147 mg chol., 404 mg sodium, 10 g carbo., 0 g fiber, 13 g pro. **Daily Values:** 19% vit. A, 0% vit. C, 30% calcium, 6% iron

MUFFINS

Fast

1¾ cups all-purpose flour
⅓ cup sugar
2 teaspoons baking powder
¼ teaspoon salt
1 beaten egg
¾ cup milk
¼ cup cooking oil

1. Grease twelve 2½-inch muffin cups or line with paper bake cups; set aside. In a medium mixing bowl combine flour, sugar, baking powder, and salt. Make a well in center of dry mixture; set aside.
2. In another mixing bowl combine egg, milk, and oil. Add egg mixture all at once to the dry mixture. Stir just till moistened (batter should be lumpy).
3. Spoon batter into prepared muffin cups, filling each ⅔ full. Bake in a 400° oven 20 minutes or till golden. Cool in muffin cups on a wire rack for 5 minutes. Remove from muffin cups; serve warm. Makes 10 to 12 muffins.

Nutrition Facts per muffin: 164 cal., 6 g total fat (1 g sat. fat), 23 mg chol., 142 mg sodium, 23 g carbo., 1 g fiber, 3 g pro. **Daily Values:** 2% vit. A, 0% vit. C, 7% calcium, 7% iron

■ **Banana Muffins:** Prepare muffins as above, except do not use paper bake cups. Reduce milk to ½ cup. Add ¾ cup mashed *banana* and ½ cup chopped *nuts* to the dry mixture with the egg mixture.

Nutrition Facts per muffin: 221 cal., 10 g total fat (2 g sat. fat)

■ **Blueberry Muffins:** Prepare muffins as above, except fold ¾

MINI TO JUMBO MUFFINS

Muffin cups are available in all shapes and sizes, including mini, regular, and jumbo. Adjust the baking time according to the pan you choose—mini muffins will bake about 8 minutes less than regular-size (2½-inch) muffins, and mega muffins will bake about 10 minutes more than regular-size muffins.

cup fresh or frozen *blueberries* and, if desired, 1 teaspoon finely shredded *lemon peel* into batter.

Nutrition Facts per muffin: 170 cal., 7 g total fat (1 g sat. fat)

■ **Cheese Muffins:** Prepare muffins as at left, except stir ¹/₂ cup shredded *cheddar or Monterey Jack cheese* (2 ounces) into dry mixture.

Nutrition Facts per muffin: 187 cal., 8 g total fat (2 g sat. fat)

■ **Cranberry Muffins:** Prepare muffins as at left, except combine 1 cup coarsely chopped *cranberries* and 2 tablespoons additional *sugar*. Fold into batter.

Nutrition Facts per muffin: 179 cal., 7 g total fat (1 g sat. fat)

■ **Oatmeal Muffins:** Prepare muffins as at left, except reduce flour to 1¹/₃ cups and add ³/₄ cup *rolled oats* to dry mixture.

Nutrition Facts per muffin: 170 cal., 7 g total fat (1 g sat. fat)

■ **Poppy Seed Muffins:** Prepare muffins as at left, except increase sugar to ¹/₂ cup and add 1 tablespoon *poppy seed* to dry mixture.

Nutrition Facts per muffin: 182 cal., 7 g total fat (1 g sat. fat)

ORANGE-YOGURT MUFFINS

PREP: 15 MINUTES   BAKE: 18 MINUTES   Oven 400°

    1³/₄ cups all-purpose flour
     ¹/₂ cup sugar
       2 teaspoons finely shredded orange peel
       1 teaspoon baking powder
     ¹/₂ teaspoon baking soda
     ¹/₄ teaspoon salt
       1 beaten egg
       1 8-ounce carton orange yogurt
     ¹/₃ cup cooking oil
       1 teaspoon vanilla
     ¹/₂ cup sifted powdered sugar
       1 to 2 teaspoons orange juice

1. Grease twelve 2½-inch muffin cups or line with paper bake cups; set aside. In a medium mixing bowl combine flour, sugar, orange peel, baking powder, baking soda, and salt. Make a well in the center of the dry mixture; set aside.

2. In another bowl combine egg, yogurt, oil, and vanilla. Add egg mixture all at once to the dry mixture. Stir just till moistened (batter should be lumpy).

3. Spoon batter into the prepared muffin cups, filling each ²⁄₃ full. Bake in a 400° oven for 18 to 20 minutes or till golden. Cool in muffin cups on a wire rack for 5 minutes. Remove muffins from muffin cups.

4. Meanwhile, stir together powdered sugar and enough orange juice to make a glaze that is easy to drizzle. Drizzle over warm muffins; serve warm. Makes 12 muffins.

■ **Lemon-Yogurt Muffins:** Prepare muffins as above, except substitute *lemon peel* for orange peel and *lemon yogurt* for orange yogurt.

Nutrition Facts per muffin: 191 cal., 7 g total fat (1 g sat. fat), 19 mg chol., 144 mg sodium, 29 g carbo., 1 g fiber, 3 g pro. **Daily Values:** 1% vit. A, 2% vit. C, 5% calcium, 6% iron

---

COFFEE CAKE MUFFINS

PREP: 20 MINUTES   BAKE: 15 MINUTES   Oven 400°

A rich ribbon of streusel fills the centers and decorates the tops of these muffins.

    3 tablespoons all-purpose flour
    3 tablespoons brown sugar
 ¼ teaspoon ground cinnamon
    2 tablespoons butter or margarine
    3 tablespoons chopped walnuts or pecans
1½ cups all-purpose flour
 ½ cup granulated sugar
1¼ teaspoons baking powder
 ½ teaspoon ground cinnamon
 ¼ teaspoon ground ginger
 ¼ teaspoon baking soda
 ¼ teaspoon salt
 ¼ cup butter or margarine
    1 beaten egg
 ½ cup buttermilk or sour milk (see tip, page 261)

1. Grease twelve 2¹/₂-inch muffin cups or line with paper bake cups; set aside.

2. For the topping, in a small mixing bowl stir together the 3 tablespoons flour, brown sugar, and the ¹/₄ teaspoon cinnamon. Cut in the 2 tablespoons butter or margarine till mixture resembles coarse crumbs. Stir in walnuts or pecans; set aside.

3. In a medium mixing bowl stir together the 1¹/₂ cups flour, granulated sugar, baking powder, the ¹/₂ teaspoon cinnamon, ginger, baking soda, and salt. Cut in the ¹/₄ cup butter or margarine till mixture resembles coarse crumbs.

4. In another medium mixing bowl combine the egg and buttermilk or sour milk. Add egg mixture all at once to the dry mixture. Stir just till moistened (batter should be lumpy).

5. Spoon half of the batter into the prepared muffin cups, filling each ¹/₃ full. Top with half of the topping, the remaining batter, and the remaining topping. Bake in a 400° oven for 15 to 18 minutes or till golden. Cool in muffin cups on a wire rack for 5 minutes. Remove muffins from muffin cups; serve warm. Makes 12 muffins.

Nutrition Facts per muffin: 177 cal., 8 g total fat (4 g sat. fat), 34 mg chol., 183 mg sodium, 25 g carbo., 1 g fiber, 3 g pro. **Daily Values:** 6% vit. A, 0% vit. C, 5% calcium, 7% iron

WHEAT BRAN MUFFINS

PREP: 10 MINUTES   BAKE: 20 MINUTES   Oven 400°

Fast   **Low-Fat**

1¹/₄ cups wheat bran or oat bran*
1 cup all-purpose flour
2 teaspoons baking powder
¹/₄ teaspoon baking soda
³/₄ cup applesauce
¹/₂ cup skim milk
¹/₃ cup honey
¹/₄ cup refrigerated egg product or frozen egg product, thawed
1 tablespoon cooking oil
¹/₂ cup raisins, snipped dried apricots, or snipped dried apples

1. Spray bottoms of twelve 2¹/₂-inch muffin cups with *nonstick spray coating;* set aside. In a mixing bowl combine wheat or oat bran, flour, baking powder, baking soda, and ¹/₄ teaspoon *salt.* Make a well in the center of the dry mixture; set aside.

2. In another bowl combine applesauce, milk, honey, egg product, and oil. Add applesauce mixture all at once to dry mixture. Stir just till moistened (batter should be lumpy). Fold in raisins.

3. Spoon batter into prepared cups, filling each $2/3$ full. Bake in a 400° oven about 20 minutes or till golden. Cool on a wire rack for 5 minutes. Remove from cups; serve warm. Makes 12 muffins.

*Note: Use 100% oat bran with no added ingredients. If oat bran isn't available, place $1^1/3$ cups *rolled oats* in a food processor bowl or blender container; process till oats are the consistency of flour. (You should have about 1 cup.)

TOASTING NUTS, SEEDS, AND COCONUT

Toasting heightens the flavor of nuts, seeds, and coconut. To toast, spread the food in a single layer in a shallow baking pan. Bake in a 350° oven for 5 to 10 minutes or till light golden brown, watching carefully and stirring once or twice so food doesn't burn.

Nutrition Facts per muffin: 126 cal., 2 g total fat (0 g sat. fat), 0 mg chol., 148 mg sodium, 28 g carbo., 2 g fiber, 4 g pro. **Daily Values:** 1% vit. A, 0% vit. C, 6% calcium, 10% iron

---

BACON-CORN MUFFINS

PREP: 20 MINUTES   BAKE: 18 MINUTES   Oven 400°

$1^1/2$ **cups all-purpose flour**
 $1/2$ **cup cornmeal**
   2 **tablespoons sugar**
   2 **teaspoons baking powder**
 $1/4$ **teaspoon baking soda**
   1 **beaten egg**
   1 **cup buttermilk or sour milk (see tip, page 261)**
 $1/3$ **cup cooking oil**
   5 **slices bacon, crisp-cooked, drained, and crumbled (about $1/4$ cup)**

1. Grease twelve $2^1/2$-inch muffin cups or line with paper bake cups; set aside. In a mixing bowl combine flour, cornmeal, sugar, baking powder, baking soda, and $\frac{1}{4}$ teaspoon *salt*. Make a well in the center of dry mixture; set aside.

2. In another bowl combine egg, buttermilk, and oil; add all at once to dry mixture. Stir just till moistened (batter should be lumpy). Fold in bacon.

3. Spoon batter into the prepared muffin cups, filling each $\frac{2}{3}$ full. Bake in a 400° oven 18 to 20 minutes or till golden. Cool on a wire rack for 5 minutes. Remove from muffin cups. Serve warm. Makes 12.

Nutrition Facts per muffin: 164 cal., 8 g total fat (2 g sat. fat), 21 mg chol., 199 mg sodium, 19 g carbo., 1 g fiber, 4 g pro. **Daily Values:** 1% vit. A, 1% vit. C, 7% calcium, and 7% iron

---

CHEDDAR-APPLE MUFFINS

PREP: 15 MINUTES   BAKE: 18 MINUTES   Oven 400°

$1\frac{1}{2}$ cups all-purpose flour
 $\frac{1}{2}$ cup finely shredded cheddar cheese (2 ounces)
 $\frac{1}{3}$ cup quick-cooking rolled oats
   2 tablespoons sugar
$2\frac{1}{2}$ teaspoons baking powder
 $\frac{1}{4}$ teaspoon salt
   1 beaten egg
 $\frac{3}{4}$ cup milk
 $\frac{1}{3}$ cup cooking oil
 $\frac{3}{4}$ cup finely chopped, peeled cooking apple (1 small)

1. Grease twelve $2\frac{1}{2}$-inch muffin cups; set aside. In a medium mixing bowl combine the flour, cheese, rolled oats, sugar, baking powder, and salt. Make a well in the center of the dry mixture; set aside.

2. In another medium mixing bowl combine the egg, milk, and cooking oil. Add egg mixture all at once to the dry mixture. Stir just till moistened (batter should be lumpy). Fold in apple.

3. Spoon batter into the prepared muffin cups, filling each $\frac{2}{3}$ full. Bake in a 400° oven 18 to 20 minutes or till golden. Cool in muffin cups on a wire rack for 5 minutes. Remove from muffin cups; serve warm. Makes 12 muffins.

Nutrition Facts per muffin: 162 cal., 9 g total fat (2 g sat. fat), 24 mg chol., 162 mg sodium, 17 g carbo., 1 g fiber, 4 g pro. **Daily Values:** 3% vit. A, 0% vit. C, 10% calcium, 6% iron

SCONES

PREP: 15 MINUTES BAKE: 12 MINUTES Oven 400°

Fast

       2 **cups all-purpose flour**
       3 **tablespoons sugar**
       1 **tablespoon baking powder**
       6 **tablespoons chilled butter**
    ¹/₄ **cup chopped nuts, toasted (see tip, page 234) (optional)**
       1 **beaten egg**
    ¹/₂ **cup half-and-half or light cream**
       1 **tablespoon half-and-half or light cream**
       2 **teaspoons sugar**

1. Combine flour, the 3 tablespoons sugar, baking powder, and ¹/₄ teaspoon *salt*. Cut in butter. If desired, stir in nuts. Combine egg and ¹/₂ cup half-and-half; add to dry mixture. Stir just till moistened.

2. Turn dough onto a floured surface. Knead 12 to 15 strokes or till nearly smooth. Pat or lightly roll to ¹/₂-inch thickness. Cut with a 2¹/₂- to 3-inch cutter.

3. Place scones 1 inch apart on an ungreased baking sheet. Brush tops with 1 tablespoon half-and-half; sprinkle with 2 teaspoons sugar. Bake in a 400° oven for 12 to 15 minutes or till golden. Remove from baking sheet and cool on a wire rack for 5 minutes; serve warm. Makes 10 to 12 scones.

Nutrition Facts per scone: 187 cal., 9 g total fat (5 g sat. fat), 45 mg chol., 244 mg sodium, 23 g carbo., 1 g fiber, 3 g pro. **Daily Values:** 9% vit. A, 0% vit. C, 10% calcium, 8% iron

■ **Dried Cherry Scones:** Prepare as above, except reduce the ¹/₂ cup half-and-half to ¹/₃ cup. Soak ¹/₂ cup *dried tart red cherries or mixed dried fruit bits* in 2 tablespoons *cherry brandy or apricot nectar* for 15 minutes. Do not drain. Add fruit mixture with egg mixture to dry ingredients.

Nutrition Facts per scone: 209 cal., 9 g total fat (5 g sat. fat)

236 B r e a d s

BUTTERMILK-CURRANT SCONES

PREP: 15 MINUTES BAKE: 12 MINUTES   Oven 400°

Fast

    2 cups all-purpose flour
 ¹/₄ cup sugar
    2 teaspoons baking powder
    1 teaspoon finely shredded orange peel
 ¹/₄ teaspoon baking soda
 ¹/₃ cup butter or margarine
    1 beaten egg
 ¹/₂ cup buttermilk or sour milk (see tip, page 261)
 ¹/₄ cup currants or raisins
    2 teaspoons sugar
 ¹/₄ teaspoon finely shredded orange peel
    1 tablespoon buttermilk or milk

1. Stir together flour, the ¹/₄ cup sugar, baking powder, the 1 teaspoon orange peel, baking soda, and ¹/₄ teaspoon *salt*. Using a pastry blender, cut in butter or margarine till mixture resembles coarse crumbs. Make a well in the center of dry mixture; set aside.

2. In another bowl, combine egg, the ¹/₂ cup buttermilk, and currants. Add egg mixture all at once to dry mixture. Using a fork, stir just till moistened.

3. Turn dough out onto a lightly floured surface. Quickly knead dough for 10 to 12 strokes or till dough is nearly smooth. Pat dough into a 7-inch circle. Cut into 12 wedges. Place wedges 1 inch apart on an ungreased baking sheet.

4. Combine 2 teaspoons sugar and ¹/₄ teaspoon orange peel. Brush wedges with 1 tablespoon buttermilk and sprinkle with sugar mixture. Bake in a 400° oven about 12 minutes or till golden. Remove from baking sheet and cool on a wire rack for 5 minutes; serve warm. Makes 12 scones.

Nutrition Facts per scone: 155 cal., 6 g total fat (3 g sat. fat), 32 mg chol., 199 mg sodium, 23 g carbo., 1 g fiber, 3 g pro. **Daily Values:** 5% vit. A, 0% vit. C, 6% calcium, 7% iron

BAKING POWDER BISCUITS

Fast

    2 cups all-purpose flour
    1 tablespoon baking powder
  ¹/₄ to ¹/₂ teaspoon salt
  ¹/₃ cup shortening
  ³/₄ cup milk

1. In a medium mixing bowl stir together flour, baking powder, and salt. Using a pastry blender, cut in shortening till mixture resembles coarse crumbs. Make a well in the center of the dry mixture. Add the milk all at once. Using a fork, stir just till moistened.

2. Turn dough out onto a lightly floured surface. Quickly knead dough by gently folding and pressing dough 10 to 12 strokes or till nearly smooth. Pat or lightly roll dough to ¹/₂-inch thickness. Cut dough with a floured 2¹/₂-inch biscuit cutter.

3. Place biscuits 1 inch apart on an ungreased baking sheet. Bake in a 450° oven for 10 to 12 minutes or till golden. Remove biscuits from baking sheet and serve hot. Makes 10 biscuits.

Nutrition Facts per biscuit: 153 cal., 7 g total fat (2 g sat. fat), 1 mg chol., 225 mg sodium, 19 g carbo., 1 g fiber, 3 g pro. **Daily Values:** 1% vit. A, 0% vit. C, 10% calcium, 8% iron

■ **Drop Biscuits:** Prepare as above, except increase milk to 1 cup. Do not knead, roll, or cut dough. Drop dough onto greased baking sheet. Bake as directed. Makes 12 biscuits.

Nutrition Facts per biscuit: 130 cal., 6 g total fat (2 g sat. fat)

■ **Buttermilk Biscuits:** Prepare as above, except stir ¹/₄ teaspoon *baking soda* into dry mixture and substitute *buttermilk or sour milk* for the milk (see tip, page 261).

Nutrition Facts per biscuit: 152 cal., 7 g total fat (2 g sat. fat)

Biscuits Supreme

PREP: 20 MINUTES   BAKE: 10 MINUTES   Oven 450°

Fast

1. Stir together 2 cups *all-purpose flour*, 1 tablespoon *baking powder*, 2 teaspoons *sugar*, ½ teaspoon *cream of tartar*, and ¼ teaspoon *salt*. Cut in ½ cup *butter, margarine, or shortening* till mixture resembles coarse crumbs. Make a well in center. Add ⅔ cup *milk* all at once; stir till moistened.

2. Turn dough out onto a lightly floured surface. Quickly knead dough by gently folding and pressing dough 10 to 12 strokes or till nearly smooth. Pat or lightly roll dough to ½-inch thickness. Cut dough with a floured 2½-inch biscuit cutter.

3. Place biscuits 1 inch apart on an ungreased baking sheet. Bake in a 450° oven for 10 to 12 minutes or till golden. Remove biscuits from baking sheet and serve hot. Makes 10 biscuits.

Nutrition Facts per biscuit: 179 cal., 10 g total fat (3 g sat. fat), 13 mg chol., 255 mg sodium, 20 g carbo., 1 g fiber, 3 g pro. **Daily Values:** 1% vit. A, 0% vit. C, 10% calcium, 8% iron

Cinnamon Breakfast Biscuits

PREP: 25 MINUTES   BAKE: 10 MINUTES   Oven 400°

  1¾ cups all-purpose flour
  ¼ cup wheat bran
  2 tablespoons granulated sugar
  1 tablespoon baking powder
  ½ teaspoon ground cinnamon
  ¼ teaspoon salt
  ½ cup butter, margarine, or shortening
  ⅔ cup milk
  ½ cup mixed dried fruit bits
  ½ cup sifted powdered sugar
  2 to 3 teaspoons orange juice, milk, or water

1. Combine flour, bran, granulated sugar, baking powder, cinnamon, and salt. Cut in the butter. Make a well in the center of dry mixture. Add the milk and fruit bits; stir just till moistened.

2. Turn dough out onto a floured surface. Quickly knead dough 10

to 12 strokes or till nearly smooth. Pat or lightly roll dough to $\frac{1}{2}$-inch thickness. Cut dough with a floured $2\frac{1}{2}$-inch biscuit cutter.

3. Place biscuits 1 inch apart on an ungreased baking sheet. Bake in a 400° oven for 10 to 12 minutes or till golden. Remove biscuits from baking sheet and cool slightly on a wire rack.

4. Meanwhile, stir together powdered sugar and enough orange juice to make an icing that is easy to drizzle. Drizzle icing over biscuits; serve warm. Makes 12 biscuits.

Nutrition Facts per biscuit: 181 cal., 8 g total fat (2 g sat. fat), 11 mg chol., 216 mg sodium, 25 g carbo., 1 g fiber, 3 g pro. **Daily Values:** 9% vit. A, 1% vit. C, 9% calcium, 7% iron

---

HEART-HEALTHY APPLE COFFEE CAKE

PREP: 20 MINUTES   BAKE: 30 MINUTES   Oven 350°

Low-Fat

For the best results when baking with margarine, be sure you select a brand that contains at least 60% vegetable oil.

Nonstick spray coating
$\frac{2}{3}$ cup all-purpose flour
$\frac{1}{2}$ cup whole wheat flour
1 teaspoon baking soda
1 teaspoon ground cinnamon
$\frac{1}{4}$ teaspoon salt
$1\frac{1}{2}$ cups finely chopped, peeled apples (2 small)
$\frac{1}{4}$ cup frozen egg product, thawed
$\frac{3}{4}$ cup granulated sugar
$\frac{1}{4}$ cup chopped walnuts or pecans
$\frac{1}{4}$ cup applesauce
$\frac{1}{4}$ cup packed brown sugar
1 tablespoon all-purpose flour
1 tablespoon whole wheat flour
$\frac{1}{2}$ teaspoon ground cinnamon
1 tablespoon margarine
$\frac{1}{4}$ cup chopped walnuts or pecans

1. Spray a 9-inch round baking pan with nonstick coating; set aside. In a small bowl stir together the $\frac{2}{3}$ cup all-purpose flour, $\frac{1}{2}$ cup whole wheat flour, baking soda, 1 teaspoon cinnamon, and salt.

2. Combine the apples and egg product. Stir in the granulated sugar, ¼ cup nuts, and applesauce. Add dry mixture; stir. Pour batter into prepared pan.

3. For topping, stir together the brown sugar, the 1 tablespoon all-purpose flour, 1 tablespoon whole wheat flour, and ½ teaspoon cinnamon. Cut in the margarine. Stir in ¼ cup nuts. Sprinkle topping over batter in pan. Bake in a 350° oven for 30 to 35 minutes or till a wooden toothpick inserted near center comes out clean. Cool in pan 10 minutes. Remove from pan; serve warm. Makes 10 servings.

Nutrition Facts per serving: 202 cal., 5 g fat (1 g sat. fat), 0 mg chol., 207 mg sodium, 37 g carbo., 2 g fiber, 3 g pro. **Daily Values:** 2% vit. A, 2% vit. C, 1% calcium, 8% iron

---

FRUIT COFFEE CAKE

PREP: 30 MINUTES   BAKE: 40 MINUTES   Oven 350°

1½ **cups chopped, peeled apple, apricots, peaches, or pineapple;**
     or 1½ cups blueberries or red raspberries
 ¼ **cup water**
 ¼ **cup sugar**
  2 **tablespoons cornstarch**
1½ **cups all-purpose flour**
 ¾ **cup sugar**
 ½ **teaspoon baking powder**
 ¼ **teaspoon baking soda**
 ¼ **cup butter or margarine**
  1 **beaten egg**
 ½ **cup buttermilk or sour milk (see tip, page 261)**
 ½ **teaspoon vanilla**
 ¼ **cup all-purpose flour**
 ¼ **cup sugar**
  2 **tablespoons butter or margarine**

1. In a medium saucepan combine fruit and water. Bring to boiling; reduce heat. Simmer,* covered, 5 minutes or till fruit is tender. Combine the ¼ cup sugar and cornstarch; stir into fruit. Cook and stir over medium heat till mixture is thickened and bubbly. Cook and stir 2 minutes more; set aside.

2. In a mixing bowl combine the 1½ cups flour, ¾ cup sugar, baking powder, and baking soda. Cut in the ¼ cup butter till mixture resembles coarse crumbs. Make a well in the center of the dry mixture; set aside.

3. In another bowl combine egg, buttermilk, and vanilla. Add egg mixture all at once to dry mixture. Using a fork, stir just till moistened (batter should be lumpy). Spread half of the batter into an ungreased 8×8×2-inch baking pan. Spread fruit mixture over batter. Drop remaining batter in small mounds atop filling.

4. Stir together the $^{1}/_{4}$ cup flour and $^{1}/_{4}$ cup sugar. Cut in the 2 tablespoons butter till mixture resembles coarse crumbs. Sprinkle atop coffee cake. Bake in a 350° oven for 40 to 45 minutes or till golden. Serve warm. Makes 9 servings.

*Note: Do not simmer raspberries.

Nutrition Facts per serving: 268 cal., 9 g total fat (2 g sat. fat), 24 mg chol., 167 mg sodium, 45 g carbo., 1 g fiber, 4 g pro. **Daily Values:** 10% vit. A, 1% vit. C, 3% calcium, 8% iron

■ **Rhubarb-Strawberry Coffee Cake:** Prepare as above, except substitute $^{3}/_{4}$ cup fresh or frozen cut-up *rhubarb* and $^{3}/_{4}$ cup frozen *unsweetened whole strawberries* for fruit. Continue as directed.

Nutrition Facts per serving: 263 cal., 9 g total fat (2 g sat. fat)

BLUEBERRY BUCKLE

PREP: 20 MINUTES   BAKE: 50 MINUTES   Oven 350°

    2 cups all-purpose flour
 2$^{1}/_{2}$ teaspoons baking powder
  $^{1}/_{4}$ teaspoon salt
  $^{1}/_{2}$ cup shortening
  $^{3}/_{4}$ cup sugar
    1 egg
  $^{1}/_{2}$ cup milk
    2 cups fresh or frozen blueberries
  $^{1}/_{2}$ cup all-purpose flour
  $^{1}/_{2}$ cup sugar
  $^{1}/_{2}$ teaspoon ground cinnamon
  $^{1}/_{4}$ cup butter or margarine

1. Grease bottom and $^{1}/_{2}$ inch up sides of a 9×9×2-inch or 8×8×2-inch baking pan; set aside. Combine the 2 cups flour, baking powder, and salt.

2. In another mixing bowl beat shortening with an electric mixer on medium speed for 30 seconds. Add the $^{3}/_{4}$ cup sugar. Beat on medium to high speed till light and fluffy. Add egg; beat well. Add dry mixture and milk alternately to beaten egg mixture, beating till smooth after each addition.

3. Spoon batter into prepared pan. Sprinkle with blueberries. Combine the $^1/_2$ cup flour, $^1/_2$ cup sugar, and cinnamon. Cut in butter till mixture resembles coarse crumbs. Sprinkle over blueberries. Bake in a 350° oven for 50 to 60 minutes or till golden. Serve warm. Makes 9 servings.

Nutrition Facts per serving: 403 cal., 18 g total fat (6 g sat. fat), 38 mg chol., 228 mg sodium, 58 g carbo., 2 g fiber, 5 g pro. **Daily Values:** 6% vit. A, 7% vit. C, 10% calcium, 12% iron

■ **Raspberry Buckle:** Prepare as above, except substitute fresh or frozen *red raspberries* for the blueberries.

Nutrition Facts per serving: 398 cal., 18 g total fat (6 g sat. fat)

BUTTERMILK COFFEE CAKE

PREP: 20 MINUTES   BAKE: 35 MINUTES   Oven 350°

Back by popular demand, this breakfast treat was known as Cowboy Coffee Cake in previous editions of this cookbook.

   $2^1/_2$ **cups all-purpose flour**
   $1^1/_2$ **cups packed brown sugar**
   $^1/_2$ **teaspoon salt**
   $^2/_3$ **cup butter, margarine, or shortening**
    2 **teaspoons baking powder**
   $^1/_2$ **teaspoon baking soda**
   $^1/_2$ **teaspoon ground cinnamon**
   $^1/_2$ **teaspoon ground nutmeg**
    2 **beaten eggs**
   $1^1/_3$ **cups buttermilk or sour milk (see tip, page 261)**
   $^1/_2$ **cup chopped nuts**

1. Grease bottom and $^1/_2$ inch up sides of a 13x9x2-inch baking pan; set aside. Combine flour, brown sugar, and salt. Cut in butter till mixture resembles coarse crumbs; set aside $^1/_2$ cup. Stir baking powder, baking soda, cinnamon, and nutmeg into remaining crumb mixture.

2. Combine eggs and buttermilk. Add egg mixture all at once to dry mixture; mix well. Spoon batter into prepared pan. Stir together reserved crumb mixture and nuts. Sprinkle atop batter. Bake in a 350° oven for 35 to 40 minutes or till a wooden toothpick inserted near the center comes out clean. Serve warm. Makes 18 servings.

Nutrition Facts per serving: 214 cal., 10 g total fat (2 g sat. fat), 33 mg chol., 228 mg sodium, 28 g carbo., 1 g fiber, 3 g pro. **Daily Values:** 7% vit. A, 0% vit. C, 6% calcium, 8% iron

CAKE DOUGHNUTS

PREP: 30 MINUTES   CHILL: 2 HOURS   FRY: 2 MINUTES PER BATCH

$3^1/_4$ cups all-purpose flour
  2 teaspoons baking powder
$^1/_2$ teaspoon ground cinnamon
$^1/_4$ teaspoon ground nutmeg
$^2/_3$ cup milk
$^1/_4$ cup butter or margarine, melted
  2 beaten eggs
$^2/_3$ cup sugar
  1 teaspoon vanilla
    Shortening or cooking oil for deep-fat frying
  1 recipe Chocolate Glaze (see page 265), granulated sugar, or
    powdered sugar (optional)

1. In a large mixing bowl combine $2^1/_4$ *cups* of the flour, baking powder, cinnamon, nutmeg, and $^1/_4$ teaspoon *salt*. In a medium mixing bowl combine milk and melted butter. In another large mixing bowl combine eggs, sugar, and vanilla; beat with an electric mixer till thick. Add dry mixture and milk mixture alternately to egg mixture, beating just till blended after each addition. Stir in remaining 1 cup flour. Cover dough; chill 2 hours.

2. Turn dough out onto a lightly floured surface. Roll dough to $^1/_2$-inch thickness. Cut dough with a floured $2^1/_2$-inch doughnut cutter, dipping cutter into flour between cuts. Reroll as necessary.

3. Fry 2 or 3 doughnuts at a time in deep hot fat (375°) about 1 minute on each side or till golden, turning once with a slotted spoon. Drain on paper towels. Repeat with remaining doughnuts and doughnut holes. If desired, drizzle warm doughnuts with Chocolate Glaze or shake warm doughnuts in a bag with granulated or powdered sugar. Cool on wire racks. Makes 13 to 15 doughnuts.

Nutrition Facts per doughnut: 288 cal., 15 g total fat (6 g sat. fat), 45 mg chol., 155 mg sodium, 33 g carbo., 1 g fiber, 4 g pro. **Daily Values:** 6% vit. A, 0% vit. C, 6% calcium, 10% iron

FRENCH TOAST

PREP: 10 MINUTES   COOK: 4 MINUTES PER SLICE

Fast

Use a nonstick skillet or griddle to limit the amount of fat required to cook the toast.

     2 beaten eggs
   $^1/_2$ cup milk
   $^1/_4$ teaspoon vanilla
   $^1/_8$ teaspoon ground cinnamon
     5 1-inch-thick slices French bread or 6 slices dry white bread
     1 tablespoon butter, margarine, or cooking oil
       Maple-flavored syrup (optional)

1. In a shallow bowl beat together eggs, milk, vanilla, and cinnamon. Dip bread into egg mixture, coating both sides (if using French bread, let soak in egg mixture about 30 seconds on each side).
2. In a skillet or on a griddle cook bread in hot butter over medium heat for 2 to 3 minutes on each side or till golden brown. Add more butter, if needed. Serve warm. If desired, serve with maple-flavored syrup. Makes 5 or 6 slices.

Nutrition Facts per slice: 133 cal., 6 g total fat (2 g sat. fat), 90 mg chol., 210 mg sodium, 15 g carbo., 0 g fiber, 6 g pro. **Daily Values:** 7% vit. A, 0% vit. C, 5% calcium, 6% iron

PANCAKES

PREP: 10 MINUTES   COOK: 4 MINUTES PER PANCAKE

Fast

Drizzle your favorite syrup or spoon fruit and whipped cream over these delicate pancakes.

1 cup all-purpose flour
1 tablespoon sugar
2 teaspoons baking powder
$^1/_4$ teaspoon salt
1 beaten egg
1 cup milk
2 tablespoons cooking oil

1. In a medium mixing bowl stir together the flour, sugar, baking powder, and salt. Make a well in the center of the dry mixture; set aside.
2. In another medium mixing bowl combine the egg, milk, and cooking oil. Add egg mixture all at once to the dry mixture. Stir just till moistened (batter should be lumpy).
3. For standard-size pancakes, pour about $^1/_4$ cup batter onto a hot, lightly greased griddle or heavy skillet. For dollar-size pancakes, pour about 1 tablespoon batter onto a hot, lightly greased griddle or heavy skillet. Cook over medium heat about 2 minutes on each side or till pancakes are golden brown, turning to second sides when pancakes have bubbly surfaces and edges are slightly dry. Serve warm. Makes 8 to 10 standard-size (4-inch) or 36 dollar-size (2-inch) pancakes (8 servings).

Nutrition Facts per 4-inch pancake: 114 cal., 5 g total fat (1 g sat. fat), 29 mg chol., 181 mg sodium, 14 g carbo., 0 g fiber, 3 g pro. **Daily Values:** 3% vit. A, 0% vit. C, 10% calcium, 6% iron

■ **Buckwheat Pancakes:** Prepare pancakes as above, except substitute $^1/_2$ cup *whole wheat flour* and $^1/_2$ cup *buckwheat flour* for the all-purpose flour; substitute *brown sugar* for the sugar.

Nutrition Facts per serving: 111 cal., 5 g total fat (1 g sat. fat)

■ **Buttermilk Pancakes:** Prepare pancakes as above, except reduce baking powder to 1 teaspoon and add $^1/_4$ teaspoon *baking soda* to dry mixture; substitute *buttermilk or sour milk* for the milk (see tip, page 261). Add additional buttermilk to thin batter, if necessary.

Nutrition Facts per serving: 111 cal., 4 g total fat (1 g sat. fat)

BLUEBERRY-BUTTERMILK PANCAKES

PREP: 10 MINUTES   COOK: 4 MINUTES PER PANCAKE

Fast

    1 cup all-purpose flour
    2 tablespoons cornmeal
    1 tablespoon sugar
    1 teaspoon baking powder
 $^1/_2$ teaspoon baking soda
 $^1/_4$ teaspoon ground cinnamon
    1 beaten egg
    1 cup buttermilk or sour milk (see tip, page 261)
    2 tablespoons cooking oil
    1 cup fresh or frozen blueberries
      Maple syrup, maple-flavored syrup, or powdered sugar
      (optional)

1. In a medium mixing bowl combine flour, cornmeal, sugar, baking powder, baking soda, $^1/_4$ teaspoon *salt*, and cinnamon. Make a well in center of dry mixture; set aside.

2. In another medium mixing bowl stir together the egg, buttermilk, and oil. Add egg mixture all at once to dry mixture. Stir just till moistened (batter should be lumpy). Gently fold in blueberries.

3. For each pancake, pour about $^1/_4$ cup of the batter onto a hot, lightly greased griddle or heavy skillet. Cook over medium heat about 2 minutes on each side or till pancakes are golden brown, turning to second sides when pancakes have bubbly surfaces and edges are slightly dry. Serve warm. If desired, pass syrup or powdered sugar. Makes 8 to 10 pancakes.

Nutrition Facts per pancake: 129 cal., 5 g total fat (1 g sat. fat), 28 mg chol., 232 mg sodium, 18 g carbo., 1 g fiber, 4 g pro. **Daily Values:** 1% vit. A, 4% vit. C, 7% calcium, 6% iron

PUFFED OVEN PANCAKE

PREP: 10 MINUTES   BAKE: 25 MINUTES   Oven 400°

   2 tablespoons butter or margarine
   3 eggs
  $^1/_2$ cup all-purpose flour
  $^1/_2$ cup milk
  $^1/_4$ teaspoon salt
   3 cups sliced fresh fruit (strawberries, nectarines, pears, or
      peeled peaches)
    Powdered sugar or whipped cream (optional)

1. Place butter in a 10-inch ovenproof skillet. Place in a 400° oven
for 3 to 5 minutes or till butter melts. In a medium mixing bowl use
a wire whisk or rotary beater to beat eggs till combined. Add flour,
milk, and salt. Beat till mixture is smooth. Immediately pour into the
hot skillet. Bake about 25 minutes or till puffed and well browned.
2. Top with fruit. If desired, sprinkle with powdered sugar or top
with whipped cream. Cut into wedges and serve warm. Makes 6
servings.

Nutrition Facts per serving: 139 cal., 7 g total fat (3 g sat. fat), 118 mg chol., 176 mg
sodium, 14 g carbo., 2 g fiber, 5 g pro. **Daily Values:** 10% vit. A, 70% vit. C, 4% calcium,
7% iron

WAFFLES

PREP: 10 MINUTES   BAKE: PER WAFFLE BAKER DIRECTIONS

Fast

*This batter works in a regular waffle baker as well as a Belgian
waffle baker.*

  $1^3/_4$ cups all-purpose flour
   1 tablespoon baking powder
  $^1/_4$ teaspoon salt
   2 egg yolks
  $1^3/_4$ cups milk
  $^1/_2$ cup cooking oil
   2 egg whites

1. In a medium mixing bowl stir together flour, baking powder, and salt. Make a well in the center of dry mixture; set aside.

2. In another medium mixing bowl beat egg yolks slightly. Stir in milk and oil. Add egg yolk mixture all at once to the dry mixture. Stir just till moistened (batter should be lumpy).

3. In a small mixing bowl beat egg whites till stiff peaks form (tips stand straight). Gently fold beaten egg whites into flour and egg yolk mixture, leaving a few fluffs of egg white. Do not overmix.

4. Pour 1 to 1¼ cups batter onto grids of a preheated, lightly greased waffle baker. Close lid quickly; do not open till done. Bake according to manufacturer's directions. When done, use a fork to lift waffle off grid. Repeat with remaining batter. Serve warm. Makes 12 to 16 (4-inch) waffles.

Nutrition Facts per waffle: 172 cal., 11 g total fat (2 g sat. fat), 38 mg chol., 164 mg sodium, 15 g carbo., 0 g fiber, 4 g pro. **Daily Values:** 7% vit. A, 0% vit. C, 11% calcium, 6% iron

■ **Easy Waffles:** Prepare as above, except do not separate eggs. In a mixing bowl beat whole eggs slightly. Beat in milk and oil. Add egg mixture all at once to dry mixture. Stir just till moistened (batter should be lumpy). Bake as directed.

Nutrition Facts per waffle: 172 cal., 11 g total fat (2 g sat. fat)

■ **Buttermilk Waffles:** Prepare as above, except reduce baking powder to 1 teaspoon and add ½ teaspoon *baking soda*. Substitute 2 cups *buttermilk or sour milk* for milk (see tip, page 261).

Nutrition Facts per waffle: 171 cal., 10 g total fat (2 g sat. fat)

OVERNIGHT WAFFLES

PREP: 10 MINUTES   CHILL: 10 HOURS   BAKE: PER WAFFLE BAKER DIRECTIONS

  2¼ cups all-purpose flour
    2 tablespoons sugar
    1 package active dry yeast
  ½ teaspoon salt
  ¼ teaspoon ground cinnamon
1¾ cups milk
    2 eggs
  ⅓ cup cooking oil

1. In a large mixing bowl stir together flour, sugar, yeast, salt, and cinnamon. Add the milk, eggs, and oil; beat till thoroughly combined. Cover loosely and refrigerate overnight.

2. Stir batter. Pour about ³⁄₄ cup batter into a preheated, lightly greased waffle baker. Close lid quickly; do not open till done. Bake according to manufacturer's directions. When done, use a fork to lift waffle off grid. Repeat with remaining batter. Serve warm. Makes about 16 (4-inch) waffles.

Nutrition Facts per waffle: 129 cal., 6 g total fat (1 g sat. fat), 29 mg chol., 88 mg sodium, 15 g carbo., 1 g fiber, 4 g pro. **Daily Values:** 28% vit. A, 0% vit. C, 3% calcium, 6% iron

■ **Overnight Cornmeal Waffles:** Prepare as above, except reduce flour to 1¹⁄₂ cups, add ³⁄₄ cup *cornmeal*, and omit cinnamon.

Nutrition Facts per waffle: 133 cal., 6 g total fat (1 g sat. fat)

POPOVERS

PREP: 10 MINUTES   BAKE: 40 MINUTES   Oven 400°

   1 tablespoon shortening or nonstick spray coating
   2 beaten eggs
   1 cup milk
   1 tablespoon cooking oil
   1 cup all-purpose flour

1. Using ¹⁄₂ teaspoon shortening for each cup, grease the bottoms and sides of six 6-ounce custard cups or cups of a popover pan. Or, spray cups with nonstick coating. Place the custard cups on a 15×10×1-inch baking pan; set aside.

2. In a mixing bowl use a wire whisk or rotary beater to beat eggs, milk, and oil till combined. Add flour and ¹⁄₄ teaspoon *salt*; beat till smooth.

3. Fill the prepared cups ¹⁄₂ full with batter. Bake in a 400° oven about 40 minutes or till very firm.

4. Immediately after removing from oven, prick each popover to let steam escape (see photo, below). Turn off the oven. For crisper popovers, return the popovers to oven for 5 to 10 minutes or till desired crispness is reached. Remove popovers from cups; serve immediately. Makes 6 popovers.

■ **Cinnamon Popovers:** Prepare as above, except add ¹/₂ teaspoon *ground cinnamon* with the flour. Continue as directed. If desired, serve with *honey* and *margarine or butter*.

Pierce each popover with a
fork to allow the steam to
escape. Steam helps
popovers rise during
baking, but it will make
them soggy if allowed to
remain inside.

CREPES

PREP: 5 MINUTES   COOK: 30 MINUTES

Low-Fat

  2 **beaten eggs**
1¹/₂ **cups milk**
  1 **cup all-purpose flour**
  1 **tablespoon cooking oil**

1. Combine eggs, milk, flour, oil, and ¹/₄ teaspoon *salt;* beat till well mixed. Heat a lightly greased 6-inch skillet; remove from heat. Spoon in 2 tablespoons batter; lift and tilt skillet to spread batter. Return to heat; brown on 1 side only. (Or, cook on a crepemaker according to manufacturer's directions.) Invert over paper towels; remove crepe. Repeat with remaining batter, greasing skillet occasionally. Makes 18 crepes.

■ **Dessert Crepes:** Prepare as above, except omit salt; add 2 tablespoons *sugar*.

HUSH PUPPIES

PREP: 10 MINUTES FRY: 3 MINUTES PER BATCH

Fast

For best results, fry just 5 or 6 at a time and allow the oil temperature to return to 375° before frying more.

 1 cup cornmeal
 ¼ cup all-purpose flour
 2 teaspoons sugar
 ¾ teaspoon baking powder
 ¼ teaspoon baking soda
 ¼ teaspoon salt
 1 beaten egg
 ½ cup buttermilk or sour milk (see tip, page 261)
 ¼ cup sliced green onion
    Shortening or cooking oil for deep-fat frying

1. Combine cornmeal, flour, sugar, baking powder, baking soda, and salt; make a well in the center of the dry mixture; set aside.
2. In another bowl, combine egg, buttermilk or sour milk, and green onion. Add egg mixture all at once to dry mixture. Stir mixture just till moistened (batter should be lumpy).
3. Drop batter by tablespoons into deep, hot fat (375°). Fry about 3 minutes or till golden, turning once. Drain on paper towels. Serve warm. Makes 14 to 18 hush puppies.

Nutrition Facts per hush puppy: 89 cal., 5 g total fat (1 g sat. fat), 16 mg chol., 94 mg sodium, 10 g carbo., 1 g fiber, 2 g pro. **Daily Values:** 1% vit. A, 0% vit. C, 2% calcium, 4% iron

CAKES

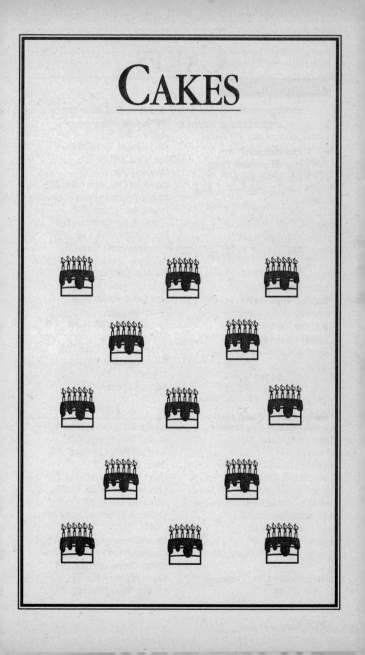

CAKES

CAKES

YELLOW CAKE

PREP: 20 MINUTES BAKE: 30 MINUTES COOL: 1 HOUR

Oven 375°

2^1/$_2$ cups all-purpose flour
2^1/$_2$ teaspoons baking powder
^{1}/$_2$ teaspoon salt
^{2}/$_3$ cup butter or margarine
1^3/$_4$ cups sugar
1^1/$_2$ teaspoons vanilla
2 eggs
1^1/$_4$ cups milk

1. Grease and lightly flour two 8×1^1/$_2$-inch or 9×1^1/$_2$-inch round baking pans or grease one 13×9×2-inch baking pan; set pan(s) aside. Combine flour, baking powder, and salt; set aside.

2. In a large mixing bowl beat butter or margarine with an electric mixer on medium to high speed for 30 seconds. Add sugar and vanilla; beat till well combined. Add eggs, one at a time, beating 1 minute after each. Add dry mixture and milk alternately to beaten mixture, beating on low speed after each addition just till combined. Pour batter into the prepared pan(s).

3. Bake in a 375° oven for 30 to 35 minutes or till a wooden toothpick comes out clean. Cool layer cakes in pans on wire racks for 10 minutes. Remove layer cakes from pans. Cool thoroughly on racks. Or, place 13×9-inch cake in pan on a wire rack; cool thoroughly. Frost with desired frosting. Serves 12.

Nutrition Facts per serving (cake only): 316 cal., 12 g total fat (7 g sat. fat), 65 mg chol., 292 mg sodium, 49 g carbo., 1 g fiber, 4 g pro. **Daily Values:** 12% vit. A, 0% vit. C, 9% calcium, 9% iron

■ **Citrus Yellow Cake:** Prepare as above, except stir 2 teaspoons finely shredded *orange peel or lemon peel* into batter.

Nutrition Facts per serving (cake only): 316 cal., 12 g total fat (7 g sat. fat)

■ **Yellow Cupcakes:** Grease and lightly flour thirty 2^1/$_2$-inch muffin cups or line with paper bake cups. Prepare cake as above. Fill each cup half full. Bake in a 375° oven for 18 to 20 minutes or till a wooden toothpick inserted in center of a cupcake comes out clean. Cool on a wire rack. Makes 30 cupcakes.

Nutrition Facts per cupcake: 127 cal., 5 g total fat (3 g sat. fat)

BEFORE YOU START

■ Use large eggs and allow them to stand at room temperature 30 minutes before using. If the eggs are to be separated, do so immediately after removing from the refrigerator.

■ Use butter or regular margarine (one that contains no less than 80% vegetable oil). Do not use whipped butter, diet or low-calorie spreads, or the soft spreadable margarines or butter blends that are sold in tubs.

■ Allow 10 minutes for your oven to preheat to the recommended baking temperature. During this time you can mix the ingredients.

■ Unless specified otherwise, grease and lightly flour baking pans for butter-type layer cakes that will be removed from their pans. Use a paper towel or pastry brush to evenly spread the shortening in the pan. Add a little flour, tilt the pan and tap it so the flour covers all the greased surfaces, then tap out the excess flour.

For butter-type cakes that will be left in their pans, grease only the bottom of the baking pan and do not coat it with flour.

Do not grease pans for angel, sponge, and chiffon cakes unless specified otherwise.

SPICE CAKE

PREP: 20 MINUTES BAKE: 35 MINUTES COOL: 1 HOUR   Oven 350°

The Browned Butter Frosting (see page 293) is a great choice for this often requested cake.

>   2 cups all-purpose flour
> 1¹/₂ teaspoons baking powder
>   ¹/₂ teaspoon baking soda
>   1 teaspoon ground cinnamon
>   ¹/₄ teaspoon ground nutmeg
>   ¹/₄ teaspoon ground cloves
>   ¹/₄ teaspoon ground ginger
>   ¹/₄ cup butter or margarine, softened
>   ¹/₄ cup shortening
> 1¹/₂ cups sugar
>   ¹/₂ teaspoon vanilla
>   2 eggs
> 1¹/₄ cups buttermilk or sour milk (see tip, page 261)

1. Grease a 13×9×2-inch baking pan or grease and lightly flour two 8×1¹/₂-inch round baking pans; set pan(s) aside. Stir together flour, baking powder, baking soda, cinnamon, nutmeg, cloves, and ginger; set aside.

2. In a large mixing bowl beat butter and shortening with an electric mixer on medium to high speed for 30 seconds. Add sugar and vanilla; beat till well combined. Add eggs, one at a time, beating well after each. Add dry mixture and buttermilk alternately to beaten mixture, beating on low speed after each addition just till combined. Pour into prepared pan(s).

3. Bake in a 350° oven for 35 to 40 minutes for 13x9-inch pan or 30 to 35 minutes for round pans or till a wooden toothpick comes out clean. Place 13x9-inch cake in pan on a wire rack; cool thoroughly. Or, cool layer cakes on wire racks for 10 minutes. Remove layer cakes from pans. Cool thoroughly on wire racks (see tip, page 285). Frost as desired. Makes 12 servings.

■ **Applesauce Spice Cake:** Prepare as above, except reduce buttermilk or sour milk to ¹/₄ cup and combine it with 1 cup *applesauce*. Add this mixture to cake alternately with dry ingredients.

■ **Pumpkin Spice Cake:** Prepare as above, except reduce buttermilk or sour milk to 1 cup and combine it with ½ cup *canned pumpkin*. Add this mixture to cake alternately with dry ingredients.

Nutrition Facts per serving (cake only): 263 cal., 9 g total fat (4 g sat. fat), 47 mg chol., 181 mg sodium, 41 g carbo., 1 g fiber, 4 g pro. **Daily Values:** 6% vit. A, 0% vit. C, 6% calcium, 7% iron

CHOCOLATE CAKE

PREP: 25 MINUTES   BAKE: 30 MINUTES   COOL: 1 HOUR   Oven 350°

Chocoholics will want to top this cake with Truffle Frosting (see page 288).

2¼ cups all-purpose flour
 1 teaspoon baking powder
¾ teaspoon baking soda
¼ teaspoon salt
⅔ cup butter or margarine
1¾ cups sugar
 2 eggs
 3 ounces unsweetened chocolate, melted and cooled
 1 teaspoon vanilla

1. Grease and lightly flour two 9×1½-inch round baking pans or grease one 13×9×2-inch baking pan; set pan(s) aside. Stir together flour, baking powder, baking soda, and salt; set aside.
2. In a large mixing bowl beat the butter or margarine with an electric mixer on medium to high speed for 30 seconds. Add sugar; beat till well combined. Add eggs, one at a time, beating well after each. Beat in chocolate and vanilla. Add dry mixture and 1¼ cups *water* alternately to beaten mixture, beating on low speed after each addition just till combined. Pour batter into the prepared pan(s).
3. Bake in a 350° oven for 30 to 35 minutes or till a wooden toothpick comes out clean. Cool layer cakes in pans on wire racks for 10 minutes. Remove layer cakes from pans. Cool thoroughly on racks (see tip, page 285). Or, place 13×9-inch cake in pan on a wire rack; cool thoroughly. Frost with desired frosting. Makes 12 servings.

Nutrition Facts per serving (cake only): 329 cal., 15 g total fat (8 g sat. fat), 63 mg chol., 269 mg sodium, 48 g carbo., 1 g fiber, 4 g pro. **Daily Values:** 11% vit. A, 0% vit. C, 3% calcium, 11% iron

■ **Chocolate Cupcakes:** Grease and lightly flour thirty 2½-inch muffin cups or line with paper bake cups. Prepare cake as above. Fill each cup half full. Bake in a 350° oven for 15 to 20 minutes or till a wooden toothpick inserted in center comes out clean. Cool on a wire rack. Makes 30 cupcakes.

Nutrition Facts per cupcake: 98 cal., 2 g total fat (1 g sat. fat)

DEVIL'S FOOD CAKE

PREP: 20 MINUTES   COOK: 35 MINUTES   COOL: 1 HOUR   Oven 350°

The reaction of the cocoa powder and baking soda gives devil's food cake its characteristic reddish brown color.

2¼ **cups all-purpose flour**
½ **cup unsweetened cocoa powder**
1½ **teaspoons baking soda**
¼ **teaspoon salt**
½ **cup shortening**
1¾ **cups sugar**
1 **teaspoon vanilla**
3 **eggs**
1⅓ **cups cold water**

1. Grease and lightly flour two 9×1½-inch round baking pans or grease one 13×9×2-inch baking pan; set pan(s) aside. Stir together flour, cocoa powder, baking soda, and salt; set aside.
2. In a large mixing bowl beat shortening with an electric mixer on medium to high speed for 30 seconds. Add sugar and vanilla; beat till well combined. Add eggs, one at a time, beating well after each. Add dry mixture and water alternately to beaten mixture, beating on low speed after each addition just till combined. Pour batter into the prepared pan(s).
3. Bake in a 350° oven for 35 to 40 minutes or till a wooden toothpick comes out clean. Cool layer cakes on wire racks for 10 minutes. Remove from pans. Cool thoroughly on wire racks (see tip, page 285). Or, place 13×9-inch cake in pan on a wire rack; cool thoroughly. Frost with desired frosting. Makes 12 servings.

Nutrition Facts per serving (cake only): 302 cal., 11 g total fat (3 g sat. fat), 53 mg chol., 219 mg sodium, 48 g carbo., 1 g fiber, 5 g pro. **Daily Values:** 2% vit. A, 0% vit. C, 4% calcium, 11% iron

GERMAN CHOCOLATE CAKE

PREP: 50 MINUTES BAKE: 30 MINUTES COOL: 1 HOUR Oven 350°

Check your oven temperature occasionally. If it's too hot, cakes may develop tunnels and cracks; if it's too cool, your cake may become coarse.

1½ cups all-purpose flour
¾ teaspoon baking soda
¼ teaspoon salt
1 4-ounce package sweet baking chocolate
¾ cup shortening
1 cup sugar
3 eggs
1 teaspoon vanilla
¾ cup buttermilk or sour milk (see tip, below)
1 recipe Coconut-Pecan Frosting (see page 262)

1. Grease and lightly flour two 8x1½-inch or 9x1½-inch round baking pans or grease one 13x9x2-inch baking pan; set pan(s) aside. Mix flour, baking soda, and salt; set aside.

2. In a saucepan combine chocolate and ½ cup *water*. Cook and stir over low heat till melted; cool.

3. In a large mixing bowl beat shortening with an electric mixer on medium to high speed 30 seconds. Add sugar; beat till fluffy. Add eggs and vanilla; beat on low speed till combined. Beat on medium speed 1 minute. Stir in chocolate mixture. Add dry mixture and buttermilk alternately to beaten mixture; beat on low speed after each addition till combined. Pour batter into the prepared pan(s).

4. Bake in a 350° oven for 30 to 40 minutes or till a wooden toothpick comes out clean. Cool layer cakes on wire racks for 10

MAKING SOUR MILK

If you don't have buttermilk on hand, substitute sour milk in the same amount. For each cup of sour milk needed, place 1 tablespoon lemon juice or vinegar in a glass measuring cup. Add enough milk to make 1 cup total liquid; stir. Let the mixture stand for 5 minutes before using it in a recipe.

minutes. Remove from pans. Cool thoroughly on wire racks (see tip, page 285). Or, place 13×9-inch cake in pan on a wire rack; cool thoroughly. Spread Coconut-Pecan Frosting over top(s) of cake, stacking round layers. Makes 12 servings.

■ **Coconut-Pecan Frosting:** In a medium saucepan slightly beat 1 *egg*. Stir in one 5-ounce can (²/₃ cup) *evaporated milk*, ²/₃ cup *sugar*, and ¹/₄ cup *butter or margarine*. Cook and stir over medium heat about 12 minutes or till thickened and bubbly. Remove from heat; stir in 1¹/₃ cups flaked *coconut* and ¹/₂ cup chopped *pecans*. Cover and cool thoroughly.

Nutrition Facts per serving (with frosting): 470 cal., 29 g total fat (11 g sat. fat), 85 mg chol., 214 mg sodium, 51 g carbo., 2 g fiber, 6 g pro. **Daily Values:** 7% vit. A, 3% vit. C, 5% calcium, 9% iron

---

WHITE CAKE

PREP: 20 MINUTES BAKE: 30 MINUTES COOL: 1 HOUR   Oven 350°

You'll get a slightly whiter cake if you use shortening instead of butter or margarine to prepare this cake.

  2 cups all-purpose flour
  1 teaspoon baking powder
¹/₂ teaspoon baking soda
¹/₈ teaspoon salt
¹/₂ cup shortening, butter, or margarine
1³/₄ cups sugar
  1 teaspoon vanilla
  4 egg whites
1¹/₃ cups buttermilk or sour milk (see tip, page 261)

1. Grease and lightly flour two 8×1¹/₂-inch or 9×1¹/₂-inch round baking pans or grease one 13×9×2-inch baking pan; set the pan(s) aside. Stir together flour, baking powder, baking soda, and salt; set aside.
2. In a large mixing bowl beat shortening, butter, or margarine with an electric mixer on medium to high speed for 30 seconds. Add sugar and vanilla; beat till well combined. Add egg whites, one at a time, beating well after each. Add dry mixture and buttermilk alternately to beaten mixture, beating on low speed after each addition just till combined. Pour batter into the prepared pan(s).
3. Bake in a 350° oven for 30 to 35 minutes or till a wooden toothpick comes out clean. Cool layer cakes in pans on wire racks for 10

minutes. Remove layer cakes from pans. Cool thoroughly on racks (see tip, page 285). Or, place 13×9-inch cake in pan on a wire rack; cool thoroughly. Frost with desired frosting. Serves 12.

Nutrition Facts per serving (cake only): 275 cal., 9 g total fat (2 g sat. fat), 1 mg chol., 149 mg sodium, 45 g carbo., 1 g fiber, 4 g pro. **Daily Values:** 0% vit. A, 0% vit. C, 5% calcium, 6% iron

■ **Coconut White Cake:** Prepare as above, except stir ¼ cup *flaked coconut* into batter.

Nutrition Facts per serving: 283 cal., 9 g total fat (3 g sat. fat)

■ **White Cupcakes:** Grease and lightly flour thirty 2½-inch muffin cups or line with paper bake cups. Prepare cake as above. Fill each cup half full. Bake in a 350° oven 20 to 25 minutes or till a wooden toothpick comes out clean. Cool on wire rack. Makes 30 cupcakes.

Nutrition Facts per cupcake: 110 cal., 4 g total fat (1 g sat. fat)

WHITE CHOCOLATE CAKE

PREP: 40 MINUTES BAKE: 25 MINUTES COOL: 1 HOUR   Oven 350°

Crowned with a fluffy frosting, this moist and tender cake is perfect for those special birthday celebrations.

     4 egg whites
  1¾ cups all-purpose flour
     2 teaspoons baking powder
     3 ounces white baking bar, chopped
   ¾ cup half-and-half, light cream, or milk
   ⅓ cup butter or margarine
     1 cup sugar
  1½ teaspoons vanilla
     4 egg yolks
     1 recipe Seven-Minute Frosting (see page 292)

1. In a mixing bowl allow egg whites to stand at room temperature for 30 minutes. Meanwhile, grease and lightly flour two 8×1½-inch round baking pans; set pans aside. Stir together flour, baking powder, and ¼ teaspoon *salt;* set aside.
2. In a small heavy saucepan melt the chopped white baking bar with ¼ *cup* of the half-and-half over very low heat, stirring con-

stantly till baking bar starts to melt. Immediately remove from heat; stir till baking bar is completely melted and smooth. Stir in remaining half-and-half; cool.

3. In a large mixing bowl beat the butter or margarine with an electric mixer on medium to high speed about 30 seconds. Add sugar and vanilla; beat till well combined. Add egg yolks, one at a time, beating till combined. Add the dry mixture and the white baking bar mixture alternately to beaten mixture, beating on low to medium speed after each addition just till combined.

4. Thoroughly wash the beaters. Beat egg whites with an electric mixer on high speed till stiff peaks form (tips stand straight). Gently fold egg whites into the batter. Spread batter in the prepared pans.

5. Bake in a 350° oven for 25 to 30 minutes or till a wooden toothpick comes out clean. Cool on wire racks for 10 minutes. Remove from pans. Cool thoroughly (see tip, page 285). Frost with Seven-Minute Frosting. Serves 12.

Nutrition Facts per serving (with frosting): 354 cal., 11 g total fat (6 g sat. fat), 90 mg chol., 155 mg sodium, 60 g carbo., 0 g fiber, 5 g pro. **Daily Values:** 17% vit. A, 1% vit. C, 8% calcium, 7% iron

---

MARBLE CAKE

PREP: 40 MINUTES BAKE: 30 MINUTES COOL: 2 HOURS   Oven 350°

      2 cups all-purpose flour
  1¹/₂ teaspoons baking powder
   ¹/₂ teaspoon baking soda
   ³/₄ cup butter or margarine
  1¹/₄ cups sugar
      2 teaspoons vanilla
      2 eggs
      1 cup milk
   ¹/₃ cup chocolate-flavored syrup
      1 recipe Chocolate Glaze (see next page)

1. Grease a 13×9×2-inch baking pan; set prepared pan aside. Combine flour, baking powder, baking soda, and ¹/₄ teaspoon *salt;* set aside.

2. In a mixing bowl beat butter for 30 seconds. Add sugar and vanilla; beat till fluffy. Add eggs, one at a time, beating well after each. Add dry mixture and milk alternately to beaten mixture, beating on low speed after each addition just till combined.

3. Transfer $1^1/_2$ *cups* of the batter to another bowl; stir in chocolate-flavored syrup. Pour light batter into the prepared pan. Spoon chocolate batter atop. Gently cut through batters to marble.

4. Bake in a 350° oven for 30 to 35 minutes or till a wooden toothpick comes out clean. Place cake in pan on a wire rack. Cool thoroughly. Drizzle with Chocolate Glaze. Makes 12 to 16 servings.

■ **Chocolate Glaze:** Melt 4 ounces *semisweet chocolate*, cut up, and 3 tablespoons *butter or margarine* over low heat, stirring frequently. Remove from heat. Stir in $1^1/_2$ cups sifted *powdered sugar* and 3 tablespoons hot *water*. Stir in additional hot water, if needed, to reach drizzling consistency. Spoon over cake.

Nutrition Facts per serving (with glaze): 412 cal., 19 g total fat (11 g sat. fat), 75 mg chol., 313 mg sodium, 60 g carbo., 1 g fiber, 5 g pro. **Daily Values:** 16% vit. A, 0% vit. C, 6% calcium, 10% iron

---

APPLE CAKE

PREP: 30 MINUTES BAKE: 1 HOUR COOL: 2 HOURS   Oven 350°

Filled with apples, nuts, and a blend of spices, this cake is a perennial autumn favorite.

   3 cups all-purpose flour
   1 teaspoon baking powder
   1 teaspoon baking soda
   1 teaspoon ground cinnamon
$^1/_4$ teaspoon ground allspice
   1 cup granulated sugar
   1 cup packed brown sugar
   1 cup cooking oil
   2 beaten eggs
   1 tablespoon vanilla
   3 cups chopped, peeled apples
   1 cup chopped pecans, toasted (see tip, page 234)
   2 teaspoons finely shredded lemon peel
     Sifted powdered sugar

1. Grease and lightly flour a 10-inch tube pan; set pan aside. Stir together flour, baking powder, baking soda, cinnamon, allspice, and $^1/_4$ teaspoon *salt;* set aside.

2. In a mixing bowl combine granulated sugar, brown sugar, oil, eggs, and vanilla. Beat with an electric mixer on medium speed for 2

minutes. Add dry mixture and beat on low speed just till combined. Fold in apples, pecans, and lemon peel. Pour batter into the prepared pan.

3. Bake in a 350° oven about 1 hour or till a wooden toothpick comes out clean. Cool cake on wire rack for 10 minutes. Remove from pan. Cool thoroughly on wire rack (see tip, page 285). Sprinkle with powdered sugar. Cover and store in refrigerator. Makes 12 servings.

Nutrition Facts per serving (with powdered sugar): 480 cal., 25 g total fat (3 g sat. fat), 36 mg chol., 195 mg sodium, 60 g carbo., 2 g fiber, 5 g pro. **Daily Values:** 1% vit. A, 3% vit. C, 4% calcium, 14% iron

---

CARROT CAKE

PREP: 20 MINUTES BAKE: 30 MINUTES COOL: 1 HOUR   Oven 350°

*Use a fine shredding surface to get very thin strips of carrots
for this classic cake.*

    2 cups all-purpose flour
    2 cups sugar
    1 teaspoon baking powder
    1 teaspoon baking soda
    1 teaspoon ground cinnamon
    3 cups finely shredded carrots
    1 cup cooking oil
    4 eggs
    1 recipe Cream Cheese Frosting (see page 290)

1. Grease and lightly flour two 9×1½-inch round baking pans or grease one 13×9×2-inch baking pan; set pan(s) aside.

2. In a large mixing bowl combine flour, sugar, baking powder, baking soda, and cinnamon. Add carrots, oil, and eggs. Beat with an electric mixer till combined. Pour batter into the prepared pan(s).

3. Bake in a 350° oven for 30 to 35 minutes for round pans or 35 to 40 minutes for 13×9-inch pan or till a wooden toothpick comes out clean. Cool layer cakes on wire racks for 10 minutes. Remove from pans. Cool thoroughly on wire racks (see tip, page 285). Or, place 13×9-inch cake in pan on a wire rack; cool thoroughly. Frost with Cream Cheese Frosting. Cover and store in refrigerator. Makes 12 to 16 servings.

■ **Pineapple-Carrot Cake:** Prepare as above, except drain one 8-ounce can *crushed pineapple.* Add drained pineapple and $^1/_2$ cup *coconut* with the shredded carrot.

BUSY-DAY CAKE WITH BROILED COCONUT TOPPING

PREP: 25 MINUTES BAKE: 25 MINUTES. BROIL: 3 MINUTES COOL: 30 MINUTES   Oven 350°

$1^1/_3$ cups all-purpose flour
$^2/_3$ cup sugar
  2 teaspoons baking powder
$^2/_3$ cup milk
$^1/_4$ cup butter or margarine, softened
  1 egg
  1 teaspoon vanilla
  1 recipe Broiled Coconut Topping (see below)

1. Grease an 8×1$^1/_2$-inch round baking pan; set the pan aside.
2. In a mixing bowl combine flour, sugar, and baking powder. Add milk, butter, egg, and vanilla. Beat on low speed till combined. Beat on medium speed for 1 minute. Pour batter into prepared pan.
3. Bake in a 350° oven for 25 to 30 minutes or till a wooden toothpick comes out clean. Spread Broiled Coconut Topping over warm cake. Broil about 4 inches from heat for 3 to 4 minutes or till golden. Cool slightly in pan on a wire rack. Serve warm. Makes 8 servings.
■ **Broiled Coconut Topping:** Beat $^1/_4$ cup packed *brown sugar* and 2 tablespoons softened *butter or margarine* till combined. Stir in 1 tablespoon *milk.* Stir in $^1/_2$ cup *flaked coconut* and, if desired, $^1/_4$ cup chopped *nuts.*

GINGERBREAD

PREP: 20 MINUTES BAKE: 35 MINUTES COOL: 30 MINUTES   Oven 350°

Drizzle warm Lemon Sauce (see page 453) over wedges of warm gingerbread.

1¹/₂ cups all-purpose flour
  ³/₄ teaspoon ground cinnamon
  ³/₄ teaspoon ground ginger
  ¹/₂ teaspoon baking powder
  ¹/₂ teaspoon baking soda
  ¹/₂ cup shortening
  ¹/₄ cup packed brown sugar
   1 egg
  ¹/₂ cup light molasses

1. Grease a 9×1¹/₂-inch round baking pan; set pan aside. In a bowl combine flour, cinnamon, ginger, baking powder, and baking soda; set aside.

2. In a large mixing bowl beat shortening with an electric mixer on medium speed for 30 seconds. Add brown sugar; beat till fluffy. Add egg and molasses; beat 1 minute. Add dry mixture and ¹/₂ cup *water* alternately to beaten mixture, beating on low speed after each addition till combined. Pour batter into pan.

3. Bake in a 350° oven for 35 to 40 minutes or till a wooden toothpick comes out clean. Cool for 30 minutes in pan on wire rack. Serve warm. Makes 9 servings.

Nutrition Facts per serving: 243 cal., 12 g total fat (3 g sat. fat), 24 mg chol., 102 mg sodium, 31 g carbo., 1 g fiber, 3 g pro. **Daily Values:** 1% vit. A, 0% vit. C, 5% calcium, 13% iron

PINEAPPLE UPSIDE-DOWN CAKE

PREP: 20 MINUTES BAKE: 30 MINUTES COOL: 30 MINUTES   Oven 350°

Carefully spoon the cake batter over the fruit in the baking pan so the fruit arrangement isn't disturbed.

  2 tablespoons butter or margarine
  ¹/₃ cup packed brown sugar
   1 tablespoon water

1 8-ounce can pineapple slices, drained and halved
  4 maraschino cherries, halved
1⅓ cups all-purpose flour
  ⅔ cup granulated sugar
  2 teaspoons baking powder
  ⅔ cup milk
  ¼ cup butter or margarine, softened
  1 egg
  1 teaspoon vanilla

1. Melt the 2 tablespoons butter or margarine in a 9×1½-inch round baking pan. Stir in brown sugar and water. Arrange pineapple and cherries in the pan. Set pan aside.

2. In a medium mixing bowl stir together flour, granulated sugar, and baking powder. Add milk, the ¼ cup butter or margarine, egg, and vanilla. Beat with an electric mixer on low speed till combined. Beat on medium speed for 1 minute. Spoon batter into the prepared pan.

3. Bake in a 350° oven for 30 to 35 minutes or till a wooden toothpick comes out clean. Cool on a wire rack for 5 minutes. Loosen sides; invert onto a plate. Serve warm. Makes 8 servings.

Nutrition Facts per serving: 286 cal., 10 g total fat (6 g sat. fat), 51 mg chol., 201 mg sodium, 47 g carbo., 1 g fiber, 4 g pro. **Daily Values:** 10% vit. A, 5% vit. C, 10% calcium, 9% iron

■ **Apricot Upside-Down Cake:** Prepare as above, except substitute one 8½-ounce can unpeeled *apricot halves,* drained and halved, or *peach slices,* drained, and 2 tablespoons toasted *coconut* for the pineapple and cherries.

Nutrition Facts per serving: 292 cal., 10 g total fat (6 g sat. fat)

■ **Pear Upside-Down Cake:** Prepare as above, except substitute one 8½-ounce can *pear slices,* drained, and 2 tablespoons *raisins or currants* for the pineapple and cherries.

Nutrition Facts per serving: 280 cal., 10 g total fat (6 g sat. fat)

ONE-BOWL CHOCOLATE CAKE

PREP: 25 MINUTES BAKE: 30 MINUTES COOL: 1 HOUR   Oven 350°

This easy one-layer cake, topped with a candylike frosting, makes just enough for dessert and a few snacks.

   1 cup all-purpose flour
   1 cup sugar
   $1/4$ cup unsweetened cocoa powder
   1 teaspoon baking powder
   $1/4$ teaspoon baking soda
   $1/4$ teaspoon salt
   $3/4$ cup milk
   $1/4$ cup shortening
   $1/2$ teaspoon vanilla
   1 egg
   1 recipe Rocky Road Frosting (see below)

1. Grease and lightly flour a 9×1½-inch round baking pan; set pan aside.

2. In a mixing bowl combine flour, sugar, cocoa powder, baking powder, baking soda, and salt. Add milk, shortening, and vanilla. Beat with an electric mixer on low speed till combined. Beat on medium speed for 2 minutes. Add egg and beat 2 minutes more. Pour batter into prepared pan.

3. Bake in a 350° oven for 30 to 35 minutes or till a wooden toothpick comes out clean. Cool cake on a wire rack for 10 minutes. Remove cake from pan. Cool thoroughly on a wire rack (see tip, page 285). Frost with Rocky Road Frosting. Makes 8 servings.

■ **Rocky Road Frosting:** In a medium saucepan combine ½ cup *tiny marshmallows;* 1 ounce *unsweetened chocolate,* cut up; 2 tablespoons *butter or margarine;* and 2 tablespoons *water.* Cook and stir over low heat till marshmallows and chocolate melt. Cool 5 minutes. Add 1¼ cups sifted *powdered sugar* and 1 teaspoon *vanilla;* beat till smooth. Stir in an additional ½ cup *tiny marshmallows* and ¼ cup coarsely chopped *walnuts.*

Nutrition Facts per serving (with frosting): 387 cal., 15 g total fat (4 g sat. fat), 28 mg chol., 208 mg sodium, 61 g carbo., 1 g fiber, 5 g pro. **Daily Values:** 6% vit. A, 0% vit. C, 9% calcium, 11% iron

■ **Mocha Cake:** Prepare as above, except add 1 to 2 tablespoons *instant coffee crystals* to the milk; stir to dissolve. Frost with desired frosting.

Nutrition Facts per serving (cake only): 240 cal., 8 g total fat (2 g sat. fat)

CAKE MIX FIX-UPS

You can create a special cake just by adding one of the following to a two-layer cake mix.

■ Add ¹/₂ cup chocolate-flavored syrup to one-third of white or yellow batter. Pour plain batter into baking pans; pour chocolate batter on top of plain batter; swirl gently.

■ Add to batter with the eggs: 1 tablespoon instant coffee crystals (dissolve in water called for in package directions), 1 teaspoon maple flavoring, or ¹/₂ teaspoon almond extract.

■ Add to mixed batter: 1 cup coconut; ¹/₂ cup finely chopped nuts; ¹/₂ cup miniature semisweet chocolate pieces; ¹/₂ cup well-drained, chopped maraschino cherries; or 1 tablespoon finely shredded orange or lemon peel.

BUTTERMILK-CHOCOLATE SHEET CAKE

PREP: 30 MINUTES   BAKE: 25 MINUTES   COOL: 1 HOUR   Oven 350°

Known to some as Texas Sheet Cake, this sinfully rich dessert often is served as brownies.

    2 cups all-purpose flour
    2 cups sugar
    1 teaspoon baking soda
¹/₄ teaspoon salt
    1 cup butter or margarine
¹/₃ cup unsweetened cocoa powder
    2 eggs
¹/₂ cup buttermilk or sour milk (see tip, page 261)
1¹/₂ teaspoons vanilla
    1 recipe Chocolate-Buttermilk Frosting (see page 272)

1. Grease a 15×10×1-inch or a 13×9×2-inch baking pan; set aside. Combine flour, sugar, baking soda, and salt; set aside.

2. In a medium saucepan combine butter, cocoa powder, and 1 cup *water*. Bring mixture just to boiling, stirring constantly. Remove from heat. Add the chocolate mixture to dry mixture and beat with an electric mixer on medium to high speed till thoroughly combined. Add eggs, buttermilk, and vanilla. Beat for 1 minute (batter will be thin). Pour batter into the prepared pan.

3. Bake in a 350° oven about 25 minutes for the 15×10-inch pan or 35 minutes for the 13×9-inch pan or till a wooden toothpick comes out clean.

4. Pour warm Chocolate-Buttermilk Frosting over the warm cake, spreading evenly. Place cake in pan on a wire rack; cool thoroughly before cutting. Makes 24 servings.

▇ **Chocolate-Buttermilk Frosting:** In a medium saucepan combine ¹/₄ cup *butter or margarine*, 3 tablespoons *unsweetened cocoa powder*, and 3 tablespoons *buttermilk*. Bring to boiling. Remove from heat. Add 2¹/₄ cups sifted *powdered sugar* and ¹/₂ teaspoon *vanilla*. Beat till smooth. If desired, stir in ³/₄ cup coarsely chopped *pecans*.

Nutrition Facts per serving (with frosting): 237 cal., 10 g total fat (6 g sat. fat), 44 mg chol., 185 mg sodium, 35 g carbo., 0 g fiber, 2 g pro. Daily Values: 9% vit. A, 0% vit. C, 2% calcium, 5% iron

▇ **Chocolate-Cinnamon Sheet Cake:** Prepare as above, except add 1 teaspoon *ground cinnamon* to the dry mixture.

Nutrition Facts per serving (with frosting): 237 cal., 10 g total fat (6 g sat. fat)

PEANUT BUTTER CAKE

PREP: 25 MINUTES BAKE: 30 MINUTES COOL: 2 HOURS   Oven 375°

Serve this tender, moist cake warm from the oven for a quick snack or breakfast treat.

  ¹/₂ cup all-purpose flour
  ¹/₂ cup packed brown sugar
  ¹/₄ cup peanut butter
   3 tablespoons butter or margarine
   2 cups all-purpose flour
   1 cup packed brown sugar

2 teaspoons baking powder
  $^1/_2$ teaspoon baking soda
  $^1/_4$ teaspoon salt
  1 cup milk
  $^1/_2$ cup peanut butter
  2 eggs
  $^1/_4$ cup butter or margarine, softened

1. Grease the bottom and $^1/_2$ inch up the sides of a 13×9×2-inch baking pan; set pan aside.

2. For topping, in a small bowl stir together the $^1/_2$ cup flour and the $^1/_2$ cup brown sugar. Using a pastry blender, cut in the $^1/_4$ cup peanut butter and the 3 tablespoons butter or margarine till mixture resembles coarse crumbs. Set aside.

3. In a large mixing bowl stir together the 2 cups flour, the 1 cup brown sugar, baking powder, baking soda, and salt. Add milk, the $^1/_2$ cup peanut butter, eggs, and the $^1/_4$ cup butter or margarine. Beat with an electric mixer on low speed till combined. Beat on medium to high speed for 3 minutes, scraping bowl frequently.

4. Spoon batter into the prepared pan, spreading evenly. Sprinkle with topping mixture. Bake in a 375° oven about 30 minutes or till a wooden toothpick comes out clean. Serve warm or cool thoroughly on a wire rack. Makes 16 servings.

Nutrition Facts per serving: 265 cal., 12 g total fat (2 g sat. fat), 28 mg chol., 256 mg sodium, 35 g carbo., 1 g fiber, 6 g pro. **Daily Values:** 8% vit. A, 0% vit. C, 7% calcium, and 10% iron

■ **Peanut Butter-Chocolate Cake:** Prepare as above, except add $^1/_4$ cup *miniature semisweet chocolate pieces* to the topping and stir $^1/_2$ cup *miniature semisweet chocolate pieces* into the batter after beating.

Nutrition Facts per serving: 297 cal., 14 g total fat (5 g sat. fat)

OATMEAL CAKE

PREP: 45 MINUTES BAKE: 40 MINUTES COOL: 1⅓ HOURS BROIL: 2 MINUTES   Oven 350°

1¼ cups boiling water
1 cup rolled oats
2 cups all-purpose flour
2 teaspoons baking powder
¾ teaspoon ground cinnamon
½ teaspoon baking soda
½ teaspoon salt
¼ teaspoon ground nutmeg
½ cup butter or margarine, softened
¾ cup granulated sugar
½ cup packed brown sugar
1 teaspoon vanilla
2 eggs
1 recipe Broiled Nut Topping (see below)

1. Grease and lightly flour a 9-inch springform pan; set pan aside. Pour boiling water over oats. Stir till combined; let stand 20 minutes. Stir together flour, baking powder, cinnamon, baking soda, salt, and nutmeg; set aside.

2. In a large mixing bowl beat butter or margarine with an electric mixer on medium to high speed for 30 seconds. Add granulated sugar, brown sugar, and vanilla; beat till well combined. Add eggs, one at a time, beating well after each. Add dry mixture and oatmeal mixture alternately to beaten mixture, beating on low speed after each addition just till combined. Pour batter into prepared pan.

3. Bake in a 350° oven for 40 to 45 minutes or till a wooden toothpick comes out clean. Cool cake in pan on a wire rack for 20 minutes. Remove sides of pan; cool on wire rack at least 1 hour more.

4. Transfer cake to a baking sheet. Spread Broiled Nut Topping over warm cake. Broil about 4 inches from heat for 2 to 3 minutes or till topping is bubbly and golden. Cool on a wire rack before serving. Makes 12 servings.

■ **Broiled Nut Topping:** In a medium saucepan combine ¼ cup *butter or margarine* and 2 tablespoons *half-and-half, light cream, or milk*. Cook and stir till butter or margarine melts. Add ½ cup packed *brown sugar;* stir till sugar dissolves. Remove from heat. Stir in ¾ cup chopped *pecans or walnuts* and ⅓ cup *flaked coconut*.

Nutrition Facts per serving (with topping): 372 cal., 18 g total fat (9 g sat. fat), 67 mg chol., 336 mg sodium, 49 g carbo., 2 g fiber, 5 g pro. **Daily Values:** 12% vit. A, 0% vit. C, 7% calcium, 13% iron

---

BANANA CAKE

PREP: 20 MINUTES BAKE: 35 MINUTES COOL: 2 HOURS   Oven 350°

2$^1/_4$ cups all-purpose flour
1$^1/_2$ cups sugar
1$^1/_2$ teaspoons baking powder
  1 teaspoon baking soda
  $^1/_2$ teaspoon salt
  1 cup mashed ripe bananas (about 3)
  $^3/_4$ cup buttermilk or sour milk (see tip, page 261)
  $^1/_2$ cup shortening
  1 teaspoon vanilla
  2 eggs

1. Grease and lightly flour two 8×1$^1/_2$-inch or 9×1$^1/_2$-inch round baking pans or grease one 13×9×2-inch baking pan; set pan(s) aside.
2. In a large mixing bowl stir together flour, sugar, baking powder, baking soda, and salt. Add bananas, buttermilk or sour milk, shortening, and vanilla. Beat with an electric mixer on low speed till combined. Add eggs; beat on medium speed for 2 minutes. Pour batter into the prepared pan(s).
3. Bake in a 350° oven for 25 to 30 minutes for round pans or about 35 minutes for 13×9-inch pan or till a wooden toothpick comes out clean. Cool layer cakes in pans on wire racks for 10 minutes. Remove layer cakes from pans. Cool thoroughly on racks (see tip, page 285). Or, place 13×9-inch cake in pan on a wire rack; cool thoroughly. Frost with desired frosting. Makes 12 to 16 servings.

Nutrition Facts per serving (cake only): 297 cal., 10 g total fat (3 g sat. fat), 36 mg chol., 267 mg sodium, 49 g carbo., 1 g fiber, 4 g pro. **Daily Values:** 1% vit. A, 4% vit. C, 5% calcium, 8% iron

FRUITCAKE

PREP: 30 MINUTES BAKE: 1¹/₄ HOURS COOL: 2 HOURS   Oven 300°

1¹/₂ cups all-purpose flour
  1 teaspoon ground cinnamon
¹/₂ teaspoon baking powder
¹/₄ teaspoon baking soda
¹/₄ teaspoon ground nutmeg
¹/₄ teaspoon ground allspice
¹/₄ teaspoon ground cloves
³/₄ cup diced mixed candied fruits and peels, or snipped mixed
     dried fruit
¹/₂ cup raisins or snipped pitted dates
¹/₂ cup candied red or green cherries, quartered
¹/₂ cup chopped pecans or walnuts
  2 eggs
¹/₂ cup packed brown sugar
¹/₂ cup orange juice or apple juice
¹/₃ cup butter or margarine, melted
  2 tablespoons light molasses
     Brandy or fruit juice

1. Grease an 8×4×2-inch loaf pan. Line bottom and sides of pan with brown paper to prevent overbrowning; grease paper. Set pan aside. In a mixing bowl stir together flour, cinnamon, baking powder, baking soda, nutmeg, allspice, and cloves. Add fruits and peels, raisins, cherries, and nuts; mix ingredients well.
2. In another mixing bowl beat eggs; stir in brown sugar, juice, butter or margarine, and molasses till combined. Stir into fruit mixture. Pour batter into the prepared pan.
3. Bake in a 300° oven for 1¹/₄ to 1¹/₂ hours or till a wooden toothpick comes out clean; cover pan loosely with foil after 1 hour of baking to prevent overbrowning. Place cake in pan on a wire rack and cool thoroughly.
4. Remove cake from pan. Wrap cake in brandy- or fruit-juice-moistened cheesecloth. Overwrap with foil. Store in the refrigerator for 2 to 8 weeks to mellow flavors. Remoisten cheesecloth about once a week or as needed. Makes 16 servings.

Nutrition Facts per serving: 202 cal., 7 g total fat (3 g sat. fat), 37 mg chol., 80 mg sodium, 32 g carbo., 1 g fiber, 3 g pro. **Daily Values:** 4% vit. A, 6% vit. C, 2% calcium, 7% iron

■ **Light Fruitcake:** Prepare as above, except omit nutmeg, allspice, and cloves and substitute *light-colored corn syrup* for the molasses. Add 1 teaspoon finely shredded *lemon peel* and 1 tablespoon *lemon juice* with the corn syrup.

Nutrition Facts per serving: 203 cal., 7 g total fat (3 g sat. fat)

HOT-MILK SPONGE CAKE

PREP: 15 MINUTES BAKE: 20 MINUTES COOL: 30 MINUTES   Oven 350°

Low-Fat

To keep this cake a low-calorie treat, dust it lightly with powdered sugar or top with fresh fruit. But if you need a sweeter fix, spread the Broiled Coconut Topping (see page 267) over the cake and pop it under the broiler.

1 cup all-purpose flour
1 teaspoon baking powder
2 eggs
1 cup sugar
$^1/_2$ cup milk
2 tablespoons butter or margarine

1. Grease a 9×9×2-inch baking pan; set pan aside. Stir together flour and baking powder; set aside.
2. In a mixing bowl beat eggs with an electric mixer on high speed about 4 minutes or till thick. Gradually add sugar, beating on medium speed for 4 to 5 minutes or till light and fluffy. Add the dry mixture; beat on low to medium speed just till combined.
3. In a small saucepan heat and stir milk and butter till butter melts; add to batter, beating till combined. Pour batter into the prepared pan.
4. Bake in a 350° oven for 20 to 25 minutes or till a wooden toothpick comes out clean. Cool cake in pan on a wire rack. Makes 9 servings.

Nutrition Facts per serving: 178 cal., 4 g total fat (2 g sat. fat), 55 mg chol., 88 mg sodium, 33 g carbo., 0 g fiber, 3 g pro. **Daily Values:** 5% vit. A, 0% vit. C, 5% calcium, 5% iron

SPONGE CAKE

PREP: 40 MINUTES BAKE: 55 MINUTES COOL: 2 HOURS   Oven 325°

Low-Fat

     6 egg yolks
     1 tablespoon finely shredded orange peel
 $^1/_2$ cup orange juice or pineapple juice
     1 teaspoon vanilla
     1 cup sugar
 $1^1/_4$ cups all-purpose flour
     6 egg whites
 $^1/_2$ teaspoon cream of tartar
 $^1/_2$ cup sugar

1. In a mixing bowl beat egg yolks with an electric mixer on high speed about 5 minutes or till thick and lemon colored. Add orange peel, orange juice, and vanilla; beat on low speed till combined. Gradually beat in the 1 cup sugar at low speed. Increase to medium speed; beat till mixture thickens slightly and doubles in volume (about 5 minutes total).

2. Sprinkle $^1/_4$ *cup* of the flour over egg yolk mixture; fold in till combined. Repeat with remaining flour, $^1/_4$ cup at a time. Set egg yolk mixture aside.

3. Thoroughly wash beaters. In a mixing bowl beat egg whites and cream of tartar on medium speed till soft peaks form (tips curl). Gradually add the $^1/_2$ cup sugar, beating on high speed till stiff peaks form (tips stand straight). Fold 1 cup of the beaten egg white mixture into the egg yolk mixture; fold egg yolk mixture into remaining egg white mixture. Pour into an ungreased 10-inch tube pan.

4. Bake in a 325° oven for 55 to 60 minutes or till cake springs back when lightly touched (see tip, page 279). Immediately invert cake (leave in pan); cool thoroughly (see tip, page 285). Loosen sides of cake from pan; remove from pan. Serves 12.

Nutrition Facts per serving: 184 cal., 3 g total fat (1 g sat. fat), 107 mg chol., 32 mg sodium, 36 g carbo., 0 g fiber, 4 g pro. **Daily Values:** 16% vit. A, 9% vit. C, 1% calcium, 6% iron

■ **Lemon Sponge Cake:** Prepare as above, except substitute 2 teaspoons finely shredded *lemon peel* for the orange peel and $^1/_4$ cup *lemon juice* plus ¹/₄ cup *water* for the orange juice or pineapple juice.

Nutrition Facts per serving: 180 cal., 3 g total fat (1 g sat. fat)

■ **Chocolate Sponge Cake:** Prepare as above, except omit orange peel. Reduce flour to 1 cup. Stir ¹/₃ cup *unsweetened cocoa powder* into flour.

Nutrition Facts per serving: 184 cal., 3 g total fat (1 g sat. fat)

■ **Almond Sponge Cake:** Prepare as above, except omit orange peel. Add ¹/₂ teaspoon *almond extract* with the orange juice or pineapple juice.

Nutrition Facts per serving: 184 cal., 3 g total fat (1 g sat. fat)

WHEN IS IT DONE?

To test whether an angel, sponge, or chiffon cake, or one made with ground nuts or crumbs is done baking, touch the top lightly. The cake is done if the top springs back. When making cakes with ground nuts or crumbs, you'll notice that they do not have domed tops like most other cakes. Instead, their tops are flat or slightly depressed.

JELLY ROLL

PREP: 30 MINUTES BAKE: 12 MINUTES COOL: 1 HOUR   Oven 375°

Low-Fat

Filled with jelly, this cake makes an impressive low-fat dessert. Choose one of the other scrumptious fillings when you want to indulge. The Chocolate Cake Roll filled with whipped cream is in the photos on page 281.

  ¹/₂ **cup all-purpose flour**
   1 **teaspoon baking powder**
   4 **egg yolks**
  ¹/₂ **teaspoon vanilla**
  ¹/₃ **cup granulated sugar**
   4 **egg whites**
  ¹/₂ **cup granulated sugar**
    Sifted powdered sugar
  ¹/₂ **cup jelly or jam**

1. Grease and lightly flour a 15×10×1-inch jelly-roll pan; set pan aside. Stir together flour and baking powder; set aside.

2. In a medium mixing bowl beat egg yolks and vanilla with an electric mixer on high speed for 5 minutes or till thick and lemon colored. Gradually add the $^1/_3$ cup granulated sugar, beating on high speed till sugar is almost dissolved.

3. Thoroughly wash the beaters. In another bowl beat egg whites on medium speed till soft peaks form (tips curl). Gradually add the $^1/_2$ cup granulated sugar, beating till stiff peaks form (tips stand straight). Fold egg yolk mixture into beaten egg whites. Sprinkle dry mixture over egg mixture; fold in gently just till combined. Spread batter evenly in the prepared pan.

4. Bake in a 375° oven for 12 to 15 minutes or till cake springs back when lightly touched (see tip, page 279). Immediately loosen edges of cake from pan and turn cake out onto a towel sprinkled with powdered sugar. Roll up towel and cake, jelly-roll style, starting from one of the cake's short sides (see photo 1, page 281). Cool on a wire rack. Unroll cake; remove towel. Spread cake with jelly or jam to within 1 inch of edges (see photo 2, page 281). Roll up cake (see photo 3, page 281). Makes 10 servings.

Nutrition Facts per serving: 162 cal., 2 g total fat (1 g sat. fat), 85 mg chol., 64 mg sodium, 33 g carbo., 0 g fiber, 3 g pro. **Daily Values:** 12% vit. A, 1% vit. C, 3% calcium, 5% iron

■ **Chocolate Cake Roll:** Prepare as above, except reduce flour to $^1/_3$ cup and omit baking powder. Add $^1/_4$ cup *unsweetened cocoa powder* and $^1/_4$ teaspoon *baking soda* to flour. Substitute 2 cups *whipped cream* or *cooled chocolate pudding* for the jelly. Roll up cake. Drizzle cake with $^1/_2$ recipe *Chocolate Glaze* (see page 265); chill up to 2 hours.

Nutrition Facts per serving: 273 cal., 15 g total fat (7 g sat. fat)

■ **Pumpkin Cake Roll:** Prepare as above, except add 2 teaspoons *pumpkin pie spice* to dry mixture and stir $^1/_2$ cup *canned pumpkin* into egg yolk and sugar mixture. Substitute 1 recipe *Cream Cheese Frosting* (see page 290) for the jelly. Sprinkle cake roll with additional sifted powdered sugar; chill.

Nutrition Facts per serving: 442 cal., 17 g total fat (10 g sat. fat)

1. Starting from a short side, roll up the warm cake and the powdered sugar-coated towel together. Let cake cool.

2. Carefully unroll the cooled cake and towel. Spread the desired filling over the cake, leaving a 1-inch border around the edges.

3. Again starting from the short side, roll up the cake and filling.

■ **Lemon Cake Roll:** Prepare as above, except substitute 1 recipe *Lemon Curd* (see page 455) for the jelly. Sprinkle cake roll with additional sifted powdered sugar; chill up to 2 hours.

Nutrition Facts per serving: 204 cal., 8 g total fat (2 g sat. fat)

■ **Ice-Cream Cake Roll:** Prepare as above, except substitute 2 cups of your favorite *ice cream*, softened, for the jelly. Store in the freezer.

Nutrition Facts per serving: 172 cal., 5 g total fat (2 g sat. fat)

BANANA NUT ROLL

Bake the filling and the cake together in one step, then roll up the cake.

   $^1/_2$ cup all-purpose flour
   $^1/_2$ teaspoon baking powder
   $^1/_4$ teaspoon baking soda
    1 8-ounce package cream cheese, softened
    1 3-ounce package cream cheese, softened
   $^1/_2$ cup sugar
    1 whole egg
    3 tablespoons milk
    4 egg yolks
   $^1/_2$ teaspoon vanilla
   $^1/_3$ cup sugar
   $^1/_2$ cup mashed ripe banana (1 large)
   $^1/_2$ cup finely chopped walnuts or pecans
    4 egg whites
   $^1/_2$ cup sugar
    1 recipe Cream Cheese Icing (below)

1. Lightly grease a 15×10×1-inch jelly-roll pan. Line bottom with waxed paper and grease paper; set pan aside. For cake, combine flour, baking powder, and baking soda; set aside.

2. For filling, in a small mixing bowl combine cream cheeses and the $^1/_2$ cup sugar. Beat with an electric mixer on medium speed till smooth. Add whole egg and milk; beat till combined. Spread in the prepared pan; set aside.

3. For cake, in a small mixing bowl beat the egg yolks and vanilla on high speed about 5 minutes or till thick and lemon colored. Gradually add the $^1/_3$ cup sugar, beating on high speed till sugar is dissolved. Stir in the mashed banana and nuts.

4. Thoroughly wash the beaters. In a large mixing bowl beat the egg whites on medium speed till soft peaks form (tips curl). Gradually add $^1/_2$ cup sugar, beating till stiff peaks form (tips stand straight). Fold egg yolk mixture into beaten egg whites. Sprinkle dry mixture evenly over egg mixture; fold in gently just till combined. Carefully spread the batter evenly over the filling in the pan.

5. Bake in a 375° oven for 15 to 20 minutes or till the cake springs back when lightly touched (see tip, page 279). Immediately loosen edges of cake from pan and turn cake out onto a towel sprinkled with powdered sugar. Carefully peel off waxed paper. Roll up cake, jelly-roll style, starting from one of the cake's short sides and using the towel as a guide. Do not roll towel into cake. Cool on a wire rack. Spread top with Cream Cheese Icing. Makes 10 servings.

■ **Cream Cheese Icing:** In a small mixing bowl combine *half* of a 3-ounce package *cream cheese,* softened, and ¹/₂ teaspoon *vanilla;* beat with an electric mixer on medium speed till light and fluffy. Gradually beat in 1 cup sifted *powdered sugar.* Beat in enough *milk* (1 to 2 tablespoons) to reach spreading consistency.

Nutrition Facts per serving (with icing): 381 cal., 19 g total fat (9 g sat. fat), 146 mg chol., 191 mg sodium, 47 g carbo., 1 g fiber, 8 g pro. **Daily Values:** 29% vit. A, 2% vit. C, 6% calcium, 8% iron

---

CHIFFON CAKE

PREP: 30 MINUTES BAKE: 65 MINUTES COOL: 2 HOURS   Oven 325°

2¹/₄ **cups sifted cake flour or 2 cups sifted all-purpose flour**
1¹/₂ **cups sugar**
  1 **tablespoon baking powder**
¹/₄ **teaspoon salt**
¹/₂ **cup cooking oil**
  7 **egg yolks**
  2 **teaspoons finely shredded orange peel**
  1 **teaspoon finely shredded lemon peel**
  1 **teaspoon vanilla**
  7 **egg whites**
¹/₂ **teaspoon cream of tartar**

1. In a large mixing bowl mix flour, sugar, baking powder, and salt. Make a well in the center of dry mixture. Add oil, egg yolks, orange and lemon peels, vanilla, and ³/₄ cup cold *water.* Beat with an electric mixer on low speed till combined. Beat on high speed for 5 minutes more or till satin smooth.

2. Thoroughly wash the beaters. In an extra-large mixing bowl beat egg whites and cream of tartar on medium speed till stiff peaks form (tips stand straight). Pour batter in a thin stream over beaten egg whites; fold in gently. Pour into an ungreased 10-inch tube pan.

3. Bake in a 325° oven for 65 to 70 minutes or till top springs back when lightly touched (see tip, page 279). Immediately invert cake (leave in pan); cool thoroughly (see tip, page 285). Loosen sides of cake from pan; remove cake. Makes 12 servings.

Nutrition Facts per serving: 298 cal., 12 g total fat (2 g sat. fat), 124 mg chol., 173 mg sodium, 42 g carbo., 0 g fiber, 5 g pro. **Daily Values:** 18% vit. A, 1% vit. C, 8% calcium, 11% iron

ANGEL FOOD CAKE

PREP: 50 MINUTES BAKE: 40 MINUTES COOL: 2 HOURS   Oven 350°

No-Fat

Loosen the cooled cake from the pan by sliding a metal spatula between the two. Constantly pressing the spatula against the pan, draw it around the pan in a continuous, not sawing, motion so you don't cut into the cake.

$1^1/_2$ cups egg whites (10 to 12 large)
$1^1/_2$ cups sifted powdered sugar
   1 cup sifted cake flour or sifted all-purpose flour
$1^1/_2$ teaspoons cream of tartar
   1 teaspoon vanilla
   1 cup granulated sugar

1. In an extra-large mixing bowl allow egg whites to stand at room temperature for 30 minutes. Meanwhile, sift powdered sugar and flour together 3 times; set aside.
2. Add cream of tartar and vanilla to egg whites. Beat with an electric mixer on medium speed till soft peaks form (tips curl). Gradually add sugar, about 2 tablespoons at a time, beating till stiff peaks form (tips stand straight).
3. Sift about *one-fourth* of the dry mixture over beaten egg whites; fold in gently. (If bowl is too full, transfer to a larger bowl.) Repeat, folding in remaining dry mixture by fourths. Pour into an ungreased 10-inch tube pan. Gently cut through batter to remove any large air pockets.
4. Bake on the lowest rack in a 350° oven for 40 to 45 minutes or till top springs back when lightly touched (see tip, page 279). Immediately invert cake (leave in pan); cool thoroughly (see tip, page 285). Loosen sides of cake from pan; remove cake. Makes 12 servings.

■ **Chocolate Angel Food Cake:** Prepare as above, except sift $^1/_4$

cup *unsweetened cocoa powder* with the flour-powdered sugar mixture.

■ **Honey Angel Food Cake:** Prepare as above, except after beating egg whites to soft peaks, gradually pour ¼ cup *honey* in a thin stream over the egg white mixture. Continue as above, except beat only ½ cup sugar into the egg whites.

Nutrition Facts per serving: 161 cal., 0 g total fat, 0 mg chol., 46 mg sodium, 37 g carbo., 0 g fiber, 4 g pro.

COOLING AND STORING CAKES

Cooling Cakes

■ Before removing a butter-type layer cake from its baking pan, allow it to cool about 10 minutes on a wire rack. To remove, loosen cake edges from pan and place an inverted wire rack on the cake layer. Turn cake and rack over and lift off the pan. Place a second rack on the cake layer and turn it over again so the baked cake is upright; cool completely. A butter-type cake left in its pan should be allowed to thoroughly cool on a wire rack.

■ Turn angel, sponge, and chiffon cakes upside down immediately after baking and let them cool completely. If your cake is too high to use the built-in legs on the baking pan, invert the pan over a metal funnel or a glass bottle that has a slim neck.

Storing Cakes

■ Refrigerate all cakes that have a frosting or filling containing whipped cream, cream cheese, sour cream or yogurt, or eggs.

■ Freeze unfrosted cakes for longer storage. To freeze a butter-type cake, place the cooled cake on a baking sheet and freeze just until firm. Wrap and seal the frozen cake in freezer wrap or seal in freezer bags or airtight freezer containers; freeze up to 4 months.

■ To freeze an unfrosted angel, sponge, or chiffon cake, place the cooled cake in a freezer bag or airtight freezer container or seal in freezer wrap; freeze up to 3 months.

SOUR CREAM POUND CAKE

PREP: 30 MINUTES BAKE: 1 HOUR COOL: 2 HOURS   Oven 325°

$^1\!/_2$ **cup butter**
3 **eggs**
$^1\!/_2$ **cup dairy sour cream**
$1^1\!/_2$ **cups all-purpose flour**
$^1\!/_4$ **teaspoon baking powder**
$^1\!/_8$ **teaspoon baking soda**
1 **cup sugar**
$^1\!/_2$ **teaspoon vanilla**

1. Allow butter, eggs, and sour cream to stand at room temperature 30 minutes. Meanwhile, grease and lightly flour an 8×4×2-inch or 9×5×3-inch loaf pan; set aside. Combine flour, baking powder, and baking soda; set aside.

2. In a mixing bowl beat butter with an electric mixer on medium to high speed for 30 seconds. Gradually add sugar, beating about 10 minutes or till very light and fluffy. Beat in vanilla. Add eggs, one at a time, beating 1 minute after each addition and scraping bowl frequently. Add dry mixture and sour cream alternately to beaten mixture, beating on low to medium speed after each addition just till combined. Pour batter into prepared pan.

3. Bake in a 325° oven for 60 to 75 minutes or till a wooden toothpick comes out clean. Cool on a rack for 10 minutes. Remove from pan; cool (see tip, right). Makes 10 servings.

Nutrition Facts per serving: 260 cal., 12 g total fat (7 g sat. fat), 93 mg chol., 141 mg sodium, 34 g carbo., 0 g fiber, 4 g pro. **Daily Values:** 12% vit. A, 0% vit. C, 2% calcium, 7% iron

■ **Lemon-Poppy Seed Pound Cake:** Prepare as above, except substitute $^1\!/_2$ cup *lemon yogurt* for sour cream. Add 1 teaspoon finely shredded *lemon peel*, 2 tablespoons *lemon juice*, and 2 tablespoons *poppy seed* to batter.

Nutrition Facts per serving: 265 cal., 12 g total fat (6 g sat. fat)

■ **Orange-Rosemary Pound Cake:** Prepare as above, except stir $1^1\!/_4$ teaspoons finely shredded *orange peel* and 1 teaspoon snipped *fresh rosemary* into the batter.

Nutrition Facts per serving: 260 cal., 12 g total fat (7 g sat. fat)

Nut Torte

Prep: 15 minutes Bake: 20 minutes Cool: 1 hour   Oven 350°

2 tablespoons all-purpose flour
1 teaspoon baking powder
1 teaspoon finely shredded orange peel
4 eggs
³/₄ cup sugar
2¹/₂ cups walnuts, pecans, or hazelnuts
1 recipe Chocolate Butter Frosting (see page 290)

1. Grease and lightly flour two 8×1¹/₂-inch round baking pans; set pans aside. Stir together the flour, baking powder, and orange peel; set aside.

2. Place eggs and sugar in a blender container or food processor bowl. Cover and blend or process till smooth. Add nuts. Blend or process about 1 minute or till nearly smooth. Add dry mixture; blend or process just till combined. Spread batter evenly in the prepared pans.

3. Bake in a 350° oven about 20 minutes or till lightly browned. Cool cakes on wire racks for 10 minutes. Remove from pans. Cool thoroughly on wire racks (see tip, page 285). Frost with Chocolate Butter Frosting. Makes 12 servings.

Nutrition Facts per serving (with frosting): 430 cal., 23 g total fat (5 g sat. fat), 85 mg chol., 108 mg sodium, 54 g carbo., 1 g fiber, 7 g pro. **Daily Values:** 8% vit. A, 1% vit. C, 9% calcium, 10% iron

Mocha Pecan Torte

Prep: 30 minutes Bake: 35 minutes Cool: 2 hours   Oven 350°

1 cup butter
1¹/₃ cups semisweet chocolate pieces
6 eggs
1 cup sugar
1¹/₂ cups pecans, toasted (see tip, page 234)
1 cup sifted unsweetened cocoa powder
¹/₄ cup coffee liqueur or strong coffee
1 recipe Mocha Glaze (see page 288)
2 ounces white baking bar, melted
³/₄ cup chopped pecans, toasted (see tip, page 234)

1. Grease a 9-inch springform pan; line bottom with parchment paper. Grease paper; dust with flour. Set aside. In a small heavy saucepan combine butter and chocolate. Stir over low heat till melted and smooth; set aside.

2. Place eggs and sugar in a blender container or food processor bowl. Cover and blend or process till smooth. Add nuts. Blend or process about 1 minute or till nearly smooth. Add melted chocolate mixture, cocoa powder, and liqueur; blend or process just till combined. Spread batter evenly in the prepared pan.

3. Bake in a 350° oven for 35 to 40 minutes or till sides are puffed and set about 2 inches in from edge of pan. Place cake on a wire rack; cool thoroughly. Loosen sides of cake; remove sides of pan. Invert cake onto rack. Remove parchment paper. Place rack with cake on baking sheet. Pour warm Mocha Glaze over cake, covering top and sides.

4. Pour melted baking bar into a plastic storage bag. Snip one corner of the bag to make a small opening. Starting at center of cake, pipe a spiral to the outer edge. Draw 8 to 10 lines with a toothpick from center of cake to edge at regular intervals to achieve a spider web effect. If necessary, chill cake till glaze is partially set but still sticky (5 to 10 minutes). Press nuts onto sides of cake. Transfer cake to plate and refrigerate. Makes 12 to 16 servings.

■ **Mocha Glaze:** In a medium heavy saucepan heat 3 tablespoons *butter* and 1 tablespoon *light-colored corn syrup* over low heat, stirring occasionally till butter melts. Add one 6-ounce package (1 cup) *semisweet chocolate pieces;* stir till melted and smooth. Remove from heat. Add 3 tablespoons *butter* and 2 tablespoons *coffee liqueur or strong coffee;* whisk till smooth.

Nutrition Facts per serving (with glaze): 664 cal., 49 g total fat (16 g sat. fat), 163 mg chol., 252 mg sodium, 54 g carbo., 1 g fiber, 9 g pro. **Daily Values:** 25% vit. A, 0% vit. C, 10% calcium, 18% iron

---

TRUFFLE FROSTING

PREP: 15 MINUTES   CHILL: 1¹/₂ HOURS

1¹/₂ **cups whipping cream**
¹/₄ **cup light-colored corn syrup**
1 **12-ounce package (2 cups) semisweet chocolate pieces**
1 **teaspoon vanilla**

1. In a medium heavy saucepan bring whipping cream and corn syrup to a simmer. Remove from heat. Stir in chocolate pieces and vanilla; let stand for 2 minutes. Whisk the mixture till smooth and melted. Cover and chill about $1^{1}/_{2}$ hours or till mixture reaches spreading consistency, stirring occasionally. Beat with an electric mixer till fluffy. This frosts tops and sides of two 8- or 9-inch layers.

Nutrition Facts per serving ($^{1}/_{12}$ of recipe): 255 cal., 19 g total fat (7 g sat. fat), 41 mg chol., 16 mg sodium, 25 g carbo., 0 g fiber, 0 g pro. **Daily Values:** 13% vit. A, 0% vit. C, 2% calcium, 6% iron

---

THE FROSTING ON THE CAKE

Decorating a cake can be as simple as a luscious, creamy frosting swirled attractively over the layers. Begin with these tips.

Get rid of loose crumbs on a cake before you frost it. Brush them off with a pastry brush or your hand.

To keep the plate clean, tuck strips of waxed paper under edge of the cake before frosting it. Spread about $^{1}/_{2}$ cup frosting on top of the first cake layer.

Place the second cake layer, top side up, on top of the frosted layer. Spread a thin coating of frosting on the sides of the cake to seal in any crumbs.

Add a thicker coating of frosting to sides of cake. Then frost sides of cake again, swirling and building up top edge about $^{1}/_{4}$ inch above the cake.

Finally, spread the remaining frosting on top of the cake, blending the frosting at the edge. Remove the strips of waxed paper once you've finished frosting the cake. When time permits, let the cake stand about an hour before slicing to allow the frosting to set up.

PENUCHE FROSTING

START TO FINISH: 15 MINUTES

1. In a saucepan melt $^{1}/_{2}$ cup *butter or margarine;* stir in 1 cup packed *brown sugar*. Cook and stir till bubbly. Remove from heat.

Add ¼ cup *milk;* beat vigorously with a wooden spoon till smooth. Add 3½ cups sifted *powdered sugar;* beat by hand till it reaches spreading consistency. Immediately frost tops of two 8- or 9-inch layers or top of one 13×9-inch cake.

Nutrition Facts per serving (⅟₁₂ of recipe): 251 cal., 8 g total fat (5 g sat. fat), 21 mg chol., 87 mg sodium, 47 g carbo., 0 g fiber, 0 g pro. **Daily Values:** 7% vit. A, 0% vit. C, 2% calcium, 2% iron

CREAM CHEESE FROSTING

START TO FINISH: 20 MINUTES

1. Beat together two 3-ounce packages *cream cheese,* softened; ½ cup *butter or margarine,* softened; and 2 teaspoons *vanilla* till light and fluffy. Gradually add 2 cups sifted *powdered sugar,* beating well. Gradually beat in 2½ to 2¾ cups additional sifted powdered sugar to reach spreading consistency. This frosts tops and sides of two 8- or 9-inch layers. Cover and store cake in refrigerator.

Nutrition Facts per serving (⅟₁₂ of recipe): 263 cal., 13 g total fat (8 g sat. fat) 36 mg chol., 120 mg sodium, 38 g carbo., 0 g fiber, 1 g pro. **Daily Values:** 13% vit. A, 0% vit. C, 1% calcium, 1% iron

BUTTER FROSTING

START TO FINISH: 20 MINUTES

  ⅓ cup butter or margarine
4½ cups sifted powdered sugar
  ¼ cup milk
1½ teaspoons vanilla
      Milk
      Food coloring (optional)

1. In a mixing bowl beat butter till fluffy. Gradually add *2 cups* of the powdered sugar, beating well. Slowly beat in the ¼ cup milk and vanilla.

2. Slowly beat in remaining powdered sugar. Beat in additional milk, if needed, to reach spreading consistency. If desired, tint with food coloring. This frosts tops and sides of two 8- or 9-inch layers.

■ **Chocolate Butter Frosting:** Prepare as above, except beat ½ cup *unsweetened cocoa powder* into butter or margarine and reduce powdered sugar to a total of 4 cups.

■ Lemon or Orange Butter Frosting: Prepare as above, except substitute fresh *lemon juice or orange juice* for the milk and add $^{1}/_{2}$ teaspoon finely shredded *lemon peel* or 1 teaspoon finely shredded *orange peel* with the juice.

■ Peanut Butter Frosting: Prepare as above, except substitute *creamy peanut butter* for the butter or margarine.

Nutrition Facts per serving ($^{1}/_{12}$ of recipe): 193 cal., 5 g total fat (3 g sat. fat), 14 mg chol., 54 mg sodium, 38 g carbo., 0 g fiber, 0 g pro. **Daily Values:** 4% vit. A, 0% vit. C, 0% calcium, 0% iron

---

CHOCOLATE-SOUR CREAM FROSTING

START TO FINISH: 25 MINUTES

    1 6-ounce package (1 cup) semisweet chocolate pieces
 $^{1}/_{4}$ cup butter or margarine
 $^{1}/_{2}$ cup dairy sour cream
 $2^{1}/_{2}$ cups sifted powdered sugar

1. In a saucepan melt chocolate and butter over low heat, stirring frequently. Cool about 5 minutes. Stir in sour cream. Gradually add powdered sugar, beating till smooth and easy to spread. This frosts tops and sides of two 8- or 9-inch cake layers. Cover and store cake in the refrigerator.

Nutrition Facts per serving ($^{1}/_{12}$ of recipe): 211 cal., 8 g total fat (3 g sat. fat), 14 mg chol., 53 mg sodium, 35 g carbo., 0 g fiber, 1 g pro. **Daily Values:** 4% vit. A, 0% vit. C, 2% calcium, 2% iron

---

POWDERED SUGAR ICING

START TO FINISH: 10 MINUTES

    1 cup sifted powdered sugar
 $^{1}/_{4}$ teaspoon vanilla
    1 tablespoon milk or orange juice

1. In a mixing bowl combine powdered sugar, vanilla, and milk or juice. Stir in additional milk or juice, 1 teaspoon at a time, till it reaches drizzling consistency. Makes $^{1}/_{2}$ cup (enough to drizzle over one 10-inch tube cake).

■ Chocolate Powdered Sugar Icing: Prepare as above, except add

2 tablespoons *unsweetened cocoa powder* to the powdered sugar. Do not use the orange juice.

Nutrition Facts per serving (¹⁄₁₂ of recipe): 33 cal., 0 g total fat, 0 mg chol., 1 mg sodium, 8 g carbo., 0 g fiber, 0 g pro.

NO-COOK FUDGE FROSTING

START TO FINISH: 20 MINUTES

Make tasty fudge frosting the easy way with this no-cook recipe.

4³⁄₄ cups sifted powdered sugar
 ¹⁄₂ cup unsweetened cocoa powder
 ¹⁄₂ cup butter or margarine, softened
 ¹⁄₃ cup boiling water
  1 teaspoon vanilla

1. Combine powdered sugar and cocoa powder. Add butter, boiling water, and vanilla. Beat with an electric mixer on low speed till combined. Beat for 1 minute on medium speed. Cool for 20 to 30 minutes or till mixture reaches spreading consistency. This frosts the tops and sides of two 8- or 9-inch cake layers.

Nutrition Facts per serving (/₁₂ of recipe): 235 cal., 8 g total fat (5 g sat. fat), 20 mg chol., 78 mg sodium, 41 g carbo., 0 g fiber, 1 g pro. **Daily Values:** 7% vit. A, 0% vit. C, 3% calcium, 3% iron

---

SEVEN-MINUTE FROSTING

START TO FINISH: 25 MINUTES

1¹⁄₂ cups sugar
 ¹⁄₃ cup cold water
  2 egg whites
 ¹⁄₄ teaspoon cream of tartar or 2 teaspoons light-colored corn
       syrup
  1 teaspoon vanilla

1. In the top of a double boiler combine sugar, cold water, egg whites, and cream of tartar or corn syrup. Beat with an electric mixer on low speed for 30 seconds.
2. Place over boiling water (upper pan should not touch water). Cook, beating constantly with the electric mixer on high speed,

about 7 minutes or till frosting forms stiff peaks. Remove from the heat; add vanilla. Beat 2 to 3 minutes more or till it reaches spreading consistency. This frosts the tops and sides of two 8- or 9-inch cake layers or one 10-inch tube cake.

Nutrition Facts per serving (¹⁄₁₂ of recipe): 100 cal., 0 g total fat, 0 mg chol., 10 mg sodium, 25 g carbo., 0 g fiber, 1 g pro.

CREAMY WHITE FROSTING

START TO FINISH: 25 MINUTES

    1 **cup shortening**
1¹⁄₂ **teaspoons vanilla**
  ¹⁄₂ **teaspoon lemon extract, orange extract, or almond extract**
4¹⁄₂ **cups sifted powdered sugar**
   3 **to 4 tablespoons milk**

1. Beat shortening, vanilla, and extract with an electric mixer on medium speed for 30 seconds. Slowly add *half* of the powdered sugar, beating well. Add *2 tablespoons* of the milk. Gradually beat in remaining powdered sugar and enough remaining milk to reach spreading consistency. This frosts the tops and sides of two 8- or 9-inch cake layers.

Nutrition Facts per serving (¹⁄₁₂ of recipe): 300 cal., 17 g total fat (4 g sat. fat), 0 mg chol., 2 mg sodium, 38 g carbo., 0 g fiber, 0 g pro.

BROWNED BUTTER FROSTING

START TO FINISH: 20 MINUTES

1. In a small saucepan heat ¹⁄₂ cup *butter* over low heat till melted. Continue heating till butter turns a delicate brown. Remove from heat; pour into small bowl. Add 4 cups sifted *powdered sugar,* 2 tablespoons *milk,* and 1 teaspoon *vanilla.* Beat with an electric mixer on low speed till combined. Beat on medium to high speed, adding additional milk, if necessary, to reach spreading consistency. This frosts tops and sides of two 8- or 9-inch cake layers.

Nutrition Facts per serving (¹⁄₁₂ of recipe): 197 cal., 8 g total fat (5 g sat. fat), 21 mg chol., 79 mg sodium, 34 g carbo., 0 g fiber, 0 g pro. **Daily Values:** 7% vit. A, 0% vit. C, 0% calcium, 0% iron

CANDY

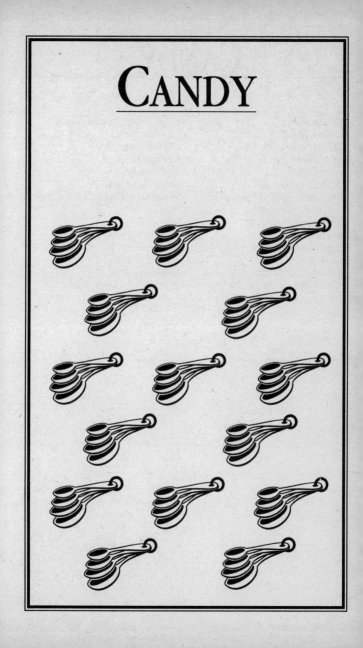

CANDY

COOKING AND TESTING CANDY MIXTURES

Cooking candy at the proper rate and then accurately determining when it is done are two very important steps in making candy successfully.

Candy mixtures should boil at a moderate, steady rate over their entire surface. To guide you, our recipes suggest range-top temperatures. However, you may need to adjust the temperature on your range in order to maintain the best rate of cooking, which ensures that the candy will cook within the recommended time. Cooking too fast or slow makes candy too hard or soft. When stirring a hot candy mixture, use a wooden spoon.

The most accurate way to test the stage of the hot mixture is to use a candy thermometer. Be sure to check the accuracy of your thermometer every time you use it. To test it, place the thermometer in a saucepan of boiling water for a few minutes, then read the temperature. If the thermometer reads above or below 212°, add or subtract the same number of degrees from the temperature specified in the recipe and cook to that temperature.

If a thermometer is not available, use the corresponding cold-water test described below. Start testing the candy shortly before it reaches the minimum cooking time.

Cold-Water Test

For the cold-water test, spoon a few drops of the hot candy mixture into a cup of very cold (but not icy) water. Using your fingers, form the drops into a ball. Remove the ball from the water; the firmness will indicate the temperature of the candy mixture. If the mixture has not reached the correct stage, continue cooking and retesting, using fresh water and a clean spoon each time.

■ **Thread stage** (230° to 233°): When a teaspoon is dipped into the hot mixture, then removed, the candy falls off the spoon in a 2-inch-long, fine, thin thread.

■ **Soft-ball stage** (234° to 240°): When the ball of candy is removed from the cold water, the candy instantly flattens and runs between your fingers.

■ **Firm-ball stage** (244° to 248°): When the ball of candy is removed from the cold water, it is firm enough to hold its shape, but quickly flattens at room temperature.

■ **Hard-ball stage** (250° to 266°): When the ball of candy is removed from the cold water, it can be deformed by pressure, but it doesn't flatten until pressed.

■ **Soft-crack stage** (270° to 290°): When dropped into the cold water, the candy separates into hard, but pliable and elastic, threads.

■ **Hard-crack stage** (295° to 310°): When dropped into the cold water, the candy separates into hard, brittle threads that snap easily.

OLD-TIME FUDGE

PREP: 20 MINUTES   COOK: 25 MINUTES   COOL: 55 MINUTES

Have a buddy handy to help you with the beating step because that's the critical part in making perfect traditional fudge.

2 cups sugar
³/₄ cup milk
2 ounces unsweetened chocolate, cut up
1 teaspoon light-colored corn syrup
2 tablespoons butter
1 teaspoon vanilla
¹/₂ cup chopped nuts (optional)

1. Line a 9×5×3-inch loaf pan with foil, extending foil over edges of pan. Butter foil; set pan aside.

2. Butter the sides of a heavy 2-quart saucepan. In saucepan combine sugar, milk, chocolate, and corn syrup. Cook and stir over medium-high heat till mixture boils. Clip a candy thermometer to side of pan. Reduce heat to medium-low; continue boiling at a moderate, steady rate, stirring frequently, till thermometer registers 234°, soft-ball stage (20 to 25 minutes).

3. Remove saucepan from heat. Add butter and vanilla, but do not stir. Cool, without stirring, to 110° (about 55 minutes).

4. Remove thermometer from saucepan. Beat mixture vigorously with a wooden spoon till fudge just begins to thicken. If desired, add nuts. Continue beating till the fudge becomes very thick and just starts to lose its gloss (about 10 minutes).

5. Immediately spread fudge in the prepared pan. Score into squares while warm. When fudge is firm, use foil to lift it out of pan. Cut fudge into squares. Store tightly covered. Makes about 1¹/₄ pounds (32 pieces).

Nutrition Facts per piece: 67 cal., 2 g total fat (1 g sat. fat), 2 mg chol., 11 mg sodium, 14 g carbo., 0 g fiber, 0 g pro. **Daily Values:** 1% vit. A, 0% vit. C, 0% calcium, 0% iron

WEATHER MAKES A DIFFERENCE

Many candies, especially divinity, are affected when the humidity is higher than 60 percent. A dry day is best for candymaking.

REMARKABLE FUDGE

PREP: 15 MINUTES   COOK: 15 MINUTES

When you include the candy bar, this fudge is even more remarkable because it's smoother.

4 **cups sugar**
2 **5-ounce cans (1$^1/_3$ cups total) evaporated milk**
1 **cup butter**
1 **12-ounce package (2 cups) semisweet chocolate pieces**
1 **7-ounce dark chocolate or milk chocolate candy bar, cut up (optional)**
1 **7-ounce jar marshmallow creme**
1 **cup chopped walnuts**
1 **teaspoon vanilla**

1. Line a 13×9×2-inch baking pan with foil, extending foil over edges of pan. Butter foil; set aside.

2. Butter sides of a heavy 3-quart saucepan. In saucepan combine sugar, evaporated milk, and butter. Cook and stir over medium-high heat till mixture boils. Reduce heat to medium; continue cooking and stirring for 10 minutes.

3. Remove pan from heat. Add chocolate pieces, cut-up chocolate bar (if desired), marshmallow creme, walnuts, and vanilla; stir till chocolate melts and mixture is combined. Beat by hand for 1 minute. Spread in the prepared pan. Score into 1-inch squares while warm. When fudge is firm, use foil to lift it out of pan. Cut fudge into squares. Store in a tightly covered container in the refrigerator. Makes about 4 pounds (96 pieces).

Nutrition Facts per piece: 84 cal., 4 g total fat (1 g sat. fat), 6 mg chol., 24 mg sodium, 13 g carbo., 0 g fiber, 1 g pro. **Daily Values:** 1% vit. A, 0% vit. C, 0% calcium, 0% iron

■ **Peanut Butter-Chocolate Fudge:** Prepare as above, except substitute 1 cup *peanut butter* for the butter and, if desired, *peanuts* for the walnuts. Do not use the optional chocolate candy bar.

Nutrition Facts per piece: 76 cal., 3 g total fat (1 g sat. fat)

PENUCHE

PREP: 20 MINUTES   COOK: 20 MINUTES   COOL: 50 MINUTES

1½ cups granulated sugar
 1 cup packed brown sugar
⅓ cup half-and-half or light cream
⅓ cup milk
 2 tablespoons butter
 1 teaspoon vanilla
½ cup chopped pecans or walnuts

1. Line an 8×4×2- or a 9×5×3-inch loaf pan with foil, extending foil over edges of pan. Butter the foil; set pan aside.

2. Butter sides of a heavy 2-quart saucepan. In saucepan combine sugars, half-and-half or cream, and milk. Cook and stir over medium-high heat till mixture boils. Clip a candy thermometer to side of pan. Reduce heat to medium-low; continue boiling at a moderate, steady rate, stirring frequently, till thermometer registers 236°, soft-ball stage (15 to 20 minutes).

3. Remove saucepan from heat. Add butter and vanilla, but do not stir. Cool, without stirring, to 110° (about 50 minutes).

4. Remove thermometer from saucepan. Beat mixture vigorously with a wooden spoon till penuche just begins to thicken. Add nuts. Continue beating till penuche becomes very thick and just starts to lose its gloss (about 10 minutes total).

5. Immediately spread penuche in the prepared pan. Score into squares while warm. When penuche is firm, use foil to lift it out of pan. Cut penuche into squares. Store tightly covered. Makes about 1¼ pounds (32 pieces).

Nutrition Facts per piece: 80 cal., 2 g total fat (1 g sat. fat), 3 mg chol., 11 mg sodium, 15 g carbo., 0 g fiber, 0 g pro.
Daily Values: 1% vit. A, 0% vit. C, 0% calcium, 1% iron

BUTTER MAKES BETTER CANDY

With all the new margarine blends and spreads that resemble margarine, our Test Kitchen recommends using only butter for candymaking. Soft margarines and spreads contain too much water and varying amounts of fat to make good homemade candy.

OPERA FUDGE

PREP: 20 MINUTES   COOK: 30 MINUTES   COOL: 55 MINUTES

  2 cups sugar
  $^1/_2$ cup milk
  $^1/_2$ cup half-and-half or light cream
  1 tablespoon light-colored corn syrup
  1 tablespoon butter
  1 teaspoon vanilla

1. Line an 8×4×2-inch loaf pan with foil, extending foil over edges of pan. Butter foil; set pan aside.

2. Butter sides of a heavy 2-quart saucepan. In pan combine sugar, milk, half-and-half, and corn syrup. Cook and stir over medium-high heat till mixture boils. Clip a candy thermometer to pan. Reduce heat to medium-low; continue boiling at a moderate, steady rate, stirring frequently, till thermometer registers 238°, soft-ball stage (25 to 35 minutes).

3. Remove saucepan from heat. Add butter and vanilla, but do not stir. Cool, without stirring, to 110° (about 55 minutes).

4. Remove thermometer from saucepan. Beat mixture vigorously till fudge becomes very thick and just starts to lose its gloss (about 10 minutes total).

5. Immediately spread fudge in prepared pan. Score into squares while warm. When firm, use foil to lift it out of pan. Cut fudge into squares. Store tightly covered. Makes about 1 pound (32 pieces).

Nutrition Facts per piece: 61 cal., 1 g total fat (1 g sat. fat), 3 mg chol., 8 mg sodium, 13 g carbo., 0 g fiber, 0 g pro. **Daily Values:** 1% vit. A, 0% vit. C, 0% calcium, 0% iron

PRALINES

PREP: 20 MINUTES   COOK: 20 MINUTES   COOL: 30 MINUTES

  $1^1/_2$ cups granulated sugar
  $1^1/_2$ cups packed brown sugar
  1 cup half-and-half or light cream
  3 tablespoons butter
  2 cups pecan halves

1. Butter sides of a heavy 2-quart saucepan. In saucepan combine sugars and half-and-half. Cook and stir over medium-high heat till mixture boils. Clip a candy thermometer to pan. Reduce heat to medium-low; continue boiling at a moderate, steady rate, stirring occasionally, till thermometer registers 234°, soft-ball stage (16 to 18 minutes).

2. Remove pan from heat. Add butter; do not stir. Cool, without stirring, to 150° (about 30 minutes).

3. Remove thermometer from saucepan. Stir in pecans. Beat vigorously with a wooden spoon till mixture just begins to thicken but is still glossy (about 3 minutes). Working quickly, drop candy by spoonfuls onto waxed paper. When firm, store in a tightly covered container. Makes about 36 pieces.

Nutrition Facts per piece: 117 cal., 6 g total fat (1 g sat. fat), 5 mg chol., 15 mg sodium, 17 g carbo., 0 g fiber, 1 g pro. **Daily Values:** 1% vit. A, 0% vit. C, 1% calcium, 2% iron

■ **Chocolate Pralines:** Prepare as above, except add 2 ounces *unsweetened chocolate*, finely chopped, with the butter.

Nutrition Facts per piece: 125 cal., 7 g total fat (2 g sat. fat)

CARAMELS

PREP: 15 MINUTES   COOK: 55 MINUTES

    1 cup chopped walnuts (optional)
    1 cup butter
    1 16-ounce package (2¼ cups) packed brown sugar
    2 cups half-and-half or light cream
    1 cup light-colored corn syrup
    1 teaspoon vanilla

1. Line an 8×8×2- or 9×9×2-inch baking pan with foil, extending foil over edges of pan. Butter the foil. If desired, sprinkle walnuts onto bottom of pan. Set pan aside.

2. In a heavy 3-quart saucepan melt butter over low heat. Add brown sugar, half-and-half or cream, and corn syrup; mix well. Cook and stir over medium-high heat till mixture boils. Clip a candy thermometer to the side of the pan. Reduce heat to medium; continue boiling at a moderate, steady rate, stirring frequently, till the thermometer registers 248°, firm-ball stage (45 to 60 minutes).

3. Remove saucepan from heat; remove thermometer. Stir in vanilla. Quickly pour the mixture into the prepared pan. When caramel mixture is firm, use foil to lift it out of pan. Use a buttered knife to cut into 1-inch squares. Wrap each piece in plastic wrap. Makes about 2 pounds (64 pieces).

Nutrition Facts per piece: 76 cal., 4 g total fat (2 g sat. fat), 10 mg chol., 38 mg sodium, 11 g carbo., 0 g fiber, 0 g pro. **Daily Values:** 3% vit. A, 0% vit. C, 1% calcium, 2% iron

■ **Shortcut Caramels:** Prepare as above, except substitute one 14-ounce can *sweetened condensed milk* for the cream. This mixture will take less time to reach 248° (about 15 to 20 minutes instead of 45 to 60 minutes).

Nutrition Facts per piece: 68 cal., 3 g total fat (2 g sat. fat)

CARAMEL APPLES

PREP: 25 MINUTES   COOK: 55 MINUTES

> 14 to 16 small tart apples
> 1 recipe Caramels or Shortcut Caramels (see above)
> 1 cup chopped peanuts (optional)

1. Wash and dry apples; remove stems. Insert a wooden skewer into the stem end of each apple. Place apples on a buttered baking sheet.
2. Prepare Caramels recipe as directed, except do not pour mixture into pan. Working quickly, dip each apple into hot caramel mixture; turn to coat. If desired, dip bottoms of apples into peanuts. Set on prepared baking sheet; chill, if desired, for up to 2 days. Makes 14 to 16 caramel apples.

Nutrition Facts per apple: 430 cal., 17 g total fat (11 g sat. fat), 48 mg chol., 174 mg sodium, 71 g carbo., 3 g fiber, 1 g pro. **Daily Values:** 17% vit. A, 13% vit. C, 7% calcium, 12% iron

SALTWATER TAFFY

For easier taffymaking, enlist one, two, or even three helpers. Have them butter their hands, then twist and pull portions of the candy until it becomes creamy and stiff.

  2 cups sugar
  1 cup light-colored corn syrup
  1 cup water
1¹/₂ teaspoons salt
  2 tablespoons butter
¹/₄ teaspoon peppermint extract, rum flavoring, or a few drops oil
      of cinnamon (optional)
      Few drops food coloring (optional)

1. Butter a 15×10×1-inch baking pan; set aside.
2. Butter sides of a heavy 2-quart saucepan. In saucepan combine sugar, corn syrup, water, and salt. Cook and stir over medium-high heat till mixture boils. Clip a candy thermometer to side of pan. Reduce heat to medium; continue boiling at a moderate, steady rate, without stirring, till thermometer registers 265°, hard-ball stage (about 40 minutes).
3. Remove saucepan from heat; remove thermometer. Stir in butter. If desired, stir in extract and food coloring. Pour into the prepared pan. Cool for 15 to 20 minutes or till taffy mixture is easy to handle.
4. Butter your hands. Twist and pull candy till it turns a creamy color and is stiff and quite difficult to pull (10 to 15 minutes). Candy is ready if it cracks when tapped on counter. Divide candy into 4 pieces; twist and pull each piece into a long strand about ¹/₂ inch thick. With buttered scissors, snip each strand of taffy into bite-size pieces. Wrap each piece in plastic wrap. Makes about 1¹/₂ pounds (100 pieces).

Nutrition Facts per piece: 27 cal., 0 g total fat, 1 mg chol., 37 mg sodium, 6 g carbo., 0 g fiber, 0 g pro.

EASY CHOCOLATE TRUFFLES

START TO FINISH: ABOUT 3 HOURS

Much of the 3 hours you put into making these candies is spent waiting for the mixture to chill. This frees you to work on other projects at the same time.

1 11½-ounce package milk chocolate pieces
⅓ cup whipping cream
¼ teaspoon almond extract
⅓ cup toasted ground almonds
8 ounces vanilla-flavored candy coating
½ cup semisweet chocolate pieces, melted

1. In a heavy saucepan combine milk chocolate pieces and whipping cream. Cook over low heat for 4 to 5 minutes or till chocolate melts, stirring frequently. Remove saucepan from heat. Cool slightly. Stir in almond extract. Beat mixture with an electric mixer on low speed till smooth. Cover and refrigerate about 1 hour or till firm.

2. Line a baking sheet with waxed paper. Shape chocolate mixture into ¾-inch balls; roll in ground almonds. Place on prepared baking sheet. Freeze for 30 minutes.

3. Meanwhile, melt candy coating (see tip, page 312). Line a baking sheet with waxed paper. Quickly dip truffles, one at a time, into coating. Let excess coating drip off truffles. Place truffles on prepared baking sheet; let stand about 30 minutes or till coating is set. Decoratively drizzle the melted chocolate over the tops of the truffles. Store in a tightly covered container in the refrigerator. Makes about 30 pieces.

Nutrition Facts per piece: 126 cal., 8 g total fat (4 g sat. fat), 4 mg chol., 19 mg sodium, 13 g carbo., 0 g fiber, 2 g pro. **Daily Values:** 2% vit. A, 0% vit. C, 3% calcium, 1% iron

DIVINITY

PREP: 25 MINUTES   COOK: 20 MINUTES

No-Fat

2½ cups sugar
½ cup light-colored corn syrup
2 egg whites
1 teaspoon vanilla
1 or 2 drops food coloring (optional)
½ cup chopped candied fruit or nuts

1. In a heavy 2-quart saucepan combine sugar, corn syrup, and ½ cup *water*. Cook and stir over medium-high heat till mixture boils. Clip a candy thermometer to the side of the pan. Reduce heat to medium; continue cooking, without stirring, till the thermometer registers 260°, hard-ball stage (10 to 15 minutes).
2. Remove pan from heat; remove thermometer. In a large mixing bowl beat egg whites with a freestanding electric mixer on medium speed till stiff peaks form (tips stand straight). Gradually pour hot mixture in a thin stream over whites, beating on high speed about 3 minutes; scrape sides of bowl occasionally. Add vanilla and, if desired, food coloring. Continue beating on high just till candy starts to lose its gloss (5 to 6 minutes). When beaters are lifted, mixture should fall in a ribbon that mounds on itself.
3. Drop a spoonful of candy mixture onto waxed paper. If it stays mounded, the mixture has been beaten sufficiently. If mixture flattens, beat ½ to 1 minute more; check again. If mixture is too stiff to spoon, beat in a few drops hot water till candy is a softer consistency. Immediately stir in fruit or nuts. Quickly drop remaining mixture onto waxed paper. Store tightly covered. Makes about 40 pieces.

Nutrition Facts per piece: 66 cal., 0 g total fat, 0 mg chol., 6 mg sodium, 17 g carbo., 0 g fiber, 0 g pro. **Daily Values:** 0% vit. A, 0% vit. C, 0% calcium, 1% iron

TOFFEE BUTTER CRUNCH

PREP: 20 MINUTES   COOK: 20 MINUTES   CHILL: 15 MINUTES

½ cup coarsely chopped almonds or pecans, toasted (see tip, page 234)

1 cup butter
1 cup sugar
3 tablespoons water
1 tablespoon light-colored corn syrup
³/₄ cup semisweet chocolate pieces
¹/₂ cup finely chopped almonds or pecans, toasted (see tip, page 234)

1. Line a 13×9×2-inch baking pan with foil, extending foil over edges of pan. Sprinkle the ¹/₂ cup coarsely chopped nuts in pan. Set pan aside.

2. Butter sides of a heavy 2-quart saucepan. In saucepan melt butter. Add sugar, water, and corn syrup. Cook and stir over medium-high heat till mixture boils. Clip a candy thermometer to side of pan. Reduce heat to medium; continue boiling at a moderate, steady rate, stirring frequently, till thermometer registers 290°, soft-crack stage (about 15 minutes). Watch carefully after 280° to prevent scorching. Remove saucepan from heat; remove thermometer. Pour candy into the prepared pan.

3. Let candy stand about 5 minutes or till firm; sprinkle with chocolate. Let stand 1 to 2 minutes. When chocolate has softened, spread over candy. Sprinkle with the ¹/₂ cup finely chopped nuts. Chill till firm. When candy is firm, use foil to lift it out of pan; break into pieces. Store tightly covered. Makes about 1¹/₂ pounds (48 servings).

Nutrition Facts per serving: 79 cal., 6 g total fat (2 g sat. fat), 10 mg chol., 39 mg sodium, 7 g carbo., 0 g fiber, 1 g pro. **Daily Values:** 3% vit. A, 0% vit. C, 0% calcium, 1% iron

---

PEANUT BRITTLE

PREP: 15 MINUTES   COOK: 50 MINUTES

Change this classic candy to feature your favorite nut, such as cashews, or try hazelnuts or fancy mixed nuts.

2 cups sugar
1 cup light-colored corn syrup
¹/₄ cup butter
2¹/₂ cups raw peanuts or other coarsely chopped nuts
1¹/₂ teaspoons baking soda, sifted

1. Butter 2 large baking sheets; set aside. Butter sides of a heavy 3-quart saucepan. In pan combine sugar, corn syrup, butter, and ¹/₂ cup *water*. Cook and stir over medium-high heat till mixture boils. Clip a candy thermometer to side of pan. Reduce heat to medium-low; continue boiling at a moderate, steady rate, stirring occasionally, till the thermometer registers 275°, soft-crack stage (about 30 minutes). Stir in nuts; continue cooking over medium-low heat, stirring frequently, till thermometer registers 295°, hard-crack stage (15 to 20 minutes more).

2. Remove pan from heat; remove thermometer. Quickly sprinkle baking soda over mixture, stirring constantly (see photo 1, below). Immediately pour onto prepared baking sheets. Use 2 forks to lift and pull candy as it cools (see photo 2, below). Cool completely; break into pieces. Store tightly covered. Makes 2¹/₄ pounds (72 servings).

Nutrition Facts per serving: 69 cal., 3 g total fat (1 g sat. fat), 2 mg chol., 37 mg sodium, 10 g carbo., 0 g fiber, 1 g pro. **Daily Values:** 0% vit. A, 0% vit. C, 0% calcium, 2% iron

1. Stir constantly as you sprinkle baking soda over candy mixture. The candy will foam as the soda reacts chemically. This makes the brittle porous.

2. As candy cools, stretch it into a thin sheet by lifting and pulling with two forks. Pull gently to avoid tearing. Stretching helps make brittle crisp.

CHOCOLATE-COVERED CHERRIES

DRAIN CHERRIES: 4 HOURS   PREP: 1¼ HOURS   CHILL: 1 HOUR

Three 10-ounce jars of cherries with stems yield about 60 cherries.

- 60 maraschino cherries with stems
- 3 tablespoons butter, softened
- 3 tablespoons light-colored corn syrup
- 2 cups sifted powdered sugar
- 1 pound chocolate-flavored candy coating

1. Drain cherries thoroughly on paper towels for several hours. Line a baking sheet with waxed paper; set baking sheet aside.

2. In a small mixing bowl combine butter and corn syrup. Stir in powdered sugar; knead mixture till smooth (chill if mixture is too soft to handle). Shape about ½ teaspoon powdered sugar mixture around each cherry. Place coated cherries, stem sides up, on the prepared baking sheet; chill about 1 hour or till firm (do not chill too long or sugar mixture will begin to dissolve).

3. Melt candy coating (see tip, page 312). Line a baking sheet with waxed paper. Holding cherries by stems, dip one at a time into coating; if necessary, spoon coating over cherries to coat. (Be sure to completely seal cherries in coating to prevent juice from leaking.) Let excess coating drip off. Place cherries, stem sides up, on prepared baking sheet.

4. Chill till coating is firm. Store in a tightly covered container in the refrigerator. Let candies ripen in refrigerator for 1 to 2 weeks before serving. (Ripening allows powdered sugar mixture around cherries to soften and liquefy.) Makes 60 pieces.

Nutrition Facts per piece: 70 cal., 3 g total fat (2 g sat. fat), 2 mg chol., 14 mg sodium, 11 g carbo., 0 g fiber, 1 g pro. **Daily Values:** 0% vit. A, 0% vit. C, 1% calcium, 0% iron

DIPPING CANDY

Both candy coating and melted chocolate are used for dipping candies. Candy coating, a chocolatelike product sometimes called almond bark, confectioner's coating, or summer coating, is probably the easiest way to coat candy. It usually comes in chocolate and vanilla flavors, doesn't speckle as it hardens, melts easily, and does not need to be tempered before dipping.

To melt candy coating for dipping, cut it up, place it in a heavy saucepan, and stir it constantly over low heat until melted and smooth. Or, you can microwave 8 ounces of the candy coating in a microwave-safe bowl, uncovered, on 100% power (high) for 1 to 3 minutes or until coating is almost melted; stir until smooth.

Semisweet and milk chocolate usually need to be tempered before dipping. This refers to the process of melting and cooling chocolate to the correct dipping temperature. Without tempering, the surface of chocolate develops speckles or gray streaks as it hardens, which affects only the appearance of the candy, not the flavor.

To quick-temper semisweet chocolate pieces, combine 1 tablespoon shortening for every 6 ounces chocolate (up to 1 pound at a time) in a 4-cup glass measure. Pour very warm water (100° to 110°) into a large glass bowl to a depth of 1 inch. Place the measure with the chocolate inside the bowl of water. The water should cover the bottom half of the measure containing the chocolate (adjust water level as necessary). It is important not to splash any water into the chocolate.

Stir chocolate mixture constantly with a rubber spatula until completely melted and smooth (15 to 20 minutes). If water begins to cool, remove measure with chocolate and replace the water in the bowl. Return measure with chocolate to warm-water bath and continue stirring. When melted and smooth, chocolate is ready for dipping. If chocolate becomes too thick during dipping, return it to the warm-water bath and stir until it again reaches dipping consistency.

Store candies that have been dipped in tempered chocolate at room temperature.

PEANUT BUTTER BALLS

PREP: 1 HOUR

- $^1/_2$ cup peanut butter
- 3 tablespoons butter
- 1 cup sifted powdered sugar
- 8 ounces chocolate-flavored candy coating

1. In a mixing bowl stir together peanut butter and butter. Gradually add powdered sugar, stirring till combined. Shape into 1-inch balls; place on waxed paper. Let stand till dry (about 20 minutes).
2. Melt candy coating (see tip, page 312). Cool slightly. Dip balls, one at a time, into coating. Let excess coating drip off peanut butter balls. Place on waxed paper; let stand till coating is firm. Store tightly covered in refrigerator. Makes about 30 pieces.

Nutrition Facts per piece: 88 cal., 6 g total fat (2 g sat. fat), 3 mg chol., 39 mg sodium, 9 g carbo., 0 g fiber, 2 g pro. **Daily Values:** 1% vit. A, 0% vit. C, 1% calcium, 0% iron

HARD CANDY

PREP: 1$^1/_4$ HOURS   COOK: 25 MINUTES

No-Fat

These tiny candies with only 12 calories each have a crystal-clear appearance.

- 2 cups sugar
- 1 cup light-colored corn syrup
- $^1/_4$ teaspoon desired food coloring
  Few drops oil of cinnamon or oil of peppermint

1. Line an 8×8×2-inch baking pan with foil, extending foil over edges of pan. Butter foil; set aside.
2. Butter sides of a heavy 2-quart saucepan. In saucepan combine sugar, corn syrup, and $^1/_2$ cup *water*. Cook and stir over medium-high heat till mixture boils, stirring to dissolve the sugar (about 5 minutes). Clip a candy thermometer to side of pan. Reduce heat to medium; continue boiling at a moderate, steady rate, stirring occasionally, till thermometer registers 290°, soft-crack stage (20 to 25 minutes).

3. Remove saucepan from heat; remove thermometer. Quickly stir in desired food coloring and flavored oil. Immediately pour mixture into the prepared pan. Let stand for 5 to 10 minutes or till a film forms over the surface of the candy.

4. Using a broad spatula or pancake turner, begin marking candy by pressing a line across surface $^{1}/_{2}$ inch from edge of pan. Do not break film on surface. Repeat along other three sides of pan, intersecting lines at corners to form squares. (If lines do not remain in candy, it is not cool enough to mark. Let candy stand a few more minutes and start again.) Continue marking lines along all sides, $^{1}/_{2}$ inch apart, till you reach center. Retrace previous lines, pressing spatula deeper but still not breaking the film on surface. Repeat till the spatula can be pressed to bottom of pan along all lines. Cool completely. Use foil to lift candy out of pan; break candy into squares. Store tightly covered. Makes $1^{1}/_{2}$ pounds (216 pieces).

Nutrition Facts per piece: 12 cal., 0 g total fat (0 g sat. fat), 0 mg chol., 1 mg sodium, 3 g carbo., 0 g fiber, 0 g pro.

SUGAR-SPICED NUTS

PREP: 20 MINUTES   BAKE: 20 MINUTES   Oven 325°

Pumpkin pie spice sweetens these nuts and gives them a rich color.

   1 **egg white**
   1 **teaspoon water**
   2 **12-ounce cans (5 cups total) mixed nuts**
   1 **cup sugar**
   1 **tablespoon pumpkin pie spice**

1. Grease a 15×10×1-inch baking pan. Set pan aside. In a large mixing bowl beat egg white and water till frothy. Add the nuts and toss to coat. Combine sugar and pumpkin pie spice. Sprinkle over nuts; toss to coat.

2. Spread nuts in a single layer in the prepared baking pan. Bake in a 325° oven for 20 minutes. Cool slightly in pan. Transfer to waxed paper to cool. Break into clusters. Store tightly covered up to 1 week. Makes 8 cups (32 servings).

Nutrition Facts per piece: 157 cal., 12 g total fat (2 g sat. fat), 0 mg chol., 4 mg sodium, 11 g carbo., 2 g fiber, 4 g pro. **Daily Values:** 0% vit. A, 0% vit. C, 2% calcium, and 4% iron

CANDIED NUTS

PREP: 20 MINUTES

*Try sprinkling some of these sweetened nuts atop a salad
in place of croutons.*

1¹/₂ cups raw or roasted cashews, peanuts, whole almonds, and/or
     pecan halves
  ¹/₂ cup sugar
  2 tablespoons butter
  ¹/₂ teaspoon vanilla

1. Line a baking sheet with foil. Butter the foil; set baking sheet
aside.
2. In a heavy 10-inch skillet combine nuts, sugar, butter, and vanilla.
Cook over medium-high heat, shaking skillet occasionally, till sugar
begins to melt. Do not stir.
3. Reduce heat to low; continue cooking till sugar is golden brown,
stirring occasionally. Remove skillet from heat. Pour nut mixture
onto the prepared baking sheet. Cool completely. Break into clusters. Store tightly covered. Makes about 10 ounces (12 servings).

Nutrition Facts per serving: 146 cal., 11 g total fat (2 g sat. fat), 5 mg chol., 21 mg
sodium, 11 g carbo., 1 g fiber, 2 g pro. **Daily Values:** 1% vit. A, 0% vit. C, 1% calcium, and
2% iron

OLD-FASHIONED POPCORN BALLS

PREP: 30 MINUTES   COOK: 25 MINUTES   Oven 300°

No-Fat

*No time to shape popcorn into balls? Spread it out on buttered foil to
cool, then break into clusters.*

  18 cups popped popcorn
   2 cups sugar
   1 cup water
  ¹/₂ cup light-colored corn syrup
   1 teaspoon vinegar
  ¹/₂ teaspoon salt
   1 tablespoon vanilla

1. Remove all unpopped kernels from popped popcorn. Put popcorn in a greased 17×12×2-inch baking or roasting pan. Keep popcorn warm in a 300° oven while making syrup.

2. For syrup mixture, butter the sides of a heavy 2-quart saucepan. In saucepan combine sugar, water, corn syrup, vinegar, and salt. Cook and stir over medium-high heat till mixture boils, stirring to dissolve sugar (about 6 minutes). Clip a candy thermometer to side of pan. Reduce heat to medium; continue boiling at a moderate, steady rate, stirring occasionally, till thermometer registers 250°, hard-ball stage (about 20 minutes).

3. Remove saucepan from heat; remove thermometer. Stir in vanilla. Pour syrup mixture over the hot popcorn and stir gently to coat. Cool till the popcorn mixture can be handled easily. With buttered hands, quickly shape the mixture into 2^1/$_2$-inch diameter balls. Wrap each popcorn ball in plastic wrap. Makes about 20 popcorn balls.

Nutrition Facts per ball: 140 cal., 0 g total fat, 0 mg chol., 60 mg sodium, 33 g carbo., 1 g fiber, 1 g pro. **Daily Values:** 0% vit. A, 0% vit. C, 0% calcium, 3% iron

CARAMEL CORN

PREP: 10 MINUTES   COOK: 15 MINUTES   BAKE: 20 MINUTES   Oven 300°

    7 to 8 cups popped popcorn
 ^{3}/$_4$ cup packed brown sugar
    6 tablespoons butter
    3 tablespoons light-colored corn syrup
 ^{1}/$_4$ teaspoon baking soda
 ^{1}/$_4$ teaspoon vanilla

1. Remove all unpopped kernels from popped popcorn. Put popcorn into a 17×12×2-inch baking or roasting pan.

2. In a medium saucepan mix brown sugar, butter, and corn syrup. Cook and stir over medium heat till mixture boils. Continue boiling at a moderate, steady rate, without stirring, for 5 minutes more.

3. Remove pan from heat. Stir in baking soda and vanilla. Pour mixture over popcorn; stir gently to coat. Bake in a 300° oven for 15 minutes. Stir mixture; bake 5 minutes more. Spread caramel corn on a large piece of buttered foil to cool. Store tightly covered. Makes 7 to 8 cups (7 servings).

Nutrition Facts per serving: 224 cal., 10 g total fat (6 g sat. fat), 26 mg chol., 157 mg sodium, 33 g carbo., 1 g fiber, 1 g pro. **Daily Values:** 9% vit. A, 0% vit. C, 2% calcium, 7% iron

---

BOURBON BALLS

PREP: 40 MINUTES   STAND: 2 OR 3 DAYS

For a no-alcohol version, substitute a mixture of 2 tablespoons water and ¹/₂ teaspoon rum or brandy flavoring for the bourbon.

    2 cups sifted powdered sugar
 1¹/₂ cups crushed vanilla wafers
 1¹/₂ cups finely chopped walnuts
  ¹/₄ cup unsweetened cocoa powder
    3 tablespoons light-colored corn syrup
    2 tablespoons bourbon or rum

1. Mix powdered sugar, vanilla wafers, nuts, and cocoa powder. Stir in corn syrup, bourbon or rum, and 3 tablespoons *water* till combined. On a surface lightly dusted with powdered sugar, pat candy mixture into an 8x6-inch rectangle; cut into 48 pieces and roll each piece in a ball. Place balls in a tightly covered container; let stand for 2 or 3 days. Before serving, roll balls in additional sifted powdered sugar. Makes about 48 pieces.

Nutrition Facts per piece: 62 cal., 3 g total fat (0 g sat. fat), 2 mg chol., 9 mg sodium, 9 g carbo., 0 g fiber, 1 g pro. **Daily Values:** 0% vit. A, 0% vit. C, 0% calcium, 1% iron

---

CREAM CHEESE MINTS

PREP: 50 MINUTES   DRY: OVERNIGHT

    1 3-ounce package cream cheese, softened
  ¹/₂ teaspoon peppermint extract
    3 cups sifted powdered sugar
      Few drops desired food coloring
      Granulated sugar

1. In a small mixing bowl stir together softened cream cheese and peppermint extract. Gradually add powdered sugar, stirring till mixture is smooth. (Knead in the last of the powdered sugar with your hands.) Add food coloring; knead till food coloring is evenly distributed.

2. Form cream cheese mixture into ³/₄-inch balls. Roll each ball in granulated sugar; place on waxed paper. Flatten each ball with the bottom of a juice glass or with the tines of a fork. (Or, sprinkle small candy molds lightly with sugar. Press about ³/₄ to 1 teaspoon cream cheese mixture into each mold. Remove from molds.) Cover mints with paper towels; let dry overnight. Store in a tightly covered container in the refrigerator or freeze up to 1 month. Makes 48 to 60 pieces.

Nutrition Facts per piece: 31 cal., 1 g total fat (0 g sat. fat), 2 mg chol., 5 mg sodium, 7 g carbo., 0 g fiber, 0 g pro.

CARAMEL SNAPPERS

PREP: 1¹/₄ HOURS

Shorten preparation time by enlisting some help to arrange the pecan halves in "trios" on the buttered foil.

> 90 pecan halves (about 1¹/₂ cups), toasted (see tip, page 234)
> ¹/₂ of a 14-ounce package vanilla caramels (about 25)
> 1 tablespoon butter
> ¹/₂ cup semisweet chocolate pieces
> 1 teaspoon shortening

1. Line a baking sheet with foil. Butter the foil. On foil, arrange pecans in groups of 3, flat sides down.
2. In a heavy saucepan combine caramels and butter. Cook and stir over low heat till melted and smooth. Remove from heat. Drop about 1 teaspoon melted caramel mixture onto each group of pecans. Let caramel pieces stand till firm (about 20 minutes).
3. In a small saucepan heat chocolate pieces and shortening over low heat, stirring constantly, till melted and smooth. Remove from heat. With a narrow spatula, spread a small amount of melted chocolate mixture over the top of each caramel piece. Let stand till firm. Remove from baking sheet. Store tightly covered. Makes 30 pieces.

Nutrition Facts per piece: 81 cal., 6 g total fat (1 g sat. fat), 1 mg chol., 21 mg sodium, 8 g carbo., 1 g fiber, 1 g pro. **Daily Values:** 0% vit. A, 0% vit. C, 1% calcium, 1% iron

MARBLED MINT CANDY

PREP: 25 MINUTES   CHILL: 30 MINUTES

With its swirls of chocolate and dots of candy cane bits, this candy makes a festive addition to a tray of sweets.

1/3 cup semisweet mint-flavored chocolate pieces or semisweet chocolate pieces
1 pound vanilla-flavored candy coating, cut up
3/4 cup finely crushed candy cane or finely crushed striped round peppermint candies

1. Line a baking sheet with foil. Set baking sheet aside. In a small saucepan heat chocolate pieces over low heat, stirring constantly, till melted and smooth. Remove saucepan from heat.
2. In a 2-quart saucepan melt candy coating (see tip, page 312). Remove saucepan from heat. Stir in crushed candy canes. Pour melted coating mixture onto the prepared baking sheet. Spread coating mixture to about a 3/8-inch thickness; drizzle with the melted chocolate. Gently zigzag a narrow metal spatula through the chocolate and peppermint layers to create a marbled effect.
3. Chill candy about 30 minutes or till firm. (Or, let candy stand at room temperature for several hours or till firm.) Use foil to lift firm candy from the baking sheet; carefully break candy into pieces. Store tightly covered for up to 2 weeks. Makes about 1 1/4 pounds (about 32 servings).

Nutrition Facts per serving: 104 cal., 5 g total fat (3 g sat. fat), 1 mg chol., 14 mg sodium, 15 g carbo., 0 g fiber, 1 g pro. **Daily Values:** 0% vit. A, 0% vit. C, 2% calcium, 1% iron

■ **Marbled Almond Candy:** Prepare as above, except use only the plain semisweet chocolate pieces and increase to 1 cup. Omit the crushed candy and stir 1 cup *whole blanched almonds,* toasted (see tip, page 234), into the melted candy coating before pouring it onto the baking sheet.

Nutrition Facts per serving: 119 cal., 7 g total fat (3 g sat. fat)

CANNING & FREEZING

CANNING & FREEZING

SYRUP FOR FRUIT

Choose the syrup that best suits the fruit and your taste.
Generally, heavier syrups are used with very sour fruits, and
lighter syrups are recommended for mild-flavored fruits. To
prepare syrup, place the specified amounts of sugar and
water in a large saucepan. Heat until the sugar dissolves. Skim
off foam, if necessary. Use the syrup hot for canned fruits and
chilled for frozen fruits. Allow $1/2$ to $2/3$ cup syrup for each 2
cups of fruit.

Type of Syrup	Sugar	Water	Yield
Very thin	1 cup	4 cups	4 cups
Thin	$1^2/3$ cups	4 cups	$4^1/4$ cups
Medium	$2^2/3$ cups	4 cups	$4^2/3$ cups
Heavy	4 cups	4 cups	$5^3/4$ cups

SAFETY REMINDER

Always boil home-canned vegetables (except tomatoes)
before tasting or using them. Bring the food to a boil and boil
for 10 minutes if you live less than 1,000 feet above sea level.
If you live more than 1,000 feet above sea level, add an
additional minute for each 1,000 feet of elevation. Add water,
if needed, to prevent sticking. If you smell an unnatural odor
as the food heats, discard the food (see "Detecting Spoilage,"
page 345).

FREEZING

Freezing is an easy way to preserve fruits and vegetables. For best
results, start with top-quality, garden-fresh products. Prepare, package, and store them as recommended and use within the suggested
storage time.

HEADSPACE MATTERS

The amount of space between the top of the food and the rim of its container is called headspace. Leaving the correct amount is essential when canning and freezing.

In canning, headspace is necessary for a vacuum to form and for the jar to seal. Use the amount specified for each food in the charts on pages 330 to 344.

In freezing, headspace allows room for the food to expand without breaking the container. When using unsweetened or dry pack (no sugar or liquid added), leave a ½-inch headspace unless otherwise directed. When using sugar, sugar-syrup, or water pack and wide-top containers with straight or slightly flared sides, leave a ½-inch headspace for pints and a 1-inch headspace for quarts. For narrow-top containers and freezing jars, leave a ¾-inch headspace for pints and a 1½-inch headspace for quarts.

EQUIPMENT

An accurate *freezer thermometer* will help you regulate your freezer temperature at 0° or below. Higher temperatures will cause food to deteriorate faster. When freezing vegetables and fruits you will need a *colander* plus a *large pot, kettle,* or *saucepan* with a *wire basket.*

A variety of *freezer containers* and materials are available. Whatever you choose should be moistureproof and vaporproof, able to withstand temperatures of 0° or below, and capable of being tightly sealed. For liquid or semiliquid foods, use rigid plastic freezer containers, freezer bags, or wide-top jars specifically designed for freezing. Regular jars are seldom tempered to withstand freezer temperatures. For solid or dry-pack foods, use freezer bags, heavy foil, plastic wrap for the freezer, or laminated freezer wrap.

GENERAL FREEZING STEPS

1. Select only the best-quality fruits and vegetables that are at their peak of maturity. Fruits should be firm yet ripe. Vegetables should be young, tender, unwilted, and garden-fresh. Hold produce in the refrigerator if it can't be frozen immediately. Rinse and drain small quantities through several changes of cold water. Lift fruits and vegetables out of the water; do not let them soak. Prepare cleaned produce as specified in the charts on pages 330 to 344.

2. Blanch vegetables (and fruits when directed) by scalding them in boiling water for a short time. This stops or slows the enzymes that cause loss of flavor and color, and toughen the food. Blanching in the microwave is not recommended because some enzymes may not be inactivated. Timings vary according to vegetable type and size.

Blanching is a heat-and-cool process. First, fill a large pot with water using 1 gallon of water per pound of prepared vegetables. Heat to boiling. Add prepared food to the boiling water (or place in a wire basket and lower into the water); cover. Start timing immediately. Cook over high heat for the time specified in the charts. (Add 1 minute if you live 5,000 feet above sea level or higher.) Near the end of the time, fill your sink or a large container with ice water. As soon as the blanching time is complete, use a slotted spoon to transfer the food from the boiling water to a colander (or lift the basket out of the water). Immediately plunge the food into the ice water. Chill for the same amount of time it was boiled; drain well.

3. Package the cooled, drained food into freezer containers, leaving the specified headspace (see "Headspace Matters," page 324).

Fruits often are frozen with added sugar or liquid for better texture and flavor. Refer to the directions in the chart on pages 330 to 334.

Unsweetened or dry pack: Add no sugar or liquid to the fruit; simply pack in a container. This works well for small whole fruits, such as berries.

Water pack: Cover the fruit with water. Do not use glass jars. Maintain the recommended headspace. Unsweetened fruit juice also can be used.

Sugar pack: Place a small amount of fruit in the container and sprinkle lightly with sugar; repeat layering. Cover and let stand about 15 minutes or until juicy; seal.

Syrup pack: Cover fruit with a syrup of sugar and water (see "Syrup for Fruit," page 323).

4. Wipe container rims. Seal according to the manufacturer's directions, pressing out as much air as possible. If necessary, use freezer tape around the edges of the lids to ensure a tight seal.

5. Label each container with its contents, the amount, and the date.

6. Add packages to the freezer in batches to make sure that the food freezes quickly and solidly. Leave some space between the packages so air can circulate around them. When frozen solid, the packages can be placed closer together.

7. Use frozen fruits and vegetables within 8 to 10 months. Post an inventory sheet near the freezer. When adding food to the freezer, write down the date, type of food, and number of packages. Cross off items as you remove them. Vegetables are best cooked from a frozen state, without thawing them first. Thaw fruits in their containers either in the refrigerator or in a bowl of cool water.

CANNING

Reaching for a jar of home-canned fruits or vegetables is a satisfying experience. To make it a reality you'll need a knowledge of canning basics, some top-quality food, and the right equipment. Plant fruit and vegetable varieties that are recommended for canning (check seed catalogs or ask a county extension service agent). Select only top-quality fruits and vegetables that are fresh, young, and tender. For best results, can food within 12 hours of harvest. Wash produce under running water or dip in several changes of clean water. If you live more than 1,000 feet above sea level, read "Altitude Adjustments," page 345, before beginning.

EQUIPMENT

Canner: Choose one of two types depending on the kind of food you are canning. A *boiling-water* (or water-bath) *canner* is used for fruits, tomatoes, pickles, relishes, jams, and jellies. It is a large kettle with a lid and a rack designed to hold canning jars. Any large cooking pot can be used if it has a rack and a tight-fitting lid and is deep enough for briskly boiling water to cover the jars by 1 inch.

A *pressure canner* must be used for vegetables and other low-acid foods. It is a large heavy pot with a rack and a tight-fitting lid that has a vent or petcock, a dial or weighted pressure gauge, and a safety fuse. It may or may not have a gasket. Pressure canners allow foods to be heated to 240° or 250° and to be held at that temperature as long as necessary. Each type of pressure canner is different; always refer to the manufacturer's instructions specific to your canner.

Jars: Use only standard canning jars. These are tempered to withstand the heat inside the canner and their mouths are specially threaded for sealing canning lids. Inspect all jars before using them; discard any that are cracked or have chipped rims. To remove mineral deposits or hard-water film, soak the empty jars in a solution of 1 cup vinegar per gallon of water. To avoid mineral deposits during processing, add $\frac{1}{4}$ cup vinegar per gallon of water in the canner.

Lids: Use screw bands and flat metal lids with a built-in sealing compound. Prepare them according to the manufacturer's directions. The flat lids are designed for one-time use only. Screw bands can be reused if they are not bent or rusty.

Other useful pieces of equipment include a *kitchen scale, wide-mouth funnel, jar lifter,* and *food mill, colander,* or *sieve.*

GENERAL CANNING STEPS

Follow these steps whether using a boiling-water canner or a pressure canner and review them before you harvest or buy the produce. Allow sufficient time to follow all directions exactly, and try to choose a time when you can work with few or no interruptions. Foods are packed into canning jars by either the *raw-pack* (cold-pack) or the *hot-pack* method. In raw packing, uncooked food is packed into the canning jar and covered with boiling water, juice, or syrup (see "Syrup for Fruit," page 323). In hot packing, food is partially cooked, packed into jars, and covered with cooking liquid. The following guidelines apply to both methods.

1. Wash empty canning jars in hot, soapy water. Rinse thoroughly. Pour boiling water over jars and let them stand in the hot water until you're ready to fill them. Sterilize jars that will be processed for 10 minutes or less by immersing them in boiling water for 10 minutes. Prepare lids and screw bands according to manufacturer's directions.

2. Start heating water in the canner.

3. Prepare only as much food as needed to fill the maximum number of jars your canner will hold at one time. Work quickly, preparing the food as specified. Keep the work area clean.

4. Place the hot jars on cloth towels to prevent them from slipping during packing.

5. Pack the food into the jars, leaving the recommended headspace.

6. Ladle or pour boiling liquid over the food, keeping the specified headspace (see photo, page 328, and "Headspace Matters," page 324).

7. Release trapped air bubbles in the jars by gently working a narrow rubber scraper or nonmetal utensil down the jars' sides. Add liquid, if needed, to maintain the necessary headspace.

8. Wipe jar rims with a clean, damp cloth. Food on the rims prevents a perfect seal.

Fill the jar, leaving the stated headspace. Then add the liquid, and measure to be sure you have maintained the correct headspace.

9. Place prepared lids on jars; add screw bands, tightening according to manufacturer's instructions.

10. Set each jar into the canner as it is filled. Be sure the jars do not touch each other.

11. Process filled jars, following the recipe's procedures and timings exactly.

12. Remove jars and place on a towel to cool. Leave at least 1 inch of space between jars to allow air to circulate, but keep the area free of drafts.

13. After the jars are completely cooled (12 to 24 hours), press the center of each lid to check the seal. If the dip in the lid holds, the jar is sealed. If the lid bounces up and down, the jar isn't sealed.

Check unsealed jars for flaws. The contents can be refrigerated and used within two to three days, frozen, or reprocessed within 24 hours. To reprocess, use a clean jar and a new lid; process for the full length of time specified. Mark the label so you can use any re-canned jars first.

If jars have lost liquid but are still sealed, the contents are safe. However, any food not covered by liquid will discolor so use these jars first.

14. Wipe the jars and lids. Remove, wash, and dry the screw bands; store for future use. Label jars with contents and date; include a batch number if you are doing more than one canner load per day (if one jar spoils, you can easily identify others from that same load). Store jars in a cool (50° to 70°), dry, dark place. Use within 1 year.

BOILING-WATER CANNING

Set the canner and rack on the range top. Fill the canner half full with water. Cover and heat over high heat. Heat additional water in another kettle.

Prepare syrup (see tip, page 323), if needed; keep it warm but not boiling. Prepare the food. When the water in the canner is hot, fill each jar and place it on the rack in the canner. Replace the canner cover each time you add a jar. After the last jar has been added, pour additional boiling water into the canner until jars are 1 inch below the water line. Cover; heat to a brisk, rolling boil. Now begin the processing timing. Keep the water boiling gently during processing, adding more boiling water if the level drops. If the water stops boiling when you add more, stop counting the time, turn up the heat, and wait for a full boil before resuming counting. At the end of the processing time, turn off the heat and remove the jars. Cool on a rack, wooden board, or towel. When jars are completely cool (12 to 24 hours), check the seals.

PRESSURE CANNING

Read the manufacturer's instructions before attempting to use the canner. Make sure all parts are clean and work properly.

If your canner has a dial gauge, have it checked yearly for accuracy. (Contact your county extension service office for the nearest testing location.) Weighted-gauge canners remain accurate from year to year.

When you're ready to start canning, check to see that the steam vent is clear. Set the canner and rack on the range top. Add 2 to 3 inches of hot water (or the amount specified by the canner manufacturer). Turn the heat to low.

Next, prepare enough food for one canner load. Fill each jar and place it in the canner. When the last jar is added, cover and lock the canner. Turn the heat to high. When steam comes out the vent, reduce the heat until the steam flows freely at a moderate rate. Let the steam flow steadily for 10 minutes or more to release all the air from inside the canner. Close the vent, or place the weighted gauge over the vent according to your canner's instructions. Start the timing when the recommended pressure is reached. Adjust the heat to maintain a constant pressure.

When the processing time is up, remove the canner from the heat and set it away from drafts on a rack or a wooden board. If the canner is too heavy to move, simply turn off the heat. Let the pressure return to normal (allow 30 to 60 minutes). Do not lift the weight, open the vent, or run water over the canner.

Follow the manufacturer's instructions for opening the canner. Be sure to lift the cover away from you to avoid a blast of steam. If the food is still boiling vigorously in the jars, wait a few minutes before

CANNING AND FREEZING FRUITS

Food	Preparation	Boiling-Water Canning, Raw Pack	Boiling-Water Canning, Hot Pack	Freezing
Apples	Allow 2½ pounds per quart. Select varieties that are crisp, not mealy, in texture. Peel and core; halve, quarter, or slice. Dip into ascorbic-acid color-keeper solution; drain.	Not recommended.	Simmer in syrup* for 5 minutes, stirring occasionally. Fill jars with fruit and syrup, leaving a ½-inch headspace. Process pints and quarts for 20 minutes.	Use a syrup, sugar, or dry pack (see step 3, page 325), leaving the recommended headspace.**
Apricots	Allow 1½ to 2½ pounds per quart. If desired, peel as for peaches, page 332. Prepare as for peaches.	See peaches, page 332.	See peaches, page 332.	Peel as for peaches, page 332. Use a syrup, sugar, or water pack (see step 3, page 325), leaving the recommended headspace.**
Berries	Allow ¾ to 1 pound per pint. Can or freeze	Fill jars with	Simmer blueberries, currants, elderberries,	Slice strawberries, if desired. Use a syrup,

blackberries, blueberries, currants, elderberries, gooseberries, huckleberries, loganberries, mulberries, and raspberries. Freeze (do not can) boysenberries and strawberries.	blackberries, loganberries, mulberries, or raspberries. Shake down gently. Add boiling syrup,* leaving a 1/2-inch headspace. Process half-pints for 15 minutes and pints for 20 minutes.	gooseberries, and huckleberries in water for 30 seconds; drain. Fill jars with berries and hot syrup,* leaving a 1/2-inch headspace. Process half-pints for 15 minutes and pints for 20 minutes.	sugar, or dry pack (see step 3, page 325), leaving the recommended headspace.**
Cherries Allow 2 to 3 pounds per quart. If desired, treat with ascorbic-acid color-keeper solution; drain. If unpitted, prick skin on opposite sides to prevent splitting.	Fill jars, shaking down gently. Add boiling syrup* or water, leaving a 1/2-inch headspace. Process pints and quarts for 25 minutes.	Add cherries to hot syrup;* bring to boiling. Fill jars with fruit and syrup, leaving a 1/2-inch headspace. Process pints for 15 minutes and quarts for 20 minutes.	Use a syrup, sugar, or dry pack (see step 3, page 325), leaving the recommended headspace.**

*See "Syrup for Fruit," page 323.
**See "Headspace Matters," page 324.

	CANNING AND FREEZING FRUITS (continued)			
Food	Preparation	Boiling-Water Canning, Raw Pack	Boiling-Water Canning, Hot Pack	Freezing
Melons	Allow about 4 pounds per quart for honeydew, cantaloupe, and watermelon.	Not recommended.	Not recommended.	Use a syrup or dry pack (see step 3, page 325), leaving the recommended headspace.**
Peaches, Nectarines	Allow 2 to 3 pounds per quart. To peel, immerse in boiling water for 20 to 30 seconds or until skins start to crack; remove and plunge into cold water. Halve and pit. If desired, slice. Treat with ascorbic-acid color-keeper solution; drain.	Fill jars, placing cut sides down. Add boiling syrup* or water, leaving a 1/2-inch headspace. Process pints for 25 minutes and quarts for 30 minutes. (Note: Hot packing gives a better product.)	Add fruit to hot syrup;* bring to boiling. Fill jars with fruit (placing cut sides down) and syrup, leaving a 1/2-inch headspace. Process pints for 20 minutes and quarts for 25 minutes.	Use a syrup, sugar, or water pack (see step 3, page 325), leaving the recommended headspace.**

Pears	Allow 2 to 3 pounds per quart. Peel, halve, and core. Treat with ascorbic-acid color-keeper solution; drain.	Not recommended.	Simmer fruit in syrup* for 5 minutes. Fill jars with fruit and syrup, leaving a 1/2-inch headspace. Process pints for 20 minutes and quarts for 25 minutes.	Not recommended.
Plums	Allow 1 1/2 to 2 1/2 pounds per quart. For best quality, let ripen at least 1 day after harvest. Prick skin on 2 sides. Freestone varieties may be halved and pitted.	Pack firmly into jars. Add boiling syrup,* leaving a 1/2-inch headspace. Process pints for 20 minutes and quarts for 25 minutes.	Simmer in water or syrup* for 2 minutes. Remove from heat. Let stand, covered, for 20 to 30 minutes. Fill jars with fruit and cooking liquid or syrup, leaving a 1/2-inch headspace. Process pints for 20 minutes and quarts for 25 minutes.	Halve and pit. Treat with ascorbic-acid color-keeper solution; drain well. Use a syrup, sugar, or dry pack (see step 3, page 325), leaving the recommended headspace.**

*See "Syrup for Fruit," page 323.

**See "Headspace Matters," page 324.

CANNING AND FREEZING FRUITS (continued)

Food	Preparation	Boiling-Water Canning, Raw Pack	Boiling-Water Canning, Hot Pack	Freezing
Rhubarb	Allow 1 to 2 pounds per quart. Discard leaves and woody ends. Cut into ½- to 1-inch pieces.	Not recommended.	In a saucepan sprinkle ½ cup sugar over each 4 cups fruit; mix well. Let stand until juice appears. Bring slowly to boiling, stirring gently. Fill jars with hot fruit and juice, leaving a ½-inch headspace. Process pints and quarts for 15 minutes.	Blanch for 1 minute; cool quickly and drain. Use a syrup or dry pack (see step 3, page 325), leaving the recommended headspace.** Or use a sugar pack of ½ cup sugar to 3 cups fruit.

*See "Syrup for Fruit," page 323.

**See "Headspace Matters," page 324.

CANNING AND FREEZING VEGETABLES

Vegetable	Preparation	Pressure Canning, Raw Pack*	Pressure Canning, Hot Pack*	Freezing
Asparagus	Allow $2^1/2$ to $4^1/2$ pounds per quart. Wash; scrape off scales. Break off woody bases where spears snap easily. Wash again. Sort by thickness. Leave whole or cut into 1-inch lengths.	Not recommended.	Not recommended.	Blanch small spears for 2 minutes, medium for 3 minutes, and large for 4 minutes; cool quickly. Fill containers; shake down, leaving no headspace.
Beans: green, Italian,	Allow $1^1/2$ to $2^1/2$ pounds per quart. Wash; remove ends and strings. Leave	Pack tightly in jars;** add boiling water, leaving a 1-inch headspace. Process	Boil for 5 minutes. Loosely fill jars with beans and cooking liquid,** leaving a	Blanch for 3 minutes; cool quickly. Fill containers; shake down, leaving a $1/2$-inch

*For a dial-gauge canner, use 11 pounds of pressure; for a weighted-gauge canner, use 10 pounds of pressure. At altitudes above 1,000 feet, see tip, page 345.

**Add salt (if desired): $1/4$ to $1/2$ teaspoon for pints, $1/2$ to 1 teaspoon for quarts.

		CANNING AND FREEZING VEGETABLES (continued)		
Vegetable	Preparation	Pressure Canning, Raw Pack*	Pressure Canning, Hot Pack*	Freezing
Beans: *(cont'd)* **snap, or wax**	whole or cut into 1-inch pieces.	pints for 20 minutes and quarts for 25 minutes.	1-inch headspace. Process pints for 20 minutes and quarts for 25 minutes.	headspace.
Beans: butter or lima	Allow 3 to 5 pounds unshelled beans per quart. Wash, shell, rinse, drain, and sort beans by size.	Fill jars with beans; do not shake down.** Add boiling water, leaving a 1-inch headspace for pints, 1½-inch for large beans in quarts, and 1½-inch for small beans in quarts. Process pints for 40 minutes and quarts for 50 minutes.	Cover beans with boiling water; return to boiling. Boil for 3 minutes. Fill jars loosely with beans and cooking liquid,** leaving a 1-inch headspace. Process pints for 40 minutes and quarts for 50 minutes.	Blanch small beans for 2 minutes, medium beans for 3 minutes, and large beans for 4 minutes; cool quickly. Fill containers loosely, leaving a ½-inch headspace.
Carrots	Allow 2 to 3 pounds per quart. Rinse, trim,	Not recommended.	Simmer for 5 minutes. Fill jars with carrots and	Blanch tiny whole carrots for 5 minutes

	Preparation	Canning	Freezing
	peel, and rinse again. Leave tiny ones whole. Slice or dice 1- to 1¼-inch diameter carrots (larger carrots may be too fibrous).	cooking liquid.** leaving a 1-inch headspace. Process pints for 25 minutes and quarts for 30 minutes.	and cut-up carrots for 2 minutes; cool quickly. Pack closely into containers, leaving a ½-inch headspace.
Corn, cream-style	Allow 2 to 3 pounds per pint. Remove husks. Scrub with a vegetable brush to remove silks. Wash and drain.	Not recommended.	Cover ears with boiling water; return to boiling and boil 4 minutes. Use a sharp knife to cut off just the kernel tips, then scrape corn with a dull knife. Cool quickly; drain. Use a sharp knife to cut off just the kernel tips, then scrape corn with a dull knife. Fill containers, leaving a ½-inch headspace.

Cover ears with boiling water; return to boiling and boil 4 minutes. Use a sharp knife to cut off just the kernel tips, then scrape corn with a dull knife. Bring to boiling 1 cup water for each 2 cups corn. Add corn; simmer 3 minutes. Fill pint jars

*For a dial-gauge canner, use 11 pounds of pressure; for a weighted-gauge canner, use 10 pounds of pressure. At altitudes above 1,000 feet, see tip, page 345.

**Add salt (if desired): ¼ to ½ teaspoon for pints, ½ to 1 teaspoon for quarts.

		CANNING AND FREEZING VEGETABLES *(continued)*		
Vegetable	Preparation	Pressure Canning, Raw Pack*	Pressure Canning, Hot Pack*	Freezing
Corn, cream-style *(cont'd)*			loosely,** leaving a 1-inch headspace. Process pints 85 minutes; do not use quart jars.	
Corn, whole kernel	Allow 4 to 5 pounds per quart. Remove husks. Scrub with a vegetable brush to remove silks. Wash and drain.	Cover ears with boiling water; boil 3 minutes. Cut corn from cobs at three-quarters depth of kernels. Pack loosely in jars (do not shake or press down).** Add boiling water, leaving a 1-inch headspace. Process pints for 55 minutes; quarts for 85 minutes.	Cover ears with boiling water; return to boiling and boil 3 minutes. Cut corn from cobs at three-quarters depth of kernels; do not scrape. Bring to boiling 1 cup water for each 4 cups corn. Add corn; simmer 5 minutes. Fill jars with corn and liquid,** leaving a 1-inch	Cover ears with boiling water; return to boiling and boil 4 minutes. Cool quickly; drain. Cut corn from cobs at two-thirds depth of kernels; do not scrape. Fill containers, leaving a 1/2-inch headspace.

| | | | | headspace. Process pints for 55 minutes and quarts for 85 minutes. | Not recommended. | Blanch small flat pods 1½ minutes or large flat pods 2 minutes. (If peas have started to develop, blanch 3 minutes. If peas are already developed, shell and follow directions for green peas.) Cool, drain, and fill containers, leaving a ½-inch headspace. |
| **Peas, edible pods** | Wash Chinese, snow, sugar, or sugar snap peas. Remove stems, blossom ends, and any strings. | Not recommended. | | | | |

*For a dial-gauge canner, use 11 pounds of pressure; for a weighted-gauge canner, use 10 pounds of pressure. At altitudes above 1,000 feet, see tip, page 345.

**Add salt (if desired): ¼ to ½ teaspoon for pints, ½ to 1 teaspoon for quarts.

Vegetable	Preparation	Pressure Canning, Raw Pack*	Pressure Canning, Hot Pack*	Freezing
Peas: English or green	Allow 2 to 2½ pounds per pint. Wash, shell, rinse, and drain.	Pack loosely in jars (do not shake or press down).** Add boiling water, leaving a 1-inch headspace. Process pints and quarts for 40 minutes.	Cover with water; heat to boiling and boil for 2 minutes. Fill jars loosely with peas and cooking liquid,** leaving a 1-inch headspace. Process pints and quarts for 40 minutes.	Blanch 1½ minutes; chill quickly. Fill containers, shaking down and leaving a ½-inch headspace.
Peppers, hot	Select firm jalapeño or other chili peppers; wash. Halve large peppers. Remove stems, seeds, and membranes. Place cut sides down on a foil-lined baking sheet.	Not recommended.	Pack in pint jars.** Add boiling water, leaving a 1-inch headspace. Process pints for 35 minutes.	Package, leaving no headspace.

Bake in a 425° oven for 20 to 25 minutes or until skin is bubbly and browned. Cover peppers or wrap in foil and let stand for 20 to 30 minutes or till cool. Pull the skin off gently and slowly using a paring knife.

Peppers, sweet	Select firm green, bright red, or yellow peppers; wash. Remove stems, seeds, and membranes.	Not recommended.	Leave small peppers whole; quarter large peppers. Cover with boiling water; boil for 3 minutes. Pack in pint jars.** Add boiling water, leaving a 1-inch	Halve or cut into 1/2-inch strips or rings. Blanch halves for 3 minutes, strips or rings for 2 minutes. Chill and drain. Fill containers, leaving a 1/2-inch

*For a dial-gauge canner, use 11 pounds of pressure; for a weighted-gauge canner, use 10 pounds of pressure. At altitudes above 1,000 feet, see tip, page 345.

**Add salt (if desired): 1/4 to 1/2 teaspoon for pints, 1/2 to 1 teaspoon for quarts.

Vegetable	Preparation	Pressure Canning, Raw Pack*	Pressure Canning, Hot Pack*	Freezing
Peppers, sweet *(cont'd)*			headspace. Process pints for 35 minutes.	headspace. Or, spread peppers in a single layer on a baking sheet; freeze till firm. Fill container, shaking to pack closely and leaving no headspace.

*For a dial-gauge canner, use 11 pounds of pressure; for a weighted-gauge canner, use 10 pounds of pressure. At altitudes above 1,000 feet, see tip, page 345.

**Add salt (if desired): $1/4$ to $1/2$ teaspoon for pints, $1/2$ to 1 teaspoon for quarts.

CANNING AND FREEZING TOMATOES

Allow 2¹/₂ to 3¹/₂ pounds tomatoes per quart. Wash unblemished tomatoes. Dip in boiling water for 30 seconds or until skins start to split. Dip in cold water; core and skin. Continue as directed below.

Tomatoes	Preparation	Boiling-Water Canning	Pressure Canning*	Freezing
Crushed	Cut into quarters; add enough to a large pan to cover bottom. Crush with a wooden spoon. Heat and stir until boiling. Slowly add remaining pieces, stirring constantly. Simmer for 5 minutes. Fill jars,** leaving a ¹/₂-inch headspace.	Process pints for 35 minutes and quarts for 45 minutes.	Process pints and quarts for 15 minutes.	Set pan of tomatoes in ice water to cool. Fill containers, leaving a 1-inch headspace.

*For a dial-gauge canner, use 11 pounds of pressure; for a weighted-gauge canner, use 10 pounds of pressure. At altitudes above 1,000 feet, see tip, page 345.

**Add bottled lemon juice: 1 tablespoon for pints, 2 tablespoons for quarts. Add salt (if desired): ¹/₄ to ¹/₂ teaspoon for pints, ¹/₂ to 1 teaspoon for quarts.

CANNING AND FREEZING TOMATOES (continued)

Tomatoes	Preparation	Boiling-Water Canning	Pressure Canning*	Freezing
Whole or halved, no added liquid	Fill jars with whole or halved tomatoes,** pressing to fill spaces with juice. Leave a 1/2-inch headspace.	Process pints and quarts for 85 minutes.	Process pints and quarts for 25 minutes.	Fill freezer containers, leaving a 1-inch headspace.
Whole or halved, water-packed	Fill jars with whole or halved tomatoes;** Add boiling water, leaving a 1/2-inch headspace. Or, heat tomatoes in saucepan with water to cover; simmer 5 minutes. Fill jars with tomatoes and cooking liquid,** leaving a 1/2-inch headspace.	Process pints for 40 minutes and quarts for 45 minutes.	Process pints and quarts for 10 minutes.	If heated, set pan of tomatoes in cold water to cool. Fill containers, leaving a 1-inch headspace.

**Add bottled lemon juice: 1 tablespoon for pints, 2 tablespoons for quarts. Add salt (if desired): 1/4 to 1/2 teaspoon for pints, 1/2 to 1 teaspoon for quarts.

removing the jars from the canner. Cool the jars 2 to 3 inches apart on a rack, wooden board, or towels in a draft-free area. Do not tighten the lids. When the jars are completely cool (12 to 24 hours), check the seals.

DETECTING SPOILAGE

Always inspect a home-canned jar carefully before serving its contents. If the jar has leaked, shows patches of mold, or has a swollen lid, or if the food has a foamy or murky appearance, discard the food and the jar. The odor from the opened jar should be pleasant. If the food doesn't look or smell right, don't use it (see "Safety Reminder," page 323).

ALTITUDE ADJUSTMENTS

Times given in this chapter are for altitudes up to 1,000 feet above sea level. For higher altitudes, make the following changes.

■ **Blanching:** Add 1 minute if you live 5,000 feet or more above sea level.

■ **Boiling-water canning:** Use a longer processing time. Call your county extension service agent for detailed instructions.

■ **Jellies and jams:** Add 1 minute to processing time for each additional 1,000 feet.

■ **Pressure canning:** Times remain the same, but different pressures must be used. For dial-gauge pressure canners, use 11 pounds of pressure if you live up to 2,000 feet above sea level; 12 pounds for 2,001 to 4,000 feet; 13 pounds for 4,001 to 6,000 feet; and 14 pounds for 6,001 to 8,000 feet.

For weighted-gauge canners, use 10 pounds of pressure if you live up to 1,000 feet above sea level. Use 15 pounds of pressure above 1,000 feet.

■ **Sterilizing jars:** Boil an additional minute for each additional 1,000 feet.

TOMATO JUICE

PREP: 50 MINUTES PROCESS: 35 TO 40 MINUTES

No-Fat

1. Wash 8 pounds ripe but firm *tomatoes*. Remove stems. Core and cut into pieces; drain. Place in an 8- or 10-quart kettle. Bring to boiling over low heat, stirring often. Cover; simmer 15 minutes or till soft, stirring often. Press tomatoes through a food mill. Discard solids. Return juice to kettle; bring to boiling. Boil gently, uncovered, for 5 minutes, stirring often. Makes 5 pints (20 half-cup servings).

■ **Boiling-Water Canning:** Add 1 tablespoon *lemon juice* and, if desired, $1/4$ teaspoon *salt* to each hot, clean pint jar. Pour hot tomato juice into jars, leaving a $1/2$-inch headspace; wipe jar rims; adjust lids. Process in a boiling-water canner for 35 minutes (start timing when water begins to boil).

■ **Freezing:** Place kettle in a sink filled with ice water; stir mixture to help it cool. Pour into wide-top freezer containers, leaving a $1/2$-inch headspace. If desired, add $1/4$ teaspoon *salt* to each container. Seal, label, and freeze for up to 10 months.

Nutrition Facts per serving: 39 cal., 0 g total fat, 0 mg chol., 16 mg sodium, 9 g carbo., 2 g fiber, 2 g pro. **Daily Values:** 11% vit. A, 60% vit. C, 0% calcium, 5% iron

CATSUP

No-Fat

So you can determine when the tomato-sugar mixture is reduced by half, be sure to measure its depth with a clean ruler after the sugar is added.

   8 **pounds tomatoes (24 medium)**
   $^1/_2$ **cup chopped onion (1 medium)**
   $^1/_4$ **teaspoon ground red pepper**
   1 **cup sugar**
   1 **cup white vinegar**
  $1^1/_2$ **inches stick cinnamon, broken**
  $1^1/_2$ **teaspoons whole cloves**
   1 **teaspoon celery seed**

1. Core and quarter tomatoes; drain. In an 8- or 10-quart kettle combine tomatoes, onion, and red pepper. Bring to boiling; cook 15 minutes, stirring often. Press through food mill or sieve. Discard seeds and skins. Return to kettle; add sugar. Bring to boiling; reduce heat. Simmer $1^1/_2$ to 2 hours or till reduced by half, stirring occasionally.

2. In a saucepan bring vinegar, cinnamon, cloves, and celery seed to boiling. Remove from heat.

3. Strain vinegar mixture into tomato mixture; discard spices. Add 1 tablespoon *salt*. Simmer for 30 minutes or to desired consistency, stirring often. Makes 4 half-pints.

■ **Boiling-Water Canning:** Ladle hot catsup into hot, clean half-pint jars, leaving a $^1/_8$-inch headspace. Wipe jar rims and adjust lids. Process in a boiling-water canner for 15 minutes (start timing when water begins to boil).

■ **Freezing:** Place kettle in ice water; stir to cool. Ladle into freezer containers, leaving a $^1/_2$-inch headspace. Seal, label, and freeze up to 10 months.

Nutrition Facts per tablespoon: 25 cal., 0 g total fat, 0 mg chol., 105 mg sodium, 6 g carbo., 1 g fiber, 1 g pro. **Daily Values:** 3% vit. A, 18% vit. C, 0% calcium, 2% iron

CHUNKY SALSA

PREP: 2 HOURS PROCESS: 35 MINUTES

No-Fat

Use vine-ripened tomatoes for this recipe-they provide the high acidity needed for safe boiling-water canning. Avoid using tomatoes from dead or frost-killed vines. If in doubt, store the salsa in the refrigerator or freezer (see below).

    7 pounds tomatoes (20 medium)
   10 Anaheim or poblano chili peppers, seeded and chopped (about
       3 cups) (see tip, below)
    3 jalapeño or serrano chili peppers, seeded and chopped (about
       $1/3$ cup) (see tip, below)
    2 cups coarsely chopped onions (2 large)
 $1/2$ cup snipped fresh cilantro or parsley
 $1/2$ cup vinegar
    5 cloves garlic, minced
    1 tablespoon sugar
    1 teaspoon salt
    1 teaspoon pepper

1. Peel, seed, and coarsely chop tomatoes (you should have about 14 cups). Place tomatoes in a large colander. Let drain about 30 minutes.

2. Place drained tomatoes in an 8-quart pot. Bring to boiling; reduce heat. Simmer, uncovered, 45 to 50 minutes or till thick and chunky; stir frequently. Add chili peppers, onions, cilantro or parsley, vinegar, garlic, sugar, salt, and pepper. Return mixture to boiling. Remove from heat. Makes 4 pints.

CHILI PEPPER PRECAUTION

Wear plastic gloves when seeding and chopping hot chili peppers to protect your hands from oils in the peppers that may burn your skin.

■ **Boiling-Water Canning:** Ladle salsa into hot, clean pint jars, leaving a $1/2$-inch headspace. Wipe jar rims and adjust lids. Process in a boiling-water canner for 35 minutes (start timing when water begins to boil).

■ **Freezing:** Place the kettle in a sink filled with ice water; stir mixture to help it cool. Spoon into wide-top freezer containers, leaving a ¹/₂-inch headspace. Seal, label, and freeze up to 6 months.

Nutrition Facts per tablespoon: 18 cal., 0 g total fat, 0 mg chol., 39 mg sodium, 4 g carbo., 1 g fiber, 1 g pro. **Daily Values:** 3% vit. A, 48% vit. C, 0% calcium, 2% iron

PICKLES AND RELISHES

The best sweet and pungent homemade pickles and relishes start with high-quality ingredients and are prepared according to tested recipes. Follow these general guidelines when making them.

INGREDIENTS

Cucumbers identified as pickling types will make crunchier pickles than table or slicing varieties. Select top-quality, unwaxed cucumbers. Use them as soon as possible (within 24 hours) after harvest. Otherwise, refrigerate cucumbers or spread them in a cool, well-ventilated spot. Just before using, remove the blossoms and a slice off the blossom end. Wash well, especially around the stem. Save the odd-shaped or more mature cucumbers for relishes and bread-and-butter-style pickles.

Granulated pickling or canning salt should be used instead of table salt, which may cause the pickles to darken or make the brine cloudy.

Cider vinegar is most often used for pickles and relishes, but white vinegar can be used for a lighter-colored product. Most importantly, choose a high-grade vinegar of 5 to 6 percent acid. Never dilute the vinegar more than is indicated in the recipe. If you want a less-sour product, add more sugar. Sugar helps keep pickles firm and plump. Use granulated white sugar unless the recipe specifies brown sugar. Spices should be as fresh as possible. If a recipe calls for a whole spice, don't substitute the ground alternative; it may cause the product to be dark and cloudy. Hard water may prevent brined pickles from curing properly; for best results, use soft or distilled water.

PROCEDURES

Use stoneware, glass, enamelware, stainless-steel, or food-grade plastic containers and utensils. Do not use aluminum, brass, copper, zinc, galvanized, or iron utensils. Process pickles and relishes in a boiling-water canner (see pages 326–329 and 345) to destroy yeasts, molds, and bacteria.

COMMON PICKLE PROBLEMS

■ **Hollow pickles:** Cucumbers poorly developed, too large, or not fresh.

■ **Shriveled pickles:** Salt, sugar, or vinegar solution too strong; cucumbers not fresh; or cucumbers overcooked.

■ **Soft or slippery pickles:** Too little salt or vinegar used, imperfect seal, blossom ends not removed, or too little processing time.

■ **Strong, bitter taste:** Vinegar too strong, too many spices, or salt substitutes used.

DILL PICKLES

PREP: 30 MINUTES   PROCESS: 10 MINUTES

No-Fat

The pickles may appear shriveled after processing. They will plump later in the sealed jars.

$2^1/4$ **pounds 4-inch pickling cucumbers (about 36)**
$3^3/4$ **cups water**
$3^3/4$ **cups cider vinegar**
  6 **tablespoons pickling salt**
12 **to 18 heads fresh dill or 6 to 8 tablespoons dillseed**
  1 **tablespoon mustard seed**

1. Thoroughly rinse cucumbers. Remove stems and cut off a slice from each blossom end. In a large saucepan combine water, vinegar, and pickling salt. Bring to boiling.

2. Pack cucumbers loosely into hot, *sterilized* pint jars, leaving a $1/2$-inch headspace. Add *2 to 3* heads of dill or *3 to 4 teaspoons* dillseed and $1/2$ *teaspoon* mustard seed to each jar. Pour hot vinegar mixture over cucumbers, leaving a $1/2$-inch headspace. Wipe jar rims and adjust lids.

3. Process in a boiling-water canner for 10 minutes (start timing when water begins to boil). Let stand 1 week. Makes 6 pints (36 servings).

■ **Kosher-Style Dill Pickles:** Prepare as above, except omit the mustard seed and add 1 clove *garlic,* halved, to each jar (6 cloves total).

BREAD AND BUTTER PICKLES

PREP: 3 HOURS, 30 MINUTES PROCESS: 10 MINUTES

No-Fat

4 quarts sliced medium cucumbers
8 medium white onions, sliced
$^1/_3$ cup pickling salt
3 cloves garlic, halved
  Cracked ice
4 cups sugar
3 cups cider vinegar
2 tablespoons mustard seed
$1^1/_2$ teaspoons turmeric
$1^1/_2$ teaspoons celery seed

1. Combine cucumbers, onions, pickling salt, and garlic. Add 2 inches of cracked ice. Refrigerate for 3 hours; drain well. Remove garlic.

2. In a large kettle combine sugar, vinegar, mustard seed, turmeric, and celery seed. Heat to boiling. Add cucumber mixture. Return to boiling. Pack cucumber mixture and liquid into hot, *sterilized* pint jars, leaving a $^1/_2$-inch headspace. Wipe jar rims; adjust lids.

3. Process in a boiling-water canner 10 minutes (start timing when water begins to boil). Makes 7 pints (70 servings).

VEGETABLE RELISH

PREP: 30 MINUTES CHILL: 16 TO 24 HOURS PROCESS: 10 MINUTES

No-Fat

8 medium tomatoes, peeled, cored, and cut up (about 2³/₄ pounds)
6 medium zucchini, quartered lengthwise (about 3 pounds)
3 large red sweet peppers, cut up
3 large green sweet peppers, cut up
2 medium onions, quartered
4 cloves garlic
¹/₄ cup pickling salt
2¹/₂ cups vinegar
2 cups sugar
1 teaspoon dried thyme, crushed
¹/₂ teaspoon pepper

1. In a food processor coarsely chop tomatoes, zucchini, sweet peppers, onions, and garlic. Measure 8 cups chopped vegetables. Place in a colander to drain excess liquid. Transfer to large nonmetal container; sprinkle with pickling salt. Cover; refrigerate 16 to 24 hours.

2. Transfer vegetable mixture to a colander; rinse and drain well. In an 8- or 10-quart pot combine vinegar, sugar, thyme, and pepper. Bring to boiling, stirring to dissolve sugar. Stir in vegetables. Return mixture to boiling. Remove from heat. Makes 8 half-pints or 4 pints.

■ **Boiling-Water Canning:** Ladle hot relish into hot, *sterilized* half-pint or pint jars, leaving a ¹/₂-inch headspace. Wipe jar rims and adjust lids. Process in a boiling-water canner 5 minutes for half-pints or 10 minutes for pints (start timing when water begins to boil).

■ **Freezing:** Place the pot in a sink of ice water; stir relish to help it cool. Ladle relish into wide-top freezer containers, leaving a ¹/₂-inch headspace. Seal, label, and freeze up to 10 months.

Nutrition Facts per tablespoon: 20 cal., 0 g total fat, 0 mg chol., 116 mg sodium, 5 g carbo., 0 g fiber, 0 g pro. **Daily Values:** 3% vit. A, 15% vit. C, 0% calcium, 1% iron

CORN RELISH

PREP: 55 MINUTES PROCESS: 15 MINUTES

No-Fat

     12 to 16 fresh ears of corn
      2 cups water
      3 cups chopped celery (6 stalks)
   1½ cups chopped red sweet peppers
   1½ cups chopped green sweet peppers
      1 cup chopped onions (2 medium)
   2½ cups vinegar
   1¾ cups sugar
      4 teaspoons dry mustard
      2 teaspoons pickling salt
      2 teaspoons celery seed
      1 teaspoon ground turmeric
      3 tablespoons cornstarch
      2 tablespoons water

1. Cut corn from cobs (do not scrape cobs). Measure 8 cups corn. In an 8- or 10-quart pot combine corn and the 2 cups water. Bring to boiling; reduce heat. Simmer, covered, for 4 to 5 minutes or till corn is nearly tender; drain.
2. In same kettle combine corn, celery, sweet peppers, and onions. Stir in vinegar, sugar, mustard, pickling salt, celery seed, and turmeric. Bring to boiling. Boil gently, uncovered, for 5 minutes, stirring occasionally. Combine cornstarch and the 2 tablespoons water; add to corn mixture. Cook and stir till bubbly; cook for 1 minute more.
3. Ladle into hot, clean pint jars, leaving a ½-inch headspace. Wipe jar rims and adjust lids. Process in a boiling-water canner for 15 minutes (start timing when water begins to boil). Makes 5 pints.

Nutrition Facts per tablespoon: 39 cal., 0 g total fat, 0 mg chol., 68 mg sodium, 16 g carbo., 1 g fiber, 0 g pro. **Daily Values:** 1% vit. A, 10% vit. C, 0% calcium, 1% iron

JELLIES AND JAMS

A variety of sweetened spreads easily can be made at home. Review these guidelines before you start.

Ingredients

Fresh fruits should be at their peak of color and flavor; canned or frozen unsweetened fruit or fruit juice can be used. Pectin is necessary for jelling. It is naturally present in some underripe fruits or can be added in a powdered or liquid form. Do not substitute one form of pectin for another, and add it exactly as the recipe specifies. Sugar must be in the correct proportion to the pectin and acid for jelling to occur. Using less pectin than the recipe suggests is likely to produce a syrup rather than a jelly or jam. Be sure to use pectin by the date indicated on its package. Lemon juice may be added to promote jelling and for flavor.

Procedures

■ Prepare only one batch at a time. Do not try to double the recipe.

■ Vigorous boiling is part of jellymaking. A full rolling boil is one so rapid that you can't stir it down. To prevent the mixture from boiling over, fill the pan no more than one-third full.

■ A mixture will sheet off a spoon when it has reached its jelling point. To test it, dip a metal spoon into the boiling mixture, then hold it over the pot. If the mixture is done, two drops will hang off the edge of the spoon, then run together. You also can use a candy thermometer to find when the jelling point is reached (8° above the boiling point of water).

■ Foam is a natural result of boiling. Quickly skim it off with a large metal spoon before ladling jelly into sterilized jars.

■ Process jellies and jams in a boiling-water canner (see instructions, pages 326–329).

■ The 5-minute processing time is for locations with altitudes below 1,000 feet above sea level. Add 1 minute for each additional 1,000 feet.

■ After processing, let jellies and jams sit for 12 to 24 hours or until set. Use within a few months.

Grape Jam

Prep: 65 minutes   Process: 5 minutes

No-Fat

3½ **pounds Concord grapes**
2 **cups water**
4½ **cups sugar**

1. Wash and stem grapes. Measure 10 cups. Remove skins from *half* of the grapes; set aside.

2. In an 8- or 10-quart pot combine the skinned and unskinned grapes. Cover and cook 10 minutes or till very soft. Press grapes through a sieve; discard seeds and cooked skins. Measure 3 cups of strained pulp; return to pot. Stir in the uncooked grape skins and water. Cook, covered, for 10 minutes. Uncover; stir in sugar. Bring mixture to a full rolling boil, stirring often. Boil, uncovered, about 12 minutes or till jam sheets off a metal spoon.

3. Remove pot from heat; quickly skim off foam with a metal spoon.

4. Ladle at once into hot, *sterilized* half-pint jars, leaving a ¼-inch headspace. Wipe jar rims and adjust lids. Process in a boiling-water canner for 5 minutes. Remove jars and cool on a rack till set. Makes 6 half-pints.

Nutrition Facts per tablespoon: 42 cal., 0 g total fat, 0 mg chol., 0 mg sodium, 11 g carbo., 0 g fiber, 0 g pro.

Pepper Jelly

Prep: 50 minutes Process: 5 minutes

No-Fat

    2 to 4 jalapeño peppers, halved and seeded (see tip, page 348)
1½ cups cranberry juice cocktail
    1 cup vinegar
    5 cups sugar
  ½ of a 6-ounce package (1 foil pouch) liquid fruit pectin
    5 tiny hot red peppers

1. In a medium saucepan combine jalapeño peppers, cranberry juice cocktail, and vinegar. Bring to boiling; reduce heat. Cover and simmer for 10 minutes. Strain mixture through a sieve, pressing with the back of a spoon to remove all the liquid (you should have 2 cups). Discard pulp.

2. In a 4-quart pot combine the 2 cups liquid and sugar. Bring to a full rolling boil over high heat, stirring constantly. Stir in pectin and tiny hot red peppers. Return to a full rolling boil; boil for 1 minute, stirring constantly. Remove from heat. Quickly skim off foam with a metal spoon.

3. Ladle at once into hot, *sterilized* half-pint jars, leaving a ¼-inch headspace and making sure each jar contains one tiny red pepper.

Wipe jar rims; adjust lids. Process in a boiling-water canner for 5 minutes (start timing when water begins to boil). Remove jars and cool on a wire rack till set (2 to 3 days). Makes 5 half-pints.

Nutrition Facts per tablespoon: 52 cal., 0 g total fat, 0 mg chol., 1 mg sodium, 14 g carbo., 0 g fiber, 0 g pro. **Daily Values:** 0% vit. A, 8% vit. C, 0% calcium, 0% iron

FRUIT JUICE JELLY

PREP: 25 MINUTES PROCESS: 5 MINUTES

No-Fat

Since this jelly starts with fruit juice it goes together quickly and easily, yet has the great taste of homemade jelly.

  4 cups cranberry juice cocktail (not low-calorie) or unsweetened apple, grape, or orange juice
 ¼ cup lemon juice
  1 1¾-ounce package powdered fruit pectin
4½ cups sugar

1. Pour cranberry and lemon juices into an 8- or 10-quart pot. Sprinkle with pectin. Let stand 1 to 2 minutes; stir to dissolve. Bring to a full rolling boil over medium-high heat, stirring frequently. Stir in sugar. Return to a full rolling boil; stir often. Boil hard 1 minute, stirring constantly. Remove from heat; quickly skim off foam with a metal spoon.
2. Ladle at once into hot, *sterilized* half-pint jars, leaving a ¼-inch headspace. Wipe jar rims and adjust lids. Process in a boiling-water canner 5 minutes. Remove jars; cool on a rack till set. Makes 6 half-pints.

Nutrition Facts per tablespoon: 43 cal., 0 g total fat, 0 mg chol., 1 mg sodium, 11 g carbo., 0 g fiber, 0 g pro.

RHUBARB-RASPBERRY JAM

PREP: 50 MINUTES

No-Fat

  6 cups fresh or frozen unsweetened sliced rhubarb
  4 cups sugar

2 cups raspberries or one 12-ounce package frozen loose-pack raspberries
1 3-ounce package raspberry-flavored gelatin (not sugar-free)

1. In a large pot combine rhubarb and sugar. Let stand 15 to 20 minutes or till sugar is moistened. Bring to boiling. Boil, uncovered, for 10 minutes, stirring often. Add berries; return to boiling. Boil hard 5 to 6 minutes or till thick, stirring often. Remove from heat. Add gelatin; stir till dissolved.

2. Ladle into half-pint freezer containers, leaving a $^1/_2$-inch headspace to allow jam to expand during freezing. Seal and label. Let stand at room temperature till set. Store up to 3 weeks in refrigerator or 1 year in freezer. Makes 5 half-pints.

Nutrition Facts per tablespoon: 46 cal., 0 g total fat, 0 mg chol., 3 mg sodium, 12 g carbo., 0 g fiber, 0 g pro. **Daily Values:** 0% vit. A, 2% vit. C, 0% calcium, 0% iron

---

BLUEBERRY-ORANGE JAM

PREP: 30 MINUTES PROCESS: 5 MINUTES

Low-Fat

   3 pints blueberries, stems removed
   1 tablespoon finely shredded orange peel
$^1/_4$ cup orange juice
   1 1$^3/_4$-ounce package powdered fruit pectin
$^1/_2$ teaspoon margarine or butter
   4 cups sugar

1. Place *1 cup* of berries in an 8-quart pot. Use a potato masher to crush berries. Continue adding berries and crushing till you have 4 cups crushed berries. Stir in orange peel, orange juice, pectin, and margarine. Heat on high, stirring constantly, till mixture comes to full rolling boil. Add sugar all at once. Return to boiling; boil 1 minute, stirring constantly. Remove from heat; quickly skim off foam.

2. Ladle at once into hot, *sterilized* half-pint jars, leaving a $^1/_4$-inch headspace. Wipe jar rims; adjust lids. Process in a boiling-water canner for 5 minutes. Remove jars; cool till set. Makes 6 half-pints.

Nutrition Facts per tablespoon: 39 cal., 0 g total fat, 0 mg chol., 1 mg sodium, 10 g carbo., 0 g fiber, 0 g pro. **Daily Values:** 0% vit. A, 2% vit. C, 0% calcium, 0% iron

STRAWBERRY JAM

PREP: 35 MINUTES PROCESS: 5 MINUTES

Low-Fat

  2 quarts fresh strawberries, hulled
  1 1³/₄-ounce package powdered pectin
  ¹/₂ teaspoon margarine or butter
  7 cups sugar

1. Crush *1 cup* of berries in an 8-quart pot. Continue adding berries and crushing till you have 5 cups crushed berries. Stir in pectin and margarine. Heat on high, stirring constantly, till mixture comes to a full rolling boil. Add sugar all at once. Return to boiling; boil 1 minute, stirring constantly. Remove from heat; skim off foam.
2. Ladle at once into hot, *sterilized* half-pint canning jars, leaving a ¹/₄-inch headspace. Wipe jar rims; adjust lids. Process in a boiling-water canner 5 minutes. Remove jars; cool. Makes 8 half-pints.

Nutrition Facts per tablespoon: 46 cal., 0 g total fat, 0 mg chol., 1 mg sodium, 12 g carbo., 0 g fiber, 0 g pro. **Daily Values:** 0% vit. A, 8% vit. C, 0% calcium, 0% iron

---

ORANGE MARMALADE

PREP: 55 MINUTES PROCESS: 5 MINUTES

No-Fat

Allow the marmalade to set up to 2 weeks before sampling this sweet-tart spread.

  4 medium oranges
  1 medium lemon
1¹/₂ cups water
  ¹/₈ teaspoon baking soda
  5 cups sugar
  ¹/₂ of a 6-ounce package (1 foil pouch) liquid fruit pectin

1. Score citrus peels into 4 lengthwise sections; remove (see photo 1, at right). Scrape off white portions (see photo 2, at right) and discard; cut peels into thin strips. Bring peels, water, and baking soda to boiling. Cover; simmer for 20 minutes. Do not drain. Section fruits, reserving juices; discard seeds. Add fruits and juices to peels; return to boiling. Cover; simmer 10 minutes. Measure 3 cups.

2. In an 8- or 10-quart pot combine fruit mixture and sugar. Bring to a full rolling boil, stirring constantly. Quickly stir in pectin; return to boiling. Boil and stir 1 minute. Remove from heat; skim off foam.

3. Ladle into hot, *sterilized* half-pint jars, leaving a ¼-inch head-space. Wipe jar rims; adjust lids. Process in a boiling-water canner 5 minutes. Remove jars and cool on a rack. Makes 6 half-pints.

Nutrition Facts per tablespoon: 50 cal., 0 g total fat, 0 mg chol., 5 mg sodium, 13 g carbo., 0 g fiber, 0 g pro. **Daily Values:** 0% vit. A, 3% vit. C, 0% calcium, 0% iron

1. After scoring a citrus fruit with a sharp knife, you can easily remove the peel with your fingers.

2. Scrape off the bitter white portions of the peels with a sharp knife. Discard white portions.

BERRY FREEZER JAM

PREP: 25 MINUTES

No-Fat

    4 cups blackberries, raspberries, or hulled strawberries
    4 cups sugar
    ¼ teaspoon finely shredded lemon peel
    ½ of a 6-ounce package (1 foil pouch) liquid fruit pectin
    2 tablespoons lemon juice

1. Crush berries till you have 2 cups blackberries or raspberries or 1¾ cups strawberries. Mix berries, sugar, and peel. Let stand for 10 minutes. Combine pectin and lemon juice. Add to berry mixture; stir for 3 minutes.

2. Ladle into half-pint freezer containers, leaving a ½-inch headspace. Seal and label. Let stand at room temperature 24 hours or till set. Store 3 weeks in refrigerator or for 1 year in freezer. Makes 4 half-pints.

Nutrition Facts per tablespoon: 53 cal., 0 g total fat, 0 mg chol., 0 mg sodium, 14 g carbo., 1 g fiber, 0 g pro. **Daily Values:** 0% vit. A, 3% vit. C, 0% calcium, 0% iron.

APPLE BUTTER

PREP: 3 HOURS PROCESS: 5 MINUTES

No-Fat

- 4¹/₂ **pounds tart cooking apples, cored and quartered (about 14 medium)**
- 4 **cups apple cider or apple juice**
- 2 **cups sugar**
- 1¹/₂ **teaspoons ground cinnamon**
- ¹/₂ **teaspoon ground cloves**
- ¹/₂ **teaspoon ground allspice**

1. In an 8- or 10-quart pot combine apples and cider or juice. Bring to boiling; reduce heat. Cover; simmer for 30 minutes, stirring occasionally. Press through a food mill or sieve till you have 9¹/₂ cups. Return to pot. Stir in sugar, cinnamon, cloves, and allspice. Bring to boiling; reduce heat. Cook, uncovered, over very low heat 1¹/₂ hours or till very thick, stirring often.

2. Ladle into hot, *sterilized* half-pint jars, leaving a ¹/₄-inch headspace. Wipe jar rims; adjust lids. Process in boiling-water canner 5 minutes (start timing when water begins to boil). Remove jars and cool on racks. Makes 8 half-pints.

Nutrition Facts per tablespoon: 35 cal., 0 g total fat, 0 mg chol., 0 mg sodium, 9 g carbo., 0 g fiber, 0 g pro. **Daily Values:** 0% vit. A, 1% vit. C, 0% calcium, 0% iron

COOKIES

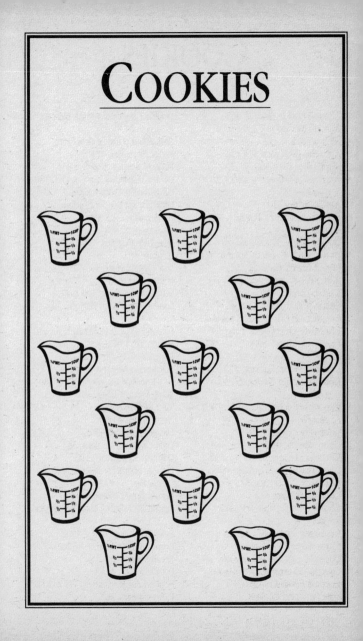

COOKIES

LEMON BARS

Bake the ultimate in bar cookies—a creamy lemon filling atop a buttery pastry crust.

$^1/_3$ **cup butter or margarine**
$^1/_4$ **cup granulated sugar**
 1 **cup all-purpose flour**
 2 **eggs**
$^3/_4$ **cup granulated sugar**
 2 **tablespoons all-purpose flour**
 2 **teaspoons finely shredded lemon peel**
 3 **tablespoons lemon juice**
$^1/_4$ **teaspoon baking powder**
  Powdered sugar (optional)

1. In a medium mixing bowl beat butter or margarine with an electric mixer on medium to high speed for 30 seconds. Add the $^1/_4$ cup granulated sugar; beat till combined. Beat in the 1 cup flour till crumbly. Press mixture into the bottom of an ungreased 8×8×2-inch baking pan. Bake in a 350° oven for 15 to 18 minutes or just till golden.
2. Meanwhile, for filling, in a small mixing bowl combine eggs, the $^3/_4$ cup granulated sugar, the 2 tablespoons flour, lemon peel, lemon juice, and baking powder. Beat 2 minutes or till combined.
3. Pour filling over baked layer. Bake 20 minutes more or till lightly browned around edges and center is set. Cool on a wire rack. If desired, sift powdered sugar over top. Cut into bars. Makes 20 bars.

Nutrition Facts per bar: 97 cal., 4 g total fat (2 g sat. fat), 29 mg chol., 42 mg sodium, 15 g carbo., 0 g fiber, 1 g pro. **Daily Values:** 3% vit. A, 2% vit. C, 0% calcium, 2% iron

---

FRUIT-FILLED OATMEAL BARS

Choose your favorite filling for these treasured lunch-box treats.

 1 **cup all-purpose flour**
 1 **cup quick-cooking rolled oats**
$^2/_3$ **cup packed brown sugar**

$^1/_4$ teaspoon baking soda
$^1/_2$ cup butter or margarine
1 recipe Apple-Cinnamon Filling, Apricot-Coconut Filling,
     Mincemeat Filling, or Raisin Filling (see below)

1. In a medium mixing bowl combine the flour, oats, brown sugar, and baking soda. Using a pastry blender or 2 knives, cut in butter or margarine till the mixture resembles coarse crumbs. Reserve $^1/_2$ cup of the crumb mixture.
2. With your fingers press remaining crumb mixture into the bottom of an ungreased 9×9×2-inch baking pan. Spread with desired filling. Sprinkle with reserved crumb mixture. Bake in a 350° oven for 30 to 35 minutes or till the top is golden. Cool on a wire rack. Cut into bars. Makes 25 bars.

■ **Apple-Cinnamon Filling:** Peel, core, and chop 2 medium *apples* (about 10 ounces). In a medium saucepan combine apples, 2 tablespoons *water*, 1 tablespoon *lemon juice*, $^1/_2$ teaspoon *ground cinnamon*, and a dash *ground cloves*. Bring apple mixture to boiling; reduce heat. Simmer, covered, for 8 to 10 minutes or till apples are tender.

Nutrition Facts per bar: 85 cal., 4 g total fat (2 g sat. fat), 10 mg chol., 52 mg sodium, 12 g carbo., 1 g fiber, 1 g pro. **Daily Values:** 3% vit. A, 1% vit. C, 0% calcium, 3% iron

■ **Apricot-Coconut Filling:** In a medium saucepan combine 1 cup snipped *dried apricots* and $^3/_4$ cup *water*. Bring apricot mixture to boiling; reduce heat. Cover and simmer for 5 minutes. Meanwhile, combine $^1/_4$ cup *sugar* and 1 tablespoon *all-purpose flour*. Stir into apricot mixture. Cook and stir about 1 minute more or till thick. Stir in $^1/_2$ cup *coconut*.

Nutrition Facts per bar: 107 cal., 4 g total fat (3 g sat. fat)

■ **Mincemeat Filling:** In a medium saucepan bring $^3/_4$ cup *water* to boiling. Add one 9-ounce package *condensed mincemeat*. Cover and simmer for 3 minutes, stirring often.

Nutrition Facts per bar: 115 cal., 4 g total fat (2 g sat. fat)

■ **Raisin Filling:** In a medium saucepan combine $^1/_2$ cup *water*, 2 tablespoons *sugar*, and 2 teaspoons *cornstarch*. Add 1 cup *raisins*. Cook and stir till thickened and bubbly.

Nutrition Facts per bar: 101 cal., 4 g total fat (2 g sat. fat)

PUMPKIN BARS

PREP: 35 MINUTES BAKE: 25 MINUTES COOL: 2 HOURS   Oven 350°

    2 cups all-purpose flour
 1¹/₂ cups sugar
    2 teaspoons baking powder
    2 teaspoons ground cinnamon
    1 teaspoon baking soda
  ¹/₄ teaspoon salt
  ¹/₄ teaspoon ground cloves
    4 beaten eggs
    1 16-ounce can pumpkin
    1 cup cooking oil
  ¹/₂ recipe Cream Cheese Frosting (see page 290)

1. In a large mixing bowl stir together the flour, sugar, baking powder, cinnamon, baking soda, salt, and cloves. Stir in the eggs, pumpkin, and oil till combined. Spread batter in an ungreased
15×10×1-inch baking pan.
2. Bake in a 350° oven 25 to 30 minutes or till a wooden toothpick
inserted near the center comes out clean. Cool for 2 hours on a wire
rack. Spread with Cream Cheese Frosting; cut into bars. Makes 48
bars.

Nutrition Facts per bar (with frosting): 116 cal., 6 g total fat (1 g sat. fat), 20 mg chol.,
64 mg sodium, 16 g carbo., 0 g fiber, 1 g pro. **Daily Values:** 22% vit. A, 0% vit. C, 1%
calcium, 3% iron

■ **Applesauce Bars:** Prepare as above, except substitute one 16-
ounce can *applesauce* for the can of pumpkin.

Nutrition Facts per bar: 161 cal., 8 g total fat (2 g sat. fat)

GRANOLA BARS

PREP: 20 MINUTES BAKE: 30 MINUTES   Oven 325°

Use purchased granola or make your own (see recipe, page 132).

    1 cup granola
    1 cup quick-cooking rolled oats
    1 cup chopped nuts
  ¹/₂ cup all-purpose flour

     $^1/_2$ cup raisins or mixed dried fruit bits
     1 beaten egg
     $^1/_3$ cup honey
     $^1/_3$ cup cooking oil
     $^1/_4$ cup packed brown sugar
     $^1/_2$ teaspoon ground cinnamon (optional)

1. Line an 8×8×2-inch baking pan with foil. Grease the foil; set pan aside. In a large mixing bowl combine granola, oats, nuts, flour, and raisins. Stir in egg, honey, oil, brown sugar, and, if desired, cinnamon. Press evenly into the prepared pan.

2. Bake in a 325° oven for 30 to 35 minutes or till lightly browned around the edges. Cool on a wire rack. Use foil to remove from pan. Cut into bars. Makes 24 bars.

Nutrition Facts per bar: 135 cal., 7 g total fat (1 g sat. fat), 9 mg chol., 14 mg sodium, 16 g carbo., 1 g fiber, 2 g pro. **Daily Values:** 0% vit. A, 0% vit. C, 1% calcium, 4% iron

---

SPICED APRICOT BARS

PREP: 15 MINUTES BAKE: 25 MINUTES COOL: 2 HOURS   Oven 350°

Low-Fat

Looking for a low-fat treat? These bars would be a good choice because applesauce is used to reduce the amount of oil needed.

     1 cup all-purpose flour
     $^1/_2$ teaspoon baking powder
     $^1/_4$ teaspoon baking soda
     $^1/_4$ teaspoon ground cardamom or $^1/_8$ teaspoon ground cloves
     1 slightly beaten egg
     $^1/_2$ cup packed brown sugar
     $^1/_2$ cup apricot nectar or orange juice
     $^1/_4$ cup unsweetened applesauce
     2 tablespoons cooking oil
     $^1/_2$ cup finely snipped dried apricots
     1 recipe Apricot Icing (see page 370)

1. In a medium mixing bowl stir together the flour, baking powder, baking soda, and cardamom or cloves; set aside. In another bowl stir together the egg, brown sugar, apricot nectar or orange juice, applesauce, and oil till combined. Add liquid mixture to dry mixture, stirring till just combined. Stir in the snipped apricots.

2. Spread batter in an ungreased 11×7×1½-inch baking pan. Bake in a 350° oven about 25 minutes or till a wooden toothpick inserted near the center comes out clean. Cool for 2 hours on a wire rack. Drizzle with the Apricot Icing. Cut into bars. Makes 24 bars.

■ **Apricot Icing:** In a small mixing bowl stir together ½ cup sifted *powdered sugar* and enough *apricot nectar or orange juice* (2 to 3 teaspoons) to make an icing that is easy to drizzle.

Nutrition Facts per bar (with icing): 63 cal., 1 g total fat (0 g sat. fat), 9 mg chol., 25 mg sodium, 12 g carbo., 0 g fiber, 1 g pro. **Daily Values:** 3% vit. A, 3% vit. C, 1% calcium, 3% iron

---

BANANA-CHOCOLATE CHIP BARS

PREP: 20 MINUTES BAKE: 25 MINUTES   Oven 350°

Here's a great way to use those bananas that have become too ripe to eat fresh.

 ¾ **cup butter or margarine, softened**
 ⅔ **cup granulated sugar**
 ⅔ **cup packed brown sugar**
 2 **teaspoons baking powder**
 ½ **teaspoon salt**
 1 **egg**
 1 **cup mashed ripe bananas (2 to 3 medium)**
 1 **teaspoon vanilla**
 2 **cups all-purpose flour**
 1 **6-ounce package (1 cup) semisweet chocolate pieces**
 ⅔ **cup chopped walnuts (optional)**

1. Grease a 15×10×1-inch baking pan; set aside. In a medium mixing bowl beat the butter or margarine with an electric mixer on medium to high speed for 30 seconds. Add the granulated sugar, brown sugar, baking powder, and salt; beat till combined. Beat in the egg, bananas, and vanilla till combined. Beat in as much of the flour as you can with the mixer. Stir in remaining flour. Stir in the chocolate pieces and, if desired, nuts.

2. Spread in the prepared baking pan. Bake in a 350° oven about 25 minutes or till golden. Cool on a wire rack. Cut into bars. Makes 36 bars.

Nutrition Facts per bar: 117 cal., 5 g total fat (2 g sat. fat), 16 mg chol., 92 mg sodium, 17 g carbo., 0 g fiber, 1 g pro. **Daily Values:** 3% vit. A, 1% vit. C, 2% calcium, 3% iron

CHOCOLATE REVEL BARS

PREP: 30 MINUTES BAKE: 25 MINUTES   Oven 350°

        1 cup butter or margarine
        2 cups packed brown sugar
        1 teaspoon baking soda
        2 eggs
        2 teaspoons vanilla
    2¹/₂ cups all-purpose flour
        3 cups quick-cooking rolled oats
    1¹/₂ cups semisweet chocolate pieces
        1 14-ounce can (1¹/₄ cups) sweetened condensed milk or low-fat
            sweetened condensed milk
      ¹/₂ cup chopped walnuts or pecans
        2 teaspoons vanilla

1. Set aside *2 tablespoons* of the butter or margarine. In a large mixing bowl beat the remaining butter or margarine with an electric mixer on medium to high speed for 30 seconds. Add the brown sugar and baking soda. Beat till combined, scraping sides of bowl occasionally. Beat in eggs and 2 teaspoons vanilla till combined. Beat in as much of the flour as you can with the mixer. Stir in remaining flour. Stir in the rolled oats.

2. For filling, in a medium saucepan combine the reserved 2 tablespoons butter or margarine, chocolate pieces, and sweetened condensed milk. Cook over low heat till chocolate melts, stirring occasionally. Remove from heat. Stir in the walnuts or pecans and 2 teaspoons vanilla.

3. Press two-thirds (about 3¹/₃ cups) of the rolled oats mixture into the bottom of an ungreased 15×10×1-inch baking pan. Spread filling evenly over the oat mixture. Dot remaining rolled oats mixture on filling (see photo, page 372).

4. Bake in a 350° oven about 25 minutes or till top is lightly browned (chocolate filling will still look moist). Cool on a wire rack. Cut into bars. Makes 60 bars.

Nutrition Facts per bar: 148 cal., 6 g total fat (2 g sat. fat), 17 mg chol., 79 mg sodium, 21 g carbo., 1 g fiber, 3 g pro. **Daily Values:** 3% vit. A, 0% vit. C, 3% calcium, 4% iron

■ **Peanut Butter-Chocolate Revel Bars:** Prepare as above, except substitute ¹/₂ cup *peanut butter* for the 2 tablespoons butter or margarine when making the chocolate filling and substitute *peanuts* for the walnuts or pecans.

Nutrition Facts per bar: 143 cal., 7 g total fat (2 g sat. fat)

■ **Whole Wheat-Chocolate Revel Bars:** Prepare as above, except reduce the all-purpose flour to 1½ cups and add 1 cup *whole wheat flour*.

Nutrition Facts per bar: 133 cal., 6 g total fat (2 g sat. fat)

Use your fingers to work the remaining oat mixture into flat pieces of various sizes; place them on the chocolate filling. Or, drop the dough from a spoon.

CHOCOLATE-PEANUT BUTTER BARS

PREP: 20 MINUTES BAKE: 27 MINUTES   Oven 350°

 2 **cups quick-cooking rolled oats**
1¾ **cups packed brown sugar**
 1 **cup all-purpose flour**
½ **cup whole wheat flour**
 1 **teaspoon baking powder**
½ **teaspoon baking soda**
 1 **cup butter or margarine**
½ **cup chopped peanuts**
 1 **12-ounce package (2 cups) semisweet chocolate pieces**
 1 **beaten egg**
 1 **14-ounce can (1¼ cups) sweetened condensed milk or low-fat sweetened condensed milk**
⅓ **cup creamy peanut butter**

1. For crumb mixture, in a large mixing bowl combine rolled oats, brown sugar, all-purpose flour, whole wheat flour, baking powder, and baking soda. Using a pastry blender, cut in the butter till mixture resembles fine crumbs. Stir in peanuts.

2. For topping, combine 1¾ cups of the crumb mixture and the chocolate pieces; set aside.

3. For crust, stir the egg into remaining crumb mixture. Press into bottom of an ungreased 15×10×1-inch baking pan. Bake in a 350° oven 15 minutes.

4. For filling, stir together sweetened condensed milk and peanut butter till well combined. Pour filling evenly over partially baked crust. Sprinkle topping evenly over filling. Bake for 12 to 15 minutes more or till lightly browned around the edges. Cool on a wire rack. Cut into bars. Makes 48 bars.

Nutrition Facts per bar: 163 cal., 9 g total fat (3 g sat. fat), 17 mg chol., 82 mg sodium, 21 g carbo., 1 g fiber, 3 g pro. **Daily Values:** 4% vit. A, 0% vit. C, 3% calcium, 4% iron

TOFFEE BARS

PREP: 25 MINUTES   BAKE: 27 MINUTES   Oven 350°

Instead of topping these bars with fudge icing, you can sprinkle one 6-ounce package (1 cup) semisweet chocolate pieces over the cookie immediately after removing it from the oven. Let pieces stand 2 to 3 minutes or till softened; spread evenly. Cool, then chill for 5 to 10 minutes or until the chocolate is set. Cut into bars.

  ½ **cup butter or margarine**
  ½ **cup granulated sugar**
  ¼ **teaspoon salt**
  1 **cup all-purpose flour**
  1 **14-ounce can (1¼ cups) sweetened condensed milk or low-fat**
    sweetened condensed milk
  2 **tablespoons butter or margarine**
  2 **teaspoons vanilla**
  1 **ounce unsweetened chocolate**
  2 **tablespoons butter or margarine**
1½ **cups sifted powdered sugar**
  1 **teaspoon vanilla**

1. In a medium mixing bowl beat the ½ cup butter or margarine, granulated sugar, and salt with an electric mixer on medium to high speed till combined. Using a wooden spoon, stir in the flour. Press into the bottom of an ungreased 13×9×2-inch baking pan. Bake in a 350° oven about 15 minutes or till the edges are lightly browned.

2. Meanwhile, in a heavy medium saucepan heat the sweetened condensed milk and 2 tablespoons butter or margarine over medium heat till bubbly, stirring constantly. Cook and stir for 5 minutes more. (Mixture will thicken and become smooth.) Stir in the 2 teaspoons vanilla. Spread over baked layer. Bake for 12 to 15 minutes or till golden.

3. For fudge icing, in a small saucepan melt chocolate and 2 tablespoons butter or margarine over low heat, stirring occasionally. Remove from heat. Stir in the powdered sugar and the 1 teaspoon vanilla. Stir in enough *hot water* (1 to 2 tablespoons) to make an icing that is easy to pour. Spread the icing evenly over the warm cookie. Immediately cut into bars. Cool on a wire rack. Makes 36 bars.

Nutrition Facts per bar: 112 cal., 5 g total fat (3 g sat. fat), 14 mg chol., 68 mg sodium, 16 g carbo., 0 g fiber, 1 g pro. **Daily Values:** 4% vit. A, 0% vit. C, 2% calcium, 1% iron

---

FUDGE BROWNIES

PREP: 15 MINUTES BAKE: 30 MINUTES   Oven 350°

Double the delight and frost the cooled brownies with half of a recipe of No-Cook Fudge Frosting (see page 292) or Chocolate Glaze (see page 265).

   ¹/₂ **cup butter or margarine**
     2 **ounces unsweetened chocolate**
     2 **eggs**
     1 **cup sugar**
     1 **teaspoon vanilla**
   ³/₄ **cup all-purpose flour**
   ¹/₂ **cup chopped nuts**

1. Grease an 8×8×2-inch baking pan; set aside. In a medium saucepan melt butter and chocolate over low heat. Remove from heat. Stir in eggs, sugar, and vanilla. Using a wooden spoon, beat lightly just till combined. Stir in flour and nuts.

2. Spread batter in prepared baking pan. Bake in a 350° oven for 30 minutes. Cool on a wire rack. Cut into bars. Makes 24 brownies.

Nutrition Facts per brownie: 113 cal., 7 g total fat (3 g sat. fat), 28 mg chol., 44 mg sodium, 12 carbo., 0 g fiber, 2 g pro. **Daily Values:** 4% vit. A, 0% vit. C, 0% calcium, 3% iron

■ **Rocky Road Fudge Brownies:** Prepare as above, except after baking, immediately sprinkle ¹/₂ cup *tiny marshmallows* and ¹/₂ cup *semisweet chocolate pieces* evenly over brownies. Bake 3 minutes more or till marshmallows are just beginning to brown and chocolate is melted.

Nutrition Facts per brownie: 133 cal., 8 g total fat (3 g sat. fat)

AMARETTO BROWNIES

PREP: 40 MINUTES   BAKE: 20 MINUTES   COOL: 2 HOURS   Oven 350°

1 cup sugar
³/₄ cup butter or margarine
¹/₂ of an 8-ounce can (about ¹/₂ cup) almond paste*
¹/₂ cup unsweetened cocoa powder
2 eggs
2 tablespoons amaretto or milk
1 teaspoon vanilla
1¹/₄ cups all-purpose flour
1 teaspoon baking powder
¹/₄ teaspoon baking soda
1 cup milk
1 recipe No-Cook Fudge Frosting (page 292)
¹/₂ cup chopped almonds, toasted (see tip, page 234)

BEYOND SQUARES

There's more than one way to cut bars and brownies. Various shapes other than squares make for an interesting presentation.

Make triangles by cutting bars or brownies into 2- or 2¹/₂-inch squares. Then cut each square in half diagonally.

For diamonds, first cut straight lines 1 or 1¹/₂ inches apart down the length of the pan. Then cut straight lines 1 to 1¹/₂ inches apart diagonally across the pan.

1. Grease a 15×10×1-inch baking pan; set aside. In a pan heat sugar, butter, almond paste, and cocoa powder over medium heat till butter melts, stirring constantly. Remove from heat. Add eggs, amaretto, and vanilla; beat with a wooden spoon just till combined. Combine flour, baking powder, and baking soda. Add flour mixture and milk alternately to chocolate mixture, beating after each.

2. Pour batter into prepared pan. Bake in a 350° oven 20 minutes or till a wooden toothpick inserted near center comes out clean. Cool on a wire rack for 2 hours. Frost with No-Cook Fudge Frosting; sprinkle with almonds. Cut into bars. Makes 48 brownies.

*Note: For best results, use an almond paste made without syrup or liquid glucose.

Nutrition Facts per brownie (with frosting): 139 cal., 7 g total fat (3 g sat. fat), 22 mg chol., 68 mg sodium, 19 g carbo., 0 g fiber, 2 g pro. **Daily Values:** 5% vit. A, 0% vit. C, 3% calcium, 3% iron

---

CAKE BROWNIES

PREP: 40 MINUTES BAKE: 20 MINUTES COOL: 2 HOURS   Oven 350°

1¹/₄ **cups sugar**
 ³/₄ **cup butter or margarine**
 ¹/₂ **cup unsweetened cocoa powder**
   2 **eggs**
   1 **teaspoon vanilla**
1¹/₂ **cups all-purpose flour**
   1 **teaspoon baking powder**
 ¹/₄ **teaspoon baking soda**
   1 **cup milk**
   1 **cup chopped walnuts or pecans**
   1 **recipe No-Cook Fudge Frosting (see page 292)**

1. Grease a 15×10×1-inch baking pan; set aside. In a pan heat sugar, butter, and cocoa powder over medium heat till butter melts, stirring constantly. Remove from heat. Add eggs and vanilla. Using a wooden spoon, beat lightly just till combined. Combine flour, baking powder, and baking soda. Add flour mixture and milk alternately to chocolate mixture, beating after each addition. Stir in nuts.

2. Pour batter into the prepared baking pan. Bake in a 350° oven about 20 minutes or till a wooden toothpick inserted near the center comes out clean. Cool 2 hours on a wire rack. Frost with No-Cook Fudge Frosting. Cut into bars. Makes 48.

Nutrition Facts per brownie (with frosting): 143 cal., 7 g total fat (3 g sat. fat), 22 mg chol., 68 mg sodium, 19 g carbo., 0 g fiber, 2 g pro. **Daily Values:** 5% vit. A, 0% vit. C, 3% calcium, 3% iron

RASPBERRY TRUFFLE BROWNIES

PREP: 40 MINUTES CHILL: 1 HOUR STAND: 1 HOUR

    1 recipe Cake Brownies (see page 376)
 2¹/₂ cups sifted powdered sugar
  ¹/₂ cup unsweetened cocoa powder
    6 tablespoons butter or margarine, softened
    2 tablespoons raspberry liqueur or melted seedless raspberry
       jam
    1 to 3 tablespoons milk
    4 ounces white chocolate baking squares, cut up and melted

1. Prepare, bake, and cool Cake Brownies as directed. For frosting, in a large mixing bowl combine powdered sugar, cocoa powder, butter or margarine, and raspberry liqueur or jam. Beat with electric mixer on medium speed, adding milk (1 tablespoon at a time) till frosting is creamy and easy to spread. Spread over brownies. Cover; chill 1 hour. Drizzle with melted white chocolate. Let stand 1 hour. Cut into bars. Makes 48 brownies.

Nutrition Facts per brownie (with frosting): 134 cal., 7 g total fat (3 g sat. fat), 21 mg chol., 65 mg sodium, 16 g carbo., 0 g fiber, 2 g pro. **Daily Values:** 4% vit. A, 0% vit. C, 3% calcium, 3% iron

■ **Mint Brownies:** Prepare as above, except increase powdered sugar to 3 cups. Omit cocoa powder, raspberry liqueur or jam, and white chocolate. To butter mixture add 2 tablespoons *crème de menthe or* ¹/₄ teaspoon *mint extract* and, if desired, a few drops *green food coloring*. Spread 1 recipe *No-Cook Fudge Frosting* (see page 292) over chilled brownies. Let stand 1 hour. Cut into bars. Makes 48 brownies.

Nutrition Facts per brownie: 182 cal., 8 g total fat (4 g sat. fat)

BLONDIES

A Southern cook's preference for brown sugar over granulated sugar resulted in these butterscotch bar cookies many years ago.

    2 cups packed brown sugar
  ²/₃ cup butter or margarine
    2 eggs
    2 teaspoons vanilla
    2 cups all-purpose flour
    1 teaspoon baking powder
  ¹/₄ teaspoon baking soda
    1 6-ounce package (1 cup) semisweet chocolate pieces
    1 cup chopped nuts

1. Grease a 13×9×2-inch baking pan; set aside. In a medium saucepan heat brown sugar and butter over medium heat till sugar dissolves, stirring constantly. Cool slightly. Stir in eggs, one at a time, and vanilla. Stir in flour, baking powder, and baking soda.

2. Spread batter in prepared baking pan. Sprinkle with chocolate and nuts. Bake in a 350° oven 25 to 30 minutes or till done. Cool slightly on a wire rack. Cut into bars while warm. Makes 36 bars.

Nutrition Facts per bar: 138 cal., 7 g total fat (2 g sat. fat), 21 mg chol., 61 mg sodium, 18 g carbo., 0 g fiber, 2 g pro. **Daily Values:** 3% vit. A, 0% vit. C, 2% calcium, 5% iron

PEANUT BUTTER-OATMEAL ROUNDS

These easy-to-make cookies make a great snack for kids.

  ³/₄ cup butter or margarine
  ¹/₂ cup peanut butter
    1 cup granulated sugar
  ¹/₂ cup packed brown sugar
    1 teaspoon baking powder
  ¹/₂ teaspoon baking soda
    2 eggs
    1 teaspoon vanilla
 1¹/₄ cups all-purpose flour

2 cups rolled oats
1 cup chopped cocktail peanuts or semisweet chocolate pieces

1. In a large mixing bowl beat butter or margarine and peanut butter with an electric mixer on medium speed about 30 seconds or till combined. Add granulated sugar, brown sugar, baking powder, and baking soda. Beat till combined, scraping the sides of bowl occasionally. Beat in the eggs and vanilla till combined. Beat in as much of the flour as you can with the mixer. Stir in remaining flour. Stir in the rolled oats and peanuts or chocolate pieces.
2. Drop dough by rounded teaspoons 2 inches apart on an ungreased cookie sheet. Bake in a 375° oven about 10 minutes or till edges are lightly browned. Transfer cookies to wire rack and let cool. Makes about 60 cookies.

Nutrition Facts per cookie: 87 cal., 5 g total fat (2 g sat. fat), 13 mg chol., 63 mg sodium, 9 g carbo., 1 g fiber, 2 g pro. **Daily Values:** 2% vit. A, 0% vit. C, 1% calcium, 2% iron

CHOCOLATE CHIP COOKIES

PREP: 25 MINUTES BAKE: 8 MINUTES PER BATCH   Oven 375°

$^1/_2$ cup shortening
$^1/_2$ cup butter or margarine
$^1/_2$ cup granulated sugar
1 cup packed brown sugar
$^1/_2$ teaspoon baking soda
2 eggs
1 teaspoon vanilla
$2^1/_2$ cups all-purpose flour
1 12-ounce package (2 cups) semisweet chocolate pieces
$1^1/_2$ cups chopped walnuts, pecans, or hazelnuts (filberts) (optional)

1. In a large mixing bowl beat the shortening and butter or margarine with an electric mixer on medium to high speed for 30 seconds. Add the granulated sugar, brown sugar, and baking soda. Beat mixture till combined, scraping sides of bowl occasionally. Beat in the eggs and vanilla till combined. Beat in as much of the flour as you can with the mixer. Stir in remaining flour. Stir in chocolate pieces and, if desired, nuts.
2. Drop dough by rounded teaspoons 2 inches apart on an ungreased cookie sheet. Bake in a 375° oven 8 to 10 minutes or till

edges are lightly browned. Transfer cookies to a wire rack and let cool. Makes about 60 cookies.

Nutrition Facts per cookie: 93 cal., 5 g total fat (1 g sat. fat), 11 mg chol., 29 mg sodium, 12 g carbo., 0 g fiber, 1 g pro. **Daily Values:** 1% vit. A, 0% vit. C, 0% calcium, 3% iron

■ **Giant Chocolate Chip Cookies:** Prepare as above, except use a $1/4$-cup measure or scoop to drop mounds of dough about 4 inches apart on an ungreased cookie sheet. Bake in a 375° oven for 11 to 13 minutes or till edges are lightly browned. Makes about 20 cookies.

Nutrition Facts per cookie: 278 cal., 15 g total fat (4 g sat. fat)

■ **Macadamia Nut and White Chocolate Chunk Cookies:** Prepare as above, except substitute chopped *white baking bars or white chocolate baking squares* for the semisweet chocolate pieces. Stir in one $3^{1}/_{2}$-ounce jar *macadamia nuts,* chopped, with the white chocolate.

Nutrition Facts per cookie: 108 cal., 6 g total fat (3 g sat. fat)

■ **Chocolate Chip Cookie Bars:** Prepare as above, except press dough into ungreased 15×10×1-inch baking pan. Bake in a 375° oven for 15 to 20 minutes or till golden. Cool on a wire rack. Cut into bars. Makes 48 bars.

Nutrition Facts per bar: 116 cal., 6 g total fat (2 g sat. fat)

■ **Chocolate Chip Cookie Pizzas:** Prepare as above, except do not stir in chocolate pieces and nuts. Press half of the dough into an ungreased 12-inch pizza pan. Sprinkle half of the chocolate pieces and nuts over the top, pressing in lightly. Repeat with a second ungreased 12-inch pizza pan and the remaining dough and toppings. Bake in a 375° oven about 15 minutes or till golden. Meanwhile, melt 4-ounces *white baking bars or white chocolate baking squares,* chopped; drizzle over baked cookie pizzas. Cut each into 8 wedges, then cut a middle circle. Makes 32 pieces total.

Nutrition Facts per piece: 193 cal., 11 g total fat (3 g sat. fat)

HERMITS

$^1/_2$ **cup butter or margarine**
$^3/_4$ **cup packed brown sugar**
$^1/_2$ **teaspoon baking soda**
$^1/_2$ **teaspoon ground cinnamon**
$^1/_4$ **teaspoon ground nutmeg**
$^1/_8$ **teaspoon ground cloves**
  1 **egg**
  2 **tablespoons milk**
  1 **teaspoon vanilla**
1$^1/_2$ **cups all-purpose flour**
  1 **cup raisins, currants, or diced mixed candied fruits and peels**
$^1/_2$ **cup chopped nuts**

1. Grease a cookie sheet; set aside. In a large mixing bowl beat butter or margarine with an electric mixer on medium to high speed for 30 seconds. Add brown sugar, baking soda, cinnamon, nutmeg, and cloves. Beat till combined, scraping sides of bowl occasionally. Beat in the egg, milk, and vanilla till combined. Beat in as much of the flour as you can with the mixer. Stir in remaining flour. Stir in raisins and nuts.

2. Drop by rounded teaspoons 2 inches apart on prepared cookie sheet. Bake in a 375° oven 10 minutes or till edges are lightly browned. Transfer cookies to a wire rack and let cool. Makes 36 cookies.

Nutrition Facts per cookie: 79 cal., 4 g total fat (2 g sat. fat), 13 mg chol., 47 mg sodium, 11 g carbo., 0 g fiber, 1 g pro. **Daily Values:** 2% vit. A, 0% vit. C, 0% calcium, 3% iron

FUDGE ECSTASIES

Prep: 20 minutes Bake: 8 minutes per batch   Oven 350°

If you like brownies, you'll love these oh-so-chocolaty cookies that are studded with nuts.

    1 12-ounce package (2 cups) semisweet chocolate pieces
    2 ounces unsweetened chocolate, chopped
    2 tablespoons butter or margarine
    2 eggs
    2/3 cup sugar
    1/4 cup all-purpose flour
    1 teaspoon vanilla
    1/4 teaspoon baking powder
    1 cup chopped nuts

1. Grease a cookie sheet; set aside. In a heavy medium saucepan heat *1 cup* of the chocolate pieces, the unsweetened chocolate, and butter or margarine till melted, stirring constantly. Add the eggs, sugar, flour, vanilla, and baking powder. Beat till combined, scraping sides of pan occasionally. Stir in remaining 1 cup chocolate pieces and nuts.

2. Drop dough by rounded teaspoons 2 inches apart on the prepared cookie sheet. Bake in a 350° oven for 8 to 10 minutes or till edges are firm and surfaces are dull and crackled. Transfer cookies to a wire rack and let cool. Makes about 36 cookies.

Nutrition Facts per cookie: 101 cal., 6 g total fat (1 g sat. fat), 14 mg chol., 13 mg sodium, 12 g carbo., 0 g fiber, 2 g pro. **Daily Values:** 1% vit. A, 0% vit. C, 0% calcium, 3% iron

OATMEAL COOKIES

Prep: 25 minutes Bake: 10 minutes per batch   Oven 375°

    3/4 cup butter or margarine
    1 cup packed brown sugar
    1/2 cup granulated sugar
    1 teaspoon baking powder
    1/4 teaspoon baking soda
    1/2 teaspoon ground cinnamon (optional)
    1/4 teaspoon ground cloves (optional)

1 egg
1 teaspoon vanilla
1³/₄ cups all-purpose flour
2 cups rolled oats

1. In a large mixing bowl beat butter or margarine with an electric mixer on medium to high speed for 30 seconds. Add brown sugar, granulated sugar, baking powder, baking soda, and, if desired, cinnamon and cloves. Beat till combined, scraping sides of bowl occasionally. Beat in the egg and vanilla till combined. Beat in as much of the flour as you can with the mixer. Stir in remaining flour. Stir in the rolled oats.

2. Drop dough by rounded teaspoons 2 inches apart on an ungreased cookie sheet. Bake in a 375° oven for 10 to 12 minutes or till edges are golden. Cool cookies on a wire rack. Makes about 48.

Nutrition Facts per cookie: 77 cal., 3 g total fat (2 g sat. fat), 12 mg chol., 46 mg sodium, 11 g carbo., 0 g fiber, 1 g pro: **Daily Values:** 2% vit. A, 0% vit. C, 1% calcium, 3% iron

■ **Oatmeal-Raisin Cookies:** Prepare as above, except, after stirring in oats, stir in 1 cup *raisins or currants*. Makes about 54 cookies.

Nutrition Facts per cookie: 70 cal., 3 g total fat (2 g sat. fat)

■ **Choose-a-Chip Oatmeal Cookies:** Prepare as above except, after stirring in oats, stir in 1 cup *semisweet chocolate, butterscotch-*

COOKIE STORAGE

■ **To store dough for dropped or shaped cookies:** Place in an airtight container; chill up to 1 week. Or, place in a freezer container; freeze up to 6 months. To use, thaw.

■ **To store dough for sliced cookies:** Wrap rolls of dough in plastic wrap. Place in an airtight container; chill up to 1 week. Or, place in a freezer container; freeze up to 6 months. To use, thaw just until soft enough to slice.

■ **To store baked cookies:** Cool cookies completely; do not frost. In an airtight or freezer container, arrange cookies in a single layer; cover with a sheet of waxed paper. Repeat layers, leaving enough air space to close container easily. Store at room temperature up to 3 days or freeze up to 8 months.

flavored, or peanut butter-flavored pieces and $^1/_2$ cup chopped *walnuts or pecans*. Makes about 54 cookies.

Nutrition Facts per cookie: 84 cal., 4 g total fat (2 g sat. fat)

LEMON TEA COOKIES

PREP: 15 MINUTES BAKE: 10 MINUTES PER BATCH   Oven 350°

Low-Fat

   $^1/_2$ **cup butter or margarine**
   $^3/_4$ **cup sugar**
    1 **teaspoon finely shredded lemon peel**
    1 **teaspoon baking powder**
   $^1/_4$ **teaspoon baking soda**
    1 **egg**
   $^1/_3$ **cup milk**
    2 **teaspoons lemon juice**
 1$^3/_4$ **cups all-purpose flour**
   $^1/_4$ **cup sugar**
    2 **tablespoons lemon juice**

1. In a large mixing bowl beat the butter or margarine with an electric mixer on medium to high speed for 30 seconds. Add the $^3/_4$ cup sugar, lemon peel, baking powder, and baking soda. Beat till combined, scraping sides of bowl occasionally. Beat in egg, milk, and the 2 teaspoons lemon juice till combined. Beat in as much of the flour as you can with the mixer. Stir in remaining flour.
2. Drop dough by rounded teaspoons 2 inches apart on an ungreased cookie sheet. Bake in a 350° oven for 10 to 12 minutes or till edges are lightly browned. Transfer cookies to a wire rack and let cool. Stir together the $^1/_4$ cup sugar and the 2 tablespoons lemon juice; brush on cookies. Makes about 48 cookies.

Nutrition Facts per cookie: 51 cal., 2 g total fat (1 g sat. fat), 10 mg chol., 36 mg sodium, 8 g carbo., 0 g fiber, 1 g pro. **Daily Values:** 2% vit. A, 0% vit. C, 0% calcium, 1% iron

■ **Citrus Bars:** Prepare as above, using *lemon, lime, or orange peel and juice.* Spread dough evenly in a greased 15x10x1-inch baking pan. Increase oven temperature to 375°. Bake for 10 to 12 minutes or till edges are lightly browned. Lightly brush with the sugar-juice mixture. Cool on a wire rack. Drizzle 1 recipe *Powdered Sugar Icing* made with lemon, lime, or orange juice (see page 291) over top. Cut into bars. Makes 60 bars.

Nutrition Facts per bar (with icing): 47 cal., 2 g total fat (1 g sat. fat)

RANGER COOKIES

PREP: 25 MINUTES BAKE: 8 MINUTES PER BATCH   Oven 375°

Low-Fat

$^1/_2$ cup butter or margarine
$^1/_2$ cup granulated sugar
$^1/_2$ cup packed brown sugar
$^1/_2$ teaspoon baking powder
$^1/_4$ teaspoon baking soda
 1 egg
 1 teaspoon vanilla
$1^1/_4$ cups all-purpose flour
 2 cups crisp rice cereal or 1 cup rolled oats
 1 $3^1/_2$-ounce can ($1^1/_3$ cups) flaked coconut
 1 cup snipped pitted whole dates or raisins

1. Beat butter 30 seconds. Add granulated sugar, brown sugar, baking powder, and baking soda; beat till combined. Beat in egg and vanilla. Beat in as much of the flour as you can. Stir in remaining flour. Stir in cereal, coconut, and dates.
2. Drop by rounded teaspoons 2 inches apart on an ungreased cookie sheet. Bake in a 375° oven about 8 minutes or till edges are golden. Cool on cookie sheet 1 minute. Transfer to a wire rack; let cool. Makes about 54.

Nutrition Facts per cookie: 61 cal., 2 g total fat (2 g sat. fat), 8 mg chol., 40 mg sodium, 10 g carbo., 1 g fiber, 1 g pro. **Daily Values:** 1% vit. A, 0% vit. C, 0% calcium, 2% iron

COCONUT-PECAN COOKIES

PREP: 25 MINUTES BAKE: 8 MINUTES PER BATCH   Oven 375°

1/4 cup shortening
1/4 cup butter or margarine
1/2 cup granulated sugar
1/4 cup packed brown sugar
1/8 teaspoon baking soda
1 egg
1 teaspoon vanilla
1 cup all-purpose flour
1 cup coconut
1 cup chopped pecans

1. In a medium mixing bowl beat shortening and butter or margarine with an electric mixer on medium to high speed for 30 seconds. Add the granulated sugar, brown sugar, and baking soda. Beat till combined, scraping sides of bowl occasionally. Beat in egg and vanilla till combined. Beat in as much of the flour as you can with the mixer. Stir in remaining flour. Stir in the coconut and pecans.
2. Drop dough by rounded teaspoons 2 inches apart on an ungreased cookie sheet. Bake in a 375° oven for 8 to 10 minutes or till edges are golden. Cool cookies on the cookie sheet for 1 minute. Transfer cookies to a wire rack and let cool. Makes about 36 cookies.

Nutrition Facts per cookie: 83 cal., 6 g total fat (2 g sat. fat), 9 mg chol., 20 mg sodium, 8 g carbo., 0 g fiber, 1 g pro. **Daily Values:** 1% vit. A, 0% vit. C, 0% calcium, 2% iron

■ **Chocolate-Peanut Cookies:** Prepare as above, except omit coconut and pecans. Add 1/3 cup *unsweetened cocoa powder* with the sugar and 3 tablespoons *milk* with the egg. After adding all the flour, stir in 1/2 cup chopped *peanuts*. Makes about 30 cookies.

Nutrition Facts per cookie: 69 cal., 4 g total fat (1 g sat. fat)

■ **Gumdrop Cookies:** Prepare as above, except omit coconut and pecans. After adding all the flour, stir in 1 cup snipped *gumdrops*. Makes about 30.

Nutrition Facts per cookie: 70 cal., 3 g total fat (1 g sat. fat)

■ **Spiced Raisin or Fruit Cookies:** Prepare as above, except omit coconut and pecans. Add ½ teaspoon *ground cinnamon* and ½ teaspoon *ground nutmeg* with the sugar. After adding all the flour, stir in 1 cup *raisins or mixed dried fruit bits*. Makes about 30 cookies.

Nutrition Facts per cookie: 66 cal., 3 g total fat (1 g sat. fat)

APPLESAUCE-OATMEAL COOKIES

PREP: 15 MINUTES BAKE: 8 MINUTES PER BATCH   Oven 375°

Low-Fat

Concerned about cholesterol? Substitute two egg whites for the whole egg.

- ⅓ cup butter or margarine, softened
- ⅔ cup packed brown sugar
- ½ teaspoon ground cinnamon
- ¼ teaspoon baking soda
- 1 egg
- ½ cup unsweetened applesauce
- 1¼ cups all-purpose flour
- 1¼ cups rolled oats

1. In medium mixing bowl beat butter or margarine with an electric mixer on medium to high speed for 30 seconds. Add the brown sugar, cinnamon, and baking soda. Beat till combined, scraping sides of bowl. Beat in egg and applesauce till combined. Beat in as much of the flour as you can with the mixer. Stir in remaining flour and the rolled oats.

2. Drop dough by rounded teaspoons 2 inches apart on an ungreased cookie sheet. Bake in a 375° oven for 8 to 10 minutes or till lightly browned. Transfer cookies to a wire rack and let cool. Makes about 30 cookies.

Nutrition Facts per cookie: 67 cal., 2 g total fat (1 g sat. fat), 13 mg chol., 35 mg sodium, 10 g carbo., 1 g fiber, 1 g pro. **Daily Values:** 2% vit. A, 0% vit. C, 0% calcium, 3% iron

CHOCOLATE-OATMEAL COOKIES

PREP: 25 MINUTES BAKE: 8 MINUTES PER BATCH   Oven 375°

*Here's a cookie that calls out for a glass of cold milk or a cup of
steaming coffee. These crispy, doubly delicious morsels
are perfect for dunking.*

    1 cup butter or margarine
1¹/₂ cups sugar
    1 teaspoon baking powder
 ¹/₂ teaspoon baking soda
    3 ounces unsweetened chocolate, melted and cooled
    1 egg
    1 teaspoon vanilla
1¹/₄ cups all-purpose flour
1¹/₂ cups quick-cooking rolled oats
    1 6-ounce package (1 cup) semisweet chocolate pieces

1. In a large mixing bowl beat butter or margarine with an electric
mixer on medium to high speed for 30 seconds. Add the sugar, baking powder, and baking soda. Beat till combined, scraping sides of
bowl occasionally. Beat in the melted chocolate, egg, and vanilla till
combined. Beat in as much of the flour as you can with the mixer.
Stir in remaining flour. Stir in the rolled oats and chocolate pieces.
2. Drop dough by slightly rounded teaspoons about 3 inches apart
on an ungreased cookie sheet. Bake in a 375° oven for 8 to 10 minutes or till edges are firm. Transfer cookies to a wire rack and let
cool. Makes about 48 cookies.

Nutrition Facts per cookie: 105 cal., 6 g total fat (3 g sat. fat), 15 mg chol., 63 mg
sodium, 13 g carbo., 0 g fiber, 1 g pro. **Daily Values:** 3% vit. A, 0% vit. C, 1% calcium, 3%
iron

CAPPUCCINO CRINKLES

PREP: 15 MINUTES BAKE: 8 MINUTES PER BATCH   Oven 350°

Low-Fat

 ¹/₃ cup butter or margarine
    1 cup packed brown sugar
 ²/₃ cup unsweetened cocoa powder
    1 tablespoon instant coffee granules

1 teaspoon baking soda
1 teaspoon ground cinnamon
2 egg whites
$^1/_3$ cup low-fat vanilla yogurt
$1^1/_2$ cups all-purpose flour
$^1/_4$ cup granulated sugar

1. In large mixing bowl beat the butter or margarine with an electric mixer on medium to high speed about 30 seconds or till softened. Add the brown sugar, cocoa powder, coffee granules, baking soda, and cinnamon. Beat till combined, scraping sides of bowl occasionally. Beat in the egg whites and yogurt till combined. Beat in as much of the flour as you can with the mixer. Stir in remaining flour.

2. Place the granulated sugar in a small bowl. Drop dough by a teaspoon into sugar and roll into balls. Place 2 inches apart on an ungreased cookie sheet. Bake in a 350° oven for 8 to 10 minutes till edges are firm. Transfer cookies to a wire rack and let cool. Makes about 40 cookies.

Nutrition Facts per cookie: 60 cal., 2 g total fat (1 g sat. fat), 4 mg chol., 52 mg sodium, 10 g carbo., 0 g fiber, 1 g pro. **Daily Values:** 1% vit. A, 0% vit. C, 2% calcium, 3% iron

---

COCONUT MACAROONS

PREP: 15 MINUTES BAKE: 20 MINUTES PER BATCH   Oven 325°

Low-Fat

2 egg whites
$^1/_2$ teaspoon vanilla
$^2/_3$ cup sugar
1 $3^1/_2$-ounce can flaked coconut ($1^1/_3$ cups)

1. Lightly grease a cookie sheet; set aside. In a medium mixing bowl beat egg whites and vanilla with an electric mixer on high speed till soft peaks form (tips curl). Gradually add sugar, about 1 tablespoon at a time, beating till stiff peaks form (tips stand straight). Fold in coconut.

2. Drop mixture by rounded teaspoons 2 inches apart on the prepared cookie sheet. Bake in 325° oven about 20 minutes or till edges are lightly browned. Transfer cookies to a wire rack and let cool. Makes about 30 cookies.

Nutrition Facts per cookie: 33 cal., 1 g total fat (1 g sat. fat), 0 mg chol., 4 mg sodium, 6 g carbo., 0 g fiber, 0 g pro.

■ **Almond Macaroons:** Prepare as above, except substitute one 8-ounce can *almond paste* (made without syrup or liquid glucose) for the coconut. Stir $1/2$ cup of the beaten egg whites into crumbled almond paste; fold this mixture into remaining egg whites. Continue as directed.

Nutrition Facts per cookie: 52 cal., 2 g total fat (0 g sat. fat)

■ **Lemon Macaroons:** Prepare as above, except substitute 1 tablespoon *lemon juice* for the vanilla and add 1 teaspoon finely shredded *lemon peel*.

Nutrition Facts per cookie: 33 cal., 1 g total fat (1 g sat. fat)

CHOCOLATE CHIP MERINGUES

PREP: 20 MINUTES   BAKE: 20 MINUTES PER BATCH   Oven 300°

Low-Fat

Crusty on the outside, soft and chewy on the inside, these low-fat treats are easy to make.

   2 **egg whites**
$1/2$ **teaspoon vanilla**
$1/8$ **teaspoon cream of tartar**
$2/3$ **cup sugar**
$2/3$ **cup miniature semisweet chocolate pieces**
   2 **ounces semisweet chocolate, melted (optional)**

1. Lightly grease a cookie sheet; set aside. In a medium mixing bowl beat egg whites, vanilla, and cream of tartar with electric mixer on high speed till soft peaks form (tips curl). Add the sugar, 1 tablespoon at a time, beating till stiff peaks form (tips stand straight). Fold in the chocolate pieces.
2. Drop mixture by rounded teaspoons 2 inches apart on the prepared cookie sheet. Bake in a 300° oven about 20 minutes or till firm and bottoms are very lightly browned. Transfer cookies to a wire rack and let cool. If desired, drizzle cookies with melted chocolate. Makes 36 cookies.

Nutrition Facts per cookie: 30 cal., 1 g total fat (0 g sat. fat), 0 mg chol., 3 mg sodium, 5 g carbo., 0 g fiber, 0 g pro.

■ **Cocoa Meringues:** Prepare as above, except stir 2 tablespoons *unsweetened cocoa powder* into the sugar; add to egg whites as directed.

Nutrition Facts per cookie: 31 cal., 1 g total fat (0 g sat. fat)

■ **Peppermint Meringues:** Prepare as above, except use ¼ teaspoon *peppermint extract* instead of vanilla. If desired, sprinkle each cookie with finely crushed *peppermint candies* before baking.

Nutrition Facts per cookie: 30 cal., 1 g total fat (0 g sat. fat)

■ **Spicy Meringues:** Prepare as above, except omit the chocolate pieces. Add ¼ teaspoon *ground ginger*, ¼ teaspoon *ground cinnamon*, and dash *ground cloves* along with the vanilla and cream of tartar.

Nutrition Facts per cookie: 16 cal., 0 g total fat

PEANUT BUTTER BLOSSOMS

PREP: 25 MINUTES   BAKE: 10 MINUTES PER BATCH   Oven 350°

For a whole wheat version, use only 1 cup all-purpose flour and add ¾ cup whole wheat flour.

½ cup shortening
½ cup peanut butter
½ cup granulated sugar
½ cup packed brown sugar
1 teaspoon baking powder
⅛ teaspoon baking soda
1 egg
2 tablespoons milk
1 teaspoon vanilla
1¾ cups all-purpose flour
¼ cup granulated sugar
  Milk chocolate kisses or stars

1. In a large mixing bowl beat the shortening and peanut butter with an electric mixer on medium speed 30 seconds. Add the ½ cup granulated sugar, brown sugar, baking powder, and baking soda. Beat till combined, scraping the sides of bowl. Beat in egg, milk, and vanilla till combined. Beat in as much of the flour as you can with the mixer. Stir in remaining flour.

2. Shape dough into 1-inch balls. Roll the balls in the ¼ cup granulated sugar. Place 2 inches apart on an ungreased cookie sheet. Bake in a 350° oven 10 to 12 minutes or till edges are firm and bottoms are lightly browned. Immediately press a chocolate kiss into each cookie's center. Transfer cookies to a wire rack; let cool. Makes about 54 cookies.

Nutrition Facts per cookie: 83 cal., 4 g total fat (2 g sat. fat), 4 mg chol., 27 mg sodium, 10 g carbo., 0 g fiber, 1 g pro. **Daily Values:** 0% vit. A, 0% vit. C, 1% calcium, 2% iron

---

CHOCOLATE CRINKLES

PREP: 25 MINUTES CHILL: 1 TO 2 HOURS BAKE: 8 MINUTES PER BATCH   Oven 375°

    3 eggs
1½ cups granulated sugar
    4 ounces unsweetened chocolate, melted
 ½ cup cooking oil
    2 teaspoons baking powder
    2 teaspoons vanilla
    2 cups all-purpose flour
      Sifted powdered sugar

1. In a mixing bowl beat eggs, granulated sugar, chocolate, oil, baking powder, and vanilla with an electric mixer till combined. Beat in as much of the flour as you can with the mixer. Stir in remaining flour. Cover and chill 1 to 2 hours or till easy to handle.

2. Shape dough into 1-inch balls. Roll balls in powdered sugar to coat generously. Place balls 1 inch apart on an ungreased cookie sheet. Bake in a 375° oven for 8 to 10 minutes or till edges are set and tops are crackled. Transfer cookies to a wire rack and let cool. If desired, sprinkle with additional powdered sugar. Makes about 48 cookies.

Nutrition Facts per cookie: 80 cal., 4 g total fat (1 g sat. fat), 13 mg chol., 19 mg sodium, 11 g carbo., 0 g fiber, 1 g pro. **Daily Values:** 0% vit. A, 0% vit. C, 1% calcium, 3% iron

SNICKERDOODLES

Prep: 25 minutes Chill: 1 hour Bake: 10 minutes per batch · Oven 375°

Cinnamon and sugar coat these old-fashioned crackled-top goodies.

$^1/_2$ **cup butter or margarine**
1 **cup sugar**
$^1/_4$ **teaspoon baking soda**
$^1/_4$ **teaspoon cream of tartar**
1 **egg**
$^1/_2$ **teaspoon vanilla**
$1^1/_2$ **cups all-purpose flour**
2 **tablespoons sugar**
1 **teaspoon ground cinnamon**

1. In a medium mixing bowl beat the butter or margarine with an electric mixer for 30 seconds. Add the 1 cup sugar, baking soda, and cream of tartar. Beat till combined, scraping sides of bowl. Beat in the egg and vanilla till combined. Beat in as much of the flour as

---

CHILLING COOKIE DOUGH

Cookie dough meant for shaping often needs to be chilled first for easier handling. The firmness of a cookie dough after chilling depends on whether it is made with butter or margarine (see "Margarine in Cookies" on page 395). Dough that is made with butter will be firmer.

To chill cookie dough, place it in the refrigerator for the time recommended in the recipe or quick-chill it in the freezer for about one-third of the refrigerator chilling time. Do not quick-chill cookie dough made with butter; it will become too firm to work with.

For shaped or sliced cookies made with margarine, chill the dough in the freezer instead of the refrigerator. For rolled cookies made with margarine, refrigerate the dough at least five hours or freeze for two hours before rolling.

---

you can with the mixer. Stir in remaining flour. Cover and chill 1 hour (see tip, page 393).

2. Combine the 2 tablespoons sugar and the cinnamon. Shape dough into 1-inch balls. Roll balls in sugar-cinnamon mixture to coat. Place 2 inches apart on an ungreased cookie sheet. Bake in a 375° oven for 10 to 11 minutes or till edges are golden. Transfer cookies to a wire rack and let cool. Makes about 36 cookies.

Nutrition Facts per cookie: 66 cal., 3 g total fat (2 g sat. fat), 13 mg chol., 36 mg sodium, 10 g carbo., 0 g fiber, 1 g pro. **Daily Values:** 2% vit. A, 0% vit. C, 0% calcium, 1% iron

---

GINGERSNAPS

PREP: 25 MINUTES   BAKE: 8 MINUTES PER BATCH   Oven 375°

2¼ cups all-purpose flour
1 cup packed brown sugar
¾ cup shortening
¼ cup molasses
1 egg
1 teaspoon baking soda
1 teaspoon ground ginger
1 teaspoon ground cinnamon
½ teaspoon ground cloves
¼ cup granulated sugar

1. In a large mixing bowl combine about *half* of the flour, brown sugar, shortening, molasses, egg, baking soda, ginger, cinnamon, and cloves. Beat with an electric mixer on medium to high speed till combined. Beat or stir in remaining flour.

2. Shape dough into 1-inch balls. Roll balls in the granulated sugar to coat. Place balls 2 inches apart on an ungreased cookie sheet. Bake in a 375° oven for 8 to 10 minutes or till edges are set and tops are crackled. Cool cookies on cookie sheet for 1 minute. Transfer cookies to a wire rack and let cool. Makes about 48 cookies.

Nutrition Facts per cookie: 72 cal., 3 g total fat (1 g sat. fat), 4 mg chol., 29 mg sodium, 10 g carbo., 0 g fiber, 1 g pro. **Daily Values:** 0% vit. A, 0% vit. C, 0% calcium, 2% iron

JAM THUMBPRINTS

PREP: 25 MINUTES CHILL: 1 HOUR BAKE: 10 MINUTES PER BATCH   Oven 375°

*Instead of jam, you can fill the centers with spoonfuls
of your favorite frosting.*

$2/3$ **cup butter or margarine**
$1/2$ **cup sugar**
  2 **egg yolks**
  1 **teaspoon vanilla**
$1^1/2$ **cups all-purpose flour**
  2 **slightly beaten egg whites**
  1 **cup finely chopped walnuts**
$1/3$ **to $1/2$ cup strawberry, cherry, or apricot jam or preserves**

1. Grease a cookie sheet; set aside. In a large mixing bowl beat butter or margarine with an electric mixer on medium to high speed for 30 seconds. Add the sugar and beat till combined, scraping sides of

MARGARINE IN COOKIES

All margarines are not equal—especially when it comes to baking cookies. For the best results, choose stick margarines containing at least 60 percent vegetable oil. Spreads with less than 60 percent vegetable oil have a high water content and do not give satisfactory results in any type of cookie, including bar and drop cookies. Also, avoid spreads labeled diet, whipped, liquid, or soft; they are intended for table use, not for baking.

Stick margarines containing corn oil will produce a soft cookie dough, so you may need to adjust the chilling instructions given in the recipe (see "Chilling Cookie Dough" on page 393).

Do not substitute cooking oil for margarine in cookie recipes. Oil is 100 percent fat; margarine is an emulsion of fat and water. Substituting an equal amount of oil for margarine will produce a cookie that tastes and feels greasy.

bowl occasionally. Beat in egg yolks and vanilla till combined. Beat in as much of the flour as you can with the mixer. Stir in remaining flour. Cover; chill dough about 1 hour or till easy to handle (see tip, page 393).

2. Shape dough into 1-inch balls. Roll balls in egg whites, then in walnuts. Place 1 inch apart on the prepared cookie sheet. Press your thumb into the center of each ball. Bake in a 375° oven for 10 to 12 minutes or till edges are lightly browned. Transfer cookies to a wire rack and let cool. Just before serving, fill centers with jam or preserves. Makes about 42 cookies.

Nutrition Facts per cookie: 79 cal., 5 g total fat (2 g sat. fat), 18 mg chol., 33 mg sodium, 8 g carbo., 0 g fiber, 1 g pro. **Daily Values:** 4% vit. A, 0% vit. C, 0% calcium, 2% iron

---

PEANUT BUTTER COOKIES

PREP: 25 MINUTES   BAKE: 7 MINUTES PER BATCH   Oven 375°

Add a new look to this classic favorite by decorating the tops of these cooled cookies with a drizzle of melted semisweet chocolate pieces.

   $^1/_2$ **cup butter or margarine**
   $^1/_2$ **cup peanut butter**
   $^1/_2$ **cup granulated sugar**
   $^1/_2$ **cup packed brown sugar or** $^1/_4$ **cup honey**
   $^1/_2$ **teaspoon baking soda**
   $^1/_2$ **teaspoon baking powder**
     1 **egg**
   $^1/_2$ **teaspoon vanilla**
   1$^1/_4$ **cups all-purpose flour**
       Granulated sugar

1. In a large mixing bowl beat the butter or margarine and peanut butter with an electric mixer on medium to high speed for 30 seconds. Add the granulated sugar, brown sugar, baking soda, and baking powder. Beat till combined, scraping sides of bowl occasionally. Beat in the egg and vanilla till combined. Beat in as much of the flour as you can with the mixer. Stir in remaining flour. If necessary, cover and chill dough till easy to handle.

2. Shape dough into 1-inch balls. Roll in additional granulated sugar to coat. Place balls 2 inches apart on an ungreased cookie sheet. Flatten by making crisscross marks with the tines of a fork. Bake in a

375° oven for 7 to 9 minutes or till bottoms are lightly browned. Transfer cookies to a wire rack and let cool. Makes about 36 cookies.

Nutrition Facts per cookie: 83 cal., 4 g total fat (2 g sat. fat), 13 mg chol., 68 mg sodium, 10 g carbo., 0 g fiber, 1 g pro. **Daily Values:** 2% vit. A, 0% vit. C, 0% calcium, 2% iron

---

BURIED CHERRY COOKIES

PREP: 30 MINUTES BAKE: 10 MINUTES PER BATCH   Oven 350°

    1 10-ounce jar maraschino cherries (42 to 48)
   1/2 cup butter or margarine
    1 cup sugar
   1/4 teaspoon baking powder
   1/4 teaspoon baking soda
    1 egg
   11/2 teaspoons vanilla
   1/2 cup unsweetened cocoa powder
   11/2 cups all-purpose flour
    1 6-ounce package (1 cup) semisweet chocolate pieces*
   1/2 cup sweetened condensed milk or low-fat sweetened
         condensed milk

1. Drain cherries, reserving juice. Halve any large cherries. In a medium mixing bowl beat butter with an electric mixer on medium to high speed for 30 seconds. Add the sugar, baking powder, baking soda, and 1/4 teaspoon *salt*. Beat till combined, scraping sides of bowl. Beat in egg and vanilla till combined. Beat in cocoa powder and as much of the flour as you can with mixer. Stir in remaining flour.

2. Shape dough into 1-inch balls. Place balls about 2 inches apart on an ungreased cookie sheet. Press your thumb into the center of each ball. Place a cherry in each center.

3. For frosting, in a small saucepan combine chocolate pieces and sweetened condensed milk. Cook and stir over low heat till chocolate is melted. Stir in *4 teaspoons* reserved cherry juice. Spoon 1 teaspoon frosting over each cherry, spreading to cover. (Frosting may be thinned with additional cherry juice, if necessary.)

4. Bake in a 350° oven 10 minutes or till edges are firm. Cool 1 minute on cookie sheet. Transfer to a wire rack and let cool. Makes 42 to 48 cookies.

*Note: Do not substitute imitation chocolate pieces for semisweet chocolate pieces.

Nutrition Facts per cookie: 98 cal., 4 g total fat (2 g sat. fat), 12 mg chol., 51 mg sodium, 15 g carbo., 0 g fiber, 1 g pro. **Daily Values:** 2% vit. A, 0% vit. C, 2% calcium, 3% iron

COOKIE SHEET CLUES

The sweet success of freshly baked cookies lies partly in choosing the right cookie sheet.

■ Opt for heavy-gauge aluminum with low sides or no sides at all.

■ Invest in lighter-colored cookie sheets. If they are too dark, cookies may overbrown.

■ For most cookies, select sheets with a dull finish so cookie bottoms brown more evenly.

■ Use shiny sheets for cookies that should not brown on bottoms, such as shortbread.

■ Use nonstick cookie sheets if you prefer to skip the greasing step. However, the dough may not spread as much, resulting in thicker cookies with smooth bottoms.

■ Use insulated cookie sheets selectively. They are fine if you want pale drop cookies with soft-set centers. You may have trouble using them for cookies high in butter, shaped cookies, and some drop cookies because the butter may start to melt, leaking out before dough is set. And because dough spreads before it sets, cookies may have thin edges.

SANDIES

PREP: 25 MINUTES BAKE: 20 MINUTES PER BATCH   Oven 325°

    1 cup butter
  ¹/₃ cup granulated sugar
    1 teaspoon vanilla
 2¹/₄ cups all-purpose flour
    1 cup chopped pecans
    1 cup sifted powdered sugar

1. Beat butter with an electric mixer on medium to high speed 30 seconds. Add granulated sugar. Beat till combined, scraping bowl. Beat in 1 tablespoon *water* and vanilla till combined. Beat in as much flour as you can with the mixer. Stir in remaining flour and pecans.

2. Shape dough into 1-inch balls or 2×½-inch logs. Place 1 inch apart on an ungreased cookie sheet. Bake in a 325° oven 20 minutes or till bottoms are lightly browned. Transfer to a rack; cool. Gently shake cooled cookies in a plastic bag with powdered sugar. Makes about 36 cookies.

Nutrition Facts per cookie: 109 cal., 7 g total fat (3 g sat. fat), 14 mg chol., 52 mg sodium, 11 g carbo., 0 g fiber, 1 g pro. **Daily Values:** 4% vit. A, 0% vit. C, 0% calcium, 2% iron

---

BRANDY SNAPS

PREP: 40 MINUTES BAKE: 5 MINUTES PER BATCH   Oven 350°

Low-Fat

 ¼ **cup packed brown sugar**
 3 **tablespoons butter or margarine, melted**
 1 **tablespoon light molasses**
 2 **teaspoons brandy**
 ⅓ **cup all-purpose flour**
 ¼ **teaspoon ground ginger**
 ¼ **teaspoon ground nutmeg**

1. Line a cookie sheet with foil. Grease foil; set aside. Combine brown sugar, butter, molasses, and brandy. Stir in flour and spices till combined.

2. Drop batter by slightly rounded teaspoonfuls 5 inches apart on prepared cookie sheet (bake 3 or 4 at a time); spread each (see tip 1, at right). Bake in a 350° oven 5 to 7 minutes or till bubbly and deep golden brown. Let stand 1 to 2 minutes or till set. Quickly shape cookies, one

IT'S A SNAP

1. Using a teaspoon, drop batter in mounds 5 inches apart on prepared baking sheet. With back of spoon, spread each to about 2 inches in diameter.

2. Quickly roll each warm cookie around a metal cone (for cone shapes) or the greased handle of a wooden spoon (for cigar shapes). As these cookies cool, they become crisp.

at a time (see tip 2, page 399); cool. (If cookies harden before you can shape them, return them to the hot oven 1 minute or till softened.) Makes 20 to 24 cookies.

Nutrition Facts per cookie: 34 cal., 2 g total fat (1 g sat. fat), 5 mg chol., 18 mg sodium, 4 g carbo., 0 g fiber, 0 g pro. **Daily Values:** 1% vit. A, 0% vit. C, 0% calcium, 1% iron

■ **Cinnamon Snaps:** Prepare as above, except substitute *honey* for the molasses and *ground cinnamon* for the ginger. Omit the nutmeg.

Nutrition Facts per cookie: 37 cal., 2 g total fat (1 g sat. fat)

■ **Pecan Snaps:** Prepare as above, except reduce flour to ¼ cup and add ⅓ cup *ground pecans or walnuts.* Omit ginger and nutmeg.

Nutrition Facts per cookie: 47 cal., 3 g total fat (1 g sat. fat)

SPICED SLICES

PREP: 25 MINUTES CHILL: 5 TO 24 HOURS BAKE: 8 MINUTES PER BATCH   Oven 375°

To make sliced oatmeal cookies, reduce flour to 1¾ cups and add 1 cup quick-cooking rolled oats.

½ cup shortening
½ cup butter or margarine
½ cup granulated sugar
½ cup packed brown sugar
1 teaspoon ground cinnamon
½ teaspoon baking soda
¼ teaspoon ground nutmeg
¼ teaspoon ground cloves
1 egg
½ teaspoon vanilla
2¼ cups all-purpose flour
½ cup sliced almonds, toasted and finely chopped (see tip, page 234)

1. Beat shortening and butter with an electric mixer on medium to high speed 30 seconds. Add granulated sugar, brown sugar, cinnamon, baking soda, nutmeg, and cloves. Beat till combined, scraping sides of bowl. Beat in egg and vanilla till combined. Beat in as much of the flour as you can. Stir in remaining flour. Stir in almonds.

Shape into two 7-inch-long rolls. Wrap in plastic wrap or waxed paper; chill 5 to 24 hours.

2. Cut rolls into ¼-inch-thick slices. Place slices 1 inch apart on an ungreased cookie sheet. Bake in a 375° oven about 8 minutes or till edges are golden. Cool on cookie sheet 1 minute. Transfer cookies to a wire rack; let cool. Makes 60 cookies.

Nutrition Facts per cookie: 63 cal., 4 g total fat (1 g sat. fat), 8 mg chol., 28 mg sodium, 7 g carbo., 0 g fiber, 1 g pro. **Daily Values:** 1% vit. A, 0% vit. C, 0% calcium, 2% iron

---

BROWN SUGAR-HAZELNUT ROUNDS

PREP: 25 MINUTES CHILL: 4 TO 48 HOURS BAKE: 10 MINUTES PER BATCH   Oven 375°

- ½ cup shortening
- ½ cup butter or margarine
- 1¼ cups packed brown sugar
- ½ teaspoon baking soda
- 1 egg
- 1 teaspoon vanilla
- 2½ cups all-purpose flour
- ¾ cup ground toasted hazelnuts or pecans (see tip, page 234)
- 1 recipe Maple-Orange Icing (see below) (optional)

1. In a mixing bowl beat shortening and butter with an electric mixer on medium to high speed 30 seconds. Add brown sugar, baking soda, and ¼ teaspoon *salt*. Beat till combined, scraping bowl. Beat in egg and vanilla till combined. Beat in as much of the flour as you can with the mixer. Stir in remaining flour and nuts.

2. Shape dough into two 10-inch-long rolls. Wrap in plastic wrap or waxed paper; chill 4 to 48 hours or till firm enough to slice.

3. Cut dough into ¼-inch-thick slices. Place slices 1 inch apart on an ungreased cookie sheet. Bake in a 375° oven about 10 minutes or till edges are firm. Transfer cookies to a wire rack and let cool. If desired, pipe a design atop each using Maple-Orange Icing. Makes about 60 cookies.

■ **Maple-Orange Icing:** Combine ½ cup sifted *powdered sugar,* ⅛ teaspoon *maple flavoring,* and 1½ teaspoons *orange juice.* Add orange juice, a few drops at a time, to reach desired consistency.

Nutrition Facts per cookie: 70 cal., 4 g total fat (1 g sat. fat), 8 mg chol., 37 mg sodium, 7 g carbo., 0 g fiber, 1 g pro. **Daily Values:** 1% vit. A, 0% vit. C, 0% calcium, 2% iron

SANTA'S WHISKERS

PREP: 20 MINUTES CHILL: 2 TO 24 HOURS BAKE: 10 MINUTES PER BATCH   Oven 375°

$^3/_4$ cup butter or margarine
$^3/_4$ cup sugar
1 tablespoon milk
1 teaspoon vanilla
2 cups all-purpose flour
$^3/_4$ cup finely chopped candied red or green cherries
$^1/_3$ cup finely chopped pecans
$^3/_4$ cup shredded coconut

1. In a large mixing bowl, beat butter with an electric mixer on medium to high speed 30 seconds. Add the sugar. Beat till combined, scraping sides of bowl. Beat in milk and vanilla till combined. Beat in as much of the flour as you can with the mixer. Stir in remaining flour. Stir in cherries and pecans. Shape into two 8-inch-long rolls. Roll in coconut. Wrap in plastic wrap or waxed paper; chill 2 to 24 hours.
2. Cut into $^1/_4$-inch-thick slices. Place 1 inch apart on an ungreased cookie sheet. Bake in a 375° oven 10 to 12 minutes or till edges are golden. Transfer cookies to a wire rack; let cool. Makes about 60.

Nutrition Facts per cookie: 57 cal., 3 g total fat (1 g sat. fat), 0 mg chol., 27 mg sodium, 7 g carbo., 0 g fiber, 1 g pro. **Daily Values:** 2% vit. A, 0% vit. C, 0% calcium, 1% iron

---

CHOCOLATE-COCONUT PINWHEELS

PREP: 30 MINUTES CHILL: 3 TO 24 HOURS BAKE: 8 MINUTES PER BATCH   Oven 375°

Low-Fat

If you often get caught with little time for baking, chill or freeze rolls of slice-and-bake cookie dough to have on hand (see tip, page 383).

1 3-ounce package cream cheese, softened
$^1/_3$ cup sugar
1 teaspoon vanilla
1 cup shredded coconut
$^1/_2$ cup finely chopped nuts
$^1/_3$ cup butter
1 cup sugar
$^1/_2$ teaspoon baking soda

1 egg
1 tablespoon milk
$^1/_4$ cup unsweetened cocoa powder
$1^1/_2$ cups all-purpose flour

1. For filling, in a small mixing bowl beat cream cheese, the $^1/_3$ cup sugar, and vanilla with an electric mixer on medium to high speed till smooth. Stir in coconut and nuts; set aside.

2. In a mixing bowl beat butter 30 seconds. Add the 1 cup sugar and baking soda. Beat till combined, scraping sides of bowl occasionally. Beat in egg and milk till combined. Beat in cocoa powder and as much of the flour as you can. Stir in remaining flour.

3. Roll half of the dough between waxed paper into a 10×8-inch rectangle. Spread half of the filling over dough. Beginning with a long side, roll up dough. Moisten edges and pinch to seal. Wrap in waxed paper. Repeat with remaining dough and filling. Chill 3 to 24 hours (see tip, page 393).

4. Grease a cookie sheet. Cut into $^1/_4$-inch-thick slices. Place slices 1 inch apart on prepared cookie sheet. Bake in a 375° oven 8 minutes or till edges are firm. Transfer cookies to a wire rack; let cool. Makes 72 cookies.

Nutrition Facts per cookie: 47 cal., 2 g total fat (1 g sat. fat), 7 mg chol., 22 mg sodium, 6 g carbo., 0 g fiber, 1 g pro. **Daily Values:** 1% vit. A, 0% vit. C, 0% calcium, 1% iron

DATE PINWHEEL COOKIES

PREP: 40 MINUTES CHILL: 2 TO 24 HOURS BAKE: 8 MINUTES PER BATCH   Oven 375°

1 8-ounce package ($1^1/_3$ cups) pitted whole dates, finely snipped
$^1/_3$ cup granulated sugar
2 tablespoons lemon juice
$^1/_2$ teaspoon vanilla
$^1/_2$ cup shortening
$^1/_2$ cup butter, softened
$^1/_2$ cup granulated sugar
$^1/_2$ cup packed brown sugar
$^1/_2$ teaspoon baking soda
1 egg
3 tablespoons milk
1 teaspoon vanilla
3 cups all-purpose flour

1. For filling, combine dates, the $1/3$ cup granulated sugar, and $1/2$ cup *water*. Bring to boiling; reduce heat. Cook and stir 2 minutes or till thick. Stir in lemon juice and the $1/2$ teaspoon vanilla; cool.

2. In a large mixing bowl beat shortening and butter with an electric mixer on medium to high speed 30 seconds. Add the $1/2$ cup granulated sugar, the brown sugar, baking soda, and $1/4$ teaspoon *salt*. Beat till combined, scraping sides of bowl. Beat in egg, milk, and the 1 teaspoon vanilla. Beat in as much of the flour as you can. Stir in remaining flour. Divide dough in half. Cover; chill for 1 hour or till easy to handle.

3. Roll half of the dough between waxed paper into a 12×10-inch rectangle. Spread with half of the filling; roll up, beginning with a long side. Moisten edges; pinch to seal. Wrap in waxed paper or clear plastic wrap. Repeat with remaining dough and filling. Chill 2 to 24 hours.

4. Grease cookie sheet. Cut rolls into $1/4$-inch-thick slices. Place slices 1 inch apart on prepared cookie sheet. Bake in 375° oven 8 to 10 minutes or till edges are lightly browned. Transfer cookies to wire rack. Makes 64 cookies.

Nutrition Facts per cookie: 73 cal., 3 g total fat (1 g sat. fat), 7 mg chol., 35 mg sodium, 11 g carbo., 0 g fiber, 1 g pro. **Daily Values:** 1% vit. A, 0% vit. C, 0% calcium, 2% iron

---

LEMON-POPPY SEED BISCOTTI

PREP: 30 MINUTES   BAKE: 36 MINUTES   COOL: 1 HOUR   Oven 375°

Low-Fat

$1/3$ **cup butter or margarine, softened**
$2/3$ **cup sugar**
  4 **teaspoons finely shredded lemon peel**
  1 **tablespoon poppy seed**
  1 **teaspoon baking powder**
$1/2$ **teaspoon baking soda**
  2 **eggs**
$2^{1}/2$ **cups all-purpose flour**

1. Beat butter or margarine with an electric mixer on medium speed 30 seconds. Add sugar, lemon peel, poppy seed, baking powder, and baking soda; beat till combined. Beat in eggs. Beat in as much of the flour as you can. Stir in remaining flour.

2. Shape dough into two 9×1$1/2$-inch rolls. Place rolls on an ungreased cookie sheet; flatten slightly. Bake in a 375° oven 20 minutes or till a wooden toothpick inserted near center comes out clean. Cool on sheet 1 hour.

3. Transfer cooled rolls to a cutting board. Cut each roll crosswise into $1/2$-inch-thick slices. Place slices, cut sides down, on cookie sheet. Bake in a 325° oven 8 minutes; turn and bake 8 minutes more or till crisp and light brown. Transfer to a wire rack and let cool. Makes about 36 cookies.

Nutrition Facts per cookie: 64 cal., 2 g total fat (1 g sat. fat), 16 mg chol., 48 mg sodium, 10 g carbo., 0 g fiber, 1 g pro. **Daily Values:** 2% vit. A, 0% vit. C, 1% calcium, 3% iron

■ **Almond Brickle Biscotti:** Prepare as above, except substitute *brown sugar* for the sugar. Omit the lemon peel and poppy seed. Stir in 1 cup *almond brickle pieces* after adding the flour.

Nutrition Facts per cookie: 86 cal., 4 g total fat (1 g sat. fat)

■ **Orange-Cranberry Biscotti:** Prepare as above, except substitute *orange peel* for lemon peel. Omit poppy seed. Stir in $1/2$ cup finely chopped *dried cranberries or tart red cherries* after adding the flour.

Nutrition Facts per cookie: 66 cal., 2 g total fat (1 g sat. fat)

DOUBLE CHOCOLATE CHUNK BISCOTTI

PREP: 30 MINUTES BAKE: 35 MINUTES COOL: 1 HOUR   Oven 375°

   $1/3$ **cup butter or margarine**
   $2/3$ **cup sugar**
   $1/4$ **cup unsweetened cocoa powder**
   2 **teaspoons baking powder**
   2 **eggs**
$1^3/4$ **cups all-purpose flour**
   4 **ounces white baking bar or white chocolate baking squares, coarsely chopped**
   3 **ounces semisweet chocolate, chopped**

1. Lightly grease a cookie sheet; set aside. Beat butter with an electric mixer on medium speed 30 seconds. Add sugar, cocoa powder, and baking powder; beat till combined. Beat in eggs. Beat in as much of the flour as you can. Stir in remaining flour. Stir in chopped white baking bar and semisweet chocolate.

2. Shape dough into two 9-inch-long rolls. Place rolls on the prepared cookie sheet; flatten slightly. Bake in a 375° oven 20 to 25
minutes or till a wooden toothpick inserted near center comes out
clean. Cool on sheet 1 hour.
3. Transfer cooled rolls to a cutting board. Cut each roll diagonally
into ¹/₂-inch-thick slices. Place slices, cut sides down, on an ungreased cookie sheet. Bake in a 325° oven 8 minutes. Turn and bake
7 to 9 minutes more or till cookies are dry and crisp (do not over-
bake). Transfer cookies to a wire rack and let cool. Makes about 32
cookies.

Nutrition Facts per cookie: 95 cal., 4 g total fat (2 g sat. fat), 13 mg chol., 52 mg sodium,
13 g carbo., 0 g fiber, 2 g pro. **Daily values:** 2% vit. A, 0% vit. C, 3% calcium, 3% iron

---

LIME ZINGERS

PREP: 30 MINUTES   BAKE: 8 MINUTES PER BATCH   Oven 350°

  1 cup butter
¹/₂ cup granulated sugar
  2 teaspoons finely shredded lime peel
¹/₄ cup lime juice (2 limes)
  1 teaspoon vanilla
2¹/₄ cups all-purpose flour
³/₄ cups finely chopped Brazil nuts or hazelnuts (filberts)
¹/₂ of an 8-ounce package cream cheese, softened
  1 cup sifted powdered sugar
  1 tablespoon lemon or lime juice
  1 teaspoon vanilla
     Food coloring

1. Beat butter with an electric mixer on medium speed 30 seconds.
Beat in granulated sugar till combined. Beat in lime peel, the ¹/₄ cup
lime juice, and 1 teaspoon vanilla. Beat in as much flour as you can.
Stir in remaining flour. Stir in nuts. Divide dough in half.
2. On a lightly floured surface roll each half of the dough to about
¹/₄ inch thick. Using 1- or 2-inch cookie cutters, cut into desired
shapes. Place on ungreased cookie sheets. Bake in a 350° oven 8 to
10 minutes or till light brown around edges. Transfer cookies to a
wire rack and let cool.
3. For frosting, beat cream cheese, powdered sugar, the 1 tablespoon lemon or lime juice, and vanilla with an electric mixer on

medium speed till smooth. Tint frosting as desired with food coloring. Frost cookies. Makes 72 cookies.

Nutrition Facts per cookie (with frosting): 62 cal., 4 g total fat (2 g sat. fat), 9 mg chol.,
31 mg sodium, 6 g carbo., 0 g fiber, 1 g pro. **Daily Values:** 3% vit. A, 0% vit. C, 0%
calcium, 1% iron

SUGAR COOKIE CUTOUTS

PREP: 30 TO 45 MINUTES CHILL: 3 HOURS (IF NECESSARY)
BAKE: 7 MINUTES PER BATCH   Oven 375°

  $^1/_3$ **cup butter or margarine**
  $^1/_3$ **cup shortening**
  $^3/_4$ **cup sugar**
  1 **teaspoon baking powder**
  1 **egg**
  1 **teaspoon vanilla**
  2 **cups all-purpose flour**
  1 **recipe Powdered Sugar Icing (see page 291) (optional)**

1. Beat butter and shortening on medium to high speed 30 seconds.
Add sugar, baking powder, and a dash *salt*. Beat till combined,
scraping bowl. Beat in egg and vanilla. Beat in as much of the flour
as you can with the mixer. Stir in remaining flour. Divide dough in
half. If necessary, cover and chill dough for 3 hours or till easy to
handle (see tip, page 393).
2. On a lightly floured surface, roll half at a time to $^1/_8$ inch thick.
Using a $2^1/_2$-inch cookie or biscuit cutter, cut into desired shapes (dip
the cutter's edge into flour to prevent sticking). Place on ungreased
cookie sheet. Bake in a 375° oven 7 to 8 minutes or till edges are
firm and bottoms are very lightly browned. Cool on a rack. If desired, frost with Powdered Sugar Icing. Makes 36 to 48.

Nutrition Facts per cookie: 74 cal., 4 g total fat (2 g sat. fat), 10 mg chol., 33 mg sodium,
9 g carbo., 0 g fiber, 1 g pro. **Daily Values:** 1% vit. A, 0% vit. C, 1% calcium, 2% iron

■ **Candy Windowpane Cutouts:** Prepare as above, except place
cutout dough on a foil-lined cookie sheet. Cut small shapes out of
cookie centers. Finely crush 3 ounces *hard candy* (about $^1/_2$ cup).
Fill each center cutout with candy. When baked, cool cookies on
foil. Store tightly covered.

Nutrition Facts per cookie: 83 cal., 4 g total fat (2 g sat. fat)

■ **Sugar Cookie Pizza:** Prepare dough as above. Spread into an ungreased 12-inch pizza pan (chilling the dough is not necessary, but may make it easier to handle). Bake in a 375° oven for 18 to 20 minutes or till edges are firm but not brown. Cool in pan on a wire rack. Prepare ¹/₂ recipe *Cream Cheese Frosting* (see page 290) *or Butter Frosting* (see page 290); carefully spread over cookie. Decorate with *candy-coated milk chocolate pieces or other candies*. Use a pizza cutter to cut cookie into wedges. Makes 16 cookie wedges.

Nutrition Facts per wedge (with frosting): 290 cal., 14 g total fat (6 g sat. fat)

GINGERBREAD CUTOUTS

PREP: 35 MINUTES CHILL: 3 HOURS BAKE: 5 MINUTES PER BATCH   Oven 375°

¹/₂ cup shortening
¹/₂ cup sugar
 1 teaspoon baking powder
 1 teaspoon ground ginger
¹/₂ teaspoon baking soda
¹/₂ teaspoon ground cinnamon
¹/₂ teaspoon ground cloves
¹/₂ cup molasses
 1 egg
 1 tablespoon vinegar
2¹/₂ cups all-purpose flour
 1 recipe Powdered Sugar Icing (see page 291) (optional)
  Decorative candies (optional)

1. In a mixing bowl beat shortening with an electric mixer on medium to high speed 30 seconds. Add sugar, baking powder, ginger, baking soda, cinnamon, and cloves. Beat till combined, scraping bowl. Beat in the molasses, egg, and vinegar till combined. Beat in as much of the flour as you can with the mixer. Stir in remaining flour. Divide dough in half. Cover and chill for 3 hours or till easy to handle (see tip, page 393).
2. Grease a cookie sheet; set aside. On a lightly floured surface, roll half of the dough at a time to ¹/₈ inch thick. Using a 2¹/₂-inch cookie cutter, cut into desired shapes (dip the cutter's edge into flour to prevent sticking). Place 1 inch apart on the prepared cookie sheet.
3. Bake in a 375° oven for 5 to 6 minutes or till edges are lightly browned. Cool on cookie sheet 1 minute. Transfer cookies to a wire

rack and let cool. If desired, decorate cookies with icing and candies. Makes 36 to 48 cookies.

Nutrition Facts per cookie: 79 cal., 3 g total fat (1 g sat. fat), 6 mg chol., 30 mg sodium, 12 g carbo., 0 g fiber, 1 g pro. **Daily Values:** 0% vit. A, 0% vit. C, 1% calcium, 4% iron

■ **Gingerbread People Cutouts:** Prepare as above, except roll dough to $1/4$ inch thick. Cut with $41/2$- to 6-inch people-shaped cookie cutters. Bake in a 375° oven for 6 to 8 minutes or till edges are lightly browned. Makes about 18 cookies.

Nutrition Facts per cookie: 157 cal., 6 g total fat (2 g sat. fat)

SHORTBREAD

PREP: 15 MINUTES BAKE: 25 MINUTES   Oven 325°

  $1^1/4$ **cups all-purpose flour**
    3 **tablespoons sugar**
  $1/2$ **cup butter**

1. In a medium mixing bowl combine flour and sugar. Using a pastry cutter, cut in butter till mixture resembles fine crumbs and starts to cling. Form the mixture into a ball and knead till smooth.

2. To make shortbread wedges,* on an ungreased cookie sheet pat or roll the dough into an 8-inch circle. Using your fingers, press to make a scalloped edge (see photo 1, page 410). Cut circle into 16 wedges (see photo 2, page 411). Leave wedges in the circle. Bake in a 325° oven for 25 to 30 minutes or till bottom just starts to brown and center is set. Cut circle into wedges again while warm. Cool on the cookie sheet for 5 minutes. Transfer to a wire rack and let cool. Makes 16 shortbread wedges.

***Note:** To make shortbread rounds, on a lightly floured surface roll dough to $1/2$ inch thick. Use a $11/2$-inch cookie cutter to cut 24 rounds. Place them 1 inch apart on an ungreased cookie sheet and bake for 20 to 25 minutes.

To make shortbread strips, on a lightly floured surface roll dough to $1/2$ inch thick (6×8 inches). Using a knife, cut into twenty-four 2×1-inch strips (see photo 3, page 411). Place 1 inch apart on an ungreased baking sheet. Bake 20 to 25 minutes.

Nutrition Facts per wedge: 92 cal., 6 g total fat (4 g sat. fat), 15 mg chol., 58 mg sodium, 9 g carbo., 0 g fiber, 1 g pro. **Daily Values:** 5% vit. A, 0% vit. C, 0% calcium, 2% iron

■ **Butter-Pecan Shortbread:** Prepare as above, except substitute *brown sugar* for the sugar. After cutting in butter, stir in 2 tablespoons finely chopped *pecans*. Sprinkle mixture with ¹/₂ teaspoon *vanilla* before kneading.

Nutrition Facts per wedge: 97 cal., 6 g total fat (4 g sat. fat)

■ **Lemon-Poppy Seed Shortbread:** Prepare as above, except stir 1 tablespoon *poppy seed* into flour mixture and add 1 teaspoon finely shredded *lemon peel* with the butter.

Nutrition Facts per wedge: 95 cal., 6 g total fat (4 g sat. fat)

■ **Oatmeal Shortbread:** Prepare as above, except reduce all-purpose flour to 1 cup. After cutting in butter, stir in ¹/₃ cup *quick-cooking rolled oats*.

Nutrition Facts per wedge: 92 cal., 6 g total fat (4 g sat. fat)

■ **Spiced Shortbread:** Prepare as above, except substitute *brown sugar* for the sugar and stir ¹/₂ teaspoon *ground cinnamon*, ¹/₄ teaspoon *ground ginger*, and ¹/₈ teaspoon *ground cloves* into the flour mixture.

Nutrition Facts per wedge: 91 cal., 6 g total fat (4 g sat. fat)

1. Using your thumb on one hand and your thumb and index finger on the other, carefully crimp a scalloped edge around the dough circle.

2. With a long, sharp knife, carefully cut the dough circle into 16 pie-shaped wedges of equal size.

3. For strips, mark the long sides of the rectangle at 1-inch intervals; mark the short sides at 2-inch intervals. Use a sharp knife or pizza cutter to cut the dough into strips.

SPRITZ

PREP: 25 MINUTES BAKE: 8 MINUTES PER BATCH   Oven 375°

$1^{1}/_{2}$ cups butter or margarine
  1 cup sugar
  1 teaspoon baking powder
  1 egg
  1 teaspoon vanilla
  $^{1}/_{4}$ teaspoon almond extract (optional)
$3^{1}/_{2}$ cups all-purpose flour
  1 recipe Powdered Sugar Icing (see page 291) (optional)

1. Beat butter with an electric mixer on medium to high speed 30 seconds. Add sugar and baking powder. Beat till combined, scraping bowl. Beat in egg, vanilla, and, if desired, almond extract till combined. Beat in as much of the flour as you can. Stir in remaining flour.

2. Force unchilled dough through a cookie press onto an ungreased

Cookies *411*

cookie sheet. Bake in a 375° oven for 8 to 10 minutes or till edges are firm but not brown. Transfer cookies to a wire rack; cool. If desired, dip tops into icing. Makes about 84.

Nutrition Facts per cookie: 56 cal., 3 g total fat (2 g sat. fat), 11 mg chol., 38 mg sodium, 6 g carbo., 0 g fiber, 1 g pro. **Daily Values:** 3% vit. A, 0% vit. C, 0% calcium, 1% iron

■ **Chocolate Spritz:** Prepare as above, except reduce all-purpose flour to 3¼ cups and add ¼ cup *unsweetened cocoa powder* with the sugar.

Nutrition Facts per cookie: 56 cal., 3 g total fat (2 g sat. fat)

■ **Nutty Spritz:** Prepare as above, except reduce sugar to ⅔ cup and flour to 3¼ cups. After adding flour, stir in 1 cup finely ground toasted *almonds or hazelnuts (filberts)* (see tip, page 234).

Nutrition Facts per cookie: 60 cal., 4 g total fat (2 g sat. fat)

ALMOND STRIPS

PREP: 25 MINUTES BAKE: 12 MINUTES PER BATCH   Oven 325°

½ cup butter or margarine
1 cup sugar
2 teaspoons baking powder
1 egg
½ teaspoon almond extract
1¾ cups all-purpose flour
   Milk
½ cup sliced almonds, coarsely chopped
1 recipe Powdered Sugar Icing (see page 291)

1. Beat butter with an electric mixer on medium to high speed 30 seconds. Add sugar and baking powder; beat till combined. Beat in egg and almond extract till combined. Beat in as much of the flour as you can. Stir in remaining flour.
2. Divide dough into 4 equal portions. Shape each portion into a 12-inch-long roll. Place 2 rolls 4 to 5 inches apart on an ungreased cookie sheet. Using your hands, slightly flatten each to 3 inches wide. Repeat with remaining rolls. Brush flattened rolls with milk and sprinkle with almonds.
3. Bake in a 325° oven for 12 to 14 minutes or till edges are lightly

browned. Cut warm cookies diagonally into 1-inch strips. Cool cookies on a wire rack. Drizzle with icing. Makes about 48 cookies.

Nutrition Facts per cookie (with icing): 64 cal., 3 g total fat (1 g sat. fat), 10 mg chol., 36 mg sodium, 10 g carbo., 0 g fiber, 1 g pro. **Daily Values:** 1% vit. A, 0% vit. C, 1% calcium, 1% iron

---

PECAN TASSIES

PREP: 30 MINUTES BAKE: 30 MINUTES   Oven 325°

$^1/_2$ cup butter or margarine, softened
1 3-ounce package cream cheese, softened
1 cup all-purpose flour
1 egg
$^3/_4$ cup packed brown sugar
1 tablespoon butter or margarine, melted
$^1/_2$ cup coarsely chopped pecans

1. For pastry, in a mixing bowl beat the $^1/_2$ cup butter and cream cheese till combined. Stir in the flour. Press a rounded teaspoon of pastry evenly into the bottom and up the sides of 24 ungreased 1$^3/_4$-inch muffin cups.
2. For pecan filling, in mixing bowl beat egg, brown sugar, and the 1 tablespoon melted butter till combined. Stir in pecans. Spoon about 1 heaping teaspoon of filling into each pastry-lined muffin cup. Bake in a 325° oven about 30 minutes or till pastry is golden and filling is puffed. Cool slightly in pan. Carefully transfer to a wire rack; cool completely. Makes 24 cookies.

Nutrition Facts per cookie: 107 cal., 7 g total fat (3 g sat. fat), 23 mg chol., 59 mg sodium, 10 g carbo., 0 g fiber, 1 g pro. **Daily Values:** 6% vit. A, 0% vit. C, 0% calcium, 3% iron

■ **Pumpkin Tassies:** Prepare as above, except, instead of pecan filling, beat together 1 egg, $^1/_2$ cup canned pumpkin, $^1/_4$ cup granulated sugar, $^1/_4$ cup milk, and 1 teaspoon pumpkin pie spice.

Nutrition Facts per cookie: 77 cal., 5 g total fat (3 g sat. fat)

DESSERTS

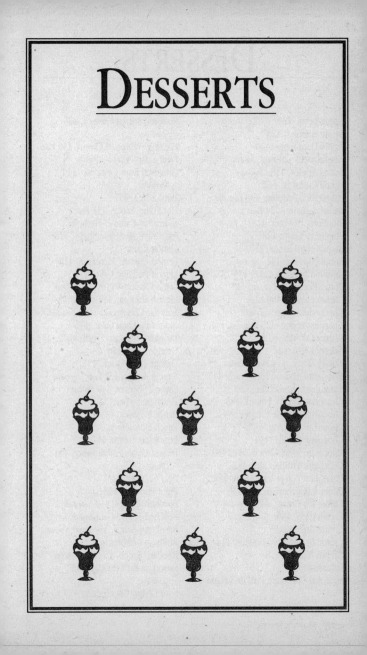

DESSERTS

BAKED APPLES

PREP: 15 MINUTES   BAKE: 40 MINUTES   Oven 350°

Low-Fat

    4 medium cooking apples, such as Rome Beauty, Granny Smith,
        or Jonathan
  1/2 cup raisins, snipped pitted whole dates, or mixed dried fruit
        bits
    2 tablespoons brown sugar
  1/2 teaspoon ground cinnamon
  1/4 teaspoon ground nutmeg
  1/3 cup apple juice or water
      Ice cream or half-and-half (optional)

1. Core apples; peel a strip from the top of each. Place apples in a
2-quart casserole. Combine the raisins, brown sugar, cinnamon, and
nutmeg; spoon into centers of apples. Pour apple juice or water into
casserole. Bake apples in a 350° oven for 40 to 45 minutes or till the
apples are tender, basting occasionally. If desired, serve warm with
ice cream or half-and-half. Makes 4 servings.

Nutrition Facts per serving: 167 cal., 1 g total fat (0 g sat. fat), 0 mg chol., 6 mg sodium,
44 g carbo., 4 g fiber, 1 g pro. **Daily Values:** 0% vit. A, 14% vit. C, 2% calcium, 6% iron

POACHED PEARS

START TO FINISH: 35 MINUTES

Low-Fat

*For the best results, use Bosc or Bartlett pears that are fairly firm
rather than those that feel soft.*

  1/3 cup sugar
  1/4 cup sweet white wine (such as Sauternes or riesling) or orange
        juice
 2 1/2 to 3 inches stick cinnamon
    1 teaspoon vanilla
    4 medium pears, peeled, halved, and cored

1. In a large skillet combine 3/4 cup *water,* sugar, wine or juice, cinnamon, and vanilla. Bring to boiling; add pears. Reduce heat. Cover

and simmer 10 to 15 minutes or till pears are tender. Remove cinnamon. Serve warm or chilled. To serve, place 2 pear halves in each of 4 dessert dishes; spoon poaching liquid over each. Makes 4 servings.

■ **Poached Apples:** Prepare as above except substitute 4 small peeled, halved, and cored *cooking apples* for the pears.

Nutrition Facts per serving: 189 cal., 1 g total fat (0 g sat. fat), 0 mg chol., 3 mg sodium, 44 g carbo., 2 g fiber, 1 g pro. **Daily Values:** 0% vit. A, 11% vit. C, 1% calcium, 3% iron

---

GINGERED FRUIT COMPOTE

PREP: 25 MINUTES   BAKE: 40 MINUTES   Oven 375°

> **Low-Fat**

  $^1/_2$ **cup dried tart cherries, dried blueberries, raisins, or currants**
  $^1/_2$ **teaspoon finely shredded orange peel**
  $^1/_2$ **cup white grape juice**
   2 **tablespoons orange liqueur or white grape juice**
  $^1/_4$ **cup packed brown sugar**
   2 **tablespoons finely chopped crystallized ginger**
   4 **cups thinly sliced, peeled peaches, nectarines, apples and/or pears**
   1 **tablespoon margarine or butter**

1. In a $1^1/_2$-quart casserole combine dried fruit, orange peel, white grape juice, orange liqueur, brown sugar, and ginger. Stir in peaches, nectarines, apples and/or pears; dot with margarine or butter.
2. Bake, covered, in a 375° oven for 40 to 45 minutes or till fruit is tender, stirring after 30 minutes of baking. Serve warm. Serves 6.

■ **Tropical Fruit Compote:** Prepare as above, except substitute 4 cups cubed *pineapple, papaya, and/or mango* for the peaches, nectarines, apples, and/or pears.

Nutrition Facts per serving: 160 cal., 2 g total fat (0 g sat. fat), 0 mg chol., 24 mg sodium, 34 g carbo., 2 g fiber, 1 g pro. **Daily Values:** 13% vit. A, 14% vit. C, 1% calcium, 5% iron

APPLESAUCE

START TO FINISH: 25 MINUTES

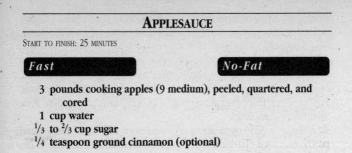

Fast   **No-Fat**

    3 pounds cooking apples (9 medium), peeled, quartered, and
       cored
    1 cup water
    1/3 to 2/3 cup sugar
    1/4 teaspoon ground cinnamon (optional)

1. In a large pot combine apples, water, sugar, and, if desired, cinnamon. Bring to boiling; reduce heat. Cover; simmer for 8 to 10 minutes or till apples are tender, adding more water if necessary.

2. Remove from heat. Mash mixture with a potato masher or process in a blender or food processor to desired texture. Serve warm or chilled. Stir before serving. Makes about 4 1/2 cups applesauce (8 servings).

Nutrition Facts per serving: 80 cal., 0 g total fat, 0 mg chol., 2 mg sodium, 21 g carbo., 2 g fiber, 0 g pro.

APPLE DUMPLINGS

PREP: 35 MINUTES   BAKE: 45 MINUTES   Oven 375°

    1 3/4 cups water
    1 1/4 cups sugar
     1/2 teaspoon ground cinnamon
     1/2 teaspoon ground nutmeg
      2 tablespoons butter or margarine
    2 1/4 cups all-purpose flour
     1/4 teaspoon salt
     2/3 cup shortening
       6 to 8 tablespoons water
       6 small cooking apples

1. For syrup, in a medium saucepan combine the 1 3/4 cups water, *1 cup* of the sugar, *1/4 teaspoon* of the cinnamon, and *1/4 teaspoon* of the nutmeg. Simmer, covered, for 5 minutes. Remove saucepan from heat; stir in the butter or margarine.

2. Meanwhile, for pastry, combine flour and salt. Cut in shortening till pieces are the size of small peas. Add water, a little at a time, mixing till all is moistened. Form dough into a ball. On a lightly floured surface, roll dough into an 18×12-inch rectangle; cut into six 6-inch squares.

3. Peel and core apples. Place an apple on each pastry square. Combine remaining sugar, cinnamon, and nutmeg; sprinkle over fruit. Moisten edges of pastry with water; fold corners to center atop fruit. Pinch to seal. Place dumplings in an 11×7×1½-inch baking pan. Pour syrup over dumplings.

4. Bake in a 375° oven about 45 minutes or till fruit is tender and pastry is brown. To serve, spoon syrup over dumplings and, if desired, serve with *ice cream*. Makes 6 servings.

Nutrition Facts per serving: 604 cal., 27 g total fat (7 g sat. fat), 0 mg chol., 46 mg sodium, 88 g carbo., 2 g fiber, 5 g pro. **Daily Values:** 5% vit. A, 5% vit. C, 1% calcium, 14% iron

■ **Peach Dumplings:** Prepare as above, except substitute small peeled, halved, and pitted *peaches or nectarines* for the apples. Place 2 peach halves (cut sides together) atop each pastry square.

Nutrition Facts per serving: 595 cal., 27 g total fat (8 g sat. fat)

FRUIT CRISP

PREP: 30 MINUTES   BAKE: 30 MINUTES   Oven 375°

   5 cups sliced, peeled cooking apples, pears, peaches, or apricots,
        or frozen unsweetened peach slices
   2 to 4 tablespoons granulated sugar
   ½ cup regular rolled oats
   ½ cup packed brown sugar
   ¼ cup all-purpose flour
   ¼ teaspoon ground nutmeg, ginger, or cinnamon
   ¼ cup butter
   ¼ cup chopped nuts or coconut
        Vanilla ice cream (optional)

1. For filling, thaw fruit, if frozen. *Do not drain*. Place fruit in a 2-quart square baking dish. Stir in the granulated sugar.

2. For topping, in a medium bowl combine the oats, brown sugar, flour, and nutmeg, ginger, or cinnamon. Cut in butter till mixture resembles coarse crumbs. Stir in the nuts or coconut. Sprinkle topping over filling.

3. Bake crisp in a 375° oven for 30 to 35 minutes (40 minutes for thawed fruit) or till fruit is tender and topping is golden. If desired, serve warm with ice cream. Makes 6 servings.

Nutrition Facts per serving: 268 cal., 12 g total fat (5 g sat. fat), 20 mg chol., 83 mg sodium, 42 g carbo., 2 g fiber, 3 g pro. **Daily Values:** 7% vit. A, 8% vit. C, 2% calcium, 7% iron

■ **Blueberry Crisp:** Prepare as above, except, for the filling, combine 4 tablespoons *sugar* and 3 tablespoons *all-purpose flour*. Toss with 5 cups *fresh or frozen blueberries.*

Nutrition Facts per serving: 343 cal., 12 g total fat (5 g sat. fat)

■ **Cherry Crisp:** Prepare Fruit Crisp as above, except, for filling, combine ¹/₂ cup *sugar* and 3 tablespoons *all-purpose flour*. Toss with 5 cups *fresh or frozen unsweetened pitted tart red cherries.*

Nutrition Facts per serving: 340 cal., 12 g total fat (5 g sat. fat)

■ **Microwave directions:** Prepare Fruit Crisp filling as above. Microwave filling, covered with vented plastic wrap, on 100% power (high) for 4 to 6 minutes or till fruit is tender, stirring twice. Prepare Fruit Crisp topping as above. Sprinkle over filling. Cook, uncovered, on high for 2 to 4 minutes or till topping is heated through, giving the dish a half-turn once.

CHERRY COBBLER

PREP: 45 MINUTES   BAKE: 20 MINUTES   Oven 400°

    1 cup all-purpose flour
    2 tablespoons sugar
1¹/₂ teaspoons baking powder
 ¹/₂ teaspoon ground cinnamon (optional)
 ¹/₄ cup butter or margarine
    6 cups fresh or frozen unsweetened pitted tart red cherries
    1 to 1¹/₄ cups sugar
    4 teaspoons cornstarch
    1 egg
 ¹/₄ cup milk
    Vanilla ice cream (optional)

1. For topping, in a medium bowl stir together flour, the 2 tablespoons sugar, baking powder, and, if desired, cinnamon. Cut in butter or margarine till mixture resembles coarse crumbs. Set aside.

2. For filling, in a saucepan combine the cherries, the 1 to 1¼ cups sugar, the cornstarch, and ¼ cup *water*. Let stand for 10 minutes (20 minutes for frozen fruit). Cook and stir till thickened and bubbly. Keep filling hot.

3. In a small bowl stir together the egg and milk. Add to flour mixture, stirring just to moisten. Transfer filling to a 2-quart square baking dish. Using a spoon, immediately drop topping into small mounds atop filling.

4. Bake cobbler in a 400° oven for 20 to 25 minutes or till a wooden toothpick inserted into topping comes out clean. If desired, serve warm with ice cream. Makes 6 servings.

■ **Rhubarb Cobbler:** Prepare as above, except substitute sliced *rhubarb* for the cherries.

Nutrition Facts per serving: 378 cal., 10 g total fat (5 g sat. fat), 57 mg chol., 187 mg sodium, 72 g carbo., 2 g fiber, 5 g pro. **Daily Values:** 22% vit. A, 4% vit. C, 10% calcium, 13% iron

■ **Blueberry or Peach Cobbler:** Prepare as above, except, for filling, in a saucepan combine ⅓ to ⅔ cup *sugar* and 1 tablespoon *cornstarch*. Add ¼ cup *water*. Stir in 4 cups *fresh or frozen blueberries or unsweetened peach slices*. Cook and stir till thickened and bubbly.

Nutrition Facts per serving: 272 cal., 10 g total fat (2 g sat. fat)

■ **Apple or Pear Cobbler:** Prepare as above, except, for filling, cook and stir 6 cups sliced, cored, and peeled *cooking apples or pears*, ⅓ to ⅔ cup *sugar*, 3 tablespoons *water*, and 1 tablespoon *lemon juice* till boiling; reduce heat. Simmer, covered, for 5 minutes or till fruit is almost tender, stirring occasionally. Combine 2 tablespoons *water* and 1 tablespoon *cornstarch*; add to filling. Cook and stir till thickened and bubbly.

Nutrition Facts per serving: 280 cal., 9 g total fat (2 g sat. fat)

BANANAS FOSTER

START TO FINISH: 15 MINUTES

Fast

$^1/_3$ **cup butter**
$^1/_3$ **cup packed brown sugar**
3 **ripe bananas, bias-sliced (2 cups)**
$^1/_4$ **teaspoon ground cinnamon**
2 **tablespoons crème de cacao or banana liqueur**
$^1/_4$ **cup rum**
2 **cups vanilla ice cream**

1. In a large skillet melt butter; stir in brown sugar till melted. Add bananas; cook and gently stir over medium heat about 2 minutes or till heated through. Sprinkle with cinnamon. Stir in crème de cacao or banana liqueur.
2. In a saucepan heat rum till it almost simmers. Ignite rum with a long match. Pour over bananas, coating evenly. Spoon sauce over ice cream; serve immediately. Makes 4 servings.

Nutrition Facts per serving: 463 cal., 23 g total fat (14 g sat. fat), 70 mg chol., 213 mg sodium, 53 g carbo., 2 g fiber, 3 g pro. **Daily Values:** 22% vit. A, 13% vit. C, 9% calcium, 5% iron

PEACH-BERRY BETTY

PREP: 15 MINUTES   BAKE: 30 MINUTES   Oven 375°

A betty is an old-fashioned baked fruit dessert made with soft bread cubes.

3 **cups fresh red raspberries or one 12-ounce package frozen red raspberries**
2 **cups sliced, peeled peaches or frozen unsweetened peach slices**
$^1/_2$ **cup sugar**
1 **tablespoon all-purpose flour**
1 **tablespoon finely chopped crystallized ginger or $^1/_8$ teaspoon ground ginger**
5 **cups soft whole wheat bread cubes (about 7 slices)**
3 **tablespoons butter or margarine, melted**
Whipped cream (optional)

1. Thaw raspberries and peaches, if frozen. *Do not drain.* For filling, in a large mixing bowl combine sugar, flour, and ginger. Add berries, peaches, and their juices; toss to coat. Add *2 cups* of the bread cubes; toss gently till combined. Transfer filling to an un-greased 2-quart square baking dish.

2. For topping, place remaining bread cubes in a medium mixing bowl. Drizzle with melted butter or margarine; toss to coat. Sprinkle topping over fruit filling. Bake in a 375° oven about 30 minutes or till fruit is tender and topping is golden. If desired, serve warm with whipped cream. Makes 6 servings.

Nutrition Facts per serving: 248 cal., 7 g total fat (4 g sat. fat), 15 mg chol., 251 mg sodium, 45 g carbo., 7 g fiber, 4 g pro. **Daily Values:** 9% vit. A, 31% vit. C, 3% calcium, 10% iron

■ **Apple Betty:** Prepare as above, except substitute 5 cups peeled, cored, and sliced *cooking apples* (5 medium) for the peaches and raspberries; $1/2$ teaspoon *ground cinnamon* for the gingerroot, and *white bread* for the whole wheat bread.

Nutrition Facts per serving: 247 cal., 7 g total fat (4 g sat. fat)

CHERRIES JUBILEE

START TO FINISH: 15 MINUTES

Fast

*If you choose to ignite the brandy in a ladle, hold it
with a pot holder.*

1. Drain a *16-ounce can pitted dark sweet cherries,* reserving $1/2$ cup syrup. Set cherries aside. In a medium saucepan or the blazer pan of a chafing dish, combine reserved syrup, $1/4$ cup *sugar,* and 1 table-spoon *cornstarch.* Cook and stir mixture till thickened and bubbly. Cook and stir for 2 minutes more. Stir in the cherries and heat through.

2. In a small saucepan heat $1/4$ cup *brandy, cherry brandy, or kirsch* till it almost simmers. (If desired, carefully pour heated brandy into a large ladle.) Carefully ignite brandy with a long match and pour over cherry mixture. Stir before serving; serve immediately over *vanilla ice cream.* Makes 6 to 8 servings.

Nutrition Facts per serving: 255 cal., 7 g total fat (5 g sat. fat), 29 mg chol., 55 mg sodium, 41 g carbo., 1 g fiber, 3 g pro. **Daily Values:** 8% vit. A, 5% vit. C, 7% calcium, 2% iron

LEMON CUSTARD MERINGUE

PREP: 40 MINUTES   BAKE/DRY: 1³/₄ HOURS CHILL: 5 TO 24 HOURS   Oven 300°

To make either the large meringue shell or individual shells ahead,
place in an airtight container and store at room temperature
for up to 3 days.

   3 egg whites
   1 teaspoon vanilla
 ¹/₄ teaspoon cream of tartar
     Dash salt
1¹/₂ cups sugar
   2 tablespoons cornstarch
   3 beaten egg yolks
 ¹/₃ cup water
   1 teaspoon finely shredded lemon peel
 ¹/₄ cup lemon juice
   1 cup whipping cream
   2 tablespoons sugar

1. For meringue, let egg whites stand in a large mixing bowl for 30 minutes. Add the vanilla, cream of tartar, and salt to egg whites. Beat with an electric mixer on medium speed till soft peaks form (tips curl). Add *1 cup* of the sugar, a tablespoon at a time, beating about 7 minutes on high speed till stiff peaks form (tips stand straight) and sugar is almost dissolved.
2. Spread meringue into a well-greased 9-inch pie plate. Build up the sides to form a shell. Bake in a 300° oven for 45 minutes. Turn off oven. Let shell dry in oven, with door closed, for at least 1 hour.
3. For custard filling, in a saucepan combine remaining ¹/₂ cup sugar and cornstarch. Stir in egg yolks, water, lemon peel, and lemon juice. Cook and stir till bubbly. Cook and stir for 2 minutes more. Remove from heat. Cover the surface with plastic wrap; cool (mixture will be very thick).
4. To assemble, spread cooled filling in meringue shell. Beat whipping cream and the 2 tablespoons sugar till soft peaks form. Spread over filling. Chill 5 to 24 hours. To serve, cut with a wet knife. Makes 8 servings.
■ **Individual Meringue Shells:** Prepare meringue as above, except cover a baking sheet with clean plain brown paper. Draw eight 3-inch circles on paper. Using a pastry bag, pipe the meringue onto

the circles on the paper, building the sides up to form shells. (Or, use the back of a spoon to spread the meringue over the circles, building up the sides.) Bake in a 300° oven for 35 minutes. Turn off oven. Let shells dry in oven, with door closed, for at least 1 hour. Remove from paper. Prepare filling and assemble shells as directed in steps 3 and 4. Or, fill shells with cut-up fresh fruit or ice cream.

Nutrition Facts per serving: 332 cal., 13 g total fat (7 g sat. fat), 121 mg chol., 52 mg sodium, 53 g carbo., 0 g fiber, 3 g pro. **Daily Values:** 25% vit. A, 6% vit. C, 2% calcium, 1% iron

---

STRAWBERRY SHORTCAKE

PREP: 25 MINUTES   BAKE: 15 MINUTES   COOL: 10 MINUTES   Oven 450°

For variety, substitute sliced peaches for the berries, or combine the two fruits.

    6 cups sliced strawberries
 ¹/₂ cup sugar
    2 cups all-purpose flour
    2 teaspoons baking powder
 ¹/₂ cup butter
    1 beaten egg
 ²/₃ cup milk
    1 cup whipping cream, whipped

1. In a small bowl stir together the berries and ¹/₄ cup of the sugar; set aside. Stir together remaining sugar, flour, and baking powder. Cut in the butter till mixture resembles coarse crumbs. Combine the egg and milk; add to dry mixture. Stir just to moisten. Spread the batter into a greased 8x1¹/₂-inch round baking pan.

2. Bake in a 450° oven for 15 to 18 minutes or till a wooden toothpick inserted near center comes out clean. Cool in pan for 10 minutes. Remove from pan. Split into 2 layers. Spoon half of the berries and whipped cream over the first layer. Top with second layer, remaining berries, and whipped cream. Serve immediately. Makes 8 servings.

Nutrition Facts per serving: 307 cal., 13 g total fat (8 g sat. fat), 59 mg chol., 227 mg sodium, 44 g carbo., 3 g fiber, 5 g pro. **Daily Values:** 13% vit. A, 105% vit. C, 11% calcium, 13% iron

CREPES SUZETTE

START TO FINISH: 1 HOUR

To make crepes ahead, layer cooled crepes with sheets of waxed paper in an airtight container; store them in the refrigerator for up to 2 days or freeze them for up to 4 months. If frozen, thaw the crepes 1 hour at room temperature before using.

1 **recipe Dessert Crepes (see page 251)**
$^1/_2$ **cup butter or margarine**
$^1/_4$ **teaspoon finely shredded orange peel**
$^1/_2$ **cup orange juice**
$^1/_3$ **cup sugar**
$^1/_4$ **cup orange liqueur**
$^1/_4$ **cup brandy**

1. Prepare crepes. Fold each crepe in half with browned side out. Fold in half again, forming a triangle. Set aside.
2. For orange sauce, in a large skillet or the blazer pan of a chafing dish, combine butter or margarine, orange peel, orange juice, sugar, and orange liqueur. Cook and stir till thickened and bubbly. Arrange folded crepes in sauce. Simmer, uncovered, for 3 to 5 minutes or just till heated through, spooning sauce over crepes occasionally.
3. In a small saucepan heat the brandy till it almost simmers. Carefully ignite brandy with a long match. Pour over crepes. Serve immediately. Makes 6 to 8 servings.

Nutrition Facts per serving: 395 cal., 21 g total fat (11 g sat. fat), 116 mg chol., 207 mg sodium, 38 g carbo., 1 g fiber, 6 g pro. **Daily Values:** 21% vit. A, 18% vit. C, 7% calcium, 8% iron

CHEESECAKE SUPREME

PREP: 40 MINUTES   BAKE: 45 MINUTES   CHILL: AT LEAST 4 HOURS   Oven 375°

Check for doneness by gently shaking the pan rather than inserting a knife, which will make a crack. When the cheesecake is done, a 1-inch area in the center still will jiggle a little; this area will firm after cooling.

$1^3/_4$ **cups finely crushed graham crackers**
$^1/_4$ **cup finely chopped walnuts**
$^1/_2$ **teaspoon ground cinnamon**

$^1/_2$ cup butter, melted
3 8-ounce packages cream cheese, softened
1 cup sugar
2 tablespoons all-purpose flour
1 teaspoon vanilla
$^1/_2$ teaspoon finely shredded lemon peel (optional)
2 eggs
1 egg yolk
$^1/_4$ cup milk

1. For crust, combine crushed graham crackers, walnuts, and cinnamon. Stir in melted butter. If desired, reserve $^1/_4$ *cup* of the crumb mixture for topping. Use a small measuring cup to press the remaining crumb mixture onto the bottom and about 2 inches up sides of an 8- or 9-inch springform pan. Set pan aside.

2. For filling, in a large mixing bowl beat cream cheese, sugar, flour, vanilla, and, if desired, lemon peel with an electric mixer till combined. Add eggs and egg yolk all at once, beating on low speed just till combined. Stir in milk.

3. Pour filling into crust-lined pan. If desired, sprinkle with reserved crumbs. Place on a shallow baking pan in oven. Bake in a 375° oven for 45 to 50 minutes for the 8-inch pan, 35 to 40 minutes for the 9-inch pan, or till center appears nearly set when shaken.

4. Cool in pan on a wire rack for 15 minutes. Loosen the crust from sides of pan with a small spatula and cool 30 minutes more. Remove the sides of the pan; cool cheesecake completely. Cover and chill at least 4 hours before serving. Makes 12 to 16 servings.

Nutrition Facts per serving: 429 cal., 32 g total fat (18 g sat. fat), 137 mg chol., 329 mg sodium, 30 g carbo., 1 g fiber, 7 g pro. **Daily Values:** 35% vit. A, 0% vit. C, 5% calcium, 10% iron

■ **Sour Cream Cheesecake:** Prepare as above, except reduce cream cheese to 2 packages and omit the milk. Add three 8-ounce cartons *dairy sour cream* with the eggs. Bake about 55 minutes for 8-inch pan (about 50 minutes for 9-inch pan).

Nutrition Facts per serving: 481 cal., 37 g total fat (21 g sat. fat)

■ **Chocolate Cheesecake:** Prepare as above, except omit lemon peel. Melt 4 ounces *semisweet chocolate*. Beat the melted chocolate into the filling mixture just before adding the eggs.

Nutrition Facts per serving: 477 cal., 35 g total fat (20 g sat. fat)

■ **Chocolate Swirl Cheesecake:** Prepare cheesecake as above, except omit lemon peel. Melt 2 ounces *semisweet chocolate*. Stir the melted chocolate into *half* of the filling. Pour chocolate filling into the crust; pour plain filling into the crust. Use a spatula to gently swirl fillings.

Nutrition Facts per serving: 451 cal., 33 g total fat (19 g sat. fat)

■ **Low-Fat Cheesecake:** Prepare as above, except reduce crushed crackers to ⅓ cup and omit walnuts, cinnamon, and butter. Sprinkle crackers on bottom and sides of a well-buttered 8- or 9-inch springform pan. Substitute three 8-ounce packages *nonfat cream cheese* for the regular cream cheese and ½ cup *refrigerated or frozen egg product* (thawed) for the eggs and egg yolk. Bake as directed. If desired, serve with fresh fruit such as *strawberries, raspberries, blueberries, and/or kiwifruit*.

Nutrition Facts per serving: 141 cal., 1 g total fat (0 g sat. fat) 10 mg chol.

CHOCOLATE SOUFFLÉ

PREP: 25 MINUTES   BAKE: 35 MINUTES   Oven 350°

Test the soufflé for doneness while it's still in the oven. If you remove the soufflé before it's done, it will fall. See page 483 for tips on serving a soufflé.

2 tablespoons butter or margarine
3 tablespoons all-purpose flour
¾ cup milk
½ cup semisweet chocolate pieces
4 beaten egg yolks
4 egg whites
½ teaspoon vanilla
¼ cup sugar
Whipped cream (optional)

1. Grease the sides of a 2-quart soufflé dish. Sprinkle sides with a little *sugar*. Set dish aside.

2. In a small saucepan melt butter or margarine. Stir in flour. Add milk all at once. Cook and stir till thickened and bubbly. Add chocolate; stir till melted. Remove from heat. Gradually stir chocolate mixture into beaten egg yolks. Set aside.

3. Beat egg whites and vanilla till soft peaks form (tips curl). Gradually add the sugar, beating till stiff peaks form (tips stand straight). Fold about *1 cup* beaten egg whites into chocolate mixture. Then fold chocolate mixture into remaining beaten whites. Transfer to prepared dish.

4. Bake in a 350° oven for 35 to 40 minutes or till a knife inserted near center comes out clean. If desired, top with whipped cream. Serve soufflé immediately. Makes 6 servings.

Nutrition Facts per serving: 212 cal., 12 g total fat (4 g sat. fat), 154 mg chol., 102 mg sodium, 22 g carbo., 0 g fiber, 6 g pro. **Daily Values:** 28% vit. A, 0% vit. C, 4% calcium, 6% iron

---

TIRAMISU

PREP: 1 HOUR   COOK: 20 MINUTES   CHILL: AT LEAST 4 HOURS

Tiramisu (tee rah MEE su), a triflelike Italian dessert, is made with mascarpone, an Italian cheese you'll find in the grocer's cheese section.

   1 **recipe Hot-Milk Sponge Cake (see page 277)**
  1/3 **cup granulated sugar**
   2 **tablespoons instant espresso powder or instant coffee crystals**
   2 **tablespoons rum**
   2 **8-ounce containers mascarpone cheese or two 8-ounce
      packages cream cheese, softened**
  1/2 **cup sifted powdered sugar**
   1 **teaspoon vanilla**
   2 **ounces semisweet chocolate, grated**
   1 **cup whipping cream**
   2 **tablespoons coffee liqueur**
  1/2 **ounce semisweet chocolate, grated**

1. Prepare Hot-Milk Sponge Cake as directed, except grease and flour the baking pan. Cool for 10 minutes in pan; remove cake from pan. Cool cake completely.

2. Meanwhile, for syrup, in a small saucepan combine granulated sugar, espresso powder or coffee crystals, and 1/3 cup *water*. Cook over medium heat to boiling. Boil for 1 minute; remove from heat and stir in rum. Cool completely.

3. For filling, in a medium bowl stir together the mascarpone or cream cheese, powdered sugar, and vanilla. Stir in the 2 ounces grated chocolate.

4. To assemble, cut cake horizontally into 3 layers. Return a cake layer to the baking pan. Brush layer in pan with *one-third* of the syrup and spread with *half* of the filling. Repeat layering with the second cake layer, *one-third* of the syrup, and remaining filling. Top with the third cake layer; brush with remaining syrup.

5. In a chilled bowl combine whipping cream and coffee liqueur. Beat with chilled beaters of an electric mixer on medium speed till soft peaks form. Spread whipped cream over top cake layer; sprinkle with the $1/2$ ounce grated chocolate. Refrigerate at least 4 hours before serving. Makes 12 to 16 servings.

Nutrition Facts per serving: 450 cal., 29 g total fat (16 g sat. fat), 117 mg chol., 96 mg sodium, 43 g carbo., 0 g fiber, 11 g pro. **Daily Values:** 12% vit. A, 0% vit. C, 5% calcium, 5% iron

---

CHOCOLATE TRUFFLE CAKE

PREP: 40 MINUTES   BAKE: 45 MINUTES   COOL: 4 HOURS   Oven 325°

Just a sliver of this chocolate dessert will satisfy—it's ultrarich.

   1 cup pecans, toasted and coarsely ground (see tip, page 234)
   1 cup graham cracker crumbs
   $1/4$ cup butter, melted
   2 tablespoons sugar
   2 8-ounce packages semisweet chocolate, cut up
   1 cup whipping cream
   6 beaten eggs
   $3/4$ cup sugar
   $1/3$ cup all-purpose flour
      Whipped cream (optional)

1. For crust, combine pecans, cracker crumbs, melted butter, and the 2 tablespoons sugar. Press onto bottom and about $1^1/2$ inches up the sides of a greased 9-inch springform pan. Set pan aside.

2. In a large saucepan cook and stir chocolate and whipping cream over low heat till the chocolate melts. Transfer the mixture to a medium mixing bowl. Set aside.

3. In a large mixing bowl combine eggs, the $3/4$ cup sugar, and flour; beat 10 minutes or till thick and lemon colored. Fold *one-fourth* of the egg mixture into the chocolate mixture; fold chocolate mixture into remaining egg mixture. Pour into crust-lined pan.

4. Bake cake in a 325° oven about 45 minutes or till puffed around edge and halfway to center (the center will be slightly soft). Cool in pan on a wire rack for 20 minutes. Remove sides of pan. Cool for 4 hours. If desired, serve with whipped cream. Cover any leftovers and store in the refrigerator. Makes 16 servings.

■ **Orange-Chocolate Truffle Cake:** Prepare as above, except stir 2 teaspoons finely shredded *orange peel* into the egg mixture after beating.

Nutrition Facts per serving: 359 cal., 24 g total fat (12 g sat. fat), 108 mg chol., 88 mg sodium, 36 g carbo., 3 g fiber, 6 g pro. **Daily Values:** 13% vit. A, 0% vit. C, 3% calcium, 11% iron

---

PLUM PUDDING

PREP: 35 MINUTES   COOK: 2¾ HOURS

Originally, plum pudding did contain plums. But today's versions use currants, raisins, or—as in this recipe—prunes instead.

  5 slices whole wheat bread, torn into small pieces
  ²/₃ cup evaporated skim milk
  2 slightly beaten egg whites
  ¹/₂ cup packed brown sugar
  ¹/₄ cup cooking oil
  ¹/₄ cup orange juice
  ¹/₂ teaspoon vanilla
  1 12-ounce package pitted prunes, snipped
  ¹/₄ cup chopped walnuts
  ³/₄ cup whole wheat flour
2¹/₂ teaspoons apple pie spice
  ¹/₂ teaspoon baking soda
  ¹/₄ teaspoon salt
    Nonstick spray coating
  1 recipe Hard Sauce (see page 457)

1. In a large bowl soak bread in evaporated milk about 3 minutes or till bread is softened. Using a fork, stir bread gently to break up the pieces. Stir in the egg whites, brown sugar, oil, orange juice, and vanilla. Stir in the snipped prunes and walnuts.

2. In a medium mixing bowl stir together the whole wheat flour, apple pie spice, baking soda, and salt. Stir in the bread mixture.

3. Spray a 6¹/₂-cup tower mold with nonstick spray coating. Pour bread mixture into the mold. Cover with foil; press foil tightly against the mold's rim.

4. Place mold on a rack in a deep kettle. Add boiling water to a depth of about 1 inch. Cover the kettle. Bring to a gentle boil and steam for 2³/₄ to 3 hours or till a long wooden pick or skewer inserted in center comes out clean. Add more boiling water to the kettle, as necessary.

5. Remove mold from kettle. Cool pudding for 10 minutes; remove pudding from mold. Serve warm with Hard Sauce. Makes 8 to 10 servings.

■ **Make-ahead directions:** Prepare as above. Cool for 10 minutes; unmold. Let stand for 30 to 40 minutes on a wire rack to cool slightly. Wrap tightly; store in the refrigerator for up to 2 weeks. To reheat, return pudding to the same mold. Cover and steam about 30 minutes or till warm. Unmold; let pudding stand till slightly cool for easier slicing.

Nutrition Facts per serving: 421 cal., 11 g total fat (1 g sat. fat), 1 mg chol., 300 mg sodium, 80 g carbo., 7 g fiber, 8 g pro. **Daily Values:** 10% vit. A, 35% vit. C, 11% calcium, 22% iron

---

BREAD PUDDING

PREP: 20 MINUTES   BAKE: 40 MINUTES   Oven 350°

Low-Fat

To dry bread cubes, place the cubes in a large pan and bake in a 350° oven for 10 to 15 minutes, stirring twice.

   4 **beaten eggs**
2¹/₄ **cups milk**
 ¹/₂ **cup sugar**
   1 **tablespoon vanilla**
   1 **teaspoon finely shredded orange peel (optional)**
 ¹/₂ **teaspoon ground cardamom or ground cinnamon**
   4 **cups dry French bread cubes or regular bread cubes**
 ¹/₃ **cup dried tart red cherries, dried cranberries, or raisins**
   1 **recipe Whiskey Sauce (see page 455) (optional)**

1. In a bowl beat together eggs, milk, sugar, vanilla, orange peel (if desired), and cardamom or cinnamon. In an ungreased 2-quart square baking dish toss together bread cubes and dried fruit; pour egg mixture evenly over bread mixture.

2. Bake in a 350° oven for 40 to 45 minutes or till a knife inserted near the center comes out clean. Cool slightly. If desired, serve warm with Whiskey Sauce. Makes 8 servings.

Nutrition Facts per serving: 194 cal., 4 g total fat (2 g sat. fat), 112 mg chol., 180 mg sodium, 30 g carbo., 0 g fiber, 7 g pro. **Daily Values:** 11% vit. A, 1% vit. C, 9% calcium, 5% iron

■ **Streusel-Topped Bread Pudding:** Prepare as above, except, for topping, in a small bowl combine ¼ cup *all-purpose flour,* ¼ cup packed *brown sugar,* and 2 tablespoons softened *butter* till mixture resembles coarse crumbs. Sprinkle over pudding before baking.

Nutrition Facts per serving: 253 cal., 7 g total fat (3 g sat. fat)

BROWNIE PUDDING CAKE

PREP: 15 MINUTES   BAKE: 30 MINUTES   Oven 350°

As this homey dessert bakes, a layer of cake magically rises to the top, leaving a sauce underneath.

  ½ **cup all-purpose flour**
  ¼ **cup sugar**
   3 **tablespoons unsweetened cocoa powder**
  ¾ **teaspoon baking powder**
  ¼ **cup milk**
   1 **tablespoon cooking oil**
  ½ **teaspoon vanilla**
  ¼ **cup chopped walnuts**
  ⅓ **cup sugar**
  ¾ **cup boiling water**

1. In a medium mixing bowl stir together flour, the ¼ cup sugar, *1 tablespoon* of the cocoa powder, and baking powder. Add milk, oil, and vanilla; stir till smooth. Stir in walnuts. Transfer batter to a 1-quart casserole.

2. Combine the remaining 2 tablespoons cocoa powder and the ⅓ cup sugar. Gradually stir in boiling water. Pour evenly over batter.

Bake in a 350° oven about 30 minutes or till a wooden toothpick inserted near the center of cake comes out clean. Serve warm. Makes 4 servings.

■ **Mocha Pudding Cake:** Prepare as above, except add 2 teaspoons *instant coffee crystals* with the boiling water.

Nutrition Facts per serving: 270 cal., 9 g total fat (1 g sat. fat), 1 mg chol., 78 mg sodium, 44 g carbo., 1 g fiber, 4 g pro. **Daily Values:** 1% vit. A, 0% vit. C, 11% calcium, 9% iron

---

LEMON PUDDING CAKE

PREP: 30 MINUTES   BAKE: 40 MINUTES   Oven 350°

$^1/_2$ cup sugar
   3 tablespoons all-purpose flour
   1 teaspoon finely shredded lemon peel
   3 tablespoons lemon juice
   2 tablespoons butter or margarine, melted
   2 slightly beaten egg yolks
   1 cup milk
   2 egg whites

1. Combine sugar and flour. Stir in lemon peel, lemon juice, and melted butter or margarine. Combine egg yolks and milk. Add to flour mixture; stir just till combined.

2. Beat egg whites till stiff peaks form (tips stand straight). Gently fold egg whites into lemon batter. Transfer batter to a 1-quart casserole. Place the casserole in a large pan on an oven rack. Pour hot water into the large pan around the casserole to a depth of 1 inch. Bake cake in a 350° oven about 40 minutes or till golden and top springs back when lightly touched near the center. Serve warm. Makes 4 servings.

Nutrition Facts per serving: 237 cal., 9 g total fat (5 g sat. fat), 126 mg chol., 120 mg sodium, 33 g carbo., 0 g fiber, 6 g pro. **Daily Values:** 25% vit. A, 10% vit. C, 7% calcium, 4% iron

SAUCEPAN RICE PUDDING

PREP: 10 MINUTES   COOK: 30 MINUTES

Low-Fat

1. In a heavy medium saucepan bring 3 cups *milk* just to boiling; stir in ⅓ cup *uncooked long grain rice* and ⅓ cup *raisins or mixed dried fruit bits*. Cover and cook over low heat for 30 to 40 minutes or till most of the milk is absorbed, stirring occasionally. (Mixture may appear curdled.)

2. Remove saucepan from heat. Stir in ¼ cup *sugar* and 1 teaspoon *vanilla*. Spoon into dessert dishes. Sprinkle with ¼ teaspoon *nutmeg*. Serve warm or chilled. Makes six ½-cup servings.

Nutrition Facts per serving: 157 cal., 2 g total fat (2 g sat. fat), 9 mg chol., 62 mg sodium, 29 g carbo., 0 g fiber, 5 g pro. **Daily Values:** 7% vit. A, 2% vit. C, 12% calcium, 4% iron

VANILLA PUDDING

PREP: 20 MINUTES   CHILL: 4 HOURS

1. In a heavy medium saucepan combine ¾ cup *sugar* and 3 tablespoons *cornstarch or flour*. Stir in 3 cups *milk*. Cook and stir over medium heat till bubbly. Cook and stir for 2 minutes more. Remove from heat. Gradually stir *1 cup* of the milk mixture into 4 beaten *egg yolks* or 2 beaten *eggs*.

2. Add egg mixture to milk mixture in saucepan. If using egg yolks, bring to a gentle boil; if using whole eggs, cook till nearly bubbly but *do not boil*. Reduce heat. Cook and stir for 2 minutes more. Remove from heat. Stir in 1 tablespoon *margarine or butter* and 1½ teaspoons *vanilla*. Pour pudding into a bowl. Place a sheet of plastic wrap on the surface of the pudding or custard before chilling it. This will prevent a "skin" from forming on the top. Chill. (Do not stir during chilling.) Serves 6.

Nutrition Facts per serving: 232 cal., 8 g total fat (3 g sat. fat), 151 mg chol., 89 mg sodium, 35 g carbo., 0 g fiber, 6 g pro. **Daily Values:** 31% vit. A, 1% vit. C, 13% calcium, 3% iron

■ **Chocolate Pudding:** Prepare as above, except add ⅓ cup *unsweetened cocoa powder* along with the sugar and use 2 tablespoons cornstarch or $\frac{1}{4}$ cup all-purpose flour, $2\frac{2}{3}$ cups milk, and 4 egg yolks (not whole eggs).

Nutrition Facts per serving: 251 cal., 8 g total fat (3 g sat. fat)

BAKED RICE PUDDING

PREP: 10 MINUTES   BAKE: 45 MINUTES   Oven 325°

Low-Fat

1. In a medium mixing bowl combine 3 *beaten eggs*, $1\frac{1}{2}$ cups *milk*, $\frac{1}{3}$ cup *sugar*, and 1 teaspoon *vanilla*. Beat till well combined but not foamy. Stir in 1 cup *cooked rice* and $\frac{1}{2}$ cup *raisins*. Pour rice mixture into a $1\frac{1}{2}$-quart casserole. If desired, sprinkle with *nutmeg or cinnamon*. Place the casserole in a 2-quart square baking dish on an oven rack. Pour boiling water into the baking dish around the casserole to a depth of 1 inch.
2. Bake in a 325° oven 45 to 55 minutes or till a knife inserted near center comes out clean, stirring after 30 minutes. Serve warm or cold. Serves 6.

Nutrition Facts per serving: 183 cal., 4 g total fat (2 g sat. fat), 111 mg chol., 64 mg sodium, 32 g carbo., 1 g fiber, 6 g pro. **Daily Values:** 8% vit. A, 1% vit. C, 7% calcium, 6% iron

COEUR À LA CRÈME HEARTS

PREP: 20 MINUTES   CHILL: 6 TO 24 HOURS

Don't let the name of this French dessert stop you from trying the recipe—it's really simple.

   6 to 8 six-inch squares 100% cotton cheesecloth
   1 8-ounce package cream cheese, softened
   $\frac{1}{2}$ teaspoon vanilla or few drops almond or lemon extract
   $\frac{1}{3}$ cup sifted powdered sugar
   $\frac{3}{4}$ cup whipping cream
   1 recipe Raspberry Sauce (see page 452)

1. Line six $\frac{1}{2}$-cup or eight $\frac{1}{3}$-cup heart-shaped or other small molds with damp cheesecloth squares, allowing the cheesecloth to hang over edges.
2. In a mixing bowl beat the cream cheese and vanilla with an elec-

tric mixer on medium speed till combined. Gradually add powdered
sugar, beating till fluffy. Set aside.

3. In another mixing bowl beat whipping cream till soft peaks form.
Fold whipped cream into the cream cheese mixture. Spoon into the
prepared molds. Cover and chill for 6 to 24 hours.

4. To serve, invert the molds onto a serving plate. Holding onto the
cheesecloth ends, remove molds. Peel the cheesecloth from the
shapes. Serve with Raspberry Sauce. Makes 6 to 8 servings.

Nutrition Facts per serving: 333 cal., 25 g total fat (15 g sat. fat), 83 mg chol., 125 mg
sodium, 26 g carbo., 3 g fiber, 4 g pro. **Daily Values:** 30% vit. A, 25% vit. C, 5% calcium,
5% iron

CHOCOLATE POTS DE CRÈME

PREP: 10 MINUTES   COOK: 12 MINUTES   CHILL: 2 TO 24 HOURS

Pots de crème (poh-duh-KREM) is a very rich, puddinglike dessert
that is served cold.

　1　cup half-and-half or light cream
　1　4-ounce package sweet baking chocolate, coarsely chopped
　2　teaspoons sugar
　3　beaten egg yolks
　$1/2$　teaspoon vanilla
　　　Whipped cream (optional)

1. In a small heavy saucepan combine half-and-half, chocolate, and
sugar. Cook and stir over medium heat about 10 minutes or till mixture comes to a full boil and thickens. Gradually stir about *half* of
the hot mixture into beaten egg yolks; add egg yolk mixture to hot
mixture in pan. Cook and stir over low heat for 2 minutes more. Remove from heat. Stir in vanilla. Pour into 4 or 6 pots de crème cups
or small dessert dishes. Cover and chill 2 to 24 hours. If desired,
serve with whipped cream. Makes 4 to 6 servings.

■ **Espresso Chocolate Pots de Crème:** Prepare as above, except
add 2 teaspoons *instant espresso powder* along with the cream.

Nutrition Facts per serving: 276 cal., 21 g total fat (11 g sat. fat), 182 mg chol., 31 mg
sodium, 22 g carbo., 2 g fiber, 5 g pro. **Daily Values:** 32% vit. A, 0% vit. C, 7% calcium,
7% iron

CREAM PUFFS

1 **cup water**
$^1/_2$ **cup butter**
$^1/_8$ **teaspoon salt**
1 **cup all-purpose flour**
4 **eggs**
Whipped cream, pudding, or ice cream
Powdered sugar (optional)

1. In a medium saucepan combine water, butter, and salt. Bring to boiling. Add flour all at once, stirring vigorously. Cook and stir till mixture forms a ball (see photo 1, top right). Remove from heat. Cool for 10 minutes. Add eggs, one at a time, beating well with a wooden spoon after each addition (see photo 2, at right).
2. Drop dough by 12 heaping tablespoons onto a greased baking sheet (see photo 3, at right). Bake in a 400° oven for 30 to 35 minutes or till golden. Cool on a wire rack.
3. Cut tops from puffs; remove soft dough from inside (see photo 4, at right). Fill with whipped cream, pudding, or ice cream. Replace tops. If desired, sift powdered sugar over tops. Makes 12 cream puffs.

Nutrition Facts per cream puff with ¼ cup whipped cream: 229 cal., 20 g total fat (12 g sat. fat), 132 mg chol., 132 mg sodium, 8 g carbo., 0 g fiber, 4 g pro. **Daily Values:** 23% vit. A, 0% vit. C, 2% calcium, 4% iron

■ **Éclairs:** Prepare as above, except spoon dough into a decorating bag fitted with a large plain round tip (about $^1/_2$-inch opening). Pipe 12 strips of dough, 3 inches apart, onto a greased baking sheet, making each strip 4 inches long, 1 inch wide, and $^3/_4$ inch high. Bake, split, and cool as above. Fill éclairs with whipped cream or pudding. Frost with 1 recipe Chocolate Glaze (see page 265). Makes 12 éclairs.

Nutrition Facts per éclair with ¼ cup whipped cream and ¹/₁₂ of glaze: 347 cal., 26 g total fat (16 g sat. fat)

1. To make cream puffs, add the flour, then stir the dough vigorously until the mixture forms a bail that doesn't separate.

2. Add the eggs, one at a time. After each addition, use a wooden spoon to beat the dough until it is smooth.

3. Using 2 spoons, drop the dough in mounds 3 inches apart on a greased baking sheet. Use second spoon to scrape the dough from the first.

4. When cool enough to handle, cut the top one-third from the baked puffs. Remove any soft dough inside puffs with a fork or spoon.

INDIVIDUAL CARAMEL FLANS

PREP: 25 MINUTES   BAKE: 30 MINUTES   Oven 325°

Caramelized sugar is poured into the cups before the custard is added. When the baked flans are unmolded, caramel spills over them like a sauce.

$^1/_3$ **cup sugar**
3 **beaten eggs**
1$^1/_2$ **cups milk**
$^1/_3$ **cup sugar**
1 **teaspoon vanilla**
   Ground nutmeg or cinnamon (optional)

1. To caramelize sugar, in a heavy 8-inch skillet cook the $^1/_3$ cup sugar over medium-high heat till sugar begins to melt, shaking the skillet occasionally to heat the sugar evenly. Do not stir. Once the sugar starts to melt, reduce heat to low and cook about 5 minutes more or till all of the sugar is melted and golden, stirring as needed with a wooden spoon. Immediately divide the caramelized sugar among four 6-ounce custard cups; tilt custard cups to coat bottoms evenly. Let stand 10 minutes.

2. Meanwhile, combine eggs, milk, the $^1/_3$ cup sugar, and vanilla. Beat till well combined but not foamy. Place the custard cups in a 2-quart square baking dish on an oven rack. Divide egg mixture among custard cups. If desired, sprinkle with nutmeg or cinnamon. Pour boiling water into the baking dish around custard cups to a depth of 1 inch. Bake in a 325° oven for 30 to 45 minutes or till a knife inserted near the centers comes out clean.

3. Remove cups from water. Cool slightly on a wire rack before serving. (Or, cool completely in custard cups. Cover and chill till serving time.) To unmold flans, loosen edges with a knife, slipping point down sides to let air in. Invert a dessert plate over each flan; turn custard cup and plate over together. Makes 4 servings.

Nutrition Facts per serving: 234 cal., 6 g total fat (2 g sat. fat), 167 mg chol., 94 mg sodium, 39 g carbo., 0 g fiber, 8 g pro. **Daily Values:** 12% vit. A, 1% vit. C, 10% calcium, 4% iron

■ **Baked Custards:** Prepare as above, except omit the $^1/_3$ cup sugar that is caramelized in step 1. Divide egg mixture among custard cups or one 3½-cup soufflé dish. Bake individual custards as directed above or bake soufflé dish for 50 to 60 minutes. Serve warm or chilled.

Nutrition Facts per serving: 170 cal., 6 g total fat (2 g sat. fat)

CRÈME BRÛLÉE

PREP: 10 MINUTES BAKE: 35 MINUTES CHILL: 1 TO 8 HOURS   Oven 325°

Our Test Kitchen turned to this method of caramelizing sugar in a skillet to avoid placing cold dishes under a hot broiler. Cold dishes can shatter in the oven.

　2　cups half-and-half or light cream
　5　slightly beaten egg yolks
　¹/₃　cup sugar
　1　teaspoon vanilla
　¹/₈　teaspoon salt
　¹/₄　cup sugar

1. In a heavy small saucepan heat half-and-half or light cream over medium-low heat just till bubbly. Remove from heat; set aside.
2. Meanwhile, in a medium mixing bowl combine egg yolks, the ¹/₃ cup sugar, vanilla, and salt. Beat with a wire whisk or rotary beater just till combined. Slowly whisk the hot half-and-half or light cream into the egg mixture.
3. Place six ³/₄-cup soufflé dishes or 6-ounce custard cups in a 3-quart rectangular baking pan. Set pan on an oven rack. Pour custard mixture evenly into the dishes or cups. Pour enough hot water into the baking pan around the dishes to reach halfway up the sides of the dishes.
4. Bake the custards in a 325° oven for 35 to 40 minutes or till a knife inserted near the center of each custard comes out clean. Remove custards from the water bath; cool on a wire rack. Cover and chill for at least 1 hour or up to 8 hours.
5. Before serving, remove custards from the refrigerator; let stand at room temperature for 20 minutes. Meanwhile, place the ¹/₄ cup sugar in a heavy 8-inch skillet. Heat skillet over medium-high heat till sugar begins to melt, shaking skillet occasionally to heat sugar evenly. Do not stir. Once the sugar starts to melt, reduce heat to low

and cook about 5 minutes more or till all of the sugar is melted and golden, stirring as needed with a wooden spoon.

6. Quickly drizzle the caramelized sugar over custards. If sugar starts to harden in the skillet, return to heat, stirring till melted. Serve immediately. Makes 6 servings.

Nutrition Facts per serving: 347 cal., 20 g total fat (11 g sat. fat), 311 mg chol., 125 mg sodium, 35 g carbo., 0 g fiber, 7 g pro. **Daily Values:** 56% vit. A, 1% vit. C, 13% calcium, 5% iron

■ **Crème Brûlée with Liqueur:** Prepare Crème Brûlée as above, except decrease half-and-half or light cream to 1¾ cups. Stir 2 tablespoons *amaretto, crème de cacao, or coffee liqueur* into the egg yolk mixture.

Nutrition Facts per serving: 231 cal., 12 g total fat (6 g sat. fat)

SECRETS TO SUCCESSFUL CUSTARDS

You can have perfect custards every time by following these easy tips.

■ The secret to smooth custard is how long you beat the eggs. Beat them just till the yolks and whites are blended. Don't beat till foamy or the custard surface will have bubbles.

■ If you're tempted to skip the hot-water bath when baking a custard, don't. The hot water helps to even out the heat so the edges won't overcook before the center is done.

■ To test baked custard for doneness, insert a clean table knife ½ inch into the custard about 1 inch from the center. If the knife comes out clean, the custard is done. If any custard clings to the knife, bake the custard a few more minutes and test again.

■ Once the custard tests done, remove it from the hot water immediately. If it remains in the hot water, it will continue to cook.

■ To test stirred custard for doneness, dip a clean metal spoon into the cooked custard. The custard should coat the spoon. Using your finger, draw a line down the center of the back of the spoon. The edges of the custard along the path drawn should hold their shape.

STIRRED CUSTARD

PREP: 15 MINUTES   CHILL: AT LEAST 1 HOUR

Low-Fat

Stir the egg mixture constantly with a figure-eight motion. This ensures even cooking and helps prevent the bottom portion from sticking or burning.

3 **beaten eggs**
2 **cups milk, half-and-half, or light cream**
$1/4$ **cup sugar**
1 **teaspoon vanilla**
Fresh fruit or sponge cake (optional)

1. In a heavy medium saucepan combine eggs; milk, half-and-half, or light cream; and sugar. Cook and stir over medium heat. Continue cooking egg mixture till it just coats a metal spoon. Remove pan from heat. Stir in vanilla.
2. Quickly cool the custard by placing the saucepan into a sink of ice water for 1 to 2 minutes, stirring constantly.
3. Pour custard mixture into a bowl. Place a sheet of plastic wrap on the surface of the custard. This will prevent a "skin" from forming on the top. Chill at least 1 hour or till serving time. If desired, serve custard over fresh fruit or cake. Makes 3 cups.

Nutrition Facts per ½ cup: 112 cal., 4 g total fat (2 g sat. fat), 113 mg chol., 72 mg sodium, 13 g carbo., 0 g fiber, 6 g pro. **Daily Values:** 9% vit. A, 1% vit. C, 9% calcium, 2% iron

■ **Flavored Stirred Custard:** Prepare as above, except substitute 2 to 3 tablespoons *amaretto, orange liqueur, coffee liqueur, rum, or brandy* for the vanilla.

Nutrition Facts per serving: 126 cal., 4 g total fat (2 g sat. fat)

TRIFLE

PREP: 40 MINUTES   CHILL: 3 TO 24 HOURS

*Save a step and use a bakery-made sponge cake or
ladyfingers for the base.*

  1 **recipe Stirred Custard (see page 445)**
  1 **recipe Hot-Milk Sponge Cake (see page 277)**
  3 **tablespoons cream sherry or brandy**
$^1/_4$ **cup strawberry preserves or currant jelly**
  2 **cups cut-up, peeled peaches or kiwifruit, or strawberries,
     raspberries, or blueberries**
  2 **tablespoons sliced almonds, toasted (see tip, page 234)**
$^1/_2$ **cup whipping cream**
  1 **tablespoon sugar**
$^1/_2$ **teaspoon vanilla**

1. Prepare Stirred Custard; cool. Cut cake into 1-inch cubes (you
should have 5 cups). Reserve remaining cake for another use.
2. In a serving bowl layer *half* of the cake cubes. Sprinkle with *half*
of the sherry. Dot with *half* of the preserves. Top with *half* of the
fruit and *half* of the almonds. Pour *half* of the Stirred Custard over
all. Repeat layers. Cover; chill for 3 to 24 hours.
3. To serve, beat cream, sugar, and vanilla till soft peaks form;
spread over trifle. Makes 8 servings.

Nutrition Facts per serving: 406 cal., 14 g total fat (6 g sat. fat), 159 mg chol., 164 mg
sodium, 61 g carbo., 1 g fiber, 9 g pro. **Daily Values:** 23% vit. A, 6% vit. C, 14% calcium,
9% iron

VANILLA ICE CREAM

PREP: 5 MINUTES   FREEZE: 40 MINUTES   RIPEN: 4 HOURS

This has the consistency of a soft-serve ice cream.

   4 **cups half-and-half, light cream, or milk**
$1^1/_2$ **cups sugar**
   1 **tablespoon vanilla**
   2 **cups whipping cream**

1. In a large bowl combine half-and-half, sugar, and vanilla. Stir till sugar dissolves. Stir in whipping cream. Freeze ice-cream mixture in a 4- or 5-quart ice-cream freezer according to the manufacturer's directions. Ripen 4 hours (see tip, page 219). Makes 2 quarts.

Nutrition Facts per ½ cup: 257 cal., 18 g total fat (11 g sat. fat), 63 mg chol., 36 mg sodium, 22 g carbo., 0 g fiber, 2 g pro. **Daily Values:** 21% vit. A, 1% vit. C, 6% calcium, 0% iron

■ **Chocolate-Almond Ice Cream:** Prepare as above, except reduce sugar to *1 cup*. Stir one 16-ounce can (1½ cups) *chocolate-flavored syrup* and ½ cup chopped *almonds,* toasted (see tip, page 234), into ice-cream mixture before freezing.

Nutrition Facts per ½ cup: 347 cal., 24 g total fat (14 g sat. fat)

■ **Strawberry or Peach Ice Cream:** Prepare as above, except in a blender container blend 4 cups fresh or frozen (thawed) unsweetened strawberries *or* cut-up, peeled *peaches* till nearly smooth. (You should have 2 cups.) Stir blended fruit into ice-cream mixture before freezing.

Nutrition Facts per ½ cup: 299 cal., 22 g total fat (14 g sat. fat)

■ **Coffee Ice Cream:** Prepare as above, except dissolve 2 to 3 tablespoons *instant coffee crystals* in the half-and-half mixture. If desired, stir ½ cup *miniature semisweet chocolate pieces* into ice-cream mixture before freezing.

Nutrition Facts per ½ cup: 314 cal., 23 g total fat (14 g sat. fat)

■ **Butter-Pecan Ice Cream:** Prepare as above, except in a heavy skillet cook ½ cup chopped *pecans,* ¼ cup *sugar,* and 1 tablespoon *butter or margarine* over medium-high heat till sugar begins to melt, shaking skillet occasionally. *Do not stir.* Reduce heat to low and cook till sugar turns golden, stirring frequently. Immediately spread on a baking sheet lined with greased foil. Cool; break into chunks. Stir nut mixture into ice-cream mixture before freezing.

Nutrition Facts per ½ cup: 329 cal., 25 g total fat (14 g sat. fat)

CHOCOLATE-CHERRY YOGURT

PREP: 30 MINUTES   FREEZE: 25 MINUTES   RIPEN: 4 HOURS

2 16-ounce cartons (3¹/₂ cups) vanilla yogurt (no gelatin added)*
2¹/₂ cups fresh or frozen unsweetened pitted dark sweet cherries
¹/₃ cup milk
¹/₃ cup light corn syrup
¹/₂ cup miniature semisweet chocolate pieces

1. In a blender container combine yogurt, *1 cup* of the cherries, the milk, and corn syrup. Cover and blend till almost smooth.

2. Freeze mixture in a 2-quart ice-cream freezer according to the manufacturer's directions. Add remaining cherries and chocolate; freeze as directed till firm. Makes 1¹/₂ quarts.

*Note: Yogurt without gelatin gives this dessert a better texture when frozen. Check the ingredient list on the carton to see if it contains gelatin.

Nutrition Facts per ½ cup: 173 cal., 4 g total fat (2 g sat. fat), 5 mg chol., 63 mg sodium, 30 g carbo., 1 g fiber, 5 g pro.
Daily Values: 1% vit. A, 4% vit. C, 10% calcium, 0% iron

RIPENING FROZEN DESSERTS

Homemade ice cream and frozen yogurt taste better and melt more slowly if they are ripened before serving. To ripen ice cream or frozen yogurt in a traditional-style ice-cream freezer, after churning, remove the lid and dasher and cover the top of freezer can with waxed paper or foil. Plug the hole in the lid with a small piece of cloth; replace the lid. Pack the outer freezer bucket with enough ice and rock salt to cover the top of the freezer can, using 4 cups ice to 1 cup salt. Ripen about 4 hours.

When using an ice-cream freezer with an insulated can, after churning, remove dasher; replace lid. Cover the lid with ice and cover with a towel. Ripen about 4 hours.

ORANGE SHERBET

PREP: 20 MINUTES   FREEZE: 40 MINUTES   RIPEN: 4 HOURS

No-Fat

1. In a saucepan combine 1¹/₂ cups *sugar* and 1 envelope *unflavored gelatin*. Stir in 3³/₄ cups *orange juice*. Cook and stir till sugar and gelatin dissolve. Remove from heat. Stir in 1 teaspoon *orange peel*, 1 cup *milk*, and a few drops *orange food coloring*. (Mixture will look curdled.)
2. Freeze in a 4-quart ice-cream freezer according to manufacturer's directions. (Or, transfer mixture to a 9×9×2-inch baking pan. Cover; freeze 2 to 3 hours or till almost firm. Break mixture into small chunks; transfer to a chilled bowl. Beat with an electric mixer till smooth but not melted. Return to pan. Cover; freeze till firm.) Makes 2 quarts.

Nutrition Facts per ¹/₂ cup: 108 cal., 0 g total fat, 1 mg chol., 9 mg sodium, 26 g carbo., 0 g fiber, 1 g pro. **Daily Values:** 2% vit. A, 49% vit. C, 2% calcium, 1% iron

■ **Lemon Sherbet:** Prepare as above, except substitute 3 cups *water* for the orange juice. Stir in ³/₄ cup *lemon juice* with the milk and substitute *lemon peel* for the orange peel and *yellow food coloring* for the orange food coloring.

Nutrition facts per ¹/₂ cup: 85 cal., 0 g total fat

STRAWBERRY DAIQUIRI SORBET

PREP: 10 MINUTES   FREEZE: 8 HOURS

No-Fat

    1 cup sugar
    8 cups strawberries
 ¹/₄ cup light rum
    2 teaspoons finely shredded lime peel
 ¹/₄ cup lime juice
    1 tablespoon orange liqueur

1. In a medium saucepan combine 1¹/₂ cups *water* and sugar. Cook and stir over high heat till mixture comes to a boil and sugar dissolves. Remove from heat and cool syrup completely.

2. Place strawberries in a food processor bowl or blender container. Cover; process or blend till nearly smooth. (For best results, puree *half* of the mixture at a time.) In a bowl stir together pureed strawberries, rum, lime peel, lime juice, and orange liqueur. Stir in the cooled syrup.

3. Freeze in a 4-quart ice-cream freezer according to the manufacturer's directions. Makes 2 quarts.

Nutrition Facts per ½ cup: 82 cal., 0 g total fat, 0 mg chol., 2 mg sodium, 18 g carbo., 1 g fiber, 0 g pro. **Daily Values:** 0% vit. A, 72% vit. C, 0% calcium, 1% iron

---

CHOCOLATY VELVET ICE CREAM

PREP: 10 MINUTES   FREEZE: 8 HOURS

You don't even need an ice-cream freezer for this.

4 cups whipping cream
1 14-ounce can (1⅓ cups) sweetened condensed milk
1 16-ounce can (1½ cups) chocolate-flavored syrup
⅔ cup coarsely chopped walnuts, cashews, or almonds

1. In a medium mixing bowl combine the whipping cream, sweetened condensed milk, and chocolate syrup. Beat with an electric mixer till soft peaks form. Fold in chopped nuts. Transfer the mixture to an 8×8×2-inch baking pan; freeze about 8 hours or till firm. Makes 2 quarts.

Nutrition Facts per ½ cup: 372 cal., 28 g total fat (15 g sat. fat), 90 mg chol., 68 mg sodium, 31 g carbo., 0 g fiber, 4 g pro. **Daily Values:** 28% vit. A, 1% vit. C, 9% calcium, 3% iron

---

CARAMEL SAUCE

START TO FINISH: 10 MINUTES

Fast

½ cup packed brown sugar
1 tablespoon cornstarch
¼ cup water
⅓ cup half-and-half or light cream
2 tablespoons light corn syrup
1 tablespoon butter
½ teaspoon vanilla

1. In a heavy saucepan combine brown sugar and cornstarch. Stir in water. Stir in half-and-half or light cream and corn syrup. Cook and stir till bubbly (mixture may appear curdled). Cook and stir for 2 minutes more. Remove saucepan from heat; stir in butter and vanilla. Serve warm or cool over ice cream, baked fruits, or cake. (Cover and chill any leftovers.) Makes 1 cup sauce.

Nutrition Facts per tablespoon: 43 cal., 1 g total fat (1 g sat. fat), 4 mg chol., 13 mg sodium, 8 g carbo., 0 g fiber, 0 g pro. **Daily Values:** 1% vit. A, 0% vit. C, 1% calcium, 1% iron

HOT FUDGE SAUCE

START TO FINISH: 15 MINUTES

To reheat this rich sauce in your microwave oven, allow 15 to 30 seconds on high power.

³/₄ **cup semisweet chocolate pieces**
¹/₄ **cup butter**
²/₃ **cup sugar**
   1 **5-ounce can (²/₃ cup) evaporated milk**

1. In a heavy small saucepan melt the chocolate and butter. Add the sugar; gradually stir in the evaporated milk. Bring mixture to boiling; reduce heat. Boil gently over low heat for 8 minutes, stirring frequently. Remove pan from heat. Cool slightly. Serve warm over ice cream. (Cover and chill any leftovers.) Makes about 1¹/₂ cups sauce.

Nutrition Facts per tablespoon: 71 cal., 4 g total fat (1 g sat. fat), 7 mg chol., 26 mg sodium, 10 g carbo., 0 g fiber, 1 g pro. **Daily Values:** 2% vit. A, 0% vit. C, 1% calcium, 1% iron

■ **Peanut Butter-Fudge Sauce:** Prepare as above, except, after cooking for 8 minutes, stir in ¹/₄ cup *peanut butter*. Makes 1³/₄ cups sauce.

Nutrition Facts per tablespoon: 75 cal., 5 g total fat (2 g sat. fat)

RHUBARB SAUCE

START TO FINISH: 20 MINUTES

Fast   **No-Fat**

You'll need about 1 pound of rhubarb to make 3 cups of sliced fruit.

   $^1/_2$ to $^2/_3$ cup sugar
   $^1/_4$ cup water
   1 strip orange peel (optional)
   3 cups sliced rhubarb

1. In a medium saucepan stir together sugar, water, and, if desired, orange peel. Bring to boiling; stir in rhubarb. Return to boiling; reduce heat. Cover and simmer about 5 minutes or till rhubarb is tender. Remove the orange peel, if using. Serve warm over cake or ice cream. Makes 2 cups sauce.

Nutrition Facts per tablespoon: 15 cal., 0 g total fat, 0 mg chol., 1 mg sodium, 4 g carbo., 1 g fiber, 0 g pro. **Daily Values:** 0% vit. A, 2% vit. C, 1% calcium, 0% iron

RASPBERRY SAUCE

START TO FINISH: 15 MINUTES

Fast   **No-Fat**

   3 cups fresh or frozen raspberries
   $^1/_3$ cup sugar
   1 teaspoon cornstarch

1. Thaw the berries, if frozen. *Do not drain.* Place *half* of the berries in a blender container or food processor bowl. Cover and blend or process till berries are smooth. Press berries through a fine-mesh sieve; discard seeds. Repeat with remaining berries. (You should have about $^1/_2$ *cup* sieved puree from *each* $1^1/_2$ cups berries.)
2. In a medium saucepan stir together sugar and cornstarch. Add sieved berries. Cook and stir over medium heat till thickened and bubbly. Cook and stir for 2 minutes more. Remove from heat. Cool to room temperature before serving. Makes about 1 cup sauce.

■ **Strawberry Sauce:** Prepare as above, except substitute *strawberries* for the raspberries and do not sieve.

Nutrition Facts per tablespoon: 30 cal., 0 g total fat, 0 mg chol., 0 mg sodium, 8 g carbo., 1 g fiber, 0 g pro. **Daily Values:** 0% vit. A, 10% vit. C, 0% calcium, 0% iron

---

LEMON SAUCE

START TO FINISH: 15 MINUTES

| Fast | Low-Fat |

Serve this sauce over gingerbread or ice cream.

- $^{1}/_{2}$ **cup water**
- $^{1}/_{4}$ **cup sugar**
- 1 **tablespoon cornstarch**
- $^{1}/_{4}$ **teaspoon finely shredded lemon peel**
- 1 **tablespoon lemon juice**
- 2 **teaspoons butter or margarine**

1. In a small saucepan combine the water, sugar, cornstarch, lemon peel, and lemon juice. Cook and stir till thickened and bubbly. Cook and stir for 2 minutes more. Remove from heat; stir in butter or margarine till melted. Serve warm. Makes $^{2}/_{3}$ cup sauce.

Nutrition Facts per tablespoon: 28 cal., 1 g total fat (0 g sat. fat), 5 mg chol., 9 mg sodium, 6 g carbo., 0 g fiber, 0 g pro. **Daily Values:** 1% vit. A, 1% vit. C, 0% calcium, 0% iron

■ **Orange Sauce:** Prepare as above, except substitute *orange peel* for lemon peel and $^{3}/_{4}$ cup *orange juice* for the lemon juice and water. Makes $^{3}/_{4}$ cup sauce.

Nutrition Facts per tablespoon: 37 cal., 1 g total fat (0 g sat. fat)

CHERRY SAUCE

Spoon this luscious topping over Angel Food Cake (see page 284) or ice cream, or use it in Cream Puffs (see page 440).

$^{1}/_{2}$ cup sugar
2 tablespoons cornstarch
$^{1}/_{2}$ cup water
2 cups fresh or frozen pitted tart cherries
1 tablespoon orange or cherry liqueur, cherry brandy, or orange juice

1. In a medium saucepan stir together sugar and cornstarch; stir in water. Add cherries. Cook and stir over medium heat till thickened and bubbly. Cook and stir for 2 minutes more. Remove saucepan from heat.
2. Stir in the liqueur, brandy, or juice. Serve warm. Or, cool to room temperature to serve. Makes 2 cups sauce.

Nutrition Facts per tablespoon: 20 cal., 0 g total fat, 0 mg chol., 0 mg sodium, 5 g carbo., 0 g fiber, 0 g pro.

VANILLA SAUCE

This sauce goes well with fresh or poached fruit, or fruit dumplings.

2 beaten egg yolks
$^{1}/_{3}$ cup milk, half-and-half, or light cream
3 tablespoons sugar
$^{1}/_{2}$ cup whipping cream
1 teaspoon vanilla

1. In a small saucepan combine egg yolks; milk, half-and-half, or light cream; and sugar. Cook and stir till mixture is thickened and bubbly. Remove from heat. Cool mixture; chill at least 1 hour.
2. Just before serving, beat the whipping cream and vanilla till soft

peaks form; fold into egg yolk mixture. (Cover and chill any left-overs.) Makes 1¹/₂ cups sauce.

Nutrition Facts per tablespoon: 30 cal., 2 g total fat (1 g sat. fat), 25 mg chol., 4 mg sodium, 2 g carbo., 0 g fiber, 0 g pro. **Daily Values:** 5% vit. A, 0% vit. C, 0% calcium, 0% iron

WHISKEY SAUCE

START TO FINISH: 10 MINUTES

Fast

Serve this bourbon-spiked sauce with Bread Pudding (see page 434).

  ¹/₄ **cup butter**
  ¹/₂ **cup sugar**
    1 **beaten egg yolk**
    2 **tablespoons water**
    1 **to 2 tablespoons bourbon**

1. In a small saucepan melt the butter. Stir in the sugar, egg yolk, and water. Cook and constantly stir the mixture over medium-low heat for 5 to 6 minutes or till sugar dissolves and mixture boils. Remove from heat; stir in bourbon. Serve warm. (Cover and chill any leftovers.) Makes ²/₃ cup sauce.

Nutrition Facts per tablespoon: 88 cal., 5 g total fat (3 g sat. fat), 34 mg chol., 47 mg sodium, 10 g carbo., 0 g fiber, 0 g pro. **Daily Values:** 7% vit. A, 0% vit. C, 0% calcium, 0% iron

LEMON CURD

PREP: 5 MINUTES   COOK: 8 MINUTES   COOL: 45 MINUTES

  ¹/₃ **cup sugar**
    2 **teaspoons cornstarch**
    2 **teaspoons finely shredded lemon peel**
  ¹/₄ **cup lemon juice**
  ¹/₄ **cup margarine or butter**
    2 **beaten eggs**

1. In a medium saucepan combine the sugar and cornstarch. Stir in lemon peel and lemon juice. Add margarine. Cook and stir till thickened and bubbly.

2. Stir *half* of the lemon mixture into the eggs. Pour egg mixture into the pan. Cook and stir for 2 minutes more. Cover with waxed paper; cool. Makes about 1 cup sauce.

■ **Orange Curd:** Prepare as above, except substitute *orange juice* for the lemon juice and *orange peel* for the lemon peel.

Nutrition Facts per tablespoon: 53 cal., 3 g total fat (1 g sat. fat), 27 mg chol., 41 mg sodium, 5 g carbo., 0 g fiber, 1 g pro. **Daily Values:** 4% vit. A, 3% vit. C, 0% calcium, 0% iron

---

WHIPPED CREAM

START TO FINISH: 10 MINUTES

Fast

1 cup whipping cream
2 tablespoons sugar
$^1/_2$ teaspoon vanilla

1. In a chilled bowl combine whipping cream, sugar, and vanilla. Beat with chilled beaters of an electric mixer on medium speed till soft peaks form. Serve atop pie, cake, or hot drinks or in cream puffs. Makes 2 cups whipped cream.

■ **Flavored Whipped Cream:** Prepare as above, except add *one* of the following along with the vanilla: 2 tablespoons *unsweetened cocoa powder plus* 1 tablespoon additional *sugar;* 2 tablespoons *amaretto or coffee, hazelnut, orange, or praline liqueur;* 1 teaspoon *instant coffee crystals;* $^1/_2$ teaspoon *almond extract;* $^1/_2$ teaspoon *finely shredded lemon, orange, or lime peel;* or $^1/_4$ teaspoon *ground cinnamon, nutmeg, or ginger.*

WHIPPED CREAM ON CALL

You don't need to get out the beaters each time you want whipped cream to top a warm dessert. Instead, when you have leftover whipped cream, freeze it for another time.

Spoon (or pipe) the extra whipped cream into mounds on a baking sheet lined with waxed paper. Freeze till firm. Transfer the frozen mounds to a container; seal, label, and freeze for up to 1 month.

When you want to use the frozen whipped cream, remove the number of mounds you need and let them stand at room temperature for 5 minutes.

Nutrition Facts per tablespoon: 29 cal., 3 g total fat (2 g sat. fat), 10 mg chol., 3 mg sodium, 1 g carbo., 0 g fiber, 0 g pro. **Daily Values:** 3% vit. A, 0% vit. C, 0% calcium, 0% iron

---

HARD SAUCE

PREP: 10 MINUTES   CHILL: 30 MINUTES

"Hard" simply means the sauce is about the consistency of butter. Try it as a topping for spice cakes or bread puddings.

$^{1}/_{4}$ **cup butter, softened**
1 **cup sifted powdered sugar**
$^{1}/_{2}$ **teaspoon vanilla**

1. In a small mixing bowl beat together butter and powdered sugar with an electric mixer on medium speed for 3 to 5 minutes or till mixture is well combined. Beat in vanilla. Spoon into a serving bowl. Chill to harden, about 30 minutes. Makes $^{2}/_{3}$ cup sauce.

■ **Brandy Hard Sauce:** Prepare as above, except substitute 1 tablespoon *brandy or rum* for the vanilla.

■ **Orange Hard Sauce:** Prepare as above, except substitute $^{1}/_{4}$ teaspoon *finely shredded orange peel* and 1 tablespoon *orange juice or orange liqueur* for the vanilla.

Nutrition Facts per tablespoon: 79 cal., 5 g total fat (3 g sat. fat), 12 mg chol., 46 mg sodium, 10 g carbo., 0 g fiber, 0 g pro. **Daily Values:** 4% vit. A, 0% vit. C, 0% calcium, 0% iron

EGGS &
CHEESE

EGGS & CHEESE

Baked Eggs, 468
Breakfast Casserole, 472
Cheese Omelet, 474 *Fast*
Cheese-and-Onion Scrambled Eggs,
    470 *Fast*
Cheese Soufflé, 482
Cheesy Brunch Roll-Ups, 484
Chili Rellenos Casserole, 486
Corn Frittata with Cheese, 478 *Fast*
Crab Benedict, 464
Crab Soufflé Roll, 481
Creamy Poached Eggs, 463 *Fast*
Deluxe Eggs Benedict, 464
Denver Omelet, 475
Denver Scrambled Eggs, 470 *Fast*
Deviled Eggs, 467
Dijon Chicken Strata, 488
Eggs Benedict, 463
French Omelet, 473 *Fast*
Fried Eggs, 467 *Fast*
Frittata, 477 *Fast*
Fruit Omelet, 474 *Fast*
Ham-Asparagus Strata, 487
Ham Soufflé Roll, 482
Hard-Cooked Eggs, 466 *Fast*
Huevos Rancheros, 465 *Fast*

Italian-Style Deviled Eggs, 468
Low-Fat Chili Rellenos Casserole,
    486 *Low-Fat*
Low-Fat Omelet, 473 *Fast Low-Fat*
Low-Fat Scrambled Eggs, 470 *Fast
    Low-Fat*
Mushroom Omelet, 473 *Fast*
Mushroom Scrambled Eggs, 470
    Fast
Oven Frittata, 477 *Fast*
Oven Omelet, 476 *Fast*
Poached Eggs, 461 *Fast Low-Fat*
Puffy Omelet, 474 *Fast*
Puffy Omelet with Ham-and-Cheese
    Sauce, 475
Quiche Lorraine, 478
Scrambled Egg Pizza, 471 *Low-Fat*
Scrambled Eggs, 469 *Fast*
Scrambled Eggs and New Potatoes,
    468 *Fast*
Soft-Cooked Eggs, 466 *Fast*
Spinach Quiche, 479
Turkey Soufflé Roll, 482
Vegetarian Quiche, 480
Welsh Rabbit, 485 *Fast*

POACHED EGGS

START TO FINISH: 10 MINUTES

Fast

Low-Fat

*Be sure to use a skillet or pan that is large enough to hold all the eggs
you want to poach. The eggs should not touch while they're cooking.*

    Cooking oil or shortening (optional)
  1 to 2 teaspoons instant chicken bouillon granules (optional)
    Eggs

1. If desired, lightly grease a medium skillet (for 3 or 4 eggs) or a
1-quart saucepan (for 1 or 2 eggs) with the oil or shortening. Add
water to half-fill the skillet or pan. If desired, stir in bouillon granules. Bring water to boiling. Reduce heat to simmering (bubbles
should begin to break the surface of the water). Break *one* of the
eggs into a measuring cup. Carefully slide egg into simmering water,
holding the lip of the cup as close to the water as possible. Repeat
with remaining eggs, allowing each egg an equal amount of space.
2. Simmer eggs, uncovered, for 3 to 5 minutes or till the whites are
completely set and yolks begin to thicken but are not hard. Remove
eggs with a slotted spoon. Season to taste with salt and pepper.
■ **Poaching pan directions:** Grease each cup of an egg-poaching
pan with oil or shortening. Place poacher cups over the pan of boiling water (water should not touch bottoms of cups). Reduce heat to
simmering. Break *one* of the eggs into a measuring cup. Carefully
slide egg into a poacher cup. Repeat with remaining eggs. Cover and
cook for 4 to 6 minutes or till the whites are completely set and
yolks begin to thicken but are not hard. Run a knife around edges to
loosen eggs. Invert poacher cups to remove eggs.

Nutrition Facts per egg: 77 cal., 5 g total fat (2 g sat. fat), 213 mg chol., 62 mg sodium, 1
g carbo., 0 g fiber, 6 g pro. **Daily Values:** 8% vit. A, 0% vit. C, 2% calcium, 4% iron

USING EGGS SAFELY

Great egg dishes depend on eggs that are in top condition.
Here are some egg-handling pointers to remember.

■ Select clean, fresh eggs from refrigerated display cases.
Don't use dirty, cracked, or leaking eggs. They may have
become contaminated with harmful bacteria.

■ When you come home from the grocery store, promptly
refrigerate the eggs with the large ends up. Store them in their
cartons because eggs easily absorb refrigerator odors. Fresh
eggs can be refrigerated for up to 5 weeks after the packing
date (a number stamped on the carton from 1 to 365, with 1
representing January 1 and 365 representing December 31).

■ To store raw egg whites, refrigerate them in a tightly
covered container for up to 4 days. Refrigerate raw yolks
covered with water in a tightly covered container for up to 2
days. Refrigerate hard-cooked eggs in their shells for up to 7
days.

■ When cracking eggs, avoid getting any eggshells in with
the raw eggs. Also, when separating eggs, don't pass the yolk
from shell half to shell half. Instead, use an egg separator so
if bacteria are present on the shell, they won't contaminate
either the yolk or the white.

■ Be sure to wash your hands, utensils, and countertop after
working with eggs.

■ Serve hot egg dishes as soon as they're cooked. Refrigerate
cold egg dishes immediately. Chill leftovers promptly and
reheat thoroughly before serving.

■ Eating uncooked or slightly cooked eggs may be harmful
because of possible bacterial contamination. The individuals
most susceptible include the elderly, infants, pregnant
women, and those who are already ill. Check with your
doctor to see if you are at risk. If you are, you probably
should avoid eating foods that contain raw or partially cooked
eggs. Healthy people should eat raw eggs with discretion.

■ For more information on handling eggs safely, call the U.S.
Department of Agriculture Meat and Poultry Hotline at
800/535-4555.

CREAMY POACHED EGGS

START TO FINISH: 20 MINUTES

Fast

Poached in a rich cheese sauce and served on toasted English muffins, these eggs make an extra-special breakfast that is quick enough to fix any day of the week.

³/₄ cup shredded American cheese (3 ounces)
  1 3-ounce package cream cheese with chives, cut up
¹/₂ cup milk
¹/₈ teaspoon pepper
  4 eggs
  2 English muffins or bagels, split and toasted

1. In a medium skillet combine American cheese, cream cheese, milk, and pepper. Cook and stir over medium heat till the cheeses melt. Remove from heat.
2. Break *one* of the eggs into a measuring cup. Carefully slide egg into cheese mixture. Repeat with remaining eggs. Cover and cook over medium-low heat for 3 to 5 minutes or till the whites are completely set and yolks begin to thicken but are not hard.
3. Top each muffin or bagel half with a cooked egg. Stir cheese mixture with a wire whisk; spoon over eggs. Makes 4 servings.

Nutrition Facts per serving: 312 cal., 20 g total fat (11 g sat. fat), 259 mg chol., 579 mg sodium, 16 g carbo., 0 g fiber, 16 g pro. **Daily Values:** 28% vit. A, 0% vit. C, 21% calcium, 12% iron

EGGS BENEDICT

START TO FINISH: 35 MINUTES

Delmonico's restaurant in Manhattan is credited with creating this famous dish when regular patrons Mr. and Mrs. LeGrand Benedict requested something new for lunch.

  4 eggs
  1 recipe Hollandaise Sauce (see page 959)
  2 English muffins, split
  4 slices Canadian-style bacon
    Paprika

1. Lightly grease a medium skillet. Add water to half-fill the skillet. Bring water to boiling. Reduce heat to simmering (bubbles should begin to break the surface of the water). Break *one* of the eggs into a measuring cup. Carefully slide egg into simmering water, holding the lip of the cup as close to the water as possible. Repeat with remaining eggs, allowing each egg an equal amount of space.

2. Simmer eggs, uncovered, for 3 to 5 minutes or till the whites are completely set and yolks begin to thicken but are not hard. Remove poached eggs with a slotted spoon and place them in a large pan of warm water to keep them warm. Prepare the Hollandaise Sauce.

3. Meanwhile, place muffin halves, cut sides up, on a baking sheet. Broil 3 to 4 inches from the heat about 1 minute or till toasted. Top each muffin half with a slice of Canadian-style bacon; broil about 1 minute more or till meat is heated.

4. To serve, top each bacon-topped muffin half with an egg; spoon Hollandaise Sauce over eggs. Sprinkle with paprika. Makes 4 servings.

Nutrition Facts per serving: 434 cal., 34 g total fat (8 g sat. fat), 386 mg chol., 829 mg sodium, 15 g carbo., 0 g fiber, 16 g pro. **Daily Values:** 61% vit. A, 11% vit. C, 8% calcium, 13% iron

■ **Crab Benedict:** Prepare as above, except substitute one 6½-ounce can *crabmeat*, drained, flaked, and cartilage removed, for the Canadian-style bacon.

Nutrition Facts per serving: 437 cal., 33 g total fat (7 g sat. fat)

■ **Deluxe Eggs Benedict:** Prepare as above, except cook 1 medium *red or green sweet pepper*, seeded and sliced into rings, and 1 small *onion*, sliced and separated into rings, in 1 tablespoon melted *margarine or butter* till crisp-tender. After broiling bacon-topped English muffin halves, top with cooked vegetable mixture. Serve as directed.

Nutrition Facts per serving: 472 cal., 37 g total fat (8 g sat. fat)

■ **Make-ahead directions:** Prepare eggs and toast English muffins as above. Place muffin halves in an 8×8×2-inch baking pan. Top each muffin half with a slice of Canadian-style bacon and 1 egg. Cover and chill for up to 24 hours. To serve, prepare *Mock Hollandaise Sauce* (see page 960); spoon sauce over eggs. Bake, covered, in a 350° oven about 20 minutes or till heated through.

Nutrition Facts per serving: 335 cal., 22 g total fat (6 g sat. fat)

HUEVOS RANCHEROS

START TO FINISH: 25 MINUTES   Oven 350°

Fast

Huevos Rancheros (WEH-vohs ran-CHER-ohs) aren't only for breakfast. Try serving this dish with refried beans and a tossed salad for a great lunch or supper.

  $^1/_2$ cup chopped onion (1 medium)
   1 tablespoon cooking oil
   1 16-ounce can tomatoes, cut up
   2 tablespoons canned diced green chili peppers, rinsed
   1 teaspoon chili powder
  $^1/_8$ teaspoon garlic powder
   3 6-inch corn tortillas
   1 teaspoon cooking oil
   6 eggs
  $^3/_4$ cup shredded Monterey Jack cheese or American cheese (3 ounces)
      Bottled hot pepper sauce

1. In a large skillet cook chopped onion in the 1 tablespoon oil till tender. Stir in *undrained* tomatoes, chili peppers, chili powder, and garlic powder. Bring to boiling; reduce heat. Simmer, uncovered, for 5 to 10 minutes or till slightly thickened.

2. Meanwhile, place tortillas on a baking sheet; brush lightly with the 1 teaspoon oil. Bake in a 350° oven about 10 minutes or till crisp. Break *one* of the eggs into a measuring cup. Carefully slide egg into simmering tomato mixture. Repeat with remaining eggs. Simmer gently, covered, for 3 to 5 minutes or till the whites are completely set and yolks begin to thicken but are not hard.

3. To serve, place each tortilla on a plate. Top each tortilla with 2 eggs; spoon tomato mixture over eggs. Sprinkle with cheese. Pass hot pepper sauce. Makes 3 servings.

Nutrition Facts per serving: 412 cal., 26 g total fat (10 g sat. fat), 449 mg chol., 729 mg sodium, 24 g carbo., 2 g fiber, 23 g pro. **Daily Values:** 39% vit. A, 67% vit. C, 29% calcium, 21% iron

Eggs & Cheese *465*

SOFT-COOKED EGGS

START TO FINISH: 10 MINUTES

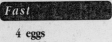

Fast

     4 eggs
     Cold water

1. Place eggs in a single layer in a medium saucepan. Add enough cold water to come 1 inch above the eggs. Bring to boiling over high heat. Reduce heat so water is just below simmering. Cover and cook for 4 to 6 minutes; drain.
2. Fill the saucepan with cold water and let stand just till the eggs are cool enough to handle. Cut off tops and serve in egg cups. Or, cut the eggs in half and use a spoon to scoop the eggs into serving dishes. Makes 4 soft-cooked eggs.

Nutrition Facts per egg: 77 cal., 5 g total fat (2 g sat. fat), 213 mg chol., 62 mg sodium, 1 g carbo., 0 g fiber, 6 g pro. **Daily Values:** 8% vit. A, 0% vit. C, 2% calcium, 4% iron

HARD-COOKED EGGS

START TO FINISH: 25 MINUTES

Fast

Sometimes hard-cooked eggs have an unattractive but harmless greenish ring around the yolk. To minimize the chances of a ring forming, time the cooking carefully. Also, cool the hard-cooked eggs in ice water.

     4 eggs
     Cold water

1. Place eggs in a single layer in a medium saucepan. Add enough cold water to come 1 inch above the eggs. Bring to boiling over high heat. Reduce heat so water is just below simmering. Cover and cook for 15 minutes; drain.
2. Run cold water over the eggs or place them in ice water till cool enough to handle; drain.
3. To peel eggs, gently tap each egg on the countertop. Roll the egg between the palms of your hands. Peel off eggshell, starting at the large end. Makes 4 hard-cooked eggs.

Nutrition Facts per egg: 77 cal., 5 g total fat (2 g sat. fat), 213 mg chol., 62 mg sodium, 1 g carbo., 0 g fiber, 6 g pro. **Daily Values:** 8% vit. A, 0% vit. C, 2% calcium, 4% iron

---

FRIED EGGS

START TO FINISH: 10 MINUTES

Fast

This simple method produces an egg similar to one cooked over-easy, but you don't need to flip it and you use less fat.

    2 **teaspoons margarine, butter, or nonstick spray coating**
    4 **eggs**
    1 **to 2 teaspoons water**

1. In a large skillet melt margarine or butter over medium heat. (Or, spray a cold skillet with nonstick coating before heating.) Break eggs into skillet. When whites are set, add water. Cover skillet and cook eggs for 3 to 4 minutes or till yolks begin to thicken but are not hard. Makes 4 fried eggs.

Nutrition Facts per egg: 92 cal., 7 g total fat (2 g sat. fat), 213 mg chol., 85 mg sodium, 1 g carbo., 0 g fiber, 6 g pro. **Daily Values:** 11% vit. A, 0% vit. C, 2% calcium, 4% iron

---

DEVILED EGGS

START TO FINISH: 35 MINUTES

    6 **Hard-Cooked Eggs (see page 466)**
   1/4 **cup mayonnaise or salad dressing**
    1 **teaspoon prepared mustard**
    1 **teaspoon vinegar**
     Paprika or parsley sprigs (optional)

1. Halve hard-cooked eggs lengthwise and remove yolks. Place yolks in a bowl; mash with a fork. Add mayonnaise, mustard, and vinegar; mix well. If desired, season with salt and pepper. Stuff egg-white halves with yolk mixture. If desired, garnish with paprika or parsley. Makes 12 servings.

Nutrition Facts per serving: 72 cal., 6 g total fat (1 g sat. fat), 109 mg chol., 63 mg sodium, 0 g carbo., 0 g fiber, 3 g pro. **Daily Values:** 4% vit. A, 0% vit. C, 1% calcium, 2% iron

■ **Italian-Style Deviled Eggs:** Prepare as above, except omit mayonnaise or salad dressing, mustard, and vinegar. Add ¼ cup *creamy Italian salad dressing* and 2 tablespoons grated *Parmesan cheese* to mashed yolks; mix well.

Nutrition Facts per serving: 66 cal., 5 g total fat (1 g sat. fat)

BAKED EGGS

PREP: 10 MINUTES BAKE: 25 MINUTES   Oven 325°

Baked eggs sometimes are referred to as shirred (SHERD) eggs.

   Margarine or butter
6 **eggs**
   Snipped fresh chives or desired herb
6 **tablespoons shredded cheddar, Swiss, or Monterey Jack cheese
   (optional)**

1. Generously grease three 10-ounce casseroles with margarine. Carefully break 2 eggs into each casserole; sprinkle with chives or desired herb, salt, and pepper. Set casseroles in a 13x9x2-inch baking pan; place on an oven rack. Pour hot water around casseroles in pan to a depth of 1 inch.
2. Bake in a 325° oven about 25 minutes or till the eggs are firm and the whites are opaque. (If desired, after 20 minutes of baking, sprinkle shredded cheese atop eggs; bake for 5 to 10 minutes more or till eggs are cooked and cheese melts.) Makes 3 servings.

Nutrition Facts per serving: 161 cal., 11 g total fat (3 g sat. fat), 426 mg chol., 186 mg sodium, 1 g carbo., 0 g fiber, 13 g pro. **Daily Values:** 21% vit. A, 1% vit. C, 4% calcium, 9% iron

---

SCRAMBLED EGGS AND NEW POTATOES

START TO FINISH: 30 MINUTES

Fast

Instead of chopping your own potatoes, use 2 cups loose-pack frozen hash browns in this hearty dish.

   2 **cups coarsely chopped tiny new potatoes or russet potatoes**
 ½ **cup chopped onion (1 medium)**

$^1/_2$ cup chopped green or red sweet pepper
2 tablespoons margarine or butter
6 eggs
$^1/_4$ cup milk
$^1/_4$ teaspoon pepper
$^1/_8$ teaspoon salt
1 cup diced fully cooked ham or Polish sausage
$^1/_2$ cup shredded cheddar cheese (2 ounces)

1. In a large nonstick or well-seasoned skillet, cook and stir the potatoes, onion, and sweet pepper, covered, in hot margarine or butter over medium-low heat for 10 to 15 minutes or till tender, stirring occasionally.

2. Meanwhile, beat together eggs, milk, pepper, and salt; stir in ham or Polish sausage. Pour egg mixture over potato mixture. Cook, without stirring, till mixture begins to set on the bottom and around edge. Using a spatula or a large spoon, lift and fold the partially cooked egg mixture so the uncooked portion flows underneath. Continue cooking about 4 minutes more or till eggs are cooked through, but are still glossy and moist.

3. Remove from heat; sprinkle with cheese. Cover; let stand 1 minute or till cheese melts. Serves 4.

Nutrition Facts per serving: 360 cal., 20 g total fat (7 g sat. fat), 354 mg chol., 751 mg sodium, 21 g carbo., 1 g fiber, 23 g pro. **Daily Values:** 27% vit. A, 41% vit. C, 14% calcium, 19% iron

SCRAMBLED EGGS

START TO FINISH: 10 MINUTES

Fast

6 eggs
$^1/_3$ cup milk, half-and-half, or light cream
$^1/_4$ teaspoon salt
Dash pepper
1 tablespoon margarine or butter

1. In a mixing bowl beat together eggs; milk, half-and-half, or light cream; salt; and pepper. In a large skillet melt margarine or butter over medium heat; pour in egg mixture. Cook over medium heat, without stirring, till mixture begins to set on the bottom and around edge.

2. Using a spatula or a large spoon, lift and fold the partially cooked eggs so the uncooked portion flows underneath. Continue cooking over medium heat for 2 to 3 minutes or till eggs are cooked through, but are still glossy and moist. Remove from heat immediately. Makes 3 servings.

Nutrition Facts per serving: 198 cal., 14 g total fat (4 g sat. fat), 428 mg chol., 362 mg sodium, 3 g carbo., 0 g fiber, 13 g pro. **Daily Values:** 25% vit. A, 0% vit. C, 7% calcium, 9% iron

■ **Cheese-and-Onion Scrambled Eggs:** Prepare as above, except cook 1 *green onion,* sliced, in the margarine or butter for 30 seconds; add egg mixture. Add ¹/₂ cup shredded *American cheese* (2 ounces) after eggs begin to set.

Nutrition Facts per serving: 253 cal., 18 g total fat (7 g sat. fat)

■ **Mushroom Scrambled Eggs:** Prepare as above, except increase the margarine or butter to 2 tablespoons. Cook ¹/₂ cup sliced *fresh mushrooms* and 1 tablespoon chopped *onion* in the margarine. Add 1 tablespoon snipped *fresh parsley,* ¹/₂ teaspoon *dry mustard,* and ¹/₄ teaspoon *Worcestershire sauce* to beaten egg mixture.

Nutrition Facts per serving: 237 cal., 18 g total fat (5 g sat. fat)

■ **Denver Scrambled Eggs:** Prepare as above, except omit salt and increase margarine to 2 tablespoons. In the skillet cook ¹/₃ cup diced *fully cooked ham;* ¹/₄ cup chopped *onion;* one 2-ounce can *mushroom stems and pieces,* drained; and 2 tablespoons finely chopped *green sweet pepper* in the margarine; add egg mixture.

Nutrition Facts per serving: 266 cal., 19 g total fat (5 g sat. fat)

■ **Low-Fat Scrambled Eggs:** Prepare as above, except replace the 6 whole eggs with 3 whole eggs and 5 *egg whites.* Substitute *skim milk* for the milk, half-and-half, or light cream. Omit the margarine or butter and spray a nonstick skillet with *nonstick spray coating* before cooking the eggs.

Nutrition Facts per serving: 147 cal., 9 g total fat (2 g sat. fat) 213 mg chol.

SCRAMBLED EGG PIZZA

Low-Fat

To give the pizza crust a decorative look, before baking make little cuts around the edge of the crust with kitchen scissors.

1   16-ounce loaf frozen whole wheat bread dough, thawed
1   cup chopped zucchini or green sweet pepper
1   cup sliced fresh mushrooms
$^1/_4$ teaspoon crushed red pepper
1   tablespoon cooking oil
8   eggs
$^1/_2$ cup milk
1   tablespoon margarine or butter
$^3/_4$ cup shredded mozzarella cheese (3 ounces)
2   strips bacon, crisp-cooked, drained, and crumbled

1. On a lightly floured surface, roll bread dough into a 14-inch circle. Transfer dough to a greased 13-inch pizza pan. Build up edges slightly. Prick dough generously with a fork. Bake in a 375° oven for 15 to 20 minutes or till light brown.

2. Meanwhile, in a large skillet cook zucchini or green sweet pepper, mushrooms, and crushed red pepper in hot oil about 5 minutes or till vegetables are almost tender. Remove vegetables and drain.

3. In a large bowl beat together eggs and milk. In the same skillet melt margarine or butter over medium heat; pour in egg mixture. Cook, without stirring, till mixture begins to set on the bottom and around edge.

4. Using a spatula or a large spoon, lift and fold partially cooked eggs so uncooked portion flows underneath. Continue cooking over medium heat for 2 to 3 minutes or till eggs are cooked through, but are still glossy and moist. Remove from heat.

5. Sprinkle *half* of the shredded cheese over the hot crust. Top with scrambled eggs, zucchini mixture, bacon, and remaining cheese. Bake for 5 to 8 minutes more or till cheese melts. Serves 10.

Nutrition Facts per serving: 238 cal., 11 g total fat (3 g sat. fat), 177 mg chol., 383 mg sodium, 24 g carbo., 2 g fiber, 14 g pro. **Daily Values:** 11% vit. A, 2% vit. C, 7% calcium, 6% iron

BREAKFAST CASSEROLE

PREP: 25 MINUTES BAKE: 20 MINUTES   Oven 375°

You can make the filling for this brunch dish up to 2 days ahead and store it in the refrigerator.

 2 packages (16) refrigerated crescent rolls
 1 cup shredded Swiss or mozzarella cheese (4 ounces)
 ½ cup chopped onion (1 medium)
 ¼ cup margarine or butter
 ⅓ cup all-purpose flour
 ¼ teaspoon dried thyme, crushed
 ¼ teaspoon pepper
 1 cup chicken broth
 ¾ cup milk
 2 cups chopped fully cooked ham
 1½ cups loose-pack frozen hash brown potatoes with onions and peppers, thawed
 5 Hard-Cooked Eggs, chopped (see page 466)
 2 tablespoons milk
 1 tablespoon sesame seed

1. For crust, separate *one* package of rolls into long rectangles. Press over the bottom and ½ inch up the sides of a 13×9×2-inch baking dish. Bake in a 375° oven for 8 to 12 minutes or till golden brown. Sprinkle cheese atop baked crust.

2. Meanwhile, for filling, cook onion in margarine or butter till tender but not brown. Stir in flour, thyme, and pepper. Add broth and ¾ cup milk all at once. Cook and stir over medium heat till thickened and bubbly. Stir in ham, potatoes, and hard-cooked eggs; heat through. Pour filling over crust.

3. Separate remaining package of crescent rolls into 8 triangles. Cover filling with triangles; brush with 2 tablespoons milk and sprinkle with sesame seed. Bake at 375° for 20 to 25 minutes more or till crust is golden brown. Makes 10 servings.

Nutrition Facts per serving: 385 cal., 24 g total fat (7 g sat. fat), 133 mg chol., 912 mg sodium, 27 g carbo., 1 g fiber, 18 g pro. **Daily Values:** 14% vit. A, 12% vit. C, 13% calcium, 11% iron

FRENCH OMELET

Fast

Make as many omelets as you need. Cover each omelet with foil to keep it warm while preparing the additional omelets.

2 eggs
1 tablespoon water
$^1/_8$ teaspoon salt
Nonstick spray coating

1. In a bowl combine eggs, water, salt, and dash *pepper*. Using a fork, beat till combined but not frothy. Spray a cold 8- or 10-inch nonstick skillet with flared sides with nonstick coating.

2. Add egg mixture to skillet; cook over medium heat. As eggs set, run a spatula around the edge of the skillet, lifting eggs so uncooked portion flows underneath. When eggs are set but still shiny, remove from the heat. Fold omelet in half. Transfer to a warm plate. Serves 1.

Nutrition Facts per serving: 152 cal., 11 g total fat (3 g sat. fat), 426 mg chol., 393 mg sodium, 1 g carbo., 0 g fiber, 13 g pro.
Daily Values: 19% vit. A, 0% vit. C, 4% calcium, 9% iron

■ **Low-Fat Omelet:** Prepare as above, except use 1 whole egg and 2 egg whites.

Nutrition Facts per serving: 111 cal., 6 g total fat (2 g sat. fat) 213 mg chol.

■ **Mushroom Omelet:** Prepare as above, except for filling, cook $^1/_3$ cup sliced *fresh mushrooms* in

EGG SUBSTITUTES

Refrigerated or frozen egg substitutes are easy to use, readily available, and enable anyone on a cholesterol-restricted diet to enjoy great-tasting egg dishes. These products are based mostly on egg whites and contain less fat than whole eggs and no cholesterol. Use $^1/_4$ cup of either the refrigerated or frozen egg product for each whole egg in scrambled egg dishes, omelets, quiches, and stratas. To replace hard-cooked eggs in salads and other recipes, cook the egg product as you would cook an omelet and cut it up.

1 tablespoon *margarine or butter* till tender. Spoon filling across center of omelet. Fold sides over.

Nutrition Facts per serving: 261 cal., 23 g total fat (5 g sat. fat)

■ **Cheese Omelet:** Prepare as above, except omit salt. For filling, sprinkle ¼ cup shredded *cheddar, Swiss, or Monterey Jack cheese* across center of omelet. Fold sides over.

Nutrition Facts per serving: 266 cal., 20 g total fat (9 g sat. fat)

■ **Fruit Omelet:** Prepare as above, except, for filling, spread 2 table-spoons *dairy sour cream or yogurt* across center of omelet. Fold sides over. Top with ¼ cup *halved strawberries; sliced, peeled peaches; or blueberries*. Sprinkle with 1 tablespoon *brown sugar*.

Nutrition Facts per serving: 267 cal., 17 g total fat (7 g sat. fat)

PUFFY OMELET

START TO FINISH: 30 MINUTES   Oven 325°

Fast

Puffy omelets are cooked on the range top until they puff and are set on the bottom. Then they're transferred to the oven until they brown and are set on the top. Fill them with a combination of shredded cheese, strips of ham or chicken, and cooked vegetables.

  4 egg whites
  2 tablespoons water
  4 beaten egg yolks
  ¼ teaspoon pepper (optional)
  ⅛ teaspoon salt
  1 tablespoon margarine or butter

1. In a bowl beat egg whites till frothy. Add water; continue beating about 1½ minutes or till stiff peaks form (tips stand straight). Fold egg yolks, pepper (if desired), and salt into egg whites.
2. In a 10-inch ovenproof skillet heat margarine or butter till a drop of water sizzles. Pour in egg mixture, mounding it slightly at the sides. Cook over low heat for 8 to 10 minutes or till puffed, set, and golden brown on the bottom. Bake in a 325° oven for 8 to 10 min-utes or till a knife inserted near the center comes out clean.

3. Loosen sides of omelet with a metal spatula. Make a shallow cut slightly off-center across the omelet. Fold smaller side of omelet over the larger side. Makes 2 servings.

Nutrition Facts per serving: 203 cal., 16 g total fat (4 g sat. fat), 426 mg chol., 324 mg sodium, 1 g carbo., 0 g fiber, 13 g pro. **Daily Values:** 71% vit. A, 0% vit. C, 4% calcium, 8% iron

■ **Puffy Omelet with Ham-and-Cheese Sauce:** Prepare as above, except while omelet is baking, melt 1 tablespoon *margarine or butter* in a saucepan. Stir in 1 tablespoon *all-purpose flour;* add ²/₃ cup *milk* all at once. Cook and stir till thickened and bubbly. Cook and stir 1 minute more. Stir in ¹/₃ cup shredded *cheddar or Swiss cheese* till melted. Stir in ¹/₄ cup diced *fully cooked ham* and one 2-ounce jar sliced *mushrooms,* drained. Heat through. Pour over folded omelet.

Nutrition Facts per serving: 425 cal., 31 g total fat (11 g sat. fat)

DENVER OMELET

START TO FINISH: 35 MINUTES   Oven 325°

The classic Denver omelet is filled with chopped ham, mushrooms, onion, and green sweet pepper.

  1 recipe Puffy Omelet (see page 474)
  1 tablespoon margarine or butter
  1 cup sliced fresh mushrooms
 ³/₄ cup chopped green sweet pepper
  4 green onions, bias sliced
 ¹/₄ teaspoon dried basil, crushed
 ¹/₂ cup fully cooked ham, cut into julienne strips
 ¹/₂ cup cherry tomatoes, quartered

1. Prepare Puffy Omelet as directed. While omelet is baking, prepare filling.
2. For filling, in a skillet melt margarine or butter; add mushrooms, sweet pepper, green onions, and basil. Cook and stir till tender but not brown. Stir in ham and cherry tomatoes; heat through.
3. Spoon filling over omelet; fold. Makes 3 servings.

Nutrition Facts per serving: 233 cal., 16 g total fat (4 g sat. fat), 296 mg chol., 547 mg sodium, 8 g carbo., 1 g fiber, 15 g pro. **Daily Values:** 59% vit. A, 58% vit. C, 4% calcium, 16% iron

OVEN OMELET

Fast

*Try cooked, sliced mushrooms and ham strips as an
alternate filling to the cheese.*

    Nonstick spray coating
12 **eggs**
$1/4$ **cup water**
$1/2$ **teaspoon salt**
$1/8$ **teaspoon pepper**
 1 **cup shredded cheddar, Monterey Jack, or colby cheese (4
    ounces)**

1. Spray a 15×10×1-inch baking pan with nonstick coating; set aside.
2. In a mixing bowl combine eggs, water, salt, and pepper. Using a
fork or a rotary beater, beat till combined but not frothy.
3. Place the prepared pan on oven rack. Carefully pour the egg mixture into the pan. Bake in a 400° oven about 7 minutes or till eggs
are set but still have a glossy surface.
4. Cut the omelet into 6 squares measuring 5×5 inches. Remove
each omelet square using a large spatula. Invert omelet squares onto
warm serving plates. Spoon some shredded cheese on half of each
omelet; fold other half over filling, forming a triangle or a rectangle.
Makes 6 servings.

Nutrition Facts per serving: 226 cal., 16 g total fat (7 g sat. fat), 446 mg chol., 421 mg
sodium, 1 g carbo., 0 g fiber, 17 g pro. **Daily Values:** 25% vit. A, 0% vit. C, 15% calcium,
10% iron

FRITTATA

Fast

A frittata is an Italian egg dish that resembles an omelet. It is cooked on top of the stove until set but still moist, and then placed under the broiler to finish cooking.

　6　**eggs**
　$1/8$　**teaspoon pepper**
　$1/4$　**cup chopped onion**
　1　**clove garlic, minced**
　1　**tablespoon margarine or butter**
　$3/4$　**cup chopped cooked vegetables or meat**
　2　**tablespoons grated Parmesan or Romano cheese**

1. Beat eggs and pepper; set aside. In a 10-inch broilerproof skillet cook onion and garlic in margarine till tender. Stir in vegetables or meat.

2. Pour egg mixture into skillet over vegetables or meat. Cook over medium heat. As mixture sets, run a spatula around edge of skillet, lifting egg mixture so the uncooked portion flows underneath. Continue cooking and lifting edges till the egg mixture is almost set (surface will be moist).

3. Place broilerproof skillet under the broiler 4 to 5 inches from the heat. Broil for 1 to 2 minutes or till top is just set. Sprinkle with cheese. Cut into wedges. Makes 3 servings.

■ **Oven Frittata:** Prepare as above, except use an ovenproof skillet. Pour egg mixture into the skillet. Bake in a 350° oven about 15 minutes or till a knife inserted near the center comes out clean.

Nutrition Facts per serving: 233 cal., 15 g total fat (5 g sat. fat), 429 mg chol., 262 mg sodium, 8 g carbo., 0 g fiber, 16 g pro. **Daily Values:** 40% vit. A, 3% vit. C, 10% calcium, 12% iron

CORN FRITTATA WITH CHEESE

START TO FINISH: 25 MINUTES

Fast

8 eggs
1 tablespoon snipped fresh basil or 1 teaspoon dried basil,
    crushed
2 tablespoons olive oil
1 cup frozen whole kernel corn or cut fresh corn
$^1/_2$ cup chopped zucchini
$^1/_3$ cup thinly sliced green onions (3)
$^3/_4$ cup chopped plum tomatoes
$^1/_2$ cup shredded cheddar cheese

1. Beat eggs and basil; set aside. In a 10-inch broilerproof skillet
heat oil. Add corn, zucchini, and onions. Cook and stir for 3 minutes. Add tomatoes. Reduce heat; simmer, uncovered, 5 minutes or
till vegetables are crisp-tender, stirring occasionally.
2. Pour egg mixture into skillet over vegetables. Cook over medium
heat. As mixture sets, run a spatula around edge of skillet, lifting egg
mixture so uncooked portion flows underneath. Continue cooking
and lifting edges till egg mixture is almost set (surface will be moist).
Sprinkle with cheese. Place broilerproof skillet under broiler 4 to 5
inches from heat. Broil 1 to 2 minutes or till top is just set. Makes 4
servings.

Nutrition Facts per serving: 314 cal., 22 g total fat (7 g sat. fat), 441 mg chol., 221 mg
sodium, 13 g carbo., 1 g fiber, 18 g pro. **Daily Values:** 29% vit. A, 23% vit. C, 13%
calcium, 14% iron

QUICHE LORRAINE

PREP: 20 MINUTES BAKE: 35 MINUTES   Oven 450°

1 recipe Pastry for Single-Crust Pie (see page 808)
6 slices bacon
1 medium onion, sliced
3 beaten eggs
1$^1/_2$ cups milk
$^1/_4$ teaspoon salt
    Dash ground nutmeg

1¹/₂ **cups shredded Swiss cheese (6 ounces)**
1 **tablespoon all-purpose flour**

1. Prepare Pastry for Single-Crust Pie. Line the unpricked pastry shell with a double thickness of foil. Bake in a 450° oven for 8 minutes. Remove foil. Bake for 4 to 5 minutes more or till pastry is set and dry. Remove from oven. Reduce oven temperature to 325°.

2. Meanwhile, in a large skillet cook bacon till crisp. Drain, reserving *2 tablespoons* drippings. Crumble bacon; set aside. Cook sliced onion in reserved drippings till tender but not brown; drain.

3. In a medium mixing bowl stir together eggs, milk, salt, and nutmeg. Stir in the crumbled bacon and onion. Toss together shredded cheese and flour. Add to egg mixture; mix well.

4. Pour egg mixture into the hot, baked pastry shell. Bake in the 325° oven for 35 to 40 minutes or till a knife inserted near the center comes out clean. If necessary, cover edge of crust with foil to prevent overbrowning. Let stand 10 minutes before serving. Makes 6 servings.

Nutrition Facts per serving: 455 cal., 31 g total fat (12 g sat. fat), 146 mg chol., 416 mg sodium, 27 g carbo., 1 g fiber, 18 g pro. **Daily Values:** 15% vit. A, 7% vit. C, 30% calcium, 11% iron

---

SPINACH QUICHE

PREP: 25 MINUTES   BAKE: 45 MINUTES   Oven 450°

No time to make your own pastry? Use a folded, refrigerated, unbaked piecrust instead.

1 **recipe Pastry for Single-Crust Pie (see page 808)**
¹/₂ **cup chopped onion (1 medium)**
6 **slices bacon, chopped**
8 **eggs**
¹/₂ **cup dairy sour cream**
¹/₂ **cup half-and-half, light cream, or milk**
¹/₄ **teaspoon salt**
¹/₈ **teaspoon white pepper**
  Dash ground nutmeg (optional)
3 **cups lightly packed chopped fresh spinach**
²/₃ **cup shredded mozzarella cheese**
¹/₂ **cup shredded Swiss cheese**

1. Prepare Pastry for Single-Crust Pie. Line the unpricked pastry shell with a double thickness of foil. Bake in a 450° oven for 8 minutes. Remove foil. Bake for 4 to 5 minutes more or till pastry is set and dry. Remove from oven. Reduce oven temperature to 325°.

2. Meanwhile, in a large skillet cook onion and bacon till onion is tender and bacon is crisp. Drain on paper towels.

3. In a medium mixing bowl beat eggs slightly with a fork. Stir in sour cream; half-and-half, light cream, or milk; salt; pepper; and, if desired, nutmeg. Stir in onion mixture, spinach, mozzarella cheese, and Swiss cheese.

4. Pour egg mixture into the hot, baked pastry shell. Bake in the 325° oven about 45 minutes or till a knife inserted near the center comes out clean. If necessary, cover edge of crust with foil to prevent overbrowning. Let stand for 10 minutes before serving. Makes 6 to 8 servings.

Nutrition Facts per serving: 479 cal., 33 g total fat (13 g sat. fat), 323 mg chol., 490 mg sodium, 24 g carbo., 2 g fiber, 21 g pro. **Daily Values:** 43% vit. A, 18% vit. C, 25% calcium, 20% iron

---

VEGETARIAN QUICHE

PREP: 35 MINUTES BAKE: 35 MINUTES   Oven 450°

Two kinds of cheese plus half-and-half make this quiche rich and creamy.

   1 **recipe Pastry for Single-Crust Pie (see page 808)**
  1/2 **cup shredded Swiss cheese**
  1/2 **cup shredded cheddar cheese**
  1/2 **cup shredded carrot**
  1/3 **cup sliced green onions (3)**
   1 **tablespoon all-purpose flour**
   4 **slightly beaten eggs**
1 1/2 **cups half-and-half, light cream, or milk**
  1/4 **teaspoon salt**
  1/8 **teaspoon pepper**
  1/8 **teaspoon garlic powder**

1. Prepare Pastry for Single-Crust Pie. Line the unpricked pastry shell with a double thickness of foil. Bake in a 450° oven for 8 minutes. Remove foil. Bake for 4 to 5 minutes more or till pastry is set and dry. Remove from oven. Reduce oven temperature to 325°.

2. Toss together Swiss cheese, cheddar cheese, carrot, green onions, and flour. Sprinkle mixture over the bottom of the pastry shell.

3. In a medium mixing bowl stir together eggs, half-and-half, salt, pepper, and garlic powder.

4. Pour egg mixture into the hot, baked pastry shell. Bake in the 325° oven for 35 to 40 minutes or till a knife inserted near the center comes out clean. If necessary, cover edge of crust with foil to prevent overbrowning. Let stand for 10 minutes before serving. Makes 6 servings.

Nutrition Facts per serving: 400 cal., 27 g total fat (12 g sat. fat), 183 mg chol., 419 mg sodium, 26 g carbo., 1 g fiber, 13 g pro. **Daily Values:** 46% vit. A, 3% vit. C, 20% calcium, 12% iron

---

CRAB SOUFFLÉ ROLL

START TO FINISH: 1¼ HOURS   Oven 375°

    3 tablespoons margarine or butter
  ⅓ cup all-purpose flour
  ⅛ teaspoon pepper
 1⅓ cups milk
    4 beaten egg yolks
    4 egg whites
  ¼ teaspoon cream of tartar
    2 tablespoons margarine or butter
    1 tablespoon all-purpose flour
  ¾ cup half-and-half, light cream, or milk
    1 6½-ounce can crabmeat, drained, flaked, and cartilage
        removed (¾ cup)
  ¼ cup sliced green onions (2)
    1 tablespoon dry sherry (optional)
    1 cup shredded Swiss cheese (4 ounces)

1. Line a 15×10×1-inch baking pan with foil, extending foil 1 inch beyond edges of pan. Grease and lightly flour the foil. Set pan aside.

2. For soufflé roll, in a medium saucepan melt the 3 tablespoons margarine or butter. Stir in the ⅓ cup flour and pepper. Add milk all at once. Cook and stir till thickened and bubbly. Remove from heat. In a medium mixing bowl slowly stir thickened mixture into beaten egg yolks. Cool slightly.

3. In a large mixing bowl beat egg whites and cream of tartar with an electric mixer on medium to high speed till stiff peaks form (tips stand straight). Fold a little of the beaten egg whites into egg yolk mixture. Fold yolk mixture into remaining beaten egg whites. Spread in prepared pan.

4. Bake in a 375° oven about 15 minutes or till soufflé is puffed, slightly set, and a knife inserted near the center comes out clean.

5. Meanwhile, for the filling, in a small heavy saucepan melt the 2 tablespoons margarine or butter. Stir in the 1 tablespoon flour. Add the half-and-half, light cream, or milk all at once. Cook and stir till thickened and bubbly. Cook and stir 1 minute more. Stir in crab-meat, green onions, and, if desired, sherry. Set filling aside.

6. Line an extra-large baking sheet with foil. Generously grease the foil. Immediately loosen the baked soufflé from pan. Place the foil-lined baking sheet over soufflé, foil side down. Invert soufflé onto baking sheet. Carefully peel foil off the top of the soufflé.

7. Sprinkle shredded cheese over soufflé; spread filling over cheese. Use foil on the baking sheet to lift and help roll up soufflé, jelly-roll style, starting from one of the short sides.

8. Transfer the soufflé roll to an ovenproof serving platter. Return soufflé roll to the oven for 10 to 15 minutes or till heated through. Makes 8 servings.

■ **Make-ahead directions:** Prepare as above through step 7. Cover and chill the soufflé roll for up to 24 hours. Bake, covered, in a 375° oven for 40 minutes or till heated through.

Nutrition Facts per serving: 249 cal., 17 g total fat (7 g sat. fat), 151 mg chol., 258 mg sodium, 8 g carbo., 0 g fiber, 15 g pro. **Daily Values:** 34% vit. A, 3% vit. C, 20% calcium, 5% iron

■ **Ham or Turkey Soufflé Roll:** Prepare as above, except substitute ³/₄ cup chopped fully cooked *ham or smoked turkey* for the crab-meat. Do not use the dry sherry.

Nutrition Facts per serving: 245 cal., 18 g total fat (7 g sat. fat)

CHEESE SOUFFLÉ

PREP: 50 MINUTES BAKE: 40 MINUTES   Oven 350°

Using a combination of the cheeses listed below makes this light and airy soufflé taste even better.

   4 egg yolks
   4 egg whites

¹/₄ cup margarine or butter
¹/₄ cup all-purpose flour
¹/₄ teaspoon dry mustard
    Dash ground red pepper
  1 cup milk
  2 cups shredded cheddar,
    colby, creamy Havarti,
    or process Swiss cheese
    (8 ounces)

1. Allow the egg yolks and egg whites to stand at room temperature for 30 minutes.

2. For cheese sauce, in a medium saucepan melt margarine or butter; stir in flour, mustard, and red pepper. Add milk all at once. Cook and stir over medium heat till thickened and bubbly. Remove from heat. Add cheese, a little at a time, stirring till melted. In a medium mixing bowl beat egg yolks with a fork till combined. Slowly add cheese sauce to egg yolks, stirring constantly. Cool slightly.

3. In a large mixing bowl beat egg whites with an electric mixer on medium to high speed till stiff peaks form (tips stand straight). Gently fold about *1 cup* of the stiffly beaten egg whites into cheese sauce.

4. Gradually pour cheese sauce over remaining stiffly beaten egg whites, folding to combine. Pour into an ungreased 1¹/₂-quart soufflé dish.

5. Bake in a 350° oven about 40 minutes or till a knife inserted near center comes out clean. Serve immediately (see tip, above). Makes 4 servings.

Nutrition Facts per serving: 463 cal., 37 g total fat (16 g sat. fat), 277 mg chol., 578 mg sodium, 10 g carbo., 0 g fiber, 23 g pro. **Daily Values:** 68% vit. A, 1% vit. C, 42% calcium, 9% iron

SERVING A SOUFFLÉ

A soufflé makes a great entrée when you're entertaining because it bakes for almost an hour, giving you time to socialize. Just make the salad and side dishes ahead, then pop the soufflé into the oven when your guests arrive. Just before the soufflé finishes baking, gather everyone around the table and wait for the oohs and ahhs.

To serve your soufflé, insert two forks back to back, and gently pull the soufflé apart. Cut into serving-size wedges in this manner. Use a large serving spoon to transfer the portions to individual plates.

CHEESY BRUNCH ROLL-UPS

PREP: 25 MINUTES   BAKE: 35 MINUTES   Oven 350°

 2 cups sliced fresh mushrooms
 $^1/_2$ cup sliced green onions (4)
 $^1/_2$ cup chopped green sweet pepper
 2 tablespoons margarine or butter
 8 7-inch flour tortillas
 $1^1/_2$ cups shredded cheddar cheese (6 ounces)
 4 beaten eggs
 2 cups milk
 1 tablespoon all-purpose flour
 $^1/_4$ teaspoon garlic powder
 Few drops bottled hot pepper sauce
 $^1/_2$ cup shredded cheddar cheese (2 ounces)

1. In a saucepan cook mushrooms, green onions, and sweet pepper in margarine or butter till tender; drain. Divide mixture evenly; spoon along center of each tortilla. Divide the $1^1/_2$ cups cheese evenly among tortillas. Roll up tortillas. Place seam sides down in a greased 2-quart rectangular baking dish. In a bowl combine eggs, milk, flour, garlic powder, and hot pepper sauce; pour over rolled-up tortillas.

2. Bake in a 350° oven for 35 to 40 minutes or till set. Sprinkle the $^1/_2$ cup cheese over the top. Let stand for 10 minutes; cut into 6 squares. Serves 6.

■ **Make-ahead directions:** Prepare as above, except do not bake. Cover and refrigerate for 2 to 24 hours. Bake, uncovered, in a 350° oven for 45 to 50 minutes or till set.

Nutrition Facts per serving: 442 cal., 25 g total fat (11 g sat. fat), 188 mg chol., 585 mg sodium, 34 g carbo., 0 g fiber, 21 g pro. **Daily Values:** 30% vit A, 13% vit C, 37% calcium, 19% iron

WELSH RABBIT

START TO FINISH: 25 MINUTES

Fast

British in origin, this sandwich known for its tangy cheese sauce often is labeled rarebit. When served with a poached egg, it may be called a golden buck. Try the sauce served over broccoli, cauliflower, or burgers, too.

  2 **English muffins, split and toasted, or 4 slices bread, toasted**
  4 **slices Canadian-style bacon, warmed, or 4 Poached Eggs (see page 461)**
  4 **slices tomato**
1¹/₂ **cups shredded cheddar or American cheese (6 ounces)**
 ³/₄ **cup regular or nonalcoholic beer or milk**
  1 **teaspoon dry mustard**
 ¹/₂ **teaspoon Worcestershire sauce**
    Dash ground red pepper
  1 **beaten egg**

1. Place an English muffin half or slice of toast on 4 plates. Top each with a slice of Canadian-style bacon and a tomato slice. (Or, if using poached eggs, top muffins or toast with tomato slices, then eggs.) Set aside.

2. For cheese sauce, in a heavy medium saucepan stir together the cheese, beer or milk, mustard, Worcestershire sauce, and red pepper. Cook over low heat, stirring constantly, till cheese melts. Slowly stir about *half* of the hot cheese sauce into beaten egg; return entire mixture to the saucepan. Cook and stir over low heat till cheese sauce thickens slightly and just bubbles.

3. To serve, spoon cheese sauce over muffin or toast stacks. Makes 4 servings.

Nutrition Facts per serving: 296 cal., 18 g total fat (10 g sat. fat), 112 mg chol., 753 mg sodium, 11 g carbo., 1 g fiber, 20 g pro. **Daily Values:** 17% vit. A, 16% vit. C, 28% calcium, 8% iron

CHILI RELLENOS CASSEROLE

PREP: 20 MINUTES BAKE: 15 MINUTES   Oven 450°

Poblano peppers are either red or dark green in color and vary in strength from medium to hot. The red peppers are slightly sweeter than the green ones.

2 large poblano peppers or green sweet peppers (8 ounces)
1 cup shredded Monterey Jack cheese with jalapeño peppers (4 ounces)
3 beaten eggs
$1/4$ cup milk
$1/3$ cup all-purpose flour
$1/2$ teaspoon baking powder
$1/4$ teaspoon ground red pepper
$1/8$ teaspoon salt
$1/2$ cup shredded cheddar cheese (2 ounces)
   Picante sauce (optional)
   Dairy sour cream (optional)

1. Quarter the peppers and remove seeds, stems, and veins (see tip, page 111). Immerse peppers into boiling water for 3 minutes; drain. Invert peppers on paper towels to drain well. Place the peppers in a well-greased 2-quart square baking dish. Top with the Monterey Jack cheese.

2. In a medium mixing bowl combine eggs and milk. Add flour, baking powder, red pepper, and salt. Beat till smooth. Pour egg mixture over peppers and cheese.

3. Bake, uncovered, in a 450° oven for 15 minutes or till a knife inserted into the egg mixture comes out clean. Sprinkle with the shredded cheddar cheese. Let stand about 5 minutes or till cheese melts. If desired, serve with picante sauce and sour cream. Makes 4 servings.

Nutrition Facts per serving: 277 cal., 18 g total fat (10 g sat. fat), 201 mg chol., 408 mg sodium, 13 g carbo., 1 g fiber, 17 g pro. **Daily Values:** 24% vit. A, 67% vit. C, 33% calcium, 106% iron

■ **Low-Fat Chili Rellenos Casserole:** Prepare as above, except substitute *reduced-fat Monterey Jack cheese with jalapeño peppers* (or reduced-fat plain Monterey Jack cheese plus 2 teaspoons chopped jalapeño peppers) and *reduced-fat cheddar cheese* for the cheeses.

Substitute ¾ cup *refrigerated or frozen egg product* (thawed) for the eggs and *skim milk* for the milk.

Nutrition Facts per serving: 221 cal., 9 g total fat (5 g sat. fat) 31 mg chol.

HAM-ASPARAGUS STRATA

PREP: 25 MINUTES CHILL: 2 TO 24 HOURS BAKE: 50 MINUTES   Oven 325°

This cheesy strata makes a great brunch dish because you can assemble it the night before and bake it in the morning.

    4 English muffins, torn or cut into bite-size pieces
    1 cup cubed fully cooked ham (6 ounces)
   ½ of a 10-ounce package frozen cut asparagus or frozen cut
         broccoli, thawed and well-drained
    6 1-ounce slices process Swiss cheese, torn
    4 beaten eggs
 1¾ cups milk
   ½ cup dairy sour cream
    2 tablespoons finely chopped onion
    1 tablespoon Dijon-style mustard
   ¼ teaspoon caraway seed (optional)
   ⅛ teaspoon pepper

1. In a greased 2-quart square baking dish layer *half* of the English muffin pieces. Top with the ham, asparagus or broccoli, and cheese. Top with the remaining English muffin pieces.
2. In a mixing bowl combine the beaten eggs, milk, sour cream, onion, mustard, caraway seed (if desired), and pepper. Pour over the layers in dish. Cover and chill in the refrigerator for 2 to 24 hours.
3. Bake, uncovered, in a 325° oven for 50 to 55 minutes or till a knife inserted near the center comes out clean. Let stand for 5 to 10 minutes before serving. Makes 6 servings.

Nutrition Facts per serving: 361 cal., 17 g total fat (9 g sat. fat), 189 mg chol., 722 mg sodium, 25 g carbo., 0 g fiber, 25 g pro. **Daily Values:** 22% vit. A, 24% vit. C, 39% calcium, 13% iron

DIJON CHICKEN STRATA

1 8-ounce loaf French bread, cut into 1-inch cubes (6 cups)
2 cups chopped cooked chicken or turkey
1 4$\frac{1}{2}$-ounce jar sliced mushrooms, drained
$\frac{1}{2}$ cup chopped green onions (4)
3 cups shredded colby-and-Monterey-Jack cheese or American
    cheese (12 ounces)
5 eggs
2$\frac{1}{2}$ cups milk
3 tablespoons Dijon-style mustard
$\frac{1}{4}$ teaspoon pepper

1. Place bread cubes in a greased 3-quart rectangular baking dish. Layer chicken, mushrooms, and green onions over bread; sprinkle with cheese.

2. In a large mixing bowl beat eggs with a rotary beater; beat in milk, mustard, and pepper. Carefully pour over layered chicken mixture. Cover and chill for 2 to 24 hours.

3. Bake, uncovered, in a 325° oven about 50 minutes or till a knife inserted near the center comes out clean. Let stand for 10 minutes before serving. Makes 10 to 12 servings.

Nutrition Facts per serving: 328 cal., 18 g total fat (9 g sat. fat), 169 mg chol., 587 mg sodium, 17 g carbo., 0 g fiber, 25 g pro. **Daily Values:** 20% vit. A, 2% vit. C, 29% calcium, 11% iron

STORING CHEESE

Airtight packaging is the key to proper cheese storage. If the cheese has a rind, leave it on to keep the cheese fresh. Wrap unused cheese tightly in foil or plastic wrap, then seal it in a plastic bag or a container with a tight-fitting lid. Store the cheese in the refrigerator.

Most cheese comes stamped with a "sell by" date on the package. In general, the softer the cheese, the shorter the storage life. If there is no date on the container, cheeses such as cottage and ricotta should be stored no longer than 5 days after purchase. Firm and hard cheeses have less moisture and can be stored for longer periods. For instance, sharp cheddar may keep for weeks in your refrigerator, if properly wrapped. For longer storage, cheese can be frozen, but semisoft and hard cheese will be more crumbly and soft cheeses may separate slightly. Because of these texture changes, it's best to use thawed cheeses for casseroles and sauces.

As cheese ages, it naturally develops more flavor and may develop surface mold. Most surface mold looks unappealing but is harmless. For firm cheese, cut away at least 1 inch around the moldy area and use the remaining cheese. Discard soft cheeses, such as cottage cheese, ricotta, and cream cheese, that have mold.

FISH & SHELLFISH

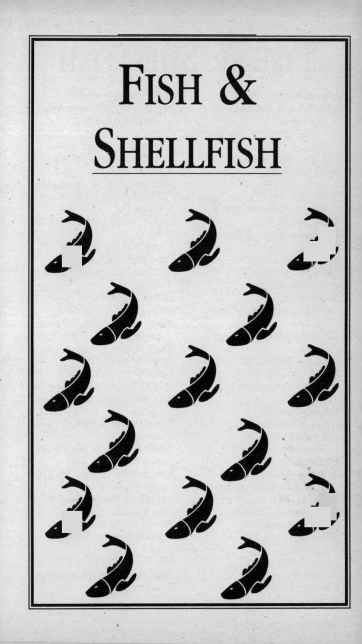

FISH & SHELLFISH

GINGERED PLUM-GLAZED HALIBUT

PREP: 15 MINUTES   BROIL: 8 MINUTES

Fast   **Low-Fat**

  1 **pound fresh or frozen halibut, swordfish, or shark steaks,**
     about 1 inch thick
  $^1/_2$ **cup red plum jam**
  1 **tablespoon lemon juice**
  $^1/_2$ **teaspoon grated gingerroot or $^1/_8$ teaspoon ground ginger**
  $^1/_8$ **to $^1/_4$ teaspoon crushed red pepper**
  $^1/_8$ **teaspoon garlic powder**
  1 **tablespoon margarine or butter, melted**

1. Thaw fish, if frozen. Rinse fish; pat dry with paper towels. Cut
into 4 serving-size pieces, if necessary. Set aside. For sauce, in a
small bowl combine jam, lemon juice, gingerroot or ginger, red pepper, and garlic powder. For glaze, in another bowl combine 3 tablespoons of the sauce with the margarine or butter. Set remaining
sauce aside.

2. Place the fish on the greased unheated rack of a broiler pan.
Lightly brush with half of the glaze. Broil 4 inches from heat for 5
minutes. Using a wide spatula, carefully turn fish over. Lightly brush
with remaining glaze. Broil for 3 to 7 minutes more or till fish flakes
easily with a fork. Serve fish with the sauce. Makes 4 servings.

Nutrition Facts per serving: 261 cal., 5 g total fat (1 g sat. fat), 36 mg chol., 100 mg
sodium, 29 g carbo., 0 g fiber, 24 g pro. **Daily Values:** 9% vit. A, 2% vit. C, 5% calcium,
9% iron

SELECTING FISH

Freshness first
Trust your eyes and nose when shopping for fish. Look for fish with:
- Clear, bright, bulging eyes
- Shiny, taut, bright skin
- Red gills that are not slippery
- Flesh that feels firm and elastic
- Moist, clean-cut fillets and steaks
- Packages that are solidly frozen

What to avoid
- Strong or fishy odor
- Dull, bloody, or sunken eyes
- Fading skin and gill color
- Ragged-cut fillets and steaks
- Frozen packages that have torn wrappers or frost or blood visible inside or out.

Common fish forms
- Whole or round: as it comes straight from the water
- Drawn: whole fish with internal organs removed; may or may not be scaled
- Dressed: ready to cook; organs, scales, head, tail, and fins have been removed
- Steak: ready to cook; crosscut slice ($\frac{1}{2}$ to 1 inch thick) from a large, dressed fish
- Fillet: ready to cook; boneless piece cut from the side and away from the backbone; may or may not be skinned
- Frozen portion: uniform-size piece cut from a large, frozen fillet block

One-serving-size equivalents
- 8 ounces of drawn or dressed fish
- 4 to 5 ounces of steaks or fillets
- 1 or 2 frozen portions

MARINATED FISH STEAKS

PREP: 15 MINUTES   MARINATE: 30 MINUTES OR 2 HOURS   BROIL: 8 MINUTES

Low-Fat

For tender, juicy fish, marinate the steaks no longer than directed. Marinating longer will cause the fish to become tough and chewy.

  1 **pound fresh or frozen salmon, swordfish, or halibut steaks, 1 inch thick**
$^1/_2$ **teaspoon finely shredded lemon peel or lime peel**
$^1/_4$ **cup lemon juice or lime juice**
  1 **tablespoon cooking oil**
  1 **tablespoon water**
  1 **tablespoon Worcestershire sauce**
$^1/_2$ **teaspoon dried rosemary or thyme, crushed**
  1 **clove garlic, minced**

1. Thaw fish, if frozen. Rinse fish steaks; pat dry with paper towels. Cut into 4 serving-size pieces, if necessary. For marinade, in a shallow dish combine lemon or lime peel, lemon or lime juice, oil, water, Worcestershire sauce, rosemary or thyme, and garlic. Add fish; turn to coat with marinade. Cover and marinate at room temperature for 30 minutes (or in the refrigerator for 2 hours), turning the steaks occasionally.

2. Drain fish, reserving marinade. Place fish on the greased unheated rack of a broiler pan. Broil 4 inches from the heat for 5 minutes. Using a wide spatula, carefully turn fish over. Brush with marinade. Broil for 3 to 7 minutes more or till fish flakes easily with a fork. Discard any remaining marinade. Makes 4 servings.

Nutrition Facts per serving: 142 cal., 7 g total fat (1 g sat. fat), 20 mg chol., 105 mg sodium, 2 g carbo., 0 g fiber, 16 g pro. **Daily Values:** 2% vit. A, 23% vit. C, 1% calcium, 6% iron

BASIL-BUTTERED SALMON STEAKS

PREP: 15 MINUTES   BROIL: 8 MINUTES

Fast

Lemon basil, a variety with a concentrated lemon flavor, makes a perfect accent for these broiled steaks.

4 fresh or frozen salmon, halibut, or sea bass steaks, 1 inch thick (about 1½ pounds total)
3 tablespoons butter, softened
1 tablespoon snipped fresh basil, lemon basil, or savory; or 1 teaspoon dried basil or savory, crushed; or 1 teaspoon snipped fresh tarragon or ¼ teaspoon dried tarragon, crushed
1 tablespoon snipped fresh parsley
2 teaspoons lemon juice

1. Thaw fish, if frozen. Rinse fish; pat dry with paper towels. Set aside. In a small mixing bowl stir together butter, basil, parsley, and lemon juice.
2. Place the fish on the greased unheated rack of a broiler pan. Lightly brush fish with some of the butter mixture. Broil 4 inches from the heat for 5 minutes. Using a wide spatula, carefully turn fish over. Lightly brush with more of the butter mixture. Broil for 3 to 7 minutes more or till fish flakes easily with a fork. Makes 4 servings.

Nutrition Facts per serving: 231 cal., 14 g total fat (7 g sat. fat), 54 mg chol., 190 mg sodium, 0 g carbo., 0 g fiber, 24 g pro. **Daily Values:** 11% vit. A, 4% vit. C, 1% calcium, 8% iron

TERIYAKI FISH STEAKS

PREP: 15 MINUTES   MARINATE: 30 MINUTES OR 2 HOURS   BROIL: 8 MINUTES

Low-Fat

If you'd like, skip the sake or sherry and increase the fruit juice to 3 tablespoons.

1 pound fresh or frozen tuna, shark, or halibut steaks, 1 inch thick
½ cup soy sauce

    2 **tablespoons orange or pineapple juice**
    1 **tablespoon cooking oil**
    1 **tablespoon sake or dry sherry**
    1 **teaspoon grated gingerroot or $\frac{1}{4}$ teaspoon ground ginger**
    1 **teaspoon honey**
    1 **clove garlic, minced**

1. Thaw fish, if frozen. Rinse fish; pat dry with paper towels. Cut steaks into 4 serving-size pieces, if necessary. Place fish in a shallow dish. For marinade, stir together the soy sauce, orange or pineapple juice, oil, sake or sherry, gingerroot, honey, and garlic. Pour over fish. Turn fish to coat with marinade. Cover and marinate at room temperature for 30 minutes (or in the refrigerator for 2 hours), turning the steaks occasionally.

2. Drain fish, reserving marinade. Place fish on the greased unheated rack of a broiler pan. Brush fish with some of the marinade. Broil 4 inches from the heat for 5 minutes. Using a wide spatula, carefully turn fish over. Brush with marinade. Broil for 3 to 7 minutes more or till fish flakes easily with a fork. Discard any remaining marinade. Makes 4 servings.

Nutrition Facts per serving: 201 cal., 7 g total fat (2 g sat. fat), 47 mg chol., 649 mg sodium, 2 g carbo., 0 g fiber, 29 g pro. **Daily Values:** 72% vit. A, 2% vit. C, 1% calcium, 10% iron

CRISPY OVEN-FRIED FISH

PREP: 15 MINUTES   BAKE: 6 MINUTES   Oven 450°

Fast   **Low-Fat**

    1 **pound fresh or frozen skinless cod, orange roughy, or catfish**
        fillets, about $\frac{1}{2}$ inch thick
  $\frac{1}{4}$ **cup milk**
  $\frac{1}{4}$ **cup all-purpose flour**
  $\frac{1}{3}$ **cup fine dry bread crumbs**
  $\frac{1}{4}$ **cup grated Parmesan cheese**
  $\frac{1}{2}$ **teaspoon dried dillweed**
  $\frac{1}{8}$ **teaspoon pepper**
    2 **tablespoons margarine or butter, melted**

1. Thaw fish, if frozen. Rinse fish; pat dry with paper towels. Cut into 4 serving-size pieces. Place milk in a shallow dish. Place flour in another shallow dish. In a third shallow dish combine bread crumbs, cheese, dillweed, and pepper. Toss with melted margarine.

2. Dip each piece of fish in the milk, then in the flour. Dip again in the milk, then in the crumb mixture to coat all sides. Place fish on a greased baking sheet. Bake, uncovered, in a 450° oven for 6 to 9 minutes or till fish flakes easily with a fork. Makes 4 servings.

Nutrition Facts per serving: 232 cal., 9 g total fat (3 g sat. fat), 51 mg chol., 316 mg sodium, 13 g carbo., 1 g fiber, 24 g pro. **Daily Values:** 10% vit. A, 1% vit. C, 10% calcium, 7% iron

---

ZESTY JALAPEÑO FISH FILLETS

START TO FINISH: 25 MINUTES

Fast   *Low-Fat*

*Low in fat and full of flavor, this quick-to-fix
recipe is a meal in one.*

  1 **pound fresh or frozen skinless red snapper, flounder, sole,
haddock, or orange roughy fillets, $^1/_2$ to 1 inch thick**
  3 **medium carrots, julienned ($1^1/_2$ cups)**
  1 **medium zucchini, julienned ($1^1/_2$ cups)**
$1^1/_2$ **cups water**
 $^1/_2$ **teaspoon instant chicken bouillon granules**
  1 **cup quick-cooking couscous**
 $^1/_3$ **cup jalapeño pepper jelly**
  1 **tablespoon white wine vinegar or vinegar**
  1 **tablespoon snipped fresh cilantro or parsley**

1. Thaw fish, if frozen. Rinse fish; pat dry. Cut fish into 4 serving-size pieces, if necessary. In a medium saucepan cook carrots, covered, in a small amount of boiling water for 2 minutes; add zucchini and cook 2 minutes more or till vegetables are crisp-tender. Drain, cover, and keep warm.

2. Measure thickness of fish. Place fish on the greased unheated rack of a broiler pan. Season with salt and pepper. Broil fish 4 inches from heat till fish flakes easily with a fork (allow 4 to 6 minutes per $^1/_2$-inch thickness of fish). Turn 1-inch-thick fillets over halfway through broiling.

3. Meanwhile, in a saucepan heat water and bouillon granules to boiling. Stir in couscous. Cover; let stand 3 to 5 minutes or till liquid is absorbed.

4. In another saucepan stir together jelly and vinegar. Heat and stir over low heat till jelly is melted.

5. To serve, use a fork to fluff the couscous; stir in the cilantro or parsley. Spoon the couscous onto each dinner plate. Top with a fillet and some of the vegetables. Drizzle with the warm jelly mixture. Makes 4 servings.

Nutrition Facts per serving: 320 cal., 2 g total fat (0 g sat. fat), 42 mg chol., 201 mg sodium, 44 g carbo., 9 g fiber, 30 g pro. **Daily Values:** 128% vit. A, 4% vit. C, 5% calcium, 7% iron

---

DIJON MUSTARD FILLETS

START TO FINISH: 15 MINUTES

Fast   **Low-Fat**

    1 **pound fresh or frozen fish fillets,** $^1/_2$ **to 1 inch thick**
       Lemon-pepper seasoning
 $^1/_4$ **cup dairy sour cream**
    1 **tablespoon milk**
    1 **tablespoon Dijon-style mustard**
    2 **teaspoons snipped fresh chives**

1. Thaw fish, if frozen. Rinse fish and pat dry with paper towels. Cut into 4 serving-size pieces, if necessary. Measure thickness of fish. Place fish on the greased unheated rack of a broiler pan. Sprinkle with lemon-pepper seasoning. Broil 4 inches from the heat till fish flakes easily with a fork (allow 4 to 6 minutes per $^1/_2$-inch thickness of fish.) Turn 1-inch-thick fillets over halfway through broiling.

2. Meanwhile, in a small saucepan stir together sour cream, milk, mustard, chives, and a dash *black pepper.* Heat through but do not boil. Serve with fish. Makes 4 servings.

Nutrition Facts per serving: 120 cal., 4 g total fat (2 g sat. fat), 49 mg chol., 183 mg sodium, 1 g carbo., 0 g fiber, 19 g pro. **Daily Values:** 4% vit. A, 2% vit. C, 2% calcium, 2% iron

PIZZA FISH FILLETS

START TO FINISH: 20 MINUTES Oven 450°

Fast   **Low-Fat**

1½ pounds fresh or frozen fish fillets, ½ to ¾ inch thick
½ teaspoon lemon-pepper seasoning
2 cups sliced fresh mushrooms
1 medium green sweet pepper, chopped (¾ cup)
1 medium onion, chopped (½ cup)
¼ cup water
1 8-ounce can pizza sauce
½ cup shredded mozzarella cheese (2 ounces)
  Hot cooked spinach fettuccine (see page 774) (optional)

1. Thaw fish, if frozen. Rinse fish; pat dry with paper towels. Cut into 6 serving-size pieces, if necessary. Measure the thickness of the fish. Place fish in a greased 2-quart rectangular baking dish, tucking under any thin edges. Sprinkle with the lemon-pepper seasoning.
2. Bake fish, uncovered, in a 450° oven till fish flakes easily with a fork (allow 4 to 6 minutes per ½-inch thickness of fish). Drain off any liquid.
3. Meanwhile, in a saucepan cook mushrooms, sweet pepper, and onion in the water, covered, 5 minutes or till tender. Drain; add pizza sauce. Heat through; spoon over fish. Sprinkle with cheese. Bake 1 minute more or till cheese melts. If desired, serve with fettuccine. Makes 6 servings.

Nutrition Facts per serving: 147 cal., 3 g total fat (1 g sat. fat), 50 mg chol., 419 mg sodium, 7 g carbo., 1 g fiber, 22 g pro. **Daily Values:** 12% vit. A, 34% vit. C, 7% calcium, 6% iron

BAKED FISH WITH MUSHROOMS

PREP: 15 MINUTES BAKE: 12 MINUTES Oven 450°

Fast **Low-Fat**

Almost any fish will taste delicious in this dish. Select the best fillets or steaks for your money.

1 **pound fresh or frozen fish fillets or steaks, $^1/_2$ to $^3/_4$ inch thick**
2 **tablespoons margarine or butter**
1 **cup sliced fresh mushrooms**
$^1/_2$ **cup sliced green onions (4)**
$^1/_4$ **teaspoon dried tarragon or thyme, crushed**
 Paprika

1. Thaw fish, if frozen. Rinse fish and pat dry with paper towels. Cut into 4 serving-size pieces, if necessary. Arrange fish in a 2-quart rectangular baking dish, turning under thin edges. Sprinkle with salt.

2. In a small saucepan melt margarine; add mushrooms, onions, and tarragon. Cook over medium heat till tender. Spoon mushroom mixture over fish; sprinkle with paprika. Bake, covered, in a 450° oven for 12 to 18 minutes or till fish flakes easily with a fork. Makes 4 servings.

Nutrition Facts per serving: 143 cal., 7 g total fat (1 g sat. fat), 45 mg chol., 131 mg sodium, 1 g carbo., 0 g fiber, 19 g pro. **Daily Values:** 10% vit. A, 6% vit. C, 1% calcium, 5% iron

STORING FISH

Sooner is better when it comes to cooking fish. When that's not possible, wrap fresh fish loosely in clear plastic wrap, store it in the coldest part of the refrigerator, and use it within 2 days. Cover and refrigerate any leftover cooked fish and use within 2 days.

If you purchase frozen fish, keep it in a freezer set at 0° or lower for up to 3 months (see "Thawing Fish" tip on page 508).

CITRUS BAKED HALIBUT

Fast

Low-Fat

For a sumptuous yet low-fat supper, serve this citrus-scented fish with a spinach salad, steamed asparagus, and boiled new potatoes.

  1 **pound fresh or frozen halibut steaks, ³/₄ inch thick**
  1 **tablespoon margarine or butter**
¹/₃ **cup finely chopped onion (1 small)**
  1 **clove garlic, minced**
  2 **tablespoons snipped fresh parsley**
¹/₂ **teaspoon finely shredded orange peel**
¹/₄ **teaspoon salt**
¹/₈ **teaspoon pepper**
¹/₄ **cup orange juice**
  1 **tablespoon lemon juice**

1. Thaw fish, if frozen. Rinse fish and pat dry with paper towels. Cut into 4 serving-size pieces, if necessary. Arrange in a 2-quart square baking dish.
2. In a small saucepan melt margarine; add onion and garlic. Cook till tender; remove from heat. Stir in parsley, orange peel, salt, and pepper; spoon over fish. Sprinkle orange and lemon juices over fish. Bake, covered, in a 400° oven for 15 to 20 minutes or till fish flakes easily with a fork. Spoon pan juices over fish. Makes 4 servings.

Nutrition Facts per serving: 167 cal., 6 g total fat (1 g sat. fat), 36 mg chol., 230 mg sodium, 4 g carbo., 0 g fiber, 24 g pro. **Daily Values:** 9% vit. A, 22% vit. C, 5% calcium, 7% iron

SPICY HALIBUT

PREP: 15 MINUTES   BAKE: 8 MINUTES   Oven 450°

Fast   **Low-Fat**

Try this Caribbean-style fish with Mango Salsa (see page 506). You also can use the spice rub on fillets, such as red snapper, orange roughy, or flounder. Allow 4 to 6 minutes baking time for each 1/2-inch thickness of fish.

  1 **pound fresh or frozen halibut steaks, 1 inch thick**
  1 **tablespoon lime juice**
  1 **teaspoon paprika**
 1/2 **teaspoon salt**
 1/4 **teaspoon ground ginger**
 1/4 **teaspoon ground allspice**
 1/4 **teaspoon pepper**
     Lime wedges and/or lime peel strips (optional)

1. Thaw fish, if frozen. Rinse; pat dry with paper towels. Cut into 4 serving-size pieces, if necessary. Brush with a mixture of lime juice and 1 tablespoon *water*. In a bowl combine paprika, salt, ginger, allspice, and pepper; rub onto fish.
2. Arrange fish in a shallow baking pan. Bake, uncovered, in a 450° oven for 8 to 12 minutes or till fish flakes easily with a fork. Brush fish with pan juices. If desired, garnish with lime wedges and/or lime peel strips. Makes 4 servings.

Nutrition Facts per serving: 127 cal., 3 g total fat (0 g sat. fat), 36 mg chol., 328 mg sodium, 1 g carbo., 0 g fiber, 24 g pro. **Daily Values:** 7% vit. A, 2% vit. C, 4% calcium, 7% iron

Fish & Shellfish **503**

SALMON IN PHYLLO

START TO FINISH: 45 MINUTES   Oven 375°

     1 pound fresh or frozen skinless salmon fillets, $1/2$ inch thick
   $1/4$ cup dairy sour cream
     2 tablespoons snipped fresh dill or 1 teaspoon dried dillweed
       Dash salt
       Dash white pepper
     8 sheets frozen phyllo dough (18x14-inch rectangles), thawed
   $1/3$ cup butter or margarine, melted
     1 recipe Mustard Cream Sauce (see below)

1. Thaw salmon, if frozen. Rinse salmon; pat dry with paper towels.
Cut salmon into 4 serving-size pieces, if necessary. Spread *1 tablespoon* of the sour cream over each salmon portion. Sprinkle with
dill, salt, and white pepper. Set aside.
2. Unfold phyllo dough; cover with a damp towel. Lay a sheet of
phyllo dough flat. Brush phyllo dough with some of the melted butter. Top with another sheet of phyllo dough. Brush with more
melted butter. Add 6 more sheets of dough, for a total of 8 sheets,
brushing each sheet with butter. Cut into four 9×7-inch rectangles.
Place a salmon fillet, sour cream side down, in the middle of each
dough rectangle. Fold a long side of the dough up over the salmon;
repeat with the other long side, brushing dough with butter and
pressing lightly. Fold up ends. Repeat with remaining rectangles,
butter, and salmon to make a total of 4 salmon-phyllo bundles.
Arrange the bundles, seam sides down, on a baking sheet. Brush the
tops with butter.
3. Bake in a 375° oven for 15 to 18 minutes or till phyllo dough is
golden and fish flakes easily with a fork. Serve with Mustard Cream
Sauce. Serves 4.
■ **Mustard Cream Sauce:** Combine $1/3$ cup *dry white wine* and 3
tablespoons finely chopped *shallots*. Bring to boiling; reduce heat.
Simmer, uncovered, for 8 to 10 minutes or till the liquid is reduced
to about 3 tablespoons, stirring occasionally. Stir 1 cup *half-and-half
or light cream* into 4 teaspoons *all-purpose flour*. Stir into wine mixture with $1/8$ teaspoon *white pepper*. Cook and stir over medium heat
till thickened and bubbly. Stir in 1 tablespoon *Dijon-style mustard*.
Cook and stir for 1 minute more.

504 Fish & Shellfish

Nutrition Facts per serving: 492 cal., 31 g total fat (17 g sat. fat), 89 mg chol., 567 mg sodium, 27 g carbo., 0 g fiber, 22 g pro. Daily Values: 36% vit. A, 2% vit. C, 8% calcium, 15% iron

FISH SANDWICH WITH BASIL MAYONNAISE

PREP: 15 MINUTES   BAKE: 4 MINUTES   Oven 500°

Fast

Baking these fillets at 500° keeps the crumb coating nice and crispy. For crumb-topped fish, toss the crumb mixture with the margarine. Brush the fillets with milk and sprinkle the crumb mixture over the top of fillets. Serve with or without the buns.

   4 **fresh or frozen skinless fish fillets, $^1/_2$ inch thick (about 1 pound total)**
 $^1/_4$ **cup milk**
 $^1/_2$ **cup fine dry bread crumbs**
 $^1/_4$ **teaspoon paprika**
 $^1/_8$ **teaspoon salt**
 $^1/_8$ **teaspoon pepper**
   2 **tablespoons margarine or butter, melted**
   4 **hamburger buns or kaiser rolls, split and toasted**
     Lettuce leaves
   1 **recipe Basil Mayonnaise (see below)**

1. Thaw fish, if frozen. Rinse fish; pat dry with paper towels. Pour milk into a shallow dish. In another shallow dish combine bread crumbs, paprika, salt, and pepper. Dip fish in milk; roll fish in crumb mixture. Place fish in a greased shallow baking pan, tucking under any thin edges. Drizzle with melted margarine or butter.

2. Bake in a 500° oven for 4 to 6 minutes or till fish flakes easily with a fork and coating is golden. Serve fish on toasted buns with lettuce and Basil Mayonnaise. Makes 4 servings.

■ **Basil Mayonnaise:** In a small mixing bowl stir together 3 tablespoons *mayonnaise or salad dressing;* 2 tablespoons *dairy sour cream;* 2 tablespoons snipped *fresh basil* or $^1/_2$ teaspoon *dried basil,* crushed; and $^1/_2$ teaspoon finely shredded *lemon peel.* Chill till serving time.

Nutrition Facts per serving: 399 cal., 22 g total fat (5 g sat. fat), 30 mg chol., 529 mg sodium, 29 g carbo., 1 g fiber, 21 g pro. Daily Values: 13% vit. A, 2% vit. C, 5% calcium, 15% iron

SAUCY SOLUTIONS

Combine one of these stir-together toppings with fish fillets or steaks prepared as you like them (see charts, pages 537–541). For additional sauces to serve with fish, see the Sauces and Relishes chapter, pages 955–975.

■ **Avocado Salsa:** In a medium mixing bowl combine 1 large *tomato,* seeded and chopped; 1 *avocado,* halved, seeded, peeled and chopped; ¹/₂ of a small *onion,* chopped; 1 clove *garlic,* minced; 1 tablespoon snipped *fresh cilantro;* 1 tablespoon *lemon or lime juice;* a few dashes *bottled hot pepper sauce;* and dash *salt.* Cover and chill 2 to 6 hours. Makes 2¹/₂ cups.

■ **Lemon Mayonnaise:** In a small mixing bowl stir together ¹/₂ cup *mayonnaise or salad dressing,* 2 tablespoons snipped fresh *chives,* 1 teaspoon finely shredded *lemon peel,* 1 tablespoon *lemon juice,* 1 tablespoon snipped *parsley,* and ¹/₄ teaspoon *coarsely cracked pepper.* Cover and chill till serving time. Makes about ²/₃ cup.

■ **Mango Salsa:** In a medium mixing bowl combine 1¹/₂ cups peeled, chopped *mangoes or peaches;* 1 medium *red sweet pepper,* seeded and finely chopped; ¹/₄ cup thinly sliced *green onions;* 1 *jalapeño pepper,* seeded and finely chopped (see tip, page 111); 3 tablespoons *olive oil or cooking oil;* ¹/₂ teaspoon finely shredded *lime peel;* 2 tablespoons *lime juice;* 1 tablespoon *vinegar;* ¹/₄ teaspoon *salt;* and ¹/₄ teaspoon *pepper.* Makes 2 cups.

■ **Pineapple Salsa:** In a small mixing bowl stir together 1 cup *chunky salsa;* one 8-ounce can crushed *pineapple* (juice pack), drained; and ¹/₄ teaspoon grated fresh *gingerroot* or dash *ground ginger.* Cover and chill till serving time; bring to room temperature to serve. Makes 1¹/₂ cups.

BROCCOLI-STUFFED SOLE

If time is short, cover the dish of rolled fish with vented plastic wrap and microwave on 100% power (high) for 8 to 10 minutes, giving the dish a half-turn once.

- 4   4-ounce fresh or frozen skinless sole, flounder, or other fish fillets, about ¼ inch thick
- 1 cup frozen cut broccoli, thawed
- 1 beaten egg
- 1 8-ounce container soft-style cream cheese with chives and onion
- ¼ cup grated Parmesan cheese
- ¾ cup herb-seasoned stuffing mix
- 2 tablespoons milk
- 2 tablespoons dry white wine

1. Thaw fish, if frozen. Rinse fish and pat dry with paper towels. For stuffing, drain broccoli, pressing out excess liquid. Combine egg, *half* of the cream cheese, and the Parmesan cheese. Stir in broccoli and stuffing mix. Spoon one-fourth of the stuffing onto an end of each fillet. Roll up, securing rolls with wooden toothpicks. Place fish in a greased 2-quart square baking dish. Bake, covered, in a 350° oven for 30 to 35 minutes or till fish flakes easily with a fork and stuffing is hot.

2. Meanwhile, for sauce, in a small saucepan cook remaining cream cheese, the milk, and wine till heated through, stirring often. Serve sauce over fish. Makes 4 servings.

Nutrition Facts per serving: 376 cal., 23 g total fat (12 g sat. fat), 172 mg chol., 500 mg sodium, 11 g carbo., 1 g fiber, 29 g pro. **Daily Values:** 23% vit. A, 20% vit. C, 14% calcium, 6% iron

FISH TACOS

Fast

1 pound fresh or frozen skinless cod, orange roughy, or other
    fish fillets
2 tablespoons margarine or butter, melted
$1/4$ teaspoon ground cumin
$1/8$ teaspoon garlic powder
2 tablespoons mayonnaise or salad dressing
2 tablespoons plain yogurt
1 teaspoon lime juice
$1^1/_2$ cups coleslaw mix or shredded cabbage, spinach, or lettuce
8 6-inch flour tortillas, warmed*
    Salsa or 1 recipe Mango Salsa (see "Saucy Solutions," page 506)
    (optional)

1. Thaw fish, if frozen. Rinse fish and pat dry with paper towels. Cut fish crosswise into $3/4$-inch thick slices. Place fish in single layer in greased shallow baking pan. Combine margarine, cumin, and garlic powder. Brush over fish. Bake in a 450° oven 4 to 6 minutes or till fish flakes easily with a fork.

2. Meanwhile, stir together mayonnaise or salad dressing, yogurt, and lime juice. Add coleslaw mix or shredded cabbage, spinach, or lettuce; toss to coat. Spoon some of the coleslaw mixture onto each tortilla; add fish slices, and, if desired, salsa. Fold tortilla over filling. Makes 4 servings.

***Note:** To warm tortillas, wrap in foil and heat in a 450° oven 5 minutes or till warm. Or, microwave tortillas. Place *half* the

THAWING FISH

To thaw fish, place the unopened package in a container in the refrigerator, allowing overnight thawing for about a 1-pound package. If necessary, you can place the wrapped package of fish under *cold* running water for 1 to 2 minutes to hasten thawing. Thawing fish at room temperature or in warm water isn't recommended, since the fish won't thaw evenly and may spoil. Do not refreeze fish.

tortillas between paper towels. Microwave on 100% power (high) for 20 to 30 seconds. Repeat with the remaining tortillas.

Nutrition Facts per serving: 427 cal., 17 g total fat (3 g sat. fat), 48 mg chol., 515 mg sodium, 42 g carbo., 1 g fiber, 24 g pro. **Daily Values:** 28% vit. A, 15% vit. C, 11% calcium, 20% iron

---

WILD RICE-STUFFED FISH

PREP: 1¼ HOURS   BAKE: 30 MINUTES   Oven 350°

Don't be misled by the long preparation period; it includes the time needed to cook the wild rice—time when you can be doing something else.

   1 2- to 2½-pound fresh or frozen dressed whitefish, lake trout, or snapper
 ⅔ cup wild rice
   1 cup sliced fresh mushrooms
 ¼ cup chopped onion
   1 clove garlic, minced
   2 tablespoons margarine or butter
1¼ cups chicken broth
   2 tablespoons dry sherry or chicken broth
   1 cup frozen peas
   2 tablespoons chopped pimiento
 ¼ teaspoon finely shredded lemon peel
   1 to 2 teaspoons cooking oil

1. Thaw fish, if frozen. Rinse fish and pat dry with paper towels. Cover and refrigerate until ready to stuff. Rinse wild rice thoroughly.
2. For stuffing, in a medium saucepan cook mushrooms, onion, and garlic in margarine or butter till tender. Stir in broth, sherry, and wild rice. Heat to boiling; reduce heat. Cover and simmer for 45 to 50 minutes or till rice is tender and liquid is absorbed. Stir in peas, pimiento, and lemon peel.
3. To stuff fish, sprinkle cavity lightly with salt. Spoon half of the stuffing into cavity; press lightly to flatten. (Place remaining stuffing in a 1-quart casserole; cover.) Tie or skewer fish closed.
4. Place stuffed fish in a greased large shallow baking pan. Brush fish lightly with oil. Cover loosely with foil. Bake stuffed fish and stuffing in casserole in a 350° oven for 30 to 40 minutes or till fish

flakes easily with a fork. Use two large spatulas to transfer the fish to a serving platter. Makes 4 or 5 servings.

Nutrition Facts per serving: 272 cal., 14 g total fat (2 g sat. fat), 68 mg chol., 398 mg sodium, 28 g carbo., 2 g fiber, 29 g pro. **Daily Values:** 10% vit. A, 16% vit. C, 2% calcium, 13% iron

POACHED FISH WITH DILL SAUCE

PREP: 25 MINUTES   COOK: 35 MINUTES

Low-Fat

*Choose a mild to moderately flavored fish, such as red snapper,
whitefish, or lake trout, for this saucy delight.*

  1 2^1/$_2$- to 3-pound fresh or frozen dressed fish
  3 lemon slices
  1 bay leaf
  ^{1}/$_2$ teaspoon salt
  2 tablespoons butter or margarine
  4 teaspoons all-purpose flour
  ^{1}/$_2$ teaspoon sugar
  ^{1}/$_2$ teaspoon dried dillweed
     Dash salt
  1 slightly beaten egg yolk

1. Thaw fish, if frozen. Rinse fish; pat dry with paper towels. In a fish poacher or a large roasting pan that has a wire rack with handles, add enough water to almost reach the rack. Remove and grease rack; set aside. To water in pan add lemon slices, bay leaf, and the ^{1}/$_2$ teaspoon salt. Place pan over two burners on range top. Bring to boiling. Reduce heat. Place fish on rack and lower into pan. Simmer, covered, 35 to 40 minutes or till fish flakes easily with a fork. Remove fish; keep warm while preparing sauce.

2. For dill sauce, strain cooking liquid, reserving 1 cup. In a small saucepan melt butter or margarine; stir in flour, sugar, dillweed, and the dash salt. Add reserved liquid. Cook and stir till thickened and bubbly. Gradually stir about ^{1}/$_2$ cup of the mixture into beaten egg yolk; pour egg yolk mixture into saucepan. Cook and stir 1 minute more. Pass dill sauce with fish. Makes 6 servings.

Nutrition Facts per serving: 241 cal., 7 g total fat (4 g sat. fat), 120 mg chol., 331 mg sodium, 2 g carbo., 0 g fiber, 40 g pro. **Daily Values:** 10% vit. A, 2% vit. C, 5% calcium, 4% iron

CHILLED SALMON STEAKS WITH LEMON-DILL DRESSING

PREP: 15 MINUTES   COOK: 8 MINUTES   CHILL: 2 HOURS

For a refreshing main course, serve these poached fish steaks on a bed of shredded lettuce.

   6 **fresh or frozen salmon or halibut steaks, 1 to 1¹/₄ inches thick (about 2 pounds total)**
1¹/₂ **cups water**
   ¹/₄ **cup lemon juice**
   1 **medium onion, sliced**
  10 **whole black peppercorns**
   3 **sprigs parsley**
   2 **bay leaves**
   ¹/₂ **teaspoon salt**
   1 **recipe Lemon-Dill Dressing (see below)**

1. Thaw fish, if frozen. Rinse fish and pat dry with paper towels; set aside. In a 12-inch skillet combine water, lemon juice, onion, peppercorns, parsley, bay leaves, and salt. Bring to boiling; add fish steaks. Cover; simmer for 8 to 12 minutes or till fish flakes easily with a fork. Remove fish from skillet; discard poaching liquid. Cover; refrigerate fish 2 hours or till chilled. Serve with Lemon-Dill Dressing. Makes 6 servings.

■ **Lemon-Dill Dressing:** In a small mixing bowl stir together ³/₄ cup *mayonnaise or salad dressing,* 3 tablespoons *buttermilk,* 2 tablespoons snipped *fresh dill* or 2 teaspoons *dried dillweed,* 1 tablespoon snipped *fresh chives,* ¹/₂ teaspoon finely shredded *lemon peel,* and 2 teaspoons *lemon juice.* Cover and chill about 1 hour.

Nutrition Facts per serving: 339 cal., 27 g total fat (4 g sat. fat), 43 mg chol., 433 mg sodium, 1 g carbo., 0 g fiber, 22 g pro. **Daily Values:** 5% vit. A, 2% vit. C, 2% calcium, 8% iron

OVEN-POACHED RED SNAPPER WITH SPINACH CREAM SAUCE

START TO FINISH: 40 MINUTES   Oven 350°

While this easy-to-fix fish is in the oven, use your stovetop to cook Rice Pilaf (see page 99) and steam some green beans.

1   2- to 3-pound dressed red snapper, lake trout, or whitefish
¼   cup sliced green onions (2)
¼   teaspoon salt
⅛   teaspoon pepper
½   cup dry white wine or chicken broth
½   cup water
⅓   cup dairy sour cream
⅓   cup mayonnaise or salad dressing
½   teaspoon dried thyme, crushed
½   teaspoon finely shredded lemon peel
¼   teaspoon dry mustard
    Dash pepper
½   cup whipping cream
¼   cup coarsely chopped fresh spinach

1. Thaw fish, if frozen. Rinse fish; pat dry with paper towels. Place fish in a 3-quart rectangular baking dish (cut tail to fit, if necessary).
2. Spoon green onions over fish; sprinkle with salt and pepper. Pour wine or broth and water around fish. Cover dish with foil. Bake in a 350° oven for 30 to 35 minutes or till fish flakes easily with a fork.
3. Meanwhile, for sauce, in a small mixing bowl stir together the sour cream, mayonnaise or salad dressing, thyme, lemon peel, dry mustard, and pepper.
4. In a medium mixing bowl beat whipping cream with an electric mixer on low speed till soft peaks form. Fold whipped cream and spinach into sour cream mixture. Serve sauce immediately with fish. Makes 4 servings.

Nutrition Facts per serving: 525 cal., 33 g total fat (12 g sat. fat), 143 mg chol., 364 mg sodium, 3 g carbo., 0 g fiber, 48 g pro. **Daily Values:** 22% vit. A, 4% vit. C, 10% calcium, 5% iron

STEAMED ORANGE ROUGHY

START TO FINISH: 20 MINUTES

Fast　　　　　　　　　　　　**Low-Fat**

Before you start, make sure your skillet is large enough to hold the steamer basket.

- 1 pound fresh or frozen orange roughy fillets, $1/2$ to $3/4$ inch thick
- 1 medium onion, sliced
- 4 celery stalks, leafy ends only
- $1/4$ teaspoon garlic salt
- 1 recipe Pineapple Salsa or Lemon Mayonnaise (for both, see "Saucy Solutions," page 506)

1. Thaw fish, if frozen. Rinse fish; pat dry with paper towels. Cut into 4 serving-size pieces, if necessary; set aside. Fill a large skillet with water to a depth of 1 inch. Bring water to boiling; reduce heat to a simmer.

2. Meanwhile, arrange onion slices in the bottom of a steamer basket; carefully place fish over onions. Lay celery over fish; sprinkle with garlic salt and a dash *pepper*. Place over simmering water. Cover skillet. Steam for 8 to 15 minutes or till fish flakes easily with a fork. Discard vegetables. Serve fish with Pineapple Salsa or Lemon Mayonnaise. Makes 4 servings.

Nutrition Facts per serving: 103 cal., 1 g total fat (0 g sat. fat), 60 mg chol., 220 mg sodium, 0 g carbo., 0 g fiber, 21 g pro. **Daily Values:** 1% vit. A, 0% vit. C, 1% calcium, 2% iron

SWEET-AND-SOUR STIR-FRIED FISH

START TO FINISH: 25 MINUTES

Fast **Low-Fat**

Use a gentle hand when stir-frying the fish to keep the pieces in nice chunks.

1 pound fresh or frozen tuna, swordfish, shark, or sea bass
   steaks or fillets
1 15^1/4-ounce can pineapple chunks (juice pack)
^{1}/4 cup packed brown sugar
^{1}/4 cup catsup
^{1}/4 cup soy sauce
3 tablespoons vinegar
3 tablespoons dry sherry or orange juice
2 tablespoons cornstarch
1 to 2 tablespoons cooking oil
1 medium green or red sweet pepper, cut into ^{3}/4-inch pieces
2 cups hot cooked rice (see page 139)

1. Thaw fish, if frozen. Rinse fish and pat dry with paper towels. Cut fish into 1-inch pieces; set aside. Drain pineapple, reserving ^{3}/4 cup juice. For sauce, combine reserved pineapple juice, brown sugar, catsup, soy sauce, vinegar, sherry or orange juice, and cornstarch; set aside.

2. Add *1 tablespoon* cooking oil to a wok or large skillet; preheat over high heat. (Add more oil as necessary during cooking.) Stir-fry the sweet pepper for 1^1/2 to 2 minutes or till crisp-tender (see step 2, page 634). Remove from wok. Stir-fry half of the fish for 3 to 5 minutes or till fish flakes easily with a fork; remove. Stir-fry remaining fish; remove. Stir sauce; add to wok (see step 4, page 634). Cook and stir till thickened and bubbly. Stir in pineapple, sweet pepper, and fish. Heat for 1 minute. Serve over rice. Makes 4 servings.

Nutrition Facts per serving: 470 cal., 10 g total fat (2 g sat. fat), 47 mg chol., 1286 mg sodium, 60 g carbo., 1 g fiber, 33 g pro. **Daily Values:** 75% vit. A, 41% vit. C, 4% calcium, 22% iron

FISH AND CHIPS

   1 **pound fresh or frozen fish fillets**
   3 **medium potatoes**
     Shortening or cooking oil for deep-fat frying
   1 **cup all-purpose flour**
 $1/2$ **teaspoon baking powder**
 $1/4$ **teaspoon salt**
   1 **cup beer or milk**
     Malt or cider vinegar (optional)

1. Thaw fish, if frozen. Rinse fish and pat dry with paper towels. Cut fish into 4 serving-size pieces, if necessary.

2. For chips, peel and cut potatoes lengthwise into $3/8$-inch-wide sticks; pat dry. In a heavy saucepan or deep-fat fryer heat 2 inches melted shortening or cooking oil to 375°. Fry potatoes in hot fat, about one-third at a time, for 4 to 6 minutes or till lightly browned. Remove and drain on paper towels. Keep warm in a 300° oven while frying fish.

3. For fish batter, combine flour, baking powder, and salt. Add beer or milk; beat till smooth. Dip fish into batter. Fry fish in hot fat, one or two pieces at a time, about 2 minutes on each side or till golden brown. Drain; keep warm in oven while frying remaining fish. If desired, serve with malt or cider vinegar. Makes 4 servings.

Nutrition Facts per serving: 552 cal., 28 g total fat (4 g sat. fat), 45 mg chol., 251 mg sodium, 47 g carbo., 2 g fiber, 24 g pro. **Daily Values:** 1% vit. A, 15% vit. C, 5% calcium, 14% iron

PAN-FRIED FISH

PREP: 12 MINUTES   FRY: 12 MINUTES   Oven 300°

Fast   **Low-Fat**

    1 pound fresh or frozen fish fillets, $^1/_2$ to 1 inch thick
    1 beaten egg
 $^2/_3$ cup cornmeal or fine dry bread crumbs
 $^1/_2$ teaspoon salt
      Dash pepper
      Shortening or cooking oil for frying

1. Thaw fish, if frozen. Rinse fish and pat dry with paper towels. Cut into 4 serving-size pieces, if necessary. Measure thickness of fish. In a shallow dish combine egg and 2 tablespoons *water*. In another dish mix cornmeal or crumbs, salt, and pepper. Dip fish into egg mixture; coat fish with cornmeal mixture.

2. In a large skillet heat $^1/_4$ inch melted shortening or oil. Add half of the fish in a single layer. (If fillets have skin, fry skin side last.) Fry fish on 1 side till golden. Allow 3 to 4 minutes per side for $^1/_2$-inch-thick fillets (5 to 6 minutes per side for 1-inch-thick fillets). Turn carefully. Fry till second side is golden and fish flakes easily with a fork. Drain on paper towels. Keep warm in a 300° oven while frying remaining fish. Makes 4 servings.

Nutrition Facts per serving: 245 cal., 9 g total fat (2 g sat. fat), 98 mg chol., 80 mg sodium, 18 g carbo., 1 g fiber, 22 g pro. **Daily Values:** 4% vit. A, 1% vit. C, 1% calcium, 10% iron

■ **Potato Chip Pan-Fried Fish:** Prepare as above, except substitute $^2/_3$ cup finely crushed *potato chips or saltine crackers* for the cornmeal or bread crumbs and omit salt.

Nutrition Facts per serving: 240 cal., 14 g total fat (3 g sat. fat)

■ **Curried Pan-Fried Fish:** Prepare as above, except add 1 tablespoon *lime or lemon juice* to egg mixture and add 2 teaspoons *curry powder* to cornmeal mixture. If desired, serve with *chutney*.

Nutrition Facts per serving: 249 cal., 9 g total fat (2 g sat. fat)

■ **Spicy Hot Pan-Fried Fish:** Prepare as above, except omit salt and pepper. Use only 2 tablespoons cornmeal and combine with $^1/_4$

cup *all-purpose flour,* $^1/_2$ to 1 teaspoon *chili powder,* $^3/_4$ to 1 teaspoon *ground red pepper,* $^1/_2$ teaspoon *garlic powder,* and $^1/_2$ teaspoon *paprika.*

Nutrition Facts per serving: 204 cal., 9 g total fat (2 g sat. fat)

PECAN-COATED CATFISH

START TO FINISH: 20 MINUTES

Fast

  1 to 1$^1/_4$ **pounds fresh or frozen catfish fillets,** $^1/_2$ **to** $^3/_4$ **inch thick**
$^1/_4$ **cup fine dry bread crumbs**
  2 **tablespoons cornmeal**
  2 **tablespoons grated Parmesan cheese**
  2 **tablespoons ground pecans**
$^1/_4$ **teaspoon salt**
$^1/_4$ **teaspoon pepper**
$^1/_4$ **cup all-purpose flour**
$^1/_4$ **cup milk**
  2 **to 3 tablespoons cooking oil**
$^1/_3$ **cup chopped pecans**

1. Thaw fish, if frozen. Rinse fish and pat dry. Cut into 4 serving-size pieces, if necessary. Set aside. In a shallow bowl mix bread crumbs, cornmeal, Parmesan cheese, ground pecans, salt, and pepper. Coat each portion of fish with flour, dip in milk, then coat evenly with crumb mixture.
2. In a large skillet fry fish in hot oil for 4 to 6 minutes on each side or till golden and fish flakes easily with a fork; keep warm.
3. Remove excess crumbs from skillet. Add additional oil, if necessary. Add chopped pecans. Cook and stir about 2 minutes or till toasted; sprinkle pecans over catfish. Makes 4 servings.

Nutrition Facts per serving: 331 cal., 18 g total fat (3 g sat. fat), 89 mg chol., 347 mg sodium, 17 g carbo., 1 g fiber, 25 g pro. **Daily Values:** 3% vit. A, 0% vit. C, 6% calcium, 8% iron

TROUT AMANDINE

PREP: 20 MINUTES   COOK: 20 MINUTES

*For sole or flounder fillets, reduce the lemon juice to 1 tablespoon
and cook the fish for 3 to 4 minutes on each side.*

  4 fresh or frozen pan-dressed trout or other pan-dressed fish
     (about 8 ounces each)
  1 beaten egg
 1/4 cup milk
 1/2 cup all-purpose flour
 1/4 teaspoon salt
 1/4 cup cooking oil
 1/4 cup sliced almonds
  2 tablespoons margarine or butter
  2 tablespoons lemon juice

1. Thaw fish, if frozen. Bone fish, if desired. Rinse fish; pat dry with
paper towels. Combine egg and milk. Stir together flour and salt.
Coat fish with flour mixture, dip into egg mixture, then coat again
with flour mixture. In a 12-inch skillet heat the oil. Fry half of the
fish in hot oil for 5 to 6 minutes on each side or till golden and crisp
and fish flakes easily with a fork. Remove fish from skillet and keep
warm while cooking remaining fish.

2. In a medium skillet cook sliced almonds in margarine or butter till
golden. Remove from heat; stir in lemon juice. Place fish on a serving platter; spoon almond mixture over fish. Makes 4 servings.

Nutrition Facts per serving: 425 cal., 28 g total fat (5 g sat. fat), 119 mg chol., 254 mg
sodium, 14 g carbo., 1 g fiber, 29 g pro. **Daily Values:** 12% vit. A, 11% vit. C, 10%
calcium, 22% iron

DEEP-DISH TUNA PIE

PREP: 25 MINUTES   BAKE: 40 MINUTES   Oven 400°

- $^1/_2$ of an 11-ounce package piecrust mix ($1^1/_3$ cups)
- 1 large onion, chopped (1 cup)
- 1 cup diced, peeled potato (1 medium)
- 1 $10^3/_4$-ounce can condensed cream of mushroom soup
- $^1/_3$ cup milk
- $^1/_3$ cup grated Parmesan cheese
- 1 tablespoon lemon juice
- $^3/_4$ teaspoon dried dillweed
- $^1/_4$ teaspoon pepper
- 1 16-ounce package frozen mixed vegetables
- 1 $9^1/_4$-ounce can tuna, drained and broken into chunks

1. Prepare piecrust mix according to package directions, except do not roll out. Cover dough; set aside. In a large skillet cook onion and potato in a small amount of boiling water, covered, about 7 minutes or till tender. Drain off liquid. Stir in soup, milk, Parmesan cheese, lemon juice, dillweed, and pepper. Cook and stir till mixture is bubbly. Gently stir in vegetables and tuna. Spoon mixture into an ungreased 2-quart casserole.

2. On a lightly floured surface, roll pastry into a circle 2 inches larger than the diameter of the top of the casserole and about $^1/_8$ inch thick. Make several 1-inch slits near the center of the pastry. Center pastry over casserole, allowing pastry to hang over edge. Trim pastry $^1/_2$ inch beyond edge of casserole. Turn pastry under; flute to the casserole edge, pressing gently. Bake in a 400° oven for 40 to 45 minutes or till crust is golden brown. Serve immediately. Makes 6 servings.

Nutrition Facts per serving: 342 cal., 15 g total fat (5 g sat. fat), 17 mg chol., 856 mg sodium, 35 g carbo., 2 g fiber, 18 g pro. **Daily Values:** 33% vit. A, 12% vit. C, 13% calcium, 16% iron

TUNA-NOODLE CASSEROLE

PREP: 20 MINUTES   BAKE: 20 MINUTES   Oven 375°

For a faster version, substitute a 10³/₄-ounce can condensed cream of mushroom soup mixed with ³/₄ cup milk for the sauce.

  3 cups medium noodles (4 ounces) or 1 cup elbow macaroni
     (3¹/₂ ounces)
¹/₄ cup fine dry bread crumbs
  1 tablespoon butter or margarine, melted
  1 cup chopped celery
¹/₄ cup chopped onion
  3 tablespoons butter or margarine
¹/₄ cup all-purpose flour
¹/₂ teaspoon dry mustard (optional)
  1 cup milk
  1 cup chicken broth
  1 9¹/₄-ounce can tuna, drained and broken into chunks, or two
     6³/₄-ounce cans skinless, boneless salmon
¹/₄ cup chopped pimiento

1. Cook noodles or macaroni according to package directions. Drain and set aside. Meanwhile, combine bread crumbs and the 1 table-spoon melted butter or margarine; set aside.
2. For sauce, in a medium saucepan cook celery and onion in the 3 tablespoons butter or margarine till tender. Stir in flour and, if de-sired, dry mustard. Add milk and chicken broth all at once; cook and stir till slightly thickened and bubbly. Combine sauce, tuna or salmon, pimiento, and cooked noodles. Transfer to a 1¹/₂-quart casserole. Sprinkle with crumb mixture. Bake, uncovered, in a 375° oven 20 minutes or till bubbly. Serves 4.

Nutrition Facts per serving: 377 cal., 15 g total fat (8 g sat. fat), 70 mg chol., 678 mg sodium, 34 g carbo., 3 g fiber, 26 g pro. **Daily Values:** 23% vit. A, 23% vit. C, 11% calcium, 19% iron

■ **Vegetable Tuna-Noodle Casserole:** Prepare as above, except add 1 cup *frozen vegetables, thawed,* with the tuna; transfer tuna mixture to a 2-quart casserole.

Nutrition Facts per serving: 392 cal., 15 g total fat (8 g sat. fat)

SALMON PATTIES

START TO FINISH: 30 MINUTES

Fast

- 1 **egg white, beaten**
- 2 **tablespoons milk**
- 1 **teaspoon dried minced onion**
- 2 **teaspoons snipped fresh dill or** $^1/_2$ **teaspoon dried dillweed**
- 1 **$7^3/_4$-ounce can salmon, drained, flaked, and skin and bones removed**
- $^1/_2$ **cup finely crushed wheat crackers**
- 1 **tablespoon cooking oil**
- 1 **tablespoon butter or margarine**
- 2 **teaspoons all-purpose flour**
- $^1/_2$ **cup milk**
- $^1/_2$ **cup shredded American cheese (2 ounces)**

1. In a medium bowl combine the egg white, milk, onion, dill, and $^1/_8$ teaspoon *pepper*. Add salmon and crushed crackers; mix well. Form mixture into three $^3/_4$-inch-thick patties. In a large skillet cook patties in hot oil over medium-low heat about 6 minutes or till golden brown, turning once. Transfer to a serving platter; keep warm.

2. For cheese sauce, in a small saucepan melt butter or margarine. Stir in flour and dash *pepper*. Add milk all at once. Cook and stir over medium heat till thickened and bubbly. Cook and stir 1 minute more. Stir in cheese till melted. Spoon sauce over patties. Makes 3 servings.

Nutrition Facts per serving: 317 cal., 21 g total fat (9 g sat. fat), 68 mg chol., 794 mg sodium, 11 g carbo., 0 g fiber, 21 g pro. **Daily Values:** 14% vit. A, 1% vit. C, 27% calcium, 7% iron

CRAB MORNAY

START TO FINISH: 30 MINUTES

Fast

Look for patty shells in the frozen food section of your grocery store.

- 4 frozen patty shells or toast points (see Lobster Newburg recipe, page 534)
- 1 cup sliced fresh mushrooms
- 2 tablespoons chopped onion
- 2 tablespoons thinly sliced celery
- 2 tablespoons butter or margarine
- 2 tablespoons all-purpose flour
- 1/8 teaspoon salt
  Dash ground red pepper
- 1 1/4 cups milk
- 1 cup shredded process Swiss or Gruyère cheese (4 ounces)
- 1 cup cooked crabmeat or one 6-ounce package frozen crabmeat, thawed and drained
- 2 tablespoons dry sherry or dry white wine
  Paprika or snipped parsley (optional)

1. Bake patty shells according to package directions. Set aside to cool.

2. Meanwhile, in a medium saucepan cook mushrooms, onion, and celery in butter or margarine till tender. Stir in flour, salt, and red pepper. Add milk all at once. Cook and stir till thickened and bubbly. Cook and stir for 1 minute more. Reduce heat. Add cheese and stir till melted. Stir in crabmeat and sherry or wine. Heat through; do not boil.

3. Serve crab mixture in patty shells or over toast points. If desired, sprinkle with paprika or parsley. Makes 4 servings.

Nutrition Facts per serving: 461 cal., 30 g total fat (9 g sat. fat), 79 mg chol., 907 mg sodium, 27 g carbo., 1 g fiber, 19 g pro. **Daily Values:** 18% vit. A, 5% vit. C, 29% calcium, 7% iron

■ **Shrimp Mornay:** Prepare as above, except substitute 8 ounces cooked, peeled, and deveined *shrimp or* two *4 1/2-ounce cans shrimp,* rinsed and drained, for crabmeat.

Nutrition Facts per serving: 470 cal., 30 g total fat (9 g sat. fat)

■ **Lobster Mornay:** Prepare as above, except substitute 1 cup cooked *lobster* or one *6¹/₂-ounce can lobster,* drained, broken into large pieces, and cartilage removed, for crabmeat.

Nutrition Facts per serving: 463 cal., 30 g total fat (9 g sat. fat)

CRAB CAKES

START TO FINISH: 25 MINUTES

Fast

Aficionados of crab cakes are quite particular about how they are served. Some insist on Tartar Sauce, and others wouldn't eat them with anything but mustard.

  1 6-ounce package frozen crabmeat or one 6-ounce can
    crabmeat, drained, flaked, and cartilage removed
  1 beaten egg
¹/₄ cup fine dry bread crumbs
  2 tablespoons finely chopped green onion (1)
  2 tablespoons mayonnaise or salad dressing
  1 tablespoon snipped fresh parsley
  2 teaspoons Dijon-style mustard
  2 teaspoons snipped fresh thyme or ¹/₂ teaspoon dried thyme,
    crushed
¹/₂ teaspoon white wine Worcestershire sauce
¹/₄ teaspoon celery salt
  2 tablespoons cornmeal
  2 tablespoons fine dry bread crumbs
  2 tablespoons cooking oil
    Lemon wedges (optional)
  1 recipe Tartar Sauce (see page 966) or Dijon-style mustard
    (optional)

1. Thaw crabmeat, if frozen; drain. In a medium mixing bowl combine egg, the ¹/₄ cup bread crumbs, the green onion, mayonnaise or salad dressing, parsley, Dijon-style mustard, thyme, Worcestershire sauce, and celery salt. Stir in crabmeat; mix well. Shape mixture into four ¹/₂-inch-thick patties.
2. Combine cornmeal and the 2 tablespoons bread crumbs. Coat patties with cornmeal mixture. In a large skillet heat oil. Add crab cakes. Cook over medium heat about 3 minutes on each side or till

golden and heated through. Add additional oil, if necessary. Serve immediately. If desired, serve with lemon wedges and Tartar Sauce or mustard. Makes 4 servings.

Nutrition Facts per serving: 229 cal., 15 g total fat (2 g sat. fat), 100 mg chol., 410 mg sodium, 11 g carbo., 1 g fiber, 12 g pro. **Daily Values:** 4% vit. A, 5% vit. C, 5% calcium, 9% iron

---

DEVILED CRAB

PREP: 20 MINUTES   BAKE: 20 MINUTES   Oven 375°

- 2 tablespoons butter or margarine
- 2 tablespoons all-purpose flour
- 1 cup milk, half-and-half, or light cream
  Several dashes bottled hot pepper sauce
- 1 6-ounce can crabmeat, drained, flaked, and cartilage removed
- 1 hard-cooked egg, chopped
- 1/2 cup shredded process Swiss cheese (2 ounces)
- 2 tablespoons chopped pimiento
- 1 tablespoon Dijon-style mustard
- 1/4 cup fine dry bread crumbs
- 1 tablespoon butter or margarine, melted
- 1/4 cup sliced almonds, toasted (see tip, page 234)

1. In a medium saucepan melt the 2 tablespoons butter or margarine. Stir in flour. Add milk, half-and-half, or light cream and hot pepper sauce all at once. Cook and stir till thickened and bubbly. Cook and stir 1 minute more. Stir in crabmeat, egg, Swiss cheese, pimiento, and mustard.
2. Spoon into four 6-ounce custard cups, 8-ounce casseroles, or large coquille shells. Toss bread crumbs with the 1 tablespoon melted butter or margarine; sprinkle over casseroles. Top with almonds. Bake in a 375° oven about 20 minutes or till the crumbs are brown. Makes 4 servings.

Nutrition Facts per serving: 297 cal., 19 g total fat (8 g sat. fat), 123 mg chol., 624 mg sodium, 13 g carbo., 1 g fiber, 19 g pro. **Daily Values:** 21% vit. A, 11% vit. C, 22% calcium, 9% iron

BROILED CRAB LEGS

START TO FINISH: 15 MINUTES

Fast

Low-Fat

For a dipping sauce, double the amount of the butter mixture and pass it with the crab legs.

- 1¹/₂ pounds fresh or frozen split crab legs
- 3 tablespoons butter or margarine, melted
- 1 tablespoon snipped fresh basil or 1 teaspoon dried basil, crushed
- ¹/₂ teaspoon finely shredded lemon peel
- 1 tablespoon lemon juice

1. Thaw crab legs, if frozen. Rinse and pat dry with paper towels. Place crab legs on the greased unheated rack of a broiler pan. Stir together butter or margarine, basil, lemon peel, and lemon juice. Brush crab legs with butter mixture.

2. Broil 4 to 6 inches from the heat for 3 to 4 minutes or till heated through. Makes 4 servings.

Nutrition Facts per serving: 176 cal., 10 g total fat (7 g sat. fat), 24 mg chol., 358 mg sodium, 4 g carbo., 0 g fiber, 16 g pro. **Daily Values:** 8% vit. A, 5% vit. C, 8% calcium, 217% iron

FRIED SOFT-SHELL CRABS

PREP: 25 MINUTES   FRY: 2¹/₂ MINUTES PER BATCH   Oven 300°

- 4 large or 8 small soft-shell crabs
- 1 beaten egg
- ¹/₄ cup milk
- ¹/₂ cup all-purpose flour
- ¹/₄ teaspoon salt
- ¹/₈ teaspoon ground red pepper
  Shortening or cooking oil for frying

1. To clean each soft-shell crab, hold the crab between the back legs. Using kitchen scissors, remove the head by cutting horizontally across the body ¹/₂ inch behind the eyes. Lift the pointed, soft top shell to expose the "devil's fingers" (the spongy projectiles). Using your fingers, push up on the devil's fingers and pull off. Replace the soft top shell over the body. Repeat on the other side. Turn crab over. Pull off the apron-shaped pieces and discard. Thoroughly rinse the crab under cold running water to remove the mustard-colored substance. Pat the crab dry with paper towels.

2. In a shallow dish combine egg and milk. In another dish combine flour, salt, and red pepper. Dip crabs in egg mixture; roll in flour mixture.

3. In an 8- or 10-inch skillet heat $1/2$ inch shortening or cooking oil. Add 2 or 3 crabs at a time, back sides down. Fry for $1^1/2$ to 2 minutes or till golden. Turn carefully. Fry for 1 to 2 minutes more or till crabs are crisp and golden and meat is done. Drain on paper towels. Keep crabs warm in a 300° oven while frying remaining crabs. Makes 4 servings.

Nutrition Facts per serving: 330 cal., 17 g total fat (4 g sat. fat), 189 mg chol., 533 mg sodium, 12 g carbo., 0 g fiber, 31 g pro. **Daily Values:** 3% vit. A, 8% vit. C, 13% calcium, 13% iron

---

SEAFOOD ENCHILADAS

PREP: 30 MINUTES   BAKE: 35 MINUTES   Oven 350°

Salad-style fish or surimi (sub REE mee) is fish flavored and formed into various seafood shapes, such as crabmeat or lobster. Most is made from Alaskan pollock, a lean, white-fleshed fish with a taste and texture similar to cod. It may be labeled "imitation crab" or "imitation lobster."

 12 ounces frozen, crab-flavored, salad-style fish
  8 $6^1/4$-inch corn tortillas
  1 medium red onion, finely chopped ($1/2$ cup)
  2 cloves garlic, minced
  1 teaspoon ground coriander
 $1/4$ teaspoon pepper
  2 tablespoons butter or margarine
  3 tablespoons all-purpose flour
  1 8-ounce carton dairy sour cream
  1 $14^1/2$-ounce can chicken broth
  1 or 2 canned jalapeño peppers, rinsed, seeded, and chopped, or
   one 4-ounce can diced green chili peppers, drained
  1 cup shredded Monterey Jack cheese (4 ounces)

1. Thaw fish, if frozen. Flake coarsely; set aside. Wrap corn tortillas in foil; place in a 350° oven for 10 to 15 minutes or till softened.

2. Meanwhile, for sauce, in a medium saucepan cook red onion, garlic, coriander, and pepper in butter or margarine till onion is tender. In a medium bowl stir flour into sour cream. Add broth; stir till combined. Add sour cream mixture to onion mixture. Stir in jalapeño or chili peppers. Cook and stir over medium heat till mixture is slightly thickened and bubbly. Remove from heat. Add *half* of the cheese; stir till melted.

3. For filling, stir 1/2 cup of the sauce into flaked fish. Place about 1/4 cup of the filling on each tortilla; roll up. Arrange rolled tortillas, seam sides down, in a lightly greased 2-quart rectangular baking dish. Top with remaining sauce.

4. Bake, covered, in a 350° oven for 30 to 35 minutes or till heated through. Sprinkle with remaining cheese. Bake, uncovered, about 5 minutes more or till cheese melts. Let stand for 10 minutes before serving. Makes 4 servings.

Nutrition Facts per serving: 529 cal., 29 g total fat (17 g sat. fat), 83 mg chol., 1,372 mg sodium, 43 g carbo., 1 g fiber, 25 g pro. **Daily Values:** 30% vit. A, 13% vit. C, 33% calcium, 13% iron

---

SHRIMP IN GARLIC BUTTER

START TO FINISH: 20 MINUTES

Fast   **Low-Fat**

> 1 pound fresh or frozen medium shrimp in shells
> 2 tablespoons butter or margarine
> 3 cloves garlic, minced
> 2 tablespoons snipped fresh parsley
> 1 tablespoon dry sherry

1. Thaw shrimp, if frozen. Peel and devein shrimp (see photos 1, 2, and 3, page 528). Rinse shrimp; pat dry with paper towels.

2. In a large skillet heat butter or margarine over medium-high heat. Add shrimp and garlic. Cook, stirring frequently, for 1 to 3 minutes or till shrimp turn pink. Stir in parsley and sherry. Serves 4.

Nutrition Facts per serving: 126 cal., 6 g total fat (4 g sat. fat), 146 mg chol., 218 mg sodium, 1 g carbo., 0 g fiber, 14 g pro. **Daily Values:** 13% vit. A, 8% vit. C, 2% calcium, 14% iron

■ **Scallops in Garlic Butter:** Prepare as above, except substitute 12 ounces fresh or frozen *scallops* for the shrimp. Thaw scallops, if frozen. Rinse scallops; pat dry with paper towels. Cut any large scallops in half. Cook and stir the scallops and garlic in butter or margarine for 3 to 5 minutes or till scallops turn opaque.

Nutrition Facts per serving: 114 cal., 6 g total fat (4 g sat. fat)

1. To peel a shrimp, open the shell lengthwise down the body. Start at the head end and peel back the shell. Gently pull on the tail to remove it.

2. To devein a shrimp, use a sharp knife to make a shallow slit along the back from the head to the tail end. Locate the black vein.

3. If the vein is visible, hold shrimp under cold running water, rinsing away the vein. Or, remove it using the tip of a knife, then rinse shrimp.

STIR-FRIED SHRIMP AND BROCCOLI

START TO FINISH: 30 MINUTES

Fast　　　　　　　　　　**Low-Fat**

This pleasing mixture of broccoli, carrots, and seasonings tastes equally delicious with shrimp or scallops. If you prefer, leave the tails on the shrimp for a striking presentation.

　1　**pound fresh or frozen medium shrimp in shells or 12 ounces fresh or frozen scallops**
　3　**tablespoons red wine vinegar**
　3　**tablespoons soy sauce**
　3　**tablespoons water**
　1　**tablespoon cornstarch**
1¹/₂　**teaspoons sugar**
　1　**tablespoon cooking oil**
　2　**cloves garlic, minced**
　2　**cups broccoli flowerets**
　1　**cup thinly bias-sliced carrots**
　1　**small onion, halved lengthwise and sliced**
　1　**cup sliced fresh mushrooms**
　8　**ounces vermicelli or fusilli, cooked and drained (see pages 775, 774) or 2 cups hot cooked rice (see page 139)**

1. Thaw shrimp or scallops, if frozen. Peel and devein shrimp if using (see photos 1, 2, and 3, at left). Rinse shrimp or scallops; pat dry with paper towels. Cut any large scallops in half. Set aside. In a small mixing bowl combine vinegar, soy sauce, water, cornstarch, and sugar; set aside.
2. Heat oil in wok or large skillet over medium-high heat. Stir-fry the garlic in the hot oil for 15 seconds. Add the broccoli, carrots, and onion. Stir-fry for 3 minutes. Add the mushrooms; stir-fry for 1 to 2 minutes more or till vegetables are crisp-tender. Remove vegetables from wok with slotted spoon. Stir vinegar mixture. Add to wok and bring to boiling. Add shrimp or scallops and cook about 3 minutes or till shrimp turn pink or scallops are opaque. Stir in vegetables; heat through. Serve with pasta or rice. Makes 4 servings.

Nutrition Facts per serving: 395 cal., 6 g total fat (1 g sat. fat), 131 mg chol., 968 mg sodium, 62 g carbo., 5 g fiber, 26 g pro. **Daily Values:** 101% vit. A, 104% vit. C, 7% calcium, 39% iron

SHRIMP CREOLE

START TO FINISH: 40 MINUTES

Low-Fat

If some family members prefer their food less hot, use the ¹/₈ teaspoon ground red pepper and pass bottled hot pepper sauce at the table.

    1   pound fresh or frozen medium shrimp in shells
    1   medium onion, chopped (¹/₂ cup)
 ¹/₂   cup chopped celery
 ¹/₂   cup chopped green sweet pepper
    2   cloves garlic, minced
    2   tablespoons margarine or butter
    1   14¹/₂-ounce can tomatoes, cut up, or one 14¹/₂-ounce can diced
          tomatoes
    2   tablespoons snipped fresh parsley
 ¹/₂   teaspoon salt
 ¹/₂   teaspoon paprika
 ¹/₈   to ¹/₄ teaspoon ground red pepper
    1   bay leaf
    2   tablespoons cold water
    4   teaspoons cornstarch
    2   cups hot cooked rice (see page 139)

1. Thaw shrimp, if frozen. Peel and devein shrimp (see photos 1, 2, and 3, page 528). Rinse shrimp; pat dry with paper towels.

2. In a large skillet cook onion, celery, sweet pepper, and garlic in margarine or butter till tender. Stir in undrained tomatoes, parsley, salt, paprika, red pepper, and bay leaf. Bring to boiling; reduce heat. Cover and simmer for 15 minutes.

3. Stir together cold water and cornstarch. Stir shrimp and cornstarch mixture into tomato mixture. Cook and stir till thickened and bubbly. Cook and stir for 1 to 3 minutes more or till shrimp turn pink. Remove bay leaf. Serve over rice. Serves 4.

Nutrition Facts per serving: 274 cal., 7 g total fat (1 g sat. fat), 131 mg chol., 692 mg sodium, 35 g carbo., 2 g fiber, 18 g pro. **Daily Values:** 23% vit. A, 56% vit. C, 7% calcium, 27% iron

■ **Fish Creole:** Prepare as above, except substitute 12 ounces fresh or frozen *fish fillets* for the shrimp. Thaw fish, if frozen. Rinse fish and cut into 1-inch pieces. Add fish to the tomato mixture after the mixture is thickened and bubbly. Cook and stir about 3 minutes or till fish flakes easily with a fork.

Nutrition Facts per serving: 272 cal., 7 g total fat (1 g sat. fat)

SPICED SHRIMP WITH RICE

START TO FINISH: 45 MINUTES

*Serve this one-pot meal along with steamed peapods
for a casual supper.*

1	pound fresh or frozen medium shrimp in shells
1	teaspoon grated gingerroot
1	teaspoon ground coriander
$^1/_2$	teaspoon five-spice powder or Homemade Five-Spice Powder (see page 532)
$^1/_2$	teaspoon paprika
$^1/_4$	teaspoon ground cumin
$^1/_4$	teaspoon ground turmeric
3	tablespoons margarine or butter
1	tablespoon cooking oil
$^1/_4$	cup finely chopped onion
3	cloves garlic, minced
1	Anaheim pepper, seeded and chopped (see tip, page 111), or 3 tablespoons canned diced green chili peppers
$1^1/_2$	cups long grain rice
$3^1/_4$	cups water or chicken broth
$^1/_2$	teaspoon salt*
3	green onions, sliced

1. Thaw shrimp, if frozen. Peel and devein shrimp (see photos 1, 2, and 3, page 528). Rinse shrimp; pat dry. In a large bowl combine shrimp, gingerroot, coriander, five-spice powder, paprika, cumin, and turmeric. Cover and let stand at room temperature for up to 30 minutes while preparing rice.
2. In a large saucepan heat margarine or butter and oil till margarine or butter is melted. Add onion, garlic, and chili pepper. Cook about 5 minutes or till onion is tender. Add rice. Stir in water and salt or chicken broth (*omit salt if using chicken broth). Bring to boiling; reduce heat. Simmer, covered, for 10 minutes (rice will not be done).
3. Stir in shrimp mixture. Return to boiling; reduce heat. Cook, cov-

ered, about 5 minutes more or till shrimp turn pink and rice is tender. Sprinkle each serving with green onions. Makes 4 servings.

■ **Homemade Five-Spice Powder:** To a blender container add 3 tablespoons *ground cinnamon,* 6 *star anise or* 2 teaspoons *aniseed,* 1 1/2 teaspoons *fennel seed,* 1 1/2 teaspoons *whole Szechwan peppers or whole black pepper,* and 3/4 teaspoon *ground cloves.* Cover and blend to a fine powder. Store in a tightly covered container. Makes 1/3 cup.

Nutrition Facts per serving: 443 cal., 13 g total fat (2 g sat. fat), 131 mg chol., 528 mg sodium, 59 g carbo., 1 g fiber, 20 g pro. **Daily Values:** 19% vit. A, 27% vit. C, 6% calcium, 38% iron

---

COQUILLES SAINT JACQUES

PREP: 30 MINUTES BAKE: 7 MINUTES   Oven 400°

    1 pound fresh or frozen scallops
  1/4 cup butter or margarine
    1 cup chopped fresh mushrooms
    2 tablespoons thinly sliced green onion
    2 tablespoons all-purpose flour
  1/8 teaspoon pepper
  2/3 cup half-and-half or light cream
    1 egg yolk, slightly beaten
    3 tablespoons dry white wine
  3/4 cup soft bread crumbs (1 slice)
    1 tablespoon butter or margarine, melted
    1 tablespoon snipped fresh parsley

1. Thaw scallops, if frozen. Rinse scallops; pat dry with paper towels. Halve any large scallops. In a large skillet cook half of the scallops in *1 tablespoon* of the 1/4 cup butter over medium heat for 1 to 3 minutes or till scallops turn opaque. Remove scallops with a slotted spoon; drain, if necessary. Repeat with remaining scallops and *1 tablespoon* of the remaining butter.

2. In the same skillet cook mushrooms and green onion in *2 tablespoons* butter till tender. Stir in flour and pepper. Add half-and-half; cook and stir till thickened and bubbly. Gradually stir hot mixture into egg yolk. Stir in scallops and wine.

3. Spoon scallop mixture into 4 coquille shells, au gratin dishes, or 6-ounce custard cups. Place in a shallow baking pan. Toss together bread crumbs, the 1 tablespoon melted butter, and parsley; sprinkle over mixture in dishes. Bake in a 400° oven for 7 to 9 minutes or till crumbs are brown. Serves 4.

Nutrition Facts per serving: 315 cal., 22 g total fat (12 g sat. fat), 140 mg chol., 399 mg sodium, 11 g carbo., 1 g fiber, 18 g pro. **Daily Values:** 32% vit. A, 5% vit. C, 11% calcium, 19% iron

OYSTERS AU GRATIN

PREP: 30 MINUTES   BAKE: 10 MINUTES   Oven 400°

    2 pints shucked oysters
    3 tablespoons butter or margarine
    1 cup sliced fresh mushrooms
    1 clove garlic, minced
    2 tablespoons all-purpose flour
  ³/₄ cup milk
  ¹/₄ cup dry white wine
    2 tablespoons snipped fresh parsley
  ¹/₂ teaspoon Worcestershire sauce
  ³/₄ cup soft bread crumbs (1 slice)
  ¹/₄ cup grated Parmesan cheese
    1 tablespoon butter or margarine, melted

1. Rinse oysters; pat dry with paper towels. In a large skillet cook and stir oysters in *1 tablespoon* of the butter or margarine for 3 to 4 minutes or till oyster edges curl; drain. Divide oysters among four 10-ounce casseroles.

2. For sauce, in the same skillet cook mushrooms and garlic in *2 tablespoons* of the butter or margarine till tender. Stir in flour. Add milk all at once. Cook and stir till thickened and bubbly. Stir in wine, parsley, and Worcestershire sauce. Spoon over oysters. Toss together the bread crumbs, Parmesan cheese, and the 1 tablespoon melted butter or margarine. Sprinkle over casseroles. Bake in a 400° oven about 10 minutes or till crumbs are brown. Makes 4 servings.

Nutrition Facts per serving: 323 cal., 19 g total fat (9 g sat. fat), 125 mg chol., 515 mg sodium, 18 g carbo., 1 g fiber, 18 g pro. **Daily Values:** 36% vit. A, 22% vit. C, 20% calcium, 82% iron

BOILED LOBSTER

PREP: 35 MINUTES   COOK: 20 MINUTES

    8 quarts water
    2 teaspoons salt
    2 1- to 1½-pound live lobsters
  ¼ cup butter

1. In a 12-quart kettle bring water and salt to boiling. Grasp each lobster just behind the eyes; rinse lobsters under cold running water. Quickly plunge lobsters headfirst into the boiling water. Return to boiling; reduce heat. Cover and simmer for 20 minutes. Drain lobsters; remove bands or pegs on large claws.
2. When cool enough to handle, place each lobster on its back. With kitchen scissors, cut the body in half lengthwise up to the tail, cutting to but not through the back shell. Cut away the membrane on the tail to expose the meat and small sand sac near the head. Remove and discard the sand sac and the black vein running through the tail. Remove the green tomalley (liver) and coral roe (found only in females); if desired, reserve to serve with the lobster. Twist the large claws away from the body. Using a nutcracker, break open the claws. Remove the meat from the claws, tail, and body.
3. Melt butter over very low heat without stirring; cool slightly. Pour off clear top layer; discard milky bottom layer. Serve with lobster. Makes 2 servings.

Nutrition Facts per serving: 298 cal., 23 g total fat (14 g sat. fat), 133 mg chol., 612 mg sodium, 1 g carbo., 0 g fiber, 21 g pro. **Daily Values:** 23% vit. A, 0% vit. C, 5% calcium, 2% iron

LOBSTER NEWBURG

START TO FINISH: 40 MINUTES

Rich and creamy, this elegant dish may be served in patty shells made from puff pastry or over toast points. To make toast points, toast 4 slices of bread, butter 1 side, and cut each slice of bread into 4 small triangles.

    4 frozen patty shells, or toast points
    2 tablespoons butter or margarine
    2 tablespoons all-purpose flour

$^1/_4$ teaspoon salt
  Dash ground red pepper
$1^1/_2$ cups half-and-half, light cream, or milk
  2 egg yolks, beaten
  2 5-ounce cans lobster, drained, broken into large pieces, and
    cartilage removed, or 10 ounces cooked lobster
  3 tablespoons Madeira or dry sherry
    Paprika
    Parsley sprigs (optional)

1. Bake patty shells according to package directions. Set aside to cool.

2. Meanwhile, in a saucepan melt butter or margarine. Stir in flour, salt, and red pepper. Add half-and-half, light cream, or milk all at once. Cook and stir till thickened and bubbly. Cook and stir 1 minute more. Stir about half of the hot mixture into egg yolks; pour egg yolk mixture into hot mixture in saucepan. Cook and stir till mixture just boils. Reduce heat. Cook and stir 2 minutes more. Stir in lobster and Madeira or sherry; heat through.

3. Spoon into patty shells or over toast points. Sprinkle with paprika. If desired, garnish with parsley sprigs. Makes 4 servings.

Nutrition Facts per serving: 502 cal., 34 g total fat (11 g sat. fat), 206 mg chol., 824 mg sodium, 25 g carbo., 0 g fiber, 21 g pro. **Daily Values:** 37% vit. A, 1% vit. C, 12% calcium, 5% iron

■ **Crab Newburg:** Prepare as above, except substitute two 7-ounce cans *crabmeat,* drained, flaked, and cartilage removed, *or* two 6-ounce packages *frozen crabmeat,* thawed and drained, for lobster.

Nutrition Facts per serving: 494 cal., 35 g total fat (13 g sat. fat)

■ **Shrimp Newburg:** Prepare as above, except substitute 8 ounces cooked, peeled, and deveined *shrimp* ($1^1/_3$ cups) for the lobster.

Nutrition Facts per serving: 505 cal., 35 g total fat (13 g sat. fat)

LOBSTER THERMIDOR

PREP: $1^1/_2$ HOURS   BAKE: 10 MINUTES   Oven 350°

If you'd rather, use 1 pound cooked lobster and omit steps 1 and 2. Stir the lobster into the sauce and spoon the mixture into four 12- to 16-ounce casseroles. Bake as directed.

4 1-pound live lobsters
1 cup sliced fresh mushrooms
2 tablespoons chopped onion
2 tablespoons butter or margarine
2 tablespoons all-purpose flour
1¼ cups half-and-half, light cream, or milk
½ cup soft bread crumbs (1 slice)
2 tablespoons dry sherry or white wine
¼ cup grated Parmesan cheese

1. In a 12-quart pot bring 8 quarts *water* and 2 teaspoons *salt* to boiling. Grasp each lobster just behind the eyes; rinse lobsters under cold running water. Quickly plunge *two* of the lobsters headfirst into the boiling water. Return to boiling; reduce heat. Cover and simmer for 20 minutes. Drain lobsters; remove bands or pegs on large claws. Repeat with remaining lobsters.

2. When lobsters are cool enough to handle, place each lobster on its back. With kitchen scissors, cut the body in half lengthwise up to the tail, cutting to but not through the back shell. Cut away the membrane on the tail to expose the meat and small sand sac near the head. Remove and discard the sand sac and the black vein running through the tail. Remove the green tomalley (liver) and coral roe (found only in females); set aside. Twist the large claws and legs away from the body. Using a nutcracker, break open the claws. Remove the meat from the claws, tail, and body. Chop meat and set aside. Wash and rinse lobster shells. Discard legs and cartilage.

3. For sauce, in a medium saucepan cook mushrooms and onion in butter till tender. Stir in flour, ⅛ teaspoon *salt,* and a dash *pepper.* Add half-and-half all at once. Cook and stir till thickened and bubbly. Cook and stir 1 minute more. Remove from heat. Gently stir in cooked lobster meat, tomalley, coral roe, bread crumbs, and sherry.

4. Place lobster shells on a shallow baking pan. Fill lobster shells with lobster mixture. Sprinkle lobster mixture with Parmesan cheese. Bake in a 350° oven about 10 minutes or till heated through. Makes 4 servings.

Nutrition Facts per serving: 321 cal., 17 g total fat (10 g sat. fat), 119 mg chol., 688 mg sodium, 13 g carbo., 1 g fiber, 27 g pro. **Daily Values:** 20% vit. A, 3% vit. C, 19% calcium, 8% iron

GUIDE TO FISH TYPES

Check this guide to become acquainted with various types of fish. Also, use the list of suggested substitutes, which can be tried in recipes. Note that the flavors range from delicate to pronounced.

Types	Fat Content*	Texture	Flavor	Substitutions
FRESHWATER FISH				
Catfish	Low	Firm	Mild	Cusk, red snapper, sea trout
Lake Trout	Moderate to high	Firm	Mild	Pike, sea trout, whitefish
Pike	Low	Firm	Mild to moderate	Cod, orange roughy, whitefish
Rainbow Trout	Moderate to high	Firm	Delicate	Salmon, pike, sea trout
Whitefish	High	Firm	Delicate	Haddock, lake trout, pike
SALTWATER FISH				
Cod	Low	Firm	Delicate	Haddock, halibut, pike, pollack
Flounder	Low	Fine	Delicate to mild	Pike, sole, whitefish, whiting
Haddock	Low	Firm	Delicate	Cod, halibut, lake trout, sole, whitefish

GUIDE TO FISH TYPES (continued)

Types	Fat Content*	Texture	Flavor	Substitutions
Halibut	Low	Firm	Delicate	Cod, flounder, sea bass, snapper, sole
Mackerel	High	Firm	Pronounced	Swordfish, tuna
Mahimahi	Moderate	Firm	Mild to moderate	Cusk
Ocean Perch	Low	Firm	Mild	Lake perch, rainbow trout, sea bass
Orange Roughy	Low	Firm	Delicate	Cod, flounder, sea bass, sole
Redfish	Low	Firm	Mild	Carp, croaker, drum
Red Snapper	Low	Firm	Mild to moderate	Lake trout, rockfish, whitefish
Rockfish	Low	Firm, chewy	Mild to moderate	Cod, drum, ocean perch, red snapper
Salmon	Moderate to high	Firm	Mild to moderate	Swordfish, tuna
Shark	Low	Firm, dense	Mild to moderate	Salmon, sea bass, swordfish, tuna

Sole	Low	Fine	Delicate to mild	Flounder, pike
Swordfish	Low to moderate	Firm, dense	Mild to moderate	Sea bass, shark, tuna
Tuna	Moderate to high	Firm	Mild to moderate	Mackerel, salmon, swordfish

*Low is less than 5% fat; moderate is 5% to 10% fat; and high is greater than 10% fat.

Cooking Fish

Minutes count when cooking fish. Use a ruler to measure the thickness of the fish in order to better estimate when to check for doneness. Properly cooked fish is opaque, begins to flake easily when tested with a fork, and comes away from the bones readily; the juices should be a milky white. Fish may be cooked while still frozen, but you will need to increase the cooking time (see directions, below). For grilling directions, see pages 594–96.

Cooking Method	Preparation	Fresh or Thawed Fillets or Steaks	Frozen Fillets or Steaks	Dressed
Bake	Place in a single layer in a greased shallow baking pan. For fillets, tuck under any thin edges. Brush with melted margarine or butter.	Bake, uncovered, in a 450° oven for 4 to 6 minutes per 1/2-inch thickness.	Bake, uncovered, in a 450° oven for 9 to 11 minutes per 1/2-inch thickness.	Bake, uncovered, in a 350° oven for 6 to 9 minutes per 1/2 pound.
Broil	Preheat broiler. Place fish on greased unheated rack of a broiler pan. For fillets, tuck under any thin	Broil 4 inches from the heat for 4 to 6 minutes per 1/2-inch thickness. If fish is 1 inch or more thick, turn it over	Broil 4 inches from the heat for 6 to 9 minutes per 1/2-inch thickness. If fish is 1 inch or more thick, turn it over	Not recommended.

Method			
	edges. Brush with melted margarine or butter.	halfway through broiling.	halfway through broiling.
Poach	Add 1½ cups water, broth, or wine to a large skillet. Bring to boiling. Add fish. Return to boiling; reduce heat.	Simmer, uncovered, for 4 to 6 minutes per ½-inch thickness.	Simmer, uncovered, for 6 to 9 minutes per ½-inch thickness.	Simmer, covered, for 6 to 9 minutes per ½ pound.
Microwave	Remove head and tail of dressed fish. Arrange fish in a single layer in a shallow baking dish. For fillets, tuck under any thin edges. Cover with vented clear plastic wrap.	Cook on 100% power (high). For ½ pound of ½-inch-thick fillets, allow 2 to 4 minutes; for 1 pound of ½-inch-thick fillets, allow 3 to 5 minutes. For 1 pound of ¾- to 1-inch-thick steaks, allow 5 to 7 minutes.	Not recommended.	Cook on 100% power (high). For two 8- to 10-ounce fish, allow 4½ to 7 minutes, giving dish a half-turn once. Let stand for 5 minutes.

Selecting and Cooking Shellfish

Refer to these directions for cooking fresh shellfish. Many types of shellfish are available partially prepared or even cooked. Ask at the fish and shellfish counter for additional information when making purchases.

Shellfish Type (Amount per serving)	Preparing	Cooking
Clams 6 clams in the shell	Scrub live clams under cold running water. For 24 clams in shells, in an 8-quart Dutch oven combine 4 quarts of cold water and 1/3 cup salt. Add clams and soak for 15 minutes; drain and rinse. Discard water. Repeat twice.	For 24 clams in shells, add 1/2 inch water to an 8-quart pot; bring to boiling. Place clams in a steamer basket. Steam, covered, 5 to 7 minutes or till clams open and are thoroughly cooked. Discard any that do not open.
Crabs 1 pound live blue crabs	Grasp live crabs from behind, firmly holding the back two legs on each side. Rinse under cold running water.	To boil 3 pounds live hard-shell blue crabs, in a 12- to 16-quart pot bring 8 quarts water and 2 teaspoons salt to boiling. Add crabs. Simmer, covered, about 15 minutes; drain and chill.
Crawfish/ Crayfish 1 pound live crawfish	Rinse live crawfish under cold running water. For 4 pounds crawfish, in a 12- to 16-quart pot combine 8 quarts cold water and 1/3 cup salt. Add crawfish. Soak for 15 minutes; rinse and drain.	For 4 pounds live crawfish, in a 12- to 16-quart pot bring 8 quarts water and 2 teaspoons salt to boiling. Add crawfish. Simmer, covered, 5 minutes or till shells turn bright red; drain.

Lobster Tails One 8-ounce frozen lobster tail (for Boiled Lobster, see recipe, page 534)	Thaw frozen lobster tails in the refrigerator.	For four 8-ounce lobster tails, in a 3-quart saucepan bring 6 cups water and $1\frac{1}{2}$ teaspoons salt to boiling. Add tails; simmer, uncovered, for 8 to 12 minutes or till shells turn bright red and meat is tender. Drain.
Mussels 12 mussels in shells	Scrub live mussels under cold running water. Using your fingers, pull out the beards that are visible between the shells. Soak as for clams, above.	For 24 mussels, add $\frac{1}{2}$ inch water to an 8-quart pot; bring to boiling. Place mussels in a steamer basket. Steam, covered, for 5 to 7 minutes or till shells open and mussels are thoroughly cooked. Discard any that do not open.
Oysters 6 oysters in shells	Scrub live oysters under cold running water. For easier shucking, chill them before opening. Shuck, reserving bottom shells, if desired.	For 24 shucked oysters, in a saucepan bring 2 cups water and $\frac{1}{2}$ teaspoon salt to boiling. Add oysters. Simmer about 5 minutes or till oysters are plump and opaque; drain.
Shrimp 6 ounces shrimp in shells or 3 to 4 ounces peeled shrimp	To peel shrimp, open the shell down the underside. Starting at the head, pull back the shell. Gently pull on the tail to remove. Use a sharp knife to remove the black vein that runs along the center of the back. Rinse under cold running water (see photos 1, 2, and 3, page 528).	For 1 pound shrimp, in a 3-quart saucepan bring 4 cups water and 1 teaspoon salt to boiling. Add shrimp. Simmer, uncovered, for 1 to 3 minutes or till shrimp turn pink, stirring occasionally. Rinse under cold running water; drain and chill.

GRILLING

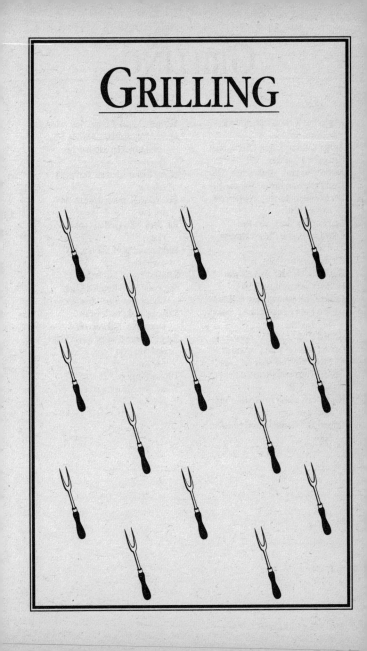

GRILLING

Reliable equipment and an appropriate fire are the basic needs for successful grilling. Choose the type of cooker you are comfortable using. The recipes in this chapter are suitable for gas, electric, or charcoal grills and include directions for both direct and indirect grilling where appropriate. Any grill can be used for direct grilling, including braziers (the basic shallow firebox on legs) and hibachis. For indirect grilling, you need a grill with a cover. These grills can be either kettle- or wagon-shaped and have gas, electric, or charcoal heat sources.

Prepare the fire

If you have a gas or electric grill, follow the manufacturer's instructions for lighting and preheating the grill. Check your owner's manual for charcoal grills, too; some recommend lining the firebox with a double layer of heavy foil and adding an inch of pea gravel or coarse grit. This promotes better air circulation so coals burn more efficiently.

A good rule of thumb for deciding how much charcoal to use is to spread the briquettes in a single layer that extends about 1 inch beyond the food to be grilled. Add a few more if the weather is humid or windy. Then mound the briquettes in the center for lighting (see tip 1, page 548).

Self-lighting briquettes can be ignited with a match and need to burn for 5 to 10 minutes before they're ready for grilling. To start other types, try an electric starter or a liquid, wax-type (solid), or jelly starter. Also consider a portable (or chimney) starter. Follow the manufacturer's directions carefully. Wait about a minute after adding a liquid, wax, or jelly starter before igniting the briquettes. Never use gasoline or kerosene as a fire starter. Standard briquettes generally take 20 to 30 minutes to heat. When ready to use, coals will appear ash gray in daylight or glowing red at night.

Arrange the coals

Before arranging the coals, know whether you're going to grill directly or indirectly (see tip, page 548). With direct grilling, the food goes on the grill rack directly over the coals. To arrange the coals, use long-handled tongs to spread them evenly in a single layer (see tip 2, page 548).

With indirect grilling, the coals are arranged around the food so that juices from the food will not reach them, reducing the chance of flare-ups. This method is used to evenly cook large cuts of meat and poultry (we suggest placing larger meat and poultry cuts on a rack in a roasting pan and omitting the drip pan). You also can indirectly grill thinner cuts such as chops or steaks.

For indirect charcoal grilling, you need a disposable drip pan. Purchase one or shape one with heavy foil. It should be large enough to cover the surface below the food. Place the drip pan in the center of the firebox. Use long-handled tongs to arrange coals around the pan (see tip 3, at right).

For a gas grill, refer to your owner's manual for specific directions on indirect cooking. Usually, for a two-burner grill, after preheating both burners, you

GRILL TIPS

1. To light charcoal briquettes, arrange them in a mound in the center of the grill rack. Placing them close together helps the fire to ignite.

2. Direct grilling: Place coals in a single layer. To test temperature, hold your hand over coals at same height food will be grilled; count as above.*

3. Indirect grilling: Move coals to add drip pan; rearrange coals as needed. To test temperature, hold your hand over coals at same height food will be grilled; count as above.*

turn off one burner and place the food over the unlit side, away from the heat source. For three-burner gas grills, you usually turn off the middle burner after preheating and place food in center of the grill. For single-burner gas grills, after preheating, you usually turn the burner to low.

Test the temperature

Different foods cook better at different temperatures. Whether you use a gas or charcoal grill, you can judge the temperature the same way. Hold your hand, palm side down, in the same location you plan to place the food for cooking (see tips 2 and 3, above). *To test for the temperature above the coals or drip pan, count "one thousand one, one thousand two," etc., for as long as you can hold your hand there. Two seconds means the coals are hot, three is medium-hot, four is medium, five is medium-slow, and six is slow.

RED WINE-MARINATED STEAK

PREP: 30 MINUTES   MARINATE: 30 MINUTES OR 6 HOURS
GRILL: 8 MINUTES

Low-Fat

*For most people, half a steak is plenty to eat. However, if you're extra
hungry, you can serve just 2 people with this recipe.*

   2 beef T-bone steaks, cut 1 inch thick; 2 beef top loin steaks, cut
      1 inch thick; or 1 pound boneless beef sirloin steak, cut 1
      inch thick
 $1/2$ cup dry red wine
 $1/3$ cup chopped onion (1 small)
   2 tablespoons olive oil or cooking oil
$1^1/2$ teaspoons snipped fresh thyme, rosemary, or marjoram, or $1/2$
      teaspoon dried thyme, rosemary, or marjoram, crushed
 $1/4$ teaspoon salt
 $1/4$ teaspoon coarsely ground pepper
   1 clove garlic, minced

1. Trim fat from meat. Place meat in a plastic bag set in a shallow
dish. For marinade, stir together wine; onion; oil; thyme, rosemary,
or marjoram; salt; pepper; and garlic. Pour over meat. Close bag.
Marinate at room temperature for 30 minutes or in the refrigerator
for up to 6 hours, turning bag occasionally.
2. Drain steaks, reserving marinade. Grill steaks on the rack of an
uncovered grill directly over
medium coals (see tip 2, page
548) to desired doneness, turning
once and brushing once with reserved marinade halfway
through. Discard any remaining
marinade. (Allow 8 to 12 minutes
for medium rare and 12 to 15
minutes for medium.) To serve,
cut steaks into serving-size
pieces. Makes 4 servings.
■ **Indirect Grilling:** In a grill
with a cover arrange preheated
coals around a drip pan. Test for

MARINADE MAINTENANCE

Marinating in a plastic bag
keeps the meat coated and
eases cleanup. First put
meat in the bag, then add
marinade. Turn several
times during chilling to
redistribute the marinade.

medium heat above the pan (see tip 3, page 548). Place the steaks on the grill rack over the drip pan. Cover and grill meat to the desired doneness, brushing once with the reserved marinade. (Allow 16 to 20 minutes for medium rare and 20 to 24 minutes for medium.)

Nutrition Facts per serving: 230 cal., 12 g total fat (4 g sat. fat), 76 mg chol., 105 mg sodium, 1 g carbo., 0 g fiber, 26 g pro. **Daily Values:** 0% vit. A, 0% vit. C, 1% calcium, 19% iron

---

BEEF TENDERLOIN WITH PEPPERCORN SAUCE

PREP: 20 MINUTES   GRILL: 14 MINUTES

To make the velvety cream sauce look even more impressive, coarsely crush multicolored peppercorns with a mortar and pestle to use in place of the coarsely ground black pepper.

    1 cup whipping cream
  $^1/_4$ cup beef broth
  $^1/_4$ teaspoon coarsely ground pepper
    1 clove garlic, minced
    1 tablespoon whiskey or brandy
    4 beef tenderloin steaks, cut $1^1/_4$ inches thick
    1 tablespoon Worcestershire sauce
    1 tablespoon coarsely ground pepper

1. For sauce, in a medium skillet combine whipping cream, beef broth, the $^1/_4$ teaspoon pepper, and garlic. Bring to a gentle boil. Reduce heat. Simmer, uncovered, about 7 minutes or till the liquid is reduced to $^1/_2$ cup, stirring occasionally. Stir in whiskey or brandy. Keep warm.

2. Meanwhile, trim fat from meat. Combine Worcestershire sauce and the 1 tablespoon pepper. Rub mixture evenly onto both sides of steaks. Grill on the rack of an uncovered grill directly over medium coals (see tip 2, page 548) to desired doneness, turning once halfway through. (Allow 14 to 18 minutes for medium rare and 18 to 22 minutes for medium.) Serve steaks with sauce. Makes 4 servings.

■ **Indirect Grilling:** In a grill with a cover arrange preheated coals around a drip pan. Test for medium heat above the pan (see tip 3, page 548). Place steaks on the grill rack over the drip pan. Cover and grill to desired doneness. (Allow 18 to 22 minutes for medium rare and 22 to 26 minutes for medium.)

Nutrition Facts per serving: 378 cal., 29 g total fat (17 g sat. fat), 145 mg chol., 157 mg sodium, 4 g carbo., 0 g fiber, 23 g pro. **Daily Values:** 26% vit. A, 15% vit. C, 4% calcium, 23% iron

STEAK TERIYAKI WITH GRILLED PINEAPPLE

PREP: 25 MINUTES   MARINATE: 6 TO 24 HOURS   GRILL: 8 MINUTES

Low-Fat

Select a plump pineapple with a sweet, aromatic scent and deep green leaves.

      1 **pound boneless beef sirloin steak, cut 1 inch thick**
  $^1/_4$ **cup soy sauce**
      2 **tablespoons dry sherry or orange juice**
      1 **tablespoon molasses**
  $1^1/_2$ **teaspoons grated gingerroot or $^1/_2$ teaspoon ground ginger**
      1 **teaspoon dry mustard**
      1 **clove garlic, minced**
      1 **small fresh pineapple**

1. Trim fat from meat. Place meat in a plastic bag set in a shallow dish. For marinade, stir together soy sauce, sherry or orange juice, molasses, gingerroot, mustard, and garlic. Pour over steak (see tip, page 549). Close bag. Marinate in the refrigerator for 6 to 24 hours, turning bag occasionally.

2. Meanwhile, use a large sharp knife to cut bottom and top off pineapple. Peel pineapple and remove eyes (see tip, page 90). Cut into quarters and core. Cut each quarter lengthwise into 3 wedges. Set aside.

3. Drain steak, discarding the marinade. Grill steak on the rack of an uncovered grill directly over medium coals (see tip 2, page 548) to desired doneness, turning once halfway through. (Allow 8 to 12 minutes for medium rare and 12 to 15 minutes for medium.) For the last 5 minutes of grilling, place the pineapple wedges across the grill rack beside the steak. Grill pineapple till heated through, turning once halfway through.

4. To serve, thinly slice the meat across the grain. Serve with pineapple wedges. Makes 6 servings.

■ **Indirect Grilling:** In a grill with a cover arrange preheated coals around a drip pan. Test for medium heat above the pan (see tip 3, page 548). Place steak on the grill rack over drip pan. Cover and grill to desired doneness. (Allow 16 to 20 minutes for medium rare and 20 to 24 minutes for medium.) For the last 8 minutes of grilling, place the pineapple wedges across the grill rack beside the steak. Grill pineapple till heated through, turning once halfway through.

Nutrition Facts per serving: 184 cal., 7 g total fat (3 g sat. fat), 50 mg chol., 382 mg sodium, 12 g carbo., 1 g fiber, 18 g pro. **Daily Values:** 0% vit. A, 20% vit. C, 1% calcium, 16% iron

---

RIB EYES WITH GRILLED GARLIC

PREP: 10 MINUTES   GRILL: 8 MINUTES

Fast

- 1 **whole bulb garlic**
- 2 **tablespoons olive oil or cooking oil**
- 1 **tablespoon snipped fresh basil or** $^1/_2$ **teaspoon dried basil, crushed**
- 1 **tablespoon snipped fresh rosemary or** $^1/_2$ **teaspoon dried rosemary, crushed**
- 2 **12-ounce rib eye steaks, cut 1 inch thick**

1. Remove papery outer layers from garlic bulb. Cut off about $^1/_2$ inch from top of bulb and discard. Place garlic in center of a 12-inch square cut from a double thickness of heavy foil. Bring foil up around garlic forming a cup. Drizzle garlic with oil; sprinkle with basil and rosemary. Twist ends of foil to completely enclose the garlic in foil.

2. Trim fat from meat. Grill steaks and garlic packet on rack of uncovered grill directly over medium coals (see tip 2, page 548) to desired doneness, turning halfway through. (Allow 8 to 12 minutes for medium rare and 12 to 25 minutes for medium.)

3. To serve, cut steaks into serving-size pieces. Drizzle oil from packet over steaks. Lift softened cloves of garlic from head; spread over steaks. If desired, season with salt and pepper. Serves 4.

 Indirect Grilling: In a grill with a cover arrange preheated coals around a drip pan. Test for medium heat above pan (see tip 3, page 548). Place steaks and garlic packet on grill rack over pan. Cover and grill to desired doneness. (Allow 16 to 20 minutes for medium rare and 20 to 24 minutes for medium.)

Nutrition Facts per serving: 366 cal., 24 g total fat (8 g sat. fat), 100 mg chol., 226 mg sodium, 2 g carbo., 0 g fiber, 34 g pro. **Daily Values:** 0% vit. A, 0% vit. C, 2% calcium, 22% iron

GRILLED BEEF SALAD

PREP: 35 MINUTES   MARINATE: 6 TO 24 HOURS   GRILL: 14 MINUTES

Low-Fat

For even more citrus flavor, add drained mandarin orange sections to the tossed greens.

12 ounces beef top loin steak, cut 1¼ inches thick
 1 teaspoon finely shredded orange peel
 ¾ cup orange juice
 ¼ cup salad oil
 1 0.7 to 1.1-ounce envelope dry honey mustard, herb, or Italian
    salad dressing mix
    Few dashes bottled hot pepper sauce
 2 tablespoons water
 4 cups torn mixed greens
 1 cup sliced fresh mushrooms
 ¾ cup thinly sliced cucumber
 8 cherry tomatoes, halved

1. Trim fat from meat. Place meat in plastic bag set in shallow dish. For marinade, stir together orange peel, orange juice, salad oil, salad dressing mix, and hot pepper sauce. Pour half the marinade over steak (see tip, page 549). Close bag. Marinate in refrigerator 6 to 24 hours, turning bag occasionally.

2. Meanwhile, for salad dressing combine the remaining marinade with the water. Cover and refrigerate till serving time. For salad, toss together mixed greens, mushrooms, cucumber, and cherry tomatoes. Divide between 4 individual salad bowls. Cover and chill till serving time.

3. Drain steak, reserving marinade. Grill steak on the rack of an uncovered grill directly over medium coals (see tip 2, page 548) to desired doneness, turning once halfway through and brushing occasionally with reserved marinade. Discard any remaining marinade. (Allow 14 to 18 minutes for medium rare and 18 to 22 minutes for medium.)

4. To serve, thinly slice the meat across the grain. Arrange the warm meat atop the salads. Drizzle with the salad dressing. Makes 4 servings.

■ **Indirect Grilling:** In a grill with a cover arrange preheated coals around a drip pan. Test for medium heat above the pan (see tip 3, page 548). Place steak on the grill rack over the drip pan. Cover and grill to desired doneness, brushing occasionally with the reserved marinade. (Allow 20 to 22 minutes for medium rare and 22 to 26 minutes for medium.)

Nutrition Facts per serving: 186 cal., 12 g total fat (2 g sat. fat), 13 mg chol., 391 mg sodium, 13 g carbo., 2 g fiber, 7 g pro. **Daily Values:** 26% vit. A, 59% vit. C, 5% calcium, 14% iron

---

CLEANING YOUR GRILL

To make the job easier, clean your grill rack right after cooking. Let the rack cool slightly, then soak it in hot sudsy water to loosen cooked-on grime. If the rack is too large for your sink, let it stand for about 1 hour wrapped in wet paper towels or newspaper, then wipe it clean. If necessary, use a stiff brush to remove stubborn burned-on food.

For gas grills, follow the steps suggested in "Controlling Flare-Ups," page 570.

TEXAS-STYLE BEEF BRISKET

PREP: 1 HOUR   GRILL: 2 HOURS

Low-Fat

    4 to 6 cups mesquite wood chips
 1/4 cup dry red wine
    4 teaspoons Worcestershire sauce
    1 tablespoon cooking oil
    1 tablespoon red wine vinegar or cider vinegar
 1/2 teaspoon ground coriander
 1/2 teaspoon hot-style mustard
      Dash ground red pepper
    1 clove garlic, minced
    2 teaspoons seasoned salt
    1 teaspoon paprika
    1 2- to 3-pound fresh beef brisket
    1 cup catsup

$^3/_4$ cup peeled, seeded, and chopped tomato (1 large)

$^1/_2$ cup chopped green sweet pepper

2 tablespoons chopped onion

2 tablespoons brown sugar

1 to 2 tablespoons steak sauce

1 to 2 tablespoons Worcestershire sauce

$^1/_2$ teaspoon garlic powder

$^1/_4$ teaspoon ground nutmeg

$^1/_4$ teaspoon ground cinnamon

$^1/_4$ teaspoon ground cloves

$^1/_8$ teaspoon ground ginger

1. At least 1 hour before grilling, soak wood chips in enough water to cover. Meanwhile, for brushing sauce, mix wine, the 4 teaspoons Worcestershire sauce, oil, vinegar, coriander, mustard, red pepper, and garlic. Set aside. For rub, combine seasoned salt, paprika, and 1 teaspoon *black pepper*.

2. Trim fat from meat. Rub paprika mixture evenly onto meat. Drain wood chips. In a grill with a cover arrange preheated coals for indirect grilling. Sprinkle some wood chips onto coals. Test for slow heat where meat will cook (see tip 3, page 548). Place meat on a rack in a roasting pan on the grill rack. Cover and grill for 2 to 2$^1/_2$ hours or till very tender. Every 30 minutes or as needed, brush meat with brushing sauce and add more briquettes and drained wood chips. Discard any remaining brushing sauce.

3. Meanwhile, for serving sauce, in a saucepan combine catsup, tomato, sweet pepper, onion, brown sugar, steak sauce, the 1 to 2 tablespoons Worcestershire sauce, garlic powder, nutmeg, cinnamon, cloves, ginger, and $^1/_8$ teaspoon *black pepper*. Bring to boiling. Reduce heat. Simmer, covered, 5 minutes or till sweet pepper is crisptender.

4. To serve, thinly slice meat across the grain. Arrange meat on plates and top with some of the serving sauce. Pass the remaining serving sauce. Makes 12 servings.

Nutrition Facts per serving: 191 cal., 9 g total fat (3 g sat. fat), 52 mg chol., 581 mg sodium, 11 g carbo., 1 g fiber, 17 g pro. **Daily Values:** 4% vit. A, 25% vit. C, 1% calcium, 14% iron

CANADIAN BACON CHEESEBURGERS

PREP: 20 MINUTES   GRILL: 16 MINUTES

If you prefer a basic burger, simply omit the
Canadian bacon and cheese.

  3 **tablespoons fine dry bread crumbs**
  2 **tablespoons catsup**
  2 **tablespoons finely chopped onion**
  1 **tablespoon Dijon-style mustard**
 $^1/_4$ **teaspoon salt**
 $^1/_8$ **teaspoon pepper**
  1 **pound lean ground beef or ground pork**
  5 **slices Canadian-style bacon**
  5 **slices American or cheddar cheese**
  5 **hamburger buns, split and toasted**

1. In a medium mixing bowl combine bread crumbs, catsup, onion, mustard, salt, and pepper. Add lean ground beef or pork; mix well. Shape the meat mixture into five $^3/_4$-inch-thick patties.

2. Grill patties on the rack of an uncovered grill directly over medium coals (see tip 2, page 548) for 14 to 18 minutes or till no pink remains, turning once halfway through. For the last 2 minutes of grilling, place the Canadian-style bacon on the grill rack beside the patties. Grill bacon till heated through, turning once halfway through.

3. Place Canadian-style bacon slices atop patties on the grill. Top with cheese slices. Grill, uncovered, about 2 minutes more or till cheese begins to melt. Serve patties on toasted hamburger buns. Makes 5 servings.

■ **Indirect Grilling:** In a grill with a cover arrange preheated coals around a drip pan. Test for medium heat above pan (see tip 3, page 548). Place patties on the grill rack over the drip pan. Cover and grill 20 to 24 minutes or till no pink remains, turning once. For last 3 minutes of grilling, place the Canadian-style bacon on the grill rack beside the patties; grill till heated through.

Nutrition Facts per serving: 389 cal., 18 g total fat (8 g sat. fat), 73 mg chol., 934 mg sodium, 28 g carbo., 1 g fiber, 27 g pro. **Daily Values:** 4% vit. A, 6% vit. C, 11% calcium, 19% iron

SHRIMP AND BEEF KABOBS

PREP: 1 HOUR   MARINATE: 3 TO 4 HOURS   GRILL: 10 MINUTES

Low-Fat

   8 ounces boneless beef sirloin steak, cut 1 inch thick
 $1/3$ cup lemon juice
 $1/4$ cup cooking oil
 $1/4$ cup white wine Worcestershire sauce
   1 tablespoon honey
 $1^1/2$ teaspoons snipped fresh basil or $1/2$ teaspoon dried basil,
      crushed
 $1^1/2$ teaspoons snipped fresh thyme or $1/2$ teaspoon dried thyme,
      crushed
 $1/8$ teaspoon garlic salt
   8 ounces fresh or frozen large shrimp in shells (10 to 16)
   1 medium onion, cut into 8 wedges
   1 small zucchini, sliced $1/2$ inch thick
   1 medium red or orange sweet pepper, cut into 1-inch pieces

1. Partially freeze beef. Thinly slice across the grain into $1/4$-inch-thick strips. Place strips in a plastic bag set in a shallow dish. For marinade, combine lemon juice, oil, Worcestershire sauce, honey, basil, thyme, garlic salt, and $1/4$ teaspoon *pepper*. Pour half of the marinade over beef (see tip, page 549). Close bag. Marinate in refrigerator 3 to 4 hours, turning bag occasionally. Chill remaining marinade. Thaw shrimp, if frozen. Peel and devein shrimp (see photos, page 528), keeping tails intact.

2. Meanwhile, in a saucepan cook onion, covered, in a small amount of boiling water for 3 minutes. Add zucchini. Cook 2 minutes more; drain.

3. Drain beef; discard marinade. On 8 long metal skewers thread meat, shrimp, and vegetables, leaving $1/4$ inch between pieces. Grill on rack of uncovered grill directly over medium coals (see tip 2, page 548) 10 to 12 minutes or till shrimp turn pink and meat is done, turning once; brush often with chilled marinade. Discard any remaining marinade. Makes 4 servings.

Nutrition Facts per serving: 201 cal., 9 g total fat (3 g sat. fat), 125 mg chol., 193 mg sodium, 7 g carbo., 1 g fiber, 23 g pro. **Daily Values:** 18% vit. A, 62% vit. C, 3% calcium, 20% iron

BARBECUED PORK SANDWICHES

PREP: 30 MINUTES   GRILL: 4 HOURS   STAND: 30 MINUTES

Double the recipe and use 2 grills to cook up a feast for 24 people.

$^1/_2$ **teaspoon salt**
$^1/_2$ **teaspoon black pepper**
$^1/_4$ **teaspoon celery seed**
$^1/_8$ **teaspoon onion powder**
$^1/_8$ **teaspoon garlic powder**
$^1/_8$ **teaspoon ground cloves**
   Dash ground red pepper
1 **4$^1/_2$- to 5-pound boneless pork shoulder roast**
1 **8-ounce can tomato sauce**
1 **cup catsup**
1 **cup chopped onion (1 large)**
$^1/_2$ **cup chopped green sweet pepper**
$^1/_4$ **cup vinegar**
2 **tablespoons brown sugar**
2 **tablespoons Worcestershire sauce**
1 **tablespoon prepared mustard**
2 **teaspoons chili powder**
1 **clove garlic, minced**
12 **French-style rolls, split and toasted**

1. For rub, in a small mixing bowl combine salt, black pepper, celery seed, onion powder, garlic powder, cloves, and red pepper.

2. Trim fat from meat. Rub seasoning mixture evenly onto meat.

3. In a grill with a cover arrange preheated coals for indirect grilling. Test for medium heat where meat will cook (see tip 3, page 548). Place the meat on a rack in a roasting pan on the grill rack. Add $^1/_2$ inch *water* to pan. Cover and grill about 4 hours or till meat is extremely tender, adding water to pan, if necessary. Remove pork roast from grill. Let pork roast stand, loosely covered with foil, for 30 minutes.

4. Meanwhile, for sauce, in a medium saucepan combine tomato sauce, catsup, onion, sweet pepper, vinegar, brown sugar, Worcestershire sauce, mustard, chili powder, and garlic. Bring to boiling. Reduce heat and simmer, covered, for 15 minutes.

5. Shred pork with 2 forks. Stir shredded pork into sauce. Heat through. Spoon pork onto toasted rolls. Makes 12 servings.

Nutrition Facts per serving: 436 cal., 19 g total fat (6 g sat. fat), 112 mg chol., 840 mg sodium, 32 g carbo., 1 g fiber, 34 g pro. **Daily Values:** 6% vit. A, 22% vit. C, 5% calcium, 23% iron

GRILLED PORK LOIN

PREP: 25 MINUTES   GRILL: 1 HOUR

Low-Fat

$^1/_4$ cup shredded onion ($^1/_2$ of a medium)
 1 tablespoon ground cinnamon
 1 tablespoon soy sauce
 1 teaspoon sugar
$^1/_2$ teaspoon salt
$^1/_4$ teaspoon pepper
 1 2- to 3-pound boneless pork top loin roast (single loin)
 2 medium cooking apples, cored and sliced into $^1/_2$-inch-thick rings
 1 cup applesauce or apple butter (optional)

1. For rub, in a small mixing bowl combine onion, cinnamon, soy sauce, sugar, salt, and pepper.

2. Trim fat from meat. Use a sharp knife to score the top and bottom of the roast in a diamond pattern, making cuts about $^1/_4$ inch deep (see tip, page 626). Rub the onion mixture evenly onto all sides of the meat. Insert a meat thermometer near the center of the roast (see tip, page 620).

3. In a grill with a cover arrange preheated coals for indirect grilling. Test for medium-slow heat where the meat will cook (see tip 3, page 548). Place the meat on a rack in a roasting pan on the grill rack. Cover and grill for 1 to $1^1/_4$ hours or till the meat thermometer registers 155°.

4. For the last 10 minutes of grilling, place apple rings on the grill rack beside the roasting pan. Grill apples till tender, turning once halfway through. Remove meat from grill. Cover with foil; let stand 15 minutes before carving. (The meat's temperature will rise 5° during standing.)

5. To serve, arrange meat and apple rings on a serving platter. If desired, serve with warm applesauce or apple butter. Makes 8 servings.

Nutrition Facts per serving: 176 cal., 8 g total fat (3 g sat. fat), 51 mg chol., 302 mg sodium, 10 g carbo., 1 g fiber, 16 g pro. **Daily Values:** 0% vit. A, 6% vit. C, 1% calcium, 7% iron

MARINATED PORK CHOPS

PREP: 10 MINUTES   MARINATE: 6 TO 24 HOURS   GRILL: 35 MINUTES

Low-Fat

Measure the beer after its foam subsides.

4 **boneless pork loin chops, cut 1¼ inches thick**
1 **cup beer or apple cider**
2 **tablespoons brown sugar**
1 **tablespoon Worcestershire sauce**
2 **teaspoons chili powder**
1 **clove garlic, minced, or ⅛ teaspoon garlic powder**

1. Trim fat from meat. Place chops in a plastic bag set in a shallow dish. For marinade, combine beer or apple cider, brown sugar, Worcestershire sauce, chili powder, and garlic. Pour marinade over chops (see tip, page 549). Close bag. Marinate in the refrigerator for 6 to 24 hours, turning occasionally.
2. Drain chops, reserving marinade. In a grill with a cover arrange preheated coals around a drip pan for indirect grilling. Test for medium heat above the pan (see tip 3, page 548). Place pork chops on grill rack over drip pan. Cover and grill for 35 to 40 minutes or till juices run clear, turning once and brushing occasionally with reserved marinade. Discard any remaining marinade. Makes 4 servings.

Nutrition Facts per serving: 214 cal., 11 g total fat (4 g sat. fat), 77 mg chol., 72 mg sodium, 2 g carbo., 0 g fiber, 24 g pro. **Daily Values:** 1% vit. A, 4% vit. C, 0% calcium, 7% iron

APPLE-AND-WALNUT-STUFFED PORK CHOPS

PREP: 30 MINUTES   GRILL: 35 MINUTES

You can make the stuffing ahead of time and chill it, but don't stuff the chops until you are ready to grill them.

$1/2$ cup herb-seasoned stuffing mix
$1/4$ cup coarsely shredded apple
   3 tablespoons chopped walnuts, toasted (see tip, page 234)
   1 tablespoon apple juice or water (optional)
   4 pork loin chops or pork rib chops, cut $1^{1}/4$ inches thick
$1/4$ cup apple jelly

1. For stuffing, in a small mixing bowl toss together stuffing mix, apple, walnuts, and, if desired, apple juice or water. Set aside.
2. Trim fat from meat. Make a pocket in each chop by cutting horizontally from the fat side almost to the bone (see photo 1, page 654). Spoon about 3 tablespoons of the stuffing into each pocket (see photo 2, page 654). If necessary, secure the opening with toothpicks (see photo 3, page 654).
3. In a grill with a cover arrange preheated coals around a drip pan for indirect grilling. Test for medium heat above the pan (see tip 3, page 548). Place chops on the grill rack over the drip pan. Cover; grill for 35 to 40 minutes or till juices run clear, turning once and brushing occasionally with apple jelly during last 5 minutes of grilling. Makes 4 servings.

Nutrition Facts per serving: 464 cal., 22 g total fat (7 g sat. fat), 128 mg chol., 239 mg sodium, 23 g carbo., 1 g fiber, 42 g pro. **Daily Values:** 0% vit. A, 4% vit. C, 1% calcium, 15% iron

APRICOT-MUSTARD PORK CHOPS

PREP: 10 MINUTES   GRILL: 35 MINUTES

If you want to use chops that are ³/₄ inch thick, just reduce the grilling time to 20 to 25 minutes.

 ¹/₃ cup apricot spreadable fruit or peach preserves
  1 tablespoon prepared mustard
 ¹/₈ teaspoon ground ginger or ground cinnamon
  4 pork loin chops or boneless pork loin chops, cut 1¹/₄ inches thick
    Salt (optional)
    Pepper (optional)

1. For glaze, in a small mixing bowl stir together spreadable fruit or preserves, mustard, and ginger or cinnamon. Set aside.

2. Trim fat from meat. If desired, season the meat lightly with salt and pepper.

3. In a grill with a cover arrange preheated coals around a drip pan for indirect grilling. Test for medium heat above the drip pan (see tip 3, page 548). Place chops on the grill rack over the drip pan. Cover and grill for 35 to 40 minutes or till juices run clear, turning once and brushing frequently with glaze the last 10 minutes of grilling. Makes 4 servings.

Nutrition Facts per serving: 406 cal., 18 g total fat (6 g sat. fat), 88 mg chol., 140 mg sodium, 19 g carbo., 0 g fiber, 41 g pro. **Daily Values:** 0% vit. A, 1% vit. C, 4% calcium, 22% iron

HAM STEAK WITH CITRUS SALSA

PREP: 20 MINUTES   GRILL: 10 MINUTES

Fast   **Low-Fat**

Because the ham already is cooked, it only needs to heat through on the grill.

> 3 oranges
>   Orange juice
> 2 tablespoons brown sugar
> 2 tablespoons snipped fresh chives or 2 teaspoons dried snipped
>   chives
> 1 teaspoon vinegar
> $\frac{1}{8}$ teaspoon pepper
> 1 1$\frac{1}{2}$- to 2-pound fully cooked center-cut ham slice, cut $\frac{1}{2}$ to $\frac{3}{4}$
>   inch thick

1. Finely shred *1 teaspoon* of peel from one of the oranges. Set aside. Peel oranges. Coarsely chop oranges, reserving any juice. Set oranges aside. Measure the reserved orange juice. If necessary, add enough additional orange juice to make 3 tablespoons total. In a small mixing bowl stir together orange juice, brown sugar, chives, vinegar, and pepper. Set aside 2 tablespoons of the juice mixture.

2. For salsa, stir together the remaining orange juice mixture, reserved chopped oranges, and reserved orange peel. Cover and refrigerate till serving time.

3. Trim fat from ham. Slash edges of ham at 1-inch intervals. Grill ham slice on the rack of an uncovered grill directly over medium-hot coals (see tip 2, page 548) for 10 to 14 minutes or till heated through, turning once halfway through and brushing occasionally with reserved juice mixture. Serve with salsa. Makes 6 servings.

■ **Indirect Grilling:** In a grill with a cover arrange preheated coals around a drip pan. Test for medium-hot heat above the pan (see tip 3, page 548). Place ham on the grill rack over the drip pan. Cover and grill for 14 to 20 minutes or till heated through, brushing occasionally with the reserved juice mixture.

Nutrition Facts per serving: 184 cal., 5 g total fat (2 g sat. fat), 54 mg chol., 1,294 mg sodium, 8 g carbo., 1 g fiber, 25 g pro. **Daily Values:** 1% vit. A, 68% vit. C, 2% calcium, 7% iron

TANGY PEANUT-SAUCED RIBS

PREP: 20 MINUTES   GRILL: 1¼ HOURS

Peanut butter, gingerroot, and crushed red pepper combine to give these ribs an exotic Oriental flavor.

    4 **pounds meaty pork spareribs or pork loin back ribs**
   ¼ **cup hot water**
   ¼ **cup peanut butter**
    2 **tablespoons lime juice**
    2 **tablespoons sliced green onion (1)**
   ½ **teaspoon grated gingerroot or ¼ teaspoon ground ginger**
   ¼ **teaspoon ground red pepper**

1. Cut the ribs into serving-size pieces (see photo, below). In a grill with a cover arrange preheated coals around a drip pan for indirect grilling. Test for medium heat above the pan (see tip 3, page 548). Place the ribs on the grill rack over the drip pan. Cover and grill for 1¼ to 1½ hours or till the ribs are tender and no pink remains.
2. Meanwhile, for sauce, in a small saucepan gradually stir hot water into peanut butter (the mixture will stiffen at first). Stir in lime juice, green onion, grated gingerroot or ground ginger, and ground red pepper. Cook and stir over low heat till heated through. Just before serving, brush ribs with sauce. Pass remaining sauce. Makes 8 servings.

Nutrition Facts per serving: 401 cal., 31 g total fat (11 g sat. fat), 107 mg chol., 120 mg sodium, 2 g carbo., 0 g fiber, 27 g pro. **Daily Values:** 0% vit. A, 2% vit. C, 3% calcium, 11% iron

With a sharp boning knife, cut between the bones to separate the ribs into serving-size portions of 2 or 3 ribs each.

GLAZED COUNTRY RIBS

PREP: 10 MINUTES GRILL: 1½ HOURS

  ½ cup catsup
  2 tablespoons finely chopped onion
  2 tablespoons cider vinegar or wine vinegar
  2 tablespoons molasses
  1 tablespoon Worcestershire sauce
  1 teaspoon chili powder
  1 clove garlic, minced
2½ to 3 pounds pork country-style ribs

1. For sauce, in a saucepan combine catsup, onion, vinegar, molasses, Worcestershire sauce, chili powder, garlic, and ¼ cup *water*. Bring to boiling. Reduce heat. Simmer, uncovered, for 10 to 15 minutes or to desired consistency, stirring often.

2. Trim fat from meat. In a grill with a cover arrange preheated coals around a drip pan for indirect grilling. Test for medium heat above pan (see tip 3, page 548). Place ribs on grill rack over drip pan. Cover; grill 1½ to 2 hours or till ribs are tender and no pink remains, brushing occasionally with the sauce during last 10 minutes of grilling. Heat remaining sauce till bubbly; serve with ribs. Makes 4 servings.

Nutrition Facts per serving: 557 cal., 37 g total fat (14 g sat. fat), 149 mg chol., 565 mg sodium, 18 g carbo., 1 g fiber, 36 g pro. **Daily Values:** 6% vit. A, 21% vit. C, 7% calcium, 22% iron

BRATWURST IN BEER

PREP: 20 MINUTES GRILL: 7 MINUTES

Fast

  6 fresh (uncooked) bratwursts
  2 12-ounce cans beer (3 cups)
 12 black peppercorns
  6 bratwurst or frankfurter buns, split and toasted

1. Pierce holes in bratwurst skins. In a large saucepan combine bratwursts, beer, and peppercorns. Bring to boiling. Reduce heat. Simmer, covered, 10 minutes or till no longer pink; drain.

2. Grill bratwursts on rack of an uncovered grill directly over medium coals (see tip 2, page 548) for 7 to 8 minutes or till skins are golden, turning often. Serve on buns with desired condiments. Makes 6 servings.

Nutrition Facts per serving: 383 cal., 24 g total fat (8 g sat. fat), 51 mg chol., 715 mg sodium, 24 g carbo., 0 g fiber, 16 g pro. **Daily Values:** 0% vit. A, 1% vit. C, 8% calcium, 16% iron

---

SPICE-AND-HERB-RUBBED LAMB CHOPS

PREP: 10 MINUTES   GRILL: 10 MINUTES

Fast   **Low-Fat**

   8 lamb loin chops, cut 1 inch thick (about $2^1/_2$ pounds total)
   1 teaspoon paprika
 $^1/_2$ teaspoon dried thyme, crushed
 $^1/_2$ teaspoon dried basil, crushed
 $^1/_4$ teaspoon coarsely ground pepper
 $^1/_8$ teaspoon ground cumin

1. Trim fat from meat; set aside. For rub, stir together all ingredients and $^1/_4$ teaspoon *salt*. Rub mixture onto both sides of chops.
2. Grill lamb chops on rack of uncovered grill directly over medium coals (see tip 2, page 548) to desired doneness (see tip, page 567), turning once halfway through. (Allow 10 to 14 minutes for medium rare; 14 to 16 minutes for medium.) Serves 4.
■ **Indirect Grilling:** In grill with a cover arrange preheated coals around a drip pan. Test for medium heat above pan (see tip 3, page 548). Place chops on grill rack over pan. Cover and grill to desired doneness. (Allow 10 to 18 minutes for medium rare and 18 to 20 minutes for medium.)

Nutrition Facts per serving: 183 cal., 9 g total fat (3 g sat. fat), 78 mg chol., 193 mg sodium, 1 g carbo., 0 g fiber, 24 g pro. **Daily Values:** 3% vit. A, 1% vit. C, 1% calcium, 17% iron

SMOKED LEG OF LAMB

PREP: 1 HOUR   GRILL: 1¾ HOURS   STAND: 15 MINUTES

If you can't find the chips called for in this recipe,
try hickory wood chips.

  4 **cups apple wood or cherry wood chips**
5½ **cups sliced fresh or frozen rhubarb (24 ounces)**
  1 **12-ounce can frozen pineapple juice concentrate or apple juice**
    concentrate
    Few drops red food coloring (optional)
  2 **tablespoons snipped fresh mint or 1 teaspoon dried mint,**
    crushed
¼ **cup corn syrup, molasses, or honey**
  1 **5- to 6-pound leg of lamb**

1. At least 1 hour before grilling, soak wood chips in enough water to cover.

2. Meanwhile, for glaze, in a medium saucepan combine rhubarb, pineapple or apple juice concentrate, and, if desired, red food coloring. Bring to boiling. Reduce heat. Cover and simmer for 15 to 20 minutes or till rhubarb is very tender. Strain, pressing liquid out of pulp. Discard pulp. Return liquid to the saucepan. Stir in mint. Bring to boiling. Reduce heat. Simmer, uncovered, for 10 to 15 minutes more or till liquid is reduced to 1 cup, stirring occasionally. Stir in corn syrup, molasses, or honey. Set glaze aside.

3. Trim fat from meat. Insert a meat thermometer into thickest part of the roast, making sure the bulb does not touch bone (see tip, page 620). In a grill with a

LAMB DONENESS

Grill a lamb chop or roast to medium rare or medium for juicy, tender meat. A lamb chop will still have a little pink in the center, but the edges will be gray to brown. Grill a roast until the thermometer registers 140° for medium rare or 155° for medium. Cover roast; let it stand 15 minutes before carving. Standing time is important because the meat continues to cook, raising the temperature 5° and bringing the meat to the doneness of your choice.

cover arrange preheated coals for indirect grilling. Drain wood chips. Sprinkle half of the wood chips onto the coals. Test for medium-slow heat where the meat will cook (see tip 3, page 548). Place meat on a rack in a roasting pan on the grill rack. Cover and grill 45 minutes. Add remaining drained wood chips and more briquettes.

4. Cover and grill the meat till thermometer registers 140° for medium rare (1 to 1½ hours) or 155° for medium (1½ to 1¾ hours) (see tip, page 567), adding briquettes every 45 minutes. For the last 20 minutes of grilling, brush meat with glaze. Remove meat from grill. Let stand, loosely covered with foil, for 15 minutes. (The meat's temperature will rise 5° during standing.) Heat remaining glaze till bubbly; pass with meat. Makes 10 to 12 servings.

Nutrition Facts per serving: 315 cal., 15 g total fat (6 g sat. fat), 72 mg chol., 60 mg sodium, 24 g carbo., 1 g fiber, 19 g pro. **Daily Values:** 1% vit. A, 33% vit. C, 7% calcium, 16% iron

---

LEMON AND GARLIC GRILLED CHICKEN

PREP: 30 MINUTES   GRILL: 1 HOUR

A clove of garlic is one section from a whole bulb of garlic.

 2 lemons
 3 tablespoons margarine or butter, melted
 1 tablespoon snipped fresh rosemary or 1 teaspoon dried
      rosemary, crushed
¼ teaspoon salt
⅛ teaspoon pepper
 1 2½- to 3-pound broiler-fryer chicken
 4 cloves garlic, halved
¾ cup chicken broth
 1 tablespoon cornstarch
 1 tablespoon margarine or butter

1. Cut *one* of the lemons into thin slices. Set aside. Finely shred *1 teaspoon* of lemon peel from the other lemon. Squeeze juice from the lemon. Measure juice. If necessary, add enough water to equal 3 tablespoons total. Set aside 1 tablespoon of the juice.

2. Stir together the lemon peel, the remaining 2 tablespoons lemon juice, the 3 tablespoons melted margarine or butter, rosemary, salt, and pepper.

3. Remove the neck and giblets from the chicken. Rinse the chicken on the outside as well as inside the body and neck cavities. Pat dry with paper towels. Place the lemon slices and garlic cloves inside the body cavity. Skewer the neck skin to the back (see photo 2, page 866). Twist wing tips under the back (see photo 4, page 867).

4. In a grill with a cover arrange preheated coals for indirect grilling. Test for medium heat where chicken will cook (see tip 3, page 548). Place the chicken, breast side up, on a rack in a roasting pan on the grill rack. Brush the chicken with the lemon-rosemary mixture. Cover and grill for 1 to 1¼ hours or till the chicken is no longer pink and the drumsticks move easily in their sockets, brushing occasionally with the lemon-rosemary mixture.

5. Meanwhile, for sauce, in a small saucepan combine the reserved lemon juice, chicken broth, and cornstarch. Cook and stir till thickened and bubbly. Cook and stir 2 minutes more. Stir in the 1 tablespoon margarine or butter. Serve with the chicken. Makes 6 servings.

Nutrition Facts per serving: 263 cal., 18 g total fat (4 g sat. fat), 66 mg chol., 337 mg sodium, 3 g carbo., 0 g fiber, 21 g pro. **Daily Values:** 12% vit. A, 9% vit. C, 1% calcium, 7% iron

---

BARBECUED CHICKEN

PREP: 20 MINUTES   GRILL: 40 MINUTES

Choose the sesame-chili sauce below or use 1 cup Barbecue Sauce (see page 963).

      ⅓ cup plum sauce or sweet-and-sour sauce
      3 tablespoons hoisin sauce or catsup
      2 tablespoons soy sauce
      2 tablespoons honey
      2 tablespoons water
  1½ teaspoons sesame seed
      1 clove garlic, minced
      1 teaspoon grated gingerroot
      ¼ teaspoon five-spice powder
        Several dashes bottled hot pepper sauce
      1 2½- to 3-pound broiler-fryer chicken, quartered

1. For sauce, in a small saucepan combine all of the ingredients except the chicken. Cook over medium heat till bubbly, stirring frequently. Reduce heat; cover and simmer for 5 minutes. Remove from heat; set aside.

2. If desired, remove skin from chicken. Rinse chicken; pat dry with paper towels. Place chicken, bone side up, on rack of an uncovered grill. Grill directly over medium coals (see tip 2, page 548) for 40 to 50 minutes or till chicken is tender and no longer pink, turning once halfway through. During the last 10 minutes of grilling, brush sauce often onto both sides of the chicken. Makes 4 servings.

■ **Indirect Grilling:** In a grill with a cover arrange preheated coals around a drip pan. Test for medium heat above the pan (see tip 3, page 548). Place chicken, bone side down, on grill rack over drip pan. Cover and grill for 50 to 60 minutes or till chicken is tender and no longer pink, brushing often with sauce the last 10 minutes of grilling.

Nutrition Facts per serving: 373 cal., 16 g total fat (4 g sat. fat), 99 mg chol., 849 mg sodium, 23 g carbo., 0 g fiber, 31 g pro. **Daily Values:** 5% vit. A, 1% vit. C, 1% calcium, 11% iron

---

CONTROLLING FLARE-UPS

Fat and meat juices dripping onto hot coals may cause sudden small blazes, called flare-ups, which can make your meat taste charred. To control flare-ups, just raise the grill rack, cover the grill, space the hot coals further apart, or remove a few coals. As a last resort, remove the food from the grill and mist the fire with water from a pump-spray bottle. When the flame subsides, return the food to the grill.

To prevent flare-ups on a gas grill, after every use turn the heat to high and let the grill run for 10 to 15 minutes with the lid closed. Then use a brass bristle brush or a grid scrubber to remove any baked-on food. This also will burn off some of the residue on the lava rock or ceramic briquettes. If the lava rock has a lot of residue, however, clean it according to your owner's manual.

MUSTARD-MARINATED CHICKEN

PREP: 15 MINUTES   MARINATE: 6 TO 8 HOURS   GRILL: 35 MINUTES

- 2 to 2¹/₂ pounds meaty chicken pieces (breasts, thighs, and drumsticks)
- ¹/₃ cup prepared mustard
- ¹/₃ cup Dijon-style mustard
- 3 tablespoons white wine vinegar or rice vinegar
- 2 tablespoons olive oil or cooking oil
- ¹/₈ teaspoon ground red pepper

1. If desired, remove skin from chicken. Rinse chicken; pat dry with paper towels. Place chicken in a plastic bag set in a shallow dish. For marinade, combine prepared mustard, Dijon-style mustard, vinegar, oil, and red pepper. Pour over chicken (see tip, page 549). Close bag. Marinate in the refrigerator 6 to 8 hours, turning bag occasionally.

2. Drain chicken, reserving marinade. Place the chicken, bone side up, on the rack of an uncovered grill. Grill directly over medium coals (see tip 2, page 548) for 35 to 45 minutes or till chicken is tender and no longer pink, turning once and brushing with marinade halfway through. Discard any remaining marinade. Makes 4 servings.

■ **Indirect Grilling:** In a grill with a cover arrange preheated coals around a drip pan. Test for medium heat above the pan (see tip 3, page 548). Place chicken, bone side down, on the grill rack over the drip pan. Cover; grill for 50 to 60 minutes or till chicken is tender and no longer pink, brushing with marinade halfway through. Discard any remaining marinade.

Nutrition Facts per serving: 362 cal., 21 g total fat (5 g sat. fat), 104 mg chol., 854 mg sodium, 2 g carbo., 0 g fiber, 35 g pro. **Daily Values:** 4% vit. A, 0% vit. C, 3% calcium, 12% iron

GRILLED HONEY-LIME CHICKEN SALAD

PREP: 30 MINUTES   GRILL: 12 MINUTES

Low-Fat

Slice the chicken breast hot from the grill and serve it atop fresh greens and fruit.

$^1/_3$ cup plain low-fat or nonfat yogurt
$^1/_3$ cup regular or lower-fat dairy sour cream
2 tablespoons honey
$1^1/_2$ teaspoons finely shredded lime peel or lemon peel
2 teaspoons lime juice or lemon juice
$^1/_4$ teaspoon salt
$^1/_4$ teaspoon pepper
4 cups shredded leaf lettuce
2 medium peaches, nectarines, or kiwifruit, sliced
1 cup small strawberries, halved
1 cup halved seedless red grapes
4 medium boneless, skinless chicken breast halves (12 ounces total)

1. For dressing, in a small mixing bowl stir together yogurt, sour cream, honey, lime or lemon peel, lime or lemon juice, salt, and pepper. Cover and chill till serving time.
2. For salad, line 4 salad plates with lettuce. Arrange peaches, nectarines, or kiwifruit; strawberries; and grapes on lettuce-lined plates. Cover and chill till serving time.
3. Rinse chicken; pat dry with paper towels. Grill chicken on the rack of an uncovered grill directly over medium coals (see tip 2, page 548) for 12 to 15 minutes or till chicken is tender and no longer pink, turning once halfway through. Let chicken stand for 5 minutes.
4. To serve, diagonally cut chicken breast halves into thin slices. Arrange warm chicken slices atop each salad. Drizzle salads with dressing. Makes 4 servings.
■ **Indirect Grilling:** In a grill with a cover arrange preheated coals around a drip pan. Test for medium heat above the pan (see tip 3, page 548). Place chicken on the grill rack over the drip pan. Cover and grill for 15 to 18 minutes or till chicken is tender and no longer pink.

Nutrition Facts per serving: 303 cal., 18 g total fat (5 g sat. fat), 57 mg chol., 424 mg sodium, 13 g carbo., 2 g fiber, 22 g pro. **Daily Values:** 27% vit. A, 65% vit. C, 5% calcium, 25% iron

---

ORIENTAL CHICKEN SANDWICHES

PREP: 10 MINUTES   MARINATE: 6 TO 24 HOURS   GRILL: 12 MINUTES

Low-Fat

Look for crinkly-leafed Chinese cabbage (also called Napa cabbage) in the produce department of your grocery store.

  4 large boneless, skinless chicken breast halves (1 pound total)
  1/4 cup water
  1/4 cup soy sauce
  1 tablespoon sesame seed, toasted (see tip, page 234)
  1 tablespoon grated gingerroot or 1 teaspoon ground ginger
  1 tablespoon toasted sesame oil or cooking oil
  1 clove garlic, minced, or 1/8 teaspoon garlic powder
  1/4 teaspoon crushed red pepper (optional)
  1 cup shredded Chinese cabbage or shredded lettuce
  4 kaiser rolls or hamburger buns, split and toasted
  4 slices tomato

1. Rinse chicken. Place chicken in a plastic bag set in a shallow dish. For marinade, combine water, soy sauce, sesame seed, gingerroot or ginger, oil, garlic, and, if desired, red pepper. Pour over the chicken (see tip, page 549). Close the bag. Marinate in the refrigerator for 6 to 24 hours, turning the bag occasionally.
2. Drain chicken, reserving marinade. Grill on the rack of an uncovered grill directly over medium coals (see tip 2, page 548) for 12 to 15 minutes or till tender and no longer pink, turning once and brushing once with marinade halfway through. Discard any remaining marinade.
3. To serve, place shredded cabbage or lettuce on kaiser rolls or hamburger buns. Top with chicken breasts and tomato slices. Makes 4 servings.
■ **Indirect Grilling:** In a grill with a cover arrange preheated coals around a drip pan. Test for medium heat above the pan (see tip 3, page 548). Place chicken on the grill rack over the drip pan. Cover and grill for 15 to 18 minutes or till chicken is tender and no longer

pink, brushing with marinade halfway through. Discard any remaining marinade.

Nutrition Facts per serving: 291 cal., 7 g total fat (1 g sat. fat), 45 mg chol., 869 mg sodium, 33 g carbo., 1 g fiber, 23 g pro. **Daily Values:** 3% vit. A, 13% vit. C, 6% calcium, 18% iron

---

PLUM-GLAZED SMOKED TURKEY

PREP: 1 HOUR   GRILL: 1²/₃ HOURS   STAND: 10 MINUTES

Low-Fat

    4 cups mesquite wood or hickory wood chips
  ³/₄ cup plum jam or seedless raspberry jam
    2 tablespoons finely chopped onion
    1 tablespoon dry sherry or orange juice
  ¹/₄ teaspoon dry mustard
    1 2- to 2¹/₂-pound bone-in turkey breast half

1. At least 1 hour before grilling, soak wood chips in enough water to cover.

2. For glaze, in a small saucepan combine jam, onion, sherry or orange juice, and dry mustard. Cook and stir over low heat just till jam is melted.

3. Rinse turkey breast half; pat dry with paper towels. Insert a meat thermometer into the thickest part of the turkey, making sure the bulb does not touch bone (see tip, page 620).

4. Drain wood chips. In a grill with a cover arrange preheated coals for indirect grilling. Sprinkle about half the chips onto coals. Test for medium heat where turkey will cook (see tip 3, page 548). Place turkey on a rack in a roasting pan on the grill rack. Cover and grill for 45 minutes. Add remaining chips and more briquettes, if necessary.

5. Cover and grill for 45 minutes to 1¹/₄ hours more or till meat thermometer registers 170°, adding briquettes every 45 minutes. Brush with glaze. Cover and grill 5 minutes. Brush again with glaze. Cover and grill 5 minutes more. Remove turkey from grill. Let turkey stand, loosely covered with foil, for 10 minutes. Pass any remaining glaze. Serves 6.

Nutrition Facts per serving: 246 cal., 3 g total fat (1 g sat. fat), 58 mg chol., 57 mg sodium, 28 g carbo., 0 g fiber, 25 g pro. **Daily Values:** 0% vit. A, 0% vit. C, 2% calcium, 10% iron

TURKEY BURGERS

PREP: 25 MINUTES   GRILL: 14 MINUTES

A glaze of mustard and fruit preserves gives these burgers a sweet-sour taste.

  1 tablespoon prepared mustard
  1 tablespoon cherry, apricot, peach, or pineapple preserves
  1 beaten egg
  $1/4$ cup quick-cooking rolled oats
  $1/4$ cup finely chopped celery
  2 tablespoons chopped dried tart cherries or snipped dried
      apricots (optional)
  1 pound ground raw turkey or ground raw chicken
  4 kaiser rolls or hamburger buns, split and toasted
     Shredded lettuce (optional)
     Chopped tomato (optional)

1. For glaze, stir together mustard and preserves. Set aside. In a medium bowl combine egg, oats, celery, cherries or apricots (if desired), $1/4$ teaspoon *salt*, and $1/8$ teaspoon *pepper*. Add turkey or chicken; mix well. Shape into four $3/4$-inch-thick patties.

2. Grill patties on the rack of an uncovered grill directly over medium coals (see tip 2, page 548) for 14 to 18 minutes or till juices run clear, turning once halfway through. For the last minute of grilling, brush glaze onto both sides of patties. Serve on rolls or buns with remaining glaze and, if desired, with lettuce and tomato. Makes 4 servings.

■ **Indirect Grilling:** In a grill with a cover arrange preheated coals around a drip pan. Test for medium heat above pan (see tip 3, page 548). Place patties on grill rack over drip pan. Cover and grill for 20 to 24 minutes or till juices run clear, turning once halfway through. For the last minute of grilling, brush glaze onto both sides of patties.

Nutrition Facts per serving: 376 cal., 13 g total fat (3 g sat. fat), 95 mg chol., 560 mg sodium, 40 g carbo., 1 g fiber, 23 g pro. **Daily Values:** 5% vit. A, 2% vit. C, 7% calcium, 24% iron

GRILLED SALMON WITH CUCUMBER SALSA

PREP: 15 MINUTES   GRILL: 8 MINUTES

Fast   **Low-Fat**

4 6- to 8-ounce fresh or frozen salmon or halibut steaks, cut 1
   inch thick
1 cup seeded and chopped cucumber
2 tablespoons white wine vinegar
2 tablespoons sliced green onion (1)
2 teaspoons snipped fresh mint or ¼ teaspoon dried mint,
   crushed
2 teaspoons olive oil or cooking oil
1 tablespoon olive oil or cooking oil
1 tablespoon lemon juice

1. Thaw fish, if frozen. Rinse fish; pat dry. For salsa, mix cucumber,
vinegar, green onion, mint, and the 2 teaspoons oil. Cover; chill till
serving time.
2. In a bowl combine 1 tablespoon oil and lemon juice; brush onto
fish. Grill fish on rack of uncovered grill directly over medium coals
(see tip 2, page 548) for 8 to 12 minutes or just till fish begins to
flake easily, turning once and brushing once with lemon mixture.
Serve salsa atop fish. Serves 4.
■ **Indirect Grilling:** In grill with a cover arrange preheated coals
around drip pan. Test for medium heat above pan (see tip 3, page
548). Place fish on grill rack over pan. Cover and grill 8 to 12 minutes or just till fish begins to flake easily, turning and brushing once
with lemon mixture.

Nutrition Facts per serving: 210 cal., 11 g total fat (2 g sat. fat), 31 mg chol., 103 mg
sodium, 2 g carbo., 0 g fiber, 24 g pro. **Daily Values:** 4% vit. A, 7% vit. C, 1% calcium, 9%
iron

WHITE WINE-MARINATED FISH

PREP: 10 MINUTES   MARINATE: 30 MINUTES OR 1 HOUR   GRILL: 8 MINUTES

Low-Fat

Store fresh fish, loosely wrapped in plastic wrap, in your refrigerator for up to 2 days.

4   5- to 6-ounce fresh or frozen swordfish, shark, or halibut
    steaks, cut 1 inch thick
^{1}/$_2$ cup dry white wine
3   tablespoons olive oil or cooking oil
2   tablespoons snipped fresh parsley
1   tablespoon white wine Worcestershire sauce
1   tablespoon snipped fresh sage, basil, or marjoram, or 1
    teaspoon dried sage, basil, or marjoram, crushed

1. Thaw fish, if frozen. Rinse fish; pat dry. Place fish in a plastic bag set in a shallow dish. For marinade, mix white wine; oil; parsley; Worcestershire sauce; sage, basil, or marjoram; and ^{1}/$_8$ teaspoon *pepper*. Pour over fish (see tip, page 549). Close bag. Marinate at room temperature for 30 minutes or in the refrigerator for up to 1 hour, turning the bag occasionally.

2. Drain fish, reserving marinade. Lightly brush grill rack with oil. Grill fish on rack of uncovered grill directly over medium coals (see tip 2, page 548) for 8 to 12 minutes or just till fish begins to flake easily, turning once and brushing once with reserved marinade halfway through. Discard any remaining marinade. Makes 4 servings.

■ **Indirect Grilling:** In a grill with a cover arrange preheated coals around a drip pan. Test for medium heat above the pan (see tip 3, page 548). Lightly brush grill rack with oil. Place fish on grill rack over drip pan. Cover and grill for 8 to 12 minutes or just till fish begins to flake easily, turning and brushing once with reserved marinade halfway through. Discard any remaining marinade.

Nutrition Facts per serving: 223 cal., 11 g total fat (2 g sat. fat), 56 mg chol., 144 mg sodium, 1 g carbo., 0 g fiber, 28 g pro. **Daily Values:** 5% vit. A, 4% vit. C, 0% calcium, 8% iron

GRILLED TUNA WITH ROASTED PEPPER SAUCE

PREP: 25 MINUTES   GRILL: 8 MINUTES

Instead of roasting the sweet peppers, use a drained 7-ounce jar of roasted red peppers to make the sauce.

   4 5- to 6-ounce fresh or frozen tuna or halibut steaks, cut 1 inch
      thick
   1 tablespoon olive oil or cooking oil
   2 roasted red sweet peppers (see Capellini with Roasted Red
      Peppers, page 770)
   3 tablespoons lime juice
   2 teaspoons snipped fresh thyme or dill, or $1/2$ teaspoon dried
      thyme, crushed, or dried dillweed
 $1/4$ teaspoon salt
 $1/8$ teaspoon pepper
   2 tablespoons margarine or butter
   4 thin slices lime (optional)

1. Thaw fish, if frozen. Rinse fish; pat dry. Brush both sides of fish with some of the oil. Grill on the rack of an uncovered grill directly over medium coals (see tip 2, page 548) for 8 to 12 minutes or just till fish begins to flake easily, turning once and brushing with remaining oil halfway through.

2. Meanwhile, for sauce, in a blender container or food processor bowl combine roasted peppers, lime juice, thyme or dill, salt, pepper, and 2 tablespoons *water*. Cover; blend or process till smooth. Pour into small saucepan. Cook and stir over low heat till heated through. Stir in margarine.

3. To serve, pour warm pepper sauce onto 4 serving plates. Top with fish steaks and, if desired, lime slices. Makes 4 servings.

■ **Indirect Grilling:** In a grill with a cover arrange preheated coals around a drip pan. Test for medium heat above pan (see tip 3, page 548). Lightly brush the fish with some of the oil. Place fish on the grill rack over drip pan. Cover and grill for 8 to 12 minutes or just till fish begins to flake easily, turning and brushing once with remaining oil halfway through.

Nutrition Facts per serving: 316 cal., 17 g total fat (3 g sat. fat), 59 mg chol., 262 mg sodium, 4 g carbo., 0 g fiber, 36 g pro. **Daily Values:** 125% vit. A, 109% vit. C, 1% calcium, 12% iron

HEALTHFUL GRILLING

Some researchers have suggested that excessive smoke and charring from fat flare-ups may be a health hazard. Although no government, health, or research organization suggests eliminating grilled foods, you may want to play it safe and always use indirect grilling. With indirect grilling, the fat from the food drips into a drip pan or an unlit area of your grill, preventing any flare-ups, excess smoke, and charring.

Because of these concerns, most of these recipes include both indirect- and direct-grilling methods. You can further reduce any risks by raising the grill rack to its highest position and thoroughly cleaning your grill after every use (see tips, pages 554 and 570).

GRILLED FISH SANDWICHES

PREP: 15 MINUTES   GRILL: 8 MINUTES

Fast

    4 4-ounce fresh or frozen fish fillets, cut 1 inch thick
    1 tablespoon lemon or lime juice
    1 teaspoon lemon-pepper seasoning, Jamaican jerk seasoning, or
         Cajun seasoning
 $^1/_4$ cup mayonnaise or salad dressing
    2 teaspoons Dijon-style mustard
    1 teaspoon honey
    4 hamburger buns or kaiser rolls, split and toasted
    4 lettuce leaves (optional)
    4 slices tomato (optional)

1. Thaw fish, if frozen. Rinse fish; pat dry. Brush fish with lemon or lime juice. Rub the seasoning evenly onto all sides of fish. Place fish in a well-greased wire grill basket. Grill on the rack of an uncovered grill directly over medium coals (see tip 2, page 548) for 8 to 12 minutes or just till fish begins to flake easily, turning once.

2. Meanwhile, in a small mixing bowl stir together mayonnaise or salad dressing, mustard, and honey; spread onto buns. Serve fish on buns. If desired, top with lettuce and tomato. Makes 4 servings.

Nutrition Facts per serving: 311 cal., 14 g total fat (2 g sat. fat), 51 mg chol., 676 mg sodium, 24 g carbo., 1 g fiber, 22 g pro. Daily Values: 2% vit. A, 4% vit. C, 3% calcium, 10% iron

---

GRILLED CORN IN HUSKS

PREP: 15 MINUTES   SOAK: 2 TO 4 HOURS   GRILL: 25 MINUTES

When cooking meat over indirect heat, place the ears of corn directly over the coals.

   4 **fresh ears of corn**
   2 **tablespoons margarine or butter, softened**
   1 **tablespoon snipped fresh chives, parsley, cilantro, or tarragon, or 1$^1/_2$ teaspoons snipped fresh dill**
  $^1/_8$ **teaspoon salt**
  $^1/_8$ **teaspoon pepper**

1. Peel back the corn husks, but do not remove. Remove the corn silks; discard. Gently rinse the ears of corn. Pull the husks back up around the corn. Using kitchen string, tie the husks shut. Cover corn with water. Soak for 2 to 4 hours.

2. Drain corn. Grill corn on the rack of an uncovered grill directly over medium coals (see tip 2, page 548) for 25 to 30 minutes or till the kernels are tender, turning once halfway through.

3. Meanwhile, in a small mixing bowl stir together margarine or butter; chives, parsley, cilantro, tarragon, or dill; salt; and pepper. Remove the string from the corn. Serve immediately with the butter mixture. Makes 4 side-dish servings.

Nutrition Facts per serving: 135 cal., 7 g total fat (1 g sat. fat), 0 mg chol., 147 mg sodium, 19 g carbo., 3 g fiber, 3 g pro. Daily Values: 9% vit. A, 8% vit. C, 0% calcium, 3% iron

---

BASIL-PARMESAN BREAD

PREP: 10 MINUTES   GRILL: 15 MINUTES

Fast

A loaf of crusty French bread heated on the grill complements most any grilled entrée.

  $^1/_4$ **cup margarine or butter, softened**
   2 **tablespoons grated Parmesan cheese**

1 tablespoon snipped fresh basil or 1 teaspoon dried basil,
  crushed
1 clove garlic, minced, or ⅛ teaspoon garlic powder
⅛ teaspoon pepper
1 16-ounce loaf unsliced French bread

1. For spread, in a small mixing bowl combine margarine or butter, Parmesan cheese, basil, garlic, and pepper.

2. Cut bread into 1-inch-thick slices, cutting to, but not through, the bottom crust. Spread cut surfaces with the spread. Tear off a 48×18-inch piece of heavy foil. Fold in half to make a double thickness of foil that measures 24×18 inches. Place bread in the center of the foil. Bring up two opposite edges of foil and seal with a double fold. Fold remaining ends to completely enclose the bread, yet leaving space for the steam to build.

3. Grill bread on the rack of an uncovered grill directly over medium coals (see tip 2, page 548) for 15 to 20 minutes or till the bread is heated through, turning once halfway through. Makes 16 side-dish servings.

Nutrition Facts per serving: 108 cal., 4 g total fat (1 g sat. fat), 1 mg chol., 220 mg sodium, 15 g carbo., 0 g fiber, 3 g pro. **Daily Values:** 3% vit. A, 0% vit. C, 2% calcium, 4% iron

---

ADJUSTING THE HEAT

■ If the coals are too hot, raise the grill rack, spread the coals apart, close the air vents halfway, or remove some briquettes. If you have a gas or electric grill, adjust the burner to a lower setting.

■ If the coals are too cool, tap ashes off the burning coals, move the coals together, add briquettes, lower the rack, or open the vents. In a gas or electric grill, adjust the burner to a higher setting.

■ Not everyone judges the temperature of coals exactly alike. Therefore, the time ranges in our recipes are recommendations. For perfectly done foods, use our timings as a guide and watch the foods closely.

DIRECT-GRILLING POULTRY

If desired, remove the skin from the poultry. Rinse poultry and pat dry with paper towels. Test for medium coals (see tip 2, page 548). Place poultry on the grill rack, bone side up, directly over the preheated coals. Grill, uncovered, for the time given below or until tender and no longer pink. (**Note:** White meat will cook slightly faster.) Turn poultry over halfway through the grilling time. If desired, during last 10 minutes of grilling, brush often with a sauce.

Type of Bird	Weight	Coal Temperature	Doneness	Direct-Grilling Time
Chicken, broiler-fryer, half	1¼ to 1½ pounds	Medium	Tender; no longer pink	40 to 50 minutes
Chicken breast half, skinned and boned	4 to 5 ounces each	Medium	Tender; no longer pink	12 to 15 minutes
Chicken quarters	2½ to 3 pounds total	Medium	Tender; no longer pink	40 to 50 minutes
Meaty chicken pieces	2 to 2½ pounds total	Medium	Tender; no longer pink	35 to 45 minutes
Turkey breast tenderloin steak	4 to 6 ounces each	Medium	Tender; no longer pink	12 to 15 minutes

Indirect-Grilling Poultry

If desired, remove skin from poultry. Rinse poultry; pat dry. In a grill with a cover arrange medium-hot coals around a drip pan; test for medium heat above the pan (see tip 3, page 548). Place unstuffed poultry, breast side up, on the grill rack directly over drip pan. Cover and grill for the time given below or until done, adding more briquettes to maintain heat as necessary. For larger poultry cuts, we suggest placing the poultry on a rack in a roasting pan and omitting the drip pan. (**Note:** Birds vary in size, shape, and tenderness. Use these times as general guides.)

To test for doneness, cut into the thickest part of the meat near a bone; juices should run clear and meat should not be pink. Or, grasp a drumstick with a paper towel. It should move up and down and twist easily in the socket. For turkeys and larger chickens, insert a meat thermometer into the center of the inside thigh muscle, not touching bone (see tip, page 620); thermometer should register 180° to 185°. In a whole or half turkey breast, thermometer should register 170°.

Type of Bird	Weight	Coal Temperature	Doneness	Indirect-Grilling Time
Chicken, broiler-fryer, half	1¼ to 1½ pounds	Medium	Tender; no longer pink	1 to 1¼ hours
Chicken, whole	2½ to 3 pounds	Medium	Tender; no longer pink	1 to 1¼ hours
	3½ to 4 pounds	Medium	Tender; no longer pink	1¼ to 1¾ hours
	4½ to 5 pounds	Medium	Tender; no longer pink	1¾ to 2 hours

Indirect-Grilling Poultry *(continued)*

Type of Bird	Weight	Coal Temperature	Doneness	Indirect-Grilling Time
Chicken breast, half (skinned and boned)	4 to 5 ounces	Medium	Tender; no longer pink	15 to 18 minutes
Chicken quarters	2½ to 3 pounds total	Medium	Tender; no longer pink	50 to 60 minutes
Cornish game hen	1½ pounds (whole) ¾ pound (half)	Medium Medium	Tender; no longer pink Tender; no longer pink	1 to 1¼ hours 40 to 50 minutes
Meaty chicken pieces	2 to 2½ pounds total	Medium	Tender; no longer pink	50 to 60 minutes
Pheasant	2 to 3 pounds	Medium	Tender; no longer pink	1 to 1½ hours
Quail	4 to 6 ounces	Medium	Tender; no longer pink	30 minutes
Squab	12 to 14 ounces	Medium	Tender; no longer pink	¾ to 1 hour
Turkey (do not stuff)	6 to 8 pounds 8 to 12 pounds 12 to 16 pounds	Medium Medium Medium	Tender; no longer pink Tender; no longer pink Tender; no longer pink	1¾ to 2¼ hours 2½ to 3½ hours 3 to 4 hours

Turkey breast, whole	4 to 6 pounds	Medium	Tender; no longer pink	1¾ to 2¼ hours
	6 to 8 pounds	Medium	Tender; no longer pink	2½ to 3½ hours
Turkey breast tenderloin steak	4 to 6 ounces	Medium	Tender; no longer pink	15 to 18 minutes
Turkey drumstick	½ to 1½ pounds	Medium	Tender; no longer pink	¾ to 1¼ hours
Turkey hindquarter	2 to 4 pounds	Medium	Tender; no longer pink	1 to 1½ hours
Turkey tenderloin	8 to 10 ounces each (¾ to 1 inch thick)	Medium	Tender; no longer pink	25 to 30 minutes
Turkey thigh	1 to 1½ pounds	Medium	Tender; no longer pink	50 to 60 minutes

Indirect-Grilling Meat

In a grill with a cover arrange medium-hot coals around a drip pan, then test for medium heat above pan (see tip 3, page 548), unless chart says otherwise. Place meat,* fat side up, on grill rack directly over drip pan, not over coals. Cover; grill for time given or until it reaches desired doneness, adding briquettes to maintain heat. For larger cuts, place the meat on a rack in a roasting pan, omitting drip pan. (*For roasts, insert a meat thermometer into meat (see tip, page 620). Grill meat until thermometer registers 5° below specified temperature. Remove meat from grill; cover with foil and let stand 15 minutes. The meat's temperature will rise 5° during this time.)

Cut	Thickness/Weight	Coal Temperature	Doneness	Indirect-Grilling Time
Beef				
Boneless chuck steak	¾ to 1 inch	Medium	Medium rare Medium	22 to 26 minutes 26 to 28 minutes
Boneless rolled rump roast	4 to 6 pounds	Medium-slow	150° to 160°	1¼ to 2½ hours
Boneless sirloin roast	4 to 6 pounds	Medium-slow	145° (medium rare) 160° (medium)	1¾ to 2¼ hours 2¼ to 2¾ hours
Boneless sirloin steak	1 inch	Medium	Medium rare Medium	22 to 26 minutes 26 to 30 minutes

	Weight or Thickness	Temperature of Coals	Doneness	Approximate Cooking Time
	1½ inches	Medium	Medium rare Medium	32 to 36 minutes 36 to 40 minutes
Eye round roast	2 to 3 pounds	Medium-slow	145° (medium rare) 160° (medium)	1 to 1½ hours 1½ to 2 hours
Flank steak	¾ to 1 inch	Medium	Medium	18 to 22 minutes
Ground meat patties	¾ inch (4 per pound)	Medium	No pink remains	20 to 24 minutes
Rib eye roast	4 to 6 pounds	Medium-slow	145° (medium rare) 160° (medium)	1 to 1½ hours 1½ to 2 hours
Rib roast	4 to 6 pounds	Medium-slow	145° (medium rare) 160° (medium)	2¼ to 2¾ hours 2¾ to 3¼ hours
Round tip roast	3 to 5 pounds 6 to 8 pounds	Medium-slow Medium-slow	145° to 160° 145° to 160°	1¼ to 2½ hours 2 to 3¼ hours
Steaks (porterhouse, rib eye, sirloin, T-bone, top loin)	1 inch 1¼ to 1½ inches	Medium Medium	Medium rare Medium Medium rare Medium	16 to 20 minutes 20 to 24 minutes 20 to 22 minutes 22 to 26 minutes
Tenderloin roast	2 to 3 pounds 4 to 6 pounds	Medium-hot Medium-hot	145° (medium rare) 145° (medium rare)	¾ to 1 hour 1¼ to 1½ hours

Indirect-Grilling Meat (continued)

Cut	Thickness/Weight	Coal Temperature	Doneness	Indirect-Grilling Time
Tenderloin steak	1 inch	Medium	Medium rare	16 to 20 minutes
			Medium	20 to 22 minutes
	1½ inches	Medium	Medium rare	18 to 22 minutes
			Medium	22 to 26 minutes
Top round roast	4 to 6 pounds	Medium-slow	145° to 160°	1 to 2 hours
	3 to 3½ pounds	Medium-slow	145° to 160°	1 to 1½ hours
Top round steak	1 inch	Medium	Medium rare	24 to 26 minutes
			Medium	28 to 30 minutes
	1½ inches	Medium	Medium rare	24 to 28 minutes
			Medium	28 to 32 minutes
VEAL				
Chop	1 inch	Medium	Medium	14 to 16 minutes
			Well-done	16 to 18 minutes
Loin roast	3 to 5 pounds	Medium-slow	160°	1¾ to 3 hours
Rib roast	3 to 5 pounds	Medium-slow	160°	1¾ to 2½ hours

LAMB				
Boneless rolled leg roast	4 to 7 pounds	Medium-slow	160° (medium)	2¼ to 3¾ hours
Boneless rolled shoulder roast	2 to 3 pounds	Medium-slow	160° (medium)	1½ to 2¼ hours
Chop	1 inch	Medium	Medium rare / Medium	16 to 18 minutes / 18 to 20 minutes
Whole leg roast	5 to 7 pounds	Medium-slow	150° (medium rare) / 160° (medium)	1¾ to 2¼ hours / 2¼ to 2½ hours
PORK*				
Boneless top loin roast	2 to 4 pounds (single loin)	Medium-slow	160°	1 to 1¼ hours
	3 to 5 pounds (double loin, tied)	Medium-slow	160°	1¼ to 2¼ hours
Bratwurst, Polish, or Italian sausages (fresh link)	3 to 4 per pound	Medium	Well-done	20 to 25 minutes
Chop	¾ inch / 1¼ to 1½ inches	Medium-hot / Medium	Medium / Medium	20 to 24 minutes / 35 to 40 minutes

INDIRECT-GRILLING MEAT (continued)

Cut	Thickness/Weight	Coal Temperature	Doneness	Indirect-Grilling Time
Ham (fully cooked)				
Boneless half	4 to 6 pounds	Medium-slow	140°	1¼ to 2½ hours
Boneless portion	3 to 4 pounds	Medium-slow	140°	1½ to 2¼ hours
Smoked picnic	5 to 8 pounds	Medium-slow	140°	2 to 3 hours
Ham slice (fully cooked)	1 inch	Medium-hot	Heated through	20 to 24 minutes
Loin blade or sirloin roast	3 to 4 pounds	Medium-slow	170° (well-done)	1¾ to 2½ hours
Loin center rib roast (backbone loosened)	3 to 5 pounds	Medium-slow	160°	1¼ to 2½ hours
Rib crown roast	6 to 8 pounds	Medium-slow	160°	2 to 3½ hours
Ribs, country-style	2 to 4 pounds	Medium	Well-done	1½ to 2 hours
Ribs, loin-back or spareribs	2 to 4 pounds	Medium	Well-done	1¼ to 1½ hours
Tenderloin	¾ to 1 pound	Medium	160°	½ to ¾ hour

*Pork should be cooked until juices run clear.

DIRECT-GRILLING MEAT

Test for the desired temperature of the coals (see tip 2, page 548). Place the meat on the rack of an uncovered grill directly over the preheated coals. Grill the meat, uncovered, for the time given below or until done, turning the meat over halfway through the grilling time.

Cut	Thickness	Coal Temperature	Doneness	Direct-Grilling Time
BEEF				
Boneless sirloin steak	1 inch	Medium	Medium rare	14 to 18 minutes
			Medium	18 to 22 minutes
	1½ inches	Medium	Medium rare	32 to 36 minutes
			Medium	36 to 40 minutes
Flank steak	¾ to 1 inch	Medium	Medium	12 to 14 minutes
Ground meat patties	¾ inch (4 per pound)	Medium	No pink remains	14 to 18 minutes
Steak (blade, chuck, top round)	1 inch	Medium	Medium rare	14 to 16 minutes
			Medium	18 to 20 minutes
	1½ inches	Medium	Medium rare	19 to 26 minutes
			Medium	27 to 32 minutes

DIRECT-GRILLING MEAT *(continued)*

Cut	Thickness	Coal Temperature	Doneness	Direct-Grilling Time
Steak (porterhouse, rib, rib eye, sirloin, T-bone, tenderloin, top loin)	1 inch 1¼ to 1½ inches	Medium Medium	Medium rare Medium Medium rare Medium	8 to 12 minutes 12 to 15 minutes 14 to 18 minutes 18 to 22 minutes
Veal Chop	1 inch	Medium	Medium	19 to 23 minutes
Lamb Chop	1 inch	Medium	Medium rare Medium	10 to 14 minutes 14 to 16 minutes
Pork* Chop	¾ inch 1¼ to 1½ inches	Medium Medium	Medium Medium	8 to 11 minutes 25 to 30 minutes

MISCELLANEOUS				
Frankfurters, smoked bratwurst, etc. (fully cooked)	(5 to 6 per pound)	Medium-hot	Heated through	3 to 5 minutes
Kabob	1-inch cubes	Medium		12 to 14 minutes

*Pork should be cooked until juices run clear.

DIRECT-GRILLING FISH

Thaw fish or shellfish, if frozen. Test for medium coals (see tip 2, page 548). For fish fillets, place in a well-greased grill basket. For fish steaks and whole fish, grease the grill rack. Place the fish on the rack directly over the preheated coals. Grill, uncovered, for the time given below or until the fish just begins to flake easily when tested with a fork; lobster, scallops, and shrimp should look opaque. Turn the fish over halfway through the grilling time. If desired, brush fish with melted margarine or butter.

Form of Fish	Weight, Size, or Thickness	Coal Temperature	Doneness	Direct-Grilling Time
Dressed fish	1/2 to 1 1/2 pounds	Medium	Flakes	7 to 9 minutes per 1/2 pound
Fillets, steaks, cubes (for kabobs)	1/2 to 1 inch thick	Medium	Flakes	4 to 6 minutes per 1/2-inch thickness
Lobster tails	6 ounces	Medium	Opaque	6 to 10 minutes
	8 ounces	Medium	Opaque	12 to 15 minutes
Sea scallops (for kabobs)	(12 to 15 per pound)	Medium	Opaque	5 to 8 minutes

Shrimp (for kabobs)			
Medium (20 per pound)	Medium	Opaque	6 to 8 minutes
Jumbo (12 to 15 per pound)	Medium	Opaque	10 to 12 minutes

Indirect-Grilling Fish

Thaw fish or shellfish, if frozen. In a grill with a cover arrange medium-hot coals around drip pan, then test for medium heat above the pan (see tip 3, page 548). For fish fillets, place in a well-greased grill basket. For fish steaks and whole fish, grease the grill rack. Place the fish on the greased grill rack over the drip pan. Cover and grill for the time given below or until the fish just begins to flake easily when tested with a fork; scallops and shrimp should look opaque. Turn fish over halfway through the grilling time. If desired, brush with melted margarine or butter.

Form of Fish	Weight, Size, or Thickness	Coal Temperature	Doneness	Indirect-Grilling Time
Dressed fish	½ to 1½ pounds	Medium	Flakes	20 to 25 minutes per ½ pound
Fillets, steaks, cubes (for kabobs)	½ to 1 inch thick	Medium	Flakes	4 to 6 minutes per ½-inch thickness
Sea scallops (for kabobs)	(12 to 15 per pound)	Medium	Opaque	5 to 7 minutes
Shrimp (for kabobs)	Medium (20 per pound)	Medium	Opaque	6 to 8 minutes
	Jumbo (12 to 15 per pound)	Medium	Opaque	8 to 10 minutes

Direct-Grilling Vegetables

Before grilling, rinse, trim, cut up, and precook vegetables as directed below. To precook vegetables, in a saucepan bring a small amount of water to boiling; add desired vegetable and simmer, covered, for the time specified in the chart. Drain well. Generously brush vegetables with olive oil, margarine, or butter before grilling to prevent vegetables from sticking to the grill rack. Test for medium or medium-hot coals (see tip 2, page 548).

To grill, place vegetables on a piece of heavy foil or on the grill rack directly over the preheated coals. If putting vegetables directly on grill rack, lay them perpendicular to wires of the rack so they won't fall into the coals. Grill, uncovered, for the time given below or until tender, turning occasionally. Monitor the grilling closely so vegetables don't char.

Vegetable	Preparation	Precooking Time	Direct-Grilling Time
Asparagus	Snap off and discard tough bases of stems. Precook, then tie asparagus in bundles with strips of cooked green onion tops.	3 to 4 minutes	3 to 5 minutes
Corn on the cob	(See recipe, page 580)		25 to 30 minutes
Eggplant	Cut off top and blossom ends. Cut eggplant crosswise into 1-inch-thick slices.	Do not precook.	8 minutes

DIRECT-GRILLING VEGETABLES *(continued)*

Vegetable	Preparation	Precooking Time	Direct-Grilling Time
Fennel	Snip off feathery leaves. Cut off stems.	10 minutes, then cut into 6 to 8 wedges	8 minutes
Fresh baby carrots	Cut off carrot tops. Wash and peel carrots.	3 to 5 minutes	3 to 5 minutes
Leeks	Cut off green tops; trim bulb roots and remove 1 or 2 layers of white skin.	10 minutes or until tender; then halve lengthwise	5 minutes
New potatoes	Halve potatoes.	10 minutes or until almost tender	10 to 12 minutes
Scallopini squash	Rinse and trim ends.	3 minutes	20 minutes
Sweet peppers	Remove stems. Quarter peppers. Remove seeds and membranes. Cut into 1-inch-wide strips.	Do not precook.	8 to 10 minutes
Zucchini or yellow summer squash	Wash; cut off ends. Quarter lengthwise.	Do not precook.	5 to 6 minutes

MEAT

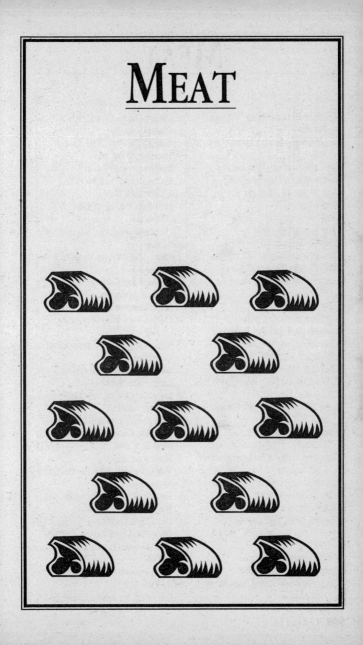

MEAT

Peach-Glazed Pork Tenderloin, 649
Low-Fat

Pizza, 707

Pizza Florentine Pie, 669

Pizza Sauce, 707

Pork and Noodles, 661 *Low-Fat*

Pork Chop Suey, 664 *Low-Fat*

Pork Chops with Black Beans, 656
Fast

Pork Crown Roast with Apple-Cherry Stuffing, 648

Pork Picante, 660 *Fast*

Pork Tenderloin Sandwiches, 650

Pot Roast in Cider, 644

Reuben Sandwiches, 705 *Fast*

Rhubarb-Glazed Pork Roast, 646
Low-Fat

Rice-and-Sage-Stuffed Pork Chops, 653

Roast Pork Sandwich with Apple Mustard, 706 *Fast*

Roast Rack of Lamb with Peach Chutney, 674

Sauerbraten, 612 *Low-Fat*

Sausage and Pepper Sandwiches, 667 *Fast*

Sloppy Joes, 695 *Fast   Low-Fat*

Smoked Pork Chops with Maple Glaze, 651 *Fast*

Spinach-Stuffed Flank Steak, 624

Spinach-Stuffed Lamb Roast, 675
Low-Fat

Standing Rib Roast, 618 *Low-Fat*

Standing Rib Roast with Oven-Browned Potatoes, 618 *Low-Fat*

Standing Rib Roast with Yorkshire Pudding, 618

Steak au Poivre, 623 *Fast*

Steak with Lemon Butter, 624 *Fast*

Stuffed Cabbage Rolls, 692

Stuffed Green Peppers, 691

Super Burritos, 693

Swedish Meatballs, 696

Sweet-and-Sour Pork, 662

Swiss Steak, 629 *Low-Fat*

Szechwan Beef Stir-Fry, 633 *Fast*
Low-Fat

Tacos, 694 *Fast*

Tortilla Roll-Ups, 705

Veal Chops with Mushroom Sauce, 638 *Fast   Low-Fat*

Veal Cordon Bleu, 636

Veal Marsala, 635

Veal Parmigiana, 639

Vegetable-Stuffed Roast, 616
Low-Fat

Venison Potpie, 685

Venison Pot Roast, 684 *Low-Fat*

Winter Pot Roast, 611 *Low-Fat*

Zesty Short Ribs, 620

VEAL

The photos here show the retail cuts of veal. The number with each one refers to the wholesale cut marked on the drawing below. The best ways to cook each meat cut also are listed.

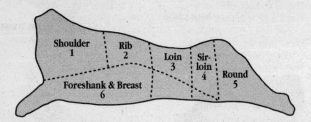

Blade steak (1)
Braise, broil, grill, panbroil

Boneless shoulder steak (1)
Braise, broil, grill, panbroil

Boneless shoulder roast (1)
Braise, roast

Rib chop (2)
Broil, grill, panfry

Rib roast (2)
Roast

Loin chop (3)
Broil, grill, panfry

Loin roast (3)
Roast

**Boneless
sirloin steak** (4)
Broil, grill, panfry

Riblet (6)
*Braise, cook in
liquid*

**Boneless breast
roast** (6)
Braise, roast

Cutlet (5)
Braise, panfry

Shank crosscut (6)
Braise, cook in liquid

Top round steak (5)
Braise, panfry

BEEF

The photos here show the retail cuts of beef. The number with each one refers to the wholesale cut marked on the drawing below. The best ways to cook each meat cut also are listed.

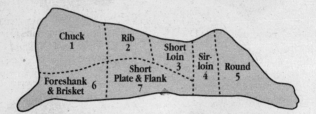

Chuck 1 | Rib 2 | Short Loin 3 | Sirloin 4 | Round 5

Foreshank & Brisket 6 | Short Plate & Flank 7

Mock tender roast (1)
Braise

Boneless chuck roast (1)
Braise

Boneless top blade steak (1)
Braise, broil, grill, panbroil, panfry, stir-fry (strips)

Boneless chuck pot roast (1)
Braise

Boneless shoulder steaks (1)
Braise

Boneless arm pot roast (1)
Braise

7-bone pot roast (1)
Braise

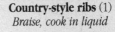

Country-style ribs (1)
Braise, cook in liquid

Short ribs (1)
Braise, cook in liquid

Rib roast (2)
Roast

Rib eye roast (2)
Roast

Rib eye steak (2)
Broil, grill, panbroil, panfry

Back ribs (2)
Braise, cook in liquid

Tenderloin roast (3)
Grill, roast

Top loin steak (3)
Broil, grill, panbroil, panfry

T-bone steak (3)
Broil, grill, panbroil

Tenderloin steak (3)
Broil, grill, panbroil, panfry

Top sirloin steak (4)
Broil, grill, panbroil, panfry

Bottom sirloin steak (4)
Broil, grill, panbroil, panfry

Sirloin steak (4)
*Broil, grill, panbroil,
panfry, stir-fry (strips)*

Top sirloin roast (4)
Roast

Tri-tip steak (5)
Broil, grill, panbroil

Tri-tip roast (5)
Broil, grill, roast

Tip steak (5)
Broil, panbroil, panfry, stir-fry (strips)

Round tip roast (5)
Braise, roast

Round steak (5)
Braise, panfry

Eye round steak (5)
Broil, grill, panfry, stir-fry (strips)

Top round steak (5)
Broil, panbroil, panfry, stir-fry (strips)

Bottom round steak (5)
Braise, panfry

Top round roast (5)
Roast

Bottom round roast (5)
Braise, roast

Eye round roast (5)
Braise, roast

Boneless rump roast (5)
Braise, roast

Brisket (6)
Braise, cook in liquid

Shank crosscut (6)
Braise, cook in liquid

Flank steak (7)
*Broil, braise, grill, panfry,
stir-fry (strips)*

Skirt steak (7)
*Braise, broil, grill, panbroil,
panfry, stir-fry (strips)*

BEEF POT ROAST

PREP: 15 MINUTES   COOK: 1³/₄ HOURS

Low-Fat

Long, moist cooking tenderizes chuck roast.

    1 2¹/₂- to 3-pound boneless beef chuck pot roast
    2 tablespoons cooking oil
  ³/₄ cup water, dry wine, or tomato juice
    1 tablespoon Worcestershire sauce
    1 teaspoon instant beef bouillon granules
    1 teaspoon dried basil, crushed
   12 ounces whole tiny new potatoes or 2 medium potatoes or
       sweet potatoes
    8 small carrots or parsnips
    2 small onions, cut into wedges
    2 stalks celery, bias-sliced into 1-inch pieces
  ¹/₂ cup cold water
  ¹/₄ cup all-purpose flour
       Salt (optional)
       Pepper (optional)

1. Trim fat from meat. In a 4- to 6-quart pot brown roast on all sides in hot oil. Drain off fat. Combine the ³/₄ cup water, wine, or tomato juice; the Worcestershire sauce; bouillon granules; and basil. Pour over roast. Bring to boiling. Reduce heat. Simmer, covered, 1 hour.

2. Meanwhile, if using new potatoes, peel a strip of skin from the center of each. If using medium potatoes or sweet potatoes, peel and quarter. Add potatoes, carrots, onions, and celery to meat. Return to boiling. Reduce heat. Simmer, covered, for 45 to 60 minutes more or till tender, adding water, if necessary. Transfer meat and vegetables to a platter, reserving juices in pot. Keep warm.

3. For gravy, measure juices; skim fat (see tip, page 882). If necessary, add enough water to juices to equal 1¹/₂ cups. Return to pot. Stir together the ¹/₂ cup cold water and flour. Stir into juices. Cook and stir over medium heat till thickened and bubbly. Cook and stir for 1 minute more. If desired, season with salt and pepper. Serve with meat and vegetables. Makes 8 to 10 servings.

■ **Oven directions:** Trim fat from meat. Brown roast as directed. Combine the ³/₄ cup water, Worcestershire sauce, bouillon granules, and basil. Pour over roast. Bake, covered, in a 325° oven for 1 hour. Prepare potatoes as directed. Add vegetables. Bake for 45 to 60 minutes more or till tender. Continue as directed.

■ **Crockery-cooker directions:** Trim fat from meat. Brown roast as directed. Thinly slice vegetables; place in a 3½- or 4-quart electric crockery cooker. Cut roast to fit; place atop vegetables. Combine the ¾ cup water, Worcestershire sauce, bouillon granules, and basil. Add to cooker. Cover and cook on low-heat setting for 10 to 12 hours. Continue as directed.

Nutrition Facts per serving: 356 cal., 12 g total fat (4 g sat. fat), 103 mg chol., 255 mg sodium, 24 g carbo., 3 g fiber, 36 g pro. **Daily Values:** 128% vit. A, 24% vit. C, 4% calcium, 35% iron

---

CARAWAY POT ROAST

PREP: 15 MINUTES   COOK: 1½ HOURS

A hearty rye bread complements this roast.

1   2½- to 3-pound boneless beef chuck pot roast
2   tablespoons cooking oil
2   medium onions, sliced and separated into rings
1   cup apple cider or apple juice
1   cup sliced carrots (2 medium)
1   teaspoon caraway seed
2   cloves garlic, minced
½   cup dairy sour cream
4   teaspoons cornstarch
    Salt (optional)
    Pepper (optional)

1. Trim fat from meat. In a 4- to 6-quart pot brown roast on all sides in hot oil. Drain off fat. Combine onions, apple cider, carrots, caraway seed, and garlic. Pour over roast. Bring to boiling. Reduce heat. Simmer, covered, for 1½ to 2 hours or till tender. Transfer meat and vegetables to a serving platter, reserving juices in pot. Keep warm.
2. For gravy, measure juices; skim fat (see tip, page 882). If necessary, add enough water to equal 1½ cups. Return to pot. Stir together sour cream and cornstarch. Stir into juices. Cook and stir over medium heat till thickened and bubbly. Cook and stir for 2 minutes

more. If desired, season to taste with salt and pepper. Serve gravy with the meat and vegetables. Makes 8 to 10 servings.

Nutrition Facts per serving: 322 cal., 15 g total fat (6 g sat. fat), 109 mg chol., 88 mg sodium, 11 g carbo., 1 g fiber, 35 g pro. **Daily Values:** 46% vit. A, 3% vit. C, 3% calcium, 28% iron

---

WINTER POT ROAST

PREP: 15 MINUTES COOK: 2¼ HOURS

Low-Fat

This roast may be labeled rolled rump roast.

- 1 3- to 3½-pound beef bottom round roast or boneless round rump roast
- 2 tablespoons cooking oil
- 2¼ cups beef broth
- 1 tablespoon finely shredded lemon peel
- 2 teaspoons dried oregano, crushed
- 2 cloves garlic, minced
- 5 medium carrots or parsnips, cut into 1½-inch pieces
- 1 large onion, cut into wedges
- 1 cup pitted prunes, halved
- ½ cup dried apricots, halved
- ⅓ cup all-purpose flour
   Hot cooked noodles (see page 729) (optional)

1. Trim fat from meat. In a 4- to 6-quart pot brown roast in hot oil. Combine broth, lemon peel, oregano, garlic, ½ teaspoon *salt,* and ¼ teaspoon *pepper.* Pour over roast. Bring to boiling. Reduce heat. Simmer, covered, for 1¾ hours.

2. Add carrots, onion, prunes, and apricots. Simmer, covered, for 30 to 40 minutes more or till meat and vegetables are tender. Transfer meat, vegetables, and

USDA HOTLINE

Have a food safety question? The USDA meat and poultry hotline is ready to help. A Registered Dietitian (R.D.) or other food professional can answer your questions on weekdays from 10 a.m. to 4 p.m. (Eastern Standard Time). Call 800/535-4555.

fruit to a platter, reserving juices in pot. If necessary, remove string. Keep warm.

3. For gravy, measure juices; skim fat (see tip, page 882). If necessary, add enough water to equal 2¾ cups. Return to pot. Combine flour and ½ cup *cold water*. Stir into juices. Cook and stir till bubbly. Cook and stir 1 minute more. Serve with meat, vegetables, fruit, and, if desired, noodles. Makes 10 to 12 servings.

Nutrition Facts per serving: 335 cal., 12 g total fat (4 g sat. fat), 93 mg chol., 357 mg sodium, 23 g carbo., 3 g fiber, 33 g pro. **Daily Values:** 93% vit. A, 5% vit. C, 3% calcium, 31% iron

---

SAUERBRATEN

PREP: 25 MINUTES MARINATE: 24 HOURS COOK: 1½ HOURS

Low-Fat

You can make homemade Spaetzle or opt for the dried variety available in the pasta section of most grocery stores.

   1 2½- to 3-pound boneless beef round rump roast
1½ cups dry red wine
   ½ cup red wine vinegar
   1 teaspoon dry mustard
   ½ teaspoon salt
   ¼ teaspoon ground cloves
   ¼ teaspoon pepper
   1 clove garlic, minced
   1 tablespoon cooking oil
   5 carrots, cut into 1-inch pieces
   1 medium onion, sliced and separated into rings
   1 cup beef broth
   ½ of a 15-ounce can tomato puree
   ¼ cup raisins
   ⅓ cup crushed gingersnaps (6)
   4 to 5 cups hot cooked Spaetzle (see page 732) (optional)

1. Trim fat from meat. Place meat in a plastic bag set in a deep bowl. For marinade, stir together the wine, wine vinegar, dry mustard, salt, cloves, pepper, and garlic. Pour over meat (see tip, page 549). Close bag. Marinate in the refrigerator for 24 hours, turning occasionally.

2. Drain meat, reserving marinade. Pat meat dry with paper towels. In a 4- to 6-quart pot brown roast on all sides in hot oil. Drain off fat. Combine 1½ cups of the reserved marinade, carrots, onion, beef broth, tomato puree, and raisins. Pour over meat. Bring to boiling. Reduce heat. Simmer, covered, for 1½ to 2 hours or till meat is tender. Transfer meat and vegetables to a serving platter, reserving juices in pot. Keep warm.

3. For gravy, measure juices; skim fat (see tip, page 882). If necessary, add enough water to juices to equal 2½ cups. Return to pot. Stir in gingersnaps. Cook and stir over medium heat till thickened and bubbly. Spoon some of the gravy over the meat and vegetables. Pass the remaining gravy. If desired, serve with Spaetzle. Serves 8 to 10.

Nutrition Facts per serving: 344 cal., 12 g total fat (4 g sat. fat), 97 mg chol., 465 mg sodium, 18 g carbo., 2 g fiber, 33 g pro. **Daily Values:** 111% vit. A, 17% vit. C, 2% calcium, 31% iron

---

OVEN-BARBECUED BEEF BRISKET

PREP: 15 MINUTES ROAST: 3 HOURS   Oven 325°

1   3- to 3½-pound fresh beef brisket
¾   cup water
½   cup chopped onion (1 medium)
3   tablespoons Worcestershire sauce
2   tablespoons cider vinegar or white wine vinegar
1   tablespoon chili powder
1   teaspoon instant beef bouillon granules
⅛   teaspoon ground red pepper
2   cloves garlic, minced
½   cup catsup
2   tablespoons brown sugar
1   tablespoon all-purpose flour

1. Trim fat from meat. Place meat in a 13×9×2-inch baking pan. Stir together water, onion, Worcestershire sauce, vinegar, chili powder, bouillon granules, red pepper, and garlic. Pour over meat. Cover with foil. Bake in a 325° oven about 3 hours or till tender, turning once. Remove meat, reserving juices. Thinly slice meat. Place on a serving platter. Keep warm.

2. For sauce, measure juices; skim fat (see tip, page 882). If necessary, add enough water to equal ¾ cup. In a saucepan stir together catsup, brown sugar, and flour. Stir in reserved juices. Cook and stir over medium heat till thickened and bubbly. Cook and stir for 1 minute more. Serve with meat. Makes 10 to 12 servings.

Nutrition Facts per serving: 276 cal., 13 g total fat (5 g sat. fat), 94 mg chol., 352 mg sodium, 8 g carbo., 1 g fiber, 30 g pro. **Daily Values:** 4% vit. A, 11% vit. C, 1% calcium, 21% iron

---

NEW ENGLAND BOILED DINNER

PREP: 15 MINUTES COOK: 2$^{1}/_{2}$ HOURS

Serve this corned beef and cabbage recipe on Saint Patrick's Day.

- 1 2- to 2$^{1}/_{2}$-pound corned beef brisket*
- 1 teaspoon whole black pepper
- 2 bay leaves
- 2 medium potatoes, peeled and quartered
- 3 medium carrots, quartered
- 2 medium parsnips or 1 medium rutabaga, peeled and cut into chunks
- 1 medium onion, cut into 6 wedges
- 1 small cabbage, cut into 6 wedges
   Prepared horseradish or mustard (optional)

1. Trim fat from meat. Place in a 4- to 6-quart pot; add juices and spices from package. Add enough water to cover meat. Add pepper and bay leaves. (*If your brisket comes with an additional packet of spices, add it and omit the pepper and bay leaves.) Bring to boiling. Reduce heat. Simmer, covered, about 2 hours or till almost tender.
2. Add potatoes, carrots, parsnips or rutabaga, and onion to meat. Return to boiling. Reduce heat. Simmer, covered, for 10 minutes. Add cabbage. Cover and cook for 15 to 20 minutes more or till tender. Discard bay leaves. Thinly slice meat across the grain. Transfer meat and vegetables to a serving platter. If desired, season to taste with salt and pepper and serve with prepared horseradish or mustard. Makes 6 servings.

Nutrition Facts per serving: 378 cal., 21 g total fat (7 g sat. fat), 104 mg chol., 1,253 mg sodium, 27 g carbo., 7 g fiber, 22 g pro. **Daily Values:** 86% vit. A, 75% vit. C, 5% calcium, 19% iron

MUSHROOM-SAUCED ROAST BEEF

PREP: 20 MINUTES   ROAST: 1½ HOURS   STAND: 15 MINUTES   Oven 325°

Low-Fat

*Whip up some Mashed Potatoes (see page 1055) to serve with this
roast and its savory sauce of mushrooms and green onions.*

  1   2- to 3-pound beef eye of round roast
  2   tablespoons Dijon-style mustard
 ½   teaspoon coarsely ground pepper
  3   cups quartered fresh mushrooms
  4   green onions, bias-sliced into ½-inch pieces
  1   clove garlic, minced
  2   tablespoons margarine or butter
 ¼   cup all-purpose flour
 ½   teaspoon dried thyme or marjoram, crushed
1½   cups beef broth
 ¼   cup light cream or milk

1. Trim fat from meat. Mix mustard and pepper. Rub onto meat.
Place meat on a rack in a shallow roasting pan. Insert a meat thermometer (see tip, page 620). Roast in a 325° oven till thermometer
registers 140° for medium rare (1½ to 2 hours) or 155° for medium
(1¾ to 2¼ hours). Cover with foil; let stand 15 minutes before carving. (The meat's temperature will rise 5° during standing.)

2. Meanwhile, for sauce, in a medium saucepan cook mushrooms,
green onions, and garlic in hot margarine till green onions are tender. Stir in flour and thyme. Gradually stir in beef broth. Cook and
stir over medium heat till thickened and bubbly. Cook and stir for 1
minute more. Stir in light cream or milk. Cook and stir till heated
through.

3. Thinly slice meat across the grain. Arrange on a serving platter.
Pour some sauce atop meat. Pass remaining sauce. Makes 8 to 10
servings.

Nutrition Facts per serving: 229 cal., 10 g total fat (3 g sat. fat), 75 mg chol., 331 mg
sodium, 5 g carbo., 1 g fiber, 29 g pro. **Daily Values:** 5% vit. A, 4% vit. C, 1% calcium,
22% iron

VEGETABLE-STUFFED ROAST

PREP: 20 MINUTES ROAST: 1½ HOURS STAND: 15 MINUTES   Oven 325°

Low-Fat

1 2- to 3-pound beef eye round roast
4 slices bacon
1 cup chopped onion (1 large)
1 cup shredded carrots or parsnips
2 cloves garlic, minced
1 tablespoon snipped fresh basil or 1 teaspoon dried basil,
    crushed

1. To butterfly roast, make a lengthwise cut down the center, cutting to within ½ inch of the opposite side. Spread open. At the center of each half, make one perpendicular slit to the right of the V and one perpendicular slit to the left. Cover with plastic wrap. Working from center to edges, pound with flat side of meat mallet to ½- to ¾-inch thickness. Remove plastic wrap; set aside.

2. Cook bacon till crisp. Drain on paper towels, reserving 2 tablespoons drippings in skillet. Cook onion, carrots, and garlic in reserved drippings over medium heat till tender. Remove from heat. Crumble bacon. Stir bacon and basil into skillet.

3. Spread bacon mixture on roast. Roll up from a short side. Tie with string. Place on a rack in a shallow roasting pan. Insert meat thermometer (see tip, page 620). Roast in a 325° oven till thermometer registers 140° for medium rare (1½ to 2 hours) or 155° for medium (1¾ to 2¼ hours). Cover with foil. Let stand 15 minutes; carve. (The meat's temperature will rise 5° during standing.) Serves 8 to 10.

Nutrition Facts per serving: 156 cal., 5 g total fat (2 g sat. fat), 57 mg chol., 95 mg sodium, 4 g carbo., 1 g fiber, 22 g pro. **Daily Values:** 38% vit. A, 6% vit. C, 1% calcium, 13% iron

BEEF WELLINGTON

PREP: 30 MINUTES ROAST: 30 MINUTES BAKE: 25 MINUTES   Oven 425°

Prepare the Bordelaise Sauce while the pastry-wrapped meat is baking.

  1   **2- to 2¹/₄-pound beef tenderloin**
1¹/₂ **cups all-purpose flour**
 ¹/₈ **teaspoon salt**
 ¹/₂ **cup shortening**
  1   **beaten egg yolk**
  3   **tablespoons cold water**
 ¹/₂ **cup deli or canned liver pâté**
  1   **beaten egg white**
  1   **recipe Bordelaise Sauce (see page 962)**
     Fresh parsley sprigs (optional)

1. If roast is long and thin, fold narrow ends under and tie. If roast is flat and wide, tie crosswise in 2 or 3 places to form a rounder roast. (The finished shape should be about 7×3¹/₂ inches.) Place meat on a rack in a shallow roasting pan. Roast in a 425° oven for 30 minutes for a 2-pound roast or 35 minutes for a 2¹/₄-pound roast. Remove from pan. (Remove strings, if tied.) Refrigerate about 10 minutes to cool surface.

2. Meanwhile, for pastry, in a medium mixing bowl stir together flour and salt. Using a pastry blender, cut in shortening till pieces are the size of small peas. Combine egg yolk and water. Add to flour mixture, tossing with a fork till all is moistened. (If necessary, add an additional 1 to 2 tablespoons cold water to moisten.) Form the dough into a ball.

3. On a lightly floured surface, roll dough into a 14×12-inch rectangle. Spread with pâté to within 1¹/₂ inches of edges. Center meat atop pastry. Fold long sides of pastry around meat, overlapping in center. Brush edges with beaten egg white and seal. Trim excess pastry from ends; fold up. Brush with egg white and seal. Place seam side down in a greased shallow baking pan. Reroll trimmings to make cutouts. Arrange cutouts on pastry. Brush pastry with remaining egg white.

4. If desired, insert a meat thermometer (see tip, page 620). Bake in a 425° oven about 25 minutes or till pastry is golden and thermometer registers 140°. Let stand 15 minutes; carve. (The meat's temperature will rise 5° during standing.) Serve with Bordelaise Sauce. If desired, garnish with parsley sprigs. Makes 8 servings.

Nutrition Facts per serving: 446 cal., 27 g total fat (8 g sat. fat), 141 mg chol., 314 mg sodium, 20 g carbo., 1 g fiber, 27 g pro. **Daily Values:** 15% vit. A, 3% vit. C, 1% calcium, 35% iron

---

STANDING RIB ROAST

PREP: 5 MINUTES ROAST: 2 HOURS STAND: 15 MINUTES   Oven 325°

Low-Fat

Yorkshire Pudding, one of three accompaniments listed below, is similar to a popover.

1 4- to 6-pound beef rib roast
1 recipe Oven-Browned Potatoes, Yorkshire Pudding, or Beef au Jus (see below)

1. Place meat, fat side up, in a 15½×10½×2-inch roasting pan. Insert a meat thermometer without touching bone (see tip, page 620). Roast in a 325° oven till the thermometer registers 140° for medium rare (2 to 2¾ hours), 155° for medium (2¼ to 3¼ hours). Cover meat with foil. Let stand 15 minutes and carve. (The meat's temperature will rise 5° during standing.)
2. Meanwhile, prepare Oven-Browned Potatoes, Yorkshire Pudding, or Beef au Jus. Serves 12 to 16.

Nutrition Facts per serving: 164 cal., 10 g total fat (4 g sat. fat), 56 mg chol., 51 mg sodium, 0 g carbo., 0 g fiber, 19 g pro. **Daily Values:** 0% vit. A, 0% vit. C, 0% calcium, 11% iron

■ **Oven-Browned Potatoes:** Peel and quarter 5 medium *potatoes*. Cook in boiling salted water for 10 minutes; drain. About 30 to 40 minutes before roast is done (the roast temperature should be about 100°), add ½ cup *water* to pan. Arrange potatoes around roast, turning to coat.

Nutrition Facts per serving: 218 cal., 10 g total fat (4 g sat. fat)

■ **Yorkshire Pudding:** After removing meat from the oven, increase oven temperature to 450°. Measure pan drippings. If necessary, add enough *cooking oil* to drippings to equal ¼ cup; return to pan. In a bowl combine 4 *eggs* and 2 cups *milk*. Add 2 cups *all-purpose flour* and $1/4$ teaspoon *salt*. Beat with an electric mixer or rotary beater till smooth. Stir into drippings in roasting pan. Bake for 20 to 25 minutes or till puffy and golden. Cut into squares. Serve at once with roast.

Nutrition Facts per serving: 319 cal., 17 g total fat (6 g sat. fat)

■ **Beef au Jus:** After removing meat from the oven, remove drippings from pan; skim fat (see tip, page 882). Add 2 cups boiling *water* to pan, stirring and scraping crusty browned bits off the bottom. Stir in pan drippings. Cook and stir till bubbly. For a richer flavor, stir in 2 teaspoons *instant beef bouillon granules*. Season to taste.

Nutrition Facts per serving: 165 cal., 9 g total fat (4 g sat. fat)

PAN GRAVY FOR ROASTED MEAT

START TO FINISH: 10 MINUTES

If you don't get $1/4$ cup fat from your roast, add enough cooking oil to equal that amount.

    Drippings from roasted meat
    Beef broth or water
$1/4$ **cup all-purpose flour**
    Salt (optional)
    Pepper (optional)

1. After removing roasted meat from pan, pour drippings into a large measuring cup, scraping out the crusty browned bits. Skim fat from drippings (see tip, page 882); reserve $1/4$ cup of the fat. Measure remaining drippings. Add enough beef broth or water to equal 2 cups.

2. In a medium saucepan combine reserved fat and flour. Gradually stir the 2 cups drippings into flour mixture. Cook and stir over medium heat till thickened and bubbly. Cook and stir for 1 minute more. If desired, season to taste with salt and pepper. Makes 2 cups (8 servings).

Nutrition Facts per serving: 75 cal., 7 g total fat (3 g sat. fat), 7 mg chol., 196 mg sodium, 3 g carbo., 0 g fiber, 1 g pro. **Daily Values:** 0% vit. A, 0% vit. C, 0% calcium, 1% iron

ZESTY SHORT RIBS

PREP: 15 MINUTES COOK: 1¹/₂ HOURS BROIL: 10 MINUTES

  3 to 4 pounds beef short ribs, cut into serving-size pieces
  ¹/₃ cup catsup
  ¹/₃ cup chili sauce
  ¹/₄ cup molasses
  3 tablespoons lemon juice
  2 tablespoons prepared mustard

1. Trim fat from meat. Place in a 4- to 6-quart pot. Add enough water to cover ribs. Bring to boiling. Reduce heat. Simmer, covered, about 1¹/₂ hours or till tender; drain.

2. For sauce, combine catsup, chili sauce, molasses, lemon juice, and mustard. Place ribs on the unheated rack of a broiler pan. Brush with some of the sauce. Broil 4 to 5 inches from the heat for 10 to 15 minutes or till heated through, turning often and brushing with sauce. Heat any remaining sauce and pass with ribs. Makes 4 servings.

Nutrition Facts per serving: 357 cal., 15 g total fat (6 g sat. fat), 70 mg chol., 691 mg sodium, 25 g carbo., 1 g fiber, 29 g pro. **Daily Values:** 5% vit. A, 18% vit. C, 6% calcium, 25% iron

---

HOW TO USE A MEAT THERMOMETER

A meat thermometer guarantees perfectly cooked meat every time. To be sure you get an accurate reading, insert the thermometer into the center of the largest muscle or thickest portion of the meat. The thermometer should not touch any fat or bone or the pan. When the meat reaches the desired doneness (see charts, pages 710 through 717), push in the thermometer a little farther. If the temperature drops, continue cooking. If it stays the same, remove the meat. Cover the meat, and let it stand about 15 minutes before carving. (It will continue to cook while standing.)

MARINATED PRIME RIB

PREP: 10 MINUTES MARINATE: 6 TO 24 HOURS ROAST: 2 HOURS STAND: 15 MINUTES
Oven 325°

Low-Fat

- $3/4$ cup dry red wine
- $1/2$ cup chopped onion (1 medium)
- $1/4$ cup water
- $1/4$ cup lemon juice
- 1 tablespoon Worcestershire sauce
- $1/2$ teaspoon dried rosemary, crushed
- $1/2$ teaspoon dried marjoram, crushed
- 4 teaspoons garlic salt
- 1 4- to 6-pound beef rib roast

1. For marinade, stir together wine, onion, water, lemon juice, Worcestershire sauce, rosemary, marjoram, and garlic salt. Place meat in a plastic bag set in a shallow dish. Pour marinade over meat (see tip, page 549). Close bag. Marinate in the refrigerator for 6 to 24 hours, turning occasionally.

2. Drain meat. Discard marinade. Place meat, fat side up, in a shallow roasting pan. Insert a meat thermometer without touching bone (see tip, page 620). Roast in a 325° oven till the thermometer registers 140° for medium rare (2 to $2^3/4$ hours), 155° for medium ($2^1/4$ to $3^1/4$ hours). Cover roast with foil. Let stand for 15 minutes; carve. (The meat's temperature will rise 5° during standing.) Makes 12 to 16 servings.

Nutrition Facts per serving: 162 cal., 9 g total fat (4 g sat. fat), 53 mg chol., 67 mg sodium, 0 g carbo., 0 g fiber, 18 g pro. **Daily Values:** 0% vit. A, 2% vit. C, 0% calcium, 11% iron

ITALIAN-STYLE PEPPER STEAK

Fast   **Low-Fat**

- 2 medium green and/or red sweet peppers, cut into thin strips
- $^1/_2$ cup chopped onion (1 medium)
- 2 cloves garlic, minced
- 1 tablespoon cooking oil
- $^3/_4$ pound beef tenderloin, sliced $^1/_2$ to $^3/_4$ inch thick, or $^3/_4$ pound beef top sirloin steak, cut $^1/_2$ to $^3/_4$ inch thick
- Salt
- $^3/_4$ cup beef broth
- $^1/_2$ teaspoon dried oregano or basil, crushed
- 2 medium tomatoes, seeded and chopped (1 cup)

1. In a large skillet cook sweet peppers, onion, and garlic in hot oil about 4 minutes or till crisp-tender. Remove from skillet. Keep warm.
2. Place meat in the same skillet. (Add more oil, if necessary.) Sprinkle with salt. Cook over medium-high heat about 4 minutes on each side or till slightly pink in center. Transfer to a serving platter, reserving drippings in skillet. Keep warm.
3. For gravy, carefully add beef broth and oregano or basil to reserved drippings. Bring to boiling. Boil gently, uncovered, over medium heat for 2 to 3 minutes or till broth is reduced to $^1/_3$ cup, scraping up crusty browned bits in pan. Remove from heat. Stir in the cooked vegetables and tomatoes. Heat through. Spoon over meat. Makes 4 servings.

Nutrition Facts per serving: 185 cal., 9 g total fat (3 g sat. fat), 48 mg chol., 223 mg sodium, 8 g carbo., 2 g fiber, 18 g pro. **Daily Values:** 6% vit. A, 82% vit. C, 1% calcium, 18% iron

STEAK AU POIVRE

START TO FINISH: 30 MINUTES

Fast

Whipping cream gives the sauce its thick, velvety richness. Do not substitute milk.

  1 tablespoon cracked black pepper
  4 beef tenderloin steaks or rib eye steaks, cut 1 inch thick (1 pound total)
  2 tablespoons margarine or butter
  2 tablespoons brandy or beef broth
  $^1/_3$ cup whipping cream
  $^1/_3$ cup beef broth
  2 teaspoons Dijon-style mustard (optional)

1. Use your fingers to press the pepper onto both sides of the steaks. In a large skillet cook steaks in hot margarine or butter over medium heat to desired doneness, turning once. (Allow 8 to 11 minutes for medium rare or 12 to 14 minutes for medium.) Transfer steaks to a serving platter, reserving the drippings in the skillet. Keep warm.

2. For sauce, stir the 2 tablespoons brandy or beef broth into drippings, scraping up crusty browned bits. Stir in whipping cream, the $^1/_3$ cup beef broth, and, if desired, mustard. Cook and stir for 4 to 5 minutes or till mixture is reduced to $^1/_3$ cup. Pour over steaks. Makes 4 servings.

Nutrition Facts per serving: 298 cal., 20 g total fat (8 g sat. fat), 91 mg chol., 246 mg sodium, 2 g carbo., 0 g fiber, 23 g pro. **Daily Values:** 15% vit. A, 3% vit. C, 2% calcium, 21% iron

STEAK WITH LEMON BUTTER

START TO FINISH: 25 MINUTES

Fast

Chill any leftover slices of lemon butter to serve on baked potatoes, burgers, and vegetables.

$^1/_4$ cup butter, softened
1 tablespoon lemon juice
1 tablespoon thinly sliced green onion
1 tablespoon snipped fresh parsley
$^1/_8$ teaspoon coarsely ground pepper
4 beef top loin, T-bone, or porterhouse steaks, cut 1 inch thick
$^1/_8$ teaspoon seasoned salt (optional)

1. Stir together butter, lemon juice, green onion, parsley, and pepper. If necessary, chill about 20 minutes or till firm enough to shape. Shape into a 1-inch-thick log. Wrap in plastic wrap; chill.
2. Slash fat on edges of the steaks at 1-inch intervals to prevent curling during broiling. If desired, sprinkle steaks with seasoned salt. Place steaks on the unheated rack of a broiler pan. Broil 3 to 4 inches from the heat to desired doneness, turning once. (Allow 10 to 12 minutes for medium rare or 12 to 15 minutes for medium.)
3. Slice lemon butter into 8 slices. Place 1 or 2 slices atop each steak. Makes 4 servings.

Nutrition Facts per serving: 425 cal., 26 g total fat (13 g sat. fat), 150 mg chol., 223 mg sodium, 0 g carbo., 0 g fiber, 45 g pro. **Daily Values:** 11% vit. A, 5% vit. C, 18% calcium, 26% iron

---

SPINACH-STUFFED FLANK STEAK

PREP: 25 MINUTES   BROIL: 12 MINUTES

6 slices bacon
1 1- to 1$^1/_2$-pound beef flank steak or top round steak
1 10-ounce package frozen chopped spinach, thawed and well drained
$^1/_4$ cup grated Parmesan cheese

1. In a large skillet cook bacon till just done but not crisp. Drain on paper towels.

2. Score meat by making shallow diagonal cuts at 1-inch intervals in a diamond pattern (see tip, page 626). Repeat on other side. Place meat between 2 pieces of plastic wrap. Working from center to edges, use flat side of a meat mallet to pound steak into a 12×8-inch rectangle. Remove plastic wrap. Sprinkle with a dash *salt* and *pepper*.

3. Arrange bacon lengthwise on steak. Spread spinach over bacon. Sprinkle with Parmesan cheese. Roll up from a short side. Secure with wooden toothpicks at 1-inch intervals, starting ½ inch from one end. Cut between toothpicks into eight 1-inch-thick slices.

4. Place slices, cut sides down, on the unheated rack of a broiler pan. Broil 3 to 4 inches from heat to desired doneness, turning once. (Allow 12 to 16 minutes for medium.) Before serving, remove toothpicks. Makes 4 servings.

Nutrition Facts per serving: 262 cal., 15 g total fat (6 g sat. fat), 66 mg chol., 408 mg sodium, 3 g carbo., 0 g fiber, 29 g pro. **Daily Values:** 38% vit. A, 15% vit. C, 13% calcium, 20% iron

---

HOW MUCH MEAT TO BUY

When buying meat, remember that cuts with large amounts of bone and fat will give fewer servings per pound. To calculate the cost per serving, divide the cost per pound of meat by the number of servings you expect to get from each pound. The chart below shows how many servings you'll get from meat cuts with different amounts of bone.

Type of Meat	Servings Per Pound
Boneless meat: ground meats, meats for soups and stews, boneless roasts and steaks, variety meats	4 or 5
Cuts with little bone: beef round cuts, or lamb or veal cutlets	3 or 4
Cuts with a medium amount of bone: whole or end cuts of beef round, loin, rump, or rib; chuck roasts; steaks; chops	2 or 3
Cuts with much bone: shanks, spareribs, short ribs	1 or 2

LONDON BROIL

PREP: 20 MINUTES   MARINATE: 4 TO 24 HOURS   BROIL: 12 MINUTES

This American creation often is served with Bearnaise Sauce or Bordelaise Sauce (see pages 960 and 962).

   1   1- to 1¹/₂-pound beef flank steak or top round steak
¹/₄   cup cooking oil
   2   tablespoons vinegar or lemon juice
¹/₄   teaspoon salt
¹/₄   teaspoon pepper
   1   clove garlic, minced

1. Score meat by making shallow diagonal cuts at 1-inch intervals in a diamond pattern (see tip, at right). Repeat on other side. Place meat in a plastic bag set in a shallow dish.

2. For marinade, combine oil, vinegar or lemon juice, salt, pepper, and garlic. Pour over meat (see tip, page 549). Close bag. Marinate in the refrigerator for 4 to 24 hours, turning occasionally.

HOW TO SCORE

Using a sharp knife, score the steak by making shallow diagonal cuts across the surface. Cutting across the grain helps tenderize the meat.

3. Drain meat. Discard marinade. Place meat on the unheated rack of a broiler pan. Broil 3 to 4 inches from the heat to desired doneness, turning once. (Allow 12 to 14 minutes for medium rare.) To serve, thinly slice meat across the grain. Makes 4 to 6 servings.

Nutrition Facts per serving: 227 cal., 15 g total fat (4 g sat. fat), 53 mg chol., 133 mg sodium, 1 g carbo., 0 g fiber, 22 g pro. **Daily Values:** 0% vit. A, 0% vit. C, 0% calcium, 14% iron

CHICKEN FRIED STEAK

PREP: 20 MINUTES COOK: 1 HOUR

Fresh basil and oregano add a new flavor twist to this country-style classic. You can find fresh herbs in the produce section of your grocery store.

1 **pound boneless beef top round steak, cut** $^1/_2$ **inch thick**
$^3/_4$ **cup fine dry bread crumbs**
$1^1/_2$ **teaspoons snipped fresh basil or oregano or** $^1/_2$ **teaspoon dried basil or oregano, crushed**
$^1/_2$ **teaspoon salt**
$^1/_4$ **teaspoon pepper**
1 **beaten egg**
1 **tablespoon milk**
2 **tablespoons cooking oil**
1 **small onion, sliced and separated into rings**
2 **tablespoons all-purpose flour**
$1^1/_3$ **cups milk**
Salt (optional)
Pepper (optional)

TENDERIZING MEATS

Less tender cuts of meat, such as beef flank steak, round steak, and chuck roast, can be tenderized in several ways before cooking. Pounding with a meat mallet, scoring (see tip, page 626), marinating, moist-heat cooking, or sprinkling with a commercial meat tenderizer will break up the connective tissue that makes meat seem chewy. (Some cuts, such as cubed steaks, have been tenderized by machine.) Slicing cooked steak thinly across the grain also will make it more tender.

1. Trim fat from meat. Cut into 4 serving-size pieces. Place meat pieces between 2 pieces of plastic wrap. Working from center to edges, pound meat lightly with the flat side of a meat mallet to $^1/_4$-inch thickness. Remove plastic wrap.

2. In a shallow dish or on waxed paper combine bread crumbs, basil or oregano, the $^1/_2$ teaspoon salt, and the $^1/_4$ teaspoon pepper. In another shallow dish combine egg and the 1 tablespoon milk. Dip meat pieces into egg mixture, then coat with the bread crumb mixture.

3. In a 12-inch skillet cook meat in hot oil over medium heat about

6 minutes or till brown, turning once. Reduce heat. Cover and cook for 45 to 60 minutes more or till meat is tender. Transfer meat to a serving platter, reserving drippings in skillet. Keep warm.

4. For gravy, cook onion in reserved drippings till tender but not brown. (Add more oil, if necessary.) Stir in flour. Gradually stir in the 1$^1/_3$ cups milk. Cook and stir over medium heat till thickened and bubbly. Cook and stir for 1 minute more. If desired, season to taste with salt and pepper. Serve with meat. Makes 4 servings.

Nutrition Facts per serving: 379 cal., 16 g total fat (4 g sat. fat), 132 mg chol., 549 mg sodium, 22 g carbo., 1 g fiber, 35 g pro. **Daily Values:** 7% vit. A, 3% vit. C, 12% calcium, 24% iron

---

CUBED STEAKS PAPRIKA

PREP: 10 MINUTES COOK: 10 MINUTES

Fast

    4 4-ounce beef cubed steaks
    2 tablespoons margarine or butter
    1 cup sliced fresh mushrooms
$^1/_2$ cup chopped onion (1 medium)
    1 clove garlic, minced
    1 tablespoon paprika
$^1/_4$ teaspoon pepper
    1 cup beef broth
$^1/_2$ cup plain yogurt
    2 tablespoons all-purpose flour
    2 cups hot cooked noodles (see page 729)

1. In a 12-inch skillet cook steaks in hot margarine or butter over medium-high heat for 5 to 8 minutes or till no pink remains, turning once. Remove meat, reserving drippings in skillet.

2. For sauce cook mushrooms, onion, garlic, paprika, and pepper in reserved drippings till mushrooms are tender. Stir in broth. Stir together yogurt and flour. Stir into skillet. Cook and stir over medium heat till thickened and bubbly. Cook and stir for 1 minute more. Return steaks to skillet with sauce; heat through. Serve with noodles. Makes 4 servings.

Nutrition Facts per serving: 377 cal., 13 g total fat (4 g sat. fat), 100 mg chol., 342 mg sodium, 29 g carbo., 2 g fiber, 34 g pro. **Daily Values:** 17% vit. A, 6% vit. C, 6% calcium, 32% iron

Swiss Steak

Prep: 25 minutes Cook: 1¼ hours

Low-Fat

Choose the cooking method—range top, crockery cooker, or oven—that best fits your schedule.

- 1 pound boneless beef round steak, cut ¾ inch thick
- 2 tablespoons all-purpose flour
- ¼ teaspoon salt
- ¼ teaspoon pepper
- 1 tablespoon cooking oil
- 1 16-ounce can tomatoes, cut up (see tip, page 999)
- 1 small onion, sliced and separated into rings
- ½ cup sliced celery (1 stalk)
- ½ cup sliced carrot (1 medium)
- ½ teaspoon dried thyme, crushed
- 2 cups hot cooked rice (see page 139) or noodles (see page 729)

1. Trim fat from meat. Cut into 4 serving-size pieces. Combine the flour, salt, and pepper. With the notched side of a meat mallet, pound flour mixture into meat.

2. In a large skillet brown meat on both sides in hot oil. Drain off fat. Add undrained tomatoes, onion, celery, carrot, and thyme. Bring to boiling. Reduce heat. Cover and simmer about 1¼ hours or till meat is tender. Skim off fat. Serve with rice or noodles. Makes 4 servings.

■ **Oven directions:** Prepare and brown meat in skillet as above. Transfer meat to a 2-quart square baking dish. In the same skillet

Freezing Meats

To store meat for longer than 1 or 2 days, freeze it according to the following guidelines.

■ If you plan to use the meat within 2 weeks after buying it, freeze it in the retail packaging. For longer storage, rewrap or overwrap the meat with moisture- and vapor-proof wrap, such as freezer paper, heavy-duty aluminum foil, or plastic wrap.

■ Freeze the meat quickly and maintain your freezer's temperature at 0° or below.

■ Thaw the frozen meat in the refrigerator on a plate or in a pan to catch any juices. Do not thaw meat at room temperature.

■ Meat also can be thawed in a microwave oven. Follow the manufacturer's directions and cook the meat right away.

combine undrained tomatoes, onion, celery, carrot, and thyme. Bring to boiling, scraping up any browned bits. Pour over meat. Cover and bake in a 350° oven about 1 hour or till tender. Serve as above.

■ **Crockery-cooker directions:** Trim fat from meat. Cut into 4 serving-size pieces. Omit flouring and pounding meat. Brown meat in hot oil. In a 3½- or 4-quart electric crockery cooker place onion, celery, and carrot. Sprinkle with thyme, 2 tablespoons *quick-cooking tapioca,* salt, and pepper. Pour undrained tomatoes over vegetables. Add meat. Cover and cook on low-heat setting for 10 to 12 hours. Serve as above.

Nutrition Facts per serving: 352 cal., 9 g total fat (2 g sat. fat), 72 mg chol., 404 mg sodium, 34 g carbo., 2 g fiber, 31 g pro. **Daily Values:** 49% vit. A, 33% vit. C, 5% calcium, 31% iron

---

BEEF AND NOODLES

PREP: 20 MINUTES   COOK: 1½ HOURS

Low-Fat

In some parts of the country, this meat and pasta combo is served over Mashed Potatoes (see recipe, page 1055).

    1 pound boneless beef round steak
    1 tablespoon cooking oil
  ½ cup chopped onion (1 medium)
    2 cloves garlic, minced
    4 cups beef broth
    2 tablespoons vinegar
  ½ teaspoon dried marjoram or basil, crushed
  ¼ teaspoon pepper
    8 ounces frozen noodles
  ¼ cup beef broth
    3 tablespoons all-purpose flour
    2 tablespoons snipped fresh parsley (optional)

1. Trim fat from meat. Cut meat into ¾-inch cubes. In a large saucepan brown half of the meat in hot oil. Remove from saucepan. Brown the remaining meat with the onion and garlic, adding more oil, if necessary. Drain off fat. Return all meat to the saucepan.
2. Stir in the 4 cups broth, vinegar, marjoram, and pepper. Bring to

boiling. Reduce heat. Simmer, covered, for 1 to 1¼ hours or till meat is tender.

3. Stir noodles into beef-broth mixture. Bring to boiling. Reduce heat. Cook, uncovered, for 25 to 30 minutes or till noodles are tender.

4. Drain meat and noodles, reserving 2½ cups of the cooking liquid. If necessary, add enough broth or water to equal 2½ cups. Return to the saucepan. Stir together the ¼ cup beef broth and the flour. Stir into the reserved broth in the saucepan. Cook and stir over medium heat till thickened and bubbly. Cook and stir for 1 minute more. Stir in beef and noodles; heat through. If desired, garnish with parsley. Makes 4 servings.

Nutrition Facts per serving: 392 cal., 11 g total fat (3 g sat. fat), 109 mg chol., 892 mg sodium, 35 g carbo., 1 g fiber, 36 g pro. **Daily Values:** 0% vit. A, 2% vit. C, 3% calcium, 34% iron

---

BEEF FAJITAS

PREP: 30 MINUTES MARINATE: 6 TO 24 HOURS
COOK: 15 MINUTES BAKE: 10 MINUTES   Oven 350°

Serve the meat sizzling hot for a traditional South Texas fajita.

  1 **pound boneless beef skirt steaks, beef flank steak, or beef round steak**
 ½ **cup Italian salad dressing**
 ½ **cup salsa**
  2 **tablespoons lime or lemon juice**
  1 **teaspoon Worcestershire sauce**
 12 **7-inch flour tortillas**
  1 **tablespoon cooking oil**
  1 **medium onion, thinly sliced and separated into rings**
  1 **medium green, red, or yellow sweet pepper, cut into thin strips**
 ⅔ **cup chopped tomato (1 medium)**
    Dairy sour cream, one recipe Guacamole (see page 69), or frozen avocado dip, thawed (optional)
    Shredded cheddar or Monterey Jack cheese (optional)
    Salsa (optional)

1. Trim fat from meat. Partially freeze. Thinly slice across grain into bite-size strips (see step 1, page 634). Place in a plastic bag set in a deep bowl.

2. For marinade, combine salad dressing, the $^1/_2$ cup salsa, lime juice, and Worcestershire sauce. Pour over meat (see tip, page 549). Close the bag. Marinate in refrigerator for 6 to 24 hours, turning occasionally.

3. Wrap tortillas in foil. Heat in a 350° oven for 10 minutes. Meanwhile, pour oil into a large skillet. (Add more oil as necessary during cooking.) Preheat over medium-high heat. Cook and stir onion in hot oil for $1^1/_2$ minutes. Add sweet pepper strips; cook and stir $1^1/_2$ minutes more or till crisp-tender. Remove from skillet.

4. Add half of the undrained beef strips to hot skillet. Cook and stir for 2 to 3 minutes or to desired doneness. Remove beef. Drain well. Repeat with remaining beef. Drain off fat. Return all beef and vegetables to skillet. Add tomato. Cook and stir for 1 to 2 minutes more or till heated through.

5. To serve, immediately fill warmed tortillas with beef mixture. If desired, add sour cream, Guacamole, or avocado dip; cheese; and additional salsa. Roll up fajitas. Makes 6 servings.

Nutrition Facts per serving: 478 cal., 23 g total fat (5 g sat. fat), 35 mg chol., 618 mg sodium, 47 g carbo., 1 g fiber, 21 g pro. **Daily Values:** 5% vit. A, 38% vit. C, 8% calcium, 27% iron

---

BEEF STROGANOFF

PREP: 25 MINUTES COOK: 10 MINUTES

  1 **pound boneless beef sirloin steak**
  1 **8-ounce carton dairy sour cream**
  2 **tablespoons all-purpose flour**
$^1/_2$ **cup water**
  2 **teaspoons instant beef bouillon granules**
$^1/_4$ **teaspoon pepper**
  2 **tablespoons margarine or butter**
$1^1/_2$ **cups sliced fresh mushrooms (4 ounces)**
$^1/_2$ **cup chopped onion (1 medium)**
  1 **clove garlic, minced**
  2 **cups hot cooked noodles (see page 729)**

1. Trim fat from meat. Partially freeze beef. Thinly slice across the grain into bite-size strips (see step 1, page 634). In a small mixing bowl stir together sour cream and flour. Stir in water, bouillon granules, and pepper. Set aside.

2. In a large skillet cook and stir half of the meat in hot margarine or butter over high heat for 2 to 3 minutes or to desired doneness. Remove from skillet. Add remaining meat, mushrooms, onion, and garlic. Cook and stir till meat reaches desired doneness. Drain off fat. Return all meat and vegetables to skillet.

3. Stir flour mixture into skillet. Cook and stir till thickened and bubbly. Cook and stir for 1 minute more. Serve over noodles. Makes 4 servings.

Nutrition Facts per serving: 480 cal., 25 g total fat (10 g sat. fat), 125 mg chol., 587 mg sodium, 29 g carbo., 2 g fiber, 33 g pro. **Daily Values:** 15% vit. A, 5% vit. C, 7% calcium, 32% iron

---

SZECHWAN BEEF STIR-FRY

PREP: 20 MINUTES COOK: 10 MINUTES

Fast   **Low-Fat**

To partially freeze the beef, place it in the freezer for about 20 minutes. If you're starting with frozen beef, thaw it until it's soft but still icy.

  $^3/_4$ pound boneless beef sirloin steak or top round steak
  3 tablespoons dry sherry or dry white wine
  3 tablespoons soy sauce
  2 tablespoons water
  2 tablespoons hoisin sauce
  2 teaspoons cornstarch
  2 teaspoons grated gingerroot
  1 teaspoon sugar
  $^1/_2$ teaspoon crushed red pepper
  $^1/_4$ teaspoon black pepper (optional)
  2 cloves garlic, minced
  1 tablespoon cooking oil
  1 cup thinly sliced carrots (2 medium)
  1 $8^3/_4$-ounce can whole baby corn, drained
  1 red sweet pepper, cut into 1-inch squares (1 cup)
  2 cups hot cooked rice (see page 139)

1. Trim fat from beef. Partially freeze beef. Thinly slice across grain into bite-size strips (see step 1, page 634). Set aside. Cut whole corn in half crosswise; set aside.
2. For sauce, stir together sherry or wine, soy sauce, water, hoisin

sauce, cornstarch, gingerroot, sugar, red pepper, black pepper (if desired), and garlic. Set aside.

3. Pour cooking oil into a wok or large skillet. (Add more oil as necessary during cooking.) Preheat over medium-high heat. Stir-fry carrots in hot oil for 2 minutes. Add baby corn and sweet pepper. Stir-fry for 1 to 2 minutes more or till vegetables are crisp-tender (see step 2, below). Remove from wok.

4. Add beef to the hot wok. Stir-fry for 2 to 3 minutes or to desired doneness. Push beef from the center of the wok (see step 3, below).

5. Stir sauce. Add sauce to the center of the wok (see step 4, below). Cook and stir till thickened and bubbly. Stir in all cooked meat and vegetables. Cook and stir 1 to 2 minutes more or till heated through. Serve with rice. Makes 4 servings.

Nutrition Facts per serving: 363 cal., 11 g total fat (4 g sat. fat), 57 mg chol., 1,396 mg sodium, 36 g carbo., 3 g fiber, 25 g pro. **Daily Values:** 108% vit. A, 65% vit. C, 3% calcium, 26% iron

---

STIR-FRY STEPS

1. Partially freezing the meat makes it easier to slice. Cutting the slices across the grain as thinly as possible makes the meat more tender.

2. To stir-fry, use a spatula or long-handled spoon, quickly turning and lifting with a folding motion until the vegetables are crisp-tender.

3. Push the cooked meat or other food away from the center of the wok so it stays warm and you have room to cook the sauce easily.

4. Before adding sauce to the wok, stir it to distribute the cornstarch. Pour sauce into center of wok. Cook and stir until thickened and bubbly.

STIR-FRYING HINTS

Stir-frying can be a quick, healthy way to cook a one-dish meal. These tips will help:

■ No wok? Use a large, deep skillet.

■ Prepare ingredients before starting to stir-fry. Some may need precooking.

■ Add the oil to the wok, lifting and tilting to distribute it evenly over the bottom. Preheat the wok over medium-high heat for 1 minute. To test the oil's hotness, add a vegetable piece; if it sizzles, start stir-frying.

■ Don't overload your wok or skillet. When too much of any item is added at once, the food stews rather than fries. Add no more than 12 ounces of meat. If your recipe calls for more meat, stir-fry half at a time.

■ Stir-fry vegetables before the meat, poultry, or seafood so you use less cooking oil.

VEAL MARSALA

START TO FINISH: 35 MINUTES

    1 pound boneless veal leg top round steak, veal sirloin steak, or
        pork tenderloin, cut ¼ inch thick
    3 tablespoons margarine or butter
    1 cup sliced fresh mushrooms
 ¼ cup dry Marsala or dry sherry
    1 teaspoon instant chicken bouillon granules
    1 tablespoon snipped fresh parsley
        Hot cooked noodles (see page 729) (optional)

1. Trim fat from meat. Cut meat into 4 serving-size pieces. Place meat between 2 pieces of plastic wrap. Working from center to edges, with the flat side of a meat mallet, pound meat to ⅛-inch thickness. Remove plastic wrap. If desired, sprinkle with salt and pepper.

2. In a large skillet cook half of the veal in *1 tablespoon* hot margarine or butter over medium heat for 2 to 3 minutes or till juices run clear, turning once. Remove from skillet, reserving drippings in skillet. Keep warm. Repeat with remaining veal and *1 tablespoon* of the margarine or butter.

3. Cook mushrooms in the remaining 1 tablespoon margarine or butter till tender. Stir in ¹/₂ cup *water,* Marsala or sherry, and bouillon granules. Bring to boiling. Boil rapidly for 3 to 4 minutes or till mixture is reduced to ¹/₃ cup. Stir in parsley. Spoon over veal. If desired, serve with noodles. Makes 4 servings.

Nutrition Facts per serving: 246 cal., 13 g total fat (3 g sat. fat), 92 mg chol., 413 mg sodium, 2 g carbo., 0 g fiber, 26 g pro. **Daily Values:** 11% vit. A, 3% vit. C, 1% calcium, 8% iron

---

VEAL CORDON BLEU

PREP: 30 MINUTES   COOK: 14 MINUTES

You can replace the veal with four skinless, boneless chicken breast halves.

  4 **thin slices fully cooked ham**
  1 **pound boneless veal leg round steak, cut ¹/₄ inch thick**
¹/₂ **cup shredded Swiss cheese (2 ounces)**
¹/₃ **cup fine dry bread crumbs**
  1 **tablespoon snipped fresh parsley**
¹/₈ **teaspoon pepper**
¹/₄ **cup all-purpose flour**
  1 **beaten egg**
  3 **tablespoons margarine or butter**

1. Trim fat from ham and veal. Cut ham into strips. Cut veal into 4 serving-size pieces. Place veal between 2 pieces of plastic wrap. Working from center to the edges, with the flat side of a meat mallet, pound veal to ¹/₈-inch thickness. Remove plastic wrap. Place ham and cheese in center. Fold in sides; overlap ends, forming bundles. Secure with wooden toothpicks.

2. In a shallow dish combine bread crumbs, parsley, and pepper. Roll veal bundles in flour. Dip into beaten egg. Roll in crumb mixture to coat.

3. In a large skillet cook meat bundles in hot margarine or butter over medium heat for 14 to 17 minutes or till golden brown, turning occasionally. (Reduce heat to medium-low if meat is browning too quickly.) Makes 4 servings.

■ **Oven directions:** Prepare bundles as above. In a large skillet brown bundles in hot margarine or butter for 5 minutes, turning occasionally. Transfer to a 2-quart rectangular baking dish. Bake in a 400° oven 18 to 20 minutes or till juices run clear.

Nutrition Facts per serving: 382 cal., 20 g total fat (7 g sat. fat), 169 mg chol., 532 mg sodium, 13 g carbo., 1 g fiber, 37 g pro. **Daily Values:** 17% vit. A, 9% vit. C, 13% calcium, 13% iron

---

OSSO BUCO

PREP: 15 MINUTES COOK: 1½ HOURS

Low-Fat

   2 to 2½ pounds veal shanks, cut into 2- to 2½-inch-thick pieces
 ¼ teaspoon lemon-pepper seasoning
   2 tablespoons all-purpose flour
   2 tablespoons cooking oil
   1 14½-ounce can tomatoes, cut up (see tip, page 999)
   1 cup chopped onion (1 large)
 ½ cup chopped celery (1 stalk)
 ½ cup chopped carrot (1 medium)
 ½ cup water
 ¼ cup dry white wine
 ½ teaspoon finely shredded orange peel
 ½ teaspoon instant beef bouillon granules
 ½ teaspoon Italian seasoning, crushed
   1 clove garlic, minced
   3 cups hot cooked rice (see page 139)
   1 tablespoon snipped fresh parsley

1. Trim fat from meat. Sprinkle with lemon-pepper seasoning. Dip into flour, coating well. In a 4- to 6-quart pot brown veal in hot oil. Drain off fat.

2. Stir together undrained tomatoes, onion, celery, carrot, water, wine, orange peel, bouillon granules, Italian seasoning, and garlic. Pour over meat. Bring to boiling. Reduce heat. Simmer, covered, for 1¼ to 1½ hours or till tender. Transfer meat to a platter, reserving broth mixture. Keep warm.

3. Boil broth mixture gently, uncovered, about 10 minutes or till desired consistency is reached. Toss rice with parsley. Arrange meat atop rice. Spoon some of the broth over meat and rice. Pass remaining broth. Makes 6 servings.

Nutrition Facts per serving: 388 cal., 10 g total fat (3 g sat. fat), 128 mg chol., 320 mg sodium, 33 g carbo., 2 g fiber, 39 g pro. **Daily Values:** 43% vit. A, 24% vit. C, 4% calcium, 20% iron

VEAL CHOPS WITH MUSHROOM SAUCE

START TO FINISH: 25 MINUTES

Fast   **Low-Fat**

Perfect with veal or pork, the mushroom sauce dresses up noodles or rice, too.

   4 veal loin chops or pork loin chops, cut ³/₄ inch thick
³/₄ cup sliced fresh mushrooms
   1 tablespoon sliced green onion (1)
   1 tablespoon margarine or butter
   1 tablespoon all-purpose flour
   2 teaspoons snipped fresh tarragon or ¹/₄ teaspoon dried tarragon, crushed
³/₄ cup milk
   2 tablespoons dry white wine or 1 tablespoon water plus 2 teaspoons white wine Worcestershire sauce

1. Place chops on the unheated rack of a broiler pan. Broil 3 to 4 inches from the heat till juices run clear, turning once. (Allow 14 to 17 minutes for veal or 8 to 10 minutes for pork.)

2. Meanwhile, for sauce, in a medium saucepan cook mushrooms and green onion in hot margarine or butter till tender. Stir in flour and tarragon. Gradually stir in milk. Cook and stir till thickened and bubbly. Cook and stir for 1 minute more. Stir in wine or water and Worcestershire sauce. If desired, season with salt and pepper.

3. Transfer chops to a serving platter. Spoon some of the sauce over the chops. Pass any remaining sauce. Makes 4 servings.

Nutrition Facts per serving: 183 cal., 9 g total fat (3 g sat. fat), 75 mg chol., 123 mg sodium, 4 g carbo., 0 g fiber, 20 g pro. **Daily Values:** 6% vit. A, 2% vit. C, 6% calcium, 6% iron

VEAL PARMIGIANA

For a shortcut, substitute a 15-ounce jar of Italian cooking sauce for the sauce ingredients.

12 ounces veal or pork scaloppini or 12 ounces boneless veal leg round steak, cut $1/4$ inch thick
$1/4$ cup all-purpose flour
2 tablespoons grated Parmesan cheese
$1/8$ teaspoon pepper
2 tablespoons olive oil or cooking oil
$1/3$ cup chopped onion (1 small)
1 clove garlic, minced
1 15-ounce can tomato sauce
$1/4$ cup dry red wine or chicken broth
1 tablespoon dried parsley, crushed
1 teaspoon dried oregano, crushed
$1/2$ teaspoon dried basil, crushed
$1/4$ teaspoon salt
$1/2$ cup shredded mozzarella cheese (2 ounces)
Fresh parsley sprigs (optional)

1. Trim fat from meat. Cut into 4 serving-size pieces. If using veal steak, place between 2 pieces of plastic wrap. Working from center to edges, pound with flat side of meat mallet to $1/8$-inch thickness. Remove plastic wrap.

2. In a shallow dish combine flour, Parmesan cheese, and pepper. Dip meat into flour mixture, coating well. In a 12-inch skillet cook meat in hot oil over medium heat for 2 to 3 minutes or till light brown, turning once. Remove meat, reserving drippings in skillet. Set meat aside.

3. For sauce, cook onion and garlic in drippings till tender. Stir in tomato sauce, wine or broth, parsley, oregano, basil, and salt. Bring to boiling. Reduce heat. Simmer, uncovered, for 5 minutes.

4. Return meat to skillet. Heat through. Remove from heat. Sprinkle with mozzarella cheese. Cover; let stand about 5 minutes or till cheese is melted. If desired, garnish with parsley. Makes 4 servings.

Nutrition Facts per serving: 296 cal., 13 g total fat (4 g sat. fat), 79 mg chol., 957 mg sodium, 16 g carbo., 2 g fiber, 26 g pro. **Daily Values:** 14% vit. A, 14% vit. C, 13% calcium, 14% iron

PORK

The photos here show the retail cuts of pork. The number with each one refers to the wholesale cut marked on the drawing below. The best ways to cook each meat cut also are listed.

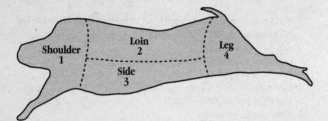

Blade steak (1)
Braise, broil, grill, panbroil, panfry

Blade roast (1)
Braise, roast

Boneless blade roast (1)
Braise, roast

Smoked picnic (1)
Cook in liquid, roast

Smoked hock (1)
Braise, cook in liquid

Smoked boneless shoulder (1)
Cook in liquid, roast

Spareribs (3)
*Braise, broil, cook in liquid,
roast*

Bacon (3)
Bake, broil, panfry

Ham (shank half) (4)
Grill, roast

Ham center slice (4)
*Broil, grill, panbroil,
panfry, roast*

Boneless smoked ham
(whole muscle) (4)
Grill, roast

Boneless smoked ham
(sectioned and formed) (4)
Grill, roast

Boneless top loin roast
(single) (2)
Grill, roast

Boneless top loin roast
(double) (2)
Grill, roast

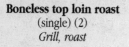

Center rib roast (2)
Grill, roast

Rib crown roast (2)
Roast

Tenderloin (2)
Grill, roast

Top loin chop (2)
*Broil, grill, panbroil, panfry,
stir-fry (strips)*

Butterfly chop (2)
*Broil, grill, panbroil,
panfry, stir-fry (strips)*

Loin chop (2)
Broil, grill, panbroil, panfry

Rib chop (2)
Broil, grill, panbroil, panfry

Boneless sirloin chop (2)
*Braise, broil, grill, panbroil,
panfry, stir-fry (strips)*

Sirloin chop (2)
*Braise, broil, grill,
panbroil, panfry*

Country-style ribs (2)
Braise, broil, cook in liquid, roast

Back ribs (2)
*Braise, broil, cook in
liquid, roast*

Canadian-style bacon (2)
Broil, panbroil, panfry, roast

Smoked loin chop (2)
*Broil, panbroil,
panfry, roast*

POT ROAST IN CIDER

PREP: 15 MINUTES   COOK: 1³/₄ HOURS

For cooking apples, try Jonathan, Rome Beauty, or Winesap varieties.

1 1¹/₂- to 2-pound boneless pork shoulder roast or pork sirloin roast
2 tablespoons cooking oil
1¹/₄ cups apple cider or apple juice
2 teaspoons instant beef bouillon granules
¹/₄ teaspoon dry mustard
¹/₄ teaspoon pepper
2 medium potatoes, peeled and quartered
2 large carrots, cut into 2-inch pieces
2 medium cooking apples, cored and cut into wedges
1 medium onion, cut into wedges
¹/₃ cup cold water
¹/₄ cup all-purpose flour

1. Trim fat from meat. In a 4- to 6-quart pot brown meat on all sides in hot oil. Drain off fat. Stir together apple cider or juice, bouillon granules, dry mustard, and pepper. Pour over meat. Bring to boiling. Reduce heat. Simmer, covered, for 1 hour.

2. Add potatoes, carrots, apples, and onion. Simmer, covered, for 30 to 40 minutes more or till meat and vegetables are tender. Transfer meat, vegetables, and apples to a serving platter, reserving juices in pot. Keep warm.

3. For gravy, measure juices; skim fat (see tip, page 882). If necessary, add enough water to juices to equal 1¹/₂ cups. Return to pot. Stir together cold water and flour. Stir into juices. Cook and stir over medium heat till thickened and bubbly. Cook and stir for 1 minute more. Serve with meat and vegetables. Makes 6 servings.

■ **Crockery-cooker directions:** Trim fat from meat. In a 4- to 6-quart pot brown meat on all sides in hot oil. Cut meat, if necessary, to fit into a 3¹/₂- or 4-quart electric crockery cooker. Place potatoes, carrots, and onion in the cooker. Add meat. Stir together apple cider or juice, bouillon granules, dry mustard, and pepper. Pour over meat and vegetables. Cover and cook on low-heat setting for 9 to 11 hours or till nearly tender. Increase heat to high. Add apple wedges. Cook, covered, for 30 to 45 minutes more or till apples are tender.

Transfer meat, vegetables, and apples to a serving platter. Keep warm. Continue as above for gravy.

Nutrition Facts per serving: 391 cal., 17 g total fat (5 g sat. fat) 78 mg chol., 379 mg sodium, 36 g carbo., 3 g fiber, 24 g pro. **Daily Values:** 85% vit. A, 22% vit. C, 3% calcium, 21% iron

---

HERB-CRUSTED PORK ROAST AND POTATOES

PREP: 15 MINUTES ROAST: 1¹/₂ HOURS STAND: 15 MINUTES   Oven 325°

Ask the butcher to loosen the backbone for you.

  1 3- to 3¹/₂-pound pork loin center rib roast, backbone loosened
  2 teaspoons dried thyme, crushed
  2 teaspoons dried rosemary, crushed
¹/₂ teaspoon ground coriander
  3 cloves garlic, slivered
24 tiny new potatoes or 4 medium potatoes
  2 tablespoons olive oil or cooking oil
  1 teaspoon dried thyme, crushed

1. Trim fat from meat. Cut 1-inch-long slits in roast. Stir together the 2 teaspoons thyme, rosemary, coriander, ¹/₄ teaspoon *salt,* and ¹/₄ teaspoon *pepper.* Rub mixture onto meat and into slits. Insert garlic slivers into slits. Place roast, rib side down, in a shallow roasting pan. Insert a meat thermometer without touching bone (see tip, page 620). Roast in a 325° oven for 1 hour.

2. Meanwhile, if using new potatoes, peel a strip of skin from the center of each. If using medium potatoes, peel and quarter. Cook potatoes in boiling salted water for 10 minutes; drain.

3. Toss potatoes with oil, the 1 teaspoon thyme, and ¹/₄ teaspoon *salt.* Place in roasting pan around pork roast. Add ¹/₄ cup *water* to the pan. Roast, uncovered, for ¹/₂ to 1 hour more or till thermometer registers 155°. Cover with foil; let stand 15 minutes before carving. (The meat's temperature will rise 5° during standing.) Makes 8 to 10 servings.

Nutrition Facts per serving: 289 cal., 13 g total fat (4 g sat. fat), 65 mg chol., 190 mg sodium, 20 g carbo., 1 g fiber, 23 g pro. **Daily Values:** 0% vit. A, 19% vit. C, 2% calcium, 17% iron

RHUBARB-GLAZED PORK ROAST

PREP: 25 MINUTES   ROAST: 1¼ HOURS   STAND: 15 MINUTES   Oven 325°

Low-Fat

Make this in the spring when rhubarb is in season or buy frozen sliced rhubarb for convenience.

- 1 2- to 3-pound boneless pork top loin roast (single loin)
- 4 cups fresh or frozen sliced rhubarb
- ½ of a 12-ounce can frozen cranberry-apple juice cocktail concentrate
- 2 tablespoons cornstarch
- 2 tablespoons cold water
- ⅓ cup honey
- 2 tablespoons Dijon-style mustard
- 1 tablespoon wine vinegar

1. Place roast on a rack in a shallow roasting pan. Insert a meat thermometer (see tip, page 620). Roast in a 325° oven for 1¼ hours to 1¾ hours or till the thermometer registers 155°.

2. Meanwhile, for glaze, in a 2-quart saucepan combine rhubarb and cranberry-apple juice cocktail concentrate. Bring to boiling; reduce heat. Cover and simmer 15 minutes or till rhubarb is very tender. Strain mixture into a 2-cup liquid measure, pressing out liquid with the back of a spoon. Add enough water to equal 1¼ cups. Discard pulp.

3. In the same saucepan stir together cornstarch and cold water. Stir in rhubarb liquid. Cook and stir over medium heat till thickened and bubbly. Cook and stir for 2 minutes more. Stir in honey, mustard, and vinegar. Heat through.

4. Brush some of the glaze onto the meat for the last 30 minutes of roasting. Cover meat with foil; let stand 15 minutes before carving. (The meat's temperature will rise 5° during standing.) Heat remaining glaze; serve with meat. Makes 6 to 8 servings.

Nutrition Facts per serving: 264 cal., 8 g total fat (3 g sat. fat), 51 mg chol., 137 mg sodium, 31 g carbo., 1 g fiber, 17 g pro. **Daily Values:** 0% vit. A, 25% vit. C, 4% calcium, 5% iron

■ **Ginger-Apricot-Glazed Pork Roast:** Prepare roast as above except substitute apricot glaze for rhubarb glaze. For apricot glaze, in a small saucepan combine ²⁄₃ cup *apricot preserves,* 4 teaspoons *lime juice,* 2 teaspoons *soy sauce,* ¹⁄₄ teaspoon grated *gingerroot* or ¹⁄₈ teaspoon *ground ginger,* and dash *ground red pepper.* Cook and stir till bubbly.

Nutrition Facts per serving: 209 cal., 7 g total fat (3 g sat. fat)

CITRUS-MUSTARD PORK ROAST

PREP: 30 MINUTES ROAST: 1³⁄₄ HOURS STAND: 15 MINUTES   Oven 325°

Low-Fat

    3 tablespoons Dijon-style mustard
    2 teaspoons finely shredded orange peel
    1 teaspoon finely shredded lemon peel
 ¹⁄₂ teaspoon pepper
    1 3- to 4-pound boneless pork top loin roast (double loin, tied)
    2 medium oranges
      Orange juice
    2 tablespoons cornstarch
    2 tablespoons honey or brown sugar
    2 tablespoons lemon juice
 ¹⁄₄ cup dry white wine or orange juice

1. In a bowl stir together *2 tablespoons* of the mustard, citrus peels, pepper, and ¹⁄₄ teaspoon *salt.*
2. Untie roast; trim fat. Spread mustard mixture on roast. Retie roast. Place on a rack in a shallow roasting pan. Insert a meat thermometer (see tip, page 620). Roast in a 325° oven for 1³⁄₄ to 2¹⁄₄ hours or till thermometer registers 155°. Cover with foil and let stand 15 minutes. (The meat's temperature will rise 5° during standing.)
3. Meanwhile, for sauce, peel and section oranges over a bowl to catch juices. Add enough orange juice to equal 1 cup. In a saucepan stir together remaining mustard, orange juice, cornstarch, honey, and lemon juice. Cook and stir till thickened and bubbly. Cook and stir 2 minutes more. Gently stir in orange sections and wine. Heat through. Serve sauce with meat. Serves 10 to 12.

Nutrition Facts per serving: 209 cal., 9 g total fat (3 g sat. fat), 61 mg chol., 214 mg sodium, 10 g carbo., 1 g fiber, 20 g pro. **Daily Values:** 0% vit. A, 35% vit. C, 1% calcium, 5% iron

PORK CROWN ROAST WITH APPLE-CHERRY STUFFING

PREP: 15 MINUTES   ROAST: 2¼ HOURS   STAND: 15 MINUTES   Oven 325°

Ask the butcher to cut this roast from the rib section of the pork loin.

  1 5½- to 6-pound pork rib crown roast (12 to 16 ribs)
  ¾ cup hot water
  ½ cup dried tart red cherries, snipped dried apricots, or dried
       cranberries
  ½ teaspoon instant chicken bouillon granules
  ½ cup sliced celery (1 stalk)
  ⅓ cup chopped onion (1 small)
  2 tablespoons margarine or butter
  4 cups dry whole wheat bread cubes (6 to 7 slices)
  1 cup chopped apple (1 medium)
  ¼ teaspoon ground sage
  ⅛ teaspoon pepper

1. Trim fat from meat. Place roast, bone tips up, on a rack in a shallow roasting pan. Make a ball of foil and press it into cavity to hold open. Wrap the bone tips with foil (see photo, top right). Roast in a 325° oven for 1½ hours.

2. Meanwhile, for stuffing, in a small mixing bowl stir together hot water; cherries, apricots, or cranberries; and bouillon granules. Let stand for 5 minutes. Do not drain.

3. In a small skillet cook celery and onion in hot margarine or butter till tender but not brown.

4. In a large mixing bowl toss together bread cubes, apple, sage, and pepper. Add fruit mixture and celery mixture. Toss gently to moisten. (If desired, add ¼ cup *water* for a moister stuffing.)

5. Remove foil from roast cavity. Loosely pack stuffing into the center of the roast. Cover stuffing loosely with foil. Insert a meat thermometer into the center of the stuffing. Place any remaining stuffing in a lightly greased casserole. Bake the stuffed roast and the stuffing in covered casserole for 45 to 60 minutes more or till thermometer in stuffing registers 160°.

6. Cover with foil and let stand for 15 minutes before carving. Serve additional stuffing in casserole along with roast. To serve, slice roast between ribs. Makes 12 servings.

Nutrition Facts per serving: 420 cal., 27 g total fat (10 g sat. fat), 74 mg chol., 201 mg sodium, 12 g carbo., 1 g fiber, 31 g pro. **Daily Values:** 5% vit. A, 2% vit. C, 2% calcium, 11% iron

To prevent the meat on the tips of the bones from drying out, cover them with small pieces of foil before roasting.

Checking Pork Doneness

Pork cooked with foods such as bacon, spinach, and tomatoes sometimes remains pink even when well-done. The same is true of grilled and smoked pork. So, when cooking pork with these ingredients, or grilling or smoking pork, rely on a meat thermometer.

Peach-Glazed Pork Tenderloin

Prep: 10 minutes   Chill: 2 to 6 hours   Roast: 25 minutes
Stand: 15 minutes   Oven 425°

Low-Fat

Save any leftovers to make tasty sandwiches.

  $^3/_4$ teaspoon dried thyme, crushed
  $^1/_4$ teaspoon salt
  $^1/_4$ teaspoon pepper
   2 teaspoons cooking oil
   1 $^3/_4$-pound pork tenderloin
  $^1/_3$ cup peach preserves or apricot preserves
   2 teaspoons Worcestershire sauce
   1 teaspoon grated gingerroot or $^1/_4$ teaspoon ground ginger

1. In a small mixing bowl stir together thyme, salt, and pepper. Rub cooking oil onto meat. Sprinkle herb mixture evenly onto meat. Rub in with fingers. Cover and refrigerate for 2 to 6 hours.
2. Meanwhile, for glaze, stir together preserves, Worcestershire sauce, and gingerroot. Set aside.

3. Place tenderloin on a rack in a shallow roasting pan. Insert a meat thermometer (see tip, page 620). Roast in a 425° oven for 15 minutes. Spoon some of the glaze over tenderloin. Roast for 10 to 15 minutes more or till thermometer registers 160°. Spoon remaining glaze over tenderloin. Cover with foil and let stand for 15 minutes before carving. Makes 4 servings.

Nutrition Facts per serving: 253 cal., 8 g total fat (2 g sat. fat), 81 mg chol., 365 mg sodium, 20 g carbo., 0 g fiber, 25 g pro. **Daily Values:** 0% vit. A, 12% vit. C, 1% calcium, 14% iron

---

PORK TENDERLOIN SANDWICHES

START TO FINISH: 35 MINUTES

This pork cut is the long, thin muscle of the loin section.

1 ³/₄-pound pork tenderloin
¹/₄ cup all-purpose flour
¹/₄ teaspoon onion powder or garlic powder
¹/₄ teaspoon pepper
1 beaten egg
1 tablespoon milk or water
1 cup finely crushed rich round crackers (about 24) or ³/₄ cup fine dry bread crumbs
1 tablespoon cooking oil
4 hamburger buns, large buns, or kaiser rolls, split and toasted
   Mustard, catsup, onion slices, and/or dill pickle slices
   (optional)

1. Cut pork crosswise into 4 serving-size slices. Place between 2 pieces of plastic wrap. Working from center, pound lightly with the flat side of a mallet to ¹/₄-inch thickness. Remove plastic wrap.
2. In a shallow dish combine flour, onion or garlic powder, and pepper. In another shallow dish combine egg and milk or water. In a third dish place crushed crackers or bread crumbs. Dip meat into the flour mixture to coat. Dip into egg mixture. Coat with crumbs.
3. In a large skillet cook 2 slices in hot oil over medium heat for 6 to 8 minutes or till no pink remains and juices run clear, turning once. Remove from skillet. Keep warm. Repeat with remaining slices, adding more oil, if necessary. Place on buns. If desired, serve with mustard, catsup, onion, and/or dill pickle slices. Makes 4 servings.

Nutrition Facts per serving: 413 cal., 16 g total fat (3 g sat. fat), 114 mg chol., 457 mg sodium, 40 g carbo., 2 g fiber, 26 g pro. **Daily Values:** 2% vit. A, 0% vit. C, 6% calcium, 21% iron

SMOKED PORK CHOPS WITH MAPLE GLAZE

START TO FINISH: 20 MINUTES

Fast

- 4 smoked pork chops, cut $^3/_4$ inch thick
- 1 tablespoon cooking oil
- $^1/_4$ cup water or apple juice
- $^1/_4$ cup maple-flavored or maple syrup
- 1 teaspoon cornstarch
- $^1/_4$ teaspoon dried sage, crushed
- $^1/_8$ teaspoon coarsely ground pepper
- $^1/_4$ cup broken pecans, toasted (see tip, page 234)

1. Trim fat from meat. In a large skillet cook chops in hot oil for 8 to 10 minutes or till hot, turning once. Transfer to a platter. Keep warm.
2. Meanwhile, for glaze, in a small saucepan combine water or juice, syrup, cornstarch, sage, and pepper. Cook and stir over medium heat till thickened and bubbly. Cook and stir for 2 minutes more. Stir in pecans. Spoon atop chops. Serves 4.

Nutrition Facts per serving: 313 cal., 15 g total fat (3 g sat. fat), 67 mg chol., 1,535 mg sodium, 17 g carbo., 0 g fiber, 27 g pro. **Daily Values:** 0% vit. A, 44% vit. C, 1% calcium, 13% iron

GINGER-GLAZED PORK CHOPS

START TO FINISH: 20 MINUTES

Fast

- 4 pork loin chops, cut $^3/_4$ inch thick
- $^1/_4$ cup honey
- 2 tablespoons soy sauce
- 2 tablespoons sliced green onion (1)
- 1 tablespoon grated gingerroot or $^1/_2$ teaspoon ground ginger
- 2 teaspoons cornstarch
- 1 clove garlic, minced
  Hot cooked rice (see page 139) (optional)

1. Trim fat from meat. Place chops on the unheated rack of a broiler pan. Broil 3 to 4 inches from heat for 8 to 10 minutes or till no pink remains and juices run clear, turning once. Transfer to a platter.

2. Meanwhile, for glaze, in a saucepan combine honey, soy sauce, green onion, ginger, cornstarch, and garlic. Cook and stir till thickened and bubbly. Cook and stir 2 minutes more. Spoon over chops. If desired, serve with rice. Makes 4 servings.

Nutrition Facts per serving: 331 cal., 15 g total fat (5 g sat. fat), 95 mg chol., 590 mg sodium, 20 g carbo., 0 g fiber, 28 g pro. **Daily Values:** 0% vit. A, 1% vit. C, 1% calcium, 8% iron

---

HANDLING AND COOKING MEAT SAFELY

Although Americans enjoy the most abundant and safest food supply in the world, it's still important to handle meat properly in the kitchen. Always follow these food safety tips:

■ Keep everything clean that food touches, including hands, utensils, surfaces, and cutting boards.

■ Always wash your hands before and after touching raw meat.

■ If you use a knife or any other utensil on raw meat, don't use it for other foods without first washing it in hot, soapy water.

■ Keep separate cutting boards for raw meats and ready-to-eat products.

■ Cook ground meat until no pink remains. Cook other cuts of beef to at least 145° and pork to at least 160°. (All recipes in this book provide directions to assure reaching these minimum temperatures.)

■ To use a marinade as a sauce, be sure to boil it for at least 2 minutes before serving.

■ Don't cook any meat, poultry, or fish in stages (partially cooking it to save time, then finishing it later). Even if you store it in the refrigerator between cooking periods, safe temperatures might not be maintained.

RICE-AND-SAGE-STUFFED PORK CHOPS

Prep: 25 minutes   Bake: 35 minutes   Oven 375°

*If you've cooked the rice in broth, omit the salt
from the stuffing mixture.*

- 1 cup cooked rice (see page 139)
- 1/3 cup shredded carrot (1 small)
- 1/4 cup sliced green onions (2)
- 1/2 teaspoon dried sage, crushed
- 1/4 teaspoon salt
- 1/8 teaspoon pepper
- 4 pork loin rib chops, cut 1 1/4 inches thick
  Dash pepper
- 1 cup sliced fresh mushrooms
- 1 tablespoon margarine or butter
- 2 teaspoons all-purpose flour
- 1/4 teaspoon salt
  Dash pepper
- 1/2 cup milk
- 1/4 cup plain yogurt or dairy sour cream
- 1 tablespoon snipped fresh parsley or
- 1 teaspoon dried parsley, crushed

1. For stuffing, in a small mixing bowl stir together rice, carrot, green onions, sage, the 1/4 teaspoon salt, and the 1/8 teaspoon pepper.

2. Trim fat from chops. Cut a pocket in each chop by cutting from the fat side almost to the bone (see photo 1, page 654). Spoon stuffing into chops (see photo 2, page 654). If necessary, secure pockets with wooden toothpicks (see photo 3, page 654). Place chops on a rack in a shallow roasting pan. Sprinkle with pepper. Bake in a 375° oven for 35 to 45 minutes or till no pink remains and juices run clear.

3. Meanwhile, for sauce, in a small saucepan cook mushrooms in hot margarine or butter till tender. Stir in flour, the 1/4 teaspoon salt, and dash pepper. Gradually stir in milk. Cook and stir over medium heat till thickened and bubbly. Cook and stir for 1 minute more. Remove from heat. Stir in yogurt or sour cream and parsley. Heat through, but do not boil. To serve, remove wooden toothpicks. Spoon sauce atop chops. Makes 4 servings.

Nutrition Facts per serving: 345 cal., 16 g total fat (5 g sat. fat), 90 mg chol., 396 mg sodium, 17 g carbo., 1 g fiber, 31 g pro. **Daily Values:** 33% vit. A, 8% vit. C, 6% calcium, 14% iron

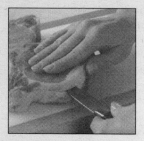

1. To cut a pocket in a chop, use a sharp knife to make a 2-inch-long slit in the fatty side. Work knife inside, cutting almost to the bone and keeping the original slit small.

2. Using a spoon, carefully push about ½ cup stuffing into each pocket. If the original slit is kept small, the stuffing will stay in better during cooking.

3. To keep the stuffing in the pockets, insert 1 or 2 wooden toothpicks diagonally into each chop near pocket opening.

CORN BREAD-STUFFED PORK CHOPS

PREP: 25 MINUTES BAKE: 35 MINUTES   Oven 375°

If you can't find jalapeño jelly, top the baked chops with
a spoonful of salsa instead.

- $^1/_4$ cup chopped onion ($^1/_2$ of a medium)
- 1 clove garlic, minced
- 1 tablespoon margarine or butter
- $^1/_2$ cup corn bread stuffing mix
- $^1/_4$ cup chopped, seeded tomato
- $^1/_2$ of a 4-ounce can diced green chili peppers, drained
- 2 tablespoons snipped fresh cilantro or parsley
- $^1/_4$ teaspoon salt
- $^1/_4$ teaspoon ground coriander
- $^1/_4$ teaspoon ground cumin
- 4 pork loin rib chops, cut $1^1/_4$ inches thick
  Red jalapeño jelly (optional)

1. For stuffing, in a small saucepan cook onion and garlic in hot margarine or butter till tender. Stir in stuffing mix, tomato, chili peppers, cilantro or parsley, salt, coriander, and cumin.
2. Trim fat from chops: Cut a pocket in each chop by cutting from fat side almost to bone (see photo 1, page 654). Spoon stuffing into chops (see photo 2, page 654). If necessary, secure with wooden toothpicks (see photo 3, page 654). Place chops on a rack in a shallow roasting pan. Bake in a 375° oven 35 to 45 minutes or till no pink remains and juices run clear.
3. Meanwhile, if desired, in a small saucepan cook and stir jalapeño jelly till heated through. Brush onto chops for the last 5 minutes of baking. To serve, remove toothpicks. Makes 4 servings.

Nutrition Facts per serving: 383 cal., 21 g total fat (7 g sat. fat), 108 mg chol., 536 mg sodium, 13 g carbo., 0 g fiber, 34 g pro. **Daily Values:** 5% vit. A, 14% vit. C, 4% calcium, 12% iron

CRANBERRY-SAUCED PORK CHOPS

START TO FINISH: 25 MINUTES

Fast	Low-Fat

This sauce is a delicious way to use up some of the cranberry sauce left over from the holidays.

6 pork loin rib chops, cut ³/₄ inch thick
  Pepper
1 tablespoon margarine or butter
¹/₂ cup apple cider or apple juice
¹/₂ of a 16-ounce can (1 cup) whole cranberry sauce
2 tablespoons sliced green onion (1)
2 teaspoons cornstarch
1 teaspoon brown sugar
¹/₂ teaspoon finely shredded orange peel

1. Trim fat from meat. Sprinkle chops lightly with pepper. In a 12-inch skillet cook chops in hot margarine or butter over medium-high heat about 4 minutes or till brown, turning once. Drain off fat.

2. Pour apple cider or juice over chops. Bring to boiling. Reduce heat. Simmer, covered, for 5 to 6 minutes or till no pink remains in pork chops and juices run clear. Transfer pork chops to a platter, reserving ¹/₂ cup juices in skillet. Keep warm.

3. For sauce, stir together cranberry sauce, green onion, cornstarch, brown sugar, and orange peel. Stir into reserved juices in skillet. Cook and stir over medium heat till thickened and bubbly. Cook and stir for 2 minutes more. To serve, spoon sauce atop chops. Makes 6 servings.

Nutrition Facts per serving: 217 cal., 9 g total fat (3 g sat. fat), 48 mg chol., 71 mg sodium, 19 g carbo., 0 g fiber, 15 g pro. **Daily Values:** 2% vit. A, 4% vit. C, 0% calcium, 5% iron

---

PORK CHOPS WITH BLACK BEANS

START TO FINISH: 20 MINUTES

Fast

4 pork loin rib chops, cut ³/₄ inch thick
¹/₈ teaspoon pepper

1 tablespoon olive oil or cooking oil
1 15-ounce can black beans, rinsed and drained, or one 15$^{1}/_{2}$-
    ounce can red kidney beans, rinsed and drained (see tip,
    page 107)
1 cup salsa
1 tablespoon snipped fresh cilantro or parsley
    Plain yogurt or dairy sour cream (optional)

1. Trim fat from meat. Rub pepper onto chops. In a skillet cook chops in hot oil over medium-high heat about 4 minutes or till brown, turning once. Remove and drain off fat.
2. In the same skillet combine beans, salsa, and cilantro or parsley. Add chops. Bring to boiling. Reduce heat. Simmer, covered, for 5 to 6 minutes or till no pink remains in pork and juices run clear.
3. To serve, top bean mixture with chops and, if desired, yogurt or sour cream. Makes 4 servings.

Nutrition Facts per serving: 276 cal., 14 g total fat (3 g sat. fat), 60 mg chol., 530 mg sodium, 18 g carbo., 5 g fiber, 26 g pro. **Daily Values:** 8% vit. A, 30% vit. C, 4% calcium, 16% iron

---

OVEN-FRIED PORK CHOPS

PREP: 10 MINUTES BAKE: 20 MINUTES   Oven 425°

Fast

4 pork loin chops, cut $^{3}/_{4}$ inch thick
2 tablespoons margarine or butter, melted
1 beaten egg
2 tablespoons milk
$^{1}/_{4}$ teaspoon pepper
1 cup herb-seasoned stuffing mix or corn bread stuffing mix,
    crushed

1. Trim fat from meat. Pour margarine or butter into a 13×9×2-inch baking pan. Combine egg, milk, and pepper. Dip chops into egg mixture. Coat with stuffing mix. Place in pan.
2. Bake in a 425° oven for 10 minutes. Turn chops. Bake about 10 minutes more or till no pink remains and juices run clear. Makes 4 servings.

Nutrition Facts per serving: 449 cal., 22 g total fat (6 g sat. fat), 139 mg chol., 432 mg sodium, 17 g carbo., 0 g fiber, 43 g pro. **Daily Values:** 10% vit. A, 1% vit. C, 5% calcium, 12% iron

OVEN-ROASTED HONEY AND BEER RIBS

PREP: 5 MINUTES BAKE: 1³/₄ HOURS   Oven 350°

2¹/₂ to 3 pounds pork country-style ribs
¹/₂ cup chopped onion (1 medium)
2 cloves garlic, minced
1 tablespoon cooking oil
³/₄ cup chili sauce
¹/₂ cup regular or nonalcoholic beer
¹/₄ cup honey
2 tablespoons Worcestershire sauce
¹/₂ teaspoon dry mustard

1. Place ribs, bone side up, in a shallow roasting pan. Bake in a 350° oven for 1 hour. Drain fat. Turn ribs meaty side up.
2. Meanwhile, for sauce, in a medium saucepan cook onion and garlic in hot oil till tender. Stir in chili sauce, beer, honey, Worcestershire sauce, and dry mustard. Bring to boiling. Reduce heat. Simmer, uncovered, for 20 minutes. (You should have about 1¹/₂ cups sauce.)
3. Spoon some sauce over ribs. Bake, covered, for 45 to 60 minutes more or till tender, adding sauce often. Pass remaining sauce. Makes 4 servings.

Nutrition Facts per serving: 445 cal., 20 g total fat (7 g sat. fat), 105 mg chol., 767 mg sodium, 33 g carbo., 1 g fiber, 30 g pro. **Daily Values:** 6% vit. A, 35% vit. C, 3% calcium, 14% iron

OVEN-ROASTED ORIENTAL-STYLE PORK RIBS

PREP: 15 MINUTES COOK: 20 MINUTES BAKE: 15 MINUTES   Oven 350°

Boiling the ribs before they're baked reduces the total cooking time.

2¹/₂ to 3 pounds pork loin back ribs or pork spareribs
3 tablespoons pineapple, peach, or apricot preserves
¹/₃ cup catsup
2 tablespoons soy sauce
1 teaspoon grated gingerroot or ¹/₄ teaspoon ground ginger
1 clove garlic, minced

1. Cut ribs into serving-size pieces (see photo, page 564). Place ribs in a 4- to 6-quart pot. Add enough water to cover. Bring to boiling.

Reduce heat. Simmer, covered, for 20 to 30 minutes or till ribs are tender; drain.

2. Meanwhile, for sauce, cut up any large pieces of fruit in the preserves. In a bowl stir together preserves, catsup, soy sauce, gingerroot, and garlic.

3. Place ribs, bone side down, in a shallow roasting pan. Brush some sauce onto ribs. Bake, uncovered, in a 350° oven for 15 to 20 minutes or till heated through. Brush with remaining sauce before serving. Makes 4 servings.

Nutrition Facts per serving: 315 cal., 19 g total fat (7 g sat. fat), 74 mg chol., 785 mg sodium, 18 g carbo., 1 g fiber, 19 g pro. **Daily Values:** 2% vit. A, 6% vit. C, 3% calcium, 10% iron

---

GREEK-STYLE PORK

PREP: 15 MINUTES COOK: 20 MINUTES

Low-Fat

A combination of cinnamon and oregano offers a delicious hint of Mediterranean flavor.

  1 **pound boneless pork sirloin**
  1 **tablespoon cooking oil**
 1/2 **of a medium onion, cut into wedges**
  1 **14¹/₂-ounce can diced tomatoes**
 1/2 **cup raisins**
 1/2 **teaspoon dried oregano, crushed**
 1/2 **teaspoon ground cinnamon**
     Hot cooked rice (see page 139) (optional)

1. Trim fat from meat. Cut into ¹/₂-inch cubes. In a large skillet brown half of the pork cubes in hot oil. Remove from skillet. Brown remaining pork and onion in skillet. Drain off fat. Return all meat and onion to skillet.

2. Stir in undrained tomatoes, raisins, oregano, and cinnamon. Bring to boiling. Reduce heat. Simmer, covered, for 20 to 25 minutes or till meat is tender. If desired, serve atop hot cooked rice. Serves 4.

Nutrition Facts per serving: 227 cal., 9 g total fat (2 g sat. fat), 47 mg chol., 457 mg sodium, 21 g carbo., 2 g fiber, 16 g pro. **Daily Values:** 7% vit. A, 28% vit. C, 4% calcium, 8% iron

PORK PICANTE

START TO FINISH: 30 MINUTES

Fast

If you like your food spicy-hot, choose hot-style salsa and hot-and-spicy vegetable juice.

- 1 **pound boneless pork sirloin**
- 1 **tablespoon cooking oil**
- ³/₄ **cup vegetable juice**
- 1 **teaspoon instant beef bouillon granules**
- 1 **cup salsa**
- ¹/₃ **cup peach, pineapple, or apricot preserves**
- 2 **tablespoons cornstarch**
  Hot cooked rice (see page 139) or hot cooked noodles (see page 729)

1. Trim fat from meat. Cut into ¹/₂-inch cubes. In a large skillet brown half of the pork in hot oil. Remove from skillet. Brown remaining. Drain off fat. Return all meat to skillet.

2. Stir in juice and bouillon granules. Bring to boiling. Reduce heat. Simmer, covered, 20 to 25 minutes or till meat is tender and no pink remains.

3. Stir together salsa, preserves, and cornstarch. Stir into skillet. Cook and stir over medium heat till thickened and bubbly. Cook and stir for 2 minutes more. Serve atop rice or noodles. Serves 4.

Nutrition Facts per serving: 386 cal., 13 g total fat (3 g sat. fat), 51 mg chol., 647 mg sodium, 51 g carbo., 0 g fiber, 20 g pro.
Daily Values: 13% vit. A, 52% vit. C, 2% calcium, 17% iron

CUE FOR CUBES

When you can't buy meat that's already cubed, buy larger cuts of beef (round or chuck roasts), veal (shoulder roasts), lamb (leg or shoulder roasts), or pork (shoulder or loin roasts). Trim and discard the fat and remove any bones. Then cut the meat into evenly sized cubes.

PORK AND NOODLES

PREP: 30 MINUTES COOK: 35 MINUTES

Low-Fat

> 1 pound boneless pork sirloin chops or pork shoulder steaks, cut ¹/₂ inch thick
> 1 tablespoon cooking oil
> ³/₄ cup chopped red sweet pepper (1 medium)
> ¹/₃ cup chopped onion (1 small)
> 1¹/₂ teaspoons instant chicken bouillon granules
> ¹/₂ teaspoon dried sage, crushed
> ¹/₄ teaspoon pepper
> 1 8-ounce carton plain yogurt or dairy sour cream
> 3 tablespoons all-purpose flour
> 1 tablespoon snipped fresh parsley (optional)
> 2 cups hot cooked noodles (see page 729)

1. Trim fat from pork. Partially freeze. Thinly slice across grain into bite-size strips (see step 1, page 634). In a large skillet brown half the meat in oil; remove. Brown remaining meat; remove. Add sweet pepper and onion; cook till tender. Drain fat.

2. Return all meat to skillet. Stir in 1 cup *water,* bouillon granules, sage, and pepper. Bring to boiling. Reduce heat. Simmer, covered, about 30 minutes or till meat is tender and no pink remains.

3. Skim fat from liquid (see tip, page 1002). Stir together yogurt or sour cream, flour, and, if desired, parsley. Stir into skillet. Cook and stir over medium heat till thickened and bubbly. Cook and stir 1 minute more. Serve over noodles. Serves 4.

Nutrition Facts per serving: 289 cal., 9 g total fat (2 g sat. fat), 74 mg chol., 394 mg sodium, 30 g carbo., 2 g fiber, 22 g pro. **Daily Values:** 14% vit. A, 54% vit. C, 9% calcium, 11% iron

CASHEW PORK AND PEA PODS

START TO FINISH: 45 MINUTES

    1 pound lean boneless pork
    $^1/_2$ cup orange juice
    $^1/_4$ cup orange marmalade
    2 tablespoons soy sauce
    1 tablespoon cornstarch
    $^1/_2$ teaspoon ground ginger
    1 tablespoon cooking oil
    2 cups fresh pea pods or one 6-ounce package frozen pea pods,
       thawed
    2 medium peaches or nectarines or 1$^1/_2$ cups cubed papaya or
       frozen peach slices, thawed
    $^1/_2$ cup cashews or peanuts
    2 cups hot cooked rice (see page 139)

1. Trim fat from meat. Partially freeze. Thinly slice across grain into
bite-size strips (see step 1, page 634). For sauce, stir together juice,
marmalade, soy sauce, cornstarch, and ginger. Set aside.
2. Pour oil into a wok or large skillet. (Add more oil as necessary
during cooking.) Preheat over medium-high heat. Add half the pork.
Stir-fry 2 to 3 minutes or till no pink remains; remove. Add remaining pork; stir-fry 2 to 3 minutes. Return all meat to wok. Stir in pea
pods and fruit. Push ingredients from center of wok (see step 3,
page 634).
3. Stir sauce; pour into center of wok (see step 4, page 634). Cook
and stir till thickened and bubbly. Cook and stir for 2 minutes. Stir in
nuts. Serve with rice. Makes 4 servings.

Nutrition Facts per serving: 486 cal., 19 g total fat (5 g sat. fat), 51 mg chol., 669 mg
sodium, 56 g carbo., 4 g fiber, 23 g pro. **Daily Values:** 3% vit. A, 75% vit. C, 4% calcium,
27% iron

SWEET-AND-SOUR PORK

PREP: 30 MINUTES   COOK: 20 MINUTES

*Keep a close eye on the temperature of your frying oil. Too low a
temperature can cause the coating to absorb more fat; too high a
temperature will burn the coating.*

1 pound lean boneless pork
1 8-ounce can pineapple chunks (juice pack)
⅓ cup sugar
¼ cup vinegar
2 tablespoons cornstarch
2 tablespoons soy sauce
1 teaspoon instant chicken bouillon granules
1 beaten egg
¼ cup cornstarch
¼ cup all-purpose flour
¼ cup water
⅛ teaspoon ground red or black pepper
    Shortening or cooking oil for deep frying
1 tablespoon cooking oil
1 cup bias-sliced carrots (2 medium)
2 cloves garlic, minced
1 large green or red sweet pepper, cut into ½-inch pieces
2 cups hot cooked rice (see page 139)

1. Trim fat from meat. Cut into ¾-inch cubes. For sauce, drain pineapple, reserving juice. Add enough water to juice to equal 1½ cups. Stir in sugar, vinegar, the 2 tablespoons cornstarch, soy sauce, and bouillon granules. Set aside.

2. For batter, in a bowl combine egg, the ¼ cup cornstarch, flour, water, and pepper. Stir till smooth. Dip pork into batter. Fry pork, one-third at a time, in hot oil (365°) for 4 to 5 minutes or till pork is no longer pink and batter is golden. Drain on paper towels.

3. Pour the 1 tablespoon oil into a wok or large skillet. (Add more oil as necessary during cooking.) Preheat over medium-high heat. Stir-fry carrots and garlic in hot oil for 1 minute. Add sweet pepper; stir-fry 1 to 2 minutes or till crisp-tender (see step 2, page 634). Push from center of wok.

4. Stir sauce. Pour into center of wok (see step 4, page 634). Cook and stir till thickened and bubbly. Cook and stir 1 minute more. Stir in pork and pineapple. Heat through. Serve over rice. Serves 5.

Nutrition Facts per serving: 500 cal., 20 g total fat (5 g sat. fat), 83 mg chol., 652 mg sodium, 62 g carbo., 2 g fiber, 18 g pro. **Daily Values:** 73% vit. A, 80% vit. C, 3% calcium, 16% iron

PORK CHOP SUEY

PREP: 30 MINUTES COOK: 15 MINUTES

Low-Fat

*For Pork Chow Mein, substitute chow mein noodles for
the hot cooked rice.*

  1 **pound lean boneless pork**
$^3/_4$ **cup water**
  3 **tablespoons soy sauce**
  2 **tablespoons cornstarch**
  2 **tablespoons dry sherry or water**
  1 **teaspoon instant chicken bouillon granules**
$^1/_4$ **teaspoon pepper**
  1 **tablespoon cooking oil**
  2 **teaspoons grated gingerroot**
  2 **stalks celery, thinly bias-sliced (1 cup)**
  2 **cups sliced fresh mushrooms**
  2 **cups fresh bean sprouts or one 16-ounce can bean sprouts,
     rinsed and drained**
10 **green onions, bias-sliced into 1-inch pieces (1 cup)**
  1 **8-ounce can sliced water chestnuts or bamboo shoots, drained**
  2 **to 3 cups hot cooked rice (see page 139)**

1. Trim fat from meat. Partially freeze pork. Thinly slice pork across the grain into bite-size strips (see step 1, page 634). For sauce, stir together water, soy sauce, cornstarch, dry sherry or water, bouillon granules, and pepper. Set aside.

2. Pour cooking oil into a wok or large skillet. (Add more oil as necessary during cooking.) Preheat over medium-high heat. Stir-fry gingerroot in hot oil for 15 seconds. Add celery; stir-fry 2 minutes. Add mushrooms, fresh bean sprouts (if using), and green onions. Stir-fry 1 to 2 minutes or till celery is crisp-tender (see step 2, page 634). Remove vegetables from wok.

3. Add half of the pork to hot wok. Stir-fry for 2 to 3 minutes or till no pink remains. Remove from wok. Add remaining pork. Stir-fry 2 to 3 minutes or till no pink remains. Return all meat to wok. Push from center of wok (see step 3, page 634).

4. Stir sauce; add to center of wok (see step 4, page 634). Cook and stir till thickened and bubbly. Add cooked vegetables, water chestnuts or bamboo shoots, and, if using, canned bean sprouts. Cook and stir till heated through. Serve with hot cooked rice. Makes 4 to 6 servings.

Nutrition Facts per serving: 363 cal., 11 g total fat (3 g sat. fat), 51 mg chol., 1,065 mg sodium, 42 g carbo., 2 g fiber, 22 g pro. **Daily Values:** 6% vit. A, 28% vit. C, 3% calcium, 24% iron

---

GLAZED HAM

PREP: 15 MINUTES   BAKE: 1³/₄ HOURS   STAND: 15 MINUTES   Oven 325°

  1 **5- to 6-pound fully cooked ham (rump half or shank portion)**
 24 **whole cloves**
  2 **teaspoons finely shredded orange peel**
  1 **cup orange juice**
¹/₂ **cup packed brown sugar**
  4 **teaspoons cornstarch**
1¹/₂ **teaspoons dry mustard**

1. Score ham by making diagonal cuts in a diamond pattern. Stud with cloves. Place on a rack in a shallow roasting pan. Insert a meat thermometer (see tip, page 620). Bake in a 325° oven till thermometer registers 125°. For rump, cook 1¹/₄ to 1¹/₂ hours; for shank, cook 1³/₄ to 2 hours.
2. For glaze, in a medium pan combine orange peel and juice, brown sugar, cornstarch, and dry mustard. Cook and stir over medium heat till thickened and bubbly. Cook and stir 2 minutes more.
3. Brush ham with some of the glaze. Bake 20 to 30 minutes more or till thermometer registers 135°. Let stand 15 minutes before carving. (The meat's temperature will rise 5° during standing.) Serve with remaining glaze. Makes 16 to 20 servings.

Nutrition Facts per serving: 351 cal., 22 g total fat (7 g sat. fat), 88 mg chol., 1,335 mg sodium, 8 g carbo., 0 g fiber, 29 g pro. **Daily Values:** 0% vit. A, 46% vit. C, 1% calcium, 14% iron

IDENTIFYING HAMS

Are you confused by the different kinds of ham at your local supermarket? Just remember the following handy definitions.

■ The most popular kind of ham is a *fully cooked ham*. It is ready to eat when you buy it. To serve the ham hot, heat it to 140° (see chart, page 715).

■ Hams labeled *cook before eating* are not completely cooked during processing and should be cooked to 160°. (If you're unsure whether a ham you've bought is fully cooked, cook it to 160°.)

■ *Country* or *country-style hams* are distinctively flavored and specially processed. They are cured, may or may not be smoked, and usually are aged. Country hams generally are saltier than other hams and often are named for the city where they are processed. Follow package directions for these hams.

■ *Turkey ham* is skinless, boneless turkey thigh meat that is smoked and cured to taste like pork ham. It's available in large pieces or as cold cuts. To serve it hot, heat it to 140°.

CURRIED HAM AND FRUIT

PREP: 20 MINUTES BAKE: 30 MINUTES   Oven 350°

Low-Fat

This sauce also tastes great over poultry or beef.

    1   1¹/₂-pound fully cooked center-cut ham slice, cut 1 inch thick
    1   8-ounce can pineapple chunks (juice pack)
  ¹/₃   cup chopped onion (1 small)
    1   tablespoon margarine or butter
1¹/₂   teaspoons curry powder
  ³/₄   cup orange juice
    1   tablespoon cornstarch
  ¹/₂   cup cranberries
    3   tablespoons brown sugar
    1   11-ounce can mandarin orange sections, drained

1. Trim fat from ham. Slash edges at 1-inch intervals to prevent curling during baking. Place on a rack in a shallow baking pan. Bake in a 350° oven about 30 minutes or till heated through.

2. Meanwhile, for sauce, drain pineapple, reserving juice. In a saucepan cook onion in hot margarine till tender. Stir in curry powder. Cook and stir for 1 minute more. Stir together reserved juice, orange juice, and cornstarch. Stir into pan. Add berries. Cook and stir over medium heat till thickened and bubbly. Cook and stir for 2 minutes more. Stir in brown sugar. Gently stir in pineapple and orange sections. Spoon atop ham. Serves 6.

Nutrition Facts per serving: 280 cal., 8 g total fat (2 g sat. fat), 60 mg chol., 1,393 mg sodium, 27 g carbo., 1 g fiber, 25 g pro. **Daily Values:** 3% vit. A, 75% vit. C, 2% calcium, 14% iron

---

SAUSAGE AND PEPPER SANDWICHES

PREP: 5 MINUTES   COOK: 20 MINUTES

Fast

Sweet sausage links also may be called mild.

  1 **pound fresh sweet Italian sausage links**
$^1/_2$ **cup water**
  1 **medium green sweet pepper, cut into 1-inch pieces (1 cup)**
  1 **medium red sweet pepper, cut into 1-inch pieces (1 cup)**
  1 **large onion, sliced and separated into rings**
  1 **tablespoon cooking oil**
$^1/_2$ **teaspoon dried oregano, crushed**
$^1/_4$ **teaspoon dried basil, crushed**
  4 **French-style rolls or hoagie buns, split and toasted**

1. In a large skillet cook sausage links over medium heat about 5 minutes or till brown, turning frequently. Add water. Bring to boiling. Reduce heat. Simmer, covered, for 15 to 20 minutes or till no longer pink. Drain sausages on paper towels. If necessary, discard any liquid remaining in skillet.

2. Add green and red sweet pepper pieces, onion, oil, oregano, and basil to skillet. Cook and stir about 5 minutes or till vegetables are crisp-tender. Return sausage links to skillet. Heat through.

3. To serve, hollow out bottoms of rolls or buns. Place sausages on roll bottoms. Top with sweet pepper mixture and roll tops. Makes 4 servings.

Nutrition Facts per serving: 436 cal., 27 g total fat (8 g sat. fat), 65 mg chol., 1,004 mg sodium, 27 g carbo., 1 g fiber, 21 g pro. **Daily Values:** 14% vit. A, 81% vit. C, 5% calcium, 17% iron

MUFFULETTA

PREP: 10 MINUTES CHILL: 4 TO 24 HOURS

Serve this big New Orleans-style sandwich at casual gatherings, picnics, or tailgate parties.

$1/2$ cup sliced pitted ripe olives
$1/2$ cup chopped pimiento-stuffed green olives
  1 tablespoon snipped fresh parsley
  2 teaspoons lemon juice
$1/2$ teaspoon dried oregano, crushed
  1 tablespoon olive oil
  1 clove garlic, minced
  1 16-ounce loaf unsliced French bread
  6 lettuce leaves
  6 ounces thinly sliced salami, pepperoni, summer sausage, fully
      cooked ham, prosciutto, or a combination
  6 ounces thinly sliced provolone, Swiss, or mozzarella cheese
  1 to 2 medium tomatoes, thinly sliced
$1/8$ teaspoon coarsely ground pepper

1. In a small mixing bowl combine the ripe olives, green olives, parsley, lemon juice, and oregano. Cover and refrigerate for 4 to 24 hours.

2. Meanwhile, stir together olive oil and garlic. Horizontally split loaf of bread. Hollow out inside of the top half, leaving a $3/4$-inch-thick shell.

3. Brush the bottom half of the bread with olive oil mixture. Top with lettuce leaves, desired meat, desired cheese, and tomato slices. Sprinkle tomato slices with pepper. Stir olive mixture. Mound atop tomato slices. Top with hollowed-out bread. To serve, slice into 6 portions. Makes 6 servings.

Nutrition Facts per serving: 476 cal., 25 g total fat (9 g sat. fat), 42 mg chol., 1,618 mg sodium, 43 g carbo., 1 g fiber, 21 g pro. **Daily Values:** 9% vit. A, 10% vit. C, 24% calcium, 19% iron

PIZZA FLORENTINE PIE

PREP: 25 MINUTES   BAKE: 30 MINUTES   STAND: 15 MINUTES   Oven 425°

You can use Pastry for Double-Crust Pie (see page 809) instead of the refrigerated piecrusts.

- 1 **15-ounce package (2 crusts) folded refrigerated unbaked piecrusts**
- 1 **tablespoon cornmeal**
- $^1/_2$ **pound bulk Italian sausage or pork sausage**
- $^1/_2$ **of a 10-ounce package frozen chopped spinach, thawed and well drained**
- 1 **4-ounce can mushroom stems and pieces, drained**
- 2 **tablespoons grated Parmesan cheese**
- 2 **cups shredded mozzarella cheese (8 ounces)**
- 1 **8-ounce can (1 cup) pizza sauce**
- 1 **teaspoon milk**

1. Let piecrusts stand at room temperature according to package directions. Lightly grease a 9-inch pie plate. Sprinkle with cornmeal. Set aside.

2. Meanwhile, in a medium skillet cook sausage till meat is no longer pink. Drain off fat. Pat dry with paper towels to remove additional fat. Stir in spinach, mushrooms, and Parmesan cheese.

3. Unfold piecrusts. Transfer 1 crust to the prepared pie plate. Sprinkle *one-third* of the mozzarella cheese onto the bottom crust. Pour *half* of the pizza sauce over the cheese. Top with the meat mixture, one-third of the mozzarella, and remaining sauce. Top with remaining mozzarella.

4. Cut slits in the remaining crust. Place crust on filling. Seal and flute edge (see steps 5, 6, and 7, page 809). Brush with milk. Bake in a 425° oven about 30 minutes or till golden and pie is heated through. Let stand for 15 minutes before serving. Cut into wedges. Makes 8 servings.

Nutrition Facts per serving: 413 cal., 26 g total fat (5 g sat. fat), 48 mg chol., 799 mg sodium, 30 g carbo., 0 g fiber, 15 g pro. **Daily Values:** 21% vit. A, 14% vit. C, 19% calcium, 4% iron

GUIDE TO SAUSAGES

How you cook sausage depends on how it has been processed. Several types of sausage are available in your supermarket. Fresh sausage comes in bulk, link, or patty form. Other sausage types come in links, rings, chunks, or slices.

■ Fresh (Uncooked): Made from fresh meat. Since fresh sausage is neither cooked nor cured, cook it well before eating.

■ Uncooked and Smoked: Made with fresh or cured meat. This sausage is smoked but not cooked. Cook it well before serving.

■ Cooked: Usually made from fresh meat that is cured during processing and fully cooked. Although these sausages are ready to eat, you can heat them before serving.

■ Cooked and Smoked: Made from fresh meat that is cured, smoked, and fully cooked. Serve these ready-to-eat sausages cold or hot.

■ Dry and Semidry: Made from fresh meat that is cured and dried during processing. Dry and semidry sausages may be smoked. Most dry sausages are salamis (highly seasoned with a characteristic fermented flavor). Most semidry sausages are a type of summer sausage (mildly seasoned and easy to store). These are all ready to eat and require no further cooking.

COOKING SAUSAGES

Different market forms of sausage require different preparation methods. Here are some cooking suggestions:

■ **Uncooked Patties:** Place $\frac{1}{2}$-inch-thick sausage patties in an unheated skillet and cook over medium-low heat for 10 to 12 minutes or until juices run clear, turning once. Drain well. Or, arrange the patties on a rack in a shallow baking pan. Bake in a 400° oven about 15 minutes or until juices run clear.

■ **Uncooked Links:** Place 1- to $1\frac{1}{4}$-inch-diameter sausage links in an unheated skillet. Add $\frac{1}{2}$ inch water. Bring to boiling; reduce heat. Cover and simmer about 15 minutes or until juices run clear; drain. Cook 1 to 2 minutes more or until browned, turning often.

■ **Fully Cooked Links:** Place sausage links in a saucepan. Cover with cold water. Bring to boiling; reduce heat. Simmer for 5 to 10 minutes or until heated through.

KIELBASA AND CABBAGE

PREP: 10 MINUTES COOK: 30 MINUTES

Limiting your fat intake? Try substituting turkey kielbasa for the pork variety.

  $^1/_3$ cup chopped onion (1 small)
   1 tablespoon margarine or butter
   1 small head green or red cabbage, cut into 12 wedges
  $^3/_4$ cup apple juice
   2 tablespoons brown sugar
   2 tablespoons red wine vinegar or cider vinegar
  12 ounces fully cooked kielbasa (Polish sausage), cut into 8 pieces
   2 medium cooking apples, cored and sliced

1. In a 12-inch skillet cook onion in hot margarine or butter till tender. Add cabbage wedges. Stir together apple juice, brown sugar, and vinegar. Pour over cabbage in skillet. Bring to boiling. Reduce heat. Simmer, covered, for 15 minutes.
2. Add kielbasa and apples. Return to boiling. Reduce heat. Simmer, covered, for 10 minutes or till sausage is hot and apple is crisp-tender. Serve with a slotted spoon. Makes 4 servings.

Nutrition Facts per serving: 423 cal., 29 g total fat (10 g sat. fat), 71 mg chol., 852 mg sodium, 22 g carbo., 6 g fiber, 12 g pro. **Daily Values:** 4% vit. A, 55% vit. C, 6% calcium, 13% iron

LAMB

The photos here show the retail cuts of lamb. The number with each one refers to the wholesale cut marked on the drawing below. The best ways to cook each meat cut also are listed.

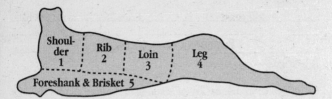

Arm chop (1)
Broil, grill, panbroil, panfry

**Boneless
shoulder roast** (1)
Braise, roast

Blade chop (1)
Broil, grill, panbroil, panfry

Rib chop (2)
*Broil, grill, panbroil,
panfry, roast*

Rib roast (2)
Grill, roast

French-style rib roast (2)
Grill, roast

Loin chop (3)
Broil, grill, panbroil, panfry, roast

Loin roast (3)
Grill, roast

Foreshank (5)
Braise, cook in liquid

Sirloin chop (4)
Broil, grill, panbroil, panfry

Top round roast (4)
Roast

Whole leg (with shank and sirloin) (4)
Grill, roast

Shank half of leg (4)
Grill, roast

Sirloin half of leg (4)
Roast

Hind shanks (4)
Braise, cook in liquid

Whole leg of lamb
(boned and tied) (4)
Grill, roast

Leg center slice (4)
Broil, grill, panbroil, panfry

ROAST RACK OF LAMB WITH PEACH CHUTNEY

PREP: 20 MINUTES ROAST: 45 MINUTES STAND: 15 MINUTES   Oven 325°

 2 1- to 1¹/₂-pound lamb rib roasts (6 to 8 ribs each), with or
       without backbone
 3 tablespoons Dijon-style mustard
 3 tablespoons lemon juice
 2 teaspoons dried rosemary or thyme, crushed
³/₄ cup soft bread crumbs (1 slice)
 1 tablespoon margarine or butter, melted
 1 recipe Peach-Ginger Chutney (page 972)

1. Trim fat from meat. Stir together mustard, lemon juice, rosemary,
and ¹/₂ teaspoon *salt*. Rub onto meat. Toss together crumbs and
melted margarine. Sprinkle onto meat.
2. Place roasts on a rack in a shallow roasting pan. Insert a meat
thermometer without touching bone (see tip, page 620). Roast in a
325° oven till thermometer registers 140° for medium rare (³/₄ to 1

hour) or 155° for medium (1 to 1½ hours). Cover with foil; let stand for 15 minutes. (The meat's temperature will rise 5° during standing.) Serve with Peach-Ginger Chutney. Makes 4 servings.

Nutrition Facts per serving: 400 cal., 22 g total fat (7 g sat. fat), 129 mg chol., 748 mg sodium, 6 g carbo., 0 g fiber, 41 g pro. **Daily Values:** 3% vit. A, 9% vit. C, 3% calcium, 23% iron

---

SPINACH-STUFFED LAMB ROAST

PREP: 30 MINUTES ROAST: 1¾ HOURS STAND: 15 MINUTES   Oven 325°

Low-Fat

The meat will remain slightly pink where it touches the stuffing. Rely on a meat thermometer to determine when the meat is done.

   ¾ cup chopped onion
   ⅓ cup chopped celery
   2 cloves garlic, minced
   2 tablespoons margarine or butter
   2 beaten eggs
   1 10-ounce package frozen chopped spinach, thawed and
      drained
   3 tablespoons snipped fresh basil or 1 tablespoon dried basil,
      crushed
   1 teaspoon snipped fresh marjoram or ¼ teaspoon dried
      marjoram, crushed
   3 cups plain croutons
   ¼ cup grated Parmesan cheese
   1 4- to 6-pound leg of lamb, boned and butterflied

1. For stuffing, in a small saucepan cook onion, celery, and garlic in margarine till tender. In a large bowl combine onion mixture, eggs, spinach, basil, and marjoram. Stir in croutons and Parmesan. Add ¼ cup *water;* toss gently to coat. Set aside.
2. Trim fat from meat. Place between 2 pieces of plastic wrap. With bone side up, pound with the flat side of a meat mallet to an even thickness. Remove wrap. If desired, sprinkle with salt and pepper. Spread the stuffing on roast. Roll up; tie securely.
3. Place roast, seam side down, on a rack in a shallow roasting pan. Insert a meat thermometer into the thickest portion of meat (see tip, page 620). Roast in a 325° oven till thermometer registers 150° (1¾

to 2½ hours). Cover with foil; let stand 15 minutes. (The meat's temperature will rise 5° during standing.) Remove strings. Makes 12 to 16 servings.

Nutrition Facts per serving: 220 cal., 9 g total fat (3 g sat. fat), 99 mg chol., 207 mg sodium, 9 g carbo., 0 g fiber, 24 g pro. **Daily Values:** 16% vit. A, 4% vit. C, 7% calcium 15% iron

---

HERB-RUBBED LEG OF LAMB

PREP: 30 MINUTES   ROAST: 2 HOURS   STAND: 15 MINUTES   Oven 325°

Low-Fat

If your grocery store doesn't regularly carry this cut, order it from the butcher a few days early.

    1 5- to 7-pound leg of lamb
       Lemon juice
    2 tablespoons snipped fresh parsley
    1 teaspoon dried mint or basil, crushed
    ½ teaspoon onion salt
    ½ teaspoon dried rosemary, crushed
    ¼ teaspoon pepper
    1 to 2 cloves garlic, slivered
       Mint jelly (optional)

1. Trim fat from meat. Cut ½-inch-wide slits into roast at 1-inch intervals. Brush meat surface and into pockets with lemon juice. Stir together parsley, mint or basil, onion salt, rosemary, and pepper. Rub parsley mixture onto meat and into pockets. Insert garlic slivers into pockets.

2. Place meat, fat side up, on a rack in a shallow roasting pan. Insert a meat thermometer without touching bone (see tip, page 620). Roast in a 325° oven till thermometer registers 140° for medium rare (2 to 2¾ hours) or 155° for medium (2½ to 3½ hours). Cover meat with foil and let stand for 15 minutes before carving. (The meat's temperature will rise 5° during standing.) If desired, serve with mint jelly. Makes 12 to 16 servings.

Nutrition Facts per serving: 121 cal., 5 g total fat (2 g sat. fat), 56 mg chol., 110 mg sodium, 0 g carbo., 0 g fiber, 18 g pro. **Daily Values:** 0% vit. A, 1% vit. C, 0% calcium, 9% iron

LAMB CHOPS WITH WALNUT-RAISIN STUFFING

PREP: 25 MINUTES BAKE: 20 MINUTES   Oven 350°

Cinnamon-raisin bread makes a fruity stuffing
for these succulent chops.

  6 slices cinnamon-raisin bread, cut into $1/2$-inch cubes
  4 boneless lamb leg sirloin chops, cut $1/2$ inch thick
  1 tablespoon margarine or butter
  $1/2$ cup sliced celery (1 stalk)
  $1/3$ cup chopped onion (1 small)
  $1/4$ cup broken walnuts
  $1/4$ to $1/3$ cup orange juice
     Orange wedges (optional)

1. Spread bread cubes in a 2-quart rectangular baking dish. Bake in a 350° oven for 15 to 20 minutes or till dry, stirring twice. (Or, let stand, loosely covered, at room temperature for 8 to 12 hours or till dry.) Set aside.

2. Trim fat from meat. In a large skillet cook chops in hot margarine or butter over medium-high heat for 3 to 4 minutes or till brown, turning once. Remove from skillet, reserving drippings in skillet. Add celery and onion to drippings. Cook and stir till onion is tender.

3. For stuffing, in a medium mixing bowl combine dried bread cubes, celery mixture, and walnuts. Add orange juice. Toss gently to moisten. Spoon into a greased 2-quart rectangular baking dish. Top with lamb chops. Cover with foil.

4. Bake in a 350° oven about 20 minutes or till the stuffing is heated through and the lamb chops are tender. If desired, garnish with orange wedges. Makes 4 servings.

Nutrition Facts per serving: 389 cal., 23 g total fat (7 g sat. fat), 63 mg chol., 252 mg sodium, 26 g carbo., 1 g fiber, 21 g pro. **Daily Values:** 4% vit. A, 17% vit. C, 4% calcium, 18% iron

LAMB CHOPS WITH MINT PESTO

PREP: 15 MINUTES BROIL: 7 MINUTES

Fast

If you can't find fresh mint leaves, use 1 cup lightly packed fresh parsley with the stems removed and 1 tablespoon dried mint.

- 1 cup lightly packed fresh mint leaves with stems removed
- 1 clove garlic
- 3 tablespoons olive oil or cooking oil
- 1 tablespoon white wine vinegar
- $^1/_4$ cup grated Parmesan cheese
- $^1/_4$ cup slivered almonds
- 8 lamb rib or loin chops, cut 1 inch thick
  Fresh mint leaves (optional)

1. For pesto, in a food processor or blender container combine mint, $^1/_8$ teaspoon *salt,* $^1/_8$ teaspoon *pepper,* and garlic. Cover and process till chopped, stopping to scrape sides. Add oil, a little at a time, processing after each addition. Add vinegar; process till nearly smooth. Add Parmesan cheese and almonds; process till nearly smooth. Set aside.

2. Trim fat from meat. Place chops on the unheated rack of a broiler pan. Broil 3 to 4 inches from heat for 7 to 11 minutes for medium doneness, turning once. Serve chops with pesto. If desired, garnish with fresh mint leaves. Makes 4 servings.

Nutrition Facts per serving: 405 cal., 26 g total fat (7 g sat. fat), 112 mg chol., 279 mg sodium, 3 g carbo., 1 g fiber, 39 g pro. **Daily Values:** 7% vit. A, 22% vit. C, 12% calcium, 42% iron

APPLE-GLAZED LAMB CHOPS

PREP: 10 MINUTES BROIL: 7 MINUTES

Fast

- $^1/_2$ cup apple jelly
- 2 teaspoons prepared mustard or Dijon-style mustard
- 8 lamb loin chops, cut 1 inch thick
- $^1/_2$ cup chopped apple ($^1/_2$ of a small)

1. For glaze, in a saucepan heat and stir jelly, mustard, $1/8$ teaspoon *salt,* and dash *pepper.*

2. Trim fat from meat. Place chops on the unheated rack of a broiler pan. Broil 3 to 4 inches from heat for 7 to 11 minutes for medium doneness, turning and brushing with some jelly mixture once.

3. Stir chopped apple into remaining jelly mixture. Bring to boiling. Reduce heat. Simmer, uncovered, for 1 minute. Serve with chops. Makes 4 servings.

Nutrition Facts per serving: 382 cal., 15 g total fat (5 g sat. fat), 103 mg chol., 202 mg sodium, 29 g carbo., 1 g fiber, 32 g pro. **Daily Values:** 0% vit. A, 4% vit. C, 2% calcium, 21% iron

---

LAMB AND PEPPERS

START TO FINISH: 25 MINUTES

Fast

  8 **lamb rib chops, cut 1 inch thick, or 4 pork rib chops, cut $1^1/4$ inches thick**

  3 **green, red, or yellow sweet peppers, cut into 1-inch pieces**

  2 **cloves garlic, minced**

  2 **bay leaves**

  1 **teaspoon dried oregano, crushed**

  2 **tablespoons olive oil or cooking oil**

$1/4$ **cup sliced pitted green or ripe olives**

  2 **tablespoons snipped fresh parsley**

1. Place chops on unheated rack of a broiler pan. Broil 3 to 4 inches from heat, turning once. Broil lamb 7 to 11 minutes or till done; broil pork 18 to 22 minutes or till no pink remains. Transfer to a serving platter.

2. Meanwhile, in a large skillet cook sweet peppers, garlic, bay leaves, and oregano in hot oil for 12 to 15 minutes or till sweet peppers are crisp-tender. Discard bay leaves. With a slotted spoon, transfer peppers to the platter, reserving drippings in skillet.

3. Add olives and parsley. Cook and stir till heated through. Spoon over chops. Makes 4 servings.

Nutrition Facts per serving: 212 cal., 14 g total fat (3 g sat. fat), 52 mg chol., 204 mg sodium, 6 g carbo., 2 g fiber, 17 g pro. **Daily Values:** 5% vit. A, 99% vit. C, 2% calcium, 14% iron

LAMB CASSOULET

PREP: 30 MINUTES   SOAK: 1 HOUR   COOK: 1½ HOURS   BAKE: 1 HOUR   Oven 325°

Cassoulet is the French name for a special bean stew. Although many French people claim their version is the only authentic one, the term is used loosely to cover just about any concoction of white beans, lamb, poultry, and sausage.

  2 cups dry navy beans
  1 pound boneless lamb, cut into 1-inch cubes
  1 cup chopped carrots (2 medium)
  ½ cup chopped green sweet pepper
  ½ cup chopped onion (1 medium)
  1 tablespoon instant beef bouillon granules
  3 cloves garlic, minced
  ¾ pound bulk pork sausage
  1 14½-ounce can tomatoes, cut up
  1 tablespoon Worcestershire sauce
  2 bay leaves
  1 teaspoon dried thyme, crushed
  ½ teaspoon salt

1. Rinse beans. In a 4- to 6-quart ovenproof pot combine the beans and 8 cups *water*. Bring to boiling. Reduce heat. Simmer for 2 minutes. Remove from heat. Cover and let stand for 1 hour. (Or, add water to beans. Cover and let stand overnight.)
2. Drain and rinse beans. Return beans to pot. Add lamb, vegetables, bouillon granules, garlic, and 6 cups *fresh water*. Bring to boiling. Reduce heat. Simmer, covered, for 1½ hours.
3. Meanwhile, shape pork sausage into small balls. In a large skillet cook the sausage till brown. Drain off fat.
4. Drain bean mixture, reserving liquid. Return bean mixture to pot. Add 1½ cups of the reserved liquid, the sausage balls, undrained tomatoes, Worcestershire sauce, bay leaves, thyme, and salt.
5. Cover and bake in a 325° oven for 1 to 1¼ hours. (Add more of the reserved liquid, if necessary.) Discard bay leaves. Skim fat. Serve in bowls. Makes 8 cups (8 servings).

Nutrition Facts per serving: 360 cal., 14 g total fat (5 g sat. fat), 48 mg chol., 855 mg sodium, 37 g carbo., 1 g fiber, 23 g pro. **Daily Values:** 46% vit. A, 30% vit. C, 10% calcium, 30% iron

LAMB SHISH KABOBS

PREP: 25 MINUTES   MARINATE: 4 TO 24 HOURS   BROIL: 6 MINUTES

Accompany these kabobs with another traditional Middle Eastern dish—Rice Pilaf (see page 99).

1 pound boneless lamb leg center slice or leg sirloin chops, cut ³/₄ inch thick
¹/₂ cup chopped onion (1 medium)
¹/₄ cup lemon juice
2 tablespoons water
2 tablespoons olive oil or cooking oil
¹/₂ teaspoon salt
¹/₂ teaspoon garlic powder
¹/₂ teaspoon dried thyme, crushed
¹/₄ teaspoon pepper
1 large zucchini, sliced ¹/₂ inch thick (1³/₄ cups)
16 large fresh mushrooms
1 large tomato, cut into 8 wedges, or 8 cherry tomatoes

1. Trim fat from meat. Partially freeze lamb. Cut into 3-inch-long strips about ¹/₄ inch thick (see step 1, page 634). Place strips in a plastic bag set in a deep bowl.
2. For marinade, stir together onion, lemon juice, water, oil, salt, garlic powder, thyme, and pepper. Pour over meat (see tip, page 549). Close bag. Marinate in the refrigerator for 4 to 24 hours, turning occasionally.
3. Drain meat, reserving marinade. In a large saucepan cook zucchini in boiling water for 2 minutes. Add the whole mushrooms. Cook for 1 minute more; drain.
4. On 4 long metal skewers alternately thread the meat accordion-style, the zucchini slices, and mushrooms, leaving ¹/₄-inch space between each piece.
5. Place kabobs on the unheated rack of a broiler pan. Broil 3 inches from the heat for 6 to 8 minutes or till tender, turning and brushing with marinade once. Add 2 tomato wedges or cherry tomatoes to the end of each skewer for the last 1 minute of broiling. Makes 4 servings.

Nutrition Facts per serving: 292 cal., 21 g total fat (7 g sat. fat), 63 mg chol., 51 mg sodium, 10 g carbo., 2 g fiber, 18 g pro. **Daily Values:** 3% vit. A, 32% vit. C, 2% calcium, 17% iron

CURRIED LAMB

PREP: 25 MINUTES COOK: 30 MINUTES

Low-Fat

*Cooking the curry powder with the onion and
garlic mellows the flavors.*

- 1 **pound boneless lamb**
- 1 **tablespoon cooking oil**
- 1 **cup coarsely chopped onion (1 large)**
- 3 **to 4 teaspoons curry powder**
- 2 **cloves garlic, minced**
- 2 **cups peeled, cored, and thinly sliced apples (2 medium)**
- ³/₄ **cup water**
- 1 **teaspoon instant chicken bouillon granules**
- ¹/₄ **cup cold water**
- 2 **tablespoons all-purpose flour**
  Salt (optional)
  Pepper (optional)
- 2 **cups hot cooked rice (see page 139)**
  Chutney (optional)
  Sliced green onions (optional)
  Raisins (optional)
  Shredded coconut (optional)
  Chopped peanuts (optional)

1. Trim fat from meat. Cut into ³/₄-inch cubes. In a large saucepan brown half of the meat in hot oil. Remove from saucepan. Brown remaining meat with onion, curry powder, and garlic till onion is tender but not brown. Return all meat to pan.

2. Stir in apples, the ³/₄ cup water, and bouillon granules. Bring to boiling. Reduce heat. Cover and simmer for 30 to 40 minutes or till meat is tender.

3. Stir together the ¹/₄ cup cold water and flour. Stir into mixture in saucepan. Cook and stir over medium heat till thickened and bubbly. Cook and stir for 1 minute more. If desired, season to taste with salt and pepper. Serve over hot cooked rice. If desired, pass chutney, green onions, raisins, coconut, and/or peanuts. Makes 4 servings.

Nutrition Facts per serving: 338 cal., 10 g total fat (3 g sat. fat), 55 mg chol., 263 mg sodium, 41 g carbo., 2 g fiber, 21 g pro. **Daily Values:** 0% vit. A, 9% vit. C, 3% calcium, 22% iron

LAMB SHANKS WITH BEANS

PREP: 30 MINUTES SOAK: 1 HOUR COOK: 1³/₄ HOURS

Choose meaty lamb pieces cut from the foreshank.

1 cup dry navy beans
4 cups water
1 medium onion, sliced and separated into rings
2 cloves garlic, minced, or ¹/₄ teaspoon garlic powder
1 tablespoon cooking oil
4 meaty lamb shanks (about 4 pounds) or meaty veal cross-cut
    shanks (about 3 pounds)
2 cups chicken broth
1 teaspoon dried thyme, crushed
¹/₂ teaspoon salt
¹/₄ teaspoon pepper
1 7¹/₂-ounce can tomatoes, cut up (see tip, page 999)
¹/₄ cup dry white wine (optional)

1. Rinse beans. In a large saucepan combine water and beans. Bring to boiling. Reduce heat. Simmer, uncovered, for 2 minutes. Remove from heat. Do not drain. Cover and let stand for 1 hour. (Or, add water to beans. Cover and let stand overnight.)

2. Drain and rinse beans. In the same pan cook onion and garlic in hot oil till tender. Add lamb or veal shanks and brown on all sides. Carefully stir in beans, chicken broth, thyme, salt, and pepper. Bring to boiling. Reduce heat. Cover and simmer for 1¹/₂ to 2 hours or till meat and beans are tender. (If necessary, add more chicken broth to keep mixture moist.)

3. Remove meat from pan. Cool slightly. When cool enough to handle, cut meat off bones and coarsely chop. Discard fat and bones.

4. Skim fat from the top of the bean mixture. Stir in the meat, tomatoes, and, if desired, white wine. Bring to boiling. Reduce heat. Simmer, covered, for 10 to 15 minutes or till heated through. Makes 6 servings.

Nutrition Facts per serving: 430 cal., 13 g total fat (4 g sat. fat), 132 mg chol., 600 mg sodium, 24 g carbo., 1 g fiber, 51 g pro. **Daily Values:** 2% vit. A, 12% vit. C, 7% calcium, 37% iron

Venison Pot Roast

PREP: 10 MINUTES   COOK: 1½ HOURS

Low-Fat

1 2- to 3-pound boneless venison shoulder or rump roast
2 tablespoons cooking oil
1 6-ounce can (⅔ cup) tomato juice
½ cup finely chopped onion (1 medium)
½ cup finely chopped carrot (1 medium)
2 teaspoons instant beef bouillon granules
3 tablespoons all-purpose flour
½ cup dairy sour cream or plain yogurt
Hot cooked noodles (see page 729) (optional)

1. Trim fat from meat. In a 4- to 6-quart pot brown meat in oil. Drain off fat. Add juice, onion, carrot, and bouillon granules. Bring to boiling. Reduce heat. Simmer, covered, for 1½ to 2 hours or till tender. Transfer meat to a platter. Keep warm.

2. For sauce, measure juices in pot; skim fat (see tip, page 882). If necessary, add enough water to equal 2 cups. Return to pot. Stir flour into sour cream or yogurt. Stir into juices in pot. Cook and stir over medium heat till thickened and bubbly. Cook and stir for 1 minute more. If desired, season to taste with salt and pepper. Serve with meat and, if desired, noodles. Makes 8 to 10 servings.

Nutrition Facts per serving: 209 cal., 8 g total fat (3 g sat. fat), 100 mg chol., 367 mg sodium, 6 g carbo., 1 g fiber, 26 g pro. **Daily Values:** 34% vit. A, 4% vit. C, 3% calcium, 22% iron

Horseradish-Rubbed Venison

PREP: 5 MINUTES   BROIL: 8 MINUTES

Fast

3 tablespoons margarine or butter, melted
½ teaspoon lemon-pepper seasoning
4 venison rib chops, cut 1 inch thick
½ cup dairy sour cream
2 tablespoons prepared horseradish
1 tablespoon snipped fresh parsley

1. In a small bowl stir together melted margarine and $^1/_4$ *teaspoon* of the lemon-pepper seasoning.

2. Trim fat from meat. Arrange chops on the unheated rack of a broiler pan. Brush with margarine mixture. Broil 3 inches from the heat to desired doneness, turning once and brushing with remaining margarine mixture. (Allow 8 to 10 minutes for medium rare, 10 to 12 minutes for medium, and 14 to 16 minutes for well-done.)

3. Meanwhile, for sauce, in a small mixing bowl stir together remaining lemon-pepper seasoning, sour cream, horseradish, and parsley. Serve with chops. Makes 4 servings.

Nutrition Facts per serving: 295 cal., 17 g total fat (6 g sat. fat), 129 mg chol., 408 mg sodium, 2 g carbo., 0 g fiber, 32 g pro. **Daily Values:** 17% vit. A, 5% vit. C, 5% calcium, 25% iron

---

VENISON POTPIE

PREP: 20 MINUTES COOK: 1$^1/_4$ HOURS BAKE: 12 MINUTES   Oven 450°

```
  1  pound lean boneless venison or beef
  2  tablespoons cooking oil
  2  cups beef broth
  1  teaspoon dried thyme, crushed
  1  10-ounce package frozen peas and carrots
  1  cup cubed turnip (¹/₂ of a medium) or parsnip (1 medium)
¹/₂  cup beef broth
¹/₃  cup all-purpose flour
³/₄  cup all-purpose flour
³/₄  teaspoon baking powder
¹/₂  teaspoon sugar
  3  tablespoons shortening
¹/₃  cup milk
```

1. Trim fat from meat. Cut into $^1/_2$-inch cubes. In a large saucepan brown half of the meat in hot oil; remove from pan. Brown remaining meat. Return all meat to pan.

2. Stir in the 2 cups broth, thyme, and $^1/_4$ teaspoon *pepper*. Bring to boiling. Reduce heat. Simmer, covered, 45 minutes. Add peas and carrots and turnip or parsnip. Simmer, covered, 15 to 30 minutes more or till meat is tender. Skim off fat (see tip, page 1002).

3. Stir together the $^1/_2$ cup beef broth and the $^1/_3$ cup flour. Stir into meat mixture. Cook and stir over medium heat till thickened and bubbly. Spoon into a 2-quart casserole. Keep warm.

4. Meanwhile, for biscuit topping, in a small mixing bowl stir together the ³/₄ cup flour, baking powder, sugar, and ¹/₄ teaspoon *salt*. Cut in shortening till mixture resembles coarse crumbs. Make a well in the center. Add milk all at once. Stir just till the dough clings together. Drop in 5 or 6 mounds atop the hot meat mixture. Bake in a 450° oven about 12 minutes or till golden. Makes 5 or 6 servings.

Nutrition Facts per serving: 359 cal., 16 g total fat (4 g sat. fat), 76 mg chol., 679 mg sodium, 28 g carbo., 4 g fiber, 26 g pro. **Daily Values:** 45% vit. A, 13% vit. C, 11% calcium, 31% iron

LIVER AND ONIONS

PREP: 10 MINUTES COOK: 10 MINUTES

Fast **Low-Fat**

This is the classic feast for those who love beef liver.

1 medium onion, sliced and separated into rings
2 tablespoons margarine or butter
1 pound sliced beef liver
Dash salt
Dash pepper
2 teaspoons water
2 teaspoons lemon juice
1 teaspoon Worcestershire sauce

1. In a large skillet cook onion in margarine or butter till tender but not brown. Remove from skillet.
2. Add liver to skillet. Sprinkle with salt and pepper. Cook over medium heat for 3 minutes; turn. Return onion to skillet. Cook for 2 to 3 minutes more or till liver is slightly pink in center. Remove liver and onion from skillet. Stir in water, lemon juice, and Worcestershire sauce. Heat through. Pour over liver and onion. Makes 4 servings.

Nutrition Facts per serving: 177 cal., 6 g total fat (2 g sat. fat), 355 mg chol., 137 mg sodium, 10 g carbo., 1 g fiber, 20 g pro. **Daily Values:** 790% vit. A, 40% vit. C, 1% calcium, 32% iron

BEER-BRAISED RABBIT

PREP: 25 MINUTES COOK: 35 MINUTES

Low-Fat

Domestic rabbit is increasingly available at grocery stores.

1 2¹/₂- to 3-pound domestic rabbit, cut up and skinned
2 tablespoons cooking oil
4 medium potatoes, quartered
4 medium carrots, cut into ¹/₂-inch pieces
1 medium onion, sliced and separated into rings
1 12-ounce can beer or 1¹/₂ cups apple juice
¹/₄ cup chili sauce
¹/₂ teaspoon salt
¹/₄ cup cold water
2 tablespoons all-purpose flour

1. If desired, sprinkle meat with salt and pepper. In a 12-inch skillet brown meat on all sides in hot oil. Drain off fat.
2. Add potatoes, carrots, and onion to skillet. Combine beer or apple juice, chili sauce, and salt. Pour over rabbit and vegetables. Bring to boiling. Reduce heat. Simmer, covered, for 35 to 45 minutes or till meat is tender. Transfer meat and vegetables to a platter. Keep warm.
3. For sauce, measure juices in skillet; skim fat. If necessary, add enough water to juices to equal 1¹/₂ cups. Return juices to skillet. Stir together the ¹/₄ cup water and flour. Stir into juices. Cook and stir over medium heat till thickened and bubbly. Cook and stir for 1 minute more. Serve sauce with meat and vegetables. Makes 4 servings.

Nutrition Facts per serving: 497 cal., 12 g total fat (3 g sat. fat), 85 mg chol., 568 mg sodium, 55 g carbo., 4 g fiber, 36 g pro. **Daily Values:** 172% vit. A, 45% vit. C, 6% calcium, 33% iron

GERMAN-STYLE RABBIT

PREP: 10 MINUTES   COOK: 45 MINUTES

If you use wild rabbit, remember that it generally is tougher and may require longer cooking than domestic rabbit.

- ¹/₄ cup all-purpose flour
- ¹/₂ teaspoon salt
- ¹/₄ teaspoon pepper
- 1 2¹/₂- to 3-pound domestic rabbit, cut up and skinned
- 2 tablespoons cooking oil
- ³/₄ cup water
- ¹/₂ cup chopped onion (1 medium)
- 2 tablespoons brown sugar
- 2 tablespoons vinegar
- 1 teaspoon caraway seed
- ¹/₄ teaspoon salt
- 8 cups shredded cabbage
- 2 medium apples, cored and coarsely chopped

1. In a plastic bag combine the flour, the ¹/₂ teaspoon salt, and pepper. Add meat, 2 or 3 pieces at a time, and shake to coat.

2. In a 12-inch skillet brown meat on all sides in hot cooking oil. Drain off fat. Add water, onion, brown sugar, vinegar, caraway seed, and the ¹/₄ teaspoon salt to meat in skillet. Bring to boiling. Reduce heat. Simmer, covered, for 35 minutes.

3. Stir cabbage and apples into skillet. Cook, covered, for 10 to 12 minutes more or till meat and cabbage are tender. Makes 4 servings.

Nutrition Facts per serving: 410 cal., 17 g total fat (17 g sat. fat), 93 mg chol., 489 mg sodium, 30 g carbo., 5 g fiber, 36 g pro. **Daily Values:** 2% vit. A, 89% vit. C, 10% calcium, 28% iron

---

BEEF AND RICE CASSEROLE

PREP: 15 MINUTES   BAKE: 1 HOUR   STAND: 10 MINUTES   Oven 350°

- 1 pound ground beef or ground pork
- 1 cup chopped celery (2 stalks)
- ¹/₂ cup chopped onion (1 medium)
- 1 cup long grain rice
- 1 14¹/₂-ounce can tomatoes, cut up

¹/₂ cup sliced pitted ripe olives
  1 4-ounce can diced green chili peppers, drained
1¹/₂ teaspoons instant beef bouillon granules
  1 teaspoon chili powder
  1 teaspoon Worcestershire sauce
  ¹/₄ teaspoon pepper
  ¹/₂ cup shredded cheddar cheese

1. In a large ovenproof skillet cook ground beef or pork, celery, and onion till meat is no longer pink and onion is tender. Drain off fat.

2. Stir in uncooked rice. Stir in 1¹/₄ cups *water*, undrained tomatoes, olives, chili peppers, bouillon granules, chili powder, Worcestershire sauce, and pepper. Bring to boiling. Remove from heat.

3. Cover and bake in a 350° oven about 1 hour or till rice is tender. Sprinkle with cheese. Let stand, covered, for 10 minutes. Makes 6 servings.

Nutrition Facts per serving: 264 cal., 15 g total fat (6 g sat. fat), 58 mg chol., 572 mg sodium, 15 g carbo., 2 g fiber, 19 g pro. **Daily Values:** 9% vit. A, 34% vit. C, 12% calcium, 17% iron

---

HAMBURGER PIE

PREP: 30 MINUTES BAKE: 20 MINUTES   Oven 375°

Homemade or instant mashed potatoes make the top "crust" for this vegetable-ground beef favorite.

  2 cups Mashed Potatoes (see page 1055) or packaged instant
      mashed potatoes (enough for 4 servings)
³/₄ pound ground beef
¹/₂ cup chopped onion (1 medium)
  1 9-ounce package frozen cut green beans or 2 cups loose-pack
      frozen mixed vegetables
¹/₄ cup water
  1 14¹/₂-ounce can Italian-style stewed tomatoes
¹/₂ of a 6-ounce can (¹/₃ cup) tomato paste
  1 teaspoon Worcestershire sauce
¹/₄ teaspoon pepper
      Paprika (optional)

1. Prepare Mashed Potatoes. Set aside. In a large skillet cook ground beef and onion till meat is no longer pink and onion is tender. Drain off fat.

2. Meanwhile, if using beans, run cold water over them to separate; drain. Stir beans or mixed vegetables and water into beef mixture. Cook, covered, for 5 to 10 minutes or till vegetables are tender. Stir in the undrained tomatoes, tomato paste, Worcestershire sauce, and pepper. Bring to boiling. Transfer the mixture to a 1¹/₂-quart casserole.

3. Drop Mashed Potatoes in mounds atop hot mixture. If desired, sprinkle with paprika. Bake in a 375° oven for 20 to 25 minutes or till heated through. Makes 4 servings.

Nutrition Facts per serving: 390 cal., 17 g total fat (5 g sat. fat), 54 mg chol., 516 mg sodium, 40 g carbo., 3 g fiber, 21 g pro. **Daily Values:** 24% vit. A, 63% vit. C, 6% calcium, 23% iron

---

MEAT AND CORN BREAD SQUARES

PREP: 20 MINUTES   BAKE: 30 MINUTES   STAND: 5 MINUTES   Oven 375°

Tote this to your next potluck—just keep it hot.

   1 **pound ground beef, ground pork, or bulk pork sausage**
   1 **tablespoon cornstarch**
   1 **tablespoon dried minced onion**
   1 **to 2 teaspoons chili powder**
¹/₂ **teaspoon garlic salt***
   1 **14¹/₂-ounce can tomatoes, cut up**
   1 **4-ounce can diced green chili peppers, drained**
³/₄ **cup all-purpose flour**
³/₄ **cup cornmeal**
   2 **teaspoons baking powder**
   2 **beaten eggs**
   1 **8¹/₂-ounce can cream-style corn**
¹/₂ **cup milk**
   3 **tablespoons cooking oil**
   1 **cup shredded cheddar cheese or Monterey Jack cheese with
      jalapeño peppers (4 ounces)**
     Salsa (optional)

1. In a large skillet cook meat till brown. Drain off fat. Stir in cornstarch, onion, chili powder, and garlic salt. Stir in undrained tomatoes and chili peppers. Cook and stir over medium heat till thickened and bubbly. Cook and stir 2 minutes more.

2. In a mixing bowl stir together flour, cornmeal, and baking powder. In another bowl combine eggs, corn, milk, and oil. Stir egg mixture into dry mixture. Add cheese. Stir just till moistened.

3. Spread half of the batter into a greased 2-quart rectangular baking dish. Spoon meat mixture atop. Top with remaining batter. Bake in a 375° oven about 30 minutes or till golden brown. Let stand for 5 minutes. To serve, cut into squares. If desired, pass salsa. Makes 6 servings.

***Note:** If using sausage, omit garlic salt.

Nutrition Facts per serving: 489 cal., 26 g total fat (9 g sat. fat), 140 mg chol., 764 mg sodium, 39 g carbo., 2 g fiber, 27 g pro. **Daily Values:** 17% vit. A, 32% vit. C, 27% calcium, 26% iron

---

STUFFED GREEN PEPPERS

PREP: 35 MINUTES   BAKE: 15 MINUTES   Oven 375°

---

   2 **large green sweet peppers**
     Dash salt (optional)
 ³/₄ **pound ground beef, ground pork, ground lamb, or bulk pork sausage**
 ¹/₃ **cup chopped onion (1 small)**
   1 **7¹/₂-ounce can tomatoes, cut up**
 ¹/₂ **cup water**
 ¹/₃ **cup long grain rice**
   1 **tablespoon Worcestershire sauce**
 ¹/₂ **teaspoon dried basil or dried oregano, crushed**
 ¹/₂ **cup shredded American cheese (2 ounces)**

1. Halve sweet peppers lengthwise, removing stem ends, seeds, and membranes. Immerse sweet peppers into boiling water for 3 minutes. If desired, sprinkle insides with a dash salt. Invert on paper towels to drain well.

2. In a large skillet cook meat and onion till meat is brown and onion is tender. Drain off fat. Stir in undrained tomatoes, water, uncooked rice, Worcestershire sauce, basil or oregano, ¹/₄ teaspoon *salt,* and ¹/₄ teaspoon *pepper.* Bring to boiling. Reduce heat. Simmer, covered, for 15 to 18 minutes or till rice is tender. Stir in ¹/₄ cup of the cheese.

3. Fill peppers with meat mixture. Place in a 2-quart square baking dish along with any remaining meat mixture. Bake in a 375° oven about 15 minutes or till heated through. Sprinkle with the remaining ¼ cup cheese. Let stand about 2 minutes or till cheese is melted. Makes 4 servings.

Nutrition Facts per serving: 290 cal., 14 g total fat (6 g sat. fat), 61 mg chol., 494 mg sodium, 20 g carbo., 1 g fiber, 21 g pro. **Daily Values:** 8% vit. A, 60% vit. C, 9% calcium, 20% iron

STUFFED CABBAGE ROLLS

PREP: 25 MINUTES   BAKE: 25 MINUTES   Oven 350°

Remove the center vein of the cabbage leaves by cutting around it in a long V shape.

   8 **medium to large cabbage leaves**
 ³/₄ **pound ground beef, ground pork, ground lamb, or bulk pork sausage**
 ¹/₃ **cup chopped onion (1 small)**
   1 **7¹/₂-ounce can tomatoes, cut up**
 ¹/₂ **cup water**
 ¹/₃ **cup long grain rice**
 ¹/₂ **teaspoon dried dillweed or thyme, crushed**
 ¹/₄ **teaspoon pepper**
 ¹/₄ **cup shredded Swiss cheese (1 ounce)**
   1 **15-ounce can tomato sauce**
   1 **teaspoon sugar**
 ¹/₂ **teaspoon dried dillweed or thyme, crushed**
 ¹/₄ **cup shredded Swiss cheese (1 ounce)**

1. Remove center veins from cabbage leaves, keeping each leaf in 1 piece. Immerse leaves, 4 at a time, into boiling water about 3 minutes or till limp. Drain well.
2. For filling, in a large skillet cook meat and onion till meat is brown and onion is tender. Drain off fat. Stir in undrained tomatoes, water, uncooked rice, ¹/₂ teaspoon dillweed or thyme, and pepper. Bring to boiling. Reduce heat. Simmer, covered, for 15 to 18 minutes or till the rice is tender. Stir in ¹/₄ cup Swiss cheese.
3. Place about ¹/₃ cup filling on each cabbage leaf. Fold in sides. Starting at an unfolded edge, carefully roll up each leaf, making sure folded sides are included in the roll.
4. For sauce, in a small mixing bowl stir together tomato sauce,

sugar, and ¹/₂ teaspoon dillweed or thyme. Pour half of the tomato mixture into a 2-quart square baking dish. Arrange cabbage rolls atop the tomato mixture. Spoon remaining tomato mixture atop. Bake, covered, in a 350° oven for 25 to 30 minutes or till heated through. Sprinkle with ¹/₄ cup Swiss cheese. Let stand about 2 minutes or till cheese is melted. Makes 4 servings.

Nutrition Facts per serving: 337 cal., 15 g total fat (7 g sat. fat), 66 mg chol., 846 mg sodium, 27 g carbo., 4 g fiber, 24 g pro. **Daily Values:** 18% vit. A, 63% vit. C, 16% calcium, 27% iron

---

SUPER BURRITOS

PREP: 30 MINUTES BAKE: 10 MINUTES   Oven 350°

    1 pound ground beef or bulk chorizo
    1 cup chopped onion (1 large)
 ¹/₂ cup chopped green sweet pepper
    1 clove garlic, minced
 ¹/₄ cup water
    1 tablespoon chili powder
 ¹/₄ teaspoon ground cumin
    1 cup cooked rice (see page 139)
    2 tablespoons canned chopped green chili peppers
    8 10-inch flour tortillas
 1¹/₂ cups shredded cheddar cheese (6 ounces)
 ²/₃ cup chopped tomato (1 medium)
    2 cups shredded lettuce
    1 recipe Burrito Sauce (see below)
    1 recipe Guacamole (see page 69) or frozen avocado dip, thawed
         (optional)

1. For filling, in a large skillet cook ground beef or chorizo, onion, sweet pepper, and garlic till meat is brown and onion is tender. Drain off fat. Stir in water, chili powder, and cumin. Cook about 5 minutes or till most of the water has evaporated. Remove from heat. Stir in rice and chili peppers.
2. Meanwhile, wrap tortillas tightly in foil. Heat in a 350° oven for 10 minutes to soften. (When ready to fill tortillas, remove only half of them at a time, keeping remaining ones warm in oven.)
3. Spoon a scant ¹/₂ cup filling onto each tortilla just below center. Set aside ¹/₂ cup of the cheese. Top filling with remaining cheese and tomato. Fold bottom edge of each tortilla up and over filling. Fold

opposite sides in, just till they meet. Roll up from the bottom. Secure with wooden toothpicks.

4. Arrange burritos on a baking sheet, seam sides down. Bake in a 350° oven for 10 to 12 minutes or till heated through. Remove toothpicks. Serve warm burritos on lettuce with Burrito Sauce, reserved cheese, and, if desired, Guacamole or avocado dip. Makes 8 servings.

▪ **Burrito Sauce:** In a medium saucepan melt 2 tablespoons *butter or margarine*. Stir in 1 tablespoon *all-purpose flour*. Gradually stir in 1 cup *chicken broth*. Cook and stir over medium heat till thickened and bubbly. Cook and stir for 1 minute more. Stir 2 tablespoons *all-purpose flour* into one 8-ounce carton *dairy sour cream*. Stir sour cream mixture and 2 tablespoons canned chopped *green chili peppers* into sauce. Cook and stir till thickened and bubbly. Cook and stir for 1 minute more.

Nutrition Facts per serving: 459 cal., 26 g total fat.(12 g sat. fat), 71 mg chol., 528 mg sodium, 34 g carbo., 1 g fiber, 22 g pro. **Daily Values:** 22% vit. A, 24% vit. C, 22% calcium, 22% iron

---

TACOS

START TO FINISH: 25 MINUTES

> *Fast*

    12 taco shells
     1 pound ground beef or ground pork
   1/2 cup chopped onion (1 medium)
     2 cloves garlic, minced
     1 4-ounce can diced green chili peppers, drained
     1 to 2 teaspoons chili powder
   1/4 teaspoon salt
       Several dashes bottled hot pepper sauce
 1 1/2 cups shredded lettuce
     1 cup chopped tomato (1 large)
     1 cup shredded sharp cheddar or Monterey Jack cheese (4 ounces)
       Salsa and/or dairy sour cream (optional)

1. Heat taco shells according to package directions. For filling, in a large skillet cook meat, onion, and garlic till meat is brown and onion is tender. Drain off fat. Stir in chili peppers, chili powder, salt, and hot pepper sauce. Heat through.

2. Fill shells with filling. Top with lettuce, tomato, and cheese. If desired, serve with salsa and/or sour cream. Makes 6 servings.

Nutrition Facts per serving: 343 cal., 20 g total fat (8 g sat. fat), 68 mg chol., 393 mg sodium, 21 g carbo., 1 g fiber, 21 g pro. **Daily Values:** 10% vit. A, 24% vit. C, 18% calcium, 17% iron

---

SLOPPY JOES

START TO FINISH: 25 MINUTES

Fast   **Low-Fat**

To keep this sandwich low in fat, use lean ground beef. Ground pork or sausage will mean a higher fat content.

   1 **pound ground beef, ground pork, or bulk pork sausage**
 $^1/_2$ **cup chopped onion (1 medium)**
 $^1/_2$ **cup chopped green sweet pepper**
   1 **$7^1/_2$-ounce can tomatoes, cut up**
   2 **tablespoons quick-cooking rolled oats**
   1 to $1^1/_2$ **teaspoons chili powder**
   1 to 2 **teaspoons Worcestershire sauce**
 $^1/_2$ **teaspoon garlic salt**
    Dash bottled hot pepper sauce
   6 **hamburger buns, split and toasted**

1. In a large skillet cook meat, onion, and sweet pepper till meat is brown. Drain off fat. Stir in undrained tomatoes, $^1/_4$ cup *water*, oats, chili powder, Worcestershire sauce, garlic salt, and hot pepper sauce. Bring to boiling. Reduce heat. Simmer, uncovered, for 5 to 10 minutes or till desired consistency is reached. Serve in buns. Serves 6.

Nutrition Facts per serving: 290 cal., 12 g total fat (4 g sat. fat), 48 mg chol., 500 mg sodium, 27 g carbo., 2 g fiber, 19 g pro. **Daily Values:** 4% vit. A, 28% vit. C, 4% calcium, 19% iron

CHILI-MAC SKILLET

PREP: 10 MINUTES COOK: 25 MINUTES

No need to boil the macaroni first. It cooks while the dish simmers.

    1 pound ground beef
    ³/₄ cup chopped onions (1¹/₂ medium)
    1 15¹/₂-ounce can red kidney beans, rinsed and drained (see tip,
        page 107)
    1 8-ounce can tomato sauce
    1 7¹/₂-ounce can tomatoes, cut up
    ¹/₂ cup elbow macaroni
    ¹/₄ cup water
    1 4-ounce can diced green chili peppers, drained
    2 to 3 teaspoons chili powder
    ¹/₂ teaspoon garlic salt
    ¹/₂ cup shredded Monterey Jack or cheddar cheese (2 ounces)

1. In a large skillet cook meat and onions till meat is brown and onions are tender. Drain off fat.

2. Stir in beans, tomato sauce, undrained tomatoes, uncooked macaroni, water, chili peppers, chili powder, and garlic salt. Bring to boiling. Reduce heat. Simmer, covered, about 20 minutes or till macaroni is tender, stirring often. Sprinkle with cheese. Cover and heat about 2 minutes more or till cheese is melted. Makes 6 servings.

Nutrition Facts per serving: 310 cal., 13 g total fat (6 g sat. fat), 56 mg chol., 726 mg sodium, 27 g carbo., 5 g fiber, 25 g pro. **Daily Values:** 11% vit. A, 26% vit. C, 11% calcium, 22% iron

SWEDISH MEATBALLS

START TO FINISH: 50 MINUTES

*To test meatballs for doneness, cut into the center of one to
see that no pink remains.*

    1 beaten egg
    ¹/₄ cup milk, half-and-half, or light cream
    ³/₄ cup soft bread crumbs (1 slice)
    ¹/₂ cup finely chopped onion (1 medium)
    ¹/₄ cup snipped fresh parsley

1/8 teaspoon ground allspice or nutmeg
1/2 pound ground beef or ground veal
1/2 pound ground pork or ground lamb
 1 tablespoon margarine or butter
 2 tablespoons all-purpose flour
 2 teaspoons instant beef bouillon granules
 2 cups milk, half-and-half, or light cream
 2 to 3 cups hot cooked noodles (see page 729)

1. In a large mixing bowl combine egg and the 1/4 cup milk, half-and-half, or light cream. Stir in bread crumbs, onion, parsley, 1/4 teaspoon *pepper*, and allspice or nutmeg. Add ground beef or veal and ground pork or lamb. Mix well. Shape into 30 meatballs.

2. In a large skillet cook meatballs in hot margarine or butter, half at a time, over medium heat about 10 minutes or till no pink remains, turning to brown evenly. Remove from skillet, reserving 2 tablespoons drippings. Drain on paper towels.

3. Stir flour, bouillon granules, and 1/8 teaspoon *pepper* into

JUDGING DONENESS OF GROUND MEAT

For safety's sake, we recommend cooking meat loaves and ground meat patties with added ingredients to 170° or until no pink remains. Ground meat patties with no other ingredients added, however, may be cooked just until their centers are brownish pink (medium doneness).

drippings. Gradually stir in the 2 cups milk, half-and-half, or light cream. Cook and stir over medium heat till thickened and bubbly. Cook and stir for 1 minute more. Return meatballs to skillet. Heat through. Serve with noodles. Makes 4 to 6 servings.

Nutrition Facts per serving: 494 cal., 24 g total fat (9 g sat. fat), 165 mg chol., 790 mg sodium, 35 g carbo., 2 g fiber, 32 g pro. **Daily Values:** 16% vit. A, 12% vit. C, 17% calcium, 21% iron

MEAT LOAF

Create your favorite meat loaf by choosing from among the ingredient options listed.

  1 **beaten egg**

  ³/₄ **cup soft bread crumbs (1 slice) or ¹/₄ cup fine dry bread crumbs**

  ¹/₄ **cup milk, beer, apple juice, or water**

  ¹/₄ **cup finely chopped onion (¹/₂ of a medium) or 1 tablespoon dried minced onion**

  ¹/₄ **cup finely chopped celery, green sweet pepper, or shredded carrot, or one 2-ounce can mushrooms, drained and chopped (optional)**

  2 **tablespoons snipped parsley (optional)**

  ¹/₂ **teaspoon dried sage, thyme, basil, or oregano, crushed, or dried dillweed**

  1 **pound ground beef or ground lamb**

  2 **tablespoons bottled barbecue sauce, chili sauce, or catsup**

1. In a mixing bowl combine egg; bread crumbs; milk, beer, apple juice, or water; onion; celery, sweet pepper, carrot, or mushrooms (if desired); parsley (if desired); sage, thyme, basil, oregano, or dillweed; ¹/₂ teaspoon *salt;* and ¹/₄ teaspoon *pepper.* Add ground meat and mix well.

2. In a shallow baking dish pat mixture into a 7×3×2-inch loaf. (Or, shape into a ring 6 inches in diameter with a 2-inch hole in the center.)

3. Bake in a 350° oven till no pink remains. Bake loaf for 45 to 50 minutes; bake the ring for 25 to 30 minutes. Transfer to a platter. Top with barbecue sauce, chili sauce, or catsup. Makes 4 servings.

Nutrition Facts per serving: 278 cal., 16 g total fat (6 g sat. fat), 126 mg chol., 456 mg sodium, 7 g carbo., 1 g fiber, 25 g pro. **Daily Values:** 4% vit. A, 2% vit. C, 4% calcium, 17% iron

HAMBURGERS

PREP: 15 MINUTES BROIL: 12 MINUTES

Fast

To speed cleanup, line your broiler pan with foil before cooking.

1 beaten egg
2 tablespoons milk or water
$^3/_4$ cup soft bread crumbs (1 slice) or $^1/_4$ cup fine dry bread
   crumbs
2 tablespoons chopped onion or $^1/_4$ teaspoon onion powder
1 tablespoon prepared mustard or $^1/_2$ teaspoon dry mustard
1 clove garlic, minced, or $^1/_8$ teaspoon garlic powder (optional)
$^1/_4$ teaspoon salt
$^1/_4$ teaspoon pepper
1 pound ground beef, ground pork, ground veal, or ground lamb
4 or 6 hamburger buns, split and toasted

1. In a large mixing bowl combine egg and milk or water. Stir in bread crumbs, onion or onion powder, mustard, garlic (if desired), salt, and pepper. Add ground meat. Mix well. Shape meat mixture into four $^3/_4$-inch-thick or six $^1/_2$-inch-thick patties.
2. Place patties on the unheated rack of a broiler pan. Broil 3 to 4 inches from the heat till no pink remains, turning once. Broil $^3/_4$-inch patties for 12 to 14 minutes; broil $^1/_2$-inch patties for 10 to 12 minutes. Serve on buns. Makes 4 or 6 servings.

Nutrition Facts per serving: 389 cal., 18 g total fat (7 g sat. fat), 125 mg chol., 506 mg sodium, 27 g carbo., 1 g fiber, 28 g pro. **Daily Values:** 2% vit. A, 1% vit. C, 5% calcium, 23% iron

■ **Cheeseburgers:** Prepare as above, except place 1 slice *American, Swiss, cheddar, mozzarella, Monterey Jack, Monterey Jack with jalapeño peppers, or Muenster cheese* atop each patty at the end of cooking time. Broil about 1 minute more or till cheese begins to melt.

Nutrition Facts per serving: 495 cal., 27 g total fat (12 g sat. fat)

■ **Burgers Oriental:** Prepare as above, except substitute *soy sauce* for the milk and omit salt. Add $^1/_4$ cup chopped *water chestnuts* and

1 teaspoon grated *gingerroot* or $^{1}/_{4}$ teaspoon *ground ginger* with the bread crumbs.

Nutrition Facts per serving: 394 cal., 18 g total fat (6 g sat. fat)

BLUE CHEESE BURGERS

PREP: 15 MINUTES BROIL: 12 MINUTES

Fast

Some popular types of blue-veined cheese include Danablu, Gorgonzola, Roquefort, and Stilton.

$^{1}/_{4}$ cup fine dry bread crumbs
  2 tablespoons crumbled blue cheese or feta cheese ($^{1}/_{2}$ ounce)
  2 tablespoons milk
  2 teaspoons prepared mustard or Dijon-style mustard
  2 teaspoons snipped fresh chives or $^{1}/_{2}$ teaspoon dried chives, crushed
$^{1}/_{2}$ teaspoon salt
$^{1}/_{8}$ teaspoon pepper
  1 pound ground beef
  4 hamburger buns, split and toasted
  1 medium tomato, sliced

1. In a large mixing bowl combine bread crumbs, blue cheese or feta cheese, milk, mustard, chives, salt, and pepper. Add meat. Mix well. Shape meat mixture into four $^{3}/_{4}$-inch-thick patties.

2. Place patties on the unheated rack of a broiler pan. Broil 3 to 4 inches from the heat for 12 to 14 minutes or till no pink remains, turning once. Serve on buns topped with a tomato slice. Makes 4 servings.

Nutrition Facts per serving: 396 cal., 18 g total fat (7 g sat. fat), 75 mg chol., 713 mg sodium, 29 g carbo., 1 g fiber, 28 g pro. **Daily Values:** 4% vit. A, 11% vit. C, 9% calcium, 26% iron

GARDEN BURGERS

PREP: 15 MINUTES BROIL: 12 MINUTES

> **Fast**

    1 beaten egg
    1 tablespoon catsup
  ¹/₂ teaspoon dried basil, crushed
  ¹/₂ teaspoon onion salt
  ¹/₄ teaspoon pepper
    1 cup frozen loose-pack chopped broccoli or shredded hash
        brown potatoes, thawed, or shredded carrot or zucchini
  ¹/₄ cup soft bread crumbs
    1 pound ground beef or ground pork
      Catsup or bottled barbecue sauce
    4 hamburger buns, split and toasted
      Mayonnaise or salad dressing
      Leaf lettuce

1. In a large mixing bowl combine egg, the 1 tablespoon catsup, the basil, onion salt, and pepper. Stir in vegetable and bread crumbs. Add meat; mix well. Shape into four ³/₄-inch-thick patties.

2. Place patties on the unheated rack of a broiler pan. Broil 3 to 4 inches from the heat for 12 to 14 minutes or till no pink remains, turning and brushing with additional catsup once. Brush again with catsup before serving.

3. Serve patties on buns with mayonnaise and lettuce. Makes 4 servings.

Nutrition Facts per serving: 433 cal., 23 g total fat (7 g sat. fat), 129 mg chol., 442 mg sodium, 28 g carbo., 2 g fiber, 28 g pro. **Daily Values:** 10% vit. A, 24% vit. C, 5% calcium, 24% iron

APPLE BREAKFAST PATTIES

PREP: 15 MINUTES COOK: 8 MINUTES

Fast   **Low-Fat**

Lean pork and egg white keep these breakfast sausages low in fat.

   1 slightly beaten egg white
   1/4 cup finely chopped onion
   1/2 cup finely chopped fresh apple
   3 tablespoons quick-cooking oats
   2 tablespoons snipped fresh parsley
   1/2 teaspoon salt
   1/2 teaspoon ground sage
   1/4 teaspoon ground nutmeg
   1/4 teaspoon pepper
      Dash ground red pepper
   1/2 pound lean ground pork or ground turkey breast
      Nonstick spray coating

1. In a medium mixing bowl combine egg white, onion, apple, oats, parsley, salt, sage, nutmeg, pepper, and ground red pepper. Add ground pork or turkey breast. Mix well. Shape the mixture into eight 2-inch-wide patties.
2. Spray a cold 10-inch skillet with nonstick coating. Preheat over medium-low heat. Cook patties over medium-low heat for 8 to 10 minutes or till meat is no longer pink and juices run clear, turning once. Drain off fat. Makes 8 patties.

Nutrition Facts per patty: 51 cal., 2 g total fat (0 g sat. fat), 13 mg chol., 151 mg sodium, 3 g carbo., 0 g fiber, 4 g pro. **Daily Values:** 0% vit. A, 3% vit. C, 0% calcium, 2% iron

---

FRENCH DIP SANDWICHES

START TO FINISH: 25 MINUTES

Fast   **Low-Fat**

A great use for either leftover or deli roast beef.

   1 small onion, sliced and separated into rings
   1 clove garlic, minced
   1 tablespoon margarine or butter

    1 14¹/₂-ounce can beef broth
 ¹/₂ teaspoon dried thyme, marjoram, or oregano, crushed
 ¹/₄ teaspoon pepper
 ³/₄ pound thinly sliced cooked beef
    4 French-style rolls, split

1. In a saucepan cook onion and garlic in hot margarine or butter till tender. Stir in broth; thyme, marjoram, or oregano; and pepper. Bring to boiling. Reduce heat. Simmer, uncovered, for 10 minutes. Add beef. Return to boiling. Reduce heat. Simmer, uncovered, 5 minutes more or till hot.

2. Remove beef slices and onion rings from liquid. Arrange atop rolls. Serve with individual dishes of broth mixture for dipping. Makes 4 servings.

Nutrition Facts per serving: 283 cal., 8 g total fat (2 g sat. fat), 59 mg chol., 654 mg sodium, 21 g carbo., 0 g fiber, 29 g pro. **Daily Values:** 3% vit. A, 2% vit. C, 4% calcium, 20% iron

CORNED BEEF HASH

START TO FINISH: 25 MINUTES

<code>Fast</code>   <code>Low-Fat</code>

Always a family favorite, this easy supper dish is a great way to use extra potatoes and beef.

    2 tablespoons margarine or butter
    2 cups finely chopped cooked potatoes or loose-pack frozen
         hash brown potatoes, thawed
 1¹/₂ cups finely chopped cooked corned beef or beef
 ¹/₂ cup chopped onion (1 medium)
    2 tablespoons snipped fresh parsley
    1 to 2 teaspoons Worcestershire sauce
 ¹/₈ teaspoon pepper
    2 tablespoons milk (optional)

1. In a large skillet melt margarine or butter. Stir in potatoes, meat, onion, parsley, Worcestershire sauce, and pepper. Spread in skillet. Cook over medium heat for 8 to 10 minutes or till brown on the bottom, turning occasionally. If desired, stir in milk; heat through. Makes 4 servings.

■ **Oven directions:** In a large skillet cook onion in hot margarine or butter till tender. Stir in remaining ingredients except milk. Transfer to a 2-quart square baking dish. Bake, covered, in a 375° oven about 30 minutes or till heated through. If desired, add milk as directed.

Nutrition Facts per serving: 259 cal., 11 g total fat (3 g sat. fat), 28 mg chol., 411 mg sodium, 32 g carbo., 3 g fiber, 8 g pro. **Daily Values:** 8% vit. A, 49% vit. C, 1% calcium, 8% iron

CREAMED CHIPPED BEEF

START TO FINISH: 20 MINUTES

Keep a package of smoked or dried beef on hand to
stir up this quick dinner.

   1 3- or 4-ounce package sliced smoked or dried beef, snipped
$^1/_2$ cup chopped green sweet pepper (optional)
   2 tablespoons margarine or butter
   2 tablespoons all-purpose flour
$^1/_8$ teaspoon pepper
$1^1/_3$ cups milk
   2 slices bread, toasted

1. If using dried beef, rinse and drain well. In a large skillet cook and stir beef and sweet pepper (if desired) in hot margarine or butter about 3 minutes or till edges of beef curl.
2. Stir in flour and pepper. Stir in milk. Cook and stir over medium heat till thickened and bubbly. Cook and stir for 1 minute more. Serve over toast. Makes 2 servings.

Nutrition Facts per serving: 326 cal., 18 g total fat (5 g sat. fat), 31 mg chol., 867 mg sodium, 26 g carbo., 1 g fiber, 17 g pro. **Daily Values:** 24% vit. A, 2% vit. C, 19% calcium, 15% iron

REUBEN SANDWICHES

PREP: 10 MINUTES COOK: 8 MINUTES

Fast

*Originally, Reubens were made with Russian dressing, but
Thousand Island is popular, too.*

- 3 tablespoons margarine or butter, softened
- 8 slices dark rye or pumpernickel bread
- 3 tablespoons Thousand Island or Russian salad dressing
- 6 ounces thinly sliced cooked corned beef, beef, pork, or ham
- 4 slices Swiss cheese (3 ounces)
- 1 cup sauerkraut, well drained

1. Spread margarine or butter on 1 side of each bread slice and
salad dressing on the other. With the margarine side down, top 4
slices with meat, cheese, and sauerkraut. Top with remaining bread
slices, dressing side down.
2. In a large skillet cook 2 of the sandwiches over medium-low heat
for 4 to 6 minutes or till bread is toasted and cheese is melted, turning once. Repeat with remaining sandwiches. Makes 4 servings.

Nutrition Facts per serving: 485 cal., 29 g total fat (9 g sat. fat), 65 mg chol., 1,531 mg
sodium, 36 g carbo., 2 g fiber, 20 g pro. **Daily Values:** 17% vit. A, 25% vit. C, 22%
calcium, 23% iron

TORTILLA ROLL-UPS

PREP: 10 MINUTES CHILL: 2 TO 24 HOURS

Enjoy these handy sandwiches as a main dish or an appetizer.

- 4 ounces soft-style cream cheese with chives and onion
- $1/4$ cup chopped, drained marinated artichoke hearts
- 2 tablespoons diced pimiento
- 2 teaspoons snipped fresh oregano or $1/2$ teaspoon dried
  oregano, crushed
- 2 10-inch flour tortillas
- 6 ounces thinly sliced fully cooked ham or prosciutto
- 4 ounces sliced Swiss or provolone cheese
- 1 large romaine lettuce leaf, rib removed

1. In a bowl stir together cream cheese, artichoke hearts, pimiento, and oregano. Spread cream cheese mixture onto the tortillas.

2. Divide remaining ingredients between tortillas. Roll up tortillas. Cover and chill, seam sides down, for 2 to 24 hours. Cut roll-ups into 1-inch-thick slices. Makes 4 main-dish or 8 appetizer servings.

Nutrition Facts per serving: 353 cal., 21 g total fat (11 g sat. fat), 78 mg chol., 825 mg sodium, 18 g carbo., 0 g fiber, 21 g pro. **Daily Values:** 19% vit. A, 33% vit. C, 27% calcium, 12% iron

---

ROAST PORK SANDWICH WITH APPLE MUSTARD

START TO FINISH: 10 MINUTES

Fast

Packaged coleslaw mix helps you put these sandwiches together fast.

$^1/_2$ cup apple butter
1 tablespoon coarse-grain mustard
8 slices marbled rye bread
$1^1/_2$ cups preshredded coleslaw mix or shredded cabbage
8 ounces thinly sliced cooked pork
4 ounces thinly sliced Swiss cheese
1 medium apple, cored and sliced into thin wedges

1. In a small bowl combine apple butter and mustard. If desired, toast bread. Spread apple butter mixture on 1 side of each bread slice. Top half of the bread slices (butter sides up) with coleslaw mix, pork, cheese, apple wedges, and the remaining bread slices (butter sides down). Serves 4.

Nutrition Facts per serving: 478 cal., 18 g total fat (8 g sat. fat), 78 mg chol., 520 mg sodium, 50 g carbo., 5 g fiber, 29 g pro. **Daily Values:** 27% vit. A, 27% vit. C, 28% calcium, 16% iron

PIZZA

Use the same dough and choice of toppings to make thin-crust pizzas, pan pizzas, or calzones.

2³/₄ to 3¹/₄ cups all-purpose flour
1 package active dry yeast
¹/₄ teaspoon salt
1 cup warm water (120° to 130°)
2 tablespoons cooking oil
1 recipe Pizza Sauce (see below) or one 15-ounce can pizza sauce
1 pound bulk Italian sausage, ground beef, or ground pork,
   cooked and drained; 6 ounces sliced pepperoni; or 1 cup
   cubed fully cooked ham or Canadian-style bacon
¹/₂ cup sliced green onions (4) or sliced pitted ripe olives
1 cup sliced fresh mushrooms or chopped green sweet pepper
2 to 3 cups shredded mozzarella cheese (8 to 12 ounces)

1. For crust, in a large mixing bowl combine *1¹/₄* cups flour, yeast, and salt. Add water and oil. Beat with an electric mixer on low speed for 30 seconds, scraping bowl. Beat on high speed for 3 minutes. Stir in as much of the remaining flour as you can. Turn out onto a lightly floured surface. Knead in enough remaining flour to make a moderately stiff dough that is smooth and elastic (6 to 8 minutes total). Divide in half. Cover and let rest for 10 minutes. Use to make Pan Pizzas, Thin Pizzas, or Calzones.

■ **Pizza Sauce:** In a medium saucepan combine one 8-ounce can *tomato sauce;* one 7¹/₂-ounce can undrained *tomatoes,* cut up (see tip, page 999); ¹/₂ cup chopped *onion;* 1 tablespoon *dried basil,* crushed; 1 teaspoon *sugar;* 1 teaspoon *dried oregano,* crushed; 2 cloves *garlic,* minced; and ¹/₄ teaspoon *pepper.* Bring to boiling. Reduce heat. Simmer, covered, about 10 minutes or till the onion is tender.

■ **Pan Pizzas:** Grease two 11×7×1¹/₂-inch or 9×9×2-inch baking pans. If desired, sprinkle with *cornmeal.* With greased fingers, pat dough onto bottoms and halfway up sides of prepared pans. Cover and let rise in a warm place till nearly double (30 to 45 minutes). Bake in a 375° oven for 20 to 25 minutes or till brown. Meanwhile, make Pizza Sauce. Spread Pizza Sauce onto hot crust. Top with meat, vegetables, and cheese. Bake for 15 to 20 minutes more or till bubbly. Serves 6.

■ **Thin Pizzas:** Make Pizza Sauce. Grease two 12-inch pizza pans or baking sheets. If desired, sprinkle with *cornmeal*. On a lightly floured surface, roll each dough portion into a 13-inch circle. Transfer to pans. Build up edges slightly. Do not let rise. Bake in a 425° oven about 12 minutes or till brown. Spread Pizza Sauce onto hot crust. Top with meat, vegetables, and cheese. Bake for 10 to 15 minutes more or till bubbly. Makes 6 servings.

■ **Calzones:** Prepare as directed for Thin Pizzas, except, after transferring dough to prepared pans, spoon sauce and meat onto half of each circle to within 1 inch of edge. Sprinkle with vegetables and cheese. Moisten edges of dough with *water*. Fold dough circles in half over filling. Seal edges by pressing with tines of a fork. Prick tops. Brush tops with *milk*. If desired, sprinkle with grated *Parmesan cheese*. Bake in a 375° oven for 30 to 35 minutes or till crusts are brown. Serves 6.

Nutrition Facts per serving: 540 cal., 26 g total fat (10 g sat. fat), 64 mg chol., 1,067 mg sodium, 49 g carbo., 3 g fiber, 27 g pro. **Daily Values:** 14% vit. A; 19% vit. C, 24% calcium, 29% iron

Pizza on the Double

For a quick version of homemade pizza, make the dough from one of the convenience products listed below. Unless otherwise specified, shape, assemble, and bake according to the instructions for the homemade dough on page 707. (To shave more time off the preparation, use the canned pizza sauce, fully cooked meats, and preshredded cheese.)

■ One 16-ounce loaf frozen bread dough, thawed and halved.

■ Two 10-ounce packages refrigerated bread dough. Do not use for Thin Pizzas. Omit the second rising time for Pan Pizzas.

■ Two 10-ounce packages refrigerated pizza dough. Omit the second rising for Pan Pizzas.

■ One 16-ounce package hot roll mix. Make according to box directions for pizza dough.

■ Packaged biscuit mix. Prepare according to package directions for pizza crust, making enough for two crusts.

■ Sixteen English muffin halves. Top with sauce, meat, vegetables, and cheese. Bake in a 425° oven about 10 minutes or until hot.

■ Eight 8-inch flour tortillas. Add toppings. Bake half the tortilla pizzas at a time in a 425° oven about 10 minutes or until hot.

Broiling Meat

Place meat on the unheated rack of a broiler pan. For cuts less than 1½ inches thick, broil 3 to 4 inches from the heat. For cuts 1½ inches thick or thicker, broil 4 to 5 inches from the heat. Broil for the time given or until done, turning meat over after half of the broiling time.

Cut	Thickness	Doneness	Time
Beef			
Flank steak	¾ inch	Medium	12 to 14 minutes
Steak (chuck, top round)	1 inch	Medium rare	14 to 16 minutes
		Medium	16 to 20 minutes
	1½ inches	Medium rare	18 to 20 minutes
		Medium	20 to 25 minutes
Steak (porterhouse, rib, rib eye, T-bone, sirloin, tenderloin, top loin)	1 inch	Medium rare	10 to 12 minutes
		Medium	12 to 15 minutes
	1½ inches	Medium rare	16 to 20 minutes
		Medium	20 to 25 minutes
Veal			
Loin/rib chop	¾ to 1 inch	Medium	14 to 16 minutes

LAMB			
Loin/rib chop	1 inch	Medium	7 to 11 minutes
Sirloin chop	3/4 to 1 inch	Medium	12 to 15 minutes
PORK			
Boneless loin chop	3/4 to 1 inch	Medium (160°)	6 to 8 minutes
	1 1/4 to 1 1/2 inches	Medium (160°)	11 to 15 minutes
Loin or rib chop	3/4 inch	Medium (160°)	8 to 10 minutes
(bone-in)	1 1/4 to 1 1/2 inches	Medium (160°)	18 to 22 minutes
Ham slice	1 inch	Heated	14 to 16 minutes
SAUSAGES			
Fresh bratwurst		Well-done	10 to 12 minutes
Frankfurters and fully cooked sausages		Heated	3 to 5 minutes
GROUND MEAT PATTIES			
Ground beef patties	1/2 inch	Medium to well-done	10 to 12 minutes
	3/4 inch	Medium to well-done	12 to 14 minutes
Ground lamb patties	1/2 inch	Medium to well-done	10 to 12 minutes
	3/4 inch	Medium to well-done	12 to 14 minutes
Ground pork patties	1/2 inch	Medium to well-done	10 to 12 minutes

ROASTING MEAT

Place meat, fat side up, on a rack in a shallow roasting pan. (Roasts with a bone do not need a rack.) For ham, if desired, score the top in a diamond pattern. Insert a meat thermometer (see tip, page 620). Do not add water or liquid, and do not cover. Roast in a 325° oven, unless chart or recipe says otherwise, for the time given and until the thermometer registers 5° below the specified temperature. Remove the roast from the oven; cover with foil and let it stand 15 minutes. The meat's temperature will rise 5° during the time it stands.

Cut	Weight	Doneness	Roasting Time
BEEF			
Boneless rolled rump roast	4 to 6 pounds	160°	1¾ to 2¾ hours
Boneless sirloin roast	4 to 6 pounds	145° medium rare 160° medium	2¼ to 3 hours 2¾ to 3½ hours
Eye round roast	2 to 3 pounds	145° medium rare 160° medium	1½ to 2 hours 1¾ to 2¼ hours
Rib eye roast (roast at 350°)	4 to 6 pounds	145° medium rare 160° medium	1½ to 2 hours 2 to 2½ hours
Rib roast (roast at 350°)	4 to 6 pounds	145° medium rare 160° medium	1¾ to 2¼ hours 2¼ to 2¾ hours

Tenderloin roast (roast at 425°)		
Half	2 to 3 pounds	145° medium rare	1/2 to 3/4 hour
Whole	4 to 6 pounds	145° medium rare	3/4 to 1 hour
Round tip roast	3 to 5 pounds	145° to 160°	1 3/4 to 2 1/2 hours
	6 to 8 pounds	145° to 160°	2 1/2 to 3 1/2 hours
Top round roast	4 to 6 pounds	145° to 160°	1 1/2 to 2 3/4 hours
Veal		
Boneless rolled breast roast	2 1/2 to 3 1/2 pounds	160°	1 3/4 to 2 1/4 hours
Boneless rolled shoulder roast	2 1/2 to 3 pounds	160°	2 to 2 3/4 hours
Loin roast	3 to 4 pounds	160°	1 3/4 to 2 1/2 hours
Rib roast	4 to 5 pounds	160°	1 3/4 to 2 1/2 hours
Lamb		
Boneless rolled leg roast	4 to 7 pounds	145° to 170°	2 to 4 hours
Boneless rolled shoulder roast	3 1/2 to 5 pounds	145° to 170°	2 to 3 1/2 hours

Roasting Meat (continued)

Cut	Weight	Doneness	Roasting Time
Whole leg roast (bone-in)	5 to 7 pounds	145° to 170°	2 to 3½ hours
	7 to 9 pounds	145° to 170°	2¼ to 3¾ hours
Shank half	3 to 4 pounds	145° to 170°	1¾ to 3 hours
Sirloin half	3 to 4 pounds	145° to 170°	1½ to 3 hours
PORK*			
Boneless top loin roast			
Single loin	2 to 3 pounds	160°	1¼ to 1¾ hours
Double loin (tied)	3 to 5 pounds	160°	1¾ to 2½ hours
Loin back ribs, spareribs	2 to 4 pounds	Well-done (until tender)	1½ to 1¾ hours
Country-style ribs (roast at 350°)	2 to 4 pounds	Well-done (until tender)	1½ to 2 hours
Blade or sirloin roast	3 to 4 pounds	170° well done	1¾ to 2½ hours
Loin center rib roast (backbone loosened)	3 to 5 pounds	160°	1½ to 2½ hours
Rib crown roast	6 to 8 pounds	160°	2 to 3½ hours

Tenderloin (roast at 425° until thermometer registers 160°)	¾ to 1 pound	160°	25 to 35 minutes
Ham (fully cooked) Boneless portion Boneless half Smoked picnic	3 to 4 pounds 4 to 6 pounds 5 to 8 pounds	140° 140° 140°	1 to 1½ hours 1¼ to 2 hours 2 to 4 hours
Ham (cook- before-eating) Bone-in portion Bone-in half	3 to 5 pounds 7 to 8 pounds	160° 160°	1¾ to 3 hours 2½ to 3¼ hours

*Pork should be cooked until the juices run clear.

Panbroiling and Panfrying Meat

To panbroil these meats, preheat a heavy skillet over high heat until extremely hot. Do not add water or fat. (For beef steaks and veal, brush skillet lightly with cooking oil before preheating.) Add meat. Do not cover. Reduce heat to medium and cook for the time given or until done, turning meat frequently. If meat browns too quickly, reduce heat to medium-low. Spoon off fat and juices as they accumulate during cooking.

To panfry these meats, in a heavy skillet melt 1 to 2 tablespoons margarine, butter, or cooking oil over medium heat. Add meat. Do not cover. Cook for time given or until done, turning meat over after half of the cooking time.

Cut	Thickness	Doneness	Panbroiling Time	Panfrying Time
BEEF				
Cubed steak	½ inch	Well-done	5 to 8 minutes	6 to 8 minutes
Steak (rib eye, sirloin, tenderloin, top loin, top round)	1 inch	Medium rare	6 to 8 minutes	8 to 11 minutes
		Medium	9 to 12 minutes	12 to 14 minutes
VEAL				
Cutlet	⅛ inch	Medium	2 to 3 minutes	3 to 4 minutes
	¼ inch	Medium	3 to 5 minutes	4 to 6 minutes
LAMB				
Chop	1 inch	Medium	8 to 10 minutes	7 to 9 minutes

PORK*

	Thickness	Doneness		
Chop	3/4 inch	Medium	7 to 9 minutes	8 to 10 minutes
		Well-done	9 to 11 minutes	11 to 13 minutes

To panbroil these meats, place meat in a cool skillet. (If using an electric range, preheat the burner for 2 to 4 minutes.) Turn heat to medium. Turn meat halfway through cooking time (for bacon, turn occasionally). If meat browns too quickly, reduce heat slightly.

Cut	Thickness	Doneness	Panbroiling Time
PORK*			
Bacon slices		Well-done	8 to 10 minutes
Canadian-style bacon	1/4 inch	Heated	3 to 5 minutes
Ham slice	1 inch	Heated	14 to 16 minutes
GROUND MEAT			
Ground meat patties (beef, lamb, pork*)	3/4 inch (4 to a pound)	Medium to Well-done	10 to 12 minutes

*Pork should be cooked until the juices run clear.

PASTA

PASTA

Baked Cavatelli, 749
Baked Ravioli with Meat Sauce, 743
Capellini with Roasted Red
  Peppers, 770
Cheesy Chicken and Tortellini
  Toss, 756 *Fast*
Classic Spaghetti Sauce, 733
Creamy Pesto Pasta, 760 *Fast*
Fettuccine Alfredo, 765
Fettuccine alla Carbonara, 738
  Fast
Fettuccine with Artichokes and
  Basil, 768 *Fast   Low-Fat*
Fettuccine with Vegetables and
  Prosciutto, 753 *Fast*
Herb-Buttered Pasta, 770 *Fast*
Homemade Pasta, 726
Lasagna, 744
Lemon-Basil Pasta with Vegetables,
  768 *Fast*
Lemon-Chive Pasta, 772 *Fast*
Lemony Fettuccine Alfredo with
  Peas, 766
Linguine with White Clam Sauce,
  734 *Fast*
Lower-Fat Pesto for Pasta, 741 *Fast*
  Low-Fat
Low-Fat Spinach Manicotti, 764
  Low-Fat
Macaroni and Cheese, 764
Mexican-Style Spaghetti, 767 *Fast*
  Low-Fat
Noodles, 729
One-Pot Spaghetti, 742 *Low-Fat*
Orange Shrimp with Fettuccine,
  759 *Fast   Low-Fat*
Orzo Pilaf, 771
Orzo with Oriental Vegetables, 772
  Fast   Low-Fat

Pasta Pizza, 747 *Low-Fat*
Pasta Primavera, 766 *Fast*
Pasta Skillet with Spicy Pepperoni
  Sauce, 750
Pasta with Bolognese Sauce, 736
Pasta with Fresh Tomato and Basil
  Sauce, 738
Pasta with Marinara Sauce, 739
Pasta with Red Clam Sauce, 735
  Low-Fat
Pasta with Scallops, 758 *Fast*
  Low-Fat
Pasta with Vegetables and Walnuts,
  766 *Fast*
Pasta with White Bean Sauce, 737
  Fast
Pesto for Pasta, 740 *Fast*
Potluck Pasta, 754 *Low-Fat*
Rainbow Rotini with Cheese Sauce,
  761 *Fast*
Salmon-Sauced Mostaccioli, 757
Saucepan Macaroni and Cheese,
  765 *Fast*
Saucy Chicken Rigatoni, 756 *Fast*
  Low-Fat
Scalloped Macaroni and Ham, 752
Southwest Couscous, 773 *Fast*
  Low-Fat
Spaetzle, 732 *Fast*
Spaghetti and Meatballs, 741
Spaghetti Pie, 748 *Low-Fat*
Spinach Lasagna, 745
Spinach Manicotti, 763
Spinach Pasta, 728
Spinach Pesto for Pasta, 741 *Fast*
Three-Cheese-Stuffed Shells, 762
  Fast
Tortellini, Chicken, and Vegetables,
  755 *Fast*

Acini di pepe

Bow ties, large (farfalle)

Bow ties, tiny

Capellini

Capellini, nested

Cavatelli

Couscous

Ditalini (thimbles)

Fettuccine

Fusilli

Gemelli

Lasagna

Linguine

Macaroni, elbow

Mafalda

Manicotti

Mostaccioli

Noodles, fine

Noodles, medium

Orzo (rosamarina)

Ravioli

Rigatoni

Rotini

Shells, jumbo

Shells, small

Spaghetti

Tortellini

Vermicelli

Vermicelli, nested

Wagon wheels (ruote)

Ziti

HOMEMADE PASTA

PREP: 1 HOUR   COOK: SEE CHART, PAGE 773

2¹/₃ cups all-purpose flour
1 teaspoon dried basil, marjoram, or sage, crushed (optional)
¹/₂ teaspoon salt
2 beaten eggs
¹/₃ cup water
1 teaspoon cooking oil or olive oil

1. In a large mixing bowl stir together *2 cups* of the flour; basil, marjoram, or sage (if desired); and salt. Make a well in the center of the dry mixture. In a small mixing bowl combine eggs, water, and oil. Add to dry mixture; mix well.

2. Sprinkle kneading surface with the remaining flour. Turn dough out onto floured surface. Knead till dough is smooth and elastic (8 to 10 minutes total). Cover and let the dough rest for 10 minutes.

3. Divide dough into 4 equal portions. On lightly floured surface, roll each portion into a 12-inch square (about ¹/₁₆ inch thick). Let stand, uncovered, about 20 minutes. Cut as desired (see photos 1, 2, or 3, right). If using a pasta machine, pass each portion through machine according to manufacturer's directions till dough is ¹/₁₆ inch thick (see photo 4, page 728). Cut as desired (see photo 5, page 728).

4. To store cut and shaped pasta, hang it from a pasta-drying rack or clothes hanger, or spread it on a wire cooling rack. Let pasta dry overnight or till completely dry; place in an airtight container and refrigerate for up to 3 days. Or, dry the pasta for at least 1 hour and seal in a freezer bag or freezer container; freeze for up to 8 months.

5. Cook homemade pasta till tender but still firm (see chart, page 773). Drain well. Makes about 1 pound fresh pasta (8 side-dish servings).

■ **Whole Wheat Pasta:** Prepare as above, except substitute *whole wheat flour* for the all-purpose flour and omit herb.

■ **Food processor directions:** Place steel blade in food processor bowl. Add flour, herb (if desired), salt, and eggs to food processor bowl. Cover and process till mixture forms fine crumbs about the consistency of cornmeal. With the processor running, slowly pour the water and oil through the feed tube. Continue processing just till the dough forms a ball. Transfer dough to a lightly floured surface. Cover; let dough rest for 10 minutes. Continue as directed.

1. For lasagna noodles, use a fluted pastry wheel or sharp knife to cut prepared dough into 2½-inch-wide strips. Cut strips into desired lengths.

Nutrition Facts per serving: 146 cal., 2 g total fat (1 g sat. fat), 53 mg chol., 150 mg sodium, 26 g carbo., 1 g fiber, 5 g pro. **Daily Values:** 2% vit. A, 0% vit. C, 1% calcium,

2. For linguine, fettuccine, or noodles, loosely roll up prepared dough jelly-roll style; cut into ⅛-inch-wide strips for linguine or ¼-inch-wide strips for fettuccine or noodles. Separate the strips and cut them into 12-inch lengths.

11% iron

3. For bow ties (farfalle), cut prepared dough into 2×1-inch rectangles. Pinch centers to form bow ties. For tripolini (not pictured), cut prepared dough into 1-inch circles; pinch centers to form rounded butterfly shapes.

4. Set a pasta machine on its widest opening; pass a dough portion through. Reset on a narrower setting; pass dough through again. Repeat till dough is ¹⁄₁₆ inch thick. Dust dough with flour to keep it from sticking.

5. To use a pasta machine to cut dough, pass a portion of rolled dough through cutting blades. Use the ⅛-inch-wide setting for linguine and the ¼-inch-wide setting for fettuccine or noodles. Cut pasta into desired lengths.

SPINACH PASTA

PREP: 1 HOUR   COOK: SEE CHART, PAGE 773

   2¾ **cups all-purpose flour**
   ½ **teaspoon salt**
   2 **beaten eggs**
   ¼ **cup water**
   ¼ **cup cooked spinach, well drained and very finely chopped**
   1 **teaspoon cooking oil or olive oil**

1. In a large mixing bowl stir together *2 cups* of the flour and the salt. Make a well in the center of the dry mixture. In a small mixing bowl combine the beaten eggs, water, spinach, and oil. Add to dry mixture; mix well.
2. Sprinkle kneading surface with the remaining flour. Turn dough out onto floured surface. Knead till dough is smooth and elastic (8 to 10 minutes total). Cover and let the dough rest for 10 minutes.
3. Divide dough into 4 equal portions. On a lightly floured surface,

roll each portion into a 12-inch square (about $1/16$ inch thick). Let stand, uncovered, about 20 minutes. Cut as desired (see photos 1, 2, or 3, page 727). If using a pasta machine, pass each portion through the machine according to manufacturer's directions till dough is $1/16$ inch thick (see photo 4, page 728). Cut as desired (see photo 5, page 728).

4. To store cut and shaped pasta, hang it from a pasta-drying rack or clothes hanger, or spread it on a wire cooling rack. Let pasta dry overnight or till completely dry; place in an air-

tight container and refrigerate for up to 3 days. Or, dry the pasta for at least 1 hour and seal in a freezer bag or freezer container; freeze for up to 8 months.

5. Cook homemade pasta till tender but still firm (see chart, page 773). Drain well. Makes about $1\frac{1}{4}$ pounds fresh pasta (10 side-dish servings).

Nutrition Facts per serving: 135 cal., 2 g total fat (0 g sat. fat), 43 mg chol., 123 mg sodium, 24 g carbo., 1 g fiber, 5 g pro. **Daily Values:** 5% vit. A, 0% vit. C, 1% calcium, 11% iron

NOODLES

PREP: 1 HOUR   COOK: $1\frac{1}{2}$ MINUTES

   2 cups all-purpose flour
$1/2$ teaspoon salt
   2 beaten egg yolks
   1 beaten egg
$1/3$ cup water
   1 teaspoon cooking oil or olive oil

1. In a large mixing bowl stir together *$1\frac{3}{4}$ cups* of the flour and the salt. Make a well in the center of the dry mixture. In a small mixing bowl combine egg yolks, egg, water, and oil. Add to dry mixture; mix well.

2. Sprinkle kneading surface with the remaining flour. Turn dough out onto floured surface. Knead till dough is smooth and elastic (8 to 10 minutes total). Cover and let the dough rest for 10 minutes.

3. Divide dough into 4 equal portions. On a lightly floured surface, roll each portion into a 12-inch square (about $^{1}/_{16}$ inch thick). Let stand, uncovered, about 20 minutes. Loosely roll up dough jelly-roll style; cut into $^{1}/_{4}$-inch-wide strips (see photo 2, page 727). Shake the strands to separate and cut into 2- to 3-inch lengths. If using a pasta machine, pass each portion through machine according to manufacturer's directions till dough is $^{1}/_{16}$ inch thick (see photo 4, page 728). Cut into $^{1}/_{4}$-inch-wide strips (see photo 5, page 728). Cut strips into 2- to 3-inch lengths.

4. To store cut noodles, spread them on a wire cooling rack. Let noodles dry overnight or till completely dry; place in an airtight container and refrigerate for up to 3 days. Or, dry the noodles for at least 1 hour and seal in a freezer bag or freezer container; freeze for up to 8 months.

5. Cook homemade noodles $1^{1}/_{2}$ to 2 minutes or till tender but still firm (see chart, page 773), allowing a few more minutes for dried or frozen noodles. Drain well. Makes about 1 pound fresh pasta (8 side-dish servings).

Nutrition Facts per serving: 134 cal., 3 g total fat (1 g sat. fat), 80 mg chol., 144 mg sodium, 22 g carbo., 1 g fiber, 4 g pro. **Daily Values:** 9% vit. A, 0% vit. C, 1% calcium, 10% iron

---

YOLKLESS NOODLES

PREP: 1 HOUR   COOK: $1^{1}/_{2}$ MINUTES

You won't find any cholesterol in these noodles since egg yolks aren't used. A little extra oil, which is also cholesterol free, is added to help make them more tender.

  2 **cups all-purpose flour**
$^{1}/_{2}$ **teaspoon salt**
  2 **beaten egg whites**
$^{1}/_{3}$ **cup water**

    2 teaspoons cooking oil or olive oil
    2 to 3 tablespoons all-purpose flour

1. In a large mixing bowl stir together the 2 cups flour and the salt. Make a well in the center of the dry mixture. In a small mixing bowl combine egg whites, water, and oil. Add to the dry mixture; mix well.

2. Sprinkle kneading surface with 1 tablespoon of the remaining flour. Turn dough out onto floured surface. Knead till dough is smooth and elastic (8 to 10 minutes total), adding 1 to 2 tablespoons additional flour as needed. Cover and let the dough rest for 10 minutes.

3. Divide dough into 4 equal portions. On a lightly floured surface, roll each portion into a 12-inch square (about $1/16$ inch thick). Let stand, uncovered, about 20 minutes. Loosely roll up dough jelly-roll style; cut into $1/4$-inch-wide strips (see photo 2, page 727). Shake the strands to separate and cut into 2- to 3-inch lengths. If using a pasta machine, pass each portion through machine according to manufacturer's directions till dough is $1/16$ inch thick (see photo 4, page 728). Cut into $1/4$-inch-wide strips (see photo 5, page 728). Cut strips into 2- to 3-inch lengths.

4. To store cut noodles, spread them on a wire cooling rack. Let noodles dry overnight or till completely dry; place in an airtight container and refrigerate for up to 3 days. Or, dry the noodles for at least 1 hour and seal in a freezer bag or freezer container; freeze for up to 8 months.

5. Cook homemade noodles for $1^1/2$ to 2 minutes or till tender but still firm (see chart, page 774), allowing a few more minutes for dried or frozen noodles. Drain noodles well. Makes about 14 ounces fresh pasta (6 to 8 side-dish servings).

Nutrition Facts per serving: 167 cal., 2 g total fat (0 g sat. fat), 0 mg chol., 197 mg sodium, 31 g carbo., 1 g fiber, 5 g pro. **Daily Values:** 0% vit. A, 0% vit. C, 0% calcium, 12% iron

SPAETZLE

Fast

*Serve these German-style noodles
or dumplings (pronounced
SHPET-sluh) as a side dish with
sauerbraten or other meats. Or,
top them with sauce when using
them as a more traditional
noodle.*

1 cup all-purpose flour
1/8 teaspoon salt
1 beaten egg
1/3 cup milk
1 tablespoon margarine or
   butter
3 tablespoons fine dry bread
   crumbs

THE LONG AND SHORT OF MEASURING PASTA

Since it's impossible to put long, uncooked spaghetti in a measuring cup, here is a handy way to measure. To make 2 cups of cooked spaghetti, use 4 ounces of dried spaghetti. If you don't have a scale, hold dried spaghetti together in a bunch. A 4-ounce portion of 10-inch-long spaghetti generally has a diameter of about 1 inch.

You can, however, use a measuring cup for short pasta such as noodles. To make 2 cups of cooked noodles, measure 2 cups (4 ounces) of dried medium noodles.

1. In a large saucepan or pot bring about 3 quarts *lightly salted water* to boiling.
2. Meanwhile, for spaetzle batter, in a medium mixing bowl stir together flour and salt. In a small mixing bowl stir together egg and milk. Stir egg mixture into dry mixture.
3. Hold a colander with large holes over the pan of boiling water; pour spaetzle batter into the colander and immediately press the batter through the holes with a wooden spoon. (Or, use a spaetzle maker following the manufacturer's directions.) Cook for 5 to 10 minutes or till spaetzle are tender but still firm, stirring occasionally. Drain well.
4. Melt margarine or butter; toss with bread crumbs. Sprinkle crumbs over hot spaetzle. Makes 4 side-dish servings.

Nutrition Facts per serving: 177 cal., 5 g total fat (1 g sat. fat), 55 mg chol., 161 mg sodium, 27 g carbo., 1 g fiber, 6 g pro. **Daily Values:** 7% vit. A, 0% vit. C, 3% calcium, 11% iron

CLASSIC SPAGHETTI SAUCE

PREP: 15 MINUTES   COOK: 40 MINUTES

To serve 4 people, cook 8 ounces of pasta; if you're serving 5, cook 10 ounces.

12 ounces ground beef or bulk pork sausage
 1 cup chopped onion (1 large)
 $^1/_2$ cup chopped green sweet pepper
 $^1/_4$ cup chopped celery
 2 cloves garlic, minced
 4 cups chopped, peeled tomatoes (6 large) or two 14$^1/_2$-ounce
     cans tomatoes, cut up
 1 6-ounce can tomato paste
 $^1/_3$ cup water
 2 tablespoons snipped fresh parsley
 1 tablespoon snipped fresh basil or 1 teaspoon dried basil,
     crushed
 1 tablespoon snipped fresh oregano or 1 teaspoon dried
     oregano, crushed
 2 teaspoons snipped fresh marjoram or $^1/_2$ teaspoon dried
     marjoram, crushed
 1 teaspoon sugar
 $^1/_2$ teaspoon salt
 $^1/_4$ teaspoon pepper
 8 or 10 ounces dried spaghetti, vermicelli, or other pasta
     Grated Parmesan cheese (optional)

1. In a large saucepan or pot cook ground beef or pork sausage, onion, sweet pepper, celery, and garlic till meat is brown. Drain fat.
2. Stir in the fresh or undrained canned tomatoes, tomato paste, water, parsley, basil, oregano, marjoram, sugar, salt, and pepper. Bring to boiling; reduce heat. Cover and simmer for 30 minutes. Uncover and simmer for 10 to 15 minutes more or to desired consistency, stirring occasionally.
3. Meanwhile, cook spaghetti for 10 to 12 minutes or till tender but still firm (see chart, page 774). Drain well. Serve sauce over spaghetti. If desired, sprinkle with Parmesan cheese. Makes 4 or 5 main-dish servings.

Nutrition Facts per serving: 503 cal., 13 g total fat (4 g sat. fat), 53 mg chol., 374 mg sodium, 71 g carbo., 6 g fiber, 28 g pro. **Daily Values:** 26% vit. A, 125% vit. C, 5% calcium, 43% iron

LINGUINE WITH WHITE CLAM SAUCE

START TO FINISH: 25 MINUTES

Fast

8 ounces dried linguine
1 pint shucked clams or two 6¹/₂-ounce cans minced clams
Half-and-half, light cream, or milk
¹/₂ cup chopped onion (1 medium)
2 cloves garlic, minced
2 tablespoons margarine or butter
¹/₄ cup all-purpose flour
2 teaspoons snipped fresh oregano or ¹/₂ teaspoon dried
   oregano, crushed
¹/₄ teaspoon salt
¹/₈ teaspoon pepper
¹/₄ cup snipped fresh parsley
¹/₄ cup dry white wine
¹/₄ cup grated Parmesan cheese

1. Cook linguine 8 to 10 minutes or till tender but still firm (see chart, page 774). Drain; keep warm.

2. Meanwhile, chop clams, reserving juice; set clams aside. Strain juice to remove bits of shell. (Or, drain canned clams, reserving the juice from 1 of the cans.) Add enough half-and-half, light cream, or milk to the reserved clam juices to equal 2 cups.

3. For sauce, in a medium saucepan cook onion and garlic in margarine or butter till tender but not brown. Stir in flour, oregano, salt, and pepper. Add half-and-half mixture all at once. Cook and stir till thickened and bubbly. Cook and stir for 1 minute more. Stir in clams, parsley, and wine. Heat through. Serve sauce over linguine. Sprinkle with Parmesan cheese. Makes 4 main-dish servings.

Nutrition Facts per serving: 475 cal., 17 g total fat (7 g sat. fat), 85 mg chol., 394 mg sodium, 59 g carbo., 1 g fiber, 21 g pro. **Daily Values:** 18% vit. A, 12% vit. C, 19% calcium, 45% iron

PASTA WITH RED CLAM SAUCE

PREP: 5 MINUTES   COOK: 35 MINUTES

Low-Fat

If you like your pasta flavored with garlic and pepper, you'll love this seafood classic.

        3   cloves garlic, minced
        1   tablespoon olive oil or cooking oil
    $^1/_4$ teaspoon coarsely ground black pepper
    $^1/_8$ to $^1/_4$ teaspoon crushed red pepper
        1   10-ounce can whole baby clams
        2   14$^1/_2$-ounce cans whole Italian-style tomatoes, cut up
        2   tablespoons snipped fresh parsley
    1$^1/_2$ teaspoons snipped fresh basil or $^1/_2$ teaspoon dried basil,
            crushed
    $^1/_2$ teaspoon anchovy paste (optional)
        3   cups dried mostaccioli or cavatelli

1. For sauce, in a large skillet cook garlic in hot oil over medium heat about 30 seconds. Add black pepper and red pepper. Cook and stir for 30 seconds more. Remove from heat.

2. Drain clams, reserving juice. Set clams aside. Add reserved clam juice and undrained tomatoes to skillet. Stir in parsley, basil, and, if desired, anchovy paste. Bring to boiling; reduce heat. Simmer, uncovered, for 30 to 35 minutes or to desired consistency. Stir in clams; heat through.

3. Meanwhile, cook mostaccioli about 14 minutes or till tender but still firm (see chart, page 774). Drain well. Serve sauce over mostaccioli. Makes 4 main-dish servings.

Nutrition Facts per serving: 325 cal., 6 g total fat (1 g sat. fat), 44 mg chol., 375 mg sodium, 55 g carbo., 2 g fiber, 15 g pro. **Daily Values:** 13% vit. A, 53% vit. C, 9% calcium, 44% iron

PASTA WITH BOLOGNESE SAUCE

PREP: 10 MINUTES   COOK: 45 MINUTES

Bolognese (boh-luh-NEEZ) sauce is full of meat and vegetables with a little red wine and cream.

- 12 ounces ground beef or bulk sweet Italian sausage
- 1 cup chopped onion
- 1/2 cup chopped green sweet pepper
- 1/4 cup chopped celery
- 2 cloves garlic, minced
- 4 cups chopped, peeled tomatoes (6 large) or two 14 1/2-ounce cans tomatoes, cut up
- 1 6-ounce can tomato paste
- 1/4 cup dry red wine
- 2 tablespoons snipped fresh parsley
- 1 tablespoon snipped fresh basil or 1 teaspoon dried basil, crushed
- 1 tablespoon snipped fresh oregano or 1 teaspoon dried oregano, crushed
- 2 teaspoons snipped fresh marjoram or 1/2 teaspoon dried marjoram, crushed
- 1 teaspoon sugar
- 3/4 cup whipping cream
- 10 to 12 ounces dried spaghetti

1. In a large saucepan or pot cook the ground beef or sausage, onion, sweet pepper, celery, and garlic till meat is brown and onion is tender. Drain fat.

2. Carefully stir in fresh or undrained canned tomatoes, tomato paste, wine, parsley, basil, oregano, marjoram, sugar, 1/2 teaspoon *salt*, and 1/4 teaspoon *pepper*. Bring to boiling; reduce heat. Cover; simmer for 30 minutes. Uncover; simmer 10 to 15 minutes more or to desired consistency, stirring occasionally. Stir in cream; heat through.

3. Meanwhile, cook spaghetti for 10 to 12 minutes or till tender but still firm (see chart, page 774). Drain well. Serve sauce over spaghetti. Makes 5 to 6 main-dish servings.

Nutrition Facts per serving: 579 cal., 24 g total fat (12 g sat. fat), 92 mg chol., 320 mg sodium, 67 g carbo., 5 g fiber, 25 g pro. **Daily Values:** 36% vit. A, 100% vit. C, 6% calcium, 38% iron

PASTA WITH WHITE BEAN SAUCE

START TO FINISH: 25 MINUTES

Fast

$^1/_2$ cup chopped onion (1 medium)
2 cloves garlic, minced
1 tablespoon margarine or butter
2 tablespoons all-purpose flour
$1^1/_3$ cups milk
$1^1/_2$ cups shredded process Swiss, Gruyère, or American cheese (6 ounces)
1 15-ounce can great Northern, navy, or white kidney beans, drained
1 4-ounce can diced green chili peppers, drained
8 ounces dried linguine or spaghetti

1. In a saucepan cook onion and garlic in hot margarine till tender. Stir in flour and $^1/_8$ teaspoon *pepper*. Add milk all at once. Cook and stir over medium heat till thickened and bubbly. Cook and stir for 1 minute more. Add cheese; stir till melted. Stir in drained beans and chili peppers; heat through.

2. Meanwhile, cook linguine for 8 to 10 minutes or till tender but still firm (see chart, page 774). Drain well. Serve the sauce over linguine. Makes 4 main-dish servings.

Nutrition Facts per serving: 525 cal., 17 g total fat (8 g sat. fat), 42 mg chol., 902 mg sodium, 71 g carbo., 6 g fiber, 28 g pro. **Daily Values:** 18% vit. A, 19% vit. C, 42% calcium, 27% iron

FETTUCCINE ALLA CARBONARA

START TO FINISH: 25 MINUTES

Fast

You can substitute pancetta for the bacon: It is cured but not smoked, with a pleasant, mild flavor.

6 slices bacon, cut into 1-inch pieces
6 ounces dried fettuccine or linguine
1 beaten egg
1 cup half-and-half, light cream, or milk
2 tablespoons margarine or butter
$^1/_2$ cup grated Parmesan or Romano cheese
$^1/_4$ cup snipped fresh parsley
    Coarsely ground pepper

1. Cook bacon till crisp. Drain on paper towels.

2. Cook fettuccine for 8 to 10 minutes or till tender but still firm (see chart, page 774). Drain well.

3. Meanwhile, for sauce, in a small saucepan combine egg, half-and-half, and margarine. Cook and stir over medium heat till egg mixture just coats a metal spoon (about 6 minutes). Immediately pour sauce over fettuccine; toss gently to coat.

4. Add Parmesan cheese and parsley; toss gently to mix. Season with pepper. Serve immediately. Makes 6 side-dish servings.

Nutrition Facts per serving: 287 cal., 15 g total fat (7 g sat. fat), 62 mg chol., 330 mg sodium, 25 g carbo., 0 g fiber, 12 g pro. **Daily Values:** 14% vit. A, 9% vit. C, 14% calcium, 10% iron

---

PASTA WITH FRESH TOMATO AND BASIL SAUCE

PREP: 20 MINUTES   COOK: 45 MINUTES

Give this sauce a Mediterranean flavor by omitting the basil and adding 3 tablespoons drained capers and 10 sliced pitted ripe olives.

$^1/_4$ cup finely chopped onion
2 cloves garlic, minced
2 tablespoons olive oil, margarine, or butter
3 pounds ripe fresh tomatoes, peeled, seeded, and chopped
    (about 4 cups)

$^1/_4$ cup snipped fresh basil or 2 teaspoons dried basil, crushed
   6 ounces dried capellini or spaghetti

1. For sauce, cook the onion and garlic in hot oil till onion is tender but not brown.

2. Carefully stir in tomatoes, $^1/_4$ teaspoon *salt*, and $^1/_4$ teaspoon *pepper*. Bring to boiling; reduce heat. Simmer, uncovered, 35 to 40 minutes or to desired consistency. Stir in basil. Cook 5 minutes more.

3. Meanwhile, cook capellini for 5 to 6 minutes or till tender but still firm (see chart, page 774). Drain well. Serve the sauce over capellini. Makes 6 side-dish servings.

Nutrition Facts per serving: 205 cal., 6 g total fat (1 g sat. fat), 0 mg chol., 111 mg sodium, 34 g carbo., 3 g fiber, 6 g pro. **Daily Values:** 14% vit. A, 73% vit. C, 1% calcium, 14% iron

---

PASTA WITH MARINARA SAUCE

PREP: 20 MINUTES   COOK: 30 MINUTES

   1 cup chopped onion (1 large)
$^1/_2$ cup chopped green sweet pepper
$^1/_4$ cup coarsely chopped carrot
$^1/_4$ cup sliced celery
   2 cloves garlic, minced
   2 tablespoons olive oil or cooking oil
   2 cups chopped, peeled tomatoes (3 large) or one 14$^1/_2$-ounce
       can tomatoes, cut up
$^1/_2$ of a 6-ounce can ($^1/_3$ cup) tomato paste
   2 teaspoons snipped fresh basil or $^3/_4$ teaspoon dried basil,
       crushed
   2 teaspoons snipped fresh oregano or $^1/_2$ teaspoon dried
       oregano, crushed
   1 teaspoon snipped fresh thyme or $^1/_4$ teaspoon dried thyme,
       crushed
$^1/_2$ teaspoon sugar
   4 ounces dried spaghetti or linguine

1. In a large skillet cook onion, sweet pepper, carrot, celery, and garlic in hot oil till tender. Stir in fresh or undrained canned tomatoes, tomato paste, basil, oregano, thyme, sugar, $^1/_4$ cup *water*, $^1/_2$ teaspoon *salt*, and $^1/_8$ teaspoon *pepper*. Bring to boiling; reduce heat.

Cover and simmer 30 minutes. If necessary, uncover and simmer 10 to 15 minutes more or to desired consistency; stir occasionally.

2. Meanwhile, cook spaghetti 10 to 12 minutes or till tender but still firm (see chart, page 774). Drain well. Serve with sauce. Makes 4 side-dish servings.

Nutrition Facts per serving: 247 cal., 8 g total fat (1 g sat. fat), 0 mg chol., 309 mg sodium, 40 g carbo., 4 g fiber, 7 g pro. **Daily Values:** 32% vit. A, 71% vit. C, 3% calcium, 18% iron

---

PESTO FOR PASTA

START TO FINISH: 30 MINUTES

Fast

What else can you do with pesto? Try serving just a little bit with soup—the Chilled Carrot Soup (see page 1021) or Cheese Soup (see page 1020) are two good choices. Or spread it on a small, thin slice of toasted French bread for an appetizer.

- 1 cup firmly packed fresh basil leaves
- $^1/_2$ cup firmly packed fresh parsley sprigs with stems removed or torn fresh spinach
- $^1/_2$ cup grated Parmesan or Romano cheese
- $^1/_4$ cup pine nuts, walnuts, or almonds
- 1 large clove garlic, quartered
- $^1/_4$ teaspoon salt
- $^1/_4$ cup olive oil or cooking oil
- 12 ounces dried fettuccine or spaghetti

1. For pesto, in a blender container or food processor bowl combine basil, parsley, Parmesan or Romano cheese, nuts, garlic, and salt. Cover and blend or process with several on-off turns till a paste forms, stopping the machine several times and scraping the sides.

2. With the machine running slowly, gradually add olive oil or cooking oil and blend or process to the consistency of soft butter.

3. Cook fettuccine 8 to 10 minutes or till tender but still firm (see chart, page 774). Drain well. Return fettuccine to pan. Toss pesto with fettuccine. Serve immediately. Makes 12 side-dish servings.

Note: If you're not serving the pesto immediately, divide it into 3 portions of about $^1/_4$ cup each. Place each portion in a small airtight container and refrigerate 1 to 2 days or freeze up to 3 months.

Nutrition Facts per serving: 188 cal., 8 g total fat (2 g sat. fat), 3 mg chol., 126 mg sodium, 23 g carbo., 0 g fiber, 7 g pro. **Daily Values:** 3% vit. A, 11% vit. C, 6% calcium, 11% iron

■ **Spinach Pesto for Pasta:** Prepare as above, except substitute torn *fresh spinach* for the fresh basil and parsley. Add 1 teaspoon *dried basil,* crushed.

Nutrition Facts per serving: 192 cal., 8 g total fat (2 g sat. fat)

■ **Lower-Fat Pesto for Pasta:** Prepare as above, except substitute torn *fresh spinach* for the fresh parsley. Decrease cheese to ¼ cup and oil to 2 tablespoons. Add 2 tablespoons *water* with the oil and continue as directed.

Nutrition Facts per serving: 161 cal., 5 g total fat (1 g sat. fat)

SPAGHETTI AND MEATBALLS

PREP: 40 MINUTES   BAKE: 15 MINUTES   Oven 350°

    1 cup sliced fresh mushrooms
   ¾ cup chopped onion
    2 cloves garlic, minced
    1 tablespoon olive oil or cooking oil
    4 cups chopped, peeled tomatoes (6 large) or two 14½-ounce
         cans tomatoes, cut up
    1 6-ounce can tomato paste
    2 tablespoons snipped fresh parsley
    2 teaspoons dried Italian seasoning, crushed
    1 teaspoon sugar
   ¼ teaspoon pepper
    1 beaten egg
   ¾ cup soft bread crumbs (1 slice)
   ¼ cup finely chopped onion
    2 tablespoons finely chopped green sweet pepper
   ¼ teaspoon dried oregano, crushed
   12 ounces ground beef or bulk pork sausage
    8 to 12 ounces dried spaghetti, linguine, or other pasta

1. For sauce, in a large pot cook mushrooms, the ¾ cup onion, and garlic in hot oil till onion is tender. Stir in the fresh or undrained canned tomatoes, tomato paste, parsley, Italian seasoning, sugar, and pepper. Bring to boiling; reduce heat. Cover and simmer for 30 minutes, stirring once or twice.

2. Meanwhile, in a large mixing bowl combine egg, bread crumbs, the $^1/_4$ cup onion, sweet pepper, oregano, and $^1/_4$ teaspoon *salt*. Add ground beef; mix well. Shape into 24 meatballs (see tip, below). Arrange meatballs in a 15×10×1-inch baking pan. Bake in a 350° oven 15 to 20 minutes or till no pink remains. Drain well.

3. Cook spaghetti for 10 to 12 minutes or till tender but still firm (see chart, page 774). Drain. Serve the sauce and meatballs over spaghetti. Makes 4 to 6 main-dish servings.

Nutrition Facts per serving: 576 cal., 18 g total fat (5 g sat. fat), 107 mg chol., 290 mg sodium, 76 g carbo., 6 g fiber, 31 g pro.
Daily Values: 28% vit. A, 121% vit. C, 7% calcium, 49% iron

MEASURING MEATBALLS

For 24 meatballs of equal size, shape meat mixture into a 6×4-inch rectangle on waxed paper. Cut into 1-inch squares; roll each square into a ball.

ONE-POT SPAGHETTI

START TO FINISH: 40 MINUTES

Low-Fat

This easy spaghetti lets you cook the pasta right in the tomato sauce, so there's one less saucepan to wash.

    8 ounces ground beef or bulk pork sausage
    1 cup sliced fresh mushrooms or one 6-ounce jar sliced
        mushrooms, drained
  $^1/_2$ cup chopped onion (1 medium)
    1 clove garlic, minced, or $^1/_8$ teaspoon garlic powder
    1 14$^1/_2$-ounce can chicken broth or beef broth
1$^3/_4$ cups water
    1 6-ounce can tomato paste
    1 teaspoon dried oregano, crushed
  $^1/_2$ teaspoon dried basil or marjoram, crushed
  $^1/_4$ teaspoon pepper
    6 ounces dried spaghetti, broken
  $^1/_4$ cup grated Parmesan cheese

1. In a large saucepan cook the ground beef or pork sausage, fresh mushrooms (if using), onion, and garlic till meat is brown and onion is tender. Drain fat.

2. Stir in the canned mushrooms (if using), chicken or beef broth, water, tomato paste, oregano, basil or marjoram, and pepper. Bring to boiling. Add the broken spaghetti, a little at a time, stirring constantly. Return to boiling; reduce heat. Boil gently, uncovered, for 17 to 20 minutes or till spaghetti is tender and sauce is of the desired consistency, stirring frequently. Serve with Parmesan cheese. Makes 4 main-dish servings.

Nutrition Facts per serving: 376 cal., 11 g total fat (4 g sat. fat), 41 mg chol., 506 mg sodium, 46 g carbo., 3 g fiber, 24 g pro. **Daily Values:** 12% vit. A, 33% vit. C, 10% calcium, 31% iron

---

BAKED RAVIOLI WITH MEAT SAUCE

PREP: 25 MINUTES   BAKE: 45 MINUTES   Oven 350°

For individual servings, layer the meat sauce, ravioli, and cheese in six 10-ounce casseroles. Bake, covered, for 25 to 30 minutes.

    8 ounces ground beef, ground pork, or bulk pork sausage
 $1/2$ cup finely chopped carrot (1 medium)
 $1/3$ cup chopped onion (1 small)
    1 clove garlic, minced
    1 $14^{1}/2$-ounce can diced tomatoes
    1 cup water*
    1 6-ounce can tomato paste
 $1/2$ cup diced fully cooked ham or crumbled, crisp-cooked bacon
    2 teaspoons sugar
    2 teaspoons dried Italian seasoning, crushed
 $1/4$ teaspoon pepper
 $1/2$ of a $27^{1}/2$- or 30-ounce package frozen cheese-filled ravioli or
      one 15- or 16-ounce package frozen cheese-filled tortellini
    1 cup shredded mozzarella cheese (4 ounces)

1. For meat sauce, in a large skillet cook ground meat, carrot, onion, and garlic till meat is brown and onion is tender. Drain fat.

2. Stir in undrained tomatoes, water, tomato paste, ham or bacon, sugar, Italian seasoning, and pepper. Bring to boiling; reduce heat. Simmer, uncovered, for 5 minutes, stirring occasionally.

3. Spoon one-third of the meat sauce into a 2-quart square baking dish. Arrange frozen ravioli or tortellini atop the meat sauce. Sprinkle with ½ *cup* of the mozzarella cheese. Top with the remaining meat sauce.

4. Bake, covered, in a 350° oven for 40 to 45 minutes or till pasta is tender. Uncover and sprinkle with remaining mozzarella cheese. Bake about 5 minutes more or till cheese melts. Makes 6 main-dish servings.

*Note: If desired, reduce the water to ¾ cup and add ¼ cup *dry red wine* to sauce.

Nutrition Facts per serving: 401 cal., 17 g total fat (9 g sat. fat), 98 mg chol., 666 mg sodium, 37 g carbo., 2 g fiber, 26 g pro. **Daily Values:** 55% vit. A, 44% vit. C, 26% calcium, 24% iron

LASAGNA

PREP: 35 MINUTES   BAKE: 30 MINUTES   STAND: 10 MINUTES   Oven 375°

```
12  ounces ground beef, ground pork, bulk pork sausage, or bulk
       Italian sausage
 1  cup chopped onion (1 large)
 2  cloves garlic, minced
 1  7½-ounce can tomatoes, cut up
 1  8-ounce can tomato sauce
 1  6-ounce can tomato paste
 2  teaspoons dried basil, crushed
 1  teaspoon dried oregano, crushed
 1  teaspoon fennel seed, crushed (optional)
 6  dried lasagna noodles
 1  beaten egg
 1  15-ounce container ricotta cheese or 2 cups cream-style cottage
       cheese, drained
¼  cup grated Parmesan or Romano cheese
 3  tablespoons snipped fresh parsley (optional)
 6  ounces sliced or shredded mozzarella cheese
    Grated Parmesan cheese (optional)
```

1. For sauce, in a medium saucepan cook meat, onion, and garlic till meat is brown. Drain fat.

2. Stir in undrained tomatoes, tomato sauce, tomato paste, basil, oregano, fennel seed (if desired), and ¼ teaspoon *pepper*. Bring to boiling; reduce heat. Cover; simmer 15 minutes, stirring occasionally.

3. Meanwhile, cook noodles for 10 to 12 minutes or till tender but still firm (see chart, page 774). Drain noodles; rinse with cold water. Drain well.

4. For filling, combine the egg, ricotta or cottage cheese, the ¼ cup Parmesan or Romano cheese, and, if desired, the parsley.

5. Layer half of the cooked noodles in a 2-quart rectangular baking dish. Spread with half of the filling. Top with half of the meat sauce and *half* of the mozzarella cheese. Repeat layers. If desired, sprinkle additional Parmesan cheese on top.

6. Bake in a 375° oven for 30 to 35 minutes or till heated through. Let stand 10 minutes before serving. Makes 8 main-dish servings.

■ **Make-ahead directions:** Prepare as above, except, after assembling, cover and refrigerate for up to 24 hours. Bake, covered, in a 375° oven for 40 minutes. Uncover; bake about 20 minutes more or till hot. Let stand for 10 minutes before serving.

Nutrition Facts per serving: 356 cal., 16 g total fat (8 g sat. fat), 87 mg chol., 495 mg sodium, 28 g carbo., 2 g fiber, 27 g pro. **Daily Values:** 23% vit. A, 27% vit. C, 32% calcium, 21% iron

---

SPINACH LASAGNA

PREP: 25 MINUTES   BAKE: 30 MINUTES STAND: 10 MINUTES   Oven 375°

The standing time allows the lasagna to set up so that it will hold its shape when cut.

   9 **dried lasagna noodles**
   1 **cup chopped onion (1 large)**
   1 **cup sliced fresh mushrooms**
   4 **cloves garlic, minced**
   2 **tablespoons margarine or butter**
   1 **7-ounce jar roasted red sweet peppers, drained and chopped***
   1 **10-ounce package frozen chopped spinach, thawed and well drained**
   1 **15-ounce container ricotta cheese**
   1 **cup shredded mozzarella cheese**
 ½ **cup grated Parmesan or Romano cheese**
   2 **beaten eggs**
   1 **teaspoon dried basil, crushed**
 ½ **teaspoon dried oregano, crushed**
   1 **30½-ounce jar meatless spaghetti sauce**
 ¼ **cup grated Parmesan or Romano cheese**

1. Cook lasagna noodles for 10 to 12 minutes or till tender but still firm (see chart, page 774). Drain noodles; rinse with cold water. Drain well.

2. Meanwhile, in a large skillet cook onion, mushrooms, and garlic in hot margarine till tender but not brown; stir in sweet peppers. Set aside.

3. Pat spinach dry with paper towels. In a medium bowl stir together spinach, ricotta cheese, mozzarella cheese, the $1/2$ cup Parmesan cheese, eggs, basil, oregano, and $1/4$ teaspoon *pepper*. Stir sweet pepper mixture into spinach mixture.

4. Spread $1/2$ *cup* of the spaghetti sauce evenly in a 3-quart rectangular baking dish. Arrange 3 lasagna noodles over sauce. Layer with half the sweet pepper-spinach mixture and 1 cup of the spaghetti sauce. Repeat layers, ending with noodles. Spoon remaining spaghetti sauce over the top. Sprinkle with the $1/4$ cup Parmesan cheese.

5. Bake, covered, in a 375° oven for 20 minutes. Uncover and bake about 10 minutes more or till heated through. Let stand 10 minutes before serving. Makes 8 main-dish servings.

*****Note:** If desired, omit the jar of roasted red peppers, and roast 2 *fresh red sweet peppers* (see Capellini with Roasted Red Peppers, page 770). Chop the roasted peppers.

Nutrition Facts per serving: 455 cal., 19 g total fat (8 g sat. fat), 105 mg chol., 980 mg sodium, 50 g carbo., 3 g fiber, 22 g pro. **Daily Values:** 62% vit. A, 111% vit. C, 38% calcium, 23% iron

---

STORING PASTA

■ Dried pasta keeps indefinitely on a shelf in a cool, dry place. Be sure the package is tightly closed.

■ Refrigerated fresh pasta should be stored in its original container following the package directions or up to 5 days. For longer storage, freeze up to 8 months.

■ Cooked pasta can be kept refrigerated for a day or two if it is sealed in an airtight container. Reheat pasta in a sauce or clear broth.

PASTA PIZZA

PREP: 30 MINUTES BAKE: 30 MINUTES   Oven 350°

Low-Fat

Instead of the typical flour-based crust, this pizza-inspired main dish has a rotini (corkscrew macaroni) "crust."

   2 cups dried rotini (5 ounces)
   1 beaten egg
 $^1/_4$ cup milk
   2 tablespoons grated Parmesan cheese
   8 ounces ground beef
 $^1/_3$ cup chopped onion (1 small)
   1 clove garlic, minced
   1 medium green or yellow sweet pepper, cut into 2-inch-long
        strips (1 cup)
   1 14$^1/_2$-ounce can Italian-style stewed tomatoes
 $^1/_2$ teaspoon dried Italian seasoning, crushed
   1 4$^1/_2$-ounce jar sliced mushrooms, drained
 $^1/_8$ to $^1/_4$ teaspoon crushed red pepper
   1 cup shredded mozzarella cheese (4 ounces)

1. Cook rotini for 8 to 10 minutes or till tender but still firm (see chart, page 774). Drain rotini; rinse with cold water. Drain well.
2. For pasta crust, in a large mixing bowl combine egg, milk, and Parmesan cheese. Stir in cooked rotini. Spread rotini mixture evenly in a greased 12-inch pizza pan. Bake in a 350° oven 20 minutes.
3. Meanwhile, in a large skillet cook ground beef, onion, and garlic till meat is brown and onion is tender. Drain fat. Add sweet pepper strips, undrained tomatoes (cut up any large pieces), and Italian seasoning to meat mixture. Bring to boiling; reduce heat. Simmer, uncovered, for 10 to 12 minutes or till sweet peppers are crisp-tender and most of the liquid is evaporated, stirring once or twice. Stir in sliced mushrooms and crushed red pepper.
4. Spoon meat mixture over baked crust. Sprinkle with mozzarella cheese. Bake in the 350° oven 10 to 12 minutes or till heated through and cheese melts. To serve, cut into wedges. Makes 6 main-dish servings.

Nutrition Facts per serving: 273 cal., 10 g total fat (5 g sat. fat), 72 mg chol., 493 mg sodium, 27 g carbo., 1 g fiber, 19 g pro. **Daily Values:** 12% vit. A, 29% vit. C, 16% calcium, 15% iron

SPAGHETTI PIE

PREP: 30 MINUTES   BAKE: 20 MINUTES   Oven 350°

Low-Fat

> *To form the crust, use two forks, a wooden spoon, or a rubber
> spatula to press the spaghetti onto the bottom and up the
> sides of the pie plate.*

4 ounces dried spaghetti
1 tablespoon margarine or butter
1 beaten egg
$^1/_4$ cup grated Parmesan cheese
8 ounces ground beef
$^1/_2$ cup chopped onion (1 medium)
$^1/_2$ cup chopped green sweet pepper
1 clove garlic, minced
$^1/_2$ teaspoon fennel seed, crushed
1 8-ounce can tomato sauce
1 teaspoon dried oregano, crushed
Nonstick spray coating
1 cup low-fat cottage cheese
$^1/_2$ cup shredded part-skim mozzarella cheese

1. Cook spaghetti for 10 to 12 minutes or till tender but still firm
(see chart, page 774). Drain well.
2. Return spaghetti to warm saucepan. Stir margarine or butter into
hot pasta till melted. Stir in egg and Parmesan cheese.
3. Meanwhile, in a medium skillet cook ground beef, onion, sweet
pepper, garlic, and fennel seed till meat is brown and onion is tender. Drain fat. Stir in tomato sauce and oregano; heat through.
4. Spray a 9-inch pie plate with nonstick coating. Press spaghetti
mixture onto bottom and up sides of pie plate, forming a crust.
Spread cottage cheese on bottom and up sides of crust. Spread meat
mixture over cottage cheese. Sprinkle with shredded mozzarella
cheese.
5. Bake in a 350° oven for 20 to 25 minutes or till bubbly. Makes 6
main-dish servings.

Nutrition Facts per serving: 276 cal., 12 g total fat (5 g sat. fat), 71 mg chol., 558 mg
sodium, 22g carbo., 1 g dietary fiber, 20 g pro. **Daily Values:** 11% vit. A, 12% vit. C, 14%
calcium, 13% iron

BAKED CAVATELLI

PREP: 25 MINUTES   BAKE: 30 MINUTES   Oven 375°

Italian sausage links are available either mild or hot—use whichever you prefer.

- 2¹/₂ **cups dried cavatelli or wagon-wheel macaroni (about 7 ounces)**
- 12 **ounces fresh Italian sausage links, sliced ¹/₂ inch thick**
- ³/₄ **cup chopped onion**
- 2 **cloves garlic, minced**
- 1 **15-ounce can tomato sauce**
- 1 **14-ounce jar spaghetti sauce with mushrooms**
- 1 **cup shredded mozzarella cheese (4 ounces)**
- 1 **teaspoon dried Italian seasoning, crushed**
- ¹/₄ **teaspoon pepper**

1. Cook cavatelli about 12 minutes or till tender but still firm (see chart, page 774). Drain well.

2. In a large skillet cook the sausage, onion, and garlic till sausage is no longer pink; remove from skillet. Drain fat.

3. In a large mixing bowl stir together the tomato sauce, spaghetti sauce, *¹/₂ cup* of the mozzarella cheese, the Italian seasoning, and pepper. Add the cooked pasta, sausage, and the onion mixture. Toss gently to combine. Spoon the mixture into a 2-quart casserole.*

4. Bake, covered, in a 375° oven for 25 minutes. Uncover and sprinkle with the remaining ¹/₂ cup mozzarella cheese. Bake for 5 to 10 minutes more or till heated through. Makes 6 main-dish servings.

*Note: To serve individual portions, spoon the mixture into 6 individual casseroles. Place the casseroles on a large baking sheet. Cover the casseroles with foil and bake for 15 minutes. Uncover, sprinkle with remaining cheese, and bake for 5 to 10 minutes more or till heated through.

Nutrition Facts per serving: 418 cal., 17 g total fat (6 g sat. fat), 50 mg chol., 1,268 mg sodium, 46 g carbo., 3 g fiber, 20 g pro. **Daily Values:** 22% vit. A, 25% vit. C, 15% calcium, 20% iron

PASTA SKILLET WITH SPICY PEPPERONI SAUCE

A little red wine boosts the flavor of the sauce.

2 cups dried cavatelli or wagon-wheel macaroni (6 ounces)
1 16-ounce can whole Italian-style tomatoes
$^1/_2$ of a 6-ounce can tomato paste ($^1/_3$ cup)
$^1/_4$ cup dry red wine or water
1 tablespoon snipped fresh basil or 1 teaspoon dried basil,
    crushed
1 teaspoon sugar
8 ounces ground turkey sausage or bulk pork sausage
$^1/_2$ cup chopped onion (1 medium)
$^1/_4$ cup chopped green sweet pepper
$^1/_2$ of a $3^1/_2$-ounce package sliced hot and spicy pepperoni,
    chopped ($^1/_2$ cup)
1 cup shredded mozzarella, provolone, or fontina cheese (4
    ounces)

1. Cook cavatelli about 12 minutes or till tender but still firm (see chart, page 774). Drain well; keep cavatelli warm.
2. Meanwhile, in a blender container or food processor bowl combine undrained tomatoes, tomato paste, red wine or water, basil, and sugar. Cover and blend or process till smooth. Set aside.
3. In a large skillet cook turkey or pork sausage, onion, and sweet pepper till sausage is no longer pink and onion is tender. Drain fat.
4. Stir in tomato mixture and pepperoni. Bring to boiling; reduce heat. Cover and simmer for 10 minutes, stirring occasionally. Stir cooked cavatelli into meat mixture in skillet. Sprinkle mozzarella cheese over pasta mixture. Cover and heat just till cheese begins to melt. Makes 4 main-dish servings.

Nutrition Facts per serving: 477 cal., 18 g total fat (8 g sat. fat), 37 mg chol., 1,029 mg sodium, 47 g carbo., 2 g fiber, 29 g pro. **Daily Values:** 17% vit. A, 53% vit. C, 20% calcium, 29% iron

TURKEY-AND-BROCCOLI-FILLED LASAGNA ROLLS

PREP: 30 MINUTES   BAKE: 30 MINUTES   Oven 375°

Instead of layering lasagna noodles in the traditional manner, this
recipe calls for rolling them around the filling in a spiral.

     4 dried lasagna noodles
     6 ounces ground raw turkey or chicken
  1/4 cup chopped onion
     1 cup chopped broccoli
  1/4 cup water
     1 beaten egg
     1 cup ricotta cheese or cream-style cottage cheese, drained
  1 1/2 teaspoons snipped fresh thyme or 1/2 teaspoon dried thyme,
          crushed
  1 1/2 cups meatless spaghetti sauce
  1/4 cup finely shredded Parmesan cheese

1. Cook lasagna noodles for 10 to 12 minutes or till tender but still
firm (see chart, page 774). Drain noodles; rinse with cold water.
Drain well.
2. Meanwhile, for filling, in a large skillet cook ground turkey and
onion till turkey is no longer pink and onion is tender. Drain fat. Stir
in chopped broccoli and water. Bring to boiling; reduce heat. Cover
and simmer about 5 minutes or till broccoli is crisp-tender; drain.
3. In a mixing bowl stir together egg, ricotta or cottage cheese, and
thyme; stir in the turkey mixture. Divide filling mixture into 4 equal
portions. Spread a portion over each lasagna noodle; roll up each
noodle. Place lasagna rolls, seam sides down, in a 2-quart square
baking dish. Spoon spaghetti sauce over lasagna rolls.
4. Bake, covered, in a 375° oven about 30 minutes or till heated
through. Uncover and sprinkle with the Parmesan cheese. Or, garnish with shaved Parmesan (use a vegetable peeler to slice thin
pieces of cheese). Makes 4 main-dish servings.

Nutrition Facts per serving: 383 cal., 16 g total fat (5 g sat. fat), 93 mg chol., 666 mg
sodium, 38 g carbo., 2 g fiber, 23 g pro. **Daily Values:** 28% vit. A, 66% vit. C, 24%
calcium, 18% iron

SCALLOPED MACARONI AND HAM

PREP: 30 MINUTES   BAKE: 30 MINUTES   Oven 350°

*Kids will really go for this homey macaroni casserole because it tastes
so good; parents will appreciate it because it's so easy to make.*

  1 cup dried elbow macaroni (4 ounces)
 ¼ cup chopped onion
  2 tablespoons margarine or butter
  2 tablespoons all-purpose flour
  1 teaspoon snipped fresh basil or ¼ teaspoon dried basil,
        crushed
 ⅛ teaspoon pepper
1½ cups milk
  1 cup diced fully cooked ham
 ½ cup frozen peas
 ½ cup soft bread crumbs
  1 tablespoon margarine or butter, melted

1. Cook macaroni about 10 minutes or till tender but still firm (see
chart, page 774). Drain well.

2. Meanwhile, for sauce, in a medium saucepan cook onion in the 2
tablespoons margarine or butter till tender but not brown. Stir in
flour, basil, and pepper. Add milk all at once. Cook and stir till thickened and bubbly. Remove from heat.

3. Stir in the cooked macaroni, ham, and frozen peas. Transfer mixture to a 1-quart casserole. Toss together the bread crumbs and the 1
tablespoon melted margarine or butter. Sprinkle crumbs atop the
macaroni mixture.

4. Bake in a 350° oven about 30 minutes or till bubbly. Makes 4
main-dish servings.

Nutrition Facts per serving: 327 cal., 13 g total fat (3 g sat. fat), 25 mg chol., 611 mg
sodium, 36 g carbo., 1 g fiber, 16 g pro. **Daily Values:** 17% vit. A, 17% vit. C, 11% calcium,
15% iron

FETTUCCINE WITH VEGETABLES AND PROSCIUTTO

START TO FINISH: 25 MINUTES

Fast

6 ounces dried fettuccine, broken
1 medium fennel bulb, trimmed and cut into 1-inch pieces (1¹/₂ cups)
1 tablespoon olive oil or cooking oil
¹/₂ pound fresh asparagus, bias-sliced into 1¹/₂-inch pieces
1¹/₂ cups peeled, seeded, and chopped tomatoes (3 medium)
2 ounces prosciutto or fully cooked ham, cut into thin strips (¹/₃ cup)
¹/₄ cup grated Parmesan cheese

1. Cook fettuccine in a large saucepan or pot for 8 to 10 minutes or till tender but still firm (see chart, page 774). Drain well. Return fettuccine to warm saucepan.

2. Meanwhile, in a medium skillet cook fennel in hot oil for 3 minutes. Add asparagus; cook about 4 minutes more or till nearly tender. Add tomatoes and prosciutto or ham; cook about 2 minutes or till heated through. Add vegetable mixture to fettuccine; toss gently to mix. Sprinkle with Parmesan cheese. Season to taste with salt and pepper. Makes 3 main-dish servings.

Nutrition Facts per serving: 418 cal., 13 g total fat (1 g sat. fat), 7 mg chol., 480 mg sodium, 58 g carbo., 3 g fiber, 19 g pro.. **Daily Values:** 14% vit. A, 77% vit. C, 11% calcium, 21% iron

USING REFRIGERATED FRESH PASTA

You can top refrigerated fresh pasta with your favorite sauce or use it in a recipe that calls for dried pasta. When buying refrigerated fresh pasta to be served with sauce, plan on 3 ounces for each main-dish serving and 1¹/₂ to 2 ounces for each side-dish serving. Or, substitute 6 to 8 ounces of the refrigerated fresh pasta for 4 ounces of the dried product. Cook the refrigerated pasta according to its package directions.

POTLUCK PASTA

PREP: 30 MINUTES   BAKE: 35 MINUTES   Oven 350°

Low-Fat

Turn this into a side dish by omitting the meat or tuna.

2 cups dried large shell macaroni or rotini or 1¼ cups dried
   elbow macaroni (about 5 ounces)
1 10-ounce package frozen chopped broccoli, frozen peas, or
   frozen mixed vegetables
⅓ cup chopped onion (1 small)
1 10¾-ounce can condensed cream of celery, chicken,
   mushroom, or cheddar cheese soup
1 8-ounce carton dairy sour cream
1 4-ounce can mushroom stems and pieces, drained
½ cup milk
½ cup shredded carrot
1 teaspoon dried oregano or basil, crushed, or dried dillweed
⅛ teaspoon pepper
2 cups cubed cooked chicken, turkey, or fully cooked ham, or
   one 12½-ounce can tuna, drained
2 tablespoons grated Parmesan cheese

1. Cook large shell macaroni for 12 to 14 minutes or till tender but still firm (see chart, page 774), adding the frozen vegetables and onion for the last 6 minutes of cooking time. Drain in a colander.
2. In a large mixing bowl stir together the condensed soup, sour cream, mushrooms, milk, carrot, desired herb, and pepper. Stir in drained pasta mixture and desired meat. Transfer to an ungreased 2-quart rectangular baking dish.
3. Bake, covered, in a 350° oven for 35 to 40 minutes or till heated through. Uncover; sprinkle with Parmesan cheese. Makes 8 main-dish servings.

■ **Make-ahead directions:** Prepare as above, except after assembling, cover and refrigerate up to 24 hours. Bake, covered, in a 350° oven for 45 to 50 minutes or till heated through. Uncover; sprinkle with Parmesan cheese.

Nutrition Facts per serving: 240 cal., 9 g total fat (4 g sat. fat), 49 mg chol., 439 mg sodium, 23 g carbo., 1 g fiber, 17 g pro. **Daily Values:** 32% vit. A, 26% vit. C, 9% calcium, 12% iron

TORTELLINI, CHICKEN, AND VEGETABLES

Fast

- 1/2 cup chopped onion (1 medium)
- 1 tablespoon margarine or butter
- 1 14 1/2-ounce can diced tomatoes
- 1/2 cup dry white or red wine
- 1 1/2 teaspoons snipped fresh thyme or 1/2 teaspoon dried thyme, crushed
- 1 teaspoon snipped fresh basil or 1/4 teaspoon dried basil, crushed
- 1 teaspoon snipped fresh oregano or 1/4 teaspoon dried oregano, crushed
- 1/4 teaspoon salt
- 1/8 teaspoon pepper
- 1 9-ounce package refrigerated fresh cheese-filled tortellini
- 2 cups loose-pack frozen mixed vegetables
- 2 cups chopped cooked chicken
- 1 tablespoon cornstarch
- 1/4 cup cold water

1. For sauce, in a medium saucepan cook onion in margarine or butter till onion is tender but not brown. Add undrained tomatoes, wine, thyme, basil, oregano, salt, and pepper. Bring to boiling; reduce heat. Cover and simmer for 10 minutes.

2. Meanwhile, in a large saucepan cook tortellini according to package directions, except stir in frozen vegetables along with tortellini. Drain cooked tortellini and vegetables; keep warm.

3. Stir chicken into sauce. Combine cornstarch and water; stir into sauce. Cook and stir till thickened and bubbly. Cook and stir for 2 minutes more. Pour sauce over tortellini and vegetables; toss well to coat. Makes 4 main-dish servings.

Nutrition Facts per serving: 441 cal., 13 g total fat (3 g sat. fat), 87 mg chol., 649 mg sodium, 47 g carbo., 1 g fiber, 32 g pro. **Daily Values:** 41% vit. A, 31% vit. C, 14% calcium, 24% iron

CHEESY CHICKEN AND TORTELLINI TOSS

START TO FINISH: 25 MINUTES

Fast

  1 cup dried cheese-filled tortellini
  3 cups broccoli flowerets or frozen cut broccoli
  1 tablespoon margarine or butter
  1 tablespoon all-purpose flour
  1 teaspoon caraway seed (optional)
  1 cup milk
  4 ounces process Swiss cheese, torn
  1 tablespoon coarse-grain brown mustard
  1 cup chopped cooked chicken or turkey, or fully cooked
      smoked turkey sausage, quartered lengthwise and sliced

1. In a large saucepan cook tortellini according to package directions, adding the broccoli for the last 5 minutes of cooking time. Drain; keep warm.

2. Meanwhile, for sauce, in a medium saucepan melt margarine or butter. Stir in flour and, if desired, caraway seed. Add milk all at once. Cook and stir till thickened and bubbly. Add Swiss cheese and mustard, stirring till cheese melts. Stir in chicken, turkey, or turkey sausage; heat through. Pour sauce over tortellini mixture; toss well to coat. Makes 4 main-dish servings.

Nutrition Facts per serving: 380 cal., 18 g total fat (7 g sat. fat), 62 mg chol., 814 mg sodium, 27 g carbo., 4 g fiber, 29 g pro. **Daily Values:** 30% vit. A, 145% vit. C, 37% calcium, 13% iron.

SAUCY CHICKEN RIGATONI

PREP: 15 MINUTES   COOK: 25 MINUTES

Fast   **Low-Fat**

  ¹/₂ cup chopped onion (1 medium)
    1 clove garlic, minced
    1 tablespoon cooking oil
    1 14¹/₂-ounce can tomatoes, cut up
    1 7¹/₂-ounce can tomatoes, cut up
    2 cups dried rigatoni or rotini (5 ounces)
 1¹/₄ cups water
    1 2¹/₂-ounce jar sliced mushrooms, drained

    1 teaspoon dried Italian seasoning, crushed
 ¹/₈ teaspoon ground red pepper (optional)
 1¹/₂ cups chopped cooked chicken or turkey

1. In a large saucepan cook onion and garlic in hot oil till tender but not brown. Stir in both cans of undrained tomatoes, rigatoni, water, mushrooms, Italian seasoning, and, if desired, ground red pepper. Bring to boiling; reduce heat. Cover and simmer about 20 minutes or till pasta is tender but still firm (see tip, page 729), stirring occasionally.
2. Stir in chicken or turkey; heat through. Makes 4 main-dish servings.

Nutrition Facts per serving: 321 cal., 9 g total fat (2 g sat. fat), 51 mg chol., 382 mg sodium, 38 g carbo., 2 g fiber, 23 g pro. **Daily Values:** 10% vit. A, 41% vit. C, 5% calcium, 22% iron

---

SALMON-SAUCED MOSTACCIOLI

PREP: 20 MINUTES   COOK: 20 MINUTES

 3¹/₂ cups dried mostaccioli or rigatoni (8 ounces)
 ¹/₂ cup chopped onion (1 medium)
 ¹/₂ of a small green or red sweet pepper, cut into bite-size strips
      (about ¹/₂ cup)
   2 tablespoons margarine or butter
 1¹/₂ cups chicken broth
   2 teaspoons snipped fresh dill or ¹/₂ teaspoon dried dillweed
 ¹/₂ cup plain low-fat yogurt
   3 tablespoons all-purpose flour
   1 15¹/₂-ounce can salmon, drained, broken into large chunks,
      and skin and bones removed
   2 tablespoons snipped fresh parsley

1. Cook mostaccioli about 14 minutes or till tender but still firm (see chart, page 774). Drain; keep warm.
2. Meanwhile, for sauce, in a medium saucepan cook onion and sweet pepper in margarine or butter till tender but not brown. Stir in *1 cup* of the broth and the dill. Bring to boiling; reduce heat. Stir together remaining broth, yogurt, and flour. Add yogurt mixture to saucepan. Cook and stir till thickened and bubbly. Cook and stir for 1 minute more. Gently stir in salmon; heat through. Serve sauce over hot mostaccioli. Sprinkle with parsley. Makes 4 main-dish servings.

Nutrition Facts per serving: 487 cal., 14 g total fat (3 g sat. fat), 63 mg chol., 990 mg sodium, 53 g carbo., 1 g fiber, 34 g pro. **Daily Values:** 10% vit. A, 17% vit. C, 25% calcium, 25% iron

PASTA WITH SCALLOPS

Fast

Low-Fat

*A tasty white wine sauce makes this pasta dish
elegant enough for company.*

  1 pound fresh or frozen sea scallops
  8 ounces dried fettuccine or linguine
  1 tablespoon margarine or butter
  1 tablespoon cooking oil
  2 to 3 cloves garlic, minced
$1^{1}/_{2}$ cups thinly bias-sliced carrots (2 large)
  2 cups sugar snap peas
$^{1}/_{3}$ cup thinly sliced green onions (3)
$^{1}/_{2}$ cup dry white wine
  1 tablespoon snipped fresh dill or 1 teaspoon dried dillweed
  1 teaspoon instant chicken bouillon granules
$^{1}/_{4}$ teaspoon crushed red pepper
  2 tablespoons cornstarch
$^{1}/_{4}$ cup grated Parmesan cheese
   Cracked black pepper

1. Thaw the sea scallops, if frozen. Halve any of the large scallops.

2. Cook fettuccine for 8 to 10 minutes or till tender but still firm (see chart, page 774). Drain well; toss with margarine or butter. Keep warm.

3. Meanwhile, pour oil into a wok or large skillet. Preheat over medium-high heat. Stir-fry garlic in hot oil for 15 seconds. Add carrots; stir-fry for 4 minutes. Add sugar snap peas and green onions. Stir-fry for 2 to 3 minutes more or till vegetables are crisp-tender. Remove vegetables from the wok.

4. Cool the wok for 1 minute. Carefully add wine, dill or dillweed, bouillon granules, crushed red pepper, and $^{1}/_{3}$ cup *water* to wok; bring to boiling. Add scallops. Reduce heat and simmer, uncovered, for 1 to 2 minutes or till scallops are opaque, stirring occasionally.

5. Stir together cornstarch and 2 tablespoons additional *water;* add to the wok. Cook and stir till thickened and bubbly. Return the vegetables to the wok. Add the fettuccine, tossing to coat; heat through.

Serve with the Parmesan cheese and black pepper. Makes 4 main-dish servings.

Nutrition Facts per serving: 467 cal., 10 g total fat (2 g sat. fat), 39 mg chol., 576 mg sodium, 61 g carbo., 4 g fiber, 28 g pro. **Daily Values:** 135% vit. A, 48% vit. C, 18% calcium, 38% iron

---

ORANGE SHRIMP WITH FETTUCCINE

START TO FINISH: 25 MINUTES

Fast   **Low-Fat**

Peel and section the oranges over a bowl to catch their juice.

12 ounces fresh or frozen peeled and deveined shrimp
6 ounces dried fettuccine or linguine
1 red or green sweet pepper, cut into ³/₄-inch squares
1 tablespoon cooking oil
¹/₂ teaspoon finely shredded orange peel
²/₃ cup orange juice
1 tablespoon cornstarch
1 teaspoon instant chicken bouillon granules
¹/₂ teaspoon toasted sesame oil
¹/₄ teaspoon salt
¹/₈ teaspoon ground red pepper
1 6-ounce package frozen pea pods, thawed
2 oranges, peeled and sectioned

1. Thaw shrimp, if frozen. Cook fettuccine for 8 to 10 minutes or till tender but still firm (see chart, page 774). Drain well; keep warm.
2. Meanwhile, in a large skillet cook sweet pepper in hot oil for 1 to 2 minutes or till crisp-tender. Remove sweet pepper. Add shrimp to skillet; cook and stir about 2 minutes or till shrimp turn pink. Remove shrimp.
3. Combine orange peel, orange juice, cornstarch, bouillon granules, sesame oil, salt, and ground red pepper; add to skillet. Cook and stir till thickened and bubbly. Return shrimp and sweet pepper to skillet; stir to coat. Gently stir in pea pods and orange sections; heat through. Serve shrimp mixture over fettuccine. Makes 4 main-dish servings.

Nutrition Facts per serving: 354 cal., 6 g total fat (1 g sat. fat), 131 mg chol., 503 mg sodium, 53 g carbo., 4 g fiber, 22 g pro. **Daily Values:** 22% vit. A, 162% vit. C, 7% calcium, 32% iron

CREAMY PESTO PASTA

START TO FINISH: 30 MINUTES

Fast

   3 cups dried rigatoni, rotini, or mostaccioli (8 ounces)
   $^1/_4$ cup chopped fresh basil or 4 teaspoons dried basil, crushed
   4 cloves garlic, minced
   1 tablespoon olive oil or cooking oil
   $^1/_2$ of an 8-ounce package reduced-fat cream cheese (Neufchâtel)
   $^1/_2$ cup low-fat cottage cheese
   $^1/_3$ cup grated Parmesan cheese
   $^1/_4$ cup snipped fresh parsley
   2 tablespoons dry white wine

1. Cook rigatoni about 15 minutes or till tender but still firm (see chart, page 774). Drain; keep warm.
2. Meanwhile, for sauce, cook basil and garlic in hot oil about 30 seconds. Reduce heat. Add cream cheese, cottage cheese, and Parmesan cheese. Heat and stir till nearly smooth. Stir in parsley, wine, and $^1/_2$ cup *water*. Cook, uncovered, for 3 minutes. Add milk or water, if necessary, to reach desired consistency. Serve sauce over rigatoni. Makes 4 main-dish servings.

Nutrition Facts per serving: 396 cal., 14 g total fat (7 g sat. fat), 31 mg chol., 388 mg sodium, 47 g carbo., 1 g fiber, 18 g pro. **Daily Values:** 13% vit. A, 9% vit. C, 15% calcium, 17% iron

VEGETARIAN PASTA

START TO FINISH: 25 MINUTES

Fast

   8 ounces dried mafalda or fettuccine, broken in half
   1 medium red, yellow, or green sweet pepper, cut into bite-size strips (1 cup)
   1 medium leek or 4 green onions, sliced
   1 cup evaporated milk
   2 teaspoons all-purpose flour
   2 teaspoons snipped fresh dill or $^1/_2$ teaspoon dried dillweed
   $^3/_4$ cup shredded Havarti or Swiss cheese
   1 small tomato, seeded and chopped

¼ cup pecan halves, toasted (see tip, page 234)
Grated Parmesan cheese (optional)

1. Cook mafalda or fettuccine 10 to 12 minutes or till tender but still firm (see chart, page 774), adding sweet pepper and leek or onions for the last 4 minutes of cooking. Drain well; keep warm.

2. Meanwhile, for sauce, in a saucepan use a fork or wire whisk to stir together evaporated milk, flour, dill, ¼ teaspoon *salt,* and ⅛ teaspoon *white pepper.* Cook and stir over medium heat till slightly thickened and bubbly. Cook and stir for 1 minute more. Add cheese; stir till melted. Stir in tomato; heat through.

3. To serve, stir ½ cup of the sauce into pasta mixture; toss gently to coat. Serve remaining sauce over pasta. Top with pecans and, if desired, Parmesan cheese. Makes 4 main-dish servings.

Nutrition Facts per serving: 469 cal., 16 g total fat (7 g sat. fat), 38 mg chol., 297 mg sodium, 61 g carbo., 3 g fiber, 20 g pro. **Daily Values:** 25% vit. A, 66% vit. C, 33% calcium, 21% iron

---

RAINBOW ROTINI WITH CHEESE SAUCE

START TO FINISH: 25 MINUTES

Fast

3½ cups dried tricolored rotini (8 ounces)
1 cup thinly bias-sliced carrots (2 medium)
1 cup coarsely chopped zucchini (1 small)
1 cup fresh whole mushrooms, quartered
2 tablespoons margarine or butter
2 tablespoons all-purpose flour
1 cup milk
¼ cup regular or nonalcoholic beer
¾ cup shredded sharp cheddar cheese (3 ounces)

1. Cook rotini for 8 to 10 minutes or till tender but still firm (see chart, page 774). Drain; keep warm.

2. Meanwhile, for sauce, in a medium saucepan cook carrots, zucchini, and mushrooms in margarine or butter till vegetables are tender. Stir in flour. Add milk all at once. Cook and stir over medium heat till thickened and bubbly. Cook and stir for 1 minute more. Add beer and heat through.

3. Remove pan from heat. Gradually add cheddar cheese, stirring just till melted. Serve sauce over rotini. Makes 4 main-dish servings.

Nutrition Facts per serving: 436 cal., 15 g total fat (6 g sat. fat), 27 mg chol., 265 mg sodium, 58 g carbo., 3 g fiber, 16 g pro. **Daily Values:** 136% vit. A, 6% vit. C, 21% calcium, 21% iron

---

TORTELLINI WITH ROSEMARY-TOMATO SAUCE

START TO FINISH: 15 MINUTES

`Fast`   `Low-Fat`

1. Cook one 9-ounce package refrigerated fresh cheese- or meat-filled *tortellini* according to package directions. Drain well; keep warm.

2. Meanwhile, for sauce, in a medium saucepan stir together one 14¹/₂-ounce can *pasta-style tomatoes,* undrained; 2 tablespoons *tomato paste;* and 2 teaspoons snipped *fresh rosemary* or ¹/₂ teaspoon *dried rosemary,* crushed. Bring to boiling; reduce heat. Simmer, uncovered, for 3 to 5 minutes or till of desired consistency. Stir in ¹/₄ cup *sliced pitted ripe olives* and ¹/₂ teaspoon finely shredded *lemon peel;* heat through. Spoon sauce over tortellini. If desired, garnish with additional *fresh rosemary.* Makes 3 main-dish servings.

Nutrition Facts per serving: 335 cal., 6 g total fat (0 g sat. fat), 47 mg chol., 1,022 mg sodium, 54 g carbo., 1 g fiber, 16 g pro. **Daily Values:** 13% vit. A, 13% vit. C, 4% calcium, 5% iron

---

THREE-CHEESE-STUFFED SHELLS

PREP: 40 MINUTES   BAKE: 25 MINUTES   Oven 350°

`Fast`

Eat up! A trio of these jumbo shells makes a generous serving.

  12 dried jumbo pasta shells
   1 beaten egg
   1 12-ounce container low-fat cottage cheese, drained
 ¹/₂ cup shredded mozzarella cheese
 ¹/₄ cup grated Parmesan cheese
   2 tablespoons snipped fresh parsley
 ¹/₂ teaspoon dried oregano, crushed
   1 14¹/₂-ounce can Italian-style stewed tomatoes, cut up

1 8-ounce can tomato sauce
Snipped fresh parsley

1. Cook pasta shells about 18 minutes or till tender but still firm (see chart, page 774). Drain well. Cool shells in a single layer on a piece of greased foil.

2. Meanwhile, for filling, stir together egg, cottage cheese, mozzarella cheese, Parmesan cheese, the 2 tablespoons parsley, and oregano. Spoon a scant ¼ cup filling into each cooked shell. Arrange filled shells in a 2-quart square baking dish.

3. Combine undrained tomatoes and tomato sauce; pour over shells in baking dish. Bake, covered, in a 350° oven for 15 minutes. Uncover and bake 10 to 15 minutes more or till heated through. Sprinkle with additional snipped parsley. Makes 4 main-dish servings.

Nutrition Facts per serving: 289 cal., 8 g total fat (4 g sat. fat), 73 mg chol., 1,247 mg sodium, 32 g carbo., 1 g fiber, 24 g pro. **Daily Values:** 22% vit. A, 29% vit. C, 22% calcium, 14% iron

---

SPINACH MANICOTTI

PREP: 40 MINUTES   BAKE: 35 MINUTES   Oven 350°

Four different cheeses—Swiss, ricotta, Parmesan, and feta—plus spinach are the major ingredients in this tasty meatless main dish.

8 dried manicotti shells
¼ cup sliced green onions (2)
1 clove garlic, minced
2 tablespoons margarine or butter
2 tablespoons all-purpose flour
1⅓ cups milk
1 cup shredded process Swiss cheese
¼ cup dry white wine or chicken broth
1 beaten egg
1 10-ounce package frozen chopped spinach, thawed and well drained
½ cup ricotta cheese
½ cup grated Parmesan cheese
½ cup crumbled feta cheese
¼ teaspoon finely shredded lemon peel
⅛ teaspoon ground nutmeg

1. Cook manicotti about 18 minutes or till tender but still firm (see chart, page 774). Drain well. Cool manicotti in a single layer on a piece of greased foil.

2. Meanwhile, for sauce, in a saucepan cook green onions and garlic in margarine or butter till tender. Stir in flour. Add milk all at once. Cook and stir till thickened and bubbly. Add Swiss cheese and wine or chicken broth, stirring till cheese melts.

3. For filling, in a mixing bowl stir together egg, spinach, ricotta cheese, Parmesan cheese, feta cheese, lemon peel, and nutmeg. Use a small spoon to fill manicotti shells with filling. Arrange filled shells in a 2-quart rectangular baking dish. Pour sauce over filled shells.

4. Bake, covered, in a 350° oven 35 to 40 minutes or till heated through. Makes 4 main-dish servings.

Nutrition Facts per serving: 551 cal., 29 g total fat (16 g sat. fat), 131 mg chol., 1,179 mg sodium, 39 g carbo., 0 g fiber, 31 g pro. **Daily Values:** 70% vit. A, 13% vit. C, 68% calcium, 20% iron

■ **Low-Fat Spinach Manicotti:** Prepare as above, except reduce margarine or butter to 1 tablespoon. Substitute *skim milk* for the milk, *reduced-fat Swiss cheese* for the Swiss cheese, an *egg white* for the egg, and *fat-free or low-fat ricotta cheese* for the ricotta and feta cheeses.

Nutrition Facts per serving: 389 cal., 11 g total fat (5 g sat. fat)

MACARONI AND CHEESE

PREP: 25 MINUTES   BAKE: 25 MINUTES   STAND: 10 MINUTES   Oven 350°

For an even richer cheese flavor, substitute natural sharp or extra-sharp cheddar cheese for half of the American cheese.

   1 cup dried elbow macaroni
 1/4 cup chopped onion
   1 tablespoon margarine or butter
   1 tablespoon all-purpose flour
     Dash pepper
1 1/4 cups milk
1 1/2 cups shredded American cheese (6 ounces)
   1 medium tomato, sliced (optional)

1. Cook macaroni in unsalted water about 10 minutes or till tender but still firm (see chart, page 774). Drain well.

2. Meanwhile, for cheese sauce, in a medium saucepan cook onion in margarine or butter till tender but not brown. Stir in flour and pepper. Add milk all at once. Cook and stir till slightly thickened and bubbly. Add American cheese, stirring till melted. Stir in cooked macaroni. Transfer mixture to a 1-quart casserole.

3. Bake in a 350° oven for 25 to 30 minutes or till hot and bubbly. If desired, arrange tomato slices atop macaroni for the last 5 minutes of baking. Let stand 10 minutes before serving. Makes 4 main-dish servings.

Nutrition Facts per serving: 342 cal., 18 g total fat (10 g sat. fat), 46 mg chol., 681 mg sodium, 29 g carbo., 0 g fiber, 16 g pro. **Daily Values:** 23% vit. A, 2% vit. C, 30% calcium, 9% iron

■ **Saucepan Macaroni and Cheese:** Prepare as above, except reduce milk to ³/₄ cup. Immediately return the drained macaroni to the saucepan in which it was cooked. Pour the cheese sauce over the macaroni; mix well. Cook over low heat for 3 to 5 minutes or till heated through, stirring frequently. Let stand 10 minutes before serving. If desired, serve with tomato slices.

Nutrition Facts per serving: 327 cal., 18 g total fat (10 g sat. fat)

FETTUCCINE ALFREDO

START TO FINISH: 35 MINUTES

Linguine or even wide noodles can be substituted for the fettuccine tossed in this classic, rich sauce of cream and Parmesan cheese.

- ¹/₃ cup half-and-half, light cream, or whipping cream
- 1 tablespoon margarine or butter
- 4 ounces dried spinach or plain fettuccine
- ¹/₃ cup grated Parmesan cheese
  Cracked black pepper
  Ground nutmeg

1. Allow half-and-half and margarine to stand at room temperature 30 minutes.

2. Meanwhile, cook fettuccine 8 to 10 minutes or till tender but still firm (see chart, page 774). Drain. Return fettuccine to warm saucepan; add half-and-half, margarine, and Parmesan cheese. Toss gently till fettuccine is well coated. Transfer to a warm serving dish. Sprinkle with pepper and nutmeg. Serve immediately. Makes 4 side-dish servings.

Nutrition Facts per serving: 203 cal., 8 g total fat (4 g sat. fat), 14 mg chol., 198 mg sodium, 24 g carbo., 0 g fiber, 8 g pro. **Daily Values:** 7% vit. A, 0% vit. C, 11% calcium, 8% iron

■ **Lemony Fettuccine Alfredo with Peas:** Prepare as above, except add ¹/₂ cup *frozen peas* to the fettuccine the last 5 minutes of cooking time. Drain well. Return fettuccine and peas to warm saucepan. Add ¹/₂ teaspoon finely shredded *lemon peel* along with the half-and-half, margarine, and Parmesan cheese. Toss gently; transfer to a warm serving dish. Omit pepper and nutmeg. If desired, sprinkle with ¹/₄ cup broken *pecans or walnuts.*

Nutrition Facts per serving: 214 cal., 8 g total fat (4 g sat. fat)

PASTA WITH VEGETABLES AND WALNUTS

START TO FINISH: 25 MINUTES

Fast

1. Cook 1 cup *dried cavatelli or medium shell macaroni* about 12 minutes or till tender but still firm (see chart, page 774), adding 2 cups *frozen cut broccoli* for the last 5 minutes of cooking time. Drain well.
2. Meanwhile, cook and stir 3 tablespoons coarsely chopped *walnuts* and 1 clove *garlic,* minced, in 2 tablespoons *margarine or butter* over low heat till nuts are toasted. Stir in ¹/₄ teaspoon *seasoned salt.* Pour over cavatelli mixture. Toss lightly to coat. Makes 4 side-dish servings.

Nutrition Facts per serving: 187 cal., 10 g total fat (1 g sat. fat), 0 mg chol., 162 mg sodium, 21 g carbo., 2 g fiber, 6 g pro. **Daily Values:** 18% vit. A, 41% vit. C, 3% calcium, 8% iron

PASTA PRIMAVERA

START TO FINISH: 25 MINUTES

Fast

  6 **ounces dried linguine or fettuccine**
  3 **tablespoons margarine or butter**

2 cups fresh broccoli flowerets
1 cup bias-sliced carrots (2 medium)
1 medium onion, cut into thin wedges
1 clove garlic, minced
1 cup fresh or frozen pea pods
$^1/_4$ to $^1/_2$ cup cashews or toasted almonds (see tip, page 234),
    coarsely chopped
$^1/_4$ cup dry white wine or chicken broth
1 teaspoon dried thyme, crushed
$^1/_4$ teaspoon pepper
$^1/_4$ cup grated Parmesan cheese

1. Cook linguine for 8 to 10 minutes or till tender but still firm (see chart, page 774). Drain well.

2. Meanwhile, in a large skillet melt *2 tablespoons* of the margarine or butter. Stir in broccoli, carrots, onion, and garlic. Cook and stir over medium-high heat about 3 minutes or till broccoli is crisp-tender.

3. Stir in pea pods. Cook 2 minutes more. Stir in cooked linguine, the remaining 1 tablespoon margarine or butter, cashews or almonds, wine or broth, thyme, and pepper. Cover and cook 1 minute more. Sprinkle with Parmesan cheese. Makes 8 side-dish servings.

Nutrition Facts per serving: 200 cal., 8 g total fat (2 g sat. fat), 2 mg chol., 161 mg sodium, 25 g carbo., 3 g fiber, 7 g pro. **Daily Values:** 69% vit. A, 60% vit. C, 7% calcium, 13% iron

MEXICAN-STYLE SPAGHETTI

START TO FINISH: 25 MINUTES

Fast   **Low-Fat**

1. Cook 4 ounces broken *dried spaghetti* 10 to 12 minutes or till tender but still firm (see chart, page 774). Drain well. Return spaghetti to pan. Add one 8$^3/_4$-ounce can *whole kernel corn,* drained; $^3/_4$ cup *chunky salsa;* $^1/_4$ cup *sliced pitted ripe olives;* and, if desired, 1 tablespoon snipped *fresh cilantro.* Toss over low heat till spaghetti is coated and mixture is hot. If desired, sprinkle with $^1/_4$ cup shredded *colby-and-Monterey-Jack cheese* and garnish with additional cilantro. Makes 4 side-dish servings.

Nutrition Facts per serving: 171 cal., 3 g total fat (0 g sat. fat), 0 mg chol., 339 mg sodium, 34 g carbo., 1 g fiber, 6 g pro. **Daily Values:** 6% vit. A, 28% vit. C, 1% calcium, 13% iron

FETTUCCINE WITH ARTICHOKES AND BASIL

START TO FINISH: 25 MINUTES

Fast   **Low-Fat**

Artichoke hearts and fresh basil dress up fettuccine for a special-occasion side dish.

- 4 ounces fettuccine or fusilli, broken
- 1 9-ounce package frozen artichoke hearts, thawed, or one 14-ounce jar or can artichoke hearts, rinsed and drained
- 1 1/2 cups chopped red or green sweet pepper (2 medium)
- 1/3 cup finely chopped onion
- 2 cloves garlic, minced
- 1 tablespoon olive oil
- 2/3 cup seeded and chopped tomato (1 medium)
- 1/4 cup snipped fresh basil or 2 teaspoons dried basil, crushed
- 2 tablespoons grated Parmesan cheese (optional)

1. Cook fettuccine 8 to 10 minutes or till tender but still firm (see chart, page 774). Drain; keep warm.
2. Meanwhile, place frozen artichoke hearts in a colander under cold running water to separate. In a large skillet cook and stir artichokes, sweet pepper, onion, and garlic in hot oil over medium-high heat about 5 minutes or till vegetables are tender.
3. Stir in tomato and basil. Cook and stir about 2 minutes more or till heated through. Add vegetable mixture to fettuccine; toss gently to mix. If desired, sprinkle each serving with Parmesan cheese. Makes 4 to 6 side-dish servings.

Nutrition Facts per serving: 256 cal., 5 g total fat (1 g sat. fat), 0 mg chol., 106 mg sodium, 47 g carbo., 1 g fiber, 11 g pro. **Daily Values:** 32% vit. A, 132% vit. C, 5% calcium, 17% iron

LEMON-BASIL PASTA WITH VEGETABLES

START TO FINISH: 30 MINUTES

Fast

- 1 cup dried rotini or bow ties (about 3 ounces)
- 1 1/2 cups loose-pack frozen broccoli, green beans, pearl onions, and red sweet peppers

   3 tablespoons margarine or butter
   1 tablespoon snipped fresh parsley
   2 teaspoons snipped fresh basil or $^1/_2$ **teaspoon** dried basil,
      crushed
   1 teaspoon finely shredded lemon peel
   1 clove garlic, minced
   Dash ground red pepper

1. Cook rotini 8 to 10 minutes or till tender but still firm (see chart, page 774), adding frozen vegetables for last 5 minutes of cooking time. Drain well.

2. Meanwhile, in a small saucepan melt the margarine or butter. Stir in parsley, basil, lemon peel, garlic, ground red pepper, and $^1/_8$ teaspoon *salt*. Pour over rotini-vegetable mixture; toss gently to coat. Makes 4 side-dish servings.

Nutrition Facts per serving: 174 cal., 9 g total fat (2 g sat. fat), 0 mg chol., 174 mg sodium, 20 g carbo., 1 g fiber, 4 g pro. **Daily Values:** 20% vit. A, 28% vit. C, 2% calcium, 8% iron

---

HOT PASTA TIPS

Hot cooked pasta that has been drained is still cooking inside. It should be used immediately so it doesn't become too soft (see tip, page 729). To keep the pasta warm for a few minutes before it is served, try one of the following suggestions.

■ Return the cooked and drained pasta to the warm cooking pan. Stir in any additional ingredients. Or, toss plain pasta with a little margarine, butter, or olive or cooking oil to help prevent it from sticking together. (If you add oil to the cooking water as suggested on page 774, it is not necessary to add more oil.) Cover the pan and let the pasta stand for no longer than 15 minutes. The heat of the pan will help keep the food warm.

■ Another option is to use a warmed serving bowl. Warm the bowl by filling it with hot water and letting it stand a few minutes to absorb the heat. Empty and dry the bowl, add the hot pasta, and serve within 5 minutes.

HERB-BUTTERED PASTA

START TO FINISH: 25 MINUTES

Fast

What could be easier and more versatile than tossing pasta with margarine or butter and an herb that complements the rest of the meal?

- 4 ounces dried spaghetti, linguine, or fettuccine
- 2 tablespoons margarine or butter, cut up, or olive oil
- 2 teaspoons snipped fresh basil, oregano, thyme, marjoram, or dill; $1/2$ teaspoon dried basil, oregano, thyme, or marjoram, crushed; or $1/2$ teaspoon dried dillweed

1. Cook spaghetti for 10 to 12 minutes or till tender but still firm (see chart, page 774). Drain well. Return spaghetti to saucepan. Add margarine, butter, or olive oil and desired herb; toss gently to coat. Season to taste with salt and pepper. Makes 4 side-dish servings.

Nutrition Facts per serving: 164 cal., 6 g total fat (1 g sat. fat), 0 mg chol., 68 mg sodium, 23 g carbo., 0 g fiber, 4 g pro. **Daily Values:** 7% vit. A, 0% vit. C, 0% calcium, 7% iron

■ **Lemon-Chive Pasta:** Prepare as above, except omit herb and add $1/4$ cup snipped *fresh chives* and 1 teaspoon finely shredded *lemon peel* with the margarine or butter.

Nutrition Facts per serving: 164 cal., 6 g total fat (1 g sat. fat)

CAPELLINI WITH ROASTED RED PEPPERS

PREP: 25 MINUTES   BAKE: 20 MINUTES   STAND: 30 MINUTES   Oven 425°

Accompany broiled chicken or fish with this colorful, delicate pasta.

- 2 large red sweet peppers
- 4 ounces dried capellini
- 2 tablespoons margarine, butter, or olive oil
- 1 cup sliced fresh mushrooms
- $1/4$ cup sliced green onions (2)
- $1/2$ teaspoon dried Italian seasoning, crushed

1 clove garlic, minced
2 tablespoons finely shredded or grated Parmesan or Romano
cheese

1. To roast sweet peppers, halve the peppers; remove and discard stems, seeds, and membranes. Cut each pepper half in half again. Place pepper, cut sides down, on a foil-lined baking sheet. Bake in a 425° oven 20 to 25 minutes or till pepper skins are blistered and dark.
2. Remove pepper skins from baking sheet; immediately wrap in foil or place in a new paper bag. Close bag and let stand about 30 minutes to steam so the skins peel away more easily. Remove skin from peppers; discard skin. Cut peppers into 1×1/2-inch strips; set aside.
3. Cook capellini for 5 to 6 minutes or till tender but still firm (see chart, page 774). Drain well; keep capellini warm.
4. Meanwhile, in a large skillet melt margarine or butter or heat olive oil. Stir in mushrooms, green onions, Italian seasoning, and garlic. Cook and stir over medium-high heat about 2 minutes or till mushrooms are tender. Remove from heat. Add the roasted pepper strips and cooked capellini to the mixture in the skillet. Toss gently to coat. Sprinkle with Parmesan or Romano cheese. Makes 4 side-dish servings.

Nutrition Facts per serving: 197 cal., 7 g total fat (1 g sat. fat), 2 mg chol., 109 mg sodium, 27 g carbo., 1 g fiber, 6 g pro. **Daily Values:** 43% vit. A, 133% vit. C, 4% calcium, 11% iron

---

ORZO PILAF

PREP: 15 MINUTES   COOK: 15 MINUTES   STAND: 5 MINUTES

Orzo, a rice-shaped pasta, also is called rosamarina.

2 cups sliced fresh mushrooms
1/2 cup chopped onion (1 medium)
2 tablespoons cooking oil
3/4 cup orzo (rosamarina)
2 cups water
1/2 cup shredded carrot (1 medium)
2 teaspoons snipped fresh marjoram or 1/2 teaspoon dried
    marjoram, crushed
1 1/2 teaspoons instant beef bouillon granules
1/8 teaspoon pepper
2 tablespoons snipped fresh parsley

1. In a large saucepan cook the mushrooms and onion in hot oil till onion is tender but not brown. Stir in the orzo. Cook and stir about 3 minutes or till orzo is lightly browned. Remove from heat.

2. Carefully stir in water, carrot, marjoram, bouillon granules, and pepper. Bring to boiling; reduce heat. Cover and simmer about 15 minutes or till orzo is tender but still firm. Remove from heat and let stand, covered, 5 minutes. Gently stir in fresh parsley with a fork. Makes 4 side-dish servings.

Nutrition Facts per serving: 214 cal., 8 g total fat (1 g sat. fat), 0 mg chol., 342 mg sodium, 31 g carbo., 2 g fiber, 6 g pro. **Daily Values:** 43% vit. A, 9% vit. C, 2% calcium, 14% iron

---

ORZO WITH ORIENTAL VEGETABLES

START TO FINISH: 20 MINUTES

Fast   **Low-Fat**

Stir some chopped cooked chicken in with the pea pods before heating to turn this side dish into a simple main dish.

  1 **cup orzo (rosamarina)**
 $^1/_2$ **cup chicken broth or water**
  2 **tablespoons soy sauce or light soy sauce**
  2 **tablespoons dry sherry**
  1 **tablespoon cornstarch**
 $^1/_4$ **teaspoon grated gingerroot or dash ground ginger**
  1 **6-ounce package frozen pea pods, thawed**
 $^1/_2$ **of an 8-ounce can sliced water chestnuts, drained**
  1 **4-ounce can sliced mushrooms, drained**

1. Cook orzo for 5 to 8 minutes or till tender but still firm (see chart, page 774). Drain well.

2. Meanwhile, in a medium saucepan stir together chicken broth or water, soy sauce, sherry, cornstarch, and gingerroot or ground ginger. Cook and stir till mixture is thickened and bubbly. Stir in pea pods, water chestnuts, and mushrooms. Cover and heat through. Spoon vegetable mixture over orzo. Makes 4 side-dish servings.

Nutrition Facts per serving: 232 cal., 1 g total fat (0 g sat. fat), 0 mg chol., 738 mg sodium, 45 g carbo., 2 g fiber, 9 g pro. **Daily Values:** 0% vit. A, 14% vit. C, 3% calcium, 21% iron

SOUTHWEST COUSCOUS

START TO FINISH: 15 MINUTES

Fast   **Low-Fat**

1 cup reduced-sodium chicken broth
$1/4$ cup sliced green onions (2)
1 4-ounce can diced green chili peppers
$1/4$ teaspoon ground turmeric
$1/8$ teaspoon pepper
$2/3$ cup quick-cooking couscous

1. In a small saucepan combine chicken broth, green onions, chili peppers, turmeric, and pepper. Bring to boiling; remove from heat. Stir in the couscous. Let stand, covered, 5 minutes. Fluff with a fork before serving. Makes 4 side-dish servings.

Nutrition Facts per serving: 128 cal., 1 g total fat (0 g sat. fat), 0 mg chol., 242 mg sodium, 25 g carbo., 5 g fiber, 5 g pro. **Daily Values:** 1% vit. A, 17% vit. C, 3% calcium, 4% iron

COOKING PASTA

For dried pasta, follow the package directions. Or, in a large saucepan or pot bring water (about 3 quarts of water for 4 to 8 ounces of pasta) to boiling. If desired, add 1 tablespoon olive oil or cooking oil to help keep the pasta separated and 1 teaspoon salt. Add the pasta a little at a time so the water does not stop boiling. Hold long pasta, such as spaghetti, at one end and dip the other end into the water. As the pasta softens, gently curl it around the pan and down into the water. Reduce the heat slightly and boil, uncovered, stirring occasionally, for the time specified or until the pasta is *al dente* (see tip, page 729). Test often for doneness near the end of the cooking time. Drain in a colander.

Homemade Pasta	Cooking Time*	Homemade Pasta	Cooking Time*
Bow ties, large	2 to 3 minutes	Noodles	1½ to 2 minutes
Bow ties, tiny	2 to 3 minutes	Ravioli	7 to 9 minutes
Fettuccine	1½ to 2 minutes	Spaetzle	5 to 10 minutes
Lasagna	2 to 3 minutes	Tagliatelle	1½ to 2 minutes
Linguine	1½ to 2 minutes	Tortellini	7 to 9 minutes
Manicotti	2 to 3 minutes	Tripolini	2 to 3 minutes

Dried Pasta	Cooking Time	Dried Pasta	Cooking Time
Acini di pepe	5 to 6 minutes	Noodles	6 to 8 minutes
Alphabets	5 to 8 minutes	Orzo (rosamarina)	5 to 8 minutes
Bow ties, large	10 minutes	Rigatoni	15 minutes
Bow ties, tiny	5 to 6 minutes	Rings (anelli)	9 to 10 minutes
Capellini	5 to 6 minutes	Rotini (corkscrew noodles)	8 to 10 minutes
Cavatelli	12 minutes	Shells, jumbo	18 minutes
Ditalini (thimbles)	7 to 9 minutes	Shells, large	12 to 14 minutes
Fettuccine	8 to 10 minutes	Shells, small	8 to 9 minutes
Fusilli	15 minutes	Spaetzle	10 to 12 minutes
Gemelli	10 minutes	Spaghetti	10 to 12 minutes
Lasagna	10 to 12 minutes	Spaghetti, thin	8 to 10 minutes
Linguine	8 to 10 minutes	Stars	5 to 8 minutes
Macaroni, elbow	10 minutes	Tortellini	15 minutes
Mafalda	10 to 12 minutes	Vermicelli	5 to 7 minutes
Manicotti	18 minutes	Wagon wheels (ruote)	12 minutes
Mostaccioli	14 minutes	Ziti	14 to 15 minutes

*If homemade pasta is dried or frozen, allow a few more minutes.

PIES & TARTS

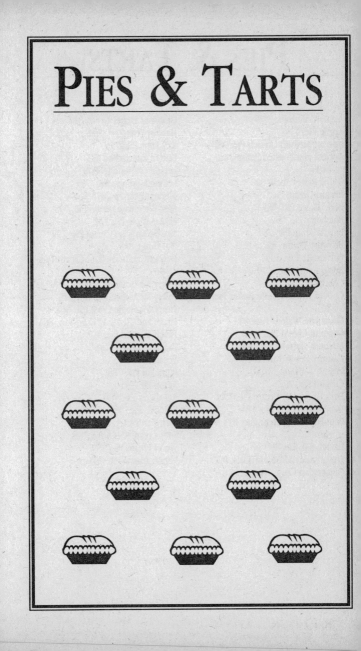

PIES & TARTS

APPLE PIE

PREP: 30 MINUTES   BAKE: 50 MINUTES   Oven 375°

Add the optional lemon juice if your apples lack tartness.

  1 **recipe Pastry for Double-Crust Pie (see page 809)**
  6 **cups thinly sliced, peeled cooking apples (about 2¹/₄ pounds)**
  1 **tablespoon lemon juice (optional)**
³/₄ **cup sugar**
  2 **tablespoons all-purpose flour**
¹/₂ **teaspoon ground cinnamon**
¹/₈ **teaspoon ground nutmeg**
¹/₂ **cup raisins or chopped walnuts (optional)**

1. Prepare and roll out Pastry for Double-Crust Pie. Line a 9-inch pie plate with half of the pastry (see step 2, page 809).
2. If desired, sprinkle apples with lemon juice. In a large mixing bowl stir together sugar, flour, cinnamon, and nutmeg. Add apple slices and, if desired, raisins or walnuts. Gently toss till coated.
3. Transfer apple mixture to the pastry-lined pie plate. Trim pastry to edge of pie plate. Cut slits in remaining pastry; place on filling and seal (see step 4, page 809). Crimp edge as desired (see steps 5, 6, and 7, page 809).
4. To prevent overbrowning, cover edge of pie with foil (see photo, page 780). Bake in a 375° oven for 25 minutes. Remove foil. Bake for 25 to 30 minutes more or till top is golden. Cool on a wire rack. Makes 8 servings.

Nutrition Facts per serving: 380 cal., 18 g total fat (4 g sat. fat), 0 mg chol., 135 mg sodium, 54 g carbo., 3 g fiber, 3 g pro. **Daily Values:** 0% vit. A, 0% vit. C, 0% calcium, 11% iron

■ **Apple Crumb Pie:** Prepare as above, except substitute 1 recipe *Pastry for Single-Crust Pie* (see page 808) for Pastry for Double-Crust Pie. Fill pastry-lined pie plate as above. Sprinkle 1 recipe *Crumb Topping* (see page 781) over apple mixture.

Nutrition Facts per serving: 390 cal., 13 g total fat (5 g sat. fat)

To protect your pie, fold a 12-inch square of foil into quarters. Cut a 7-inch hole out of the center. Unfold and loosely mold the foil ring over the pie's edges.

MINCE-APPLE PIE

PREP: 30 MINUTES   BAKE: 50 MINUTES   Oven 375°

Instead of ice cream, serve this yummy pie with homemade Hard Sauce (see page 457).

 1 **recipe Pastry for Double-Crust Pie (see page 809)**
 1 **27-ounce jar mincemeat**
 3 **cups thinly sliced, peeled cooking apples (about 1 pound)**
¹⁄₄ **cup packed brown sugar**
 2 **tablespoons orange juice or brandy**

1. Prepare and roll out Pastry for Double-Crust Pie. Line a 9-inch pie plate with half of the pastry (see step 2, page 809).
2. In a large mixing bowl stir together mincemeat, apples, brown sugar, and orange juice or brandy.
3. Transfer apple mixture to the pastry-lined pie plate. Trim pastry to edge of pie plate. Cut slits in remaining pastry; place on filling and seal (see step 4, page 809). Crimp edge as desired (see steps 5, 6, and 7, page 809).
4. To prevent overbrowning, cover edge of the pie with foil (see photo, above). Bake in a 375° oven for 25 minutes. Remove foil. Bake for 25 to 30 minutes more or till top is golden. Cool on a wire rack. Makes 8 servings.

Nutrition Facts per serving: 517 cal., 19 g total fat (4 g sat. fat), 0 mg chol., 428 mg sodium, 86 g carbo., 1 g fiber, 4 g pro. **Daily Values:** 0% vit. A, 2% vit. C, 3% calcium, 20% iron

APRICOT-ALMOND CRUNCH PIE

PREP: 35 MINUTES BAKE: 45 MINUTES   Oven 375°

To peel or not to peel the apricots -it's up to you.

    1 recipe Pastry for Single-Crust Pie (see page 808)
    1 recipe Crumb Topping (see below)
  ³/₄ cup sugar
  ¹/₃ cup all-purpose flour
    4 cups sliced, pitted apricots (about 1³/₄ pounds)
    2 tablespoons amaretto or ¹/₂ teaspoon almond extract plus 2
        tablespoons water
  ¹/₄ cup slivered almonds

1. Prepare and roll out Pastry for Single-Crust Pie. Line a 9-inch pie plate with the pastry (see step 2, page 809). Trim (see step 3, page 809) and crimp edge as desired (see steps 5, 6, and 7, page 809). Prepare Crumb Topping; set aside.

2. In a large mixing bowl combine sugar and flour. Add apricots and amaretto. Gently toss till coated.

3. Transfer apricot mixture to pastry-lined pie plate. Sprinkle Crumb Topping over the filling. Sprinkle with almonds.

4. To prevent overbrowning, cover edge of the pie with foil (see photo, page 780). Bake in a 375° oven for 25 minutes. Remove foil. Bake for 20 to 25 minutes more or till top is golden. Cool on a wire rack. Makes 8 servings.

■ **Crumb Topping:** Stir together ¹/₂ cup *all-purpose flour* and ¹/₂ cup packed *brown sugar*. Using a pastry blender, cut in 3 tablespoons *butter* till mixture resembles coarse crumbs.

Nutrition Facts per serving: 412 cal., 15 g total fat (5 g sat. fat), 12 mg chol., 115 mg sodium, 65 g carbo., 3 g fiber, 5 g pro. **Daily Values:** 29% vit. A, 16% vit. C, 3% calcium, 15% iron

BLUEBERRY PIE

PREP: 30 MINUTES   BAKE: 45 MINUTES   Oven 375°

   1 **recipe Pastry for Double-Crust Pie (see page 809)**
  ³/₄ **cup sugar**
  ¹/₃ **cup all-purpose flour**
   2 **teaspoons finely shredded lemon peel**
   1 **tablespoon lemon juice**
   5 **cups fresh or frozen blueberries**
     Milk (optional)
     Sugar (optional)

1. Prepare and roll out Pastry for Double-Crust Pie. Line a 9-inch pie plate with half of the pastry (see step 2, page 809).

2. In a large mixing bowl stir together the ³/₄ cup sugar, flour, lemon peel, and lemon juice. Add blueberries. Gently toss till coated. (If using frozen fruit, let mixture stand for 15 to 30 minutes or till fruit is partially thawed, but still icy.)

3. Transfer berry mixture to pastry-lined pie plate. Trim pastry to edge of pie plate. Cut slits in remaining pastry; place on filling and seal (see step 4, page 809). Crimp edge as desired (see steps 5, 6, and 7, page 809). If desired, brush top with milk and sprinkle with sugar.

4. To prevent overbrowning, cover edge of the pie with foil (see photo, page 780). Bake in a 375° oven for 25 minutes for fresh fruit (50 minutes for frozen fruit). Remove foil. Bake for 20 to 25 minutes more for fresh fruit (20 to 30 minutes for frozen fruit) or till top is golden. Cool on a wire rack. Makes 8 servings.

Nutrition Facts per serving: 397 cal., 18 g total fat (4 g sat. fat), 0 mg chol., 140 mg sodium, 57 g carbo., 3 g fiber, 4 g pro. **Daily Values:** 0% vit. A, 22% vit. C, 1% calcium, 11% iron

---

CHERRY PIE

PREP: 1¹/₄ HOURS   BAKE: 50 MINUTES   Oven 375°

Good varieties of tart pie cherries include Montmorency, Early Richmond, and English Morello. They're available in June and July.

   1 **recipe Pastry for Double-Crust Pie (see page 809)**
 1¹/₄ **to 1¹/₂ cups sugar**

2 tablespoons quick-cooking tapioca
5 cups fresh or frozen unsweetened pitted tart red cherries
1/4 teaspoon almond extract

1. Prepare and roll out Pastry for Double-Crust Pie. Line a 9-inch pie plate with half of the pastry (see step 2, page 809).

2. In a large mixing bowl stir together sugar and tapioca. Add cherries and almond extract. Gently toss till coated. Let mixture stand about 15 minutes or till a syrup forms, stirring occasionally. (If using frozen fruit, let mixture stand about 1 hour.)

3. Stir cherry mixture. Transfer cherry mixture to pastry-lined pie plate. Trim pastry to edge of pie plate. Cut slits in remaining pastry; place on filling and seal (see step 4, page 809). Crimp edge as desired (see steps 5, 6, and 7, page 809).

4. To prevent overbrowning, cover edge of the pie with foil (see photo, page 780). Bake in a 375° oven for 25 minutes for fresh fruit (50 minutes for frozen fruit). Remove foil. Bake for 25 to 35 minutes more for fresh fruit (about 30 minutes for frozen fruit) or till top is golden. Cool on a wire rack. Makes 8 servings.

■ **Lattice Cherry Pie:** Prepare as on page 805, except follow directions for Pastry for Lattice-Top Pie (see page 810).

CHOOSING A PIE PLATE

You need to use a standard glass or dull metal pie plate if you want your pie to be as nicely browned on the bottom as it is on the top. Shiny metal pie pans—which work just fine for crumb-crust pies—can cause the bottom pastry crust to turn out soggy.

Check the size of ceramic or pottery pie plates; they may not be standard. A standard-size plate holds about 3¾ cups liquid. If your pie plate holds more or less liquid, you may need to adjust the amount of filling and the baking time for our recipes.

Disposable foil pie pans usually are smaller than standard pie plates, although foil deep-dish pie pans are closer to the norm.

Nutrition Facts per serving: 417 cal., 18 g total fat (4 g sat. fat), 0 mg chol., 135 mg sodium, 63 g carbo., 2 g fiber, 4 g pro. **Daily Values:** 6% vit. A, 2% vit. C, 1% calcium, 11% iron

BRANDY PLUM PIE

PREP: 35 MINUTES   BAKE: 45 MINUTES   Oven 375°

    1 recipe Pastry for Single-Crust Pie (see page 808)
    1 recipe Crumb Topping (see page 781)
  ³/₄ cup packed brown sugar
  ¹/₄ cup all-purpose flour
  ¹/₄ cup brandy or apple juice
  ¹/₈ teaspoon nutmeg (optional)
    4 cups sliced, pitted plums (1³/₄ pounds)
  ¹/₃ cup chopped almonds or pecans

1. Prepare and roll out Pastry for Single-Crust Pie. Line a 9-inch pie plate with pastry (see step 2, page 809). Trim (see step 3, page 809) and crimp edge as desired (see steps 5, 6, and 7, page 809). Prepare Crumb Topping; set aside.

2. Mix brown sugar, flour, brandy, and, if desired, nutmeg. Add plums. Gently toss till coated.

3. Transfer plum mixture to the pastry-lined pie plate. Sprinkle Crumb Topping over filling. Sprinkle with chopped nuts.

4. To prevent overbrowning, cover edge of the pie with foil (see photo, page 780). Bake in a 375° oven for 25 minutes. Remove foil. Bake for 20 to 25 minutes more or till top is golden. Cool on a wire rack. Makes 8 servings.

Nutrition Facts per serving: 464 cal., 20 g total fat (6 g sat. fat), 15 mg chol., 147 mg sodium, 65 g carbo., 2 g fiber, 5 g pro. **Daily Values:** 5% vit. A, 16% vit. C, 5% calcium, 15% iron

DEEP-DISH PEACH PIE

PREP: 30 MINUTES   BAKE: 55 MINUTES   Oven 375°

  ¹/₂ to ³/₄ cup sugar
    3 tablespoons all-purpose flour
    7 cups thinly sliced, peeled peaches (3¹/₂ pounds)
  ¹/₈ teaspoon almond extract
    1 recipe Pastry for Single-Crust Pie (see page 808)

1. In a large mixing bowl stir together sugar and flour. Add peaches and almond extract. Gently toss till coated. Transfer filling to a 1¹/₂-quart casserole.

2. Prepare and roll out Pastry for Single-Crust Pie, except roll pastry 1 inch larger than the top of the casserole. Cut slits in pastry. Place pastry on filling. Seal and crimp to the rim of the casserole as desired (see steps 5, 6, and 7, page 809).

3. To prevent overbrowning, cover edge of pie with foil (see photo, page 780). Place casserole on a baking sheet. Bake in a 375° oven for 25 minutes. Remove foil. Bake 30 to 35 minutes more or till top is golden. Cool on a wire rack. Makes 8 servings.

Nutrition Facts per serving: 263 cal., 9 g total fat (2 g sat. fat), 0 mg chol., 67 mg sodium, 45 g carbo., 3 g fiber, 3 g pro. **Daily Values:** 7% vit. A, 16% vit. C, 0% calcium, 7% iron

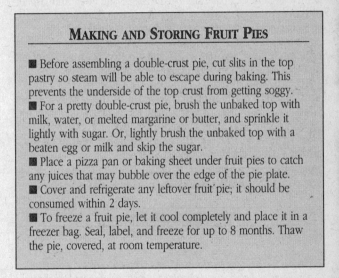

MAKING AND STORING FRUIT PIES

■ Before assembling a double-crust pie, cut slits in the top pastry so steam will be able to escape during baking. This prevents the underside of the top crust from getting soggy.

■ For a pretty double-crust pie, brush the unbaked top with milk, water, or melted margarine or butter, and sprinkle it lightly with sugar. Or, lightly brush the unbaked top with a beaten egg or milk and skip the sugar.

■ Place a pizza pan or baking sheet under fruit pies to catch any juices that may bubble over the edge of the pie plate.

■ Cover and refrigerate any leftover fruit pie; it should be consumed within 2 days.

■ To freeze a fruit pie, let it cool completely and place it in a freezer bag. Seal, label, and freeze for up to 8 months. Thaw the pie, covered, at room temperature.

RASPBERRY PIE

PREP: 25 MINUTES   BAKE: 50 MINUTES   Oven 375°

Stir raspberries gently to prevent them from being crushed.

    1 **recipe Pastry for Double-Crust Pie (see page 808)**
  1/2 **to 3/4 cup sugar**
    3 **tablespoons all-purpose flour**
    5 **cups fresh or frozen unsweetened red raspberries**

1. Prepare and roll out Pastry for Double-Crust Pie. Line a 9-inch pie plate with half of the pastry (see step 2, page 809).

2. In a large mixing bowl stir together sugar and flour. Add raspberries. Gently toss till coated. (If using frozen fruit, let mixture stand 15 to 30 minutes or till fruit is partially thawed, but still icy.)

3. Transfer berry mixture to the pastry-lined pie plate. Trim pastry to edge of pie plate. Cut slits in remaining pastry; place on filling and seal (see step 4, page 809). Crimp edge as desired (see steps 5, 6, and 7, page 809).

4. To prevent overbrowning, cover edge of the pie with foil (see photo, page 780). Bake in a 375° oven for 25 minutes for fresh fruit (50 minutes for frozen fruit). Remove foil. Bake for 25 to 30 minutes more for fresh fruit (about 30 minutes for frozen fruit) or till top is golden. Cool on a wire rack. Makes 8 servings.

Nutrition Facts per serving: 351 cal., 18 g total fat (4 g sat. fat), 0 mg chol., 134 mg sodium, 45 g carbo., 4 g fiber, 4 g pro. **Daily Values:** 1% vit. A, 32% vit. C, 1% calcium, 12% iron

---

RHUBARB PIE

PREP: 25 MINUTES   BAKE: 45 MINUTES   Oven 375°

This recipe calls for a crumb topping. You can use the filling in a double-crust pastry, too. Follow the directions on page 808 for the pastry, then bake as directed in step 4.

    1 **recipe Pastry for Single-Crust Pie (see page 808)**
    1 **recipe Crumb Topping (see page 781)**
  3/4 **cup sugar**
  1/4 **cup all-purpose flour**
  1/2 **teaspoon ground cinnamon (optional)**
    4 **cups fresh or frozen unsweetened, sliced rhubarb**

1. Prepare and roll out Pastry for Single-Crust Pie. Line a 9-inch pie plate with the pastry (see step 2, page 809). Trim (see step 3, page 809) and crimp edge as desired (see steps 5, 6, and 7, page 809). Prepare Crumb Topping; set aside.

2. In a large mixing bowl stir together sugar, flour, and, if desired, cinnamon. Add rhubarb. Gently toss till coated. (If using frozen fruit, let mixture stand for 15 to 30 minutes or till fruit is partially thawed, but still icy.)

3. Transfer rhubarb mixture to the pastry-lined pie plate. Sprinkle Crumb Topping over filling.

4. To prevent overbrowning, cover edge of the pie with foil (see photo, page 780). Bake in a 375° oven for 25 minutes for fresh fruit (50 minutes for frozen fruit). Remove foil. Bake for 20 to 25 minutes more for fresh fruit (20 to 30 minutes for frozen fruit) or till top is golden. Cool on a wire rack. Makes 8 servings.

Nutrition Facts per serving: 345 cal., 13 g total fat (5 g sat. fat), 12 mg chol., 117 mg sodium, 54 g carbo., 2 g fiber, 4 g pro. **Daily Values:** 4% vit. A, 8% vit. C, 5% calcium, 11% iron

---

BERRY GLACÉ PIE

PREP: 1 HOUR   CHILL: 1 TO 2 HOURS

   1 **recipe Baked Pastry Shell (see page 808)**
   8 **cups medium strawberries**
   $^2/_3$ **cup sugar**
   2 **tablespoons cornstarch**
     Several drops red food coloring (optional)
     Whipped cream (optional)

1. Prepare Baked Pastry Shell and set aside. Meanwhile remove stems from strawberries. Cut any large strawberries in half lengthwise; set aside.

2. For glaze, in a blender container or food processor bowl combine *1 cup* of the strawberries and $^2/_3$ cup *water*. Cover and blend or process till smooth. Add enough additional water to the mixture to equal $1^1/_2$ cups. In a medium saucepan combine sugar and cornstarch; stir in blended berry mixture. Cook and stir over medium heat till mixture is thickened and bubbly. Cook and stir 2 minutes more. If desired, stir in red food coloring. Cool for 10 minutes without stirring.

3. Spread about ¼ cup of the glaze over bottom and sides of Baked Pastry Shell. Arrange half of the remaining strawberries, stem end down, in the pastry shell.

4. Carefully spoon half of the remaining glaze over fruit, thoroughly covering each piece of fruit. Arrange remaining fruit over first layer. Spoon remaining glaze over fruit, covering each piece. Chill for 1 to 2 hours. (After 2 hours, filling may begin to water out.) If desired, garnish with whipped cream. Makes 8 servings.

■ **Peach Glacé Pie:** Prepare as on page 787, except substitute 6 cups sliced, peeled *peaches* for the strawberries and omit the food coloring.

Nutrition Facts per serving: 258 cal., 9 g total fat (2 g sat. fat), 0 mg chol., 70 mg sodium, 43 g carbo., 3 g fiber, 3 g pro. **Daily Values:** 0% vit. A, 140% vit. C, 2% calcium, 9% iron

---

PUMPKIN PIE

PREP: 25 MINUTES   BAKE: 50 MINUTES   Oven 375°

Rather than measuring individual spices, you can use 1½ teaspoons pumpkin pie spice instead.

   1 **recipe Pastry for Single-Crust Pie (see page 808)**
   1 **16-ounce can pumpkin**
⅔ **cup sugar**
   1 **teaspoon ground cinnamon**
½ **teaspoon ground ginger**
½ **teaspoon ground nutmeg**
   3 **slightly beaten eggs**
   1 **5-ounce can (⅔ cup) evaporated milk**
½ **cup milk**

1. Prepare and roll out Pastry for Single-Crust Pie. Line a 9-inch pie plate with the pastry (see step 2, page 809). Trim (see step 3, page 809); crimp edge as desired (see steps 5, 6, and 7, page 809).

2. For filling, in a mixing bowl combine pumpkin, sugar, cinnamon, ginger, and nutmeg. Add eggs. Beat lightly with a rotary beater or fork just till combined. Gradually stir in evaporated milk and milk; mix well.

3. Place the pastry-lined pie plate on the oven rack. Carefully pour filling into pastry shell.

4. To prevent overbrowning, cover edge of the pie with foil (see photo, page 780). Bake in a 375° oven for 25 minutes. Remove foil. Bake about 25 minutes more or till a knife inserted near the center comes out clean. Cool on a wire rack. Refrigerate within 2 hours; cover for longer storage. Makes 8 servings.

Nutrition Facts per serving: 286 cal., 13 g total fat (4 g sat. fat), 86 mg chol., 120 mg sodium, 38 g carbo., 2 g fiber, 7 g pro. **Daily Values:** 130% vit. A, 9% vit. C, 7% calcium, 13% iron

---

SWEET POTATO PIE

PREP: 1¼ HOURS   BAKE: 50 MINUTES   COOL: 30 MINUTES
CHILL: AT LEAST 2 HOURS   Oven 450°

This Southern favorite is not as sweet as pumpkin pie, but has a similar appearance.

 3 **medium sweet potatoes (about 1 pound) or one 17-ounce can sweet potatoes, drained and mashed**
 1 **recipe Pastry for Single-Crust Pie (see page 808)**
 ½ **cup sugar**
 ½ **teaspoon ground cinnamon**
 ¼ **teaspoon ground allspice**
 ¼ **teaspoon ground nutmeg**
 ⅛ **teaspoon salt**
 3 **slightly beaten eggs**
 1 **cup buttermilk or dairy sour cream**
   Whipped cream (optional)

1. Scrub sweet potatoes thoroughly with a brush. Pat dry; prick potatoes with a fork. Bake in a 450° oven for 40 to 50 minutes or till very tender. Cool till easy to handle.
2. Meanwhile, prepare and roll out Pastry for Single-Crust Pie. Line a 9-inch pie plate with the pastry (see step 2, page 809). Trim (see step 3, page 809) and crimp edge as desired (see steps 5, 6, and 7, page 809). Line pastry with a double thickness of foil (see photo, page 795). Bake pastry shell in a 450° oven for 8 minutes. Remove foil. Bake for 4 to 5 minutes more or till set and dry.
3. For filling, cut baked potatoes in half and scoop pulp into a large mixing bowl. Use a potato masher to mash pulp (you should have about 2 cups). Stir sugar, cinnamon, allspice, nutmeg, and salt into mashed potatoes. Add eggs. Beat lightly with a rotary beater or fork

just till combined. Gradually stir in buttermilk or sour cream; mix well.

4. Place the partially baked pastry shell on the oven rack. Carefully pour filling into pastry shell.

5. To prevent overbrowning, cover edge of pie with foil (see photo, page 780). Reduce oven temperature to 375° and bake for 25 minutes. Remove foil. Bake for 25 to 30 minutes more or till a knife inserted near the center comes out clean. Cool on a wire rack for 30 minutes. Chill at least 2 hours before serving; cover for longer storage. If desired, top with whipped cream. Makes 8 servings.

Nutrition Facts per serving: 276 cal., 11 g total fat (3 g sat. fat), 81 mg chol., 161 mg sodium, 39 g carbo., 2 g fiber, 6 g pro. **Daily Values:** 100% vit. A, 18% vit. C, 5 mg calcium, 9% iron

---

PECAN PIE

PREP: 25 MINUTES   BAKE: 45 MINUTES   Oven 350°

---

    1 recipe Pastry for Single-Crust Pie (see page 808)
    3 slightly beaten eggs
    1 cup corn syrup
  ²/₃ cup sugar
  ¹/₃ cup margarine or butter, melted
    1 teaspoon vanilla
 1¹/₄ cups pecan halves or chopped macadamia nuts

1. Prepare and roll out pastry for Single-Crust Pie. Line a 9-inch pie plate with the pastry (see step 2, page 809). Trim (see step 3, page 809); crimp edge as desired (see steps 5, 6, and 7, page 809).

2. For filling, combine eggs, corn syrup, sugar, margarine or butter, and vanilla. Mix well. Stir in pecan halves.

3. Place the pastry-lined pie plate on the oven rack. Carefully pour the filling into the pastry shell.

4. To prevent overbrowning, cover edge of the pie with foil (see photo, page 780). Bake in a 350° oven for 25 minutes. Remove foil. Bake for 20 to 25 minutes more or till a knife inserted near the center comes out clean. Cool on a wire rack. Refrigerate within 2 hours; cover for longer storage. Makes 8 servings.

Nutrition Facts per serving: 541 cal., 30 g total fat (8 g sat. fat), 100 mg chol., 197 mg sodium, 67 g carbo., 2 g fiber, 6 g pro. **Daily Values:** 10% vit. A, 0% vit. C, 2% calcium, 11% iron

RAISIN PIE

    1 **recipe Pastry for Double-Crust Pie (see page 808)**
 ¹/₂ **cup sugar**
    2 **tablespoons all-purpose flour**
    2 **cups raisins**
1¹/₃ **cups water**
 ¹/₂ **teaspoon finely shredded lemon peel**
    3 **tablespoons lemon juice**
 ¹/₂ **cup chopped walnuts**

1. Prepare and roll out Pastry for Double-Crust Pie. Line a 9-inch pie plate with half of the pastry (see step 2, page 809).

2. In a saucepan stir together sugar and flour. Stir in raisins, water, lemon peel, and lemon juice. Cook and stir till thickened and bubbly. Cook and stir 1 minute more. Remove from heat; stir in nuts.

3. Transfer raisin mixture to the pastry-lined pie plate. Trim pastry to edge of pie plate. Cut slits in remaining pastry. Place pastry on filling and seal (see step 4, page 809). Crimp edge as desired (see steps 5, 6, and 7, page 809).

4. To prevent overbrowning, cover edge of the pie with foil (see photo, page 780). Bake in a 375° oven for 25 minutes. Remove foil. Bake for 20 to 25 minutes more or till top is golden. Cool on a wire rack. Makes 10 servings.

Nutrition Facts per serving: 375 cal., 18 g total fat (4 g sat. fat), 0 mg chol., 112 mg sodium, 53 g carbo., 2 g fiber, 4 g pro. **Daily Values:** 0% vit. A, 5% vit. C, 2% calcium, 12% iron

CUSTARD PIE

PREP: 25 MINUTES   BAKE: 40 MINUTES   Oven 450°

1 **recipe Pastry for Single-Crust Pie (see page 808)**
4 **eggs**
$^1/_2$ **cup sugar**
1 **teaspoon vanilla**
$^1/_8$ **teaspoon salt**
$2^1/_2$ **cups milk**
  Ground nutmeg

MAKING AND STORING CUSTARD PIES

■ To avoid spills, place the pie shell on the oven rack before adding the filling.
■ Because the filling continues to set after it is removed from the oven, a custard pie is done if liquid area in the center is smaller than a quarter. Or, insert a knife near the center. If it comes out clean, the pie is done. (The knife test may cause the filling to crack.)
■ Pies that contain eggs or dairy products should be refrigerated within 2 hours of being removed from the oven.

1. Prepare and roll out Pastry for Single-Crust Pie. Line 9-inch pie plate with pastry (see step 2, page 809). Trim (see step 3, page 809); crimp edge as desired (see steps 5, 6, and 7, page 809). Line pastry with a double thickness of foil (see photo, page 795). Bake in a 450° oven 8 minutes. Remove foil. Bake 4 to 5 minutes more or till set and dry.
2. Meanwhile, for filling, in a mixing bowl slightly beat eggs with a rotary beater or fork. Stir in sugar, vanilla, and salt. Gradually stir in milk. Mix well.
3. Place the partially baked pastry shell on the oven rack. Carefully pour filling into the pastry shell. Sprinkle with nutmeg.
4. To prevent overbrowning, cover edge of pie with foil (see photo, page 780). Reduce oven temperature to 350° and bake for 25 minutes. Remove foil. Bake for 15 to 20 minutes more or till a knife inserted near the center comes out clean. Cool on a wire rack. Refrigerate within 2 hours; cover for longer storage. Makes 8 servings.

Nutrition Facts per serving: 266 cal., 13 g total fat (4 g sat. fat), 112 mg chol., 170 mg sodium, 30 g carbo., 0 g fiber, 8 g pro. **Daily Values:** 9% vit. A, 1% vit. C, 9% calcium, 8% iron

■ **Coconut Custard Pie:** Prepare as above, except stir in ¹/₂ cup toasted *coconut* with the milk.

Nutrition Facts per serving: 287 cal., 14 g total fat (5 g sat. fat)

PEACH CUSTARD PIE

PREP: 25 MINUTES   BAKE: 45 MINUTES   Oven 450°

  1 recipe Pastry for Single-Crust Pie (see page 808)
  3 cups sliced, peeled peaches
  2 eggs
 ¹/₂ cup sugar
  3 tablespoons all-purpose flour
  1 teaspoon vanilla
 ¹/₈ teaspoon ground nutmeg
 ³/₄ cup milk

1. Prepare and roll out Pastry for Single-Crust Pie. Line a 9-inch pie plate with pastry (see step 2, page 809). Trim (see step 3, page 809); crimp as desired (see steps 5, 6, and 7, page 809). Line pastry with a double thickness of foil (see photo, page 795). Bake in a 450° oven 8 minutes. Remove foil; bake 4 to 5 minutes more or till set and dry. Layer peaches in pastry shell; set aside.

2. For filling, slightly beat eggs with a rotary beater or fork. Stir in sugar, flour, vanilla, and nutmeg. Gradually stir in milk. Mix just till combined.

3. Place partially baked pastry shell on oven rack. Carefully pour filling over sliced fruit in pastry shell.

4. To prevent overbrowning, cover edge of pie with foil (see photo, page 780). Reduce oven temperature to 350° and bake for 25 minutes. Remove foil. Bake for 20 to 25 minutes more or till a knife inserted near center comes out clean. Cool on a wire rack. Refrigerate within 2 hours; cover for longer storage. Makes 8 servings.

Nutrition Facts per serving: 266 cal., 11 g total fat (3 g sat. fat), 55 mg chol., 94 mg sodium, 39 g carbo., 2 g fiber, 5 g pro. **Daily Values:** 8% vit. A, 9% vit. C, 3% calcium, 8% iron

BUTTERMILK CHESS PIE

PREP: 25 MINUTES BAKE: 35 MINUTES   Oven 450°

There are many versions of the classic chess pie, but one thing they all have in common is a thin top "crust" that rises to the surface of the lemony butter filling.

  1   recipe Pastry for Single-Crust Pie (see page 808)
1½   cups sugar
  2   tablespoons cornmeal
  4   eggs
½   cup buttermilk
¼   cup margarine or butter, melted and cooled
  1   tablespoon finely shredded lemon peel
¼   cup lemon juice
  1   teaspoon vanilla

1. Prepare and roll out Pastry for Single-Crust Pie. Line a 9-inch pie plate with pastry (see step 2, page 809). Trim (see step 3, page 809); crimp as desired (see steps 5, 6, and 7, page 809). Line pastry with a double thickness of foil (see photo, at right). Bake in a 450° oven 8 minutes. Remove foil; bake 4 to 5 minutes more or till set and dry.
2. Meanwhile, for filling, in a small mixing bowl stir together sugar and cornmeal. In a large mixing bowl beat the eggs with an electric mixer on high speed about 5 minutes or till thick and light colored. Add the sugar mixture; mix well. Gradually stir in buttermilk, melted margarine or butter, lemon peel, lemon juice, and vanilla. Mix well.
3. Place partially baked pastry shell on the oven rack. Carefully pour the filling into the pastry shell.
4. To prevent overbrowning, cover edge of pie with foil (see photo, page 780). Reduce oven temperature to 350° and bake for 25 minutes. Remove foil. Bake 10 to 15 minutes more or till a knife inserted near the center comes out clean. Cool on a wire rack. Refrigerate within 2 hours; cover for longer storage. Makes 8 servings.

Nutrition Facts per serving: 390 cal., 17 g total fat (7 g sat. fat), 122 mg chol., 173 mg sodium, 55 g carbo., 1 g fiber, 6 g pro. **Daily Values:** 10% vit. A, 7% vit. C, 3% calcium, 8% iron

To prevent pastry from shrinking during baking, line it with a double thickness of regular foil or one layer of heavy-duty foil.

LEMON MERINGUE PIE

PREP: 40 MINUTES   BAKE: 15 MINUTES   COOL: 1 HOUR   CHILL: 3 TO 6 HOURS   **Oven 350°**

- 1 recipe Baked Pastry Shell (see page 808)
- 3 eggs
- 1¹/₂ cups sugar
- 3 tablespoons all-purpose flour
- 3 tablespoons cornstarch
- 2 tablespoons margarine or butter
- 1 to 2 teaspoons finely shredded lemon peel
- ¹/₃ cup lemon juice
- 1 recipe Meringue for Pie (see page 813)

1. Prepare Baked Pastry Shell. Separate egg yolks from whites; set whites aside for meringue.

2. Meanwhile, for filling, mix sugar, flour, cornstarch, and dash *salt*. Gradually stir in 1¹/₂ cups *water*. Cook and stir over medium-high heat till thickened and bubbly. Reduce heat; cook and stir 2 minutes more. Remove from heat. Slightly beat egg yolks with a rotary beater or fork. Gradually stir about 1 cup of the hot filling into yolks. Pour egg yolk mixture into remaining hot filling in saucepan. Bring to a gentle boil. Cook and stir 2 minutes more. Remove from heat. Stir in margarine and lemon peel. Gently stir in lemon juice. Keep filling warm; prepare Meringue for Pie.

3. Pour warm filling into Baked Pastry Shell. Spread meringue over warm filling; seal to edge. Bake in a 350° oven 15 minutes. Cool on wire rack 1 hour. Chill 3 to 6 hours before serving; cover for longer storage. Makes 8 servings.

Nutrition Facts per serving: 395 cal., 14 g total fat (5 g sat. fat), 88 mg chol., 139 mg sodium, 65 g carbo., 1 g fiber, 5 g pro. **Daily Values:** 14% vit. A, 8% vit. C, 1% calcium, 8% iron

KEY LIME PIE

PREP: 25 MINUTES   BAKE: 45 MINUTES   COOL: 1 HOUR   CHILL: 3 TO 6 HOURS   Oven 325°

Key limes grow only in Florida and the Caribbean, but Persian limes grow in many locales and are available in most markets.

1 **recipe Pastry for Single-Crust Pie (see page 808)**
3 **eggs**
1 **14-ounce can (1¼ cups) sweetened condensed milk**
½ **to ¾ teaspoon finely shredded Key lime peel or 1½ teaspoons finely shredded Persian lime peel**
½ **cup water**
⅓ **cup lime juice (8 to 10 Key limes or 2 to 3 Persian limes)**
   Several drops green food coloring (optional)
1 **recipe Meringue for Pie (see page 813)**

1. Prepare and roll out Pastry for Single-Crust Pie. Line a 9-inch pie plate with pastry (see step 2, page 809). Trim (see step 3, page 809) and crimp edge as desired (see steps 5, 6, and 7, page 809).

2. Separate egg yolks from whites; set whites aside for meringue. For filling, in a medium mixing bowl beat egg yolks with a rotary beater or fork. Gradually stir in sweetened condensed milk and lime peel. Add water, lime juice, and, if desired, food coloring. Mix well (mixture will thicken).

3. Spoon thickened filling into pastry-lined pie plate. Bake in a 325° oven 30 minutes. Meanwhile, prepare Meringue for Pie. Remove pie from oven. Increase the oven temperature to 350°. Spread meringue over hot filling; seal to edge. Bake in 350° oven for 15 minutes. Cool on a wire rack for 1 hour. Chill 3 to 6 hours before serving; cover for longer storage. Makes 8 servings.

Nutrition Facts per serving: 370 cal., 15 g total fat (6 g sat. fat), 97 mg chol., 157 mg sodium, 51 g carbo., 0 g fiber, 8 g pro. **Daily Values:** 8% vit. A, 7% vit. C, 13% calcium, 8% iron

VANILLA CREAM PIE

PREP: 1 HOUR   BAKE: 25 MINUTES   COOL: 1 HOUR   CHILL: 3 TO 6 HOURS   Oven 325°

*If you wish, skip the meringue and top the chilled pie
with whipped cream.*

- 1 **recipe Baked Pastry Shell (see page 808)**
- 4 **eggs**
- ³/₄ **cup sugar**
- ¹/₄ **cup cornstarch or ¹/₂ cup all-purpose flour**
- 3 **cups milk**
- 1 **tablespoon margarine or butter**
- 1¹/₂ **teaspoons vanilla**
  Four-Egg-White Meringue (see page 814)

1. Prepare Baked Pastry Shell. Separate egg yolks from whites; set whites aside for meringue.

2. Meanwhile, for filling, combine sugar and cornstarch. Gradually stir in milk. Cook and stir over medium-high heat till thickened and bubbly. Cook and stir for 2 minutes more. Remove from heat. Slightly beat egg yolks with a rotary beater or fork. Gradually stir about 1 cup of the hot filling into yolks. Pour egg yolk mixture into hot filling in pan. Bring to a gentle boil. Cook and stir 2 minutes more. Remove from heat. Stir in margarine and vanilla. Keep filling warm; prepare meringue.

3. Pour warm filling into Baked Pastry Shell. Spread meringue over warm filling; seal to edge. Bake in a 325° oven for 25 to 30 minutes or till lightly browned. Cool on a wire rack for 1 hour. Chill 3 to 6 hours before serving; cover for longer storage. Makes 8 servings.

Nutrition Facts per serving: 377 cal., 14 g total fat (4 g sat. fat), 113 mg chol., 161 mg sodium, 54 g carbo., 1 g fiber, 8 g pro. **Daily Values:** 23% vit. A, 1% vit. C, 10% calcium, 8% iron

■ **Coconut Cream Pie:** Prepare as above, except stir in 1 cup *flaked coconut* with margarine or butter and vanilla. Sprinkle another ¹/₃ cup *flaked coconut* over meringue before baking.

Nutrition Facts per serving: 428 cal., 17 g total fat (7 g sat. fat)

■ **Banana Cream Pie:** Prepare as above, except, before adding filling, arrange 3 medium *bananas,* sliced (about 2¹/₄ cups), over bottom of shell.

Nutrition Facts per serving: 425 cal., 15 g total fat (4 g sat. fat)

■ **Dark Chocolate Cream Pie:** Prepare as on page 797, except increase the sugar to 1 cup. Stir in 3 ounces *unsweetened chocolate,* cut up, with the milk.

Nutrition Facts per serving: 463 cal., 20 g total fat (7 g sat. fat)

■ **Milk Chocolate Cream Pie:** Prepare as on page 797, except stir in 3 ounces *semisweet chocolate,* cut up, with the milk.

Nutrition Facts per serving: 436 cal., 18 g total fat (6 g sat. fat)

■ **Sour Cream-Raisin Pie:** Prepare as on page 797, except increase the cornstarch to $1/3$ cup (or increase flour to $2/3$ cup). Fold in 1 cup *raisins* and $1/2$ cup *dairy sour cream* with the margarine or butter and vanilla.

Nutrition Facts per serving: 476 cal., 18 g total fat (6 g sat. fat)

BUTTERSCOTCH PIE

PREP: 1 HOUR   BAKE: 15 MINUTES   COOL: 1 HOUR   CHILL: 3 TO 6 HOURS   Oven 350°

For easier cutting, before you slice this and other meringue-topped pies, dip your knife into hot water.

   1 **recipe Baked Pastry Shell (see page 808)**
   3 **eggs**
$1^1/2$ **cups packed brown sugar**
 $1/3$ **cup all-purpose flour**
$2^1/4$ **cups milk**
   2 **tablespoons margarine or butter**
   1 **teaspoon vanilla**
   1 **recipe Meringue for Pie (see page 813)**

1. Prepare Baked Pastry Shell; set aside. Separate egg yolks from egg whites; set the egg whites aside for meringue.
2. Meanwhile, for filling, in a saucepan stir together brown sugar and flour. Gradually stir in milk. Cook and stir over medium heat till thickened and bubbly. Cook and stir for 1 minute more. Remove from heat. Slightly beat egg yolks with a rotary beater or fork. Gradually stir about 1 cup of the hot filling into egg yolks. Pour egg yolk mixture into hot filling in saucepan. Bring to a gentle boil. Cook and

stir for 2 minutes more. Remove from heat. Stir in margarine and vanilla. Keep filling warm; prepare Meringue for Pie.

3. Pour warm filling into Baked Pastry Shell. Spread meringue over warm filling; seal to edge. Bake in a 350° oven for 15 minutes. Cool on a wire rack for 1 hour. Chill for 3 to 6 hours before serving; cover for longer storage. Makes 8 servings.

Nutrition Facts per serving: 410 cal., 15 g total fat (5 g sat. fat), 93 mg chol., 164 mg sodium, 63 g carbo., 1 g fiber, 7 g pro. **Daily Values:** 18% vit. A, 1% vit. C, 10% calcium, 13% iron

MOCHA BAVARIAN CREAM PIE

PREP: 25 MINUTES   CHILL: 8 HOURS

1 **recipe Nut Crust (see page 812) or Baked Pastry Shell (see page 808)**
¹/₂ **cup sugar**
1 **envelope unflavored gelatin**
2 **cups milk**
2 **ounces unsweetened chocolate, cut up**
2 **teaspoons instant coffee crystals (optional)**
4 **egg yolks**
1 **teaspoon vanilla**
1 **cup whipping cream**

1. Prepare Nut Crust; set aside.

2. For filling, in a heavy saucepan combine sugar and gelatin; stir in milk. Add chocolate and, if desired, coffee crystals. Cook and stir over medium heat till gelatin dissolves and chocolate melts.

3. In a mixing bowl slightly beat egg yolks with a rotary beater or fork. Gradually stir about half of the hot mixture into yolks. Pour yolk mixture into hot filling in pan. Bring to a gentle boil. Cook and stir 2 minutes more. Remove from heat. Stir in vanilla. Chill gelatin mixture 30 minutes.

4. Beat whipping cream till soft peaks form; fold whipped cream into gelatin mixture. Chill again till mixture mounds when spooned. Transfer filling to Nut Crust. Cover and chill about 8 hours or till set. If desired, garnish with *chocolate curls*. Serves 8.

Nutrition Facts per serving: 465 cal., 37 g total fat (12 g sat. fat), 152 mg chol., 63 mg sodium, 29 g carbo., 2 g fiber, 11 g pro. **Daily Values:** 33% vit. A, 3% vit. C, 11% calcium, 10% iron

FRENCH SILK PIE

PREP: 35 MINUTES   CHILL: 5 TO 24 HOURS

1. Prepare *Baked Pastry Shell* (see page 808); set shell aside.
2. For filling, in a large mixing bowl beat $^3/_4$ cup *sugar* and $^3/_4$ cup *butter* with an electric mixer on medium speed about 4 minutes or till fluffy. Stir in one 6-ounce package (1 cup) melted and cooled *semisweet chocolate pieces* and 1 teaspoon *vanilla*. Gradually add $^3/_4$ cup *refrigerated or frozen egg product,* thawed, beating on high speed and scraping sides of bowl constantly till light and fluffy.
3. Transfer filling to Baked Pastry Shell. Cover and chill for 5 to 24 hours. If desired, garnish with *whipped cream* and *chocolate curls.* Serves 10.

Nutrition Facts per serving: 378 cal., 24 g total fat (10 g sat. fat), 37 mg chol., 229 mg sodium, 38 g carbo., 0 g fiber, 4 g pro. **Daily Values:** 21% vit. A, 0% vit. C, 3% calcium, 9% iron

---

LEMON CHIFFON PIE

PREP: $1^1/_4$ HOURS   CHILL: 4 HOURS

  1 **recipe Graham Cracker Crust (see page 812) or Baked Pastry
      Shell (see page 808)**
  2 **envelopes unflavored gelatin**
$1^1/_2$ **cups sugar**
$1^1/_2$ **cups refrigerated or frozen egg product, thawed**
  2 **teaspoons finely shredded lemon peel**
$^3/_4$ **cup lemon juice**
$^3/_4$ **cup whipping cream**

1. Prepare Graham Cracker Crust; set aside.
2. For filling, in a small saucepan soften gelatin in $^1/_2$ cup *cold water.* Cook and stir over low heat just till gelatin dissolves. Remove from heat; transfer to a large mixing bowl. Stir in $^1/_2$ cup *cold water,* sugar, egg product, lemon peel, and lemon juice (mixture may appear curdled). Chill till mixture mounds when spooned, stirring occasionally.
3. Beat gelatin mixture with an electric mixer on medium to high speed for 4 to 5 minutes or till mixture becomes light and frothy. Immediately beat whipping cream till soft peaks form; fold whipped cream into gelatin mixture. Chill again till mixture mounds when

spooned. Transfer filling to Graham Cracker Crust. Cover and chill about 4 hours or till firm. Makes 8 servings.

Nutrition Facts per serving: 456 cal., 22 g total fat (11 g sat. fat), 52 mg chol., 251 mg sodium, 59 g carbo., 1 g fiber, 8 g pro. **Daily Values:** 22% vit. A, 20% vit. C, 4% calcium, 10% iron

---

CHOCOLATE AND PEANUT BUTTER PIE

PREP: 15 MINUTES   CHILL: 2 HOURS

    1 recipe Chocolate Wafer Crust (see page 812)
    1 8-ounce package cream cheese, cut up
 ³/₄ cup peanut butter
    1 cup sifted powdered sugar
    2 tablespoons milk
    1 teaspoon vanilla
    1 cup whipping cream
    2 tablespoons sifted powdered sugar
 ³/₄ cup miniature semisweet chocolate pieces

1. Prepare Chocolate Wafer Crust; set aside.

2. For filling, beat cream cheese and peanut butter till smooth. Add the 1 cup powdered sugar, milk, and vanilla; beat till combined.

3. In a chilled mixing bowl beat whipping cream and the 2 tablespoons powdered sugar till soft peaks form. Gently fold about one-third of the whipped cream into the peanut butter mixture. Fold remaining whipped cream and miniature chocolate pieces into peanut butter mixture. Spoon into Chocolate Wafer Crust. If desired, sprinkle with *peanuts*. Cover and chill about 2 hours or till set. Makes 10 servings.

Nutrition Facts per serving: 538 cal., 38 g total fat (14 g sat. fat), 58 mg chol., 336 mg sodium, 46 g carbo., 1 g fiber, 9 g pro. **Daily Values:** 27% vit. A, 0% vit. C, 5% calcium, 10% iron

BROWNIE-WALNUT PIE

PREP: 40 MINUTES BAKE: 50 MINUTES   Oven 350°

  - $^1/_2$ cup butter or margarine
  - 3 ounces unsweetened chocolate, cut up
  - 1 recipe Pastry for Single-Crust Pie (page 808)
  - 3 beaten eggs
  - $1^1/_2$ cups sugar
  - $^1/_2$ cup all-purpose flour
  - 1 teaspoon vanilla
  - 1 cup chopped walnuts
  - 1 recipe Hot Fudge Sauce (see page 451) or fresh fruit such as
        raspberries, sliced strawberries, or sliced peaches (optional)

1. For filling, in a small heavy saucepan melt butter or margarine and chocolate over low heat, stirring frequently. Cool 20 minutes.
2. Meanwhile, prepare and roll out Pastry for Single-Crust Pie. Line a 9-inch pie plate with the pastry (see step 2, page 809). Trim (see step 3, page 809) and crimp edge as desired (see steps 5, 6, and 7, page 809).
3. Combine eggs, sugar, flour, and vanilla; stir in the cooled chocolate mixture and walnuts.
4. Pour filling into a pastry-lined pie plate. Bake in a 350° oven for 50 to 55 minutes or till a knife inserted near the center comes out clean. Cool on a wire rack. If desired, serve with Hot Fudge Sauce or fresh fruit. Makes 8 servings.

Nutrition Facts per serving: 591 cal., 37 g total fat (13 g sat. fat), 111 mg chol., 209 mg sodium, 63 g carbo., 2 g fiber, 8 g pro. **Daily Values:** 14% vit. A, 0% vit. C, 3% calcium, 17% iron

---

COUNTRY PEACH TART

PREP: 30 MINUTES BAKE: 40 MINUTES COOL: 30 MINUTES   Oven 375°

  - 1 recipe Pastry for Single-Crust Pie (see page 808)
  - $^1/_4$ cup granulated sugar
  - 4 teaspoons all-purpose flour
  - $^1/_4$ teaspoon ground nutmeg
  - 3 cups sliced, peeled peaches or nectarines ($1^1/_2$ pounds)
  - 1 tablespoon lemon juice
  - 1 beaten egg
      Powdered sugar

1. Prepare pastry for Single-Crust Pie; set aside. Line a baking sheet with foil; sprinkle lightly with flour. Roll pastry to 13-inch circle atop baking sheet.

2. Mix granulated sugar, the 4 teaspoons flour, and nutmeg; stir in peaches and lemon juice. Mound peach mixture in center of crust, leaving a 2-inch border. Fold border up over peaches. Combine egg and 1 tablespoon *water;* brush onto the top and sides of the crust.

3. Bake in a 375° oven for 40 to 45 minutes or till crust is golden. To prevent overbrowning, cover edge with foil the last 10 to 15 minutes of baking (see photo, page 780). Cool 30 minutes on the baking sheet. Dust edges with powdered sugar. If desired, serve with *whipped cream.* Serves 8.

Nutrition Facts per serving: 207 cal., 9 g total fat (2 g sat. fat), 27 mg chol., 75 mg sodium, 28 g carbo., 2 g fiber, and 3 g pro. **Daily Values:** 4% vit. A, 8% vit. C, 0% calcium, and 7% iron

---

APRICOT AND TOASTED PECAN TART

PREP: 1 HOUR   BAKE: 13 MINUTES   CHILL: 3 HOURS   Oven 450°

Nectarine slices also work well in this tart.

  1 **recipe Rich Tart Pastry (see page 811)**
  1 **10-ounce jar apricot spreadable fruit**
  3 **tablespoons orange juice or apple juice**
  1 **teaspoon finely shredded lemon peel**
 12 **apricots, peeled, pitted, and halved (1 pound)**
 $1/4$ **cup chopped pecans, toasted (see tip, page 234)**

1. Prepare and roll out Rich Tart Pastry. Line a 10- or 11-inch tart pan with a removable bottom with pastry. Press pastry into fluted sides of tart pan; trim edges. Line pastry with double thickness of foil (see photo, page 795). Bake in a 450° oven for 8 minutes. Remove foil. Bake for 5 to 8 minutes more or till golden. Cool on a wire rack.

2. Meanwhile, for glaze, in a small saucepan combine spreadable fruit, orange or apple juice, and lemon peel. Cook and stir over low heat just till spread melts. Spread thin layer of glaze on bottom of cooled tart shell, reserving some glaze. Arrange apricot halves, cut sides down, atop glaze. Drizzle remaining glaze over fruit. Sprinkle with pecans. Chill 3 hours. To serve, remove sides of tart pan. If desired, top with *whipped cream.* Makes 10 servings.

■ **Peach and Toasted Pecan Tart:** Prepare as on page 803, except substitute 4 peeled and sliced *peaches* for the apricots.

Nutrition Facts per serving: 298 cal., 15 g total fat (7 g sat. fat), 57 mg chol., 118 mg sodium, 42 g carbo., 2 g fiber, 3 g pro. **Daily Values:** 28% vit. A, 14% vit. C, 1% calcium, 8% iron

---

HARVEST FRUIT TART

PREP: 35 MINUTES   BAKE: 45 MINUTES   Oven 375°

  1 recipe Pastry for Lattice-Top Pie (see page 810)
1²/₃ cups apple juice or apple cider
  ³/₄ cup snipped dried apricots or peaches
  ³/₄ cup bite-size pitted prunes
  ¹/₂ cup dried tart cherries or raisins
  ¹/₃ cup packed brown sugar
  ¹/₄ cup all-purpose flour
  ¹/₄ teaspoon ground nutmeg
  1 cup chopped cooking apple or pear
  ¹/₂ cup broken walnuts

1. Prepare and roll out Pastry for Lattice-Top Pie, except roll pastry half for bottom crust into a 12-inch circle. Line a 10- or 11-inch tart pan with a removable bottom with pastry. Press pastry into fluted sides of tart pan and trim edges. Save remaining pastry for lattice top.
2. For filling, in a medium saucepan combine apple juice, apricots, prunes, and cherries or raisins. Bring to boiling; reduce heat. Simmer, covered, 10 minutes. Remove from heat. Meanwhile, stir together brown sugar, flour, and nutmeg; add chopped apple or pear and walnuts. Gradually stir dried fruit mixture into apple mixture.
3. Transfer filling to pastry-lined tart pan. Top with a lattice crust (see photos 1 through 4, at right). Bake in 375° oven about 45 minutes or till fruit is bubbly and pastry is golden. Cool on wire rack. To serve, remove sides of tart pan. Makes 10 servings.

Nutrition Facts per serving: 375 cal., 18 g total fat (4 g sat. fat), 0 mg chol., 113 mg sodium, 52 g carbo., 3 g fiber, 4 g pro. **Daily Values:** 12% vit. A, 1% vit. C, 2% calcium, 15% iron

1. Lay *half* of the pastry strips atop the filling at 1-inch intervals.

2. Fold alternate pastry strips back halfway. Place another pastry strip in the center of the tart across the strips already in place.

3. Unfold folded strips; fold back remaining strips. Place another pastry strip parallel to strip in center. Repeat weaving steps until lattice covers filling.

4. Use your fingers and the edge of the tart pan to trim pastry strips even with pan. Press strips against the pan to seal.

ORANGE-CRANBERRY SOUR CREAM TART

PREP: 45 MINUTES   BAKE: 15 MINUTES   COOL: 1 HOURCHILL: 4 TO 24 HOURS   Oven 450°

*For a delightful change, omit the cranberry sauce and orange slices,
and try fresh strawberries or blueberries with
melted jam atop the tart.*

    1 recipe Rich Tart Pastry (see page 811)
    2 eggs
1¹/₄ cups dairy sour cream
  ¹/₃ cup sugar
    2 tablespoons all-purpose flour
    2 tablespoons milk
    1 teaspoon vanilla
    1 cup cranberries
  ²/₃ cup sugar
  ¹/₂ teaspoon finely shredded orange peel (set aside)
  ¹/₂ cup orange juice
    2 medium oranges, peeled and sliced crosswise

1. Prepare and roll out Rich Tart Pastry. Line a 10- or 11-inch tart
pan with a removable bottom with pastry. Press pastry into fluted
sides of tart pan and trim edges. Line pastry with a double thickness
of foil (see photo, page 795). Bake in a 450° oven for 8 minutes. Remove foil. Bake 4 to 5 minutes more or till set and dry.
2. Meanwhile, for filling, in a mixing bowl slightly beat eggs with a
rotary beater or fork. Stir in sour cream, the ¹/₃ cup sugar, flour, milk,
and vanilla.
3. Place the partially baked tart shell on the oven rack. Carefully
pour the filling into the tart shell. Reduce oven temperature to 350°
and bake for 15 to 20 minutes or till a knife inserted near the center
comes out clean. Cool on a wire rack for 1 hour. Cover and chill 4 to
24 hours.
4. Meanwhile, for sauce, in a small saucepan combine cranberries, the
²/₃ cup sugar, and orange juice. Bring to boiling; reduce heat. Boil
gently about 5 minutes or till slightly thickened. Stir in orange peel.
Cover and chill sauce 4 to 24 hours. To serve, remove sides of tart
pan. Arrange sliced oranges around tart. Serve with sauce. Serves 10.

Nutrition Facts per serving: 333 cal., 17 g total fat (10 g sat. fat), 111 mg chol., 144 mg
sodium, 40 g carbo., 1 g fiber, 5 g pro. **Daily Values:** 20% vit. A, 13% vit. C, 4% calcium,
8% iron

FRESH FRUIT AND CREAM TARTS

PREP: 45 MINUTES   BAKE: 13 MINUTES   COOL: 1 HOUR   CHILL: 4 HOURS   Oven 450°

Use the fruits suggested or mix a variety of colors and shapes of other fruits for your own combination.

      1 **recipe Rich Tart Pastry (see page 811)**
    $^1/_2$ **cup sugar**
      2 **tablespoons cornstarch**
  $1^3/_4$ **cups milk**
      2 **beaten egg yolks**
    $^1/_2$ **teaspoon vanilla**
      2 **cups fresh fruit such as sliced strawberries; raspberries; blackberries; peeled, sliced papaya; and/or peeled, sliced kiwifruit**

1. Prepare Rich Tart Pastry; divide pastry into 6 portions. On a lightly floured surface, use your hands to slightly flatten 1 portion. Roll dough from center to edges into a circle about 6 inches in diameter. Line a 4-inch tart pan with a removable bottom with pastry. Press pastry into fluted sides of tart pan; trim edges. Prick bottom and sides of pastry. Repeat with remaining 5 portions of pastry. Line pastry shells with a double thickness of foil (see photo, page 795). Bake pastry shells in a 450° oven for 8 minutes. Remove foil. Bake for 5 to 6 minutes more or till pastry shells are golden. Cool pastry shells on a wire rack.

2. Meanwhile, for filling, in a medium saucepan stir together sugar and cornstarch. Gradually stir in milk. Cook and stir over medium heat till thickened and bubbly. Cook and stir for 2 minutes more. Remove from heat. Stir about 1 cup of the hot mixture into the egg yolks. Pour egg yolk mixture into hot filling in saucepan. Bring to a gentle boil. Cook and stir for 2 minutes more. Remove from heat. Stir in vanilla. Cover surface of filling with plastic wrap; chill about 4 hours or till cold.

3. Divide the chilled filling among the pastry shells. Arrange strawberries, raspberries, blackberries, papaya, or kiwifruit atop filling. To serve, remove sides of tart pans. Makes 6 servings.

Nutrition Facts per serving: 564 cal., 29 g total fat (17 g sat. fat), 229 mg chol., 293 mg sodium, 67 g carbo., 2 g fiber, 10 g pro. **Daily Values:** 51% vit. A, 72% vit. C, 14% calcium, 16% iron

PASTRY FOR SINGLE-CRUST PIE

PREP: 10 MINUTES

Butter-flavored shortening also works well in this recipe.

1¼ **cups all-purpose flour**
⅓ **cup shortening**
4 **to 5 tablespoons cold water**

1. Stir together flour and ¼ teaspoon *salt*. Using a pastry blender, cut in shortening till pieces are pea-size (see step 1, page 809).

2. Sprinkle *1 tablespoon* of the water over part of the mixture; gently toss with a fork. Push moistened dough to the side of the bowl. Repeat moistening dough, using 1 tablespoon of the water at a time, till all the dough is moistened. Form dough into a ball.

3. On a lightly floured surface, use your hands to slightly flatten dough. Roll dough from center to edges into a circle about 12 inches in diameter.

4. To transfer pastry, wrap it around the rolling pin. Unroll pastry into a 9-inch pie plate. Ease pastry into pie plate, being careful not to stretch pastry (see step 2, page 809).

5. Trim pastry to ½ inch beyond edge of pie plate. Fold under extra pastry (see step 3, page 809). Crimp edge as desired (see steps 5, 6, and 7, page 809). Do not prick pastry. Bake as directed in individual recipes. Makes 8 servings.

■ **Food processor directions:** Prepare as above, except place steel blade in food processor bowl. Add flour, shortening, and ¼ teaspoon *salt*. Cover and process with on/off turns till most of mixture resembles cornmeal, but a few larger pieces remain. With food processor running, quickly add 3 tablespoons *water* through feed tube. Stop processor as soon as all water is added; scrape down sides. Process with 2 on/off turns (mixture may not all be moistened). Remove dough from bowl; shape into a ball.

■ **Baked Pastry Shell:** Prepare as above, except generously prick bottom and sides of pastry in pie plate with a fork. Prick all around where bottom and sides meet. Line pastry with a double thickness of foil (see photo, page 795). Bake in a 450° oven for 8 minutes. Remove foil. Bake 5 to 6 minutes more or till golden. Cool on a wire rack.

Nutrition Facts per serving: 141 cal., 9 g total fat (2 g sat. fat), 0 mg chol., 67 mg sodium, 14 g carbo., 0 g fiber, 2 g pro. **Daily Values:** 0% vit. A, 0% vit. C, 0% calcium, 5% iron

TO PREPARE PIE CRUST

1. Use a pastry blender to cut the shortening into the dry mixture until the pieces are the size of small peas.

2. Starting at one side, unroll pastry over a pie plate. Ease pastry into the plate without stretching it; this prevents it from shrinking while baking.

3. Trim pastry to ½ inch beyond the edge of the pie plate. Fold the extra pastry under, even with the plate's rim, to build up the edge.

4. For a double-crust pie, place top pastry on the filling. Lift the edge of the bottom pastry away from the plate; fold the excess top pastry underneath.

5. For a rope edge, pinch the pastry, pushing forward on a slant with your bent index finger and pulling back with your thumb.

6. For a fluted edge, place your thumb against the inside of the pastry; press dough around your thumb with your other hand's thumb and index finger.

7. For a petal edge, flute the pastry as directed in step 6. Press the tines of a fork lightly into the center of each flute.

PASTRY FOR DOUBLE-CRUST PIE

PREP: 15 MINUTES

2 cups all-purpose flour
⅔ cup shortening
6 to 7 tablespoons cold water

1. Stir together flour and ½ teaspoon *salt*. Using a pastry blender, cut in shortening till pieces are pea-size (see step 1, above).

2. Sprinkle *1 tablespoon* of the water over part of the mixture; gently toss with a fork. Push moistened dough to side of bowl. Repeat, using 1 tablespoon water at a time, till all the dough is moistened. Divide in half. Form each half into a ball.

3. On lightly floured surface, flatten 1 dough ball. Roll from center to edges into 12-inch circle.

4. To transfer pastry, wrap it around the rolling pin; unroll into a 9-inch pie plate. Ease pastry into pie plate, being careful not to stretch pastry (see step 2, page 809). Transfer filling to pastry-lined pie plate. Trim pastry even with rim of pie plate.

5. Roll remaining dough into a circle about 12 inches in diameter. Cut slits to allow steam to escape. Place remaining pastry on filling; trim ½ inch beyond edge of plate. Fold top pastry under bottom pastry (see step 4, page 809). Crimp edge as desired (see steps 5, 6, and 7, page 809). Bake as directed in individual recipes. Makes 8 servings.

■ **Food processor directions:** Prepare as above, except place steel blade in processor bowl. Add flour, shortening, and ½ teaspoon *salt*. Cover; process with on/off turns till most of mixture resembles cornmeal, but with a few larger pieces. With processor running, quickly add ¼ cup *water* through feed tube. Stop processor when all water is added; scrape down sides. Process with 2 on/off turns (mixture may not all be moistened). Remove dough from bowl; shape into a ball. Divide in half.

■ **Pastry for Lattice-Top Pie:** Prepare as above, except trim bottom pastry to ½ inch beyond edge of pie plate. Roll out remaining pastry

PASTRY KNOW-HOW

■ Measure accurately. Too much flour makes the pastry tough, too much shortening makes the pastry crumbly, and too much water makes the pastry tough and soggy.

■ To roll pastry dough out with little sticking, use a stockinette cover for your rolling pin and a pastry cloth. Lightly flour both the stockinette and the pastry cloth.

■ Use a glass or dull metal pie plate so your pastry browns evenly (see tip, page 780).

■ If pastry is to be baked without a filling, prick it well with the tines of a fork. This prevents it from puffing up. (Do not prick pastry if filling and pastry will be baked together.)

■ Be sure your oven temperature is accurate. If it's too low, the bottom crust will be soggy.

and cut into $1/2$-inch-wide strips. Fill pastry-lined pie plate with desired filling. Weave strips over filling for lattice crust (see photos 1, 2, and 3, page 805). Press ends of strips into crust rim. Fold bottom pastry over strips; seal and crimp edge. For a quick lattice, roll out top pastry. Use a mini-cookie or canapé cutter to make cutouts an equal distance apart from pastry center to edge. Place pastry on filling and seal (see steps 4 and 5, page 809). Bake as directed.

Nutrition Facts per serving: 256 cal., 17 g total fat (4 g sat. fat), 0 mg chol., 134 mg sodium, 22 g carbo., 1 g fiber, 3 g pro. **Daily Values:** 0% vit. A, 0% vit. C, 0% calcium, 8% iron

---

RICH TART PASTRY

PREP: 15 MINUTES

$1/2$ cup cold butter
$1^1/4$ cups all-purpose flour
1 beaten egg yolk
2 to 3 tablespoons ice water

1. In a mixing bowl cut butter into flour till pieces are pea-size (see step 1, page 809). Stir together egg yolk and *1 tablespoon* of the ice water. Gradually stir egg yolk mixture into flour mixture. Add remaining water, 1 tablespoon at a time, till all the dough is moistened. Gently knead the dough just till a ball forms. If necessary, cover dough with plastic wrap and refrigerate for 30 to 60 minutes or till dough is easy to handle.
2. On a lightly floured surface, use your hands to slightly flatten the dough. Roll dough from center to edges into a circle 12 inches in diameter.
3. To transfer pastry, wrap it around the rolling pin. Unroll pastry into a 10-inch tart pan with a removable bottom. Ease pastry into pan, being careful not to stretch pastry (see step 2, page 809). Press pastry into fluted sides of tart pan and trim edges. Do not prick pastry. Bake as directed in individual recipes. Makes 10 servings.

Nutrition Facts per serving: 173 cal., 12 g total fat (7 g sat. fat), 57 mg chol., 117 mg sodium, 14 g carbo., 0 g fiber, 2 g pro. **Daily Values:** 14% vit. A, 0% vit. C, 0% calcium, 6% iron

GRAHAM CRACKER CRUST

PREP: 10 MINUTES   CHILL: 1 HOUR

   $^1/_3$ **cup butter**
   $^1/_4$ **cup sugar**
   1$^1/_4$ **cups finely crushed graham crackers (about 18)**

1. Melt butter; stir in sugar. Add crushed crackers; toss to mix well. Spread evenly into a 9-inch pie plate. Press onto bottom and sides to form a firm, even crust. Chill about 1 hour or till firm. (Or, bake in a 375° oven for 4 to 5 minutes or till edge is lightly browned. Cool on a wire rack before filling.) Makes 8 servings.

Nutrition Facts per serving: 150 cal., 9 g total fat (5 g sat. fat), 20 mg chol., 149 mg sodium, 17 g carbo., 0 g fiber, 1 g pro. **Daily Values:** 6% vit. A, 0% vit. C, 0% calcium, 3% iron

■ **Chocolate Wafer Crust:** Prepare as above, except omit sugar and substitute 1$^1/_2$ cups finely crushed *chocolate wafers* (about 25) for the crushed graham crackers. Do not bake.

Nutrition Facts per serving: 148 cal., 10 g total fat (5 g sat. fat)

■ **Gingersnap Crust:** Prepare as above, except omit the sugar and substitute 1$^1/_4$ cups finely crushed *gingersnaps* (20 to 22) for the crushed graham crackers.

Nutrition Facts per serving: 142 cal., 9 g total fat (6 g sat. fat)

NUT CRUST

PREP: 10 MINUTES   BAKE: 10 MINUTES   Oven 375°

If you use the blender for this recipe, process only half the nuts and sugar at a time.

   2 **cups walnuts, almonds, or pecans**
   3 **tablespoons sugar**
   2 **slightly beaten egg whites**

1. Place nuts and sugar in a blender container or food processor bowl. Cover and blend or process till nuts are finely ground. Stir together ground nut mixture and egg whites. Using a spatula, press mixture onto bottom and sides of a 9-inch pie plate. Bake in a 375° degree oven for 10 to 12 minutes or till crust appears dry. Cool on a wire rack before filling. Makes 8 servings.

Nutrition Facts per serving: 215 cal., 19 g total fat (2 g sat. fat), 0 mg chol., 17 mg sodium, 10 g carbo., 1 g fiber, 5 g pro. **Daily Values:** 0% vit. A, 1% vit. C, 2% calcium, 4% iron

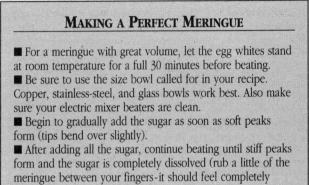

MAKING A PERFECT MERINGUE

■ For a meringue with great volume, let the egg whites stand at room temperature for a full 30 minutes before beating.
■ Be sure to use the size bowl called for in your recipe. Copper, stainless-steel, and glass bowls work best. Also make sure your electric mixer beaters are clean.
■ Begin to gradually add the sugar as soon as soft peaks form (tips bend over slightly).
■ After adding all the sugar, continue beating until stiff peaks form and the sugar is completely dissolved (rub a little of the meringue between your fingers-it should feel completely smooth).

MERINGUE FOR PIE

STAND: 30 MINUTES   PREP: 10 MINUTES

No-Fat

    3 egg whites
 ¹/₂ teaspoon vanilla
 ¹/₄ teaspoon cream of tartar
    6 tablespoons sugar

1. Allow egg whites to stand at room temperature for 30 minutes. In a large mixing bowl combine egg whites, vanilla, and cream of tartar. Beat with an electric mixer on medium speed about 1 minute or till soft peaks form (tips curl).
2. Gradually add sugar, *1 tablespoon* at a time, beating on high speed about 4 minutes more or till mixture forms stiff, glossy peaks (tips stand straight) and sugar dissolves.

3. Immediately spread meringue over hot pie filling, carefully sealing to edge of pastry to prevent shrinkage. Bake as directed in individual recipes. Makes 8 servings.

Nutrition Facts per serving: 39 cal., 0 g total fat, 0 mg chol., 21 mg sodium, 8 g carbo., 0 g fiber, 1 g pro.

■ **Four-Egg-White Meringue:** Prepare as above, except use 4 *egg whites,* 1 teaspoon *vanilla,* ¹/₂ teaspoon *cream of tartar,* and ¹/₂ cup *sugar.* Beat about 5 minutes or till stiff, glossy peaks form. Continue as directed.

Nutrition Facts per serving: 59 cal., 0 g total fat

POULTRY

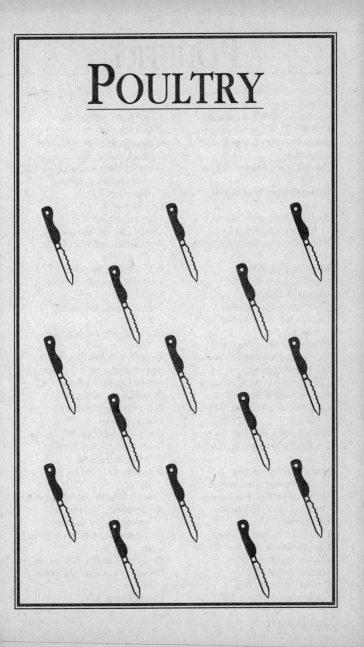

PEPPER-LIME CHICKEN

PREP: 10 MINUTES   BROIL: 25 MINUTES

Low-Fat

    2 to 2¹/₂ pounds meaty chicken pieces (breasts, thighs, and
         drumsticks)
 ¹/₂ teaspoon finely shredded lime peel
 ¹/₄ cup lime juice
    1 tablespoon cooking oil
    2 cloves garlic, minced
    1 teaspoon dried thyme or basil, crushed
 ¹/₂ to 1 teaspoon cracked black pepper
 ¹/₄ teaspoon salt

1. Skin chicken. Rinse chicken; pat dry. Place chicken pieces, bone
sides up, on the unheated rack of a broiler pan. Broil 4 to 5 inches
from the heat about 20 minutes or till lightly browned.
2. Meanwhile, for glaze, in a bowl stir together lime peel, lime juice,
oil, garlic, thyme or basil, pepper, and salt. Brush chicken with
glaze. Turn chicken; brush with more glaze. Broil for 5 to 15 minutes
more or till chicken is tender and no longer pink, brushing often
with glaze during the last 5 minutes of cooking. Makes 6 servings.

Nutrition Facts per serving: 153 cal., 7 g total fat (2 g sat. fat), 61 mg chol., 145 mg
sodium, 1 g carbo., 0 g fiber, 20 g pro. **Daily Values:** 0% vit. A, 6% vit. C, 1% calcium, 6%
iron

LEMON-MUSTARD CHICKEN

PREP: 10 MINUTES   BROIL: 25 MINUTES

Low-Fat

    2 to 2¹/₂ pounds meaty chicken pieces (breasts, thighs, and
         drumsticks)
    2 tablespoons cooking oil
    1 tablespoon Dijon-style mustard
    1 tablespoon lemon juice
 1¹/₂ teaspoons lemon-pepper seasoning
    1 teaspoon dried oregano or basil, crushed
 ¹/₈ teaspoon ground red pepper

1. Skin chicken. Rinse chicken; pat dry. Place chicken pieces, bone sides up, on the unheated rack of a broiler pan. Broil 4 to 5 inches from the heat about 20 minutes or till lightly browned.

2. Meanwhile, for glaze, in a bowl stir together oil, mustard, lemon juice, lemon-pepper seasoning, oregano or basil, and red pepper. Brush chicken with glaze. Turn chicken; brush with remaining glaze. Broil for 5 to 15 minutes more or till chicken is tender and no longer pink. Makes 6 servings.

Nutrition Facts per serving: 174 cal., 10 g total fat (2 g sat. fat), 61 mg chol., 390 mg sodium, 1 g carbo., 0 g fiber, 20 g pro. **Daily Values:** 1% vit. A, 2% vit. C, 1% calcium, 6% iron

---

HANDLING POULTRY SAFELY

Follow these simple guidelines to safely handle fresh poultry (see also "Poultry Hotline," page 829).

■ Always wash your hands, work surfaces, and utensils in hot soapy water after handling raw poultry to prevent spreading bacteria to other foods.

■ When cutting raw poultry, use a plastic cutting board because it's easier to clean and disinfect than a wooden one.

■ Rinse and pat poultry dry with paper towels before cooking.

■ When grilling, never use the same plate to transfer uncooked and cooked poultry to and from the grill.

■ Always marinate poultry in the refrigerator.

■ Any marinade or basting sauce in the bottom of the pan that is to be served alongside grilled or broiled poultry must be heated to boiling before serving because of the raw meat juices in it and the possibility of contamination by bacteria from the uncooked poultry. Or, before you start basting, set some of the sauce aside.

■ Serve poultry immediately after cooking it. Don't let it stand at room temperature longer than 1 hour or bacteria will form—especially in warm weather. Refrigerate leftovers as soon as possible.

■ Reheat leftover gravy to a rolling boil (about 185°) in a covered saucepan for best taste and food safety.

BROILED CHICKEN WITH SESAME-GINGER GLAZE

PREP: 15 MINUTES   BROIL: 27 MINUTES

Low-Fat

Whenever you broil poultry, meat, or fish, preheat only the broiler unit. Preheating the pan and rack can cause them to warp and the food to stick to the rack.

2 to 2½ pounds meaty chicken pieces (breasts, thighs, and
    drumsticks)
⅓ cup plum sauce or sweet-and-sour sauce*
3 tablespoons hoisin sauce
2 tablespoons soy sauce
4 teaspoons honey
4 teaspoons water
1½ teaspoons sesame seed
1 teaspoon grated gingerroot or ¼ teaspoon ground ginger
¼ teaspoon five-spice powder
1 clove garlic, minced
    Several dashes bottled hot pepper sauce

1. Skin chicken. Rinse chicken; pat dry. Place chicken pieces, bone sides up, on the unheated rack of a broiler pan. Broil 4 to 5 inches from heat about 20 minutes or till lightly browned.
2. Meanwhile, for glaze, in a small saucepan combine plum sauce or sweet-and-sour sauce, hoisin sauce, soy sauce, honey, water, sesame seed, gingerroot or ground ginger, five-spice powder, garlic, and hot pepper sauce. Bring to boiling; reduce heat. Simmer, uncovered, for 2 minutes.
3. Turn chicken. Broil for 5 to 15 minutes more or till chicken is tender and no longer pink. Brush with glaze; broil 2 minutes more. Makes 6 servings.
*Note: If desired, use the Sweet-and-Sour Sauce recipe on page 964.

Nutrition Facts per serving: 191 cal., 5 g total fat (1 g sat. fat), 61 mg chol., 560 mg sodium, 14 g carbo., 0 g fiber, 20 g pro. **Daily Values:** 1% vit. A, 1% vit. C, 1% calcium, 6% iron

FRIED CHICKEN WITH CREAM GRAVY

PREP: 25 MINUTES COOK: 45 MINUTES

You can keep just-fried chicken hot in a 250° oven while making gravy.

  2 to 2¹/₂ pounds meaty chicken pieces (breasts, thighs, and
     drumsticks)
¹/₄ cup all-purpose flour or ¹/₂ cup fine dry bread crumbs
  1 teaspoon paprika, curry powder, poultry seasoning, chili
     powder; or dried basil or marjoram, crushed; or ¹/₂
     teaspoon garlic powder or onion powder
¹/₂ teaspoon salt
¹/₄ teaspoon pepper
  2 tablespoons cooking oil
  1 recipe Cream Gravy (see below)

1. Rinse chicken; pat dry. In a plastic bag combine flour or crumbs, herb, salt, and pepper. Add chicken pieces, a few at a time, shaking to coat.

2. In a 12-inch skillet heat oil. Add chicken to the skillet, placing meaty pieces toward the center. Cook, uncovered, over medium heat for 15 minutes, turning to brown evenly. Reduce heat; cover tightly. Cook for 25 minutes. Uncover and cook for 5 to 10 minutes more or till chicken is tender and no longer pink. Drain on paper towels, reserving drippings for gravy. Transfer chicken to a serving platter; keep warm. Prepare Cream Gravy. Serve gravy with chicken. Makes 6 servings.

■ **Oven directions:** Rinse chicken; pat dry. Coat chicken as above. Brown chicken in a 12-inch ovenproof skillet. (Or, brown chicken in a regular skillet; transfer, skin side up, to a 15×10×1-inch baking pan.) Place in a 375° oven. Bake, uncovered, for 35 to 40 minutes or till chicken is tender and no longer pink. Do not turn.

■ **Cream Gravy:** Pour off drippings in skillet, reserving 2 tablespoons. Return reserved drippings to skillet. Add 2 tablespoons *all-purpose flour;* ¹/₈ teaspoon *pepper;* and, if desired, 1 teaspoon instant *chicken bouillon granules,* stirring till smooth. Add 1²/₃ cups *milk* all at once. Cook and stir over medium heat till thickened and bubbly. Cook and stir for 1 minute more. (If necessary, thin with a little additional milk.) Makes 1²/₃ cups.

Nutrition Facts per serving: 273 cal., 14 g total fat (4 g sat. fat), 74 mg chol., 417 mg sodium, 9 g carbo., 0 g fiber, 25 g pro. **Daily Values:** 8% vit. A, 1% vit. C, 8% calcium, 9% iron

CORNMEAL BATTER-FRIED CHICKEN

START TO FINISH: 1 HOUR

Be sure to drain and dry chicken pieces well after simmering so the batter will cling evenly.

2 to 2¹/₂ pounds meaty chicken pieces (breasts, thighs, and drumsticks)
²/₃ cup all-purpose flour
¹/₃ cup cornmeal
¹/₂ teaspoon baking powder
¹/₂ teaspoon garlic salt
¹/₂ teaspoon poultry seasoning
¹/₈ teaspoon ground red pepper
1 beaten egg
¹/₂ cup milk
2 tablespoons cooking oil
Shortening or cooking oil for deep-fat frying

1. Skin and rinse chicken. In a large saucepan cover chicken with *lightly salted water*. Bring to boiling; reduce heat. Cover and simmer for 20 minutes; drain. Pat chicken dry with paper towels.
2. For batter, in a mixing bowl combine flour, cornmeal, baking powder, garlic salt, poultry seasoning, and red pepper. Stir together egg, milk, and the 2 tablespoons oil. Add to flour mixture; beat till smooth.
3. Meanwhile, in a heavy 3-quart saucepan or deep-fat fryer heat 1¹/₄ inches shortening or oil to 365°. Dip chicken pieces, 1 at a time, into batter, gently shaking off excess. Carefully lower into the hot oil. Fry 2 or 3 pieces at a time for 2 to 3 minutes or till golden, turning once. Carefully remove and drain well. Keep warm while frying remaining chicken. Makes 6 servings.

Nutrition Facts per serving: 342 cal., 19 g total fat (5 g sat. fat), 98 mg chol., 278 mg sodium, 17 g carbo., 1 g fiber, 23 g pro. **Daily Values:** 4% vit. A, 0% vit. C, 5% calcium, 12% iron

■ **Herbed Batter-Fried Chicken:** Prepare as above, except omit poultry seasoning. Stir 1 teaspoon dried *thyme, savory, marjoram, Italian seasoning, or sage,* crushed, into flour mixture.

Nutrition Facts per serving: 342 cal., 19 g total fat (5 g sat. fat)

■ **Parmesan Batter-Fried Chicken:** Prepare as above, except omit garlic salt and poultry seasoning. Stir ¹/₄ cup grated *Parmesan cheese,* 2 tablespoons snipped *fresh parsley,* and ¹/₄ teaspoon *garlic powder* into the flour mixture. Increase the milk to ²/₃ cup.

Nutrition Facts per serving: 364 cal., 21 g total fat (6 g sat. fat)

OVEN-FRIED CHICKEN

PREP: 20 MINUTES   BAKE: 45 MINUTES   Oven 375°

Low-Fat

  1 beaten egg
  3 tablespoons milk
  1 cup finely crushed saltine crackers (about 28)
  1 teaspoon dried thyme, crushed
  ¹/₂ teaspoon paprika
  ¹/₈ teaspoon pepper
  2 to 2¹/₂ pounds meaty chicken pieces (breasts, thighs, and
     drumsticks)
  2 tablespoons margarine or butter, melted

1. In a small bowl combine egg and milk. For coating mixture, in a shallow dish combine crushed crackers, thyme, paprika, and pepper. Set aside. Skin chicken. Rinse chicken; pat dry. Dip chicken pieces into egg mixture; coat with crumb mixture.

2. In a greased 15×10×1-inch or 13×9×2-inch baking pan, arrange chicken so the pieces don't touch. Drizzle chicken pieces with the melted margarine or butter.

3. Bake in a 375° oven for 45 to 55 minutes or till chicken is tender and no longer pink. Do not turn chicken pieces while baking. Makes 6 servings.

Nutrition Facts per serving: 240 cal., 12 g total fat (5 g sat. fat), 107 mg chol., 296 mg sodium, 11 g carbo., 0 g fiber, 22 g pro. **Daily Values:** 8% vit. A, 0% vit. C, 3% calcium, 12% iron

■ **Oven-Fried Parmesan Chicken:** Prepare as on page 823, except omit crushed crackers and thyme. For the coating mixture, combine 1/2 cup grated *Parmesan cheese,* 1/4 cup fine dry *bread crumbs,* and 1 teaspoon *dried oregano,* crushed, with the paprika and pepper.

Nutrition Facts per serving: 233 cal., 12 g total fat (6 g sat. fat)

TURKEY GRUYÈRE

START TO FINISH: 30 MINUTES

Fast

   4 **turkey breast tenderloin steaks (about 1 pound total)**
 1/3 **cup all-purpose flour**
   2 **teaspoons lemon-pepper seasoning**
 1/4 **teaspoon ground nutmeg**
   2 **beaten eggs**
   1 **tablespoon dry sherry, white wine, or water**
 3/4 **cup finely shredded natural Gruyère, Jarlsberg, or Swiss cheese**
 1/2 **cup fine dry seasoned bread crumbs**
 1/4 **cup snipped fresh parsley**
 1/4 **cup margarine or butter**
     Lemon wedges (optional)

1. Rinse turkey; pat dry. Stir together flour, lemon-pepper seasoning, and nutmeg; set aside. In a shallow dish stir together eggs and dry sherry, wine, or water; set aside. Stir together shredded cheese, bread crumbs, and parsley. Coat turkey steaks with flour mixture, dip into egg mixture, then coat evenly with bread crumb mixture.

2. In a 12-inch skillet melt *2 tablespoons* of the margarine or butter. Cook turkey over medium heat about 8 minutes or till turkey is tender and no longer pink, turning once. Add remaining margarine or butter as needed. If desired, serve with lemon wedges. Makes 4 servings.

Nutrition Facts per serving: 414 cal., 23 g total fat (8 g sat. fat), 175 mg chol., 1,192 mg sodium, 19 g carbo., 0 g fiber, 30 g pro. **Daily Values:** 29% vit. A, 8% vit. C, 22% calcium, 12% iron

CHICKEN KIEV

PREP: 20 MINUTES   CHILL: 1 TO 24 HOURS   BAKE: 15 MINUTES   Oven 400°

    4 skinless, boneless chicken breast halves (about 1 pound total)
    1 tablespoon chopped green onion (1)
    1 tablespoon snipped fresh parsley
    1 clove garlic, minced
  1/2 of a 1/4-pound stick of butter, chilled
    1 beaten egg
    1 tablespoon water
  1/4 cup all-purpose flour
  1/4 cup fine dry bread crumbs
    1 tablespoon butter
    1 tablespoon cooking oil

1. Rinse chicken; pat dry. Place each breast half between 2 pieces of plastic wrap. Pound lightly into a rectangle about 1/8 inch thick. Remove plastic wrap. Sprinkle with salt and pepper. Combine green onion, parsley, and garlic; sprinkle on chicken.

2. Cut chilled 1/2 stick of butter into four 2 1/2x1/2-inch sticks. Place a stick of butter in center of each chicken piece. Fold in sides; roll up jelly-roll style, pressing edges to seal. Stir together egg and water. Coat rolls with flour, dip in egg mixture, then coat with bread crumbs. Cover and chill 1 to 24 hours.

3. In a large skillet melt the 1 tablespoon butter; add oil. Add chilled chicken rolls. Cook over medium-high heat about 5 minutes or till golden brown, turning to brown all sides. Transfer to a 2-quart rectangular baking dish. Bake in a 400° oven for 15 to 18 minutes or till chicken is no longer pink. Spoon drippings over rolls. Makes 4 servings.

Nutrition Facts per serving: 348 cal., 23 g total fat (11 g sat. fat), 152 mg chol., 263 mg sodium, 11 g carbo., 0 g fiber, 25 g pro. **Daily Values:** 17% vit. A, 2% vit. C, 2% calcium, 10% iron

■ **Cheesy Chicken Rolls:** Prepare as above, except substitute sticks of *caraway, cheddar, Gruyère, or blue cheese* for the butter.

Nutrition Facts per serving: 300 cal., 15 g total fat (6 g sat. fat)

CHICKEN DIJON

START TO FINISH: 25 MINUTES

Fast  **Low-Fat**

- ³/₄ cup long grain rice or one 4.5-ounce package herb-flavored rice mix
- 4 skinless, boneless chicken breast halves (about 1 pound total)
- 1 teaspoon lemon-pepper seasoning
- ¹/₄ teaspoon onion powder
- 2 tablespoons margarine or butter
  Milk, half-and-half, or light cream
- ¹/₄ cup milk, half-and-half, or light cream
- 2 teaspoons all-purpose flour
- 1 tablespoon Dijon-style mustard
  Tomato wedges (optional)
  Snipped fresh parsley (optional)

1. Cook rice or herb-flavored rice mix according to package directions.

2. Meanwhile, rinse chicken; pat dry. Sprinkle both sides of chicken with lemon-pepper seasoning and onion powder. In a large skillet cook chicken in margarine or butter over medium heat for 8 to 10 minutes or till chicken is tender and no longer pink, turning once. Transfer to a serving platter; keep warm.

3. For sauce, measure pan juices; add milk, half-and-half, or light cream to make ²/₃ cup liquid. Return to the skillet. Stir the ¹/₄ cup milk, half-and-half, or light cream into flour till smooth; add to juice mixture in skillet. Stir in mustard. Cook and stir till thickened and bubbly. Cook and stir for 1 minute more. Spoon some sauce over chicken; pass remaining sauce. If desired, garnish with tomato wedges and parsley and serve with hot cooked rice. Makes 4 servings.

Nutrition Facts per serving: 332 cal., 10 g total fat (3 g sat. fat), 63 mg chol., 511 mg sodium, 31 g carbo., 0 g fiber, 26 g pro. **Daily Values:** 10% vit. A, 0% vit. C, 6% calcium, 15% iron

CHICKEN CORDON BLEU

START TO FINISH: 40 MINUTES

In food terms, cordon bleu refers to chicken or veal that has been pounded thin, layered with Swiss cheese and ham, rolled, breaded, and sautéed until golden brown.

4 skinless, boneless chicken breast halves (about 1 pound total)
4 slices prosciutto or fully cooked ham
4 slices Swiss cheese (3 ounces total)
3 tablespoons margarine or butter
1 cup sliced fresh mushrooms
1 clove garlic, minced
2 tablespoons all-purpose flour
$^{1}/_{4}$ teaspoon ground nutmeg
1 cup milk
2 tablespoons dry white wine
Hot cooked noodles (see page 774) (optional)

1. Rinse chicken; pat dry. Place each breast half between 2 pieces of plastic wrap. Pound lightly into a rectangle about $^{1}/_{8}$ inch thick. Remove plastic wrap.

2. Place a slice of prosciutto or ham and a slice of cheese on each chicken piece. Fold in the bottom and sides; roll up jelly-roll style. Secure with wooden toothpicks.

3. In a 10-inch skillet cook rolls in *1 tablespoon* of the hot margarine or butter over medium-low heat for 20 minutes or till tender and juices run clear. Turn to brown evenly. Remove toothpicks.

4. Meanwhile, for sauce, in a small saucepan melt the remaining 2 tablespoons margarine or butter. Add mushrooms and garlic. Cook and stir till tender. Stir in flour and nutmeg. Add milk all at once. Cook and stir till thickened and bubbly. Cook and stir 2 minutes more. Stir in wine.

5. If desired, serve chicken rolls atop hot cooked noodles. Top with sauce. Makes 4 servings.

Nutrition Facts per serving: 400 cal., 24 g total fat (7 g sat. fat), 83 mg chol., 617 mg sodium, 8 g carbo., 0 g fiber, 36 g pro. **Daily Values:** 20% vit. A, 2% vit. C, 24% calcium, 8% iron

CHICKEN MARSALA

START TO FINISH: 25 MINUTES

Fast **Low-Fat**

4 skinless, boneless chicken breast halves (about 1 pound total)
$1/4$ cup all-purpose flour
$1/4$ teaspoon dried marjoram, crushed
$1/8$ teaspoon salt
1 cup sliced fresh mushrooms
2 tablespoons sliced green onion (1)
3 tablespoons margarine or butter
$1/4$ cup chicken broth
$1/4$ cup dry Marsala or dry sherry
Snipped fresh parsley (optional)

1. Rinse chicken; pat dry. Place each breast half between 2 pieces of plastic wrap. Pound lightly to $1/8$-inch thickness. Remove plastic wrap. Stir together flour, marjoram, salt, and $1/8$ teaspoon *pepper*. Lightly press chicken pieces into flour mixture on both sides; shake off excess.

2. In a large skillet cook mushrooms and green onion in *1 tablespoon* of the margarine till tender; remove from skillet. In the same skillet cook chicken pieces in remaining margarine over medium-high heat for 4 minutes, turning to brown evenly. Remove skillet from heat. Return mushrooms and green onion to skillet. Carefully add broth and Marsala. Cook, uncovered, for 2 to 3 minutes or till mushroom mixture thickens slightly, stirring occasionally. Transfer chicken to a serving platter. Spoon mushroom mixture over chicken. If desired, sprinkle with parsley. Makes 4 servings.

Nutrition Facts per serving: 251 cal., 12 g total fat (3 g sat. fat), 60 mg chol., 270 mg sodium, 8 g carbo., 0 g fiber, 23 g pro. **Daily Values:** 11% vit. A, 2% vit. C, 1% calcium, 10% iron

BROILED CHICKEN SANDWICH

PREP: 15 MINUTES   MARINATE: 4 HOURS   BROIL: 7 MINUTES

Low-Fat

- ¹/₃ cup orange juice
- 2 tablespoons reduced-sodium soy sauce
- 2 tablespoons honey
- 2 teaspoons lemon-pepper seasoning
- 1 teaspoon ground ginger
- ¹/₄ teaspoon garlic powder
- 4 skinless, boneless chicken breast halves (about 1 pound total)
- 4 whole wheat hamburger buns, split and toasted
- 4 lettuce leaves
- 4 tomato slices

1. For marinade, in a shallow, nonmetallic dish combine orange juice, soy sauce, honey, lemon-pepper seasoning, ginger, and garlic powder. Set marinade aside.

2. Rinse chicken; pat dry. Place each breast half between 2 pieces of plastic wrap. Pound lightly to an even thickness. Remove plastic wrap. Place chicken pieces in marinade. Cover and marinate in the refrigerator for 4 to 6 hours or overnight.

3. Remove chicken from marinade, reserving marinade. Place chicken on the unheated rack of a broiler pan. Broil 4 to 5 inches from the heat about 7 minutes or till tender and no longer pink, turning and brushing chicken with reserved marinade once. Serve chicken breasts on buns with lettuce and tomato. Makes 4 servings.

POULTRY HOTLINE

For answers to your questions about chicken handling or safety, call the U.S. Department of Agriculture's Meat and Poultry Hotline, 800/535-4555 (447-3333 in the Washington, D.C., area). Consumer specialists at the hotline take calls from 10 a.m. to 4 p.m. (Eastern Standard Time).

Nutrition Facts per serving: 297 cal., 6 g total fat (1 g sat. fat), 59 mg chol., 1,066 mg sodium, 34 g carbo., 1 g fiber, 26 g pro. **Daily Values:** 2% vit. A, 23% vit. C, 4% calcium, 15% iron

CURRIED CHICKEN

PREP: 20 MINUTES COOK: 28 MINUTES

Low-Fat

12 ounces skinless, boneless chicken breast halves
 1 tablespoon cooking oil
 1 to 2 teaspoons curry powder
 1 cup chicken broth
 1 cup thinly sliced celery
 1 medium onion, cut into thin wedges
 1 cup coarsely chopped apple (1 large)
 1 tablespoon cornstarch
 2 cups hot cooked rice (see page 139)
   Chutney, raisins, coconut, and peanuts (optional)

1. Rinse chicken; pat dry. Cut chicken into 1-inch pieces; set aside.
2. In a large skillet heat oil over medium-high heat. Add curry powder; cook and stir for 30 seconds. Add chicken; cook and stir till chicken is browned. Slowly add broth, celery, onion, and ⅛ teaspoon *pepper.* Bring to boiling; reduce heat. Cover; simmer 15 minutes. Add apple. Cover; cook 5 minutes.
3. Combine cornstarch and ¼ cup *cold water;* add to skillet. Cook and stir till thickened and bubbly. Cook and stir for 2 minutes more. Serve with rice and, if desired, condiments. Makes 4 servings.

Nutrition Facts per serving: 277 cal., 7 g total fat (1 g sat. fat), 45 mg chol., 278 mg sodium, 33 g carbo., 2 g fiber, 20 g pro. **Daily Values:** 1% vit. A, 9% vit. C, 3% calcium, 14% iron

POLLO RELLENO

Low-Fat

Expect oohs and aahs when you serve these chicken rolls; each has a cheese-stuffed chili pepper inside.

6 **skinless, boneless chicken breast halves (about 1½ pounds total)**
⅓ **cup cornmeal**
½ **of a 1¼-ounce package (2 tablespoons) taco seasoning mix**
1 **egg**
1 **4-ounce can whole green chili peppers, rinsed, seeded, and cut in half lengthwise (6 pieces total)**
2 **ounces Monterey Jack cheese, cut into six 2×½-inch sticks**
2 **tablespoons snipped fresh cilantro or fresh parsley**
¼ **teaspoon black pepper**
¼ **teaspoon crushed red pepper**
1 **8-ounce jar taco sauce or salsa**
½ **cup shredded Monterey Jack or cheddar cheese (optional)**
Fresh cilantro sprigs (optional)

1. Rinse chicken; pat dry. Place each breast half between 2 pieces of plastic wrap. Pound lightly into a rectangle about ⅛ inch thick. Remove plastic wrap.
2. In a bowl combine cornmeal and taco seasoning mix. Place egg in another bowl; beat lightly.
3. For each roll, place a chili pepper half on a chicken piece. Place a cheese stick atop chili pepper near an edge. Sprinkle with some of the cilantro or parsley, black pepper, and red pepper. Fold in sides; roll up jelly-roll style, starting from edge with cheese.
4. Dip rolls into egg and coat with cornmeal mixture. Place rolls, seam sides down, in a shallow baking pan. Bake, uncovered, in a 375° oven for 25 to 30 minutes. Heat taco sauce. If desired, sprinkle chicken with shredded cheese. Serve with taco sauce or salsa. If desired, garnish with cilantro sprigs. Makes 6 servings.

Nutrition Facts per serving: 235 cal., 10 g total fat (3 g sat. fat), 103 mg chol., 769 mg sodium, 13 g carbo., 0 g fiber, 28 g pro. **Daily Values:** 6% vit. A, 34% vit. C, 10% calcium, 13% iron

TURKEY IN TORTILLAS

PREP: 20 MINUTES   MARINATE: 1 HOUR   BROIL: 6 MINUTES

- 1/4 **cup snipped fresh cilantro or parsley**
- 2 **tablespoons olive oil or cooking oil**
- 1 **teaspoon finely shredded lemon peel**
- 2 **tablespoons lemon juice**
- 1 **teaspoon chili powder**
- 1/2 **teaspoon ground cumin**
- 12 **ounces turkey breast tenderloin steaks**
- 8 **8-inch flour tortillas, warmed***
- 2 **cups shredded lettuce**
- 1/2 **cup shredded cheddar cheese**
- 1 **large tomato, chopped**
- 1/4 **cup sliced pitted ripe olives (optional)**
  Salsa (optional)

1. In a shallow, nonmetallic dish combine cilantro, oil, lemon peel, lemon juice, chili powder, cumin, and 1/2 teaspoon *pepper*. Rinse turkey; pat dry. Place turkey in marinade, turning to coat. Cover and marinate in the refrigerator about 1 hour.

2. Remove turkey from marinade, reserving marinade. Place turkey on the unheated rack of a broiler pan. Broil 4 to 5 inches from the heat for 6 to 8 minutes or till tender and no longer pink, turning and brushing with reserved marinade once.

3. Cut turkey into bite-size strips. Fill each tortilla with some of the turkey, lettuce, cheese, tomato, and, if desired, olives. Fold tortillas over filling. If desired, serve with salsa. Makes 4 servings.

*Note: To warm tortillas, wrap in foil and heat in a 350° oven for 5 minutes.

Nutrition Facts per serving: 447 cal., 19 g total fat (5 g sat. fat), 52 mg chol., 470 mg sodium, 43 g carbo., 1 g fiber, 26 g pro. **Daily Values:** 10% vit. A, 22% vit. C, 18% calcium, 26% iron

HONEY-GLAZED CHICKEN STIR-FRY

START TO FINISH: 25 MINUTES

Fast   **Low-Fat**

Frozen vegetables save on the preparation time.

12 ounces skinless, boneless chicken breast halves or skinless,
      boneless chicken thighs
 2 tablespoons honey
 2 tablespoons vinegar
 2 tablespoons orange juice
 1 tablespoon soy sauce
 1 teaspoon cornstarch
 2 tablespoons cooking oil
 2 cups loose-pack frozen mixed vegetables
   Hot cooked rice (see page 139) (optional)

1. Rinse chicken; pat dry. Cut chicken into 1-inch pieces; set aside.
For sauce, in a small bowl stir together honey, vinegar, orange juice,
soy sauce, and cornstarch; set aside.

2. Pour cooking oil into a wok or large skillet. (Add more oil as necessary during cooking.) Preheat over medium-high heat. Stir-fry
frozen vegetables for 3 minutes or till vegetables are crisp-tender.
Remove vegetables from wok. Add chicken to hot wok. Stir-fry for 3
to 4 minutes or till chicken is no longer pink. Push chicken from the
center of the wok. Stir sauce; add to center of the wok. Cook and
stir till thickened and bubbly.

3. Return cooked vegetables to wok. Stir all ingredients together to
coat. Cook and stir about 1 minute more or till heated through. If desired, serve immediately over rice. Makes 4 servings.

Nutrition Facts per serving: 232 cal., 9 g total fat (2 g sat. fat), 45 mg chol., 322 mg
sodium, 20 g carbo., 0 g fiber, 18 g pro. **Daily Values**: 30% vit. A, 10% vit. C, 2% calcium,
8% iron

CHICKEN KABOBS

PREP: 25 MINUTES   BROIL: 8 MINUTES

Low-Fat

If you use bamboo skewers, soak them in water for 30 minutes before using so they won't burn.

  1 8-ounce can pineapple chunks (juice pack)
$1/4$ cup bottled chili sauce
  1 tablespoon brown sugar
  1 tablespoon lime juice
$1/4$ teaspoon salt
$1/4$ teaspoon ground ginger
$1/4$ teaspoon ground allspice
$1/4$ to $1/2$ teaspoon ground red pepper
  4 skinless, boneless chicken breast halves (about 1 pound total)
  1 large red or green sweet pepper, cut into 1-inch pieces

1. Drain pineapple, reserving 2 tablespoons juice; set chunks aside. For sauce, in a small mixing bowl combine reserved pineapple juice, chili sauce, brown sugar, lime juice, salt, ginger, allspice, and red pepper; set aside.
2. Rinse chicken; pat dry. Cut chicken breasts lengthwise into 1-inch-wide strips. On 8 long metal skewers, alternately thread chicken strips, accordion-style, with sweet pepper and pineapple chunks.
3. Place skewers on the unheated rack of a broiler pan; brush with sauce. Broil 4 to 5 inches from the heat for 5 minutes. Turn chicken; brush with sauce. Broil 3 to 5 minutes more or till chicken is tender and no longer pink. Makes 4 servings.

Nutrition Facts per serving: 198 cal., 3 g total fat (1 g sat. fat), 59 mg chol., 391 mg sodium, 19 g carbo., 1 g fiber, 23 g pro. **Daily Values:** 21% vit. A, 86% vit. C, 2% calcium, 8% iron

THAI CHICKEN STIR-FRY

START TO FINISH: 35 MINUTES

Low-Fat

Fish sauce is a thin, brown liquid made from salted fish that adds a bold, salty flavor to Oriental dishes. Look for it at your supermarket, specialty food store, or Oriental grocery.

3 tablespoons dry sherry
2 tablespoons soy sauce
1 tablespoon fish sauce (optional)
1 tablespoon water
1 teaspoon cornstarch
$1/2$ teaspoon crushed red pepper
12 ounces skinless, boneless chicken breast halves
1 tablespoon cooking oil
1 teaspoon grated gingerroot
2 cloves garlic, minced
1 cup bias-sliced carrots
2 cups fresh pea pods, tips and strings removed, or one 6-ounce package frozen pea pods, thawed
4 green onions, bias-sliced into 1-inch pieces ($1/2$ cup)
$1/3$ cup dry roasted peanuts
Hot cooked rice (see page 139) (optional)

BUYING AND STORING POULTRY

Poultry is highly perishable and should be purchased and stored carefully. Check the "sell by" date on the package label. That is the last day the product should be sold. (If properly refrigerated, poultry will retain its freshness for a few days after that date.) Store fresh poultry in the coldest part of your refrigerator as soon as you get it home. Plan to use the fresh poultry within 1 to 2 days. Poultry that's packaged in supermarket trays can be refrigerated in its original wrapping.

1. For sauce, in a small bowl stir together sherry, soy sauce, fish sauce, water, cornstarch, and red pepper. Set sauce aside.
2. Rinse chicken; pat dry. Cut chicken into 1-inch pieces; set aside.
3. Pour cooking oil into a wok or large skillet. (Add more oil as necessary during cooking.) Preheat over medium-high heat. Stir-fry gingerroot and garlic in hot oil for 15 seconds. Add carrots; stir-fry for 2 minutes. Add pea pods and green onions; stir-fry for 2 to 3 minutes or till crisp-tender. Remove vegetables from wok or skillet.
4. Add chicken to hot wok. Stir-fry for 3 to 4 minutes or till chicken is no longer pink. Push chicken from center of wok. Stir sauce; add

to center of wok. Cook and stir till thickened and bubbly. Return vegetables to wok. Add peanuts. Stir all ingredients together to coat with sauce. Cook and stir 1 to 2 minutes more or till heated through. If desired, serve at once with rice. Makes 4 servings.

Nutrition Facts per serving: 254 cal., 12 g total fat (2 g sat. fat), 45 mg chol., 679 mg sodium, 13 g carbo., 4 g fiber, 22 g pro. **Daily Values:** 77% vit. A, 48% vit. C, 4% calcium, 16% iron

GARLIC CHICKEN

START TO FINISH: 50 MINUTES

Low-Fat

*For added convenience, use bottled minced garlic i
nstead of whole cloves.*

   1 cup water
 ¹/₄ cup soy sauce
   2 tablespoons dry white wine
   2 teaspoons cornstarch
  12 ounces skinless, boneless chicken breast halves
   2 tablespoons cooking oil
  10 green onions, bias-sliced into 1-inch pieces (1¹/₄ cups)
   1 cup thinly sliced fresh mushrooms
  10 cloves garlic, peeled and finely chopped (3 tablespoons)
 ¹/₂ cup sliced water chestnuts
     Hot cooked rice (see page 139) or fried rice sticks

1. For marinade, in a bowl stir together water, soy sauce, white wine, and cornstarch; set aside.
2. Rinse chicken; pat dry. Cut chicken into ¹/₂-inch pieces. In a bowl stir together the chicken pieces and *half* of the marinade. Cover and marinate in the refrigerator for 30 minutes. Drain chicken, discarding marinade.
3. Pour oil into a wok or large skillet. (Add more oil as necessary during cooking.) Preheat over medium-high heat. Stir-fry green onions, mushrooms, and garlic in hot oil for 1 to 2 minutes or till tender. Remove from wok or skillet. Add chicken to hot wok. Stir-fry for 2 to 3 minutes or till no longer pink. Push chicken from center of wok. Stir remaining marinade; add to center of wok. Cook and stir till thickened and bubbly.

4. Return cooked vegetables to wok. Add water chestnuts. Stir all ingredients together to coat. Cook and stir about 1 minute more or till heated through. Serve immediately with hot cooked rice or rice sticks. Makes 4 servings.

Nutrition Facts per serving: 291 cal., 10 g total fat (2 g sat. fat), 45 mg chol., 560 mg sodium, 30 g carbo., 1 g fiber, 20 g pro. **Daily Values:** 6% vit. A, 14% vit. C, 3% calcium, 16% iron

■ **Chicken with Cashews:** Prepare as above, except stir ¹/₂ teaspoon *crushed red pepper* into marinade. Reduce garlic to 2 cloves (or 1¹/₂ teaspoons bottled minced garlic). Stir-fry 1 cup *raw cashews* with onion mixture.

Nutrition Facts per serving: 479 cal., 25 g total fat (5 g sat. fat)

EASY CHICKEN AND VEGETABLE STIR-FRY

START TO FINISH: 25 MINUTES   Oven 350°

Fast

       1 3-ounce can chow mein noodles or rice noodles
       2 tablespoons soy sauce
       1 tablespoon apricot or peach jam or preserves
       1 tablespoon vinegar
       1 teaspoon cornstarch
      12 ounces skinless, boneless chicken thighs or skinless, boneless
             chicken breast halves
       1 tablespoon cooking oil
       3 cups loose-pack frozen broccoli, green beans, onions, and red
             peppers

1. Pour noodles onto an ungreased baking pan; heat in a 350° oven for 5 minutes.
2. Meanwhile, for sauce, in a small mixing bowl stir together soy sauce, jam or preserves, vinegar, and cornstarch; set aside.
3. Rinse chicken; pat dry. Cut chicken into 1-inch pieces. Pour cooking oil into a wok or large skillet. (Add more oil as necessary during cooking.) Preheat over medium-high heat. Stir-fry frozen vegetables for 2 to 3 minutes or till crisp-tender. Remove vegetables from wok. Add chicken to hot wok. Stir-fry for 3 to 4 minutes or till chicken is no longer pink. Push chicken from the center of the wok. Stir sauce; add to center of wok. Cook and stir till thickened and bubbly.

4. Return cooked vegetables to wok. Stir all ingredients together to coat with sauce. Cook and stir about 1 minute more or till heated through. Serve immediately over noodles. Makes 4 servings.

Nutrition Facts per serving: 280 cal., 14 g total fat (3 g sat. fat), 41 mg chol., 660 mg sodium, 23 g carbo., 3 g fiber, 16 g pro. **Daily Values:** 19% vit. A, 45% vit. C, 4% calcium, 16% iron

---

CHICKEN AND ARTICHOKE SAUTÉ

START TO FINISH: 20 MINUTES

Fast　　　　　　　　　　**Low-Fat**

If juices are clear when chicken is cut, it's done; if juices are pink, cook a little longer and test again.

　　4　skinless, boneless chicken breast halves (about 1 pound total)
$^1/_4$　cup all-purpose flour
$^1/_4$　teaspoon salt
$^1/_4$　teaspoon ground sage
$^1/_8$　teaspoon pepper
　　2　tablespoons cooking oil
$^1/_2$　cup dry white wine
　　1　14-ounce can artichoke hearts, drained and halved
　　1　4-ounce can sliced mushrooms, drained
　　2　tablespoons grated Parmesan or Romano cheese
　　2　tablespoons snipped fresh parsley

1. Rinse chicken; pat dry. In a shallow bowl stir together flour, salt, sage, and pepper; reserve 1 tablespoon of the flour mixture. Dip chicken in remaining flour mixture to coat.

2. In a large skillet cook chicken in hot oil over medium-high heat about 6 minutes or till chicken is tender and no longer pink, turning once. Remove chicken from skillet; cover and keep warm. Drain off any excess oil in skillet.

3. For sauce, stir together reserved flour mixture and wine. Add wine mixture, artichoke hearts, and mushrooms to skillet, scraping up crusty bits from pan. Cook and stir till thickened and bubbly. Cook and stir for 2 minutes more. Pour sauce over chicken. Sprinkle with cheese and parsley. Serve immediately. Makes 4 servings.

Nutrition Facts per serving: 281 cal., 11 g total fat (3 g sat. fat), 62 mg chol., 495 mg sodium, 14 g carbo., 4 g fiber, 26 g pro. **Daily Values:** 3% vit. A, 14% vit. C, 7% calcium, 15% iron

GREEK-STYLE TURKEY PITAS

PREP: 20 MINUTES   MARINATE: 6 TO 24 HOURS   COOK: 10 MINUTES

Turkey breast tenderloins are skinless, boneless cuts of turkey from the inside of the breast. The steaks are the same cut, split lengthwise.

4 turkey breast tenderloin steaks (about 1 pound total)
$^1/_4$ cup mayonnaise or salad dressing
$^1/_4$ cup clear Italian salad dressing
1 tablespoon olive oil or cooking oil
1 recipe Cucumber-Yogurt Sauce (see below)
2 whole wheat pita bread rounds, halved crosswise
$^1/_2$ cup chopped tomato
$^1/_4$ cup crumbled feta cheese

1. Rinse turkey; pat dry. Place turkey steaks in a plastic bag set in a shallow dish.

2. For marinade, combine mayonnaise or salad dressing and Italian salad dressing; pour over turkey. Close bag. Marinate in refrigerator for 6 to 24 hours, turning occasionally.

3. Drain turkey, discarding marinade. In a large skillet cook turkey steaks in hot oil over medium heat about 10 minutes or till turkey is tender and no longer pink. Cool slightly; cut into thin strips.

4. Stir turkey strips into Cucumber-Yogurt Sauce. Divide turkey mixture among pita rounds. Top with tomato and feta cheese. Makes 4 servings.

■ **Cucumber-Yogurt Sauce:** In a small mixing bowl combine $^1/_2$ cup plain *fat-free yogurt;* $^1/_4$ cup chopped, seeded *cucumber;* 1 tablespoon finely chopped *onion;* 1 tablespoon snipped *fresh parsley;* $^1/_2$ teaspoon *lemon juice;* and $^1/_8$ teaspoon *garlic powder.* Cover and chill the sauce till serving time. Makes $^3/_4$ cup.

Nutrition Facts per serving: 335 cal., 15 g total fat (4 g sat. fat), 66 mg chol., 466 mg sodium, 23 g carbo., 0 g fiber, 29 g pro. **Daily Values:** 4% vit. A, 12% vit. C, 13% calcium, 8% iron

OVEN-BARBECUED CHICKEN

PREP: 5 MINUTES   BAKE: 45 MINUTES   Oven 375°

Low-Fat

> 2 to 2¹/₂ pounds meaty chicken pieces (breasts, thighs, and
>   drumsticks)
> ¹/₂ cup chopped onion (1 medium)
> 1 clove garlic, minced
> 1 tablespoon cooking oil
> ³/₄ cup bottled chili sauce
> 2 tablespoons honey
> 2 tablespoons soy sauce
> 1 tablespoon prepared mustard
> ¹/₂ teaspoon prepared horseradish
> ¹/₄ teaspoon crushed red pepper

1. Skin chicken, if desired. Rinse chicken; pat dry. Arrange chicken
pieces, meaty sides down, in a 15×10×1-inch baking pan. Bake in a
375° oven for 25 minutes. Drain off fat.

2. Meanwhile, for sauce, in a saucepan cook onion and garlic in hot
oil till tender but not brown. Stir in chili sauce, honey, soy sauce,
mustard, horseradish, and red pepper; heat through.

3. Turn chicken skin side up. Brush about half of the sauce over the
chicken. Bake for 20 to 30 minutes more or till chicken is tender and
no longer pink. Reheat remaining sauce and pass with chicken.
Makes 6 servings.

Nutrition Facts per serving: 255 cal., 11 g total fat (3 g sat. fat), 69 mg chol., 807 mg
sodium, 15 g carbo., 0 g fiber, 24 g pro. **Daily Values:** 7% vit. A, 8% vit. C, 1% calcium,
9% iron

TRIPLE-CHEESE-STUFFED CHICKEN BREASTS

PREP: 20 MINUTES   BAKE: 45 MINUTES   Oven 375°

*Stuffed with lots of cheese and fresh herbs, these chicken breasts
make a great recipe for entertaining.*

> 6 medium chicken breast halves (about 3 pounds total)
> ¹/₂ cup ricotta cheese
> ¹/₂ cup shredded fontina or mozzarella cheese (2 ounces)
> ¹/₃ cup grated Parmesan or Romano cheese

2 teaspoons snipped fresh basil or $^{1}/_{2}$ teaspoon dried basil, crushed

1 teaspoon snipped fresh oregano or $^{1}/_{4}$ teaspoon dried oregano, crushed

$^{1}/_{4}$ teaspoon lemon-pepper seasoning

1 teaspoon olive oil or cooking oil

1. Rinse chicken; pat dry. With your fingers, gently separate the skin from the meat along rib edge (see photo 1, below).

2. For stuffing, combine cheeses, basil, oregano, and lemon-pepper seasoning. Stuff a little less than $^{1}/_{4}$ cup stuffing between the skin and meat of each breast (see photo 2, below). Place the chicken, skin side up, in a 13×9×2-inch baking dish. Brush chicken lightly with oil. Bake in a 375° oven for 45 to 55 minutes or till chicken is tender and no longer pink. Makes 6 servings.

Nutrition Facts per serving: 290 cal., 15 g total fat (6 g sat. fat), 105 mg chol., 319 mg sodium, 1 g carbo., 0 g fiber, 36 g pro. **Daily Values:** 9% vit. A, 0% vit. C, 16% calcium, 8% iron

1. To prepare Triple-Cheese-Stuffed Chicken Breasts, leave skin attached at breast bone when separating skin from meat along rib edge.

2. Use a spoon to stuff a scant $^{1}/_{4}$ cup of the cheese mixture into each breast half, placing the mixture between skin and meat of the chicken.

FIESTA CHICKEN BAKE

PREP: 10 MINUTES   BAKE: 50 MINUTES   Oven 375°

6 chicken legs (thigh-drumstick pieces) (3 to 3¹/₂ pounds total)
¹/₂ cup chopped onion (1 medium)
1 tablespoon cooking oil
1 14¹/₂-ounce can tomatoes, cut up
1 8³/₄-ounce can whole kernel corn, drained
1 4-ounce can diced green chili peppers, drained
1 teaspoon chili powder
¹/₂ teaspoon paprika
¹/₄ teaspoon ground cumin
¹/₈ teaspoon pepper
Several dashes bottled hot pepper sauce
¹/₂ cup shredded cheddar cheese
2 tablespoons sliced pitted ripe olives
Hot cooked rice (see page 139) (optional)

1. Skin chicken. Rinse chicken; pat dry. Arrange chicken in a 3-quart rectangular baking dish. Bake in a 375° oven for 30 minutes. Drain off fat.

2. Meanwhile, for sauce, in a saucepan cook onion in hot cooking oil till onion is tender but not brown. Stir in undrained tomatoes, drained corn, chili peppers, chili powder, paprika, cumin, pepper, and hot pepper sauce.

3. Pour sauce over chicken. Bake in the 375° oven for 20 to 30 minutes more or till chicken is tender and no longer pink, basting occasionally with sauce. Sprinkle chicken with cheese and olives. If desired, serve over hot cooked rice. Serves 6.

Nutrition Facts per serving: 298 cal., 15 g total fat (5 g sat. fat), 100 mg chol., 408 mg sodium, 11 g carbo., 1 g fiber, 31 g pro. **Daily Values:** 12% vit. A, 33% vit. C, 10% calcium, 16% iron

SPICY CHICKEN AND RICE

Low-Fat

2 to 2¹/₂ pounds meaty chicken pieces (breasts, thighs, and
    drumsticks)
¹/₂ cup chopped onion (1 medium)
¹/₂ cup chopped green sweet pepper
2 cloves garlic, minced
1 tablespoon cooking oil
1 14¹/₂-ounce can tomatoes, cut up
1 15-ounce can black beans, rinsed and drained
1 cup tomato juice
1 cup frozen whole kernel corn
²/₃ cup long grain rice
1 teaspoon chili powder
¹/₂ teaspoon salt
¹/₄ teaspoon ground red pepper
   Paprika

1. Skin chicken. Rinse; pat dry. Set chicken aside.
2. In a large saucepan cook onion, sweet pepper, and garlic in hot
oil till tender but not brown. Stir in undrained tomatoes, drained
black beans, tomato juice, corn, uncooked rice, chili powder, salt,
and ground red pepper. Bring to boiling. Transfer rice mixture to a
3-quart rectangular baking dish. Arrange chicken pieces atop rice
mixture. Sprinkle chicken with paprika.
3. Bake, covered, in a 375° oven for 50 to 60 minutes or till chicken
is tender and no longer pink and rice is tender. Makes 6 servings.

Nutrition Facts per serving: 326 cal., 8 g total fat (2 g sat. fat), 61 mg chol., 736 mg
sodium, 40 g carbo., 5 g fiber, 28 g pro. **Daily Values:** 9% vit. A, 41% vit. C, 6% calcium,
23% iron

CHICKEN FRICASSEE

PREP: 35 MINUTES   COOK: 35 MINUTES

Low-Fat

This old-fashioned chicken dish also tastes great made with herbs other than basil—try marjoram, oregano, or thyme.

$^1/_4$ **cup all-purpose flour**
1 **teaspoon paprika**
$^1/_4$ **teaspoon salt**
$^1/_4$ **teaspoon pepper**
2 **to 2$^1/_2$ pounds meaty chicken pieces (breasts, thighs, and drumsticks)**
1 **tablespoon cooking oil or shortening**
1 **cup halved fresh mushrooms**
$^1/_3$ **cup chopped green or red sweet pepper or celery**
$^1/_3$ **cup sliced green onions (3)**
1 **cup chicken broth**
$^1/_4$ **teaspoon dried basil, crushed**
$^1/_4$ **cup milk**
1 **tablespoon all-purpose flour**
Hot cooked noodles or spaetzle (see page 774) (optional)

1. In a plastic or paper bag combine the $^1/_4$ cup flour, paprika, salt, and pepper; set aside.

2. Skin chicken. Rinse chicken; pat dry. Add chicken, 2 or 3 pieces at a time, to the bag, shaking to coat well.

3. In a 12-inch skillet cook chicken in hot oil over medium heat about 10 minutes or till lightly browned, turning to brown evenly (add more oil, if necessary). Remove chicken from skillet; set aside. Drain fat, reserving 2 tablespoons of the drippings in the skillet.

4. Add mushrooms, sweet pepper or celery, and green onions to skillet. Cook and stir for 2 minutes. Stir in chicken broth and basil. Bring to boiling, scraping up browned bits from the bottom of the skillet. Return chicken to the skillet. Bring to boiling; reduce heat. Cover and simmer for 35 to 40 minutes or till chicken is tender and no longer pink. Transfer chicken and vegetables to a serving platter; keep warm.

5. Skim fat from pan juices; measure $^3/_4$ cup of the pan juices and return to the skillet. Stir milk into the 1 tablespoon flour; stir into pan juices. Cook and stir till thickened and bubbly. Cook and stir for 1 minute more.

6. Spoon some of the sauce over chicken; pass remaining sauce. If desired, serve with hot cooked noodles or spaetzle. Makes 6 servings.

Nutrition Facts per serving: 208 cal., 10 g total fat (2 g sat. fat), 62 mg chol., 279 mg sodium, 7 g carbo., 0 g fiber, 22 g pro. **Daily Values:** 5% vit. A, 10% vit. C, 2% calcium, 10% iron

---

CHICKEN PAPRIKASH

PREP: 30 MINUTES   COOK: 35 MINUTES

Don't be surprised by the amount of paprika in this creamy Hungarian dish. You can use the mild supermarket variety or the hot Hungarian type available in ethnic markets.

   2 to 2¹/₂ pounds meaty chicken pieces (breasts, thighs, and drumsticks)
   1 tablespoon cooking oil
     Salt
     Pepper
   1 cup chopped onion (1 large)
   3 to 4 teaspoons paprika
   ³/₄ cup chicken broth
   ¹/₄ cup dry white wine or chicken broth
   1 8-ounce carton dairy sour cream
   2 tablespoons all-purpose flour
   3 cups hot cooked noodles (see page 774) or rice (see page 139)

1. Skin chicken. Rinse chicken; pat dry. In a 12-inch skillet cook chicken in hot oil about 15 minutes or till lightly browned, turning to brown evenly. Sprinkle with salt and pepper. Remove chicken from skillet; set aside.

2. Add onion and paprika to skillet; cook till onion is tender. Return chicken to skillet, turning pieces to coat with paprika mixture. Add broth and wine to skillet. Bring to boiling; reduce heat. Cover and simmer for 35 to 40 minutes or till chicken is tender and no longer pink. Transfer chicken to a serving platter; keep warm.

3. For sauce, skim fat from pan juices. Measure 1¹/₂ cups juices, adding water, if necessary. In a mixing bowl stir together sour cream and flour; gradually stir into pan juices. Pour into skillet. Cook and stir till thickened and bubbly. Cook and stir for 1 minute more.

4. Spoon some of the sauce over chicken; pass remaining sauce. Serve with hot cooked noodles or rice. Makes 6 servings.

Nutrition Facts per serving: 366 cal., 16 g total fat (7 g sat. fat), 103 mg chol., 198 mg sodium, 26 g carbo., 2 g fiber, 26 g pro. **Daily Values:** 16% vit. A, 4% vit. C, 6% calcium, 13% iron

---

FREEZING AND THAWING TIPS

If you can't use your fresh poultry within 2 days, freeze it at 0° or below. First, rinse the poultry and pat it dry. For individual poultry pieces or cubed poultry, spread the meat on a tray and freeze until firm; transfer to freezer bags. Press out air, seal, label, and freeze. For best flavor and texture, keep frozen, uncooked whole turkeys or chickens no longer than a year, chicken pieces up to 9 months, and frozen uncooked turkey pieces up to 6 months. Never freeze stuffed poultry.

The refrigerator is the best place to thaw poultry. Place poultry on a tray in your refrigerator. Allow 5 hours of thawing time for every pound of poultry. Cold-water thawing is another safe way to defrost poultry. Place poultry in its freezer wrapping in a sink or large bowl of cold water. Allow about 30 minutes of thawing time for every pound of poultry, changing the water every 30 minutes.

Never thaw poultry on your kitchen countertop. Bacteria that can cause food poisoning multiply rapidly at room temperature.

COQ AU VIN

PREP: 35 MINUTES   COOK: 35 MINUTES

The name of this classic French recipe literally means chicken cooked in wine. Serve this chicken, smothered in a rich, wine-flavored gravy, with a lettuce salad and a loaf of French bread.

2 to 2¹/₂ pounds meaty chicken pieces (breasts, thighs, and
      drumsticks)
   2 tablespoons cooking oil
      Salt
      Pepper
  12 to 18 pearl onions or shallots, peeled
1¹/₄ cups burgundy
   1 cup whole fresh mushrooms
   1 cup thinly sliced carrots (2 medium)
   1 tablespoon snipped fresh parsley
   2 cloves garlic, minced
 ¹/₂ teaspoon dried marjoram, crushed
 ¹/₂ teaspoon dried thyme, crushed
   1 bay leaf
   2 tablespoons all-purpose flour
   2 tablespoons margarine or butter, softened
   2 slices bacon, crisp-cooked, drained, and crumbled
      Snipped fresh parsley (optional)
      Hot cooked noodles (see page 774) (optional)

1. Skin chicken. Rinse chicken; pat dry. In a 12-inch skillet cook
chicken in hot oil about 15 minutes or till lightly browned, turning to
brown evenly. Sprinkle with salt and pepper. Add onions or shallots,
burgundy, mushrooms, carrots, the 1 tablespoon parsley, garlic, marjoram, thyme, and bay leaf. Bring to boiling; reduce heat. Cover and
simmer for 35 to 40 minutes or till chicken is tender and is no longer
pink. Transfer chicken and vegetables to a serving platter; keep
warm. Discard the bay leaf.

2. In a mixing bowl stir together flour and softened margarine or
butter to make a smooth paste. Stir into burgundy mixture in skillet.
Cook and stir till thickened and bubbly. Cook and stir for 1 minute
more. Season to taste with salt and pepper.

3. Pour thickened burgundy mixture over chicken and vegetables.
Sprinkle with bacon. If desired, top with additional parsley and serve
with hot cooked noodles. Makes 6 servings.

Nutrition Facts per serving: 285 cal., 14 g total fat (3 g sat. fat), 63 mg chol., 205 mg
sodium, 9 g carbo., 2 g fiber, 22 g pro. **Daily Values:** 62% vit. A, 7% vit. C, 2% calcium,
11% iron

CHICKEN COUNTRY CAPTAIN

START TO FINISH: 55 MINUTES

Low-Fat

This Anglo-Indian dish gets its name from the nickname of the British army captain who brought the recipe home from India. The officer blended the two cuisines—combining curry from India and chicken and tomatoes from England.

- 2 to 2¹/₂ pounds meaty chicken pieces (breasts, thighs, and drumsticks)
- 1 14¹/₂-ounce can chunky-style stewed tomatoes
- ¹/₄ cup snipped fresh parsley
- ¹/₄ cup currants or raisins
- 1 tablespoon curry powder
- ¹/₂ teaspoon instant chicken bouillon granules
- ¹/₂ teaspoon ground mace or nutmeg
- ¹/₄ teaspoon sugar
- 1 tablespoon cornstarch
- 1 tablespoon cold water
  Hot cooked rice (see page 139) (optional)
- 2 tablespoons slivered almonds, toasted (see tip, page 234) (optional)

1. Skin chicken. Rinse chicken; pat dry. In a large skillet stir together undrained tomatoes, parsley, currants or raisins, curry powder, bouillon granules, mace or nutmeg, and sugar. Place chicken pieces in skillet. Spoon tomato mixture over chicken. Bring to boiling; reduce heat. Cover and simmer for 35 to 45 minutes or till chicken is tender and no longer pink. Using a slotted spoon, remove chicken from the skillet; keep warm.

2. For sauce, skim fat from tomato mixture in skillet (see tip, page 882). In a small mixing bowl stir together cornstarch and cold water; add to skillet. Cook and stir till mixture is thickened and bubbly. Cook and stir for 2 minutes more. If desired, serve chicken and sauce with hot cooked rice and sprinkle with almonds. Makes 6 servings.

Nutrition Facts per serving: 186 cal., 5 g total fat (1 g sat. fat), 61 mg chol., 423 mg sodium, 13 g carbo., 1 g fiber, 21 g pro. **Daily Values:** 7% vit. A, 19% vit. C, 3% calcium, 11% iron

CHICKEN CACCIATORE

START TO FINISH: 1 HOUR

Low-Fat

    2 to 2¹/₂ pounds meaty chicken pieces (breasts, thighs, and
        drumsticks)
    2 tablespoons olive oil
    1 medium onion, sliced
    1 clove garlic, minced
    1 7¹/₂-ounce can tomatoes, cut up
    1 6-ounce can tomato paste
  ³/₄ cup dry white wine
    1 4-ounce can mushroom stems and pieces, drained
    2 tablespoons snipped fresh parsley
    1 teaspoon sugar
  ¹/₂ teaspoon salt
  ¹/₂ teaspoon dried rosemary, crushed
  ¹/₂ teaspoon dried thyme, crushed
  ¹/₄ teaspoon dried oregano, crushed
        Hot cooked spaghetti (see page 774) (optional)

1. Skin chicken. Rinse chicken; pat dry. In a 12-inch skillet cook chicken in hot oil about 15 minutes or till lightly browned, turning to brown evenly. Add onion and garlic the last 5 minutes of cooking. Drain off fat.

2. Meanwhile, in a medium mixing bowl combine undrained tomatoes, tomato paste, wine, mushrooms, parsley, sugar, salt, rosemary, thyme, oregano, and ¹/₈ teaspoon *pepper*. Pour over chicken in skillet. Bring to boiling; reduce heat. Cover and simmer for 35 to 40 minutes or till chicken is tender. Turn once during cooking. If desired, serve over hot cooked spaghetti. Makes 6 servings.

Nutrition Facts per serving: 208 cal., 7 g total fat (2 g sat. fat), 61 mg chol., 393 mg sodium, 11 g carbo., 2 g fiber, 22 g pro. **Daily Values:** 10% vit. A, 33% vit. C, 3% calcium, 15% iron

CHICKEN AND DUMPLINGS

Prep: 30 minutes   Cook: 45 minutes

  2 to 2$^{1}/_{2}$ pounds meaty chicken pieces (breasts, thighs, and
      drumsticks)
  3 cups water
  1 medium onion, cut into wedges
  1 teaspoon dried basil, crushed
$^{1}/_{2}$ teaspoon salt
$^{1}/_{4}$ teaspoon dried marjoram, crushed
$^{1}/_{4}$ teaspoon pepper
  1 bay leaf
  1 cup sliced celery
  1 cup thinly sliced carrots (2 medium)
$^{1}/_{2}$ cup sliced fresh mushrooms
  1 cup all-purpose flour
  1 tablespoon snipped fresh parsley
  2 teaspoons baking powder
$^{1}/_{4}$ teaspoon salt
$^{1}/_{4}$ teaspoon dried oregano, crushed
  1 beaten egg
$^{1}/_{4}$ cup milk
  2 tablespoons cooking oil
$^{1}/_{2}$ cup cold water
$^{1}/_{4}$ cup all-purpose flour

1. Skin chicken, if desired. Rinse chicken. In a large pot combine chicken, the 3 cups water, onion, basil, the $^{1}/_{2}$ teaspoon salt, marjoram, pepper, and bay leaf. Bring to boiling; reduce heat. Cover and simmer for 25 minutes. Add celery, carrots, and mushrooms. Return mixture to boiling; reduce heat. Cover and simmer about 10 minutes more or till chicken and vegetables are tender. Discard bay leaf.

2. For dumplings, in a mixing bowl combine the 1 cup flour, parsley, baking powder, the $^{1}/_{4}$ teaspoon salt, and oregano. In another bowl combine the egg, milk, and oil; add to flour mixture. Stir with a fork just till moistened. Drop batter onto the hot chicken in broth, making 6 dumplings. Do not drop batter into the liquid. Return to boiling; reduce heat. Cover and simmer for 10 to 12 minutes or till a wooden toothpick inserted into a dumpling comes out clean. Do not lift cover while simmering. Transfer chicken, dumplings, and vegetables to a serving platter; keep warm.

3. For gravy, pour broth into a large measuring cup. Skim fat from broth (see tip, page 882); discard fat. Measure 2 cups of the broth; return to pot. Combine the ½ cup cold water and the ¼ cup flour; stir into the broth. Cook and stir till mixture is thickened and bubbly. Cook and stir for 1 minute more. Serve gravy over chicken and vegetables with dumplings. Makes 6 servings.

Nutrition Facts per serving: 342 cal., 14 g total fat (3 g sat. fat), 105 mg chol., 513 mg sodium, 25 g carbo., 2 g fiber, 27 g pro. **Daily Values:** 62% vit. A, 7% vit. C, 14% calcium, 19% iron

---

CHICKEN AND NOODLES

PREP: 20 MINUTES   COOK: 1¼ HOURS

This home-style dish uses the thigh and drumstick pieces for the cooked chicken.

 3 **chicken legs (thigh-drumstick piece) (about 2 pounds total)**
 4 **cups water**
 ½ **cup chopped celery leaves**
 2 **tablespoons snipped fresh parsley**
 1 **bay leaf**
 1 **teaspoon dried thyme, crushed**
 1 **teaspoon salt**
 ¼ **teaspoon pepper**
 1½ **cups chopped onions**
 2 **cups sliced carrots**
 1 **cup sliced celery**
 3 **cups wide noodles**
 1 **cup loose-pack frozen peas**
 2 **cups milk**
 2 **tablespoons all-purpose flour**

1. Skin chicken. Rinse chicken. In a 4½-quart pot place chicken, water, celery leaves, parsley, bay leaf, thyme, salt, and pepper. Bring to boiling; reduce heat. Cover and simmer for 30 minutes. Add onions, carrots, and celery. Cover and simmer about 30 minutes more or till chicken is tender and no longer pink. Remove from heat. Discard the bay leaf. Remove chicken; cool slightly. Remove meat from bones; discard bones. Chop the chicken and set aside.

2. Bring broth mixture to boiling. Add noodles; cook for 5 minutes. Stir in frozen peas and 1½ cups of the milk.

3. In a screw-top jar combine the remaining ½ cup milk and the flour. Cover and shake till smooth; stir into noodle mixture. Cook and stir till thickened and bubbly. Stir in chopped chicken. Cook and stir for 1 to 2 minutes more or till mixture is heated through. Makes 6 servings.

Nutrition Facts per serving: 424 cal., 8 g total fat (3 g sat. fat), 97 mg chol., 546 mg sodium, 63 g carbo., 4 g fiber, 24 g pro. **Daily Values:** 166% vit. A, 17% vit. C, 15% calcium, 30% iron

---

MEDITERRANEAN CHICKEN AND VEGETABLES

PREP: 20 MINUTES   COOK: 45 MINUTES

Low-Fat

Couscous, a ricelike grain in the shape of tiny beads, is commonly used in place of rice in North African cooking.

      2 to 2½ pounds meaty chicken pieces (breasts, thighs, and
          drumsticks)
      2 tablespoons olive oil or cooking oil
      1 medium onion, sliced and separated into rings
      2 cloves garlic, minced
      1 14½-ounce can stewed tomatoes
      1 small eggplant (about 1 pound), cut into 1-inch chunks (3
          cups)
      1 medium zucchini, cut into ½-inch chunks (1¼ cups)
      1 medium green sweet pepper, cut into 1-inch pieces (1 cup)
      1 2¼-ounce can sliced pitted ripe olives, drained
      1 teaspoon dried oregano, crushed
    ½ teaspoon dried thyme, crushed
    ½ teaspoon salt
    ¼ teaspoon pepper
      Hot cooked couscous or orzo (see page 774) (optional)

1. Skin chicken. Rinse chicken; pat dry. In a 4½-quart pot cook chicken in hot oil over medium heat about 10 minutes or till chicken is lightly browned, turning to brown evenly. Remove chicken; set aside.

2. Add onion and garlic to drippings in pot. Cook about 5 minutes or till tender but not brown. Stir in undrained tomatoes, eggplant, zucchini, sweet pepper, olives, oregano, thyme, salt, and pepper. Return chicken to pot.

3. Bring to boiling; reduce heat. Cover and simmer for 35 to 40 minutes or till chicken is tender and no longer pink, stirring occasionally. Spoon off excess fat, if necessary. Transfer chicken to a serving bowl; keep warm.

4. Simmer tomato mixture, uncovered, for 5 to 10 minutes more or till slightly thickened. Pour sauce over chicken. If desired, serve with hot cooked couscous or orzo. Makes 6 servings.

Nutrition Facts per serving: 235 cal., 12 g total fat (2 g sat. fat), 61 mg chol., 478 mg sodium, 12 g carbo., 3 g fiber, 22 g pro. **Daily Values:** 6% vit. A, 34% vit. C, 4% calcium, 13% iron

---

CHICKEN LIVER SAUTÉ

START TO FINISH: 25 MINUTES

Fast

    1 **pound chicken livers, cut in half**
    4 **slices bacon**
    1 **medium onion, cut into thin wedges**
  $1/8$ **teaspoon pepper**
  $1/4$ **cup chicken broth**
     Hot cooked fettuccine or linguine (see page 774) (optional)
    1 **tablespoon snipped fresh parsley**

1. Rinse chicken livers; pat dry. Set livers aside. In a large skillet cook bacon till crisp. Remove bacon from skillet, reserving 2 tablespoons of the drippings. Crumble bacon; set aside.

2. Cook onion in reserved bacon drippings till tender but not brown. Stir in chicken livers and pepper. Cover and cook over medium heat about 5 minutes or till center of livers are only slightly pink, stirring occasionally. Stir in crumbled bacon and chicken broth. Cook and stir about 1 minute more or till heated through. If desired, serve over pasta. Sprinkle with parsley. Makes 4 servings.

Nutrition Facts per serving: 217 cal., 13 g total fat (5 g sat. fat), 455 mg chol., 186 mg sodium, 3 g carbo., 0 g fiber, 20 g pro. **Daily Values:** 346% vit. A, 26% vit. C, 1% calcium, 41% iron

VEGETABLE-STUFFED TURKEY LOAF

PREP: 25 MINUTES BAKE: 1 HOUR Oven 350°

Low-Fat

To microwave the stuffing, combine the vegetables in a 1-quart microwave-safe casserole. Microwave on 100% power (high) for 2 to 3 minutes or until crisp-tender; drain. Stir in Parmesan cheese.

    1   slightly beaten egg
$^1/_2$ cup fine dry bread crumbs
$^1/_2$ cup finely chopped onion (1 medium)
$^1/_4$ cup milk
$^1/_2$ teaspoon dried thyme, crushed
$^1/_4$ teaspoon dried rosemary, crushed
$^1/_4$ teaspoon garlic salt
$^1/_4$ teaspoon pepper
$1^1/_2$ pounds ground raw turkey
    1   cup chopped broccoli
$^2/_3$ cup shredded carrots
$^1/_3$ cup chopped red sweet pepper
    2   tablespoons grated Parmesan cheese
    2   tablespoons currant jelly, melted

1. In a medium mixing bowl combine egg, bread crumbs, onion, milk, thyme, rosemary, garlic salt, and pepper. Add turkey; mix well. On waxed paper pat turkey mixture into a 12×8-inch rectangle; set aside.

2. For vegetable stuffing, in a saucepan cook broccoli, carrots, and sweet pepper, covered, in a small amount of boiling water for 3 to 4 minutes or till crisp-tender. Drain well. Stir in Parmesan cheese.

3. Spread vegetable stuffing over turkey mixture to within 1 inch of sides. Beginning at a short end, roll turkey tightly using waxed paper to lift mixture. Peel waxed paper away as you roll. Place in a 9×5×3-inch loaf pan.

4. Bake in a 350° oven for 1 to 1¼ hours or till no longer pink (meat thermometer registers 180°). Transfer to a serving platter; brush with melted jelly. Makes 6 servings.

Nutrition Facts per serving: 242 cal., 11 g total fat (3 g sat. fat), 80 mg chol., 272 mg sodium, 17 g carbo., 2 g fiber, 19 g pro. **Daily Values:** 63% vit. A, 63% vit. C, 7% calcium, 14% iron

CHICKEN BURGERS

START TO FINISH: 35 MINUTES

    Mayonnaise Sauce (below) (optional)
1 **beaten egg**
$1/2$ **cup finely chopped celery**
$1/2$ **cup finely chopped green sweet pepper**
$1/3$ **cup fine dry seasoned bread crumbs**
2 **tablespoons finely chopped onion**
1 **tablespoon snipped fresh parsley**
1 **teaspoon Worcestershire sauce**
1 **pound ground raw chicken**
2 **tablespoons cooking oil**
4 **Kaiser rolls, split and toasted**
4 **lettuce leaves**
1 **large tomato, sliced**

1. If desired, prepare Mayonnaise Sauce.

2. For burgers, in a medium mixing bowl combine egg, celery, sweet pepper, bread crumbs, onion, parsley, and Worcestershire sauce. Add chicken and mix well. Shape into four $3/4$-inch-thick patties.

3. In a large skillet cook chicken patties in hot oil over medium heat for 10 to 12 minutes or till no longer pink, turning once.

4. To serve, if desired, spread cut sides of Kaiser rolls with some of the sauce. Top with chicken patties, lettuce, and tomato. Makes 4 servings.

Nutrition Facts per serving: 403 cal., 16 g total fat (3 g sat. fat), 100 mg chol., 650 mg sodium, 41 g carbo., 1 g fiber, 22 g pro. **Daily Values:** 8% vit. A, 36% vit. C, 7% calcium, 22% iron

■ **Mayonnaise Sauce:** In a small bowl combine $1/4$ cup *mayonnaise or salad dressing*, 1 tablespoon finely chopped *green onion*, 1 teaspoon snipped *fresh parsley*, $1/4$ teaspoon *dried Italian seasoning*, crushed, and a dash *pepper*. Cover and chill till serving time. Makes $1/2$ cup.

Nutrition Facts per tablespoon: 99 cal., 11 g total fat (2 g sat. fat)

■ **Broiled Hawaiian Chicken Burgers:** Prepare as above, except do not use the Mayonnaise Sauce. For chicken patties, omit Worcestershire sauce and tomato slices. Add 3 tablespoons finely chopped *water chestnuts* and ³/₄ teaspoon *ground ginger* to the bread crumb mixture. Place burgers on the unheated rack of a broiler pan. Broil 4 inches from the heat for 12 to 14 minutes or till no longer pink, turning once and brushing with about 2 tablespoons bottled *sweet-and-sour sauce* during the last 5 minutes of broiling.

Meanwhile, place 4 canned *pineapple slices* on broiler pan. Broil for 1 to 2 minutes, turning as needed. Serve patties on toasted Kaiser rolls with lettuce. Brush patties with an additional 2 tablespoons bottled sweet-and-sour sauce and top with pineapple slices. Makes 4 servings.

Nutrition Facts per serving: 319 cal., 15 g total fat (3 g sat. fat)

CHICKEN DIVAN CASSEROLE

PREP: 20 MINUTES   BAKE: 20 MINUTES   Oven 350°

Low-Fat

    1 10-ounce package frozen cut broccoli, thawed
    2 cups chopped cooked chicken or turkey (see tip, page 857)
    1 4¹/₂-ounce can sliced mushrooms, drained
    1 10³/₄-ounce can reduced-fat and reduced-salt condensed cream
         of chicken, cream of celery, or cream of mushroom soup or
         regular condensed cream of chicken, cream of celery, or
         cream of mushroom soup
 ¹/₂ cup plain low-fat yogurt
 ¹/₄ cup chicken broth
 ¹/₄ teaspoon dry mustard
 ¹/₄ teaspoon curry powder (optional)
    1 cup corn bread stuffing mix or herb-seasoned stuffing mix
    2 tablespoons grated Parmesan cheese
 ¹/₄ teaspoon paprika

1. Place broccoli in the bottom of a 2-quart square baking dish; top with cooked chicken or turkey and mushrooms.

2. In a medium saucepan combine soup, yogurt, chicken broth, dry mustard, and, if desired, curry powder. Heat through but do not boil. Pour the soup mixture over broccoli, chicken, and mushrooms in baking dish. Sprinkle stuffing mix over soup mixture; top with Parmesan cheese. Sprinkle with paprika.

3. Bake in a 350° oven for 20 to 25 minutes or till heated through. Makes 4 servings.

Nutrition Facts per serving: 334 cal., 10 g total fat (3 g sat. fat), 78 mg chol., 943 mg sodium, 31 g carbo., 3 g fiber, 31 g pro. **Daily Values:** 15% vit. A, 25% vit. C, 13% calcium, 17% iron

COUNTRY CHICKEN BAKE WITH DUMPLINGS

PREP: 25 MINUTES   BAKE: 45 MINUTES
Oven 400°

    2¹/₂ cups chopped cooked
            chicken or turkey (see
            tip, at right)
      1 14³/₄-ounce can cream-style
            corn
      1 cup frozen peas and
            carrots
      1 4¹/₂-ounce can sliced
            mushrooms, drained
    ¹/₂ cup milk
    ¹/₂ cup shredded cheddar
            cheese
    ¹/₄ cup sliced green onions (2)
      1 tablespoon Worcestershire
            sauce
    ¹/₂ teaspoon pepper
    ²/₃ cup all-purpose flour
    ²/₃ cup yellow cornmeal
      2 tablespoons grated
            Parmesan cheese
      2 tablespoons snipped fresh
            parsley
      2 teaspoons baking powder
    ¹/₄ teaspoon salt
    ¹/₂ cup milk
    ¹/₄ cup cooking oil

1. In a large mixing bowl combine chicken, corn, peas and carrots, mushrooms, ¹/₂ cup milk,

QUICK-COOKED CHICKEN

If you need cooked chicken for a recipe but don't have any leftovers, one solution is to purchase a deli-roasted chicken. A cooked chicken will yield 1¹/₂ to 2 cups boneless chopped meat.

Or, poach chicken breasts. In a large skillet place 12 ounces skinless, boneless *chicken breasts* and 1¹/₂ cups *water*. Bring to boiling; reduce heat. Cover and simmer for 12 to 14 minutes or until chicken is tender and no longer pink. Drain well. Cut up the chicken. The 12 ounces boneless breasts will yield about 2 cups cubed, cooked chicken.

For chilled chicken, cover the cut-up chicken and put it in the refrigerator for 2 hours or until thoroughly chilled. Or, quick-chill by putting the chicken in the freezer for 30 minutes.

cheddar cheese, green onions, Worcestershire sauce, and pepper. Transfer to a greased 2-quart rectangular baking dish. Bake, covered, in a 400° oven for 25 to 30 minutes or till bubbly.

2. Meanwhile, for dumplings, in a mixing bowl combine flour, cornmeal, Parmesan cheese, parsley, baking powder, and salt. Combine $1/2$ cup milk and oil; add to flour mixture. Stir till just combined. Uncover casserole; drop batter from a tablespoon into 6 mounds directly atop the bubbling chicken mixture.

3. Bake, uncovered, for 20 to 25 minutes more or till a wooden toothpick inserted into dumplings comes out clean. Let stand 10 minutes before serving. Makes 6 servings.

Nutrition Facts per serving: 440 cal., 19 g total fat (6 g sat. fat), 71 mg chol., 713 mg sodium, 41 g carbo., 3 g fiber, 28 g pro. **Daily Values:** 27% vit. A, 20% vit. C, 23% calcium, 21% iron

---

TURKEY CRUNCH CASSEROLE

PREP: 20 MINUTES   BAKE: 30 MINUTES   Oven 350°

Use a rolling pin to crush the chow mein noodles in a plastic bag.

   2 cups chopped cooked turkey or chicken (see tip, page 857)
   1 10³/₄-ounce can reduced-fat and reduced-salt condensed cream
         of chicken soup
 ³/₄ cup chopped celery
 ³/₄ cup light mayonnaise or salad dressing
 ¹/₂ cup slivered almonds, toasted (see tip, page 234)
   2 Hard-Cooked Eggs, chopped (optional) (see recipe, page 466)
   1 2-ounce jar diced pimiento, drained
   2 tablespoons chopped onion
1¹/₂ cups chow mein noodles, slightly crushed

1. In a large mixing bowl combine turkey or chicken, cream of chicken soup, celery, mayonnaise or salad dressing, almonds, eggs (if desired), pimiento, and onion. Transfer to a 2-quart rectangular baking dish. Sprinkle with chow mein noodles.

2. Bake in a 350° oven about 30 minutes or till heated through. Makes 6 servings.

Nutrition Facts per serving: 362 cal., 25 g total fat (4 g sat. fat), 50 mg chol., 539 mg sodium, 16 g carbo., 2 g fiber, 18 g pro. **Daily Values:** 11% vit. A, 16% vit. C, 4% calcium, 13% iron

ARTICHOKE-TURKEY CASSEROLE

PREP: 45 MINUTES BAKE: 40 MINUTES STAND: 10 MINUTES   Oven 350°

Low-Fat

You can use a reduced-fat and reduced-sodium condensed soup in this colorful, company-special casserole and no one will know the difference.

    1/2 cup chopped carrot
    1/2 cup chopped red sweet pepper
    1/4 cup sliced green onions (2)
      1 tablespoon margarine or butter
      1 10³/₄-ounce can condensed cream of chicken soup
      1 9-ounce package frozen artichoke hearts, thawed and cut up
  1 1/2 cups chopped cooked turkey or chicken (see tip, page 857)
      1 cup cooked wild rice and/or long grain rice (see page 139)
    1/2 cup shredded mozzarella cheese
    1/2 cup milk
      2 tablespoons dry sherry or milk
      2 slices bacon, crisp-cooked, drained, and crumbled
      3 tablespoons grated Parmesan cheese

1. In a large skillet cook carrot, sweet pepper, and green onions in hot margarine or butter till crisp-tender. Remove from heat and stir in chicken soup, artichoke hearts, turkey or chicken, rice, mozzarella cheese, milk, sherry, and bacon. Transfer turkey mixture to a 2-quart rectangular baking dish. Sprinkle with Parmesan cheese.

2. Bake, covered, in a 350° oven for 20 minutes. Uncover and bake about 20 minutes more or till bubbly. Let stand 10 minutes before serving. Makes 6 servings.

■ **Make-ahead directions:** Prepare as above, except after assembling, cover and refrigerate for up to 24 hours. Bake, covered, in a 350° oven for 30 minutes. Uncover and bake about 20 minutes more or till bubbly.

Nutrition Facts per serving: 257 cal., 11 g total fat (4 g sat. fat), 44 mg chol., 651 mg sodium, 19 g carbo., 4 g fiber, 20 g pro. **Daily Values:** 72% vit. A, 34% vit. C, 15% calcium, 13% iron

CHICKEN POTPIES

PREP: 50 MINUTES   BAKE: 12 MINUTES   Oven 450°

Pastry for Double-Crust Pie (see page 808)
1 10-ounce package frozen peas and carrots
1/2 cup chopped onion (1 medium)
1/2 cup chopped fresh mushrooms
1/4 cup margarine or butter
1/3 cup all-purpose flour
1/2 teaspoon salt
1/2 teaspoon dried sage, marjoram, or thyme, crushed
1/8 teaspoon pepper
2 cups chicken broth
3/4 cup milk
3 cups cubed cooked chicken or turkey (see tip, page 857)
1/4 cup snipped fresh parsley
1/4 cup diced pimiento

1. Prepare Pastry for Double-Crust Pie; set aside. Cook peas and carrots according to package directions; drain.

2. In a saucepan cook onion and mushrooms in margarine or butter till tender. Stir in flour; salt; sage, marjoram, or thyme; and pepper. Add chicken broth and milk all at once. Cook and stir till thickened and bubbly. Stir in drained peas and carrots, chicken or turkey, parsley, and pimiento; cook till bubbly.

3. Pour mixture into six 10-ounce casseroles. (Or, use a 2-quart rectangular baking dish.)

4. Roll pastry into a 15×10-inch rectangle. Cut into six 5-inch circles and place atop the 10-ounce casseroles. (Or, roll pastry into a 13×9-inch rectangle. Place over the rectangular baking dish.) Flute edges of pastry and cut slits in the top for steam to escape. Bake in a 450° oven for 12 to 15 minutes or till pastry is golden brown. Makes 6 servings.

Nutrition Facts per serving: 638 cal., 38 g total fat (9 g sat. fat), 70 mg chol., 820 mg sodium, 43 g carbo., 3 g fiber, 31 g pro. **Daily Values:** 52% vit. A, 25% vit. C, 6% calcium, 27% iron

■ **Biscuit-Topped Chicken Potpies:** Prepare as above, except omit pastry. Cut 1 package (6) *refrigerated biscuits* into quarters and arrange atop bubbly chicken mixture in individual casseroles or the baking dish. Bake in a 400° oven about 15 minutes or till biscuits are golden.

Nutrition Facts per serving: 390 cal., 19 g total fat (5 g sat. fat)

Chicken Jambalaya

Prep: 15 minutes   Cook: 25 minutes

Low-Fat

$^1/_3$ cup chopped celery
$^1/_4$ cup chopped onion
$^1/_4$ cup chopped green sweet pepper
2 tablespoons margarine or butter
1 14$^1/_2$-ounce can tomatoes, cut up
1$^1/_2$ cups chicken broth
$^2/_3$ cup long grain rice
1 teaspoon dried basil or thyme, crushed
$^1/_4$ teaspoon garlic powder
$^1/_4$ teaspoon pepper
$^1/_4$ to $^1/_2$ teaspoon bottled hot pepper sauce
1 bay leaf
2 cups cubed cooked chicken or turkey (see tip, page 857)

1. In a large skillet cook celery, onion, and sweet pepper in margarine or butter till vegetables are tender but not brown.
2. Stir in undrained tomatoes, chicken broth, uncooked rice, basil or thyme, garlic powder, pepper, hot pepper sauce, and bay leaf. Bring to boiling; reduce heat. Cover and simmer about 20 minutes or till rice is tender. Stir in chicken or turkey; heat through. Discard bay leaf. Makes 4 servings.

Nutrition Facts per serving: 354 cal., 12 g total fat (3 g sat. fat), 68 mg chol., 610 mg sodium, 32 g carbo., 2 g fiber, 27 g pro. **Daily Values:** 15% vit. A, 37% vit. C, 5% calcium, 22% iron

CHICKEN À LA KING

START TO FINISH: 25 MINUTES

Fast

   1 cup sliced fresh mushrooms
 ¼ cup chopped green sweet pepper
 ¼ cup chopped onion
   3 tablespoons margarine or butter
   2 tablespoons all-purpose flour
 ½ teaspoon salt
 ½ teaspoon paprika
2½ cups half-and-half or light cream
   3 beaten egg yolks
   2 tablespoons dry sherry
   1 tablespoon lemon juice
   2 cups cubed cooked chicken (see tip, page 857)
   2 tablespoons diced pimiento
  24 toast points or 6 baked patty shells

1. In a large saucepan cook mushrooms, sweet pepper, and onion in margarine or butter till tender but not brown. Stir in flour, salt, and paprika. Add half-and-half or light cream all at once. Cook and stir till thickened and bubbly.

2. Stir about 1 cup of the thickened sauce into the beaten egg yolks; return to saucepan. Cook and stir over medium heat till bubbly. Stir in sherry and lemon juice. Add chicken and pimiento; heat through. Serve over toast points or in patty shells. Makes 6 servings.

Nutrition Facts per serving: 424 cal., 26 g total fat (11 g sat. fat), 200 mg chol., 474 mg sodium, 21 g carbo., 1 g fiber, 25 g pro. **Daily Values:** 39% vit. A, 15% vit. C, 13% calcium, 15% iron

CHICKEN TETRAZZINI

PREP: 30 MINUTES   BAKE: 15 MINUTES   Oven 350°

This perennial favorite is said to have been named for an opera singer.

    8 ounces spaghetti or linguine
    2 cups sliced fresh mushrooms
  $^1/_2$ cup sliced green onions (4)
    2 tablespoons margarine or butter
  $^1/_4$ cup all-purpose flour
  $^1/_8$ teaspoon coarsely ground pepper
  $^1/_8$ teaspoon ground nutmeg
    1 cup chicken broth
    1 cup milk, half-and-half, or light cream
    2 cups chopped cooked chicken or turkey (see tip, page 857)
    2 tablespoons dry sherry
  $^1/_4$ cup grated Parmesan cheese
  $^1/_4$ cup sliced almonds
    2 tablespoons snipped fresh parsley

1. Cook spaghetti or linguine according to package directions; drain.
2. Meanwhile, in a large saucepan cook mushrooms and green onions in hot margarine or butter till tender. Stir in flour, pepper, and nutmeg. Add chicken broth and milk all at once. Cook and stir till thickened and bubbly. Stir in chicken or turkey, sherry, and *half* of the Parmesan cheese. Add cooked spaghetti or linguine; toss to coat.
3. Transfer chicken mixture to a 2-quart rectangular baking dish. Sprinkle with the remaining Parmesan cheese and almonds.
4. Bake in a 350° oven for 15 to 20 minutes or till heated through. Sprinkle with parsley. Serves 6.

Nutrition Facts per serving: 383 cal., 13 g total fat (3 g sat. fat), 51 mg chol., 318 mg sodium, 39 g carbo., 1 g fiber, 26 g pro. **Daily Values:** 11% vit. A, 7% vit. C, 12% calcium, 22% iron

CHICKEN ENCHILADAS

PREP: 25 MINUTES   BAKE: 40 MINUTES   Oven 350°

$\frac{1}{4}$ cup chopped pecans
$\frac{1}{4}$ cup chopped onion
 2 tablespoons margarine or butter
 1 4-ounce can diced green chili peppers, drained
 1 3-ounce package cream cheese, softened
 1 tablespoon milk
$\frac{1}{4}$ teaspoon ground cumin
 2 cups chopped cooked chicken (see tip, page 857)
12 7-inch flour tortillas
 1 10$\frac{3}{4}$-ounce can condensed cream of chicken or cream of
       mushroom soup
 1 8-ounce carton dairy sour cream
 1 cup milk
$\frac{3}{4}$ cup shredded Monterey Jack or cheddar cheese (3 ounces)
 2 tablespoons chopped pecans

1. In a skillet cook the $\frac{1}{4}$ cup pecans and the onion in margarine or butter over medium heat till onion is tender and pecans are lightly toasted. Remove skillet from heat. Stir in *1 tablespoon* of the canned green chili peppers.

2. In a medium mixing bowl combine softened cream cheese, the 1 tablespoon milk, and cumin; add nut mixture and chicken. Stir till combined. Spoon about 3 tablespoons of the chicken mixture onto each tortilla near an edge; roll up. Place filled tortillas, seam sides down, in a greased 3-quart rectangular baking dish.

3. In a medium mixing bowl combine soup, sour cream, the 1 cup milk, and remaining canned chili peppers. Pour the soup mixture evenly over the tortillas in the baking dish. Cover with foil and bake in a 350° oven about 35 minutes or till heated through. Remove foil. Sprinkle enchiladas with Monterey Jack cheese and the 2 tablespoons pecans. Return to oven and bake about 5 minutes more or till cheese melts. Makes 6 servings.

Nutrition Facts per serving: 664 cal., 39 g total fat (15 g sat. fat), 97 mg chol., 1,034 mg sodium, 50 g carbo., 1 g fiber, 30 g pro. **Daily Values**: 29% vit. A, 12% vit. C, 29% calcium, 25% iron

■ **Lower-Fat Chicken Enchiladas:** Prepare as above, except use *fat-free cream cheese* (4 ounces), *lower-sodium soup, fat-free dairy* *sour cream, skim milk,* and *reduced-fat Monterey Jack cheese.* Omit the 2 tablespoons pecans and top the baked enchiladas with $^1/_2$ cup chopped *tomatoes.*

Nutrition Facts per serving: 555 cal., 22 g total fat (4 g sat. fat), 61 mg chol., 823 mg sodium

---

ROAST TURKEY WITH OLD-FASHIONED BREAD STUFFING

PREP: 1 HOUR ROAST: $3^1/_4$ HOURS STAND: 20 MINUTES   Oven 325°

If you have questions about making stuffing, read "Stuffing Tips" on page 873.

>   1 cup chopped celery
>   1 cup sliced fresh mushrooms or one 4-ounce can sliced
>   mushrooms, drained (optional)
> $^1/_2$ cup chopped onion (1 medium)
> $^1/_3$ cup margarine or butter
>   1 teaspoon poultry seasoning or ground sage
> $^1/_4$ teaspoon pepper
> $^1/_8$ teaspoon salt
>   8 cups dry bread cubes
> $^1/_2$ to $^3/_4$ cup chicken broth or water
>   1 10- to 12-pound turkey
>   Cooking oil

1. For stuffing, in a large skillet cook celery; fresh mushrooms, if using; and onion in margarine or butter till tender but not brown; remove from heat. Stir in poultry seasoning or sage, pepper, and salt. Place dry bread cubes in a large mixing bowl; add onion mixture and, if using, canned mushrooms. Drizzle with enough broth or water to moisten, tossing lightly.

2. Rinse turkey on the outside as well as inside body and neck cavities; pat dry. Season body cavity with salt. Spoon some of the stuffing loosely into neck cavity (see photo 1, page 866). Pull the neck skin to the back; fasten with a skewer (see photo 2, page 866).

3. Lightly spoon more stuffing into the body cavity. Use no more than $^3/_4$ cup stuffing per pound of turkey. (Place any remaining stuffing in a casserole, cover, and chill. Bake stuffing alongside turkey for 30 to 45 minutes or till heated through.) Tuck the ends of the drumsticks under the band of skin across the tail (see photo 3, right). If the band of skin is not present, tie the drumsticks securely to the tail. Twist wing tips under the back (see photo 4, right).

4. Place turkey, breast side up, on a rack in a shallow roasting pan. Brush with oil. Insert a meat thermometer into the center of one of the inside thigh muscles (see photo 5, right). The thermometer bulb should not touch the bone. Cover turkey loosely with foil.

5. Roast turkey in a 325° oven for $3^1/_4$ to $3^1/_2$ hours or till thermometer registers 180° to 185°, juices run clear, and the center of the stuffing registers at least 165°. After $2^1/_2$ hours, cut band of skin or string between drumsticks so thighs cook evenly. When done, drumsticks should move very easily in their sockets and their thickest parts will feel soft when pressed. Uncover the last 30 minutes of roasting.

6. Remove turkey from oven. Cover; let stand 15 to 20 minutes before carving. Use a spoon to remove stuffing from turkey; place in a serving bowl. Carve turkey (see tip, page 870). Makes 12 to 14 servings.

Nutrition Facts per serving: 392 cal., 19 g total fat (5 g sat. fat), 121 mg chol., 343 mg sodium, 14 g carbo., 1 g fiber, 38 g pro. **Daily Values:** 15% vit. A, 2% vit. C, 6% calcium, 23% iron

1. Lightly spoon some stuffing into neck cavity. Do not pack stuffing tightly or it won't be hot enough when turkey is cooked. Use no more than ¾ cup stuffing per pound.

2. After adding stuffing to the neck cavity, pull the neck skin over the stuffing onto the back of the turkey and secure with a small skewer.

3. Loosely fill body cavity with stuffing, allowing for it to cook thoroughly and expand during roasting. Tuck legs under band of skin, if present, or tie legs to tail with string.

4. For a neat appearance and to prevent wing tips from overbrowning, twist the wing tips under the back of the turkey.

5. Insert a meat thermometer into center of an inside thigh muscle. Its tip should not touch bone. After roasting, use an instant-read thermometer to check thigh in several places and the stuffing.

GLAZED CHICKEN AND VEGETABLES

1 2½- to 3-pound whole broiler-fryer chicken
   Cooking oil
2 medium potatoes, peeled and quartered
6 carrots, bias-sliced ½ inch thick
½ cup honey
¼ cup prepared mustard
2 tablespoons margarine or butter
2 tablespoons finely chopped onion
2 teaspoons curry powder
½ teaspoon garlic salt
¼ teaspoon crushed red pepper
¼ teaspoon ground ginger
2 medium apples, cored

1. Rinse chicken; pat dry. Skewer neck skin to back (see photo 2, left); tie legs to tail. Twist wing tips under back (see photo 4, left). Place breast side up on a rack in a shallow roasting pan. Brush with oil. If desired, insert a meat thermometer into center of an inside thigh muscle (see photo 5, page 867). Roast, uncovered, in a 375° oven for 1 hour.
2. Meanwhile, cook vegetables in boiling water for 20 to 25 minutes or till nearly tender; drain.
3. For glaze, in a saucepan combine honey and the next 7 ingredients. Bring to boiling, stirring constantly. Remove from heat; set glaze aside.
4. Discard fat in roasting pan. Cut apples into wedges. Arrange potatoes, carrots, and apples around chicken in pan. Spoon glaze over poultry, vegetables, and apples. Roast for 15 to 20 minutes more or till chicken is no longer pink and meat thermometer registers 180° to 185°. Serves 6.

Nutrition Facts per serving: 422 cal., 17 g total fat (4 g sat. fat), 66 mg chol., 456 mg sodium, 46 g carbo., 4 g fiber, 23 g pro. **Daily Values:** 179% vit. A, 11% vit. C, 4% calcium, 14% iron

HONEY-MUSTARD GLAZED TURKEY BREAST

PREP: 15 MINUTES   ROAST: 1¼ HOURS   Oven 325°

Low-Fat

1 1³/₄- to 2-pound bone-in turkey breast portion
1 tablespoon cooking oil
¼ teaspoon salt
1 recipe Honey-Mustard Glaze (see below)

1. Rinse turkey; pat dry. Place turkey, skin side up, on a rack in a shallow roasting pan. Brush with oil; sprinkle with salt and ⅛ teaspoon *pepper*. Insert a meat thermometer into thickest part of the breast. The thermometer bulb should not touch the bone.

2. Roast turkey, uncovered, in a 325° oven for 1¼ to 1½ hours or till juices run clear and the thermometer registers 170°, brushing with Honey-Mustard Glaze several times during the last 15 minutes of roasting.

3. Transfer turkey to a cutting board; let stand 10 to 15 minutes before carving. Heat any remaining glaze; serve with turkey. Makes 6 servings.

■ **Honey-Mustard Glaze:** In a small mixing bowl stir together ¼ cup *honey*, 1 tablespoon *Dijon-style mustard*, 1 tablespoon *white wine Worcestershire sauce*, and 1 tablespoon *margarine or butter*, melted.

Nutrition Facts per serving: 257 cal., 11 g total fat (3 g sat. fat), 67 mg chol., 253 mg sodium, 12 g carbo., 0 g fiber, 26 g pro. **Daily Values:** 2% vit. A, 0% vit. C, 2% calcium, 9% iron

CARVING A ROASTED BIRD

To carve poultry with confidence, use a sharp knife and follow these directions.

■ When the bird is done, remove it from the oven and cover it with foil. Let it stand for 15 to 20 minutes before beginning to carve. Standing lets the bird's flesh firm up, allowing the carved slices to hold together better.

■ Place the bird on a cutting board. Remove the stuffing. Grasp the tip of one drumstick and pull it away from the body. Cut through the skin and meat between the thigh and the body (see illustration 1, at right). Repeat on the other side.

■ With the tip of the knife, separate the thighbone from the backbone by cutting through the joint. Repeat on the other side.

■ To separate the thighs and drumsticks, cut through the joints where the drumstick bones and thighbones meet.

■ To carve the meat from the drumsticks, hold each drumstick vertically by the tip with the large end resting on the cutting board. Slice the meat parallel to the bone and under some tendons, turning the leg to get even slices. Slice the thigh meat the same way.

■ To carve the breast meat, make a deep horizontal cut into the breast above each wing (see illustration 2, at right). This cut marks the end of each breast meat slice. Beginning at the outer top edge of each breast, cut slices from the top down to the horizontal cut (see illustration 3, at right). Cut the final smaller slices following the curve of the breastbone.

■ Remove wings by cutting through the joints where the wing bones and backbone meet.

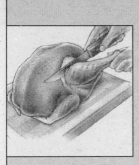

1. Pull a leg away from the bird; cut through the meat between the thigh and the body.

2. Steady the bird with a large fork. Make a deep cut into the breast just above each wing.

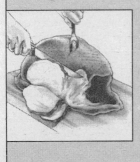

3. Cut from the top down to the deep horizontal cut, cutting thin, even slices from the breast.

CORNISH GAME HENS WITH CORN BREAD STUFFING

PREP: 15 MINUTES   ROAST: 1 HOUR   Oven 375°

2 cups crumbled corn bread*
¼ cup chopped pecans, toasted (see tip, page 234)
¼ cup chopped green sweet pepper
2 tablespoons dried currants or raisins
¼ cup sliced green onions (2)
2 teaspoons snipped fresh sage or ½ teaspoon dried sage, crushed
1 tablespoon margarine or butter, melted
½ cup chicken broth
2 1¼- to 1½-pound Cornish game hens, split
2 teaspoons cooking oil
¼ teaspoon salt
¼ teaspoon paprika
⅛ teaspoon ground cumin

1. For stuffing, combine corn bread, pecans, sweet pepper, currants or raisins, green onions, and sage. Drizzle with melted margarine and broth to moisten, tossing lightly. Place stuffing in a 1-quart casserole. Cover and chill.

2. Use a long, heavy knife or kitchen shears to halve Cornish hens lengthwise. Cut through the breast bone, just off center. Cut through the center of the backbone. (If desired, ask a butcher to split the hens.) Rinse hens, pat dry.

3. Twist wing tips under back (see photo 4, page 867). Place hen halves, cut sides down, in a 3-quart rectangular baking dish. Combine cooking oil, salt, paprika, and cumin; brush over Cornish hens.

4. Bake, covered, in a 375° oven for 35 minutes. Add covered casserole of stuffing to oven; uncover hens. Bake hens and stuffing about 25 minutes more or till hens are tender and no longer pink and stuffing is heated through.

5. To serve, divide stuffing into 4 equal mounds on individual plates. Place a hen half on top of each mound of stuffing. Makes 4 servings.

*Note: Prepare one 8½-ounce package corn muffin mix or 1 recipe Corn Bread (see page 226); freeze any leftover corn bread for another use.

Nutrition Facts per serving: 511 cal., 33 g total fat (5 g sat. fat), 116 mg chol., 532 mg sodium, 23 g carbo., 1 g fiber, 34 g pro. **Daily Values:** 6% vit. A, 10% vit. C, 4% calcium, 6% iron

STUFFING TIPS

■ To make dry bread cubes for stuffing, cut bread into ½-inch-square pieces. (You'll need 12 to 14 slices of bread for 8 cups of dry cubes.) Spread in a single layer in a shallow baking pan. Bake in a 300° oven for 10 to 15 minutes or until dry, stirring twice; cool. (Bread will continue to dry and crisp as it cools.) Or, let stand, loosely covered, at room temperature for 8 to 12 hours.

■ Never stuff poultry until just before roasting.

■ You'll need no more than ¾ cup stuffing for each pound of ready-to-cook turkey.

■ Spoon the stuffing into the turkey loosely so there will be room for it to expand during roasting. If the stuffing is too tightly packed, it will not reach a safe temperature by the time the turkey is done. Put remaining stuffing in a casserole and heat thoroughly.

■ Stuffing temperatures should reach at least 165°. Since there is no visual doneness test, use a meat thermometer. Insert it through the body cavity into the thickest part of the stuffing; let it stand 5 minutes. Or, after removing from oven, use an instant-read thermometer to check the temperature of the stuffing.

■ To bake an entire recipe of stuffing, place in a casserole and bake, covered, in a 325° oven for 40 to 45 minutes or in a 375° oven about 30 minutes.

HERB-ROASTED CHICKEN

PREP: 15 MINUTES ROAST: 1 HOUR Oven 375°

    1 2¹/₂- to 3-pound whole broiler-fryer chicken
    2 tablespoons margarine or butter, melted
    2 cloves garlic, minced
    1 teaspoon dried basil, crushed
  ¹/₂ teaspoon salt
  ¹/₂ teaspoon ground sage
  ¹/₂ teaspoon dried thyme, crushed
  ¹/₄ teaspoon lemon-pepper seasoning or pepper

1. Rinse chicken; pat dry. Skewer neck skin to back (see photo 2, page 866); tie legs to tail. Twist wings under back (see photo 4, page 867). Place chicken, breast side up, on a rack in a shallow roasting pan. Brush with melted margarine or butter; rub garlic over bird.

2. In a small bowl stir together basil, salt, sage, thyme, and lemon-pepper seasoning; rub onto bird (see photo, below). If desired, insert a meat thermometer into center of an inside thigh muscle (see photo 5, page 867). Do not allow thermometer bulb to touch bone. Roast, uncovered, in a 375° oven for 1 to 1¹/₄ hours or till drumsticks move easily in their sockets, chicken is no longer pink, and meat thermometer registers 180° to 185°. Remove chicken from oven, cover, and let stand 10 minutes before carving. Makes 6 servings.

Nutrition Facts per serving: 210 cal., 14 g total fat (3 g sat. fat), 79 mg chol., 326 mg sodium, 1 g carbo., 0 g fiber, 20 g pro. **Daily Values:** 18% vit. A, 1% vit. C, 1% calcium, 9% iron

APRICOT-HONEY-GLAZED DUCKLING

PREP: 20 MINUTES   ROAST: 1¾ HOURS   Oven 375°

1 4- to 5-pound domestic duckling
½ teaspoon dried oregano, crushed
½ teaspoon onion salt
½ teaspoon garlic salt
¼ teaspoon pepper
⅓ cup apricot preserves
2 tablespoons honey
½ teaspoon finely shredded lemon peel (set aside)
2 tablespoons lemon juice
½ cup chicken broth
2 teaspoons cornstarch
2 teaspoons soy sauce
   Hot cooked wild rice (see page 139) (optional)

1. Rinse duck; pat dry. In a small mixing bowl combine oregano, onion salt, garlic salt, and pepper. Sprinkle body cavity of duck with some of the oregano mixture; rub remaining mixture onto skin of duck. Skewer neck skin to back (see photo 2, page 866); tie legs to tail with string. Twist wings under back (see photo 4, page 867). Prick skin all over with a fork.

2. Place duck, breast side up, on a rack in a shallow roasting pan. Roast in a 375° oven for 1¾ to 2¼ hours or till the drumsticks move easily in their sockets and duck is no longer pink, spooning off fat occasionally.

3. Meanwhile, for glaze, in a small saucepan heat apricot preserves, honey, and lemon juice just till preserves melt. Baste duck with about half of the glaze during the last 10 minutes of roasting.

4. For sauce, combine chicken broth and cornstarch; stir into remaining glaze in saucepan along with lemon peel and soy sauce. Cook and stir till thickened and bubbly. Cook and stir for 2 minutes more. Serve sauce with duck. If desired, serve with wild rice. Makes 4 servings.

Nutrition Facts per serving: 557 cal., 37 g total fat (13 g sat. fat), 109 mg chol., 806 mg sodium, 30 g carbo., 0 g fiber, 26 g pro. **Daily Values:** 8% vit. A, 7% vit. C, 2% calcium, 26% iron

SAUSAGE STUFFING

PREP: 20 MINUTES   BAKE: SEE CHART, PAGES 887–89

*For the corn bread needed in this stuffing, you can make the Corn
Bread recipe on page 226 or bake two 8¹/₂-ounce
packages corn muffin mix.*

12 **ounces bulk pork sausage**
³/₄ **cup finely chopped onion**
¹/₂ **cup chopped green sweet pepper**
¹/₂ **cup chopped celery**
¹/₂ **cup margarine or butter**
 2 **beaten eggs**
 1 **teaspoon poultry seasoning**
¹/₈ **teaspoon pepper**
 5 **cups dry white bread cubes (see tip, page 873)**
 5 **cups crumbled corn bread**
³/₄ **cup chopped pecans, toasted (see tip, page 234)**
 1 **to 1¹/₂ cups chicken broth**

1. In a large skillet cook sausage till brown. Drain fat. Set sausage
aside.
2. In the same skillet cook onion, sweet pepper, and celery in hot
margarine or butter till tender but not brown; set aside.
3. In a large mixing bowl combine eggs, poultry seasoning, and
pepper. Add bread cubes and corn bread; toss till coated. Add
cooked sausage, onion mixture, and pecans. Add enough broth to
moisten (³/₄ to 1 cup), tossing lightly to mix.
4. Use to stuff one 10- to 12-pound turkey. (See tip, page 873, and
roasting chart, pages 887–89, for doneness temperatures of turkey
and stuffing.) Place any remaining stuffing in a casserole and drizzle
with enough of the remaining chicken broth (¹/₄ to ¹/₂ cup) to make
a stuffing of desired moistness; cover and chill till ready to bake.
Bake, covered, in a 325° oven for 30 to 35 minutes or till hot. Makes
12 cups (12 to 14 servings).

Nutrition Facts per serving: 426 cal., 25 g total fat (4 g sat. fat), 73 mg chol., 772 mg
sodium, 43 g carbo., 1 g fiber, 11 g pro. **Daily Values:** 11% vit. A, 6% vit. C, 8% calcium,
13% iron

CLASSIC GIBLET STUFFING

PREP: 15 MINUTES   BAKE: SEE CHART, PAGES 887-89

Substitute the giblet cooking broth for the chicken broth or water for a flavorful alternative.

  1 cup finely chopped celery
$^1/_2$ cup chopped onion (1 medium)
$^1/_2$ cup margarine or butter
$^1/_2$ cup chopped, cooked poultry giblets (see Giblet Gravy, step 1, page 881)
  1 teaspoon poultry seasoning or ground sage
$^1/_4$ teaspoon pepper
$^1/_8$ teaspoon salt
  8 cups dry bread cubes (see tip, page 873)
  1 to 1$^1/_3$ cups chicken broth or water

1. In a small saucepan cook celery and onion in margarine or butter till tender but not brown; remove from heat. Stir in giblets, poultry seasoning or sage, pepper, and salt.

2. Place dry bread cubes in a large mixing bowl; add the onion mixture. Drizzle with enough broth or water to moisten, tossing lightly to mix. Use to stuff one 8- to 10-pound turkey. (See tip, page 873, and roasting chart, pages 887-89, for doneness temperatures of turkey and stuffing.) Makes 8 cups (10 to 12 servings).

Nutrition Facts per serving: 210 cal., 11 g total fat (2 g sat. fat), 29 mg chol., 444 mg sodium, 21 g carbo., 1 g fiber, 12 g pro. **Daily Values:** 27% vit. A, 2% vit. C, 4% calcium, 12% iron

■ **Oyster Stuffing:** Prepare as above, except omit the giblets. Add 1 pint *shucked oysters,* drained and chopped, or two 8-ounce cans *whole oysters,* drained and chopped, to the cooked vegetables. Cook and stir 2 minutes more. Stir in seasonings. Reduce broth to $^3/_4$ to 1 cup. If desired, substitute *oyster liquid* for chicken broth or water.

Nutrition Facts per serving: 288 cal., 15 g total fat (3g sat. fat)

■ **Chestnut Stuffing:** Prepare as above, except omit the giblets. With a knife, cut an X in the shells of 1 pound *fresh chestnuts* (3 cups). Roast chestnuts on a baking sheet in a 400° oven for 15 minutes; cool. Peel and coarsely chop. (Or, use one 8-ounce jar whole peeled chestnuts, chopped.) Add chestnuts with seasonings.

Nutrition Facts per serving: 385 cal., 14 g total fat (3 g sat. fat)

BULGUR STUFFING

PREP: 30 MINUTES   BAKE: SEE CHART, PAGES 887–89

$1^1/2$ **cups bulgur**
$1^1/2$ **cups chopped onions (3 medium)**
 1 **cup sliced celery**
 $1/4$ **cup margarine or butter**
$1^1/2$ **cups snipped dried apricots**
 1 **cup raisins**
 $1/2$ **cup chicken broth**
 1 **teaspoon ground cinnamon**
 $1/2$ **teaspoon ground coriander**
 $1/2$ **teaspoon ground cumin**
 $1/8$ **teaspoon ground cloves**
$1^1/2$ **cups chopped walnuts**
 $1/4$ **cup orange liqueur or orange juice**

1. Cook bulgur according to package directions; set aside. In a large skillet cook onions and celery in margarine or butter till tender but not brown. Add apricots, raisins, chicken broth, cinnamon, coriander, cumin, and cloves. Bring to boiling; reduce heat. Cover and simmer for 10 minutes, stirring the mixture occasionally.
2. Transfer to a large mixing bowl. Add cooked bulgur, walnuts, and orange liqueur or orange juice. Toss lightly to combine.
3. Use to stuff one 10- to 12-pound turkey.* (See tip, page 873, and roasting chart, pages 887–89, for doneness temperatures of turkey and stuffing.) Place any remaining stuffing in a covered casserole; chill. Bake, covered, alongside the turkey for the last 30 minutes of roasting time or till heated through. Makes 10 cups (12 to 14 servings).

Nutrition Facts per serving: 298 cal., 14 g total fat (2 g sat. fat), 0 mg chol., 100 mg sodium, 41 g carbo., 7 g fiber, 6 g pro. **Daily Values:** 16% vit. A, 6% vit. C, 4% calcium, 14% iron

HARVEST STUFFING

PREP: 20 MINUTES   BAKE: SEE CHART, PAGES 887–89

    1 cup shredded carrots
    1 cup chopped celery
    $^{1}/_{2}$ cup chopped onion (1 medium)
    $^{1}/_{2}$ cup margarine or butter
    $^{1}/_{4}$ teaspoon salt
    $^{1}/_{4}$ teaspoon ground nutmeg
    $^{1}/_{4}$ teaspoon pepper
    8 cups dry bread cubes (see tip, page 873)
    2 cups finely chopped peeled apples
    $^{1}/_{2}$ cup chopped walnuts
    $^{1}/_{4}$ cup toasted wheat germ
    $^{1}/_{2}$ to 1 cup chicken broth

1. In a large skillet cook carrots, celery, and onion in margarine or butter till tender but not brown. Stir in salt, nutmeg, and pepper.
2. In a large mixing bowl combine bread cubes, apples, walnuts, and wheat germ; add carrot mixture. Drizzle with enough broth to moisten, tossing lightly. Use to stuff one 10- to 12-pound turkey.*
(See tip, page 873, and roasting chart, pages 887–89, for doneness temperatures of turkey and stuffing.) Makes about 11 cups (12 to 14 servings).

*Note: If desired, place all of the stuffing in a 3-quart casserole. Cover and bake in a 325° oven for 40 to 45 minutes or till heated through.

Nutrition Facts per serving: 221 cal., 12 g total fat (3 g sat. fat), 0 mg chol., 363 mg sodium, 24 g carbo., 1 g fiber, 5 g pro. **Daily Values:** 33% vit. A, 2% vit. C, 4% calcium, 10% iron

WILD RICE STUFFING

PREP: 15 MINUTES   COOK: 50 MINUTES

No-Fat

If desired, spoon this nutty stuffing into a 1-quart casserole and chill for up to 24 hours. Stir in ¼ cup water and bake in a 375° oven for about 30 minutes or until heated through.

  ¼ cup wild rice
1¼ cups water
  ¼ cup brown rice
1½ teaspoons instant chicken bouillon granules
  ⅛ to ¼ teaspoon ground sage or nutmeg
  2 cups sliced fresh mushrooms
  ½ cup chopped celery
  3 green onions, sliced
  ¼ cup slivered almonds or pine nuts, toasted (see tip, page 234)
      (optional)

1. Rinse wild rice in a strainer under cold water about 1 minute. In a medium saucepan combine wild rice, the 1¼ cups water, brown rice, bouillon granules, and sage or nutmeg. Bring to boiling; reduce heat. Cover and simmer for 20 minutes.

2. Add mushrooms, celery, and green onions. Cook, covered, over medium-low heat for 25 minutes more or till vegetables are just tender, stirring frequently. If desired, stir in almonds or pine nuts. Serve immediately or use to stuff one 2½- to 3-pound broiler-fryer chicken. (See tip, page 873, and roasting chart, pages 887–89, for doneness temperatures of turkey and stuffing.) Makes 2½ cups (6 servings).

Nutrition Facts per serving: 64 cal., 0 g total fat, 0 mg chol., 233 mg sodium, 13 g carbo., 1 g fiber, 2 g pro. **Daily Values:** 1% vit. A, 5% vit. C, 1% calcium, 5% iron

GIBLET GRAVY

PREP: 15 MINUTES   COOK: 1¹/₂ HOURS

Giblets are the edible internal organs of poultry—the liver, heart, and gizzard.

  4 ounces turkey or chicken giblets and neck
  1 stalk celery with leaves, cut up
  ¹/₂ small onion, cut up
    Pan drippings from roast turkey or chicken
  ¹/₄ cup all-purpose flour
  ¹/₄ teaspoon salt
  ¹/₈ teaspoon pepper
  1 Hard-Cooked Egg, chopped (optional) (see recipe, page 466)

1. Rinse giblets and neck. Refrigerate liver till needed. In a medium saucepan combine remaining giblets, neck, celery, onion, and enough *lightly salted water* to cover. Bring to boiling; reduce heat. Cover and simmer about 1 hour or till tender. Add liver; simmer 20 to 30 minutes more for turkey (5 to 10 minutes more for chicken) or till tender. Remove giblets and finely chop. Discard neck bones. Strain broth (see photo, page 979). Discard vegetables. Chill the giblets and broth while the poultry roasts.
2. After transferring roast turkey or chicken to a serving platter, pour pan drippings into a large measuring cup. Skim and reserve fat from drippings (see tip, page 882). Pour ¹/₄ cup of the fat into the saucepan (discard remaining fat).
3. Stir in flour, salt, and pepper. Add the reserved broth to the drippings in the measuring cup to equal 1¹/₂ cups; add all at once to flour mixture in the saucepan.
4. Cook and stir over medium heat till thickened and bubbly. Cook and stir for 1 minute more. Stir in chopped giblets. If desired, stir in chopped egg. Heat through. Makes 2 cups (8 to 10 servings).

Nutrition Facts per serving: 97 cal., 7 g total fat (2 g sat. fat), 44 mg chol., 173 mg sodium, 4 g carbo., 0 g fiber, 4 g pro. **Daily Values**: 16% vit. A, 1% vit. C, 0% calcium, 6% iron

PAN GRAVY

START TO FINISH: 10 MINUTES

Follow these same steps—and use meat drippings and beef broth—to make gravy for roasted meat.

Pan drippings from roast poultry
¹/₄ cup all-purpose flour
Chicken broth or water

1. After transferring roast poultry to a serving platter, pour pan drippings into a large measuring cup. (Also scrape the browned bits into the cup.) Skim and reserve fat from drippings.

2. Pour ¹/₄ cup of the fat into a medium saucepan (discard remaining fat). Stir in flour. Add enough broth or water to remaining drippings in the measuring cup to equal 2 cups; add all

SKIMMING THE FAT

To skim off fat from poultry or meat drippings, tip the container and use a metal spoon to remove the oily liquid (fat) that rises to the top.

at once to flour mixture in saucepan. Cook and stir over medium heat till thickened and bubbly. Cook and stir for 1 minute more. Season to taste with salt and pepper. Makes 2 cups (8 to 10 servings).

Nutrition Facts per serving: 80 cal., 7 g total fat (2 g sat. fat), 6 mg chol., 194 mg sodium, 3 g carbo., 0 g fiber, 2 g pro.

BROILING POULTRY

If desired, remove the skin from the poultry. Rinse and pat dry with paper towels. If desired, sprinkle with salt and pepper.

Remove the broiler pan from the oven and preheat the broiler for 5 to 10 minutes. Arrange the poultry on the unheated rack of the broiler pan with the bone side up. If desired, brush poultry with cooking oil.

Place the pan under the broiler so the surface of the poultry is 4 to 5 inches from the heat; chicken and Cornish game hen halves should be 5 to 6 inches from the heat. Turn the pieces over when browned on 1 side, usually after half of the broiling time. Chicken halves and meaty pieces should be turned after 20 minutes. Brush again with oil. The poultry is done when the meat is no longer pink and the juices run clear. Brush with a sauce the last 5 minutes of cooking, if desired.

Type of Bird	Weight	Broiling Time
Chicken, broiler-fryer, half	1¼ to 1½ pounds	28 to 32 minutes
Chicken breast halves, skinned and boned	4 to 5 ounces	12 to 15 minutes
Chicken breast halves, thighs, and drumsticks	2 to 2½ pounds total	25 to 35 minutes
Chicken kabobs (boneless breast, cut into 2×1/2-inch strips and threaded loosely onto skewers)	1 pound	8 to 10 minutes
Cornish game hen, half	10 to 12 ounces	30 to 40 minutes

Broiling Poultry *(continued)*

Type of Bird	Weight	Broiling Time
Turkey breast steak or slice	2 ounces	6 to 8 minutes
Turkey breast tenderloin steak	4 to 6 ounces	8 to 10 minutes
Turkey patties (ground raw turkey)	3/4 inch thick	10 to 12 minutes

DEFROSTING POULTRY IN THE MICROWAVE

Place a whole bird, unwrapped and breast side down, in a microwave-safe baking dish. Remove the metal clamp, if present, and the giblets packet as soon as possible. Place unwrapped poultry pieces in a microwave-safe baking dish.

Defrost on 30% power (medium-low) for the time specified. After half of the defrosting time, turn a whole bird breast side up. Or, separate, rearrange, and turn pieces over, putting icy parts near the dish edges. If some areas thaw faster, shield them with small pieces of foil (check your owner's manual to see if foil is allowed in your oven). If the poultry starts to cook on the edges, immediately remove it from the oven and place it in cold water for the specified standing time.

If giblets are loosened but difficult to remove during standing time, run cool water into cavity. Poultry must be completely thawed before cooking. It should feel soft and moist but still cold. Cook poultry immediately after defrosting because some areas may have started to cook.

Type of Bird	Amount	Defrosting Time	Standing Time
Chicken, broiler-fryer, cut up	One 2½- to 3-pound bird	13 to 17 minutes	10 minutes
Chicken, broiler-fryer, whole	One 2½- to 3-pound bird	18 to 25 minutes	30 minutes
Chicken, roasting, whole	One 3½- to 4-pound bird	23 to 30 minutes	30 minutes

Defrosting Poultry in the Microwave (continued)

Type of Bird	Amount	Defrosting Time	Standing Time
Chicken breast, whole	One 12-ounce breast	5 to 7 minutes	15 minutes
	Two 12-ounce breasts	11 to 14 minutes	15 minutes
Chicken drumsticks	2 drumsticks	4 to 7 minutes	5 minutes
	6 drumsticks	8 to 12 minutes	5 minutes
Chicken pieces (about 3/4 inch thick)	1 pound	7 to 12 minutes	
Cornish game hen, whole	One 1 1/4- to 1 1/2-pound bird	8 to 10 minutes	30 minutes
	Two 1 1/4- to 1 1/2-pound birds	12 to 15 minutes	30 minutes
Turkey, ground, raw	1 pound	8 to 12 minutes	5 minutes
Turkey breast, half	One 3- to 4-pound half	15 to 25 minutes	40 to 45 minutes
Turkey breast tenderloin steaks	Four 4-ounce steaks	6 to 10 minutes	
Turkey drumstick	One 1-pound drumstick	8 to 11 minutes	

ROASTING POULTRY

Since birds vary in size, shape, and tenderness, use the times as general guides.

1. Rinse a whole bird thoroughly on outside as well as inside the body and neck cavities. Pat dry. If desired, rub inside of the body cavity with salt.

2. For an *unstuffed bird*, if desired, place quartered onions and celery in body cavity. Pull neck skin to back and fasten with a skewer. If a band of skin crosses tail, tuck drumsticks under band. If there is no band, tie drumsticks to tail. Twist wing tips under the back. For a *stuffed bird* (see tip, page 873), just before cooking, spoon some stuffing loosely into the neck cavity; fasten neck skin as for an unstuffed bird. Lightly spoon stuffing into body cavity. Secure drumsticks and wings.

3. Place bird, breast side up, on a rack in a shallow roasting pan; brush with cooking oil and, if desired, sprinkle with a crushed dried herb such as thyme or oregano. (When cooking a domestic duckling or goose, prick skin well all over and omit cooking oil.) For large birds, insert a meat thermometer into center of one of the inside thigh muscles. The bulb should not touch the bone.

4. Cover Cornish game hen, quail, squab, and turkey with foil, leaving air space between bird and foil. Press foil lightly at ends of drumsticks and neck. Leave all other types of poultry uncovered.

5. Roast in an uncovered pan. Baste occasionally with pan drippings. When bird is two-thirds done, cut band of skin or string between drumsticks. Uncover bird for last 45 minutes of cooking (leave quail covered for entire cooking time). Continue roasting till the meat thermometer registers 180° to 185° (check temperature of thigh in several places), or till drumsticks move easily in their sockets and juices run clear. Center of stuffing should register at least

165°. (In a whole or half turkey breast, thermometer should register 170°.) Remove bird from the oven and cover it with foil. Let large birds stand for 15 to 20 minutes before carving.

Type of Bird	Weight	Oven Temperature	Roasting Time
Capon	5 to 7 pounds	325°	1³/₄ to 2¹/₂ hours
Chicken, whole	2¹/₂ to 3 pounds	375°	1 to 1¹/₄ hours
	3¹/₂ to 4 pounds	375°	1¹/₄ to 1³/₄ hours
	4¹/₂ to 5 pounds	375°	1¹/₂ to 2 hours
	5 to 6 pounds	325°	1³/₄ to 2¹/₂ hours
Cornish game hen	1¹/₄ to 1¹/₂ pounds	375°	1 to 1¹/₄ hours
Duckling, domestic	3 to 5 pounds	375°	1³/₄ to 2¹/₄ hours
Goose, domestic	7 to 8 pounds	350°	2 to 2¹/₂ hours
	8 to 10 pounds	350°	2¹/₂ to 3 hours
	10 to 12 pound	350°	3 to 3¹/₂ hours
Pheasant	2 to 3 pounds	350°	1¹/₂ to 1³/₄ hours
Quail	4 to 6 ounces	375°	30 to 50 minutes
Squab	12 to 14 ounces	375°	45 to 60 minutes
Turkey, boneless whole	2¹/₂ to 3¹/₂ pounds	325°	2 to 2¹/₂ hours
	4 to 6 pounds	325°	2¹/₂ to 3¹/₂ hours

Turkey, unstuffed*	8 to 12 pounds	325°	2³/₄ to 3 hours
	12 to 14 pounds	325°	3 to 3³/₄ hours
	14 to 18 pounds	325°	3³/₄ to 4¹/₄ hours
	18 to 20 pounds	325°	4¹/₄ to 4¹/₂ hours
	20 to 24 pounds	325°	4¹/₂ to 5 hours
Turkey breast, whole	4 to 6 pounds	325°	1¹/₂ to 2¹/₄ hours
	6 to 8 pounds	325°	2¹/₄ to 3¹/₄ hours
Turkey drumstick	1 to 1¹/₂ pounds	325°	1¹/₄ to 1³/₄ hours
Turkey thigh	1¹/₂ to 1³/₄ pounds	325°	1¹/₂ to 1³/₄ hours

*Stuffed birds generally require 15 to 45 minutes more roasting time than unstuffed birds. Always verify doneness temperatures of poultry and stuffing with a meat thermometer or an instant-read thermometer.

Microwaving Poultry

To microwave a *whole bird*, rinse thoroughly and pat the bird dry. Tie the legs to the tail and twist the wing tips under the back (see photo 4, page 867). Place the bird, breast side down, on a rack in a microwave-safe baking dish. Brush with melted margarine or butter. Cover with waxed paper. Microwave on the power specified and for the time given or till done. After half of the cooking time, turn the breast side up and brush again with melted margarine or butter. (If desired, insert a temperature probe into the thigh, but don't let it touch the bone.)

The bird is done when the drumsticks move easily in their sockets, the temperature is 185° in several spots, no pink remains, and the juices run clear. If the wing and leg tips or other areas are done before the rest, shield these areas with small pieces of foil (check your owner's manual to see if foil is allowed in your oven). Let cooked birds weighing more than 2 pounds stand, covered with foil, for 15 minutes.

To microwave *poultry parts*, rinse thoroughly and pat dry. Arrange pieces in a microwave-safe baking dish with meaty portions toward edges of dish, tucking under thin boneless portions. If pieces are crowded in the dish, omit the neck, back, and wings. Cover with waxed paper. (Or, for skinless poultry, cover with a lid or vented plastic wrap.) Microwave on the power level specified and for the time given or till done, rearranging, stirring, and turning pieces over after half of the cooking time.

Type of Bird	Amount	Power Level	Cooking Time
Chicken, broiler-fryer, cut up	One 2½- to 3-pound bird	100% (high)	9 to 17 minutes
Chicken, broiler-fryer, whole	One 2½- to 3-pound bird	50% (medium)	30 to 37 minutes
Chicken breasts, halved	Two 12-ounce breasts	100% (high)	8 to 10 minutes
	Two 16-ounce breasts	100% (high)	8 to 11 minutes
Chicken breast, whole	One 12-ounce breast	100% (high)	5 to 7 minutes
	Two 12-ounce breasts	100% (high)	13 to 15 minutes
Chicken drumsticks	2 drumsticks	100% (high)	2½ to 5 minutes
	6 drumsticks	100% (high)	6 to 10 minutes
Chicken pieces	1 pound	100% (high)	2½ to 5 minutes
Cornish game hen, whole	One 1¼- to 1½-pound bird	100% (high)	7 to 10 minutes
	Two 1½- to 1½-pound birds	100% (high)	13 to 18 minutes
Turkey, ground, raw	1 pound	100% (high)	4 to 7 minutes
Turkey breast, half	One 3- to 4-pound half	50% (medium)	40 to 55 minutes
Turkey breast tenderloin steaks	Four 4-ounce steaks	100% (high)	5 to 8 minutes
Turkey drumstick	One 1-pound drumstick	100% (high)	7 to 9 minutes

SALADS &
DRESSINGS

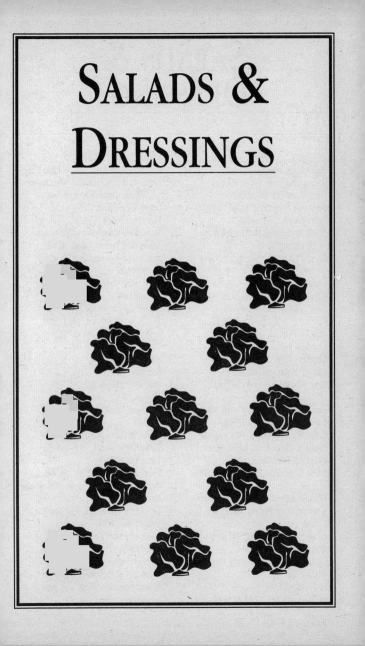

Salads & Dressings

CHICKEN SALAD

PREP: 20 MINUTES   CHILL: 1 HOUR

$1^1/2$ cups finely chopped cooked chicken or turkey (see tip, page 857)
$^1/2$ cup chopped celery (1)
$^1/2$ cup thinly sliced green onions (4)
1 tablespoon lemon juice
2 Hard-Cooked Eggs, chopped (see recipe, page 466)
$^1/3$ cup mayonnaise or salad dressing
2 tablespoons sweet pickle relish or chopped green sweet pepper
2 teaspoons prepared mustard
4 medium tomatoes or lettuce leaves

1. In a mixing bowl combine chicken, celery, green onions, lemon juice, and $^1/8$ teaspoon *pepper*. Stir in eggs, mayonnaise, pickle relish or sweet pepper, and mustard. Cover; chill at least 1 hour.
2. Meanwhile, if using tomatoes, cut a thin slice off stem end of each tomato. Using a spoon, scoop out the centers of tomatoes, leaving $^1/4$ to $^1/2$-inch-thick shells. Reserve pulp for another use. Serve salad in tomato shells or on lettuce leaves. Makes 4 main-dish servings.

Nutrition Facts per serving: 333 cal., 25 g total fat (5 g sat. fat), 157 mg chol., 248 mg sodium, 9 g carbo., 2 g fiber, 20 g pro. **Daily Values:** 16% vit. A., 47% vit. C, 2% calcium, 12% iron

■ **Ham Salad:** Prepare as above, except substitute finely chopped *cooked ham* for the chicken.

Nutrition Facts per serving: 286 cal., 22 g total fat (4 g sat. fat)

■ **Salmon Salad:** Prepare as above, except substitute one $7^3/4$-ounce can *salmon*, drained, flaked, and skin and bones removed, for the chicken. Omit pickle relish and mustard; add $^1/2$ teaspoon *dried dillweed* with the eggs.

Nutrition Facts per serving: 278 cal., 22 g total fat (4 g sat. fat)

■ **Tuna Salad:** Prepare as above, except substitute one $6^1/2$-ounce can *tuna*, drained and broken into chunks, for the chicken. Omit mustard.

Nutrition Facts per serving: 260 cal., 19 g total fat (4 g sat.fat)

CHEF'S SALAD

START TO FINISH: 30 MINUTES

Fast

Personalize this salad by choosing a different green, meat, cheese, vegetable, and dressing every time you make it.

3 cups torn iceberg or leaf lettuce
3 cups torn romaine or spinach
4 ounces cooked ham, chicken, turkey, beef, pork, or lamb, cut into bite-size strips
1 cup cubed Swiss, cheddar, American, provolone, or Gruyère cheese or crumbled blue cheese (4 ounces)
2 Hard-Cooked Eggs, sliced (see recipe, page 466)
2 medium tomatoes, cut into wedges, or 8 cherry tomatoes, halved
1 small green or red sweet pepper, cut into rings
1/3 cup thinly sliced green onions (3)
1 cup Bagel Croutons (see tip, page 917) or purchased croutons (optional)
3/4 cup Creamy French Dressing (see page 942), Buttermilk Dressing (see page 943), Creamy Italian Dressing (see page 944), Oil-Free Herb Dressing (see page 946), or other salad dressing

1. In a large salad bowl toss together lettuce and romaine or spinach. Arrange meat, cheese, eggs, tomatoes, sweet pepper rings, and green onions atop the greens. If desired, sprinkle with Bagel Croutons. Pour Creamy French Dressing or other salad dressing over all, tossing to coat. Makes 4 main-dish servings.

■ **Individual Chef's Salads:** Toss together lettuce and romaine or spinach; divide among four individual salad bowls. Top each serving with *one-fourth* of the meat, cheese, eggs, tomatoes, sweet pepper rings, and green onions. If desired, sprinkle each serving with 1/4 cup of the Bagel Croutons. Pass the Creamy French Dressing or other salad dressing.

Nutrition Facts per serving: 432 cal., 35 g total fat (10 g sat. fat), 147 mg chol., 532 mg sodium, 13 g carbo., 2 g fiber, 19 g pro. **Daily Values:** 34% vit. A, 94% vit. C, 26% calcium, 14% iron

GUIDE TO GREENS

Type/Description	Weight as Purchased	Amount After Preparation	Preparation and Storage*
Arugula	1 ounce	1½ cups torn	Rinse thoroughly in cold water to remove all sand; pat dry. Refrigerate in plastic bag for up to 2 days.
Bok Choy	1¼ pounds (1 head)	7 cups sliced stems and shredded leaves	Trim base; pull stalks apart. Rinse in cold water; pat dry. Refrigerate in plastic bag and use within a few days.
Cabbage	2 pounds (1 head)	12 cups shredded; 10 cups coarsely chopped	Rinse in cold water; pat dry. Refrigerate in plastic bag for up to a week.
Collard Greens	8 ounces	4 cups torn	Wash in cold water; pat dry. Refrigerate in plastic bag for up to 5 days.

Endive, Belgian		4 ounces (1 head)	20 leaves	Cut off bottom core. Rinse in cold water; pat dry. Refrigerate in plastic bag for up to 3 days.
Endive, Curly		12 ounces (1 head)	10 cups torn	Rinse in cold water; pat dry. Refrigerate in plastic bag for up to 3 days.
Escarole		8 ounces (1 head)	7 cups torn	Rinse in cold water; pat dry before using. Refrigerate, tightly wrapped, for up to 3 days.
Kale		8 ounces	7 cups torn	Wash in cold water; pat dry. Refrigerate in plastic bag for up to 3 days; longer storage increases the bitterness.
Lettuce, Butterhead (Bibb or Boston)		12 ounces (1 head)	4 cups torn	Cut off bottom core. Rinse in cold water; pat dry. Refrigerate in plastic bag for up to 5 days.

Guide to Greens (continued)

Type/Description		Weight as Purchased	Amount After Preparation	Preparation and Storage*
Lettuce, Iceberg		1¼ pounds (1 head)	10 cups torn 12 cups shredded	Remove core. Rinse (core side up) under cold running water; invert to drain. Refrigerate in plastic bag for up to 5 days.
Lettuce, Leaf		12 ounces (1 head)	8 cups torn	Cut off bottom core. Rinse in cold water; pat dry. Refrigerate in plastic bag for up to 5 days.
Mustard Greens		8 ounces	12 cups torn	Rinse in cold water; pat dry. Refrigerate in plastic bag for up to 3 days.
Radicchio		8 ounces (1 head)	5½ cups torn	Rinse in cold water; pat dry. Refrigerate in plastic bag for up to 1 week.

Romaine		1 pound (1 head)	6 cups torn	Cut off bottom core. Rinse leaves in cold water; pat dry. Refrigerate in plastic bag for up to 5 days.
Sorrel		1 ounce	1 cup torn	Rinse in cold water; pat dry. Refrigerate in plastic bag for up to 3 days.
Spinach		1 pound	12 cups torn, stems removed	Rinse thoroughly in cold water to remove all sand; pat dry. Refrigerate in plastic bag for up to 3 days.
Swiss Chard		1 pound	12 cups	Rinse in cold water; pat dry. Refrigerate in plastic bag for up to 3 days.
Watercress		4 ounces	2⅓ cups, stems removed	Rinse in cold water. Wrap in damp paper towels; refrigerate in plastic bag for 1 or 2 days.

*Note: Always choose the freshest-looking greens. To store, line a plastic bag or airtight container with a paper towel. Discard leaves that are bruised, discolored, or wilted.

TACO SALAD

PREP: 30 MINUTES   BAKE: 15 MINUTES   Oven 350°

*Rinse ground beef to remove even more fat than just draining the
meat. To do so, place drained, cooked ground beef in a strainer set
over a bowl or sink. Pour boiling water over the meat.*

- 1 **recipe Tortilla Cups (see below)**
- 8 **ounces lean ground beef or ground raw turkey**
- 3 **cloves garlic, minced**
- 1 **15-ounce can dark red kidney beans, rinsed and drained (see
    tip, page 107)**
- 1 **8-ounce jar taco sauce**
- $^3/_4$ **cup frozen whole kernel corn (optional)**
- 1 **tablespoon chili powder**
- 6 **cups shredded leaf or iceberg lettuce**
- 2 **medium tomatoes, chopped**
- 1 **large green sweet pepper, chopped**
- $^1/_2$ **cup thinly sliced green onions (4)**
- 1 **medium avocado, pitted, peeled, and sliced (optional)**
- $^3/_4$ **cup shredded sharp cheddar cheese (3 ounces)**
  Dairy sour cream (optional)
  Taco sauce or salsa (optional)

1. Prepare Tortilla Cups; set aside. In a medium skillet cook ground
beef or turkey and garlic till juices run clear. Drain off fat. Stir in kidney beans, taco sauce, corn (if desired), and chili powder. Bring to
boiling; reduce heat. Cover and simmer for 10 minutes.

2. Meanwhile, in a large bowl combine lettuce, tomatoes, sweet
pepper, and green onions. To serve, divide lettuce mixture among
the Tortilla Cups. (Or, if desired, omit Tortilla Cups and serve on individual salad plates.) Top each serving with some of the meat mixture and, if desired, avocado. Sprinkle with cheese. If desired, serve
with sour cream and additional taco sauce or salsa. Makes 6 main-
dish servings.

■ **Tortilla Cups:** Lightly brush six 9- or 10-inch *flour tortillas* with a
small amount of *water* or spray *nonstick spray coating* onto 1 side of
each tortilla. Spray nonstick coating into six small oven-safe bowls or
six 16-ounce individual casseroles. Press tortillas, coated sides up,
into bowls or casseroles. Place a ball of foil in each tortilla cup. Bake
in a 350° oven for 15 to 20 minutes or till light brown. Remove the

foil; cool. Remove Tortilla Cups from the bowls. Serve cups immediately or store in an airtight container for up to 5 days.

Nutrition Facts per serving: 366 cal., 14 g total fat (5 g sat. fat), 39 mg chol., 738 mg sodium, 47 g carbo., 6 g fiber, 21 g pro. **Daily Values:** 18% vit. A, 101% vit. C, 17% calcium, 30% iron

---

ITALIAN-STYLE PASTA TOSS

PREP: 25 MINUTES CHILL: 4 TO 24 HOURS

To cut preparation time, substitute ⅔ cup bottled Italian dressing for the homemade dressing.

    6 **ounces rotini or medium macaroni shells (2¼ cups)**
    1 **cup cubed mozzarella or provolone cheese (4 ounces)**
    4 **ounces sliced salami, cut into strips**
    1 **cup thinly sliced cauliflower flowerets and/or thinly sliced zucchini**
    ½ **cup chopped green or red sweet pepper (1 small)**
    1 **small onion, thinly sliced and separated into rings**
    ⅓ **cup sliced pitted ripe olives**
    ¼ **cup snipped fresh parsley**
    ⅓ **cup olive oil or salad oil**
    ⅓ **cup wine vinegar**
    2 **cloves garlic, minced**
    2 **teaspoons dried basil, crushed**
    1 **teaspoon dried oregano, crushed**
    ½ **teaspoon sugar**
    ½ **teaspoon pepper**
    2 **small tomatoes, cut into wedges**
    2 **tablespoons finely shredded Parmesan cheese**

1. Cook pasta according to package directions. Drain pasta. Rinse with cold water; drain again. In a bowl toss together cooked pasta, cubed cheese, salami, cauliflower and/or zucchini, green or red sweet pepper, onion rings, olives, and parsley.

2. For dressing, in a screw-top jar combine oil, vinegar, garlic, basil, oregano, sugar, and pepper. Cover and shake well. Pour over salad. Toss to coat. Cover; chill 4 to 24 hours. To serve, add tomatoes; toss gently. Sprinkle with Parmesan cheese. Makes 6 main-dish servings.

Nutrition Facts per serving: 387 cal., 25 g total fat (7 g sat. fat), 31 mg chol., 565 mg sodium, 29 g carbo., 2 g fiber, 14 g pro. **Daily Values:** 9% vit. A, 67% vit. C, 12% calcium, 15% iron

GREEK-STYLE SALADS

START TO FINISH: 35 MINUTES

   3 cups torn curly endive and/or romaine
1½ cups torn iceberg lettuce or spinach
   8 ounces cooked lean lamb, pork, chicken, turkey, or beef, cut
        into bite-size strips (1½ cups)
   1 medium tomato, chopped
  ½ of a small cucumber, thinly sliced
  ½ cup crumbled feta cheese (2 ounces)
   6 radishes, thinly sliced (¼ cup)
  ¼ cup thinly sliced green onions (2)
   2 tablespoons sliced pitted ripe olives
   1 recipe Greek Vinaigrette (see below)
   4 anchovy fillets, drained, rinsed, and patted dry (optional)

1. In large mixing bowl toss together curly endive and/or romaine and lettuce or spinach. Divide greens among 4 salad plates. Arrange *one-fourth* of the meat, tomato, cucumber, feta cheese, radishes, green onions, and olives on each plate of greens. Prepare Greek Vinaigrette and drizzle about 2 tablespoons over each salad. If desired, top each with anchovy fillet. Makes 4 main-dish servings.

■ **Greek Vinaigrette:** In a screw-top jar combine 3 tablespoons *olive oil or salad oil;* 3 tablespoons *lemon juice;* 1 tablespoon *anchovy paste;* 1 tablespoon snipped *fresh oregano or* 1 teaspoon *dried oregano,* crushed; 2 large *cloves garlic,* minced; and ⅛ teaspoon *pepper.* Cover and shake well. Makes about ½ cup.

Nutrition Facts per serving: 329 cal., 24 g total fat (8 g sat. fat), 83 mg chol., 543 mg sodium, 8 g carbo., 2 g fiber, 23 g pro. **Daily Values:** 16% vit. A, 32% vit. C, 17% calcium, 16% iron

24-HOUR CHICKEN FIESTA SALAD

PREP: 30 MINUTES   CHILL: 4 TO 24 HOURS

*Chilling the salad for up to 24 hours allows the flavors to blend.
Layer the ingredients one evening and have a
ready-to-serve meal the next.*

4 cups torn iceberg, Boston, or Bibb lettuce
$^1/_2$ cup shredded Monterey Jack cheese with jalapeño peppers (2
    ounces)
1 8-ounce can red kidney beans, rinsed and drained, or $^1/_2$ of a
    15-ounce can garbanzo beans, rinsed and drained (1 cup)
    (see tip, page 107)
1$^1/_2$ cups chopped cooked chicken or turkey (about 8 ounces) (see
    tip, page 857)
2 small tomatoes, cut into thin wedges
$^1/_2$ of a small jicama (about 4 ounces), cut into bite-size strips (1
    cup)
$^1/_2$ cup sliced pitted ripe olives (optional)
1 recipe Avocado Dressing (see below)
$^3/_4$ cup slightly crushed tortilla chips

1. Place the lettuce in a large salad bowl. Layer ingredients in the
following order atop lettuce: cheese, beans, chicken or turkey, tomatoes, jicama, and, if desired, olives. Spread Avocado Dressing evenly
over the top of the salad, sealing to the edge of the bowl. Cover
salad tightly with plastic wrap. Chill for 4 to 24 hours. To serve, toss
lightly to mix; sprinkle with the crushed tortilla chips. Makes 4 main-
dish servings.

■ **Avocado Dressing:** In a blender container or food processor
bowl combine 1 small *avocado,* pitted, peeled, and cut up; $^1/_4$ cup
mayonnaise or salad dressing; 2 tablespoons chopped canned *green
chili peppers;* 2 tablespoons *lemon juice;* 1 tablespoon *honey;* $^1/_2$ teaspoon *chili powder;* $^1/_4$ teaspoon *salt;* and 1 clove *garlic,* minced.
Cover and blend or process till smooth. Makes about $^3/_4$ cup.

Nutrition Facts per serving: 480 cal., 31 g total fat (7 g sat. fat), 71 mg chol., 511 mg
sodium, 30 g carbo., 6 g fiber, 27 g pro. **Daily Values:** 15% vit. A., 46% vit. C, 14%
calcium, 20% iron

SALAD NIÇOISE

PREP: 45 MINUTES   CHILL: 2 TO 24 HOURS

*You can cook and chill the beans and potatoes for this
French salad a day before serving.*

$^1/_2$ **pound green beans**
$^3/_4$ **pound whole tiny new potatoes, scrubbed and sliced**
$^1/_4$ **cup olive oil or salad oil**
$^1/_4$ **cup white wine vinegar or white vinegar**
  1 **teaspoon sugar**
  1 **teaspoon snipped fresh tarragon or $^1/_4$ teaspoon dried
      tarragon, crushed**
$^1/_8$ **teaspoon dry mustard**
     Dash pepper
     Boston or Bibb lettuce leaves
$1^1/_2$ **cups flaked cooked tuna or salmon ($^1/_2$ pound) or one $9^1/_4$-
      ounce can chunk white tuna (water-pack), drained and
      broken into chunks**
  2 **medium tomatoes, cut into wedges**
  2 **Hard-Cooked Eggs, sliced (see recipe, page 466)**
$^1/_2$ **cup pitted ripe olives (optional)**
$^1/_4$ **cup thinly sliced green onions (2)**
  4 **anchovy fillets, drained, rinsed, and patted dry (optional)**
     Fresh chervil (optional)

1. Wash green beans; remove ends and strings. In a large covered
saucepan or pot cook green beans and potatoes in a small amount
of boiling water for 15 to 20 minutes or just till tender. Drain; place
vegetables in a medium bowl. Cover and chill for 2 to 24 hours.
2. For dressing, in a screw-top jar combine oil, vinegar, sugar, tarragon, dry mustard, and pepper. Cover and shake well. To serve,
line 4 salad plates with lettuce leaves. Arrange chilled vegetables,
tuna or salmon, tomatoes, eggs, and, if desired, olives on the lettuce-
lined plates. Sprinkle each serving with green onions. If desired, top
each salad with an anchovy fillet and garnish with chervil. Shake
dressing well; pour some over each salad. Makes 4 main-dish servings.

Nutrition Facts per serving: 378 cal., 20 g total fat (4 g sat. fat), 134 mg chol., 79 mg
sodium, 28 g carbo., 2 g fiber, 24 g pro. **Daily Values:** 56% vit. A, 49% vit. C, 5% calcium,
22% iron

SEAFOOD LOUIS SALAD

START TO FINISH: 25 MINUTES

Fast   **Low-Fat**

Substituting low-fat cottage cheese for the mayonnaise and whipping cream in the original recipe results in half as many calories and 30 grams less fat per serving in this updated version.

- ¹/₂ cup low-fat cottage cheese
- 2 tablespoons skim milk
- 1 tablespoon tomato paste
- 2 tablespoons chopped red sweet pepper or diced pimiento
- 1 tablespoon thinly sliced green onion
- ¹/₈ teaspoon salt
- ¹/₈ teaspoon pepper
- 6 cups torn romaine
- 1 cup shredded red cabbage
- ¹/₂ cup shredded carrot (1 medium)
- 1 6-ounce can lump crabmeat, drained and cartilage removed, or one 6¹/₃-ounce can crab-flavored fish chunks
- 1 6-ounce package frozen, peeled, cooked shrimp, thawed
- 2 tomatoes, cut into thin wedges
- 3 thin lemon wedges, halved (optional)

1. For dressing, in a blender container or food processor bowl, combine the cottage cheese, the 2 tablespoons skim milk, and tomato paste. Cover and blend or process till smooth. Transfer to a small bowl. Stir in red sweet pepper or pimiento, green onion, salt, pepper, and enough additional skim milk to make dressing of desired consistency. Cover and chill till serving time.

2. In a large bowl toss together romaine, cabbage, and carrot; divide among 3 salad plates. If desired, reserve a small amount of seafood for topping. Arrange one-third of the remaining seafood and tomatoes atop each plate of greens. Top salads with dressing. If desired, top with reserved seafood and garnish with lemon wedges. Makes 3 main-dish servings.

Nutrition Facts per serving: 188 cal., 2 g total fat (1 g sat. fat), 119 mg chol., 987 mg sodium, 13 g carbo., 4 g fiber, 29 g pro. **Daily Values:** 93% vit. A., 123% vit. C, 13% calcium, 26% iron

BEEF AND VEGETABLE SALAD

PREP: 30 MINUTES   CHILL: 30 MINUTES OR 24 HOURS

For ease in preparing this pasta salad, use leftover beef or pork roast.

   1 cup rotini, wagon-wheel macaroni, or shell pasta
   2 cups cut-up broccoli or one 10-ounce package frozen cut
       broccoli
   2 cups cubed or bite-size strips cooked lean beef or pork
   $^{1}/_{2}$ cup shredded carrot (1 medium)
   $^{1}/_{2}$ cup sliced fresh mushrooms
   $^{3}/_{4}$ cup bottled creamy cucumber dressing or $^{3}/_{4}$ cup Oil-Free
       Creamy Onion Dressing (see page 947)
   $^{1}/_{2}$ cup cherry tomato halves

1. Cook pasta according to package directions; drain. Place cooked pasta in a colander and rinse with cold water; drain well. If using frozen broccoli, thaw while pasta cooks by placing in colander and rinsing with cool water till thawed; drain well.
2. In a large bowl combine the cooked pasta, broccoli, beef or pork, carrot, and mushrooms. Add dressing; toss lightly to coat. Cover and chill for 30 to 45 minutes or overnight. To serve, stir in the cherry tomato halves. Makes 4 main-dish servings.

Nutrition Facts per serving: 443 cal., 29 g total fat (5 g sat. fat), 49 mg chol., 635 mg sodium, 25 g carbo., 3 g fiber, 25 g pro. **Daily Values:** 47% vit. A., 80% vit. C, 2% calcium, 19% iron

---

HAM AND PEAR SALAD

START TO FINISH: 25 MINUTES

Fast

Low-Fat

Either yellow Bartlett or green Anjou pears work well in this salad.

   5 cups torn leaf lettuce and/or spinach
   2 medium pears, unpeeled, rinsed, cored, and chopped (2 cups)
   8 ounces lean cooked ham, cut into bite-size strips ($1^{1}/_{2}$ cups)
   $^{1}/_{2}$ cup sliced carrot (1 medium)
   $^{1}/_{4}$ cup thinly sliced green onions (2)
   1 recipe Pineapple-Mint Vinaigrette (see recipe, above right)
       Fresh pineapple mint or mint sprigs (optional)

1. In a large salad bowl combine leaf lettuce and/or spinach, pears, ham, carrot, and green onions. Toss to mix. Pour enough Pineapple-Mint Vinaigrette over salad to moisten. Toss lightly to coat. Pass any remaining dressing or store in refrigerator up to 1 week. If desired, garnish with fresh pineapple mint or mint sprigs. Makes 4 main-dish servings.

■ **Pineapple-Mint Vinaigrette:** In a screw-top jar combine ½ cup *unsweetened pineapple juice,* 2 tablespoons *white wine vinegar,* 2 tablespoons *salad oil,* and 1 tablespoon snipped *fresh mint or* 1 teaspoon *dried mint,* crushed. Cover; shake well.

Nutrition Facts per serving: 229 cal., 11 g total fat (2 g sat. fat), 30 mg chol., 694 mg sodium, 22 g carbo., 4 g fiber, 13 g pro. **Daily Values:** 53% vit. A., 56% vit. C, 6% calcium, 16% iron

---

CHICKEN CABBAGE SALAD

PREP: 20 MINUTES BAKE: 5 MINUTES   Oven 350°

Fast

    1 3-ounce package ramen noodles
  ¼ cup slivered or sliced almonds
    2 tablespoons sesame seed
    3 cups shredded Napa or green cabbage (about ½ of a 1-pound
        head)
    2 cups chopped cooked chicken or turkey (see tip, page 857)
  ¼ cup thinly sliced green onions (2)
  ¼ cup chopped red sweet pepper (optional)
    3 tablespoons salad oil
    2 tablespoons white wine vinegar or rice vinegar
    2 tablespoons soy sauce
    1 teaspoon sugar
  ½ teaspoon toasted sesame oil (optional)

1. Reserve seasoning packet from noodles for another use. Break up the noodles; place in a 15×10×1-inch baking pan along with the almonds and sesame seed. Bake in a 350° oven for 5 to 8 minutes or till golden. Remove from oven.

2. In large salad bowl combine cabbage, cooked chicken or turkey, green onions, and, if desired, red sweet pepper; toss to mix.

3. For dressing, in a screw-top jar combine oil, vinegar, soy sauce, sugar, and, if desired, sesame oil. Cover and shake well. Pour over cabbage mixture. Add toasted noodle mixture; toss to coat. Serve immediately. Makes 4 main-dish servings.

Nutrition Facts per serving: 430 cal., 27 g total fat (4 g sat. fat), 83 mg chol., 531 mg sodium, 21 g carbo., 2 g fiber, 27 g pro. **Daily Values:** 9% vit. A., 27% vit. C, 7% calcium, 19% iron

---

HEALTHY SALAD CHOICES

Salads made with vegetables, fruits, and/or whole grains are an important part of a healthy eating plan. They provide necessary vitamins, minerals, and dietary fiber. Many salads (but not all) also are low in calories, fat, and sodium.

Boost the nutritional impact of a simple bowl of lettuce by adding healthful extras. For example, add colorful sliced carrots, broccoli flowerets, or strips of bright red sweet peppers. The type of salad dressing you choose is especially important. Many fat-free and light choices can be purchased or made at home (see recipes, pages 946–47).

Healthful eating means you should be aware of the total amount of fat consumed over several days. It does not mean focusing on fat in a single food. Learn to balance high-fat favorites with lower-fat choices for a more reasonable approach to eating. Try these fat-reducing ideas.

■ Use avocados, olives, nuts, sausage, cheeses, and other high-fat ingredients less often or in smaller amounts.

■ Combine a favorite high-fat, side-dish salad with a lean main dish, such as broiled fish or chicken.

■ Make a main-dish salad with lean meats, poultry, fish, and reduced-fat cheeses. Serve with bread sticks or baguettes instead of crackers or croissants.

■ If a recipe calls for mayonnaise or salad dressing or dairy sour cream, try a reduced-fat or nonfat variety instead.

LAYERED TUNA AND PASTA SALAD

PREP: 45 MINUTES   CHILL: 4 TO 24 HOURS

Use reduced-fat mayonnaise or salad dressing plus low-fat yogurt and cheese to cut calories and fat in the dressing.

- 1⅓ cups cavatelli or medium shell macaroni
- 4 cups shredded iceberg lettuce
- 1 cup chopped, seeded cucumber
- 1 cup chopped, seeded tomato
- 1 9¼-ounce can chunk white tuna (water-pack), drained and broken into chunks, or 8 ounces flaked cooked tuna
- 1 cup frozen peas
- 1 2¼-ounce can sliced ripe olives, drained
- 2 Hard-Cooked Eggs, sliced (see recipe, page 466)
- 2 tablespoons sliced green onion (1)
- 1 recipe Herb Dressing (see below)
- ½ cup shredded cheddar or American cheese (2 ounces)

1. Cook pasta according to package directions; drain. Rinse with cold water; drain again.

2. Place shredded lettuce in a 3-quart salad bowl. Layer atop lettuce in the following order: cooked pasta, cucumber, tomato, tuna, peas, olives, egg slices, and green onion.

3. Carefully spread Herb Dressing evenly over top of salad, sealing to the edge of the bowl. Sprinkle with cheese. Cover tightly with plastic wrap. Chill for 4 to 24 hours. To serve, toss lightly. Makes 6 main-dish servings.

■ **Herb Dressing:** In a small bowl combine ½ cup *mayonnaise or salad dressing*, ⅓ cup *plain yogurt*, ¼ cup snipped *fresh parsley*, 1 tablespoon snipped *fresh chives*, 1 tablespoon *lemon juice*, 1 tablespoon *Dijon-style mustard*, and ⅛ teaspoon *pepper*. Makes about 1 cup.

Nutrition Facts per serving: 384 cal., 23 g total fat (5 g sat. fat), 105 mg chol., 499 mg sodium, 24 g carbo., 2 g fiber, 21 g pro. **Daily Values:** 16% vit. A, 28% vit. C, 11% calcium, 19% iron

CRAB-STUFFED PAPAYAS

START TO FINISH: 30 MINUTES

Fast **Low-Fat**

A medium cantaloupe may be substituted for the papayas. Halve and seed the melon, and chop ½ cup of it to stir into the crab mixture. Thinly slice the remaining cantaloupe, arranging slices on serving plates. Top with the crab mixture.

- 2 **large ripe papayas**
  Lemon juice
- 2 **cups red raspberries or one 10-ounce package frozen red raspberries, thawed**
- ⅓ **cup vanilla yogurt**
- 2 **tablespoons milk**
- 1 **12-ounce package frozen crabmeat, thawed, or two 8-ounce packages crab-flavored, salad-style fish, thawed**
  Shredded Boston or Bibb lettuce
- ¼ **cup sliced almonds or chopped pecans, toasted (see tip, page 234)**

1. Halve papayas lengthwise. Scoop out seeds; scoop out pulp, leaving a ½-inch-thick shell. Peel papaya. Brush shells with lemon juice. Chop enough pulp to measure ½ cup; set aside. If using frozen raspberries, drain off juice.

2. For dressing, in a medium mixing bowl stir milk into yogurt till of desired consistency. Stir chopped papaya, raspberries, and crabmeat into dressing.

3. Arrange shredded lettuce on 4 salad plates. Spoon crab mixture into papaya shells. Place papaya shells atop lettuce. Sprinkle each serving with nuts. Makes 4 main-dish servings.

Nutrition Facts per serving: 209 cal., 6 g total fat (1 g sat. fat), 86 mg chol., 252 mg sodium, 20 g carbo., 4 g fiber, 21 g pro.
Daily Values: 20% vit. A., 122% vit. C, 14% calcium, 10% iron

CHILLED SALAD

Most salads taste best when served refreshingly cold. Here are a few cool tips:

- ■ Chill all of the ingredients thoroughly before you make the salad.
- ■ Prepare the salad but do not add the dressing. Cover and chill for at least 1 hour.
- ■ For a quick cooldown, cover the salad and place it in the freezer for 20 minutes.

LENTIL-RICE SALAD

PREP: 30 MINUTES   CHILL: 2 TO 24 HOURS

This refreshing lemon-kissed salad can be served as a main dish when summertime begs for lighter meals.

$^1/_2$ **cup dry lentils**
2 **cups water**
$^1/_2$ **cup long grain rice**
$^1/_2$ **cup chopped red or green sweet pepper**
$^1/_3$ **cup shredded carrot**
$^1/_4$ **cup thinly sliced green onions (2)**
3 **tablespoons olive oil**
$^1/_2$ **teaspoon finely shredded lemon peel**
3 **tablespoons lemon juice**
$1^1/_2$ **teaspoons snipped fresh basil or $^1/_2$ teaspoon dried basil, crushed**
$^1/_4$ **teaspoon salt**
Lettuce leaves (optional)
1 **medium tomato, cut into 8 wedges**
4 **ounces cheddar cheese, sliced**

1. Rinse and drain lentils. Transfer to medium saucepan; add water. Bring to boiling; reduce heat. Simmer, covered, for 5 minutes. Add uncooked rice. Cover and simmer 15 minutes more. Remove from heat. Let stand, covered, for 10 minutes; drain. Rinse with cold water; drain again.

2. In a large mixing bowl combine lentil mixture, red or green sweet pepper, carrot, and green onions. Set aside.

3. For dressing, in a screw-top jar combine oil, lemon peel, lemon juice, basil, and salt. Cover and shake well. Pour over lentil mixture; toss to coat. Cover and chill for 2 to 24 hours.

4. To serve, if desired, line 4 salad plates with lettuce leaves. Spoon lentil mixture onto lettuce leaves; arrange tomato wedges and cheese slices on each plate. Makes 4 main-dish servings.

Nutrition Facts per serving: 385 cal., 20 g total fat (7 g sat. fat), 30 mg chol., 193 mg sodium, 38 g carbo., 3 g fiber, 14 g pro. **Daily Values:** 50% vit. A, 54% vit. C, 20% calcium, 23% iron

WILTED SPINACH SALAD

START TO FINISH: 25 MINUTES

Fast   **Low-Fat**

6 cups torn spinach or romaine
1 cup sliced fresh mushrooms
1/4 cup thinly sliced green onions (2)
   Dash pepper (optional)
3 slices bacon
3 tablespoons vinegar
1 teaspoon sugar
1/4 teaspoon dry mustard
1 cup sliced strawberries and/or drained mandarin orange
   sections
1 Hard-Cooked Egg, chopped (see recipe, page 466)

1. In a large bowl combine spinach, mushrooms, and green onions.
If desired, sprinkle with pepper; set aside.
2. For dressing, in a 12-inch skillet cook bacon till crisp. Remove bacon, reserving 2 tablespoons drippings in skillet. (Or, if desired, substitute 2 tablespoons *salad oil* for bacon drippings.) Crumble bacon;
set aside. Stir vinegar, sugar, and dry mustard into drippings. Bring
to boiling; remove from heat. Add the spinach mixture. Toss mixture
in skillet for 30 to 60 seconds or till spinach is just wilted.
3. Transfer mixture to a serving dish. Add the strawberries and/or
orange sections. Top salad with chopped egg and crumbled bacon.
Serve salad immediately. Makes 4 side-dish servings.

Nutrition Facts per serving: 86 cal., 4 g total fat (1 g sat. fat), 57 mg chol., 159 mg
sodium, 8 g carbo., 3 g fiber, 6 g pro. **Daily Values:** 59% vit. A, 80% vit. C, 8% calcium,
19% iron

SPINACH TOSS

PREP: 20 MINUTES   CHILL: 2 HOURS

Low-Fat

For a change, try this same salad with ¹/₃ cup Honey-Lime Dressing
(see page 949).

  1 **recipe Oil-Free Orange-Poppy Seed Dressing (see page 948)**
  5 **cups torn spinach**
³/₄ **cup sliced strawberries**
¹/₂ **cup sliced fresh mushrooms**

1. Prepare dressing. Cover; refrigerate for 2 hours. Meanwhile, prepare remaining ingredients.
2. To serve, place spinach in a large salad bowl. Add the strawberries, mushrooms, and dressing. Toss lightly to coat. Makes 4 side-dish servings.

Nutrition Facts per serving: 63 cal., 1 g total fat (0 g sat. fat), 0 mg chol., 62 mg sodium, 14 g carbo., 3 g fiber, 3 g pro. **Daily Values:** 47% vit. A., 81% vit. C, 6% calcium, 15% iron

24-HOUR VEGETABLE SALAD

PREP: 30 MINUTES   CHILL: 2 TO 24 HOURS

You don't have to allow this salad to chill 24 hours. But it's perfect
when you need a dish that can be made ahead.

  4 **cups torn iceberg lettuce, romaine, leaf lettuce, Bibb lettuce,**
    and/or spinach
  1 **cup sliced fresh mushrooms, broccoli flowerets, or frozen peas**
  1 **cup shredded carrots (2 medium)**
  2 **Hard-Cooked Eggs, sliced (see recipe, page 466)**
  6 **slices bacon, crisp-cooked, drained, and crumbled (¹/₄ pound)**
³/₄ **cup shredded Swiss, American, or cheddar cheese (3 ounces)**
¹/₄ **cup thinly sliced green onions (2)**
³/₄ **cup mayonnaise or salad dressing**
1¹/₂ **teaspoons lemon juice**
¹/₂ **teaspoon dried dillweed (optional)**

1. Place lettuce in a 3-quart salad bowl. If desired, sprinkle with salt and pepper. Layer atop lettuce in the following order: mushrooms, broccoli, or peas; carrots; eggs; bacon; ½ cup of the cheese; and green onions.

2. For dressing, in small bowl combine the mayonnaise or salad dressing, lemon juice, and, if desired, dillweed. Spread dressing over top of salad, sealing to edge of bowl. Sprinkle with the remaining ¼ cup cheese. Cover and chill for 2 to 24 hours. Before serving, toss to coat vegetables. Makes 6 to 8 side-dish servings.

Nutrition Facts per serving: 330 cal., 31 g total fat (7 g sat. fat), 105 mg chol., 326 mg sodium, 5 g carbo., 1 g fiber, 9 g pro. **Daily Values:** 62% vit. A, 11% vit. C, 13% calcium, 6% iron

---

CAESAR SALAD

PREP: 25 MINUTES   CHILL: 2 TO 24 HOURS   BAKE: 15 MINUTES   Oven 300°

Traditional Caesar Salad contains raw eggs, which are unsafe to eat. Our cooked-egg version puts this classic back on the menu.

1 egg
⅓ cup chicken broth
3 anchovy fillets
3 tablespoons olive oil
2 tablespoons lemon juice
    Few dashes white wine
    Worcestershire sauce
1 clove garlic, halved
10 cups torn romaine (see tip, right)
½ cup Parmesan Croutons (see right) or purchased garlic croutons
¼ cup grated Parmesan cheese
    Freshly ground black pepper

DE-RIBBING ROMAINE

Before tearing the romaine, cut the fibrous rib from the larger leaves. Place the leaf on a cutting board and slice along both sides of the rib with a small, sharp knife.

1. For dressing, in a blender container or food processor bowl, combine egg, broth, anchovy fillets, oil, lemon juice, and Worcestershire sauce. Cover and blend or process till smooth. Transfer dressing to a small saucepan. Cook and stir the dressing over low heat for 8 to 10 minutes or till thickened. Do not boil. Transfer to a bowl. Cover surface with plastic wrap; chill for 2 to 24 hours.

2. To serve, rub inside of a wooden salad bowl with cut edges of the garlic clove; discard garlic clove. Add romaine, Parmesan Croutons, and Parmesan cheese to bowl. Pour dressing over salad. Toss lightly to coat. To serve, divide salad among 6 individual salad plates; sprinkle pepper over each salad. Makes 6 side-dish servings.

Nutrition Facts per serving: 147 cal., 12 g total fat (3 g sat. fat), 41 mg chol., 275 mg sodium, 5 g carbo., 2 g fiber, 6 g pro. **Daily Values:** 29% vit. A, 41% vit. C, 9% calcium, 9% iron

---

BAGEL CROUTONS

Croutons make an ordinary salad more exciting by adding crunch and flavor. Toss these dill-flavored croutons onto your next salad for a special treat. Two tablespoons of the croutons will add 50 calories and 3 grams of fat to your salad.

■ Cut 2 *plain, whole wheat, or onion bagels* into ¼-inch-thick wedges. In large skillet melt ¼ cup *margarine or butter*. Stir in ½ teaspoon *dried dillweed* and ⅛ teaspoon *garlic or onion powder*. Add wedges, stirring to coat.

■ Spread wedges in a single layer in a baking pan. Bake in a 300° oven for 10 minutes. Stir; bake about 15 minutes more or till dry and crisp. Let cool. To store, place croutons in an airtight container and refrigerate for up to 1 month. Bring to room temperature before serving. Makes 2 cups.

■ **Parmesan Croutons:** Cut four ½-inch-thick slices *French bread* into ¾-inch cubes; set aside. In a large skillet melt ¼ cup *margarine or butter*. Remove from heat. Stir in 3 tablespoons grated *Parmesan cheese* and ⅛ teaspoon *garlic powder*. Add bread cubes, stirring till cubes are coated with margarine mixture. Spread bread cubes in a single layer in a shallow baking pan. Bake in a 300° oven for 10 minutes; stir. Continue baking about 5 minutes more or till bread cubes are dry and crisp. Cool completely before using. Store, tightly covered, up to 1 week. Makes about 2 cups (sixteen 2-tablespoon servings).

■ **Chicken Caesar Salad:** Prepare as at left, except add 2 cups chopped cooked *chicken* with the romaine. Makes 6 main-dish servings.

Nutrition Facts per serving: 242 cal., 15 g total fat (4 g sat. fat)

MARINATED VEGETABLE SALAD

PREP: 20 MINUTES   CHILL: 4 TO 24 HOURS

Low-Fat

2 cups small cauliflower flowerets
2 cups green beans, bias-sliced into 1-inch pieces, or 2 cups broccoli flowerets
1 cup thinly sliced carrots (2 medium)
1 cup coarsely chopped green sweet pepper (1 medium)
1 medium onion, sliced and separated into rings
1 small zucchini, thinly sliced (1 cup)
$^1/_4$ cup halved pitted ripe olives (optional)
$^1/_2$ cup white wine vinegar
$^1/_4$ cup salad oil
1 tablespoon sugar
1 tablespoon snipped fresh oregano or 1 teaspoon dried oregano, crushed
$^1/_4$ teaspoon salt
$^1/_4$ teaspoon pepper

1. In a large saucepan cook cauliflower, beans or broccoli, carrots, sweet pepper, and onion in a small amount of boiling water for 5 minutes or till crisp-tender. Drain; transfer to a bowl. Stir in zucchini and, if desired, olives.

2. For marinade, in a screw-top jar combine vinegar, oil, sugar, oregano, salt, and pepper. Cover and shake well. Pour marinade over vegetables; stir lightly. Cover and chill for 4 to 24 hours, stirring occasionally. Serve with a slotted spoon. Makes 8 side-dish servings.

Nutrition Facts per serving: 65 cal., 4 g total fat (1 g sat. fat), 0 mg chol., 48 mg sodium, 8 g carbo., 2 g fiber, 2 g pro. **Daily Values:** 45% vit. A, 32% vit. C, 2% calcium, 4% iron

MARINATED CUCUMBERS

PREP: 15 MINUTES   CHILL: 2 HOURS TO 5 DAYS

No-Fat

1. For marinade, in a covered container combine ¼ cup *vinegar or lemon juice,* 1 to 2 tablespoons *sugar,* and ¼ teaspoon *celery seed.* Add 1 large *cucumber,* halved lengthwise and thinly sliced (3 cups), and 1 small *onion,* thinly sliced and separated into rings. Toss to coat with marinade. Cover and chill for 2 hours or up to 5 days, stirring occasionally. Makes 6 side-dish servings.

Nutrition Facts per serving: 20 cal., 0 g total fat, 0 mg chol., 2 mg sodium, 5 g carbo., 0 g fiber, 1 g pro. **Daily Values:** 1% vit. A., 6% vit. C, 1% calcium, 1% iron

---

MARINATED ROASTED PEPPERS AND BROCCOLI

PREP: 20 MINUTES   CHILL: 4 TO 24 HOURS

    2 pounds broccoli
  ⅓ cup white vinegar
  ⅓ cup olive oil or salad oil
    2 tablespoons sugar
  ½ teaspoon dried tarragon, crushed
  ½ teaspoon dried thyme, crushed
  ½ teaspoon dry mustard
    1 7-ounce jar roasted red sweet peppers or whole pimiento,
      drained and cut into bite-size pieces

1. Wash broccoli; trim off tough ends. Cut broccoli into spears. Cook broccoli, covered, in a small amount of boiling salted water about 8 minutes or till crisp-tender; drain. Cover; chill 4 to 24 hours.
2. For marinade, combine vinegar, oil, sugar, tarragon, thyme, mustard, and ½ teaspoon *salt.* Stir in the roasted peppers. Cover; chill 4 to 24 hours. Arrange broccoli on a platter lined with *lettuce.* Spoon pepper mixture atop. Serves 8 to 10.

Nutrition Facts per serving: 125 cal., 9 g total fat (1 g sat. fat), 0 mg chol., 158 mg sodium, 10 g carbo., 4 g fiber, 3 g pro. **Daily Values:** 28% vit. A, 201% vit. C, 4% calcium, 9% iron

VINAIGRETTE COLESLAW

PREP: 20 MINUTES CHILL: 2 TO 24 HOURS

    3 tablespoons vinegar
    3 tablespoons salad oil
    2 to 3 tablespoons sugar
    ¼ teaspoon dry mustard
    ¼ teaspoon caraway seed (optional)
    ⅛ to ¼ teaspoon pepper
    Several dashes bottled hot pepper sauce (optional)
    3 cups shredded green cabbage
    1 cup shredded red or green cabbage
    1 cup shredded carrots (2 medium)
    ¼ cup thinly sliced green onions (2)

1. In a screw-top jar combine vinegar, oil, sugar, mustard, caraway seed (if desired), pepper, hot pepper sauce (if desired), and ¼ teaspoon *salt*. Cover; shake well. In a large bowl combine the cabbage, carrots, and green onions. Pour vinaigrette over cabbage mixture. Toss lightly to coat. Chill 2 to 24 hours. Makes 4 to 6 side-dish servings.

Nutrition Facts per serving: 149 cal., 10 g total fat (2 g sat. fat), 0 mg chol., 157 mg. sodium, 15 g carbo., 2 g fiber, 1 g pro. **Daily Values:** 79% vit. A, 76% vit. C, 4% calcium, 5% iron

CREAMY COLESLAW

PREP: 20 MINUTES CHILL: 2 TO 24 HOURS

1. In a bowl stir together ½ cup *mayonnaise or salad dressing*, 1 tablespoon *vinegar*, 1 to 2 teaspoons *sugar*, ½ teaspoon *celery seed*, and ¼ teaspoon *salt*.
2. In a large bowl combine 3 cups shredded *green cabbage*, 1 cup shredded *red or green cabbage*, 1 cup shredded *carrots* (2 medium), and ¼ cup thinly sliced *green onions* (2). Pour mayonnaise mixture over cabbage mixture. Toss lightly to coat. Cover; chill 2 to 24 hours. Makes 4 to 6 side-dish servings.

Nutrition Facts per serving: 236 cal., 22 g total fat (3 g sat. fat), 16 mg chol., 314 mg sodium, 10 g carbo., 2 g fiber, 2 g pro. **Daily Values:** 81% vit. A, 76% vit. C, 4% calcium, 6% iron

THREE-BEAN SALAD

PREP: 15 MINUTES   CHILL: 4 TO 24 HOURS

Low-Fat

1 16-ounce can cut wax beans, drained; one 16-ounce can lima beans, drained; or one 15-ounce can garbanzo beans, drained

1 8-ounce can cut green beans, drained, or one 8-ounce can black beans, drained

1 8-ounce can red kidney beans, drained

$^1/_2$ cup chopped onion (1 medium)

$^1/_2$ cup chopped green sweet pepper

$^1/_2$ cup vinegar

$^1/_4$ cup salad oil

2 tablespoons sugar

$^1/_2$ teaspoon celery seed

$^1/_2$ teaspoon dry mustard

1 clove garlic, minced

1. In a bowl combine wax beans, green beans, red kidney beans, onion, and sweet pepper.

2. For dressing, in a screw-top jar combine the vinegar, oil, sugar, celery seed, dry mustard, and garlic. Cover and shake well. Pour over vegetables; stir lightly. Cover and chill for 4 to 24 hours, stirring often. Makes 6 side-dish servings.

Nutrition Facts per serving: 72 cal., 2 g total fat (0 g sat. fat), 0 mg chol., 201 mg sodium, 11 g carbo., 3 g fiber, 3 g pro. **Daily Values:** 2% vit. A, 18% vit. C, 2% calcium, 6% iron

■ **Creamy Three-Bean Salad:** Prepare as above, except reduce vinegar to 1 tablespoon and omit salad oil and sugar. For dressing, combine $^1/_3$ cup *mayonnaise or salad dressing* with 1 tablespoon vinegar, the celery seed, dry mustard, and garlic.

Nutrition Facts per serving: 137 cal., 11 g total fat (2 g sat. fat)

BLACK BEANS AND CORN WITH SALSA DRESSING

PREP: 15 MINUTES   CHILL: 2 TO 24 HOURS

- 1 15-ounce can black beans, rinsed and drained (see tip, page 107)
- 1 cup cooked whole kernel corn
- 1 red sweet pepper, cut into $1/2$-inch pieces ($3/4$ cup)
- 1 celery stalk with leaves, sliced ($2/3$ cup)
- 1 tablespoon snipped cilantro or parsley
- 1 recipe Salsa Dressing (see below)
  Lettuce leaves (optional)
- $1/2$ of a medium avocado, pitted, peeled, and sliced (optional)

1. In a large bowl combine beans, corn, sweet pepper, celery, and cilantro. Add dressing. Toss to coat. Cover; chill 2 to 24 hours. If desired, serve in salad bowls lined with lettuce leaves and garnish with avocado slices. Makes 6 side-dish servings.

◼ **Salsa Dressing:** In a small bowl combine $1/4$ cup *plain yogurt,* $1/4$ cup *mayonnaise or salad dressing,* and $1/4$ cup *salsa.* Cover and store in the refrigerator for up to 1 week. Makes about $3/4$ cup.

Nutrition Facts per serving: 154 cal., 8 g total fat (1 g sat. fat), 6 mg chol., 281 mg sodium, 19 g carbo., 4 g fiber, 6 g pro. **Daily Values:** 12% vit. A., 43% vit. C, 3% calcium, 7% iron

---

BARLEY AND BEAN SALAD

PREP: 20 MINUTES   COOK: 10 MINUTES   CHILL: 4 TO 24 HOURS

- $1^1/4$ cups chicken broth or water
- 1 cup quick-cooking barley
- $1/2$ of a 15-ounce can garbanzo beans, rinsed and drained (1 cup)
- 1 cup frozen peas
- $1/2$ of a red sweet pepper, cut into strips
- $1/2$ cup chopped cucumber
- $1/4$ cup thinly sliced green onions (2)
- 1 tablespoon snipped fresh rosemary or 1 teaspoon dried rosemary, crushed
- $1/4$ cup Italian Vinaigrette (see page 949)

1. In saucepan combine broth or water and barley. Bring to boiling; reduce heat. Cover; simmer 10 to 12 minutes or till liquid is absorbed. In a bowl combine barley, beans, frozen peas, sweet pepper, cucumber, green onions, and rosemary. Pour vinaigrette over barley mixture; toss to coat. Cover; chill for 4 to 24 hours. Makes 4 to 6 side-dish servings.

Nutrition Facts per serving: 330 cal., 9 g total fat (1 g sat. fat), 1 mg chol., 510 mg sodium, 52 g carbo., 54 g fiber, 12 g pro. **Daily Values:** 18% vit. A, 54% vit. C, 4% calcium, 19% iron

CREAMY CUCUMBERS

PREP: 20 MINUTES   CHILL: 2 TO 24 HOURS

Low-Fat

$^1/_2$ cup dairy sour cream or plain yogurt
1 tablespoon vinegar
1 teaspoon sugar
$^1/_4$ teaspoon dried dillweed
$^1/_4$ teaspoon salt
1 large cucumber, halved lengthwise and thinly sliced (about 3 cups)
1 small onion, thinly sliced and separated into rings

1. In a covered container stir together the sour cream, vinegar, sugar, dillweed, salt, and dash pepper. Add cucumber and onion; toss to coat. Cover and chill for 2 to 24 hours, stirring often. Stir before serving. Makes 6 side-dish servings.

Nutrition Facts per serving: 41 cal., 3 g total fat (2 g sat. fat), 8 mg chol., 10 mg sodium, 4 g carbo., 0 g fiber, 1 g pro. **Daily Values:** 3% vit. A, 6% vit. C, 2% calcium, 1% iron

PEAS AND CHEESE SALAD

PREP: 20 MINUTES   CHILL: 4 TO 24 HOURS

1 10-ounce package frozen peas or one 17-ounce can peas, drained
2 Hard-Cooked Eggs, chopped (see recipe, page 466)
$^3/_4$ cup cubed cheddar cheese (3 ounces)
$^1/_4$ cup chopped celery
2 tablespoons chopped onion
2 tablespoons diced pimiento or red sweet pepper
$^1/_4$ cup mayonnaise or salad dressing
$^1/_4$ teaspoon salt
4 medium tomatoes (optional)
Leaf lettuce (optional)

1. Rinse frozen peas in a colander under cool water to thaw; drain. In a large bowl combine thawed peas, eggs, cheese, celery, onion, and pimiento or sweet pepper. In a small bowl combine the mayonnaise or salad dressing, salt, and $1/8$ teaspoon *pepper*. Add to pea mixture; toss to coat.

2. Cover; chill 4 to 24 hours. Stir mixture before serving. If desired, cut each tomato into 8 wedges, cutting just to the bottom; place tomatoes atop lettuce. Fill center of each tomato with pea mixture. Makes 4 side-dish servings.

Nutrition Facts per serving: 283 cal., 21 g total fat (7 g sat. fat), 137 mg chol., 442 mg sodium, 12 g carbo., 3 g fiber, 12 g pro. **Daily Values:** 18% vit. A, 21% vit. C, 15% calcium, 12% iron

---

CLASSIC POTATO SALAD

PREP: 40 MINUTES CHILL: 6 TO 24 HOURS

  6 **medium potatoes (2 pounds) (see tip, page 927)**
$1^1/4$ **cups mayonnaise or salad dressing**
  1 **tablespoon prepared mustard (optional)**
$1/2$ **teaspoon salt**
$1/4$ **teaspoon pepper**
  1 **cup thinly sliced celery (2 stalks)**
$1/3$ **cup chopped onion (1 small)**
$1/2$ **cup chopped sweet or dill pickles or sweet or dill pickle relish**
  6 **Hard-Cooked Eggs, coarsely chopped (see recipe, page 466)**
    Lettuce leaves (optional)
    Paprika (optional)

1. Place potatoes in a medium saucepan; add water to cover and, if desired, $1/4$ teaspoon *salt*. Bring to boiling; reduce heat. Simmer, covered, for 20 to 25 minutes or till just tender. Drain well; cool slightly. Peel and cube potatoes.

2. Meanwhile, for dressing, in a large mixing bowl combine the mayonnaise or salad dressing, mustard (if desired), the $1/2$ teaspoon salt, and pepper.

3. Stir in the celery, onion, and chopped pickles or pickle relish. Add the potatoes and eggs. Toss lightly to coat. Cover and chill for 6 to 24 hours.

4. To serve, if desired, line a salad bowl with lettuce leaves. Transfer the potato salad to the bowl. If desired, sprinkle with paprika. Makes 12 side-dish servings.

Nutrition Facts per serving: 285 cal., 21 g total fat (4 g sat. fat), 120 mg chol., 297 mg sodium, 20 g carbo., 1 g fiber, 5 g pro. **Daily Values:** 6% vit. A, 18% vit. C, 2% calcium, 12% iron

---

MARINATED POTATO SALAD

PREP: 35 MINUTES   COOK: 15 MINUTES   CHILL: 4 TO 24 HOURS

Vary the flavors of this salad each time you make it by using a different herb in the homemade Vinaigrette of your choice (see recipes, page 949).

$3/4$ **pound whole tiny new potatoes (see tip, page 927)**
$1/2$ **cup Vinaigrette (see page 949) or other oil-and-vinegar salad dressing**
  1 **9-ounce package artichoke hearts, thawed, drained, halved**
  1 **small green sweet pepper, cut into strips**
  6 **cherry tomatoes, halved**
$1/2$ **of a small red onion, sliced and separated into rings**
$1/4$ **cup halved pitted ripe olives**
$1/4$ **cup snipped fresh parsley**
   Kale leaves (optional)

1. Place potatoes in a medium saucepan; add water to cover and, if desired, $1/4$ teaspoon *salt*. Bring to boiling; reduce heat. Simmer, covered, for 15 to 20 minutes or till just tender. Drain well. Cut potatoes into quarters and place in a large bowl. Pour Vinaigrette or other dressing over potatoes. Add artichoke hearts, sweet pepper, tomatoes, red onion, olives, and parsley. Toss gently to mix.

2. Cover and chill for 4 to 24 hours, stirring salad occasionally. To serve, if desired, line a salad bowl with kale leaves. Transfer potato salad to the bowl. Makes 6 side-dish servings.

Nutrition Facts per serving: 167 cal., 9 g total fat (1 g sat. fat), 0 mg chol., 80 mg sodium, 21 g carbo., 4 g fiber, 4 g pro. **Daily Values:** 4% vit. A, 43% vit. C, 3% calcium, 13% iron

GERMAN-STYLE POTATO SALAD

START TO FINISH: 45 MINUTES

Low-Fat

For added color, 12 small red potatoes can be substituted for the regular potatoes. Cook the unpeeled, whole potatoes for 12 to 15 minutes. Cut into 1/4-inch-thick slices, leaving peel intact.

- 4 **medium potatoes (1¹/₄ pounds) (see tip, right)**
- 4 **slices bacon**
- ¹/₂ **cup chopped onion (1 medium)**
- 1 **tablespoon all-purpose flour**
- 1 **tablespoon sugar**
- ¹/₂ **teaspoon salt**
- ¹/₂ **teaspoon celery seed**
- ¹/₂ **teaspoon dry mustard**
- ¹/₈ **to ¹/₄ teaspoon pepper**
- ²/₃ **cup water**
- ¹/₄ **cup vinegar**
- 1 **Hard-Cooked Egg, chopped (see recipe, page 466)**
- 2 **tablespoons snipped fresh parsley or 2 slices bacon, crisp-cooked, drained, and crumbled (optional)**

1. Place potatoes in a saucepan; add water to cover and, if desired, ¹/₄ teaspoon *salt*. Bring to boiling; reduce heat. Simmer, covered, for 20 to 25 minutes or till just tender; drain well. Cool potatoes slightly. Halve, peel, and cut potatoes into ¹/₄-inch-thick slices. Set aside.

2. For dressing, in a large skillet cook the 4 slices bacon over medium heat till crisp. Remove bacon, reserving 2 tablespoons drippings in skillet. Drain bacon on paper towels. Crumble the bacon and set aside.

3. Add chopped onion to the reserved drippings. Cook over medium heat till tender. Stir in the flour, sugar, the ¹/₂ teaspoon salt, celery seed, dry mustard, and pepper. Stir in the ²/₃ cup water and vinegar. Cook and stir till thickened and bubbly. Stir in the potatoes and bacon. Toss to mix. Cook, stirring gently, for 1 to 2 minutes more or till heated through. Transfer to a serving bowl. Garnish with egg and, if desired, parsley or crumbled bacon. Makes 4 to 6 side-dish servings.

Nutrition Facts per serving: 113 cal., 5 g total fat (2 g sat. fat), 59 mg chol., 387 mg sodium, 14 g carbo., 1 g fiber, 5 g pro. **Daily Values:** 2% vit. A, 9% vit. C, 1% calcium, 4% iron

---

SALAD SPUDS

When buying potatoes to use in salads, it's important to select a variety that keeps its shape when cooked. Potatoes classified as waxy, such as long whites and round reds, have a moist, smooth texture and perform well for this purpose. New potatoes are not a type of potato, but are just young, small potatoes—often the round red variety—making them another good choice for salads.

POTLUCK PASTA SALAD

PREP: 30 MINUTES   CHILL: 2 TO 24 HOURS

  4 ounces wagon-wheel macaroni or desired pasta (1¹/₂ cups)
  4 ounces tricolored rotini or desired pasta (1¹/₂ cups)
  1 teaspoon crushed red pepper
  1 medium red sweet pepper, cut into strips
  1 medium yellow summer squash and/or zucchini, halved
       lengthwise and sliced (2 cups)
  1 10-ounce package frozen peas, thawed, or 1¹/₂ cups shelled peas,
       cooked and cooled (see page 1092–93)
  1 6-ounce can pitted ripe olives, drained
  1 cup cubed smoked cheddar cheese or cheddar cheese (4
       ounces)
  1 cup unblanched whole almonds, toasted (see tip, page 234)
¹/₂ cup thinly sliced green onions (4)
  2 tablespoons snipped fresh tarragon, oregano, basil, or dill; or 2
       teaspoons dried tarragon, oregano, basil, crushed; or dried
       dillweed
  1 8-ounce bottle regular or nonfat Italian salad dressing

1. Cook pasta according to package directions, except add red pepper to cooking water. Drain pasta. Rinse with cold water; drain again.

2. In a large bowl combine pasta and remaining ingredients except dressing. Add dressing to pasta mixture; toss gently to coat. Cover and chill 2 to 24 hours. Makes 12 side-dish servings.

Nutrition Facts per serving: 309 cal., 22 g total fat (4 g sat. fat), 10 mg chol., 323 mg sodium, 24 g carbo., 3 g fiber, 9 g pro. **Daily Values:** 14% vit. A, 26% vit. C, 10% calcium, 12% iron

---

BASIL TORTELLINI SALAD

PREP: 25 MINUTES   CHILL: 4 TO 24 HOURS

1 7-ounce package frozen cheese tortellini or 3^1/$_2$ ounces (2 cups) packaged cheese-filled tortellini
1 small red sweet pepper, cut into bite-size strips
1 cup broccoli flowerets
^{3}/$_4$ cup thinly sliced carrot (1 large)
^{1}/$_2$ cup mayonnaise or salad dressing
2 tablespoons grated Parmesan cheese
1 tablespoon snipped fresh basil or 1 teaspoon dried basil, crushed
1 tablespoon milk
^{1}/$_4$ teaspoon pepper
1 clove garlic, minced
^{1}/$_4$ cup pine nuts or chopped walnuts, toasted (see tip, page 234)

1. Cook pasta according to package directions. Drain pasta. Rinse with cold water; drain again. In a large mixing bowl combine pasta, sweet pepper, broccoli, and carrot.
2. For dressing, in a small bowl stir together the mayonnaise or salad dressing, Parmesan cheese, basil, milk, pepper, and garlic. Pour the dressing over the pasta mixture. Toss lightly to coat. Cover and chill for 4 to 24 hours.
3. Before serving, stir in nuts and, if necessary, more milk to moisten. Makes 6 side-dish servings.

Nutrition Facts per serving: 326 cal., 22 g total fat (3 g sat. fat), 13 mg chol., 448 mg sodium, 24 g carbo., 1 g fiber, 10 g pro. **Daily Values:** 55% vit. A, 38% vit. C, 13% calcium, 9% iron

FRUIT AND PASTA SALAD

PREP: 30 MINUTES   CHILL: 4 TO 24 HOURS

Low-Fat

2 slightly beaten egg yolks
$^1/_3$ cup orange juice
3 tablespoons honey
2 tablespoons lemon juice
$^1/_8$ teaspoon ground cardamom
1 cup bow-tie pasta or $^2/_3$ cup wagon-wheel macaroni (about 2 ounces)
1 cup sliced, peeled peaches, orange sections, or cubed cantaloupe or honeydew melon
$^1/_2$ cup sliced celery
$^1/_2$ cup sliced strawberries
1 kiwifruit, peeled and sliced

1. For dressing, in a small saucepan mix egg yolks, orange juice, honey, lemon juice, and cardamom. Cook and stir over medium heat till thickened and bubbly. Cool slightly. Cover and chill.

2. Cook the pasta according to package directions. Drain pasta. Rinse with cold water; drain again. Combine the cooked pasta; peaches, orange sections, or melon; and celery. Add dressing; toss to coat. Cover; chill for 4 to 24 hours. Before serving, stir in the strawberries and kiwifruit. Makes 6 side-dish servings.

Nutrition Facts per serving: 121 cal., 2 g total fat (1 g sat. fat), 71 mg chol., 13 mg sodium, 24 g carbo., 1 g fiber, 3 g pro. **Daily Values:** 12% vit. A, 52% vit. C, 1% calcium, 5% iron

FRESH VEGETABLE PASTA SALAD

START TO FINISH: 25 MINUTES

Fast

This salad contains less dressing than most pasta salads. To keep it moist, it's best to serve it soon after making it. The pasta will absorb too much of the dressing if it sits too long.

- $1/4$ cup loosely packed fresh parsley sprigs
- 2 tablespoons salad oil
- 2 tablespoons wine vinegar
- 2 tablespoons water
- 1 to 2 cloves garlic
- $1/2$ teaspoon dry mustard
- $1/4$ teaspoon salt
- $1/4$ teaspoon pepper
- 2 ounces dried linguine, broken
- 1 large carrot, cut into thin strips
- 1 small turnip, cut into thin strips
- 1 small zucchini, cut into thin strips
- $1/2$ cup chopped red sweet pepper
- $1/2$ cup frozen peas, thawed
- $1/2$ cup cubed part-skim mozzarella, Gruyère, or Swiss cheese (2 ounces)

1. For dressing, in a blender container combine parsley sprigs, oil, wine vinegar, water, garlic, mustard, salt, and pepper. Cover and blend till combined. Set aside.

2. Cook dried pasta according to package directions, adding carrot and turnip the last 3 to 4 minutes of cooking. Drain pasta and vegetables. Rinse with cold water; drain again.

3. In a large salad bowl combine the cooked pasta and vegetables, the zucchini, sweet pepper, peas, and cheese. Add the dressing; toss lightly to coat. Makes 6 side-dish servings.

Nutrition Facts per serving: 155 cal., 7 g total fat (1 g sat. fat), 27 mg chol., 166 mg sodium, 18 g carbo., 2 g fiber, 6 g pro. **Daily Values:** 42% vit. A, 40% vit. C, 6% calcium, 7% iron

MACARONI SALAD

PREP: 30 MINUTES   CHILL: 4 TO 24 HOURS

Make the flavor of this creamy pasta salad sweet or sour by using either sweet or dill pickle relish or pickles.

  1 cup elbow macaroni or wagon-wheel macaroni (3 ounces)
  $^3/_4$ cup cubed cheddar or American cheese (3 ounces)
  $^1/_2$ cup thinly sliced celery (1 stalk)
  $^1/_2$ cup frozen peas
  $^1/_2$ cup thinly sliced radishes
  2 tablespoons thinly sliced green onion or chopped onion
  $^1/_2$ cup mayonnaise or salad dressing
  $^1/_4$ cup sweet or dill pickle relish or chopped sweet or dill pickles
  2 tablespoons milk
  $^1/_4$ teaspoon salt
     Dash ground pepper
  2 Hard-Cooked Eggs, coarsely chopped (see recipe, page 466)

1. Cook pasta according to package directions. Drain pasta. Rinse with cold water; drain again. In a large mixing bowl combine cooked pasta, cheese, celery, peas, radishes, and green onion.
2. For dressing, in a small bowl stir together the mayonnaise or salad dressing, pickle relish or pickles, milk, salt, and pepper.
3. Pour dressing over pasta mixture. Add chopped eggs. Toss lightly to coat. Cover and chill for 4 to 24 hours. Before serving, if necessary, stir in additional milk to moisten. Makes 6 side-dish servings.

Nutrition Facts per serving: 298 cal., 22 g total fat (6 g sat. fat), 97 mg chol., 409 mg sodium, 18 g carbo., 1 g fiber, 9 g pro. **Daily Values:** 10% vit. A, 7% vit. C, 10% calcium, 9% iron

Lentil and Bulgur Salad with Bacon-Walnut Dressing

Start to finish: 30 minutes

Fast

   $^1/_2$ cup dry lentils
    2 cups water or chicken broth
   $^1/_3$ cup bulgur
    3 slices bacon, chopped
   $^1/_3$ cup chopped onion (1 small)
   $^1/_2$ cup chopped fresh mushrooms
   $^1/_4$ cup chopped walnuts
    1 tablespoon cider vinegar
   $^1/_4$ teaspoon dried oregano, crushed
    2 cups shredded spinach or romaine
    1 small tomato, chopped

1. Rinse and drain the lentils; transfer to a medium saucepan. Add the water or chicken broth and bulgur. Bring to boiling; reduce heat. Cover and simmer for 20 minutes; drain. Rinse with cold water; drain again. Transfer to a large bowl.

2. For dressing, in a skillet cook bacon and onion over medium heat till bacon is done and onion is tender. Add mushrooms, walnuts, vinegar, and oregano; heat through. Add to lentils and bulgur; add spinach. Toss lightly to mix. Garnish with chopped tomato. Makes 4 to 6 side-dish servings.

Nutrition Facts per serving: 210 cal., 8 g total fat (1 g sat. fat), 4 mg chol., 109 mg sodium, 27 g carbo., 5 g fiber, 11 g pro. **Daily Values:** 21% vit. A, 30% vit. C, 4% calcium, 25% iron

TABBOULEH

Prep: 25 minutes Chill: 4 to 24 Hours

Bulgur is the result of soaking, cooking, drying, and cracking whole wheat kernels. There is no need to cook the bulgur further for this salad—the dressing softens the wheat while the salad chills.

$^3/_4$ **cup bulgur**
$^1/_2$ **cup chopped, seeded cucumber**
$^1/_2$ **cup snipped fresh parsley**
  2 **tablespoons thinly sliced green onion**
$^1/_4$ **cup olive oil or salad oil**
$^1/_4$ **cup lemon juice**
  1 **tablespoon snipped fresh mint or 1 teaspoon dried mint, crushed**
$^1/_4$ **teaspoon salt**
$^1/_2$ **cup chopped, seeded tomato (1 small)**

1. Place bulgur in a colander; rinse with cold water and drain. In a medium bowl combine bulgur, cucumber, parsley, and green onion.
2. For dressing, in a screw-top jar combine the oil, lemon juice, mint, salt, and $^1/_8$ teaspoon *pepper*. Cover and shake well. Pour the dressing over the bulgur mixture. Toss lightly to coat. Cover; chill for 4 to 24 hours. Before serving, stir tomato into the bulgur mixture. Makes 4 to 6 side-dish servings.

Nutrition Facts per serving: 223 cal., 14 g total fat (2 g sat. fat), 0 mg chol., 144 mg sodium, 23 g carbo., 6 g fiber, 4 g pro. **Daily Values:** 6% vit. A, 39% vit. C, 2% calcium, 10% iron

CHUTNEY-FRUIT RICE SALAD

PREP: 40 MINUTES   CHILL: 2 TO 24 HOURS

Cut 20 minutes off the preparation time by using leftover white rice in this salad.

1½ cups cooked long grain rice (see page 139)
  1 medium orange, peeled and cut into bite-size pieces
  1 cup chopped apple (1 large or 2 small)
 ½ cup seedless grapes, halved
 ½ cup plain yogurt
 ½ cup mayonnaise or salad dressing
 ¼ cup chutney, chopped
 ½ to 1 teaspoon curry powder
 ⅛ teaspoon garlic powder
 ⅛ teaspoon pepper
 ½ cup coarsely chopped peanuts
  6 lettuce leaves (optional)

1. In a large salad bowl combine the cooked rice, orange, apple, and grapes. For dressing, in a small bowl combine the yogurt, mayonnaise, chutney, curry powder, garlic powder, and pepper. Pour over fruit mixture; toss to coat. Cover and chill for 2 to 24 hours. If necessary, add *milk* to moisten. Before serving, stir in peanuts. If desired, serve on lettuce leaves. Makes 6 side-dish servings.

Nutrition Facts per serving: 323 cal., 21 g total fat (3 g sat. fat), 13 mg chol., 123 mg sodium, 29 g carbo., 2 g fiber, 6 g pro. **Daily Values:** 3% vit. A, 15% vit. C, 5% calcium, 7% iron

CAJUN-STYLE RICE SALAD

PREP: 20 MINUTES   CHILL: 4 TO 24 HOURS

For 4 main-dish servings, double the amount of shrimp used in the recipe.

  2 cups cooked rice (see page 139)
  1 cup chopped green sweet pepper
  4 ounces cooked shrimp, coarsely chopped, or one 4½-ounce can shrimp, rinsed and drained
 ½ cup sliced fresh mushrooms

1 Hard-Cooked Egg, finely chopped (see recipe, page 466)
2 tablespoons snipped fresh parsley
$^{1}/_{4}$ cup water
$^{1}/_{4}$ cup salad oil
$^{1}/_{4}$ cup vinegar
2 teaspoons paprika
2 teaspoons prepared horseradish
$^{1}/_{2}$ teaspoon onion salt
$^{1}/_{8}$ teaspoon ground red pepper
6 lettuce leaves

1. In mixing bowl gently stir together rice, sweet pepper, shrimp, mushrooms, egg, and parsley; set aside.

2. For dressing, in a screw-top jar combine the water, oil, vinegar, paprika, horseradish, onion salt, and red pepper. Cover; shake well. Pour over rice mixture; toss to coat. Cover; chill 4 to 24 hours. Serve on lettuce leaves. Makes 6 side-dish servings.

Nutrition Facts per serving: 195 cal., 11 g total fat (2 g sat. fat), 72 mg chol., 208 mg sodium, 19 g carbo., 1 g fiber, 8 g pro. **Daily Values:** 10% vit. A, 48% vit. C, 2% calcium, 12% iron

---

BROWN RICE AND VEGETABLE SALAD

PREP: 50 MINUTES   CHILL: 4 TO 24 HOURS

$1^{1}/_{2}$ cups cooked brown rice (see page 139)
$1^{1}/_{4}$ cups coarsely chopped, seeded tomato
2 medium carrots, julienned (1 cup)
$^{1}/_{2}$ cup frozen peas
$^{1}/_{4}$ cup thinly sliced green onions (2)
1 tablespoon snipped fresh parsley
1 tablespoon snipped fresh dill or basil or 1 teaspoon dried
    dillweed or basil, crushed
1 recipe Mustard Vinaigrette (see below)
Lettuce leaves

1. In a large bowl stir together the cooked rice, tomato, carrots, peas, green onions, parsley, and dill or basil. Pour vinaigrette over rice mixture. Toss lightly to coat. Cover and chill 4 to 24 hours.

2. To serve, line a salad bowl with lettuce leaves. Transfer salad to bowl. Makes 6 side-dish servings.

■ **Mustard Vinaigrette:** In a screw-top jar combine 3 tablespoons *olive oil or salad oil,* 3 tablespoons *red wine vinegar,* 2 teaspoons *Dijon-style mustard,* 1¹/₂ teaspoons *sugar,* and ¹/₈ teaspoon *pepper.* Cover and shake well.

Nutrition Facts per serving: 151 cal., 8 g total fat (1 g sat. fat), 0 mg chol., 68 mg sodium, 19 g carbo., 3 g fiber, 3 g pro. **Daily Values:** 72% vit. A, 24% vit. C, 1% calcium, 6% iron

---

FIVE-CUP FRUIT SALAD

PREP: 10 MINUTES   CHILL: 2 TO 24 HOURS

    1 8-ounce can pineapple chunks
    1 11-ounce can mandarin orange sections, drained
    1 cup coconut
    1 cup tiny marshmallows
    1 8-ounce carton dairy sour cream
    2 tablespoons chopped pecans

1. Drain pineapple chunks, reserving *1 tablespoon* juice. In a bowl combine reserved juice, pineapple chunks, mandarin orange sections, coconut, marshmallows, and sour cream. Cover and chill for 2 to 24 hours. Before serving, sprinkle with pecans. Makes 6 side-dish servings.

Nutrition Facts per serving: 224 cal., 14 g total fat (9 g sat. fat), 17 mg chol., 30 mg sodium, 26 g carbo., 1 g fiber, 2 g pro. **Daily Values:** 9% vit. A, 5% vit. C, 4% calcium, 4% iron

---

WALDORF SALAD

PREP: 15 MINUTES   CHILL: 2 TO 24 HOURS

    2 cups chopped apples or pears
 1¹/₂ teaspoons lemon juice
  ¹/₄ cup chopped celery
  ¹/₄ cup chopped walnuts or pecans, toasted (see tip, page 234)
  ¹/₄ cup raisins, snipped pitted whole dates, or dried tart cherries
  ¹/₄ cup seedless green grapes, halved (optional)
  ¹/₃ cup whipping cream or ²/₃ cup frozen whipped dessert
       topping, thawed
  ¹/₄ cup mayonnaise or salad dressing
       Ground nutmeg

1. In a bowl toss apples or pears with lemon juice. Stir in celery; nuts; raisins, dates, or dried tart cherries; and, if desired, the grapes.
2. For dressing, if using whipping cream, in a chilled mixing bowl whip cream to soft peaks. Fold mayonnaise or salad dressing into the whipped cream or dessert topping. Spread dressing over the top of the apple mixture. Sprinkle with nutmeg. Cover and chill for 2 to 24 hours. To serve, fold dressing into the apple mixture. Makes 4 to 6 side-dish servings.

Nutrition Facts per serving: 284 cal., 23 g total fat (7 g sat. fat), 35 mg chol., 94 mg sodium, 20 g carbo., 2 g fiber, 2 g pro. **Daily Values:** 10% vit. A, 10% vit. C, 2% calcium, 4% iron

---

GINGERED FRUIT SALAD

START TO FINISH: 25 MINUTES

Fast

After cutting the apple and peach, toss the pieces with a mixture of a little lemon juice and some water to prevent the fruit from darkening.

    2 cups cubed cantaloupe
    1 medium orange, peeled and sectioned
    1 medium apple, cored and coarsely chopped
    1 medium peach, peeled, pitted, and thinly sliced
    1 cup blueberries
  ¹/₂ cup halved strawberries
    1 8-ounce carton pineapple yogurt
    2 tablespoons mayonnaise or salad dressing
    2 teaspoons brown sugar
    1 teaspoon grated gingerroot or ¹/₄ teaspoon ground ginger

1. In a large bowl combine the melon, orange, apple, peach, blueberries, and strawberries.
2. For dressing, stir together yogurt, mayonnaise or salad dressing, brown sugar, and gingerroot. If desired, line 4 salad plates with *lettuce leaves*. Divide fruit among plates. Top each serving with dressing. Makes 4 side-dish servings.

Nutrition Facts per serving: 206 cal., 7 g total fat (1 g sat. fat), 6 mg chol., 84 mg sodium, 35 g carbo., 3 g fiber, 4 g pro. **Daily Values:** 29% vit. A, 101% vit. C, 9% calcium, 3% iron

TROPICAL FRUIT SALAD

START TO FINISH: 35 MINUTES

Low-Fat

To toast coconut, spread it in a shallow baking pan; bake in a 350°
oven 5 to 10 minutes or until light golden brown,
stirring once or twice.

$^1/_2$ cup vanilla yogurt
1 ripe medium banana, cut up
2 tablespoons pineapple juice
1 medium papaya, seeded, peeled, and sliced
$^1/_2$ medium mango, seeded, peeled, and chopped
2 cups honeydew melon and/or cantaloupe balls
$^1/_4$ cup coconut, toasted (see above)
Fresh mint sprigs (optional)

1. For dressing, in blender container or food processor bowl, combine yogurt, banana, and pineapple juice. Cover and blend or
process till smooth. Transfer to covered container and refrigerate
while preparing fruit.
2. Arrange the sliced papaya and chopped mango on 4 salad plates.
Mound $^1/_2$ cup of the melon balls atop each plate. Spoon 2 tablespoons dressing over each. Sprinkle each with *1 tablespoon* of the
toasted coconut. If desired, garnish with fresh mint sprigs. Makes 4
side-dish servings.

Nutrition Facts per serving: 178 cal., 2 g total fat (0 g sat. fat), 2 mg chol., 38 mg sodium, 40 g
carbo., 4 g fiber, 3 g pro. **Daily Values:** 14% vit. A, 181% vit. C, 6% calcium, 3% iron

PEACH-BERRY FROZEN SALAD

PREP: 15 MINUTES   FREEZE: 8 TO 24 HOURS

1 8-ounce container soft-style cream cheese or one 8-ounce
    package Neufchâtel cheese, softened
2 8-ounce cartons peach yogurt
1 4-ounce container frozen whipped dessert topping, thawed
1 cup chopped, peeled fresh or frozen unsweetened peaches or
    one 8$^3/_4$-ounce can peach slices, drained and chopped
1 cup fresh or frozen unsweetened raspberries or blueberries
$^1/_4$ cup slivered almonds, toasted (see tip, page 234)

1. In a medium bowl combine cream cheese and yogurt. Beat with an electric mixer on medium speed till smooth. Stir in the whipped topping, peaches, berries, and almonds.

2. Pour into a 2-quart square baking dish. Cover and freeze 8 to 24 hours or till firm.

3. To serve, let stand at room temperature about 30 minutes to thaw slightly. Cut into squares. Makes 9 side-dish servings.

Nutrition Facts per serving: 186 cal., 14 g total fat (7 g sat. fat), 29 mg chol., 121 mg sodium, 11 g carbo., 1 g fiber, 5 g pro. **Daily Values:** 6% vit. A, 8% vit. C, 12% calcium, 1% iron

---

TOMATO-VEGETABLE ASPIC

PREP: 20 MINUTES   CHILL: 6 TO 24 HOURS

No-Fat

> 2 envelopes unflavored gelatin
> 1 cup beef broth
> 3 cups tomato juice
> $1/2$ cup chopped cucumber, celery, or green sweet pepper
> $1/4$ cup chopped onion (1 small)
> 1 tablespoon brown sugar
> 2 teaspoons Worcestershire sauce
> 1 teaspoon dried basil, crushed
> 1 bay leaf
> 2 tablespoons lemon juice
> Dash bottled hot pepper sauce

1. In a small saucepan combine gelatin and $1/2$ cup of the beef broth. Let stand 5 minutes.

2. Meanwhile, in a saucepan combine *1 cup* of the tomato juice, the cucumber, onion, brown sugar, Worcestershire sauce, basil, and bay leaf. Simmer for 5 minutes. Strain mixture through several layers of 100% cotton cheesecloth. Discard vegetables and herbs.

3. Add gelatin mixture to hot tomato juice mixture; stir to dissolve. Stir in remaining broth and tomato juice, the lemon juice, and hot pepper sauce. Pour into a 4- or $4^{1}/_2$-cup mold. Cover and chill for 6 to 24 hours. Unmold salad onto a plate (see photo, page 941). Makes 8 to 10 side-dish servings.

Nutrition Facts per serving: 36 cal., 0 g total fat, 0 mg chol., 444 mg sodium, 7 g carbo., 1 g fiber, 3 g pro. **Daily Values:** 5% vit. A, 38% vit. C, 1% calcium, 6% iron

CRANBERRY RELISH RING

PREP: 10 MINUTES   CHILL: 4³/₄ HOURS

No-Fat

- ¹/₂ cup sugar
- 1 3-ounce package cherry-flavored gelatin
- 1 3-ounce package raspberry-flavored gelatin
- 1¹/₂ cups boiling water
- 1 12-ounce can lemon-lime carbonated beverage
- 1 8¹/₄-ounce can crushed pineapple
- 1 small orange, quartered and seeded
- 2 cups cranberries

1. In a bowl combine sugar and gelatin. Add boiling water; stir till dissolved. Add carbonated beverage and undrained pineapple. Chill 45 minutes or till partially set (the consistency of egg whites).

2. Using a food processor or food grinder with a coarse blade, grind unpeeled orange and cranberries. Fold the cranberry mixture into partially set gelatin. Pour the cranberry-gelatin mixture into a 6¹/₂-cup ring mold or a 12×7¹/₂×2-inch dish. Chill 4 hours or till firm. Unmold onto a serving plate (see photo, right). Makes 12 side-dish servings.

Nutrition Facts per serving: 121 cal., 0 g total fat, 0 mg chol., 45 mg sodium, 30 g carbo., 1 g fiber, 2 g pro. **Daily Values:** 0% vit. A, 16% vit. C, 0% calcium, 1% iron

■ **Shortcut Cranberry Relish Ring:** Prepare as at lower left, except reduce sugar to ¹/₄ cup and substitute two 10-ounce packages *frozen cranberry-orange relish,* thawed, for ground orange and cranberries.

Nutrition Facts per serving: 174 cal., 0 g total fat

BERRY SALAD

PREP: 10 MINUTES   CHILL: 4³/₄ HOURS

No-Fat

- 1 10-ounce package frozen sliced strawberries, thawed
- 1 10-ounce package frozen red raspberries, thawed
- 1 6-ounce package strawberry- or raspberry-flavored gelatin
- 1¹/₄ cups boiling water

$^1/_2$ **cup cranberry juice cocktail or apple juice**
1 **tablespoon lemon juice**

1. Drain strawberries and raspberries, reserving syrup. In a mixing bowl combine gelatin and boiling water, stirring till gelatin dissolves. Stir in reserved syrup, cranberry juice cocktail and lemon juice. Chill about 45 minutes or till partially set (the consistency of unbeaten egg whites).
2. Fold in berries. Pour into a 5- or 5$^1/_2$-cup mold. Cover; chill 4 hours or till firm. Unmold salad onto a serving plate (see photo, below). Makes 8 side-dish servings.

Nutrition Facts per serving: 141 cal., 0 g total fat, 0 mg chol., 32 mg sodium, 36 g carbo., 5 g fiber, 2 g pro. **Daily Values:** 0% vit. A, 46% vit. C, 0% calcium, 3% iron

To unmold gelatin salads, set mold in a bowl or sink filled with warm water for several seconds or until the salad edges appear to separate from the mold.

MAYONNAISE

START TO FINISH: 15 MINUTES

Fast

Classic homemade mayonnaise contains raw eggs, which contain harmful bacteria. We used egg product in this version so you can make it safely.

1. In a small mixer bowl combine $^1/_2$ teaspoon *dry mustard*, $^1/_4$ teaspoon *salt*, $^1/_4$ teaspoon *paprika* (if desired), and $^1/_8$ teaspoon *ground red pepper*. Add $^1/_4$ cup *refrigerated or frozen egg product*, thawed, and 2 tablespoons *vinegar or lemon juice*. Beat mixture with an electric mixer on medium speed till combined.
2. With mixer running, add 2 tablespoons *salad oil*, 1 teaspoon at a time. Slowly add an additional 1$^3/_4$ cups plus 2 tablespoons *salad oil*,

in a thin, steady stream. (This should take about 5 minutes.) Cover; store in the refrigerator for up to 2 weeks. Makes about 2 cups.

■ **Food processor directions:** In a food processor bowl combine all ingredients except oil; process till combined. With the processor running, add oil in a thin, steady stream. (When necessary, stop processor and scrape down sides of bowl.)

■ **Blender directions:** Use only *half* of each ingredient, except use the ¼ cup egg product. In a blender container combine all ingredients except oil. Cover and blend for 5 seconds. With blender running slowly, add 1 cup salad oil in a thin, steady stream. (When necessary, stop blender and use a rubber scraper to scrape the sides of the blender.) Makes 1 cup.

Nutrition Facts per tablespoon: 124 cal., 14 g total fat (2 g sat. fat), 0 mg chol., 20 mg sodium, 0 g carbo., 0 g fiber, 0 g pro.

CREAMY FRENCH DRESSING

START TO FINISH: 15 MINUTES

> ### Fast

   3 tablespoons vinegar
   2 tablespoons sugar
   2 teaspoons paprika
   1 teaspoon Worcestershire sauce (optional)
   ¼ teaspoon salt
   ¼ teaspoon dry mustard
   ⅛ teaspoon garlic powder
      Dash ground red pepper
   ¾ cup salad oil or olive oil

1. In a small mixing bowl, blender container, or food processor bowl, combine vinegar, sugar, paprika, Worcestershire sauce (if desired), salt, dry mustard, garlic powder, and red pepper. With mixer, blender, or food processor running, slowly add oil in a thin, steady stream. (This should take 2 to 3 minutes.) Continue mixing, blending, or processing till mixture is thick.

2. Serve immediately or cover and store in the refrigerator for up to 2 weeks. Stir before serving. Makes about 1⅓ cups.

Nutrition Facts per tablespoon: 71 cal., 7 g total fat (1 g sat. fat), 0 mg chol., 24 mg sodium, 1 g carbo., 0 g fiber, 0 g pro. **Daily Values:** 1% vit. A, 0% vit. C, 0% calcium, 0% iron

BUTTERMILK DRESSING

PREP: 10 MINUTES   CHILL: 30 MINUTES

1. In a small bowl stir together ³/₄ cup *buttermilk;* ¹/₂ cup *mayonnaise or salad dressing or light mayonnaise or light salad dressing;* 1 tablespoon snipped *fresh parsley or* 1 teaspoon *dried parsley,* crushed; ¹/₄ teaspoon *pepper;* ¹/₄ teaspoon *onion powder;* ¹/₄ teaspoon *dry mustard;* and 1 *clove garlic,* minced. If necessary, add additional buttermilk to make dressing of desired consistency.
2. Cover and chill dressing for 30 minutes before serving. Cover and store in the refrigerator for up to 1 week. Makes 1¹/₄ cups.

Nutrition Facts per tablespoon: 44 cal., 5 g total fat (1 g sat. fat), 2 mg chol., 38 mg sodium, 1 g carbo., 0 g fiber, 0 g pro.

THOUSAND ISLAND DRESSING

START TO FINISH: 20 MINUTES

Fast

1. In a small bowl combine 1 cup *mayonnaise or salad dressing* and ¹/₄ cup *chili sauce.* Stir in 2 tablespoons finely chopped *pimiento-stuffed olives,* 2 tablespoons finely chopped *green or red sweet pepper,* 2 tablespoons finely chopped *onion,* 1 teaspoon *Worcestershire sauce or prepared horseradish* (if desired), and 1 *Hard-Cooked Egg* (see recipe, page 466), finely chopped.
2. Serve immediately or cover and refrigerate for up to 1 week. Before serving, if necessary, stir in 1 to 2 tablespoons *milk* to make dressing of desired consistency. Makes 1¹/₂ cups.

Nutrition Facts per tablespoon: 73 cal., 8 g total fat (1 g sat. fat), 14 mg chol., 104 mg sodium, 1 g carbo., 0 g fiber, 1 g pro. **Daily Values:** 1% vit. A, 2% vit. C, 4% calcium, 0% iron

BLUE CHEESE DRESSING

START TO FINISH: 10 MINUTES

Fast

1. In a blender container or food processor bowl combine ½ cup *plain yogurt or dairy sour cream,* ¼ cup *cream-style cottage cheese,* ¼ cup *mayonnaise or salad dressing,* and ¼ cup crumbled *blue cheese.* Cover and blend or process till smooth. Stir in ½ cup crumbled *blue cheese.* If necessary, stir in 2 to 3 tablespoons *milk* to make the dressing of the desired consistency.
2. Serve immediately or cover and store in the refrigerator up to 2 weeks. Makes about 1¼ cups.

Nutrition Facts per tablespoon: 45 cal., 4 g total fat (1 g sat. fat), 6 mg chol., 101 mg sodium, 1 g carbo., 0 g fiber, 2 g pro. **Daily Values:** 1% vit. A, 0% vit. C, 3% calcium, 0% iron

CREAMY ITALIAN DRESSING

START TO FINISH: 15 MINUTES

Fast

   ¾ **cup mayonnaise or salad dressing**
   ¼ **cup dairy sour cream**
   2 **teaspoons white wine vinegar or white vinegar**
   ¼ **teaspoon dry mustard**
   ¼ **teaspoon dried basil, crushed**
   ¼ **teaspoon dried oregano, crushed**
   ⅛ **teaspoon salt**
   ⅛ **teaspoon garlic powder**
   1 **to 2 tablespoons milk (optional)**

1. In a small mixing bowl stir together mayonnaise or salad dressing, sour cream, vinegar, mustard, basil, oregano, salt, and garlic powder.
2. Serve immediately or cover and store in the refrigerator for up to 2 weeks. Before serving, if necessary, stir in milk to make dressing of desired consistency. Makes about 1 cup.
■ **Creamy Garlic Dressing:** Prepare as above, except omit oregano and garlic powder. Add 2 *cloves garlic,* minced.
■ **Creamy Parmesan Dressing:** Prepare as above, except omit the

dry mustard, dried oregano, and salt. Stir in 3 tablespoons grated *Parmesan cheese* and, if desired, $^{1}/_{2}$ teaspoon *cracked black pepper.*

Nutrition Facts per tablespoon: 82 cal., 9 g total fat (2 g sat. fat), 8 mg chol., 77 mg sodium, 1 g carbo., 0 g fiber, 0 g pro. **Daily Values:** 1% vit. A, 0% vit. C, 0% calcium, 0% iron

RUSSIAN DRESSING

START TO FINISH: 10 MINUTES

> *Fast*

$^{1}/_{4}$ **cup salad oil**
$^{1}/_{4}$ **cup catsup**
1 **tablespoon sugar**
1 **tablespoon white wine vinegar or vinegar**
1 **tablespoon lemon juice**
1 **teaspoon Worcestershire sauce**
$^{1}/_{2}$ **teaspoon paprika**
$^{1}/_{4}$ **teaspoon salt**
$^{1}/_{8}$ **teaspoon pepper**

1. In a screw-top jar combine the oil, catsup, sugar, vinegar, lemon juice, Worcestershire sauce, paprika, salt, and pepper. Cover; shake well.

2. Serve immediately or cover and store in the refrigerator for up to 2 weeks. Shake before serving. Makes $^{2}/_{3}$ cup.

Nutrition Facts per tablespoon: 56 cal., 5 g total fat (1 g sat. fat), 0 mg chol., 136 mg sodium, 3 g carbo., 0 g fiber, 0 g pro. **Daily Values:** 1% vit. A, 6% vit. C, 0% calcium, 1% iron

GREEN GODDESS DRESSING

START TO FINISH: 15 MINUTES

Fast

³/₄ cup packed fresh parsley sprigs
¹/₃ cup mayonnaise or salad dressing
¹/₃ cup dairy sour cream or plain yogurt
 1 green onion, cut up
 1 tablespoon vinegar
 1 teaspoon anchovy paste or 1 anchovy fillet, cut up
¹/₄ teaspoon dried basil, crushed
¹/₈ teaspoon garlic powder
¹/₈ teaspoon dried tarragon, crushed
 1 to 2 tablespoons milk

1. In a blender container or food processor bowl combine parsley, mayonnaise or salad dressing, sour cream, green onion, vinegar, anchovy paste or anchovy, basil, garlic powder, and tarragon. Cover and blend or process till smooth.

2. Serve immediately or cover and store in refrigerator for up to 2 weeks. Before serving, stir in milk to make dressing of desired consistency. Makes about 1 cup.

Nutrition Facts per tablespoon: 45 cal., 5 g total fat (1 g sat. fat), 5 mg chol., 40 mg sodium, 1 g carbo., 0 g fiber, 0 g pro. **Daily Values:** 3% vit. A, 6% vit. C, 1% calcium, 1% iron

OIL-FREE HERB DRESSING

PREP: 15 MINUTES   CHILL: 30 MINUTES

No-Fat

 1 tablespoon powdered fruit pectin for lower-sugar recipes
³/₄ teaspoon snipped fresh oregano, basil, thyme, tarragon,
     savory, or dill, or ¹/₄ teaspoon dried herb, crushed
¹/₂ teaspoon sugar
¹/₈ teaspoon dry mustard
¹/₈ teaspoon pepper
 1 tablespoon vinegar
 1 small clove garlic, minced

1. In a small mixing bowl stir together pectin, desired herb, sugar, dry mustard, and pepper. Stir in vinegar, garlic, and ¼ cup *water*. Cover and chill for 30 minutes before serving. Cover and store remaining dressing in the refrigerator for up to 3 days. Makes about ½ cup.

Nutrition Facts per tablespoon: 8 cal., 0 g total fat, 0 mg chol., 3 mg sodium, 2 g carbo., 0 g fiber, 0 g pro.

■ **Oil-Free Creamy Onion Dressing:** Prepare as above, except increase the sugar to 1 tablespoon. Stir in ¼ cup thinly sliced *green onions* (2) and ¼ cup *plain yogurt* with the vinegar, garlic, and ¼ cup *water*. Makes about ¾ cup.

Nutrition Facts per tablespoon: 12 cal., 0 g total fat

OIL-FREE FRENCH DRESSING

PREP: 10 MINUTES CHILL: 30 MINUTES

No-Fat

    1 8-ounce can tomato sauce
 ¼ cup light-colored corn syrup
    2 tablespoons chopped onion
    1 tablespoon vinegar
    1 teaspoon paprika
 ¼ teaspoon garlic powder
    Dash ground red pepper

1. In a blender container combine tomato sauce, corn syrup, onion, vinegar, paprika, garlic powder, and red pepper. Cover; blend till well combined. Transfer dressing to a jar with a tight-fitting lid; refrigerate 30 minutes to blend flavors before serving. Store any remaining dressing in refrigerator up to 3 days. Makes 1 cup.

Nutrition Facts per tablespoon: 20 cal., 0 g total fat, 0 mg chol., 89 mg sodium, 5 g carbo., 0 g fiber, 0 g pro. **Daily Values:** 2% vit. A, 1% vit. C, 0% calcium, 2% iron

LOW-CALORIE THOUSAND ISLAND DRESSING

START TO FINISH: 15 MINUTES

Fast   **Low-Fat**

- 1/3 cup plain low-fat yogurt
- 2 tablespoons light mayonnaise or salad dressing
- 2 tablespoons chili sauce
- 1 tablespoon finely chopped green or red sweet pepper
- 1 tablespoon finely chopped onion
- 1 tablespoon skim milk
- 1/2 teaspoon paprika
- 1 hard-cooked egg white, finely chopped (optional)

1. In a small mixing bowl stir together the yogurt, mayonnaise or salad dressing, and chili sauce. Stir in the chopped sweet pepper, onion, milk, paprika, and, if desired, chopped egg white. Serve immediately or cover and store in the refrigerator for up to 1 week. Makes about 3/4 cup.

Nutrition Facts per tablespoon: 17 cal., 1 g total fat (0 g sat. fat), 1 mg chol., 57 mg sodium, 1 g carbo., 0 g fiber, 0 g pro. **Daily Values:** 1% vit. A, 2% vit. C, 1% calcium, 0% iron

---

OIL-FREE ORANGE-POPPY SEED DRESSING

PREP: 10 MINUTES   CHILL: 2 HOURS

No-Fat

*Look for powdered fruit pectin with the jam-making supplies
in the grocery store.*

- 1/4 teaspoon finely shredded orange peel
- 1/3 cup orange juice
- 1 tablespoon powdered fruit pectin for lower-sugar recipes
- 1 tablespoon honey
- 1/4 teaspoon poppy seed

1. In a small mixing bowl stir together orange peel, orange juice, pectin, honey, and poppy seed. Cover and chill for 2 hours before serving. Cover and store remaining dressing for up to 3 days. Makes about 1/2 cup.

Nutrition Facts per tablespoon: 18 cal., 0 g total fat, 0 mg chol., 3 mg sodium, 5 g carbo., 0 g fiber, 0 g pro. Daily Values: 0% vit. A, 8% vit. C, 0% calcium, 0% iron

HONEY-LIME DRESSING

START TO FINISH: 15 MINUTES

Fast

$^1/_3$ cup honey
$^1/_2$ teaspoon finely shredded lime peel
$^1/_4$ cup lime juice
$^1/_8$ teaspoon ground nutmeg
$^3/_4$ cup salad oil

1. In a small mixing bowl combine honey, lime peel, lime juice, and nutmeg. Beating with an electric mixer on medium speed, add oil to honey mixture in a thin, steady stream. Continue beating till mixture is thick. Serve immediately or cover and store in the refrigerator up to 2 weeks. Makes about $1^1/_3$ cups.

Nutrition Facts per tablespoon: 86 cal., 8 g total fat (1 g sat. fat), 0 mg chol., 0 mg sodium, 5 g carbo., 0 g fiber, 0 g pro. Daily Values: 0% vit. A, 1% vit. C, 0% calcium, 0% iron

VINAIGRETTE

START TO FINISH: 10 MINUTES

Fast

$^1/_3$ cup salad oil
$^1/_3$ cup white wine vinegar or vinegar
1 tablespoon sugar (optional)
2 teaspoons snipped fresh thyme, oregano, or basil, or $^1/_2$ teaspoon dried thyme, oregano, or basil, crushed
$^1/_2$ teaspoon paprika
$^1/_4$ teaspoon dry mustard or 1 teaspoon Dijon-style mustard (optional)

1. In a screw-top jar combine oil, vinegar, sugar (if desired), herb, paprika, mustard (if desired), and $^1/_8$ teaspoon *pepper*. Cover; shake well. Serve immediately or cover and store in refrigerator up to 2 weeks. Shake before serving. Makes about $^3/_4$ cup.

■ **Italian Vinaigrette:** Prepare as above, except use oregano for the herb and use the mustard. Add 2 tablespoons grated *Parmesan cheese,* $^1/_4$ teaspoon *celery seed,* and 1 *clove garlic,* minced.

■ **Red Wine Vinaigrette:** Prepare as on page 949, except reduce vinegar to 3 tablespoons. Use half *thyme* and half *oregano* for the herb. Add 2 tablespoons dry *red wine* and 1 *clove garlic,* minced.

■ **Garlic Vinaigrette:** Prepare as on page 949, except omit the herb and paprika. Add 2 large *cloves garlic,* minced.

Nutrition Facts per tablespoon: 54 cal., 6 g total fat (1 g sat. fat) 0 mg chol., 0 mg sodium, 1 g carbo., 0 g fiber, 0 g pro.

HERB VINEGAR

PREP: 15 MINUTES   STAND: 2 WEEKS

No-Fat

Allow 2 weeks between preparation and use of this flavorful alternative to plain vinegar.

$^1/_2$ **cup tightly packed fresh tarragon, thyme, mint, rosemary, or basil leaves**
2 **cups white wine vinegar**

1. Wash desired herbs; pat dry with paper towels. In a small stainless-steel or enamel saucepan combine the herbs and vinegar. Bring almost to boiling. Remove from heat and cover loosely with 100% cotton cheesecloth; cool. Pour mixture into a clean 1-quart jar. Cover jar tightly with a nonmetallic lid (or cover the jar with plastic wrap and tightly seal with a metal lid). Let stand in a cool, dark place for 2 weeks.

2. Line a colander with several layers of 100% cotton cheesecloth. Pour vinegar mixture through the colander and let it drain into a bowl. Discard herbs.

3. Transfer strained vinegar to a clean 1$^1/_2$-pint jar or bottle. If desired, add sprig of fresh herb to the jar. Cover jar with a nonmetallic lid (or cover with plastic wrap and tightly seal with a metal lid). Store vinegar in a cool, dark place for up to 6 months. Makes about 2 cups.

Nutrition Facts per tablespoon: 0 cal., 0 g total fat, 0 mg chol., 0 mg sodium, 1 g carbo., 0 g fiber, 0 g pro.

SALAD OIL GLOSSARY

Choosing the right oil is easier when you know the distinguishing characteristics of each. In general, use milder-flavored oils with mild greens, such as Boston, sorrel, oak-leaf, and Bibb lettuce. Use a stronger oil with arugula, radicchio, and other hearty greens.

■ **Nut oil:** Almond oil is clear and pale with a delicate, sweet flavor. Hazelnut and walnut oils are golden-colored with rich aromas and pronounced nut flavors. All usually are used in small amounts and should be refrigerated. Hold bottle under warm water to liquefy the oil before using. If stored for more than a couple of months, check for an "old" odor before using.

■ **Olive oil:** A versatile oil, it is made from pressed olives and sold by grade from "pure" (a blend of lower- and higher-quality oils) to "extra virgin" (richest in aroma and flavor). Color also indicates a flavor difference. Green to greenish gold olive oil is pressed from semiripe olives and tastes slightly sharp. Golden olive oil is pressed from ripe olives and has a more delicate flavor. Store at room temperature for up to 6 months or refrigerate for up to 1 year. If it gets too thick to pour, let it stand at room temperature for a few minutes or run warm water over the bottle.

■ **Salad oil or vegetable oil:** A variety of these oils are made from soybeans, sunflowers, corn, peanuts, canola, and safflower. All are light yellow and have a neutral flavor. They can be stored at room temperature and are best used within 6 to 9 months.

■ **Sesame oil:** This pale yellow oil is made from untoasted sesame seed and has a mild sesame flavor. It is best stored in the refrigerator to delay rancidity.

■ **Toasted sesame oil:** Also called Oriental sesame oil, this thick, brown oil is made from toasted sesame seed. It has a concentrated flavor and is used in small amounts. Refrigerate to keep oil from turning rancid.

VINEGAR GLOSSARY

Due to its acidity, vinegar can be stored at room temperature almost indefinitely. Check these descriptions for a flavor to meet your salad dressing needs.

■ **Balsamic:** Sweet, dark brown vinegar made from the boiled-down juice of a white grape. According to Italian law, balsamic vinegars that are labeled as *aceto balsamico tradizionale* cannot contain any wine vinegar and must be aged at least 12 years.

■ **Cider:** Golden brown with a strong bite and a faint apple flavor.

■ **Fruit:** Made by steeping berries or other fruits in cider or white wine vinegar (see recipe, below).

■ **Herb:** Made by infusing tarragon, basil, dill, or other herbs in cider or white wine vinegar (see recipe, page 950).

■ **Rice:** Clear to pale gold and made from rice wine or sake; has a subtle tang and slightly sweet taste.

■ **White or Distilled:** Colorless vinegar made from grain alcohol; the strongest and sharpest flavored of all vinegars.

■ **Wine:** The color and flavor reflect the source: white, red, or rosé wine; champagne; or sherry.

FRUIT VINEGAR

PREP: 15 MINUTES   STAND: 2 WEEKS

No-Fat

Create your own salad dressings by combining equal amounts of oil and this vinegar.

> 1 cup fresh or frozen unsweetened tart red cherries, blueberries, or raspberries
> 2 cups white wine vinegar

1. Thaw fruit, if frozen. In a small stainless-steel or enamel saucepan combine fruit and vinegar. Bring to boiling; reduce heat. Boil gently, uncovered, for 3 minutes. Remove from heat and cover loosely with 100% cotton cheesecloth; cool.

2. Pour mixture into a clean 1-quart jar. Cover jar tightly with a non-metallic lid (or cover with plastic wrap and tightly seal with a metal lid). Let stand in a cool, dark place for 2 weeks.

3. Line a colander with several layers of 100% cotton cheesecloth. Pour vinegar mixture through the colander and let it drain into a bowl. Discard the fruit.

4. Transfer strained vinegar to a clean 1-pint jar or bottle. If desired, add a few pieces of fresh fruit to the jar or bottle. Cover the jar or bottle tightly with a nonmetallic lid (or cover with plastic wrap and tightly seal with a metal lid).

5. Store vinegar in a cool, dark place for up to 6 months. Makes about $1^1/_2$ cups.

Nutrition Facts per tablespoon: 3 cal., 0 g total fat, 0 mg chol., 0 mg sodium, 2 g carbo., 0 g fiber, 0 g pro. **Daily Values:** 0% vit. A, 1% vit. C, 0% calcium, 1% iron

SAUCES &
RELISHES

SAUCES & RELISHES

WHITE SAUCE

START TO FINISH: 15 MINUTES

> **Fast**

      1 tablespoon butter or margarine
      1 tablespoon all-purpose flour
    $^1/_8$ teaspoon salt
      Dash pepper
    $^3/_4$ cup milk

1. In a small saucepan melt butter or margarine. Stir in flour, salt, and pepper (see photo 1, page 958). Stir in milk all at once (see photo 2, page 958). Cook and stir over medium heat till thickened and bubbly (see photo 3, page 958). Cook and stir 1 minute more. Makes $^3/_4$ cup sauce.

■ **Microwave directions:** In a microwave-safe 2-cup measure, microwave butter or margarine, uncovered, on 100% power (high) for 30 to 40 seconds or till melted. Stir in flour, salt, and pepper. Reduce milk to $^2/_3$ cup; add all at once and stir to combine. Cook, uncovered, on high 2 to 4 minutes or till thickened and bubbly, stirring every 30 seconds.

Nutrition Facts per tablespoon: 18 cal., 1 g total fat (1 g sat. fat), 4 mg chol., 40 mg sodium, 1 g carbo., 0 g fiber, 1 g pro. **Daily Values:** 1% vit. A, 0% vit. C, 1% calcium, 0% iron

■ **Cheese Sauce:** Prepare as above, except omit salt. Over low heat, stir $^3/_4$ cup shredded *process Swiss, American, or Gruyère cheese* or $^1/_4$ cup crumbled *blue cheese* into the cooked sauce till melted. Serve with vegetables. Makes about 1 cup sauce.

Nutrition Facts per tablespoon: 34 cal., 2 g total fat (2 g sat. fat)

■ **Curry Sauce:** Prepare as above, except cook $^1/_2$ to 1 teaspoon *curry powder* in the melted butter or margarine for 1 minute. If desired, stir 1 tablespoon chopped *chutney* into the cooked sauce. Serve with fish or poultry.

Nutrition Facts per tablespoon: 18 cal., 1 g total fat (1 g sat. fat)

■ **Herb-Garlic Sauce:** Prepare as above, except cook 1 clove *garlic*, minced, in the melted butter or margarine for 30 seconds. Stir in $^1/_4$

WHITE SAUCES

White sauces provide the base for numerous recipes. The recipe on page 957 is considered a medium white sauce because of the proportions of flour to milk. It is used for scalloped dishes and creamed dishes as well as many sauces. A thin white sauce is necessary for cream soups and creamed vegetables. To make a thin white sauce, prepare the recipe at left using 1 cup milk. Use the directions below to ensure a successful sauce, free of lumps.

1. Use a heavy saucepan and a wooden spoon. Cook and stir flour and seasonings into melted fat over low heat until evenly combined, making a roux.

2. After the fat and flour are combined with no lumps, stir in the milk all at once. Stir constantly to evenly distribute fat-flour mixture.

3. Stir the sauce over medium heat until the mixture bubbles across the entire surface. Cook and stir for 1 minute longer to completely cook the flour.

teaspoon *caraway seed or celery seed, or dried basil, oregano, or sage,* crushed, with the flour. Serve with vegetables or poultry.

Nutrition Facts per tablespoon: 19 cal., 1 g total fat (1 g sat. fat)

■ **Lemon-Chive Sauce:** Prepare as above, except stir in 1 tablespoon snipped *fresh chives* and ¹/₂ teaspoon finely shredded *lemon peel* with the flour. Serve with vegetables, poultry, or fish.

Nutrition Facts per tablespoon: 18 cal., 1 g total fat (1 g sat. fat)

■ **Parmesan Sauce:** Prepare as above left, except omit salt. Over low heat, stir ¹/₄ cup grated *Parmesan cheese* into the cooked sauce till melted. Serve with beef, pork, poultry, or vegetables.

Nutrition Facts per tablespoon: 28 cal., 2 g total fat (1 g sat. fat)

■ **Sherry Sauce:** Prepare as at left, except stir 1 to 2 tablespoons *dry sherry or dry white wine* into the cooked sauce. Serve with veal.
Nutrition Facts per tablespoon: 20 cal., 1 g total fat (1 g sat. fat)

HOLLANDAISE SAUCE

START TO FINISH: 15 MINUTES

Fast

Well known for its presence in classic Eggs Benedict, this sauce is best when made in a double boiler to prevent overheating it.

¹/₂ **cup butter**
  3 **beaten egg yolks**
  1 **tablespoon water**
  1 **tablespoon lemon juice**
    Dash salt
    Dash white pepper

1. Cut the butter into thirds and bring it to room temperature.
2. In the top of a double boiler combine egg yolks, water, lemon juice, salt, and pepper. Add a piece of the butter. Place over boiling water (upper pan should not touch water). Cook, stirring rapidly with a whisk, till butter melts and sauce begins to thicken. Add the remaining butter, a piece at a time, stirring constantly till melted. Continue to cook and stir till sauce thickens (about 2 minutes more).

Immediately remove from heat. If sauce is too thick or curdles, immediately whisk in 1 to 2 tablespoons *hot water*. Serve with cooked vegetables, poultry, fish, or eggs. Makes ³/₄ cup sauce.

Nutrition Facts per tablespoon: 83 cal., 9 g total fat (5 g sat. fat), 74 mg chol., 91 mg sodium, 0 g carbo., 0 g fiber, 1 g pro. **Daily Values:** 17% vit. A, 0% vit. C, 0% calcium, 0% iron

MOCK HOLLANDAISE SAUCE

START TO FINISH: 10 MINUTES

Fast

  ¹/₄ **cup dairy sour cream**
  ¹/₄ **cup mayonnaise or salad dressing**
  1 **teaspoon lemon juice**
  ¹/₂ **teaspoon prepared mustard**

1. In a small saucepan combine sour cream, mayonnaise or salad dressing, lemon juice, and mustard. Cook and stir over low heat till hot. Serve with vegetables, poultry, fish, or eggs. Makes ¹/₂ cup sauce.

Nutrition Facts per tablespoon: 65 cal., 7 g total fat (2 g sat. fat), 7 mg chol., 47 mg sodium, 1 g carbo., 0 g fiber, 0 g pro. **Daily Values:** 2% vit. A, 0% vit. C, 0% calcium, 0% iron

BEARNAISE SAUCE

START TO FINISH: 15 MINUTES

Fast

  ¹/₂ **cup butter**
  3 **tablespoons white wine vinegar**
  1 **teaspoon finely chopped green onion**
  1 **teaspoon snipped fresh tarragon or ¹/₄ teaspoon dried tarragon, crushed**
  ¹/₄ **teaspoon snipped fresh chervil or pinch dried chervil, crushed**
  ¹/₈ **teaspoon white pepper**
  4 **beaten egg yolks**
  1 **tablespoon water**

1. Cut butter into thirds; bring it to room temperature. In a small saucepan combine vinegar, green onion, tarragon, chervil, and pepper. Bring to boiling; boil, uncovered, on high for 2 minutes or till reduced by about half.

2. In the top of a double boiler combine vinegar mixture, egg yolks, and water. Add a piece of the butter. Place over boiling water (upper pan should not touch water). Cook, stirring rapidly with a whisk, till butter melts and sauce begins to thicken. Add the remaining butter, a piece at a time, stirring constantly till melted. Continue to cook and stir till sauce is thickened (1 to 2 minutes more). Immediately remove saucepan from heat. If sauce is too thick or curdles, immediately whisk in 1 to 2 tablespoons *hot water.* Serve with beef, pork, or poultry. Makes $3/4$ cup sauce.

Nutrition Facts per tablespoon: 88 cal., 9 g total fat (5 g sat. fat), 92 mg chol., 92 mg sodium, 0 g carbo., 0 g fiber, 1 g pro. **Daily Values:** 20% vit. A, 0% vit. C, 0% calcium, 1% iron

---

CREAMY MUSHROOM SAUCE

START TO FINISH: 20 MINUTES

Fast

   1 cup sliced fresh mushrooms
 $1/4$ cup chopped onion
   1 tablespoon butter or margarine
   1 tablespoon all-purpose flour
 $1/4$ teaspoon salt
 $1/8$ teaspoon pepper
 $2/3$ cup milk
 $1/2$ cup dairy sour cream or plain yogurt

1. In a medium saucepan cook mushrooms and onion in butter or margarine till tender. Stir in flour, salt, and pepper. Stir in milk all at once. Cook and stir over medium heat till thickened and bubbly. Cook and stir for 1 minute more. Stir in sour cream or yogurt; heat through, but do not boil. Serve with beef or poultry. Makes about $1^1/2$ cups sauce.

Nutrition Facts per tablespoon: 21 cal., 2 g total fat (1 g sat. fat), 4 mg chol., 33 mg sodium, 1 g carbo., 0 g fiber, 1 g pro. **Daily Values:** 1% vit. A, 0% vit. C, 1% calcium, 0% iron

BORDELAISE SAUCE

START TO FINISH: 30 MINUTES

Fast

 $1^1/2$ cups water
 $^3/4$ cup dry red wine
 2 tablespoons finely chopped shallot or onion
 1 teaspoon instant beef bouillon granules
 $^1/2$ teaspoon dried thyme, crushed
 1 bay leaf
 3 tablespoons butter or margarine, softened
 2 tablespoons all-purpose flour
 1 tablespoon snipped fresh parsley

1. In a medium saucepan combine water, red wine, shallot or onion, bouillon granules, thyme, and bay leaf. Bring to boiling; reduce heat. Simmer, uncovered, for 15 to 20 minutes (you should have about $1^1/3$ cups). Remove bay leaf. Stir together butter or margarine and flour. Add to wine mixture. Cook and stir till thickened and bubbly. Cook and stir for 1 minute more. Stir in parsley. Serve with broiled or grilled meats. Makes about 1 cup sauce.

Nutrition Facts per tablespoon: 32 cal., 2 g total fat (1 g sat. fat), 6 mg chol., 87 mg sodium, 1 g carbo., 0 g fiber, 0 g pro. **Daily Values:** 4% vit. A, 0% vit. C, 0% calcium, 1% iron

---

SUCCESSFUL SAUCES

For a perfect sauce every time, follow the recipe directions and remember these tips.
■ Prevent lumps in sauces thickened with cornstarch or flour by stirring constantly. If lumps do form, beat the sauce briskly with a wire whisk or a rotary beater.
■ Cook sauces over low to medium heat unless the recipe says otherwise. And, cook your sauces no longer than the time specified. High heat and lengthy cooking can cause sauces to curdle or break down.
■ If it's necessary to leave the sauce during cooking, remove the sauce from the heat.

SAUCE PROVENÇALE

START TO FINISH: 30 MINUTES

Fast

*Tomatoes, garlic, and olive oil associate this sauce
with Provence, France.*

  3 medium tomatoes, peeled, seeded, and chopped (about 1
        pound)
$^1/_2$ teaspoon sugar
$^1/_4$ cup sliced green onions (2)
  1 clove garlic, minced
  1 tablespoon olive oil or cooking oil
$^1/_2$ cup dry white wine
  2 tablespoons snipped fresh parsley

1. Sprinkle chopped tomatoes with sugar; set aside. In a medium
saucepan cook green onions and garlic in olive oil till tender. Stir in
tomato mixture, wine, and parsley. Bring to boiling; reduce heat.
Boil gently, uncovered, for 10 minutes (you should have about 1$^1/_4$
cups). Serve with beef or pork. Makes 1$^1/_4$ cups sauce.

Nutrition Facts per tablespoon: 16 cal., 1 g total fat (0 g sat. fat), 0 mg chol., 3 mg sodium,
1 g carbo., 0 g fiber, 0 g pro. **Daily Values:** 1% vit. A, 8% vit. C, 0% calcium, 1% iron

---

BARBECUE SAUCE

START TO FINISH: 20 MINUTES

Fast   **No-Fat**

*Vary the hotness by adjusting the amount of hot pepper sauce
that's added.*

  1 cup catsup
$^1/_2$ cup water
$^1/_4$ cup finely chopped onion or 1 tablespoon dried minced onion
$^1/_4$ cup vinegar
  1 to 2 tablespoons sugar
  1 tablespoon Worcestershire sauce
$^1/_4$ teaspoon celery seed
$^1/_4$ teaspoon salt
        Several dashes bottled hot pepper sauce

1. In a saucepan combine catsup, water, onion, vinegar, sugar, Worcestershire sauce, celery seed, salt, and hot pepper sauce. Bring to boiling; reduce heat. Simmer, uncovered, 10 to 15 minutes or to desired consistency. Brush on beef, pork, or poultry during last 10 to 20 minutes of grilling or roasting. If desired, pass any remaining sauce. Makes 1³/₄ cups sauce.

■ **Hot Barbecue Sauce:** Prepare as above, except add 1 teaspoon *chili powder* and ¹/₂ teaspoon *ground red pepper* with the catsup.

■ **Tangy Mustard Barbecue Sauce:** Prepare as above, except omit celery seed. Add 2 tablespoons *prepared mustard* and ¹/₄ teaspoon *garlic powder* with the catsup.

Nutrition Facts per tablespoon: 13 cal., 0 g total fat, 0 mg chol., 140 mg sodium, 4 g carbo., 0 g fiber, 0 g pro. **Daily Values:** 1% vit. A, 4% vit. C, 0% calcium, 0% iron

---

SWEET-AND-SOUR SAUCE

START TO FINISH: 20 MINUTES

Fast　　　　　　　　　　**No-Fat**

¹/₂ cup packed brown sugar
4 teaspoons cornstarch
¹/₂ cup chicken broth
¹/₃ cup red wine vinegar
¹/₄ cup finely chopped green sweet pepper
2 tablespoons chopped pimiento
2 tablespoons corn syrup
2 tablespoons soy sauce
2 teaspoons grated gingerroot
1 clove garlic, minced

1. In a small saucepan combine brown sugar and cornstarch. Stir in chicken broth, vinegar, sweet pepper, pimiento, corn syrup, soy sauce, gingerroot, and garlic. Cook and stir till thickened and bubbly. Cook and stir for 2 minutes more. Serve warm. Makes about 1¹/₃ cups sauce.

Nutrition Facts per tablespoon: 26 cal., 0 g total fat, 0 mg chol., 119 mg sodium, 7 g carbo., 0 g fiber, 0 g pro. **Daily Values:** 0% vit. A, 3% vit. C, 0% calcium, 1% iron

COCKTAIL SAUCE

START TO FINISH: 10 MINUTES

Fast   **No-Fat**

3/4 **cup bottled chili sauce**
2 **tablespoons lemon juice**
2 **tablespoons thinly sliced green onion (1)**
1 **tablespoon prepared horseradish**
2 **teaspoons Worcestershire sauce**
   Several dashes bottled hot pepper sauce

1. In a mixing bowl combine chili sauce, lemon juice, green onion, horseradish, Worcestershire sauce, and hot pepper sauce. Cover and store in refrigerator for up to 2 weeks. Serve with fish or seafood. Makes about 1 cup sauce.

Nutrition Facts per tablespoon: 13 cal., 0 g total fat, 0 mg chol., 167 mg sodium, 3 g carbo., 0 g fiber, 0 g pro. **Daily Values:** 1% vit. A, 6% vit. C, 0% calcium, 0% iron

---

HORSERADISH SAUCE

START TO FINISH: 10 MINUTES

Fast

1/2 **cup whipping cream**
2 **to 3 tablespoons prepared horseradish**

1. In a mixing bowl beat whipping cream till soft peaks form. Fold in horseradish. Cover and store in the refrigerator for up to 24 hours. Serve with beef or pork. Makes 1 cup sauce.

Nutrition Facts per tablespoon: 26 cal., 3 g total fat (2 g sat. fat), 10 mg chol., 23 mg sodium, 0 g carbo., 0 g fiber, 0 g pro. **Daily Values:** 3% vit. A, 0% vit. C, 0% calcium, 0% iron

■ **Mustard Sauce:** Prepare as above, except substitute 2 tablespoons *Dijon-style mustard* for the horseradish.

Nutrition Facts per tablespoon: 28 cal., 3 g total fat (2 g sat. fat)

TARTAR SAUCE

PREP: 10 MINUTES   CHILL: 2 HOURS

Save a little time by using ¼ cup drained sweet or dill pickle relish instead of chopping whole pickles.

   1 cup mayonnaise or salad dressing
   ¼ cup finely chopped sweet pickle or dill pickle
   1 tablespoon finely chopped onion
   1 tablespoon snipped fresh parsley
   1 tablespoon diced pimiento
   1 teaspoon lemon juice

1. In a bowl combine the mayonnaise or salad dressing, pickle, onion, parsley, pimiento, and lemon juice. Cover; chill for at least 2 hours before serving. Store in the refrigerator up to 2 weeks. Serve with fish or seafood. Makes 1¼ cups sauce.

Nutrition Facts per tablespoon: 84 cal., 9 g total fat (1 g sat. fat), 6 mg chol., 96 mg sodium, 2 g carbo., 0 g fiber, 0 g pro. **Daily Values:** 1% vit. A, 1% vit. C, 0% calcium, 0% iron

■ **Low-Fat Tartar Sauce:** Prepare as above, except substitute ⅔ cup *light mayonnaise or salad dressing* and ⅓ cup *plain yogurt* for the mayonnaise or salad dressing. Omit lemon juice.

Nutrition Facts per tablespoon: 34 cal., 3 g total fat (1 g sat. fat)

SAUCE VÉRONIQUE

START TO FINISH: 20 MINUTES

Fast   **No-Fat**

Véronique (vay roh NEEK) indicates a dish prepared or garnished with seedless grapes.

   1 cup chicken broth
   ⅓ cup milk, half-and-half, or light cream
   1 tablespoon all-purpose flour
   ¼ teaspoon finely shredded lemon peel
      Dash ground nutmeg
   ½ cup seedless grapes, halved

1. In a medium saucepan bring chicken broth to boiling; reduce heat. Boil gently, uncovered, for 4 to 5 minutes (you should have ¹/₂ cup). Combine the milk, flour, lemon peel, and nutmeg; stir into chicken broth. Cook and stir over medium heat till thickened and bubbly. Stir in grapes. Cook and stir 1 minute more. Serve with fish or poultry. Makes 1¹/₄ cups sauce.

Nutrition Facts per tablespoon: 8 cal., 0 g total fat, 0 mg chol., 41 mg sodium, 1 g carbo., 0 g fiber, 0 g pro.

PLUM SAUCE

START TO FINISH: 15 MINUTES

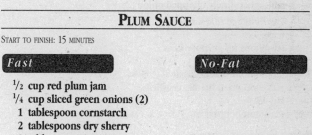

Fast   No-Fat

¹/₂ cup red plum jam
¹/₄ cup sliced green onions (2)
 1 tablespoon cornstarch
 2 tablespoons dry sherry
 2 tablespoons soy sauce
 1 tablespoon vinegar

1. In a small saucepan combine jam, green onions, and cornstarch. Stir in sherry, soy sauce, and vinegar. Cook and stir till thickened and bubbly. Cook and stir 2 minutes more. Serve with beef, pork, or poultry. Makes ³/₄ cup sauce.

Nutrition Facts per tablespoon: 44 cal., 0 g total fat, 0 mg chol., 173 mg sodium, 11 g carbo., 0 g fiber, 0 g pro. **Daily Values:** 0% vit. A, 0% vit. C, 0% calcium, 1% iron

DEMI-GLACÉ SAUCE

START TO FINISH: 1 HOUR

This spin-off of the traditional French brown sauce is worth the time it takes to prepare. If you make it ahead, chill the sauce for up to 24 hours and reheat it over low heat.

- ¹/₂ cup onion, chopped (1 medium)
- ¹/₂ cup sliced carrot (1 medium)
- ¹/₄ cup butter or margarine
- 2 teaspoons sugar
- 4 teaspoons all-purpose flour
- 1¹/₂ cups beef broth
- 2 tablespoons tomato paste
- ¹/₂ teaspoon dried thyme, crushed
- 1 bay leaf
- ¹/₈ teaspoon pepper

1. In a medium saucepan cook onion and carrot in butter or margarine over medium heat till tender. Stir in sugar. Cook and stir for 10 minutes or till vegetables are translucent and onions are turning golden brown. Stir in the flour. Cook and stir for 6 to 8 minutes more or till flour is brown. Add the beef broth, tomato paste, thyme, bay leaf, and pepper. Bring broth mixture to boiling. Reduce heat; simmer, uncovered, for 30 minutes or till mixture is reduced to about 1¹/₃ cups. Strain out and discard vegetables. Serve with beef, pork, or lamb. Makes about 1 cup sauce.

Nutrition Facts per tablespoon: 38 cal., 3 g total fat (2 g sat. fat), 8 mg chol., 108 mg sodium, 3 g carbo., 0 g fiber, 1 g pro. **Daily Values:** 17% vit. A, 2% vit. C, 0% calcium, 1% iron

---

YOGURT-DILL SAUCE

START TO FINISH: 5 MINUTES

Fast   **No-Fat**

- 1 8-ounce carton plain yogurt or dairy sour cream
- 1 tablespoon snipped fresh dill or 1 teaspoon dried dillweed
- ¹/₄ teaspoon pepper
- ¹/₈ teaspoon garlic powder

1. In a mixing bowl combine yogurt or sour cream, dill, pepper, and garlic powder. Chill till serving time. Serve with fish or seafood. Makes about 1 cup sauce.

Nutrition Facts per tablespoon: 9 cal., 0 g total fat, 1 mg chol., 10 mg sodium, 1 g carbo., 0 g fiber, 1 g pro. **Daily Values:** 0% vit. A, 0% vit. C, 2% calcium, 0% iron

■ **Yogurt-Cucumber-Mint Sauce:** Prepare as above, except omit dill. Pat ¹/₂ cup shredded *cucumber* with a paper towel to remove excess liquid. Stir into yogurt mixture along with ¹/₄ teaspoon *dried mint*, crushed. Serve with lamb.

Nutrition Facts per tablespoon: 10 cal., 0 g total fat

CRANBERRY SAUCE

START TO FINISH: 20 MINUTES

Fast	No-Fat

1 cup sugar
1 cup water
2 cups cranberries (8 ounces)

1. In a medium saucepan combine sugar and water. Bring to boiling, stirring to dissolve sugar. Boil rapidly for 5 minutes. Add cranberries. Return to boiling; reduce heat. Boil gently, uncovered, over medium-high heat for 3 to 4 minutes or till skins pop, stirring occasionally. Remove from heat. Serve warm or chilled with poultry or pork. Makes about 2 cups sauce.

■ **Molded Cranberry Sauce:** Prepare as above, except gently boil cranberry mixture for 13 to 16 minutes or till a drop gels on a cold plate. Pour into a 1¹/₂-cup mold and chill till firm.

Nutrition Facts per tablespoon: 28 cal., 0 g total fat, 0 mg chol., 0 mg sodium, 7 g carbo., 0 g fiber, 0 g pro. **Daily Values:** 0% vit. A, 1% vit. C, 0% calcium, 0% iron

CHERRY SAUCE

START TO FINISH: 20 MINUTES

Fast　　　　　　　　　　**No-Fat**

3 tablespoons brown sugar
4 teaspoons cornstarch
1/4 teaspoon ground cinnamon
Dash ground cloves
1 cup apple juice
1 tablespoon vinegar
Few drops red food coloring (optional)
1 16-ounce can pitted tart red cherries (water pack), drained

1. In a medium saucepan combine brown sugar, cornstarch, cinnamon, and cloves. Stir in apple juice, vinegar, and, if desired, food coloring. Cook and stir over medium heat till thickened and bubbly. Cook and stir for 2 minutes more. Stir in drained cherries. Heat through. Serve warm with ham, pork, or poultry. Makes 2 1/4 cups sauce.

Nutrition Facts per tablespoon: 17 cal., 0 g total fat, 0 mg chol., 1 mg sodium, 4 g carbo., 0 g fiber, 0 g pro. **Daily Values:** 0% vit. A, 0% vit. C, 0% calcium, 1% iron

---

ORANGE SAUCE

START TO FINISH: 20 MINUTES

Fast

For an easy variation, stir in 1/2 cup seedless red or green grapes along with the orange sections.

2 medium oranges
1 tablespoon cornstarch
1 tablespoon butter or margarine
1 teaspoon honey
1/2 teaspoon instant chicken bouillon granules

1. Finely shred 1 teaspoon *orange peel;* set aside. Peel and section *one* orange over a bowl to catch juice; set aside. Squeeze juice from remaining orange. Measure orange juice; add enough water to equal 2/3 cup.

2. In a small saucepan stir juice mixture into cornstarch. Add butter or margarine, honey, and bouillon granules. Cook and stir till thickened and bubbly. Cook and stir 2 minutes more. Stir in orange peel and orange sections. Heat through. Serve with fish, pork, or poultry. Makes 1 cup sauce.

Nutrition Facts per tablespoon: 16 cal., 1 g total fat (0 g sat. fat), 2 mg chol., 34 mg sodium, 2 g carbo., 0 g fiber, 0 g pro. **Daily Values:** 0% vit. A, 12% vit. C, 0% calcium, 0% iron

PICKLED BEETS

PREP: 10 MINUTES   COOL: 30 MINUTES   CHILL: 8 HOURS

No-Fat

When fresh beets are available, use 2 cups sliced, cooked fresh beets instead of canned beets.

  $^{1}/_{3}$ **cup vinegar**
  $^{1}/_{4}$ **cup sugar**
  $^{1}/_{4}$ **cup water**
  $^{1}/_{2}$ **teaspoon ground cinnamon**
  $^{1}/_{4}$ **teaspoon salt**
  $^{1}/_{4}$ **teaspoon ground cloves**
   1 **16-ounce can sliced beets, drained**

1. In a medium saucepan combine vinegar, sugar, water, cinnamon, salt, and cloves. Bring to boiling, stirring occasionally. Stir in drained beets. Return to boiling; reduce heat. Cover and simmer for 5 minutes. Cool for 30 minutes. Chill beets in liquid at least 8 hours before serving. Cover and store in liquid in the refrigerator up to 1 month. Drain before serving. Makes 8 servings.

Nutrition Facts per serving: 34 cal., 0 g total fat, 0 mg chol., 82 mg sodium, 9 g carbo., 1 g fiber, 0 g pro. **Daily Values:** 0% vit. A, 2% vit. C, 0% calcium, 2% iron

MANGO-GINGER CHUTNEY

PREP: 20 MINUTES   COOK: 15 MINUTES

No-Fat

When you make this colorful chutney with mangoes, you easily can prepare the mangoes by following these steps. Slide a sharp knife next to the seed along one side of the mango, cutting through the fruit. Repeat on the other side of the seed to divide into two large pieces. Then cut away all of the meat that remains around the seed. Remove all of the peel and chop the meat.

- ¹/₂ **cup packed brown sugar**
- ¹/₂ **cup dried tart cherries, dried cranberries, or raisins**
- ¹/₃ **cup vinegar**
- ¹/₄ **cup chopped onion**
- 1 **teaspoon grated gingerroot**
- ¹/₄ **teaspoon crushed red pepper**
- 3 **cups chopped, peeled mangoes (about 3 mangoes)**

1. In a medium saucepan combine brown sugar, dried cherries, vinegar, onion, gingerroot, and crushed red pepper. Bring to boiling; reduce heat. Simmer, uncovered, for 15 minutes, stirring occasionally. Stir in mangoes; heat through. Let cool. Cover and store in the refrigerator up to 4 weeks. Or, freeze up to 12 months. Serve with beef, pork, ham, lamb, or poultry. Makes about 2¹/₂ cups.

Nutrition Facts per tablespoon: 19 cal., 0 g total fat, 0 mg chol., 1 mg sodium, 5 g carbo., 0 g fiber, 0 g pro. **Daily Values:** 4% vit. A, 3% vit. C, 0% calcium, 0% iron

■ **Peach-Ginger Chutney:** Prepare as above, except substitute chopped peeled *fresh peaches or frozen peach slices*, thawed and chopped, for the mangoes.

Nutrition Facts per tablespoon: 19 cal., 0 g total fat

SPICED APPLE RINGS

START TO FINISH: 1 HOUR

No-Fat

- 4 **small cooking apples**
- ¹/₃ **cup red cinnamon candies***

$^1/_4$ **cup sugar**
2 **cups water**

1. If desired, peel apples; core and cut crosswise into $^1/_2$-inch rings.
2. For syrup, in a large skillet combine cinnamon candies and sugar; stir in water. Cook and stir over medium heat till liquid boils and candies dissolve. Add apples to syrup. Bring to boiling; reduce heat. Simmer, uncovered, for 10 to 15 minutes or till tender, spooning syrup over apples occasionally. Cool apples in syrup. Cover and store in syrup in the refrigerator up to 1 month. Drain before serving. Serve with ham, pork, or poultry. Makes 6 servings.
*Note: If desired, substitute 6 inches *stick cinnamon*, broken, for the cinnamon candies and increase sugar to $^3/_4$ cup. Cook and stir over medium heat till boiling. Cover and simmer 5 minutes. Add apples to syrup and continue as directed.

Nutrition Facts per serving: 129 cal., 0 g total fat, 0 mg chol., 3 mg sodium, 34 g carbo., 2 g fiber, 0 g pro. **Daily Values:** 0% vit. A, 8% vit. C, 0% calcium, 1% iron

---

CRANBERRY RELISH

PREP: 15 MINUTES   CHILL: 2 HOURS

Low-Fat

$^3/_4$ **cup apple juice or orange juice**
$^1/_2$ **to $^2/_3$ cup sugar**
$^1/_4$ **teaspoon ground cinnamon**
$^1/_4$ **teaspoon ground nutmeg**
   Dash ground cloves
1 **12-ounce package (3 cups) cranberries**
$^1/_2$ **cup light raisins**
$^1/_2$ **cup chopped pecans**

1. In a saucepan combine apple juice, sugar, cinnamon, nutmeg, and cloves. Cook and stir over medium heat till sugar is dissolved. Add the cranberries and raisins. Bring to boiling; reduce heat. Cook and stir for 3 to 4 minutes or till cranberries pop. Remove from heat. Stir in pecans. Cover and chill at least 2 hours before serving. Serve with poultry, pork, or ham. Store in the refrigerator up to 2 days. Makes about 2$^1/_2$ cups relish.

Nutrition Facts per tablespoon: 31 cal., 1 g total fat, (0 g sat. fat), 0 mg chol., 1 mg sodium, 6 g carbo., 1 g fiber, 0 g pro. **Daily Values:** 0% vit. A, 2% vit. C, 0% calcium, 0% iron

REFRIGERATOR CORN RELISH

START TO FINISH: 1 HOUR

No-Fat

1 10-ounce package frozen whole kernel corn
1/3 cup sugar
1 tablespoon cornstarch
1/2 cup vinegar
1/4 cup chopped celery
1/4 cup chopped green or red sweet pepper
2 tablespoons chopped pimiento
1 tablespoon dried minced onion
1 teaspoon ground turmeric
1/2 teaspoon dry mustard

1. Cook corn according to package directions; drain. In a pan combine sugar and cornstarch; stir in vinegar and 1/3 cup *cold water*. Stir in corn, celery, sweet pepper, pimiento, onion, turmeric, mustard, and 1/4 teaspoon *salt*. Cook and stir till thickened and bubbly. Cook and stir for 2 minutes more; cool. Cover; store in the refrigerator up to 4 weeks. Serve with beef, pork, or poultry. Makes about 2 1/2 cups relish.

Nutrition Facts per tablespoon: 15 cal., 0 g total fat, 0 mg chol., 15 mg sodium, 4 g carbo., 0 g fiber, 0 g pro. **Daily Values:** 0% vit. A, 3% vit. C, 0% calcium, 0% iron

SAUERKRAUT RELISH

PREP: 15 MINUTES CHILL: 2 HOURS

No-Fat

1/4 cup sugar
1/2 teaspoon prepared mustard
1/4 cup vinegar
1/8 teaspoon garlic powder
1/8 teaspoon pepper
1 8-ounce can sauerkraut, drained
1/4 cup chopped green or red sweet pepper
1/4 cup chopped cucumber
1/4 cup chopped onion

1. In a bowl combine sugar and mustard. Stir in vinegar, garlic powder, and pepper. Stir in sauerkraut, sweet pepper, cucumber, and onion. Cover and chill at least 2 hours before serving. Serve with frankfurters or bratwurst. Store in the refrigerator up to 2 days. Makes about 2 cups relish.

Nutrition Facts per tablespoon: 8 cal., 0 g total fat, 0 mg chol., 48 mg sodium, 2 g carbo., 0 g fiber, 0 g pro. **Daily Values:** 0% vit. A, 3% vit. C, 0% calcium, 0% iron

CUCUMBER-RADISH RELISH

PREP: 20 MINUTES   CHILL: 8 HOURS

No-Fat

Instead of using traditional radishes, try daikons in this fiery relish. A daikon is a long, carrot-shaped Japanese radish. Its flesh is juicy and white with a mildly spicy, radishlike flavor.

    1 cup finely chopped seeded cucumber
    1 cup finely chopped radishes or daikons
  1/4 cup finely chopped onion
    3 tablespoons lime juice
    1 tablespoon sugar
    1 teaspoon grated gingerroot
  1/4 teaspoon salt
  1/4 to 1/2 teaspoon chili oil
    1 clove garlic, minced

1. In a medium mixing bowl combine cucumber, radishes or daikons, onion, lime juice, sugar, gingerroot, salt, chili oil, and garlic. Cover and chill at least 8 hours before serving, stirring once or twice. Serve with hamburgers or frankfurters. Store in the refrigerator up to 2 days. Makes 1³/₄ cups relish.

Nutrition Facts per tablespoon: 4 cal., 0 g total fat, 0 mg chol., 20 mg sodium, 1 g carbo., 0 g fiber, 0 g pro. **Daily Values:** 0% vit. A, 1% vit. C, 0% calcium, 0% iron

SOUPS & STEWS

SOUPS & STEWS

CHICKEN BROTH

PREP: 20 MINUTES COOK: 2 HOURS

An unpeeled yellow onion will add a rich color to this broth.

2½ **pounds bony chicken pieces (wings, backs, and necks)**
3 **stalks celery with leaves, cut up**
2 **carrots, cut up**
1 **large onion, cut up**
2 **sprigs fresh parsley**
½ **teaspoon dried thyme, sage, or basil, crushed**
2 **bay leaves**

1. In a large pot place chicken pieces, celery, carrots, onion, parsley, thyme, bay leaves, 1 teaspoon *salt*, and ¼ teaspoon *pepper*. Add 6 cups cold *water*. Bring to boiling; reduce heat. Cover and simmer for 2 hours. Remove chicken.

2. Strain broth (see photo, below). Discard vegetables and seasonings. If desired, clarify broth.* If using the broth while hot, skim fat. Or chill, then lift off fat (see tip, page 1002). If desired, when bones are cool enough to handle, remove meat from bones and reserve meat for another use. Discard bones. Refrigerate broth and any reserved meat in separate covered containers up to 3 days or freeze up to 6 months. Makes about 6 cups broth and about 2½ cups meat.

*Note: To clarify, combine ¼ cup cold *water* and 1 *egg white;* stir into hot, strained broth in the pot or kettle. Bring to boiling. Remove from heat; let stand 5 minutes. Strain broth.

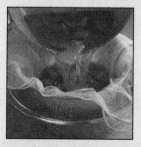

Line a large colander or sieve with 2 layers of 100% cotton cheesecloth. Set colander in a large heatproof bowl; carefully pour broth through it.

■ **Crockery-cooker directions:** In a 3½- or 4-quart electric crockery cooker (see tip, page 985) combine chicken pieces, celery, carrots, onion, parsley, thyme, bay leaves, 1 teaspoon *salt,* and ¼ teaspoon *pepper.* Add only 4 cups *water.* Cover and cook on low-heat setting 8 to 10 hours or on high-heat setting 4 to 5 hours. Remove chicken. Strain; store broth and meat as above. Makes about 5½ cups broth and about 2½ cups meat.

Nutrition Facts per cup broth: 30 cal., 2 g total fat (1 g sat. fat), 5 mg chol., 435 mg sodium, 1 g carbo., 0 g fiber, 2 g pro. **Daily Values:** 0% vit. A, 0% vit. C, 1% calcium, 1% iron

---

BEEF BROTH

PREP: 30 MINUTES   BAKE: 30 MINUTES   COOK: 3½ HOURS   Oven 450°

Add the leftover cooked meat to soups, stews, or casseroles.

  4 **pounds meaty beef soup bones (beef shank crosscuts or short ribs)**
  3 **carrots, cut up**
  2 **medium onions, cut up**
  2 **stalks celery with leaves, cut up**
  8 **sprigs fresh parsley**
 10 **black peppercorns**
  1 **tablespoon dried basil or thyme, crushed**
  4 **bay leaves**
  2 **cloves garlic, halved**

1. Place soup bones in a large shallow roasting pan. Bake in a 450° oven about 30 minutes or till well browned, turning once. Place soup bones in a large pot. Pour ½ cup *water* into the roasting pan, scraping up crusty browned bits. Add water mixture to pot. Add carrots, onions, celery, parsley, black peppers, basil, bay leaves, garlic, and 1½ teaspoons *salt.* Add 10 cups *water.* Bring to boiling; reduce heat. Cover and simmer for 3½ hours. Remove soup bones.

2. Strain broth (see photo, page 979). Discard vegetables and seasonings. If desired, clarify broth (see note page 979). If using the broth while hot, skim fat. Or chill, then lift off fat (see tip, page 1002). If desired, when bones are cool enough to handle, remove meat from bones and reserve meat for another use. Discard bones. Refrigerate broth and any reserved meat in separate covered containers up to 3 days or freeze up to 6 months. Makes about 8 cups broth and about 2 cups meat.

■ **Crockery-cooker directions:** Reduce soup bones to 3 pounds. In a large skillet brown soup bones on all sides in 1 tablespoon *cooking oil*. In a 4- or 5-quart electric crockery cooker (see tip, page 985) combine carrots, onions, celery, parsley, black peppers, basil, bay leaves, garlic, and 1½ teaspoons *salt*. Add soup bones and only 6 cups *water*. Cover and cook on low-heat setting 10 to 12 hours or on high-heat setting for 5 to 6 hours. Remove soup bones. Strain and store broth and meat as above. Makes about 7 cups broth and 1½ cups meat.

Nutrition Facts per cup broth: 20 cal., 1 g total fat (1 g sat. fat), 5 mg chol., 409 mg sodium, 1 g carbo., 0 g fiber, 2 g pro. **Daily Values:** 0% vit. A, 0% vit. C, 1% calcium, 1% iron

---

OLD-FASHIONED BEEF STEW

PREP: 20 MINUTES   COOK: 1½ HOURS

Low-Fat

    2 tablespoons all-purpose flour
    1 pound beef or pork stew meat, cut into ³/₄-inch cubes
    2 tablespoons cooking oil
    3 cups vegetable juice
    1 cup water
    1 medium onion, cut into thin wedges
    1 teaspoon instant beef bouillon granules
    1 teaspoon Worcestershire sauce
  ½ teaspoon dried marjoram, crushed
  ½ teaspoon dried oregano, crushed
    1 bay leaf
2½ cups cubed potatoes (about 3 medium)
    1 cup frozen cut green beans
    1 cup frozen whole kernel corn
    1 cup sliced carrots (2 medium)

1. Place flour in a plastic bag. Add meat cubes, a few at a time, shaking to coat. In a large saucepan or pot brown meat, half at a time, in hot oil. Drain fat. Return all meat to saucepan. Stir in the vegetable juice, water, onion, bouillon granules, Worcestershire sauce, marjoram, oregano, bay leaf, and ¼ teaspoon *pepper*. Bring to boiling; reduce heat. Cover and simmer for 1 to 1¼ hours for beef (about 30 minutes for pork) or till meat is nearly tender. Stir in potatoes, green beans, corn, and carrots. Bring to boiling; reduce heat. Cover and simmer about 30 minutes more or till meat and vegetables are tender. Discard bay leaf. Makes about 9 cups (6 main-dish servings).

■ **Crockery-cooker directions:** Prepare and brown meat as above. In the bottom of a 3¹/₂- or 4-quart electric crockery cooker (see tip, page 985) layer meat, onion, potatoes, green beans, corn, and carrots. Decrease vegetable juice to 2 cups. Combine vegetable juice, water, bouillon granules, Worcestershire sauce, marjoram, oregano, bay leaf, and ¹/₄ teaspoon *pepper*. Pour over meat and vegetables in crockery cooker. Cover and cook on low-heat setting for 10 to 12 hours or on high-heat setting for 5 to 6 hours or till meat and vegetables are tender.

Nutrition Facts per serving: 281 cal., 6 g total fat (2 g sat. fat), 48 mg chol., 655 mg sodium, 35 g carbo., 2 g fiber, 22 g pro. **Daily Values:** 72% vit. A, 81% vit. C, 4% calcium, 28% iron

BROTH SUBSTITUTIONS

When a recipe calls for chicken broth or beef broth, you can make your own using one of the recipes on pages 979, 980. But if you're in a hurry, choose from one of several broth substitutes that are available.

Canned chicken and beef broth are ready to use straight from the can (low-sodium versions are available, too). Instant bouillon granules or cubes can be purchased in beef, chicken, or vegetable flavors. One teaspoon of granules or 1 cube mixed with 1 cup water makes an easy broth. Cans of condensed chicken or beef broth also can be used, but remember to dilute them according to the label directions.

HAMBURGER-VEGETABLE SOUP

PREP: 20 MINUTES   COOK: 15 MINUTES

Low-Fat

  1 pound ground beef or ground pork
$^1/_2$ cup chopped onion (1 medium)
$^1/_2$ cup chopped green sweet pepper
  4 cups beef broth (see tip, below)
  1 cup frozen whole kernel corn
  1 7$^1/_2$-ounce can tomatoes, cut up (see tip, page 999)
$^1/_2$ of a 9-ounce package frozen lima beans
$^1/_2$ cup chopped, peeled potato or $^1/_2$ cup loose-pack frozen hash-
    brown potatoes
  1 medium carrot, julienned ($^1/_2$ cup)
  1 tablespoon snipped fresh basil or 1 teaspoon dried basil,
    crushed
  1 teaspoon Worcestershire sauce
  1 bay leaf

1. In a large saucepan or pot cook ground beef or pork, onion, and
sweet pepper till meat is brown and onion is tender. Drain fat. Stir in
beef broth, corn, undrained tomatoes, lima beans, potato, carrot,
basil, Worcestershire sauce, bay leaf, and $^1/_8$ teaspoon *pepper*. Bring
to boiling; reduce heat. Cover and simmer for 15 to 20 minutes or till
vegetables are tender. Discard bay leaf. Makes about 8 cups (6 main-
dish servings).

Nutrition Facts per serving: 243 cal., 10 g total fat (4 g sat. fat), 48 mg chol., 652 mg
sodium, 19 g carbo., 3 g fiber, 20 g pro. **Daily Values:** 33% vit. A, 60% vit. C, 3% calcium,
18% iron

CHILI

PREP: 20 MINUTES   COOK: 20 MINUTES

Low-Fat

You can prepare this hearty soup on the range top to save time or slowly in a crockery cooker.

  12 **ounces ground beef**
   1 **cup chopped onion (1 large)**
 1/2 **cup chopped green sweet pepper**
   2 **cloves garlic, minced**
   1 **14¹/₂-ounce can tomatoes, cut up (see tip, page 999)**
   1 **15-ounce can dark red kidney beans, rinsed and drained (see tip, page 107)**
   1 **8-ounce can tomato sauce**
   2 **to 3 teaspoons chili powder**
 1/2 **teaspoon dried basil, crushed**
 1/4 **teaspoon pepper**

1. In a large saucepan cook ground beef, onion, sweet pepper, and garlic till meat is brown and onion is tender. Drain fat. Stir in undrained tomatoes, kidney beans, tomato sauce, chili powder, basil, and pepper. Bring to boiling; reduce heat. Cover and simmer for 20 minutes. Makes about 5 cups (4 main-dish servings).

■ **Crockery-cooker directions:** Cook meat, onion, sweet pepper, and garlic as above. Drain fat. In a 3¹/₂- or 4-quart electric crockery cooker (see tip, right) combine meat mixture, undrained tomatoes, beans, tomato sauce, chili powder, basil, and pepper. Cover; cook on low-heat setting for 8 to 10 hours or on high-heat setting for 4 to 5 hours.

Nutrition Facts per serving: 308 cal., 11 g total fat (4 g sat. fat), 53 mg chol., 755 mg sodium, 31 g carbo., 9 g fiber, 26 g pro. **Daily Values:** 17% vit. A, 66% vit. C, 6% calcium, 29% iron

■ **Cincinnati Chili:** Prepare as above, except omit kidney beans in chili mixture and add ¹/₄ teaspoon *ground cinnamon*. While chili is simmering, cook 6 ounces dried *spaghetti or fettuccine,* broken into 4-inch lengths (see page 774); drain pasta. Heat one 8-ounce can *dark red kidney beans* separately; drain. After simmering chili, stir in ¹/₂ ounce *unsweetened chocolate* till melted. To serve, divide pasta among 4 serving plates. Make an indentation in center of each pasta portion. Top each serving with some of the chili and beans. Divide 1 cup shredded *American cheese* and ½ cup chopped *onion* among servings. Makes 4 main-dish servings.

Nutrition Facts per serving: 564 cal., 23 g total fat (11 g sat. fat)

CROCKERY COOKERS

There are two basic types of crockery cookers (see illustrations A and B below). The recipes in this book were tested only in the type shown in illustration A. This type of cooker has a crockery insert and two temperature settings: low (about 200°) and high (about 300°). The heating coils wrap around the sides of the cooker. This allows for the continuous slow cooking needed for our recipes. The cooker in illustration B has an adjustable thermostat, indicating temperature in degrees. The heating coil is located in the bottom of the cooker—the only place heat is applied. Since the heat element cycles on and off, our recipes will not work in this type of cooker.

The following tips are helpful when using your crockery cooker.

■ If you chop vegetables or do other make-ahead preparations, wrap and store the food items in the refrigerator until you're ready to start the cooker.

■ Add only thawed or partially precooked foods, such as browned meat, to a crockery cooker. Do not place frozen meats or vegetables in a cold cooker.

- ■ If you're using an automatic timer to start the cooker while you are gone, make sure it is set to start within 2 hours and that the food is thoroughly chilled when it is placed in the cooker.
- ■ Avoid peeking into the pot or stirring during cooking. Since the cooker works at low temperatures, lost heat is not easily or quickly recovered.
- ■ After cooking, transfer any leftover food as quickly as possible to containers and store it in the refrigerator or freezer.

MEATBALL SOUP

PREP: 35 MINUTES   COOK: 11 MINUTES

Low-Fat

Accompany this hearty meat-and-pasta soup with a fresh-fruit salad.

- 1 beaten egg white
- $1/2$ cup soft bread crumbs
- $1/4$ cup finely chopped onion
- $1/8$ teaspoon garlic powder
- $1/8$ teaspoon pepper
- 8 ounces lean ground beef
  Nonstick spray coating
- $3^1/2$ cups water
- 1 15-ounce can garbanzo beans, rinsed and drained (see tip, page 107)
- 1 $14^1/2$-ounce can Italian-style stewed tomatoes
- 1 cup sliced fresh mushrooms
- 1 teaspoon instant beef bouillon granules
- 1 teaspoon dried Italian seasoning, crushed
- $1/4$ cup tiny bow-tie pasta
- 3 cups torn fresh spinach or $1/2$ of a 10-ounce package frozen chopped spinach, thawed and well drained

1. In a medium mixing bowl combine egg white, bread crumbs, onion, garlic powder, and pepper. Add ground beef; mix well. Shape meat mixture into thirty-six $^3/_4$-inch meatballs.

2. Spray a large skillet with nonstick coating. Cook meatballs over medium heat about 8 minutes or till no pink remains, turning occasionally to brown evenly. Cover and keep warm over low heat.

3. In a large saucepan stir together water, garbanzo beans, undrained tomatoes, mushrooms, bouillon granules, and Italian seasoning. Bring to boiling. Add pasta. Return to boiling; reduce heat. Cover and simmer for 10 to 12 minutes or till pasta is tender. Stir in spinach and meatballs. Cook for 1 to 2 minutes more or just till spinach is wilted. Makes about $7^1/_2$ cups (5 main-dish servings).

Nutrition Facts per serving: 218 cal., 6 g total fat (2 g sat. fat), 31 mg chol., 860 mg sodium, 26 g carbo., 5 g fiber, 16 g pro. **Daily Values:** 29% vit. A, 40% vit. C, 8% calcium, 30% iron

---

BEEF BOURGUIGNONNE

PREP: 40 MINUTES   COOK: 1$^1/_4$ HOURS

    1 pound boneless beef chuck roast, cut into $^3/_4$-inch cubes
    2 tablespoons cooking oil
    1 cup chopped onion (1 large)
    1 clove garlic, minced
 1$^1/_2$ cups burgundy
  $^3/_4$ cup beef broth (see tip, page 980)
    1 teaspoon dried thyme, crushed
  $^3/_4$ teaspoon dried marjoram, crushed
  $^1/_2$ teaspoon salt
  $^1/_4$ teaspoon pepper
    2 bay leaves
    3 cups whole fresh mushrooms
    4 medium carrots, cut into $^3/_4$-inch pieces
    8 ounces pearl onions or 2 cups frozen small whole onions
    2 tablespoons all-purpose flour
  $^1/_4$ cup water
    2 slices bacon, crisp-cooked, drained, and crumbled
    3 cups hot cooked noodles (see page 774)

1. In a large pot cook *half* of the meat in *1 tablespoon* of the hot oil till meat is brown; remove meat from pan. Add remaining oil, remaining meat, the chopped onion, and garlic. Cook till meat is brown and onion is tender. Drain fat. Return all meat to pot.

2. Stir in burgundy, beef broth, thyme, marjoram, salt, pepper, and bay leaves. Bring to boiling; reduce heat. Cover and simmer 45 minutes. Add mushrooms, carrots, and the pearl onions. Return to boiling; reduce heat. Cover and cook for 25 to 30 minutes more or till tender. Discard bay leaves.

3. Combine flour and water; stir into meat mixture. Cook and stir till thickened and bubbly. Cook and stir 1 minute more. Stir in bacon. Serve with noodles. Makes about 8 cups (6 main-dish servings).

■ **Crockery-cooker directions:** Brown meat, chopped onion, and garlic in hot oil as above. In a 3½- or 4-quart electric crockery cooker (see tip, page 985) layer mushrooms, carrots, and pearl onions. Sprinkle with 3 tablespoons *quick-cooking tapioca*. Place meat mixture atop vegetables. Add thyme, marjoram, salt, pepper, and bay leaves. Pour only 1¼ cups burgundy and ½ cup beef broth over meat. Cover; cook on low-heat setting 10 to 12 hours or on high-heat setting 5 to 6 hours or till tender. Discard bay leaves. Stir in bacon.

Nutrition Facts per serving: 405 cal., 13 g total fat (3 g sat. fat), 83 mg chol, 434 mg sodium, 38 g carbo., 5 g fiber, 26 g pro. **Daily Values:** 157% vit. A, 12% vit. C, 5% calcium, 35% iron

VEGETABLE-BEEF SOUP

PREP: 30 MINUTES   COOK: 2¹/₂ HOURS

Low-Fat

How much meat you include in this soup depends on the meatiness of your beef shanks. If you prefer, use 1 pound beef stew meat, cut into ¹/₂-inch cubes.

    2 to 3 pounds meaty beef shank crosscuts
    1 tablespoon cooking oil
    2 tablespoons instant beef bouillon granules
    1 teaspoon dried oregano, crushed
  ¹/₂ teaspoon dried marjoram, crushed
  ¹/₄ teaspoon pepper
    2 bay leaves
    2 cups chopped, peeled tomatoes or one 14¹/₂-ounce can
        tomatoes, cut up (see tip, page 999)
    1 10-ounce package frozen whole kernel corn
 1¹/₂ cups cubed, peeled potatoes
    1 cup frozen cut green beans
    1 cup sliced carrots (2 medium)
    1 cup sliced celery (2 stalks)
  ¹/₂ cup chopped onion (1 medium)

1. In a large pot brown meat, *half* at a time, in hot oil, adding more oil if necessary. Drain fat. Return all meat to pot. Add bouillon granules, oregano, marjoram, pepper, bay leaves, and 8 cups *water*. Bring to boiling; reduce heat. Cover and simmer for 2 hours. Remove meat.

2. Strain broth (see photo, page 979). Discard seasonings. Skim fat (see tip, page 1002); return broth to pot. When cool enough to handle, remove meat from bones and coarsely chop. Discard bones.

3. Stir chopped meat, fresh or undrained tomatoes, corn, potatoes, green beans, carrots, celery, and onion into the broth. Return to boiling; reduce heat. Cover and simmer about 30 minutes or till vegetables are crisp-tender. Season broth to taste with salt and pepper. Makes about 14 cups (8 main-dish servings).

Nutrition Facts per serving: 201 cal., 5 g total fat (1 g sat. fat), 33 mg chol., 730 mg sodium, 24 g carbo., 2 g fiber, 18 g pro. **Daily Values:** 64% vit. A, 31% vit. C, 4% calcium, 19% iron

STEAK SOUP

START TO FINISH: 35 MINUTES

Low-Fat

Sometimes called minute steaks, beef cubed steaks are thin pieces of meat that usually are tenderized. They're a good choice for this soup because they cook quickly.

- 2 4-ounce beef cubed steaks
- ¼ teaspoon garlic salt
- ⅛ teaspoon pepper
- 1 tablespoon cooking oil
- ½ cup chopped onion (1 medium)
- ½ cup chopped celery (1 stalk)
- 4 cups water
- 1 10-ounce package frozen mixed vegetables
- 1 tablespoon instant beef bouillon granules
- 1 tablespoon Worcestershire sauce
- 1 teaspoon dried basil, crushed
- 1 7½-ounce can tomatoes, cut up (see tip, page 999)
- ½ cup water
- ⅓ cup all-purpose flour

1. Sprinkle steaks with garlic salt and pepper. In a large saucepan cook steaks over medium-high heat in hot oil about 3 minutes or till done, turning once. Remove steaks from pan; reserve meat drippings. Cut meat into cubes; set aside.

2. In the same pan cook onion and celery in meat drippings over medium heat till tender. Stir in meat, the 4 cups water, frozen vegetables, bouillon granules, Worcestershire sauce, and basil. Bring to boiling; reduce heat. Cover and simmer about 5 minutes or till vegetables are crisp-tender. Stir in undrained tomatoes.

3. In a screw-top jar shake together the ½ cup water and the flour; add to the saucepan. Cook and stir till thickened and bubbly. Cook and stir for 1 minute more. Makes about 7½ cups (5 main-dish servings).

Nutrition Facts per serving: 177 cal., 5 g total fat (1 g sat. fat), 29 mg chol., 784 mg sodium, 18 g carbo., 1 g fiber, 14 g pro. **Daily Values:** 26% vit. A, 26% vit. C, 4% calcium, 16% iron

BARLEY-BEEF SOUP

PREP: 25 MINUTES   COOK: 1¼ HOURS

Low-Fat

If desired, substitute ¼ cup regular pearl barley for quick-cooking barley; add it with the water.

  ³/₄ **pound beef or lamb stew meat, cut into 1-inch cubes**
  1 **tablespoon cooking oil**
  4 **cups water**
  1 **cup chopped onion (1 large)**
  ¹/₂ **cup chopped celery (1 stalk)**
  2 **teaspoons instant beef bouillon granules**
  2 **cloves garlic, minced**
  1 **teaspoon dried oregano or basil, crushed**
  ¹/₄ **teaspoon pepper**
  1 **bay leaf**
  1 **cup frozen mixed vegetables**
  1 **cup parsnips, cut into ¹/₂-inch slices, or peeled potatoes, cut into ¹/₂-inch cubes**
  1 **7¹/₂-ounce can tomatoes, cut up (see tip, page 999)**
  ¹/₄ **cup quick-cooking pearl barley**

1. In a large pot brown meat in hot oil. Drain fat. Stir in water, onion, celery, bouillon granules, garlic, oregano or basil, pepper, and bay leaf. Bring to boiling; reduce heat. Cover and simmer 1 hour for beef (45 minutes for lamb).

2. Stir in frozen vegetables, parsnips or potatoes, undrained tomatoes, and quick-cooking barley. Return to boiling; reduce heat. Cover and simmer about 15 minutes more or till meat and vegetables are tender. Discard bay leaf. Makes about 6 cups (4 main-dish servings).

Nutrition Facts per serving: 289 cal., 9 g total fat (3 g sat. fat), 58 mg chol., 596 mg sodium, 30 g carbo., 4 g fiber, 24 g pro. **Daily Values:** 18% vit. A, 31% vit. C, 6% calcium, 23% iron

LAMB AND VEGETABLE STEW

PREP: 40 MINUTES   COOK: 50 MINUTES

If lamb stew meat isn't available, buy a lamb shoulder roast, trim off the fat, and cut it into cubes.

1 pound lamb stew meat, cut into $^3/_4$-inch cubes
2 teaspoons cooking oil
1 14$^1/_2$-ounce can beef broth
1$^1/_4$ cups dry red wine or beef broth
2 cloves garlic, minced
1 tablespoon snipped fresh thyme or 1 teaspoon dried thyme, crushed
1 bay leaf
2 cups cubed, peeled butternut squash
1 cup parsnips cut into $^1/_2$-inch slices
1 cup chopped, peeled sweet potatoes
1 cup sliced celery (2 stalks)
1 medium onion, cut into thin wedges
$^1/_2$ cup plain low-fat yogurt or dairy sour cream
3 tablespoons all-purpose flour

1. In a large saucepan or pot brown meat, *half* at a time, in hot oil. Drain fat. Return all meat to pan. Stir in beef broth, wine or broth, garlic, thyme, and bay leaf. Bring to boiling; reduce heat. Cover and simmer for 20 minutes.
2. Stir in squash, parsnips, sweet potatoes, celery, and onion. Return to boiling; reduce heat. Cover and simmer about 30 minutes more or till meat and vegetables are tender. Discard bay leaf.
3. In a small mixing bowl combine yogurt or sour cream and flour. Stir $^1/_2$ cup of the hot liquid into the yogurt mixture. Return entire mixture to saucepan. Cook and stir till thickened and bubbly. Cook and stir 1 minute more. Season to taste with salt and pepper. Makes about 6$^1/_2$ cups (4 main-dish servings).

Nutrition Facts per serving: 407 cal., 17 g total fat (7 g sat. fat), 65 mg chol., 532 mg sodium, 31 g carbo., 5 g fiber, 22 g pro. **Daily Values:** 103% vit. A, 40% vit. C, 12% calcium, 22% iron

HAM AND BEAN SOUP

PREP: 20 MINUTES   SOAK: 1 HOUR   COOK: 1¼ HOURS

Low-Fat

    1 cup dry navy beans
    1 to 1½ pounds meaty smoked pork hocks or one 1- to 1½-
       pound meaty ham bone
1½ cups sliced celery (3 stalks)
    1 cup chopped onion (1 large)
¾ teaspoon dried thyme, crushed
¼ teaspoon pepper
    1 bay leaf

1. Rinse beans. In a large saucepan combine beans and 4 cups *water*. Bring to boiling; reduce heat. Simmer for 2 minutes. Remove from heat. Cover and let stand for 1 hour. (Or, place beans in water in pan. Cover and let soak in a cool place for 6 to 8 hours or overnight.) Drain and rinse beans.

2. In the same pan combine beans, pork hocks or ham bone, celery, onion, thyme, pepper, bay leaf, and 4 cups fresh *water*. Bring to boiling; reduce heat. Cover and simmer about 1 hour or till beans are tender. Remove meat. When cool enough to handle, cut meat off bones; coarsely chop meat. Discard bones and bay leaf. Slightly mash beans in saucepan. Return meat to saucepan. Heat through. Makes about 8 cups (5 main-dish servings).

■ **Crockery-cooker directions:** Prepare beans as above; drain and rinse. In a 3½- or 4-quart electric crockery cooker (see tip, page 985) combine pork hocks or ham bone, celery, onion, thyme, pepper, and bay leaf. Stir in beans and 4 cups fresh *water*. Cover and cook on low-heat setting for 8 to 10 hours or on high-heat setting for 4 to 5 hours. Discard bay leaf. Remove meat; coarsely chop. Slightly mash beans in crockery cooker. Return meat to crockery cooker. Cover; cook on high-heat setting 5 to 10 minutes more or till heated through.

Nutrition Facts per serving: 177 cal., 2 g total fat (1 g sat. fat), 15 mg chol., 379 mg sodium, 26 g carbo., 1 g fiber, 14 g pro. **Daily Values:** 0% vit. A, 17% vit. C, 7% calcium, 19% iron

■ **Ham and Bean Soup with Vegetables:** Prepare as above, except, after mashing beans, stir in 2 cups chopped *parsnips or rutabaga*

Soups & Stews   **993**

and 1 cup sliced *carrot*. Return to boiling; reduce heat. Simmer, covered, about 15 minutes or till vegetables are tender. Stir in chopped meat and one 10-ounce package *frozen chopped spinach,* thawed and well drained. Heat through. Season to taste with salt and pepper. Makes about 9½ cups (5 or 6 main-dish servings).

Nutrition Facts per serving: 248 cal., 2 g total fat (1 g sat. fat)

BLACK BEAN SOUP WITH SAUSAGE

PREP: 30 MINUTES   SOAK: 1 HOUR   COOK: 1¼ HOURS

Low-Fat

*Hot cooked rice (see page 139) makes a tasty
accompaniment for this soup.*

   1 cup dry black beans
   6 cups water
   2 cups chicken broth (see tip, page 979)
   2 cups water
   1 cup chopped onion (1 large)
   1 cup chopped celery (2 stalks)
   4 cloves garlic, minced
   1 teaspoon ground coriander
¼ teaspoon salt
⅛ to ¼ teaspoon ground red pepper
   8 ounces fully cooked smoked turkey sausage or Polish sausage,
       chopped
   3 tablespoons dry sherry (optional)
       Dairy sour cream or shredded Monterey Jack cheese (optional)
       Snipped fresh parsley (optional)

1. Rinse beans. In a large saucepan or pot combine beans and the 6 cups water. Bring to boiling; reduce heat. Simmer for 2 minutes. Remove from heat. Cover and let stand for 1 hour. (Or, place beans in water in pan. Cover and let soak in a cool place for 6 to 8 hours or overnight.) Drain and rinse beans.
2. In the same pan combine beans, chicken broth, the 2 cups water, onion, celery, garlic, coriander, salt, and ground red pepper. Bring to boiling; reduce heat. Cover and simmer for 1 to 1½ hours or till beans are tender.
3. If desired, mash beans slightly. Stir in sausage and, if desired, dry

sherry. Cook 2 to 3 minutes more or till heated through. If desired, garnish with sour cream or shredded cheese and parsley. Makes about 8 cups (6 main-dish servings).

■ **Crockery-cooker directions:** Prepare beans as directed above in step 1. In a 3½- or 4-quart electric crockery cooker (see tip, page 985) combine chicken broth, the 2 cups water, onion, celery, garlic, coriander, salt, and ground red pepper. Stir in beans. Cover and cook on low-heat setting for 8 to 10 hours or on high-heat setting for 4 to 5 hours. Stir in sausage and, if desired, dry sherry. Cover and cook on high-heat setting about 30 minutes more or till heated through.

Nutrition Facts per serving: 178 cal., 4 g total fat (1 g sat. fat), 24 mg chol., 689 mg sodium, 22 g carbo., 2 g fiber, 15 g pro. **Daily Values:** 0% vit. A, 5% vit. C, 6% calcium, 16% iron

■ **Shortcut Black Bean Soup with Sausage:** Prepare as on page 994, except omit dry black beans and the 6 cups soaking water. Decrease chicken broth to 1½ cups. Rinse and drain two 15-ounce cans *black beans* (see tip, page 107); add to saucepan with broth, the 2 cups water, vegetables, and seasonings. Bring to boiling; reduce heat. Cover and simmer about 15 minutes or till vegetables are tender. Makes about 6 cups (4 main-dish servings).

Nutrition Facts per serving: 175 cal., 4 g total fat (1 g sat. fat), 974 mg sodium

---

ITALIAN SAUSAGE-NAVY BEAN STEW

PREP: 30 MINUTES SOAK: 1 HOUR COOK: 1½ HOURS

Low-Fat

Cabbage, tomatoes, onion, and sausage turn this bean soup into a hearty, home-style stew.

  1 **pound dry navy beans (2⅓ cups)**
  2 **14½-ounce cans beef broth**
 ¾ **cup water**
  1 **pound Italian sausage links, cut into ½-inch-thick slices**
  3 **cups chopped cabbage**
  1 **14½-ounce can tomatoes, cut up (see tip, page 999)**
  1 **cup chopped onion (1 large)**
  1 **teaspoon dried oregano, crushed**
  1 **clove garlic, minced**
  2 **bay leaves**

1. Rinse beans. In a large saucepan or pot combine beans and 6 cups *water*. Bring to boiling; reduce heat. Simmer for 2 minutes. Remove from heat. Cover and let stand for 1 hour. (Or, place beans in water in pan. Cover and let soak in a cool place for 6 to 8 hours or overnight.) Drain and rinse beans.

2. In the same pan combine beans, beef broth, the ³/₄ cup water, uncooked sausage slices, cabbage, undrained tomatoes, onion, oregano, garlic, and bay leaves. Bring to boiling; reduce heat. Cover and simmer about 1¹/₂ hours or till beans are tender, stirring occasionally. Discard the bay leaves. Skim off fat (see tip, page 1002). Season to taste with salt and pepper. Makes about 11 cups (8 main-dish servings).

■ **Crockery-cooker directions:** Prepare beans as above; drain and rinse. In a 3¹/₂-, 4-, or 5-quart electric crockery cooker (see tip, page 985) combine beans, beef broth, water, uncooked sausage slices, cabbage, undrained tomatoes, onion, oregano, garlic, and bay leaves. Cover and cook on high-heat setting for 6 to 8 hours. Discard bay leaves. Skim off fat (see tip, page 1002). Season to taste with salt and pepper.

Nutrition Facts per serving: 353 cal., 12 g total fat (4 g sat. fat), 32 mg chol., 808 mg sodium, 41 g carbo., 1 g fiber, 22 g pro. **Daily Values:** 3% vit. A, 38% vit. C, 11% calcium, 30% iron

---

CHICKEN NOODLE SOUP

START TO FINISH: 35 MINUTES

Low-Fat

4¹/₂ cups chicken broth (see tip, page 979)

¹/₂ cup chopped onion (1 medium)

2 teaspoons snipped fresh basil or ¹/₂ teaspoon dried basil, crushed

2 teaspoons snipped fresh oregano or ¹/₂ teaspoon dried oregano, crushed

¹/₄ teaspoon pepper

1 bay leaf

1 10-ounce package frozen mixed vegetables

¹/₂ cup medium noodles or other small pasta

2 cups cubed cooked chicken or turkey (see tip, page 857)

1 14¹/₂-ounce can tomatoes, cut up (see tip, page 999)

1. In a large saucepan combine chicken broth, onion, basil, oregano, pepper, and bay leaf. Stir in vegetables. Bring to boiling; stir in uncooked noodles. Return to boiling; reduce heat. Cover; simmer 8 minutes or till noodles are tender but still firm and vegetables are crisp-tender. Discard bay leaf. Stir in chicken or turkey and undrained tomatoes; heat through. Makes 8 cups (6 main-dish servings).

Nutrition Facts per serving: 190 cal., 5 g total fat (1 g sat. fat), 50 mg chol., 754 mg sodium, 14 g carbo., 1 g fiber, 21 g pro. **Daily Values:** 24% vit. A, 21% vit. C, 4% calcium, 14% iron

---

CHICKEN STEW WITH DUMPLINGS

START TO FINISH: 40 MINUTES

- 1 14^1/$_2$-ounce can chicken broth
- 1 10-ounce package frozen mixed vegetables
- 1 cup frozen small whole onions
- ^{1}/$_2$ cup water
- 2 teaspoons snipped fresh basil, oregano, or dill; or ^{1}/$_2$ teaspoon dried basil or oregano, crushed; or ^{1}/$_2$ teaspoon dried dillweed
- ^{1}/$_8$ teaspoon garlic powder
- ^{1}/$_8$ teaspoon pepper
- 1 cup milk
- ^{1}/$_3$ cup all-purpose flour
- 2 cups cubed cooked chicken or turkey (see tip, page 857) or two 5-ounce cans chunk-style chicken or turkey
- 1 recipe Dumplings for Stew (see below)

1. In a large saucepan combine chicken broth, frozen vegetables, onions, water, herb, garlic powder, and pepper. Bring to boiling. Meanwhile, combine milk and flour; stir into vegetable mixture. Stir in chicken or turkey. Cook and stir till thickened and bubbly.

2. Drop dumpling mixture from a tablespoon to make 4 to 8 mounds atop the bubbling stew. Cover (do not lift cover) and simmer over low heat for 10 to 12 minutes or till a toothpick inserted in a dumpling comes out clean. Makes about 6 cups (4 main-dish servings).

■ **Dumplings for Stew:** Combine ^{2}/$_3$ cup *all- purpose flour;* 1 tablespoon snipped *fresh parsley;* 1 teaspoon *baking powder;* 1 teaspoon snipped *fresh basil or dill or* ^{1}/$_8$ teaspoon *dried basil,* crushed, *or* ^{1}/$_8$

teaspoon *dried dillweed;* and ¹/₈ teaspoon *salt.* Combine ¹/₄ cup *milk* and 2 tablespoons *cooking oil;* pour into flour mixture. Stir just till combined. (Or, for a shortcut, combine 1 cup *packaged biscuit mix,* ¹/₃ cup *milk,* and ¹/₂ teaspoon *dried parsley flakes.*)

Nutrition Facts per serving: 418 cal., 15 g total fat (4 g sat. fat), 74 mg chol, 614 mg sodium, 38 g carbo., 1 g fiber, 32 g pro. **Daily Values:** 35% vit. A, 9% vit. C, 18% calcium, 22% iron

CREAM OF CHICKEN SOUP

START TO FINISH: 30 MINUTES

Fast

1. Cut 8-ounces skinless, boneless *chicken breast halves* into bite-size strips. In a large saucepan cook and stir chicken, 1 cup sliced *fresh mushrooms,* and ¹/₄ cup sliced *green onions* in 3 tablespoons *margarine or butter* about 4 minutes or till chicken is no longer pink and onions are tender.

2. Stir in ¹/₄ cup *all-purpose flour* and, if desired, 1 teaspoon snipped *fresh thyme or tarragon or* ¹/₄ teaspoon *dried thyme or tarragon,* crushed. Stir in 2 cups *chicken broth* (see tip, page 979), 1¹/₂ cups *milk,* ¹/₂ cup *half-and-half, light cream, or milk,* and ¹/₈ teaspoon *pepper.* Cook and stir till mixture is thickened and bubbly. Cook and stir for 1 minute more.

3. In a small bowl combine ¹/₂ cup *half-and-half, light cream, or milk* and 1 *egg yolk;* add to saucepan. Cook and stir till mixture comes to a boil. Makes about 5¹/₂ cups (4 main-dish servings).

Nutrition Facts per serving: 327 cal., 21 g total fat (8 g sat. fat), 113 mg chol., 588 mg sodium, 14 g carbo., 1 g fiber, 20 g pro. **Daily Values:** 33% vit. A, 5% vit. C, 16% calcium, 10% iron

TURKEY FRAME SOUP

PREP: 30 MINUTES   COOK: 2 HOURS

Low-Fat

Whenever you roast a whole turkey, use the leftover bones for this comforting soup.

  1 meaty turkey frame
  8 cups water

1 large onion, quartered
$^{1}/_{2}$ teaspoon garlic salt
  Chopped cooked turkey
1 14$^{1}/_{2}$-ounce can tomatoes, cut up (see tip, below)
1 tablespoon instant chicken bouillon granules
1$^{1}/_{2}$ teaspoons dried oregano, basil, marjoram, or thyme, crushed
$^{1}/_{4}$ teaspoon pepper
3 cups (any combination) sliced celery, carrots, parsnips, or
  mushrooms; chopped onions or rutabagas; or broccoli or
  cauliflower flowerets
1$^{1}/_{2}$ cups medium noodles

1. Break turkey frame or cut in half with kitchen shears. Place in a large pot. Add water, onion, and garlic salt. Bring to boiling; reduce heat. Cover and simmer for 1$^{1}/_{2}$ hours.

2. Remove turkey frame. When cool enough to handle, cut meat off bones; coarsely chop meat. If necessary, add enough turkey to equal 2 cups. Set aside. Discard bones. Strain broth (see photo, page 979); skim fat from broth (see tip, page 1002).

3. Return broth to pot. Stir in undrained tomatoes, bouillon granules, herb, and pepper. Stir in vegetables. Return to boiling; reduce heat. Cover and simmer for 15 minutes. Stir in uncooked noodles. Simmer for 8 to 10 minutes more or till noodles are tender but still firm and vegetables are crisp-tender. Stir in turkey; heat through. Makes about 9$^{1}/_{2}$ cups (6 main-dish servings).

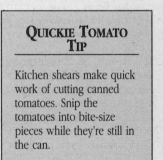

QUICKIE TOMATO TIP

Kitchen shears make quick work of cutting canned tomatoes. Snip the tomatoes into bite-size pieces while they're still in the can.

Nutrition Facts per serving: 260 cal., 6 g total fat (2 g sat. fat), 75 mg chol., 848 mg sodium, 31 g carbo., 3 g fiber, 20 g pro.
Daily Values: 9% vit. A, 29% vit. C, 8% calcium, 22% iron

CHICKEN AND SAUSAGE GUMBO

PREP: 30 MINUTES   COOK: 15 MINUTES

*Filé (fee-LAY) powder will thicken and lend a
thymelike flavor to this stew.*

- $1/3$ cup all-purpose flour
- $1/4$ cup cooking oil
- $1/2$ cup chopped onion (1 medium)
- $1/2$ cup chopped celery (1 stalk)
- $1/2$ cup chopped green sweet pepper
- 4 cloves garlic, minced
- $1/4$ teaspoon black pepper
- $1/4$ teaspoon ground red pepper
- 1 $14^1/2$-ounce can chicken broth, heated
- $1^1/4$ cups water, heated
- $1^1/2$ cups chopped cooked chicken or turkey (see tip, page 857)
- 8 ounces andouille sausage or fully cooked smoked sausage
  links, halved lengthwise and cut into $1/2$-inch slices
- $1^1/2$ cups sliced fresh okra or one 10-ounce package frozen cut okra
- 2 bay leaves
- 3 cups hot cooked rice (see page 139)
  Filé powder (optional)

1. For roux, in a large heavy saucepan or pot combine flour and oil till smooth. Cook over medium-high heat for 5 minutes, stirring constantly. Reduce heat to medium. Cook and stir for 10 to 15 minutes more or till the roux is dark reddish brown (see tip, right).

2. Stir in onion, celery, sweet pepper, garlic, black pepper, and ground red pepper. Cook over

> ## ROUX RULES
>
> Roux is ready when its color matches that of a penny. Stir the roux constantly so it doesn't scorch; if it does, it won't thicken your gumbo.

medium heat for 3 to 5 minutes or till vegetables are just crisp-tender, stirring often.

3. Gradually stir in hot chicken broth, hot water, chicken or turkey, sausage, okra, and bay leaves. Bring to boiling; reduce heat. Cover and simmer about 15 minutes or till okra is tender. Discard bay leaves. Serve in bowls with rice. If desired, stir $^1/_4$ to $^1/_2$ teaspoon filé powder into each serving. Makes about 7 cups (6 main-dish servings).

Nutrition Facts per serving: 422 cal., 25 g total fat (7 g sat. fat), 60 mg chol., 618 mg sodium, 30 g carbo., 2 g fiber, 21 g pro. **Daily Values:** 4% vit. A, 26% vit. C, 5% calcium, 13% iron

---

EASY MULLIGATAWNY SOUP

PREP: 25 MINUTES   COOK: 20 MINUTES

Low-Fat

This is a simplified version of the classic, curry-flavored Indian soup.

  $2^1/_2$ cups chicken broth (see tip, page 979)
   1 cup chopped apples (2 small)
   1 cup chopped carrots (2 medium)
   1 $7^1/_2$-ounce can tomatoes, cut up (see tip, page 999)
  $^1/_2$ cup chopped celery (1 stalk)
  $^1/_3$ cup long grain rice
  $^1/_4$ cup chopped onion
  $^1/_4$ cup raisins
   1 tablespoon snipped fresh parsley
   1 to $1^1/_2$ teaspoons curry powder
   1 teaspoon lemon juice
  $^1/_4$ teaspoon coarsely ground pepper
  $^1/_8$ teaspoon ground mace or ground nutmeg
  $1^1/_2$ cups chopped cooked chicken or turkey (see tip, page 857)

1. In a large saucepan combine chicken broth, apples, carrots, undrained tomatoes, celery, uncooked rice, onion, raisins, parsley, curry powder, lemon juice, pepper, mace or nutmeg, and 1 cup *water*. Bring to boiling; reduce heat. Cover and simmer about 20 minutes or till rice is tender. Stir in chicken or turkey; heat through. Makes about 6 cups (4 main-dish servings).

Nutrition Facts per serving: 275 cal., 6 g total fat (2 g sat. fat), 51 mg chol., 677 mg sodium, 34 g carbo., 4 g fiber, 22 g pro. **Daily Values:** 122% vit. A, 23% vit. C, 5% calcium, 19% iron

CHICKEN SOUP WITH LENTILS AND BARLEY

PREP: 25 MINUTES   COOK: 40 MINUTES

Low-Fat

- 1 cup sliced leeks or chopped onion
- ¹/₂ cup chopped red or green sweet pepper
- 1 clove garlic, minced
- 2 tablespoons margarine or butter
- 2 14¹/₂-ounce cans chicken broth
- 1¹/₂ cups water
- ¹/₂ cup dry lentils, rinsed and drained
- ¹/₂ teaspoon dried basil, crushed
- ¹/₄ teaspoon dried oregano, crushed
- ¹/₄ teaspoon dried rosemary, crushed
- 1¹/₂ cups chopped cooked chicken or turkey (see tip, page 857)
- 1¹/₂ cups sliced carrots (3 medium)
- ¹/₂ cup quick-cooking barley
- 1 14¹/₂-ounce can tomatoes, cut up (see tip, page 999)

1. In a large saucepan cook leeks or onion, sweet pepper, and garlic in margarine or butter till tender. Carefully stir in broth, water, lentils, basil, oregano, rosemary, and ¹/₄ teaspoon *pepper*. Bring to boiling; reduce heat. Cover and simmer for 20 minutes.
2. Stir in the chicken, carrots, and uncooked barley. Cover and sim-

SKIMMING FAT OFF THE TOP

Make your homemade soups as fat- and calorie-trimmed as possible by skimming off extra fat. To remove fat from hot soup or broth, use a large metal spoon and skim off the fat that rises to the top. You also can cover and refrigerate the soup or broth for 6 to 8 hours or until the fat solidifies on the surface. Then use a spoon to lift off the hardened fat.

In addition, there are utensils that will help you remove fat. A good one is a fat-skimming ladle that has slots near the upper edge of its bowl to skim off fat; the fat drains into the bowl of the ladle. Also useful is a large fat-separating pitcher that has a spout near the bottom. After the soup stands a few minutes in the pitcher, the fat rises to the top. You then pour off the broth, leaving the fat in the pitcher.

mer about 20 minutes more or just till carrots are tender. Add the undrained tomatoes; heat through. Makes about 8 cups (6 main-dish servings).

Nutrition Facts per serving: 292 cal., 8 g total fat (2 g sat. fat), 34 mg chol., 659 mg sodium, 34 g carbo., 5 g fiber, 21 g pro. **Daily Values:** 101% vit. A, 47% vit. C, 6% calcium, 26% iron

---

MANHATTAN CLAM CHOWDER

PREP: 25 MINUTES   COOK: 30 MINUTES

Low-Fat

    1 pint shucked clams or two 6¹/₂-ounce cans minced clams
    1 cup chopped celery (2 stalks)
    1 cup chopped green or red sweet pepper
  ¹/₄ cup chopped carrot (1 small)
    2 tablespoons sliced green onion (1)
    2 cups finely chopped, peeled potatoes
    1 14¹/₂-ounce can tomatoes, cut up (see tip, page 999)
    1 cup chicken broth (see tip, page 979)
  ¹/₂ teaspoon dried basil, crushed
  ¹/₈ teaspoon ground red pepper (optional)
    2 tablespoons snipped fresh parsley

1. Chop clams, reserving juice; set clams aside. Strain clam juice to remove bits of shell. (Or, drain canned clams, reserving juice.) If necessary, add enough water to reserved juice to equal 1¹/₂ cups.

2. In a large saucepan combine the juice mixture, celery, sweet pepper, carrot, and green onion. Bring to boiling; reduce heat. Cover and simmer about 10 minutes or till vegetables are tender. Stir in potatoes, undrained tomatoes, chicken broth, basil, ground red pepper (if desired), and ¹/₈ teaspoon *black pepper.* Bring to boiling; reduce heat. Cover and simmer for 10 minutes. Stir in clams. Return to boiling; reduce heat. Cook for 1 to 2 minutes more. Sprinkle with parsley. Makes about 7¹/₂ cups (4 main-dish servings).

Nutrition Facts per serving: 175 cal., 2 g total fat (0 g sat. fat), 29 mg chol., 464 mg sodium, 26 g carbo., 3 g fiber, 15 g pro. **Daily Values**: 55% vit. A, 113% vit. C, 8% calcium, 89% iron

NEW ENGLAND CLAM CHOWDER

PREP: 30 MINUTES   COOK: 10 MINUTES

Low-Fat

To save time and retain nutrients, don't peel the potatoes—scrub them and chop finely.

    1 pint shucked clams or two 6½-ounce cans minced clams
    2 slices bacon, halved
 2½ cups finely chopped, peeled potatoes (about 3 medium)
    1 cup chopped onion (1 large)
    1 teaspoon instant chicken bouillon granules
    1 teaspoon Worcestershire sauce
  ¼ teaspoon dried thyme, crushed
  ⅛ teaspoon pepper
    2 cups milk
    1 cup half-and-half or light cream
    2 tablespoons all-purpose flour

1. Chop clams, reserving juice; set clams aside. Strain clam juice to remove bits of shell. (Or, drain canned clams, reserving juice.) If necessary, add water to reserved clam juices to equal 1 cup. Set juice mixture aside.

2. In a large saucepan cook bacon till crisp. Remove bacon, reserving 1 tablespoon drippings in pan. Drain bacon on paper towels. Crumble bacon and set aside.

3. Stir reserved clam juice mixture, potatoes, onion, bouillon granules, Worcestershire sauce, thyme, and pepper into saucepan. Bring to boiling; reduce heat. Cover and simmer about 10 minutes or till potatoes are tender. With the back of a fork, mash potatoes slightly against the side of the pan.

4. Stir together milk, half-and-half or light cream, and flour; add to potato mixture. Cook and stir till slightly thickened and bubbly. Stir in clams. Return to boiling; reduce heat. Cook for 1 to 2 minutes more. Sprinkle each serving with some crumbled bacon. Makes about 7 cups (4 main-dish servings).

Nutrition Facts per serving: 336 cal., 12 g total fat (6 g sat. fat), 62 mg chol., 420 mg sodium, 37 g carbo., 2 g fiber, 20 g pro. **Daily Values:** 22% vit. A, 42% vit. C, 22% calcium, 85% iron

CIOPPINO

PREP: 1 HOUR   COOK: 25 MINUTES

Low-Fat

*Italian immigrant fishermen in the San Francisco Bay
area created this stew.*

- 8 fresh or frozen clams in shells
- 8 ounces fresh or frozen fish fillets (red snapper, perch, sea bass, or halibut)
- 8 ounces fresh or frozen peeled and deveined shrimp
- $1/2$ cup sliced fresh mushrooms
- $1/3$ cup chopped green or red sweet pepper
- $1/4$ cup chopped onion
- 2 cloves garlic, minced
- 1 tablespoon olive oil or cooking oil
- 1 $14^1/2$-ounce can tomatoes, cut up (see tip, page 999)
- $1/3$ cup dry red or white wine
- 2 tablespoons snipped fresh parsley
- 2 tablespoons tomato paste
- 1 tablespoon lemon juice
- $1^1/2$ teaspoons snipped fresh basil or $1/2$ teaspoon dried basil, crushed
- $1^1/2$ teaspoons snipped fresh oregano or $1/2$ teaspoon dried oregano, crushed
- 1 teaspoon sugar
- $1/8$ teaspoon crushed red pepper

1. Thaw clams, if frozen. Scrub fresh clam shells under cold running water using a stiff brush. In a large pot or bowl combine 8 cups *water* and 3 tablespoons *salt*. Add clams; soak 15 minutes. Drain and rinse. Discard water. Repeat the soaking, draining, and rinsing steps 2 more times.

2. Thaw fish and shrimp, if frozen. Remove and discard fish skin, if present. Cut fish into $1^1/2$-inch pieces. Cover and refrigerate fish pieces and shrimp till needed.

3. In a large saucepan cook mushrooms, sweet pepper, onion, and garlic in hot oil till tender but not brown. Stir in undrained tomatoes, wine, parsley, tomato paste, lemon juice, basil, oregano, sugar, crushed red pepper, $1/4$ cup *water,* and $1/4$ teaspoon *salt*. Bring to boiling; reduce heat. Cover and simmer for 20 minutes.

4. Add clams, fish pieces, and shrimp to saucepan. Cover and simmer for 5 to 10 minutes more or till clams open, fish flakes easily, and shrimp are opaque. Discard any unopened clams. Makes about 6 cups (4 main-dish servings).

Nutrition Facts per serving: 231 cal., 6 g total fat (1 g sat. fat), 127 mg chol., 478 mg sodium, 12 g carbo., 2 g fiber, 30 g pro. **Daily Values:** 18% vit. A, 60% vit. C, 8% calcium, 71% iron

OYSTER STEW

START TO FINISH: 20 MINUTES

Fast

For a richer stew, use more half-and-half or light cream and less milk.

- $^1/_4$ **cup finely chopped onion or sliced leek**
- 2 **teaspoons margarine or butter**
- 1 **pint shucked oysters**
- $^1/_2$ **teaspoon salt**
- 2 **cups milk**
- 1 **cup half-and-half or light cream**
- 1 **tablespoon snipped fresh parsley**
- 1 **tablespoon diced pimiento (optional)**
- $^1/_4$ **teaspoon white pepper**
  Margarine or butter (optional)

1. In a large saucepan cook onion or leek in hot margarine or butter till tender but not brown. Stir in the undrained oysters and salt. Cook over medium heat about 5 minutes or till oysters curl around the edges, stirring occasionally.
2. Stir in the milk, half-and-half or light cream, parsley, pimiento (if desired), and white pepper. Heat through. If desired, top each serving with margarine or butter. Makes about 6 cups (4 main-dish servings).

Nutrition Facts per serving: 240 cal., 14 g total fat (7 g sat. fat), 93 mg chol., 502 mg sodium, 14 g carbo., 0 g fiber, 14 g pro. **Daily Values:** 29% vit. A, 15% vit. C, 22% calcium, 52% iron

■ **Vegetable-Oyster Stew:** Prepare as above, except increase margarine or butter to 2 tablespoons. Cook $^1/_2$ cup shredded *carrot* and

$^{1}/_{2}$ cup finely chopped *celery* along with the onion or leek in the margarine or butter. Stir in 1 teaspoon *Worcestershire sauce* with the milk, half-and-half, or light cream, and seasonings. Makes about 6 cups (4 main-dish servings).

Nutrition Facts per serving: 285 cal., 18 g total fat (8 g sat. fat)

TUNA-CORN CHOWDER

START TO FINISH: 25 MINUTES

Fast **Low-Fat**

$^{1}/_{4}$ cup chopped onion
3 tablespoons margarine or butter
$^{1}/_{4}$ cup all-purpose flour
$^{1}/_{2}$ teaspoon dried dillweed
$^{1}/_{4}$ teaspoon pepper
2 cups milk
1 cup chicken broth (see tip, page 979)
1 cup water
1 11-ounce can whole kernel corn with sweet peppers or whole kernel corn, drained
1 6-ounce can tuna, drained and broken into chunks
Snipped fresh parsley (optional)

1. In a large saucepan cook onion in hot margarine or butter till tender but not brown. Stir in flour, dillweed, and pepper. Add the milk, chicken broth, and water all at once. Cook and stir till thickened and bubbly. Cook and stir for 1 minute more. Stir in the corn and tuna; heat through. If desired, sprinkle with parsley. Makes about $5^{1}/_{2}$ cups (4 main-dish servings).

Nutrition Facts per serving: 286 cal., 12 g total fat (3 g sat. fat), 21 mg chol., 785 mg sodium, 28 g carbo., 2 g fiber, 18 g pro. **Daily Values:** 20% vit. A, 15% vit. C, 14% calcium, 12% iron

SEAFOOD STEW

PREP: 20 MINUTES COOK: 15 MINUTES

Low-Fat

This easy gumbo omits the traditional roux and uses frozen seafood and Cajun-seasoned tomatoes.

  1 **cup chopped green sweet pepper**
  $^1/_2$ **cup chopped onion (1 medium)**
  1 **tablespoon cooking oil**
  1 **tablespoon cornstarch**
  1 **$14^1/_2$-ounce can Cajun-style stewed tomatoes**
  1 **6-ounce can hot-style tomato juice**
  1 **cup frozen cut okra**
  1 **8-ounce package frozen, peeled, cooked shrimp**
  $^1/_2$ **of an 8-ounce package crab-flavored, flake-style fish (about 1 cup)**
  $^3/_4$ **cup quick-cooking rice**

1. In a large pot cook sweet pepper and onion in hot oil till tender; stir in cornstarch. Add the undrained tomatoes and tomato juice all at once. Cook and stir till bubbly; add okra. Bring mixture to boiling; reduce heat. Cover; simmer 10 minutes.
2. Stir in shrimp, crab-flavored fish, uncooked rice, and $1^1/_4$ cups *water*. Return mixture to boiling. Remove from heat. Cover and let stand about 5 minutes or till rice is tender, stirring occasionally. Makes about 7 cups (4 main-dish servings).

Nutrition Facts per serving: 246 cal., 4 g total fat (1 g sat. fat), 93 mg chol., 931 mg sodium, 35 g carbo., 1 g fiber, 17 g pro. **Daily Values:** 17% vit. A, 67% vit. C, 6% calcium, 21% iron

VEGETARIAN CHILI

PREP: 20 MINUTES COOK: 20 MINUTES

Low-Fat

Although they save a lot of time, canned beans and tomatoes contribute significant amounts of sodium to a recipe. If you're interested in reducing sodium in your diet, see "Sodium Sense" on page 1011 and the tip on page 107.

3 cloves garlic, minced
1 tablespoon cooking oil
2 14¹/₂-ounce cans chunky chili-style tomatoes or low-sodium
    stewed tomatoes
1 12-ounce can beer or nonalcoholic beer
1 cup water
1 8-ounce can low-sodium tomato sauce
3 to 4 teaspoons chili powder
1 tablespoon snipped fresh oregano or 1 teaspoon dried
    oregano, crushed
1 tablespoon Dijon-style mustard
1 teaspoon ground cumin
¹/₂ teaspoon pepper
    Several dashes bottled hot pepper sauce (optional)
1 15-ounce can lower-sodium pinto beans, rinsed and drained
1 15-ounce can white kidney beans, rinsed and drained
1 15-ounce can lower-sodium red kidney beans, rinsed and
    drained
1¹/₂ cups fresh or frozen whole kernel corn
1¹/₂ cups chopped zucchini or yellow summer squash
³/₄ cup shredded cheddar or Monterey Jack cheese (3 ounces)
    (optional)

1. In a 4-quart pot cook garlic in hot oil for 30 seconds. Stir in the undrained tomatoes, beer, water, tomato sauce, chili powder, oregano, mustard, cumin, pepper, and, if desired, hot pepper sauce. Stir in pinto beans, white kidney beans, and red kidney beans. Bring to boiling; reduce heat. Cover and simmer for 10 minutes.

2. Stir in corn and zucchini or yellow summer squash. Simmer, covered, about 10 minutes more or till vegetables are tender. If desired, top each serving with *2 tablespoons* of the shredded cheese. Makes about 10 cups (6 main-dish servings).

Nutrition Facts per serving: 256 cal., 4 g total fat (0 g sat. fat), 0 mg chol., 1,006 mg sodium, 54 g carbo., 12 g fiber, 15 g pro. **Daily Values**: 27% vit. A, 40% vit. C, 10% calcium, 28% iron

LENTIL SOUP

PREP: 25 MINUTES   COOK: 20 MINUTES

Low-Fat

- 1 cup dry lentils, rinsed and drained
- 1 cup chopped green sweet pepper
- 1 cup sliced carrots (2 medium)
- ¹/₂ cup chopped onion (1 medium)
- 2 teaspoons instant chicken bouillon granules
- 2 teaspoons snipped fresh sage or ¹/₂ teaspoon dried sage, crushed
- ¹/₈ teaspoon ground red pepper
- 2 cloves garlic, minced
- 6 ounces fully cooked smoked sausage links, quartered lengthwise and sliced

1. In a large pot mix lentils, sweet pepper, carrots, onion, bouillon granules, sage, ground red pepper, garlic, and 5 cups *water*. Bring to boiling; reduce heat. Cover and simmer for 20 to 25 minutes or till vegetables and lentils are tender. Stir in sausage and heat through. Makes about 7 cups (5 main-dish servings).

Nutrition Facts per serving: 267 cal., 11 g total fat (4 g sat. fat), 24 mg chol., 696 mg sodium, 28 g carbo., 2 g fiber, 15 g pro. **Daily Values:** 69% vit. A, 34% vit. C, 3% calcium, 29% iron

SPLIT PEA SOUP

PREP: 20 MINUTES   COOK: 1¹/₃ HOURS

Low-Fat

- 2 cups chicken broth (see tip, page 979)
- 1 cup dry split peas, rinsed and drained
- 1 to 1¹/₂ pounds meaty smoked pork hocks or one 1- to 1¹/₂-pound meaty ham bone
- ¹/₄ teaspoon dried marjoram, crushed
- 1 bay leaf
- ¹/₂ cup chopped carrot (1 medium)
- ¹/₂ cup chopped celery (1 stalk)
- ¹/₂ cup chopped onion (1 medium)

1. In a large saucepan combine broth, split peas, pork hocks or ham bone, marjoram, bay leaf, 2 cups *water*, and dash pepper. Bring to boiling; reduce heat. Cover and simmer for 1 hour, stirring occasionally. Remove meat. When cool enough to handle, cut meat off bones; coarsely chop meat. Discard bones. Return meat to saucepan. Stir in carrot, celery, and onion. Return to boiling; reduce heat. Cover and simmer for 20 to 30 minutes more or till vegetables are tender. Discard bay leaf. Makes about 5½ cups (4 main-dish servings).

■ **Crockery-cooker directions:** In a 3½- or 4-quart electric crockery cooker (see tip, page 985) combine split peas, pork hocks, marjoram, bay leaf, carrot, celery, onion, and dash pepper. Pour chicken broth and 2 cups *water* over all. Cover and cook on low-heat setting for 10 to 12 hours or on high-heat setting for 5 to 6 hours. Discard bay leaf. Remove meat; coarsely chop. Return meat to crockery cooker. Cover and cook on high-heat setting 5 to 10 minutes more or till heated through.

Nutrition Facts per serving: 264 cal., 3 g total fat (1 g sat. fat), 19 mg chol., 863 mg sodium, 37 g carbo., 3 g fiber, 23 g pro. **Daily Values:** 60% vit. A, 19% vit. C, 5% calcium, 22% iron

MINESTRONE

PREP: 30 MINUTES   COOK: 30 MINUTES

> **Low-Fat**

- 1 14¹/₂-ounce can chicken broth
- 1 14¹/₂-ounce can low-sodium tomatoes, cut up (see tip, page 999)
- 1 cup chopped onion (1 large)
- 1 cup shredded cabbage
- ³/₄ cup tomato juice
- ¹/₂ cup chopped carrot (1 medium)
- ¹/₂ cup sliced celery (1 stalk)
- 1 tablespoon snipped fresh basil or 1 teaspoon dried basil, crushed
- ¹/₄ teaspoon garlic powder
- 1 15-ounce can white kidney beans or great Northern beans, rinsed and drained (see tip, page 107)
- 1 medium zucchini, sliced ¹/₄ inch thick (1¹/₄ cups)
- ¹/₂ of a 9-ounce package frozen Italian green beans
- 2 ounces spaghetti or linguine, broken (about ¹/₂ cup)
- 2 tablespoons finely shredded Parmesan cheese

1. In a pot mix broth, undrained tomatoes, onion, cabbage, tomato juice, carrot, celery, basil, garlic powder, and 1¹/₄ cups *water*. Bring to boiling; reduce heat. Cover; simmer 20 minutes. Stir in kidney beans, zucchini, green beans, and spaghetti. Return to boiling; reduce heat. Cover; simmer 10 to 15 minutes more or till vegetables and pasta are tender. Top each serving with Parmesan cheese. Makes about 8¹/₂ cups (4 main-dish servings).

Nutrition Facts per serving: 225 cal., 3 g total fat (0 g sat. fat), 3 mg chol., 751 mg sodium, 44 g carbo., 9 g fiber, 15 g pro. **Daily Values:** 54% vit. A, 62% vit. C, 12% calcium, 23% iron

---

CORN CHOWDER

PREP: 40 MINUTES   COOK: 20 MINUTES

For a slightly thicker chowder, blend or process half of the corn until it's smooth before adding it to the soup. If you want a cheesy chowder, add ¹/₂ cup shredded cheddar cheese with the bacon and stir until it melts.

6 **fresh medium ears of corn** or 3 cups frozen whole kernel corn, thawed
¹/₂ **cup chopped onion** (1 medium)
¹/₂ **cup chopped green sweet pepper**
1 **tablespoon cooking oil**
1 **14¹/₂-ounce can chicken broth**
1 **cup cubed, peeled potato** (1 medium)
1 **cup milk**
1 **tablespoon all-purpose flour**
¹/₄ **teaspoon salt**
¹/₄ **teaspoon pepper**
2 **slices bacon,** crisp-cooked, drained, and crumbled
2 **tablespoons snipped fresh parsley** (optional)

1. If using fresh corn, use a sharp knife to cut the kernels off the cobs (you should have about 3 cups corn) (see photo, below).

2. In a large saucepan cook onion and sweet pepper in hot oil till onion is tender but not brown. Stir in chicken broth and potato. Bring to boiling; reduce heat. Cover and simmer for 10 minutes. Stir in the corn. Cook, uncovered, about 10 minutes more or till potato and corn are tender, stirring the mixture occasionally.

3. In a small bowl combine milk, flour, salt, and pepper; stir into corn mixture. Cook and stir till thickened and bubbly. Cook and stir for 1 minute more. Add bacon; cook and stir till heated through. If desired, garnish each serving with parsley. Makes about 5¹/₂ cups (6 side-dish servings).

Nutrition Facts per serving: 180 cal., 6 g total fat (1 g sat. fat), 5 mg chol., 376 mg sodium, 29 g carbo., 4 g fiber, 7 g pro. **Daily Values:** 4% vit. A, 27% vit. C, 5% calcium, 6% iron

Hold the ear of corn so an end rests on a cutting board. Using a sharp knife, cut across the base of the kernels from the top of the ear toward the board.

VEGETABLE-CHEESE CHOWDER

START TO FINISH: 30 MINUTES

Fast

Pair this soup with a grilled chicken sandwich for a hearty lunch or supper.

  1 10-ounce package frozen cauliflower or cut broccoli
  $^1/_2$ cup shredded carrot (1 medium)
  $^1/_2$ cup water
  2 cups milk
  $^1/_3$ cup all-purpose flour
  $^1/_8$ teaspoon pepper
  1 14$^1/_2$-ounce can chicken broth
  $^3/_4$ cup shredded American cheese (3 ounces)
  $^3/_4$ cup shredded sharp cheddar cheese (3 ounces)
  2 tablespoons snipped fresh parsley

1. In a medium saucepan combine cauliflower or broccoli, carrot, and water. Bring to boiling; reduce heat. Cover and simmer about 4 minutes or just till vegetables are crisp-tender. Do not drain. Cut up any large pieces of cauliflower or broccoli.

2. In a screw-top jar shake together the milk, flour, and pepper; add to saucepan. Stir in broth. Cook and stir till thickened and bubbly. Stir in shredded cheeses and parsley. Cook and stir over low heat till cheeses melt and chowder is heated through. Makes about 6$^1/_2$ cups (4 main-dish servings).

Nutrition Facts per serving: 296 cal., 17 g total fat (10 g sat. fat), 52 mg chol., 842 mg sodium, 18 g carbo., 2 g fiber, 18 g pro. **Daily Values:** 61% vit. A, 42% vit. C, 37% calcium, 9% iron

WILD RICE-MUSHROOM SOUP

PREP: 20 MINUTES   COOK: 45 MINUTES

To rinse wild rice, place it in a pan of warm water, stir, and remove particles that float to the top. Drain and repeat rinsing; drain before using.

  3 cups chicken broth (see tip, page 979)
  $^1/_3$ cup wild rice, rinsed and drained

½ cup thinly sliced green onions (4)
1 cup half-and-half or light cream
2 tablespoons all-purpose flour
1 teaspoon snipped fresh thyme or ¼ teaspoon dried thyme, crushed
⅛ teaspoon pepper
½ cup sliced fresh mushrooms
1 tablespoon dry sherry

1. In a medium saucepan combine the chicken broth and uncooked wild rice. Bring to boiling; reduce heat. Cover and simmer for 40 minutes. Stir in green onions; cook for 5 to 10 minutes more or till rice is tender.

2. Combine half-and-half or light cream, flour, thyme, and pepper. Stir into rice mixture along with mushrooms. Cook and stir till thickened and bubbly. Cook and stir for 1 minute more. Stir in sherry; heat through. Makes about 3½ cups (4 side-dish servings).

Nutrition Facts per serving: 185 cal., 8 g total fat (5 g sat. fat), 23 mg chol., 609 mg sodium, 19 g carbo., 1 g fiber, 9 g pro. **Daily Values:** 10% vit. A, 7% vit. C, 6% calcium, 12% iron

FRENCH ONION SOUP

START TO FINISH: 30 MINUTES

Fast

2 tablespoons margarine or butter
2 cups thinly sliced onions (2 large)
4 cups beef broth (see tip, page 980)
2 tablespoons dry sherry or dry white wine (optional)
1 teaspoon Worcestershire sauce
Dash pepper
6 slices French bread, toasted
¾ cup shredded Swiss, Gruyère, or Jarlsberg cheese (3 ounces)

1. In a large saucepan melt margarine or butter. Stir in onions. Cook, covered, over medium-low heat for 8 to 10 minutes or till tender and golden, stirring occasionally. Stir in beef broth, dry sherry or wine (if desired), Worcestershire sauce, and pepper. Bring to boiling; reduce heat. Cover and simmer for 10 minutes.

2. Meanwhile, sprinkle toasted bread with shredded cheese. Place bread under broiler till cheese melts and turns light brown. To serve, ladle soup into bowls and float bread atop. Makes about 4¹/₂ cups (6 side-dish servings).

Nutrition Facts per serving: 195 cal., 9 g total fat (4 g sat. fat), 13 mg chol., 765 mg sodium, 20 g carbo., 1 g fiber, 9 g pro. **Daily Values:** 8% vit. A, 7% vit. C, 14% calcium, 7% iron

GAZPACHO

PREP: 30 MINUTES   CHILL: 2 TO 24 HOURS

Low-Fat

  4 cups chopped, peeled tomatoes (4 large)
  1 cup tomato juice or vegetable juice
  1 cup beef broth (see tip, page 980)
¹/₂ cup chopped, seeded cucumber
¹/₄ cup finely chopped green sweet pepper
¹/₄ cup finely chopped onion
  2 tablespoons snipped fresh basil or 1 teaspoon dried basil, crushed
  1 tablespoon olive oil or cooking oil
  1 tablespoon lemon juice or lime juice
  1 clove garlic, minced
¹/₂ teaspoon ground cumin (optional)
¹/₄ teaspoon bottled hot pepper sauce
    Croutons (optional)

1. In a large mixing bowl combine tomatoes, tomato juice, beef broth, cucumber, sweet pepper, onion, basil, oil, lemon or lime juice, garlic, cumin (if desired), and hot pepper sauce. Cover and chill for 2 to 24 hours.
2. To serve, ladle soup into chilled bowls or mugs. If desired, top each serving with croutons. Makes about 6 cups (6 to 8 side-dish servings).

Nutrition Facts per serving: 68 cal., 3 g total fat (0 g sat. fat), 0 mg chol., 286 mg sodium, 10 g carbo., 2 g fiber, 2 g pro. **Daily Values:** 12% vit. A, 70% vit. C, 1% calcium, 7% iron

PREP: 30 MINUTES   COOK: 20 MINUTES   CHILL: 4 TO 24 HOURS

1. In a medium saucepan cook ¹/₂ cup sliced *leeks or* chopped *onion* in 1 tablespoon *margarine or butter* till tender but not brown. Stir in 1¹/₂ cups sliced, peeled *potatoes;* 1 cup *chicken broth* (see tip, page 979); ¹/₈ teaspoon *salt;* and dash *white pepper.* Bring to boiling; reduce heat. Cover and simmer for 20 to 25 minutes or till potatoes are tender. Cool slightly. Place half of the potato mixture in a blender container or food processor bowl. Cover and blend or process till smooth; transfer to a bowl. Repeat with remaining potato mixture. Stir ³/₄ cup *milk* and ¹/₂ cup *whipping cream* into the potato mixture. If necessary, add more *milk* to make of desired consistency. Cover and chill 4 to 24 hours. If desired, garnish with snipped *fresh chives.* Makes about 4 cups (4 side-dish servings).

Nutrition Facts per serving: 223 cal., 15 g total fat (8 g sat. fat), 44 mg chol., 336 mg sodium, 18 g carbo., 2 g fiber, 5 g pro. **Daily Values:** 19% vit. A, 11% vit. C, 8% calcium, 5% iron

ORIENTAL HOT-AND-SOUR SOUP

START TO FINISH: 35 MINUTES

Low-Fat

    8 ounces fresh or frozen peeled and deveined shrimp
 3¹/₂ cups chicken broth (see tip, page 979)
  ¹/₂ of a 15-ounce jar whole straw mushrooms, drained and halved
         lengthwise, or sliced fresh straw mushrooms (optional)
  ¹/₄ cup rice vinegar or white vinegar
    2 tablespoons soy sauce
    1 teaspoon sugar
    1 teaspoon grated gingerroot
    4 ounces tofu, cut into bite-size pieces
    1 tablespoon cornstarch
    1 cup fresh pea pods, halved crosswise, or ¹/₂ of a 6-ounce
         package frozen pea pods, thawed and halved crosswise
    1 beaten egg
    2 tablespoons thinly sliced green onion

1. Thaw shrimp, if frozen. In a large saucepan or pot combine chicken broth, mushrooms (if desired), vinegar, soy sauce, sugar, gingerroot, and $^1/_2$ teaspoon *pepper*. Bring to boiling; reduce heat. Cover and simmer for 2 minutes. Add shrimp and tofu. Simmer, covered, for 1 minute more.

2. Stir together cornstarch and 1 tablespoon *cold water*. Stir into chicken broth mixture along with pea pods. Cook and stir till slightly thickened and bubbly. Cook and stir for 2 minutes more. Pour the egg into the soup in a steady stream while stirring 2 or 3 times to create shreds. Remove from heat. Stir in green onion. Makes about 6 cups (6 side-dish servings).

Nutrition Facts per serving: 109 cal., 4 g total fat (1 g sat. fat), 94 mg chol., 876 mg sodium, 6 g carbo., 1 g fiber, 14 g pro. **Daily Values:** 4% vit. A, 12% vit. C, 5% calcium, 25% iron

---

FRESH TOMATO SOUP

PREP: 30 MINUTES   COOK: 20 MINUTES

Low-Fat

With only 1 gram of fat and no cholesterol, this soup is a great, heart-healthy way to enjoy a bumper crop of summer tomatoes.

   3 **medium tomatoes, peeled and quartered, or one 14$^1/_2$-ounce can tomatoes, cut up**
1$^1/_2$ **cups water**
 $^1/_2$ **cup chopped onion (1 medium)**
 $^1/_2$ **cup chopped celery (1 stalk)**
 $^1/_2$ **of a 6-ounce can tomato paste ($^1/_3$ cup)**
   2 **tablespoons snipped fresh cilantro or parsley**
   2 **teaspoons instant chicken bouillon granules**
   2 **teaspoons lime juice or lemon juice**
   1 **teaspoon sugar**
     Few dashes bottled hot pepper sauce
     Snipped fresh cilantro or parsley (optional)

1. If desired, seed the fresh tomatoes. In a large saucepan combine fresh tomatoes or undrained canned tomatoes, water, onion, celery, tomato paste, the 2 tablespoons cilantro or parsley, bouillon granules, lime juice or lemon juice, sugar, and hot pepper sauce. Bring to boiling; reduce heat. Cover and simmer about 20 minutes or till celery and onion are very tender. Cool slightly.

2. Place half of the tomato mixture in a blender container or food processor bowl. Cover and blend or process till smooth. Repeat with the remaining mixture. Return all to the saucepan; heat through. If desired, garnish with the additional cilantro or parsley. Makes about 4 cups (4 side-dish servings).

Nutrition Facts per serving: 59 cal., 1 g total fat (0 g sat. fat), 0 mg chol., 480 mg sodium, 13 g carbo., 3 g fiber, 2 g pro. **Daily Values:** 11% vit. A, 52% vit. C, 2% calcium, 8% iron

---

CREAM OF VEGETABLE SOUP

START TO FINISH: 20 MINUTES (PLUS VEGETABLE COOKING TIME)

Cook desired vegetables according to the cooking charts on pages 1082 through 1096 or according to the package directions. Drain vegetables well. You should have 2 cups cooked vegetables to add to the soup. Add the seasonings suggested with each vegetable. All of the soups have similar nutrition information.

Cooked vegetable (see variations, below)
1 1/2 cups chicken broth (see tip, page 979)
1 tablespoon margarine or butter
1 tablespoon all-purpose flour
Seasonings (see variations, below)
1/8 teaspoon salt
Dash pepper
1 cup milk, half-and-half, or light cream

1. In a blender container or food processor bowl, combine the cooked vegetable and 3/4 cup of the chicken broth. Cover and blend or process about 1 minute or till smooth. Set aside.

2. In a medium saucepan melt margarine or butter. Stir in flour, seasonings, salt, and pepper. Add milk all at once. Cook and stir till slightly thickened and bubbly. Cook 1 minute more. Stir in vegetable mixture and remaining broth. Cook and stir till heated through. If necessary, stir in additional milk to make of desired consistency. Season to taste with salt and pepper. Makes about 3 1/2 cups (3 or 4 side-dish servings).

■ **Cream of Asparagus Soup:** 3 cups cut *asparagus or* one 10-ounce package *frozen cut asparagus,* 1/2 teaspoon finely shredded *lemon peel,* and 1/8 teaspoon *ground nutmeg.*

■ **Cream of Broccoli Soup:** 3 cups *broccoli flowerets or* one 10-

ounce package *frozen cut broccoli* and 1 teaspoon snipped *fresh thyme or* ¹/₄ teaspoon *dried thyme,* crushed.

■ **Cream of Cauliflower Soup:** 3 cups *cauliflower flowerets or* one 10-ounce package *frozen cauliflower* and ¹/₂ to ³/₄ teaspoon *curry powder.*

■ **Cream of Mushroom Soup:** 5 cups sliced *fresh mushrooms;* 1 teaspoon snipped *fresh thyme or* ¹/₈ teaspoon *dried thyme,* crushed; and, if desired, 1 tablespoon *dry sherry.*

■ **Cream of Potato Soup:** 3 medium *potatoes,* peeled and cubed, *or* 1³/₄ cups mashed, cooked *potatoes* and 1 teaspoon snipped *fresh dill or* ¹/₄ teaspoon *dried dillweed.*

■ **Cream of Pumpkin Soup:** 1 cup canned *pumpkin* and ¹/₄ teaspoon *ground ginger or ground nutmeg.*

■ **Cream of Squash Soup:** 1¹/₄ pounds *acorn squash* (scrape the flesh from peel after cooking; you should have 1¹/₂ cups) and ¹/₄ teaspoon *ground ginger or ground nutmeg.*

Nutrition Facts per serving: 119 cal., 6 g total fat (2 g sat. fat), 6 mg chol., 317 mg sodium, 11 g carbo., 0 g fiber, 7 g pro. **Daily Values:** 16% vit. A, 23% vit. C, 10% calcium, 7% iron

---

CHEESE SOUP

START TO FINISH: 25 MINUTES

Fast

   ¹/₂ cup chopped carrot (1 medium)
   ¹/₂ cup sliced celery (1 stalk)
   ¹/₂ cup chopped red sweet pepper
   ¹/₄ cup thinly sliced green onions (2)
    1 cup water
    3 cups milk
   ¹/₃ cup all-purpose flour
   ¹/₂ teaspoon instant chicken bouillon granules
   ¹/₄ teaspoon white pepper
  1¹/₂ cups shredded sharp cheddar cheese (6 ounces)
  1¹/₂ cups shredded American cheese (6 ounces)

1. In a saucepan cook carrot, celery, sweet pepper, and green onions, covered, in water for 5 minutes or till tender. Do not drain.

2. Gradually stir about *1 cup* of the milk into the flour. Add flour-

milk mixture to cooked vegetables in saucepan along with the remaining milk, the bouillon granules, and white pepper.
3. Cook and stir mixture till thickened and bubbly. Cook and stir for
1 minute more. Stir in cheddar cheese and American cheese till
cheese melts. Makes about 5¹/₂ cups (6 to 8 side-dish servings).

Nutrition Facts per serving: 313 cal., 21 g total fat (13 g sat. fat), 66 mg chol., 732 mg
sodium, 14 g carbo., 1 g fiber, 18 g pro. **Daily Values:** 57% vit. A, 27% vit. C, 44%
calcium, 5% iron

CHILLED CARROT SOUP

PREP: 15 MINUTES   COOK: 20 MINUTES   CHILL: 2 TO 24 HOURS

*Cold soups like this one are a real advantage when you're
entertaining. They can be made the night before and
chilled until serving time.*

1 **pound carrots, chopped (3 cups)**
1 **14¹/₂-ounce can chicken broth**
¹/₄ **teaspoon white pepper**
  Dash ground ginger
¹/₂ **cup dairy sour cream**
  Celery leaves (optional)

1. In a medium saucepan cook carrots in boiling water for 20 to 25
minutes or till very tender. Drain in a colander. Transfer carrots and
¹/₂ cup of the chicken broth to a blender container or food processor
bowl. Cover and blend or process till carrots are smooth.
2. Transfer carrots to a large mixing bowl. Stir in remaining chicken
broth, white pepper, and ginger. Cover and chill for 2 to 24 hours.
3. Before serving, stir in sour cream. If desired, top each serving
with celery leaves. Makes 3¹/₂ cups (4 to 6 side-dish servings).

Nutrition Facts per serving: 127 cal., 7 g total fat, (4 g sat. fat), 13 mg chol., 411 mg
sodium, 13 g carbo., 4 g fiber, 4 g pro. **Daily Values:** 262% vit. A, 4% vit. C, 5% calcium,
6% iron

CHILLED PEACH-YOGURT SOUP

PREP: 10 MINUTES   CHILL: 2 TO 24 HOURS

Low-Fat

This refreshing, cool soup works well as an appetizer or a dessert.

   2 cups sliced, peeled peaches or frozen unsweetened peach slices
  ³/₄ cup peach or apricot nectar
1¹/₂ teaspoons lemon juice
  ¹/₄ teaspoon ground cinnamon
   1 8-ounce carton vanilla yogurt
    Fresh mint sprigs (optional)
    Raspberries (optional)

1. Thaw peaches, if frozen; do not drain. Place peach slices, peach or apricot nectar, lemon juice, and cinnamon in a blender container or food processor bowl. Cover and blend or process till peaches are smooth.

2. If desired, reserve *2 tablespoons* of the yogurt for garnish. In a large mixing bowl stir a little of the peach mixture into the remaining yogurt, stirring till smooth. Stir in the remaining peach mixture. Cover and chill for 2 to 24 hours.

3. If desired, garnish each serving with the reserved yogurt, mint sprigs, and raspberries. Makes about 2¹/₂ cups (4 side-dish servings).

Nutrition Facts per serving: 115 cal., 1 g total fat (1 g sat. fat), 3 mg chol., 36 mg sodium, 25 g carbo., 1 g fiber, 3 g pro. **Daily Values:** 6% vit. A, 15% vit. C, 6% calcium, 1% iron

TROPICAL FRUIT SOUP

PREP: 20 MINUTES   CHILL: 4 TO 24 HOURS

No-Fat

This chilled fruit soup is the perfect way to start a springtime brunch.

   2 cups cubed, peeled cantaloupe, papaya, mango, and/or guava
1 1/2 cups cubed pineapple
   3/4 cup papaya, pear, or guava nectar
   2 teaspoons snipped fresh mint
   3/4 cup lime-flavored seltzer water, chilled
      Sliced strawberries (optional)
      Mint leaves (optional)

1. Place *half* of the fruit, *half* of the nectar, and *1 teaspoon* of the mint in a blender container or food processor bowl. Cover and blend or process till nearly smooth; transfer to a large mixing bowl. Repeat with remaining fruit, nectar, and mint. Cover and chill for 4 to 24 hours.

2. Just before serving, stir in the seltzer water. If desired, garnish each serving with strawberries and mint. Makes about 4 cups (4 to 6 side-dish servings).

Nutrition Facts per serving: 99 cal., 0 g total fat, 0 mg chol., 12 mg sodium, 25g carbo., 1 g fiber, 1 g pro. **Daily Values:** 26% vit. A, 74% vit. C, 1% calcium, 4% iron

VEGETABLES

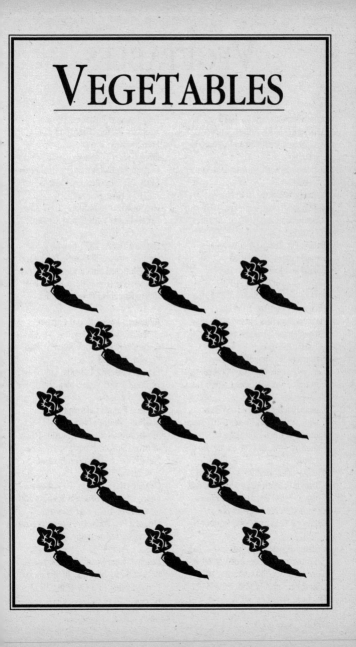

VEGETABLES

ARTICHOKES WITH BUTTER SAUCE

START TO FINISH: 35 MINUTES

    2 artichokes (about 10 ounces each)
      Lemon juice
 1/4 cup butter or margarine
    1 teaspoon snipped fresh dill, tarragon, oregano, or chervil, or
      1/4 teaspoon dried dillweed, tarragon, oregano, or chervil,
      crushed
    1 tablespoon lemon juice

1. Wash artichokes; trim stems and remove loose outer leaves. Cut
off 1 inch from each top; snip off the sharp leaf tips (see photo,
right). Brush the cut edges with a little lemon juice. In a large
saucepan or pot bring a large amount of lightly salted water to boiling. Add artichokes and return to boiling. Reduce heat and simmer,
covered, for 20 to 30 minutes or till a leaf pulls out easily. Drain artichokes upside down on paper towels.
2. Meanwhile, for butter sauce, melt butter or margarine. Stir in the
desired herb and the 1 tablespoon lemon juice. Turn artichokes right
side up and serve with the butter sauce.* Makes 2 servings.
*Note: To eat artichokes, pull off one leaf at a time and dip base of
leaf into sauce. Turn leaf upside down and draw it through your
teeth, scraping off only tender flesh at base of leaf. Discard remainder of leaf. Continue removing leaves until the fuzzy choke appears.
Remove the choke by scooping it out with a spoon; discard choke. If
you have trouble getting the choke out with a spoon, try loosening it
with a grapefruit knife and then pulling it out with the spoon. Eat
the remaining heart with a fork, dipping each piece into the sauce.

Nutrition Facts per serving: 264 cal., 23 g total fat (14 g sat. fat), 61 mg chol., 346 mg
sodium, 15 g carbo., 4 g fiber, 5 g pro. **Daily Values:** 23% vit. A, 31% vit. C, 5% calcium,
11% iron

■ **Artichokes with Sour Cream Sauce:** Prepare artichokes as in
step 1, above. Chill thoroughly. For sour cream sauce, omit butter or
margarine and the 1 tablespoon lemon juice. Reduce the dried herb
(if using) to 1/8 teaspoon. Combine the fresh or dried herb with 1/2
cup *dairy sour cream,* 1 1/2 teaspoons *milk,* 1/2 teaspoon *Dijon-style
mustard,* and dash *onion powder.* Cover and chill at least 2 hours
before serving with chilled artichokes.

Nutrition Facts per serving: 188 cal., 12 g total fat (8 g sat. fat)

■ **Artichokes with Citrus Mayonnaise:** Prepare artichokes as in step 1, page 1028. Chill thoroughly. Omit butter sauce. For citrus mayonnaise, combine ¼ cup *mayonnaise or salad dressing;* 2 teaspoons *orange juice concentrate,* thawed; and ⅛ teaspoon *lemon-pepper seasoning.* Cover and chill at least 2 hours before serving with chilled artichokes.

Nutrition Facts per serving: 269 cal., 22 g total fat (3 g sat. fat)

Using kitchen shears, cut 1 inch from the top of each artichoke. Next, carefully snip off sharp tips of leaves.

ARTICHOKES AU GRATIN

PREP: 30 MINUTES   BAKE: 20 MINUTES   Oven 350°

  1 9-ounce package frozen artichoke hearts
  1 tablespoon grated Parmesan cheese
  1 tablespoon fine dry bread crumbs
 ¼ teaspoon paprika
  1 teaspoon margarine or butter, softened
  1 cup sliced fresh mushrooms
  1 tablespoon margarine or butter
  1 tablespoon all-purpose flour
  1 teaspoon Dijon-style mustard
 ⅛ teaspoon salt
 ⅛ teaspoon dried marjoram or thyme, crushed
    Dash pepper
 ⅔ cup milk

1. Cook artichoke hearts according to package directions; drain. Combine cheese, bread crumbs, and paprika; stir in the 1 teaspoon softened margarine. Set aside artichokes and crumb mixture.

2. For sauce, in a medium saucepan cook mushrooms in the 1 tablespoon margarine over medium-high heat about 3 minutes or till almost tender. Stir in flour, mustard, salt, marjoram, and pepper. Add milk all at once. Cook and stir till thickened and bubbly. Cook and stir 1 minute more. Stir in the artichoke hearts.

3. Transfer mixture to a 1-quart casserole. Sprinkle crumb mixture over the artichoke hearts. Bake, uncovered, in a 350° oven about 20 minutes or till bubbly. Makes 3 servings.*

*Note: To make 6 servings, double the ingredients and prepare as above, except use a large saucepan. Transfer to a 1½-quart casserole and bake, uncovered, about 25 minutes or till bubbly.

Nutrition Facts per serving: 223 cal., 8 g total fat (2 g sat. fat), 6 mg chol., 407 mg sodium, 31 g carbo., 0 g fiber, 12 g pro. **Daily Values:** 15% vit. A, 24% vit. C, 13% calcium, 14% iron

---

ASPARAGUS DIJON

START TO FINISH: 15 MINUTES

Fast

An easy way to remove scales from asparagus spears is with a vegetable peeler.

1½ **pounds asparagus spears or two 10-ounce packages frozen**
    asparagus spears
¼ **cup whipping cream**
2 **tablespoons mayonnaise or salad dressing**
2 **tablespoons sliced green onion (1)**
3 **to 4 teaspoons Dijon-style mustard**
1 **hard-cooked egg, finely chopped (optional)**

1. Snap off and discard woody bases from fresh asparagus (see photo, at right). If desired, scrape off scales. Cook fresh asparagus, covered, in a small amount of boiling water for 4 to 6 minutes or till crisp-tender. (Or, cook frozen asparagus according to the package directions.) Drain; keep warm.

2. Meanwhile, for sauce, beat whipping cream just till stiff peaks form. Fold in mayonnaise, green onion, mustard, and, if desired, egg. Spoon sauce atop asparagus. Serve immediately. Serves 6.

Nutrition Facts per serving: 90 cal., 8 g total fat (3 g sat. fat), 16 mg chol., 96 mg sodium, 4 g carbo., 2 g fiber, 2 g pro. **Daily Values:** 11% vit. A, 36% vit. C, 2% calcium, 3% iron

Starting at the base and working toward the tip, bend the spear several times until you find a place where it breaks easily; snap off there.

SESAME ASPARAGUS

START TO FINISH: 20 MINUTES

Fast

³/₄ **pound asparagus spears or one 10-ounce package frozen cut asparagus**
1 **tablespoon margarine or butter**
1 **tablespoon sesame seed**
1 **cup sliced fresh mushrooms**
1 **teaspoon lemon juice**
¹/₄ **teaspoon toasted sesame oil (optional)**

1. Snap off and discard woody bases from fresh asparagus (see photo, above). If desired, scrape off scales. Cut asparagus into 1-inch pieces. Cook fresh asparagus, covered, in a small amount of boiling water for 4 to 6 minutes or till crisp-tender. (Or, cook frozen asparagus according to package directions.) Drain; remove from pan.
2. In the same pan melt margarine or butter; add sesame seed. Cook and stir over medium heat till seed is toasted. Add mushrooms; cook and stir about 4 minutes or till tender. Add lemon juice and, if desired, sesame oil. Add asparagus, tossing to coat; heat through. Makes 4 servings.

Nutrition Facts per serving: 56 cal., 4 g total fat (1 g sat. fat), 0 mg chol., 37 mg sodium, 4 g carbo., 2 g fiber, 2 g pro. **Daily Values:** 7% vit. A, 25% vit. C, 1% calcium, 5% iron

GREEN BEANS AMANDINE

START TO FINISH: 30 MINUTES

Fast

$^1/_2$ **pound green beans or one 9-ounce package frozen cut or**
   French-cut green beans
  2 **tablespoons slivered almonds**
  1 **tablespoon margarine or butter**
  1 **teaspoon lemon juice**

1. Cut fresh beans into 1-inch pieces or lengthwise (French-cut) slices. Cook fresh green beans, covered, in a small amount of boiling water 20 to 25 minutes (10 to 15 minutes for French-cut beans) or till crisp-tender. (Or, cook frozen beans according to package directions.) Drain; keep warm.

2. Meanwhile, cook and stir almonds in melted margarine or butter over medium heat till golden. Remove from heat; stir in lemon juice. Stir almond mixture into beans. Makes 3 servings.

Nutrition Facts per serving: 85 cal., 6 g total fat (1 g sat. fat), 0 mg chol., 47 mg sodium, 7 g carbo., 2 g fiber, 3 g pro. **Daily Values:** 9% vit. A, 13% vit. C, 4% calcium, 7% iron

GREEN BEANS WITH SHERRY CREAM SAUCE

START TO FINISH: 35 MINUTES

  1 **pound green beans or two 9-ounce packages frozen cut green**
   beans
$^1/_2$ **cup sliced fresh mushrooms**
$^1/_4$ **cup chopped onion**
  1 **clove garlic, minced**
  1 **tablespoon margarine or butter**
  1 **tablespoon all-purpose flour**
$^1/_8$ **teaspoon salt**
$^1/_8$ **teaspoon coarsely cracked black pepper**
$^1/_4$ **cup beef broth**
$^1/_4$ **cup half-and-half, light cream, or milk**
  2 **tablespoons dry sherry, dry white wine, or beef broth**

1. Cut fresh green beans into 1-inch pieces. Cook fresh green beans, covered, in a small amount of boiling water for 20 to 25 minutes or till crisp-tender. (Or, cook frozen beans according to package directions.) Drain; return beans to saucepan.

2. Meanwhile, for sauce, in a small saucepan cook and stir mushrooms, onion, and garlic in margarine or butter about 4 minutes or till tender. Stir in flour, salt, and pepper. Carefully add beef broth and half-and-half all at once. Cook and stir till thickened and bubbly. Cook and stir for 1 minute more. Stir in sherry. Stir sauce into cooked beans in saucepan; heat through. Makes 4 to 6 servings.

Nutrition Facts per serving: 110 cal., 5 g total fat (2 g sat. fat), 6 mg chol., 159 mg sodium, 13 g carbo., 3 g fiber, 3 g pro. **Daily Values:** 12% vit. A, 20% vit. C, 6% calcium, 11% iron

---

HOME-STYLE GREEN BEAN BAKE

PREP: 20 MINUTES   BAKE: 25 MINUTES   Oven 350°

    2 9-ounce packages frozen French-cut green beans or two 16-
        ounce cans French-cut green beans, drained
    1 10³/₄-ounce can condensed cream of celery or cream of
        mushroom soup
  ¹/₂ cup shredded cheddar or American cheese (2 ounces)
    1 2-ounce jar diced pimiento, drained
    1 16-ounce can cut wax beans, drained
  ¹/₂ of a 2.8-ounce can French-fried onions (³/₄ cup) or ³/₄ cup
        croutons, coarsely crushed

1. Cook frozen green beans according to package directions; drain well.

2. In a 1¹/₂-quart casserole combine the soup, cheese, and pimiento. Stir in green beans and wax beans. Bake in a 350° oven for 20 to 25 minutes or till bubbly. Sprinkle with French-fried onions or croutons. Bake 5 minutes more. Makes 6 servings.

Nutrition Facts per serving: 147 cal., 9 g total fat (3 g sat. fat), 16 mg chol., 599 mg sodium, 14 g carbo., 1 g fiber, 5 g pro. **Daily Values:** 12% vit. A, 29% vit. C, 11% calcium, 9% iron

HARVARD BEETS

START TO FINISH: 1 HOUR

Low-Fat

Store unwashed fresh beets in an open plastic bag. They will last up to a week in the refrigerator.

 4 **medium beets (1 pound) or one 16-ounce can sliced or diced beets**
 2 **tablespoons sugar**
 2 **tablespoons vinegar**
 2 **teaspoons cornstarch**
 1 **tablespoon margarine or butter**

1. Cut off all but 1 inch of fresh beet stems and roots; wash. Do not peel. Cook, covered, in boiling water for 40 to 50 minutes or till tender. Drain, reserving $\frac{1}{3}$ cup liquid; cool beets slightly. Slip skins off beets and slice or dice. (Or, drain canned beets, reserving $\frac{1}{3}$ cup liquid.)

2. In a medium saucepan combine reserved beet liquid, sugar, vinegar, and cornstarch. Cook and stir till thickened and bubbly. Cook and stir 2 minutes more. Stir in beets and margarine or butter; heat through. Makes 4 servings.

Nutrition Facts per serving: 85 cal., 3 g total fat (1 g sat. fat), 0 mg chol., 82 mg sodium, 15 g carbo., 4 g fiber, 1 g pro. **Daily Values:** 3% vit. A, 9% vit. C, 1% calcium, 4% iron

---

ORANGE-GLAZED BEETS

START TO FINISH: 1 HOUR

Low-Fat

 4 **medium beets (1 pound) or one 16-ounce can sliced beets, drained**
 1 **tablespoon margarine or butter**
 1 **tablespoon brown sugar**
 1 **teaspoon cornstarch**
 $\frac{1}{4}$ **teaspoon finely shredded orange peel**
 $\frac{1}{4}$ **cup orange juice**

1. Cut off all but 1 inch of fresh beet stems and roots; wash. Do not peel. Cook, covered, in boiling water for 40 to 50 minutes or till tender. Drain and cool slightly. Slip skins off beets and slice.

2. In a medium saucepan melt margarine or butter. Stir in brown sugar and cornstarch. Stir in orange peel and orange juice. Cook and stir till thickened and bubbly. Stir in cooked or canned sliced beets; heat through. Makes 4 servings.

Nutrition Facts per serving: 70 cal., 3 g total fat (1 g sat. fat), 0 mg chol., 73 mg sodium, 10 g carbo., 3 g fiber, 1 g pro. **Daily Values:** 3% vit. A, 20% vit. C, 1% calcium, 3% iron

---

BROCCOLI ORIENTAL

START TO FINISH: 15 MINUTES

Fast

When broccoli stems are tough, use a sharp knife to peel away the outer portion.

> 1 **pound broccoli, cut up (4 cups), or one 10-ounce package frozen cut broccoli**
> ¹/₂ **cup sliced water chestnuts**
> 2 **tablespoons margarine or butter**
> 4 **teaspoons soy sauce**
>   **Dash ground red pepper**

1. In a medium saucepan cook fresh broccoli and water chestnuts, covered, in a small amount of boiling water for 8 to 12 minutes or till crisp-tender. (Or, cook frozen broccoli and water chestnuts according to broccoli package directions.) Drain; transfer to a bowl and keep warm.

2. In the same saucepan melt margarine. Stir in soy sauce and red pepper; heat through. Pour over broccoli mixture, tossing to coat. Makes 3 servings.

Nutrition Facts per serving: 126 cal., 8 g total fat (2 g sat. fat), 0 mg chol., 588 mg sodium, 11 g carbo., 5 g fiber, 5 g pro. **Daily Values:** 30% vit. A, 188% vit. C, 6% calcium, 10% iron

CURRIED BROCCOLI CASSEROLE

PREP: 15 MINUTES   BAKE: 30 MINUTES   Oven 350°

1 1/2 pounds broccoli, cut up (6 cups), or one 16-ounce package
     frozen cut broccoli
  1 cup fresh or frozen sliced carrots
  1 10 3/4-ounce can condensed cream of chicken or cream of
     celery soup
1/2 cup shredded American cheese (2 ounces)
  2 tablespoons milk
1/2 to 1 teaspoon curry powder
1/4 cup crushed rich round crackers

1. Cook fresh broccoli and carrots, covered, in a small amount of
boiling water about 8 minutes or till crisp-tender. (Or, cook frozen
broccoli and carrots according to package directions.) Drain vegetables well.

2. In a 1 1/2-quart casserole combine soup, cheese, milk, and curry
powder. Stir in broccoli and carrots. Sprinkle with crushed crackers.
Bake, uncovered, in a 350° oven about 30 minutes or till heated
through. Makes 6 servings.

Nutrition Facts per serving: 140 cal., 7 g total fat (3 g sat. fat), 13 mg chol., 609 mg
sodium, 14 g carbo., 4 g fiber, 7 g pro. **Daily Values:** 75% vit. A, 118% vit. C, 11% calcium,
9% iron

CREAMY BRUSSELS SPROUTS

START TO FINISH: 30 MINUTES

| Fast |

  2 cups Brussels sprouts or one 10-ounce package frozen Brussels
     sprouts
1/4 cup chopped onion
  1 tablespoon margarine or butter
1/2 cup milk
1/4 cup dairy sour cream or plain yogurt
  2 teaspoons all-purpose flour
1/2 teaspoon Dijon-style, brown, or horseradish mustard
1/8 teaspoon salt

1. Trim stems and remove any wilted outer leaves from fresh Brussels sprouts; wash. Cut any large Brussels sprouts in half lengthwise.
2. Cook fresh Brussels sprouts, covered, in a small amount of boiling water for 10 to 12 minutes or till crisp-tender. Drain; remove from pan. (Or, cook frozen sprouts according to package directions. Drain; remove from pan. Halve large sprouts.)
3. In the same saucepan cook onion in margarine or butter till tender. Combine milk, sour cream or yogurt, flour, mustard, and salt; stir into saucepan. Cook and stir till thickened and bubbly. Stir in Brussels sprouts; heat through. Makes 4 servings.

Nutrition Facts per serving: 104 cal., 7 g total fat (3 g sat. fat), 9 mg chol., 152 mg sodium, 9 g carbo., 3 g fiber, 3 g pro. **Daily Values:** 13% vit. A, 65% vit. C, 6% calcium, 5% iron

PENNSYLVANIA RED CABBAGE

START TO FINISH: 15 MINUTES

Fast

2 tablespoons brown sugar
2 tablespoons vinegar
2 tablespoons water
1 tablespoon cooking oil
1/4 teaspoon caraway seed
2 cups shredded red or green cabbage
3/4 cup coarsely chopped apple (1 small)

1. In a large skillet combine the brown sugar, vinegar, water, oil, caraway seed, 1/4 teaspoon *salt*, and dash *pepper*. Cook for 2 to 3 minutes or till hot, stirring occasionally. Stir in the cabbage and apple. Cook, covered, over medium-low heat about 5 minutes or till cabbage is crisp-tender, stirring occasionally. Makes 3 to 4 servings.

Nutrition Facts per serving: 90 cal., 5 g total fat (1 g sat. fat), 0 mg chol., 184 mg sodium, 13 g carbo., 2 g fiber, 1 g pro. **Daily Values:** 0% vit. A, 32% vit. C, 2% calcium, 3% iron

BROWN SUGAR-GLAZED CARROTS

START TO FINISH: 25 MINUTES

Fast　　　　　　　　　　**Low-Fat**

 ³/₄ **pound medium carrots, parsnips, or turnips, peeled**
  1 **tablespoon margarine or butter**
  1 **tablespoon brown sugar**
    Dash salt

1. Cut the carrots or parsnips in half, both crosswise and lengthwise. (Or, cut the turnips into ¹/₂-inch cubes.)
2. In a medium saucepan cook carrots, parsnips, or turnips, covered, in a small amount of boiling water 8 to 10 minutes for carrots or parsnips, or 10 to 12 minutes for turnips, or till crisp-tender. Drain; remove from pan.
3. In the same saucepan combine margarine or butter, brown sugar, and salt. Stir over medium heat till combined. Add carrots, parsnips, or turnips. Cook, uncovered, about 2 minutes or till glazed, stirring frequently. Season to taste with pepper. Makes 4 servings.

Nutrition Facts per serving: 71 cal., 3 g total fat (1 g sat. fat), 0 mg chol., 86 mg sodium, 11 g carbo., 3 g fiber, 1 g pro. **Daily Values:** 195% vit. A, 3% vit. C, 2% calcium, 3% iron

SWEET-AND-SOUR CARROTS

START TO FINISH: 25 MINUTES

Fast

  3 **cups sliced carrots (4 large) or loose-pack frozen crinkle-cut carrots**
  4 **green onions, cut into ¹/₂-inch pieces**
 ¹/₄ **cup unsweetened pineapple juice**
  2 **tablespoons honey**
  2 **tablespoons margarine or butter**
  1 **tablespoon vinegar**
  1 **teaspoon cornstarch**
  1 **teaspoon soy sauce**

1. In a medium saucepan cook fresh carrots, covered, in a small amount of boiling water for 7 to 9 minutes or till crisp-tender. (Or, cook frozen carrots according to package directions.) Drain; remove from pan.

2. In same saucepan combine onions, pineapple juice, honey, margarine, vinegar, cornstarch, and soy sauce. Cook and stir till thickened and bubbly. Add carrots, tossing to coat; heat through. Serves 4.

Nutrition Facts per serving: 120 cal., 6 g total fat (1 g sat. fat), 0 mg chol., 188 mg sodium, 17 g carbo., 2 g fiber, 1 g pro. **Daily Values:** 137% vit. A, 8% vit. C, 2% calcium, 3% iron

TINY CARROTS WITH DILL BUTTER

START TO FINISH: 15 MINUTES

Fast

If you use baby carrots (those with the tops still on), they need to be peeled and may not have to cook as long as the slightly larger carrots sold in bags.

  1 **16-ounce package (3$^1/_2$ cups) tiny whole carrots**
  2 **tablespoons margarine or butter, softened**
  1 **tablespoon snipped fresh dill or $^1/_2$ teaspoon dried dillweed**
  1 **tablespoon lemon juice**
  $^1/_4$ **teaspoon salt**
  $^1/_8$ **teaspoon pepper**

1. In a medium saucepan cook carrots, covered, in a small amount of boiling water about 10 minutes or till crisp-tender; drain. Stir margarine or butter, dill, lemon juice, salt, and pepper into carrots; toss lightly to coat. Makes 4 servings.

Nutrition Facts per serving: 99 cal., 6 g total fat (1 g sat. fat), 0 mg chol., 269 mg sodium, 11 g carbo., 4 g fiber, 1 g pro. **Daily Values:** 263% vit. A, 7% vit. C, 3% calcium, 4% iron

CAULIFLOWER IN CHEESE SAUCE

START TO FINISH: 30 MINUTES

Fast

Place any extra cauliflower you might have in a plastic bag and chill for up to 4 days.

- 2 cups cauliflower flowerets
- 1 tablespoon margarine or butter
- 1 tablespoon all-purpose flour
  Dash pepper
- 1/2 cup milk
- 1/2 cup shredded American cheese (2 ounces)
- 1 4-ounce can sliced mushrooms, drained

1. In a saucepan cook cauliflower, covered, in a small amount of boiling water for 8 to 10 minutes or till crisp-tender. Drain; remove from pan.

2. In the same pan melt margarine or butter. Stir in flour and pepper. Add milk all at once. Cook and stir till thickened and bubbly. Add cheese, stirring till melted. Stir in the cauliflower and mushrooms; heat through. Makes 4 servings.

Nutrition Facts per serving: 116 cal., 8 g total fat (4 g sat. fat), 16 mg chol., 375 mg sodium, 6 g carbo., 2 g fiber, 6 g pro. **Daily Values:** 10% vit. A, 36% vit. C, 11% calcium, 3% iron

---

BREADED CAULIFLOWER

PREP: 25 MINUTES   BAKE: 20 MINUTES   Oven 400°

Besides cauliflower, this seasoned coating is great on broccoli flowerets and tiny carrots.

- 4 cups cauliflower flowerets
- 1/2 cup fine dry seasoned bread crumbs
- 2 tablespoons grated Parmesan cheese
- 1/4 teaspoon pepper
- 1 slightly beaten egg
- 1 tablespoon milk
- 1 tablespoon butter or margarine, melted

1. Lightly grease a 15×10×1-inch baking pan; set aside. In a large saucepan cook cauliflower, covered, in a small amount of boiling water for 8 to 10 minutes or till crisp-tender. Drain well.

2. Meanwhile, in a plastic bag combine bread crumbs, Parmesan cheese, and pepper. In a small mixing bowl combine egg and milk.

3. Toss 1 cup of the flowerets in the egg mixture; add flowerets to the plastic bag. Close bag and shake to coat well. Place coated flowerets on the prepared baking sheet. Repeat with remaining flowerets. Drizzle melted butter over flowerets.

4. Bake in a 400° oven 20 minutes or till golden, stirring twice. Serve immediately. Makes 6 servings.

Nutrition Facts per serving: 88 cal., 4 g total fat (2 g sat. fat), 42 mg chol., 321 mg sodium, 10 g carbo., 1 g fiber, 4 g pro. **Daily Values:** 4% vit. A, 48% vit. C, 4% calcium, 3% iron

---

CORN AND GREEN CHILI SOUFFLÉ

PREP: 35 MINUTES   BAKE: 45 MINUTES   Oven 350°

*For the best volume, be sure to preheat your oven before
starting this cheesy soufflé.*

   1/4 **cup chopped onion**
   1/4 **cup finely chopped green or red sweet pepper**
    1 **clove garlic, minced**
    3 **tablespoons margarine or butter**
    3 **tablespoons all-purpose flour**
   1/8 **teaspoon ground red pepper**
   3/4 **cup milk**
    1 **cup shredded sharp cheddar cheese (4 ounces)**
    1 **8³/4-ounce can whole kernel corn, drained**
    1 **4-ounce can diced green chili peppers, drained**
    3 **egg yolks**
    3 **egg whites**

1. In a medium saucepan cook onion, sweet pepper, and garlic in margarine or butter till tender. Stir in flour, ground red pepper, and 1/4 teaspoon *salt*. Add milk all at once. Cook and stir till thickened and bubbly. Remove from heat. Add cheese and stir till melted. Stir in corn and green chili peppers.

2. In a medium mixing bowl beat egg yolks with a fork till combined. Gradually add corn mixture, stirring constantly; set aside.

3. In a large mixing bowl beat egg whites till stiff peaks form (tips stand straight). Gently fold about 1 cup of the beaten egg whites into the corn mixture to lighten it. Gradually pour corn mixture over remaining beaten egg whites, folding to combine. Pour into an ungreased 1½-quart soufflé dish.

4. Bake in a 350° oven for about 45 minutes or till a knife inserted near the center comes out clean. Serve immediately (see tip, page 483). Makes 6 servings.

Nutrition Facts per serving: 216 cal., 15 g total fat (6 g sat. fat), 129 mg chol., 474 mg sodium, 10 g carbo., 1 g fiber, 10 g pro. **Daily Values:** 20% vit. A, 17% vit. C, 16% calcium, 6% iron

---

SCALLOPED CORN

PREP: 20 MINUTES   BAKE: 40 MINUTES   STAND: 10 MINUTES   Oven 325°

- ½ cup chopped red or green sweet pepper
- ½ cup chopped onion (1 medium)
- ⅓ cup shredded carrot
- ¼ cup water
- 1 14¾- or 16-ounce can cream-style corn
- 1 8¾-ounce can whole kernel corn, drained
- 1 cup milk
- 1 cup coarsely crushed saltine crackers (about 20 crackers)
- ¾ cup shredded cheddar cheese (3 ounces)
- 2 slightly beaten eggs
- ¼ cup shredded cheddar cheese (1 ounce)

1. Grease a 2-quart square baking dish; set aside. In a small saucepan combine red or green sweet pepper, onion, carrot, and water. Bring to boiling; reduce heat. Simmer, covered, for 5 to 7 minutes or till vegetables are crisp-tender. Drain well, pressing out excess liquid.

2. Meanwhile, in a large mixing bowl stir together the cream-style corn, whole kernel corn, milk, crushed crackers, the ¾ cup shredded cheddar cheese, and eggs. Stir in the cooked vegetables. Transfer mixture to the prepared baking dish.

3. Bake, uncovered, in a 325° oven for 40 to 45 minutes or till center is set. Sprinkle with the ¼ cup shredded cheddar cheese. Let stand 10 minutes before serving. Makes 8 servings.

Nutrition Facts per serving: 174 cal., 7 g total fat (3 g sat. fat), 68 mg chol., 419 mg sodium, 22 g carbo., 1 g fiber, 8 g pro. **Daily Values:** 24% vit. A, 25% vit. C, 11% calcium, 1% iron

---

EGGPLANT PARMIGIANA

PREP: 20 MINUTES   BAKE: 10 MINUTES   Oven 400°

Fast

Eggplants look sturdier than they really are—refrigerate them only up to 2 days.

  1 **small eggplant ($^3/_4$ pound)**
  1 **beaten egg**
$^1/_4$ **cup all-purpose flour**
  2 **tablespoons cooking oil**
$^1/_3$ **cup grated Parmesan cheese**
  1 **cup meatless spaghetti sauce**
  1 **cup shredded mozzarella cheese (4 ounces)**

1. Wash and peel eggplant; cut crosswise into $^1/_2$-inch-thick slices. Dip eggplant into egg, then into flour, turning to coat both sides. In a large skillet cook eggplant, half at a time, in hot oil for 4 to 6 minutes or till golden, turning once. (If necessary, add additional oil.) Drain on paper towels.
2. Place eggplant slices in a single layer in a 2-quart rectangular baking dish.* (If necessary, cut slices to fit.) Sprinkle with Parmesan cheese. Top with spaghetti sauce and mozzarella cheese. Bake in a 400° oven for 10 to 12 minutes or till heated through. Makes 4 servings.
*Note: If desired, omit the baking step. Wipe the skillet with paper towels. Arrange the fried eggplant slices in the skillet; sprinkle with the Parmesan cheese. Top with spaghetti sauce and mozzarella cheese. Cook, covered, over medium-low heat for 5 to 7 minutes or till heated through.

Nutrition Facts per serving: 307 cal., 19 g total fat (8 g sat. fat), 92 mg chol., 594 mg sodium, 21 g carbo., 3 g fiber, 13 g pro. **Daily Values:** 21% vit. A, 16% vit. C, 24% calcium, 9% iron

CREAMED FENNEL

START TO FINISH: 30 MINUTES

Fast

You're probably familiar with the licorice-like taste of fennel seed, which is used to flavor sausages, breads, and cookies. But the less familiar aromatic parent plant, fennel, offers delicious eating, too.

1 fennel bulb (about 1 pound)
1 cup water
1 teaspoon instant chicken bouillon granules
2 tablespoons fine dry bread crumbs
1 tablespoon snipped fresh oregano or $1/2$ teaspoon dried
    oregano, crushed
    Dash pepper
2 tablespoons margarine or butter
2 tablespoons grated Parmesan cheese
$1/4$ cup half-and-half, light cream, or milk
2 teaspoons cornstarch
    Dash paprika
1 tablespoon dry white wine

1. Cut off and discard upper stalks of fennel. Remove any wilted outer layers; cut off a thin slice from fennel base. Wash fennel and cut into quarters lengthwise. In a medium saucepan bring water and bouillon to boiling; add fennel. Cover; simmer for 6 to 10 minutes or till tender. Drain fennel, reserving $1/4$ cup cooking liquid. Transfer fennel to a serving dish; keep warm.

2. Meanwhile, in a small skillet over medium heat cook and stir the bread crumbs, oregano, and pepper in hot margarine or butter for 1 to 2 minutes or till crumbs are toasted. Stir in Parmesan cheese.

3. For sauce, in same saucepan used for fennel combine reserved cooking liquid; half-and-half, light cream, or milk; cornstarch; and paprika. Cook and stir till thickened and bubbly. Cook and stir 2 minutes more. Stir in wine. Spoon sauce over fennel. Sprinkle with crumb mixture. Makes 4 servings.

Nutrition Facts per serving: 116 cal., 9 g total fat (3 g sat. fat), 8 mg chol., 226 mg sodium, 7 g carbo., 0 g fiber, 3 g pro. **Daily Values:** 9% vit. A, 6% vit. C, 6% calcium, 1% iron

KOHLRABI WITH HONEY BUTTER

START TO FINISH: 30 MINUTES

Fast　　　　　　　　　　　　**Low-Fat**

　4　small kohlrabies (about 1 pound), peeled (see photo, below)
　　　and cut into ¼-inch-thick strips
　1　medium carrot, cut into ⅛-inch-thick strips (½ cup)
¼　teaspoon finely shredded lemon peel
　1　tablespoon lemon juice
　1　tablespoon snipped fresh chives or parsley
　2　teaspoons honey
　1　tablespoon margarine or butter

1. Cook kohlrabies and carrot, covered, in a small amount of boiling
water for 6 to 8 minutes or till crisp-tender. Drain; keep warm.
2. Combine lemon peel and juice, chives, honey, and ⅛ teaspoon
pepper. Pour over hot vegetables; add margarine, tossing to coat.
Makes 4 servings.

Nutrition Facts per serving: 79 cal., 3 g total fat (1 g sat. fat), 0 mg chol., 69 mg sodium,
13 g carbo., 3 g fiber, 2 g pro. **Daily Values:** 46% vit. A, 106% vit. C, 3% calcium, 4% iron

Using a sharp knife, pull off strips of
kohlrabi peel from top to bottom to
remove woody fibers.

MUSHROOMS

The many kinds of mushrooms you find in the produce aisle can be bewildering. The following information might help solve some of those mysteries.

Fresh Mushrooms

■ **Button:** Includes white, cream, and brown varieties. Used for commercial production and sometimes referred to as the common mushroom. It has a mild flavor and a cap that ranges from $1/2$ inch to 3 inches in diameter.

■ **Chanterelle** (shan-tuh-REL): Looks like a trumpet with a large, flowerlike cap. It has a golden to yellow-orange color and a delicate, yet meaty flavor.

■ **Enoki** (ee-NO-key): An Oriental variety with a tiny cap and long, slender stems attached to a central base. The enoki mushroom has a mild flavor and is good raw.

■ **Oyster:** An Oriental variety with a pale cream to gray color that has a large, oyster-shell-like cap and a short, fat stem. Cooking helps enhance the flavor.

■ **Portobello** (por-toh-BEHL-loh): A giant-size mushroom that is actually a mature brown mushroom. Cooking brings out its hearty beef flavor.

■ **Shiitake** (shih-TOCK-ee): A brown Japanese mushroom with a large, floppy cap and a rich, meaty flavor. Use only the caps.

■ **Straw:** An Oriental variety grown on straw made from rice plants. These brown, umbrella-shaped mushrooms have a mild flavor and a meaty texture.

Dried Mushrooms

Despite being shriveled, dried mushrooms swell into tender, flavorful morsels ready to toss into pasta, stir-fries, soups, and sauces. To rehydrate, simply soak them in warm water for 30 minutes; rinse, squeeze out the excess water, and remove and discard the tough stems. All Oriental mushrooms mentioned above are available dried, as well as these varieties:

■ **Cèpe** (sehp): Also called porcino (porcini for plural), this Italian mushroom has a rich hazelnut or anise flavor.

■ **Morel:** The elongated cap looks like a sponge with veins. It has a rich, meaty flavor.

MUSHROOM MEDLEY AU GRATIN

PREP: 35 MINUTES   BAKE: 20 MINUTES

Oven 350°

2 tablespoons grated Parmesan cheese
2 tablespoons fine dry bread crumbs
2 teaspoons margarine or butter, softened
$^1/_2$ pound fresh shiitake mushrooms
$^1/_4$ pound fresh oyster mushrooms
1 pound fresh button mushrooms, sliced
1 clove garlic, minced
2 tablespoons margarine or butter
2 tablespoons all-purpose flour
2 teaspoons Dijon-style mustard
$1^1/_2$ teaspoons snipped fresh thyme or $^1/_2$ teaspoon dried thyme, crushed
$^1/_4$ teaspoon salt
$^2/_3$ cup milk

1. In a small mixing bowl stir together the Parmesan cheese, bread crumbs, and the 2 teaspoons margarine or butter; set aside.

2. Separate caps and stems from shiitake and oyster mushrooms. Reserve stems to use in stocks or discard. Slice mushroom caps.

3. In a large skillet cook button mushrooms and garlic in the 2 tablespoons margarine or butter over medium-high heat about 5 minutes or till tender and most of the liquid has evaporated, stirring occasionally. Remove mushrooms, reserving drippings. Add the shiitake and oyster mushrooms to the skillet. Cook for 7 to 8 minutes or till tender and most liquid has evaporated, stirring occasionally. Stir in the flour, mustard, thyme, and salt. Add the milk all at once. Cook and stir till thickened and bubbly. Cook and stir for 1 minute more. Stir in the button mushrooms.

4. Transfer the mushroom mixture to a 1-quart casserole. Sprinkle with the bread crumb mixture. Bake in a 350° oven about 20 minutes or till bubbly. Makes 4 servings.

Nutrition Facts per serving: 184 cal., 11 g total fat (3 g sat. fat), 5 mg chol., 391 mg sodium, 18 g carbo., 3 g fiber, 8 g pro. **Daily Values:** 12% vit. A, 13% vit. C, 9% calcium, 25% iron

HERB-BUTTERED MUSHROOMS

START TO FINISH: 20 MINUTES

Fast

Serve these basil-and-sherry-flavored mushrooms with
broiled steaks or pork chops.

　1　pound fresh mushrooms
1/4　cup chopped onion
　2　cloves garlic, minced
　2　tablespoons margarine or butter
　2　tablespoons dry sherry
　1　tablespoon snipped fresh basil or 1 teaspoon dried basil,
　　　crushed
1/4　teaspoon lemon-pepper seasoning or cracked black pepper

1. Halve mushrooms (quarter any large ones). In a large skillet cook mushrooms, onion, and garlic in margarine or butter over medium-high heat about 5 minutes or till mushrooms are tender, stirring occasionally. Stir in the sherry, basil, and lemon-pepper seasoning or cracked black pepper; heat through. Makes 4 servings.

Nutrition Facts per serving: 98 cal., 6 g total fat (1 g sat. fat), 0 mg chol., 138 mg sodium, 8 g carbo., 2 g fiber, 3 g pro. **Daily Values:** 7% vit. A, 9% vit. C, 1% calcium, 13% iron

PORTOBELLO MUSHROOMS WITH TERIYAKI MARINADE

PREP: 20 MINUTES　MARINATE: 2 TO 4 HOURS　COOK: 18 MINUTES

These magnificent mushrooms are so rich and beef-flavored, you
can serve them as your meat course.

　1　pound fresh portobello mushrooms
　2　tablespoons brown sugar
　2　tablespoons cooking oil
　2　tablespoons lemon juice
　2　tablespoons soy sauce
1/2　teaspoon dry mustard
1/2　teaspoon ground ginger

2 cups shredded Chinese cabbage
2 tablespoons sliced green onion (1)
1 tablespoon snipped fresh cilantro

1. Cut off the mushroom stems even with the caps. Discard stems. Place mushrooms in a large plastic bag set in a bowl. For teriyaki marinade, whisk together the brown sugar, oil, lemon juice, soy sauce, mustard, and ginger. Pour teriyaki marinade over mushrooms; close bag. Refrigerate for 2 to 4 hours, turning the bag several times.
2. Place mushrooms and marinade in a 3-quart saucepan. Cover and simmer about 15 minutes or till mushrooms are just tender. Uncover and simmer for 3 to 5 minutes more or till most of the liquid has evaporated; cool slightly. Cut the mushrooms into ¼-inch-thick slices.
3. To serve, place mushroom slices atop cabbage. Drizzle with any remaining cooking liquid. Sprinkle with green onion and cilantro. Makes 6 to 8 servings.

Nutrition Facts per serving: 84 cal., 5 g total fat (1 g sat. fat), 0 mg chol., 348 mg sodium, 9 g carbo., 1 g fiber, 2 g pro. **Daily Values:** 3% vit. A, 20% vit. C, 2% calcium, 10% iron

SMOTHERED OKRA

PREP: 20 MINUTES   COOK: 20 MINUTES

½ cup chopped onion (1 medium)
½ cup chopped green sweet pepper
2 cloves garlic, minced
2 tablespoons margarine or butter
½ pound whole okra, cut into ½-inch-thick pieces (2 cups) or one 10-ounce package frozen cut okra, thawed
2 large tomatoes, peeled and chopped (2 cups)
½ teaspoon salt
⅛ teaspoon ground black pepper
⅛ teaspoon ground red pepper (optional)
2 slices bacon, crisp-cooked, drained, and crumbled (optional)

1. In a large skillet cook and stir the onion, sweet pepper, and garlic in margarine or butter about 5 minutes or till tender. Stir in okra, tomatoes, salt, black pepper, and, if desired, red pepper. Bring to boiling. Reduce heat and simmer, covered, 20 to 30 minutes for fresh okra (15 minutes for thawed okra) or till okra is very tender. If desired, sprinkle with bacon. Serves 4.

Nutrition Facts per serving: 106 cal., 6 g total fat (1 g sat. fat), 0 mg chol., 344 mg sodium, 12 g carbo., 2 g fiber, 3 g pro. **Daily Values:** 16% vit. A, 61% vit. C, 5% calcium, 5% iron

---

CAJUN FRIED OKRA

PREP: 15 MINUTES   COOK: 3 MINUTES PER BATCH

Fast

*Keep fried okra warm in a 300° oven while you fry
the remaining batches.*

- $1/3$ cup all-purpose flour
- $1/3$ cup yellow cornmeal
- 1 tablespoon Cajun seasoning
- 1 slightly beaten egg
- 1 tablespoon milk
- $1/2$ pound whole okra, cut into $1/2$-inch-thick pieces (2 cups)
  Cooking oil or shortening for deep-fat frying
  Salsa (optional)

1. In a plastic bag combine the flour, cornmeal, and Cajun seasoning. In a small mixing bowl combine the egg and milk. Toss okra pieces in egg mixture. Add one-fourth of the okra to the plastic bag; close bag and shake to coat okra well. Remove coated okra. Repeat with remaining okra.
2. In a large skillet heat $1/4$ inch oil or melted shortening. Fry okra, one-fourth at a time, over medium-high heat 3 to 4 minutes or till golden, turning once. Remove from oil; drain on paper towels. Serve warm, with salsa, if desired. Serves 4.

Nutrition Facts per serving: 370 cal., 29 g total fat (5 g sat. fat), 54 mg chol., 160 mg sodium, 24 g carbo., 2 g fiber, 5 g pro. **Daily Values:** 14% vit. A, 22% vit. C, 6% calcium, 12% iron

CARAMELIZED ONIONS

START TO FINISH: 25 MINUTES

Fast

2 large white or red onions, cut into ¾-inch chunks (2 cups)
2 tablespoons margarine or butter
4 teaspoons brown sugar

1. In a medium skillet cook onions, covered, in hot margarine or butter over medium-low heat for 13 to 15 minutes or till onions are tender. Uncover; add brown sugar. Cook and stir over medium-high heat for 4 to 5 minutes or till onions are golden. Serve hot over burgers, prime rib, or beef steaks. Makes ¾ cup (4 to 6 servings).

Nutrition Facts per serving: 91 cal., 6 g total fat (1 g sat. fat), 0 mg chol., 70 mg sodium, 10 g carbo., 1 g fiber, 1 g pro. **Daily Values:** 7% vit. A, 5% vit. C, 1% calcium, 1% iron

---

GLAZED HONEY-MUSTARD ONIONS

START TO FINISH: 20 MINUTES

Fast   **Low-Fat**

2 medium mild yellow or white onions
2 teaspoons margarine or butter
1 tablespoon bourbon or water
1 tablespoon honey mustard or Dijon-style mustard
1 tablespoon honey
1 teaspoon lemon juice

1. Cut each onion into 8 wedges. In a large saucepan cook onions in a small amount of boiling water for 5 minutes; drain well.
2. In a large skillet cook the onion wedges in margarine over medium-high heat about 6 minutes or till onions begin to turn golden, stirring frequently.
3. Meanwhile, combine bourbon, mustard, honey, and lemon juice. Pour sauce over onions, stirring to coat. Cook and stir 1 minute. Makes 4 servings.

Nutrition Facts per serving: 71 cal., 2 g total fat (0 g sat. fat), 0 mg chol., 119 mg sodium, 10 g carbo., 1 g fiber, 1 g pro. **Daily Values:** 2% vit. A, 5% vit. C, 1% calcium, 1% iron

PARSNIP PUFF

PREP: 30 MINUTES   BAKE: 35 MINUTES   Oven 375°

    1 pound parsnips, peeled and sliced ¹/₂ inch thick (about 3 cups)
  ³/₄ cup thinly sliced carrot (1 large)
  ¹/₄ cup chopped onion
    2 tablespoons margarine or butter
  ¹/₂ teaspoon salt
  ¹/₄ teaspoon pepper
  ¹/₈ teaspoon ground nutmeg
  ¹/₃ cup soft bread crumbs
    2 slightly beaten eggs

1. Lightly grease a 1-quart casserole; set aside. Cook parsnips, carrot, and onion, covered, in a small amount of boiling water about 12 minutes or till very tender; drain. Add margarine or butter, salt, pepper, and nutmeg to vegetables. Mash with a potato masher or beat with an electric mixer on low speed. Add bread crumbs and eggs; mash or beat till smooth.

2. Transfer vegetable mixture to the prepared casserole. Bake, uncovered, in a 375° oven for 35 to 40 minutes or till a knife inserted near the center comes out clean. Makes 4 to 6 servings.

Nutrition Facts per serving: 210 cal., 9 g total fat (2 g sat. fat), 107 mg chol., 147 mg sodium, 29 g carbo., 7 g fiber, 5 g pro. **Daily Values:** 75% vit. A, 27% vit. C, 6% calcium, 8% iron

■ **Turnip Puff:** Prepare as above, except substitute *turnips,* peeled and cut into ¹/₂-inch cubes, for the parsnips.

Nutrition Facts per serving: 135 cal., 9 g total fat (2 g sat. fat)

SCALLOPED PARSNIPS

PREP: 30 MINUTES   BAKE: 15 MINUTES   Oven 350°

For a scalloped vegetable combo, use ¹/₂ pound parsnips and ¹/₂ pound sweet potatoes, peeled and sliced. Cook potatoes in boiling water 8 minutes, then add parsnips and continue as directed.

    1 pound parsnips, peeled and sliced ¹/₄ inch thick (about 3 cups)
  ¹/₄ cup chopped onion
    2 tablespoons margarine or butter

2 tablespoons all-purpose flour
1/4 teaspoon salt
1/4 teaspoon dried thyme or oregano, crushed
1/2 cup chicken broth
1/2 cup milk
1/4 cup fine dry bread crumbs
1 tablespoon margarine or butter, melted

1. Cook parsnips, covered, in a small amount of boiling water for 7 to 9 minutes or just till crisp-tender; drain.

2. Meanwhile, for sauce, cook onion in the 2 tablespoons margarine or butter till tender. Stir in flour, salt, and thyme or oregano. Add chicken broth and milk all at once. Cook and stir till thickened and bubbly. Stir parsnips into sauce. Transfer to a 1-quart casserole.

3. Combine bread crumbs and the 1 tablespoon margarine or butter; sprinkle over casserole. Bake, uncovered, in a 350° oven about 15 minutes or till heated through. Makes 4 servings.

Nutrition Facts per serving: 225 cal., 10 g total fat (2 g sat. fat), 2 mg chol., 415 mg sodium, 31 g carbo., 5 g fiber, 4 g pro. **Daily Values:** 12% vit. A, 23% vit. C, 8% calcium, 8% iron

---

DILLED PEAS AND WALNUTS

START TO FINISH: 35 MINUTES

2 cups shelled peas or one 10-ounce package frozen peas
1/4 cup chopped onion
1 tablespoon margarine or butter
1 1/2 teaspoons snipped fresh dill or 1/2 teaspoon dried dillweed
1/4 cup broken walnuts, toasted (see tip, page 234)

1. Cook the fresh peas and onion, covered, in a small amount of boiling water for 10 to 12 minutes or till crisp-tender. (Or, cook frozen peas and onion according to the pea package directions.) Drain well. Stir in the margarine or butter, dill, 1/4 teaspoon *salt,* and 1/4 teaspoon *pepper;* heat through. Sprinkle with walnuts. Makes 4 servings.

Nutrition Facts per serving: 136 cal., 8 g total fat (1 g sat. fat), 0 mg chol., 170 mg sodium, 13 g carbo., 3 g fiber, 5 g pro. **Daily Values:** 7% vit. A, 17% vit. C, 2% calcium, 8% iron

■ **Peas and Mushrooms:** Prepare as on page 1053, except cook 1 cup sliced *fresh mushrooms* with the peas and onion. Omit dill and walnuts. If desired, stir 1 tablespoon diced *pimiento* into cooked peas and mushrooms.

Nutrition Facts per serving: 91 cal., 3 g total fat (1 g sat. fat), 0 mg chol., 170 mg sodium, 13 g carbo., 3 g fiber, 4 g pro. **Daily Values:** 8% vit. A, 22% vit. C, 1% calcium, 9% iron

ORIENTAL PEA PODS

START TO FINISH: 20 MINUTES

Fast   **Low-Fat**

To lower the sodium in this colorful side dish, use reduced-sodium soy sauce.

  2 cups fresh snow pea pods or one 6-ounce package frozen snow
       pea pods, thawed
 $^1/_4$ cup cold water
  1 tablespoon soy sauce
  1 teaspoon cornstarch
  1 teaspoon sugar
 $^1/_2$ teaspoon grated gingerroot
 $^1/_8$ teaspoon pepper
  1 tablespoon cooking oil
 $^1/_2$ cup thinly sliced carrot (1 medium)
  1 8-ounce can sliced water chestnuts, drained

1. Remove strings and tips from pea pods. For sauce, combine water, soy sauce, cornstarch, sugar, gingerroot, and pepper. Set aside pods and sauce.
2. Pour oil into a wok or medium skillet. Preheat over medium-high heat. Stir-fry carrot in hot oil 2 minutes. Add pea pods; stir-fry 2 to 3 minutes or till vegetables are crisp-tender. Stir in water chestnuts. Push vegetables from center of wok.
3. Stir sauce. Carefully add sauce to center of wok. Cook and stir till thickened and bubbly. Stir all ingredients together to coat with sauce. Cook and stir about 1 minute more or till heated through. Serve immediately. Makes 4 servings.

SUGAR SNAP PEAS WITH ORANGE-GINGER BUTTER

START TO FINISH: 25 MINUTES

Fast   **Low-Fat**

Sugar snap peas (sometimes called sugar peas) are sweet, tender pods that have fully developed, plump, rounded peas inside. Refrigerate sugar snap peas in a plastic bag for up to 3 days.

　　3 **cups fresh or frozen loose-pack sugar snap peas**
　　2 **tablespoons orange marmalade**
　　$^1/_2$ **teaspoon cider vinegar**
　　$^1/_8$ **teaspoon ground ginger**
　　1 **tablespoon margarine or butter**

1. Remove strings and tips from peas. Cook fresh peas, covered, in a small amount of boiling salted water 2 to 4 minutes or till crisp-tender. (Or, cook frozen peas according to package directions.) Drain well.

2. Meanwhile, in a small saucepan heat and stir orange marmalade just till melted. Stir in vinegar, ginger, and $^1/_8$ teaspoon *pepper*. Pour sauce over hot cooked sugar snap peas. Add margarine or butter, tossing lightly to coat. Makes 4 servings.

Nutrition Facts per serving: 85 cal., 3 g total fat (1 g sat. fat), 0 mg chol., 38 mg sodium, 13 g carbo., 3 g fiber, 3 g pro. **Daily Values:** 4% vit. A, 64% vit. C, 3% calcium, 11% iron

MASHED POTATOES

START TO FINISH: 35 MINUTES

　　3 **medium baking potatoes (1 pound), such as russet, round**
　　　　white, or yellow
　　2 **tablespoons margarine or butter**
　　2 to 4 **tablespoons milk**

1. Peel and quarter potatoes. Cook, covered, in a small amount of boiling lightly salted water for 20 to 25 minutes or till tender; drain. Mash with a potato masher or beat with an electric mixer on low speed. Add margarine or butter. Season to taste with salt and pepper. Gradually beat in enough milk to make light and fluffy. Makes 4 servings.

Nutrition Facts per serving: 139 cal., 6 g total fat (1 g sat. fat), 1 mg chol., 209 mg sodium, 20 g carbo., 1 g fiber, 2 g pro. **Daily Values:** 7% vit. A, 12% vit. C, 1% calcium, 2% iron

■ **Duchess Potatoes:** Prepare Mashed Potatoes as on page 1055, except decrease milk to 1 to 2 tablespoons. After adding milk, let mashed potatoes cool slightly. With an electric mixer on low speed, beat in 1 *egg*. Using a decorating bag with a large star tip, pipe potatoes into 4 mounds on a greased 15×10×1-inch baking pan. (Or, spoon 4 mounds onto the baking pan.) Drizzle with 2 tablespoons melted *margarine or butter*. Bake in a 500° oven for 10 to 12 minutes or till lightly browned.

Nutrition Facts per serving: 168 cal., 7 g total fat (2 g sat. fat), 53 mg chol., 124 mg sodium, 23 g carbo., 1 g fiber, 4 g pro. **Daily Values:** 9% vit. A, 13% vit. C, 1% calcium, 3% iron

■ **Potato Patties:** Prepare Mashed Potatoes as on page 1055, except after adding the milk, chill mashed potatoes. In a large skillet cook $1/3$ cup sliced *green onions* in 1 tablespoon *margarine or butter*. Using a slotted spoon, remove onions; reserve drippings. Combine the mashed potatoes, onions, and 1 slightly beaten *egg*. Shape into four $3^{1}/_{2}$- to 4-inch-round patties. In the skillet cook patties in reserved drippings and 2 tablespoons melted *margarine or butter* over medium heat 10 minutes or till golden brown, turning once.

Nutrition Facts per serving: 245 cal., 16 g total fat (3 g sat. fat), 54 mg chol., 224 mg sodium, 23 g carbo., 2 g fiber, 4 g pro. **Daily Values:** 21% vit. A, 16% vit. C, 2% calcium, 3% iron

· MASHED POTATO CASSEROLE

PREP: 35 MINUTES   CHILL: UP TO 24 HOURS   BAKE: 45 MINUTES   Oven 350°

*Perfect for entertaining, these sure-to-please potatoes can
be made the day ahead.*

6 **medium baking potatoes (2 pounds), such as russet, round
white, or yellow**
$^1/_3$ **cup sliced green onions (3)**
1 **or 2 cloves garlic, minced**
2 **tablespoons margarine or butter**
1 **8-ounce carton dairy sour cream**
4 **to 5 tablespoons milk**
   Snipped fresh parsley (optional)

1. Grease a $1^1/_2$-quart casserole; set aside. If desired, peel potatoes.
Quarter potatoes. Cook, covered, in boiling salted water for 20 to 25
minutes or till tender; drain.
2. Meanwhile, in a small skillet cook the green onions and garlic in
margarine or butter till tender. Mash the drained potatoes with a
potato masher or beat with an electric mixer on low speed. Add the
onion mixture, sour cream, $^1/_2$ teaspoon *salt,* and $^1/_4$ teaspoon *pepper.*
Gradually beat in enough milk to make smooth and fluffy. Transfer
to prepared casserole. Cover and chill up to 24 hours.
3. To serve, bake, uncovered, in a 350° oven for 45 to 50 minutes or
till heated through. If desired, sprinkle with parsley. Makes 6 servings.

Nutrition Facts per serving: 267 cal., 12 g total fat (6 g sat. fat), 18 mg chol., 259 mg
sodium, 36 g carbo., 2 g fiber, 5 g pro. **Daily Values:** 15% vit. A, 35% vit. C, 6% calcium,
17% iron

SCALLOPED POTATOES

For a main dish, sprinkle 2 cups chopped fully cooked ham between the layers of potatoes.

$^1/_2$ cup chopped onion (1 medium)
  1 clove garlic, minced
  2 tablespoons margarine or butter
  2 tablespoons all-purpose flour
$^1/_4$ teaspoon pepper
    Dash salt
$1^1/_4$ cups milk
  3 medium potatoes (1 pound), such as long white, round white, round red, or yellow

1. Grease a $1^1/_2$-quart casserole; set aside. For sauce, in a small saucepan cook onion and garlic in margarine till tender but not brown. Stir in flour, pepper, and salt. Add milk all at once. Cook and stir over medium heat till thickened and bubbly.
2. Thinly slice potatoes. Place half the sliced potatoes in the prepared casserole. Cover with half the sauce. Repeat potato and sauce layers.
3. Bake, covered, in a 350° oven for 40 minutes. Uncover and bake about 30 minutes more or till potatoes are tender. Makes 4 to 6 servings.

Nutrition Facts per serving: 228 cal., 7 g total fat (2 g sat. fat), 6 mg chol., 148 mg sodium, 35 g carbo., 1 g fiber, 6 g pro. **Daily Values:** 11% vit. A, 31% vit. C, 9% calcium, 11% iron

■ **Cheesy Scalloped Potatoes:** Prepare as above, except stir $^3/_4$ cup shredded *white cheddar, American, or processed Gruyère cheese* (3 ounces) into thickened sauce till melted. If desired, sprinkle 3 slices crisp-cooked, drained, and crumbled *bacon* over the first layer of potatoes and sauce.

Nutrition Facts per serving: 313 cal., 14 g total fat (6 g sat. fat)

BAKED POTATOES

PREP: 5 MINUTES   BAKE: 40 MINUTES   Oven 425°

No-Fat

> 4 medium baking potatoes (6 to 8 ounces each)
> Shortening, margarine, or butter (optional)

1. Scrub potatoes thoroughly with a brush; pat dry. Prick potatoes with a fork. (If desired, for soft skins, rub potatoes with shortening or wrap each potato in foil.)

2. Bake potatoes in a 425° oven for 40 to 60 minutes (or in a 350° oven for 70 to 80 minutes) or till tender. Roll each potato gently under your hand. Using a knife, cut a crisscross in each top. Press in and up on ends of each potato. Serves 4.

■ **Baked Sweet Potatoes:** Prepare as above except substitute *sweet potatoes* for baking potatoes.

Nutrition Facts per serving: 149 cal., 0 g total fat, 0 mg chol., 10 mg sodium, 35 g carbo., 3 g fiber, 3 g pro. **Daily Values:** 0% vit. A, 37% vit. C, 0% calcium, 4% iron

---

VEGETABLE-TOPPED SAUCY POTATOES

PREP: 15 MINUTES   BAKE: 40 MINUTES   Oven 425°

Low-Fat

Use the herbed yogurt as a dip for your favorite vegetable crudités.

> 1 recipe Baked Potatoes (see above)
> 2 medium zucchini or yellow summer squash, halved lengthwise and thinly sliced (about 2 cups)
> 1 cup sliced fresh mushrooms
> 1/4 cup thin red onion wedges
> 1 tablespoon margarine or butter
> 1 8-ounce carton plain low-fat yogurt
> 1 tablespoon snipped fresh thyme
> 1 tablespoon snipped fresh parsley
> 1/2 teaspoon celery seed

1. Bake potatoes as directed. In a skillet cook zucchini, mushrooms, onion wedges, and 1/4 teaspoon *salt* in hot margarine till onion is tender but not brown and liquid is evaporated, stirring often.

2. Stir together the yogurt, thyme, parsley, and celery seed. Spoon yogurt mixture atop potatoes; add vegetable mixture. Makes 4 main-dish servings.

Nutrition Facts per serving: 265 cal., 4 g total fat (1 g sat. fat), 3 mg chol., 223 mg sodium, 48 g carbo., 2 g fiber, 8 g pro. Daily Values: 6% vit. A, 50% vit. C, 11% calcium, 19% iron

---

TWICE-BAKED POTATOES

PREP: 25 MINUTES   BAKE: 1 HOUR   Oven 425°

  1   **recipe Baked Potatoes (see page 1059)**
  $1/2$ **cup dairy sour cream or plain yogurt**
  $1/4$ **teaspoon garlic salt**
  $1/8$ **teaspoon pepper**
      Milk (optional)
  2   **slices American cheese, halved diagonally (optional)**

1. Bake potatoes as directed. Cut a lengthwise slice from the top of each baked potato; discard skin from slice and place pulp in a bowl. Scoop pulp out of each potato, leaving a $1/4$-inch thick shell. Add the pulp to the bowl.
2. Mash the potato pulp with a potato masher or an electric mixer on low speed. Add sour cream or yogurt, garlic salt, and pepper; beat till smooth. (If necessary, stir in 1 to 2 tablespoons milk to make of desired consistency.) Season to taste with salt and pepper. Spoon the mashed potato mixture into the potato shells. Place in a 2-quart rectangular or square baking dish.
3. Bake, uncovered, in a 425° oven for 20 to 25 minutes or till lightly browned. If desired, place cheese slices atop potatoes. Bake for 2 to 3 minutes more or till cheese melts. Makes 4 servings.

Nutrition Facts per serving: 230 cal., 6 g total fat (4 g sat. fat), 13 mg chol., 155 mg sodium, 41 g carbo., 0 g fiber, 4 g pro. Daily Values: 6% vit. A, 42% vit. C, 3% calcium, 4% iron

BAKED POTATO FANS

PREP: 10 MINUTES   BAKE: 65 MINUTES   Oven 350°

Make cleanup easy by lining your baking dish with aluminum foil.

   4 **medium baking potatoes, such as russet (6 to 8 ounces each)**
   3 **tablespoons margarine or butter, melted**
   3 **tablespoons snipped fresh chives or green onion tops**
 $^1/_4$ **teaspoon garlic salt**
 $^1/_4$ **cup shredded cheddar cheese (1 ounce)**
   2 **tablespoons grated Parmesan cheese**

1. Scrub potatoes thoroughly with a brush. Pat dry. Cut potatoes crosswise into thin slices, but do not cut all the way through (see photo, below). Place in a shallow baking dish or pan. Using your fingers to separate slices, fan potatoes slightly.
2. Combine melted margarine, chives, and garlic salt; drizzle over potatoes. Cover with foil and bake in a 350° oven for 50 minutes. Uncover and bake about 15 minutes more or till tender. Transfer potatoes to a serving platter. Sprinkle with cheddar cheese and Parmesan cheese. Let stand 5 minutes or till cheeses melt. Makes 4 servings.

Nutrition Facts per serving: 277 cal., 12 g total fat (4 g sat. fat), 10 mg chol., 343 mg sodium, 36 g carbo., 1 g fiber, 7 g pro. **Daily Values:** 14% vit. A, 39% vit. C, 9% calcium, 13% iron

---

NEW POTATOES WITH LEMON AND CHIVES

START TO FINISH: 25 MINUTES

Fast

Team these fresh and flavorful potatoes with grilled fish or poultry.

  10 **to 12 whole tiny new potatoes (1 pound)**
   2 **tablespoons margarine or butter**
   1 **tablespoon snipped fresh chives or green onion tops**
   1 **tablespoon lemon juice**
 $^1/_8$ **to $^1/_4$ teaspoon pepper**

1. Scrub potatoes thoroughly with a stiff brush. Cut potatoes in halves or quarters. In a large saucepan cook potatoes in a small amount of boiling, lightly salted water 15 to 20 minutes or till tender; drain.

2. Add the margarine, chives, lemon juice, pepper, and ¹/₈ teaspoon *salt* to the potatoes, tossing gently to coat. Makes 4 servings.

Nutrition Facts per serving: 162 cal., 6 g total fat (1 g sat. fat), 0 mg chol., 142 mg sodium, 25 g carbo., 1 g fiber, 3 g pro. **Daily Values:** 7% vit. A, 28% vit. C, 1% calcium, 12% iron

---

MUSTARD-SAUCED POTATOES

START TO FINISH: 25 MINUTES

Fast

   10 to 12 whole tiny new potatoes (1 pound)
    2 tablespoons finely chopped onion
    2 tablespoons margarine or butter
    2 teaspoons all-purpose flour
 ¹/₈ to ¹/₄ teaspoon pepper
  ³/₄ cup milk
    1 tablespoon Dijon-style mustard
    1 teaspoon prepared horseradish

1. Scrub potatoes thoroughly with a stiff brush. Cut potatoes in halves or quarters. In a large saucepan cook potatoes in a small amount of boiling, lightly salted water 15 to 20 minutes or till tender; drain.

2. For sauce, cook the onion in margarine till tender. Stir in the flour, pepper, and ¹/₈ teaspoon *salt*. Add milk all at once. Cook and stir till thickened and bubbly. Cook and stir 1 minute more. Stir in mustard and horseradish. Pour sauce over potatoes, tossing gently to coat. Makes 4 servings.

Nutrition Facts per serving: 195 cal., 7 g total fat (2 g sat. fat), 3 mg chol., 273 mg sodium, 29 g carbo., 1 g fiber, 5 g pro. **Daily Values:** 9% vit. A, 26% vit. C, 6% calcium, 13% iron

EASY ROASTED POTATOES

PREP: 10 MINUTES   BAKE: 55 MINUTES Oven 325°

To speed it up, roast potatoes, uncovered, in a 450° oven 30 minutes, stirring occasionally.

   3 medium potatoes (1 pound), quartered, or 10 to 12 whole tiny new potatoes (1 pound), quartered
   2 tablespoons olive oil or margarine or butter, melted
   $1/2$ teaspoon onion powder
   $1/4$ teaspoon garlic salt
   $1/4$ teaspoon pepper
   $1/8$ teaspoon paprika

1. Place potatoes in a greased 9×9×2-inch baking pan. Combine oil and seasonings. Drizzle over potatoes, tossing to coat. Bake, covered, in a 325° oven 45 minutes. Stir potatoes. Bake, uncovered, 10 to 20 minutes more or till potatoes are tender and brown on edges. Makes 4 servings.

Nutrition Facts per serving: 171 cal., 7 g total fat (1 g sat. fat), 0 mg chol., 137 mg sodium, 25 g carbo., 1 g fiber, 3 g pro. **Daily Values:** 0% vit. A, 24% vit. C, 1% calcium, 12% iron

HASHED BROWN POTATOES

START TO FINISH: 30 MINUTES

`Fast`

   3 medium potatoes (1 pound), such as russet or yellow
   $1/4$ cup finely chopped onion
   $1/4$ teaspoon salt
   $1/8$ teaspoon pepper
   3 tablespoons margarine or butter

1. Peel potatoes; coarsely shred to make 3 cups. Rinse the shredded potatoes and pat dry with paper towels. Combine shredded potatoes, onion, salt, and pepper.
2. In a large skillet melt margarine or butter. Using a pancake turner, pat potato mixture into skillet. Cook over medium-low heat about 10

minutes or till bottom is crisp. Cut into 4 wedges; turn. Cook for 8 to 10 minutes more or till golden. Makes 4 servings.

Nutrition Facts per serving: 165 cal., 9 g total fat (2 g sat. fat), 0 mg chol., 106 mg sodium, 21 g carbo., 1 g fiber, 2 g pro. **Daily Values:** 10% vit. A, 13% vit. C, 1% calcium, 2% iron

---

FRENCH FRIES

PREP: 15 MINUTES   COOK: 5 MINUTES PER BATCH   Oven 300°

4 medium baking potatoes, such as russet
  Cooking oil or shortening for deep-fat frying
  Salt or seasoned salt (optional)

1. If desired, peel potatoes. To prevent darkening, immerse peeled potatoes in a bowl of cold water till ready to cut. Cut potatoes lengthwise into ³/8-inch-wide strips. Return strips to bowl of water.
2. In a heavy, deep, 3-quart saucepan or deep-fat fryer, heat oil or shortening to 375°. To prevent splattering, pat potatoes dry. Using a spoon, carefully add potato strips, a few at a time, to hot oil. Fry for 5 to 6 minutes or till crisp and golden brown, turning once.
3. Using a slotted spoon, carefully remove potatoes from hot oil. Drain on paper towels. If desired, sprinkle with salt or seasoned salt. Keep potatoes warm in a 300° oven while frying remaining potatoes. Makes 4 to 6 servings.

Nutrition Facts per serving: 263 cal., 12 g total fat (2 g sat. fat), 0 mg chol., 12 mg sodium, 36 g carbo., 1 g fiber, 4 g pro. **Daily Values:** 0% vit. A, 37% vit. C, 1% calcium, 12% iron

■ **Shoestring Potatoes:** Prepare as above, except cut potatoes into long strips and fry for 3 to 4 minutes.

Nutrition Facts per serving: 307 cal., 17 g total fat (2 g sat. fat)

COTTAGE FRIED POTATOES

START TO FINISH: 25 MINUTES

Fast

> 3 tablespoons margarine or butter
> 3 medium potatoes (1 pound), thinly sliced
> 1/4 teaspoon salt
> 1/8 teaspoon garlic powder
> 1/8 teaspoon pepper
> 1 small onion, thinly sliced and separated into rings

1. In a large skillet melt margarine or butter. (If necessary, add additional margarine during cooking.) Layer potatoes into skillet. Sprinkle with salt, garlic powder, and pepper. Cook, covered, over medium heat for 8 minutes. Add onion rings. Cook, uncovered, for 8 to 10 minutes more or till potatoes are tender and browned, turning frequently. Makes 4 servings.

Nutrition Facts per serving: 194 cal., 9 g total fat (2 g sat. fat), 0 mg chol., 243 mg sodium, 27 g carbo., 1 g fiber, 3 g pro. **Daily Values:** 10% vit. A, 25% vit. C, 2% calcium, 12% iron

■ **Baked Parmesan Cottage Potatoes:** Prepare as above, except arrange potatoes and onion in a thin layer in a greased 15×10×1-inch baking pan. Melt margarine or butter; drizzle over potatoes. Omit salt. Combine garlic powder, pepper, and 1/4 cup grated *Parmesan cheese;* sprinkle over the potatoes. Bake in a 450° oven about 25 minutes or till browned.

Nutrition Facts per serving: 225 cal., 11 g total fat (3 g sat. fat),

CANDIED SWEET POTATOES

PREP: 40 MINUTES BAKE: 30 MINUTES   Oven 375°

Low-Fat

    3 medium sweet potatoes or yams (1 pound) or one 18-ounce
        can sweet potatoes, drained
    3 tablespoons brown sugar
    1 tablespoon margarine or butter
  1/4 to 1/2 cup chopped nuts or tiny marshmallows (optional)

1. Cook fresh sweet potatoes, covered, in enough boiling water to
cover, for 25 to 35 minutes or till tender. Drain; cool slightly. Peel
potatoes; cut into 1/2-inch-thick slices. (Or, cut up canned potatoes.)
2. In a 1-quart casserole layer half of the potatoes, *half* of the brown
sugar, and *half* of the margarine. Repeat layers. Bake, uncovered, in
a 375° oven for 30 to 35 minutes or till potatoes are glazed, spooning liquid over potatoes once or twice. If desired, sprinkle with nuts
or marshmallows and bake for 5 minutes more. Makes 4 servings.

Nutrition Facts per serving: 148 cal., 3 g total fat (1 g sat. fat), 0 mg chol., 45 mg
sodium, 30 g carbo., 3 g fiber, 2 g pro. **Daily Values:** 196% vit. A, 36% vit. C, 2% calcium,
3% iron

■ **Peachy Sweet Potatoes:** Prepare Candied Sweet Potatoes as
above, except stir 1/8 teaspoon *ground ginger* into the brown sugar.
Drain and cut up one 8³/4-ounce can *peach slices;* layer with sweet
potatoes.

Nutrition Facts per serving: 195 cal., 3 g total fat (1 g sat. fat)

SWEET POTATO SWIRLS

PREP: 45 MINUTES BAKE: 20 MINUTES   Oven 350°

*Yams, a tropically grown tuber with brownish skin and yellow to
white starchy flesh, are not widely available in the United States.
However, many times, the vegetables labeled yams in supermarkets
are a type of sweet potato. In any case, either yams or sweet potatoes
are a suitable choice for these recipes.*

    6 medium sweet potatoes or yams (2 pounds)
  1/4 cup margarine or butter

1 to 2 tablespoons milk (optional)
2 eggs
2 tablespoons margarine or butter, melted

1. Peel and quarter potatoes. Cook potatoes, covered, in a small amount of boiling water for 25 to 35 minutes or till tender; drain.
2. Mash potatoes with a potato masher or beat with an electric mixer on low speed. Beat in the 1/4 cup margarine. Add salt and pepper to taste. If necessary, beat in enough of the milk to make potato mixture fluffy; cool slightly. Beat eggs into cooled mixture. Using a pastry bag with a large star tip, pipe potatoes into 8 mounds on a greased 15×10×1-inch baking pan. (Or, spoon 8 mounds onto baking pan.)
3. To bake, drizzle the potato mounds with the melted margarine or butter. Bake in a 350° oven about 20 minutes or till light brown. Serves 8.
■ **Make-ahead directions:** Prepare as at lower left, except cover unbaked mounds and chill up to 4 hours or freeze up to 1 month. Bake as directed.

Nutrition facts per serving: 186 cal., 10 g total fat (2 g sat. fat), 53 mg chol., 125 mg sodium, 22 g carbo., 3 g fiber, 3 g pro. **Daily Values:** 205% vit. A, 36% vit. C, 2% calcium, 3% iron

SPAGHETTI SQUASH MARINARA

PREP: 20 MINUTES   BAKE: 30 MINUTES   Oven 350°

Low-Fat

Spaghetti squash is a tasty, low-calorie, high-vitamin substitute for spaghetti.

1 medium spaghetti squash (2 1/2 to 3 pounds)
1/4 cup chopped onion
2 cloves garlic, minced
1 tablespoon cooking oil
1 16-ounce can tomatoes, cut up
1 teaspoon dried Italian seasoning, crushed
1/8 teaspoon fennel seed, crushed (optional)
Grated Parmesan cheese (optional)

1. Halve squash lengthwise; scoop out seeds. Place squash, cut sides down, in a large baking dish. Using a fork, prick the skin all over. Bake in a 350° oven for 30 to 40 minutes or till tender.

2. Meanwhile, for sauce, cook onion and garlic in hot oil till onion is tender. Stir in the undrained tomatoes, Italian seasoning, fennel seed (if desired), and $1/4$ teaspoon each *salt and pepper*. Bring to boiling. Reduce heat; simmer, uncovered, 10 to 15 minutes or to desired consistency, stirring often.

3. To serve, remove the squash pulp from shell with a fork, carefully raking the pulp into spaghetti-like strands. Spoon sauce over squash. If desired, sprinkle with grated Parmesan cheese. Makes 6 servings.

Nutrition Facts per serving: 80 cal., 3 g total fat (0 g sat. fat), 0 mg chol., 236 mg sodium, 13 g carbo., 3 g fiber, 1 g pro. **Daily Values:** 6% vit. A, 28% vit. C, 4% calcium, 7% iron

---

CANDIED ACORN SQUASH

PREP: 10 MINUTES   BAKE: 50 MINUTES   Oven 350°

Low-Fat

> 1 **medium acorn squash (about 1 pound)**
> 3 **tablespoons brown sugar**
> 1 **tablespoon margarine or butter**
> 1 **teaspoon lemon juice or water**
> $1/8$ **teaspoon ground cinnamon or nutmeg**

1. Cut squash into 4 rings; discard seeds. Arrange rings in a single layer in a 2-quart square baking dish. If desired, sprinkle with salt and pepper. Bake, covered, in a 350° oven for 40 minutes.

2. In a saucepan combine brown sugar, margarine, lemon juice, and cinnamon. Cook and stir till bubbly; spoon over squash. Bake, uncovered, 10 minutes or till tender, basting often. Makes 4 servings.

Nutrition Facts per serving: 95 cal., 3 g total fat (1 g sat. fat), 0 mg chol., 40 mg sodium, 18 g carbo., 2 g fiber, 1 g pro. **Daily Values:** 70% vit. A, 24% vit. C, 4% calcium, 5% iron

---

SCALLOPED TOMATOES

PREP: 30 MINUTES   BAKE: 20 MINUTES   Oven 350°

> 3 **slices bread, toasted**
> 2 **tablespoons margarine or butter**
> $1/2$ **cup chopped celery (1 stalk)**

½ cup chopped onion (1 medium)
3 medium tomatoes, peeled and cut up (about 2 cups), or one 16-ounce can tomatoes, cut up
2 tablespoons water
1 tablespoon all-purpose flour
1 teaspoon sugar
½ teaspoon dried marjoram or basil, crushed
Grated Parmesan cheese (optional)

1. Spread toast with *1 tablespoon* of the margarine. Cut toast into cubes; set aside. Cook celery and onion in remaining margarine till crisp-tender. Add fresh or undrained canned tomatoes. Bring to boiling. Reduce heat and simmer, covered, 8 minutes.

2. Combine water, flour, sugar, marjoram, ¼ teaspoon *salt*, and ⅛ teaspoon *pepper*. Stir into tomatoes. Cook and stir till bubbly. Stir two-thirds of the toast cubes into tomato mixture. Pour into a 1-quart casserole. Top with remaining toast cubes. If desired, sprinkle with cheese. Bake in a 350° oven 20 minutes or till bubbly. Makes 4 servings.

Nutrition Facts per serving: 143 cal., 7 g total fat (1 g sat. fat), 0 mg chol., 315 mg sodium, 19 g carbo., 2 g fiber, 3 g pro. **Daily Values:** 12% vit. A, 32% vit. C, 3% calcium, 8% iron

---

CRUMB-TOPPED TOMATOES

START TO FINISH: 25 MINUTES   Oven 375°

Fast

If your fresh tomatoes need to ripen, store them at room temperature in a brown paper bag. Don't stand them in the sun—they'll get mushy.

2 large tomatoes
2 tablespoons fine dry bread crumbs
2 tablespoons grated Parmesan cheese
1 tablespoon margarine or butter, melted
1½ teaspoons snipped fresh basil, oregano, or thyme; or ½ teaspoon dried basil, oregano, or thyme, crushed; or 1 tablespoon snipped fresh parsley or chives
⅛ teaspoon pepper
Dash garlic salt or onion salt

1. Remove stems and cores from tomatoes; halve tomatoes cross-wise. Place tomatoes, cut sides up, in a 2-quart square baking dish. Combine bread crumbs, cheese, margarine or butter, herb, pepper, and garlic salt or onion salt. Sprinkle atop tomatoes. Bake in a 375° oven 15 to 20 minutes or till heated. Makes 4 servings.

Nutrition Facts per serving: 62 cal., 4 g total fat (1 g sat. fat), 2 mg chol., 151 mg sodium, 5 g carbo., 1 g fiber, 2 g pro.
Daily Values: 7% vit. A, 14% vit. C, 4% calcium, 2% iron

FRIED GREEN TOMATOES

START TO FINISH: 35 MINUTES

> 3 medium firm green
>   tomatoes
> ¼ to ⅓ cup milk
> ½ cup all-purpose flour
> 2 beaten eggs
> ¾ cup fine dry bread crumbs
> ¼ cup cooking oil

1. Cut unpeeled tomatoes into ½-inch-thick slices. Sprinkle both sides with salt and pepper. Dip slices in milk, then flour. Dip in eggs, then bread crumbs.
2. In a skillet fry half the slices at a time in hot oil over medium heat 8 to 10 minutes on each side or till brown. (If tomatoes begin to brown too quickly, reduce heat to medium-low.) Add more oil, if needed. Season with salt and pepper. Serves 6.

DRIED TOMATOES

Intensely flavored dried tomatoes are great for cooking because of their rich taste. The process of drying tomatoes originated in Italy, where ripe plum tomatoes were dried in the sun. Today, most dried tomatoes are mechanically dehydrated. They are available as dried halves or bits, plain, or marinated in oil.

■ To plump dried halves, pour boiling water over the tomatoes in a bowl. Let stand about 2 minutes, then drain. Pat dry and, if desired, snip into pieces with kitchen shears. Ready-to-use dried tomato bits and marinated dried tomatoes do not require plumping.

■ To store the dried form, keep the tomatoes in an airtight container in a cool, dry place for up to one year. You can store marinated dried tomatoes in the refrigerator for up to 6 months after opening, but make sure the oil covers the tomatoes.

Nutrition Facts per serving: 176 cal., 11 g total fat (2 g sat. fat), 72 mg chol., 87 mg sodium, 14 g carbo., 1 g fiber, 5 g pro. **Daily Values:** 7% vit. A, 24% vit. C, 2% calcium, 7% iron

LEMON-BUTTERED TURNIPS

START TO FINISH: 25 MINUTES

Fast

    3 medium turnips (1 pound)
    2 tablespoons margarine or butter
    2 tablespoons sliced green onion (1)
    2 teaspoons lemon juice

1. Peel turnips; cut into $1/2$-inch cubes or $2\times1/2$-inch sticks. Cook, covered, in boiling water 10 to 12 minutes or till crisp-tender; drain. Stir in remaining ingredients. Season with salt and pepper. Serves 4.

Nutrition Facts per serving: 71 cal., 6 g total fat (1 g sat. fat), 0 mg chol., 121 mg sodium, 6 g carbo., 3 g fiber, 1 g pro. **Daily Values:** 7% vit. A, 23% vit. C, 2% calcium, 1% iron

BROILED ZUCCHINI SLICES

START TO FINISH: 20 MINUTES

Fast

    2 cloves garlic, minced
    2 tablespoons olive oil, margarine, or butter
    1 tablespoon snipped fresh rosemary or $1/2$ teaspoon dried
        rosemary, crushed
 $1/2$ teaspoon cracked black pepper
    2 medium zucchini and/or yellow summer squash, cut
        lengthwise into $1/4$-inch-thick slices

1. In a saucepan over medium heat cook garlic in oil 30 seconds. Stir in rosemary, pepper, and $1/8$ teaspoon *salt*. Drizzle mixture over zucchini; toss to coat. Arrange zucchini in a single layer in a 15×10×1-inch baking pan. Broil about 5 inches from heat 5 to 6 minutes or till tender, turning once. Serves 4.

Nutrition Facts per serving: 72 cal., 7 g total fat (1 g sat. fat), 0 mg chol., 69 mg sodium, 3 g carbo., 1 g fiber, 0 g pro. **Daily Values:** 1% vit. A, 5% vit. C, 1% calcium, 2% iron

ITALIAN ZUCCHINI-TOMATO SKILLET

START TO FINISH: 20 MINUTES

Fast

- 1 clove garlic, minced
- 1 tablespoon cooking oil
- 2 medium zucchini and/or yellow summer squash, halved lengthwise and cut into $1/4$-inch slices ($2^2/3$ cups)
- 6 green onions, bias-sliced into 1-inch lengths ($3/4$ cup)
- 1 cup halved red and/or yellow baby pear tomatoes or cherry tomatoes (12)
- 3 tablespoons snipped fresh parsley (optional)
- 1 tablespoon snipped fresh basil or 1 teaspoon dried basil, crushed
- 2 tablespoons grated Parmesan cheese

1. In a large skillet cook and stir garlic in hot oil 30 seconds. Stir in zucchini. Cook and stir $1^1/2$ minutes. Add green onions; cook and stir $1^1/2$ minutes more or till vegetables are crisp-tender.

2. Stir in tomatoes, parsley (if desired), and basil. Cook and stir 1 minute more or till heated through. Transfer to a serving dish; sprinkle with Parmesan cheese. Serve immediately. Makes 4 servings.

Nutrition Facts per serving: 68 cal., 5 g total fat (1 g sat. fat), 2 mg chol., 65 mg sodium, 5 g carbo., 2 g fiber, 2 g pro. **Daily Values:** 7% vit. A, 26% vit. C, 4% calcium, 3% iron

BROCCOLI-CARROT STIR-FRY

START TO FINISH: 25 MINUTES

Fast

If you don't have a wok, use a 10-inch skillet when stir-frying. If you have more than 4 cups of ingredients, you'll need a 12-inch skillet.

- $1/3$ cup orange juice
- 1 tablespoon dry sherry
- 1 teaspoon cornstarch
- 1 tablespoon cooking oil
- 1 teaspoon grated gingerroot
- $1^1/2$ cups thinly bias-sliced carrots (3 medium)

1 cup broccoli flowerets
2 tablespoons chopped walnuts

1. For sauce, in a bowl stir together orange juice, dry sherry, and cornstarch; set aside.

2. Pour oil into a wok or large skillet. (Add more oil as necessary during cooking.) Preheat over medium-high heat. Stir-fry gingerroot in hot oil 15 seconds. Add carrots; stir-fry 1 minute. Add broccoli and stir-fry 3 to 4 minutes or till crisp-tender (see step 2, page 634). Push vegetables from center of wok (see step 3, page 634).

3. Stir sauce. Add the sauce to the center of wok (see step 4, page 634). Cook and stir till thickened and bubbly. Stir all ingredients together to coat with sauce. Cook and stir 1 minute more or till heated through. Sprinkle with nuts. Serve immediately. Makes 4 servings.

Nutrition Facts per serving: 106 cal., 6 g total fat (1 g sat. fat), 0 mg chol., 45 mg sodium, 11 g carbo., 3 g fiber, 2 g pro. **Daily Values:** 133% vit. A, 67% vit. C, 3% calcium, 5% iron

---

ORANGE-GLAZED BRUSSELS SPROUTS AND CARROTS

START TO FINISH: 30 MINUTES

Fast **Low-Fat**

2 cups Brussels sprouts (³/₄ pound) or one 10-ounce package frozen Brussels sprouts
3 medium carrots, quartered lengthwise and cut into 1-inch-long pieces (1¹/₂ cups)
¹/₃ cup orange juice
1 teaspoon cornstarch
¹/₂ teaspoon sugar
¹/₄ teaspoon ground nutmeg (optional)
¹/₄ teaspoon salt

1. Halve large fresh Brussels sprouts. In a medium saucepan cook fresh sprouts and carrots, covered, in a small amount of boiling water for 10 to 12 minutes or till crisp-tender. Drain well; return vegetables to pan. (Or, cook frozen sprouts separately according to package directions. Drain; halve any large sprouts. Combine sprouts and cooked carrots in same saucepan.)

2. Combine orange juice, cornstarch, sugar, nutmeg (if desired), and salt. Stir into the vegetables. Cook and stir over medium heat till thickened and bubbly. Cook and stir 1 minute more. Serves 4.

Nutrition Facts per serving: 70 cal., 1 g total fat (0 g sat. fat), 0 mg chol., 188 mg sodium, 16 g carbo., 5 g fiber, 3 g pro. **Daily Values:** 149% vit. A, 99% vit. C, 4% calcium, 8% iron

CARROT AND ONION COMBO

START TO FINISH: 20 MINUTES

Fast

- 2 cups tiny whole carrots or 4 medium carrots, cut into 1-inch-long pieces
- 2 cups frozen loose-pack small whole onions
- 2 tablespoons margarine or butter
- 2 tablespoons brown sugar
- 1/4 teaspoon salt
- 1/8 teaspoon pepper
- 1/8 teaspoon ground mace or nutmeg

1. In a medium saucepan cook carrots and onions, covered, in a small amount of boiling water 8 to 10 minutes or till crisp-tender. Drain; remove from pan.

2. In the same saucepan combine the margarine, brown sugar, salt, pepper, and mace. Cook and stir about 1 minute or till combined. Stir in cooked vegetables, tossing gently to coat. Makes 4 servings.

Nutrition Facts per serving: 125 cal., 6 g total fat (1 g sat. fat), 0 mg chol., 249 mg sodium, 18 g carbo., 3 g fiber, 1 g pro. **Daily Values:** 177% vit. A, 6% vit. C, 3% calcium, 4% iron

JULIENNED PARSNIPS AND CARROTS

START TO FINISH: 20 MINUTES

Fast   **Low-Fat**

- 2 medium parsnips or turnips, julienned (2 cups)
- 4 medium carrots, julienned (2 cups)
- 2 tablespoons snipped fresh parsley
- 1 tablespoon margarine or butter
- 1/4 teaspoon dried thyme, crushed
- 1/8 teaspoon salt
- 1/8 teaspoon pepper

1. In a medium saucepan cook parsnips and carrots, covered, in a small amount of boiling water 7 to 9 minutes or till crisp-tender; drain. Stir in the parsley, margarine, thyme, salt, and pepper. Serves 4.

Nutrition Facts per serving: 105 cal., 3 g total fat (1 g sat. fat), 0 mg chol., 132 mg sodium, 19 g carbo., 5 g fiber, 2 g pro. **Daily Values:** 89% vit. A, 22% vit. C, 3% calcium, 5% iron

---

ASPARAGUS-TOMATO STIR-FRY

START TO FINISH: 25 MINUTES

Fast

³⁄₄ **pound asparagus spears or one 10-ounce package frozen cut asparagus**

¹⁄₄ **cup chicken broth**

2 **teaspoons soy sauce**

1 **teaspoon cornstarch**

1 **tablespoon cooking oil**

¹⁄₂ **teaspoon grated gingerroot**

4 **green onions, bias-sliced into 1-inch lengths (¹⁄₂ cup)**

1¹⁄₂ **cups sliced fresh mushrooms**

2 **small tomatoes, cut into thin wedges**

1. Snap off and discard woody bases from fresh asparagus (see photo, page 1031). If desired, scrape off scales. Bias-slice asparagus into 1-inch-long pieces. (Or, thaw and drain frozen asparagus.) For sauce, combine broth, soy sauce, and cornstarch.

2. Pour cooking oil into a wok or large skillet. (Add more oil as necessary during cooking.) Preheat over medium-high heat. Stir-fry gingerroot in hot oil 30 seconds. Add asparagus and green onions; stir-fry 3 minutes. Add mushrooms; stir-fry 1 minute more or till asparagus is crisp-tender (see step 2, page 634).

3. Push the vegetables from center of wok (see step 3, page 634). Stir sauce; add to center of wok (see step 4, page 634). Cook and stir till thickened and bubbly. Add tomatoes. Stir to coat vegetables with sauce; heat through. Serves 4.

Nutrition Facts per serving: 70 cal., 4 g total fat (1 g sat. fat), 0 mg chol., 227 mg sodium, 7 g carbo., 2 g fiber, 3 g pro. **Daily Values:** 10% vit. A, 46% vit. C, 1% calcium, 8% iron

CAULIFLOWER-BROCCOLI BAKE

PREP: 25 MINUTES BAKE: 12 MINUTES Oven 375°

- 1 10-ounce package frozen cauliflower
- 1 10-ounce package frozen cut broccoli
- 1 17-ounce can cream-style corn
- 1 10³/₄-ounce can condensed cream of celery or cream of mushroom soup
- 1¹/₂ cups shredded American or process Swiss cheese (6 ounces)
- 1 4-ounce can sliced mushrooms, drained
- 1 tablespoon dried minced onion
- ¹/₂ teaspoon dried thyme, marjoram, or savory, crushed
- 2 tablespoons margarine or butter, melted
- 1 cup soft bread crumbs

1. Cook cauliflower and broccoli according to package directions. Drain; remove from pan.
2. In the same saucepan combine corn, soup, cheese, mushrooms, onion, and herb. Cook and stir till bubbly. Stir in cooked cauliflower and broccoli. Transfer mixture to a 2-quart casserole.
3. Combine margarine and bread crumbs; sprinkle atop casserole. Bake in a 375° oven 12 to 15 minutes or till bubbly. Makes 10 to 12 servings.

Nutrition Facts per serving: 154 cal., 8 g total fat (3 g sat. fat), 13 mg chol., 705 mg sodium, 18 g carbo., 3 g fiber, 6 g pro. **Daily Values:** 12% vit. A, 34% vit. C, 11% calcium, 6% iron

---

RATATOUILLE

PREP: 25 MINUTES COOK: 25 MINUTES

This Mediterranean dish featuring eggplant and tomatoes is equally delicious served cold.

- ¹/₂ cup finely chopped onion (1 medium)
- 1 clove garlic, minced
- 1 tablespoon olive oil or cooking oil
- 2 cups cubed, peeled eggplant
- 1 small zucchini or yellow summer squash, halved lengthwise and cut into ¹/₄-inch-thick slices (1 cup)

1 cup peeled, chopped tomatoes or one 7$\frac{1}{2}$-ounce can tomatoes, cut up
$\frac{1}{2}$ cup chopped green sweet pepper
2 tablespoons dry white wine or water
1$\frac{1}{2}$ teaspoons snipped fresh basil or $\frac{1}{2}$ teaspoon dried basil, crushed
$\frac{1}{2}$ cup shredded Swiss cheese (optional)

1. In a large skillet cook onion and garlic in hot oil till onion is tender. Stir in the vegetables, wine, basil, $\frac{1}{8}$ teaspoon *salt*, and $\frac{1}{8}$ teaspoon *pepper*. Bring to boiling. Reduce heat; simmer, covered, 20 minutes or till tender. Uncover; cook 5 to 10 minutes or till thickened, stirring occasionally. If desired, sprinkle with cheese. Makes 4 servings.

Nutrition Facts per serving: 77 cal., 4 g total fat (1 g sat. fat), 0 mg chol., 75 mg sodium, 10 g carbo., 3 g fiber, 1 g pro. **Daily Values:** 4% vit. A, 37% vit. C, 1% calcium, 4% iron

---

CREAMED PEAS AND NEW POTATOES

START TO FINISH: 40 MINUTES

10 to 12 whole tiny new potatoes (1 pound)
1$\frac{1}{2}$ cups shelled peas or frozen loose-pack peas
$\frac{1}{4}$ cup chopped onion
1 tablespoon margarine or butter
1 tablespoon all-purpose flour
1 cup milk

1. Scrub potatoes; cut any large potatoes in half. If desired, remove a narrow strip of peel from around the center of each potato. In a medium saucepan cook potatoes in a small amount of boiling salted water for 8 minutes. Add peas and cook 10 to 12 minutes more or till tender; drain.
2. Meanwhile, in a medium saucepan cook onion in margarine till tender. Stir in flour, $\frac{1}{2}$ teaspoon *salt*, and dash *pepper*. Add milk all at once. Cook and stir till thickened and bubbly. Cook and stir 1 minute more. Stir in potatoes and peas; heat through. Season to taste. Makes 4 servings.

Nutrition Facts per serving: 210 cal., 4 g total fat (1 g sat. fat), 5 mg chol., 340 mg sodium, 37 g carbo., 3 g fiber, 7 g pro. **Daily Values:** 9% vit. A, 35% vit. C, 8% calcium, 17% iron

SUCCOTASH

START TO FINISH: 25 MINUTES

Fast

    2 cups cut fresh corn or one 10-ounce package frozen whole
        kernel corn
    2 cups fresh baby lima beans or one 10-ounce package frozen
        baby lima beans
 1/4 cup chopped onion
 1/4 cup chopped red or green sweet pepper
    1 tablespoon margarine or butter
 1/4 teaspoon salt
 1/8 teaspoon pepper

1. In a large saucepan cook fresh or frozen corn and lima beans in a small amount of boiling, lightly salted water for 10 minutes. Add onion and sweet pepper; cook 5 to 10 minutes more or till vegetables are tender; drain well. Stir in margarine or butter, salt, and pepper. Makes 4 to 6 servings.

Nutrition Facts per serving: 311 cal., 5 g total fat (1 g sat. fat), 0 mg chol., 184 mg sodium, 56 g carbo., 8 g fiber, 16 g pro. **Daily Values:** 9% vit. A, 26% vit. C, 2% calcium, 30% iron

---

LEMON-GLAZED VEGETABLES WITH DILL

START TO FINISH: 40 MINUTES

Low-Fat

    8 whole tiny new potatoes, halved, or 2 medium red-skinned
        potatoes, quartered
    1 medium rutabaga, peeled and cut into 1-inch pieces (1 1/2 cups)
    2 medium carrots, sliced (1 cup)
    1 medium turnip, peeled and cut into 1-inch pieces (1 1/4 cups)
    1 medium parsnip, peeled and sliced (1 cup)
    1 small onion, cut into wedges
    1 tablespoon margarine or butter
    3 tablespoons brown sugar
    1 teaspoon cornstarch
 1/2 teaspoon finely shredded lemon peel
    3 tablespoons lemon juice
    2 teaspoons snipped fresh dill or 1/2 teaspoon dried dillweed

1. In a saucepan cook potatoes and rutabaga, covered, in boiling, lightly salted water 10 minutes. Add carrots, turnip, parsnip, and onion. Return to boiling. Reduce heat; cook, covered, 7 to 9 minutes or till tender. Drain; return vegetables to saucepan.

2. Meanwhile, in a small saucepan melt margarine. Stir in brown sugar and cornstarch. Stir in lemon peel and juice, dill, ¼ cup *water,* ½ teaspoon *salt,* and ¼ teaspoon *pepper.* Cook and stir till thickened and bubbly. Cook and stir 2 minutes more. Pour over vegetables in pan. Cook and stir 3 to 4 minutes or till vegetables are heated through. Serves 6.

Nutrition Facts per serving: 140 cal., 2 g total fat (0 g sat. fat), 0 mg chol., 241 mg sodium, 29 g carbo., 4 g fiber, 2 g pro. **Daily Values:** 59% vit. A, 38% vit. C, 4% calcium, 9% iron

---

VEGETABLES WITH TOMATO-PEPPER BUTTER

START TO FINISH: 20 MINUTES

Fast

    2 tablespoons butter or margarine, softened
    1 tablespoon finely snipped oil-packed dried tomatoes or roasted
        sweet peppers, drained
    1 clove garlic, minced (optional)
  ⅛ teaspoon coarsely ground black pepper
    4 cups hot cooked broccoli flowerets, cauliflower flowerets,
        green beans, asparagus spears, sugar snap peas or snow pea
        pods, or tiny whole carrots

1. Combine margarine or butter, dried tomatoes or sweet peppers, garlic (if desired), and pepper. Add butter mixture to desired cooked vegetables, tossing gently to coat. Makes 4 servings.

Nutrition Facts per serving: 97 cal., 7 g total fat (4 g sat. fat), 15 mg chol., 103 mg sodium, 8 g carbo., 5 g fiber, 5 g pro. **Daily Values:** 26% vit. A, 196% vit. C, 6% calcium, 8% iron

GARDEN-VEGETABLE STIR-FRY

START TO FINISH: 30 MINUTES

Fast

    2 tablespoons cold water
1¹/₂ teaspoons cornstarch
    2 tablespoons soy sauce
    1 tablespoon dry sherry or orange juice
    2 teaspoons sugar
    1 cup green beans, bias-sliced into 1-inch pieces
1¹/₂ cups cauliflower, cut into ¹/₂-inch flowerets
    1 tablespoon cooking oil
    1 medium onion, cut into thin wedges
 ¹/₂ cup thinly bias-sliced carrot (1 medium)
    1 small zucchini, halved lengthwise and cut into ¹/₄-inch slices (1
      cup)

1. Combine water and cornstarch. Stir in soy sauce, sherry, sugar, and dash *pepper;* set aside.

2. Cook beans, covered, in boiling, salted water 2 minutes. Add cauliflower; return to boiling. Reduce heat. Simmer, covered, 1 minute; drain.

3. Pour oil into a wok or large skillet. (Add more oil as necessary during cooking.) Preheat over medium-high heat. Add onion and carrot; stir-fry 2 minutes. Add beans, cauliflower, and zucchini; stir-fry 3 to 4 minutes or till vegetables are crisp-tender (see step 2, page 634). Push vegetables from center of wok (see step 3, page 634).

4. Stir sauce. Add sauce to the center of wok (see step 4, page 634). Cook and stir till thickened and bubbly. Stir to coat vegetables with sauce. Cook and stir 1 minute or till heated through. Makes 4 servings.

Nutrition Facts per serving: 97 cal., 4 g total fat (1 g sat. fat), 0 mg chol., 530 mg sodium, 14 g carbo., 2 g fiber, 3 g pro. **Daily Values:** 54% vit. A, 49% vit. C, 3% calcium, 7% iron

OVEN-ROASTED VEGGIES

PREP: 20 MINUTES   BAKE: 65 MINUTES   Oven 325°

    3 medium potatoes (1 pound), peeled and cut into 1-inch pieces
    1 medium turnip, peeled, quartered, and sliced ¹/₂ inch thick
    1 cup tiny whole carrots or 2 medium carrots, halved lengthwise
         and cut into 2-inch pieces
    1 medium onion, cut into wedges
  ¹/₄ cup olive oil, or margarine or butter, melted
    1 tablespoon snipped fresh basil or oregano, or 1 teaspoon dried
         basil or oregano, crushed
    1 tablespoon lemon juice
    3 cloves garlic, minced
    1 teaspoon salt
  ¹/₂ teaspoon coarsely ground black pepper
    1 medium red and/or green sweet pepper, cut into ¹/₂-inch-wide
         strips

1. In a greased 13×9×2-inch baking pan combine potatoes, turnip, carrots, and onion.
2. Combine oil, herb, lemon juice, garlic, salt, and pepper. Drizzle over vegetables; toss to coat. Bake, covered, in a 325° oven 45 minutes, stirring once.
3. Increase oven temperature to 450°. Add sweet pepper strips to baking pan; toss. Bake, uncovered, about 20 minutes or till vegetables are tender and brown on edges, stirring occasionally. Serves 6.

Nutrition Facts per serving: 235 cal., 14 g total fat (4 g sat. fat), 0 mg chol., 396 mg sodium, 26 g carbo., 5 g fiber, 3 g pro. **Daily Values:** 57% vit. A, 33% vit. C, 2% calcium, 7% iron

COOKING FRESH VEGETABLES

There are several ways to cook fresh vegetables—on the range top, in the oven, and in the microwave oven. Keep in mind that cooking and steaming times may vary depending on the particular vegetable. The amounts given on the chart yield enough cooked vegetables for 4 servings, except where noted.

To steam vegetables, place the steamer basket in a saucepan. Add water to just below the bottom of the steamer basket. Bring to boiling. Add vegetables. Cover and reduce heat. Steam for the time specified in the chart or until desired doneness.

To microwave vegetables, use a microwave-safe baking dish or casserole and follow the directions in the chart.

Vegetable Amount	Preparation	Conventional Cooking Directions	Microwave Cooking Directions
Artichokes Two, 10 ounces each (2 servings)	Wash; trim stems. Cut off 1 inch from tops, and snip off sharp leaf tips (see photo, page 1029). Brush cut edges with lemon juice.	Cook, covered, in a large amount of boiling salted water for 20 to 30 minutes or till a leaf pulls out easily. (Or, steam for 20 to 25 minutes.) Invert artichokes to drain.	Place in a casserole with 2 tablespoons water. Microwave, covered, on 100% power (high) for 7 to 9 minutes or till a leaf pulls out easily, rearranging artichokes once. Invert to drain.

Artichokes, baby 1 pound (6 to 8 whole)	Trim stems; cut off the top ¼ of the artichoke. Remove outer leaves till pale green petals are reached. Cut into halves or quarters. Cut out fuzzy centers, if necessary.	Cook, covered, in a large amount of boiling salted water for 15 minutes or till tender. (Or, steam for 15 to 20 minutes.)	Place in a casserole with 2 tablespoons water. Microwave, covered, on 100% power (high) for 6 to 9 minutes or till tender.
Asparagus 1 pound (2 cups pieces)	Wash; break off woody bases where spears snap easily (see photo, page 1031). Scrape off scales. Leave spears whole or cut into 1-inch pieces.	Cook spears or pieces, covered, in a small amount of boiling salted water for 4 to 6 minutes or till crisp-tender. (Or, steam spears or pieces for 4 to 6 minutes.)	Place in a baking dish or casserole with 2 tablespoons water. Microwave spears or pieces, covered, on 100% power (high) for 3 to 6 minutes or till crisp-tender, rearranging or stirring once.
Beans (green, Italian green, purple, yellow wax) ¾ pound (2¼ cups pieces)	Wash; remove ends and strings. Leave whole or cut into 1-inch pieces. For French-cut beans, slice lengthwise.	Cook, covered, in a small amount of boiling salted water for 20 to 25 minutes for whole or cut beans (10 to 15 minutes for	Place in a casserole with 2 tablespoons water. Microwave, covered, on 100% power (high) for 10 to 13 minutes for whole or

Cooking Fresh Vegetables (continued)

Vegetable Amount	Preparation	Conventional Cooking Directions	Microwave Cooking Directions
		French-cut beans) or till tender. (Or, steam whole, cut, or French-cut beans for 18 to 22 minutes.)	cut beans (9 to 12 minutes for French-cut beans) or till tender, stirring once.
Beets 1 pound (2¼ cups cubes)	For whole beets, cut off all but 1 inch of stems and roots; wash. Do not peel. (For microwaving, prick the skins of whole beets.) Or, peel beets; cube or slice.	Cook, covered, in boiling salted water for 40 to 50 minutes for whole beets (about 20 minutes for cubed or sliced beets) or till crisp-tender. Slip skins off whole beets.	Place in a casserole with 2 tablespoons water. Microwave whole, cubed, or sliced beets, covered, on 100% power (high) for 9 to 12 minutes or till crisp-tender, rearranging or stirring once. Slip skins off whole beets.
Broccoli ¾ pound (3 cups flowerets)	Wash; remove outer leaves and tough parts of stalks. Cut lengthwise into spears or cut into ½-inch	Cook, covered, in a small amount of boiling salted water for 8 to 12 minutes or till crisp-tender. (Or,	Place in a baking dish with 2 tablespoons water. Microwave, covered, on 100% power (high) for 5 to

		steam for 8 to 12 minutes.	8 minutes or till crisp-tender, rearranging or stirring once.
	flowerets.		
Brussels Sprouts 3/4 pound (3 cups)	Trim stems and remove any wilted outer leaves; wash. Cut large sprouts in half lengthwise.	Cook, covered, in a small amount of boiling salted water for 10 to 12 minutes or till crisp-tender. (Or, steam for 10 to 15 minutes.)	Place in a casserole with 2 tablespoons water. Microwave, covered, on 100% power (high) for 5 to 7 minutes or till crisp-tender, stirring once.
Cabbage Half of a 1- to 1½-pound head (4 cups pieces)	Remove wilted outer leaves; wash. Cut into 4 wedges or 1-inch pieces.	Cook, uncovered, in a small amount of boiling water for 2 minutes. Cover; cook for 6 to 8 minutes for wedges (3 to 5 minutes for pieces) or till crisp-tender. (Or, steam wedges for 10 to 12 minutes.)	Place in a baking dish or casserole with 2 tablespoons water. Microwave, covered, on 100% power (high) for 9 to 11 minutes for wedges (4 to 6 minutes for pieces) or till crisp-tender, rearranging or stirring once.
Carrots	Wash, trim, and peel or scrub. Cut into ¼-inch-	Cook, covered, in small amount of boiling salted	Place in a casserole with 2 tablespoons water.

COOKING FRESH VEGETABLES (continued)

Vegetable Amount	Preparation	Conventional Cooking Directions	Microwave Cooking Directions
1 pound (3 cups slices)	thick slices or into strips.	water for 7 to 9 minutes for slices (5 to 7 minutes for strips) or till crisp-tender. (Or, steam slices for 8 to 10 minutes or strips for 6 to 8 minutes.)	Microwave, covered, on 100% power (high) for 6 to 9 minutes for slices (5 to 7 minutes for strips) or till crisp-tender, stirring once.
Carrots, tiny whole 1 pound (3½ cups)	Wash; trim and scrub if necessary.	Cook, covered, in boiling salted water for 8 to 10 minutes or till crisp-tender. (Or, steam for 8 to 10 minutes.)	Place in a casserole with 2 tablespoons water. Microwave, covered, on 100% power (high) for 7 to 9 minutes or till crisp-tender, stirring once.
Cauliflower ¾ pound (3 cups flowerets)	Wash; remove leaves and woody stem. Leave whole or break into flowerets.	Cook, covered, in a small amount of boiling salted water for 10 to 15 minutes for head (8 to 10 minutes for flowerets) or till crisp-	Place in a casserole with 2 tablespoons water. Microwave, covered, on 100% power (high) for 9 to 11 minutes for head (6½

	tender. (Or, steam head or flowerets for 8 to 12 minutes.)	to 10 minutes for flowerets) or till tender, turning, rearranging, or stirring once.
Celeriac 1 pound (2½ cups strips)	Wash; trim off the leaves and ends. Peel off hairy brown skin. Cut into strips.	Cook, covered, in a small amount of boiling salted water for 5 to 6 minutes or till crisp-tender. (Or, steam for 5 minutes.)	Place in a casserole with 2 tablespoons water. Microwave, covered, on 100% power (high) for 3 to 4 minutes or till crisp-tender, stirring once.
Celery 5 stalks (2½ cups slices)	Remove leaves; wash stalks. Cut into ½-inch-thick slices.	Cook, covered, in a small amount of boiling salted water for 6 to 9 minutes or till tender. (Or, steam for 7 to 10 minutes.)	Place in a casserole with 2 tablespoons water. Microwave, covered, on 100% power (high) for 6 to 10 minutes or till tender, stirring once.
Chayote 1½ medium (15 ounces) (2 cups cubes)	Wash, peel, halve lengthwise, and remove seed; cube.	Cook, covered, in a small amount of boiling salted water about 5 minutes or till tender. (Or, steam	Place in a casserole with 2 tablespoons water. Microwave, covered, on 100% power (high) for 5 to

Cooking Fresh Vegetables *(continued)*

Vegetable Amount	Preparation	Conventional Cooking Directions	Microwave Cooking Directions
		about 8 minutes.)	6 minutes or till tender, stirring once.
Corn 2 cups	Remove husks from fresh ears of corn. Scrub with a stiff brush to remove silks; rinse. Cut kernels from cob.	Cook, covered, in a small amount of boiling salted water for 4 minutes. (Or, steam for 4 to 5 minutes.)	Place in a casserole with 2 tablespoons water. Microwave, covered, on high for 5 to 6 minutes, stirring once.
Corn on the cob (1 ear equals 1 serving)	Remove husks from fresh ears of corn. Scrub with a stiff brush to remove silks; rinse.	Cook, covered, in a small amount of lightly salted boiling water (or in enough boiling water to cover) for 5 to 7 minutes or till tender.	Wrap each ear in waxed paper; place on microwave-safe paper towels in the microwave. Microwave on 100% power (high) for 3 to 5 minutes for 1 ear; 5 to 7 minutes for 2 ears; or 9 to 12 minutes for 4 ears, rearranging once.

Eggplant 1 medium (1 pound) (5 cups cubes)	Wash and peel. Cut into ¾-inch cubes.	Cook, covered, in a small amount of boiling water for 4 to 5 minutes or till tender. (Or, steam for 4 to 5 minutes.)	Place in a casserole with 2 tablespoons water. Microwave, covered, on 100% power (high) for 6 to 8 minutes or till tender, stirring once.
Fennel 2 bulbs (2½ cups quarters)	Cut off and discard upper stalks, including feathery leaves. Remove wilted outer layer of stalks; cut off a thin slice from base. Wash; cut fennel into quarters lengthwise.	Cook, covered, in a small amount of boiling water for 6 to 10 minutes or till tender. (Or, steam for 6 to 8 minutes.)	Place in a casserole with ¼ cup water. Microwave, covered, on 100% power (high) for 6 to 8 minutes or till tender, rearranging once.
Greens (beet, collard, kale, mustard, turnip) ¾ pound (12 cups torn)	Wash thoroughly in cold water; drain well. Remove stems; trim bruised leaves.	Cook, covered, in a small amount of boiling salted water for 9 to 12 minutes or till tender.	Not recommended.
Jerusalem Artichokes (sunchokes)	Wash, trim, and peel or scrub. Cut into ¼-inch-thick slices.	Cook, covered, in a small amount of boiling salted water for 8 to 10 minutes	Place in a casserole with 2 tablespoons water. Microwave, covered, on

Vegetable Amount	Preparation	Conventional Cooking Directions	Microwave Cooking Directions
1 pound (2 cups slices)		or till tender. (Or, steam for 10 to 12 minutes.)	100% power (high) for 5 to 7 minutes or till tender, stirring once.
Jicama 10 ounces (2 cups cubes)	Wash, trim, and peel. Cut into ½-inch cubes.	Cook, covered, in a small amount of boiling salted water about 5 minutes or till hot and crisp-tender. (Or, steam about 5 minutes.)	Place in a casserole with 2 tablespoons water. Microwave, covered, on 100% power (high) for 5 minutes or till crisp-tender, stirring once.
Kohlrabi 1 pound (3 cups strips)	Cut off leaves; wash. Peel; chop or cut into strips.	Cook, covered, in a small amount of boiling salted water for 6 to 8 minutes or till tender. (Or, steam about 8 minutes.)	Place in a casserole with 2 tablespoons water. Microwave, covered, on 100% power (high) for 6-to 8 minutes or till tender, stirring once.
Leeks	Wash well; remove any tough outer leaves. Trim	Cook, covered, in a small amount of boiling salted	Place in a casserole with 2 tablespoons water.

1½ pounds (3 cups slices)	roots from base. Slit lengthwise and wash well. Cut into ½-inch-thick slices.	water for 5 minutes or till tender. (Or, steam slices about 5 minutes.)	Microwave, covered, on 100% power (high) for 4 to 5 minutes or till tender, stirring once.
Mushrooms 1 pound (6 cups slices)	Wash mushrooms with a damp towel or paper towel. Leave whole or cut into slices.	Cook sliced mushrooms, covered, in 2 tablespoons margarine or butter about 5 minutes. (Or, steam whole mushrooms for 10 to 12 minutes.)	Place mushrooms in a casserole with 2 tablespoons margarine or butter. Microwave, covered, on 100% power (high) about 4 minutes, stirring twice.
Okra ½ pound	Wash; cut off stems. Cut into ½-inch-thick slices.	Cook, covered, in a small amount of boiling salted water for 8 to 10 minutes or till tender.	Place in a casserole with 2 tablespoons water. Microwave, covered, on 100% power (high) for 4 to 6 minutes or till tender, stirring once.
Onion, boiling or pearl 8 ounces boiling onions (10 to 12) 8 ounces pearl	Peel boiling onions. (Pearl onions are easier to peel after cooking.)	Cook, covered, in small amount of boiling salted water for 10 to 12 minutes for boiling onions, 8 to 10	Place in a casserole with 2 tablespoons water. Microwave, covered, on 100% power (high) for 2 to

Cooking Fresh Vegetables *(continued)*

Vegetable Amount	Preparation	Conventional Cooking Directions	Microwave Cooking Directions
onions (20 to 24, 2 cups)		for pearl onions. (Or, steam 12 to 15 minutes for boiling onions, 10 to 12 minutes for pearl onions.)	4 minutes.
Parsnips 3/4 pound (2 cups slices)	Wash, trim, and peel or scrub. Cut into 1/4-inch-thick slices.	Cook, covered, in a small amount of boiling salted water for 7 to 9 minutes or till tender. (Or, steam for 8 to 10 minutes.)	Place in a casserole with 2 tablespoons water. Microwave, covered, on 100% power (high) for 4 to 6 minutes or till tender, stirring once.
Peas, edible pod (snow peas or sugar snap peas) 1/2 pound (2 cups)	Remove tips and strings; wash.	Cook, covered, in a small amount of boiling salted water for 2 to 4 minutes or till crisp-tender. (Or, steam for 2 to 4 minutes.)	Place in a casserole with 2 tablespoons water. Microwave, covered, on 100% power (high) for 3 to 5 minutes or till crisp-tender, stirring once.

Peas, green 2 pounds (3 cups shelled)	Shell and wash.	Cook, covered, in a small amount of boiling salted water for 10 to 12 minutes or till crisp-tender. (Or, steam for 12 to 15 minutes.)	Place in a casserole with 2 tablespoons water. Microwave, covered, on 100% power (high) for 6 to 8 minutes or till crisp-tender, stirring once.
Peppers, sweet 2 large (2½ cups rings or strips)	Remove stems. Wash and remove seeds and ribs. Cut into rings or strips.	Cook, covered, in a small amount of boiling salted water for 6 to 7 minutes or till crisp-tender. (Or, steam for 6 to 7 minutes.)	Place rings or strips in a casserole with 2 tablespoons water. Microwave, covered, on 100% power (high) for 4 to 6 minutes or till crisp-tender, stirring once.
Potatoes 1 pound (2¾ cups cubes)	Wash and peel. Remove eyes, sprouts, or green areas. Cut into quarters or cubes.	Cook, covered, in a small amount of boiling salted water for 20 to 25 minutes or till tender. (Or, steam about 20 minutes.)	Place in a casserole with 2 tablespoons water. Microwave, covered, on 100% power (high) for 8 to 10 minutes or till tender, stirring once.
Rutabagas	Wash and peel. Cut into ½-inch cubes.	Cook, covered, in a small amount of boiling salted	Place in a casserole with 2 tablespoons water.

Vegetable Amount	Preparation	Conventional Cooking Directions	Microwave Cooking Directions
1 pound (2¾ cups cubes)		water for 18 to 20 minutes or till tender. (Or, steam for 18 to 20 minutes.)	Microwave, covered, on 100% power (high) for 11 to 13 minutes or till tender, stirring 3 times.
Spinach 1 pound (12 cups torn)	Wash and drain; remove stems.	Cook, covered, in a small amount of boiling salted water for 3 to 5 minutes or till tender, beginning timing when steam forms. (Or, steam for 3 to 5 minutes.)	Place in a casserole with 2 tablespoons water. Microwave, covered, on 100% power (high) for 4 to 6 minutes or till tender, stirring once.
Squash (acorn, delicata, golden nugget, sweet dumpling) 1 pound (2 servings)	Wash, halve, and remove seeds.	Place squash halves, cut sides down, in a baking dish. Bake in a 350° oven for 30 minutes. Turn cut sides up. Bake, covered, for 20 to 25 minutes more	Place squash halves, cut sides down, in a baking dish with 2 tablespoons water. Microwave, covered, on 100% power (high) for 6 to 9 minutes or till

		or till tender.	tender, rearranging once. Let stand, covered, 5 minutes.
Squash (banana, buttercup, butternut, Hubbard, turban) One 1½-pound or a 1½-pound piece	Wash, halve squash lengthwise, and remove seeds.	Place squash halves, cut sides down, in a baking dish. Bake in a 350° oven for 30 minutes. Turn cut sides up. Bake, covered, for 20 to 25 minutes more or till tender.	Place squash halves, cut sides down, in a baking dish with 2 tablespoons water. Microwave, covered on 100% power (high) for 9 to 12 minutes or till tender, rearranging once.
Squash (pattypan, sunburst, yellow, zucchini) ¾ pound (2½ cups slices)	Wash; do not peel. Cut off ends. Cut into ¼-inch-thick slices.	Cook, covered, in a small amount of boiling salted water for 3 to 5 minutes or till crisp-tender. (Or, steam for 4 to 6 minutes.)	Place in a casserole with 2 tablespoons water. Microwave, covered, on 100% power (high) for 4 to 5 minutes or till crisp-tender, stirring twice.
Squash, spaghetti One 2½- to 3-pound	Wash, halve lengthwise, and remove seeds.	Place squash halves, cut sides down, in a baking dish. Bake in a 350° oven for 30 to 40 minutes or till	Place halves, cut sides down, in a baking dish with ¼ cup water. Microwave, covered, on

COOKING FRESH VEGETABLES *(continued)*

Vegetable Amount	Preparation	Conventional Cooking Directions	Microwave Cooking Directions
		tender.	100% power (high) 15 to 20 minutes or till tender, rearranging once.
Sweet potatoes 1 pound	Wash and peel. Cut off woody portions and ends. Cut into quarters or cube. (For microwaving, cut into quarters.)	Cook, covered, in enough boiling salted water to cover for 25 to 35 minutes or till tender. (Or, steam for 20 to 25 minutes.)	Place in a casserole with ½ cup water. Microwave, covered, on 100% power (high) for 10 to 13 minutes or till tender, stirring once.
Turnips 1 pound (2½ cups cubes)	Wash and peel. Cut into ½-inch cubes or strips.	Cook, covered, in a small amount of boiling salted water for 10 to 12 minutes or till tender. (Or, steam for 10 to 15 minutes.)	Place in a casserole with 2 tablespoons water. Microwave, covered, on 100% power (high) for 10 to 12 minutes or till tender, stirring once.

INDEX

HOW TO USE THE INDEX

This comprehensive, full-service index includes not just all the recipes from the New Cook Book, but the cooking tips from our Test Kitchen as well.

■ Recipes are sorted by food category and often by title.

■ Tips are sorted by subject matter. You'll find them among the recipe titles.

■ Fast, low-fat, and no-fat symbols accompany the recipe listings in the index, just as on the recipe pages.

M

Macaroni. *See Pasta.*

Macaroons, 389 *Low-Fat*

Malts, 156 *Fast*

Mangoes.
  about, 22
  choosing and storing, 13
  Mango-Ginger Chutney, 972
    No-Fat
  Mango Salsa, 506

Manicotti.
  Low-Fat Spinach Manicotti,
    764 *Low-Fat*
  Spinach Manicotti, 763

Marble Cake, 264

Margarine, 5

Margaritas, Frozen, 161 *Fast*
    No-Fat

Marinara Sauce, Pasta with, 739

Marinating, using bag for, 549

Marmalade, Orange, 358 *No-Fat*

Mayonnaise. *See also Dressings.*
  Basil Mayonnaise, 505 *Fast*
  Citrus Mayonnaise, 1029
  Lemon Mayonnaise, 506
  Mayonnaise, 941 *Fast*
  Mayonnaise Sauce, 855

Meal planning.
  diet and nutrition, 33–39
  dining etiquette, 44
  food labels, 35
  low-fat cooking, 38
  menus, guide to, 41–44
  recipe timing, 40
  saving time, 40
  serving sizes, 35
  shopping, 38

Measuring tips, 50

Meat. *See also Beef; Lamb; Pork;
    Poultry; Rabbit; Veal;
    Venison.*
  amount needed, 625
  broiling, 710
  cubing, 660

  freezing and thawing, 629
  grilling, 586–593
  handling, 652
  panbroiling and panfrying,
    716
  roasting, 712–715
  serving size, 35
  stir-frying, 635
  tenderizing, 627
  thermometer for, 620
  USDA hotline for questions,
    611

Meatballs.
  forming, 742
  Meatball Soup, 986 *Low-Fat*
  Polynesian Meatballs, 90
  Spaghetti and Meatballs, 741
  Swedish Meatballs, 696

Meat Loaf, 698

Melon.
  choosing and storing, 14
  freezing, 332
  Melon and Prosciutto, 95 *Fast*
    Low-Fat
  Tropical Fruit Salad, 938
    Low-Fat

Menus, 41

Meringue.
  Chocolate Chip Meringues,
    390 *Low-Fat*
  Cocoa Meringues, 391
    Low-Fat
  Lemon Custard Meringue,
    426
  Lemon Meringue Pie, 795
  Meringue Shells, Individual,
    426
  Peppermint Meringues, 391
    Low-Fat
  pies, for, 813 *No-Fat*
  Spicy Meringues, 391 *Low-Fat*

Metric information, 1147

Mexican-style foods. *See also
    Burritos; Enchiladas;
    Salsas; Tacos; Tortillas.*

Q

R

METRIC COOKING HINTS

By making a few conversions, cooks in Australia, Canada, and the United Kingdom can use the recipes in *Better Homes and Gardens® New Cook Book* with confidence. The charts on this page provide a guide for converting measurements from the U.S. customary system, which is used throughout this book, to the imperial and metric systems. There also is a conversion table for oven temperatures to accommodate the differences in oven calibrations.

Product Differences: Most of the ingredients called for in the recipes in this book are available in English-speaking countries. However, some are known by different names. Here are some common American ingredients and their possible counterparts:

■ Sugar is granulated or castor sugar.

■ Powdered sugar is icing sugar.

■ All-purpose flour is plain household flour or white flour. When self-rising flour is used in place of all-purpose flour in a recipe that calls for leavening, omit the leavening agent (baking soda or baking powder) and salt.

■ Light corn syrup is golden syrup.

■ Cornstarch is cornflour.

■ Baking soda is bicarbonate of soda.

■ Vanilla is vanilla essence.

■ Green, red, or yellow sweet peppers are capsicums.

■ Sultanas are golden raisins.

Volume and Weight: Americans traditionally use cup measures for liquid and solid ingredients. The chart, below, shows the approximate imperial and metric equivalents. If you are accustomed to weighing solid ingredients, the following approximate equivalents will be helpful.

■ 1 cup butter, castor sugar, or rice = 8 ounces = about 250 grams

■ 1 cup flour = 4 ounces = about 125 grams

■ 1 cup icing sugar = 5 ounces = about 150 grams

Spoon measures are used for smaller amounts of ingredients. Although the size of the tablespoon varies slightly in different countries, for practical purposes and for recipes in this book, a straight substitution is all that's necessary.

Measurements made using cups or spoons always should be level unless stated otherwise.

EQUIVALENTS: U.S. = AUSTRALIA/U.K.

$1/8$ teaspoon = 0.5 ml
$1/4$ teaspoon = 1 ml
$1/2$ teaspoon = 2 ml
1 teaspoon = 5 ml
1 tablespoon = 1 tablespoon
$1/4$ cup = 2 tablespoons = 2 fluid ounces = 60 ml
$1/3$ cup = $1/4$ cup = 3 fluid ounces = 90 ml
$1/2$ cup = $1/3$ cup = 4 fluid ounces = 120 ml
$2/3$ cup = $1/2$ cup = 5 fluid ounces = 150 ml
$3/4$ cup = $2/3$ cup = 6 fluid ounces = 180 ml
1 cup = $3/4$ cup = 8 fluid ounces = 240 ml
$1^{1}/4$ cups = 1 cup
2 cups = 1 pint
1 quart = 1 litre
$1/2$ inch = 1.27 cm
1 inch = 2.54 cm

BAKING PAN SIZES

American	Metric
8×1½-inch round baking pan	20×4-centimetre cake tin
9×1½-inch round baking pan	23×3.5-centimetre cake tin
11×7×1½-inch baking pan	28×18×4-centimetre baking tin
13×9×2-inch baking pan	30×20×3-centimetre baking tin
2-quart rectangular baking dish	30×20×3-centimetre baking tin
15×10×2-inch baking pan	30×25×2-centimetre baking tin (Swiss roll tin)
9-inch pie plate	22×4- or 23×4-centimetre
7- or 8-inch springform pan	18- or 20-centimetre springform or loose-bottom cake tin
9×5×3-inch loaf pan	23×13×7-centimetre or 2-pound narrow loaf tin or paté tin
1½-quart casserole	1.5-litre casserole
2-quart casserole	2-litre casserole

Oven Temperature Equivalents

Fahrenheit Setting*	Celsius Setting	Gas Setting
300°F	150°C	Gas Mark 2 (slow)
325°F	160°C	Gas Mark 3 (moderately slow)
350°F	180°C	Gas Mark 4 (moderate)
375°F	190°C	Gas Mark 5 (moderately hot)
400°F	200°C	Gas Mark 6 (hot)
425°F	220°C	Gas Mark 7
450°F	230°C	Gas Mark 8 (very hot)
Broil		Grill

*Electric and gas ovens may be calibrated using Celsius. However, for an electric oven, increase the Celsius setting 10 to 20 degrees when cooking above 160°C. For convection or forced-air ovens (gas or electric), lower the temperature setting 10°C when cooking at all heat levels.

Weights and Measures

3 teaspoons = 1 tablespoon

4 tablespoons = $1/4$ cup

$5^{1}/_{3}$ tablespoons = $1/3$ cup

8 tablespoons = $1/2$ cup

$10^{2}/_{3}$ tablespoons = $2/3$ cup

12 tablespoons = $3/4$ cup

16 tablespoons = 1 cup

1 tablespoon = $1/2$ fluid ounce

1 cup = 8 fluid ounces

1 cup = $1/2$ pint

2 cups = 1 pint

4 cups = 1 quart

2 pints = 1 quart

4 quarts = 1 gallon

1 teaspoon = 5 milliliters

1 tablespoon = 15 milliliters

1 cup = 240 milliliters

1 quart = 1 liter

1 ounce = 28 grams

1 pound = 454 grams

MICROWAVE HINTS

■ **Bacon:** Place bacon on a microwave-safe rack or a plate lined with paper towels. Cook on 100% power (high) till done. Allow 1½ to 2 minutes for 2 slices, 2½ to 3½ minutes for 4 slices, and 4 to 5 minutes for 6 slices.

■ **Butter or margarine, melting:** In a bowl heat butter or margarine, uncovered, on 100% power (high) 35 to 45 seconds for 2 tablespoons, 45 to 60 seconds for ¼ cup, or 1 to 1½ minutes (about 45 seconds in high-wattage ovens) for ½ cup.

■ **Butter or margarine, softening:** In a bowl heat ½ cup butter or margarine, uncovered, on 10% power (low) for 1½ to 2½ minutes (about 45 seconds in high-wattage ovens) or till softened.

■ **Chicken:** Arrange 12 ounces skinless, boneless chicken breasts in a baking dish, tucking under thin portions. Cover with clear plastic wrap; fold back one corner, leaving about a 1-inch opening. Cook on 100% power (high) for 4 to 6 minutes or till chicken is tender and no longer pink, rearranging pieces after 2 minutes. This makes enough for 2 cups cubed, cooked chicken.

■ **Chocolate, melting:** In a bowl heat chocolate, uncovered, on 100% power (high) 1 to 2 minutes for 1 ounce (1½ to 2½ minutes for 1 cup chocolate pieces) or till soft enough to stir smooth, stirring every minute.

■ **Coconut, toasting:** In a 2-cup measure cook 1 cup coconut, uncovered, on 100% power (high) for 2½ to 3½ minutes or till toasted, stirring after 1 minute, then stirring every 30 seconds.

Cream cheese, softening: In a bowl heat cream cheese, uncovered, on 100% power (high) 15 to 30 seconds for 3 ounces (30 to 60 seconds for 8 ounces) or till softened.

■ **Ice cream, softening:** Heat 1 pint solidly frozen ice cream in a container, uncovered, on 100% power (high) for 15 seconds or till soft.

■ **Ice-cream topping, heating:** Heat chilled topping, uncovered, on 100% power (high) 1 to 1½ minutes for ½ cup or 1 to 2 minutes for 1 cup.

■ **Lemons, juicing:** Halve or quarter 1 lemon. Heat on 100% power (high) 20 to 45 seconds. Squeeze out juice.

■ **Meat, ground:** Crumble 1 pound ground meat into a 1½-quart casserole. Cook, covered, on 100% power (high) till no pink remains, stirring once or twice. Allow 3 to 5 minutes for beef or pork and 4 to 6 minutes for chicken or turkey. Drain off fat.

■ **Muffins and rolls, reheating:** Place muffins or rolls on a plate. Heat, uncovered, on 100% power (high) for 10 to 20 seconds for 1 or 2 muffins or 30 to 60 seconds for 4 muffins.

■ **Nuts, toasting:** In a 2-cup measure cook nuts, uncovered, on 100% power (high) till toasted, stirring every minute for the first 2 minutes, then stirring every 30 seconds. Allow 2 to 3 minutes for ½ cup almonds or pecans, 2 to 3 minutes for 1 cup almonds, 3 to 4 minutes for 1 cup pecans, 3 to 4 minutes for ½ cup raw peanuts or walnuts, and 3½ to 5 minutes for 1 cup raw peanuts or walnuts. Whole nuts may toast first on the inside, so open a few to check for doneness. At the first sign of toasting, spread whole or chopped nuts on paper towels to cool. They will continue to toast as they stand. Let them stand for at least 15 minutes.

■ **Pancake syrup, heating:** Heat syrup, uncovered, on 100% power (high) 20 to 30 seconds for ½ cup (30 to 60 seconds for 1 cup) or till warm.

■ **Pie (fruit), warming:** Place one slice of fruit pie on a plate. Heat, uncovered, on 100% power (high) for 45 to 60 seconds (about 20 seconds in high-wattage ovens).

■ **Potatoes, baking:** Prick medium potatoes (6 to 8 ounces each) with a fork. Cook, uncovered, on 100% power (high) till almost tender, rearranging once. Allow 4 to 6 minutes for 1 potato, 6 to 9 minutes for 2 potatoes, and 10 to 15 minutes for 4 potatoes. Let potatoes stand for 5 minutes.

■ **Tortillas, softening:** Place four 6- to 7-inch flour tortillas between paper towels. Heat on 100% power (high) for 20 to 30 seconds or till softened.

Emergency Substitutions

If you don't have:	Substitute:
Apple pie spice, 1 teaspoon	$1/2$ teaspoon ground cinnamon plus $1/4$ teaspoon ground nutmeg, $1/8$ teaspoon ground allspice, and dash ground cloves or ginger
Baking powder, 1 teaspoon	$1/2$ teaspoon cream of tartar plus $1/4$ teaspoon baking soda
Bread crumbs, fine dry, $1/4$ cup	$3/4$ cup soft bread crumbs; $1/4$ cup cracker crumbs; or $1/4$ cup cornflake crumbs
Broth, beef or chicken, 1 cup	1 teaspoon or 1 cube instant beef or chicken bouillon plus 1 cup hot water
Buttermilk, 1 cup	1 tablespoon lemon juice or vinegar plus enough milk to make 1 cup (let stand 5 minutes before using); or 1 cup plain yogurt
Cajun spice, 1 tablespoon	$1/2$ teaspoon white pepper, $1/2$ teaspoon garlic powder, $1/2$ teaspoon onion powder, $1/2$ teaspoon ground red pepper, $1/2$ teaspoon paprika, and $1/2$ teaspoon black pepper
Chocolate, semisweet, 1 ounce	3 tablespoons semisweet chocolate pieces; or 1 ounce unsweetened chocolate plus 1 tablespoon granulated sugar
Chocolate, sweet baking, 4 ounces	$1/4$ cup unsweetened cocoa powder plus $1/3$ cup granulated sugar and 3 tablespoons shortening

Ingredient	Substitution
Chocolate, unsweetened, 1 ounce	3 tablespoons unsweetened cocoa powder plus 1 tablespoon cooking oil or shortening, melted
Cornstarch, 1 tablespoon (for thickening)	2 tablespoons all-purpose flour
Corn syrup, 1 cup	1 cup granulated sugar plus $1/4$ cup water
Egg, 1 whole	2 egg whites; 2 egg yolks; or $1/4$ cup frozen egg product, thawed
Flour, cake, 1 cup	1 cup minus 2 tablespoons all-purpose flour
Flour, self-rising, 1 cup	1 cup all-purpose flour plus 1 teaspoon baking powder, $1/2$ teaspoon salt, and $1/4$ teaspoon baking soda
Garlic, 1 clove	$1/2$ teaspoon bottled minced garlic; or $1/8$ teaspoon garlic powder
Gingerroot, grated, 1 teaspoon	$1/4$ teaspoon ground ginger
Half-and-half or light cream, 1 cup	1 tablespoon melted butter or margarine plus enough whole milk to make 1 cup
Herb, dried, 1 teaspoon	$1/2$ teaspoon ground herb
Herb, snipped fresh, 1 tablespoon	$1/2$ to 1 teaspoon dried herb, crushed
Honey, 1 cup	$1 1/4$ cups granulated sugar plus $1/4$ cup water
Lemon juice, 1 teaspoon	$1/2$ teaspoon vinegar
Margarine, 1 cup	1 cup butter; or 1 cup shortening plus $1/4$ teaspoon salt, if desired
Milk, whole, 1 cup	$1/2$ cup evaporated milk plus $1/2$ cup water; or 1 cup water plus $1/3$ cup nonfat dry milk powder

EMERGENCY SUBSTITUTIONS (continued)

If you don't have:	Substitute:
Molasses, 1 cup	1 cup honey
Mustard, dry, 1 teaspoon	1 tablespoon prepared mustard (in cooked mixtures)
Onion, chopped, 1 small ($\frac{1}{3}$ cup)	1 teaspoon onion powder; or 1 tablespoon dried minced onion
Poultry seasoning, 1 teaspoon	$\frac{3}{4}$ teaspoon dried sage, crushed, plus $\frac{1}{4}$ teaspoon dried thyme or marjoram, crushed
Pumpkin pie spice, 1 teaspoon	$\frac{1}{2}$ teaspoon ground cinnamon plus $\frac{1}{4}$ teaspoon ground ginger, $\frac{1}{4}$ teaspoon ground allspice, and $\frac{1}{8}$ teaspoon ground nutmeg
Sour cream, dairy, 1 cup	1 cup plain yogurt
Sugar, granulated, 1 cup	1 cup packed brown sugar; or 2 cups sifted powdered sugar
Tomato juice, 1 cup	$\frac{1}{2}$ cup tomato sauce plus $\frac{1}{2}$ cup water
Tomato sauce, 2 cups	$\frac{3}{4}$ cup tomato paste plus 1 cup water
Yeast, active dry, 1 package	1 cake compressed yeast